Peter D. Mosses Mogens Nielsen
Michael I. Schwartzbach (Eds.)

TAPSOFT '95: Theory and Practice of Software Development

6th International Joint Conference CAAP/FASE
Aarhus, Denmark, May 22-26, 1995
Proceedings

Springer

Series Editors

Gerhard Goos
Universität Karlsruhe
Vincenz-Priessnitz-Straße 3, D-76128 Karlsruhe, Germany

Juris Hartmanis
Department of Computer Science, Cornell University
4130 Upson Hall, Ithaca, NY 14853, USA

Jan van Leeuwen
Department of Computer Science, Utrecht University
Padualaan 14, 3584 CH Utrecht, The Netherlands

Volume Editors

Peter D. Mosses
Mogens Nielsen
Michael I. Schwartzbach
BRICS, Department of Computer Science, University of Aarhus
Ny Munkegade, Bldg. 540, DK-8000 Aarhus C, Denmark

CR Subject Classification (1991):D.2.1-2, D.2.4-7, D.2.10, D.3.1-4, F.1.1-2, F.2.2, F.3.1-3, F.4.1-3, K.6.3, B.2.3

ISBN 3-540-59293-8 Springer-Verlag Berlin Heidelberg New York

CIP data applied for

Printed in Germany

Typesetting: Camera-ready by author
SPIN: 10485773 06/3142-543210 - Printed on acid-free paper

Preface

TAPSOFT '95 is the Sixth International Joint Conference on the Theory and Practice of Software Development. It is to take place at the University of Aarhus, Denmark, 22–26 May, 1995.

The TAPSOFT series was started in Berlin in 1985, on the initiative of Hartmut Ehrig, Bernd Mahr, and Christiane Floyd (among others). Since then TAPSOFT has been held biennially, in Pisa (1987), Barcelona (1989), Brighton (1991), and Orsay (1993). The overall aim of TAPSOFT was formulated as:

> *to bring together theoretical computer scientists and software engineers (researchers and practitioners) with a view to discussing how formal methods can usefully be applied in software development.*

As part of TAPSOFT '95, Ehrig, Mahr, and Floyd review what has been achieved within the TAPSOFT area during the past decade, and consider prospects for the future. Moreover, there is to be a session to debate the general organization of European Spring Conferences on Software Science (including TAPSOFT). This 10th anniversary of the start of TAPSOFT looks as if it will be a significant turning point in the development of the series.

TAPSOFT traditionally comprises three parts:

- **Invited Lectures:**
  by leading researchers, on a variety of relevant topics;
- **CAAP:** Colloquium on Trees in Algebra and Programming
  covering a wide range of topics in theoretical computer science;
- **FASE:** Colloquium on Formal Approaches in Software Engineering
  with the emphasis on practical applicability.

In recognition of the importance of support tools for practical use of formal approaches in software development, TAPSOFT '95 includes a fourth part:

- **TOOLS:**
  two plenary sessions for tool demonstrations, as well as facilities for individual demonstrations.

Satellite Meetings

The following three satellite meetings are to take place in conjunction with TAPSOFT '95: *TACAS* (Workshop on Tools and Algorithms for the Construction and Analysis of Systems, 19–20 May); *TPA* (Workshop on Types for Program Analysis, 26–27 May); and *COMPASS WG Day* (for Members of ESPRIT BR Working Group 6112, 26–27 May).

TAPSOFT Steering Committee:

André Arnold, Pierpaolo Degano, Hartmut Ehrig, Marie-Claude Gaudel, Tom Maibaum, Ugo Montanari, Maurice Nivat, Fernando Orejas.

Invited Lectures

In their paper *A Decade of TAPSOFT: Aspects of Progress and Prospects in Theory and Practice of Software Development*, Hartmut Ehrig and Bernd Mahr discuss the general background of TAPSOFT, and focus on specific aspects of theory and practice which seem to them to be typical of TAPSOFT: the support of software development by algebraic methods, techniques and tools. They also give their expectations for the future of TAPSOFT and its topics.

In *Theory and Practice of Software Development – Stages in a Debate*, Christiane Floyd discusses the place of formal methods in software development. She distinguishes two notions of theory: the mathematical science of computation and the treatment of computing as a human activity. Fundamental assumptions underlying formal methods and their relation to emancipatory approaches such as participatory design are discussed. The paper closes with a call for a dialogical framework for further pursuing these questions.

In *Testing Can Be Formal, Too*, Marie-Claude Gaudel presents a theory of program testing based on formal specifications. The formal semantics of the specification is the basis for a notion of an exhaustive test set. She also considers the problem of observability of the results of a program with respect to its specification, and proposes a solution in the case of algebraic specifications.

In the paper *Formal Methods and Social Context in Software Development*, Joseph Goguen and Luqi explore some reasons why formal methods have not been accepted to the expected extent. One major problem has been that formal methods have not taken sufficient account of the social context of computer systems. To better understand social context, they discuss ethnomethodology, a branch of sociology, and situated abstract data types, which help bridge the gap between the technical and the social. The paper concludes with discussions of software composition and a new paradigm of "Domain Specific Formal Methods".

Set constraints have been used extensively in program analysis and type inference. In *Rational Spaces and Set Constraints*, Dexter Kozen investigates the topological structure of the spaces of solutions to systems of set constraints. He develops the theory of rational spaces and derives generalizations and proofs from topological principles of some results in the literature on set constraints.

Vaughan Pratt has been closely involved with analysing the significance of the recently revealed bug in the Intel Pentium computer chip. His topical paper on the *Anatomy of the Pentium Bug* presents general background and new results. The software engineering implications of the bug include the observations that the method of exercising reachable components cannot detect reachable components mistakenly believed unreachable, and that hand-checked proofs build false confidence.

In his other invited paper, *Rational Mechanics and Natural Mathematics*, Pratt works with so-called Chu spaces, which have found applications in computer science, mathematics, and physics. He uses Chu spaces and residuation to derive all causal interaction, both between and within two planes, from a uniform and algebraically rich theory of between-plane interaction alone, and addresses fundamental philosophical questions.

CAAP '95: Colloquium on Trees in Algebra and Programming

Programme Committee:

André Arnold	(France)	Jan Willem Klop	(Netherlands)
Bruno Courcelle	(France)	Ugo Montanari	(Italy)
Josep Díaz	(Spain)	Mogens Nielsen	(chair, Denmark)
Volker Diekert	(Germany)	Colin Stirling	(Britain)
Hartmut Ehrig	(Germany)	Wolfgang Thomas	(Germany)
Juhani Karhumäki	(Finland)	Sophie Tison	(France)

This colloquium series was originally devoted to the algebraic and combinatorial properties of trees, and their rôle in various fields of computer science. The importance of trees in computer science is now firmly established, and the study of their algebraic, logical, and combinatorial properties has made significant progress. Many other structures such as graphs are playing similar roles and deserve similar theoretical studies. In keeping with CAAP's traditions while accounting for these new trends, CAAP '95 covers algebraic, logical and combinatorial properties of discrete structures and their applications to computer science.

Out of 71 submitted papers, the programme committee selected 23 for presentation at the conference. These are grouped into sessions on trees and automata, concurrency, logic and specification, formal languages, rewriting systems, and semantics.

FASE '95: Colloquium on Formal Approaches in Software Engineering

Programme Committee:

Egidio Astesiano	(Italy)	Bernd Mahr	(Germany)
David Basin	(Germany)	Fernando Orejas	(Spain)
Véronique Donzeau-Gouge	(France)	Don Sannella	(Britain)
Marie-Claude Gaudel	(France)	Michael Schwartzbach	(chair, Denmark)
Bengt Jonsson	(Sweden)	Bernhard Steffen	(Germany)
Paul Klint	(Netherlands)	Reinhard Wilhelm	(Germany)

This colloquium aims at being a forum where different formal approaches to problems of software specification, development, and verification are presented, compared, and discussed.

Out of 76 submitted papers, the programme committee selected 21 for presentation at the conference. These are grouped into sessions on types, tools, static analysis, case studies, transformations, concurrency, and specifications.

TOOLS

The two plenary TOOLS sessions at TAPSOFT '95 are to provide demonstrations of nine relevant systems altogether. Moreover, there are to be facilities for further demonstrations of these and other systems in the breaks and during the parallel sessions. It is hoped that this will give the TAPSOFT participants a useful opportunity to assess some of the main tools that are currently available, and that tool demonstrations will be a regular feature of future TAPSOFT conferences. The demonstrations are documented by 2-page summaries, printed at the back of this proceedings.

Acknowledgments

The organizers gratefully acknowledge the following support:

The TAPSOFT Steering Committee made the decision to hold TAPSOFT '95 in Aarhus in good time, and gave a lot of useful advice about organization.

The CAAP and FASE Programme Committee members had the difficult task of selecting papers from a satisfyingly large number of submissions; fortunately most of them (20 out of 24) were able to attend the selection meeting. Almost 300 referees, listed on the following pages, provided reports on the submitted papers. Michael Schwartzbach developed the system by which referee reports could be submitted directly to a database using WWW forms, with programme committee members being automatically informed of any major differences of assessment on particular papers.

The invited lecturers have written a varied and exciting collection of full papers to support their lectures. Special thanks to Vaughan Pratt for the paper on the Pentium bug, which was a last-minute addition to the TAPSOFT '95 programme.

Karen K. Møller has efficiently managed the preparation of the proceedings, as well as many other aspects of the organization; her assistance has been (and still is!) indispensable.

Alfred Hofmann at Springer-Verlag kindly agreed to publish the proceedings in the Lecture Notes in Computer Science series, and helped with its preparation.

BRICS (Centre for Basic Research in Computer Science: a centre established in cooperation between the Danish National Research Foundation, the University of Aarhus and Aalborg University) is the host for TAPSOFT '95.

The following organizations are sponsoring TAPSOFT '95:

- **COMPASS:** ESPRIT Basic Research Working Group 6112: a COMPrehensive Algebraic approach to System Specification and development
- **DAIMI:** Department of Computer Science, University of Aarhus, Denmark
- **EATCS:** European Association for Theoretical Computer Science
- **SNF:** Danish Science Research Council
- **University of Aarhus:** Faculty of Science, University of Aarhus, Denmark

TAPSOFT '95 Organizing Committee: Karen K. Møller, Peter D. Mosses (chair), Mogens Nielsen, Michael I. Schwartzbach.

Aarhus, February 1995

Peter D. Mosses

Referees

P. Abdulla
J.R. Abrial
M. Alt
R. Amadio
T. Amtoft
M. Ancona
H.R. Andersen
P. Anderson
S. Anderson
R. Andonov
M.-V. Aponte
K. Apt
P. Audebaud
S.J. van Bakel
H. Baumeister
J. Beauquier
M. Bellia
K. Bennacer
B. Bérard
R. Berghammer
J.A. Bergstra
E. Best
J. Bétréma
M. Bidoit
P. Binderup
J. Blanco
J. Blom
A. Bockmayr
F.S. de Boer
M. Boreale
D. Bosscher
A. Bouali
P. Boullier
J. Boyar
J. Bradfield
M.G.J. van den Brand
F. Brandenburg
G.S. Brodal
M. Broy
G. Bruns
A. Bundy
O. Burkart
I. Castellani
P. Casteran
M. Cerioli
A. Cheng
C. Choppy
I. Christoff
L. Christoff
A. Claßen
M. Clerbout
S. Clérici
E. Contejean
F. Cornelius
A. Corradini
G. Costa
M. Dam
O. Danvy
M. Dauchet
R. De Nicola
P. Degano
M. Deininger
J. Delacroix
F. Denis
J. Desel
A. Deutsch
P. Devienne
R. DiCosmo
A. Dicky
K. Didrich
S. Diehl
G. Dowek
C. Dubois
W. Ebinger
U. Engberg
U.H. Engberg
J. Engelfriet
J. Esparza
P. Facon
R. Fagerberg
P. Feautrier
C. Fecht
C. Ferdinand
G. Ferrari
A. Finkel
G. Florin
M. Fokkinga
G. Frandsen
D. de Frutos Escrig
M. Fuchs
J. Gabarro
F. Gadducci
H. Ganzinger
R. Gavalda
G. Germano
A. Geser
G. Ghelli
S. Gilmore
R. Glas
S. Gnesi
W. Goerigk
M. Goldwurm
W. Grieskamp
A. Griffault
J.F. Groote
M. Grosse-Rhode
G. Guaiana
S. Gündel
A. Habel
N. Halbwachs
C. Hankin
H. Hansen
M. Hanus
T. Hardin
K. Havelund
A. Heckler
J. Heering
A. Hense
C. Hermida
D. Hofbauer
J. Honkala
F. Honsell
O.I. Hougaard
J. Hromkovic
M. Huhn
H. Hungar
H. Hüttel
J.M. Ilie
P. Inverardi
D. Janin
M. Jantzen
C. Jard
K. Jensen
T. Jensen
M. Jerrum
B. Josko
M. Jourdan
S. Kahrs
R. Kaivola
K. Kalorkoti
J.F.T. Kamperman
L. Kempe
R. Kennaway
M. Kindahl
P. King
C. Kirchner
H. Kirchner
N. Klarlund

S. Klusener
J. Knoop
M. Korff
H. Kroeger
R. Kuiper
A. van Lamsweerde
C. Laneve
B. Lang
K.G. Larsen
M. Latteux
B. Le Saëc
H. Lescow
J.J. Lévy
G. Luettgen
D. Lutzebäck
C. Lynch
G. Mélançon
A. Maggiolo
K. Malmkjær
J. Marcinkowski
T. Margaria
J.Y. Marion
B. Marre
N. Martí-Oliet
M. Martelli
P.-E. Martin
C. Martinez
S. Martini
A. Masini
A. Mateescu
D. Matthews
S. Matthews
B. Mayoh
L. Meertens
E. Meijer
P.-A. Mellies
E. Mikk
H. Millroth
K. Mitchell
E. Moggi
B. Möller
R. Monroy
F. Morando
P.D. Mosses
F. Mourlin
A. Muscholl
M. Navarro
F. Nielson
H.R. Nielson
A. Nonnengart
O. Nurmi
S.-O. Nyström
E. Ohlebusch
J. van Oosten
V. van Oostrom
Y. Ortega Mallén
F. Otto
J. Padberg
C. Palamidessi
J. Palsberg
H. Partsch
R. Peña
D. Peled
R.P. Perez
H. Petersen
C. Petersohn
A. Petit
P. Pettersson
B. Pierce
G. Pighizzini
G. Plateau
D. Plump
A. Podelski
A. Poetzsch-Heffter
A. Potthoff
D. Pym
P. Quaglia
C. Queinnec
G. Reggio
K. Reinhardt
L. Rigeiro
U. Roesler
J. Roman
F. Rouaix
G. Rünger
O. Ruthing
J. Rutten
M. Ryan
G. Saake
N. Saheb
P. Sallé
A. Salomaa
K. Salomaa
D. Sangiorgi
V. Sassone
H.J. Schneider
T. Schöbel-Theuer
H. Seidl
L. Seinturier
M.J. Serna
M. Siegel
J. Sifakis
F. Simon
H. Sips
A. Skou
A. Smaill
L. Staiger
P. Steckler
P. Stevens
K. Stoelen
M. Sudholt
K. Sunesen
A. Tönne
P.S. Thiagarajan
R. Tolksdorf
J. Trescher
D. Troeger
Y.-K. Tsay
D. Turi
J. Underwood
F.W. Vaandrager
E. Valkema
B. Victor
G. Vidal-Naquet
L. Vigano
E. Visser
W. Vogler
F. Voisin
G. Wall
H.R. Walters
A. Weber
K. Weihrauch
C. Weise
W. Weisweber
R. Whitty
S. Wiebrock
T. Wilke
M. Wirsing
M. Wolf
U. Wolter
D. Wolz
K. Yi
W. Yi
P. Zeitz
S. Zhou
W. Zielonka
E. Zucca

Table of Contents

I Invited Lectures 1

A Decade of TAPSOFT: Aspects of Progress and Prospects in Theory and Practice of Software Development 3
H. Ehrig, B. Mahr

Theory and Practice of Software Development – Stages in a Debate . . . 25
C. Floyd

Rational Spaces and Set Constraints 42
D. Kozen

Formal Methods and Social Context in Software Development 62
J.A. Goguen, Luqi

Testing Can Be Formal, Too 82
M.-C. Gaudel

Anatomy of the Pentium Bug 97
V. Pratt

Rational Mechanics and Natural Mathematics 108
V. Pratt

II CAAP 123

CAAP-1: Trees & Automata

First-Order Logic on Finite Trees 125
A. Potthoff

Decidability of Equivalence for Deterministic Synchronized Tree Automata 140
K. Salomaa

The Equivalence Problem for Letter-to-Letter Bottom-up Tree Transducers is Solvable 155
Y. André, F. Bossut

CAAP-2: Concurrency I

πI: A Symmetric Calculus based on Internal Mobility 172
D. Sangiorgi

Complete Inference Systems for Weak Bisimulation Equivalences in the π-Calculus 187
H. Lin

Reasoning about Higher-Order Processes 202
R.M. Amadio, M. Dam

Confluence of Processes and Systems of Objects 217
X. Liu, D. Walker

CAAP-3: Logic & Specification

An Algebraic Approach to Temporal Logic 232
B. von Karger

On Behavioural Abstraction and Behavioural Satisfaction in Higher-Order Logic 247
M. Hofmann, D. Sannella

Assumption/Guarantee Specifications in Linear-Time Temporal Logic (Extended Abstract) 262
B. Jonsson, Y.-K. Tsay

CAAP-4: Formal Languages

Fine Hierarchy of Regular ω-Languages 277
V. Selivanov

Computing the Wadge Degree, the Lifschitz Degree, and the Rabin Index of a Regular Language of Infinite Words in Polynomial Time 288
T. Wilke, H. Yoo

Semi-Trace Morphisms and Rational Transductions 303
P.-A. Wacrenier

Nonfinite Axiomatizability of Shuffle Inequalities 318
S.L. Bloom, Z. Ésik

CAAP-5: Concurrency II

On the Category of Petri Net Computations 334
V. Sassone

High Undecidability of Weak Bisimilarity for Petri Nets 349
P. Jančar

Polynomial Algorithms for the Synthesis of Bounded Nets 364
E. Badouel, L. Bernardinello, Ph. Darondeau

CAAP-6: Rewriting Systems

Semi-Completeness of Hierarchical and Super-Hierarchical Combinations of Term Rewriting Systems 379
M.R.K. Krishna Rao

Lazy Narrowing: Strong Completeness and Eager Variable Elimination (Extended Abstract) 394
S. Okui, A. Middeldorp, T. Ida

On the Expressive Power of Algebraic Graph Grammars with Application Conditions 409
A. Wagner

CAAP-7: Semantics

Generated Models and the ω-Rule: The Nondeterministic Case 424
M. Walicki, S. Meldal

CPO Models for a Class of GSOS Languages 439
L. Aceto, A. Ingólfsdóttir

Statecharts, Transition Structures and Transformations 454
A. Peron

III FASE 469

FASE-1: Types

An Imperative Object Calculus 471
M. Abadi, L. Cardelli

A Refinement of Import/Export Declarations in Modular Logic Programming and Its Semantics 486
I. Karali, C. Halatsis

Strictness and Totality Analysis with Conjunction 501
K.L. Solberg

FASE-2: Tools

Generic Techniques for Source-Level Debugging and Dynamic Program Slicing 516
F. Tip

Reasoning with Executable Specifications 531
Y. Bertot, R. Fraer

Calculating Software Generators from Solution Specifications 546
R.B. Kieburtz, F. Bellegarde, J. Bell, J. Hook, J. Lewis, D. Oliva, T. Sheard, L. Walton, T. Zhou

FASE-3: Static Analysis

Comparing Flow-Based Binding-Time Analyses 561
J. Palsberg

Can you Trust your Data? 575
P. Ørbæk

Static and Dynamic Processor Allocation for Higher-Order Concurrent Languages 590
H.R. Nielson, F. Nielson

FASE-4: Case Studies

Mechanized Inductive Proof of Properties of a Simple Code Optimizer . . 605
A. Geser

Describing a Signal Analyzer in the Process Algebra PMC
– A Case Study 620
H.R. Andersen, M. Mendler

A Gentle Introduction to Specification Engineering Using
a Case Study in Telecommunications 636
S. Kleuker

FASE-5: Transformations

Precise Interprocedural Dataflow Analysis with Applications
to Constant Propagation 651
M. Sagiv, T. Reps, S. Horwitz

Formal Specification and Prototyping of a Program Specializer 666
S. Blazy, Ph. Facon

Proving the Correctness of Recursion-Based Automatic
Program Transformations 681
D. Sands

FASE-6: Concurrency

Reactive System Specification and Refinement 696
K. Lano

Measuring Concurrency of Regular Distributed Computations 711
C. Bareau, B. Caillaud, C. Jard, R. Thoraval

Non-Speculative and Upward Invocation of Continuations in
a Parallel Language 726
L. Moreau

FASE-7: Specifications

A Model Inference System for Generic Specification
with Application to Code Sharing 741
D. Bert, C. Oriat

Relations as Abstract Datatypes: An Institution to Specify Relations
Between Algebras 756
H. Baumeister

Performance-Oriented Formal Specifications – the LotoTis Approach . . . 772
I. Schieferdecker

IV TOOLS 787

TOOLS-1

SIGNAL: A Formal Design Environment for Real-Time Systems 789
EP-ATR Project

The META-Frame: An Environment for Flexible Tool Management . . . 791
B. Steffen, T. Margaria, A. Claßen

STeP: The Stanford Temporal Prover 793
Z. Manna, N. Bjørner, A. Browne, E. Chang, M. Colón, L. de Alfaro, H. Devarajan, A. Kapur, J. Lee, H. Sipma, T. Uribe

The HOL-UNITY Verification System 795
F. Andersen, U. Binau, K. Nyblad, K.D. Petersen, J.S. Pettersson

PLATO: A Tool to Assist Programming as Term Rewriting and Theorem Proving 797
A.J. Sampaio, A.M. Haeberer, C.T. Prates, C.D. Ururahy, M.F. Frias, N.C. Albuquerque

TOOLS-2

LOFT: A Tool for Assisting Selection of Test Data Sets from Algebraic Specifications 799
B. Marre

The SMoLCS ToolSet 801
E. Astesiano, G. Reggio, F. Morando

The ASF+SDF Meta-Environment: Documentation Tools for Free! 803
M.G.J. van den Brand, E. Visser

The B-Toolkit Demonstration 805
B-Core (UK) Ltd.

TOOLS-3

Object Oriented Semantics Directed Compiler Generation: A Prototype 807
L.C.C. Guedes, E.H. Haeusler, J.L. Rangel

Author Index 809

Part I

Invited Lectures

A Decade of TAPSOFT:
Aspects of Progress and Prospects in Theory and Practice of Software Development

Hartmut Ehrig
Bernd Mahr
Technical University of Berlin
Franklinstraße 28 / 29, 10587 Berlin
e-mail: {ehrig, mahr}@ cs.tu-berlin.de

Abstract. The relationship between theory and practice of software development on the background of the driving forces in the 70'ies and 80'ies was the main topic of the first TAPSOFT conference in 1985. After a decade of TAPSOFT the intention of this survey is not so much to give a complete review of the TAPSOFT conferences but to discuss the general background and to focus on specific aspects of theory and practice which seem to be typical for TAPSOFT: The support of software development by algebraic methods, techniques and tools, in particular corresponding activities at TU Berlin. The survey in this paper shows that there is quite a different kind of progress in the decades before and after TAPSOFT'85: Before 1985 the focus was more on the development of new concepts while consolidation and attempts to adapt to practical needs was dominant after 1985.

Finally the expectations for the future of theory and practice of software development are discussed on the background of the driving forces in the 90'ies hoping that TAPSOFT will be able to meet these requirements.

Contents

1. History, Aims and Expectations of TAPSOFT
2. Driving Forces of Software Development and its Major Concepts in the 70'ies and 80'ies
3. Support of Software Development by Algebraic Methods, Techniques and Tools
4. Algebraic Specification and Graph Transformation at TU Berlin
5. Theory and Practice of Software Development in the 90'ies
6. References

1 History, Aims and Expectations of TAPSOFT

The idea to have a joint conference on theory and practice of software development was born following the offer to organize the 1985 Colloquium on Trees in Algebra and Programming (CAAP) in Berlin. At that time a joint seminar on the role of formal methods in software development was organized by Christiane Floyd and Hartmut Ehrig. Although it was most difficult to understand each others' terminology and intentions, all of us in the seminar were convinced that it would be desirable to understand each others research aims and to launch joint projects to bridge theory and practice in software development.

Since there was already an offer to have CAAP'85 in Berlin we proposed that it might be a good idea to combine CAAP'85 with a corresponding Colloquium on Software Engineering (CSE). Discussing this proposal in Ugo Montanari's office in 1983 Maurice Nivat advocated that we should have a third part "An Advanced Seminar on the Role of Semantics in Software Development": The idea of TAPSOFT was born. Last but not least Jim Thatcher was enthusiastic about this idea and joined us to organize the "Joint Conference on Theory and Practice of Software Development", short TAPSOFT, in Berlin 1985.

Although the organization of TAPSOFT'85 with 12 invited speakers for the advanced seminar was not at all easy from the financial and the organizational point of view it finally turned out to be a real success. In fact, it was remarkable to have most distinguished invited speakers like John Backus, Peter Naur, Rod Burstall, John Reynolds, Manfred Broy, Ugo Montanari, Dave Parnas, Cliff Jones, Jim Horning and A. P. Ershov at the same conference, interesting contributions in CAAP and CSE including a session on industrial experience, an extra evening session on social responsibility and several working groups on specific topics.

1.1 Aims and Expectations of TAPSOFT

The overall aim of TAPSOFT was formulated in the call for papers in 1985 as

> "to bring together theoretical computer scientists and software engineers (researchers and practitioners) with a view to discussing how formal methods can usefully be applied in software development"

This overall aim includes two different aspects. The first one is to bring together researchers and practitioners within one conference to discuss each others problems. The second one is the relevance of formal methods for software development. Both of these aspects were lively discussed during TAPSOFT'85.

In fact, TAPSOFT'85 brought together more than 400 participants from research and practice, and a discussion of problems of mutual impact was started at least in some cases. We will discuss below whether this first aim of TAPSOFT could really be fulfilled in the last decade.

Concerning the second aspect let us have a closer look at the aims and expectations formulated in the position papers by Christiane Floyd and Hartmut Ehrig in the proceedings of TAPSOFT'85 [Ehr 85], [Flo 85] and the contributions of the organizers during the panel at TAPSOFT'85.

The main statements in the position papers and during the TAPSOFT panel concerning the relevance of formal methods in software development are more or less the following:

Maurice Nivat pointed out that direct applicability of formal techniques is not his main problem. However, his students should learn formal methods, because good mathematical knowledge of a person leads to good computer science capabilities.

Jim Thatcher reported on his experience within IBM and came to the conclusion that formal specification techniques for large companies like IBM are almost hopeless.

Christiane Floyd discussed the relevance of formal methods in her position paper. She criticized several of the claims in favor of formal methods, but admitted that there are at least some useful aspects. However, the essential part of software development - according to her statement during the panel - is the human interface, which cannot be improved by formal methods.

Hartmut Ehrig focused in his position paper on the question "In what way can formal specification methods and languages improve the software development process?" His conclusion during the panel was that there is a good chance that formal methods will improve the software development process at least in the long run.

So the influence of theory on practice and vice versa was considered quite differently among the panelists. It also turned out that these different views which do in fact not contradict each other were shared by different groups in the audience.

Before we discuss the role of formal methods and the progress of TAPSOFT in the next sections let us have a closer look at the focus of the TAPSOFT conferences during the last decade.

1.2 A Decade of TAPSOFT

After the initial TAPSOFT conference in 1985 combining CAAP, CSE and the advanced seminar "On the Role of Semantics in Software Development" it was decided to continue TAPSOFT every two years combing CAAP with some more applied conference and a suitable advanced seminar. The proceedings of the TAPSOFT conferences have been published as separate volumes of "Springer Lecture Notes in Computer Science".

The focus of TAPSOFT'87 in Pisa, organized by Ugo Montanari and Pierpaolo Degano, shifted from general software engineering to new programming paradigms, a "Colloquium on Functional and Logic Programming" (CFLP). The advanced seminar was on "Innovative Software Development".

TAPSOFT'89, organized by Fernando Orejas and Joseph Diaz in Barcelona, combined CAAP with a "Colloquium on Current Issues in Programming Languages" (CCIPL) and an advanced seminar on "Foundations of Innovative Software Development".

Tom Maibaum and Samson Abramsky organized TAPSOFT'91 in Brighton and combined CAAP with a "Colloquium on Combining Paradigms for Software Development" (CCPSD) and an advanced course on "Advances in Distributed Computing".

The concept of TAPSOFT'93 in Orsay, organized by Marie-Claude Gaudel and Jean-Pierre Jouannaud, was to combine CAAP with a "Colloquium on Formal Approaches in Software Engineering" (FASE) and to have invited talks on a variety of relevant topics. The same concept is being used now for TAPSOFT'95 in Aarhus, organized by Peter Mosses, Mogens Nielsen and Michael Schwartzbach.

While the contents of the CAAP part was more or less stable from 1985 to 1995, covering in addition to trees a wide range of topics in theoretical computer science, the focus of the second colloquium has shifted from general software engineering, via new programming paradigms to formal approaches in software engineering, especially to algebraic methods, techniques and tools.

Accordingly the focus concerning participants has changed from "general software engineers" to "theoretical software engineers", i.e. to those software engineers, who are already convinced of formal methods and try to find suitable theoretical foundations of software engineering.
This means that the first aspect of the overall aims of TAPSOFT "to bring together researchers and practitioners within one conference to discuss each others problems" has not been fulfilled in the last decade.

Is this already a failure of TAPSOFT? Does this imply a failure of formal methods? In order to find an answer to these questions let us have a closer look at the driving forces of software development and at the relationship between theory and practice. It will become clear that the shift from general to theoretical software engineering was natural and that formal methods had a steady influence on concepts and development in software specification and programming.

2 Driving Forces of Software Development and its Major Concepts in the 70'ies and 80'ies

Already in the late 60'ies it was seen that software could not be produced as fast as desired, in a predictable way, and with guarantees comparable to those customary for other goods like cars or electronic equipment. There was common agreement on the fact that the engineering process of software development was not well enough understood and that methods, techniques and tools were missing to support this process appropriately. Moreover, there was agreement, though only to a lesser extent, that theory and formal methods would show a way out of the so called 'software crisis'. But in any case it was also quite clear that new techniques had to be developed and better means of abstraction had to be found which would allow to cope with the tremendous complexity of large software systems.

2.1 The Situation in the 70'ies

The 70'ies have then seen an enormous progress in concepts and tools for systems development and programming which laid the ground for most of the achievements in the next decade. Economically, hardware was still the dominant factor in information technology but the awareness grew that software would have a growing market in the future and that productivity of software development was a major aspect to be regarded in research and development.

From a systems point of view, emphasis was on operating systems, compilers, programming tools and interfaces, data bases, information systems as well as application programming and simulation and control. The theories of parsing and translation, program semantics, program verification, queuing theory, data base theory and fundamental concepts for information systems and information retrieval have in the 70'ies been the topics of major concern. Research on Petri nets as a model for concurrency started in this decade and first concepts for parallel programming and synchronization have been developed. Software engineering was established as a new discipline focussing on the software life cycle as a model for the software development process and on programming, specification and verification. The reason for errors in software were analyzed and most of the concepts, languages, tools, and organizational schemata discussed in the 70'ies were seen under the aspect of correctness, effectiveness and rational control of programming and software development. While on the one hand it was enthusiastically discussed how programming could be understood, as a craft, a discipline or an art, the basic fundaments for abstract data types and modularization were laid in the papers by Hoare [Ho 72] and Parnas [Pa 72]. Both, abstract data types and modularization have deeply influenced the design of new more high level programming languages like CLU, MODULA and later ADA as well as the theory of abstract data types and their specification, resulting in specification languages like CLEAR, ACT or ASL.

Also in the 70'ies the study of efficient algorithms and complexity flourished, mainly motivated from the papers by Cook [Co 71] and Strassen [St 69].

Typical for the 70'ies is a new relationship between theory and practice: existing mathematical theories like algebra, logic, probability theory, computability theory, category theory, and theorem proving were found useful in information technology and have been applied yielding new methods and techniques, usually in a less machine dependent way and with all means of abstraction. However, the distance between the newly developed concepts and theories on the one hand, and commercial software development on the other was by no means bridged. Instead there was a steady diffusion of originally theoretical results into systems, systems development and programming. This could be seen in the domains of operating systems, data bases, programming languages and compilers.

2.2 The Situation in the 80'ies

The 80'ies have been different in many respects. The 'software crisis' more and more became an economic problem: a shortage in manpower, low productivity rate, demands for application software that could not be met. The spendings for hardware and software became almost equal and there was a vision for an even further growing market in the future. Information systems, simulation and computer control became weapons in a cold technology war and in a race for the leading position in the world market. The Japanese 5th generation project, proclaimed 1981, threatened the community with an offensive in super-computing and natural language processing based on unification grammars and PROLOG. The United States responded with their strategic computing and strategic defense initiatives SCI and SDI in 1983. The information processing requirements for the proposed developments in these initiatives were immense. The proposals heavily relied on advances in artificial intelligence and software engineering. Feasibility studies argued in any direction, but increased activities also in Europe, namely in the EUREKA and ESPRIT programs, lead to strong support in parallel computing, information systems and basic research.

The concepts and theories originating from the 70'ies were further elaborated and applied and new programming and specification techniques were developed on their basis. In as much as there was a general belief in the potentials of the theoretical and conceptual developments for their effective use in practical software production, there was a growing scepticism in the adequacy of the software life cycle model (starting from ideas via requirements and design specification to implementation and validation) and in the usefulness of formal methods in software development. The relationship between theory and practice became a matter of concern resulting in an emphasis on prototyping and on tools in software engineering. Theoretical and conceptual developments had to prove their applicability in the implementation of tools, prototypes and in case studies. The rigor of a mathematical treatment was no longer unanimously seen as a value in its own right.

An interesting phenomenon in the 80'ies was the role of the software life cycle model. While it still strongly influenced the theoretical work on programming languages, specification languages and requirement specifications as well as on formal implementation and program transformation concepts, it was objected by those seeing software development mainly as a social process and by those who developed techniques and tools which should support the software life cycle as a whole. The experience from large scale software production showed the need for a much more open process model and the means for general modularization adequate to allow for revision, portability, reusability and unrestricted ways of abstraction to separate concerns. Based on this understanding modular and object-oriented design techniques and architectures, building on object and class libraries, became fashionable and popular.

2.3 New Concepts of Programming

In the 80'ies several new programming paradigms were studied, elaborated and widely applied. Some built on mathematical concepts, others on operational models different from that of the von-Neumann computer:

Functional Programming has its roots in LISP, denotational semantics and a functional style of programming. Backus' Turing Award lecture [Ba 78], in which he presents FP, was a starting point for many researchers in this field. Another source of inspiration was ML that grew out of a meta language for theorem proving and employed strong typing checkable at compile-time. There are also close connections between ML and algebraic specifications. Today ML is a full grown programming language available on PCs.

Logic Programming dates back to the paper by Colmerauer [Col 70] and became known through Kowalski [Ko 79]. But it was the 5th generation project in 1981 that created awareness and world wide activities. Origins of Logic Programming are two-level grammars as used in the definition of ALGOL 68 and theorem proving. Efficient implementations are available now and Logic Programming has proven its usefulness in prototyping and in certain applications like natural language processing.

Object-Oriented Programming originates from the SIMULA class concept [DN 66] and is motivated from abstract data types. Objects have an autonomous behaviour and cooperate through message passing or shared variables. Objects encapsulate a state and data and have methods for operation. Methods may be inherited from classes or other objects. Object-orientation starting with the SMALLTALK language [GR 83] became strongly influential to system design and system architectures and today plays an important role in software engineering. Since the general concept of object is weakly determined and there are various approaches and interpretations, a common and accepted theoretical foundation of object-oriented systems is still an unsettled question.

Process-Oriented Programming is based on process models which define the means for communication of sequential processes. In the models of Hoare [Ho 78] and Milner [Mil 80] communication takes place via ports or channels in a static communication topology. While process-oriented programming has not yet found its way into practical programming, it originated deep studies of process calculi and process semantics.

Data flow Programming which is based on the asynchronous execution of function application in a static interconnection topology and thereby supports the single assignment principle of programming grew out of the data flow operational model [AA 82]. Computers operating on the data flow principle have been built and shown to be adequate. The architectural concepts of these computers have influenced other approaches, like the LINDA approach to coordination.

A key question in the 80'ies has been to deal with concurrent systems and to gain operational speed by the use of parallel languages. This was also a major motivation for functional and logic programming which by their declarative nature could avoid unwanted sequentialization. The support of software development by formal methods in the 80'ies had its contribution in tools for programming and specification. Conceptually the integration of these tools and their suitability for concurrent systems have been the most prominent topics. From a mathematical and a theoretical point of view the major achievements have come from type theory, rewriting, semantic models and general frameworks for logics and specification. The gap between theory and practice in software development, however, could not be closed, though the influence of conceptual and theoretical work on techniques and tools in practice was, as it seems, very strong.

3 Support of Software Development by Algebraic Methods, Techniques, and Tools

Support of software development by algebraic methods, techniques, and tools concerns the specification phases of the life cycle. A detailed survey and annotated bibliography is given in [BKLOS 91] within the ESPRIT Basis Research Action COMPASS. We here will discuss some of the main concepts and results occurring in different algebraic approaches and look at the progress during the 70'ies to 90'ies, the relation to corresponding mathematical theories, their relevance for software development in theory resp. practice and aspects for acceptance in practice. To be precise, the main focus of algebraic specification techniques in the 70'ies was the specification of abstract data types. The focus was shifted to specification of software systems only in the 80'ies and 90'ies.

3.1 Models and Semantics

The predominant interest in the 70'ies was on "initial" and "terminal" semantics of algebraic specifications, i.e. one model for each specification up to isomorphism. The initial algebra approach, initiated by the ADJ-group [GTW 76], was especially useful for the specification of basic abstract data types, like natural numbers, characters, strings, stacks and queues. It can be characterized by the slogans "no junk" and "no confusion". The main idea of terminal semantics in contrast is to have one model in the sense of "fully abstract semantics" considered for programming languages.

The next step in the development of algebraic specifications for abstract data types was to consider "loose" semantics, i.e. the class of all models of a given algebraic specification. This was especially useful for requirements specifications within early stages of the software development process and for formal parameters of parameterized specifications, like **data** in **stack(data)**. The focus in the 80'ies then was to consider loose semantics with different kinds of constraints, like generating and free generating constraints, which allow to restrict the semantics to all those algebras satisfying specific properties for suitable subparts of the specification.

Motivated by operational aspects and the idea of hidden states different kinds of behavioural semantics of algebraic specifications have been studied in the late 80'ies and 90'ies, although behavioural semantics had been introduced already by Reichel [Rei 81] as a unifying concept for initial and final semantics. The main idea in behavioural semantics is to define some notion of observation and to consider all models which satisfy the observable consequences of the axioms, but not necessarily the axioms themselves. Behavioural semantics is an important concept to model state oriented systems, where the state is nonobservable.

These different kinds of models and semantics for algebraic specifications were studied in the context of compositionality as well as consistency and completeness w.r.t. corresponding logical calculi. Different models and semantics are seen relevant in different stages of software development from the theoretical point of view, but they are certainly a burden for acceptance in practice because of the large variety of existing approaches and the formal difficulties of the mainly mathematical constructions.

3.2 Logic of Specifications

In the 70'ies and begin of the 80'ies the main focus of research was on many sorted algebras and equational axioms, especially in the initial algebra approach [GTW 76, EM 85]. In [MM 82/84] it was shown that the logic of universal Horn formulas was the most general one within first order logic to admit initial semantics. Problems with error handling in [GTW 76] have motivated to study order-sorted specifications in the 80'ies which also allow to model partiality. In addition algebraic specifications of partial algebras have been studied in the Munich CIP Group [BW 82] focussing on semantics of programming languages.

The intention to have a unified framework to define semantics for different kinds of programming languages has motivated the concept of action semantics and unified algebras [Mos 89] which can be seen as an extension of order sorted specifications and polymorphism. In the late 80'ies the demand to specify higher order functions as they appear in functional programming was the motivation to incorporate higher-order functions into algebraic specifications ([MTW 88]).

Another demand extending algebraic specifications was to deal with problems of concurrency. To consider processes as special data types which interact with each other was adopted in the SMoLCS approach [AR 87] together with corresponding concurrent calculi. In other approaches algebraic specifications are combined with metrics, stream processing functions, Petri nets and modal or temporal logic. All these logics were introduced and studied in view of their semantics and proof calculi in order to support different specification styles and demands as the ones mentioned above.

In order to deal with the different kinds of logic in a unified framework the informal notion of a logical system has been formalized by Goguen and Burstall through the concept of "institutions" [GB 84]. This and other concepts, like "specification frame", have been used in the 80'ies and

90'ies to formulate logic, semantics and structuring of algebraic specifications in a unified way, independent of a specific logic. This was an important step to unify the various theories of specification. Meseguer and others have extended the concept of "institution" by an entailment relation and proof calculus leading to the concepts of "general logics" and "logical systems" thereby following to study the interrelationships between different logics [MM 94]. This is certainly a most important theoretical contribution for the theory of specifications and also for the mathematical theory of logic within the last decade. On the other hand the categorical formulation of these concepts may be an additional burden for its adoption in more practical approaches to specification.

3.3 Structuring and Refinement of Specifications

Structuring concepts for specifications were considered to be important for data types already in the 70'ies. Horizontal structuring concepts allow to build up large specifications from small pieces, while vertical refinement and implementation means transformation steps between different abstraction levels of specifications, e.g. from requirements to design specification. These structuring and refinement concepts are most important for the software development process. In the 80'ies parameterization concepts have been studied for different kinds of semantics and logics and compatibility results were shown for different notions of refinement. In the second half of the 80'ies and in the 90'ies different modularization concepts were studied w.r.t. compatibility and compositionality [BEP 87, EM 90]. The relationship between module concepts in specification and programming was considered in [LEFJ 91] and especially for ML by Sannella and Tarlecki [ST 86]. They also provided a systematic study of implementations in an institutional framework [ST 87]. Moreover parameterization and modularization was extended to behavioural semantics. By now most structuring and refinement concepts are formulated in institutions or specification frames, s.t. they are independent of the underlying logic. This again is elegant from a theoretical point of view but an additional burden for people with more practical intentions usually not familiar with categorical methods.

3.4 Correctness by Verification and Transformation

For the development of correct software systems suitable notions of correctness and corresponding verification techniques are most important. However, one has to make clear which kind of correctness one has in mind and how to verify it.

On one hand there is "internal" correctness of a specification w.r.t. a given base-specification, which means completeness and consistency of new operations w.r.t. the base operations. This notion is important mainly for constructive specifications, like those with initial semantics, and has been studied in the 80'ies and 90'ies based on techniques and results from term rewriting in the case of equations, conditional equations and order sorted equations.

On the other hand there is correctness of refinement or implementation steps between different abstraction levels of specifications. In the case of loose semantics one has to show the inclusion of model classes. For this purpose a proof is required which shows that the axioms of the more abstract specification are derivable from those of the more concrete one. This can be done by correctness preserving transformations or by techniques of theorem proving which, however, are in general very inefficient for first order logic. In the last decade some improvements have been made on the theoretical level concerning computer-aided proof checking. In spite of advances in methods for automatic theorem proving in special cases it seems to be more reasonable to concentrate on interactive proof checkers for verification in the near future. Some examples are the LCF theorem proving system, the theorem prover of LARCH [GG 89], the Boyer/Moore theorem prover, the Edinburgh Logical Framework, Isabelle, and KIV (Karlsruhe Interactive

Verifier) which have been developed or improved during the last decade.

An alternative to verification of correctness of a refinement step between specifications is the use of correctness preserving transformations. Corresponding techniques for program transformation have been developed by Burstall and Darlington and the CIP-group in Munich in the 70'ies and begin of the 80'ies. In the last decade these techniques have been extended to correctness preserving transformations of specifications, for example in the ESPRIT project PROSPECTRA in which the PROSPECTRA transformation system [Kri 90] has been developed. Today such transformation systems are still highly user interactive and experts are needed to achieve the desired results.

A third important notion of correctness is that of specifications w.r.t. programs in a suitable programming language. In some restricted cases there are compilers from specifications into imperative languages, like Pascal [GHM 87]. The more promising way is to transform algebraic specifications into functional programming languages like ML or OPAL, for which efficient compilers exist or have been constructed recently [FGGP 93]. Correctness of specifications w.r.t. programs can be considered as a special case of model correctness where results on induced model correctness [EM 85] are important to construct models for large specifications from those of the components.

3.5 Specification Executability, Language and Tool Support

Executability of specifications is a most important property from the practical point of view because it allows early prototyping on a very high level. The prototyping tools for algebraic specifications are mainly based on term rewriting and narrowing where significant improvements have been achieved during the last decade. For the efficient implementation of functional programming and term rewriting languages graph reduction is a common place technique, where terms are represented as graphs so that common subterms are shared and graph transformations is used.

The need for specification languages to support the construction of specifications for data types and software systems was clear from the very beginning.

The first specification languages for algebraic specifications like CLEAR, OBJ, LOOK, ASL, ACT ONE, PLUSS and LARCH were developed in the late 70'ies and early 80'ies, where OBJ and ACT ONE are based on initial and the others on loose semantics. In the last decade several new algebraic specification languages have been developed to support new specification concepts: Extended ML to support functional programming in standard ML, OBJ2 and 3 for order sorted specifications, ACT TWO for module specifications, SPECTRAL and SPECTRUM for higher order types and TROLL light for object orientation. Especially important from the practical point of view is tool support for specifications including editors, analyser, interpreters, compilers, theorem proving and graphical visualization tools. Experimental versions of several tools were developed before 85, but more advanced versions and the development of support environments were done only in the last decade. Typical examples are the RAP system, the ACT system and ASSPEGIQUE supporting specification in ASL, ACT ONE and PLUSS respectively.

3.6 Development Methodology and Integration of Techniques

It was pointed out in section 2 that an important aspect of software development from the practical point of view is a suitable development methodology for the software development process including all stages and steps from informal problem description, via formal requirement and design specifications to efficient implementation in suitable programming languages. In the 70'ies and early 80'ies the methodology problem was discussed at most on an informal level but in the last decade it has gained more and more importance, especially in ESPRIT projects with industrial partners. Today it is considered an integral part of most joint projects between academic institutes and industrial companies. In the KORSO-methodology [PW 94] one of the main problems is to provide a suitable description of all the activities and the technical documents which are created and updated during the development process. Especially it indicates how this process can be supported by graph transformations. While formal specification techniques have focussed on the phase between formal requirement and design specifications in the 70'ies and early 80'ies the problem of requirements engineering with formal methods has been considered in the last decade [DP 89]. Meanwhile it turned out that the acceptance of formal methods can be increased considerably if it is possible to extend semi-formal methods to formal ones [GM 87] or to integrate well-established semi-formal methods used in practice with suitable formal specification techniques (see next section for more detail). The last topic was the subject of the GI-workshop "Integration of semi-formal and formal methods for software development" during the IFIP-world congress in Hamburg in 1994. Another topic which is most important for applicability and acceptance of formal methods in practice is the integration of different formal specification techniques. Presently it is a deficiency of algebraic specification techniques, in contrast to model oriented techniques based on VDM and Z, that there are too many different approaches which are not sufficiently integrated with each other.

In fact, it would be of great importance for the acceptance of formal methods in practice if there would be a suitable integration of model-oriented and algebraic techniques. A first indication that this is possible from the semantical point of view is given by Hodges in [Hod 94] where specific semantical constructions corresponding to the different approaches are shown to be natural isomorphic functors. Concerning integration of specification techniques for concurrency like CCS and Petri nets with algebraic ones we refer to LOTOS [LOTOS 88] and algebraic high level nets [EPR 94]. Although these integrated concepts are not yet fully developed it seems to be a major progress within the last decade that their fundament could be worked out.

4 Algebraic Specification and Graph Transformation at TU Berlin

Berlin was among the first places in Europe which strongly emphazised the field of software development from a practical point of view mainly influenced by Kees Koster in the 70'ies and Christiane Floyd in the 80'ies. Research on mathematical concepts and theoretical foundations of data types and software systems started also in the early 70'ies concentrating on graph transformation and algebraic specification, and in the 80'ies on software development in its various phases and on the integration of specification techniques in the 90'ies.

In both cases, algebraic specification and graph transformation, the main idea was to study fundamental properties first, using constructions and results from category theory in the context of total algebras and homomorphisms. In a second phase the results were generalized in a categorical framework s.t. not only the total, but also the partial case as well as other cases interesting from an applications point of view could be handled as explicit examples of the general case. Moreover the integration of algebraic specification with graph grammars was studied as an interesting example for the integration of different specification techniques relevant for practical applications.

4.1 Algebraic Specification

Research on algebraic specification techniques in Berlin started in the late 70'ies. We were mainly influenced by the ADJ-group to follow the initial algebra approach, especially concerning parameterization and implementation of algebraic specifications. The state of the art of our specification techniques at TU Berlin in 1985 is more or less given in our first EATCS-Volume

[EM 85] on "Fundamentals of Algebraic Specification: Equations and Initial Semantics". In fact, this approach was still within the spirit of universal algebra and varieties leading to a clean mathematical theory of specification and correctness of abstract data types using algebraic specifications with initial algebra semantics. Moreover, it included parameterized specifications and parameter passing techniques as the main concepts of our algebraic specification language ACT ONE.

The restriction to total algebras, equational axioms and initial semantics in [EM 85] is nice for an introduction into the theory but turned out to be not fully appropriate for practical applications in software development. This became clear in the ESPRIT-projects SEDOS and LOTOSPHERE where ACT ONE was used for the data type part of the language LOTOS for specification of concurrent and distributed systems. This observation has motivated several extensions of ACT ONE during the last decade, including partiality, constraints and shared subtypes. Some of these, especially operational semantics and tool support are presented in our AMAST-book [CEW 93].

Another major development in Berlin - in cooperation with the universities in Dortmund and Los Angeles (USC) - was the concept of algebraic module specification, where in addition to the parameter part of a parameterized specification explicit import and export interfaces have been introduced. It could be shown that there are powerful interconnection mechanisms, like composition, union and actualization with important compositionality results concerning correctness and semantics. Our second EATCS-Volume [EM 90] presents this theory of module specifications as well as a theory of constraints which is most useful for the interfaces in practical applications. The language ACT TWO is purely based on these concepts [Fey 88] and a more practical variant, called Π-language, was developed and implemented in the Eureka Software Factory (ESF) project and the Fraunhofer Institute (ISST) in Berlin. There the module concept was extended to study module and configuration families and the relationship to module concepts in programming languages [LEFJ 91].

A third major development at TU Berlin within the last decade was a generalization of parameterized and module specifications on the level of specification logics or frames in the sense of indexed categories [EBCO 91]. In fact, specification frames can be considered as a variant of institutions in the sense of Burstall and Goguen, which define directly model categories for specifications without explicit satisfaction relation. There are four important existence properties - to be stated as axioms - which allow to obtain the main results of parameterized and module specifications given in [EM 85] and [EM 90] for abstract specifications within a specification frame [EBCO 91, EG 94]: Pushouts, Free Constructions, Amalgamation, and Extension.

In fact, some of the results need only part of these properties and amalgamation implies extension. These properties are valid for equational algebraic specifications as considered in [EM 85, 90] and a large number of variations, including algebraic specifications with conditional equations, universal Horn axioms, partial algebraic specifications, projection specifications and in a restricted sense also behavioural specifications. It is worthwhile to mention, that a variant of behavioural specifications, called view specifications, does not satisfy amalgamation but only extension, so that only part of the general theory can be applied.

The main reason for these general studies is the fact that most of the constructions and proofs in [EM 85, 90] have been given already on a categorical level, which justifies from today's point of view the restricted kind of models and logics used in 1985 in [EM 85]. It turns out that the same results are now applicable to specification techniques that are much more general and suitable from an applications point of view.

Most recently interesting extensions of algebraic specifications and abstract data types meant to model systems with dynamic behaviour have been introduced by Gaudel, Astesiano and others, where dynamic operations are modelled by transformations between algebras and abstract data types. This motivated us to propose a concept of dynamic abstract data types in [EO 94] which seems to be promising for the future development of algebraic specifications and their integration with other specification techniques (see 4.3).

Finally let us mention two other activities at TU Berlin: the design and efficient implementation of the language OPAL (by the group of Peter Pepper) which can be considered as a significant progress towards algebraic programming languages [DFG+ 94] useful as target languages for the transformation of algebraic specification with efficient implementations.

Motivated from the need for a unified approach to the various algebraic specification techniques and from studies of semantics in natural language processing a general type theoretic framework for specification and type disciplines was proposed and investigated in the group of Bernd Mahr [Ma 93]. This framework also allows for selfapplicable functions, reflexive domains and an intensional theory of non-well-founded sets.

4.2 Graph Transformations

The algebraic approach of graph grammars has been created at TU Berlin in 1973 and developed in cooperation with B. Rosen (IBM Yorktown Heights) in the 70'ies and early 80'ies as a graph transformation technique with various applications in Computer Science and Biology [Ehr 79]. At the time of TAPSOFT'85 there was already a well-developed theory for algebraic graph transformations including results about independence, parallelism, concurrency, amalgamation, and embedding of derivations and canonical derivation sequences. In this approach a direct derivation is defined via two pushouts in the category of graphs and total graph morphisms. For this reason it is also called "double pushout approach".

Within the last decade the algebraic approach to graph transformations was extended in several ways. First of all distributed graph transformations have been introduced where a distributed state can be modelled by a family of local state graphs which share suitable interfaces. A distributed derivation is a family of local derivations which preserve the interfaces or change them in a compatible way. This concept was later integrated into an approach for modular graph transformations [EE 94], which also includes an inheritance concept and an import-export concept in analogy to algebraic module specifications.

Another important step was the development of high-level-replacement (short HLR) systems [EHKP 91] which allow to handle transformation systems for several variants of graphs, like hypergraphs, graphs with partially ordered labels, relational structures, algebraic signatures and algebraic specifications, in a uniform way. The main idea was to reformulate the double-pushout approach in a general category instead of the category of graphs, and to formulate specific categorical properties for their use in the constructions and proofs, as axioms for the theory of HLR-systems. These HLR-properties have to be checked for the corresponding application categories. In addition to the examples mentioned above HLR-systems have been applied to different kinds of Petri nets leading to net transformation systems which allow a rule-based change of the net structure in addition to the token game [EPR 94].

A third important step in the last decade was the development of the "single-pushout approach" for graph transformations in the PhD Thesis of M. Löwe [at TU Berlin, 1990]. The idea to formulate graph rewriting by a single-pushout is due to Raoult [Rao 84] and was reformulated by Kennaway [Ken 87] but the appropriate mathematical formulation as a basis for a powerful theory is due to Löwe [Löw 93]. The single-pushout approach is based on the idea that a graph rule is given by a partial graph homomorphism and a graph transformation is given by a (single) pushout in the category of graphs and partial graph morphisms. The explicit single-pushout construction for partial morphisms is much more complex than the double-pushout construction for total graph morphisms but avoids the specific applicability condition of the double-pushout approach, called gluing condition. This admits a wider range of applicability, e.g. in information systems with implicit deletion, but can also be restricted to simulate exactly the double-pushout approach.

Although the explicit construction of a derivation step in the single-pushout approach is in general more complex than in the double-pushout approach it turned out that the theory concerning independence, parallelism, concurrency and amalgamation is easier in the single-pushout approach due to the categorical treatment of one instead of two pushouts. The single-pushout and the double-pushout approach have both been implemented in the AGG-System and the GRADE-ONE-System at TU Berlin and have been used in several projects.

Finally let us mention a new interesting development for graph transformations in cooperation of Pisa and Berlin. Petri nets are well-known as a powerful concept for true concurrency. Nevertheless there are some limitations concerning the modelling of states and transitions which are avoided in algebraic graph grammars, like graph structure of states instead of sets of markings and context conditions for graph transformations.

In [CELMR 94] we have started to develop an event structure semantics for graph grammars similar to that for place transition nets which is a first step towards a theory of graph grammars as a new model for true concurrency.

4.3 Integration of Specification Concepts

In the 70'ies and begin of the 80'ies specification techniques, like algebraic and model theoretic ones, CCS, Petri nets and graph transformations have been developed more or less independently so that there was almost no integration of different concepts.

In the last decade it became more and more important to integrate techniques for process specification with those for data types in order to handle practical applications in an adequate way.

At TU Berlin we were involved since 1985 in the development of the language LOTOS within the ESPRIT projects SEDOS and LOTOSPHERE, where process specifications based on CCS were combined with data type specifications based on ACT ONE. Although this integration is not fully satisfactory from todays point of view it was an important step leading to an international standardization of LOTOS and to several practical applications in the area of communication protocols. Another important step was the integration of Petri nets with algebraic specifications, leading to the notion of algebraic high-level nets, a specific version of coloured nets and high-level nets in the sense of Jensen. Our approach in [Hum 89, DHP 91] and [EPR 94], influenced by Vautherin [Vau 87] and Reisig [Rei 91], allows to extend structuring and compositionality results from algebraic specifications to algebraic high-level nets.

An application of HLR-systems (see above) to algebraic high-level nets leads to the concept of algebraic high-level net transformation systems which are an interesting integration of Petri nets with graph transformation techniques [PER 93]. This has been applied to improve the requirement analysis phase of a larger case study in the BMFT-project KORSO.

Another application of HLR-systems to algebraic specification led to the notion of algebraic specification grammars which have been used by Parisi-Presicce for a rule-based approach to modular system design.

An integration of graph grammars with algebraic specification yields the concept of attributed graph grammars [LKW 93] which is suitable to model the graphical and the data type parts of system states in a unified framework. This integration of graphical and data type features within a single formal method seems to be very important for the acceptance of formal methods in practice. In fact, most of the semi-formal methods used in practice combine graphical and textual parts and it is therefore promising to develop techniques which allow a smooth integration of semi-formal methods and attributed graph transformation techniques. A first step in this direction is taken in [CLWW 94] where the static aspects of entity relationship diagrams are modelled by attributed graphs and the dynamic ones by attributed graph transformations. Moreover, this technique has been used to define dynamic abstract data types based on algebraic graph transformations [ELO 94/95] and has been applied to the problem of shipping software in [EB 94].

5 Theory and Practice of Software Development in the 90'ies

Following the considerations in the previous sections we summarize now the achievements in the 70'ies and 80'ies and discuss the contributions of TAPSOFT in the last decade. Finally we formulate our expectations for the future based on a discussion of driving forces in the 90'ies and the role of software development and formal methods in a true application context.

5.1 Achievements in the 70'ies and 80'ies

The relationship between theory and practice of software development in the 70'ies and 80'ies was not stable and appeared under different perspectives in a quite different light. In retrospective one can say that, no matter what the causes of the software crisis were, there was a definite lack of theory and conceptualization of the software development process. But it is at the same time clear that not all aspects of this process are accessible by formal methods. It is fruitless to debate which aspects are more important, those which can be addressed by a mathematically based theory or those which concern social, psychological or cognitive phenomena of the development process. With the advance of technology also the characteristics of the software crisis changed. It is therefore not surprising, that the cure for the deficiencies seen in the 70'ies did not equally apply in the 80'ies or even 90'ies. In fact, progress in theory and formal methods became effective in a pace slower than progress in hardware, in end user facilities and in means of communication, and at the same time pressure from the market and from applications for quick solutions grew strongly. As a consequence the distance between theory and formal methods on one side and practice of software development on the other widened and became increasingly harder to bridge.

On the other hand, the achievements in theory and formal methods, in the 70'ies and 80'ies had an essential influence on the practice in software development. The study of abstract data types in an algebraic framework is a good example. It influenced not only the features of new programming languages but also lead to the abstraction techniques of modularization and object-orientation which are key elements in todays software development and architectures. But also vice versa, the practical requirements had an essential influence on the theory. The development of specification techniques, for example, reflected the need for improved expressiveness, higher flexibility, integration of concepts and availability in the form of tools. It also turned out that abstract frameworks, like institutions or specification frames, were not only motivated from a purely theoretical point of view, but also from considerations of applicability of formalisms, namely when these formalisms had to be changed.

In summary one can say that there was a mutual influence in theory and practice of software development in the 70'ies and 80'ies. Major conceptual developments fall in the 70'ies, while the progress in theory and formal methods in the 80'ies is to a large extent due to elaboration and consolidation of results from the previous decade. The expectation of some people that formal methods could be applied directly and with considerable benefit in practical software development, however, turned out to be too optimistic. First, because the state of development of these methods had not even in the 80'ies reached a point where they could readily be used by the software writers in competitive environments of industry or application sites, and secondly, because failure or success of software development was dependent on many other factors, which relativised the role of formal methods in the opinion of those having responsibilities in the development process. On the other hand formal methods are of increasing importance for specification and verification of safety critical systems.

5.2 The Contribution of TAPSOFT

Looking back now at the series of TAPSOFT conferences and the effect this series had on theory and practice in software development, one may come to the following conclusion: TAPSOFT had started in a time where the pressure on science and academia was very high to contribute to ways out of the software crisis. This pressure was an international phenomenon and TAPSOFT'85 reflected this not only in its technical part but also in its panel discussions. The expectations expressed with this conference turned the open questions at that time into a program. The position statements of Jim Thatcher, Christiane Floyd, Maurice Nivat and Hartmut Ehrig, however, already express the difficulties to be faced. It turns out that, in retrospect, all four have made a good point and seen clear enough the reasons why a bridge between theory and practice in software development was hard to build and to maintain.

On the other hand, the idea of "bringing together researchers and practitioners within one conference to discuss each others problems" was still appealing and, in a sense, unavoidable if one wanted to address the relationship between theory and practice in software development. In the run of the series TAPSOFT has made a shift from "general software engineering" to "theoretical software engineering". The counterpart to CAAP as the theory component of the joint conference became a series of conferences which from a theoretical point of view were more applied, but from a practical point of view were still very theoretical. The choice of topics reflects the focus of research of the time proceeding. The contribution of TAPSOFT is therefore in line with the general progress in the late 80'ies and early 90'ies. But TAPSOFT is not a forum for the difficult topic of theory and true practice of software development and also it does not cover the full spectrum of formal methods. Instead, TAPSOFT is successful in combining true theory with applied topics.

5.3 Driving Forces in the 90'ies

The driving forces for software development in the 90'ies have changed again. The idea of reusability of software became critical and for reasons of productivity and cost effectiveness by far more challenging than initially expected:

Migration of existing software to other new hardware or software platforms, interoperability with existing and often as stand alone systems designed components, and systems re-engineering and code transformation are industrial and application demands with the potential of large economic losses or wins.

New systems development is today more like the configuration of existing components rather than design and implementation from scratch. The large amounts of available software products have lead to software life cycle phases which follow strategies completely different to those of the old 'waterfall'-model of the 70'ies and 80'ies.

Also the landscape of software applications has changed since the 80'ies:
Communication nets, the processing and transfer of data of different mediality, like text, image, film, video, sound, and the progress made with end user facilities have broadened the range of computer support in a revolutionary way. Functionality of systems can no longer be seen in isolation, but is tightly connected with processes of real life enterprises. Widespread or even world wide networks have introduced the concepts of autonomy of system components, of heterogenity and of openness in the most extreme sense. Software development in this context requires new techniques and organizational structures since systems borders can not be assumed to be fixed and no central authority can be presupposed which controls the consistency of the systems behaviours.

Another type of application has gained increasing importance. Safety critical applications with extreme requirements on timeliness, security, operability and correctness, namely in the field of embedded systems, appear more frequently and require assurances for which appropriate and reliable techniques are not yet ready at hand.

Now, after two decades of conceptual development an abundance of methods, techniques and tools has been created to support the various phases of software development. Their practical usability is proven in most cases but the questions of their use in an industrial context in daily routine and of their contribution to system quality are still open to a large extend. Even though the limitations in most of the underlying concepts were seen, the theoretical and conceptual achievements form a rich basis suitable for pragmatic approaches to build on. This is already visible in object-orientation which became the most prominent and successful concept of todays software and systems development. It grew out of the search for a flexible modularization technique and is appropriate to cope with dynamic topologies of interconnection, heterogenity and openness. It applies to several of the software life cycle phases and is the key for standardization of architectures, interfaces and behaviour.

Theory and practice today have further separated and the pressure for marketable solutions and routine application has increased. But again, it seems that new technology can not be thought without the contributions from theoretical and conceptual work. The question is therefore anew what formal methods can do in the future.

5.4 Software Development and Formal Methods in a True Application Context

Software development is not an isolated activity but is bound to certain intentions and usually embedded in a competitive environment. In one extreme the development of software is part of the production of a product to be marketed. In another extreme the development is part of the realization of a particular application in a real life enterprise. In both cases the development is strongly influenced by factors outside the life cycle model, but also in both cases the rationality of the development process is an important aspect which among others is crucial for the developments success. The following example is of the second type and shows well the relationship of theory and practice of software development in the beginning 90'ies , and the potentials and deficiencies of formal methods.

In 1989 the Project Group Medicine Informatics at the German Heart Institut and the Technical University in Berlin was established, headed by the cardiologist Eckart Fleck and by Bernd Mahr. The group, directed by Horst Hansen, developed a distributed information management system for the integration of heterogeneous networks, system components and patient related data and documents (called HDMS). The system was designed to be open and to evolve with increasing integration, new applications and extended use [FHMO 91]. Based on TCP / IP protocols the session layer and the application layer of the ISO reference model were implemented by communication libraries upon which the core of the management system, the so-called object machines with their object societies were placed. The HDMS object model was designed to meet the requirements of the medical environment and allowed for integration of heterogeneous software components and data, see [Ku 94]. It is conceptually based on type-theoretic considerations and implemented in ML. The prototype implementation was used as the management component which on the one side integrated the extremely heterogeneous and distributed complex infrastructure in the German Heart Institute, and on the other side served as a platform for the various medical applications including medical documentation, image processing and archiving. Two integrated medical application systems, an in-house information system and a net interconnecting cardiological practitioners and hospitals with the German Heart Institute were implemented and ran on the HDMS platform.

The described work was preceded by a thorough document-oriented analysis of the data and data flow in the clinic. Among the investigated 120 documents and clinical processes several were used in the implemented applications. These applications were later reimplemented on a more conventional data base-oriented platform, using DCE as a network operating system, and the HDMS development was no longer continued. The reasons for abandoning this line of development were manifold and can be explained by the time and the environment in which it took place. The more practical the system became the more it became a subject of economical and strategical considerations disregarding the conceptual advantages and potentials it has proven in its clinical routine use. The basic concepts of HDMS, however, have been used as a fundament for the next generation of integrated medical applications [Fl 94] developed by the PMI.

An interesting question is that of formal methods in the HDMS development. Most of the project group members were mathematicians and well-trained in formal methods. The systems implementation, however, was not preceded by a formal specification phase. It was mainly the pressure from the application site and from the German Telecom which funded the project, that not sufficient time was found to proceed that way. On the other hand the development was based on mathematically well-founded theoretical concepts and the functional language ML was used for its advanced type discipline, higher-order functions and modularization features.

But there is another activity which relates HDMS and formal methods: In 1992 the KORSO-project, funded by the German Minister of Research and Technology, has chosen HDMS for a case study on formal methods in correct software development (see [BJ 94], [CHL 94]). For this reason an abstract version of some of the medical applications were formulated, called HDMS-A, and then used to study the use of algebraic specification techniques and issues of correctness. The choice of HDMS-A focussed on some of the key documents of the patient record and their interconnection as well as their processing in the clinical procedures. In case studies these were specified and investigated. This mainly included the following activities (see [CHL 94]):

1. Based on the document-oriented analysis of the data and data flow in the clinic, a semi-formal state-oriented system definition of HDMS-A was given using the algebraic specification language SPECTRUM for the static data types and condition event nets for the dynamic processing.
2. Using the technique of "functional essence" by McMenamim and Palmer, the semi-formal description of data by entity relationship diagrams and of data flow by data flow diagrams was given.
3. Entity relationship diagrams and data flow diagrams were then transformed into a formal requirement specification in SPECTRUM, using axioms for integrity constraints and stream-processing functions for data flow diagrams [Nic 93].
4. Safety and security aspects have been added to the SPECTRUM specification using the PASCAL-like language of the Karlsruhe Interactive Verifier (KIV).
5. The integration of pre-existing components, which are not formally specified, was considered and two possible solutions have been proposed: Either by an event driven specification of the user interface in SPECTRUM, or by translating parts of the formally specified system as standard system calls of the non-specified system.

As a result of this case study one can conclude that means of formal specification are at hand to tackle in principle the problem of formally describe complex systems like HDMS, or at least components of it in some phases of the life cycle model. But the integration of specification techniques is still not available in a satisfactory way and the steps from semi-formal to formal specification still need careful consideration.

At the level of requirements these observations have motivated a second case study, called HDMS-AHL, executed at TU Berlin. Based on the SPECTRUM specification of data types and condition event nets of the dynamic processing an integrated specification was produced using algebraic high-level (AHL) nets and net transformations as considered in [Rei 91] and [EPR 94]. In [PRCE 93] the process of a heart catheter examination is specified and the steps from the state-oriented system specification to the formal requirements specification is modelled and it is shown how to apply structuring and transformation techniques, concurrency properties and compatibility results from the theory of AHL-nets [PER 93].

This case study demonstrates well the suitability of theoretical concepts and results, already in the early phases of the software life cycle model.

The experience around HDMS shows both advantages and difficulties of formal methods in software development and hints at ways of further research and at the same time teaches the limitations of formal methods in regard to the overall task of software development.

5.5 Expectations for the Future

In [CGR 93] a report is given on an international survey of industrial applications of formal methods, which was provided by the National Institute of Science and Technology (NIST) in the United States.

In the NIST survey twelve projects have been analysed using different formal specification techniques. The main conclusions are the following:

1. Formal methods are maturing, slowly but steadily from small case studies to systems of significant scale and importance.
2. The primary uses of formal methods, as shown in the case studies, are re-engineering existing systems.
3. Tool support, while necessary for the full industrialization process, has been found neither necessary nor sufficient for the successful application of formal methods in the case studies. But for the future a software development tool suite is needed.
4. The current educational base in the U.S. is weak in teaching formal methods for software development but several organizations have formal methods technology transfer efforts in progress. Added emphasis on developing notations more suitable to use by individuals not experts in formal methods or mathematical logic is required.
5. There is a clear need for improved integration of formal methods techniques with other software engineering practices and computing science trends, such as visualization, multimedia, object-oriented programming and CASE.

These observations fit very well to the analysis and report in this paper. They also hint at the future direction of research and development in formal methods. But the focus here is more closely on the use of formal specification methods and not on the wider topic of theory and practice in software development. It seems that additional requirements must be stated if this wider spectrum is taken into consideration:

Software configuration and reusability create new types of questions which, as it seems, are in principle tractable by theoretical considerations and formal models. The abstraction techniques of modularization and object-orientation seem suitable to apply. But the practical problems of software migration and re-engineering are major problems at the code level and are highly dependent on the system and application context so that techniques bound to particular specification formalisms do not suffice.

The trend to general concepts of modularization and encapsulation of behaviour in object-orientation is at the same time producing an uncontrolled variety of variants which differ only slightly, but have large effects in practice. Ways out of this diversity have to be found if the requirements of todays software development can be met.

In the light of open systems which today gain world wide influence, standardization is necessary in both, the way to look at the systems and the interfaces for systems interconnection. Powerful standardization organizations have developed recommendations and frameworks which, sometimes even formally, prescribe components, features and architectures of systems, like ISO, SGML or ODP. There is no sufficient theoretical treatment of these models which evolve at the borderline of established research communities but are widely considered in practical software development.

We hope that the TAPSOFT conferences in the next decade will be able to meet these expectations for the future.

6 References

[AA 82] Agerwala, T., Arwind, C.: Data Flow Systems. Computer 15,2 (1982)

[AR 87] E. Astesiano and G. Reggio: SMoLCS-driven concurrent calculi. In H. Ehrig, R. Kowalski, G. Levi, and U. Montanari, eds. Proc TAPSOFT'87, Vol 1, no 249, LNCS, 1987, pp. 169-201, Springer Verlag Berlin

[Ba 78] Backus, J.: Can programming be liberated from the von-Neumann style?, a functional style and its algebra of programs. Communication of the ACM 21,8 (1978)

[BEP 87] Blum, E.K.; Ehrig, H.; Parisi-Presicce, F.: Algebraic Specification of Modules and Their Basic Interconnections, JCSS 34,2/3 (1987), 293-339

[BJ 94] Broy, M., Jähnichen, S. (eds.): KORSO: Correct Software by Formal Methods Draft Version, Univ. Bremen 1994, to appear in Springer LNCS

[BKLOS 91] Bidoit, M., Kreowski, H.-J., Lescanne, P., Orejas, F., Sannella, D. (eds.): Algebraic System Specification and Development: A Survey and Annotated Bibliography, Springer LNCS 501, 1991

[BW 82] Broy, M.; Wirsing, M.: Partial abstract data types. Acta Informatica 18 (1982), 47-64

[CELMR 84] Corradini, A., Ehrig, H., Löwe, M., Montanari, U., Rossi, F.: An Event Structure Semantics for Safe Graph Grammars. Proc. PROCOMET'94, IFIP TC2 Working Conf., San Miniato 1994, 412-439

[CEW 93] Claßen, I., Ehrig, H., Wolz, D.: Algebraic Specification Techniques and Languages for Software Development - The ACT Approach. World Scientific Pub. 1993

[CGR 93] Craigen, D., Gerhart, S., Ralston, T.: An International Survey of Industrial Applications of Formal Methods, National Institute of Science and Technology, US Dept. of Commerce, NIST GCR 93/626, 1993

[CHL 94] Cornelius, F., Hußmann, H., Löwe, M.: The KORSO Case Study for Software Engineering with Formal Methods: A Medical Information System. In [BJ 94]

[CLWW 94] Claßen I., Löwe, M., Waßerroth, S., Wortmann, J.: Static and Dynamic Semantics of Entity-Relationship Models Based on Algebraic Methods. Proc. GI-Fachgespräche, Hamburg 1994

[Co 71] Cook, S.: The complexity of theorem-proving. Proc. 3rd ACM Symposium on Theory of Computing (1971)

[Col 70] Colmerauer, A.: Les systems-Q on une formalisme pour analyser et synthetise des phrases sur ordinateur. Internal Report 43, Department d'Informatique, Université de Montreal, Canada (1970)

[DFG+94] Didrich, K., Fett, A., Gerke, C., Grieskamp, W., Pepper, P.: OPAL: Design and Implementation of an Algebraic Programming Language. Proc. Conf. Progr. Lang. and Syst. Architecture 1994

[DHP 91] Dimitrovici, C., Hummert, U., Petrucci, L.: Composition and net properties of algebraic high-level nets. In Advances of Petri Nets, vol. 483 LNCS, Springer Berlin 1991

[DN 66] Dahl, O.-J., Nygaard, K.: Simula - An Algol-based simulation language. Communications of the ACM 9,9 (1966)

[DP 89] van Diepen, N., Partsch, H.: Some aspects of formalizing informal requirements. Proc. METEOR Workshop, Mierlo, 1989

[EB 94] Ehrig, H., Bardohl, R.: Specification Techniques Using Dynamic Abstract Data Types and Application to Shipping Software. Proc. Int. Workshop on Advanced in Software Technology, Shanghai Workshop 1994

[EBCO 91] Ehrig, H., Baldamus, M., Cornelius, F., Orejas, F.: Theory of Algebraic Module Specifications Including Behavioural Semantics, Constraints and Aspects of Generalized Morphisms. Proc. 2nd AMAST Conf., Iowa (U.S.A.) 1991

[EE 94] Ehrig, H., Engels, G.: Towards a Module Concept for Graph Transformation Systems: The Software Engineering Perspective. Proc. Graph Grammar Workshop, Mallorca 1994, to appear

[EG 94] Ehrig, H., Große-Rhode, M.: Functorial Theory of Parameterized Specifications in a General Specification Framework, accepted for TCS 1994

[EHKP 91] Ehrig, H., A. Habel, H.-J. Kreowski, F. Parisi-Presicce: From Graph Grammars to High-Level Replacement Systems, Proc. 4th Int. Workshop on Graph Grammars and Application to Computer Science, Springer LNCS 532 (1991) pp. 269-291

[Ehr 79] Ehrig, H.: Introduction to the algebraic theory of graph grammars (A Survey) in: Graph Grammars and Their Application to Computer Science and Biology, Springer LNCS 73, (1979), 1-69

[Ehr 85] Ehrig, H.: Introduction. Springer LNCS 185 (1985), 1-3

[ELO 94/95] Ehrig, H., Löwe, M., Orejas, F.: Dynamic Abstract Data Types Based on Algebraic Graph Transformations. Proc. ADT-COMPASS Workshop 1994, to appear in Springer LNCS 1995

[EM 85] Ehrig, H.; Mahr, B.: Fundamentals of Algebraic Specification 1. Equations and Initial Semantics. EATCS Monographs on Theoretical Computer Science, Vol. 6, Springer (1985)

[EM 90] Ehrig, H.; Mahr, B.: Fundamentals of Algebraic Specification 2. Module Specifications and Constraints. EATCS Monographs on Theoretical Computer Science, Vol. 21, Springer-Verlag (1990)

[EO 94] Ehrig, H., Orejas, F.: Dynamic Abstract Data Types: An Informal Proposal. Bull. EATCS 53 (1994), 162-169

[EPR 94] Ehrig, H., Padberg, J., Ribeiro, L.: Algebraic High-Level Nets: Petri nets revisited. Springer LNCS 785 (1994), 188-206

[Fey 88] Fey, W.: Pragmatics, Concepts, Syntax, Semantics, and Correctness Notions of ACT TWO: An Algebraic Module Specification and Interconnection Language, Diss. TU Berlin, 1988

[FGGP] Fett, A., Gierke, C., Grieskamp, W., Pepper, P.: Algebraic Programming in OPAL, Bull. EATCS 50 (1993), 171-181

[FHMO 91] Fleck, E., Hansen, H., Mahr, B., Oswald, H.: Systementwicklung für die Integration und Kommunikation von Patientendaten und -dokumenten. Forschungsbericht 02-91, PMI am DHZB, 1991

[Fl 94] Fleck, E.(ed.): Open Systems in Medicine, IOS Press, 1994

[Flo 85] Floyd, Ch.: Introduction On the Relevance of Formal Methods to Software Development, Springer LNCS 186 (1986), 1-11

[GB 84] Goguen, J.A.; Burstall, R.M.: Introducing institutions. Proc. Logics of Programming Workshop, Carnegie-Mellon. LNCS 164, Springer (1984), 221-256

[GG 89] Garland, S.J., Guttag, J.V.: An overview of LP, the Larch Prover. Proc. 3rd Conf. on Rewriting Techniques and Applications, Chapel Hill, North Carolina, Springer LNCS 355, 137-151 (1989)

[GHM 87] Geser, A., Hußmann, H., Mueck, A.: A compiler for a class of conditional rewrite systems. Proc. Int. Workshop on Conditional Term Rewriting, Orsay. Springer LNCS 308, 84-90 (1987)

[GM 87] Goguen, J. A., Meseguer, J.: Models and Equality for Logic Programming, Springer LNCS 250 (1987), 1-22

[GR 83] Goldberg, A., Robson, D.: Smalltalk 80: The language and its implementation. Addison-Wesley (1983)

[GTW 76] Goguen, J.A.; Thatcher, J.W.; Wagner, E.G.: An initial algebra approach to the specification, correctness and implementation of abstract data types. IBM Research Report RC 6487, 1976. Also: Current Trends in Programming Methodology IV: Data Structuring (R. Yeh, ed.), Prentice Hall (1978), 80-144

[Ho 72] Hoare, C.A.R.: Proof of correctness of data representation. Acta Informatica 1 (1972)

[Ho 78] Hoare, C.A.R.: Communicating sequential processes. Communications of the ACM 21,8 (1978)

[Hod 94] Hodges, W.: The Meaning of Specifications I: Domains and initial models, accepted for TCS 1994

[Hum 89] Hummert, U.: Algebraische High-Level Netze. PhD thesis, TU Berlin, Dept. of Comp. Sci., 1989

[Ken 87] Kennaway, R.: On "on graph rewriting", TCS 52 (1987), 37-58

[Ko 79] Kowalski, R.: Logic for problem solving. North Holland (1979)

[Kri 90] Krieg-Brückner, B.: PROgram development by SPECification and TRAnsformation. Technique et Science Informatiques. Special Issue on Advanced Software Engineering in ESPRIT (1990)

[Ku 94] Kutsche, R.: An Application-Oriented Object Model and Concepts of its Formal Foundation, PhD Thesis, TU Berlin, 1994

[LEFJ 91] Löwe, M., Ehrig, H., Fey, W., Jacobs, D.: On the Relationship Between Algebraic Module Specifications and Program Modules, Springer LNCS 494 (1991), 83-98

[LKW 93] Löwe, M., Korff, M., Wagner, A.: An Algebraic Framework for the Transformation of Attributed Graphs. In M.R. Sleep et. al. eds. Term Graph Rewriting: Theory and Practice, Wiley 1993, 185-199

[LOTOS 88] Brinksma, E.(ed.): Information processing systems - open systems interconnection. LOTOS: a formal description technique based on the temporal ordering of observational behaviour, International Standard, ISO 8807 (1988)

[Löw 93] Löwe, M.: An Algebraic Approach to Single-Pushout Graph Transformations. TCS 109 (1993), 181-224

[Ma 93] Mahr, B.: Applications of Type Theory. In Proc. of TAPSOFT'93, LNCS 668, pp. 343-355, Springer Verlag, 1993

[Mil 80] Milner, R.: A Calculus of Communicating Systems. Springer LNCS Vol. 92 (1980)

[MM 82/84] Mahr, B.; Makowski, J.A.: Characterizing specification languages which admit initial semantics. Technion Techn. Report 232, Haifa 1982, and TCS 31 (1984), 49-59

[MM 94] Marti-Oliet, N., Meseguer, J.: General Logics and Logical Frameworks. In: What is a Logical System? (D.M. Gabbay ed.), Oxford University Press, 1994

[Mos 89] Mosses, P.D.: Unified Algebras and Institutions. LICS'89, Proc. 4th Ann. Symp. on Logic in Comp. Sci., IEEE, 1989, 304-312

[MTW 88] Möller, B., Tarlecki, A., Wirsing, M.: Algebraic specifications of reachable higher-order algebras. Recent Trends in Data Type Specification, Selected Papers from the 5th Workshop on Specification of Abstract Data Types, Gullane, Scotland. Springer LNCS 332, 154-169 (1988)

[Nic 93] Nickel, F.: Ablaufspezifikation durch Datenflußmodellierung und stromverarbeitende Funktionen, Techn. Report TUM-9334, TU München 1993

[Pa 72] Parnas, D.C.: A technique for software module specification with examples. Communications of the ACM 15,5 (1972). On the criteria to be used in decomposing systems into modules. Communications of the ACM 15,12 (1972)

[PER 93] Padberg, J., Ehrig, H., Ribeiro, L.: Algebraic high-level net-transformation systems. Techn. Report No. 93-12, TU Berlin, 1993; revised version in MSCS

[PRCE 93] Padberg, J., Ribeiro, L., Cornelius, F., Ehrig, H.: Formal Requirements Analysis Using Algebraic High-Level Nets and Transformations, Techn. Report TU Berlin No. 93-34 (1993)

[PW 94] Pepper, P., Wirsing, M. (eds.): KORSO: A Methodology for the Development of Correct Software, in [BJ 94]

[Rao 84] Raoult, J.C.: On Graph Rewriting. TCS 32 (1984), 1-24

[Rei 81] Reichel, H.: Behavioural equivalence - a unifying concept for initial and final specification methods. In Proc. 3rd Hungarian Comp. Sci. Conf., Budapest, pp. 27-39, 1981

[Rei 91] Reisig, W.: Petri nets and algebraic specifications. TCS 80:1-34, 1991

[St 69] Strassen, V.: Gaussian elimination is not optimal. Numerische Mathematik 13 (1969)

[ST 86] Sannella, D.T.; Tarlecki, A.: Extended ML: an institution-independent framework for formal program development. Proc. Workshop on Category Theory and Comp. Programming, Guildford. LNCS 240, Springer (1986), 364-389

[ST 87] Sannella, D.T.; Tarlecki, A.: Toward formal development of programs from algebraic specifications: implementations revisited. Extended abstract in: Proc. Joint Conf. on Theory and Practice of Software Development, Pisa, LNCS 249, Springer (1987), 96-110; full version to appear in Acta Informatica

[Vau 87] Vautherin, J.: Parallel specification with coloured Petri nets and algebraic data types. In Proc. of the 7th Europ. Workshop on Appl. and Theory of Petri Nets, 5-23, Oxford, 1987

Theory and Practice of Software Development
- Stages in a Debate -

Christiane Floyd

Department of Computer Science
University of Hamburg
Vogt-Kölln-Straße 30, 22527 Hamburg
e-mail: floyd@informatik.uni-hamburg.de

Abstract. Starting from the experience gained in organizing TAPSOFT'85, the paper discusses the place of formal methods in software development. It distinguishes two notions of theory: the mathematical science of computation and the treatment of computing as a human activity. An adequate software theory needs to take both theoretical perspectives into account. Therefore, the paper explores the borderline of formalization and human activity in several directions: concerning the role and scope of formalized procedures, the relation between formal models and situated use, the process of learning in software development and the ways computer programs become effective in use. Fundamental assumptions underlying formal methods and their relation to emancipatory approaches such as participatory design are discussed. The paper closes with calling for a dialogical framework for further pursuing these questions.

1 Starting a dialogue in 1985

As a co-organizer of the original TAPSOFT conference held at the Technical University of Berlin in March 1985, I have been invited to make a contribution to the tenth anniversary of the ensuing movement. So, let me start by congratulating all those who have participated in the TAPSOFT effort during the past decade, for having achieved a highly successful series of scientific events. And I hope, that it will continue in the future.

Assessing the success of my own involvement in TAPSOFT is a little more difficult. When Hartmut Ehrig originally approached me about co-organizing a conference on formal methods, he wanted me to bring in the practice perspective - the "P". Though we probably did not have the same notion of "P" in mind, I agreed and suggested to discuss the *relevance of formal methods* in software development. And he, in turn, agreed to that. Thus, we created a field of tension between two scientific communities, one focussing on formal approaches and their foundations, and the other reflecting the role of formal approaches in practice, and we set the stage for a controversial discussion. The resulting conference organization is explained in detail in the contribution by Ehrig and Mahr in this volume [EhM 95]. It comprised three parts: two colloquia and an advanced seminar.

However, the discussion we planned for did not actually come about. In the context of the individual colloquia, the members of each community discussed largely among themselves. In the plenary sessions, there were impressive talks from both sides, but no dialogue. My role as a hostess kept me from bringing in a strong position myself. In retrospect I believe, I may have been the only one to consider this dialogue an essential element of TAPSOFT. I also arranged an evening discussion on responsibility. This, I believe, was an important event for quite a few people who were able to voice and exchange their human concerns. The discussion there was very lively, but it took place outside the scientific program.

As soon as the conference organization moved from Berlin to Pisa, the outlook has changed. Since then, I have come to think of the TAPSOFT conferences simply as of a platform for promoting formal methods.

Now I am happy to see that Peter Mosses wishes to take up the discussion again. When inviting me, he encouraged me to say something about my work on software development and reality construction. He also expressed his hope that I might promote an exchange between the formal methods group and the system development group at the University of Aarhus, both very prominent in the international discussion in their respective fields of interest. Therefore, I will focus here on the limits and borderlines of formalization. I will not concentrate on the technical issues in programming, but on the place of formalization in design.

Looking back at TAPSOFT'85 once more, I would like to bring out two reasons for the lack of actual discussion. On one hand, it is a question of personal motivation and of an appropriate *style of interaction*. TAPSOFT was a very friendly gathering, but the conference took place at a time, when controversies on formalization (both oral and written) tended to be put forth in a hostile and arrogant manner on both sides. This experience may have made the participants unwilling to speak up and carry on an open dispute in a large group. If we want dialogue, we need to cultivate an attitude of mutual respect.

Even more important, however, in my opinion, was the absence of a *common level of reference* that would allow the two parties to engage in a fruitful exchange. I remember taking part in a panel discussion where I suggested that we needed a theory of the human processes involved in software development. This was met with strong rebuke by another panel member from the formalist community - he took it entirely for granted that "theory" must refer to mathematical theory and thus misunderstood completely what I tried to say.

Between 1985 and 1995, some basic elements of the theory I was looking for have been formulated. Therefore, I have now taken up the challenge to make a dialogical contribution to TAPSOFT'95.

In doing so, it seems natural to start from the position I presented shortly after TAPSOFT'85 at the conference on *Development and Use of Computer-based Systems and Tools - in the Context of Democratization of Work* held at the University of Aarhus in August 1985, leading to the publication of [BEK 87]. This conference was also a highly successful scientific event and thus there is another ten years' anniversary I wish to commemorate here.

The Aarhus 85 conference was like a scientific watershed in my life. On one hand, it gave me the opportunity to present a theoretical basis for my own work in software engineering. The positive reaction to this greatly encouraged me to delve into studying the epistemological foundations of software development. This became my predominant area of research for several years. On the other hand, it was one of the first events to make explicit that there was an emerging scientific community dealing with human and social issues in computing. Thus, the role of this conference in promoting encounters and forming alliances was similar to that of TAPSOFT, only for a different group.

At this conference, I also became acquainted with the work on *model monopoly* and *dialogue* by Stein Bråten [Brå 73], which has been very helpful to me ever since. In the context of the present paper, I would like to apply his ideas to the interaction between two theoretical paradigms dealing with software development. In 1985, the *mathematical science of computation* was already well under way, while only fragmentary attempts for understanding *computing as a human activity* had been published (cf. section 2).

Thus, the formalist community held what Bråten calls a model monopoly on software theory. If, in a situation of model monopoly, two partners engage in a dialogue, this cannot be symmetric, since one actor is *model-strong*, while the other is *model-weak*. The model-weak actor has to try to express his or her concerns in the terms proposed by the model-strong actor. This can only lead to further strengthening the position of the model-strong actor. This is well in keeping with my impressions from TAPSOFT and other attempts at discussion at that time. The formalist community wanted to change practice by introducing formal approaches. They did not see the need to understand practice in its own right. On the other side, the practice-oriented community seemed pre-occupied with fighting off formal approaches as though they were a threat. But they were not in a position to offer an alternative.

What is needed to resolve the model monopoly is to formulate an alternative position and allow the two to interact. The aim of the present paper is to sketch such a platform for dialogue about theory and practice of software development, as seen from my side.

Another prerequisite for dialogue is to clarify our mutual positions. I would like to illustrate this by reference to the specific debate about formal methods. The success story reported by Ehrig and Mahr in [EhM 95] is impressive. But it smoothes out the original controversy.

At the time of TAPSOFT, the idea put forth by the formalist community was that a complete and strictly formal (for example, algebraic) specification should be prepared beforehand as a basis for implementation. This was considered necessary, in keeping with the idea of providing formal semantics for the program.

I suppose that from the formalist point of view the main point of interest here is the use of formal concepts in dealing with a practical problem. But from the human activity point of view, a formalized procedure is implied, prescribing at what time and for what purposes these concepts are supposed to be worked with in software development projects. When and how this can or must be done, makes all the difference. In my argumentation, I never opposed formal concepts as such, but I spent a lot of energy objecting to what I still consider senseless manners of proceeding in using them.

Instead, I argued for partial formalization, for the flexible, semi-formal use of formal concepts [Flo 85]. Reading [EhM 95], it is not entirely clear to me any more, what the proponents now mean by using formal methods in software development. In particular, the success reported from the practical project relies on semi-formal use of formal approaches - exactly along the lines that I have advocated and practiced in 1985. The paper shows that many of the original claims associated with formal methods could not be fulfilled. Thus, the success reported rests on *restating more realistic claims* with respect to formal methods and on subsuming large parts of basic software engineering and programming languages research into the TAPSOFT movement.

So, what are we talking about? What was really the part contributed by strictly formal methods to the success reported? And why are the objections raised by critics like myself not quoted as having been confirmed by practical experience?

Once an alternative model is available, we have the conditions for a symmetric dialogue - at least in principle. In practice, conducting such a dialogue depends on the willingness of the participants. On creating and maintaining environments and on allocating resources for allowing it to take place. I believe that this task is ahead of the computer science community as a whole now and in the near future.

2 Two notions of theory about computing

In my paper *Outline of a Paradigm Change in Software Engineering* in [Flo 87], I contrast two perspectives on software development:

- The *product-oriented perspective* regards software as a product standing on its own, consisting of a set of programs and related defining texts.
- The *process-oriented perspective*, on the other hand, views software in connection with human learning, work and communication, taking place in an evolving world with changing needs.

The notion of "product" is used in a very general sense here. It refers to any tangible result of human activity, while the notion of "process" denotes the unfolding activity in the situation. Bringing out these complementary perspectives is helpful for understanding many spheres of human activity. For most contexts of interest in software development, the relevant products are *formal artifacts,* such as programs or defining documents. Processes are carried out by individuals working on their own or, more often, by groups of developers and users and other people responsible for embedding these artifacts in *human context.*

The two perspectives can be expressed concretely for concepts such as programs, quality and method. In any software development project both the product- and the process-oriented perspectives need to be adopted and reconciled. I criticize the established software engineering tradition for focussing almost exclusively on the product-oriented perspective and declaring a concern with the process-oriented perspective to be outside the realm of computer science. I suggest that a shift of emphasis is needed, giving greater priority to the process-oriented perspective.

Taking these two perspectives seriously, we are also lead to reexamine the very idea of "theory and practice of software development". It is no longer adequate to distinguish "formal theory" from "informal practice" to which this theory is applied, we are now faced with two different notions of theory and their respective relation to practice.

In what follows, I shall address three levels:

- software development as a (collection of) human process(es) giving rise to formal artifacts and their embedding in human contexts,
- the theoretical frameworks needed for dealing with these aspects, and their potential interleavement,
- the nature of the discipline concerned with software development in computer science, a question which belongs to the philosophy of science.

In investigating the relation of theory and practice, I will draw extensively on a very interesting book [CFR 93] on program verification, whose aim is to make a contribution to the philosophy of computer science. Colburn, one of the editors, shows in his introduction [CFR 93, p.7], how for several sciences the philosophy of that science centers around a basic reductionist question. For example in biology, the controversy between vitalism and mechanism deals with the question, whether or not life can be explained in terms of inorganic processes. Colburn suggests: *Can Computer Science be reduced to a branch of mathematics?* as the basic reductionist question for our discipline. The book contains an excellent selection of articles from the proponents of the mathematical paradigm on one hand, and from some of the most prominent critics on the other. I have the pleasure that [Flo 87] is also included.

The mathematical is traced back to John McCarthy. In his seminal paper *Towards a mathematical science of computation*, [McC 63], he asks "What are the entities with which computer science deals?" and gives the answer "These are problems, procedures, data spaces, programs representing procedures in particular programming languages, and computers". While some of these entities are expressed in terms that nowadays are no longer in use, the formal research programme initiated by McCarthy, and continued by Floyd, Hoare, Dijkstra and so many other great proponents stayed on the course that was laid out here.

It is interesting to look at the collection of entities (latin for "beings") a little closer. What kind of an entity is a problem? What is its ontological status? Does it have a way of existing on its own? Whose problem is it and who decides on the options for solutions? Surely, the problems considered here must have been posed by someone and passed on in the community. Similarly for procedures: can we consider a procedure as an entity without referring to the class of human activities it is meant to standardize? On the other hand, what kind of entity is a computer here? Can we treat it as a formal automaton with no concern for its technical counterpart? It is clear that the mathematical science proposed by McCarthy should treat these entities as formal objects with no reference to their human and technical context. And it does. But all of these entities, even the elusive problems, are *artifacts*, resulting from human activity and used within human activity.

So, the mathematical paradigm stands for the product-oriented theory perspective about software. In principle, no way of organizing human activity is associated with the mathematical paradigm. But in practice, many authors rely on recommending predefined processes such as top-down development. Thus product-formalization and process-formalization tend to be combined. I shall denote this combination as formal methods approach for the time being, but eventually argue for a separation of these two aspects.

In contrast, I would like to denote the process-oriented theory perspective by *computing: a human activity*, the title chosen by Peter Naur for his recent book [Nau 92], which contains a collection of his articles written in the course of the past three decades. It starts with "The Place of Programming in a World of Problems, Tools and People" [Nau 92, pp. 1-8], published in 1965. Here, we find some of McCarthy's entities again - but what a shift of emphasis. It is not a science about formal objects any more, but about the activity of programming considered in its context, and about problems seen in connection with people on one hand and with tools on the other. Naur applied this view both to the use of computers in human activity and to the activity of software development itself. Thus, amongst other issues, he is concerned with the place of formalization in human insight. He is also the most-featured author in Colburn et al., since he has published articles both with and as a critic of the mathematical paradigm.

The two notions of theory suggested here differ in many ways, and yet they are closely related:

- They are inherently complementary, one cannot be treated without implying the basis for the other. This is exemplified in the very titles. When arguing for a mathematical science, McCarthy needs to refer to the human activity "computation", and conversely, when denoting the human activity of interest, Naur calls on the nucleus of mathematical science, "computing".
- Their historical development is quite different. McCarthy's article started a research programme, the mathematical paradigm was taken up and pursued hotly by many researchers from the 1960s onwards and came to full bloom in the seventies and eighties. The resulting theory has a strong coherence, enabling the community to take a common scientific stand. By contrast, the theory about computing as a human activity was slow in starting. For a long time, it manifested itself in critical positions formulated by individuals in different contexts, and only started gaining momentum in the mid-eighties. There is no central theme here, but a network of individual and related views.
- The relation of these notions of theory to the practice of computing is different. While the formal theory of computing deals with an ideal practice, the human activity approach rests on actual practical experience in developing and using formal artifacts in human contexts. Thus, the nature of one is prescriptive and that of the other reflective.
- The foundations of these theories are different: one rests on formal logic and mathematics, while the other rests on approaches in the humanities for understanding human learning and communication, individual and cooperative work.

The gist of my contribution is that an adequate treatment of software development must comprise both theoretical perspectives. Thus, I take a stand on Colburn's reductionist question. In what follows, I shall not argue for intermingling these perspectives into one common super-theory, but for *creating a dialogical framework*, taking both perspectives into account. Such a framework has to allow for the formal properties of software on one hand and for the human context of their development and use on the other. I will refer to such a framework as *software theory*. This conversational use of the term theory is in keeping with the ideas proposed in Germany under the name "Theorie der Informatik" [CNPRSSS 92].

3 Basic questions for a software theory

In this and the following sections, I shall take you on something like a guided tour through the world of human activities associated with computing. We shall concern ourselves with the *stuff that software is made of*, in particular with the borderlines between the formal and the informal, the static and the dynamic, the controlled and the unfolding aspects of it.

In order to examine these borderlines, we need to address questions such as: How does software emerge? How is it embedded in human contexts? What can and should be formalized? How do we decide what to model? How do we relate the model to reality? How are operational models effective? How do we judge software quality? How should humans interact with computers? Let me start by pointing out that when thinking in this way about software we always imply assumptions on the nature of human thinking, on the being of formal objects and on desirable ways of handling human affairs. In doing so, whether or not we admit it, we draw on epistemology, ontology and ethics. Moreover, we also refer to ourselves and to our professional role. To the claims we make about computing in society. To the way we deal with power, hierarchy and control.

Some of the basic works addressing these questions from various angles have appeared since the mid-eighties.

Many of these contributions come from Scandinavian countries, including Naur's work which has already been mentioned. On the basis of a study of Scandinavian approaches [FMRSW 89] I have come to the conclusion that the focus of computer science in the Scandinavian countries has been different from the beginning. It is not primarily concerned with technical innovation and formal artifacts as such, but with their explicit orientation to human use. It is also characterized by cooperation between researchers working in different fields.

This is evidenced by Simula, for example, a language that had a profound influence on programming methodology, but at the same time addressed itself towards a particular class of applications. Simula was developed by Ole Johan Dahl and Kristen Nygaard, a member of the formalist community and an application-oriented scientist. As we know, Simula created the technical basis for object-orientation and for user-oriented modelling. Also, the connection between computing and work design was already studied in the early 1960s in Norway - much earlier than anywhere else.

The ideas and the technology developed by scientists in the generation of Naur, Dahl and Nygaard had a profound influence on the younger scientists in Scandinavia, as they were passed on through education. Most Scandinavians I know refer to their programming practice with Simula sooner or later, when they try to explain the way they think. The borderline between what is in and outside of computer science becomes quite different when taking this approach.

Kristen Nygaard was also the pioneer in studying the social nature of software development, pointing out *perspectivity* as fundamental in what we consider relevant for modelling and programming [Nyg 86]. And he is responsible for founding a whole school of "systems development" in Oslo and here in Aarhus which has made many important contributions to studying the human activity of computing. For example, Susanne Bødker gave an excellent theoretical treatment of human computer interface [Bød 87]. Pelle Ehn came up with basic guidelines for designing computer based artifacts for supporting human work [Ehn 88]. Bo Dahlbom and Lars Mathiassen treated computers in context in philosophical terms [DM 93]. And so on.

By now, these approaches have acquired a great significance in the international discussion. "A Scandinavian Challenge" was the subtitle chosen by [BEK 87], the book resulting from the Aarhus conference in 1985. This challenge has been taken up by many researchers elsewhere, since meaningful ways of applying information technology are now a dominant concern. For the rest of us working in this field, it is sometimes a bit strange to be considered part of the "Scandinavian school".

In the United States, the discussion centered along the philosophical assumptions embodied in computer science. While the early classic Dreyfus mainly focussed on artificial intelligence, Winograd and Flores set the stage with [WF 86], their well-known book on philosophical foundations for design. From an anthropological point of view, Lucy Suchman showed in [Suc 87] how to think about software use in terms of situated action.

My own project was to study the epistemological foundations of software development. In cooperation with a number of colleagues in Germany, I arranged a small interdisciplinary workshop held in September 1988 under the name of *Software Development and Reality Construction.* This suggestive phrase was used to indicate a range of philosophical questions pertaining to the practice of software development and use. The participants were scientists from several fields in computer science and from other disciplines, such as linguistics, philosophy, psychology and sociology. The resulting book [FZBKS 92] discusses the nature of computer science as a scientific discipline and the theoretical foundations and systemic practice required for human-oriented system design. It comprises a series of contributions by different authors, arranged so as to form a coherent whole.

As I pointed out in [Flo 92], there is a *Leitmotiv* underlying this whole line of research: How do we understand people in relation to computers? This comes up in different ways: Are human beings in their cognitive faculties similar to computers? Can computers, in principle, be likened to human beings? How should computers be allowed to interfere with human affairs?

Computer science has inherited fundamental views equating humans with computers. Even in formulating his basic theoretical concepts, Turing explained the functioning of his universal machine by likening it to a man proceeding according to rules. The overall social context of the emerging computer science was taylorism as a way of rationalizing and optimizing human work by rules, so that groups performing work would behave like machines. A very interesting analysis of the interplay of the theoretical basis of computer science and the socio-cultural developments in the 1920s and 1930s is given in [Hei 93].

While equating humans and computers is explicit in artificial intelligence, it is also implied by many approaches in software engineering and human-computer interface, whenever we rely solely on rule-based human thinking and predictable functional behaviour. There is a direct connection between these questions and formalization, since what can be formalized can also be mechanized. Formalizing and automating human activity is inherent in computing.

To characterize the specific way in which formalization occurs in computing, I shall use the term *operational form*. By this, I mean an abstract characterization of the informational basis and the functional content of defined human activity. Note that this terminology avoids reducing human activity to operational form. It merely aims at characterizing that aspect of human activity that is amenable to being formalized and automated. The practice of computing, in particular software development, always involves bringing out and automating operational form. This presumes routine in human activity and a modelling process in which this routine is explicitly defined. It rests on characterizing the objects we work with by informational attributes and our dealing with them as manipulation of these attributes.

A program executed on a computer can then be seen as *auto-operational form*. What is of basic interest to the theory I have in mind, is how operational form, and in particular, auto-operational form, relates to situated human activity.

My aim in the following sections is to sketch different orientations for research in a dialogical framework drawing on both the formalist and the human activity oriented theoretical perspectives. I will support my arguments by some of the positions taken by different authors mentioned in this section. Rather than discussing their individual contributions one by one, I would like to group them according to the issues involved.

4 The role and scope of formalized procedures

Computing invariably has to do with identifying and standardizing discrete operational steps and grouping them into complex formalized procedures, which give rise to algorithmic structures to be executed on a computer.

Thus, the basic way of thinking in our discipline involves several instances:

- an instance to *set up rules*: a human, who makes or identifies rules (for example the software developer complying with the wishes of the customer, the method developer prescribing how to proceed in software development and so on),
- an instance to *impose rules*, often a non-human agent (the computer controlling work processes or technical systems), and
- an instance to *carry out rules*, either human or technical.

It is difficult to write about these instances without equating people and computers, since we have to choose between "which" and "who". This seemingly linguistic triviality reflects the fact that the mutual "rights" of these instances depend entirely on our views of their interaction and thus on decisions taken in systems design. There is, however, little concern in computer science with how to embed formalized procedures in human activity.

Imposing automated formalized procedures leads to basic questions, since the computer brings about a new quality. While in general, the rules imposed on human activity have to be sufficiently clear and unambiguous for humans to follow, here they must be formulated in machine-interpretable terms. While humans interpret rules as they apply to the needs of the specific situation, programs always operate according to their predefined model. And while humans tend to associate rules with exceptions, computers do not.

As was first pointed out by Lehman in [Leh 80], automating a sphere of human activity is not a problem that can be specified in formal terms, thus the need to distinguish between "specification-based" S-programs and "embedded" E-programs. One important borderline to explore in software theory is the scope and the limits of process formalization and to develop criteria for design choices here. This is connected with the identification and the connection between the individual operation steps to be automated, with the possibility for humans to interfere and with the organization of computer-supported work. We find these questions arising both in the process of software development, and in concepts for software application.

Thus the instance setting up the rules must have a mental picture of the class of possible situations and a sufficiently rich understanding to allow for any potentially relevant activity at any time. There are two basic options for embedding formalized procedures in the richness of human situations. One is to rely on a formal model of the class of use situations, and to automate a set of rules for how to proceed according to this model. The other is to leave the use context open and to offer a repertoire of resources to use in self-organizing work. In this way, I shall differentiate between "centralized control" and "situated coordination" of cooperative work.

The choice between these options arises at many levels in computing. For example: how do we view the embedding of computers in work processes? The design of human-computer interfaces? The automation of the software development process with CASE tools? Or the application of formal methods in software development?

Because of their basic importance for computers in connection with work design, many authors have addressed these questions. For example, I have implicitly referred to Lucy Suchman's discussion in [Suc 87] just now: rather than as rule systems to be followed, she suggests that plans could be seen as *resources* to be relied on. Related is Reinhard Keil-Slawik's design guideline: *avoid all unnecessary sequencing* of predefined work steps in [K-S 92]. The common theme here is that formalized procedures should not be imposed, but be available for flexible use in cooperative work.

Closely connected are the perspectives and metaphors used in design, ranging from *machine*, to *tool*, *media* and so on. An excellent overview has been given by Susanne Maaß and Horst Oberquelle [MO 92]. They show, how different perspectives embody views on how humans should interact with computers. Examples of specific metaphors include the *tools and materials metaphor* first elaborated by Reinhard Budde and Heinz

Züllighoven in [BZ 92], and the *subject-oriented approach to information systems* put forth by Markku Nurminen [Nur 92]. I suggest, we should investigate how formal approaches can be combined with using such metaphors.

5 Formal models in situated use

Since all operational form rests on reductionist models of entities carrying informational attributes, another borderline to explore is the relation of formal models to reality. This involves various levels: How do we decide which aspects are relevant for being included into a model? How do our modelling concepts shape how we think about the world? What kind of being do we ascribe to modelled entities? What claims do we associate with models? How are different models connected? How do models become operational in use?

The underlying assumptions of modelling can be expressed with reference to various philosophical schools dealing with ontology and epistemology. This is particularly relevant in connection with global data models in enterprises. It also has direct bearings to how computer based systems are used to control technical and social processes.

Heinz Klein and Kalle Lyytinen address in [KL 92] the *social process of model building*, in particular data modelling in organizations as one of negotiation. Data models appear like laws, codifying the informational work basis in a specific manner. Modelling involves making choices. It also involves the power and authorization for making these choices. Thus, it is *essential who participates* in the processes leading to formal models.

Naur gives a careful account of what he calls the mystique of formal models [Nau 92, pp. 468-479]. He addresses specifically the relation between what is to be modelled, the *modellee*, the *concepts used for modelling* and the *modelling process.*

Starting from a different angle, Brian Cantwell Smith discusses *the relevance of formal models for use* in his thoughtful paper on the limits of correctness in computers [Smi 85]. He contrasts formal correctness (i.e. logical consistency) with suitability or adequacy in the situation. Since formal approaches do not help us with suitability, the connection between the model and its use remains unresolved. Only humans can take the responsibility for bridging the gap.

A basic distinction made by several authors is between modelling *structure and behaviour as such*, and modelling *with a view to human use*. In the former case we adopt the stand that attributes for formal entities can be described in a context-free manner, while in the latter, the entities to be modelled are perceived in the context of the work to be performed with them. If we want to use models, like plans, as resources in situated activity, this requires an understanding of their relation to use.

Therefore, Michaela Reisin understands a *reference theory* in software development as centering around the *use-meaning* of software. The use-meaning must be anticipated in cooperative design processes involving developers and users [Rei 92]. Similarly, Budde and Züllighoven regard programs as *things to use* and formulate their object-oriented concepts in terms of how things are used in work processes [BZ 92]. Use-oriented modelling rests on understanding the human activity to be supported.

We can identify various semantic dimensions of modelling in software development. This requires a holistic approach, relying on different notions of semantics. That is, we need to concern ourselves with *individuals forming personal meaning*, with *groups relying on conventional meaning* in their respective technical language, and with the relation of these two *to the formal meaning* specified for the attributes and operations in formal models and implemented in programs. Since embedded programs dominate in practice, we are faced with the emergence of insights on software issues on the part of the people involved as constitutive for the formal artifacts to be developed.

We can also distinguish different ways in which auto-operational form becomes effective in use. Is it supportive or controlling? Is it informative or instructive? Is it simulative or does it directly affect reality? I don't know a good classification here, but we need to work in this direction, as we populate the world with auto-operational entities of various kinds. Perhaps we need something akin to the speech-act theory in the philosophy of language: an operational model-effect theory that would provide us with conceptual categories for discussing how computers interfere with human activity in situated use.

In these fields, I see important avenues for joint research combining the formalist and the human activity perspective.

6 Formal methods as resources in software development

Naur's radical statement: *There is no right method for theory building* refers to an understanding of "method" as a formalized procedure. Instead, he argues in [Nau 92, pp. 37-48], we should master a repertoire of concepts for modelling to be used as needed in the situation.

This is quite similar to Goguen's argumentation in [Gog 92]. He deals with the idea of error-free programming as treated by the "Dijkstra School". He criticizes the tendency to apply formal methods in a rigid top-down hierarchical manner and argues for using them in flexible non-ideological ways. He also considers bugs in programs as interesting and important in themselves: they define the boundary between what is understood and what is not. Since errors in programming are a major reason for advocating formal methods, it is illuminating how this topic is addressed by different authors.

In formal approaches, errors are defined as deviances between the program and its specification. By contrast, Don Knuth has reported on his own errors in developing TEX in [Knu 92]. The most amazing thing to me is his classification of errors., He analyzes his errors in terms of how he saw them in relation to what would have been desirable. Thus, his error categories range from "blunder, botch" to "quest for quality". There is no way of expressing all of these errors in terms such as "right" and "wrong" with respect to a formal specification. Rather, *errors refer to mismatches between actual and desirable decisions taken during programming*, where no frame of reference is available for judging what is right and wrong.

The connection between errors and formalization is a subtle one. On one hand, formal approaches provide us with conceptual means that enable suitable ways of abstraction and avoid certain categories of errors altogether. Thus, they greatly improve the logical consistency of our programs. On the other hand, they introduce new sources of blunders.

And they give us no hint about quality. Whether or not we make suitable decisions with respect to the context. Whether we tackle the right problem, so to speak.

The formalist notion of errors is based on the idea of considering software development as the construction of a defined product, it is not compatible with the idea of a learning process in design. Here, errors have the constructive role of learning events, a point which is made by several authors in [FZBKS 92], in particular by [K-S 92], as well as by [WF 86] and by many others. In [Flo 87], I argue that errors need to be understood in terms of the human processes where they originate.

This leads to the question on how formalization is embedded in other modes of thinking and being. [Sie 92] gives hints by showing how formal statements need to be communicated in informal ways. This too is a point stressed by Naur repeatedly. In [Bur 92], Rod Burstall gives a fascinating account of the states of mind associated with computing. He concludes that we need to free ourselves from "being entrapped by a limited perspective based on desire for control and exclusive reliance on conceptual thought". Admittedly, this danger of single-mindedness is inherent in whatever approach to system development we adopt. But strictly formal methods introduce yet another level of expertise, control and potential alienation that we have to deal with.

There is by now a wealth of literature dealing with human processes in software development. Basically, it is a question of how insight is to be reached. The dissatisfaction with the original phase models formalizing the software process has given rise to the movement of prototyping and evolutionary development, where the basic idea is understanding and supporting the communication involved with an orientation to feedback and constructive ways of viewing human errors.

Adopting such a view leads us to examine the following issues:

- What is the place of formalization in contexts of multiperspectivity and evolving insight?
- When should we formalize, how and why?
- Is the nature of program verification one of using formal proofs or one of context-oriented argumentation?
- How can we use formal concepts as modelling tools?
- How can we adapt methods cooperatively rather than following rules?

I am passionate in these questions, since they reflect my own area of research. Allow me therefore, to point to [Flo 87] once more and also to our work on STEPS which is a methodical framework accommodating for various approaches. In particular, you can also take a formal approach in STEPS, if you find ways for incorporating this in an overall evolutionary process ([FRS 89], see also [K-S 92]).

In the meantime, I have also gained extensive experience in working with emancipatory approaches in software development. With participatory design, for example, with democratic work organization and with self-organization. It remains an open question to me, how formal methods could be used as resources in this context. While software developers can and should learn to master formal methods by better education, users cannot. We have to find ways how formalization can be used without interfering in the human process of shaping technology for human use.

7 An invitation to continued dialogue

In this paper, I have named some of the issues of interest in treating computing as a human activity, but I have not treated them in depth. There are several reasons for this. One is the scope and time available. If you want to delve into these issues I have raised, be sure to look at some of the books I have suggested. Another reason is the context. I am not primarily addressing the human-activity community here, but those of the formalist community who are interested in cooperating on these questions in a dialogical way across boundaries. Note that in this paper I have not drawn on any philosophical school for founding my arguments.

Essentially, I argue that the stuff that software is made of, is a web of human views. Software does not only embody facts amenable to logical analysis, it also *reifies decisions on how human affairs should be handled*, resulting as compromises in processes of learning, communication and negotiation. This is often soft stuff, as the name software suggests, the validity of our formal models depending on subjective judgements. Inspite of its name, we are *not always* engaged in *computing* in our profession.

Therefore, I plead for a serious concern with theories from the humanities as an integral part of computer science education and for admitting such theories as basis for foundation in computer science research. Furthermore, I propose to create conditions in universities that would enable students to gain experience in communicative software practice during their education and to understand the interplay between the formal and the human activity dimensions of software development.

In 1985, I was engaged in building up a research group at the Technical University of Berlin. Technical and formal aspects of software development were considered there against the background of the human processes giving rise to them. Thus, the students in our department were exposed to formal methods as taught by Ehrig's group on one hand and to reflections on communicative practice in our group on the other hand.

I cannot agree to the overall harmonious interpretation of TAPSOFT given by Ehrig and Mahr. As seen from my side, it stands for conflict as well. TAPSOFT has marked the beginning of a profound change at my former home university with a strong shift of emphasis in the direction of formal methods. Eventually this became so forceful that the values and belief systems inherent in formal methods left no room for other views. I am not blaming this on any individual, it was a qualitative shift in culture. Based on my experience in the years following TAPSOFT, I have come to conclude that formalization issues are not just topics of academic dispute. Only at the surface are we talking about the merits and the limits of formal methods. Underneath, human convictions and scientific power struggle are at play. Decisions must be taken relating to curricula and learning forms. To positions to be created, to criteria for filling them and to money to be allocated for research. There are battles to be fought here, and they are hard, since they involve us.

Within a few years, the tensions became so strong that my willingness for continuing the dialogue came to an end. My continued personal friendship with Hartmut Ehrig was not sufficient as a basis for maintaining a dialogical milieu. So, inspite of my remaining loyalty to the department, I left Berlin and rebuilt my existence in Hamburg. As far as I am concerned, my move was one of professional emancipation.

I remember TAPSOFT'85 as a rare and valuable example for scientific cooperation across boundaries of theoretical perspectives and associated values and belief systems. And I consider my mission here at TAPSOFT'95 to formulate an invitation for joint research. Let us strive for a new dialogue on equal terms, while taking both perspectives seriously. Let us engage in common projects, aiming at bringing out and reconciling the different points of view.

As for maintaining a dialogical milieu: Though we have failed in the long run in Berlin, I wish good luck to our hosts for intensifying their dialogue here in Aarhus.

But dialogue is not confined to taking place within one university site. It is a question of forming alliances and networks of individuals between people from different communities sharing the same concerns.

Acknowledgements

I would like to thank Cliff Jones for sharing with me at TAPSOFT'85 his experience in putting VDM into practice, and to commemorate with pleasure the contributions made by Rod Burstall and Joseph Goguen to Software Development and Reality Construction. I am very grateful to Dirk Siefkes for a continued stream of discussion throughout the past decade on the issues raised here. The present paper draws to some extent on the work of Uli Piepenburg on "Softwareentwicklung als Semantikerstellung" and that of Guido Gryczan on "Situierte Koordination" to be published in their doctoral theses this year.

References

[BEK 87] Bjerknes, G., Ehn, P., and Kyng, M. (eds.): Computers and Democracy. A Scandinavian Challenge. Avebury, Aldershot, UK, 1987.

[Bur 92] Burstall, R.M.: Computing: Yet Another Reality Construction. In [FZBKS 92]: 45-51.

[Bød 87] Bødker, S. (1987). Through the Interface. A Human Activity Approach to User Interface Design. Aarhus University, Aarhus, 1987.

[BZ 92] Budde, R., Züllighoven, H.: Software Tools in a Programming Workshop. In [FZBKS 92]: 252-268.

[Brå 73] Bråten, S.: Model monopoly and communication: Systems theoretical notes on democratization. Acta Sociologica, 16(2): 98-107.

[CFR 93] Colburn, T. R., Fetzer, J. H., and Rankin T. L. (eds.): Program Verification. Kluwer Academic Publishers, Dordrecht/Boston/London, 1993.

[CNPRSSS 92]
Coy, W., Nake, F., Pflüger, J.-M., Rolf, A., Seetzen, J., Siefkes, D., Stransfeld, R. (eds.): Sichtweisen der Informatik. Vieweg-Verlag, Braunschweig/Wiesbaden, 1992.

[DM 93] Dahlbom, B., Mathiassen, L.: Computers In Context - The Philosophy and Practice of Systems Design. Blackwell Publishers. Cambridge, Massachusetts, 1993.

[EhM 95] Ehrig, H., Mahr, B.: A Decade of TAPSOFT: Aspects of Progress and Prospects in Theory and Practice of Software Development. This volume.

[Ehn 88] Ehn, P.: Work-oriented Design of Computer Artifacts. Almquist and Wiksell International, Stockholm, 1988.

[Flo 85] Floyd, C.: On the Relevance of Formal Methods to Software Development. In Springer LNCS 186 (1986): 1-11.

[Flo 87] Floyd, C.: Outline of a Paradigm Change in Software Engineering. In [BEK 87]: 191-210.

[Flo 92] Floyd, C.: Human Questions in Computer Science. In [FZBKS 92]: 15-27.

[FMRSW 89]
Floyd, C., Mehl, W.-M., Reisin, F.-M., Schmidt, G., and Wolf, G.: Out of Scandinavia: Alternative approaches to software design and system development. Human-Computer Interaction, 4(4): 253-349.

[FRS 89] Floyd, C., Reisin, F.-M., Schmidt, G.: STEPS to Software Development with Users. In: Ghezzi, C. and McDermid, J.A. (eds.): ESEC'89, Springer LNCS 387: 48-64.

[FZBKS 92] Floyd, C., Züllighoven, H., Budde, R., Keil-Slawik, R. (eds.): Software Development and Reality Construction. Springer-Verlag, Berlin, Heidelberg, New York, Tokio, 1992.

[Gog 92] Goguen, J.: The denial of Error. In [FZBKS 92]: 193-202.

[Hei 93] Heintz, B.: Die Herrschaft der Regel. Zur Grundlagengeschichte des Computers. Campus Verlag, Frankfurt/New York, 1993.

[KL 92] Klein, H. K., Lyytinen, K.: Towards a New Understanding of Data Modelling. In [FZBKS 92]: 203-219.

[Knu 92] Knuth, D.E.: Learning from our Errors. In [FZBKS 92]: 28-30.

[K-S 92] Keil-Slawik, R.: Artifacts in Software Design. In [FZBKS 92]: 168-188.

[Leh 80] Lehmann, M.: Programs, life cycles, and laws of software evolution. Proceedings of the IEEE, 86(9): 1060-1076.

[McC 63] Towards a Mathematical Science of Computation. In [CFR 93]: 35-56.

[MO 92] Maaß, S., Oberquelle, H.: Perspectives and Metaphors for Human-Computer Interaction. In [FZBKS 92]: 233-251.

[Nau 92] Naur, P.: Computing: A Human Activity. ACM-Press, New York, 1992.

[Nur 92] Nurminen, M. I.: A Subject-Oriented Approach to Information Systems. In [FZBKS 92]: 302-311.

[Nyg 86] Nygaard, K.: Program development as social activity. In Kugler, H. G. (ed.): Information Processing 86 - Proceedings of the IFIP 10th World Computer Congress. North-Holland, Amsterdam, 189-198.

[Rei 92] Reisin, F.-M.: Anticipating Reality Construction. In [FZBKS 92]: 312-325.

[Sie 92] Siefkes, D.: How to Communicate Proofs or Programs. In [FZBKS 92]: 140-154.

[Smi 85] Smith, B.C.: Limits of Correctness in Computers. Reprinted in [CFR 92]: 275-293.

[Suc 87] Suchman, L.A.: Plans and Situated Actions - The Problem of Human-Machine Communication. Cambridge University Press, Cambridge, UK, 1987.

[WF 86] Winograd, T., Flores, F.: Understanding Computers and Cognition - A new Foundation for Design. Ablex, Norwood, NJ, 1986.

Rational Spaces and Set Constraints

Dexter Kozen

Computer Science Department
Cornell University
Ithaca, New York 14853-7501, USA
kozen@cs.cornell.edu

Abstract. Set constraints are inclusions between expressions denoting sets of ground terms. They have been used extensively in program analysis and type inference. In this paper we investigate the topological structure of the spaces of solutions to systems of set constraints. We identify a family of topological spaces called *rational spaces*, which formalize the notion of a topological space with a regular or self-similar structure, such as the Cantor discontinuum or the space of runs of a finite automaton. We develop the basic theory of rational spaces and derive generalizations and proofs from topological principles of some results in the literature on set constraints.

1 Introduction

Set constraints are inclusions between expressions denoting sets of ground terms. They have been used extensively in program analysis and type inference for many years [3, 4, 12, 14, 15, 22, 23, 24, 26]. Considerable recent effort has focussed on the complexity of the satisfiability problem [1, 2, 5, 6, 7, 8, 10, 11, 13, 25]. Set constraints have also recently been used to define a constraint logic programming language over sets of ground terms that generalizes ordinary logic programming over an Herbrand domain [19].

Set constraints exhibit a rich mathematical structure. There are strong connections to automata theory [10, 11], type theory [20, 21], first-order monadic logic [6, 7], Boolean algebras with operators [16, 17], and modal logic [18]. There are algebraic and topological formulations, corresponding roughly to "soft" and "hard" typing respectively, which are related by Stone duality [18].

Many results in the literature on set constraints are topological in flavor. For example, Aiken *et al.* [2] prove that mixed positive and negative set constraints are strictly more expressive than positive constraints alone. The proof of this result is based on a compactness lemma which states that a system of positive constraints is satisfiable if and only if all finite subsets are satisfiable. It is well known that the compactness of classical propositional and predicate logic is essentially a topological result: logical compactness is equivalent to the topological compactness of a dual space. This is also the case here.

In [10], Gilleron *et al.* introduce *tree set automata*. Among other results, they establish various closure properties of these automata and show that every satisfiable finite system of set constraints has a regular solution. The space of runs of a tree set automaton can be viewed as a topological space, and analogs of these results hold in a more general context.

One might wish to incorporate these observations into a theory from which such results can be derived from general topological principles. This quest leads us to the definition of *rational spaces.* This definition is meant to capture the idea of a topological space with a regular or self-similar structure. The Cantor discontinuum is a simple example of such a space. Another example is provided by the space of runs of a Büchi automaton or tree set automaton. Sets of solutions to (finite) systems of set constraints can also be represented as (finitary) rational spaces.

Once this definition has been made and the basic theory developed, it is possible to rederive some of the results mentioned above from general principles, and in some cases give generalizations. For example, the result of [10] that every satisfiable finite system of set constraints has a regular solution is tantamount to the fact that every nonempty finitary rational space contains a rational point. (A *rational point* is a finitary singleton rational subspace.) In fact, every finitary rational space is a complete metric space, and is the completion of its rational points. The significance of this statement in terms of set constraints is that every finite system of set constraints is determined by its regular solutions.

This paper is organized as follows. In §2, we review the basic definitions of set constraints, termset algebras, regular sets, hypergraphs, and tree set automata. In §3 we introduce rational spaces, give several examples, and develop their basic theory, including the notions of rational maps, rational subspaces, rational products, and rational equivalence. In §4 we prove our main theorem, which characterizes the spaces of solutions of systems of set constraints in terms of rational spaces. In §5, we give several applications. Finally, in §6 we draw conclusions and discuss future work.

2 Preliminary Definitions

2.1 Set Expressions and Set Constraints

Let Σ be a finite ranked alphabet consisting of symbols f, each with an associated finite arity. Symbols in Σ of arity 0, 1, 2, and n are called *nullary, unary, binary,* and *n-ary*, respectively. Nullary elements are called *constants.* To avoid trivial special cases, we assume throughout that Σ contains at least one constant and at least one nonconstant. The use of the expression $f(x_1, \ldots, x_n)$ carries the implicit assumption that f is of arity n.

The set of ground terms over Σ is denoted T_Σ. If $X = \{x, y, \ldots\}$ is a set of variables, then $T_\Sigma(X)$ denotes the set of terms over Σ and X, considering the elements of X as symbols of arity 0.

Let $\mathrm{B} = (\cup, \cap, \sim, 0, 1)$ be the usual signature of Boolean algebra. Other Boolean operators such as $-$ (set difference) and $\oplus$ (symmetric difference) are defined as usual. Let $\Sigma + \mathrm{B}$ denote the signature consisting of the disjoint union of Σ and B. A *set expression* over variables X is any element of $T_{\Sigma+\mathrm{B}}(X)$.

A *positive set constraint* is a formal inclusion $\varphi \subseteq \psi$, where φ and ψ are set expressions. We also allow equational constraints $\varphi = \psi$, although inclusions and equations are interdefinable. A *negative set constraint* is the negation of a positive set constraint: $\psi \not\subseteq \psi$ or $\varphi \neq \psi$.

We interpret set expressions over the powerset 2^{T_Σ} of T_Σ. This forms an algebra of signature $\Sigma + \mathrm{B}$, where the Boolean operators have their usual set-theoretic interpretations and elements $f \in \Sigma$ are interpreted as functions

$$\begin{aligned} f &: (2^{T_\Sigma})^n \to 2^{T_\Sigma} \\ f(A_1, \ldots, A_n) &= \{f(t_1, \ldots, t_n) \mid t_i \in A_i,\ 1 \leq i \leq n\} . \end{aligned} \tag{1}$$

A *set valuation* is a map $\sigma : X \to 2^{T_\Sigma}$ assigning a subset of T_Σ to each variable in X. Any set valuation σ extends uniquely to a $(\Sigma + \mathrm{B})$-homomorphism

$$\sigma : T_{\Sigma+\mathrm{B}}(X) \to 2^{T_\Sigma}$$

by induction on the structure of set expressions. We say that the set valuation σ *satisfies* the positive constraint $\varphi \subseteq \psi$ if $\sigma(\varphi) \subseteq \sigma(\psi)$, and satisfies the negative constraint $\varphi \not\subseteq \psi$ if $\sigma(\varphi) \not\subseteq \sigma(\psi)$. We write $\sigma \models \alpha$ if the set valuation σ satisfies the constraint α. A system $\mathcal{S}$ of set constraints is *satisfiable* if there is a set valuation σ that satisfies all the constraints in $\mathcal{S}$; in this case we write $\sigma \models \mathcal{S}$ and say σ is a *solution* of $\mathcal{S}$. We write $\mathcal{S} \models \alpha$ if $\sigma \models \alpha$ whenever $\sigma \models \mathcal{S}$, and say α is a *logical consequence* of $\mathcal{S}$. We write $\mathcal{S} \models \mathcal{S}'$ if $\mathcal{S} \models \alpha$ for all $\alpha \in \mathcal{S}'$. We say $\mathcal{S}$ and $\mathcal{S}'$ are *logically equivalent* if $\mathcal{S} \models \mathcal{S}'$ and $\mathcal{S}' \models \mathcal{S}$.

2.2 Termset Algebras

Termset algebras were introduced in [18]. These are structures of signature $\Sigma + \mathrm{B}$ satisfying axioms (2)–(6):

$$\text{axioms of Boolean algebra} \tag{2}$$

$$f(\ldots, x \cup y, \ldots) = f(\ldots, x, \ldots) \cup f(\ldots, y, \ldots) \tag{3}$$

$$f(\ldots, x - y, \ldots) = f(\ldots, x, \ldots) - f(\ldots, y, \ldots) \tag{4}$$

$$\bigcup_{f \in \Sigma} f(1, \ldots, 1) = 1 \tag{5}$$

$$f(1, \ldots, 1) \cap g(1, \ldots, 1) = 0 , \quad f \neq g . \tag{6}$$

A termset algebra is called *entire*[1] if it satisfies (7).

$$f(x_1, \ldots, x_n) = 0 \to \bigvee_{i=1}^{n} (x_i = 0) . \tag{7}$$

The ellipses in (3) and (4) indicate that the explicitly given arguments occur in corresponding places, and that implicit arguments in corresponding places agree.

[1] The term *closed* was used in [18]. This terminology will be unsuitable in the present context because of the potential of confusion with topological closure.

The algebra 2^{T_Σ} discussed in §2.1 forms a model of these axioms. Another model is given by the subalgebra Reg_Σ of regular subsets of T_Σ described in §2.3 below.

Some immediate consequences of (2)–(6) are

$$\begin{aligned}
f(\ldots,0,\ldots) &= 0 &(8)\\
f(\ldots,\sim x,\ldots) &= f(\ldots,1,\ldots) - f(\ldots,x,\ldots) &(9)\\
f(\ldots,x\oplus y,\ldots) &= f(\ldots,x,\ldots)\oplus f(\ldots,y,\ldots) &(10)\\
f(\ldots,x\cap y,\ldots) &= f(\ldots,x,\ldots)\cap f(\ldots,y,\ldots) &(11)\\
f(x_1\cap y_1,\ldots,x_n\cap y_n) &= f(x_1,\ldots,x_n)\cap f(y_1,\ldots,y_n) &(12)\\
x\subseteq y \Rightarrow f(\ldots,x,\ldots) &\subseteq f(\ldots,y,\ldots) &(13)\\
\sim f(x_1,\ldots,x_n) &= \bigcup_{g\neq f} g(1,\ldots,1)\\
&\quad \cup \bigcup_{i=1}^{n} f(\underbrace{1,\ldots,1}_{i-1},\sim x_i,\underbrace{1,\ldots,1}_{n-i})\,. &(14)
\end{aligned}$$

Property (14) is called the *generalized DeMorgan law.*

Let X be a fixed set of variables. Let F be a subset of $T_{\Sigma+\mathrm{B}}(X)$ closed under subexpressions. Let F' denote the set of conjunctions of elements of F and their negations. A *literal* is a variable or a negation of a variable.

Proposition 1. *Any set constraint all of whose subexpressions are in F is equivalent under the termset algebra axioms (2)–(6) to a finite system of constraints of the form $\varphi\cap f(\varphi_1,\ldots,\varphi_n)=0$, where $f\in\Sigma$, $\varphi,\varphi_1,\ldots,\varphi_n\in F'$, and φ is a conjunction of literals.*

Proof. If the constraint is an equation, write it as two inclusions. Write an inclusion $\varphi\subseteq\psi$ as $\varphi\cap\sim\psi=0$. Use the DeMorgan laws and the law $\sim\sim\varphi=\varphi$ of Boolean algebra to push negations occurring outside the scope of any $f\in\Sigma$ down until any such negation is applied to a variable or an expression $f(\varphi_1,\ldots,\varphi_n)$. Use the generalized DeMorgan law (14) at the outermost level only to transform the expression $\sim f(\varphi_1,\ldots,\varphi_n)$ to a disjunction of expressions $g(\psi_1,\ldots,\psi_m)$, where each ψ_i is either $\sim\varphi_j$ or 1. Note both of these expressions are in F' (1 is the null conjunction). The expression is now a monotone Boolean combination of literals and expressions $f(\varphi_1,\ldots,\varphi_n)$, where $\varphi_1,\ldots,\varphi_n\in F'$. Use the distributive laws of Boolean algebra outside the scope of any $f\in\Sigma$ only to transform the expression to disjunctive normal form. Break the resulting disjunction up into several constraints, one for each disjunct, using the rule $\varphi\cup\psi=0\iff\varphi=0\wedge\psi=0$. Discard any constraint containing $f(\varphi_1,\ldots,\varphi_n)$ and $g(\psi_1,\ldots,\psi_m)$, $f\neq g$, because the constraint is automatically true by (6). In each of the remaining constraints, combine all non-literals into one expression using (12); *i.e.*, replace $f(\varphi_1,\ldots,\varphi_n)\cap f(\psi_1,\ldots,\psi_n)$ with $f(\varphi_1\cap\psi_1,\ldots,\varphi_n\cap\psi_n)$. Replace any constraint $\varphi=0$, where φ is a conjunction of literals alone, with the constraints $\varphi\cap f(1,\ldots,1)=0$ for all $f\in\Sigma$, as justified by (5). The resulting constraints are of the desired form.

2.3 Regular Sets

A subset of T_Σ is *regular* if it is described by a finite bottom-up tree automaton [9]; equivalently, if it is some set x_1 described by a system of simultaneous set equations of the form

$$x_i = \varphi_i(x_1, \ldots, x_m) \ , \quad 1 \leq i \leq n \tag{15}$$

in which each variable x_i occurs on the left hand side of exactly one equation and each right hand side is a disjunction of set expressions of the form $f(y_1, \ldots, y_n)$, where $f \in \Sigma$ and $y_i \in \{x_1, \ldots, x_m\}$, $1 \leq i \leq n$. It can be proved by induction on the depth of terms that any such system has a unique solution. The family of regular sets over Σ is denoted Reg_Σ. For example, the system

$$x = a \cup g(y) \qquad y = g(x) \tag{16}$$

has the unique regular solution

$$\sigma(x) = \{g^n(a) \mid n \text{ even}\} \qquad \sigma(y) = \{g^n(a) \mid n \text{ odd}\} \ .$$

2.4 Tree Set Automata and Hypergraphs

Tree set automata were introduced in [10]. They are strongly related to the *hypergraphs* introduced in [1], the only essential difference being the inclusion of an acceptance condition in the former. The relation of finite tree set automata and finite hypergraphs to set constraints has been well studied [1, 2, 10, 11, 19, 25].

Definition 2. Let Σ be a finite ranked alphabet. A *Σ-hypergraph* is a pair (D, E), where D is a set (not necessarily finite) and E is an indexed collection of hyperedges

$$E_f : D^n \to 2^D \ , \quad n = \mathrm{arity}(f) \ ,$$

one for each $f \in \Sigma$.

Thus E_a gives a subset of D for constants a, E_g is an ordinary binary edge relation for unary g, *etc.*

Definition 3. A hypergraph (D, E) is said to be *entire*[2] if every $E_f(d_1, \ldots, d_n)$ is nonempty, *deterministic* if every $E_f(d_1, \ldots, d_n)$ is a singleton, and *unrestricted* if every $E_f(d_1, \ldots, d_n) = D$.

Definition 4. A *run* of the hypergraph (D, E) is a map $\theta : T_\Sigma \to D$ such that for all $f(t_1, \ldots, t_n) \in T_\Sigma$,

$$\theta(f(t_1, \ldots, t_n)) \in E_f(\theta(t_1), \ldots, \theta(t_n)) \ . \tag{17}$$

[2] The term *closed* was used in [1, 2, 18, 19, 25]. This also corresponds to the condition $COND_\omega$ of [10].

There exists a run in $(D,\ E)$ if and only if $(D,\ E)$ has an entire induced subhypergraph: an entire induced subhypergraph on $D' \subseteq D$ allows the definition of a run $\theta : T_\Sigma \rightarrow D'$ by induction; conversely, for any run θ, the induced subhypergraph on the image $\theta(T_\Sigma)$ is entire.

Definition 5. Let X be a set of variables. A *Σ, X-tree set automaton* $\mathcal{M}$ is a tuple $(D,\ E,\ A)$, where $(D,\ E)$ is a Σ-hypergraph and A is an indexed family A_x, $x \in X$ of subsets of D, called *accept sets.* A tuple L_x, $x \in X$ of subsets of T_Σ is *accepted* by $\mathcal{M}$ if there exists a run θ such that $L_x = \{t \mid \theta(t) \in A_x\}$, $x \in X$.

In previous work [1, 2, 10, 11, 19, 25], D and X are assumed to be finite, but we will find it convenient not impose these restrictions.

3 Rational Spaces

3.1 Definition of Rational Spaces

Let Σ be a fixed finite ranked alphabet.

Definition 6. A *topological Σ-hypergraph* is a Σ-hypergraph $(D,\ E)$, finite or infinite, endowed with a topology on D whose hyperedges

$$\{(d, d_1, \ldots, d_n) \mid d \in E_f(d_1, \ldots, d_n)\}$$

are closed in the product topology on D^{n+1}.

Definition 7. A *space of runs* over Σ is the space $\mathcal{R}(\mathcal{D})$ of runs of a topological Σ-hypergraph $\mathcal{D}$, where the topology on $\mathcal{R}(\mathcal{D})$ is inherited from the product topology on $\mathcal{D}^{T_\Sigma}$. The space $\mathcal{R}(\mathcal{D})$ is called *finitary* if $\mathcal{D}$ is finite.

Recall that the product topology on $\mathcal{D}^{T_\Sigma}$ is the smallest topology such that all projections $\pi_t : \theta \mapsto \theta(t)$ are continuous. In other words, it is generated by subbasic open sets

$$\{\theta \mid \theta(t) \in x\}\ , \quad t \in T_\Sigma\ , \quad x \text{ open in } \mathcal{D}. \tag{18}$$

The space $\mathcal{R}(\mathcal{D})$ of runs of $\mathcal{D}$, being a space of functions $T_\Sigma \rightarrow \mathcal{D}$, is a subspace of this space. The topology is thus generated by subbasic open sets (18) restricted to $\mathcal{R}(\mathcal{D})$.

Definition 8. A *rational space* is a space of runs $\mathcal{R}(\mathcal{D})$ such that $\mathcal{D}$ is compact and Hausdorff.

We remark here that rational spaces are more than just Cantor spaces; the representation in terms of $\mathcal{D}$ is germane. Formally, this will be reflected in the restricted class of morphisms defined below, called *rational maps.* First, however, let us look at some examples of rational spaces.

Example 1. A simple but revealing example is the *Cantor discontinuum.* This space can be constructed by starting from the closed real unit interval $[0, 1]$ and applying the following operation: delete the "middle third", *i.e.*, the open interval $(\frac{1}{3}, \frac{2}{3})$; then delete the middle thirds of the remaining intervals; and so on. The Cantor discontinuum consists of points that are never deleted.

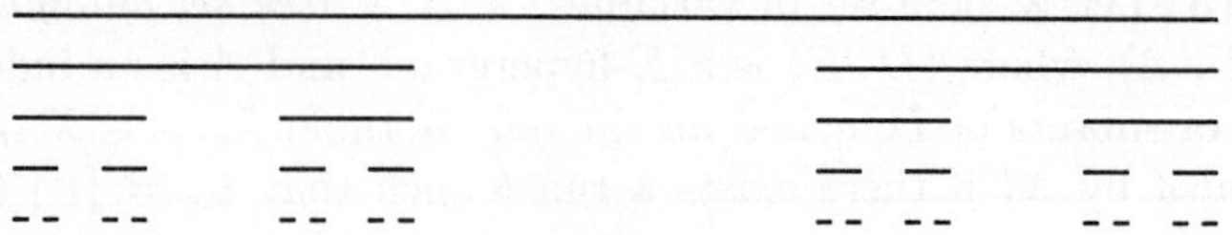

Equivalently, these are all real numbers in the unit interval whose ternary (base 3) expansion does not contain the digit 1. This is a classical example of an uncountable nowhere dense set of reals.

The topology on the Cantor discontinuum is inherited from the usual topology on the real line. With that topology, it is homeomorphic to the topological product 2^ω, or the space of infinite paths of the infinite binary tree with the intervals as basic open sets, where in this context an *interval* is a set consisting of all extensions of some finite prefix.

The Cantor discontinuum has a representation as a finitary rational space over $\Sigma = \{a, g\}$, where a is a constant and g is unary. For $\mathcal{D}$ we take the discrete space $\{0, 1, 2\}$ with $E_g(d) = E_a(\,) = \{0, 2\}$. Corresponding to each point x we take the run whose value on $g^n(a)$ is the nth digit in the ternary expansion of x.

Example 2. Consider an infinite tree that is binary branching at even levels and ternary branching at odd levels. The basic open sets are the intervals. Equivalently, take the subspace of the real unit interval consisting of all numbers whose ternary expansion contains no 2 in an even position. This space has a representation as a finitary rational space with $\Sigma = \{a, g\}$, $\mathcal{D}$ the discrete space $\{0, 1, 2\} \times \{0, 1\}$, and

$$E_a(\,) = E_g((d, 1)) = \{(0, 0),\ (1, 0)\}$$
$$E_g((d, 0)) = \{(0, 1),\ (1, 1),\ (2, 1)\}\ .$$

The value on $g^n(a)$ of the run corresponding to x is $(d, n \bmod 2)$, where d is the nth digit in the ternary expansion of x.

Examples (1) and (2) exhibit a treelike structure, because there is only one nonconstant symbol and it is unary. Already with two unary symbols, this intuitive picture is no longer accurate.

Example 3. The following is an example of a non-finitary rational space. Let X be a set of variables ranging over subsets of T_Σ, and consider the family of set valuations $\sigma : X \to 2^{T_\Sigma}$. Endow this set with smallest topology whose closed sets include all sets of the form $\{\sigma \mid \sigma \models S\}$ for S a system of set constraints over X. One can show that the topology on this space is generated by subbasic clopen (closed and open) sets $\{\sigma \mid \sigma \models t \subseteq x\}$ and $\{\sigma \mid \sigma \models t \subseteq {\sim} x\}$ for $t \in T_\Sigma$ and $x \in X$. It was shown in [2] that this space is compact.

We will show in §4 below that this space has the following representation as a rational space. Take $\mathcal{D}$ to be the topological product 2^X with $E_f(d_1,\ldots,d_n) = \mathcal{D}$. (If X is countable, $\mathcal{D}$ is just the Cantor discontinuum.) Associate with every set valuation σ the run

$$\lambda t.\lambda x.\begin{cases} 1 \text{ , if } t \in \sigma(x) \\ 0 \text{ , otherwise.} \end{cases} \tag{19}$$

This space is not finitary unless X is finite. However, it is a product of finitary spaces, one for each $x \in X$, as can be seen by reversing the binding order of t and x in the λ-expression (19).

Example 4. Every termset algebra has a set-theoretic representation as a *topological term automaton* whose topology is Stone [18]. These automata were introduced in [20, 21]. They differ from tree set automata in that they are top-down instead of bottom-up, but they have a naturally defined hypergraph structure in which the hyperedges are closed, giving rational spaces.

3.2 Basic Properties

Proposition 9. *Let $\mathcal{R}(\mathcal{D})$ be a space of runs.*

(i) If $\mathcal{D}$ is Hausdorff, then so is $\mathcal{R}(\mathcal{D})$.
(ii) If $\mathcal{D}$ is compact, then so is $\mathcal{R}(\mathcal{D})$.
(iii) If $\mathcal{D}$ is finite and discrete (all sets are open), then $\mathcal{R}(\mathcal{D})$ is a complete metric space (all Cauchy sequences converge) under the metric

$$d(\theta,\eta) = 2^{-\text{depth}(t)} , \tag{20}$$

where t is a term of minimal depth on which θ and η differ, or 0 if no such term exists.

Proof. (i) Any product of Hausdorff spaces is Hausdorff and any subspace of a Hausdorff space is Hausdorff, and $\mathcal{R}(\mathcal{D})$ is a subspace of the product $\mathcal{D}^{T_\Sigma}$.

(ii) Regarding E_f as an $(n+1)$-ary relation, we can write

$$\mathcal{R}(\mathcal{D}) = \bigcap_{f(t_1,\ldots,t_n)\in T_\Sigma} \{\theta \in \mathcal{D}^{T_\Sigma} \mid (\theta(f(t_1,\ldots,t_n)),\theta(t_1),\ldots,\theta(t_n)) \in E_f\} .$$

The set in this conjunction corresponding to $f(t_1,\ldots,t_n)$ is the continuous preimage of the closed set E_f under the projection $(\pi_{f(t_1,\ldots,t_n)},\pi_{t_1},\ldots,\pi_{t_n}) : \mathcal{D}^{T_\Sigma} \to D^{n+1}$, thus is closed. By Tychonoff's Theorem, $\mathcal{D}^{T_\Sigma}$ is compact, and any closed subspace of a compact space is compact, therefore $\mathcal{R}(\mathcal{D})$ is compact.

(iii) It is easily verified that $d(\theta,\eta) = 0$ iff $\theta = \eta$, $d(\theta,\eta) = d(\eta,\theta)$, and the triangle inequality holds. The two topologies coincide: every basic open neighborhood in the metric topology is open in the product topology, since

$$N_\epsilon(\theta) = \{\eta \mid d(\eta,\theta) < \epsilon\} = \bigcap_{\text{depth}(t)\leq -\log\epsilon} \{\eta \mid \eta(t) = \theta(t)\} ,$$

and vice-versa, since if $\theta(t) = u$, then

$$\{\eta \mid \eta(t) = u\} \supseteq \{\eta \mid d(\eta, \theta) < 2^{-\text{depth}(t)}\} = N_{2^{-\text{depth}(t)}}(\theta) .$$

The space $\mathcal{R}(\mathcal{D})$ is complete because it is compact by (ii), and any compact metric space is complete.

Corollary 10. *Every rational space is compact and Hausdorff. Every finitary rational space is a complete metric space under the metric (20).*

3.3 Rational Maps

The spaces of Examples 1 and 2 are homeomorphic, since both spaces are compact Hausdorff spaces with countable clopen bases and no isolated points, and all such spaces are homeomorphic. This is a consequence under Stone duality of the fact that all countable atomless Boolean algebras are isomorphic. Indeed, the space of paths in a tree that is binary branching at prime levels and ternary branching at nonprime levels is also homeomorphic to the Cantor space, but it is not clear at all how to assign a finitary rational space structure to it.

The homeomorphisms relating these spaces apparently do not preserve the structure inherent in the representation as spaces of runs. Thus the relation of *homeomorphism* is too coarse. Reflecting on this observation, one is led to the realization that rational spaces cannot be defined independent of some representation; *i.e.*, there is no purely topological definition.

These observations motivate the definition of a restricted class of maps called *rational maps*, which are continuous maps preserving the rational structure. We take these maps as our morphisms in the category of rational spaces.

Definition 11. Let $\mathcal{R}(\mathcal{D})$ and $\mathcal{R}(\mathcal{E})$ be rational spaces over Σ. A *rational map* $\mathcal{R}(\mathcal{D}) \rightarrow \mathcal{R}(\mathcal{E})$ is a function $\widehat{h} : \theta \mapsto h \circ \theta$ defined by a continuous map $h : \mathcal{D} \rightarrow \mathcal{E}$ such that

$$h(E_f^{\mathcal{D}}(d_1, \ldots, d_n)) \subseteq E_f^{\mathcal{E}}(h(d_1), \ldots, h(d_n)) . \tag{21}$$

A rational map $\mathcal{R}(\mathcal{D}) \rightarrow \mathcal{R}(\mathcal{E})$ is called a *rational embedding* if it is injective, and a *refinement* if it is bijective.

Note that the terms "injective" and "bijective" in this definition refer to $\widehat{h}$, not to h. There exist rational embeddings and refinements in which h is not one-to-one.

Any rational embedding or refinement is a homeomorphism between its domain and image, since any continuous bijection from a compact space to a Hausdorff space is a homeomorphism.

We mention in particular two special kinds of rational embeddings:

Narrowing If $\mathcal{D} = (D, E)$ and $\mathcal{D}' = (D, E')$ are two hypergraphs on the same set of vertices D, and if all $h(E_f(d_1, \ldots, d_n)) \subseteq E'_f(h(d_1), \ldots, h(d_n))$, then the identity map $D \rightarrow D$ induces an embedding $\mathcal{R}(\mathcal{D}) \rightarrow \mathcal{R}(\mathcal{D}')$. Such an $\mathcal{R}(\mathcal{D})$ is called a *narrowing* of $\mathcal{R}(\mathcal{D}')$.

Induced Subspaces If $\mathcal{D} = (D,\ E)$ is the induced subhypergraph of $\mathcal{D}' = (D',\ E')$ on some subset $D \subseteq D'$, *i.e.* if $E_f(d_1, \ldots, d_n) = E'_f(d_1, \ldots, d_n) \cap D$ for all $d_1, \ldots, d_n \in D$, then the inclusion map $D \to D'$ induces an embedding $\mathcal{R}(\mathcal{D}) \to \mathcal{R}(\mathcal{D}')$. Such an $\mathcal{R}(\mathcal{D})$ is called an *induced subspace* of $\mathcal{R}(\mathcal{D}')$.

Example 5. The map $h((d,0)) = 0$, $h((d,1)) = 2$ gives a rational map from the space of Example 2 into the space of Example 1. The image consists of the single point $.020202\cdots$. This is not a rational embedding, since it is not injective.

Example 6. The hypergraph with vertices $\{0,1,2\}$ and hyperedges

$$E_a(\,) = E_g((d,1)) = \{(0,0)\}$$
$$E_g((d,0)) = \{(0,1),\ (2,1)\}$$

constitutes a narrowing of the space of Example 2. This is the subspace consisting of all numbers whose ternary expansion contains no 1 or 2 in an even position or 1 in an odd position.

Example 7. The induced subhypergraph of $\{0,1,2\}$ on $\{0,1\}$ generates an induced subspace of the space of Example 2. This is the subspace of all numbers whose ternary expansion contains no 2.

Example 8. Here is an example of a rational embedding which is neither a narrowing nor an induced subspace. Let $\Sigma = \{a, g\}$, where a is a constant and g is unary. Consider the following hypergraph:

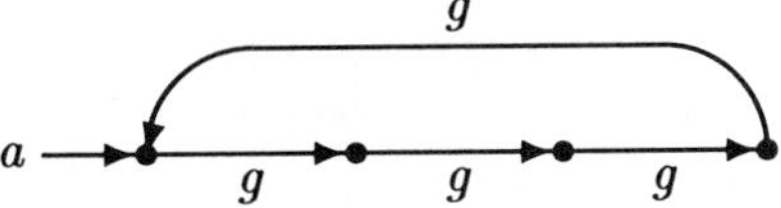

Map the first three vertices to 0 and the last vertex to 2. This gives a rational embedding of a singleton finitary rational space into the Cantor discontinuum. The image is the rational number $.000200020002\cdots$.

Example 9. The induced subspace on the subhypergraph $\{0,2\}$ is a refinement of the Cantor discontinuum, as is the subspace of Example 7 under the map $d \mapsto 2d$.

3.4 Rational Products

Definition 12. The *rational product* of any indexed family $\mathcal{R}(\mathcal{D}_x)$ of rational spaces is the space $\mathcal{R}(\Pi_x \mathcal{D}_x)$, where

$$E_f^{\Pi_x \mathcal{D}_x}(d_1, \ldots, d_n) = \Pi_x E_f^{\mathcal{D}_x}(\pi_x(d_1), \ldots, \pi_x(d_n)) .$$

Intuitively, the runs in each factor space can develop independently. The topological product $\Pi_x \mathcal{D}_x$ is Hausdorff and compact by Tychonoff's Theorem, and $E_f^{\Pi_x \mathcal{D}_x}$ is closed in the product topology, thus $\mathcal{R}(\Pi_x \mathcal{D}_x)$ is a rational space.

Strictly speaking, the rational product $\mathcal{R}(\Pi_x \mathcal{D}_x)$ is not the same as the set-theoretic (Cartesian) product $\Pi_x \mathcal{R}(\mathcal{D}_x)$, although the two are in one-to-one correspondence, as can be seen by exchanging the order of λ-bindings as in Example 3.

The projections $\pi_y : \Pi_x \mathcal{D}_x \to \mathcal{D}_y$ induce projections $\widehat{\pi}_y : \mathcal{R}(\Pi_x \mathcal{D}_x) \to \mathcal{R}(\mathcal{D}_y)$, which are rational maps.

A finite rational product of finitary spaces is finitary.

3.5 Rational Subspaces and Rational Points

Definition 13. A *rational subspace* of a rational space is any embedded image of another rational space. In other words, a subspace $\mathcal{R}$ of a rational space $\mathcal{R}(\mathcal{E})$ is a *rational subspace* if there exists a rational space $\mathcal{R}(\mathcal{D})$ and a rational embedding $\widehat{h} : \mathcal{R}(\mathcal{D}) \to \mathcal{R}(\mathcal{E})$ such that $\mathcal{R} = \widehat{h}(\mathcal{R}(\mathcal{D}))$.

A rational subspace is *entire* if it is the embedded image of a rational space defined on an entire hypergraph.

Definition 14. A *rational point* of a rational space is a finitary singleton rational subspace.

Example 10. The rational points of the Cantor discontinuum are the rational numbers, *i.e.*, real numbers whose ternary expansion is ultimately periodic.

Proposition 15. *Let $\mathcal{R}(\mathcal{D})$ be any rational space. For any closed set $x \subseteq \mathcal{D}$ and $t \in T_\Sigma$, the closed set $\pi_t^{-1}(x) = \{\theta \mid \theta(t) \in x\}$ is a rational subspace of $\mathcal{R}(\mathcal{D})$. Moreover, if $\mathcal{R}(\mathcal{D})$ is finitary, then so is $\pi_t^{-1}(x)$.*

Proof. Let F be the set of subterms of t. Let $*$ be a new element not in F, and let $D_* = F \cup \{*\}$. Let $\mathcal{D}_*$ be the discrete hypergraph on this set with hyperedges

$$E_f(t_1, \ldots, t_n) = \begin{cases} \{f(t_1, \ldots, t_n)\} \text{ , if } f(t_1, \ldots, t_n) \text{ is a subterm of } t \\ * \text{ ,} \qquad\qquad\qquad\qquad \text{otherwise.} \end{cases}$$

Now take the rational product $\mathcal{R}(\mathcal{D}_*) \times \mathcal{R}(\mathcal{D})$, then take the induced subspace obtained by discarding the open set consisting all vertices of the form (t, d) for $d \notin x$.

Proposition 16. *The intersection of two (finitary) rational subspaces is again a (finitary) rational subspace.*

Proof. Let $h_1 : \mathcal{D}_1 \to \mathcal{E}$, $h_2 : \mathcal{D}_2 \to \mathcal{E}$ be maps inducing rational maps $\widehat{h}_1 : \mathcal{R}(\mathcal{D}_1) \to \mathcal{R}(\mathcal{E})$, $\widehat{h}_2 : \mathcal{R}(\mathcal{D}_2) \to \mathcal{R}(\mathcal{E})$. Construct the rational product $\mathcal{R}(\mathcal{D}_1) \times \mathcal{R}(\mathcal{D}_2)$ with projections $\pi_i : \mathcal{D}_1 \times \mathcal{D}_2 \to \mathcal{D}_i$, $i \in \{1, 2\}$, and restrict to the diagonal set $\mathcal{C} = \{(d_1, d_2) \mid h_1(d_1) = h_2(d_2)\}$. Let $\mathcal{R}(\mathcal{C})$ be the induced rational subspace. The map $h((d_1, d_2)) = h_1(d_1) = h_2(d_2)$ gives the desired intersection.

Definition 17. The *essential subspace* of a rational space $\mathcal{R}(\mathcal{D})$ is the induced subspace on the set $\bigcup_{\theta \in \mathcal{R}(\mathcal{D})} \theta(T_\Sigma)$.

In other words, we discard vertices not appearing in any run. The essential subspace of $\mathcal{R}(\mathcal{D})$ is a refinement of $\mathcal{R}(\mathcal{D})$.

3.6 Rational Equivalence

Definition 18. Two spaces are *rationally equivalent* if they have a common refinement.

Proposition 19. *Rational equivalence is transitive.*

Proof. It suffices to show the following *Diamond Lemma*: if $\mathcal{R}(\mathcal{D}_1)$ and $\mathcal{R}(\mathcal{D}_2)$ are both refinements of $\mathcal{R}(\mathcal{E})$, then $\mathcal{R}(\mathcal{D}_1)$ and $\mathcal{R}(\mathcal{D}_2)$ have a common refinement. Let $\mathcal{R}(\mathcal{C})$ be the space constructed in the proof of Proposition 16. The rational maps $\mathcal{R}(\mathcal{C}) \to \mathcal{R}(\mathcal{D}_1)$ and $\mathcal{R}(\mathcal{C}) \to \mathcal{R}(\mathcal{D}_2)$ induced by the restriction of π_1 and π_2 to domain $\mathcal{C}$ are bijective, thus $\mathcal{R}(\mathcal{C})$ is the desired common refinement.

4 A Characterization of Set Constraints

In this section we give a complete characterization of the sets of solutions to systems of set constraints in terms of rational spaces. Our main result is a one-to-one correspondence, up to logical equivalence on one side and rational equivalence preserving X on the other, between (finite) systems of set constraints over variables X and certain (finitary) subspaces of a certain rational space (Theorem 21).

Let Σ be a fixed finite ranked alphabet and let X be a fixed set of variables (finite or infinite). Let $\mathcal{S}$ be a finite system of set constraints over Σ and X. In [1] it was shown how to construct a finite hypergraph (D, E) whose runs are in one-to-one correspondence with the solutions $\sigma : X \to 2^{T_\Sigma}$ of $\mathcal{S}$, where X is the set of variables occurring in $\mathcal{S}$. This result is also implicit in [10]. One can construct (D, E) by various alternative methods [2, 18, 19]. Here is yet another method.

Let F be any subset of $T_{\Sigma+\mathrm{B}}(X)$ (finite or infinite) containing X and closed under subexpressions. Let 2^F be the topological product of F copies of the discrete space $2 = \{0, 1\}$.

The space of all unrestricted runs $\theta : T_\Sigma \to 2^F$ is homeomorphic to the space of all functions $\sigma : F \to 2^{T_\Sigma}$, taking the product topology on each. This can be seen by writing

$$\begin{aligned} \theta &: T_\Sigma \to F \to 2 \\ \sigma &: F \to T_\Sigma \to 2 \end{aligned} \tag{22}$$

and exchanging the order of λ-binding. Their respective topologies are generated by subbasic clopen sets

$$\{\theta \mid \theta(t)(\varphi) = b\} \qquad \{\sigma \mid \sigma(\varphi)(t) = b\}$$

for $b \in \{0, 1\}$, $t \in T_\Sigma$ and $\varphi \in F$.

Note that the set of all functions $\sigma : F \to 2^{T_\Sigma}$ includes some that are not partial set valuations. In order to be a partial set valuation, σ must be a $(\Sigma + \mathrm{B})$-homomorphism on its domain, *i.e.*, must satisfy the following requirements for expressions in F:

$$\sigma(\varphi \cup \psi) = \sigma(\varphi) \cup \sigma(\psi) \tag{23}$$

$$\sigma({\sim}\varphi) = {\sim}\sigma(\varphi) \tag{24}$$

$$\sigma(f(\varphi_1, \ldots, \varphi_n)) = \{f(t_1, \ldots, t_n) \mid t_i \in \sigma(\varphi_n),\ 1 \leq i \leq n\}\ . \tag{25}$$

Likewise, the set of functions $\theta : T_\Sigma \to 2^F$ is the unrestricted rational space $\mathcal{R}(2^F)$. Let us narrow this space as follows.

Let $\mathcal{S}$ be any system of set constraints all of whose subexpressions are in F. Let F' denote the set of conjunctions of elements of F and their negations. For each $d \in 2^F$, let $d' \subseteq F'$ be the smallest set of expressions including d and $\{{\sim}\varphi \mid \varphi \in F - d\}$ and closed under conjunction. Call a set expression φ *$\mathcal{S}$-consistent* if $\varphi = 0$ is not a logical consequence of $\mathcal{S}$ and the equational axioms (2)–(6) of termset algebra. Define the hyperedges

$$E_f^{\mathcal{S}}(d_1, \ldots, d_n) = \{d \mid \text{for every } \varphi \in d' \text{ and } \varphi_i \in d_i',\ 1 \leq i \leq n,\ \varphi \cap f(\varphi_1, \ldots, \varphi_n) \text{ is } \mathcal{S}\text{-consistent}\}\ .$$

The $(n+1)$-ary relation $E_f^{\mathcal{S}}$ is closed, as is any set

$$\{u \mid \text{for all basic open neighborhoods } x \text{ of } u,\ P(x)\}$$

in any topological space for any property P of open sets whatsoever. Denote the resulting rational space by $\mathcal{R}(2^F, \mathcal{S})$.

Theorem 20. *Let the function $\sigma : F \to 2^{T_\Sigma}$ correspond to the unrestricted run $\theta : T_\Sigma \to 2^F$ under the correspondence (22). Let $\mathcal{S}$ be any system of set constraints all of whose subexpressions are in F. Then σ is a partial set valuation satisfying $\mathcal{S}$ if and only if θ is a run of $\mathcal{R}(2^F, \mathcal{S})$.*

Proof. If σ is a partial set valuation on F, then it extends uniquely by induction to a total set valuation $\sigma' : T_{\Sigma+\mathrm{B}}(X) \to 2^{T_\Sigma}$. Such a map is a $(\Sigma + \mathrm{B})$-homomorphism and its image is a subalgebra $\mathcal{A}$ of the set-theoretic termset algebra 2^{T_Σ}. Moreover, since $\sigma \models \mathcal{S}$, $\mathcal{A}$ satisfies the equations and inequalities in $\mathcal{S}$.

Let $f(t_1, \ldots, t_n)$ be any ground term. For any $\varphi \in \theta(f(t_1, \ldots, t_n))'$ and $\varphi_i \in \theta(t_i)'$, $1 \leq i \leq n$, by (22) we have $f(t_1, \ldots, t_n) \in \sigma'(\varphi)$ and $t_i \in \sigma'(\varphi_i)$, $1 \leq i \leq n$, thus $f(t_1, \ldots, t_n) \in \sigma'(\varphi \cap f(\varphi_1, \ldots, \varphi_n))$. Then $\varphi \cap f(\varphi_1, \ldots, \varphi_n)$ is $\mathcal{S}$-consistent, since it is nonzero in the termset algebra $\mathcal{A}$. Since the $\varphi, \varphi_1, \ldots, \varphi_n$ were arbitrary, $\theta(f(t_1, \ldots, t_n)) \in E_f^{\mathcal{S}}(\theta(t_1), \ldots, \theta(t_n))$, and since $f(t_1, \ldots, t_n)$ was arbitrary, θ is a run of $\mathcal{R}(2^F, \mathcal{S})$.

Conversely, suppose θ is a run of $\mathcal{R}(2^F, \mathcal{S})$. Under the correspondence (22), the properties (23)–(25) become

$$\varphi \cup \psi \in \theta(t) \iff \varphi \in \theta(t) \text{ or } \psi \in \theta(t) \tag{26}$$

$${\sim}\varphi \in \theta(t) \iff \varphi \notin \theta(t) \tag{27}$$

$$f(\varphi_1, \ldots, \varphi_n) \in \theta(t) \iff \exists t_1, \ldots, t_n\ t = f(t_1, \ldots, t_n) \text{ and } \varphi_i \in \theta(t_i)\ ,\quad 1 \leq i \leq n \tag{28}$$

for expressions $\varphi \cup \psi$, $\sim\varphi$, and $f(\varphi_1, \ldots, \varphi_n) \in F$. The first two of these follow immediately from fact that $\theta(t)'$ is consistent with the laws of Boolean algebra (2). For (28), suppose first that $f(\varphi_1, \ldots, \varphi_n) \in \theta(t)$. For any $g \in \Sigma$,

$$\begin{aligned} t = g(t_1, \ldots, t_m) &\Rightarrow \theta(t) \in E_g^{\mathcal{S}}(\theta(t_1), \ldots, \theta(t_m)) \\ &\Rightarrow f(\varphi_1, \ldots, \varphi_n) \cap g(1, \ldots, 1) \text{ is } \mathcal{S}\text{-consistent} \\ &\Rightarrow m = n \text{ and } f = g \qquad\qquad \text{by (6).} \end{aligned}$$

Thus $t = f(t_1, \ldots, t_n)$ and $\theta(t) \in E_f^{\mathcal{S}}(\theta(t_1), \ldots, \theta(t_n))$. Now each $\theta(t_i)'$ contains some $\psi_i \in \{\varphi_i, \sim\varphi_i\}$, and $f(\varphi_1, \ldots, \varphi_n) \cap f(\psi_1, \ldots, \psi_n)$ must be $\mathcal{S}$-consistent. By properties (8) and (12), the only $\mathcal{S}$-consistent possibility is $\varphi_i = \psi_i$, $1 \le i \le n$, thus $\varphi_i \in \theta(t_i)$, $1 \le i \le n$.

For the other direction of (28), suppose $\varphi_i \in \theta(t_i)$, $1 \le i \le n$. Since θ is a run, for any $\psi \in \theta(f(t_1, \ldots, t_n))'$, $\psi \cap f(\varphi_1, \ldots, \varphi_n)$ is $\mathcal{S}$-consistent. But $\theta(f(t_1, \ldots, t_n))'$ contains at least one of $f(\varphi_1, \ldots, \varphi_n)$, $\sim f(\varphi_1, \ldots, \varphi_n)$, and the former is the only $\mathcal{S}$-consistent choice. Therefore $f(\varphi_1, \ldots, \varphi_n) \in \theta(f(t_1, \ldots, t_n))$.

Finally we show that $\sigma \models \mathcal{S}$. If not, then by Proposition 1, there exists a logical consequence $\varphi \cap f(\varphi_1, \ldots, \varphi_n) = 0$ of $\mathcal{S}$, $\varphi, \varphi_1, \ldots, \varphi_n \in F'$, such that $\sigma'(\varphi \cap f(\varphi_1, \ldots, \varphi_n)) \neq 0$. No term with head symbol $g \neq f$ can be in $\sigma'(\varphi \cap f(\varphi_1, \ldots, \varphi_n))$, thus there must be a term $f(t_1, \ldots, t_n) \in \sigma'(\varphi \cap f(\varphi_1, \ldots, \varphi_n))$. Then $f(t_1, \ldots, t_n) \in \sigma'(\varphi)$ and $t_i \in \sigma'(\varphi_i)$, $1 \le i \le n$, and by the correspondence (22), $\varphi \in \theta(f(t_1, \ldots, t_n))'$ and $\varphi_i \in \theta(t_i)'$, $1 \le i \le n$. But since θ is a run, $\theta(f(t_1, \ldots, t_n)) \in E_f^{\mathcal{S}}(\theta(t_1), \ldots, \theta(t_n))$, therefore $\varphi \cap f(\varphi_1, \ldots, \varphi_n)$ is $\mathcal{S}$-consistent. This is a contradiction.

Theorem 20 implies that if $F_1 \subseteq F_2$, where F_1 and F_2 are subexpression-closed families of set expressions over X, and if $\mathcal{S}$ is any system of set constraints over F_1, then $\mathcal{R}(2^{F_2}, \mathcal{S})$ is a refinement of $\mathcal{R}(2^{F_1}, \mathcal{S})$ under the natural projection $2^{F_2} \to 2^{F_1}$. In particular, for every subexpression-closed family F of set expressions over X, $\mathcal{R}(2^F, \emptyset)$ is a refinement of $\mathcal{R}(2^X, \emptyset)$.

Similarly, if $\mathcal{S}_1$ and $\mathcal{S}_2$ are systems of set constraints over F and $\mathcal{S}_1 \models \mathcal{S}_2$, then any logical consequence of $\mathcal{S}_2$ is a logical consequence of $\mathcal{S}_1$, therefore $\mathcal{R}(2^F, \mathcal{S}_1)$ is a narrowing of $\mathcal{R}(2^F, \mathcal{S}_2)$.

Combining these observations, we see that every $\mathcal{R}(2^F, \mathcal{S})$ is a rational subspace of $\mathcal{R}(2^X, \emptyset)$, since $\mathcal{R}(2^F, \mathcal{S})$ is a narrowing of $\mathcal{R}(2^F, \emptyset)$, which in turn is a refinement of $\mathcal{R}(2^X, \emptyset)$.

For $x \in X$, let us denote also by x the clopen set $\{d \mid x \in d\}$ of any hypergraph 2^F. Let us say that a rational embedding between spaces $\mathcal{R}(2^F, \mathcal{S})$ *preserves* X if the map h on the underlying hypergraphs satisfies $x = h^{-1}(x)$ for all $x \in X$. Note that both the refinement $\mathcal{R}(2^{F_2}, \mathcal{S}) \to \mathcal{R}(2^{F_1}, \mathcal{S})$ and the narrowing $\mathcal{R}(2^F, \mathcal{S}_1) \to \mathcal{R}(2^F, \mathcal{S}_2)$ preserve X in this sense. Let us say that a rational equivalence *preserves* X if the functions $h_1 : \mathcal{C} \to 2^{F_1}$ and $h_2 : \mathcal{C} \to 2^{F_2}$ from the hypergraph underlying the common refinement $\mathcal{R}(\mathcal{C})$ satisfy the property that $h_1^{-1}(x) = h_2^{-1}(x)$ for all $x \in X$.

The following is our main theorem.

Theorem 21. *Let X be any set of variables. Up to logical equivalence on one side and rational equivalence preserving X on the other, the systems $\mathcal{S}$ of set constraints over X are in one-to-one correspondence with the rational subspaces $\mathcal{R}(2^F, \mathcal{S})$ of $\mathcal{R}(2^X, \emptyset)$. If X is finite, then the finite systems of set constraints correspond to the finitary subspaces of $\mathcal{R}(2^X, \emptyset)$. The correspondence preserves the partial orders of logical entailment on one side and X-preserving rational embedding on the other.*

Proof. For any system of set constraints $\mathcal{S}$, let $F_\mathcal{S}$ be the smallest subexpression-closed subset of $T_{\Sigma+\mathrm{B}}(X)$ containing X and all cxpressions occurring in $\mathcal{S}$. Consider the map $\mu : \mathcal{S} \mapsto \mathcal{R}(2^{F_\mathcal{S}}, \mathcal{S})$.

First we show that up to X-preserving rational equivalence on the right hand side, the map μ is well-defined on logical equivalence classes on the left hand side. Suppose $\mathcal{S}_1 \models \mathcal{S}_2$ and $\mathcal{S}_2 \models \mathcal{S}_1$. Let $F_1 = F_{\mathcal{S}_1}$, $F_2 = F_{\mathcal{S}_2}$, and $F = F_1 \cup F_2$. Then $\mathcal{R}(2^F, \mathcal{S}_1)$ is a refinement of $\mathcal{R}(2^{F_1}, \mathcal{S}_1)$ and $\mathcal{R}(2^F, \mathcal{S}_2)$ is a refinement of $\mathcal{R}(2^{F_2}, \mathcal{S}_2)$. But since $\mathcal{S}_1$ and $\mathcal{S}_2$ have the same logical consequences, the two spaces $\mathcal{R}(2^F, \mathcal{S}_1)$ and $\mathcal{R}(2^F, \mathcal{S}_2)$ coincide, thus form a common refinement of $\mathcal{R}(2^{F_1}, \mathcal{S}_1)$ and $\mathcal{R}(2^{F_2}, \mathcal{S}_2)$. Moreover, the natural refinements $\mathcal{R}(2^F, \mathcal{S}_1) \to \mathcal{R}(2^{F_1}, \mathcal{S}_1)$ and $\mathcal{R}(2^F, \mathcal{S}_2) \to \mathcal{R}(2^{F_2}, \mathcal{S}_2)$ preserve X.

To show that the map μ is one-to-one, suppose $\mathcal{R}(2^{F_1}, \mathcal{S}_1)$ and $\mathcal{R}(2^{F_2}, \mathcal{S}_2)$ have a common refinement $\mathcal{R}(\mathcal{D})$ with underlying maps $h_1 : \mathcal{D} \to 2^{F_1}$, $h_2 : \mathcal{D} \to 2^{F_2}$ such that $h_1^{-1}(x) = h_2^{-1}(x)$, $x \in X$. It follows that for any run θ of $\mathcal{R}(\mathcal{D})$, $t \in T_\Sigma$, and $x \in X$,

$$\widehat{h}_1(\theta)(t) \in x \iff \widehat{h}_2(\theta)(t) \in x \ .$$

Thus under the correspondence (22), the runs of $\mathcal{R}(2^{F_1}, \mathcal{S}_1)$ and $\mathcal{R}(2^{F_2}, \mathcal{S}_2)$ correspond to the same family of set valuations. By Theorem 20, $\mathcal{S}_1$ and $\mathcal{S}_2$ have the same set of solutions, thus are logically equivalent.

Suppose X is finite. If $\mathcal{S}$ is finite, then $\mathcal{R}(2^{F_\mathcal{S}}, \mathcal{S})$ is finitary. Conversely, if $\mathcal{R}(2^{F_\mathcal{S}}, \mathcal{S})$ is finitary, then by Proposition 1, $\mathcal{S}$ is logically equivalent to a finite system.

Finally, let $\mathcal{S}_1$ and $\mathcal{S}_2$ be two systems of set constraints, and let $F_1 = F_{\mathcal{S}_1}$, $F_2 = F_{\mathcal{S}_2}$, and $F = F_1 \cup F_2$. As argued above, if $\mathcal{S}_1 \models \mathcal{S}_2$ then $\mathcal{R}(2^F, \mathcal{S}_1)$ is a narrowing of $\mathcal{R}(2^F, \mathcal{S}_2)$, therefore gives a rational embedding preserving X. Conversely, if $\widehat{h} : \mathcal{R}(2^{F_1}, \mathcal{S}_1) \to \mathcal{R}(2^{F_2}, \mathcal{S}_2)$ is a rational embedding preserving X induced by $h : 2^{F_1} \to 2^{F_2}$, then for any run θ of $\mathcal{R}(2^{F_1}, \mathcal{S}_1)$ and $t \in T_\Sigma$,

$$\theta(t) \in x \iff h(\theta(t)) \in h(x) \iff \widehat{h}(\theta)(t) \in x \ .$$

Thus under the correspondence (22), the set valuation corresponding to the run θ of $\mathcal{R}(2^{F_1}, \mathcal{S}_1)$ also corresponds to the run $\widehat{h}(\theta)$ of $\mathcal{R}(2^{F_2}, \mathcal{S}_2)$. By Theorem 20, every solution of $\mathcal{S}_1$ is also a solution of $\mathcal{S}_2$, thus $\mathcal{S}_1 \models \mathcal{S}_2$.

We remark that the Stone dual $\mathbf{St}(F_X/\mathcal{S})$ of the free termset algebra on generators X modulo $\mathcal{S}$ [18], embedded in $2^{T_{\Sigma+\mathrm{B}}(X)}$ in the natural way, gives rise to an induced subspace $\mathcal{R}(\mathbf{St}(F_X/\mathcal{S}))$ of $\mathcal{R}(2^{T_{\Sigma+\mathrm{B}}(X)}, \mathcal{S})$.

5 Applications

In this section we apply the theory of rational spaces to set constraints. We rederive several results in the literature on set constraints and tree set automata in terms of rational spaces. In many cases we are able to generalize the results and give shorter proofs that reveal the topological principles at work.

5.1 Positive and Negative Constraints

In [2], Aiken *et al.* prove that mixed positive and negative set constraints are strictly more expressive than positive constraints alone. The proof of this result is based on a compactness lemma which states that a system of positive constraints is satisfiable if and only if all finite subsets are satisfiable. Under the correspondence of Theorem 21, the compactness lemma of [2] is equivalent to the compactness of the space $\mathcal{R}(2^X, \emptyset)$.

However, the fact that negative constraints can express something that positive constraints alone cannot is a simple consequence of the observation that all systems of positive set constraints define closed sets, whereas the set of solutions of $x \neq 0$ is not closed: if $\sigma_n(x) = \{t \mid \text{depth}(t) > n\}$, then σ_n is a Cauchy sequence, each of whose elements satisfies $x \neq 0$ but whose limit does not.

5.2 Entire Subspaces

In §2.4, we argued that a hypergraph has a run iff it has an entire induced subhypergraph. This essential fact is used in several algorithms for satisfiability of set constraints [1, 2, 10, 11, 25]. Similarly, a rational space is nonempty if and only if it contains an entire subspace. This can be generalized as follows.

Theorem 22. *Every (finitary) rational space is a (finite) union of entire subspaces. Over a language with only constants and unary function symbols, every rational space is essentially entire.*

Proof. The essential subspace of $\mathcal{R}(\mathcal{D})$ is

$$\mathcal{R}\Big(\bigcup_{\theta \in \mathcal{R}(\mathcal{D})} \theta(T_\Sigma)\Big) = \bigcup_{\theta \in \mathcal{R}(\mathcal{D})} \mathcal{R}(\theta(T_\Sigma)) , \tag{29}$$

and $\theta(T_\Sigma)$ is entire. This union is finite if $\mathcal{D}$ is, since there are only finitely many induced subspaces. Any entire subspace of $\mathcal{R}(\mathcal{D})$ is a rational subspace of an entire induced subspace of $\mathcal{R}(\mathcal{D})$.

Over a language with only constants and unary function symbols, the union $\bigcup_x \mathcal{D}_x$ of any family $\mathcal{D}_x$ of entire induced subhypergraphs of $\mathcal{D}$ is an entire induced subhypergraph of $\mathcal{D}$. (Note, however, that in general $\mathcal{R}(\bigcup_x \mathcal{D}_x) \neq \bigcup_x \mathcal{R}(\mathcal{D}_x)$! A counterexample is given below in §5.4.) Applied to (29), this says that the essential subspace of $\mathcal{R}(\mathcal{D})$ is entire.

5.3 Density of Rational Points

Gilleron *et al.* [10] prove that every satisfiable finite system of set constraints has a regular solution. Under the correspondence of Theorem 21, this reduces to the following fact about finitary rational spaces:

Proposition 23. *Every nonempty finitary rational space contains a rational point.*

Proof. If $\mathcal{R}(\mathcal{D})$ is nonempty, then $\mathcal{D}$ has an entire induced subspace $\mathcal{R}(\mathcal{D}')$. In turn, $\mathcal{R}(\mathcal{D}')$ has a deterministic narrowing $\mathcal{R}(\mathcal{D}'')$, which is a rational point.

A rational point corresponds to a deterministic tree set automaton, which has a unique run. Such automata accept regular sets, as can be seen by writing down a system of regular equations of the form (15), one variable for each state.

However, there are more rational points in a finitary rational subspace than just those obtained by narrowings of entire induced subspaces. Indeed, there are only finitely many narrowings of entire induced subspaces, whereas the number of rational points is infinite in general. For example, the Cantor discontinuum contains countably many rational numbers. An example of a rational point of the Cantor discontinuum that is not a narrowing of an entire induced subspace is given in Example 8. This subspace cannot be represented on a hypergraph of fewer than four vertices.

The following result says that the rational points of any nonempty finitary rational space are dense. In terms of set constraints, the significance of this theorem is that every finite system of positive set constraints is determined by its regular solutions.

Theorem 24. *Every finitary rational space is the completion of its rational points.*

Proof. Let $\mathcal{R}(\mathcal{D})$ be a finitary rational space. Recall that $\mathcal{R}(\mathcal{D})$ is a complete metric space. For any $x \subseteq \mathcal{D}$ and $t \in T_\Sigma$, by Proposition 15 the subbasic open set $\{\theta \mid \theta(t) \in x\}$ is a finitary rational subspace of $\mathcal{R}(\mathcal{D})$. Any basic open set A of $\mathcal{R}(\mathcal{D})$ is a finite intersection of subbasic open sets, and A is a finitary rational subspace of $\mathcal{R}(\mathcal{D})$ by Proposition 16. By Proposition 23, any nonempty such A contains a rational point. Thus the set of rational points is dense in $\mathcal{R}(\mathcal{D})$, and its closure is $\mathcal{R}(\mathcal{D})$.

5.4 Closure Properties of Tree Set Automata

In [10], it is claimed without proof that the family of languages accepted by tree set automata is closed under (finite) union, intersection, and cylindrification.

Closure under intersection can be shown as follows. Let $\mathcal{D}_x$ be an indexed family of tree set automata with tuples A_x of accept sets. The tuple A_x is an indexed family A_{xi} of subsets of $\mathcal{D}_x$. Take the induced subspace of the product

$\Pi_x \mathcal{D}_x$ consisting of points $\bigcap_i \Pi_x A_{xi}$. The resulting automaton gives the desired intersection.

Cylindrification is effected as follows. If $\mathcal{D}$ is a tree set automaton, take the rational product $\mathcal{D} \times \{0,1\}$ of $\mathcal{D}$ with a two-element unrestricted hypergraph. For A an accept set in $\mathcal{D}$, take $A' = \pi_1^{-1}(A)$, and add the new accept set $\pi_2^{-1}(1)$.

Contrary to the claim of [10], the family of languages accepted by tree set automata is only closed under union for signatures Σ containing at most one constant or at least one symbol of arity two or greater. In those cases, a marked union $\bigcup_x \mathcal{D}_x \times \{x\}$ of the hypergraphs with the naturally induced hyperedges will give the desired union of sets of runs: in the case of one constant symbol a, if $\theta(a) \in \mathcal{D}_x$ then the entire image of θ must be contained in $\mathcal{D}_x$; and in the case of at least one symbol f of arity two or greater, there can be no run θ taking a value $d \in \mathcal{D}_x$ and $e \in \mathcal{D}_y$ for $x \neq y$, since $E_f(d,e) = \emptyset$, so the run cannot be completed.

For Σ containing at least two constants a, b and no symbol of arity greater than one, the family of languages accepted by tree set automata is not closed under union. Consider the two systems of set constraints $\{x = 1\}$ and $\{x = 0\}$. Let $\mathcal{M}$ be any tree set automaton accepting at least the union of the two sets of solutions. Because $\mathcal{M}$ accepts the solutions of the first system, it must admit a run θ with $\theta(T_\Sigma) \subseteq A_x$. Because $\mathcal{M}$ accepts the solutions of the second system, it must admit a run η with $\eta(T_\Sigma) \subseteq A_{\sim x}$. Let H denote any composition of unary functions. Then the function

$$\lambda t. \begin{cases} \theta(t) \text{ , if } t = H(a) \text{ for some } H, \\ \eta(t) \text{ , if } t = H(b) \text{ for some } H \end{cases}$$

is a legal run of $\mathcal{M}$, but does not satisfy either of the constraints $x = 1$ or $x = 0$.

6 Conclusion

In this paper we have investigated the topological structure of the spaces of solutions of systems of set constraints. We have identified a family of topological spaces called *rational spaces*, which formalize the notion of a topological space with a regular or self-similar structure, such as the Cantor discontinuum. We have developed the basic theory of rational spaces and applied this theory to understand more fully the structure of set constraints.

In a subsequent paper, we will apply these results further to provide a Gentzen-style axiomatization involving sequents $\Phi \vdash \Psi$, where Φ and Ψ are finite sets of set constraints, and give completeness and incompleteness results for this system.

Acknowledgements

The support of the National Science Foundation under grant CCR-9317320 and the U.S. Army Research Office through the ACSyAM branch of the Mathematical Sciences Institute of Cornell University under contract DAAL03-91-C-0027 is gratefully acknowledged.

References

1. A. Aiken, D. Kozen, M. Vardi, and E. Wimmers, *The complexity of set constraints*, in Proc. 1993 Conf. Computer Science Logic (CSL'93), E. Börger, Y. Gurevich, and K. Meinke, eds., vol. 832 of Lect. Notes in Comput. Sci., Eur. Assoc. Comput. Sci. Logic, Springer, September 1993, pp. 1–17.
2. A. Aiken, D. Kozen, and E. Wimmers, *Decidability of systems of set constraints with negative constraints*, Infor. and Comput., (1995). To appear. Also Cornell University Tech. Report 93-1362, June, 1993.
3. A. Aiken and B. Murphy, *Implementing regular tree expressions*, in Proc. 1991 Conf. Functional Programming Languages and Computer Architecture, August 1991, pp. 427–447.
4. ——, *Static type inference in a dynamically typed language*, in Proc. 18th Symp. Principles of Programming Languages, ACM, January 1991, pp. 279–290.
5. A. Aiken and E. Wimmers, *Solving systems of set constraints*, in Proc. 7th Symp. Logic in Computer Science, IEEE, June 1992, pp. 329–340.
6. L. Bachmair, H. Ganzinger, and U. Waldmann, *Set constraints are the monadic class*, in Proc. 8th Symp. Logic in Computer Science, IEEE, June 1993, pp. 75–83.
7. W. Charatonik and L. Pacholski, *Negative set constraints with equality*, in Proc. 9th Symp. Logic in Computer Science, IEEE, July 1994, pp. 128–136.
8. ——, *Set constraints with projections are in NEXPTIME*, in Proc. 35th Symp. Foundations of Computer Science, IEEE, November 1994, pp. 642–653.
9. J. Englefriet, *Tree automata and tree grammars*, Tech. Rep. DAIMI FN-10, Aarhus University, April 1975.
10. R. Gilleron, S. Tison, and M. Tommasi, *Solving systems of set constraints using tree automata*, in Proc. Symp. Theor. Aspects of Comput. Sci., vol. 665, Springer-Verlag Lect. Notes in Comput. Sci., February 1993, pp. 505–514.
11. ——, *Solving systems of set constraints with negated subset relationships*, in Proc. 34th Symp. Foundations of Comput. Sci., IEEE, November 1993, pp. 372–380.
12. N. Heintze, *Set Based Program Analysis*, PhD thesis, Carnegie Mellon University, 1993.
13. N. Heintze and J. Jaffar, *A decision procedure for a class of set constraints*, in Proc. 5th Symp. Logic in Computer Science, IEEE, June 1990, pp. 42–51.
14. ——, *A finite presentation theorem for approximating logic programs*, in Proc. 17th Symp. Principles of Programming Languages, ACM, January 1990, pp. 197–209.
15. N. D. Jones and S. S. Muchnick, *Flow analysis and optimization of LISP-like structures*, in Proc. 6th Symp. Principles of Programming Languages, ACM, January 1979, pp. 244–256.
16. B. Jónsson and A. Tarski, *Boolean algebras with operators*, Amer. J. Math., 73 (1951), pp. 891–939.
17. ——, *Boolean algebras with operators*, Amer. J. Math., 74 (1952), pp. 127–162.
18. D. Kozen, *Logical aspects of set constraints*, in Proc. 1993 Conf. Computer Science Logic (CSL'93), E. Börger, Y. Gurevich, and K. Meinke, eds., vol. 832 of Lect. Notes in Comput. Sci., Eur. Assoc. Comput. Sci. Logic, Springer, September 1993, pp. 175–188.
19. ——, *Set constraints and logic programming (abstract)*, in Proc. First Conf. Constraints in Computational Logics (CCL'94), J.-P. Jouannaud, ed., vol. 845 of Lect.

Notes in Comput. Sci., ESPRIT, Springer, September 1994, pp. 302–303. Full version available as: *Set constraints and logic programming*, Tech. Rep. 94-1467, Cornell University, November 1994.

20. D. Kozen, J. Palsberg, and M. I. Schwartzbach, *Efficient recursive subtyping*, in Proc. 20th Symp. Princip. Programming Lang., ACM, January 1993, pp. 419–428.
21. ———, *Efficient inference of partial types*, J. Comput. Syst. Sci., 49 (1994), pp. 306–324.
22. P. Mishra, *Towards a theory of types in PROLOG*, in Proc. 1st Symp. Logic Programming, IEEE, 1984, pp. 289–298.
23. P. Mishra and U. Reddy, *Declaration-free type checking*, in Proc. 12th Symp. Principles of Programming Languages, ACM, 1985, pp. 7–21.
24. J. C. Reynolds, *Automatic computation of data set definitions*, in Information Processing 68, North-Holland, 1969, pp. 456–461.
25. K. Stefánsson, *Systems of set constraints with negative constraints are NEXPTIME-complete*, in Proc. 9th Symp. Logic in Computer Science, IEEE, June 1994, pp. 137–141.
26. J. Young and P. O'Keefe, *Experience with a type evaluator*, in Partial Evaluation and Mixed Computation, D. Bjørner, A. P. Ershov, and N. D. Jones, eds., North-Holland, 1988, pp. 573–581.

Formal Methods and Social Context in Software Development*

Joseph A. Goguen

Programming Research Group, Oxford University Computing Lab

Luqi

Naval Postgraduate School, Monterey California

Abstract: Formal methods have not been accepted to the extent for which many computing scientists hoped. This paper explores some reasons for that fact, and proposes some ways to make progress. One major problem has been that formal methods have not taken sufficient account of the social context of computer systems. For example, social context causes a continuous evolution of requirements for large complex systems. This implies that designs, specifications and code must also evolve with requirements, and that traceability is important. We discuss a traceability technique called hyper-requirements. To better understand social context, we discuss ethnomethodology, a branch of sociology, and situated abstract data types, which help bridge the gap between the technical and the social. These attempt to provide a scientific basis for requirements capture. Some case studies are briefly described. We distinguish between small, large and huge grain formal methods, arguing that small grain methods do not scale up. This motivates our discussions of software composition and a new paradigm of "Domain Specific Formal Methods."

1 Introduction

Failures of large software development projects are common today, due to the ever increasing size, complexity and cost of software systems. Although billions are spent each year on software in the US alone, many software systems do not actually satisfy users' needs. Moreover, many systems that are built are never used, and even more are abandoned before completion. Many systems once thought adequate no longer are. To remedy this situation, we recommend a two-fold approach: take better account of the social context of computing; and use formal models as a basis for computer support of software evolution.

Experience shows that many failures of large software projects arise from social, political or cultural factors. Hence it is crucial to take account of the

*The research reported in this paper has been supported in part (for J. Goguen) by British Telecommunications plc, the CEC under ESPRIT-2 BRA Working Group 6071, IS-CORE (Information Systems COrrectness and REusability), and Fujitsu Laboratories Limited, and (for Luqi) by the National Science Foundation and the Army Research Office under grant numbers CCR-9058453 and ARO-145-91.

social context of computer-based systems, in addition to the usual technical factors. Social context appears in requirements, where the properties a system must have in order to succeed are determined [11]. The requirements phase of a large system development project is the most error-prone, and these errors are the most expensive to correct [3, 5], so improvements here will have the greatest economic leverage. Unfortunately, requirements are one of the least developed areas of software engineering. Sections 2.2 and 3.1 discuss ethnomethodology, a promising branch of sociology, and situated abstract data types, a new concept that helps bridge the gap between computer technology and its social context. These attempt to provide a scientific basis for requirements capture. Some case studies are given in Section 3.2.

Taking better account of the social context of computing can also lead to faster and more effective system development. For example, requirements for large complex systems are usually wrong initially, and they evolve continually. This has important implications for methodology: first, any methods used to implement requirements should be flexible, so that they can accommodate the ongoing flood of requirements changes, and second it should be easy to trace design changes back to the requirements that triggered them. Section 5.1 describes a technique for traceability called *hyper-requirements.*

We distinguish between formal methods and formal models, in that *formal methods* try to handle some large class of systems (such as information systems), or even all possible systems, whereas *formal models* guide the construction and use of a single system, or a narrow class. We suggest using mechanically processable formal models for building and integrating tools to produce software faster, cheaper, and more reliably, by increasing automation and decreasing inconsistency. This contrasts with formal methods that call for mathematical rigor throughout the development process, usually through a formal notation with a precise mathematical semantics. Section 4.3 distinguishes between small, large and huge grain formal methods, and explains why small grain methods, which are the most common, fail to scale up. The Domain Specific Formal Methods in Section 4.4 illustrate the use of formal models.

2 Social Context and Requirements

Requirements are properties that a system should have in order to succeed in the environment where it will be used [11]. This refers to the system's context of use, and thus to the social as well as the technical. Much of the information that requirements engineers need is embedded in the social worlds of users and managers, and is extracted through interaction with them. This information is informal and dependent on its social context for interpretation. Moreover, much information needed for requirements is *tacit*, i.e., cannot be verbalized by the members who have that information. On the other hand, the representations that appear in constructing computer-based systems are defined by formal rules. Both the formal, context insensitive, and the informal, socially situated aspects of information are crucial to the success of requirements engineering; these two aspects are called "the dry" and "the wet" in [11], which says that the essence of requirements engineering is to reconcile them.

2.1 Video-Based Requirements Elicitation

The Video-Based Requirements Elicitation project the Centre for Requirements and Foundations at Oxford University is exploring techniques from sociology to reveal tacit, interactional work practices that are invisible to standard requirements methods. The following are some goals of this project:

1. To develop an effective new requirements method that can be used by ordinary computer scientists in actual projects.
2. To reduce the risk of delivering inappropriate systems by discovering what work practices must actually be supported.
3. To ease the introduction of new systems by understanding where disruptions might and might not be tolerable.
4. To help manage user expectations by determining where users might want a new system to give a better service than the old one, through analysis of current work practices.

In this project, audio-visual recordings of actual work are analyzed using principles from ethnomethodology, to better understand social and interactional practices in the workplace.

2.2 Ethnomethodology

Traditional sociology is much influenced by what it considers to be orthodox science, where the scientist first formulates a theory, on the basis of which predictions are made, and then tested empirically. The aim is to achieve *objectivity*, in the sense that the desires and biases of the scientist cannot affect the conclusions. Hence, there is a rigid separation between subject and object, between observer and observed. Since modern physics has already moved far from this kind of objectivity, it should not be surprising if sociology, and the social aspects of computing, had to go even further. In particular, if objective information is replaced by situated information, then orthodox techniques for formulating and testing hypotheses, e.g., statistical sampling, are not valid, because the events observed can no longer be assumed statistically independent. However, statistical methods are the foundation for much sociology, e.g., the design and evaluation of questionnaires. This is not to say that statistics and questionnaires are never useful, but that they are *not always valid*, and in particular, that they should not be used where context plays a significant role.

Ethnomethodology can be seen as a reaction against the "scientific" approach of traditional sociology. Ethnomethodology reconciles a radical empiricism with the situatedness of social data, by looking closely at how competent members of a group actually organize their behavior. A basic principle underlying ethnomethodology is that members are held *accountable* for certain actions by their social groups; moreover, exactly those actions are considered socially significant by those groups. A member performing such an action can always to be asked for an account, that is, a justification[1]. Let us call this the *principle of accountability*. From this follows the *principle of orderliness*, that social interaction is *orderly*, in the sense that it can be understood. This follows from the fact that the participants themselves understand it, because of accountability; therefore analysts should also be able to understand it, if they can discover the methods and categories that members themselves use to make sense of their interactions. This implies it is important to use "naturally occurring" data, collected in a situation where members are engaged in activities that they regularly and ordinarily do; otherwise, the basic principle of accountability will not apply, and we cannot be sure that events in the data have any natural social significance. For example, data collected from interviews cannot be used.

Ethnomethodology tries to determine the *categories* and *methods* that members use to render their actions intelligible to one another; this contrasts with presupposing that the categories and methods of the analyst are necessarily superior to those of members. The methods and categories of members are identifiable through the ways that members are held socially accountable by other members of their group. Through immersion in data from some particular social group (such as stock brokers), particular competencies are gradually acquired that enable an analyst to be a sensitive, effective "measuring instrument" in that domain. In this way, subjectivity is harnessed rather than rejected.

Unfortunately, ethnomethodology can be hard to understand; relatively comprehensible expositions of some important points are in [16], [24], and [11], which we have followed here. Conversation analysis studies details of timing, overlap, response, interruption, repair, etc. in ordinary conversation [21], while interaction analysis uses video data.

We can now be more precise about what it means to say that social interaction is *situated*: it means that the events in some interaction can only be fully understood in relation to the concrete situation in which they actually occur. The following *qualities of situatedness* (from [11], inspired in part by Suchman [24]) may help to further clarify this point:

1. *Emergent:* Social events cannot be understood at the level of the individual, that is, in terms of individual (cognitive) psychology, because they are jointly constructed as social events by the members of some group through their on-going interactions.

2. *Local:* Actions and their interpretations are constructed in some particular context, including a particular time and place.

3. *Contingent:* The construction and interpretation of events depends upon the current situation (potentially including the current interpretation of

[1]This does not mean that such accounts are always, or even usually, requested by members of the group, or that they are necessarily given when requested.

prior events). In particular, interpretations are subject to *negotiation*, and relevant rules are interpreted locally, and can even be modified locally.

4. *Embodied:* Actions are linked to bodies that have particular physical contexts, and to the particular way that bodies are embedded in a context may be essential to the social interpretation of some events.

5. *Open:* Theories of social events cannot in general be given a final and complete form, but must remain open to revision in the light of further analyses and further events.

6. *Vague:* Practical information is only elaborated to the degree that it is useful to do so; the rest is left grounded in tacit knowledge.

We will see that these qualities give rise to basic limitations of formalization.

2.3 An Hypothesis and Some Consequences

The *retrospective hypothesis* [11] says that it only becomes clear what the requirements really are when the system is successfully operating in its social and organizational context. This explains why it can be so difficult to manage the requirements of a large system. The retrospective hypothesis also explains why it can be so difficult to enforce rigid process models on actual software projects: it is difficult even to know what phase a given action fits into until some coherence has emerged retrospectively. Note that it takes work by members to achieve a retrospective reconstruction, and that this work is often not done in real projects because of the effort required.

We can now understand why it is impossible to completely formalize requirements: it is because they cannot be fully separated from their social context. More specifically, the qualities of situatedness explain why the lifecycle phases cannot be fully formalized or separated. Indeed, the activities that are necessary for a successful system development project cannot be expected always to fit in a natural way into any system of pre-given categories, and practising software engineers often report that they have to spend much of their time circumventing narrowly prescriptive plans and rules [4]. In general, abstract representations have only a practical utility, and must be interpreted concretely in order for that utility to be made manifest [24]; this includes software production plans and process models.

These considerations have consequences for software engineering. Perhaps the most important is that tools must provide very strong support for retrospective revision; in particular, they must be very flexible, to accommodate the frequent changes in requirements and their links with other objects. Another consequence is that degrees of formalization are needed, ranging from raw data to mathematical formulae. Moreover, information that is heavily situated should come with pointers into its context (e.g., background ethnographic information, audio and video clips of work and interviews, questionnaires and their analyses, sample documents from the work environment, etc.), in order to make it understandable by those who have not had direct contact with the client group.

3 Requirements Elicitation

This section discusses a new approach (from [11]) for transferring information from requirements analysts to system developers, using concepts from both sociology and computing science. Two case studies are briefly described.

3.1 Situated Abstract Data Types

In ordinary social interaction, including cooperative work, there are many structures that participants use and represent in a variety of ways, e.g., with verbal descriptions, drawings, tables, graphs, etc. For example, consider sporting events. Figure 1 shows a table from a newspaper representing the order and participants in a boat race, the Henley Regatta, while Figure 2 shows the same information in the form of a tree. This structure could also be conveyed by a table on a scoreboard, or a sequence of phrases in spoken English. Thus there is a precise structure that is independent of how it happens to be represented; i.e., we have an *abstract data type*, abbreviated *ADT*. As in [11], we use order sorted initial algebra semantics (see [12]) to formalize this structure. A complete formal specification of the Henley Regatta ADT is given in the appendix, using the specification language OBJ3 [14]. This specification has been executed. (Experience shows it is necessary to test all but the most trivial specifications in order to eliminate bugs.) The Henley Regatta example was inspired by Toulmin [25], although Toulmin only used concrete representations without realizing they were algebras, that different representations give isomorphic algebras, or that there is no unique best representation.

Visitors' Cup. Heat 1: Jesus, Cambridge *v.* Christ Church; Heat 2: Oriel *v.* New College; ... Heat 8: Lady Margaret *v.* winner of Heat 1; ... Heat 26: Winner of Heat 23 *v.* winner of Heat 24; Final: Winner of Heat 25 *v.* winner of Heat 26.

Figure 1: A Draw for the Henley Regatta

Several different kinds of entity are involved in a regatta. Some of these can be arranged in a hierarchical classification scheme according to the subsort relation. Sorts correspond to an important class of members' categories, although not every members' category is formalized by a sort; for example, heats are not formalized this way. We will say that boats have sort `Boat`, completed regattas have sort `Reg`, possibly not yet specified boats have sort `Boat?` (a supersort of `Boat`), and possibly not yet completed regattas have the supersort `Reg?`; the latter includes all draws. It is convenient to assume that `Boat` is a subsort of `Reg` and that `Boat?` is a subsort of `Reg?`; these assumptions imply that there are trivial regattas consisting of just one boat, which could even be the unknown boat, denoted "?". Some sorts are *built in*, in the sense that they are already

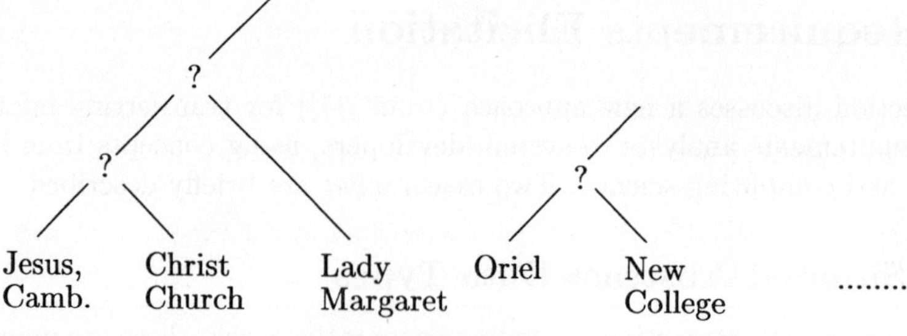

Figure 2: Tree for the Henley Regatta Draw

defined. Two examples are integers and identifiers. The latter have sort `Id` from the built in module `QID` that provides identifiers, here used for naming boats by letting `Id` be a subsort of `Boat`.

Since members use a variety of representations, we should ask how to avoid being tied to any particular representation. The key is to focus on the *methods* that members use to describe (or construct) representations. We distinguish two kinds of method: *constructors*, for building representations from more primitive parts, and *selectors*, for extracting particular information[2]. For regattas, the most important method is a constructor that adds a new heat; it must specify the two contestants, and also provide a slot for the winner. In Figure 2, each non-tip node represents a heat, where the two contestants are the winners of subregattas, or else are given boats; the query mark represents a not yet determined winner. In general, if `R` and `R'` are regattas and `B` is a boat, then `heat(R,R',B)` constructs a new regatta, by adding a heat in which the winners of the subreggatas `R` and `R'` race against each other, with `B` the winner of that heat. Selectors correspond to certain categories used by members. For example, there is a selector that extracts the winner of a given regatta by taking the winner of its final heat.

Methods respect the sorts of representations. For example, the `heat` method takes three inputs, two of which are regattas, and one of which is a boat; it is not meaningful to give a regatta, or an integer, for its third input. In addition, there can be "constants" that do not have any inputs, but do have an output sort; for example, the unknown boat "?" has output sort `Boat?`. We think of these as methods with no input. For example, the method that adds a new heat to a regatta is a function

```
heat : Reg? Reg? Boat? -> Reg?
```

which takes two regatta representations and a boat, and constructs the new regatta where the winners of the subregattas race against each other. Similarly, the selector that gives the winner of a regatta is a function

```
winner : Reg? -> Boat?
```

from regattas to boats.

[2]In object oriented programming, "methods" are operations that can modify; this use of "method" is roughly consistent with that of ethnomethodology. Also, "attributes" are operations that extract information; here these are called "selectors."

Given a particular representation, say by trees, we can collect the possible structures of that representation into an *algebra*, where each sort corresponds to the set of representations of that sort, and the methods correspond to functions that map representations to other representations (or else to built in values, such as numbers). If A is a given algebra, then A_s is its set of representations of sort s. If s' is a subsort of s, then $A_{s'}$ is a subset of A_s (see [12]). Constant methods (such as "?") designate particular representations in an algebra.

It is convenient to overload a method for not yet completed structures with another for completed structures. For example, in addition to `heat` as defined above, we may also have

```
heat : Reg Reg Boat -> Reg
```

for constructing completed regattas.

A set of sorts (with their subsort relations) and a set of methods are together called a *signature* Given a signature, we construct its terms as follows: all constants are terms; and if m is a method with input sorts $s_1, ..., s_n$ and $t_1, ..., t_n$ are terms such that t_i has output sort s_i, then $m(t_1, ..., t_n)$ is a term, with the same output sort as m. For example,

```
heat(heat('JesusCam, 'ChristCh, ?), 'LadyM, ?)
```

is a term, using OBJ3-style identifiers as constants for the names of boats; these begin with a quote and contain no spaces (also we have further abbreviated the boat names).

Given any term t and algebra A over the same signature, that term denotes a unique representation in A. This value or denotation of t is determined by finding the values in A of any constants in t, then applying the functions in A that correspond to the methods in t to those values, then applying further functions to further values, etc., until a final value is obtained. For example, the above term denotes the left subtree in the representation shown in Figure 2. More technically, the denotation of terms is A is given by the *unique homomorphism* from the term algebra to A.

Now we can say that two representation systems are "essentially the same," in the sense that they can represent exactly the same things, if and only if the two algebras are *isomorphic.*

But we are still dealing with representations. How can we obtain structures that are truly independent of how they are represented? The answer has two steps. The first is to describe the *equations* that necessarily hold among the given methods. For example, the fact that the winner of any regatta of the form `heat(R,R',B)` is `B` is expressed by the equation

```
winner(heat(R,R',B)) = B .
```

This is a relationship between the category `winner` and the constructor `heat`.

The second step has to do with limiting the possible models of these equations. So far, we have described an ADT by giving a set of sorts with subsort relations, a set of methods, and a set of equations; let us call these three together a *specification.* Then a *model* of such a specification is an algebra, providing sets for sorts (with subsets for subsorts) and functions for methods, such that all the equations are satisfied. The elements of such a model are a system of representations for the categories and methods in the signature. We now have a way of specifying representations that is truly abstract, in that it says nothing at all about the representations themselves. But unfortunately, there are too many models, and they are not isomorphic to each other. We need one more principle to get what we want; it is called *initiality*, and amounts to the following:

1. *No junk*: every representation in the algebra can be constructed using methods in the given signature.
2. *No confusion*: two terms denote the same representation if and only if they can be proved equal using the given equations.

So now we take as models only those algebras that satisfy not only the equations, but also the two principles above. Such models are called *initial models*, and it can be shown that any two initial algebras are necessarily isomorphic. This gives us the representation independent way of specifying structures that we wanted.

We should distinguish between the object and meta levels of description of this example; a different language is used at each level, for a different purpose. The object level language involves boats, heats, and so on, and its terms construct draws, announce winners, etc. The meta language involves sorts, methods, equations, etc.; at this level we can add new methods, revise equations, etc.

The complexity of the specification in the appendix may seem surprising. But the Henley Regatta really does have boats, heats, regattas, winners, not yet determined boats, etc., and the relationships among them really are rather complex. Also, we know from experience that it can take quite some effort to learn how some unfamiliar sport is structured. It is clear that the methods for constructing and restructuring regattas really are rather complex. Moreover, this kind of complexity is not unique to this example, but is typical of sporting events, games, and many other social phenomena.

Now let us consider what *situatedness* means for this example. First, we must distinguish between the "actual" situated ADT and its formalization in OBJ. The formal code is fixed: it has 3 modules, 32 lines, etc. The structure of an actual Henley Regatta is much more elusive. No doubt there is a rule book; but there are also disgreements, which are negotiated by Stewards and other officials. Any actual Henley Regatta is *emergent* from the myriad interactions among members of a large group, and much of what goes on is *contingent* upon the *local* details of that particular context. It is *open*, in that we cannot hope to formalize everything that could potentially occur, and it is *vague*, because much of what goes on is unarticulated (tacit) and perhaps unarticulatable.

The qualities of situatedness impose limits on the utility of any formal specification. It is doubtful if the Henley Stewards would be interested in the OBJ code, and certainly the sports fans would not be. On the other hand, the code could be useful in designing a computer system to store and display the results of races. The trouble with the formal specification is that it is *too* precise and rigid; it fails to incorporate the richness and flexibility of an actual sporting event. But it does help bridge the huge gap between the rich situatedness of social interaction and the needs of those who develop systems.

Finally, we consider how a situated ADT could be justified by ethnographic data. Since we claim that members recognize that the "same information" is present in different representations, it is natural to find support for the structure in actual instances of such recognitions. Because these would likely be rare in naturally occurring data, requirements engineers could provoke such events by directly posing appropriate questions to members.

3.2 Two Case Studies

This section discusses two case studies done at Oxford using video-based requirements elicitation and situated abstract data types. They are based on live interactions, as opposed to the artificial case study of the Henley Regatta sketched above. The fieldwork was done by Marina Jirotka with help from Jonathan Hindmarsh, and the analysis was done by them with Joseph Goguen, Christian Heath, and Paul Luff. The situated ADT analyses are due to Goguen.

3.2.1 Financial Dealing Rooms

Financial dealers buy and sell financial instruments, such as stocks, bonds and futures. The process of recording a deal is called "deal capture." In the sites studied, this is done by the dealer writing the information on a ticket, often in a very rapid and abbreviated script; this is both time consuming and error prone. Moreover, errors in this task can be extremely costly to correct. A deal is officially a 6-tuple, consisting of the stock (or other financial instrument) name, quantity, date, buyer, seller, and price. Although this ADT is adequate for the legal purpose of registering a deal, it was found to be far from adequate for situations in the dealing room where one deal is part of a complex package of deals negotiated simultaneously, e.g., buying the same stock on one market and selling it on another, with a concomitant foreign exchange transaction.

Over the years, many technical systems have been proposed for making deal capture more accurate and less time consuming. Unfortunately, most systems have failed. These failures can be spectacular, as dealers, who may be angry, tense and very busy, simply throw the new equipment at the wall and then resume business in the old way. This has motivated increasingly radical suggestions for new technology.

One group believed that voice recognition could be used to automate deal capture, and was designing a system based on that technology. They claimed that a very limited number of words needed to be recongized, including numbers and some jargon. However, a detailed video-based analysis of several dealing rooms showed that voice recognition could not support the complex interactions that actually occur in this highly competitive environment [15]. This research potentially saved about a million pounds for prototyping and testing a system that could not succeed. A promising alternative is an active document system, possibly based on a touch sensitive LCD desktop, and virtual reality is promising for the long term.

3.2.2 A Telecommunications Central Operations Unit

A second case study considered a new integrated database for the Fault Restoration Office of a telecommunications Central Operations Unit. This office tries to restore service when lines go down, by finding and connecting alternative lines. Analysis showed that the new database being designed might actually make it harder to get the required information and do the job. An interesting ADT was found to be used by personnel, namely a directed labelled graph showing the faulty route and possible alternatives, labelling edges and nodes with capacities, locations, relevant phone numbers, etc.

It was also found that it would be counter-productive to use the huge video wall in the Central Operations Unit, because this could not support the kind of cooperative work that is actually done. For example, personnel often point at particular items, but pointing at a distant image does not enable co-present personnel to tell which item is indicated. A smaller display located on or above a desk, such that information can be accessed by touching relevant parts of the appropriate graph, should support cooperative work practices in a highly productive way.

4 Formal Methods

After discussing what formalization is, we discuss some limitations of formal methods, building on our previous discussion of the social context of computing. We then discuss the granularity of formal methods, and an emerging paradigm.

4.1 What is Formalization?

According to Webster's Dictionary, "*formal*" means definite, orderly, and methodical; it does not necessarily entail logic or proofs of correctness. Everything that computers do is formal in the sense that syntactic structures are manipulated according to definite rules. Formal methods are syntactic in essence but semantic in purpose.

The prototypical example of a formal notation is first order logic. This notation encodes the semantics of first order model theory with certain formal rules of deduction that are provably sound and complete. Unfortunately, theorem provers for first order logic can be difficult to work with. Formal notations can also capture higher levels of meaning, e.g., they can express certain requirements, but such notations will be much harder to work with, and will have fewer nice properties. By contrast, equational logic is simpler and computationally easier than first order logic, and has many pleasant properties.

The orderliness of social life (due to accountability, as discussed in Section 2.2) and the example in Section 3.1 suggest that social interaction might be formalizable; but there are limits to how successful any such formalization can be. In particular, it will not be easy to formalize domains where there are many *ad hoc* special cases, or where much of the knowledge is tacit. Formalization will be more successful on narrow and orderly domains, such as sporting events, that have long traditions, rule books, referees, regulating bodies, etc. For example, it would be more difficult to formalize a children's game than a boat race, and much more difficult still to formalize human political behavior. There are degrees of formalization, from dry to wet, and it can be important not to formalize beyond the appropriate degree. Cooking recipes are an interesting example, showing how an intermediate degree of formalization is possible and helpful, whereas a very formal treatment would be unhelpful, if it were even possible.

In the driest formalizations, the meta language is also formalized, so that the object level model is a formal theory in the meta language. In less fully formalized models, the meta language may simply be a natural language, or a somewhat stylized dialect. Note that there can be rules at both the object and meta levels. Rules at the object level are part of the model, while rules at the meta level define the language that is used for formalization. Any use of a formalism is situated. Therefore the qualities of situatedness impose basic limitations on any formalization: it will necessarily be emergent, contingent, local, open, and vague. All this is illustrated by the Henley Regatta example.

4.2 Limits and Problems

This section discusses six problems with formal methods:

(1) Formal notation is alien to most programmers, who have little training or skill in higher mathematics. This problem seems to be worse in the U.S. than Europe. For example, set theoretic notation is better accepted in Europe. This may be due to the higher level of mathematics education in Europe.

(2) Another problem is that some advocates of formal methods take a very dogmatic position, that absolutely everything must be proved, to the highest possible degree of mathematical rigor; it must at least be machine checked by a program that will not allow any errors or gaps, and preferably the proof should be produced by a machine. However, mathematicians hardly ever achieve, or even strive for, such rigor; published proofs in mathematics are highly informal, and often have small errors; they never explicitly mention rules of inference from logic (unless they are proving something *about* such rules). In fact, there are various levels of formality, and the most rigorous levels are very expensive; such efforts are only warranted for critical aspects of systems.

(3) A major problem is that formal methods tend to be inflexible; in particular, it is difficult to adapt a formal proof of one statement to prove another, slightly different statement. Since requirements and specifications are constantly changing in the real world, such adaptations are frequently necessary. But classical formal methods have great difficulty in dealing with such changes; we might say that they are a discontinuous function of how the hypotheses to be proved are formulated.

(4) Another problem is that formal methods papers and training often deal only with toy examples, and often these examples have been previously treated

in other formal methods papers. Although it may not be possible to give a detailed treatment of a realistic example in a research paper or a classroom, it is still necessary that such examples exist for a method to have credibility. To be effective, training in formal methods should treat some parts of a realistic (difficult) application.

(5) A technical deficiency of many formal methods is that first order logic is inadequate for loop invariants, as noted long ago by Engeler [6]. However, second order logic is adequate, and has been used by the authors for some years in teaching and research at Oxford [10] and the Naval Postgraduate School [2].

(6) Finally, the fundamental limits imposed by the qualities of situatedness imply that without human intervention, a formalization will often be inadequate for its intended application.

4.3 Small, Large and Huge Grain Methods

It is useful to distinguish among small, large, and huge grain formal methods. This distinction refers to the size of the atomic components that are used, rather than the size of the system itself. The "classic" formal methods fall into the small grain category. These methods have a mathematical basis at the level of individual statements and small programs, but rapidly hit a complexity barrier when programs get large. In particular, pre- and post- conditions, Hoare axioms, weakest preconditions, predicate transformers and transformational programming all have small size atomic units, and fail to scale up because they do not provide structuring or encapsulation. In general, small grain methods have great difficulty handling change, and thus fit poorly into the lifecycle of large complex projects. Transformational programming is less resistant to change than other small grain methods, but has the particular problem that there is no bound to the number of transformations that may be needed; this restricts its use to relatively small and well understood domains (see Section 4.4).

The main techniques of large grain programming involve module composition. We briefly describe an approach based on module expressions, theories, views, and a distinction among sorts for values, classes for objects, and modules for encapsulation. This allows expressing designs and high level system properties in a modular way, and allows the parameterization, composition and reuse of designs, specifications, and code.

The main programming unit is the *module*, which allows multiple classes to be declared together. Module composition features include renaming, sum, parameterization, instantiation, and importation. These constitute *parameterized programming* [8], which can be seen as functional programming with modules as values, theories as types, and module expressions as (functional) programs. *Renaming* allows the sorts, classes, attributes and methods of modules to get new names, while *sum* is a kind of parallel composition of modules that takes account of sharing. The interfaces of parameterized modules are defined by *theories*, which declare both syntactic and semantic properties. *Instantiation* is specified by a *view* from an interface theory to an actual module, describing a binding of parts in the theory to parts in the actual module; *default views* can be used to give "obvious" bindings. A design for a system (or subsystem) is described by a *module expression*, which can be parameterized, and can be evaluated to produce an executable version of the system. *Importation* gives multiple inheritance at the module level. Parameterized programming is implemented in OBJ [14], has a rigorous semantics based on category theory, and has influenced the designs of ML and Ada. Much of the power of parameterized programming comes from treating theories and views as first class citizens. For example, it can provide a higher order capability in a first order setting.

A major advantage of parameterized programming is its support for *design* in the same framework as specification and coding. Designs are expressed as module expressions, and they can be executed symbolically if specifications of a suitable form are available. This gives a convenient form of prototyping. Alternatively, prototypes for the modules involved can be composed to give a prototype for the system, again by evaluating the module expression for the design. An interesting feature of the approach is to distinguish between horizontal and vertical structuring. *Vertical structure* relates to layers of abstraction, where lower layers implement or support higher layers. *Horizontal structure* is concerned with module aggregation, enrichment and specialization. Both kinds of structure can appear in module expressions, and both are evaluated when a module expression is evaluated. We can also support rather efficient prototyping through *built-in* modules, which can be composed just like other modules, and give a way to combine symbolic execution with access to an underlying implementation language.

Parameterized programming is considerably more general than the module systems of languages like Ada, CLU and Modula-3, which provide only limited support for module composition. For example, interfaces in these languages can express at most purely syntactic restrictions on actual arguments, cannot be horizontally structured, and cannot be reused. LILEANNA [26] implements many ideas of parameterized programmming, including horizontal and vertical composition (following LIL [7]) for the Ada language. In [13], some further features are described: dynamic binding with views, abstract classes, private class inheritance, and dynamic integration of components from different libraries.

CAPS [19] is a rapid prototyping system with a data flow like semantics supporting hard real time constraints. It has module composition and powerful facilities to retrieve software components [17] and to support evolution [18].

Developing systems with huge grain components is qualitatively very different from working with small and large grain components. For example, very different ways to handle errors are needed. In systems with huge components, correcting errors in the components is generally impossible; such errors must be accepted and worked around. For example, a network protocol such as TCP/IP may have been obtained from an external vendor, so that the developers of the larger system will not have access to the code. If the version being used has a bug, there is no choice but to find some way to avoid that bug. This is often possible because of the multiplicity of features provided in such components.

4.4 Domain Specific Formal Methods

There is much more to formal methods than suggested by the themes dominant in the past, namely synthesis and correctness proofs for algorithms. Although both remain interesting for theoretical research, their impact on the practice of large scale software development is limited. A number of successful recent tools suggest a new formal methods paradigm having the following attributes:

1. A narrow, well defined, well understood problem domain is addressed; there may already be a successful library for this domain.

2. There is a community of users who understand the domain, have good communication among themselves, and have potential financial resources.

3. The tool has a graphical user interface that is intuitive to the user community, embodying their own language and conventions.

4. The tool takes a large grain approach; rather than synthesizing procedures out of statements, it synthesizes systems out of modules; it may use a library of components and synthesize code for putting them together.

5. Inside the tool is a powerful engine that encapsulates formal methods concepts and/or algorithms; it may be a theorem prover or a code generator; users do not have to know how it works, or even that it is there.

Some systems that fit this description are: CAPS [19]; ControlH and MetaH [27]; AMPHION [23]; Panel [22]; and DSDL [1]. This emerging paradigm might be *Domain Specific Formal Methods*, in recognition of the role played by the user community and their specific domain. This falls into the category of large grain methods, and can potentially be extended to huge grain problems.

4.5 Education

Teaching a formal method while ignoring the social, political and cultural problems that necessarily arise in real projects can have a negative impact. For example, students may be taught programming from formal specifications, but not that specifications come from requirements, and that requirements are always changing. As a result, they are not prepared for the rapid pace of evolution found in real industrial work. A related problem is that many students feel that formal methods turn programming from a creative activity into a boring formal exercise. The failure of teachers to deal with these problems has caused students to leave computing science.

Students need to know how to deal with real programs having thousands or even millions of lines of code. Carefully crafted correctness proofs of simple algorithms give an entirely misleading impression of what real programming is like. Most of the examples in textbooks and the classroom are very small, and most of the techniques are small grain.

Reliable formal method based tools can let students do problems that would be impossible by hand; this should increase their confidence. Teachers could also present methods and tools that work on large grain units, that is, on modules, rather than on small grain units like statements, functions and procedures, because such methods can scale up, whereas the small grain methods can not. It is desirable to develop suites of sample problems that systematically show how and when to apply formal methods, and how to combine them with informal approaches.

5 Software Evolution

A traditional view is that software evolution only occurs after initial development is completed. For example, software evolution has been defined to consist of the activities required to keep a software system operational and responsive after it is accepted and placed into production; this is synonymous with maintenance, but avoids the deadly negative connotation of that word. Evolution has the connotation of life, and if used in the context of an alternative software lifecycle like prototyping, it captures the dynamic aspects of all activities from requirements specification and system construction to updating operational systems [18].

Difficulties associated with evolution are not purely technical; social, political and cultural factors are important, and can dominate cost. Tools based on formal models can help with both technical and management tasks. They can maintain the integrity of a software development project by scheduling tasks, monitoring deadlines, assigning tasks to programmers, keeping on-line documentation, maintaining relations among system components, tracking versions, variations and dependencies of components, and merging changes to programs. These problems are especially important when a large group of programmers work concurrently on a large complex system.

An important practical problem is dealing with so-called "legacy code," i.e., old code that is poorly structured, poorly documented, and often in an obsolete language. For example, many banks depend on huge COBOL programs, but find it extremely difficult to modify these programs when business conditions change.

5.1 Hyper-Requirements

The Centre for Requirements and Foundations at Oxford has a project on improving the *traceability*, *accessibility*, *modularity*, and *reusability* of the numerous objects that arise and are manipulated during software development. An initial study administered a detailed two-stage questionnaire to requirements engineers at a large firm. Analysis of the results showed that there are many different traceability problems. Major distinctions are between pre-RS (Requirements Specification) traceability and post-RS traceability, and between forward and backward traceability. Analysis also showed that "access to users" was a very common difficulty. Further investigation revealed certain policies and traditions that restrict communication within the firm, so that requirements engineers often could not discover what users really needed. One problem was an "internal market" which restricted communication between "vendors" and "clients" within the firm. Abolition of the internal market for requirements projects and improving the openness of information could potentially save enormous sums for such firms.

A major aspect of the traceability problem is the difficulty of maintaining the huge mass of dependencies among components in a large system development effort. Often the components are not adequately defined, e.g., module boundaries may be incorrectly drawn, or not even explicitly declared; also, module interfaces may be poorly chosen and badly documented. Without formal models of dependencies and tool support for managing them, it is impossible to know what effect a change to a component will have, and in particular, to know what other components may have to be changed to maintain consistency.

The second phase of this project is designing a flexible object oriented database to support links among related objects [20], in order to ground decisions in the prior objects that justify them, and to track module dependencies. These links may be of a variety of different kinds, which are user-definable, and the objects may be in different media. Particular subproblems include formalizing dependencies, developing methods to calculate dependencies, and propagating the implications of a change. We intend to support the *situatedness* of requirements decisions, as well as their *traceability* through an idealized chain of stages. This associates related objects into what are called *module clusters* in hyperprogramming [9]. Techniques of parameterized programming, as described in Section 4.3, should improve reuse, and a generalized notion of *view* should help with organizing links. These techniques should be useful for design, when specifications are produced from requirements, as well for coding and maintenance.

A Formal Specification for the Henley Regatta

This appendix gives a formal specification for the Henley Regatta, using the executable part of the programming and specification language OBJ3, which is described in detail in [14]. First we give a rough overview of the specification below. There are three modules, beginning with the keyword "`obj`" and ending with the keyword "`endo`." Immediately after "`obj`" comes the name of the module. Sorts, operations (for methods), subsorts, variables, and equations are declared after fairly obvious keywords; also, "`cq`" indicates a conditional equation, while "`pr`" and "`dfn`" indicate module importations, the latter with a renaming of the principle sort (in this case, from `List` to `Index`).

The first module, named "`12`", merely introduces two constants, "`1`" and "`2`", used to indicate the two boats in a heat. Note that this is an abstract data type, in the sense that we could have chosen different representations for the two boats, such as "`A`" and "`B`", or "`1st`" and "`2nd`"; any such choice will yield an isomorphic (two element) initial algebra. The second module, named "`LIST`", is a *parameterized module* for forming lists of anything; the list constructor has the syntax "_ _" for placing a new element at the head of a list; `nil` is the empty list. Inside the third module, we form and import the module `LIST[12]`, renaming its principal sort `List` to be `Index`; these lists are used for picking out particular instances of a boat racing in a regatta; a typical term of sort `Index` is "`1 1 2 nil`". This module also introduces the constructor `heat` for regattas, the method `swin` for setting winners of heats, and the selector `winner`.

```
obj 12 is sort 12 .
  ops 1 2 : -> 12 .
endo

obj LIST[X :: TRIV] is sort List .
  op nil : -> List .
  op _ _ : Elt List -> List .
endo

obj HENLEY is
  sorts Boat Reg Boat? Reg? .
  pr QID .
  subsorts Id < Boat < Reg Boat? < Reg? .
  dfn Index is LIST[12].

  op ? : -> Boat? .
  op heat : Reg? Reg? Boat? -> Reg? .
  op heat : Reg Reg Boat -> Reg .

  var B B' : Boat? .
  vars R R' R'' : Reg? .
  var I : Index .

  op winner : Reg? Index -> Boat? .
  eq winner(heat(R,R',B), nil) = B .
  eq winner(heat(R,R',B), 1 I) = winner(R,I) .
  eq winner(heat(R,R',B), 2 I) = winner(R',I) .
  eq winner(B,nil) = B .
  cq winner(B,I) = ? if I =/= nil .

  op swin : Reg? Index -> Reg? .
  eq swin(heat(R,R',B), nil) = heat(R,R',B).
  eq swin(heat(R,R',B), 1 nil) = heat(R,R',winner(R,nil)).
  eq swin(heat(R,R',B), 2 nil) = heat(R,R',winner(R',nil)).
  cq swin(heat(R,R',B), 1 I) = heat(swin(R,I),R',B) if I =/= nil .
  cq swin(heat(R,R',B), 2 I) = heat(R,swin(R',I),B) if I =/= nil .
  eq swin(B,I) = ? .
endo
```

This code, with many test cases, has actually been run in OBJ3.

References

[1] Jeffrey Bell, Richard Kieburtz, *et al.* Software design for reliability and reuse: a proof-of-concept demonstration. Technical report, Department of Computer Science and Engineering, Oregon Graduate Institute, 1994.

[2] Valdis Berzins and Luqi. *Software Engineering with Abstractions.* Addison-Wesley, 1990.

[3] Barry Boehm. *Software Engineering Economics.* Prentice-Hall, 1981.

[4] Graham Button and Wes Sharrock. Occasioned practises in the work of implementing development methodologies. In Marina Jirotka and Joseph Goguen, editors, *Requirements Engineering: Social and Technical Issues*, pages 217–240. Academic Press, 1994.

[5] Alan M. Davis. *Software Requirements: Analysis & Specification.* Prentice-Hall, 1990.

[6] Erwin Engeler. Structure and meaning of elementary programs. In Erwin Engeler, editor, *Symposium on Semantics of Algorithmic Languages*, pages 89–101. Springer, 1971. Lecture Notes in Mathematics, Volume 188.

[7] Joseph Goguen. Reusing and interconnecting software components. *Computer*, 19(2):16–28, February 1986. Reprinted in *Tutorial: Software Reusability*, Peter Freeman, editor, IEEE Computer Society, 1987, pages 251–263, and in *Domain Analysis and Software Systems Modelling*, Rubén Prieto-Díaz and Guillermo Arango, editors, IEEE Computer Society, 1991, pages 125–137.

[8] Joseph Goguen. Principles of parameterized programming. In Ted Biggerstaff and Alan Perlis, editors, *Software Reusability, Volume I: Concepts and Models*, pages 159–225. Addison Wesley, 1989.

[9] Joseph Goguen. Hyperprogramming: A formal approach to software environments. In *Proceedings, Symposium on Formal Approaches to Software Environment Technology.* Joint System Development Corporation, Tokyo, Japan, January 1990.

[10] Joseph Goguen. Proving and rewriting. In Hélène Kirchner and Wolfgang Wechler, editors, *Proceedings, Second International Conference on Algebraic and Logic Programming*, pages 1–24. Springer, 1990. Lecture Notes in Computer Science, Volume 463.

[11] Joseph Goguen. Requirements engineering as the reconciliation of social and technical issues. In Marina Jirotka and Joseph Goguen, editors, *Requirements Engineering: Social and Technical Issues*, pages 165–200. Academic Press, 1994.

[12] Joseph Goguen and José Meseguer. Order-sorted algebra I: Equational deduction for multiple inheritance, overloading, exceptions and partial operations. *Theoretical Computer Science*, 105(2):217–273, 1992.

[13] Joseph Goguen and Adolfo Socorro. Module composition and system design for the object paradigm. *Journal of Object Oriented Programming*, to appear 1995.

[14] Joseph Goguen, Timothy Winkler, José Meseguer, Kokichi Futatsugi, and Jean-Pierre Jouannaud. Introducing OBJ. In Joseph Goguen, editor, *Algebraic Specification with OBJ: An Introduction with Case Studies.* Cambridge, to appear.

[15] Christian Heath, Marina Jirotka, Paul Luff, and Jon Hindmarsh. Unpacking collaboration: the interactional organisation of trading in a city dealing room. In *European Conference on Computer Supported Cooperative Work '93*. IEEE, 1993.

[16] Steven Levinson. *Pragmatics.* Cambridge University, 1983.

[17] Luqi. Normalized specifications for identifying reusable software. In *Proceedings of the 1987 Fall Joint Computer Conference*, pages 46–49. IEEE, October 1987.

[18] Luqi. A graph model for software evolution. *IEEE Transactions on Software Engineering*, 16(8):917–927, 1990.

[19] Luqi. Real-time constraints in a rapid prototyping language. *Journal of Computer Languages*, 18(2):77–103, 1993.

[20] Francisco Pinheiro. TOOR: An object oriented tool for hypermedia requirements, 1994.

[21] Harvey Sacks, Emanuel Schegloff, and Gail Jefferson. A simplest systematics of the organization of turn-taking in conversation. *Language*, 504:696–735, 1974.

[22] Jacob T. Schwartz and W. Kirk Snyder. Design of languages for multimedia applications development. In *Proceedings of 1994 Monterey Workshop: Increasing the Practical Impact of Formal Methods for Computer-Aided Software Development*, pages 46–55, 1994.

[23] Mark Stickel, Richard Waldinger, Michael Lowry, T. Pressburger, and I. Underwood. Deductive composition of astronomical software from subroutine libraries. In *Conference on Automated Deduction*, volume 12, 1994.

[24] Lucy Suchman. *Plans and Situated Actions: The Problem of Human-machine Communication.* Cambridge University, 1987.

[25] Stephen Toulmin. *The Uses of Argument.* Cambridge University, 1958.

[26] Will Tracz. Parameterized programming in LILEANNA. In *Proceedings, Second International Workshop on Software Reuse*, March 1993. Lucca, Italy.

[27] Steve Vestal. Integrating control and sopftware views in a CACE/CASE toolset. In *Proceedings, Symposium on Computer-Aided Control Systems*, 1994.

Testing can be formal, too

Marie-Claude Gaudel

LRI, URA 410 du CNRS
Université de Paris-Sud, Batiment 490
91405 Orsay, France

Abstract. The paper presents a theory of program testing based on formal specifications. The formal semantics of the specifications is the basis for a notion of an exhaustive test set. Under some minimal hypotheses on the program under test, the success of this test set is equivalent to the satisfaction of the specification.
The selection of a finite subset of the exhaustive test set can be seen as the introduction of more hypotheses on the program, called selection hypotheses. Several examples of commonly used selection hypotheses are presented.
Another problem is the observability of the results of a program with respect to its specification: contrary to some common belief, the use of a formal specification is not always sufficient to decide whether a test execution is a success. As soon as the specification deals with more abstract entities than the program, program results may appear in a form which is not obviously equivalent to the specified results. A solution to this problem is proposed in the case of algebraic specifications.

1 Introduction

This paper is a survey of a research activity which has been led for several years in the area of program testing [5, 6, 7], and a presentation of some recent results [2, 3, 22].

There has been surprisingly little research on the foundations of program testing. Some notable exceptions are the early paper by Goodenough and Gerhart [18] where the notion of testing criteria was first introduced and the work of Gourlay [19] who proposed a formal definition of a test method and pointed out the role of specifications in the testing process. More recently, the growing interest in the use of formal methods has raised several works on testing based on formal specifications. It turns out that formal specifications are quite fundamental to a rigourous and systematic approach of program testing. For instance, an application area where testing has been extensively studied is the area of communication protocols [8, 15, 27], etc: all these works are based on formal models of the protocol to be tested, generally finite state machines or transition systems.

First, let us make more precise the background of the works reported here. The aim of a testing activity is to detect some faults in a program. The use of the verb *detect* is important here, since locating and correcting the faults are generally regarded as out of the scope of testing: they require different data and techniques.

Several approaches of testing are possible: in this work we consider dynamic testing, i.e. the execution of the program under test on a finite subset of its input domain and the interpretation of the obtained results. Other approaches are inspections or analysis of the text of the program; they are often called static techniques.

Obviously, testing methods strongly depend on the nature of the faults which are searched for. We consider here a large class of faults, namely discrepancies between the behaviour of a program and some functional specification. It means that non functional aspects such as performance or robustness are currently not considered in our framework.

There exist numerous criteria and strategies to guide the choice of the test data, i.e. the *selection* of a finite subset of the input domain called the test set. A test data criterion is a predicate *C(P, S, T)* which characterises those test sets *T* which are adequate for testing a program *P* with respect to a specification *S* according to the criterion. An example of a common (and weak) criterion is that *T* must ensure the execution of all the statements in *P*. When a criterion is only based on the text of the program, as in this example, the corresponding testing strategy is said to be structural. When the criterion is only based on the specification, the strategy is called functional. The program is considered as a "black-box" and the way it is written does not influence the test. Clearly, structural testing and black-box testing are complementary: structural testing cannot detect omissions; black-box testing cannot test every detail of the program. Currently, most research results on software testing are related to structural testing for historical reasons: without formal specifications it was difficult to study functional testing on theoretical grounds. It is this problem which is addressed in this paper.

Most test methods, and the corresponding selection criteria, consist in dividing the input domain of the program into subdomains and require the test set to include at least one element from each subdomain (these subdomains are not always disjoint, it is the case for the "all-statements" criterion mentioned above). Reasoning by cases on a formal specification seems a very natural way to define such subdomains. The approach presented here follows this idea. It is based on algebraic specifications and has been experimented on several significant case studies. Some underlying ideas have been reused for other kinds of formal specification or model: VDM in [13], finite state automata and labelled transition systems in [26], and Lustre programs [21].

The interpretation of the results of a test is often very difficult. This difficulty is known as the *oracle problem*: deciding whether the result of a test execution is acceptable or not requires a procedure (manual, automated, or both) which relies upon a knowledge of the expected results. For some problems, the expected results are not known for the whole input domain (for instance, it happens in numerical analysis); in some other cases the decision problem is undecidable (for instance the equivalence of the source and object programs when testing a compiler).

But even in less extreme situations, the problem is difficult as soon as the program yields the results in a way which may depend on some representation choices and makes the comparison with the specified results difficult. This is an important issue in the case of black-box testing, since the test is based on a specification which is (normally) more abstract than the program. Thus program results may appear in a form which is not obviously equivalent to the specificied results. This contradicts a common belief that the existence of a formal specification is sufficient to directly decide whether a test is a success: some more work is often needed. A solution to this problem is proposed in the case of algebraic specifications. It is based on a notion of observational equivalence of the specification and the program [28, 20].

The paper is organized as follows: part 2 presents a theory of black-box testing based on formal specifications and both the test data selection problem and the oracle problem are addressed in the case of algebraic specifications; part 3 reports briefly several applications: some case studies in algebraic specifications and the use of some aspects of the approach for other formalisms.

2 A Theory of Testing

2.1 Specifications and Programs

Algebraic specifications are characterized as usual by a signature $\Sigma = (S, F)$, where S is a finite set of sorts and F a finite set of operation names with arity in S, and some axioms, i.e. a finite set Ax of Σ-formulas. We consider positive conditional axioms, i.e. the following form of formulas:

$$(v_1 = w_1 \wedge \ldots \wedge v_k = w_k) \Rightarrow v = w$$

with $k \geq 0$, where v_i, w_i, v and w are Σ-terms with S-variables.

A subset S_{obs} of observable sorts is distinguished among the sorts of S.

Let SP be such a specification and P be a program under test. Since we consider dynamic testing, we are interested by the properties of the computations by P of the operations mentioned in Σ; P must provide some procedure or function for executing these operations; the question is whether they satisfy the axioms of SP. Given a ground Σ-term t, we note t_P the result of its computation by P. We define now how to test P against a Σ-equation.

Definition 1: Given a Σ-equation ε, and a program P which provides an implementation for every operation name of Σ,
• a *test* for ε is any ground instantiation $t = t'$ of ε;
• a *test experiment* of P against $t = t'$ consists of the evaluation of t_P and t'_P and the comparison of the resulting values.

The generalization of this definition to positive conditional axioms is straightforward. In the following, we say that a test experiment is successful if it concludes to the satisfaction of the test by P, and we note it $P \models \Gamma$ where Γ is the test, i.e. a ground formula (deciding whether $P \models \Gamma$ is the oracle problem mentioned in the introduction; we postpone the discussion on the way it can be realised to section 2.3).

We can now introduce the definition of an exhaustive test of a program P against a specification SP.

Definition 2: Given a specification $SP = (\Sigma, Ax)$, the ***exhaustive test set*** for SP, noted $Exhaust_{SP}$ is the set of all well-sorted ground instances of all the Σ-axioms:

$$Exhaust_{SP} = \{ \Phi\sigma \,/\, \Phi \in Ax,\ \sigma = \{\sigma_s : var(\Phi)_s \rightarrow T_{\Sigma s} \,/\, s \in S\} \}$$

An exhaustive test of P against SP is the set of all the test experiments of P against the formulas of $Exhaust_{SP}$.

The definition of $Exhaust_{SP}$ is very close to (and is derived from) the notion of satisfaction of a set of Σ-equations by a Σ-algebra as it has been defined for a long time [17]. In particular, the fact that each axiom can be tested independently comes from this definition. But several points prevent the success of an exhaustive test of *P* against *SP* from being equivalent to the satisfaction of *SP* by *P*. This is true under some conditions on *P* which are discussed below.

It seems natural and convenient to consider *P* as defining a Σ-algebra, and we assume it for the moment. But this is far from being a weak assumption. It means that there is no influence of any internal state on the procedures which implement the operations of Σ: they behave as mathematical functions. As it has been pointed out in [22], it is possible to weaken this hypothesis on *P*. This point is related to the oracle problem and is discussed in section 2.3.

A second point is that in definition 2, the substitutions σ assign ground Σ-terms to the variables. It means that $Exhaust_{SP}$ is exhaustive with respect to the specification, not always with respect to the program. Thus, such a test ensures the satisfaction of *SP* by *P* only if all the values computable by *P* are reachable by T_Σ. These two points define a class of programs for which the result of an exhaustive test would be meaningful.

Definition 3: Given a signature Σ, a program *P* is *Σ-testable* if it defines a finitely generated Σ-algebra A_P. The Σ-testability of *P* is called the *minimal hypothesis* H_{min} of an exhaustive test of *P* against a specification of signature Σ.

The definitions of $Exhaust_{SP}$ and H_{min} provide a framework for developing a theory of black-box testing from algebraic specifications. Practical test criteria (i.e. those which correspond to a finite test set) will be described as stronger hypotheses on the program. Important properties such as *unbias* (correct programs are not rejected) and *validity* (only correct programs are accepted) can be characterized. This is done in the following subsections. Now, we list some remarks on these definitions where we discuss their adequacy and suggest some variants.

Remark 1: Strictly speaking, definition 1 above defines a *tester* rather than a test data: a test $t = t'$ is nothing else than the abstract definition of a program which evaluates *t* and *t'* via the relevant calls to the procedures of a program and compares the results; a test experiment of *P* is an execution of this tester linked to *P*. There is an interesting analogy with Brinksma's work on protocol testing [8]: there, from the specification of the process under test is derived a specification of a "canonical tester process"; the concurrent execution of the two processes performs the test experiment.

Remark 2: As said above, the definition of $Exhaust_{SP}$ comes from the notion of satisfaction of [17]. However, it does not correspond exactly to initial semantics of algebraic specifications since inequalities are not tested: it rather corresponds to loose semantics. It is possible to choose another definition. For instance, as suggested in [4] and applied by Dong and Frankl in the ASTOOT system [14], another possibility is to consider the algebraic specification as a rewriting system, following a "normal-form" semantics. Under the condition that the specification defines a ground-convergent rewriting system, it leads to an alternative definition of the exhaustive test set:

$$Exhaust'_{SP} = \{ t = t{\downarrow} \,/\, t \in T_\Sigma \}$$

where $t{\downarrow}$ is the unique normal form of *t*. In [14] a bigger exhaustive test set is mentioned (but not used) which includes for every ground term the inequalities with other normal forms, following the definition of initial semantics.

Remark 3: An open question is how to deal with the case of test experiments which do not terminate (more precisely, the evaluation of t_P or t'_P does not terminate). Given the kind of specification that is considered here, where performance issues are not addressed, there is no way to make a decision in such a case... In practice, it is generally not a problem since more information is available on the expected behaviour of the system.
Remark 4: The generalization of the theory presented here to partial operations is possible when the specification provides definition predicates which are completely specified, i.e. they are defined for all the ground terms. In this case, it is possible to define the exhaustive test set as the restriction of $Exhaust_{SP}$ to those formulas which only contain equations with defined terms. This means that the exhaustive test checks the axioms for all the terms which must be defined. Other definitions of $Exhaust_{SP}$ are possible, depending on the considered semantics (for instance all partial algebras or only minimally defined ones [9]) and on some conventions on what is a correct behaviour of the program for undefined terms.

2.2 Selection and Hypotheses

$Exhaust_{SP}$ is obviously not usable in practice since it is generally infinite. One way to make it finite is to introduce stronger hypotheses on the behaviour of P. These *selection hypotheses* are the formal counterpart of some common test methods: for instance, the subdomain-based selection criteria mentioned in the introduction correspond to the determination of subdomains of the variables where the program is supposed to have the same behaviour. Assuming that, it is no more necessary to have all the ground instances of the variables but only one by subdomain. Such criteria are modelled in our framework by uniformity hypotheses.

Definition 4: Given a formula $\Phi(X)$ where X is a variable, a ***uniformity hypothesis*** on a subdomain D for a program P is the assumption:

$$(\forall t_0 \in D)\ (P \models \Phi(t_0) \Rightarrow (\forall t \in D)\ (P \models \Phi(t)\ )$$

The generalization to several variables is straightforward.

In the framework of black-box testing, the determination of such subdomains is guided by the specification, as we will see later. Other kinds of selection criterion correspond to other forms of hypothesis. For instance regularity hypotheses express the fact that it is sometimes enough to test a formula for terms under a certain "size".

Definition 5: Given a formula $\Phi(X)$ where X is a variable, and a function of interest $|t|$ from ground terms into natural numbers, a *regularity hypothesis* for a program P is the assumption:

$$((\forall t \in T_\Sigma)\ (\ |t| \leq k \Rightarrow P \models \Phi(t)\ ))\ \Rightarrow\ (\forall t \in T_\Sigma)\ (P \models \Phi(t))$$

Some other kinds of useful hypothesis will be mentioned in section 3. The choice of the hypotheses is nothing else than the determination of a test strategy, of a test selection criteria. But the advantage of the notion of hypothesis is that it makes explicit the assumptions on the program which correspond to one strategy. A test set T should never be presented independently of its selection hypotheses: thus we use the notion of a *testing context* which is a pair (H, T) of a set of hypotheses and a set of tests. Now, we define some important properties which are required for testing contexts:

Definition 6: Given a specification $SP = (\Sigma, Ax)$, a testing context (H, T) is *valid* if, for all Σ-testable programs P

$$H \Rightarrow (P \models T \Rightarrow P \models Exhaust_{SP})$$

Definition 7: Given a specification $SP = (\Sigma, Ax)$, a testing context (H, T) is *unbiased* if, for all Σ-testable programs P,

$$H \Rightarrow (P \models Exhaust_{SP} \Rightarrow P \models T)$$

Assuming H, validity ensures that any incorrect program is rejected and unbias prevents the rejection of correct programs. By construction, the testing context $(H_{min}, Exhaust_{SP})$ is valid and unbiased. Another extreme valid and unbiased testing context is $(H_{min} \wedge P \models Exhaust_{SP}, \emptyset)$, which states that assuming that the program is correct, an empty test set is sufficient.

An interesting fact is that any context (H, T) where T is a subset of $Exhaust_{SP}$ is unbiased. Conversely, if T contains a test which is not a consequence of SP, or which is in contradiction with it, any context (H, T) is biased.

It is clear that the interesting testing contexts are valid and unbiased and they are compromises between the two extreme examples given above. Intuitively, weak hypotheses correspond to large test sets and conversely. This naturally leads to the definition of a preorder on testing contexts [2]:

Definition 8: Let $TC1 = (H1, T1)$ and $TC2 = (H2, T2)$ be two testing contexts. $TC1 \leq TC2$ (pronounce "*TC2* refines *TC1*") iff:

(i) $H2 \Rightarrow H1$

(ii) $H2 \Rightarrow (P \models T2 \Rightarrow P \models T1)$

$\leq$ means that in the refined testing context the hypotheses on the program are stengthened, and, assuming these refined hypotheses, the refined test set reveals as many faults as the original one. $\leq$ is reflexive, transitive, but not anti-symmetric. It makes it possible to build valid contexts since it preserves validity:

Proposition: If $(H_{min}, Exhaust_{SP}) \leq (H, T)$, then (H,T) is valid.

The proof results directly from the definitions. This proposition and the above remarks on unbiased contexts provide the bases of a method to obtain valid and unbiased testing contexts: the starting point is $(H_{min}, Exhaust_{SP})$ and by successive refinements, new hypotheses are added, and the test set is restricted to a subset of the previous one (thus of $Exhaust_{SP}$); for every step the property (ii) of definition 8 must be verified.

The choice of the selection hypotheses can be guided by the specification. For instance, given an axiom of the form: $(v_1 = w_1 \wedge \ldots \wedge v_k = w_k) \Rightarrow f(\tau(X)) = w$, where X is a list of variables also occuring in the v_i, w_i and w, the domain defined by the precondition can be considered as a uniformity subdomain. This gives one test for the axiom, and the instantiations of the variables are any solution of the set of equations of the precondition. If this coverage of the axiom is considered not sufficient, weaker uniformity hypotheses on subdomains can be obtained by *unfolding* the axiom.

We just give an example of one unfolding step and send the reader to [3] for a formal presentation. Assume that v_1 is of the form $g(\mu(X))$, that there is no other occurrence of g in the axiom, and that there is the following axiom somewhere in the specification: $cond(Y) \Rightarrow g(\nu(Y)) = w'$; then it is possible to compose the preconditions of the two axioms, and it will result in a more complicated axiom, namely: $cond(Y) \wedge \mu(X) = \nu(Y) \wedge w' = w_1 \wedge ... \wedge v_k = w_n \Rightarrow f(\tau(X)) = w$. Note that this axiom is never explicitly constructed: the specification remains unchanged. Unfolding is just used to build smaller uniformity subdomains by composition of the preconditions of the axioms. There will be as many tests of the original axiom as possible unfoldings and a set of weaker uniformity hypotheses. Now the problem of choosing uniformity subdomains is transformed into the problem of deciding when to stop unfolding, since it is well-known that unfolding recursive definitions of functions on recursive domains results in the enumeration of the domain. One possible way is to introduce some regularity hypothesis or some other uniformity hypotheses.

This kind of symbolic manipulation of the specification is implemented by a tool, the LOFT system [23]. The kernel of this system is an equational resolution procedure since the implementation of uniformity hypotheses requires to solve conjunctions of equations in the theory defined by the specification.

2.3 The Oracle Problem

In definition 1, we have stated that a test experiment of P against $t = t'$ consists of the evaluation of t_P and t'_P and the comparison of the resulting values. This comparison is obvious to perform when the sort s of t and t' corresponds exactly to a type of the programming language. Under the (weak) hypothesis that this comparison is correctly implemented by the compiler, we can use the equality of the programming language, noted $eq_{s,P}$ as a valid and unbiased oracle, i.e. test whether $P /= t = t'$ by computing $eq_{s,P}(t_P, t'_P)$.

We call such an hypothesis an *oracle hypothesis*. Some sorts for which it is sound to assume that their equality is correctly implemented are the predefined sorts of the programming languages (booleans, integers, ...). We distinguish these sorts as *observable*: as in [20] they will be used to observe the implementation of the other sorts.

It is more problematic to have such an hypothesis on data types defined by the programmer to represent more elaborated sorts of the specification. Even if an equality function is available for these sorts, it is a part of the program under test and it is possible for this function or the representation to be erroneous. The naive idea of testing the equality of all the observable components of the representation is wrong: the folk literature on abstract data types provide numerous examples where different representations correspond to the same abstraction (see [3] for a nasty variant of the good old stack example).

One solution is to refer to an observational equivalence for defining such equalities: an observation is a computation which has a non observable value as argument and returns an observable value. Clearly, if there is a way, using P, to get different results from the same observation of two non observable values, these values are different. Conversely, if there is no observable difference, they can be considered as equal.

Definition 9: Given a signature Σ, a *Σ-context* is a Σ-term which contains *exactly one* variable. If the variable is of s sort, we say it is a *Σ-context over s*. We call an *observable context* a context of observable sort where the variable is of non observable sort and we note $OC_\Sigma[s]$ the set of observable contexts over s for a signature Σ.

Given the non observable test $t = t'$ where t and t' are of sort s, it can be transformed into an (often infinite) set of observable tests:

$$\{ C(t) = C(t') \,/\, C \in OC_{\Sigma}[s] \}$$

It is possible to only consider minimal observable contexts, i.e. those which do not contain any observable context, assuming that the implementation of the operations of the observable sorts preserves equality. It is a slightly stronger oracle hypothesis than the correctness of the equality implementation, but even stronger ones, such as the correctness of the implementation of observable sorts, are very likely to be sound if, as suggested above, the observable sorts correspond to the predefined types of the programming languages.

Anyway, the set of observable tests is very likely to be infinite. A natural way to get finite observable test sets is to follow a similar approach as in the previous section: we may introduce some hypotheses to reduce the infinite set of contexts to a finite one. However, an erroneous decision in favor of equality has different consequences depending on the position of the considered equation in the axiom:

- if the equation is the *conclusion* of a positive conditional axiom, if the oracle hypotheses are not satisfied by the program, the finite set of observable tests may be successful for an incorrect program;
- if the equation occurs in the *precondition* of an axiom, and if its test is erroneously decided successful, the conclusion of the axiom is required to be valid despite the fact that it is not required by the specification, and there is a risk to reject correct programs.

The first case is acceptable in our framework since there is no problem of bias, and the validity of the testing context is preserved (remind that validity is defined by: *assuming the hypotheses*, the success of the test set implies the satisfaction of the specification). But the second one is not acceptable since it corresponds to a biased testing context. This leads to a restriction on the kind of considered algebraic specifications: it is possible to use observable contexts as oracle only for those positive conditional specifications where all the equations in preconditions are of observable sorts. Under this condition, we define an observable exhaustive test set for a specification:

Definition 10: Given a positive conditional specification $SP = (\Sigma, Ax)$, where is distinguished a subset S_o of observable sorts, where all the equations occuring in the preconditions of the axioms of Ax are of observable sort, the *observable exhaustive test set* for SP, noted Obs_{SP} is:

$$\begin{aligned} Obs_{SP} = \{ & L \Rightarrow C(t) = C(u) \,/\, L \Rightarrow t = u \in Exhaust_{SP}, \\ & t \text{ and } u \text{ of sort } s \notin S_o,\ C \in OC_{\Sigma}[s] \} \cup \\ \{ & L \Rightarrow t = u \,/\, L \Rightarrow t = u \in Exhaust_{SP},\ t \text{ and } u \text{ of sort } s \in S_o \} \end{aligned}$$

An *observable exhaustive test* of P against SP is the set of all the test experiments of P against the formulas of Obs_{SP}.

The notion of Σ-testability (definition 3) must be revised accordingly in order to ensure that the success of an observable exhaustive test set is meaningful: the conditions on the observable sorts must be added; H_{min} can be weakened (the definition given in [3] turned out to be too strong as pointed out in [22]). It must be noted that stating definition 10, we have changed the notion of satisfaction of a specification SP by a program P into a notion of behavioural satisfaction (more precisely, the "behavioural satisfaction I" of [25]), and we have kept the fact that the exhaustive test only considers those values which are finitely generated by Σ. Thus there is no more need that *P* defines a finitely generated Σ-algebra: it is sufficient that it can be observed as a finitely generated Σ-algebra via the observable contexts.

Definition 11: Given a signature Σ where is distinguished a subset S_o of observable sorts, a program *P* is *OΣ-testable* if:

- for every observable sort *so*, *P* provides a correct implementation of equality;
- the behaviour of *P* is observationally equivalent via the observable contexts to a finitely generated Σ-algebra.

The OΣ-testability of *P* is called the *minimal hypothesis* $OBSH_{min}$ of an observable exhaustive test of *P*.

We are now in the position of defining validity and unbias of testing contexts in this new framework:

Definition 12: Given a positive conditional specification $SP = (\Sigma, Ax)$, where is distinguished a subset S_o of observable sorts, where all the equations occuring in the preconditions of the axioms of *Ax* are of observable sort, a testing context *(H, T)* is *observationally valid* if, for all OΣ-testable program *P*

$$H \Rightarrow (P /= T \Rightarrow P /= Obs_{SP})$$

Definition 13: Given a specification $SP = (\Sigma, Ax)$, a testing context *(H, T)* is *observationally unbiased* if, for all OΣ-testable programs *P*,

$$H \Rightarrow (P /= Obs_{SP} \Rightarrow P /= T)$$

Similarly to the previous subsection, the testing context ($OBSH_{min}$, Obs_{SP}) can be used as a starting point to build observationally valid and unbiased testing contexts by addition of new hypotheses and restriction of the test set in a way satisfying requirement (ii) of definition 8: any testing context *(H,T)* where *T* is a subset of Obs_{SP} is observationally unbiased, and the ≤ preorder preserves observational validity.

Remark 5: It has been suggested to choose the observable sorts among the predefined types of the programming language. It is clear that other possibilities can arise: it may be possible to correctly decide whether two values of a type are equal even is there is not a built-in equality operation in the programming language.
Remark 6: It is interesting to note that the restriction on the form of the specification introduced by definition 10 is mentioned in [25] as necessary to have a sensible definition of behavioural satisfaction based on the concept of observable consequence (our $C(t) = C(t')$ are observable consequences of *SP*). It is clear that, depending on the kind of considered program, other observable exhaustive test sets could be defined, with some other kind of observation and thus a different notion of behavioural satisfaction. In such cases, there is no reason to have the same restriction.
Remark 7: Another reasonable requirement on the specification is that it should be hierarchically consistent with respect to the specification of the observable sorts. However, in our theory, it is quite possible to test a program against an inconsistent specification, but the observable exhaustive test fails as soon as the program satisfies $OBSH_{min}$.
Remark 8: Practically, Σ-testability requires that the program provides an implementation of every operation of Σ, which must behave as a function; moreover the values computable by the program must be finitely generated by Σ. One way to ensure functional behaviours of the operations is to forbid the use of global variables

and any side effects in the program. One way to ensure the last point is to require, as in [3], that the program exports exactly the operations of Σ. These conditions are sufficient but too strong to be realistic and it is important to look at more flexible ones. OΣ-testability slightly relaxes the constraint of a functional behaviour of the operations into an "observational" functional behaviour. Besides, it is clearly possible to allow the program to define the operations of Σ up to a renaming; it is also possible to allow the program to export more operations, or less operations (if some hidden operations are used in the specification). A first discussion of the conditions under which it is possible can be found in [22].

Remark 9: These minimum hypotheses are static properties of the program. Some of them are (or could be) checkable: currently the tools for static checking of programs are often independent of the specifications. However, [16] reports some promising experiments on the use of specifications for statically detecting violations of abstraction barriers.

2.4 Equational test sets

When the specification is sufficiently complete with respect to the observable sorts, it is possible to consider another exhaustive test set where all the elementary tests are equations [2].

Definition 14: Given a positive conditional specification $SP = (\Sigma, Ax)$, where is distinguished a subset S_o of observable sorts, where all the equations occuring in the preconditions of the axioms of Ax are of observable sort, the *exhaustive observable equational test set* for SP, noted $EqObs_{SP}$ is:

$$EqObs_{SP} = \{ t = u \,/\, t_1 = u_1 \wedge \ldots \wedge t_k = u_k \Rightarrow t = u \in Obs_{SP}, \\ \forall i = 1, \ldots, k,\ Ax \vdash_{EQ} t_i = u_i \}$$

where $\vdash_{EQ}$ corresponds to the usual equational calculus.

The testing context $(OBSH_{min}, EqObs_{SP})$ is observationally unbiased and valid if SP is sufficiently complete. Thus it can be use as a starting point for the selection of finite test sets by the addition of selection hypotheses as shown in section 2.2. It is what is done by the LOFT system.

3 Applications

This part of the paper briefly reports some case studies and experiments related to the theory presented here. Some of them were performed at LRI, some of them elsewhere. The first subsection is devoted to studies based on algebraic specifications. The second one reports some interesting attempts to transport some aspects of the theory to other formal approaches, namely VDM, automata, and Lustre.

3.1 Some Case Studies with Algebraic Specifications

A first experiment, performed at LRI by Pierre Dauchy and Bruno Marre, was on the on-board part of the driving system of an automatic subway. An algebraic specification was written [12] . Then two modules of the specification were used for experiments with LOFT. The experiment is reported in details in [11]. We just give the conclusions here. It must be noted that this work was performed with the certification agency (INRETS), not with the development team of the system.

The first module was the control of the door opening; there were 25 axioms, some of them with rather long and complex preconditions. The choice of the uniformity subdomains was done in a standard way: for instance unfolding ≤ into = and < and stopping, unfolding false conjunctions and true disjunctions into three cases, but forbidding any decomposition leading to meaningless enumerations. The total number of tests turned out to be reasonable: 254. The good surprise was that 230 of these tests were related to the emergency stop, and that some of them presented some conjunctions of cases which were not yet considered in the certification process.

The second module was the overspeed control. There were 6 axioms in the main module which used 4 other modules. A first experiment was performed with the same choices as for the previous module, and reasonable test sets were selected for most of the axioms (between 1 to 40); but some problems arose when trying to treat the following axiom:

limspeed(S) = min4 (target-speed(S), stop-speed(S), imposed-lim-speed(S), way-speed(S))

where *S* is the state of the train and *min4* is the minimum of its four arguments. A brute application of the same strategy as above to the four arguments of *min4* would lead to 25920 tests... The point is that a lot of useless decompositions are performed, for instance if *target-speed(S)* is the minimum, it is useless to test all the possible orders on the three other speeds. Thus another testing strategy was tried: first perform the decomposition of the *target-speed* operation, then add to the obtained subdomains the three equations describing the comparisons with the other speeds and return one value in this domain. This example demonstrates that the choice of a testing context is an interactive process: the LOFT system aims at assisting this process, by guiding the choice of the uniformity subdomains and yielding unbiased and valid testing contexts.

A second experiment is reported in [24] and was performed within a collaboration between LRI and the LAAS laboratory in Toulouse. Our colleagues from LAAS have a good experience in evaluating the quality of test sets by mutation. The experiment was performed on a rather small piece of software written in C, which was extracted from a nuclear safety shutdown system. It was the filtering procedure which aims at checking the validity of successive measures in order to eliminate doubtful ones. For some previous work, 1345 mutants of this procedure have been built by the LAAS team using classical fault injection methods.

The algebraic specification was written in a data-flow like style and contained 30 axioms. 5 different test sets of 282 tests were selected using the LOFT system, with the same hypotheses: we were interested in studying both the quality and the stability of the method with respect to the arbitrary choices in the uniformity subdomains. The score, i.e. the rate of rejected mutants, turned out to be rather stable, from 0.9651 to 0.9784, and good for a black-box strategy. These results were better than the ones of the all-paths structural strategy, which is supposed to be the most powerful structural testing strategy.

The Software Engineering Laboratory at EPFL in Lausanne has developed and is continually extending a library of components in Ada. The components are used for teaching and in industry; most of them have been released as publicly available software. A characteristic of this library is the existence of numerous variants (with respect to parameter passing, storage properties, etc) of some components. Such a set of variants is called a family. An experiment of "intensive" testing of a family have been led by Didier Buchs and Stéphane Barbey [1]. First an algebraic specification of the component was reengineered: the signature was derived from the package specifications of the family, and the axioms were written manually. Then the LOFT system was used with a standard choice of hypotheses [23].

The ASTOOT approach has been developped by Phyllis Frankl and her team at the Polytechnic University in New York [14]. The addressed problem is the test of object-oriented programs: classes are tested against algebraic specifications. A set of tools has been developed; we focus here on the test cases generation issues. As mentioned in remark 2, a different choice has been made for the exhaustive test set, which is the set of equalities of every closed term with its normal form. Thus, the specification must define a convergent term rewriting system. Moreover, there is a restriction to classes such that their operations have no side effects on their parameters and functions have no side effects: it corresponds to a notion of testability. The oracle problem is solved by introducing a notion of observational equivalence between objects of user-defined classes, which is based on minimal observational contexts, and by approximating it. The test case selection is guided by an analysis of the conditions occuring in the axioms; the result is a set of constraints which must be solved manually. It is encouraging to note that this project was led independently from our research, but that it turned out, a posteriori, that the theory presented here nicely fits to describe it, even when different basic choices were made.

3.2 Other Formalisms

In section 2 we followed several times the same procedure to build slightly different formal bases for program testing against an algebraic specification: we stated a notion of test, a notion of exhaustive test and some minimal hypotheses to ensure validity and unbias. A reasonable conjecture is that this procedure is applicable to other kinds of formal specification. In the case of VDM, a first interesting step has been performed by Jeremy Dick and Alain Faivre within a project, led at Bull Corporate Research Centre, on automating the generation of test cases from VDM-SL specifications [13].

The formulae of the specification are relations on states decribed by operations (in the sense of VDM, i.e. state modifications). They are expressed in first-order predicate calculus. These relations are reduced to a disjunctive normal form (DNF), creating a set of disjoint sub-relations. Each sub-relation yields a set of constraints which describe a single test domain. The reduction to DNF is the equivalent of the axioms unfolding presented in section 2.2. Uniformity and regularity hypotheses appear in relation with this partition analysis.

As VDM is state-based, it is not enough to partition the operations domains: thus the authors give a method of extracting a finite state automaton from a specification. This method uses the results of the partition analysis of the operations to perform a partition analysis of the states. This led to a set of disjoint classes of states, each of which corresponds either to a precondition or a postcondition of one of the above subrelations. Thus, a finite state automaton can be defined, where the states are some equivalence classes of states of the specifications. From this automaton, some *test suites* are produced such that they ensure a certain coverage of the automaton paths. The notion of test suites is strongly related to the state orientation of the specification: it is necessary to test the state evolution in presence of sequences of data, the order being important.

A tool has been developed to assist this process. However, since the kind of considered formula is more general than in our case, it is not possible, in general, to solve the returned constraints: the tool is more a test cases generator than a test data generator.

This work makes numerous references to some of the important notions and techniques presented in section 2: uniformity and regularity hypotheses, unfolding. What is currently missing is a notion of exhaustive test set, and its connex concepts, testability, validity and unbias. A very tentative idea is to consider that a specification defines an infinite automaton, and to take the test suites which exercise all the paths of this automaton as an exhaustive test set. Clearly, it deserves more investigation and more thought about the kind of semantics to be considered.

In a thesis prepared at the France-Telecom CNET laboratory in Lannion [26], Marc Phalippou has studied conformance testing of telecommunication systems with respect to a formal model. His work is based on IOSM, as Input-Output State Machines, which are a variant of labelled transition systems. He has systematically studied the kinds of selection hypothesis which are used, or could be useful in this framework. First he shows that most existing methods for generating test data from automata are based on regularity hypotheses (more exactly, on the counterpart, in the automata framework, of the definition presented here: its form is rather different). Then he shows how uniformity hypotheses can be seen as congruence on automata, and he introduces two variants, weak and strong uniformities. He suggests several other kinds of hypothesis which provide a formal expression of some interesting testing strategies. One of them, the fairness hypothesis is of quite general interest since it corresponds to a notion of testability for non deterministic systems.

In another thesis, prepared jointly at CEA and LRI, the use the LOFT system to assist the test of Lustre programs has been investigated [21]. Lustre is a description language for reactive systems which is based on the synchronous approach [10]. An algebraic semantics of Lustre has been stated and entered as a specification in LOFT. A Lustre program is considered as an enrichment of this specification, just a specific axiom to be tested. It is too early to decide of the practical interest of this work, but this way of adapting new formalisms to the system is interesting.

Acknowledgements

The content of this article is directly indebted to joint work and many stimulating discussions with Gilles Bernot, Bruno Marre and Pascale Le Gall. Bruno Marre has been very helpful in the preparation of this paper. The discussions with Phyllis Frankl during her visit to Orsay in June 94 influenced this presentation in a significant way.

References

1. Barbey S., Buchs D., Testing Ada abstract data types using formal specifications, in Ada in Europe, proc. 1st Int. Eurospece-Ada-Europe Symposium, Copenhagen, Sept. 1994, LNCS n°887, Springer-Verlag, 1994, pp. 76-89.
2. Bernot G., Testing against formal specifications: a theoretical view, TAPSOFT'91 CCPSD proceedings, LNCS n° 494, Springer-Verlag, Brighton, 1991, pp. 99-119.
3. Bernot G., Gaudel M-C., Marre B., Software testing based on formal specifications : a theory and a tool, Software Engineering Journal, vol. 6, n° 6, Nov. 1991.
4. Bernot G., Gaudel M-C, Marre B., A Formal Approach to Software Testing, 2nd International Conference on Algebraic Methodology and Software Technology (AMAST), Iowa City, May 1991, Workshops in Computing Series, Springer-Verlag, 1992.
5. Bougé L., A contribution to the theory of program testing, Theoretical Computer Science, vol. 37, 1985, pp. 151-181.
6. Bougé L., Choquet N., Fribourg L., Gaudel M.-C., Application of PROLOG to test sets generation from algebraic specifications, TAPSOFT'85 proceedings, LNCS n°186, Springer-Verlag, Berlin, 1985, pp. 246-260.
7. Bougé L., Choquet N., Fribourg L., Gaudel M.-C., Test set generation from algebraic specifications using logic programming, Journal of Systems and Software, vol. 6, n°4, pp. 343-360, 1986.
8. Brinksma E., A theory for the derivation of tests, 8th International Conference on Protocol Specification, Testing and Verification, Atlantic City, North-Holland, 1988.
9. Broy M., Wirsing M., Partial Abstract Types. Acta Informatica, 3, 1982, pp. 47-64.
10. Caspi P., Halbwachs N., Pilaud D., Plaice J., Lustre: a declarative language for programming synchronous systems, 14th ACM symposium on Principle of Programming Languages, Munich, 1987, pp. 178-188.
11. Dauchy P., Gaudel M-C, Marre B., Using Algebraic Specifications in Software Testing : a case study on the software of an automatic subway, Journal of Systems and Software, vol. 21, n° 3, June 1993, pp. 229-244.
12. Dauchy P., Ozello P., Experiments with Formal Specifications on MAGGALY, Second International Conference on Applications of Advanced Technologies in Transportation Engineering, Minneapolis, Aug. 1991.
13. Dick J., Faivre A., Automating the generation and sequencing of test cases from model-based specifications, FME'93, LNCS n°670, Springer-Verlag, 1993, pp. 268-284.
14. Dong R. K., Frankl Ph. G., The ASTOOT approach to testing object-oriented programs, ACM Transactions on Software Engineering and Methodology, vol. 3, n° 2, Apr. 1994.
15. Dssouli R., Bochmann G., Conformance testing with multiple observers, in Protocol Specification Testing and Verification VI, North-Holland 1987, pp. 217-229.
16. Evans D., Using specifications to check source code, Master thesis, MIT Laboratory for Computer Science, 1994.

17. Goguen, J.A., Thatcher, J.W. and Wagner E.G., An initial algebra approach to the specification, correctness and implementation of abstract data types, in Current Trends in Programming Methodology, Vol.4: Data Structuring, edited by R.T. Yeh, pp. 80-149, Prentice-Hall, 1978.
18. Goodenough J. B., Gerhart S., Towards a theory of test data selection, IEEE Transactions on Software Engineering, vol. SE-1, n° 2, June 1975.
19. Gourlay J., A mathematical framework for the investigation of testing, IEEE Transactions on Software Engineering, vol. SE-9, n° 6, pp. 686-709, Nov. 1983.
20. Hennicker R., Observational implementations of algebraic specifications, Acta Informatica, vol. 28, n° 3, pp. 187-230, 1991.
21. Hsiao N. C., Sélection de test de propriétés de sûreté à partir d'une modélisation algébrique de programme Lustre, Thèse de l'Université de Paris-Sud, Orsay, 1994.
22. Le Gall P., Les Algèbres étiquetées : une sémantique pour les spécifications algébriques fondée sur une utilisation systématique des termes. Application au test de logiciel avec traitement d'exceptions, Thèse de l'université de Paris-Sud, LRI, Orsay, 1993.
23. Marre B., LOFT, a tool for assisting test data selection from algebraic specifications, in these proceedings.
24. Marre B., Thévenod-Fosse P., Waeselink H., Le Gall P., Crouzet Y., An experimental evaluation of formal testing and statistical testing, SAFECOMP'92, Zürich, Oct. 1992.
25. Orejas F., Implementation and behavioural equivalence: a survey, 8th WADT/3rd COMPASS Workshop, Doudan, 1991, LNCS n° 655, Springer-Verlag, 1993, pp. 93-125.
26. Phalippou M., Relations d'implantation et hypothèses de test sur des automates à entrées et sorties, Thèse de l'université de Bordeaux 1, Sept. 1994.
27. Pitt D.H., Freestone D., " The derivation of conformance tests from LOTOS specifications", IEEE Transactions on Software Engineering, vol. 16, n°12, Dec. 1990, pp. 1337-1343.
28. Sannella D. T., Tarlecki A., On observational equivalence of algebraic specifications, J.C.S.S., vol.34, pp. 150-178, 1987.

Anatomy of the Pentium Bug

Vaughan Pratt*

Dept. of Computer Science, Stanford University, Stanford, CA 94305-2140
pratt@cs.stanford.edu

Abstract. The Pentium computer chip's division algorithm relies on a table from which five entries were inadvertently omitted, with the result that 1738 single precision dividend-divisor pairs yield relative errors whose most significant bit is uniformly distributed from the 14th to the 23rd (least significant) bit. This corresponds to a rate of one error every 40 billion random single precision divisions. The same general pattern appears at double precision, with an error rate of one in every 9 billion divisions or 75 minutes of division time.
These rates assume randomly distributed *data.* The distribution of the faulty pairs themselves however is far from random, with the effect that if the data is so nonrandom as to be just the constant 1, then random *calculations* started from that constant produce a division error once every few minutes, and these errors will sometimes propagate many more steps. A much higher rate yet is obtained when dividing small (< 100) integers "bruised" by subtracting one millionth, where every 400 divisions will see a relative error of at least one in a million.
The software engineering implications of the bug include the observations that the method of exercising reachable components cannot detect reachable components mistakenly believed unreachable, and that hand-checked proofs build false confidence.

1 Background

The Intel Pentium[2] microprocessor makes occasional errors in floating point divisions due to five missing entries from a lookup table of quotient digits. Relative errors as large as 2^{-14} are possible. The errors depend only on the mantissas of the operands and not their exponents. In the space of all operand pairs, one in nine billion pairs generate an error in the quotient exceeding the usual double precision errors; of these, one in 40 billion generates an error exceeding single precision errors.

The error was first noticed within Intel and independently by Prof. Thomas Nicely at Lynchburg College, Virginia, in the course of an ongoing project to estimate the sum of the reciprocals of the twin primes, known to exist but not known to much accuracy. Nicely publicized his discovery at the end of October, and it quickly became a *cause célèbre* on the Internet.

* This work was supported by ONR under grant number N00014-92-J-1974

[2] Pentium is a trademark of Intel Corporation

In early December 1994 Intel put on their World-Wide Web home page their White Paper [SB94]. The paper described in broad outline the nature of the bug, and estimated that the average user would encounter the error once every 27,000 years.

Intel was initially reluctant to replace processors, and attempted to distinguish those with a genuine need. This proved unreliable and eventually Intel agreed to exchange processors with no requirement that any test be passed.

This paper gives a considerably more detailed account of the bug than can be inferred from the White Paper. We are indebted to Tim Coe, a floating point hardware designer at Vitesse Semiconductor for unearthing some of these details. Coe constructed a model of the bug that predicted most of the errors, and also found much larger errors than Nicely did, most notably 4195835/3145727 which the Pentium computes with a relative error of 2^{-14}. The bug renders visible many details of the Pentium's floating point division process that are invisible in the absence of the bug. In this respect the bug is like a linear accelerator with the errors being the analogue of scattered particles. We have duplicated Coe's model and modified it slightly to account for additional errors, exposing more architectural details.

A workaround for the bug has been developed by Terje Mathisen and Cleve Moler. The workaround is to detect those divisors at risk of an error and to scale both operands by a suitable constant to move the operands out of danger before performing the division. With this precaution the Pentium never performs an erroneous division, not even as an intermediate step in getting the correct result. These and other aspects of the bug have very recently been written up [CMMP95].

The natural software engineering question is, what did this bug teach us? For example, what could have been done differently that would have avoided this bug? The following points seem to us to be of general interest, not so much for their novelty as for their relevance to the Pentium bug.

1. An Achilles' heel for testing. One thinks of testing as being as good as verification *if* one could test all possible cases. As a weakened version of this, a comprehensive test should exercise every device and/or line of code in the system.

The Pentium bug reveals a serious limitation of this approach. There is of course no data that can exercise unreachable code or table entries. Thus if one believes that the five "missing" entries are unreachable, then no attempt will be made to produce a test for this case. Hence missing entries are likely to be overlooked by any *fabricated* set of test cases. Randomly generated test cases have a better chance of reaching a supposedly unreachable part of the system.

2. Manual verification has negative value. In contrast to computer proof checking, manual proof checking is a notoriously unreliable process. Nevertheless one may feel reassured after having proved manually that an algorithm works in every detail, and hence attach little incremental value to a machine-checked proof. This opens the way to $475,000,000 errors, Intel's estimate of the cost of the bug.

2 The SRT division algorithm

The SRT[3] division algorithm adapts the familiar process of long division to computer hardware, for an arbitrary radix $r \geq 2$. On binary computers (as opposed to say decimal), SRT happens to work particularly well at radix 4, which we now assume.

Division problems involving negative operands may be reduced to divisions involving only nonnegative operands, via the identities $(-y)/x = y/(-x) = -(y/x)$ and $(-y)/(-x) = y/x$. This lets us concentrate on nonnegative operands.

The basis for the radix 4 SRT algorithm is the following navigational strategy permitting a microbot, Robby, to determine his position to any desired accuracy when placed on the main diagonal of Figure 1.

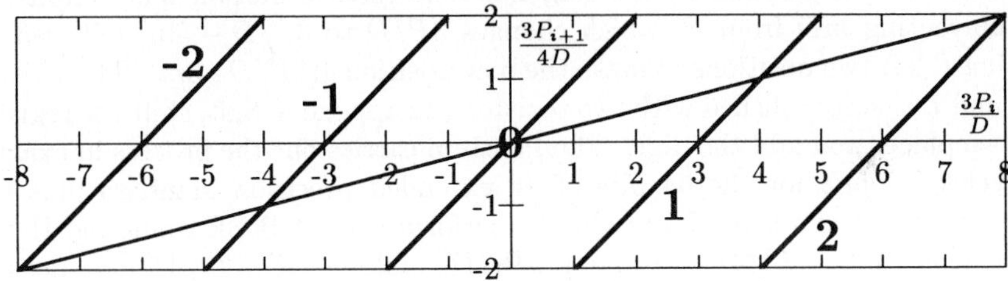

Figure 1. An easily navigated rectangle.

Robby walks around while writing down two numbers R and L in radix 4 from left to right. He begins by walking north or south so as to reach one of the five steep line segments (without leaving the rectangle), then appends one digit to each of R and L. (The first digit of each goes in the units position, so after four digits we can have 2.102 or 0.021 but not 12.02. The convention before anything is written is that R and L are zero.) One digit is zero, the other is the absolute value of the segment's label, which if nonzero is appended to R or L according to whether the segment is on the right or left (positive or negative label) respectively. Robby completes this cycle of his walk by returning to the main diagonal via a horizontal trajectory.

After c such cycles, Robby asserts the horizontal coordinate of his original position (as a vector in the plane) to be $3(R-L)+e/4^c$ where e is the horizontal coordinate of his current position. He interprets $3(R-L)$ as his estimate of his position and $e/4^c$ as the error of that estimate.

Robby's assertion is proved by induction as follows. Initially $c = 0$, $R = L = 0$, and the current error is his initial position, verifying his assertion for the basis case of the induction. Now assume that the assertion holds at cycle c, and suppose that label m is encountered on the next cycle. It suffices to show that the estimate increases by $3m/4^c$ and the error decreases by that amount.

For the former, appending one of m or $-m$ at the c-th position of one of R or L respectively increases $R-L$ by $m/4^c$ in either case, whence $3(R-L)$ increases by $3m/4^c$.

[3] The SRT algorithm is named for its independent inventors Sweeney at IBM, Robinson at the University of Illinois [Rob58], and Tocher at Imperial College [Toc58].

For the latter, imagine Robbie detours (still traveling vertically) to segment 0 (extended if necessary) on the way to m. Leaving from $(e, e/4)$, he must arrive at (e, e) on segment 0 due to its 45 degree slope. Segment 0 being $3m$ above segment m, he reaches the latter at the point $(e, e-3m)$. The trip back to the main diagonal simply sets the horizontal coordinate to four time the vertical, so his position at the end of the cycle is $(4(e-3m), e-3m)$. This completes cycle $c+1$, making his error his new position $4(e-3m)$ divided by 4^{c+1}, namely $(e-3m)/4^c$. This is $3m/4^c$ less than before, and with this we have completed the proof of the assertion.

Given a dividend P_0 and a divisor D, the Pentium solves the problem of estimating P_0/D by the above method. P_0 is loaded[4] into a register P, and before and after each cycle of the division $3P/D$ corresponds to the horizontal coordinate of the position on the diagonal. The vertical motion is accomplished by subtracting mD from P, which changes $3P/D$ to $3P/D - 3m$, followed by shifting P left two positions to make the new position $4(3P/D-3m)$. The writing of R and L is accomplished with two registers; to append a digit, shift the register left two places and add the digit. The Pentium carries out the process in exactly 34 cycles, enough for the 64 bits of an extended precision mantissa plus the guard, round, and sticky bits needed to perform correct IEEE rounding. Hence when done, $3(R-L)/4^{34}$ estimates $3P_0/D$, making $(R-L)/4^{34}$ the desired quotient P_0/D.

The hard part is to determine m. This is accomplished by computing an approximation to P/D by sampling a few of the leading bits of P and D to yield P' and D', the *chopped* partial remainder and divisor respectively. We then use these to index a table of integer approximations to P'/D' called the *PD-plot* [Atk68]. According to the White Paper [SB94] the Pentium chops P down to $P' = \lfloor 8P \rfloor/8$, and chops D down to $D'' = \lfloor 16D \rfloor/16$. These approximations correspond to sampling the first 7 significant bits of P, the first bit being the sign bit and the binary point following the first four bits, and to sampling the first 5 significant bits of D, this being the number of bits in an integer in $[16, 32)$.

Since D is in $[1, 2)$, it follows that P is in $[-16/3, 16/3]$ (consider D near 2), whence $\lfloor 8P \rfloor$ ranges from $\lfloor -128/3 \rfloor = -43$ to $\lfloor 128/3 \rfloor = 42$, a total of 86 distinct values. And for D in $[1, 2)$, $\lfloor 16D \rfloor$ ranges from 16 to 31, a total of 16 distinct values.

Coe has conjectured to us that the Pentium approximates D more coarsely than this by taking $D' = 3\lfloor 16D/3 \rfloor/16$, on the ground that it works and makes the table nearly one-third the size. This has the effect of coalescing the 16 samples in twos and threes to form six groups, corresponding to the six possible values of $\lfloor 16D/3 \rfloor$ when $D \in [1, 2)$. We assume Coe's conjecture for the sequel.

The Pentium's PD-plot is depicted on the next page as an 89×6 array of cells (this may be one or two more rows than are physically present in the Pentium).

[4] At the start of the process P_0 and D are assumed to have previously been normalized to lie in the interval $[1, 2)$, whence P_0 lies in $(D/2, 2D)$. The division process confines P to the interval $[-8D/3, 8D/3]$, which P starts out in because $(D/2, 2D)$ is a subinterval.

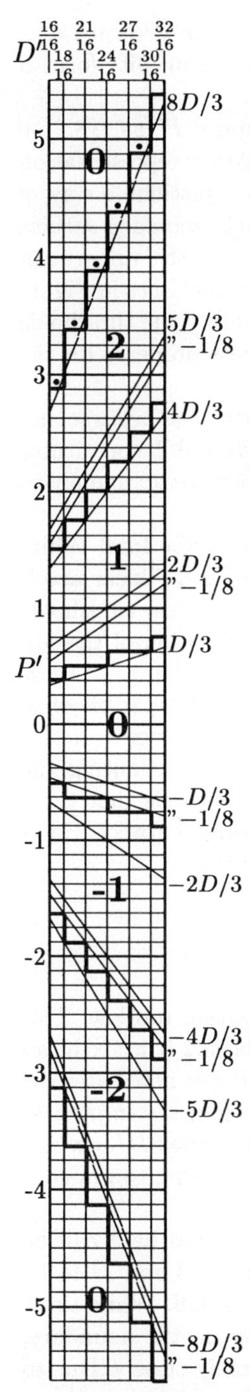

Figure 2.
The PD-plot

The P and D dimensions are both drawn at a scale of one unit per 16mm. Cells hold integers in $[-2, 2]$, and are grouped into homogeneous regions in each of which all cells contain the same value. (The cells would reasonably be coded with two bits, with the sign of the entries implicit and inferrable from that of P'.) The regions are delimited in the diagram by the bold jagged lines, called *thresholds*, and the common value in the cells of a region is given by the large boldface number in the center of that region.

The PD-plot can be viewed simultaneously as a physical discrete table indexed by P' and D' and as a continuum (to within extended precision) indexed by P and D. This permits the chopping process to be visualized as taking place in the diagram: chopping P moves it to the lower edge of the containing cell while chopping D moves it to the left edge.

The crucial property is that *the m obtained with P' and D' from the table is such that P lies in the interval* $[(m - 2/3)D, (m + 2/3)D]$. These five intervals determine 10 boundaries, which are depicted in the figure as the lines $8D/3$ and so on (ignore for now the lower line of any pair of parallel lines 1/8 apart). The crucial fact proving this property is that *the thresholds lie in the intersection of their corresponding intervals.*

For those locations corresponding to no possible P and D one arbitrarily sets m to whatever minimizes power consumption, apparently $m = 0$.

Complicating all this greatly is that the number P is represented in the Pentium in carry-save form, namely as a pair S, C of numbers satisfying $S + C = P$. This representation has the property that a quantity such as the divisor can be added or subtracted with a small bound on the time for carry propagation that is independent of the word length.

Initially S is set to P_0 and C to 0. To add D to P, form $S = S \oplus C \oplus D$ (exclusive or), $C = (S \wedge C) \vee (C \wedge D) \vee (D \wedge S)$ in parallel, that is, both right hand sides are evaluated before performing either assignment to the left hand side. Then shift C left one place. To subtract D, add the logical complement of D, that is, $-D - 1$, as above. Then compensate for the -1 by setting to 1 the low order bit of C, which had been cleared to 0 by the shift.

The underlying principle is that these bit-vector operations implement a full adder at every bit position. A full adder has three inputs, and its two outputs, called *sum* and *carry*, record as a two-bit binary numeral the number of 1's on its inputs. The sum bits form S and the carry bits C.

This complicates the computation of m. We now compute P' as $(\lfloor 8S \rfloor + \lfloor 8C \rfloor)/8$. Previously $P' \leq P < P' + 1/8$. The redundant carry-save representation weakens this to $P' \leq P < P' + 1/4$. A simple yet rigorously justifiable way of accommodating the additional 1/8 is to lower by 1/8 *every boundary serving to bound a threshold from above but not from below.* All but the uppermost threshold have such boundaries, leading to the five pairs of parallel lines in Figure 2. Observe that even after so narrowing the regions of uncertainty the thresholds still lie completely within those regions, the crucial correctness property for the PD-plot.

It should be pointed out that the technique of accumulating the positive and negative contributions to the quotient in separate registers R and L constitutes a redundant representation of the quotient serving the same purpose, namely to avoid having to wait for carries to propagate.

The thresholds of Figure 2 cannot be inferred directly from the Intel White Paper's explanation. However using the bug described below as a "linear accelerator" it becomes possible to test whether any other settings of these thresholds predicts the errors experienced by the Pentium. With the exception of the uppermost threshold, which is low by 1 in the Pentium, all other settings of these thresholds turn out to generate errors in the model that are incompatible with the Pentium's observed behavior. In making these measurements one can also measure the length of the P register as having at least 68 bits counting the sign bit. It is not possible however to use it to test Coe's hypothesis that there are only six "chopped" divisors D'; the bug cannot distinguish between Coe's hypothesis and the 16 chopped divisors shown in the White Paper.

3 Nature of the bug

The bug is that the top threshold in Figure 2 is set one position too low. This sets to 0 five accessible entries in the table that should have been 2 (the sixth can remain zero because $D < 2$), dotted in Figure 2. The White Paper attributes the error to a script that incorrectly copied values; one is nevertheless tempted to wonder whether the rule for lowering thresholds was applied to the $8D/3$, which would be an incorrect application because that boundary is serving to bound a threshold from below.

The effect of taking the quotient digit to be 0 when it should be 2 can be understood by first considering P to be the boundary case $8D/3$ and D to be one of the boundary cases 18/16, 21/16, 24/16, 27/16, and 30/16. While these cases themselves are unreachable by virtue of being actually on the boundary, there are reachable cases that approach the boundary extremely closely. Due to obscure vagaries of carry-save arithmetic, in order to reach a missing entry D must lie in $[T - 2^{-10}, T]$ where $16T$ is an integer multiple of 3. Since $D \in [1, 2)$ there are only five possible T's, namely $16T = 18$, 21, 24, 27, or 30.

For $D = 18/16$, $P = 8/3 \cdot 18/16 = 3$. This quantity should have been reduced to $3/4$ by subtraction of $2D = 9/4$. Instead nothing is subtracted and then P is scaled by 4 to become 12. Because the sign bit has weight 8 here, 12 is read as -4. But this is below the table's lower limit, at $D = 18/16$, of $P = -8/3 \cdot 18/16 = -3$. Hence a second subtraction is skipped and P is further scaled to -16, which is mistaken for 0. We have now lost the whole of P, which was 3. Simply subtracting 3 from P before these two cycles would have yielded the exact same sequence of choices of quotient digit. This therefore gives a clean characterization of the error in this boundary case: it is equivalent to subtracting 3, scaled by a suitable power of 2, from the original dividend. It follows that $y - (y/x)x$ will be 3 so scaled, to within the precision normally achieved by division.

For $D = 21/16$, $P = 8/3 \cdot 21/16 = 7/2$. This quantity should have been reduced to $7/8$ then scaled to $7/2$. Instead it is scaled to 14 and then mistaken for -2. This puts it within P's safe operating range. Hence the effect is the same as if we had started with $P = -1/2$. But this represents a loss of 4 from P. Hence $y - (y/x)x$ will be a power of two. Continuing these calculations for the remaining three boundary cases of D, we find a similar loss of 4 in every case.

A perturbation of D and P sufficiently small that the missing table entry is still hit will not be sufficient to change the gross loss of bits from the high end of the partial remainder. Hence $y - (y/x)x$ will continue to be 3 times a power of 2 when D is near $18/16$ and a power of 2 for other D.

4 Rate of Errors

The highly nonuniform distribution of erroneous operands makes it exceedingly difficult to predict the error rate of any given application. For many applications however it is helpful to know the general characteristics of the bug.

We list here a table of the number of errors caused by the bug, as a function of the precision of the operands and the quotient. The operand precision affects mainly the number of operands defining the total population from which the errors are sampled.

Table 1. Number of Pentium Errors, by precision of operands and quotient

Operand Precision	Quotient Precision Single	Double	Extended	TOTAL
Single	1738	7863	9915	7.037×10^{13}
Double	5.009×10^{20}	2.266×10^{21}	2.858×10^{21}	2.028×10^{31}
Extended	2.101×10^{27}	9.502×10^{27}	1.199×10^{28}	8.507×10^{37}
ERROR RATE	2.470×10^{-11}	1.117×10^{-10}	1.409×10^{-10}	

The quotient precision affects the number of errors of a given magnitude. The 1738 single precision quotient errors are a subset of the 7863 double precision errors, and the latter are in turn a subset of the 9915 extended precision errors.

The errors turn out to be uniformly distributed with regard to the cycle on which they happen (and hence with regard to the logarithm (exponent) of the corresponding relative error), starting with the first cycle at which an error is possible, namely cycle 9, and continuing on to cycle 34, the last cycle of the Pentium division algorithm. The relative number of errors in each column of the above table can be roughly predicted given the number of bits of mantissa for each, namely 23, 52, and 63 (not counting the most significant bit in any of these cases). The following table classifies all 9915 errors tabulated above; we have clearly missed some 600 errors at cycles 33 and 34, whose small size makes them hard to distinguish from normal truncation error.

Table 2. Classification of errors

	18	21	24	27	30	Total
9	96	35	16	12	16	175
10	128	43	95	28	26	320
11	108	52	96	56	102	414
12	121	46	88	45	94	394
13	139	51	99	51	95	435
14	140	54	91	45	95	425
15	128	54	109	52	97	440
16	139	52	99	50	86	426
17	136	54	104	47	98	439
18	138	54	102	47	91	432
19	134	57	104	37	85	417
20	140	46	103	44	83	416
21	127	50	101	38	89	405
22	132	54	100	45	68	399
23	140	49	95	43	92	419
24	138	53	101	49	89	430
25	134	50	99	46	91	420
26	131	53	95	42	82	403
27	132	48	94	41	94	409
28	134	51	95	40	86	406
29	137	50	92	46	93	418
30	134	55	100	39	85	413
31	128	54	102	41	80	405
32	135	53	96	40	83	407
33	0	48	81	46	73	248
34	0	0	0	0	0	0
Total	3149	1266	2357	1070	2073	9915

5 Random Computation

We may think of the uniform-distribution model as amounting to a program consisting of just the instruction FDIV, with random data. A natural counterpoint to this is a single datum, for simplicity the number 1, operated on with random instructions.

To explore this dual point of view we initialized a database to contain just the number 1. We then randomly added, subtracted, multiplied, and divided numbers, some from this database, some being more copies of the number 1, and put the results into the database. When the database reached its capacity of 750,000 numbers, further incoming numbers displaced existing numbers removed from randomly selected locations in the database.

To prevent "database meltdown" through cumulative error, we kept track of how many times a number had been "put through the mill" and discarded numbers that had been operated on more than 100 times. More precisely, the depth of incoming 1's was taken to be 0, and the depth of constructed numbers was taken to be 1 plus the maximum depth of its operands. At depths of 200, cumulative errors on the order of 10^{-6} were produced and depth 300 resulted in "total meltdown." Limiting the depth to 100 largely avoided cumulative errors greater than 10^{-12}.

To simulate the typed discipline of a real database we assumed that the 1's were counts of kumquats, and distinguished kumquats, square kumquats, etc. Types were limited to kumquat^i for i ranging from -3 to 3, and operations that added kumquats to square kumquats or produced illegal types were discarded.

Two databases were maintained, clean and dirty. The difference was that divisions destined for the clean database were computed using the Mathisen-Moler bug workaround. Any discrepancies larger than 10^{-16} between the two databases were logged, giving the time (in cycles and ticks), clean and dirty values, relative error, depth, type, and cause of the discrepancy as a number. The first appearance of cause number n indicates the n-th FDIV error to occur during the computation. Subsequent appearances of n indicate relative errors larger than 10^{-16} resulting from operating on a number influenced by the n-th FDIV error.

The output from a typical run is given in Table 3.

The time is given in cycles consisting of 750,000 ticks, a tick being the production of one number passing all tests for membership in the database. The above table records all errors logged in the first 400 cycles. It is particularly noteworthy that no errors at all were logged during the second half of those 400 cycles. But then at cycle 402 the 13th FDIV error occurred, and half a cycle later combined with one of the offspring of the 5th error. A flurry of errors attributed to the 5th and 7th division errors then started up, and for the next thirty cycles a storm ensued reaching rates of up to ten errors per second. Gradually the storm calmed down, and at cycle 430, 1700 errors later, died out altogether. In all that time not a single fresh FDIV error had been logged, and the 14th FDIV error did not occur until cycle 512.

Table 3. Output from a typical run

__TIME__	_________DATA________					
Cycle:Tick	Clean	Dirty	Error	Depth	Type	Cause
17:497981	0.16666668154	0.16666667905	1.5e-08	58	-1	1
17:616863	5.9999994647	5.9999995541	-1.5e-08	59	2	1
17:665562	-8561.0008917	-8561.0008917	-2.9e-13	59	-1	1
37:257439	-0.6666667262	-0.66666671626	1.5e-08	99	0	2
37:527542	-0.6666667262	-0.66666671626	1.5e-08	100	1	2
40:656817	0.83333330718	0.83333203561	1.5e-06	95	-2	3
41:702595	0.16666666668	0.16666666668	1.5e-11	98	-2	4
42:22138	0.16666666668	0.16666666668	1.5e-11	99	-3	4
42:116157	0.33333333336	0.33333333336	1.5e-11	100	0	4
44:669106	-0.33333333345	-0.33333333343	5.8e-11	90	0	5
45:135182	1.3082215759	1.3082215758	5.8e-11	99	3	5
45:181839	-1.3333332431	-1.3333332431	-1.5e-11	100	0	5
45:388059	1.3082215759	1.3082215758	5.8e-11	100	2	5
46:344255	-0.58333332942	-0.58333301153	5.4e-07	98	2	6
46:519308	-61017.845279	-61017.845279	-1.3e-15	100	3	5
46:740247	-0.58333332942	-0.58333301153	5.4e-07	99	0	6
47:138389	1.2215684139	1.2215684138	6.2e-11	100	3	5
47:275623	-0.497968866	-0.49796854811	6.4e-07	100	0	6
48:372879	-1.833333333	-1.8333332535	4.3e-08	99	0	7
51:277507	-0.66666690447	-0.66666686473	6e-08	92	1	8
94:659253	0.1666666669	0.16666666686	2.3e-10	98	-1	9
95:17753	0.1666666669	0.16666666686	2.3e-10	99	0	5
95:57593	-5.1666666669	-5.1666666669	7.5e-12	100	0	7
116:611163	-0.45833333333	-0.45833333333	6.6e-13	39	2	10
138:230655	-228378.66667	-228378.66667	7e-13	59	1	11
138:268063	-4.3786926e-06	-4.3786926e-06	-7e-13	60	0	7
138:502339	-228377.66667	-228377.66667	7e-13	60	1	7
138:521008	-4.3787118e-06	-4.3787118e-06	-7e-13	61	0	7
195:80147	3.6666666667	3.6666666667	6.6e-13	17	-1	12
195:103551	3.6666666667	3.6666666667	6.6e-13	18	0	12
195:114214	0.60604609328	0.60604609328	-6.6e-13	100	0	5
195:358813	-21.853931025	-21.853931025	6.6e-13	76	-2	7
196:231884	-22.853931025	-22.853931025	6.3e-13	77	-2	7

However a total of 12 FDIV errors had occurred during the 300 million ticks comprising the first 400 cycles, 50 million of which were divisions. This corresponds to an error rate of one in 4 million. This is a thousand times greater than the rate predicted by the uniform-distribution model.

Of greater concern is the tendency of errors to propagate through a database. This example graphically illustrates the chaotic nature of this propagation: errors may have one or two descendants over a very long period, but then errors that one assumes must have been flushed completely out of the system by now can suddenly reappear like the creature from Aliens and wreak havoc. When the 1700 indirectly caused errors are added to the 12 direct errors, the total error rate rises to one in 30,000 divisions!

On the domain of small bruised integers the error rate rises several more orders of magnitude. Choose two integers from 1 to 100 with equal probability, subtract 10^{-6} from each, and divide one by the other. The probability of encountering a cycle 10 error (the second largest possible) is 0.08%, for a cycle 11 error it is 0.15%, and for cycle 12, 0.17%.

A good example of this is given by 4.999999/14.999999. This should be 0.33333329, but on the Pentium it turns out to be 0.333329, a cycle 10 error.

References

[Atk68] D.E. Atkins. Higher-radix division using estimates of the divisor and partial remainders. *IEEE Transactions on Computers*, C-17(10), October 1968.

[CMMP95] T. Coe, T. Mathisen, C. Moler, and V. Pratt. Computational aspects of the Pentium affair. *IEEE J. Computational Sci. and Eng.*, March 1995.

[Rob58] J.E. Robertson. A new class of digital division methods. *IRE Transactions on Electronic Computers*, EC-7:218–222, September 1958.

[SB94] H.P. Sharangpani and M.L. Barton. Statistical analysis of floating point flaw in the Pentium^{TM} processor (1994). Available on World-Wide Web as http://www.intel.com/product/pentium/white11/index.html, November 1994.

[Toc58] T.D. Tocher. Techniques of multiplication and division for binary computers. *Quarterly J. of Applied Math*, 2:364–384, 1958.

Rational Mechanics and Natural Mathematics

Vaughan Pratt*

Dept. of Computer Science, Stanford University, Stanford CA 94305-2140
pratt@cs.stanford.edu

Abstract. Chu spaces have found applications in computer science, mathematics, and physics. They enjoy a useful categorical duality analogous to that of lattice theory and projective geometry. As natural mathematics Chu spaces borrow ideas from the natural sciences, particularly physics, while as rational mechanics they cast Hamiltonian mechanics in terms of the interaction of body and mind.

This paper addresses the chief stumbling block for Descartes' 17th-century philosophy of mind-body dualism, how can the fundamentally dissimilar mental and physical planes causally interact with each other? We apply Cartesian logic to reject not only divine intervention, preordained synchronization, and the eventual mass retreat to monism, but also an assumption Descartes himself somehow neglected to reject, that causal interaction within these planes is an easier problem than between. We use Chu spaces and residuation to derive all causal interaction, both between and within the two planes, from a uniform and algebraically rich theory of between-plane interaction alone. Lifting the two-valued Boolean logic of binary relations to the complex-valued fuzzy logic of quantum mechanics transforms residuation into a natural generalization of the inner product operation of a Hilbert space and demonstrates that this account of causal interaction is of essentially the same form as the Heisenberg-Schrödinger quantum-mechanical solution to analogous problems of causal interaction in physics.

1 Cartesian Dualism

The Chu construction [Bar79] strikes us as extraordinarily useful, more so with every passing month. Elsewhere we have described the application of Chu spaces to process algebra [GP93], metamathematics [Pra93, Pra94a], and physics [Pra94b]. Here we make a first attempt at applying them to philosophy.

It might seem that traditional philosophical questions would be beyond the scope of TAPSOFT. Bear in mind however that Boolean logic as the basis for computer circuits was born of philosophy (and a little statistics). Only slightly more recently, program verification has drawn heavily on more sophisticated logics such as first order, modal, and higher order. Computers being thinking machines, computer science should not neglect the philosophical literature on thinking. It is easy to dismiss "all that stuff" as obsoleted by technology. However

* This work was supported by ONR under grant number N00014-92-J-1974

good truths, like good wine, must be served at the proper time. We would like to think of our application of Chu spaces to Descartes' inspiring yet short-lived theory of mind-body dualism as a convincing example.

Cartesianism is a "philosophy of everything" founded by René Descartes in the 1630's. Its point of departure was to reject all authority and question everything including the questioner's existence. Descartes resourcefully bootstrapped himself back into existence with an instance of the liar paradox, the absurdity of questioning his own questioning, constructivized as *Cogito, ergo sum.* Emboldened by this success, Descartes posed many more questions whose imaginative answers formed the basis of Cartesianism. This rationalist philosophy flourished for half a century until the march of science contradicted too many of its answers for it to remain a viable grand unified theory of anything. Some of the questions however remain philosophically challenging even today.

A central tenet of Cartesianism is mind-body dualism, the principle that mind and body are the two basic substances of which reality is constituted. Each can exist separately, body as realized in inanimate objects and lower forms of life, mind as realized in abstract concepts and mathematical certainties. According to Descartes the two come together only in humans, where they undergo *causal interaction*, the mind reflecting on sensory perceptions while orchestrating the physical motions of the limbs and other organs of the body.

The crucial problem for the causal interaction theory of mind and body was its mechanism: how did it work?

Descartes hypothesized the pineal gland, near the center of the brain, as the seat of causal interaction. The objection was raised that the mental and physical planes were of such a fundamentally dissimilar character as to preclude any ordinary notion of causal interaction. But the part about a separate yet joint reality of mind and body seemed less objectionable, and various commentators offered their own explanations for the undeniably strong correlations of mental and physical phenomena.

Malebranche insisted that these were only correlations and not true interactions, whose appearance of interaction was arranged in every detail by God by divine intervention on every occasion of correlation, a theory that naturally enough came to be called occasionalism. Spinoza freed God from this demanding schedule by organizing the parallel behavior of mind and matter as a preordained apartheid emanating from God as the source of everything. Leibniz postulated *monads*, cosmic chronometers miraculously keeping perfect time with each other yet not interacting.

These patently untestable answers only served to give dualism a bad name, and it gave way in due course to one or another form of monism: either mind *or* matter but not both as distinct real substances. Berkeley opined that matter did not exist and that the universe consisted solely of ideas. Hobbes ventured the opposite: mind did not exist except as an artifact of matter. Russell [Rus27] embraced *neutral* monism, which reconciled Berkeley's and Hobbes' viewpoints as compatible dual accounts of a common neutral Leibnizian monad.

This much of the history of mind-body dualism will suffice as a convenient point of reference for the sequel. R. Watson's Britannica article [Wat86] is a conveniently accessible starting point for further reading.

The thesis of this paper is that mind-body dualism can be made to work via a theory that we greatly prefer to its monist competitors. Reflecting an era of reduced expectations for the superiority of humans, we have implemented causal interaction not with the pineal gland but with machinery freely available to all classical entities, whether newt, pet rock, electron, or theorem (but not quantum mechanical wavefunction, which is sibling to if not an actual instance of our machinery).

2 Dualism via Chu Spaces

We propose to reduce complex mind-body interaction to the elementary interactions of their constituents. Events of the body interact with states of the mind. This interaction has two dual forms. A physical event a in the body A *impresses* its occurrence on a mental state x of the mind X, written $a \dashv x$. Dually, in state x the mind *infers* the prior occurrence of event a, written $x \models a$. States may be understood as corresponding more or less to the possible worlds of a Kripke structure, and events to propositions that may or may not hold in different worlds of that structure.

With regard to orientation, impression is *causal* and its direction is that of time. Inference is *logical*, and logic swims upstream against time. Prolog's backward-chaining strategy dualizes this by viewing logic as primary and time as swimming upstream against logic, but this amounts to the same thing. The basic idea is that time and logic flow in opposite directions.

Can a body meet a body? Only indirectly. All direct interaction in our account of Cartesian dualism is between mind and body. Any hypothesized interaction of two events is an inference from respective interactions between each of those events and all possible states of the mind. Dually, any claimed interaction of two states is inferred from their respective interactions with all possible events of the body.

The general nature of these inferences depends on the set K of values that events can impress on states. The simplest nontrivial case is $K = 2 = \{0, 1\}$, permitting the simple recording of respectively nonoccurrence or occurrence of a given event in a given state. In this case body-body and mind-mind interactions are computed via a process called residuation. Specifically, event a *necessarily precedes* event b when every state x witnessing the occurrence of b also witnesses a. This inferred relationship is calculated formally by left residuation, which we describe in detail later. The dual calculation, right residuation, *permits* a transition from state x to state y when every event a impressing itself on x does so also on y. That is, any transition is permitted just so long as it forgets no event. These simple-minded criteria are the appropriate ones for the small set $K = 2$.

For $K = 3$ more complex rules for inferring necessary precedence and possible transition obtain, including the possibility of forgetting (to be written up). At

$K \doteq 8$ we have groups and semigroups, the latter embedding all *abstract* category theory [PT80]. For K the set (not field) of complex numbers, right and left residuation are naturally taken to be the respective products $\langle\varphi|\psi\rangle$ or $\varphi^*\psi$ and $|\psi\rangle\langle\varphi|$ or $\psi\varphi^*$, corresponding to respectively inner product and its dual outer product in a Hilbert space.

This conveys the flavor of our proposal. We now equip these general ideas with enough algebraic structure and properties to make the proposal interesting, useful, and we hope convincing.

The following analogy serves to fix ideas. The numbers ± 1 are connected in two ways, algebraic and geometric. The algebraic connection is via the operation of negation, an involution ($- - x = x$) that connects them logically by interchanging them. The geometric connection is via the interval $[-1, 1]$ of reals lying between these numbers, a closed convex space connecting them topologically. We refer to these connections as respectively the *duality* and *interaction* of -1 and 1. The connections themselves might respectively be understood as mental and physical, but this takes us beyond our present story.

We regard each point of the interval as a weighted sum of the endpoints, assuming nonnegative weights p, q normalized via $p + q = 1$, making each point the quantity $p - q$. An important property of interaction is that it includes the endpoints, namely as the special cases where one of p or q is zero. An important property of duality is that it extends to interaction, namely via the calculation $q - p = -(p - q)$.

We shall arrange for Cartesian dualism to enjoy the same two basic connections and the two associated properties, with mind and body in place of -1 and 1 respectively. Ideally the duality would be a negation-like involution that interchanges their roles; no information is lost in this transformation, and the original mind or body is recovered when the transformation is repeated. And ideally the interaction would turn out to be the long-sought solution to dualism's main conceptual hurdle. Chu spaces achieve both of these in a very satisfactory way.

The counterparts to ± 1 in our Chu space formulation of Cartesian dualism are the respective categories **Set** and $\mathbf{Set}^{\mathrm{op}}$. That is, at 1 we place the class of all sets, each understood as a pure body. At -1 we place what would appear at first sight to be the same sets, which we propose to construe as pure minds.

Our first distinction between body and mind will be the trivial one of using different variables to range over these sets: A, B over bodies, X, Y over minds. The second distinction will be in how the two kinds of sets transform into each other. Later we make a third distinction within the objects themselves by realizing the two kinds as Chu spaces with dual form factors: sets tall and thin, antisets short and wide.

Bodies transform with functions. We turn the class of bodies into **Set** by first superimposing on it the graph whose edges comprise all functions, with each function $f : A \to B$ connecting the set A to the set B. We then promote this graph to a category by equipping it with the standard composition rule for functions, as an instance of composition of binary relations, along with an identity function $1_A : A \to A$ at every set A.

Minds transform with *antifunctions.* An antifunction $g^\perp : X \to Y$ is a binary relation from X to Y whose converse is a function $g : Y \to X$. Adopting the composition rule for binary relations as with **Set** then yields a category dual to **Set**, one that is equivalent, in fact isomorphic, to $\mathbf{Set}^{\mathrm{op}}$ (the result of merely reversing all the edges of **Set**), which we simply identify with $\mathbf{Set}^{\mathrm{op}}$.

These graphs are not isomorphic, even without their respective compositions. A quick way to tell them apart is to look for a vertex whose only edge to it is a self-loop. This vertex occurs only in **Set**, namely as the empty set. Or look for a vertex whose only edge *from* it is a self-loop; this too is the empty set, but in $\mathbf{Set}^{\mathrm{op}}$. The reader will think of other tests.[2]

We now argue that sets are physical and antisets mental. Since the only difference is in how they transform, any distinction between mental and physical must be either dynamic in the sense of being transformational, or algebraic in the sense that structure regulates transformation. We present both types of argument (which themselves can be understood as respectively operational hence mental and denotational hence physical).

Functions identify and adjoin. The function $F : A \to B$ identifies just when it fails to be injective: $f(a) = f(b)$ means that f identifies a and b. It adjoins just when it fails to be surjective: $f : A \to B$ first transforms A *onto* $f(A)$, then adjoins to it $B - f(A)$ to become *into*.

Antifunctions copy and delete. The antifunction $g^\perp : X \to Y$ makes multiple copies just when its converse $g : Y \to X$ fails to be injective: $g(y) = g(y')$ means that $g^\perp$ sends copies of $g(y)$ to both y and y', *inter alia*. It deletes just when g fails to be surjective: $g^\perp : Y \to X$ deletes exactly $Y - g(X)$.

Identifying and adjoining are canonically denotational tasks that mathematicians are accustomed to performing on their spaces, groups, and other algebraic objects. This is the realm of the physical.

Copying and deleting are canonically operational tasks that logicians and computer scientists are accustomed to performing on their proofs, spreadsheets, and other symbolic objects. This is the realm of the mental.

In additional to these transformational arguments we can contrast the discrete or dust-like physical structure of sets with the rigidly intermeshed mental structure of Boolean algebras.

A set is an algebra with no language at all, and no equational theory beyond the equational tautologies $x = x$. There is therefore no mental plane to speak of in sets, making them the most physical of all the objects of traditional concrete (set-based) mathematics, if not of all category theory (and perhaps even there, cf. [RW94]).

$\mathbf{Set}^{\mathrm{op}}$ is equivalent to the category of complete atomic Boolean algebras (CABA's). But the free CABA generated by the set X is the power set 2^{2^X}. Hence the Boolean operations of each arity X, X empty, finite, or infinite, con-

---

[2] Example: look for any vertex having exactly one edge to it from each vertex, and infinitely many edges out. There are lots of these in **Set**, namely the many singletons, all isomorphic, but none in $\mathbf{Set}^{\mathrm{op}}$.

sist of *all* functions from 2^X to 2. This is the maximum possible language compatible with CABA homomorphisms; not only is every arity represented but every operation of that arity.[3] Furthermore the equational theory of CABA's is maximally consistent in the sense that no new equation can be added without collapsing the entire algebra to a singleton. A CABA as the ultimate know-it-all is as mental as any object of traditional concrete mathematics can be.

We have thus established that the two isolated points **Set** and $\mathbf{Set}^{\mathrm{op}}$ represent respectively the physical and the mental. We now proceed with the promised construction. At this point the situation is as for ± 1 on their own: we have two isolated graphs, and we seek a duality and an interaction.

The duality analogous to negation is simply the converse operation for binary relations, which evidently interchanges **Set** and $\mathbf{Set}^{\mathrm{op}}$.

The interaction analogous to the interval $[-1, 1]$, which includes the points it connects as part of the interval, consists of all Chu spaces and a graph superimposed on them, which includes as subgraphs **Set** and $\mathbf{Set}^{\mathrm{op}}$. That is, the interaction consists of adding further vertices and edges, in addition to those already present, to populate an interval from $\mathbf{Set}^{\mathrm{op}}$ to **Set**.

A *Chu space* $\mathcal{A} = (A, X, \models)$ *over* a set K consists of a set A of *points*, an antiset X of *states*, and an $X \times A$ matrix $\models$ with entries drawn from K.[4] These provide the vertices of the interval.

This ontogeny of the Chu space recapitulates the phylogeny we are working towards. A and X are respectively the body or object and mind or menu of the space, $\models$ is their interaction, and matrix transposition is the duality interchanging mind and body to yield the dual Chu space $\mathcal{A}^{\perp} = (X, A, \models^{\smile})$.

Points have *necessary* existence, all being present simultaneously in the physical object A. States are *possible*, making a Chu space a kind of a Kripke structure [Gup93]: only one state at a time may be chosen from the menu X of alternatives.

Lafont and Streicher [LS91] were the first to single out Chu spaces as a case of the more general Chu construction $\mathbf{Chu}(V, k)$ [Bar79, Bar91], namely $V = \mathbf{Set}$, worthy of separate attention as a natural model of linear logic [Gir87] embedding topological spaces, vector spaces, and coherent spaces. They referred to these objects as games, understanding $\models$ as the payoff matrix of a von-Neumann-Morgenstern two-person game.

There is a chicken-and-egg question here as to whether Chu spaces are more naturally understood as a game or a player of a game. As players, the spaces $\mathcal{A}$ and $\mathcal{B}$ play the *interaction game* $\mathcal{A} \otimes \mathcal{B}$, their tensor product. This interaction has featured prominently in our own research as an operation we called *orthocurrence* [Pra85, Pra86]. We originally identified orthocurrence as ordinary product in a cartesian closed category of partially ordered multisets (pomsets), but subsequently generalized it to the tensor product of any closed category [CCMP91, Pra93, GP93, Pra94a]. In all cases we took as our basic example

[3] One can add further operations, for example modal logic adds $\diamond$. However CABA homomorphisms respect none of these additional operations whatsoever.

[4] Contrast this with a vector space over a field k, which requires k to be equipped with the four rationals; here K is simply a set with no additional structure.

the interaction of trains and stations described on the train station wall by the daily schedule. Whereas ordinary product must be capable of being projected *consistently* onto either component, tensor product requires only that each row or column of the resulting rectangular body of the space (how stations appear to conductors, and trains to stationmasters) meet all the constraints imposed on each of the two constituents of the product, the concept of bilinearity. The tensor product constitutes a larger Chu space, which can in turn be a player in a yet larger game.

The representation $\mathcal{A}\otimes\mathcal{B}$ takes the physical viewpoint. The logic of the game may be understood in terms of its dual $(\mathcal{A}\otimes\mathcal{B})^{\perp}$, which is equivalent to either of $\mathcal{A}\multimap\mathcal{B}^{\perp}$ or $\mathcal{B}\multimap\mathcal{A}^{\perp}$. In the former, we take Alice's point of view as our premises and view Bob as the goal. This view dualizes Bob to make his body, which Bob proudly thinks of as his strong points, appear to Alice as Bob's possible Achilles' heels (wrists, etc.). At the same time Bob's mind, which Bob thinks of as his possible options, are seen by Alice as Bob's tricks, all of which she must be simultaneously on her guard against.

A *Chu transform* $(f,g) : (A,X,\models) \to (A',X',\models')$ consists of a function $f : A \to A'$ and an antifunction $g^{\perp} : X \to X'$, namely the converse of a function $g : X' \to X$, satisfying the *continuity condition* $g(x') \models a \;=\; x' \models' f(a)$ for all $a \in A$ and $x' \in X'$. These provide the edges of the graph on the interval of all Chu spaces running from $\mathbf{Set}^{\mathrm{op}}$ to $\mathbf{Set}$. They compose via $(f',g')(f,g) = (f'f, gg')$ to make the graph a category, denoted $\mathbf{Chu}_K$.

The function f transforms the body of the space denotationally, identifying some points and adjoining others, but neither deleting nor duplicating any. At the same time the antifunction g transforms the mind of the space operationally, i.e. as a symbolic object such as a program or a proof, deleting some states to further constrain the degrees of freedom of the space and copying some as needed so as not to infringe on the degrees of freedom of the newly adjoined points (transformations need only preserve the structure of what they transform and cannot be held responsible for what goes on in the adjoined points). However g never identifies states, which would be logically inconsistent for states having distinct rows, and never adjoins states having new rows, which would be logically unsound (the image could enter a state not permitted its source).

To understand better this last point, let $\mathrm{row} : X \to (A \to K)$ and dually $\mathrm{col} : A \to (X \to K)$ denote the functions satisfying $\mathrm{row}(x)(a) \;=\; x{\models}a \;=\; \mathrm{col}(a)(x)$. Continuity may then be rephrased in terms of rows: $\mathrm{row}(g(x')) \;=\; \mathrm{row}'(x') \circ f$, verified via $\mathrm{row}(g(x'))(a) \;=\; g(x'){\models}a \;=\; x'{\models'}f(a) \;=\; (\mathrm{row}'(x'){\circ}f)(a)$. That is, every row of B when composed with f must be some row of A, with g a function selecting a suitable row index. When $K = 2$ this is equivalent to requiring that g behave as f^{-1} on rows viewed as characteristic functions of subsets of A'. But then the requirement that every row of $\mathcal{A}'$ be mapped by f^{-1} to some row of $\mathcal{A}$ is recognizable as the condition for a function between topological spaces to be continuous, where rows are understood as open sets.

For technical reasons Chu transforms are usually associated with a fixed K, calling for a distinct category $\mathbf{Chu}_K$ of Chu spaces for each set K. A set theorist should have no difficulty with Chu spaces over different K's transforming into each other, but the resulting category would to begin with lack a tensor unit, an annoying omission when one begins to press the rich algebraic structure of $\mathbf{Chu}_K$ into service.

The structure of $\mathbf{Chu}_K$ is that of linear logic [Gir87], which can be understood as the logic of four key structural properties of $\mathbf{Chu}_K$: it is concrete, complete, closed, and self-dual (which therefore makes it also cocomplete and coconcrete). The associated linear logic connectives are respectively $!A$, $A \oplus B$ (and unit 0), $A \multimap B$ (and left unit 1), and $A^\perp$, which form a complete basis for linear logic. $\mathbf{Chu}_K$ is complete but perhaps for syntactic simplicity linear logic weakens completeness to finite products. Furthermore it is not yet agreed whether induction is a necessary element of concreteness.

Just as $\{-1,1\} \subseteq [-1,1]$, so are sets and antisets made part of the category of Chu spaces, as follows. The set A is identified with the Chu space $\mathcal{A} = (A, K^A, \gamma)$ where for each $x : A \to K$, $\gamma(x,a)$ denotes the application $x(a)$. The function $f : A \to A'$ is identified with the pair $(f, f^\perp) : (A, K^A, \gamma) \to (A', K^{A'}, \gamma)$ where $f^\perp : K^{A'} \to K^A$ is defined by $f^\perp(g)(a) = g(f(a))$. When $K = 2$, $f^\perp$ can be seen to be the usual inverse-image function f^{-1}, making this topology's continuity condition as remarked earlier. We call the Chu space $\mathcal{A}$ a *realization*[5] of the set A in $\mathbf{Chu}_2$.

Dually the antiset X is identified with $(K^X, X, \gamma^\smallsmile)$ where $\gamma^\smallsmile$ is converse application, satisfying $\gamma^\smallsmile(x,a) = a(x)$, and the antifunction $g^\perp : X \to X'$ (i.e. the function $g : X' \to X$) is identified with the pair (f,g) where $f : K^X \to K^{X'}$ is defined at each $h : X \to K$ by $f(h)(x') = h(g(x'))$. This constitutes a realization of $\mathbf{Set}^{\mathrm{op}}$ in $\mathbf{Chu}_2$.

Just as the duality of ± 1 extended to $[-1,1]$, so does the mind-body duality of $\mathbf{Set}$ and $\mathbf{Set}^{\mathrm{op}}$ extend to $\mathbf{Chu}_K$. The dual of $\mathcal{A} = (A, X, \models)$ is $\mathcal{A}^\perp = (X, A, \dashv\!\!|)$, while the dual of the Chu transform (f,g) is (g,f). Moreover the duality of sets and antisets achieved via converse of their transforming binary relations is also achieved via Chu duality for their realizations in $\mathbf{Chu}_K$.

To each finite Chu space $\mathcal{A}$ we associate integers P and Q measuring respectively the *discipline* and *versatility* of $\mathcal{A}$, in terms of the amount by which the space fails to be a set or an antiset respectively. Write $\|A\|$ for the number of *distinct* columns of the matrix, and likewise $\|X\|$ for the number of distinct rows. Let $P = K^{\|A\|} - \|X\|$ and $Q = K^{\|X\|} - \|A\|$, both nonnegative. For $K \geq 2$ these cannot vanish simultaneously or we would have an integer solution to $K^{K^A} = A$. Hence we can safely define nonnegative reals $p = P/(P+Q)$, $q = Q/(P+Q)$ satisfying $p + q = 1$. We take $p - q$ as the location of $\mathcal{A}$ in the interval $[-1,1]$ itself, giving a sense in which $\mathbf{Chu}_K$ lies between $\mathbf{Set}^{\mathrm{op}}$ and $\mathbf{Set}$. Notice that this procedure assigns sets and antisets to 1 and -1 respectively, while exactly square Chu spaces are sent to 0.

[5] A *representation* is a full embedding of one category in another, i.e. a full and faithful functor $F : C \to D$. A *realization* is a concrete representation; that is, C and D are concrete categories, meaning they have underlying set functors $U_C : C \to \mathbf{Set}$ and $U_D : D \to \mathbf{Set}$, with which F commutes, $U_D F = U_C$, i.e. the realizing object has the same underlying set as the object it realizes [PT80, p.49].

Although the position of a Chu space in $[-1,1]$ gives some indication of its form factor, these positions turn out not to populate $[-1,1]$ densely. For example at $K=2$ the intervals $[\frac{1}{3},\frac{1}{2})$ and $(\frac{1}{2},\frac{2}{3}]$ contain no Chu spaces, since Chu spaces that are only one away from being square are below $\frac{1}{3}$ or above $\frac{2}{3}$, and indeed the interval is riddled with such holes. One imagines being able to distribute Chu spaces more uniformly along $[-1,1]$ with the help of say $\|A\|/\|X\|$, but in choosing such a formula it would help to have some reason for wanting a dense distribution.

This viewpoint is a compromise between those of set theory and category theory. Set theory monistically constructs everything from the single category of pure sets. Category theory pluralistically constructs a plethora of categories. Chu spaces are like sets in that there is only one category $\mathbf{Chu}_K$ of them (modulo the parameter K). $\mathbf{Chu}_K$ is dualistic in that it postulates the two categories **Set** and $\mathbf{Set}^{\mathrm{op}}$, neither of which is singled out as having priority over the other, and connects them via interaction to form the single much larger category $\mathbf{Chu}_K$. Some impression of its size may be had from the theorem [Pra93, p.153-4] that $\mathbf{Chu}_{2^k}$ realizes the category of *all* k-ary relational structures and their homomorphisms standardly defined. For example Chu_8 realizes the category of ternary relational structures, which in turn realizes the category of groups and group homomorphisms (since its multiplication is the ternary relation $xy=z$), and realization is transitive.

3 The Meaning of Interaction

Thus far we have constructed interaction as no more than a formal notion. We now relate it to our intuitions about causal interaction.

It is ironic that Cartesian philosophy, whose guiding dictum was to question everything, should question causal interaction *between* the mental and physical planes before that *within* the planes. The latter problems must have posed an insufficient challenge to the Cartesians. We argue that the converse is the case: between is actually easier than within!

We interpret interaction as causality. Causality is directional, but the direction depends on whether we have in mind physical or mental causality. We interpret $x \models a$ ambiguously as the time elapsed between the occurrence of the physical a and its impression on the mental state x, and as the truth value of a as a proposition.[6] The former is physical causality or *impression*, flowing forward in time from events to states. The latter is mental causality or *inference*, flowing backwards in time from the thought of a to the inference of a's occurrence. In this way time flows forward (from the usual point of view) while logic flows

[6] The reader may be understandably concerned at this identification of physical events and ostensibly mental propositions. However a Boolean proposition about events in A is of type 2^{2^A} and *each exponentiation* dualizes, whence two of them return us to the physical plane. The truly mental propositions are the constituent descriptive clauses of a physical DNF formula, each describing a possible world.

backward. This is *primary* interaction, and it occurs only *between* the mental and physical plane.

We thus see that the seat of causal interaction in Cartesian duality is not the pineal gland but the identification of impression and inference. We write $x \models a$ as expressing equally the impression of event a on subsequent state x and the deduction by state x of the prior occurrence of event a. The Cartesian dictum *cogito, ergo sum* is the case of this where x is the thinker's state and a the event of his or her existence.

As a proponent of more dynamic logics than traditionally contemplated in logic [Pra76, Pra90a] we point out the atemporal quality of this dictum, a hallmark of classical logic. Examined closely, our analysis shows that Descartes' dictum properly tensed becomes *cogito, ergo eram* (I was), an epitaph both of whose tenses the liar paradox renders true in perpetuity. Our thoughts follow from our events but not conversely and hence may survive them without logical contradiction. A particularly good one may far outlive its source.

We pass now to interaction *within* each plane, whether physical or mental, which we derive as *secondary* interaction from the primary form with the aid of *residuation*, a pair of operations on binary relations that constitutes dynamic implications forwards and backwards in time;. For $K = 2$, $\Dashv$ as a matrix of 0's and 1's is an ordinary binary relation: the event a either is or is not related to state x. This relation is understood ambiguously as a two-valued distance in either time space ($a \Dashv x$, physical) or information space ($x \models a$, mental).

Given any two contrary binary relations $R \subseteq U \times V$, $T \subseteq U \times W$, their *right residual* $R\backslash T$ [WD39, Jón82, Pra90b] can be defined equivalently as follows.

(i) As the operation satisfying $R;S \subseteq T$ iff $S \subseteq R\backslash T$. (Think of this as defining division on the left by R, with inequalities where one would expect an equality. The case $R = 0$, all entries 0, requires no special attention.)

(ii) As the largest relation $S \subseteq V \times W$ such that $R;S \subseteq T$.

(iii) As the set of all pairs (v, w) in $V \times W$ such that $uRv \rightarrow uTw$ for all $u \in U$.

(iv) As that operation monotone in its right hand argument that satisfies modus ponens, $R;(R\backslash T) \vdash T$, and also $T \vdash R\backslash(R;T)$, where $\vdash$ is read as $\subseteq$. This makes $R;-$ and $R\backslash -$ pseudoinverse operations which when composed either decrease or increase their argument depending on the order of composition.

(v) As the relation $(R^{\smile};T^{-})^{-}$ where $R^{\smile}$ is converse (transpose) and T^{-} is complement (change all 0's to 1's in the matrix and vice versa). This can be written more neatly as $(T\dagger;R)\dagger$ where $T\dagger$ denotes $T^{-\smile}$. If we think of residuation $R\backslash T$ as a form of implication $R \rightarrow T$, and composition as a form of conjunction, and allow for the noncommutativity of relational composition (relative product), then this corresponds to the classical principle $A \rightarrow B \equiv \neg(A \wedge \neg B)$, as well as to linear logic's $A \multimap B \equiv (A \otimes B^{\perp})^{\perp}$.

It is a straightforward exercise to show the equivalence of these definitions; see [Pra90a] for further discussion.

Definition (v) reveals the contravariance of the operation in R, and its covariance in T, composition being monotone in each argument, a form of bilinearity.

We therefore call residuation *sesquilinear*, in anticipation of the next section.

Now consider $\Dashv\backslash\Dashv$ in the light of condition (iii). This instance of residuation is a binary relation on X. For all x, y in X, $x(\Dashv\backslash\Dashv)y$ holds just when row x implies (is a subset of) row y for every event, i.e. when $x \rightarrow y$ is valid. Now $x \rightarrow y$ says that in order to be able to get from x to y, every event a whose occurrence is recorded in x must still be recorded in y. Thus $\Dashv\backslash\Dashv$ consists of those pairs (x, y) which as transitions do not entail taking back the claim that an event has already happened.

This makes $\Dashv\backslash\Dashv$ the natural transition relation on X. This is a partially ordered *automaton*. Elsewhere we have used higher dimensional automata to argue that automata could be reliably paired up as the dual of schedules [Pra92]. We find Chu spaces a very appealing extension of this duality.

The left residual T/S, where $T \subseteq U \times W$, $S \subseteq V \times W$, is the dual of the right. We settle for defining T/S as the set of all pairs (u, v) in $U \times V$ such that $vSw \rightarrow uTw$ for all $w \in W$ (cf. (iii)), and ask the reader to infer the other four equivalent formulations corresponding to (i)-(v) above.

The left residual $\Dashv/\Dashv$ is, by dual reasoning to $\Dashv\backslash\Dashv$, that binary relation on A containing (a, b) just when for all $x \in X$, $b\Dashv x$ implies $a\Dashv x$. This makes it the natural temporal precedence relation on events, namely a *schedule* of events, an alternative to automata theory and Kripke structures that has attracted our attention as a reliable model of true concurrency since 1982 [Pra82].

When we unravel the primitive causal links contributing to secondary causal interaction we find that two events, or two states, communicate with each other by interrogating *all* entities of the opposite type. Thus event a deduces that it precedes event b not by broaching the matter with b directly, but instead by consulting the record of every state to see if there is any state volunteering a counterexample. When none is found, the precedence is established. Conversely when a Chu space is in state x and desires to pass to state y, it inquires as to whether this would undo any event that has already occurred. If not then the transition is allowed.

If one truly believed that the universe proceeded via state transitions, this might seem a roundabout and inefficient way of implementing those transitions. However it seems to us, particularly in view of the considerations of the following section, that the more likely possibility is that the universe only *seems* to proceed via state transitions, due perhaps to our ancestors having ill-advisedly chosen monism as the natural world view, perhaps millennia before the rise of Cartesianism, perhaps only some years after its decline. What we conjecture actually happens is that events signal states forward in time, or equivalently that states infer events backwards in time, and the world we imagine we live in is simply what that process looks like to its inhabitants when interpreted monistically.

Why this theory as opposed to any other? Well, certainly no other theory has satisfactorily explained the causal interaction of real mental and physical planes as conceived by Descartes. Whether monism is an equally satisfactory alternative for Descartes' problem is a good question. But for the other applications of Chu spaces considered here, namely concurrency, metamathematics, quantum mechanics, and logic (see below), it seems to us that monism simply cannot compete with dualism.

4 Quantum Mechanics

When time and truth are complex-valued as in quantum mechanics, right residuation is replaced by the sesquilinear operation of inner product $\langle\varphi|\psi\rangle$. This is a complex-valued *correlation* between wavefunctions $\langle\varphi|$ and $|\psi\rangle$, which are given as points of a *Hilbert space*, a metrically complete vector space which is made an inner product space with this operation.

The correspondence with Chu spaces is as follows. Any given choice of basis of Hilbert space defines a set of propositions, one per basis vector. Each coordinate of a given state vector relative to that basis is interpreted as the complex truth value of the corresponding proposition in that state. Relative to that basis, a state vector then corresponds to a row of $\models$, or a column of $=\!|$. Right residuation is defined even for one-state spaces, and is in form the logical counterpart to inner product. The right residual of a one-state space with itself is simply the identity relation on that state, this being the only partial order possible. The inner product of a wavefunction with itself is a scalar, namely its length squared, but quantum mechanics is a projective system where lengths are only physically meaningful in proportion: the length of a single state is no more informative in QM than is the identity partial order on a singleton.

A *mixed state* is a set of pure states and a distribution giving their relative probabilities. Such a distribution can be understood as a quantitative form of disjunction, making a mixed state the quantum mechanical counterpart of a Chu space. Here $\langle\varphi|\psi\rangle$ for mixed states corresponds to the right residual of two Chu spaces. The inner product of a mixed state with itself yields a square matrix of transition probabilities between its constituent pure states. The right residual of a Chu space with itself yields a square matrix of transition *possibilities* when $K = 2$, and a suitably richer relation for larger K, where the possibilities begin to depend on choice of quantale for K, taking us beyond the scope of this paper.

The outer product $|\psi\rangle\langle\varphi|$ produces an operator which transforms Hilbert space. Viewed as a transformation of basis vectors of Hilbert space, such an operator establishes correlations between attributes. The corresponding operation on Chu spaces is left residuation, which likewise produces a (two-valued) correlation between events, which we may identify with attributes.

This perspective leads to the following reconstruction of the emergence of modern quantum mechanics in 1925-26. Classical physics, and the old quantum mechanics, took between-state correlations as basic. Newton's laws, or their expression in terms of Lagrange's equations and the energy-difference Langrangian, were couched in terms of space and time, with velocity v being the derivative of position with respect to time, and momentum being mv. Hamilton made the bold move of taking momentum to be an independent quantity in its own right, observing that two equations per dimension based on a total-energy Hamiltonian yielded an elegantly symmetric reformulation of Langrange's one equation per dimension. From the perspective of classical physics this was no more than an ingeniously symmetric but otherwise unimproved variant of the basic laws of motion.

The new quantum mechanics made Hamilton's "causal interaction" of momentum and position primitive, and derived the classical laws as secondary. Furthermore they used the same logic, only as a complex-valued fuzzy logic rather than a two-valued logic, to achieve this end. This made momentum-space interaction a simple interaction, and the derived momentum-momentum and space-space interactions more complex. These can be understood as having to go both backwards and forwards in time for their complete effect, the basis for Cramer's transactional account of quantum mechanics [Cra86], which Leslie Lamport drew to my attention in 1987.

5 Conclusion

We have advanced a mechanism for the causal interaction of mind and body, and argued that separate additional mechanisms for body-body and mind-mind interaction can be dispensed with; mind-body interaction is all that is needed. This is a very different outcome from that contemplated by 17th century Cartesianists, who took body-body and mind-mind interaction as given and who could find no satisfactory passage from these to mind-body interaction. Even had they found a technically plausible solution to their puzzle, mind-body interaction would presumably still have been regarded as secondary to body-body interaction. We have reversed that priority.

One might not expect mind-body duality as a mere philosophical problem to address any urgent need outside of philosophy. Nevertheless we have offered solutions to the following practical problems that could be construed as particular applications of our general solution to Descartes' mind-body problem, broadly construed to allow scarecrows and everything else to have minds.

What is the conceptual basis of concurrent computation? What is the essence of quantum mechanics? On what foundation should mathematics be based? What is the right logic to reason with?

Concepts for concurrent computation. Our research focus since 1980 has been concurrent computation. Our conclusion is that programmers should be able to move as freely as possible between declarative and imperative modes of thought about the same program. We are now convinced that the duality of schedules and automata, as the realization of the duality of body and mind respectively in the world of programming, provides a better conceptual foundation for concurrent programming than any other model.

Essence of quantum mechanics. We claim that quantum mechanics has not previously been reduced to lay terms by physicists, who have been content to leave the subject as a mysterious jumble of properties of Hilbert space that the working physicist can become acclimatized to and even confident with after sufficient exposure. Mind-body duality and interaction explains respectively complementarity and the inner product in relatively elementary terms making a clear connection with other structures such as the above model of computation and the following foundation for mathematics. The central role of the mental plane in this account of quantum mechanics makes it a *rational* mechanics.

Foundations of mathematics. We implicitly settle for relational structures as the objects of mathematics when we so restrict the models of first-order logic. But this has the unfortunate side effect of excluding some popular mathematical structures, most notably topology, which would appear to require a second order theory. Chu spaces over 2^k realize all k-ary relational structures [Pra93, p.154-3] as well as topological spaces when $K = 2$ [LS91], all as objects of the one category, yielding a novel degree of morphism-sensitive typelessness for foundations. The above connection with quantum mechanics suggests that mathematics based on Chu spaces be thought of as *natural* mathematics, sharing with nature the essential principles of duality and interaction.

Choice of logic. We envision two logics, elementary and transformational. Elementary logic has its usual meaning as the logic of individual objects such as sets, groups, and Boolean algebras. It serves to reason about relationships between elements of such objects. These objects are traditionally understood as relational structures but they can also more generally be understood as Chu spaces as per the preceding paragraph.

Transformational logic bears superficial resemblances to elementary logic but serves to reason about interactions between objects rather than relationships within objects. The structural basis for object interaction is the homomorphism or structure-preserving morphism, from which flows all other interaction structure such as duality, limits, tensor products, homsets, and size (cardinality or concreteness).

The most promising transformational logic seems to us to be Girard's linear logic [Gir87]. $\mathbf{Chu}_K$ is a constructive model of linear logic in the sense that it interprets the sequents of linear logic as sets of proofs rather than as Boolean or intuitionistic truth values. Nonconstructive models of linear logic such as phase spaces seem to us at best a curiosity. As to alternative constructive models, for want of any convincing counterexamples we conjecture mildly that these can all be satisfactorily subsumed by Chu spaces, the case $V = \mathbf{Set}$ of the general Chu construction $\mathbf{Chu}(V, k)$. We have yet to be shown a V that improves on **Set** for any significant application of the Chu construction.

References

[Bar79] M. Barr. *$*$-Autonomous categories, LNM 752.* Springer-Verlag, 1979.

[Bar91] M. Barr. $*$-Autonomous categories and linear logic. *Math Structures in Comp. Sci.*, 1(2), 1991.

[CCMP91] R.T Casley, R.F. Crew, J. Meseguer, and V.R. Pratt. Temporal structures. *Math. Structures in Comp. Sci.*, 1(2):179–213, July 1991.

[Cra86] J.G. Cramer. The transactional interpretation of quantum mechanics. *Reviews of Modern Physics*, pages 647–687, 1986.

[Gir87] J.-Y. Girard. Linear logic. *Theoretical Computer Science*, 50:1–102, 1987.

[GP93] V. Gupta and V.R. Pratt. Gates accept concurrent behavior. In *Proc. 34th Ann. IEEE Symp. on Foundations of Comp. Sci.*, pages 62–71, November 1993.

[Gup93] V. Gupta. Concurrent Kripke structures. In *Proceedings of the North American Process Algebra Workshop, Cornell CS-TR-93-1369*, August 1993.

[Jón82] B. Jónsson. Varieties of relation algebras. *Algebra Universalis*, 15:273–298, 1982.

[LS91] Y. Lafont and T. Streicher. Games semantics for linear logic. In *Proc. 6th Annual IEEE Symp. on Logic in Computer Science*, pages 43–49, Amsterdam, July 1991.

[Pra76] V.R. Pratt. Semantical considerations on Floyd-Hoare logic. In *Proc. 17th Ann. IEEE Symp. on Foundations of Comp. Sci.*, pages 109–121, October 1976.

[Pra82] V.R. Pratt. On the composition of processes. In *Proceedings of the Ninth Annual ACM Symposium on Principles of Programming Languages*, January 1982.

[Pra85] V.R. Pratt. Some constructions for order-theoretic models of concurrency. In *Proc. Conf. on Logics of Programs, LNCS 193*, pages 269–283, Brooklyn, 1985. Springer-Verlag.

[Pra86] V.R. Pratt. Modeling concurrency with partial orders. *Int. J. of Parallel Programming*, 15(1):33–71, February 1986.

[Pra90a] V.R. Pratt. Action logic and pure induction. In J. van Eijck, editor, *Logics in AI: European Workshop JELIA '90, LNCS 478*, pages 97–120, Amsterdam, NL, September 1990. Springer-Verlag.

[Pra90b] V.R. Pratt. Dynamic algebras as a well-behaved fragment of relation algebras. In *Algebraic Logic and Universal Algebra in Computer Science, LNCS 425*, pages 77–110, Ames, Iowa, June 1988, 1990. Springer-Verlag.

[Pra92] V.R. Pratt. Event spaces and their linear logic. In *AMAST'91: Algebraic Methodology and Software Technology*, Workshops in Computing, pages 1–23, Iowa City, 1992. Springer-Verlag.

[Pra93] V.R. Pratt. The second calculus of binary relations. In *Proceedings of MFCS'93*, pages 142–155, Gdańsk, Poland, 1993. Springer-Verlag.

[Pra94a] V. Pratt. Chu spaces: complementarity and uncertainty in rational mechanics. Technical report, TEMPUS Summer School, Budapest, July 1994. Manuscript available as pub/bud.tex.Z by anonymous FTP from Boole.Stanford.EDU.

[Pra94b] V.R. Pratt. Chu spaces: Automata with quantum aspects. In *Proc. Workshop on Physics and Computation (PhysComp'94)*, Dallas, 1994. IEEE.

[PT80] A. Pultr and V. Trnková. *Combinatorial, Algebraic and Topological Representations of Groups, Semigroups, and Categories.* North-Holland, 1980.

[Rus27] B. Russell. *The analysis of matter.* Paul, Trench, Trubner (also Dover 1955), 1927.

[RW94] R. Rosebrugh and R.J. Wood. An adjoint characterization of the category of sets. *Proc. Amer. Math. Soc.*, 122(2):409–413, 1994.

[Wat86] R.A. Watson. Descartes and Cartesianism. In *The New Encylopaedia Britannica.* Encyclopaedia Britannica, Inc., 1986.

[WD39] M. Ward and R.P. Dilworth. Residuated lattices. *Trans. AMS*, 45:335–354, 1939.

Part II

CAAP

First-Order Logic on Finite Trees *

Andreas Potthoff

IRISA, Campus de Beaulieu
F-35042 Rennes Cedex
e-mail: potthoff@irisa.fr

Abstract. We present effective criteria for first-order definability of regular tree languages. It is known that over words the absence of modulo counting (the "noncounting property") characterizes the expressive power of first-order logic (McNaughton, Schützenberger), whereas noncounting regular tree languages exist which are not first-order definable. We present new conditions on regular tree languages (more precisely, on tree automata) which imply nondefinability in first-order logic. One method is based on tree homomorphisms which allow to deduce nondefinability of one tree language from nondefinability of another tree language. Additionly we introduce a structural property of tree automata (the so-called $\wedge$-$\vee$-patterns) which also causes tree languages to be undefinable in first-order logic. Finally, it is shown that this notion does not yet give a complete characterization of first-order logic over trees. The proofs rely on the method of Ehrenfeucht-Fraïssé games .

1 Introduction

Regular word languages as well as many subclasses of regular word languages can be defined using very different formalisms, e.g. finite automata, regular expressions and monadic second-order formulas. An important example is the class of star-free word languages that has been investigated by McNaughton and Schützenberger [10, 15]. In particular it was shown by McNaughton that this class coincides with the class of first-order definable word languages and from Schützenberger we know that a regular word language is star-free iff the language is aperiodic. (A word language L is called aperiodic if there exists $n \in \mathbb{N}$ such that for all $u, v, w \in \Sigma^*$ we have $uv^n w \in L \iff uv^{n+1} w \in L$.) Since aperiodicity is decidable for a regular word language by inspecting the minimal deterministic automaton accepting this language, also first-order definability turns out to be decidable.

In the introduction to [1] Büchi wrote: "The extension from unary algebras to n-ary algebras (tree automata) sometimes is obvious and sometimes requires additional ideas." The "obvious extension" applies well to the definition of regular tree languages in the above mentioned formalisms whereas the notions of

* The present work was supported by EBRA Working Group 6317 "Algebraic and Syntactic Methods in Computer Science (ASMICS 2)" and by a fellowship of the EC program "Human, Capital and Mobility".

star-freeness, aperiodicity and first-order definability introduced by Thomas [18] yield different classes of regular tree languages. In [14] it was shown that every regular tree language over an alphabet without unary symbols is star-free and in [8] that there exist aperiodic tree languages which are not first-order definable. Thus aperiodicity is only a necessary criterion for first-order definability.

Up to now, the only way to prove that an aperiodic tree language is not first-order definable is to apply the well-known Ehrenfeucht-Fraïssé game [4, 6]. In the present context this game is played by two players on two trees. Trees satisfy the same set of first-order formulas of a certain quantifier-depth n if and only if the second player has a winning strategy in the play with n rounds on these trees. Thus a tree language T is not first-order definable if there exists a sequence $(s_n, t_n)_{n \in \mathbb{N}}$ of trees such that for all $n \in \mathbb{N}$: $s_n \in T$, $t_n \notin T$, and the second player has a winning strategy in the n-round play on s_n and t_n. As can be seen in [8] it is often difficult to construct such a sequence and to verify the required properties.

The aim of this paper is to provide effective necessary conditions for first-order definability. We show that certain mappings on trees (nondeleting linear tree homomorphisms [5]) preserve winning strategies of the second player and thus allow to deduce nondefinability of one tree language from nondefinability of another tree language. We also apply these mappings to show that it suffices to deal with languages of binary trees in order to find a decision procedure for definability in first-order logic.

In [12] it was shown that a certain set of partial boolean expressions is aperiodic, but not first-order definable. From this example we extract the notion of an $\wedge$-$\vee$-pattern which is a condition on state transformations in the corresponding minimal tree automaton. We show that this notion provides a quite powerful necessary condition for first-order definability but still does not characterize the class of first-order definable tree languages. The example language proving that the absence of an $\wedge$-$\vee$-pattern does not suffice to insure first-order definability also corrects an error in [18] by showing that there exists an aperiodic tree language that is definable in chain logic but not in first-order logic.

The remainder of this paper has 5 sections. In Section 2 we introduce regular tree languages in terms of tree automata and monadic second-order formulas. In Section 3 we present an Ehrenfeucht-Fraïssé game for first-order logic on finite trees and recall some basic facts on this game. In Sections 4 we investigate tree homomorphisms and in Section 5 $\wedge$-$\vee$-patterns. An outline of future work will be given in Section 6. For lack of space some proofs have to be omitted which can be found in [13].

2 Notation

Let $\Sigma = \Sigma_0 \cup \ldots \cup \Sigma_r$ be a *finite ranked alphabet* where Σ_i denotes the set of all symbols of arity i. Let furthermore V denote a set of 0-ary variables. The set of all trees over Σ with variables in V, denoted by $T_\Sigma(V)$, is inductively defined as follows: every 0-ary symbol $a \in \Sigma_0$ and every variable $c \in V$ belongs to $T_\Sigma(V)$

and with $b \in \Sigma_i$ and $t_1, \ldots, t_i \in T_\Sigma(V)$ also $b(t_1, \ldots, t_i)$ belongs to $T_\Sigma(V)$. T_Σ denotes the set of trees over Σ without any variables. $T \subseteq T_\Sigma$ is called a tree language over Σ. If additionally $\Sigma = \Sigma_0 \cup \Sigma_2$ we call a tree language over Σ binary. In the remainder of this section we denote by a always a 0-ary symbol, by c a variable and by b a symbol of positive arity. The labelling of the leaves of a tree t from left to right is denoted $yield(t)$, e.g. $yield(a) = a$, $yield(c) = c$ and $yield(b(t_1, \ldots, t_i)) = yield(t_1) \cdot \ldots \cdot yield(t_i)$. With each tree we associate a prefix closed set $dom(t) \subset \{1, \ldots, r\}^*$ called the domain of t and defined by $dom(a) = dom(c) = \{\varepsilon\}$ and $dom(b(t_1, \ldots, t_i)) = \{\varepsilon\} \cup \bigcup_{k=1,\ldots,i} k \cdot dom(t_k)$. $<$ denotes the partial prefix ordering on the domain of a tree. We refer to the set of leaves of a tree t by $front(t) \subseteq dom(t)$. For $k \in dom(t)$ we denote by $t(k) \in \Sigma$ the label of node k in t. t^k denotes the tree obtained from t by removing all nodes that are not greater than k, i.e. $dom(t^k) = \{\, l \mid kl \in dom(t)\,\}$ and $t^k(l) = t(kl)$ for all $l \in dom(t^k)$.

We will now introduce a concatenation on trees via replacement of variables. Let $T, T_1, \ldots, T_m \subseteq T_\Sigma(V)$ and $\{c_1, \ldots, c_m\} \subseteq V$, then we denote by $T[c_1 \leftarrow T_1, \ldots, c_m \leftarrow T_m]$ the set of all trees obtained from trees in T by replacing all variables c_i by possibly different trees in the corresponding tree language T_i, more formally we put $T[\bar{c} \leftarrow \bar{T}] = \bigcup_{t \in T} t[\bar{c} \leftarrow \bar{T}]$ with $a[\bar{c} \leftarrow \bar{T}] = a$ for $a \in \Sigma_0 \cup V \setminus \{c_1, \ldots, c_m\}$, $c_i[\bar{c} \leftarrow \bar{T}] = T_i$ and $b(t_1, \ldots, t_i)[\bar{c} \leftarrow \bar{T}] = \{b(t'_1, \ldots, t'_i) \mid t'_j \in t_j[\bar{c} \leftarrow \bar{T}] \text{ for } j = 1, \ldots, i\}$. For $T \subseteq T_\Sigma(V)$ and $c \in V$ we put $T^{*,c} = \bigcup_{i \geq 0} T^{c,i}$ with $T^{c,0} = \{c\}$ and $T^{c,i+1} = T^{c,i} \cup T^{c,i}[c \leftarrow T]$.

A tree $s \in T_\Sigma(\{c\})$ with exactly one leaf labelled c is called a *special tree*. The set of all special trees is denoted by S_Σ. For $s \in S_\Sigma$ and $t \in T_\Sigma \cup S_\Sigma$ we write $s \cdot t$ instead of $s[c \leftarrow t]$. $(S_\Sigma, \cdot, c)$ is a monoid that serves to extend the notions of Nerode-congruence and aperiodicity from word languages to tree languages. Let $T \subseteq T_\Sigma$ and $t, t' \in T_\Sigma$. t and t' are called (Nerode-)congruent with respect to T ($t \cong_T t'$) iff $\forall s \in S_\Sigma \; s \cdot t \in T \iff s \cdot t' \in T$. T is called aperiodic iff $\exists n \in \mathbb{N} \; \forall s', s \in S_\Sigma \forall t \in T_\Sigma \; s' \cdot s^n \cdot t \in T \iff s' \cdot s^{n+1} \cdot t \in T$.

A *deterministic bottom-up tree automaton (DBA)* $\mathcal{A} = (Q, \Sigma, \delta, F)$ consists of a finite set of states Q, a set of final states $F \subseteq Q$, a ranked alphabet Σ and a transition function $\delta : \bigcup_{k=0,\ldots,r} \Sigma_k \times Q^k \to Q$. We can extend δ in the usual way to a mapping $\delta : T_\Sigma \to Q$. The tree language accepted by $\mathcal{A}$ is $T(\mathcal{A}) = \{t \in T_\Sigma \mid \delta(t) \in F\}$. A tree language T is called *regular* if $T = T(\mathcal{A})$ for a DBA $\mathcal{A}$. Let $p \in Q$, $s \in S_\Sigma$ and $t \in T_\Sigma$ with $\delta(t) = p$. Then we put $\delta(s, p) = \delta(s \cdot t)$.

As in the case of regular word languages there exists a *minimal* DBA for every regular tree language which is unique up to state renaming and which is characterized by the following two conditions: $\forall q \in Q \; \exists t \in T_\Sigma \; \delta(t) = q$ and $\forall p, q \in Q \;\; p \neq q \Rightarrow \exists s \in S_\Sigma \;\; \delta(s, p) \in F \iff \delta(s, q) \notin F$. Furthermore the minimal DBA can be computed effectively from an arbitrary DBA accepting the tree language. The states of this minimal DBA correspond to the equivalence classes of the Nerode-congruence, thus a tree language is regular iff the Nerode-congruence has finite index. Furthermore, if $\mathcal{A}$ is a minimal DBA accepting T

we have that T is aperiodic iff there exists $n \in \mathrm{IN}$ such that for all $s \in S_\Sigma$ and for all $q \in Q$ we have $\delta(s^n, q) = \delta(s^{n+1}, q)$. Therefore we obtain that aperiodicity is decidable for regular tree languages. For a more detailed introduction in tree language theory see [7].

We will now describe tree languages in terms of monadic second-order logic. With every tree t we associate a relational structure $t = (dom(t), <, S_1, \ldots, S_r, (P_a)_{a \in \Sigma})$ where $<$ denotes the partial prefix ordering on $dom(t)$ and S_i denotes the i-th successor relation (with kS_ik' iff $ki = k'$). P_a consists of all nodes labelled a.

We use x, y, ... to denote variables ranging over nodes and X, Y, ... to denote variables ranging over sets of nodes. Atomic formulas are the following: $x < y$, $x = y$, xS_iy, Xx and P_ax. From the atomic formulas we build up the set of all monadic second-order formulas using the boolean connectives $\wedge$, $\vee$, $\neg$, and the quantifiers $\exists$ and $\forall$ for both kinds of variables. We denote by $\varphi(x_1, \ldots, x_n, X_1, \ldots, X_m)$ a formula with free variables among $x_1, \ldots, x_n$ and $X_1, \ldots, X_m$. The satisfaction relation $(t, k_1, \ldots, k_n, K_1, \ldots, K_m) \models \varphi(x_1, \ldots, x_n, X_1, \ldots, X_m)$ is defined as usual. By FO we denote the set of first-order formulas, i.e. formulas without any set variables. The quantifier-depth of a first-order formula is inductively defined as follows: $qd(\varphi) = 0$ for all atomic formulas φ, $qd(\varphi \vee \psi) = qd(\varphi \wedge \psi) = max\,\{qd(\varphi), qd(\psi)\}$, $qd(\neg\varphi) = qd(\varphi)$ and $qd(\exists x\varphi) = qd(\forall x\varphi) = qd(\varphi) + 1$. Every formula φ without free variables defines a tree language $T(\varphi) = \{t \mid t \models \varphi\}$. A tree language is called monadic second-order definable (first-order definable) if there exists a monadic second-order formula (first-order formula) φ such that $T = T(\varphi)$. Regular and monadic second-order definable tree languages are related by the following theorem:

Theorem 1. *[2, 17] A tree language T is regular iff T is monadic second-order definable.*

Chain logic and antichain logic have been introduced by Thomas [18] as fragments of monadic second-order logic. In chain logic set quantifiers range only over chains, i.e. sets of nodes that are totally ordered by the partial prefix ordering. An antichain in a tree is a set of nodes such that no two nodes in this set are comparable in the partial prefix ordering. Antichain formulas (where set quantifiers are restricted to range over antichains) define exactly the class of star-free tree languages.

The following theorems summarize the relations between the notions of star-freeness, aperiodicity and first-order definability:

Theorem 2. *[14] Every regular binary tree language is star-free.*

Theorem 3. *[8] Every first-order definable tree language is aperiodic, but there exist aperiodic tree languages that are not first-order definable.*

The only difference between word languages and tree languages of unary trees is that word automata process a word starting from the minimal node in the usual ordering whereas bottom-up tree automata start at the maximal node in the partial prefix ordering. Since regular word languages are closed against reversing we can apply the results of Schützenberger and McNaughton to sets of unary trees. In [11] Perrin presents an effective construction of a star-free expression defining all words which effect the same transformation on the states of an aperiodic word automaton. Star-free expressions on words can be rewritten syntactically to a first-order formula defining the same word language. With a technique of restricting the range of quantifiers we finally arrive at the following proposition:

Lemma 4. *Let $\mathcal{A} = (Q, \Sigma, \delta, F)$ be an aperiodic DBA and $m : Q \to Q$. Then there exists a first-order formula $\varphi_m(x)$ such that for all $t \in T_\Sigma$ we have: $(t, k) \models \varphi_m(x)$ iff the maximal unary subtree above x effects state transformation m.*

3 An Ehrenfeucht-Fraïssé Game

Ehrenfeucht-Fraïssé games are widely used in the literature to show that certain properties of relational structures are not expressible in a given logic [3, 4, 6]. In this section we recall the rules of the first-order game played on trees as introduced in [8]. Furthermore we enumerate some basic facts on this game. Most proofs can be found in [8, 12, 13] and are therefore omitted here.

The Ehrenfeucht-Fraïssé game is played on two trees by two players, here called player I and player II, with the aim of player I to show that the given trees are different. By $G_n((t, k_1, \ldots, k_m), (t', k'_1, \ldots, k'_m))$ we denote a play with n rounds on two trees t and t' with a sequence of m specified nodes in both trees. In each move player I chooses a node in t or t' and player II reacts by choosing a node in the other tree. Let k_{m+i} resp. k'_{m+i} be the nodes chosen in t resp. t' in the i-th round. Player II wins the play if the nodes $k_1, \ldots, k_{n+m}$ in t and $k'_1, \ldots, k'_{n+m}$ in t' define a partial isomorphism from t to t', i.e. if we have for all $1 \leq i, j \leq m+n$, for all $a \in \Sigma$ and for all $1 \leq l \leq r$: $k_i = (<, S_l)\, k_j \iff k'_i = (<, S_l)\, k'_j$ and $P_a k_i \iff P_a k'_i$. Since we deal with finite trees either player I or player II has a winning strategy. This fact yields to the following definition:

Definition 5. Let T_Σ^m denote the set of all trees in T_Σ with a sequence of m specified nodes and let FO^m denote the set of all first-order formulas with m free variables. For $(t, \bar{k}), (t', \bar{k}') \in T_\Sigma^m$ we denote by $(t, \bar{k}) \approx_n (t', \bar{k}')$ that player II has a winning strategy in the play $G_n((t, \bar{k}), (t', \bar{k}'))$.

$\approx_n$ and $\approx_{n+1}$-equivalence are related by the so-called back and forth property:

Lemma 6. *Let $(t, \bar{k}), (t', \bar{k}') \in T_\Sigma^m$.*
$(t, \bar{k}) \approx_{n+1} (t', \bar{k}')$ *iff*
$\forall k \in dom(t)\, \exists k' \in dom(t') \quad (t, \bar{k}, k) \approx_n (t', \bar{k}', k')$ *and*
$\forall k' \in dom(t')\, \exists k \in dom(t) \quad (t, \bar{k}, k) \approx_n (t', \bar{k}', k')$

From this property the following theorem can be deduced easily:

Theorem 7. *[8] The relations $\approx_n$ are equivalence relations of finite index on T_Σ^m and we have for all $(t,\bar{k}),(t',\bar{k}') \in T_\Sigma^m$:*

$(t,\bar{k}) \approx_n (t',\bar{k}')$ *iff*

$\forall \varphi(\bar{x}) \in FO^m \; qd(\varphi(\bar{x})) \leq n \Rightarrow [(t,\bar{k}) \models \varphi(\bar{x}) \iff (t',\bar{k}') \models \varphi(\bar{x})]$

We will use the last theorem in the following way to prove that a tree language is not first-order definable:

Corollary 8. *$T \subseteq T_\Sigma$ is not first-order definable iff there exists a sequence $(s_n,t_n)_{n\in\mathbb{N}}$ such that $s_n \in T$, $t_n \notin T$ and $s_n \approx_n t_n$ for all $n \in \mathbb{N}$.*

We will construct such sequences of pairs of trees by induction. For the inductive step we need some technical propositions that allow us to construct $\approx_{n+1}$-equivalent trees from $\approx_n$-equivalent ones. The first proposition states that winning strategies of player II on certain parts of two trees can be combined to get a winning strategy for the whole trees.

Lemma 9 (Composition Lemma).
Let $s,t \in S_\Sigma$ with $s(l)=t(k)=c$ and $s',t' \in T_\Sigma$.

$$\begin{array}{lccc} & (s,l_1,\ldots,l_m,l) & \approx_n & (t,k_1,\ldots,k_m,k) \\ \wedge & (s',\varepsilon,l'_1,\ldots,l'_r) & \approx_n & (t',\varepsilon,k'_1,\ldots,k'_r) \\ & & \iff & \end{array}$$

$$(s\cdot s',l_1,\ldots,l_m,l,ll'_1,\ldots,ll'_r) \approx_n (t\cdot t',k_1,\ldots,k_m,k,kk'_1,\ldots,kk'_r)$$

The previous lemma allows us to weaken the precondition of Corollary 8.

Remark 10. *Let T be a regular tree language. T is not first-order definable iff there exists a sequence $(s_n,t_n)_{n\in\mathbb{N}}$ such that $s_n \not\cong_T t_n$ and $s_n \approx t_n$ for all $n \in \mathbb{N}$.*

Proof. The direction from left to right follows directly from Corollary 8. For the reverse direction we use that the Nerode-congruence has finite index. Thus there exists a subsequence $(s'_n,t'_n)_{n\in\mathbb{N}}$ such that $s'_n \cong_T s'_m$ and $t'_n \cong_T t'_m$ for all $n,m \geq 0$. From the definition of this congruence we obtain a special tree s such that $s\cdot s'_n \in T \iff s\cdot t'_n \notin T$ for all $n \in \mathbb{N}$. The Composition Lemma 9 shows that either the sequence $(s(s'_n),s(t'_n))_{n\in\mathbb{N}}$ or the sequence $(s(t'_n),s(s'_n))_{n\in\mathbb{N}}$ proves nondefinability of T according to Corollary 8.

A more powerful method to combine winning strategies is formulated in the following proposition.

Lemma 11 (Substitution Lemma). *[13]*
Let $(u,l_1,\ldots,l_m),(v,k_1,\ldots,k_m) \in T_\Sigma^m(\{c_1,\ldots,c_r\})$ and $T_1,\ldots,T_r \subseteq T_\Sigma$ such that

$(u,l_1,\ldots,l_m) \approx_n (v,k_1,\ldots,k_m)$ *and*
$(s,\varepsilon) \approx_n (s',\varepsilon)$ *for all $s,s' \in T_i$ $(i=1,\ldots,r)$.*

Then $(t,l_1,\ldots,l_m) \approx_n (t',k_1,\ldots,k_m)$ for all $t \in u[c_1 \leftarrow T_1,\ldots,c_r \leftarrow T_r]$ and $t' \in v[c_1 \leftarrow T_1,\ldots,c_r \leftarrow T_r]$.

The following remark describes exactly the way how sequences of pairs of trees as required in Corollary 8 are constructed in the sequel.

Remark 12. *Let* $u, v \in T_\Sigma(\{c_1, \ldots, c_r\})$, $t_1, t_1', \ldots, t_r, t_r' \in T_\Sigma$, $s \in u[c_i \leftarrow \{t_i, t_i'\} \mid 1 \leq i \leq r]$ *and* $t \in v[c_i \leftarrow \{t_i, t_i'\} \mid 1 \leq i \leq r]$ *such that*

(1) $(u, \varepsilon) \approx_{n+1} (v, \varepsilon)$

(2) $(t_i, \varepsilon) \approx_n (t_i', \varepsilon)$ *for* $1 \leq i \leq r$

(3) $\forall k \in front(u)\ \exists k' \in front(v) \quad (u, \varepsilon, k) \approx_n (v, \varepsilon, k') \wedge s^k = t^{k'}$

$\forall k' \in front(v)\ \exists k \in front(u) \quad (u, \varepsilon, k) \approx_n (v, \varepsilon, k') \wedge s^k = t^{k'}$

Then we have $(s, \varepsilon) \approx_{n+1} (t, \varepsilon)$.

4 Tree Homomorphisms

In this section we introduce tree homomorphisms (see also [5]) and show that these mappings preserve winning strategies of player II. Then we use tree homomorphisms to show that it suffices to deal with binary tree languages in order to obtain a decidability result for first-order logic.

Definition 13. In order to define tree homomorphisms we extend the notion of special trees. The set of *n-special trees*, denoted by S^n_Σ, consists of all trees $t \in T_\Sigma(\{c_1, \ldots, c_n\})$ such that $yield(t) \in \Sigma_0^* c_1 \Sigma_0^* \ldots \Sigma_0^* c_n \Sigma_0^*$. For $t \in S^n_\Sigma$ and $t_1, \ldots, t_n \in T_\Sigma$ we abbreviate $t[c_1 \leftarrow t_1, \ldots, c_n \leftarrow t_n]$ by $t(t_1, \ldots, t_n)$.

A *tree homomorphism* from T_Σ to T_Ω assigns to a symbol $b \in \Sigma_k$ a k-special tree $h(b) \in S^k_\Omega$, i.e. $h : \bigcup_{k=0,\ldots,r} \Sigma_k \rightarrow S^k_\Omega$. h induces a mapping $h^* : T_\Sigma \rightarrow T_\Omega$ by $h^*(a) = h(a)$ for $a \in \Sigma_0$ and $h^*(b(t_1, \ldots, t_k)) = h(b)(h^*(t_1), \ldots, h^*(t_k))$ for $b \in \Sigma_i$. In the sequel we will identify h and h^*.

Since copying (multiple occurences of a variable c_i) is not allowed for tree homomorphisms we can transfer a winning strategy of player II on two trees to the images of these trees. At first we show that the restriction to noncopying mappings is indeed necessary.

Example 1. Let $\Sigma = \Sigma_0 \cup \Sigma_1$ with $\Sigma_0 = \{a\}$ and $\Sigma_1 = \{b\}$, $T \subset T_\Sigma$ the set of all trees (words) of even height, $\Omega = \Omega_0 \cup \Omega_2$ with $\Omega_0 = \{a\}$ and $\Omega_2 = \{b\}$ and finally $T_{even} \subset T_\Omega$ the set of all trees that contain a path of even length.

T is periodic and therefore not first-order definable. Let $h : T_\Sigma \rightarrow T_\Omega$ be defined by $h(a) = a$ and $h(b) = b(c_1, c_1)$. Then h is syntactic for T and T_{even}, but T_{even} is first-order definable.

We call the path that starts at node k and contains all nodes in the set $k(12)^*(1 \cup \varepsilon)$ the "zig-zag" path starting at k. This path has even length if the final node belongs to the set $k(12)^*$ and has odd length otherwise. It is easy to construct a first-order formula $\varphi_{even}(x)$ which is satisfied by all nodes k with a zig-zag path of even length starting at k. A tree contains a least one path of even length and one path of odd path of length iff there exists a node k such that all path below the left successor of k have even length and all path below the right successor have odd length or vice versa. In particular $\varphi_{even}(x)$ applies to $k1$ iff $\varphi_{even}(x)$ does not apply to $k2$ in this case. Hence we are able to define the set of all trees that contain at least one path of even length and one path of odd length. If a tree has only paths of even length or only paths of odd length, then also the zig-zag path starting at the root has even length or odd length respectively. So a disjunction of two formulas defines T_{even}, one defining the set of trees with paths of even and odd length and the other one defining the trees with a zig-zag path of even length starting at the root.

Lemma 14. *Let $h : T_\Sigma \to T_\Omega$ be a tree homomorphism and $t, t' \in T_\Sigma$. Then we have $t \approx_{n+1} t' \Rightarrow h(t) \approx_n h(t')$.*

Proof. Let us call a subtree in $h(t)$ or $h(t')$ resulting from a node labelled a in t or t' an a-segment. Suppose player I chooses a node l in $h(t)$. Let k be the preimage of this node in t. Then player II chooses a node k' in t' according to his winning strategy in the $n+1$-round game on t and t'. If the node k in t is labelled with a then also k' in t' is labelled with a. In a last step player II computes the a-segment which is the image of k' in $h(t')$ and chooses in this segment the same node as player I. The strategy of player II is shown in the following picture.

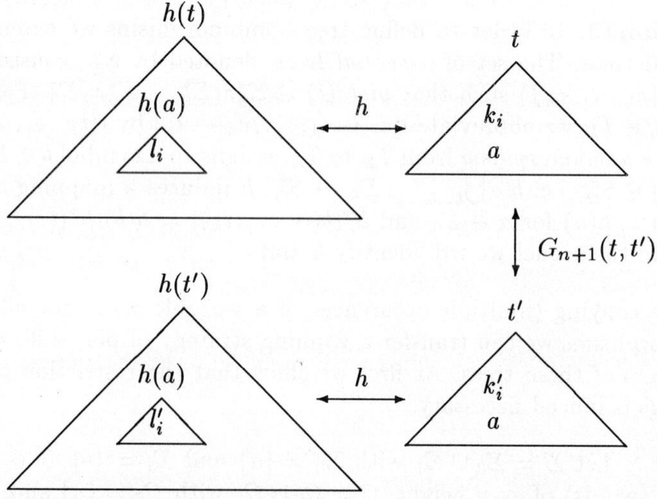

After n moves the game ends with n chosen nodes in $h(t)$, $h(t')$, t and t'. Let us call these nodes l_i, l'_i, k_i and k'_i for $i = 1, \ldots, n$. Now we have to verify the winning conditions for player II . We only show the most difficult condition to verify, i.e. $l_i < l_j \iff l'_i < l'_j$.

So let $l_i < l_j$. If l_i and l_j belong to the same segment, i.e. $k_i = k_j$, then also $k'_i = k'_j$ and since player II has chosen the same nodes in corresponding segments, we also have $l'_i < l'_j$.

It remains to investigate the case that l_i and l_j do not belong to the same segment. Thus we have $k_i < k_j$ and $k'_i < k'_j$. From this fact we can not deduce directly that $l'_i < l'_j$ because not all nodes in the segment belonging to k'_i are predecessors of all nodes in the segment belonging to k'_j. Let $k_i r$ be the direct successor of k_i above k_j, i.e. $k_i r \leq k_j$. Thus l_i is a predecessor of the segment belonging to the r-th successor of k_i and so is l'_i for the segment belonging to $k'_i r$. Since player II has played in t and t' according to his winning strategy in the game with $n+1$ moves and up to know only n moves a played, we can deduce that also $k'_i r \leq k'_j$. Thus l'_i is a predecessor of all nodes in the segment of k'_j, in particular of l'_j.

In order to be able to transfer nondefinability from a tree language T to another tree language T' using a tree homomorphism we need an additional condition stating that the tree homomorphism respects the Nerode-congruences of T and T'.

Definition 15. A tree homomorphism $h : T_\Sigma \longrightarrow T_\Omega$ is called syntactic for $T \subseteq T_\Sigma$ and $T' \subseteq T_\Omega$ iff for all $t, t' \in T_\Sigma \quad t \not\approx_T t' \Rightarrow h(t) \not\approx_{T'} h(t')$.

Lemma 14 and Remark 10 yield immediately:

Theorem 16. *Let $T \subseteq T_\Sigma$ and $T' \subseteq T_\Omega$ be regular tree languages. If T is not first-order definable and if $h : T_\Sigma \longrightarrow T_\Omega$ is a syntactic tree homomorphism for T and T', then T' is not first-order definable.*

One application of tree homomorphisms is the proof of the following theorem, stating that the decidability problem for first-order logic can be reduced to binary tree languages over a one letter alphabet.

Theorem 17. *[13] For every regular tree language T, we are able to construct effectively a regular binary tree language T' over a one letter alphabet such that T is first-order definable iff T' is first-order definable.*

Proof. The proof can be divided into two parts. In the first part we eliminate unary symbols. Therefore state transformations obtained from unary subtrees are shifted to minimal nonunary nodes below. Then we code non-unary symbols in a binary one letter alphabet. The correctness of these transformations is shown using tree homomorphisms and manipulations of first-order formulas.

The next lemma states that it is decidable whether a syntactic tree homomorphism between two regular binary tree languages exists. The restriction to binary tree languages is motivated by Theorem 17 and also simplifies the proof. Thus in order to obtain decidability of first-order logic it would suffice to find a recursively enumerable set of regular binary tree languages such that every other nondefinable regular tree language is related via a syntactic tree homomorphism to one of these tree languages. It can be shown that at least no finite set of tree languages has this property.

Lemma 18. *Let T and T' be regular binary tree languages. Then it is decidable if there exists a syntactic tree homomorphism for T and T'.*

Proof of Lemma 18. Let $\mathcal{A} = (Q, \Sigma, \delta, F)$ and $\mathcal{A}' = (Q', \Omega, \delta', F')$ be minimal DBA accepting T and T' respectively. Every tree homomorphism h induces a mapping $H : Q \to 2^{Q'}$ defined by $H(q) = \{\delta(h(t)) | \delta(t) = q\}$ with the following properties: (i) $H(q) \neq \emptyset$ for $q \in Q$, (ii) $\delta'(h(a)) \in H(\delta(a))$ for all $a \in \Sigma_0$, (iii) $\delta'(h(b), H(p_1), H(p_2)) \subseteq H(\delta(b, p_1, p_2))$ for all $b \in \Sigma_2$ and all $p_1, p_2 \in Q$. h is syntactic if additionly (iv) $H(p) \cap H(q) = \emptyset$ for all $p \neq q$.

Condition (ii) can be satisfied for all H that already satisfy condition (i). Thus it suffices to test all mappings H which satisfy conditions (i) and (iv) whether for all $b \in \Sigma_2$ there exists $t_b \in S^2_\Omega$ such that $\delta'(t_b, H(p_1), H(p_2)) \subseteq H(\delta(b, p_1, p_2))$ for all $p_1, p_2 \in Q$. Therefore we only have to show that we can compute all binary mappings $m : Q \times Q \to Q$ effected by any tree in S^2_Ω. Every 2-special tree can be decomposed in 3 special trees and a binary symbol as shown in the following picture.

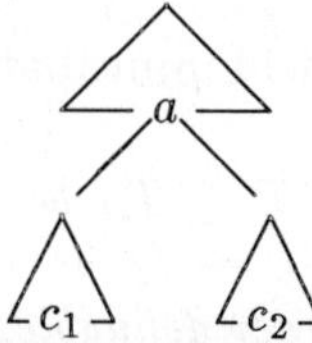

Thus it suffices to compute all state transformations obtained from special trees and then to combine these transformations with all binary symbols in all possible ways as indicated in the previous picture.

An application of Theorem 16 will be given in the next chapter.

5 ∧-∨-Patterns

In [12] it was shown that a certain set of partial boolean expressions is not first-order definable. The simplicity of this particular tree language allows us to transfer the proof of nondefinability in first-order logic of this tree language to all tree languages that satisfy a certain condition (called ∧-∨-pattern) on state transformations in the corresponding minimal DBA. We first recall the definition of this tree language.

Definition 19. Let $\Sigma^B = \Sigma^B_0 \cup \Sigma^B_2$ with $\Sigma^B_0 = \{0, 1\}$ and $\Sigma^B_2 = \{\wedge, \vee\}$. Let $\mathcal{A}_{\wedge,\vee}$ be the DBA over Σ^B with set of states $\{0, 1, \bot\}$, set of final states $\{1\}$ and the transition function γ with $\gamma(0) = 0$ and $\gamma(1) = 1$. For $\wedge$ and $\vee$ we define γ in the following tables:

∧	0	1	⊥
0	⊥	0	⊥
1	0	1	⊥
⊥	⊥	⊥	⊥

∨	0	1	⊥
0	0	1	⊥
1	1	⊥	⊥
⊥	⊥	⊥	⊥

We denote $T(\mathcal{A}_{\wedge,\vee})$ by $T_{\wedge,\vee}$.

It is easy to see that $T_{\wedge,\vee}$ is aperiodic, because ∧ and ∨ are monoton on 0 and 1. Now we introduce the notion of an ∧-∨-pattern.

Definition 20. Let $\mathcal{A} = (Q, \Omega, \delta, F)$ be a DBA and let t_q denote an arbitrary tree with $\delta(t_q) = q$ for all $q \in Q$. We say that $\mathcal{A}$ contains an $\wedge$-$\vee$-pattern if there exists a nonempty, irreflexive and symmetrical relation $R \subseteq Q \times Q$ such that there exists for all $(p, p') \in R$ a tree $t_{p,p'} \in T_\Omega(\{x_{r,r'}, y_{r,r'} \mid (r, r') \in R\})$ such that

(i) $\delta(t_{p,p'}[x_{r,r'} \leftarrow t_r, y_{r,r'} \leftarrow t_r]) = p$,
(ii) $\delta(t_{p,p'}[x_{r,r'} \leftarrow t'_r, y_{r,r'} \leftarrow t_r]) = p'$ and
(iii) $\delta(t_{p,p'}[x_{r,r'} \leftarrow t_r, y_{r,r'} \leftarrow t'_r]) = p'$.

The following remark justifies the notion $\wedge$-$\vee$-pattern by showing that $t_{p,p'}$ acts as a generalized $\vee$ for $p = 0$ and $p' = 1$.

Remark 21. *Let $\mathcal{A} = (Q, \Omega, \delta, F)$ be a DBA and let t_q be a tree with $\delta(t_q) = q$ for all $q \in Q$. Let furthermore $R \subseteq Q \times Q$ and $t_{p,p'} \in T_\Omega(\{x_{r,r'}, y_{r,r'} \mid (r, r') \in R\})$ for all $(p, p') \in R$ as in the previous definition. We define simultaneously for all $(p, p') \in R$ a mapping $g_{p,p'} : T_{\Sigma^B}(\{c\}) \to T_\Omega(\{c_{r,r'} \mid (r, r') \in R\})$ by*

$$g_{p,p'}(0) = t_p,\ g_{p,p'}(1) = t_{p'},\ g_{p,p'}(c) = c_{p,p'},$$

$$g_{p,p'}(\vee(t_1, t_2)) = t_{p,p'}[x_{r,r'} \leftarrow g_{r,r'}(t_1), y_{r,r'} \leftarrow g_{r,r'}(t_2)] \text{ and}$$

$$g_{p,p'}(\wedge(t_1, t_2)) = t_{p',p}[x_{r,r'} \leftarrow g_{r',r}(t_1), y_{r,r'} \leftarrow g_{r',r}(t_2)].$$

Then we have for all $t \in T_{\Sigma^B}$ and all $(p, p') \in R$:

$$\gamma(t) = 0 \Rightarrow \delta(g_{p,p'}(t)) = p \text{ and } \gamma(t) = 1 \Rightarrow \delta(g_{p,p'}(t)) = p'.$$

The conclusion in the previous remark does not depend on a particular choice of the trees $g_{p,p'}(0)$ and $g_{p,p'}(1)$ whereas the definition of these mappings does. Therefore we will denote mappings obtained from different choices with the same name and specify $g_{p,p'}(0)$ and $g_{p,p'}(1)$ more precisely when necessary.

Now we turn to the main result of this section stating that the existence of an $\wedge$-$\vee$-pattern implies nondefinability in first-order logic. In the proof we will use the trees $u_i \in T_{\Sigma^B}(\{c\})$ for $i \in \mathbb{N}$ defined as follows: $u_0 = c$ and $u_m = \wedge(u_{m-1}, u_{m-1})$ if m is even and $u_m = \vee(u_{m-1}, u_{m-1})$ if m is odd.

Lemma 22. *[12] Let l, l', l'' be leaves in u_m $(m \geq 2)$ which are not neighbours. Then we can label all leaves of u_m with 0 and 1 in two different ways such that the resulting trees v_m and w_m have the following properties:*

- *$v_m(k) = w_m(k)$ for all leaves k except l*
- *$v_m(l) = v_m(l') = w_m(l') = 0$*
- *$w_m(l) = v_m(l'') = w_m(l'') = 1$*
- *$\gamma(v_m) = 0$ and $\gamma(w_m) = 1$*

Theorem 23. *Let $\mathcal{A} = (Q, \Omega, \delta, F)$ be a minimal DBA that contains an $\wedge$-$\vee$-pattern. Then $T(\mathcal{A})$ is not first-order definable.*

Proof. Let $R \subseteq Q \times Q$ and $t_{p,p'} \in T_\Omega(\{x_{r,r'}, y_{r,r'} \mid (r, r') \in R\})$ for all $(p, p') \in R$ as in Definition 20. We will construct simultaneously for all $(p, p') \in R$ a sequence

$(s_n^{p,p'}, t_n^{p,p'})_{n\in\mathbb{N}}$ such that $\delta(s_n^{p,p'}) = p$, $\delta(t_n^{p,p'}) = p'$ and $(s_n^{p,p'}, \varepsilon) \approx_n (t_n^{p,p'}, \varepsilon)$. Then we obtain nondefinability of $T(\mathcal{A})$ directly from Remark 10.

For $n = 0$ we put $s_0^{p,p'} = g_{p,p'}(\vee(0,0))$ and and $t_0^{p,p'} = g_{p,p'}(\vee(0,0))$ where $g_{p,p'}(0)$ and $g_{p,p'}(1)$ are arbitrary with $\delta(g_{p,p'}(0)) = p$ and $\delta(g_{p,p'}(1)) = p'$.

For the induction step let us assume that $s_n^{r,r'}$ and $t_n^{r,r'}$ have the required properties for all $(r, r') \in R$ and let $(p, p') \in R$ be fixed in the sequel. Now we apply $g_{p,p'}$ to the trees u_m. For $l \in front(u_m)$ let us denote by M_l the set of images of l in $g_{p,p'}(u_m)$. From finiteness of the $\approx_n$-equivalence relation on $T_\Omega(\{c_{r,r'} \mid (r,r') \in R\})$ we obtain that for sufficiently large m there exist $l, l', l'' \in dom(u_m)$ such that:
$(*)$ $\forall k \in M_l \; \exists k' \in M_{l'} \; \exists k'' \in M_{l''}$

$$(g_{p,p'}(u_m), \varepsilon, k) \approx_n (g_{p,p'}(u_m), \varepsilon, k') \approx_n (g_{p,p'}(u_m), \varepsilon, k'').$$

Let v_m and w_m as in Lemma 22. We put $s_{p,p'}^{n+1} = g_{p,p'}(v_m)$ and $t_{p,p'}^{n+1} = g_{p,p'}(w_m)$ with $g_{r,r'}(0) = s_{r,r'}^n$ and $g_{r,r'}(1) = t_{r,r'}^n$ for all $(r,r') \in R$. From Remark 21 we obtain immediately that $\delta(s_{p,p'}^{n+1}) = p$ and $\delta(t_{p,p'}^{n+1}) = p'$.

In order to prove $\approx_{n+1}$-equivalence of $s_{p,p'}^{n+1}$ and $t_{p,p'}^{n+1}$ using Remark 12 let us first mention that $s_{p,p'}^{n+1}, t_{p,p'}^{n+1} \in g_{p,p'}(u_m)[c_{r,r'} \leftarrow \{s_{r,r'}^n, (t_{r,r'}^n\} \mid (r,r') \in R]$ and that ${s_{p,p'}^{n+1}}^k = {t_{p,p'}^{n+1}}^k$ for all $k \in front(g_{p,p'}(u_m)) \setminus M_l$. Thus it remains to verify condition (c) of Remark 12 for $k \in M_l$. But this condition is guaranteed by the choice of l, l', l'' satisfying $(*)$ and the construction of v_m and w_m.

It remains to state effectiveness of this condition.

Lemma 24. *It is decidable whether an $\wedge$-$\vee$-pattern exists in a DBA $\mathcal{A}$.*

Proof. There is only a finite number of relations $R \subseteq Q \times Q$, hence it suffices to decide whether an $\wedge$-$\vee$-pattern for a fixed R exists. We can assign to every tree $t \in T_\Omega(\{x_{r,r'}, y_{r,r'} \mid (r,r') \in R\})$ three states according to the equations (i)-(iii) in Definition 20. Now let us enumerate all trees in $T_\Omega(\{x_{r,r'}, y_{r,r'} \mid (r,r') \in R\})$ by increasing height and collect the corresponding tupels of states until all trees of a certain height $m \leq |Q|^3$ do not add any new tupel to the collection. Then it remains to test whether for each pair $(p,p') \in R$ there exists a tupel (p,p',p') in the computed set. This is the case if and only if there exists an $\wedge$-$\vee$-pattern for R.

The following examples show applications of Theorem 16 and Theorem 23.

Example 2. The first tree language known to be aperiodic and not first-order definable was introduced by Heuter [8]. The proof of the latter property was quite difficult. In this example we obtain the same result using a tree homomorphism.

Let $\Sigma = \Sigma_0 = \Sigma_2 = \{a, b\}$. A set of nodes in a tree is called a cut if this set is an antichain that is maximal with respect to set inclusion. The labelling of a cut C is the labelling of the nodes of C in the lexicographical ordering. Let $T_{\Sigma^* aa \Sigma^*} = \{t \in T_\Sigma \mid$ every cut of size greater than 1 has a labelling in $\Sigma^* aa \Sigma^*\}$. Let $T \subset T_{\Sigma^B}$ be the set of boolean expressions with value 1 where $\wedge$

and $\vee$ are totally defined, i.e. $\wedge(0,0) = 0$ and $\vee(1,1) = 1$. Finally let h be the tree homomorphism defined as follows: $h(0) = a(b,b)$, $h(1) = a$,

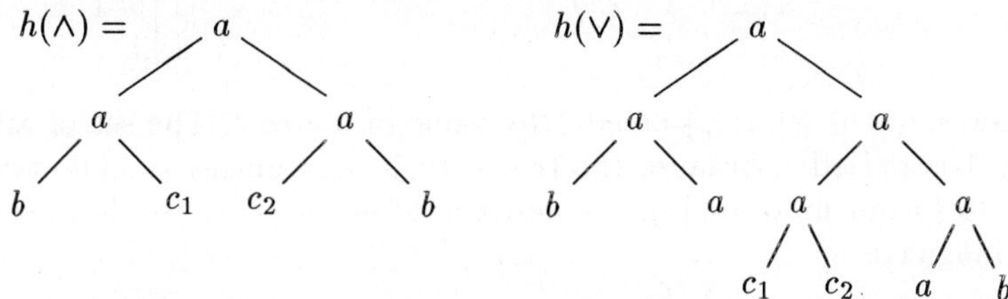

By induction on the height of t, we are able to show:

If $t \in T$ then $h(t) \in T_{\Sigma^* aa \Sigma^*}$ and if $t \in T$ then $h(t)$ contains a cut with labelling in $b\Sigma^* b \setminus \Sigma^* aa \Sigma^*$. Thus h is syntactic for T and $T_{\Sigma^* aa \Sigma^*}$ and therefore we obtain that $T_{\Sigma^* aa \Sigma^*}$ is not first-order definable.

Example 3. Let $\Sigma = \Sigma_0 \cup \Sigma_2$ with $\Sigma_2 = \{\vee, \overset{\neg}{=}\}$ and $\Sigma_0 = \{0,1\}$ where $\vee$ and $\overset{\neg}{=}$ are defined in the following tables:

$\overset{\neg}{=}$	0	1	$\bot$
0	1	$\bot$	$\bot$
1	$\bot$	0	$\bot$
$\bot$	$\bot$	$\bot$	$\bot$

$\vee$	0	1	$\bot$
0	0	1	$\bot$
1	1	$\bot$	$\bot$
$\bot$	$\bot$	$\bot$	$\bot$

The following trees show that the minimal automaton (with set of states $\{0,1,\bot\}$) accepting the set of expressions with value 1 contains an $\wedge$-$\vee$-pattern. Let $R = \{(0,1),(1,0)\}$ and

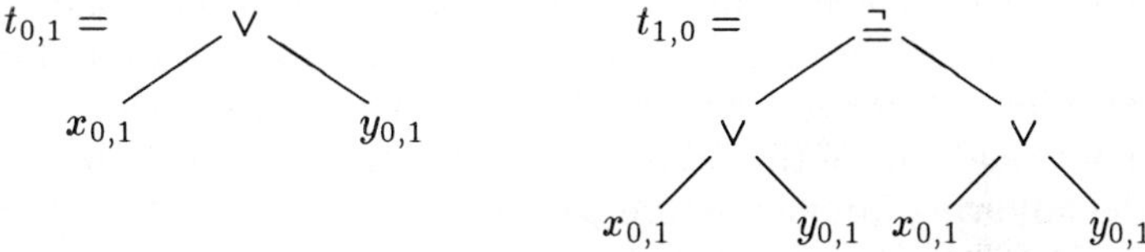

In order to verify that these trees match the required properties, one only has to replace $x_{0,1}$ and $y_{0,1}$ by 0 and 1 respectively and to compute the value of the tree. So we obtain easily that this tree language is not first-order definable.

Many aperiodic tree languages that are not first-order definable can be treated this way. But the tree language introduced in the next definition shows that the absence of an $\wedge$-$\vee$-pattern does not guarantee first-order definability. This tree language is aperiodic, contains no $\wedge$-$\vee$-pattern and is chain definable, but not first-order definable. Thus we also correct a proposition in [18] stating that every aperiodic and chain definable tree language is already first-order definable.

Definition 25. Let $\Sigma = \Sigma_2 \cup \Sigma_0$ with $\Sigma_2 = \{\overset{\neg}{=}, \leftrightarrow\}$ and $\Sigma_0 = \{0,1\}$. The binary symbols $\overset{\neg}{=}$ and $\leftrightarrow$ denote partial boolean functions defined in the following tables:

$\overset{\neg}{=}$	0	1	$\bot$
0	1	$\bot$	$\bot$
1	$\bot$	0	$\bot$
$\bot$	$\bot$	$\bot$	$\bot$

$\leftrightarrow$	0	1	$\bot$
0	1	0	$\bot$
1	0	1	$\bot$
$\bot$	$\bot$	$\bot$	$\bot$

Let $val(t) \in \{0, 1, \bot\}$ denote the value of a tree t. The set of all trees with value 1 is periodic, because the tree $\leftrightarrow(c, 0)$ is counting modulo two. Thus we have to forbid unlimited direct nestings of $\leftrightarrow$ in order to obtain an aperiodic tree language.

Let $T' = \left(\overset{\neg}{=}(c, \leftrightarrow(c, c)) \right)^{*,c} \cdot^c \{0,1\}$ and let $T = T' \cap \{t \mid val(t) = 1\}$.

Theorem 26. *T is aperiodic, contains no $\wedge$-$\vee$-pattern and is chain definable.*

Proof. T is regular, because it is an intersection of a first-order definable tree language and a regular tree language. It is also easy to see that T is aperiodic and contains no $\wedge$-$\vee$-pattern because the leftmost path of a tree in T' consists of inner nodes only labelled $\overset{\neg}{=}$ and already determines the value of the tree in the following sense: if this path is of even length then the value of the tree is $\bot$ or the value of the leftmost leaf, if the path is of odd length then the value of the tree is $\bot$ or the complement of the value of the leftmost leaf. The property of a path to be of even length can be easily expressed in chain logic. Thus we can construct a formula $\varphi_1(x)$ expressing that the leftmost path below node x determines the value of the subtree at node x to be 1 or $\bot$. Then we can define T by the following formula, where $\varphi_{T'}$ describes T':

$$\varphi_{T'} \wedge \exists x \forall x' \, (x \leq x' \wedge \varphi_1(x)) \wedge$$
$$\forall x \forall x_2 \forall x_{11} \forall x_{12} [P_{\overset{\neg}{=}} x \wedge x S_2 x_2 \wedge x_2 S_1 x_{21} \wedge x_2 S_2 x_{22}] \Rightarrow$$
$$[(\varphi_1(x) \iff (\neg \varphi_1(x_{21}) \iff \varphi_1(x_{22}))].$$

Theorem 27. *[13] T is not first-order definable*

The proof of this theorem is rather technical and is therefore omitted.

6 Conclusion

The notions of tree homomorphisms and $\wedge$-$\vee$-patterns introduced here provide effective and powerful criteria for first-order definability of regular tree languages. Nevertheless the problem of deciding first-order definability remains unsolved.

We want to mention some other possibilities to investigate this problem. Whereas we decrease the alphabet of tree automata and increase the number of states in the proof of Theorem 17, one can also try the opposite direction, i.e. to define operations on tree automata that decrease the number of states but preserve nondefinability of the accepted tree language. A more algebraic approach may result from the notion of tree language variety defined in [16] since the class of first-order definable tree languges build such a variety.

References

1. J.R.Büchi, *Finite automata, their algebras and grammars*, D.Siefkes, ed. (Springer Verlag, New York, 1989).
2. J.Doner, Tree acceptors and some of their applications, Journal of Computer and System Sciences **4** (1970) 406-451.
3. H.-D.Ebbinghaus, J.Flum, W.Thomas, *Mathematical Logic* (Springer Verlag, New York, Berlin, Heidelberg, Tokyo, 1984).
4. A.Ehrenfeucht, An application of games to the completeness problem for formalized theories, Fundamenta Mathematicae **49** (1961) 129-141.
5. J.Engelfriet, Bottom-up and top-down tree transformations - a comparison, Mathematical Systems Theory **9** (1975) 198-231.
6. R.Fraïssé, Sur quelques classifications des systèmes de relations, basés sur des isomorphismes restreints, Publications Scientifique de l'Université d'Alger, Série A **1** (1954) 35-182.
7. F.Gecség, M.Steinby, *Tree Automata* (Akadémiai Kiadó, Budapest, 1984).
8. U.Heuter, First-order properties of trees, star-free expressions and aperiodicity, RAIRO Theoretical Informatics and Applications **25** (1991) 125-145.
9. R.Ladner, Applications of model theoretic games to discrete linear orders and finite automata, Information and Control **33** (1977), 281-303.
10. R.McNaughton, S.Papert, *Counter-free Automata* (The M.I.T. Press, Cambridge, Massachusetts, 1971).
11. D.Perrin, Finite Automata, in: *Handbook of Theoretical Computer Science, Vol. B*, J.v.Leeuwen, ed. (Elsevier , Amsterdam, 1990) 3-57.
12. A.Potthoff, Modulo counting quantifiers over finite trees, TCS **126** (1994) 97-112.
13. A.Potthoff, Logische Klassifizierung regulärer Baumsprachen, (Dissertation, Kiel, 1994).
14. A.Potthoff, W.Thomas, Regular tree languages without unary symbols are star-free, in: *9th International Conference on Fundamentals of Computation Theory*, Zoltán Ésik, ed., Lecture Notes in Computer Science **710** (1993) 396-405.
15. M.P.Schützenberger, On monoids having only trivial subgroups, Information and Control **8** (1965) 190-194.
16. M.Steinby, A theory of tree language varieties, in *Tree automata and languages*, M.Nivat, A.Podelski, eds., Studies in Computer Science and Artifical Intelligence Vol. **10** (Elsevier, Amsterdam, 1992) 57-81.
17. J.W.Thatcher, J.B.Wright, Generalized finite automata theory with an application to a decision problem of second-order logic, Mathematical Systems Theory **2** (1968) 57-81.
18. W.Thomas, Logical aspects in the study of tree languages, in: *9th Colloquium on Trees in Algebra and Programming*, B.Courcelle, ed. (Cambridge University Press, Cambridge, 1984) 31-51.
19. W.Thomas, On the Ehrenfeucht-Fraïssé game in theoretical computer science, in: *18th Colloquium on Trees in Algebra and Programming*, M.C.Gaudel, J.P.Jouannaud, eds., Lecture Notes in Computer Science **668** (1993) 559-568.

Decidability of Equivalence for Deterministic Synchronized Tree Automata

Kai Salomaa

Department of Mathematics, University of Turku
FIN-20500 Turku, Finland
E-mail: ksalomaa@sara.cc.utu.fi

Abstract. Synchronized tree automata allow limited communication between computations in independent subtrees of the input. This enables them to verify, for instance, the equality of two unary subtrees of unlimited size. The class of tree languages recognized by synchronized tree automata is strictly included in the context-free tree languages. As our main result we show that equivalence of tree languages recognized by deterministic synchronized tree automata can be effectively decided. This contrasts the earlier undecidability result for the equivalence problem for nondeterministic synchronized tree automata.

1 Introduction

The recognition capability of finite tree automata is restricted by the fact that computations in independent subtrees of the input are not allowed to communicate with each other. The restriction is especially severe for deterministic top-down tree automata which recognize a proper subfamily of the regular tree languages. Because of this handicap, various extensions of the finite tree automaton model have been proposed. Top-down tree automata augmented with different types of look-ahead capabilities are considered in [4,5,6,16,17]. Other natural extensions of the finite tree automaton model are the automata with constraints and encompassment automata studied in [1,2,3].

A top-down synchronized tree automaton allows a simple limited form of communication between independent computations. Some states of the automaton contain synchronizing symbols, these are called synchronizing states. The synchronization condition requires that the sequences of synchronization symbols produced along any two paths of the input are in the prefix relation, i.e, one is a prefix of the other. In the equality-synchronized computation mode we require that the synchronization sequences corresponding to all paths of the input are the same. Intuitively, the synchronization condition can be interpreted by saying that when the automaton enters a synchronizing state, it must stop and wait until all other computations in independent subtrees either terminate successfully or enter a synchronizing state containing the same synchronizing symbol.

The above notion of synchronization was originally introduced for alternating machines by Hromkovič [9]. Synchronization has turned out to be a very useful notion in the study of parallel computations, see [10,11,12] and the references listed there. Synchronized tree automata were first considered in [14]. In spite of the similarity of the definitions, the notion of synchronization is essentially different, respectively, for alternating machines and for tree automata. In the former case one synchronizes parallel computations on the same input but in the case of tree automata synchronization represents communication between different parts of the input. Alternating tree automata [13,15] combine these two notions of parallelism. It is not clear what would be the right way to define synchronization for alternating tree automata.

The inclusion relations between the families of tree languages defined by deterministic and nondeterministic prefix- and equality-synchronized tree automata were established in [14]. Furthermore, it was shown that all synchronized tree language families are properly included in the context-free tree languages. This implies that emptiness is decidable for synchronized tree languages. On the other hand, equivalence turns out to be undecidable for nondeterministic synchronized tree automata. Contrasting this result it was established in [14] that equivalence of deterministic equality-synchronized automata can be decided effectively. This question was reduced to the equivalence problem for deterministic multitape finite automata which is known to be decidable [8]. An essential part of the proof was the so called normalization property for equality-synchronized automata. A normalized automaton recognizes as its extended tree language exactly the set of prefix-trees of the tree language defined by the automaton. A similar property could not be established for prefix-synchronized computations.

As our main result here we show that equivalence of deterministic prefix-synchronized automata is decidable. As a tool for our proof we consider so called globally deterministic synchronized tree automata. Globally deterministic synchronized alternating machines are considered in [11]. We use slightly weaker conditions to define the notion of global determinism than the conditions of the definition of [11].

Globally deterministic automata can recognize the set of so called two-pruned prefix-trees of a deterministic synchronized tree automaton. The (nontrivial part of the) equivalence problem for deterministic synchronized automata can be reduced to the question of equivalence of the corresponding sets of two-pruned prefix-trees. Although we do not know whether equivalence of globally deterministic tree automata in general is decidable, we can effectively decide the equivalence of the specific automata used in our proof.

The tree language families defined, respectively, by the deterministic prefix-synchronized and equality-synchronized automata are incomparable. However, a prefix-synchronized automaton can simulate arbitrary equality-synchronized computations provided that we allow the use of end-markers at the leaves of the input. This means that the decidability of equivalence for deterministic prefix-synchronized automata gives as an immediate corollary the corresponding decidability result for equality-synchronized automata.

The synchronized tree automata recognize only a small subfamily of the context-free tree languages. However, even a deterministic synchronized automaton can, for instance, determine the equality of unary subtrees of unlimited height. In view of this fact the above decidability results seem to be of some interest. Note that the automata with constraints considered in [1,2,3] can verify much more general properties of the inputs, but for them equivalence is undecidable. Without certain restrictions even the question of emptiness is undecidable for these automata.

2 Preliminaries

Here we fix some notations and briefly recall definitions concerning trees that will be used in the later sections.

The set of positive integers is denoted by $\mathbb{N}$ and $\mathbb{N}_0 = \mathbb{N} \cup \{0\}$. Let A be a set. The power set of A is $\mathcal{P}(A)$. If A is finite we denote its cardinality by $\#A$. The set of finite words over A is denoted by A^* and λ is the empty word. Also, $A^+ = A^* - \{\lambda\}$. For $w \in A^*$ and $L \subseteq A^*$, the quotient of L by w is $w^{-1}L = \{v \in A^* \mid wv \in L\}$. The length of a word w is denoted by $|w|$.

If $w_2 = w_1 u$, $w_1, w_2, u \in A^*$, we say that w_1 is a prefix of w_2 and denote $w_1 \preceq w_2$. The *prefix relation* $\simeq_{\mathrm{pr}} \subseteq A^* \times A^*$ is defined by setting $w_1 \simeq_{\mathrm{pr}} w_2$ if and only if $w_1 \preceq w_2$ or $w_2 \preceq w_1$. Let W be a finite subset of A^* such that $w_1 \simeq_{\mathrm{pr}} w_2$ for all $w_1, w_2 \in W$. Then $\max_{\preceq}(W)$ denotes the unique word $w \in W$ such that $w' \preceq w$ for all $w' \in W$.

A *tree domain* D is a nonempty finite subset of $\mathbb{N}^*$ that satisfies the following two conditions: (i) If $u \preceq v \in D$, then $u \in D$. (ii) For every $u \in D$ there exists $\mathrm{rank}_D(u) \in \mathbb{N}_0$ such that $ui \in D$ for $i = 1, \ldots, \mathrm{rank}_D(u)$ and $ui \notin D$ for $i > \mathrm{rank}_D(u)$.

Let A be a set. An A-labeled tree is a mapping $t : \mathrm{dom}(t) \to A$, where $\mathrm{dom}(t)$ is a tree domain. A node $u \in \mathrm{dom}(t)$ is said to be labeled by $t(u) \in A$. A node v is a *child* of a node u ($u, v \in \mathrm{dom}(t)$) if $v = uj$, $j \in \mathbb{N}$.

We use symbols Σ and Ω to denote finite ranked alphabets. The set of symbols of Σ of rank m, $m \geq 0$, is denoted by Σ_m. Let Y be a set of auxiliary symbols. The set of ΣY-trees (or ΣY-terms), $F_\Sigma(Y)$, is the smallest set such that $\Sigma_0 \cup Y \subseteq F_\Sigma(Y)$ and $\sigma(t_1, \ldots, t_m) \in F_\Sigma(Y)$ for all $m \geq 1$, $\sigma \in \Sigma_m$, $t_1, \ldots, t_m \in F_\Sigma(Y)$. By choosing above $Y = \emptyset$ we obtain the definition of the set of Σ-trees F_Σ.

In the natural way, a given ΣY-tree can be viewed as a $(\Sigma \cup Y)$-labeled tree $t : \mathrm{dom}(t) \to \Sigma \cup Y$ that satisfies the condition that every node of rank m is labeled by an m-ary symbol. In the following, we use interchangeably the above algebraic definition of a tree and the notion of a labeled tree defined using a tree domain.

We denote by $X = \{x_1, x_2, \ldots\}$ a fixed countably infinite set of variables. We assume that notions such as the height, the root, a leaf and a subtree of a ΣX-tree t are known. The set of leaves of t is denoted $\mathrm{leaf}(t) \subseteq \mathrm{dom}(t)$. The set of leaves of t labeled by elements of Σ_0 is $\mathrm{leaf}_\Sigma(t)$ and $\mathrm{leaf}_X(t)$ is the set of leaves labeled by variables of X. The set of variables appearing in a tree $t \in F_\Sigma(X)$ is $\mathrm{var}(t)$ and we say that t is *linear* (in variables X) if t has only one occurrence of any variable of X. The set of linear ΣX-trees is denoted $\text{lin}(\Sigma, X)$. For our purposes the names of the variables of a ΣX-tree are irrelevant and we identify trees that are obtained from each other by renaming variables.

Let $t, t_1, \ldots, t_m \in F_\Sigma(X)$ and $x_1, \ldots, x_m \in \text{var}(t)$. Then $t(x_1 \leftarrow t_1, \ldots, x_m \leftarrow t_m)$ denotes the ΣX-tree obtained from t by replacing each occurrence of the variable x_i with t_i, $i = 1, \ldots, m$.

Let $t \in F_\Sigma$. We define the set of *prefix-trees* of t, $\text{pref}(t)$, to consist of all $r \in \text{lin}(\Sigma, X)$ with $\text{var}(r) = \{x_1, \ldots, x_m\}$, $m \geq 0$, such that there exist $r_1, \ldots, r_m \in F_\Sigma$ such that $r(x_1 \leftarrow r_1, \ldots, x_m \leftarrow r_m) = t$. The set $\text{pref}(t)$ consists of all linear ΣX-trees that are obtained from t by replacing a set of independent subtrees by distinct variables.

To conclude this section we define notations concerning paths in trees that will be used when considering synchronization conditions for tree automata. Let t be an A-labeled tree for some set A. A *path* of t from the root to a node $u_m \in \text{dom}(t)$ is a word

$$t(u_1) \cdots t(u_m) \in A^+, \tag{1}$$

where $u_1 = \lambda$, and u_{i+1} is a child of u_i, $i = 1, \ldots, m-1$. A path (1) is denoted $\text{path}(t, u_m)$. The set of paths of the tree t consists of all paths from the root of t to a leaf and we denote

$$\text{path}(t) = \{\text{path}(t, u) \mid u \in \text{leaf}(t)\}.$$

The *domain* of $\text{path}(t, u_m)$ as in (1) is defined by $\text{PATH}(t, u_m) = \{u_1, \ldots, u_m\}$.

Let $t \in F_\Sigma(X)$ and $u \in \text{leaf}(t)$. The set of variable nodes corresponding to the path $\text{path}(t, u)$, $\text{varnd-path}(t, u)$, consists of all nodes $v \in \text{leaf}_X(t)$ such that v is a child of a node of $\text{PATH}(t, u)$ and $v \notin \text{PATH}(t, u)$. Thus $\text{varnd-path}(t, u)$ consists of all nodes "branching out" from the path that are labeled by variables.

Let $t \in F_\Sigma$ and u_1, u_2 be two distinct leaves of t. Denote $P(u_1, u_2) = \text{PATH}(t, u_1) \cup \text{PATH}(t, u_2)$. The *two-pruned tree* $\text{2pr}(t, u_1, u_2)$ is the linear ΣX-tree r determined by the below conditions (i) and (ii).

(i) $\text{dom}(r)$ is the subset of $\text{dom}(t)$ containing the set $P(u_1, u_2)$ and all children of the nodes of $P(u_1, u_2)$.

(ii) If $u \in P(u_1, u_2)$, then $r(u) = t(u)$. If u is a child of a node of $P(u_1, u_2)$ not belonging to $P(u_1, u_2)$, then u is labeled by a variable.

Intuitively, $\text{2pr}(t, u_1, u_2)$ is obtained from t by cutting off all subtrees branching out from the paths leading to u_1 and u_2 and replacing each subtree by a distinct variable. The tree $\text{2pr}(t, u_1, u_2)$ is defined uniquely by the above conditions because we consider trees obtained from each other by a renaming of variables to be identical. Note that, in general, the paths from the root to the leaves u_1 and u_2 may contain a common prefix.

The set of two-pruned trees corresponding to $t \in F_\Sigma$ is $\text{2pr}(t) = \{\text{2pr}(t, u_1, u_2) \mid u_1, u_2 \in \text{leaf}(t),\ u_1 \neq u_2\}$, and,

$$\text{2pr}(\Sigma) = \bigcup_{t \in F_\Sigma} \text{2pr}(t). \tag{2}$$

3 Synchronized Tree Automata

We recall the definition of synchronized tree automata from [14]. Roughly speaking, they are top-down finite tree automata where the computations corresponding to independent subtrees of the input can communicate by way of so called synchronizing symbols. Here we give only the definitions that are needed for the decidability results in the last section. For more details and examples of synchronized tree automata see [14].

A *nondeterministic top-down tree automaton, nta,* is a four-tuple $\mathcal{A} = (\Sigma, Q, Q_0, g)$, where Σ is a ranked alphabet of input symbols, Q is a finite set of states, $Q_0 \subseteq Q$ is a set of initial states, and g determines the state transitions by associating to each $\sigma \in \Sigma_m$, $m \geq 0$, a mapping $\sigma_g : Q \to \mathcal{P}(Q^m)$. The automaton $\mathcal{A}$ is *deterministic, dta,* if $Q_0 = \{q_0\}$ is a singleton set and for all $q \in Q$, $\sigma \in \Sigma_m$, $m \geq 1$, $\#\sigma_g(q) \leq 1$. The class of nondeterministic (respectively, deterministic) top-down tree automata is denoted *nt* (respectively, *dt*.)

We make the notational convention that m-tuples $q_1, \ldots, q_m$ belonging to $\sigma_g(q)$, $\sigma \in \Sigma_m$, $m \geq 1$, $q \in Q$, are denoted using square brackets: $[q_1, \ldots, q_m] \in \sigma_g(q)$. This is done for easier readability because synchronized automata will have states with several components. By a computation step we mean a pair (q, σ), $q \in Q$, $\sigma \in \Sigma$. A computation step (q, σ) is said to be *deterministic* if $\#\sigma_g(q) \leq 1$, and otherwise it is a *nondeterministic computation step.*

Definition 3.1 *Let* $\mathcal{A} = (\Sigma, Q, Q_0, g) \in nt$ *and* $t \in F_\Sigma$. *A* (successful) computation *of* $\mathcal{A}$ *on the input* t *is a* Q*-labeled tree* $r : dom(t) \to Q$ *satisfying the following three conditions:*

(i) $r(\lambda) \in Q_0$.
(ii) *Let* $u \in dom(t)$, $t(u) = \sigma \in \Sigma_m$, $m \geq 1$, *and let* $u_1, \ldots, u_m$ *be the children of the node* u. *Then* $[r(u_1), \ldots, r(u_m)] \in \sigma_g(r(u))$.
(iii) *If* $u \in leaf(t)$ *and* $t(u) = \sigma \in \Sigma_0$, *then* $r(u) \in \sigma_g$.

The set of computations of $\mathcal{A}$ on a tree t is denoted $\mathrm{com}_\mathcal{A}(t)$. If $\mathcal{A}$ is deterministic, then $\#\mathrm{com}_\mathcal{A}(t) \leq 1$ for every $t \in F_\Sigma$. The tree language *recognized* by $\mathcal{A}$ is $L(\mathcal{A}) = \{t \in F_\Sigma \mid \mathrm{com}_\mathcal{A}(t) \neq \emptyset\}$. We denote the tree language families recognized by nondeterministic and deterministic (top-down) tree automata, respectively, NT and DT. It is well known that DT is strictly included in NT [7].

Definition 3.2 *[14] A* nondeterministic synchronized tree automaton, nsta, *is a top-down tree automaton* $\mathcal{A} = (\Sigma, Q, Q_0, g)$ *where the state set is of the form*

$$Q = Q_1 \cup (Q_2 \times S). \tag{3}$$

The set S *is the* synchronization alphabet *and elements of* S *are called* synchronizing symbols, *(sync-symbols for short). States belonging to* $Q_2 \times S$ *are said to be the* synchronizing states *of the automaton. When referring to an nsta* $\mathcal{A}$, *unless otherwise mentioned, we always assume that the state set of* $\mathcal{A}$ *is as in (3) and* S *denotes the synchronization alphabet.*

The above automaton $\mathcal{A}$ is a deterministic synchronized tree automaton, dsta, *if it is a deterministic top-down tree automaton. We denote the class of nondeterministic (respectively, deterministic) synchronized tree automata by* nst *(respectively,* dst*).*

We define a morphism $h_{\mathcal{A}} : Q^* \to S^*$ by setting $h_{\mathcal{A}}(q_1) = \lambda$ and $h_{\mathcal{A}}((q_2, s)) = s$ for all $q_i \in Q_i$, $i = 1, 2$, $s \in S$. Let $t \in F_\Sigma$. The set of synchronized computations *(or* prefix-synchronized computations*) of $\mathcal{A}$ on $t \in F_\Sigma$ is*

$$scom_{\mathcal{A}}(t) = \{r \in com_{\mathcal{A}}(t) \mid (\forall u, v \in path(r))\ h_{\mathcal{A}}(u) \simeq_{pr} h_{\mathcal{A}}(v)\}. \qquad (4)$$

The set of equality-synchronized *computations of $\mathcal{A}$ on the tree t is defined as*

$$s_e com_{\mathcal{A}}(t) = \{r \in com_{\mathcal{A}}(t) \mid (\forall u, v \in path(r))\ h_{\mathcal{A}}(u) = h_{\mathcal{A}}(v)\}.$$

The tree language (prefix-)synchronized recognized *by $\mathcal{A}$ is defined as*

$$L_s(\mathcal{A}) = \{t \in F_\Sigma \mid scom_{\mathcal{A}}(t) \neq \emptyset\},$$

and the tree language equality-synchronized recognized *by $\mathcal{A}$ is*

$$L_e(\mathcal{A}) = \{t \in F_\Sigma \mid s_e com_{\mathcal{A}}(t) \neq \emptyset\}.$$

The families of tree languages synchronized recognized by nondeterministic and deterministic automata are denoted, respectively, NST and DST. The corresponding families defined by the equality-synchronized computation mode are $\mathrm{N_eST}$ and $\mathrm{D_eST}$. Here we are mainly concerned with the prefix-synchronized computation mode and we call prefix-synchronized computations simply synchronized computations.

We will need the following result concerning string languages defined as synchronizing sequences of computations of tree automata. Let $\mathcal{A} = (\Sigma, Q, Q_0, g) \in nst$, $t \in F_\Sigma$ and $r \in \mathrm{scom}_{\mathcal{A}}(t)$ be a synchronized computation on t. The (maximal) *synchronizing sequence* of the computation r is $\mathrm{seq}(r) = \max_{\simeq}(h_{\mathcal{A}}(\mathrm{path}(r)))$. The right side exists by the definition of synchronized computations. The set of synchronizing sequences corresponding to the input t is $\mathrm{seq}(\mathcal{A}, t) = \{\mathrm{seq}(r) \mid r \in \mathrm{scom}_{\mathcal{A}}(t)\}$ and the *synchronization language* of $\mathcal{A}$ is $\mathrm{sync}(\mathcal{A}) = \bigcup_{t \in F_\Sigma} \mathrm{seq}(\mathcal{A}, t)$.

Theorem 3.1 *[14] The language sync($\mathcal{A}$) is a regular word language for every $\mathcal{A} \in nst$.*

For our decidability results it turns out to be useful to consider automata that locally allow nondeterministic choices in the computation, but where the global computation on any given input is deterministic via the synchronization condition. We define these automata similarly as the globally deterministic synchronized alternating machines of [11].

Definition 3.3 *Let $\mathcal{A} = (\Sigma, Q, Q_0, g) \in nst$, $t \in F_\Sigma$ and let $r \in scom_{\mathcal{A}}(t)$ be a synchronized computation of $\mathcal{A}$ on t. For each $i \in \{1, \ldots, |seq(r)|\}$, the ith* synchronization cut *of r is the set $scut(r, i)$ consisting of all nodes $u \in dom(r)$ such that u is labeled by a synchronizing state of $\mathcal{A}$ and $|h_{\mathcal{A}}(path(r, u))| = i$.*

The set scut(r,i) consists of exactly all nodes where the computation reaches the ith synchronizing state in different branches of the input. From the definition of synchronized computations it follows that every node of a given synchronization cut scut(r,i) contains the same sync-symbol.

Definition 3.4 *An automaton* $\mathcal{A} = (\Sigma, Q, Q_0, g) \in nst$, $Q = Q_1 \cup (Q_2 \times S)$, *is* globally deterministic, gdsta, *if it has a unique initial state* $Q_0 = \{q_0\}$ *and the following conditions hold.*

(i) *For every nondeterministic computation step* (q, σ), $q \in Q$, $\sigma \in \Sigma_m$, $m \geq 1$, *the set* $\sigma_g(q)$ *consists of m-tuples of synchronizing states,* $\sigma_g(q) = \{[(q_1^i, s_i), \ldots, (q_m^i, s_i)] \mid i = 1, \ldots, k,\ k \geq 2\}$, *and* $s_i \neq s_j$ *when* $i \neq j$, $1 \leq i, j \leq k$.

(ii) *Let* $t \in F_\Sigma$ *and* $r \in scom_{\mathcal{A}}(t)$. *Let* $scut(r,i)$ *be a synchronization cut of* r *and let* s *be the sync-symbol appearing in the nodes of* $scut(r,i)$. *Then* s *is the only sync-symbol that can be produced by* all *the nondeterministic computation steps at the parent nodes of the synchronization cut* $scut(r,i)$.

The condition (i) requires that in all nondeterministic computation steps of $\mathcal{A}$ the different nondeterministic decisions must be connected with a choice of different sync-symbols. Thus all computation steps producing nonsynchronizing states are deterministic. Condition (ii) guarantees that, for every synchronization cut among all the nondeterministic choices, there is only one that does not immediately violate the synchronization condition. This means that the global computation is in fact deterministic. Note that (ii) above is weaker than the corresponding condition in the definition of globally deterministic synchronized computations in [11]. There it is required that every synchronization cut of a successful computation contains a node where the corresponding sync-symbol is enforced deterministically. Our condition (ii) requires only that the sync-symbol is enforced deterministically as the only common choice for all the nondeterministic steps in question. The automaton we use in the construction for the decidability proof will have only this weaker property.

Combining the above observations it is easy to prove the following lemma. An analogous result for synchronized alternating machines appears in [11].

Lemma 3.1 *Let* $\mathcal{A} = (\Sigma, Q, q_0, g)$ *be a gdsta and* $t \in F_\Sigma$. *Then* $scom_{\mathcal{A}}(t)$ *consists of a unique computation or is empty.*

Condition (ii) of Definition 3.4 requires that a certain property has to be satisfied for all synchronization cuts of all successful computations of $\mathcal{A}$. Given an automaton $\mathcal{A}$, it is not immediately obvious whether $\mathcal{A}$ satisfies the condition (ii). It can be shown that we can effectively decide whether a given nst $\mathcal{A}$ is globally deterministic. In any case, for the globally deterministic automata that we use in the constructions of the next section the conditions of Definition 3.4 can be immediately verified.

The class of globally deterministic automata as given in Definition 3.4 is denoted *gdst* and the corresponding tree language family is denoted GDST. The above definition of a gdsta $\mathcal{A}$ uses explicitly the prefix-synchronized computation mode. Similarly, by considering equality-synchronized computations of the automaton we can define ***globally deterministic equality-synchronized tree automata, gd$_e$sta's.*** Again, the corresponding family of tree languages is denoted GD_eST.

Note that if a given nsta $\mathcal{A}$ is globally deterministic in the sense of Definition 3.4 (a gdsta), then $\mathcal{A}$ is always a globally deterministic equality-synchronized automaton, gd$_e$sta. This follows from the observation that for every tree t, $s_e com_{\mathcal{A}}(t) \subseteq scom_{\mathcal{A}}(t)$. However, it is easy to see (using similar examples as in [14]) that GDST is not a subfamily of GD_eST. This is because of course usually $L_e(\mathcal{A}) \neq L_s(\mathcal{A})$.

The inclusions between the tree language families defined by the various classes of synchronized tree automata are depicted in Figure 1. In the figure a line indicates strict inclusion and unconnected classes are incomparable. CFT denotes the family of context-free tree languages and REC is the family of recognizable tree languages. All relations of the figure not involving the families defined by globally deterministic automata are proved in [14]. We leave the remaining relations as an exercise.

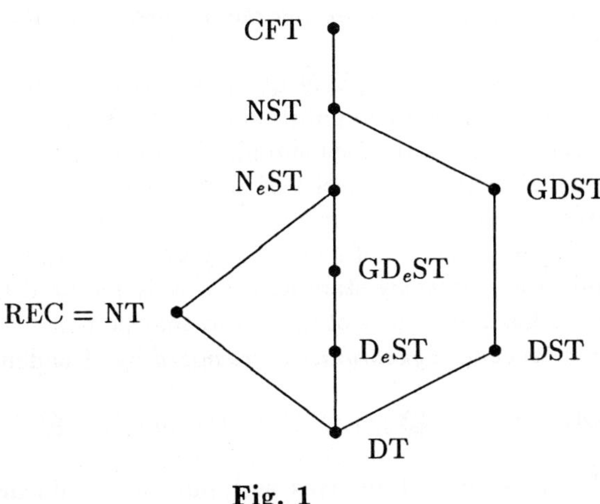

Fig. 1

4 Decidability of Equivalence

The equivalence problem for nondeterministic prefix- and equality-synchronized tree automata is undecidable [14]. Here we will prove that equivalence is decidable for DST. It was established in [14] that equivalence is decidable for D_eST. This result follows now as a corollary of the decidability result for DST since a prefix-synchronized automaton can simulate arbitrary equality-synchronized computations provided that the input trees are augmented with end-markers on each path before the leaf node [14].

A central tool for proving the decidability of equivalence for D_eST was the so called normalization condition. A synchronized tree automaton $\mathcal{A}$ is said to be normalized if any synchronized partial computation ending at leaves labeled by variables can be completed successfully, assuming that one substitutes suitably chosen Σ-trees for the variables. Intuitively, we can say that a normalized automaton does not produce synchronizing sequences that do not appear in any successful computation. Given a dst $\mathcal{A}$ we can effectively construct a normalized dst $\mathcal{B}$ such that $L_e(\mathcal{B}) = L_e(\mathcal{A})$ [14], that is, equality-synchronized automata can be assumed to be normalized. A normalized automaton $\mathcal{A}$ recognizes as its extended tree language exactly the set of prefix trees of the tree language defined by $\mathcal{A}$. Using this observation we can reduce the equivalence problem for deterministic normalized automata to deciding equivalence of deterministic multitape finite automata. However, an analogous normalization result does not hold for prefix-synchronized tree automata, see [14].

Here we will show that the set of two-pruned prefix-trees of a tree language defined by a prefix-synchronized deterministic automaton can be recognized using a *globally deterministic* synchronized tree automaton. This "quasi-normalization" condition turns out to be sufficient for carrying out the rest of the decidability proof. The crucial observation is that the automaton operating on prefix-trees does not need to be deterministic, the weaker requirement of global determinism suffices.

We view a computation of $\mathcal{A} = (\Sigma, Q, Q_0, g) \in nst$ on a tree having variables as an intermediate stage of a computation that is to be continued from the nodes labeled by variables. The set of synchronized computations of $\mathcal{A} \in$ nst on $t \in F_\Sigma(X)$, $\text{scom}_\mathcal{A}(t)$, is defined to consist of all labeled trees $r : \text{dom}(t) \to Q$ that satisfy the three conditions of Definition 3.1 and the synchronization condition given by (4). Thus, at leaves of t labeled by variables, the computations of $\text{scom}_\mathcal{A}(t)$ can end in an arbitrary state and it is only required that the synchronization condition has not been violated up to that point.

The *extended tree language synchronized recognized* by $\mathcal{A}$ is denoted

$$M_s(\mathcal{A}) = \{t \in F_\Sigma(X) \cap \text{lin}(\Sigma, X) \mid \text{scom}_\mathcal{A}(t) \neq \emptyset\}.$$

We restrict the ΣX-trees that $\mathcal{A}$ receives as inputs to be linear and we do not distinguish between trees that differ only in the names of the variables. The automaton $\mathcal{A}$ treats every leaf labeled by a variable identically. Clearly, $L_s(\mathcal{A}) = M_s(\mathcal{A}) \cap F_\Sigma$ and $\text{pref}(L_s(\mathcal{A})) \subseteq M_s(\mathcal{A})$. Note that this inclusion is, in general, strict since there is no guarantee that the computations from variables of $t \in M_s(\mathcal{A})$ can be continued without violating the synchronization condition.

Let Σ be a ranked alphabet. We denote by $\text{un}(\Sigma)$ the set of all unary Σ-trees, that is, trees containing only symbols of rank at most one. The decision algorithm for the equivalence problem will be based on the following lemma.

Lemma 4.1 *Let $\mathcal{A}_i = (\Sigma, Q_i, q_{i0}, g_i) \in dst$, $i = 1, 2$. Denote $Y_i = pref(L_s(\mathcal{A}_i)) \cap 2pr(\Sigma)$ (see (2)) and $Z_i = L_s(\mathcal{A}_i) \cap un(\Sigma)$, $i = 1, 2$.*

Then $L_s(\mathcal{A}_1) = L_s(\mathcal{A}_2)$ if and only if $Y_1 = Y_2$ and $Z_1 = Z_2$.

Proof. The proof is similar to the proof of Lemma 5.5 of [14]. □

We want to show that for arbitrary dst's $\mathcal{A}_i$, $i = 1, 2$, we can construct globally deterministic automata that are equivalent if and only if $Y_1 = Y_2$, where $Y_i = \text{pref}(L_s(\mathcal{A}_i)) \cap 2\text{pr}(\Sigma)$. We still need some technical lemmas.

We say that $\mathcal{A} = (\Sigma, Q, q_0, g) \in$ dst has the *end-marker property* if there exists $\$ \in \Sigma_1$ such that for every $t \in L_s(\mathcal{A})$ the following holds.

(EM1) Every subtree of t of height one is of the form $\$(\sigma)$, $\sigma \in \Sigma_0$, and the symbol $\$$ does not appear in t except in subtrees of height one.

(EM2) The unique computation of $\text{scom}_{\mathcal{A}}(t)$ enters each of the leaves of t in a synchronizing state.

If $\mathcal{A}$ has the end-marker property, then $\mathcal{A}$ ends the computation in each branch of the input by producing a synchronizing symbol. The following lemma states that, when considering the equivalence problem for DST, without restriction we can assume that the given automata have the end-marker property.

Lemma 4.2 *Let $\mathcal{A}_i = (\Sigma, Q, q_{i0}, g_i) \in$ dst, $i = 1, 2$. We can effectively construct automata $\mathcal{B}_i = (\Omega, P, p_{i0}, h_i) \in$ dst having the end-marker property, $i = 1, 2$, such that $L_s(\mathcal{B}_1) = L_s(\mathcal{B}_2)$ if and only if $L_s(\mathcal{A}_1) = L_s(\mathcal{A}_2)$.*

Proof. Define Ω by setting $\Omega_1 = \Sigma_1 \cup \{\$\}$ and $\Omega_m = \Sigma_m$ when $m \neq 1$. Here $\$ \notin \Sigma$. Let $\alpha : F_\Sigma \to F_\Omega$ be the tree homomorphism that replaces every leaf labeled by $\sigma \in \Sigma_0$ with the subtree $\$(\sigma)$. We construct $\mathcal{B}_i$ such that $L_s(\mathcal{B}_i) = \alpha(L_s(\mathcal{A}_i))$, $i = 1, 2$. The tree language $\alpha(L_s(\mathcal{A}_i))$ clearly satisfies the condition (EM1) so it is sufficient to show that the automaton $\mathcal{B}_i$, $1 \leq i \leq 2$, can be made to satisfy (EM2).

Without restriction we can assume that the initial state q_{i0} of $\mathcal{A}_i$ is a synchronizing state. Thus we can write $q_{i0} = (r_0, s_0)$ where s_0 is a sync-symbol. On an input $t \in F_\Omega$ the automaton $\mathcal{B}_i$ exactly simulates the computation of $\mathcal{A}_i$ except that along each path of t it delays the production of the synchronizing sequence by one step. Thus the initial state of $\mathcal{B}_i$ is not synchronizing and $\mathcal{B}_i$ produces the sync-symbol s_0 when $\mathcal{A}_i$ would produce the next sync-symbol s_1 on a given path. $\mathcal{B}_i$ then stores s_1 in its finite-state memory (the nonsynchronizing component of the states) and produces s_1 when $\mathcal{A}_i$ would produce the following sync-symbol. When $\mathcal{B}_i$ reaches a unary symbol $\$$ it produces the previous sync-symbol of the computation of $\mathcal{A}_i$ that it is simulating. Finally, $\mathcal{B}_i$ simulates the computation step of $\mathcal{A}_i$ on the leaf below. The operation of $\mathcal{B}_i$ is completely deterministic. For every $t \in F_\Sigma$, the unique computation of $\mathcal{B}_i$ on $\alpha(t)$ is synchronized if and only if the computation of $\mathcal{A}_i$ on t is synchronized. □

We want to develop a criterion for deciding whether a given two-pruned tree is a prefix-tree of the tree language recognized by a dsta. In the following let $\mathcal{A} = (\Sigma, Q, q_0, g) \in$ dst. For $q \in Q$ we denote

$$\mathcal{A}(q) = (\Sigma, Q, q, g).$$

$\mathcal{A}(q)$ is the dsta obtained from $\mathcal{A}$ by changing the initial state to be q.

Let $t \in M_s(\mathcal{A}) \cap 2\text{pr}(\Sigma)$ and let $r \in \text{scom}_{\mathcal{A}}(t)$ be the unique synchronized computation of $\mathcal{A}$ on t. Let u_1 and u_2 be the two nodes of t labeled by elements of Σ_0 and denote $w_i = h_{\mathcal{A}}(\text{path}(r, u_i))$, $i = 1, 2$. Thus w_i is the synchronization sequence corresponding to the node u_i. Let $v \in \text{varnd-path}(t, u_i)$, $1 \leq i \leq 2$, that is, v is a node labeled by a variable "corresponding" to the path determined by u_i. Denote $v = v'j$, $j \in \mathbb{N}$. Assume that, in the computation r, $\mathcal{A}$ reaches the node v in state q_v, that is, $r(v) = q_v$. Denote $w_{v'} = h_{\mathcal{A}}(\text{path}(r, v'))$. Then clearly $w_{v'} \preceq w_i$. We define the *residue* of v with respect to u_i in the computation r by setting

$$\text{res}(v, u_i) = w_{v'}^{-1} w_i.$$

Let $w_M = \max_{\simeq}\{w_1, w_2\}$. The word w_M is just the longer one of the two synchronization sequences corresponding to the nodes u_1 and u_2. Clearly, the synchronization sequence corresponding to v' is a prefix of w_M, $w_{v'} \preceq w_M$. We define the *residue* of v (with respect to both u_1 and u_2) as

$$\text{res}(v) = w_{v'}^{-1} w_M.$$

The computation continuing from the variable at node v can be completed successfully (with a suitable choice of the subtree to be substituted there) if and only if $\text{res}(v)$ is in the prefix-relation with some word $w_v \in \text{sync}(\mathcal{A}(q_v))$. The tree t is a prefix-tree of $L_s(\mathcal{A})$ if and only if the words w_v can be chosen so that, additionally, they are all pairwise in the prefix-relation. We note that if we choose $w_v \in \text{sync}(\mathcal{A}(q_v))$ to be a prefix of the word $\text{res}(v)$ then w_v does not affect the possible choices for the computations beginning from the remaining variables of t. We say that a node $v \in \text{leaf}_X(t)$ is *relevant* with respect to the computation r if $\text{sync}(\mathcal{A}(q_v))$ does not contain any prefix of $\text{res}(v)$. Recall that q_v is the state where $\mathcal{A}$ reaches the node v. Combining the above observations, we have proved the following lemma.

Lemma 4.3 *Let $\mathcal{A} = (\Sigma, Q, q_0, g) \in dst$ and $t \in M_s(\mathcal{A}) \cap 2pr(\Sigma)$. Let r be the unique computation in $scom_{\mathcal{A}}(t)$. Denote by REL the set of all relevant variable nodes of t in the computation r. Then $t \in pref(L_s(\mathcal{A}))$ if and only if there exist words*

$$w_v \in res(v)^{-1} sync(\mathcal{A}(r(v))), \quad v \in REL, \tag{5}$$

such that the words w_v are pairwise in the prefix-relation.

Note that if for some relevant variable node v, $\text{res}(v)^{-1}\text{sync}(\mathcal{A}(r(v))) = \emptyset$, then $t \notin \text{pref}(L_s(\mathcal{A}))$, i.e., the computation cannot be continued successfully from t. By Theorem 3.1 the languages $\text{sync}(\mathcal{A}(q))$, $q \in Q$, are regular. Denote

$$\Xi(\mathcal{A}) = \{w^{-1}\text{sync}(\mathcal{A}(q)) \mid w \in S^*,\ q \in Q\}.$$

Here S is the synchronization alphabet of the automaton $\mathcal{A}$. Then all the languages belonging to $\Xi(\mathcal{A})$ are regular and $\Xi(\mathcal{A})$ contains only finitely many different languages.

Let Σ be a ranked alphabet. The *look-ahead alphabet* corresponding to Σ is the ranked alphabet Σ^{LA} defined by setting

$$(\Sigma^{LA})_m = \{\sigma[z_1,\ldots,z_m] \mid \sigma \in \Sigma_m,\ z_1,\ldots,z_m \in \Sigma \cup \{*\}\},$$

$m \geq 0$. We define the mapping $\beta : \Sigma^{LA} \to \Sigma$ by setting $\beta(\sigma[z_1,\ldots,z_m]) = \sigma$, $\sigma \in \Sigma_m$, $m \geq 0$. The relabeling $F_{\Sigma^{LA}}(X) \to F_\Sigma(X)$ induced by β is denoted also simply by β.

A tree $t \in F_{\Sigma^{LA}}(X)$ is said to be *well-formed* if it satisfies the following condition. Let $u \in \mathrm{dom}(t)$ be a node of rank $m \geq 1$. Then $t(u) = \sigma[z_1,\ldots,z_m]$, where for $j = 1,\ldots,m$,

$$z_j = \begin{cases} \beta(t(uj)) & \text{if } t(uj) \in \Sigma^{LA}, \\ * & \text{if } t(uj) \in X. \end{cases}$$

The set of well-formed $\Sigma^{LA}X$-trees is denoted by $F^{\mathrm{wf}}_{\Sigma^{LA}}(X)$. Intuitively, in a well-formed $\Sigma^{LA}X$-tree the label of each node contains the "look-ahead one" information about the labels of the children. Clearly for every $t \in F_\Sigma(X)$ there exists a unique tree $r \in F^{\mathrm{wf}}_{\Sigma^{LA}}(X)$ such that $\beta(r) = t$. We denote by β_{wf} the restriction of β to the set of well-formed trees. Then β_{wf} is a bijection $F^{\mathrm{wf}}_{\Sigma^{LA}}(X) \to F_\Sigma(X)$.

The set of well-formed two-pruned trees $F^{\mathrm{wf}}_{\Sigma^{LA}}(X) \cap 2\mathrm{pr}(\Sigma^{LA})$ can obviously be recognized by a deterministic top-down tree automaton $\mathcal{A}$. Also, the tree language families DT and GDST are closed with respect to intersection with a tree language belonging to DT. Thus in the below Lemmas 4.4 and 4.5, without further mention, we assume that the input belongs to $F^{\mathrm{wf}}_{\Sigma^{LA}}(X) \cap 2\mathrm{pr}(\Sigma^{LA})$ and the automata need not verify this property.

Lemma 4.4 *Let $\mathcal{A} = (\Sigma, Q, q_0, g)$ be a dsta. Then there exists a deterministic top-down tree automaton $\mathcal{B} = (\Sigma^{LA}, P, p_0, h)$ such that for every $t \in F^{\mathrm{wf}}_{\Sigma^{LA}}(X) \cap 2pr(\Sigma^{LA})$ the automaton $\mathcal{B}$ reaches the two nonvariable leaves u of t in a state that contains (as its second component) a set $\Lambda(u) \subseteq \Xi(\mathcal{A})$ defined as follows. Denote $\beta_{\mathrm{wf}}(t) = t'$, $t' \in F_\Sigma(X)$. Since β_{wf} is a relabeling we can identify the nodes of t and t'. Let r be the unique computation of $\mathcal{A}$ on t'.*

Then $\Lambda(u)$ contains all elements

$$res(v,u)^{-1} sync(\mathcal{A}(r(v))),$$

where $v \in varnd\text{-}path(t,u)$ and

$$sync(\mathcal{A}(r(v))) \text{ does not contain any prefix of } res(v,u). \qquad (6)$$

Proof. The states of $\mathcal{B}$ contain two components. When reading an input symbol $\sigma \in \Sigma^{LA}$, the first component simulates directly the computation step of $\mathcal{A}$ on $\beta(\sigma)$. The second component is a subset of $\Xi(\mathcal{A})$. When the simulated computation of $\mathcal{A}$ enters a variable node v in a state q, the automaton $\mathcal{B}$ ads the element $\mathrm{sync}(\mathcal{A}(q))$ to the second component of the state in the brother node of v that belongs to the path leading to a nonvariable leaf. Note that since t is well-formed, the look-ahead capability enables $\mathcal{B}$ to know which child nodes are labeled by variables. On the paths labeled by symbols of Σ^{LA}, always when the simulated computation of $\mathcal{A}$ produces a sync-symbol s, $\mathcal{B}$ updates the elements of the second component by replacing a language L with $s^{-1}L$. If some language L contains the empty word, it means that the negation of the condition (6) holds for the variable nodes whose synchronization language is represented by L. Such languages will be discarded from the subset of $\Xi(\mathcal{A})$ appearing in the second component. It is clear that at the leaves u corresponding to the nonvariable paths of t the second component of $\mathcal{B}$ will contain exactly the set $\Lambda(u)$. □

In the above proof, note that $\Xi(\mathcal{A})$ consists of a finite number of regular languages, and thus each subset of $\Xi(\mathcal{A})$ can be presented using, for instance, a constant number of finite automata. These can be stored in the finite-state memory of $\mathcal{B}$. Also, for each $L \in \Xi(\mathcal{A})$ the operations $s^{-1}L$, where s is a sync-symbol, can be finitely specified.

Lemma 4.5 *Let $\mathcal{A} = (\Sigma, Q, q_0, g) \in dst$. Then there exists a gdsta $\mathcal{C} = (\Sigma^{LA}, P, p_0, h)$ such that*

$$M_s(\mathcal{C}) = \beta_{\mathrm{wf}}^{-1}(\mathit{pref}(L_s(\mathcal{A}))) \cap \mathit{2pr}(\Sigma^{LA}).$$

Proof. The states of $\mathcal{C}$ have two components. On an input tree t the first component simulates the computation of $\mathcal{A}$ on $\beta_{\mathrm{wf}}(t)$ and verifies that $\beta_{\mathrm{wf}}(t) \in M_s(\mathcal{A})$. Let $\mathcal{B}$ be the dta constructed corresponding to $\mathcal{A}$ as in Lemma 4.4. The second component of $\mathcal{C}$ simulates the computation of $\mathcal{B}$. Since $\mathcal{B}$ is just a finite tree automaton, the two components of $\mathcal{C}$ can operate independently in parallel.

The second component reaches the two nonvariable nodes u_1 and u_2 of t in states containing the subsets of $\Xi(\mathcal{A})$, $\Lambda(u_1)$ and $\Lambda(u_2)$, as defined in Lemma 4.4. Assume that in the computation r of $\mathcal{A}$ on $\beta_{\mathrm{wf}}(t)$ the synchronization sequence corresponding to u_1 is a prefix of the synchronization sequence corresponding to u_2. If we assume that the automaton can transfer the state $\Lambda(u_1)$ to the corresponding position in the computation on the path to u_2, then it can reach the leaf u_2 with a subset of $\Xi(\mathcal{A})$ consisting of all the languages $\mathrm{res}(v)^{-1}\mathrm{sync}(\mathcal{A}(r(v)))$, where v is a relevant node of t in the computation r. This means that the automaton can decide whether the condition (5) of Lemma 4.3 holds and, thus, it can decide whether $t \in \beta_{\mathrm{wf}}^{-1}(\mathrm{pref}(L_s(\mathcal{A})))$. Since the languages of $\Xi(\mathcal{A})$ are regular, given an arbitrary subset $\{\mu_1, \ldots, \mu_k\} \subseteq \Xi(\mathcal{A})$, we can decide effectively whether there exist words $w_i \in \mu_i$, $i = 1, \ldots, k$, that are all pairwise in the prefix relation. The answer for each of the finitely many subsets of $\Xi(\mathcal{A})$ can then be stored in the states of $\mathcal{C}$.

Thus it is sufficient to show that when simulating the synchronized computation of $\mathcal{A}$, the gdsta $\mathcal{C}$ can transfer a finite amount of information from the node u_1 to u_2, where u_1 is the leaf corresponding to the shorter synchronization sequence. By Lemma 4.2, we can assume that $\mathcal{A}$ has the end-marker property. Thus the computation of $\mathcal{A}$ produces a sync-symbol when entering the node u_1.

The automaton $\mathcal{C}$ can take care of the transfer of information by allowing nondeterministic guesses always when $\mathcal{A}$ produces a sync-symbol s. In the left path of t the guesses are defined as follows. If the input symbol is not the end-marker, the possibilities are: (i) s (representing the guess that also the right path is not yet at the end-marker), (ii) (s, χ, right) for all $\chi \subseteq \Xi(\mathcal{A})$ (representing the guess that the right path is at the end-marker with $\Lambda(u) = \chi$). If the input is the end-marker, the sync-symbol produced will be (s, χ, left) where χ is the corresponding state of the automaton $\mathcal{B}$. In the right path, if the input is not the end-marker the possibilities are (i) s and (ii) (s, χ, left) for all $\chi \subseteq \Xi(\mathcal{A})$. At the end-marker of the right path one has also two possibilities: (i) (s, χ, right) where χ is the corresponding state of $\mathcal{B}$, and (ii) (s, χ, left) for all $\chi \subseteq \Xi(\mathcal{A})$. The last choice corresponds to the guess that the left path is simultaneously at the end-marker. It is easy to verify that in all cases there is exactly one global choice for the two paths that does not violate the synchronization condition. Thus $\mathcal{C}$ is globally deterministic. □

Now we can prove our main result.

Theorem 4.1 *Given $\mathcal{A}_1$, $\mathcal{A}_2 \in dst$ we can effectively decide whether $L_s(\mathcal{A}_1) = L_s(\mathcal{A}_2)$.*

Proof. Without loss of generality we can assume that the automata $\mathcal{A}_1$ and $\mathcal{A}_2$ have the same input alphabet Σ. By Lemma 4.1, to prove the claim it is suffient to show that the condition

$$\text{pref}(L_s(\mathcal{A}_1)) \cap 2\text{pr}(\Sigma) = \text{pref}(L_s(\mathcal{A}_2)) \cap 2\text{pr}(\Sigma) \tag{7}$$

can be decided effectively. The other condition appearing in Lemma 4.1 concerning unary trees is clearly decidable. By Lemma 4.5, there exist globally deterministic automata $\mathcal{C}_i$, $i = 1, 2$, such that

$$M_s(\mathcal{C}_i) = \beta_{\text{wf}}^{-1}(\text{pref}(L_s(\mathcal{A}_i))) \cap 2\text{pr}(\Sigma^{LA}).$$

By coding two-pruned trees into two strings we can simulate the computations of $\mathcal{C}_i$ using a deterministic two-tape finite automaton $\mathcal{D}_i$. This is done similarly as in the proof of Lemma 5.6 of [14]. The only difference is that instead of deterministic synchronized automata we are considering globally deterministic automata. However, this does not change anything because the finite control of $\mathcal{D}_i$ has reading heads on both tapes (representing the paths of a two-pruned tree), and thus corresponding to an arbitrary synchronization cut, from the nondeterministic choices of $\mathcal{C}_i$ on the two paths, $\mathcal{D}_i$ can deterministically make the unique possible global choice. Thus $\mathcal{D}_1$ and $\mathcal{D}_2$ accept the same inputs if and only if $M_s(\mathcal{C}_1) = M_s(\mathcal{C}_2)$.

Since equivalence of deterministic multitape automata is decidable [8], it follows that we can effectively decide whether $M_s(\mathcal{C}_1) = M_s(\mathcal{C}_2)$. Since the mapping β_{wf} is bijective, it follows that also the condition (7) is decidable. □

Using the easy Lemma 3.3 of [14], we see that the above theorem implies also the decidability of equivalence for D_eST. This result was established differently in [14].

Corollary 4.1 *Equivalence is decidable for deterministic equality-synchronized tree automata.*

We have established that for deterministic prefix- and equality-synchronized automata equivalence is decidable and it is undecidable in the nondeterministic cases. The family of tree languages defined by globally deterministic synchronized automata lies strictly between the corresponding nondeterministic and deterministic families. It is an open question whether equivalence of globally deterministic tree automata can be decided effectively.

References

1. B. Bogaert and S. Tison, Equality and disequality constraints on direct subterms in tree automata, in: *Proc. of the 9th Symposium on Theoretical Aspects of Computer Science*, Lect. Notes Comput. Sci. **577**, Springer-Verlag, 1992, pp. 161–171.
2. A.-C. Caron, J.-L. Coquidé and M. Dauchet, Encompassment properties and automata with constraints, in: *Proc. of 5th RTA,* Lect. Notes Comput. Sci. **690**, Springer-Verlag, 1993, pp. 328–342.
3. A.-C. Caron, H. Comon, J.-L. Coquidé, M. Dauchet and F. Jacquemard, Pumping, cleaning and symbolic constraints solving, in: *Proc. of 21st ICALP,* Lect. Notes Comput. Sci. **820**, Springer-Verlag, 1994, pp. 436–449.
4. Z. Fülöp and S. Vágvölgyi, Variants of top-down tree transducers with look-ahead, *Math. Systems Theory* **21** (1989) 125–145.
5. Z. Fülöp and S. Vágvölgyi, Iterated deterministic top-down look-ahead, in: *Proc. of 7th FCT,* Lect. Notes Comput. Sci. **380**, Springer-Verlag, 1989, pp. 175–184.
6. Z. Fülöp and S. Vágvölgyi, A characterization of irreducible sets modulo left-linear term rewriting systems by tree automata, *Fundam. Inf.* **13** (1990) 211-226.
7. F. Gécseg and M. Steinby, *Tree automata,* Akadémiai Kiadó, Budapest, 1984.
8. T. Harju and J. Karhumäki, The equivalence problem of multitape finite automata, *Theoret. Comput. Sci.* **78** (1991) 347–355.
9. J. Hromkovič, How to organize the communication among parallel processes in alternating computations, unpublished manuscript, Comenius University, Bratislava, 1986.
10. J. Hromkovič, J. Karhumäki, B. Rovan and A. Slobodová, On the power of synchronization in parallel computations, *Discrete Appl. Math.* **32** (1991) 155–182.
11. J. Hromkovič, B. Rovan, A. Slobodová, Deterministic versus nondeterministic space in terms of synchronized alternating machines, *Theoret. Comput. Sci.* **132** (1994) 319–336.
12. O. Ibarra and N. Trân, Synchronized finite automata and 2DFA reductions, *Theoret. Comput. Sci.* **115** (1993) 261–275.
13. K. Salomaa, Yield-languages recognized by alternating tree recognizers, *RAIRO Inform. Théor.* **22** (1988) 319–339.
14. K. Salomaa, Synchronized tree automata, *Theoret. Comput. Sci.* **127** (1994) 25–51.
15. G. Slutzki, Alternating tree automata, *Theoret. Comput. Sci.* **41** (1985) 305–318.
16. G. Slutzki and S. Vágvölgyi, A hierarchy of deterministic top-down tree transformations, in: *Proc. of 9th FCT,* Lect. Notes Comput. Sci. **710**, Springer-Verlag, 1993, pp. 440–451.
17. S. Vágvölgyi, Top-down tree transducers with two-way tree walking look-ahead, *Theoret. Comput. Sci.* **93** (1992) 43–74.

The Equivalence Problem for Letter-to-Letter Bottom-up Tree Transducers is Solvable*

Yves ANDRE and Francis BOSSUT

L.I.F.L., U.R.A. 369 C.N.R.S.
University of Lille 1, 59655 Villeneuve d'Ascq Cedex. France.
e-mail:{andre, bossut} @ lifl.lifl.fr

Abstract. Letter-to-letter bottom-up tree transducers are investigated in this paper. With an encoding of the so defined tree transformations into relabelings, we establish the decidability of equivalence for this class of tree transducers. Some extensions are next given.

1 Introduction

From a general point of view, tree transducers investigate computations on structured objects. Consider a concrete algorithm A taking terms from T_Σ as input and producing terms of T_Δ, where Σ and Δ are finite sets of operators. Abstracting from the meaning of the operators, A turns into a symbolic algorithm which is a tree transducer transforming elements of T_Σ into elements of T_Δ.
Finite state tree transducers, which are a generalization of Generalized Sequential Machines in the word case, were introduced by Rounds and Thatcher [13, 15] in order to give an algebraic formalism for the theory of syntax-directed translation. Let us give some examples. In compiler construction finite state transducers can be used to express simple transformations of abstract syntactical trees. Attribute grammars with only synthesized attributes correspond closely to deterministic top-down finite state transducers.
For the description of a larger class of operations on tree more subtle devices are needed as macro tree transducers [8]; general operations on trees (primitive recursive functions) can be defined in term of modular tree transducers [9].
For the formal language point of view the question arises whether or not results obtained for such transformations in the word case can be transferred in the tree case, especially decidability of equivalence (i) and closure properties with respect to composition (ii). The situation is more complex because we have to distinguish two main classes of finite state tree transducers: top-down transducers which process the input trees from the root to the leaves and bottom-up transducers for which, on the contrary, the computations begin at the leaves and finish at the root (a comparison between these two classes can be found in [6]). As noteworthy characteristics in the bottom-up case, let us point out the fact that since some variables can be missing, the image of a correctly parsed subtree can be deleted.

* Supported in part by the PRC-GDR "Mathématiques et Informatique" and the Basic Research Working Group ESPRIT 6317 ASMICS II

(i) Two transducers are called equivalent if they define the same translation. It is well-known that equivalence is, in general, undecidable for non-deterministic tree transducers and that it is decidable for deterministic transducers, in the bottom-up case (Z. Zachar [16]) as in the top-down one (Z. Esik [10]). More recently, H. Seidl established the decidability of equivalence for finite-valued bottom-up transducers [14].
(ii) The class of top-down tree transformation is not closed under composition. In 1977, J. Engelfriet defined the notion of top-down tree transducer with regular look-ahead in order to get nice properties with respect to composition [7]. These top-down transducers are able to inspect a subtree before deleting it. Moreover, he showed that the class of top-down tree transducers with regular look-ahead is a subset of the class of transformation realized by composition of bottom-up and top-down transducers. Many classes of top-down tree transducers with look-ahead have been studied. Let us quote the works of Z. Fülöp and S. Vágvölgyi ([11] for instance).
This paper is part of a study of letter-to-letter tree transducers. Informally, trees which appear in the rules of these transducers are reduced to one letter in the right-hand side as in the left-hand one. By means of an example, we first illustrate this kind of transducers.

Example 1 Let us consider some rules[1] of a bottom-up letter-to-letter transducer, which realizes simplifications of formulae of propositional logic

$$
\begin{array}{rll}
1 \rightarrow q_1(1) & \neg(q_\perp(x)) \rightarrow q_\perp(\neg(x)) & \wedge(q_0(x), q_\perp(y)) \rightarrow q_0(0) \\
0 \rightarrow q_0(0) & \wedge(q_\perp(x), q_\perp(y)) \rightarrow q_\perp(\wedge(x,y)) & \wedge(q_\perp(x), q_0(y)) \rightarrow q_0(0) \\
v \rightarrow q_\perp(v)^2 & \wedge(q_1(x), q_\perp(y)) \rightarrow q_\perp(y) & \wedge(q_0(x), q_1(y)) \rightarrow q_0(0) \\
\neg(q_1(x)) \rightarrow q_0(0) & \wedge(q_\perp(x), q_1(y)) \rightarrow q_\perp(x) & \wedge(q_1(x), q_0(y)) \rightarrow q_0(0) \\
\neg(q_0(x)) \rightarrow q_1(1) & \wedge(q_1(x), q_1(y)) \rightarrow q_1(1) & \wedge(q_0(x), q_0(y)) \rightarrow q_0(0)
\end{array}
$$

This transducer is letter-to-letter, deterministic and linear but it is deleting. The sequence

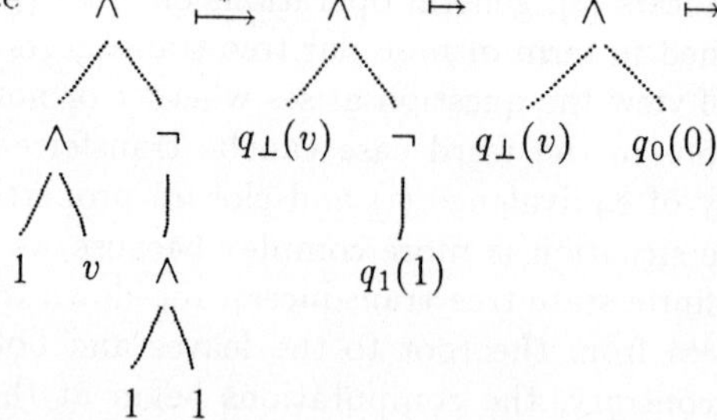

is an example of computations.

[1] The reader can easily find the rules involving the operator "or" ($\vee$).
[2] for any atomic proposition symbol v

In previous works [1, 2, 3], we established the decidability of equivalence for linear transducers and for non-deleting transducers in the top-down case. Here, we prove the decidability of equivalence for letter-to-letter bottom-up transducers. As a corollary of this result and previous ones, we can deduce the decidability of equivalence for some subclasses of letter-to-letter transducers with regular look-ahead.
Some authors (Coquidé et al. [5], for instance) showed that, in some particular cases, one can construct a bottom-up tree pushdown automata computing normal forms of ground terms with respect to a rewrite system. As one may view a bottom-up tree pushdown automaton as a transducer that outputs its pushdown, a subject of further investigation should be to study letter-to-letter rewrite systems; especially, the properties of the associated letter-to-letter transducer.

2 Basic Definitions and Properties

In this section, we just recall definitions and properties used in the sequel. We refer the reader to [6, 7] for tree transducers and to [12] for tree automata.

A *ranked alphabet* is a pair (Σ, ρ) where Σ is a finite alphabet and ρ is a mapping from Σ to $\mathbb{N}$. Usually, we will write Σ for short. For any σ of Σ, $\rho(\sigma)$ is called the *rank* of σ. For any integer n, Σ_n denotes the subset of Σ of letters of rank n. For any $k \geq 1$, X_k denotes the set of variables $\{x_1, .., x_k\}$.
Given a ranked alphabet Σ and a denumerable set X of variables, $T_\Sigma(X)$ denotes the set of all *terms* (*trees*) over Σ and indexed by X. In the particular case of an empty set of variables, we will write T_Σ instead of $T_\Sigma(\emptyset)$. A tree $t_o(x_1, .., x_n)$ is a *prefix* of a term t if there exist $t_1, .., t_n$ such that $t = t_o(t_1, .., t_n)$. For any tree t of $T_\Sigma(X)$, the *height* of t, denoted by $\pi(t)$, is defined by $\pi(t) = 0$ if $t \in \Sigma_0$ or $t \in X$ and $\pi(t) = 1 + max\{\pi(t_1), .., \pi(t_n)\}$ if $t = \sigma(t_1, .., t_n)$.
For any $p \in \mathbb{N}$, $[p]$ denotes the set $\{1, .., p\}$. A *torsion* θ from $[p]$ to $[q]$ is a mapping from $[p]$ to $[q]$. We denote it by $< q; \theta(1), .., \theta(p) >$. By $id_{[n]}$ we denote the identity mapping on $[n]$.

A finite state *bottom-up tree transducer* is a 5-tuple $B =< \Sigma, \Delta, Q, F, R >$ where Σ and Δ are ranked alphabets of respectively input and output symbols, Q is a finite set of unary symbols called *states*, F is the subset of Q of *final* states and R is a finite set of rules of the form $\sigma(q_1(x_1), .., q_n(x_n)) \mapsto q(t)$ with $q, q_1, .., q_n \in Q$, $\sigma \in \Sigma_n$ and $t \in T_\Delta(X_n)$ or of the form $\sigma \mapsto q(t)$ with $\sigma \in \Sigma_0$ and $t \in T_\Delta$. In this paper, these rules will be denoted by $\sigma(q_1(x_1), .., q_n(x_n)) \rightarrow q(\delta(x_{\theta(1)}, .., x_{\theta(p)}))$ with $\delta \in T_\Delta(X_n)$ and θ torsion from $[p]$ to $[n]$ (if $n = 0$ we write $\sigma \rightarrow q(\delta)$). So torsions θ will express permutations, duplications or deletions of subtrees. A transducer is *letter-to-letter* if, for every rule, δ belongs to Δ.

The rules define patterns for rewriting trees, so we write $t \mapsto u$ if t is rewritten in u in one step. By $\overset{*}{\longmapsto}$ we denote the reflexive and transitive closure of $\mapsto$. A sequence of rewriting steps $t \overset{*}{\longmapsto} q(u)$ is called a *computation*.

Let B be a bottom-up transducer and $\mathcal{D}$ be a computation on a term $t = \sigma(t_1, .., t_m)$, $\mathcal{D}$: $\sigma(t_1, .., t_m) \overset{*}{\longmapsto} \sigma(q_1(u_1), .., q_m(u_m)) \mapsto q(\delta(u_{\theta(1)}, .., u_{\theta(n)}))$. The triple (σ, δ, θ) is called the *final transformation*.

Let B be a bottom-up transducer, q and E be respectively a state and a set of states of B and let (σ, δ, θ) be a final transformation. $\widehat{B}_q$ denotes the set $\{(t, u) \in T_\Sigma \times T_\Delta \mid t \overset{*}{\longmapsto} q(u)\}$, $\widehat{B}_E = \cup_{q \in E} \widehat{B}_q$ and we denote by $\widehat{B}_{q_{(\sigma,\delta,\theta)}}$ the set $\{(t, u) \mid t = \sigma(t_1, .., t_m)$ and $t \overset{*}{\longmapsto}_B \sigma(q_1(u_1), .., q_m(u_m) \mapsto q(\delta(u_{\theta(1)}, .., u_{\theta(n)})) = q(u)\}$. Obviously $\widehat{B}_{E_{(\sigma,\delta,\theta)}} = \cup_{q \in E} \widehat{B}_{q_{(\sigma,\delta,\theta)}}$. Finally we denote by $\widehat{B}$ the tree transformation associated with B: $\widehat{B} = \widehat{B}_F$ (where F is the set of final states).

Two sets of states E and F of a transducer B are *globally equivalent* if and only if $\widehat{B}_E = \widehat{B}_F$. Two transducers B and B' are *equivalent* if and only if $\widehat{B} = \widehat{B}'$. The *domain* of a tree transformation $\widehat{B}$, denoted by $dom(\widehat{B})$, is the regular language $\{t \in T_\Sigma \,/\, \exists u \in T_\Delta,\ (t, u) \in \widehat{B}\}$. The *range* of a tree transformation $\widehat{B}$, denoted by $range(\widehat{B})$, is the set $\{u \in T_\Delta \,/\, \exists t \in T_\Sigma,\ (t, u) \in \widehat{B}\}$. A tree transformation $\widehat{B}$ is *of finite range* if its range is finite. We extend the last definition to any subset of a tree transformation: a subset S of a tree transformation $\widehat{B}$ is *of finite range* if the set $\{u \mid \exists t$ such that $(t, u) \in S\}$ is finite.
A state q of a transducer B is *infinitary* if and only if $\widehat{B}_q$ is of infinite range. A transducer all states of which are infinitary is said to be *infinitary*. A bottom-up tree transducer is *deterministic* if and only if the set of final states is a singleton and there are no two rules with the same left-hand side.
A transducer is *linear* (respectively *non-deleting, torsion-free*) if and only if for each rule the torsion θ is injective (respectively surjective, the identity mapping). A torsion-free letter-to-letter transducer is also called a *relabeling*.

Property 1. *For any letter-to-letter tree transducer B, for any couple of trees (t, u) of $\widehat{B}$, we have $\pi(t) = \pi(u)$ if B is non-deleting and $\pi(t) \geq \pi(u)$ in the other cases.*

We denote by **B-LL** the class of all bottom-up letter-to-letter tree transducers. By **LB-LL** (respectively **NdB-LL, B-LAB**), we will denote the subclass of **B-LL** of Linear transducers (resp. Non-deleting transducers, relabelings).

Symmetrically, we define a *top-down tree transducer* as a 5-tuple $T =< \Sigma, \Delta, Q, I, R >$ where I is the subset of Q of *initial* states and R is a finite set of rules of the form $q(\sigma(x_1, .., x_n)) \to \delta(q_1(x_{\theta(1)}), .., q_p(x_{\theta(p)}))$ or of the form $q(\sigma) \to \delta$. **T-LL** is the class of all top-down letter-to-letter tree transducers.

A *top-down tree transducer with regular look-ahead* is a 5-tuple $T =< \Sigma, \Delta, Q, I, R >$ where Σ, Δ , Q and I are defined as for classical top-down transducers and R is a finite set of rules of the form $t \to t', D$ where $t \to t'$ is a classical rule and D is a mapping from the set of variables occurring in t to recognizable subsets of T_Σ (more details can be found in [7]).

The class of all top-down transducers with regular look-ahead is denoted by $\mathbf{T^R}$**-FST** (for Finite State Transformation). Here, we will use $\mathbf{T^R}$**-LL** for the subclass of $\mathbf{T^R}$**-FST** of letter-to-letter transducers.

Remark For easier exposition, we will restrict ourselves to letters of rank at most 2. It is the typical case from which constructions and results to be discussed below are easily transferred to the general situation (with adaptations in the statement of some lemmas).

3 Equivalence of bottom-up transducers

In this section, we show that the equivalence problem for letter-to-letter bottom-up tree transducers can be reduced to the equivalence of relabelings.
The main problem, which is illustrated by the following example, is that even if two transducers are equivalent, for some trees, different torsions must be necessarily applied in the computations.

Example 2 Let B_1 and B_2 be the transducers defined by the following rules:

$$\begin{array}{lll}
B_1 : \bar{a} \to q_1(e) & \bar{a} \to q'_1(\bar{\alpha}) & a(q''_1(x)) \to q_1(e) \\
\quad\;\; \bar{a} \to q_2(e) & \bar{a} \to q'_2(\bar{\beta}) & a(q'_2(x)) \to q_2(e) \\
\quad\;\; a(q'_1(x)) \to q''_1(\alpha(x)) & a(q''_1(x)) \to q'_1(\alpha(x)) & a(q'_2(x)) \to q'_2(\beta(x)) \\
\quad\;\; \sigma(q_1(x_1), q_2(x_2)) \to q(\delta(x_1, x_2)) & &
\end{array}$$

The transducer B_2 is defined in the same way. The only difference is that we have $\sigma(q_1(x_1), q_2(x_2)) \to k(\delta(x_2, x_1))$ instead of the rule $\sigma(q_1(x_1), q_2(x_2)) \to q(\delta(x_1, x_2))$. We have $\widehat{B}_{1_q} = \widehat{B}_{2_k} = \{(\sigma(a^{2n}(\bar{a}), a^m(\bar{a})), \delta(e, e)) \mid n, m \in I\!N\}$. But, different final transformations are applied in the computations reaching state q and those reaching state k. We first show that this phenomenon only occurs for output trees of "bounded depth".

3.1 Final transformations

For technical reasons, only infinitary transducers are investigated in the first lemma. Next, a generalization is given.

Lemma 1. *Let q and k be two equivalent states of an infinitary transducer B. For any final transformation (σ, δ, θ), the difference $\widehat{B}_{q_{(\sigma,\delta,\theta)}} - \widehat{B}_{k_{(\sigma,\delta,\theta)}}$ is of finite range.*

PROOF: Let σ be a letter of rank 2. According to the rank of δ we will distinguish two cases: δ of rank 2 and δ of rank 1. θ is a mapping from $\rho(\delta)$ to [2].

First case: δ is a letter of rank 2.
First, assume that θ is the identity mapping on [2] and so the rules are of the

form $\sigma(q_i(x_1), q_i'(x_2)) \rightarrow q(\delta(x_1, x_2))$ (the case $\theta =< 2; 2, 1 >$ is quite similar).
Let n be the number of rules of the form $\sigma(q_i(x_1), q_i'(x_2)) \rightarrow q(\delta(x_1, x_2))$, and m be the number of rules of the form $\sigma(k_i(x_1), k_i'(x_2)) \rightarrow k(\delta(x_1, x_2))$.
The difference $\widehat{B}_{q_{(\sigma,\delta,\theta)}} - \widehat{B}_{k_{(\sigma,\delta,\theta)}}$ is considered.
We denote by $\mathcal{Q}$ the set $\bigcup_{i \in [n]} \widehat{B}_{q_i} \times \widehat{B}_{q_i'}$ and similarly $\mathcal{K} = \bigcup_{j \in [m]} \widehat{B}_{k_j} \times \widehat{B}_{k_j'}$.
So we have $(\sigma(u, u'), \delta(v, v')) \in \widehat{B}_{q_{(\sigma,\delta,\theta)}} - \widehat{B}_{k_{(\sigma,\delta,\theta)}} \Leftrightarrow ((u, v), (u', v')) \in \mathcal{Q} - \mathcal{K}$.
Elementary properties of the theory of sets allow us to express $\mathcal{Q} - \mathcal{K}$ in terms of $\widehat{B}_{q_i}$, $\widehat{B}_{q_i'}$, $\widehat{B}_{k_j}$, $\widehat{B}_{k_j'}$, $\overline{B}_{k_j}$ and $\overline{B}_{k_j'}$ ($\overline{B}_{k_j}$ is the complementation of $\widehat{B}_{k_j}$ in $T_\Sigma \times T_\Delta$).

$$\mathcal{Q} - \mathcal{K} = (\bigcup_{i \in [n]} \widehat{B}_{q_i} \times \widehat{B}_{q_i'}) - (\bigcup_{j \in [m]} \widehat{B}_{k_j} \times \widehat{B}_{k_j'})$$

$$= \bigcup_{i \in [n]} (\bigcup_{J \subseteq [m]} (\widehat{B}_{q_i} \cap (\bigcap_{j \in J} (\overline{B}_{k_j}))) \times (\widehat{B}_{q_i'} \cap (\bigcap_{l \in [m]-J} (\overline{B}_{k_l'})))).$$

Assume that the difference $\widehat{B}_{q_{(\sigma,\delta,\theta)}} - \widehat{B}_{k_{(\sigma,\delta,\theta)}}$ is not of finite range. In this case, there would exist at least $i \in [n]$ and $J \subseteq [m]$ such that $\widehat{B}_{q_i} \cap (\bigcap_{j \in J} (\overline{B}_{k_j}))$ or $\widehat{B}_{q_i'} \cap (\bigcap_{l \in [m]-J} (\overline{B}_{k_l'}))$ is not of finite range. Suppose now that $\widehat{B}_{q_i} \cap (\bigcap_{j \in J} (\overline{B}_{k_j}))$ is not of finite range.
Thus for every couple (u', v') in $\widehat{B}_{q_i'} \cap (\bigcap_{l \in [m]-J} (\overline{B}_{k_l'}))$, we could find a couple (u, v) of $\widehat{B}_{q_i} \cap (\bigcap_{j \in J} (\overline{B}_{k_j}))$ such that $\pi(v) > \pi(u')$ (B is an infinitary transducer) that is to say a couple $(\sigma(u, u'), \delta(v, v')) \in \widehat{B}_{q_{(\sigma,\delta,\theta)}} - \widehat{B}_{k_{(\sigma,\delta,\theta)}}$ with $\pi(v) > \pi(u')$.
Because q and k are equivalent states, there would exist another torsion μ ($\mu \neq \theta$) such that $(\sigma(u, u'), \delta(v, v')) \in \widehat{B}_{k_{(\sigma,\delta,\mu)}}$. The torsion μ should be of one of the following forms: $\mu =< 2; 2, 1 >$, $\mu =< 2; 1, 1 >$ or $\mu =< 2; 2, 2 >$. Each case leads to a contradiction.
If $\mu =< 2; 2, 1 >$, for instance, we should have $\sigma(u, u') \overset{*}{\longmapsto} \sigma(k_j(v'), k_j'(v)) \mapsto k(\delta(v, v'))$. Such computations are impossible because we should have $\pi(v) \leq \pi(u')$ (property 1) when we chose $\pi(v) > \pi(u')$.

The same result is obtained for $\theta =< 2; 1, 1 >$ or $\theta =< 2; 2, 2 >$ and so we conclude that the difference $\widehat{B}_{q_{(\sigma,\delta,\theta)}} - \widehat{B}_{k_{(\sigma,\delta,\theta)}}$ is of finite range when σ and δ are of rank 2.

Second case: δ is of rank 1.
The rules are now of the form $\sigma(q_i(x_1), q_i'(x_2)) \rightarrow q(\delta(x_{\theta(1)}))$ where θ is either $< 2; 1 >$ or $< 2; 2 >$. Let $\theta =< 2; 1 >$; the other case is quite similar.
Let us suppose that $\widehat{B}_{q_{(\sigma,\delta,\theta)}} - \widehat{B}_{k_{(\sigma,\delta,\theta)}}$ is not of finite range. Then there would exist an infinite number of trees v such that we can find u and u' in T_Σ with $(\sigma(u, u'), \delta(v)) \notin \widehat{B}_{k_{(\sigma,\delta,\theta)}}$. In particular, there would exist v and u' such that $\pi(v) > \pi(u')$.

Now q and k are equivalent states and so there exists an other torsion μ such that $(\sigma(u,u'),\delta(v)) \in \widehat{B}_{k_{(\sigma,\delta,\mu)}}$. Here we would have $\mu =< 2;2 >$ and $\sigma(u,u') \overset{*}{\longmapsto} \sigma(k_i(w),k'_i(v)) \mapsto k(\delta(v))$. Such computations cannot be realized because we should have $\pi(v) > \pi(u')$ and $\pi(v) \leq \pi(u')$.

Therefore, in all cases, for any final transformation (σ,δ,θ) the difference $\widehat{B}_{q_{(\sigma,\delta,\theta)}} - \widehat{B}_{k_{(\sigma,\delta,\theta)}}$ is of finite range. □

Corollary 1. *Let B be a letter-to-letter bottom-up transducer. There exists a natural number, denoted by Λ, such that for any globally equivalent sets of states E and F, for any final transformation (σ,δ,θ), as soon as $\pi(u) > \Lambda$, we have $(t,u) \in \widehat{B}_{E_{(\sigma,\delta,\theta)}} \Leftrightarrow (t,u) \in \widehat{B}_{F_{(\sigma,\delta,\theta)}}$.*

PROOF: A result analogous to lemma 1 is obtained when we consider globally equivalent sets of states E and F (instead of equivalent states) of an infinitary transducer: for any final transformation (σ,δ,θ), the difference $\widehat{B}_{E_{(\sigma,\delta,\theta)}} - \widehat{B}_{F_{(\sigma,\delta,\theta)}}$ is of finite range and so, obviously, there exists a natural number $\lambda_{(E,F),(\sigma,\delta,\theta)}$, such that as soon as $\pi(u) > \lambda_{(E,F),(\sigma,\delta,\theta)}$, we have $(t,u) \in \widehat{B}_{E_{(\sigma,\delta,\theta)}} \Leftrightarrow (t,u) \in \widehat{B}_{F_{(\sigma,\delta,\theta)}}$.
To extend this result to a transducer some states of which are finitary, we take $\lambda_{(E,F),(\sigma,\delta,\theta)}$ greater than the number of finitary states of this transducer. Now let λ be an upper-bound for these integers $\lambda_{(E,F),(\sigma,\delta,\theta)}$ obtained for all globally equivalent sets of states and for all final transformations (σ,δ,θ) and let N_F be the number of finitary states of B. We define Λ as the integer $Sup(\lambda, N_F)$. □

As in the top-down case [1, 2, 3], in order to eliminate these differences $\widehat{B}_{E_{(\sigma,\delta,\theta)}} - \widehat{B}_{F_{(\sigma,\delta,\theta)}}$ in the computations of some elements of $\widehat{B}_E$ (equal to $\widehat{B}_F$) we will consider as atomic any term an output tree of which is a ground term of height less than or equal to Λ. We do not compute this bound Λ but, even if the construction is defined for any natural number ν, the correctness of the results is connected to a large enough value of this integer.

3.2 ν-Semi-normalized Forms

For any natural number ν, we associate with any transducer B its ν-semi-normalized form, denoted by B^ν, and for which any couple of trees (or subtrees) (t,u) with $\pi(t), \pi(u) \leq \nu$ is considered as atomic, that is to say is considered as a couple of new letters.
Let $B =< \Sigma, \Delta, Q, F, R >$, $B^\nu =< \Sigma^\nu, \Delta^\nu, Q^\nu, F^\nu, R^\nu >$ is constructed as follows:

- $Q^\nu = \{q^{<\nu}$ and $q^\nu \mid q \in Q\}$ and $F^\nu = \{q^{<\nu}$ and $q^\nu \mid q \in F\}$.
- Rules of R^ν which simulate computations producing trees of height $\leq \nu$:

[1] and there is no computation $t_0(q_1(x_1),..,q_n(x_n)) \overset{*}{\longmapsto}_B t'(q'_1(t'_1),..,q'_m(t'_m))$ where t' is a prefix of t_0 and such that $t'(q'_1(x_1),..,q'_m(x_m)) \overset{*}{\longmapsto}_B q(u)$

Computations in B	New letters and associated rules of B^ν
$t \overset{*}{\longmapsto}_B q(u)$ $\pi(t) = \pi(u) < \nu$	$t \rightarrow q^{<\nu}(u) \ \in R^\nu$ $t \in \Sigma^\nu$ and $u \in \Delta^\nu$
$t \overset{*}{\longmapsto}_B q(u)$ $\pi(t) = \pi(u) = \nu$	$t \rightarrow q^{\nu}(u) \ \in R^\nu$ $t \in \Sigma^\nu$ and $u \in \Delta^\nu$
$t_0(q_1(x_1), .., q_n(x_n)) \overset{*}{\longmapsto}_B q(u)$ $\pi(t_0(x_1, .., x_n)) = \pi(u) < \nu$.[1]	$t_0(q_1^\diamond(x_1), .., q_n^\diamond(x_n)) \rightarrow q^{<\nu}(u) \in R^\nu$ $q_i^\diamond$ is either $q_i^{<\nu}$ or q_i^ν, $t_0 \in \Sigma_n^\nu$ and $u \in \Delta_0^\nu$
$t_0(q_1(x_1), .., q_n(x_n)) \overset{*}{\longmapsto}_B q(u)$ $\pi(t_0(x_1, .., x_n)) = \pi(u) = \nu$[1]	$t_0(q_1^\diamond(x_1), .., q_n^\diamond(x_n)) \rightarrow q^{\nu}(u) \in R^\nu$ $q_i^\diamond$ is either $q_i^{<\nu}$ or q_i^ν, $t_0 \in \Sigma_n^\nu$ and $u \in \Delta_0^\nu$

- In order to control the depth of the trees which are transformed, for any rule $\sigma(q_1(x_1), .., q_n(x_n)) \rightarrow q(\delta(x_{\theta(1)}, .., x_{\theta(m)}))$ in R we will have in R^ν the rules $\sigma(q_1^\diamond(x_1), .., q_n^\diamond(x_n)) \rightarrow q^\nu(\delta(x_{\theta(1)}, .., x_{\theta(m)}))$ where
  - $\sigma \in \Sigma_n^\nu$ and $\delta \in \Delta_m^\nu$
  - there exists at least $j \in [n]$ such that $q_j^\diamond$ is of the form q_j^ν and for any $i \in [n]$ with $i \neq j$, $q_i^\diamond$ is either $q_i^{<\nu}$ or q_i^ν.

  So, these non-ground rules only apply for output terms of height greater than ν.

Example 2 (*continued*) For $\nu = 1$, the ν-semi-normalized form of B_1 (page 5) is defined by:

Rules producing ground terms:

$\bar{a} \rightarrow q_1^{<1}(e)$ $\quad \bar{a} \rightarrow q_2^{<1}(e)$ $\quad a(q_1''^{<1}(x)) \rightarrow q_1^{<1}(e)$ $\quad a(q_1''^{1}(x)) \rightarrow q_1^{<1}(e)$

$\bar{a} \rightarrow q_1'^{<1}(\bar{\alpha})$ $\quad \bar{a} \rightarrow q_2'^{<1}(\bar{\beta})$ $\quad a(q_2'^{<1}(x)) \rightarrow q_2^{<1}(e)$ $\quad a(q_2'^{1}(x)) \rightarrow q_2^{<1}(e)$

$\boxed{a(\bar{a})} \rightarrow q_1''^{1}(\boxed{\alpha(\bar{\alpha})})$ $\qquad \boxed{\sigma(.,\bar{a})}\, q_1^{<1}(x) \rightarrow q^1(\boxed{\delta(e,e)})$

$\boxed{a(\bar{a})} \rightarrow q_2'^{1}(\boxed{\beta(\bar{\beta})})$ $\qquad \boxed{\sigma(\bar{a},.)}\, q_2^{<1}(x) \rightarrow q^1(\boxed{\delta(e,e)})$

$\boxed{\sigma(\bar{a},\bar{a})} \rightarrow q^1(\boxed{\delta(e,e)})$ $\qquad \sigma(q_1^{<1}(x), q_2^{<1}(y)) \rightarrow q^1(\boxed{\delta(e,e)})$

Other rules: $\begin{cases} a(q_1'^{1}(x)) \rightarrow q_1''^{1}(\alpha(x)) \quad a(q_1''^{1}(x)) \rightarrow q_1'^{1}(\alpha(x)) \\ a(q_2'^{1}(x)) \rightarrow q_2'^{1}(\beta(x)) \end{cases}$

Trees written into boxes are now considered as new letters. Note that we just mention the usable rules □.

Lemma 2. *Let B be a letter-to-letter bottom-up transducer. There exists a natural number Λ such that, for any couple (E, F)*[1] *of globally equivalent sets of states, for any final transformation (σ, δ, θ), $\widehat{B}^{\Lambda}_{E_{(\sigma,\delta,\theta)}} = \widehat{B}^{\Lambda}_{F_{(\sigma,\delta,\theta)}}$.*

PROOF: Immediate from corollary 1 and the previous construction. □

---

[1] To avoid a multiplication of notations, for any set E of states of B, the set of states $\{q^\nu, q^{<\nu} \mid q \in E\}$ of B^ν is also denoted by E.

We now prove that, when ν is large enough, for equivalent states of this ν-semi-normalized form, the same torsions can be applied (except eventually for subtrees which are next deleted). In order to formalize this fact, from the transducer B^ν we introduce a new form, denoted by $B^{\nu,d}$, for which the torsions applied in a computation are encoded in the nodes of the output tree (the nodes of the output trees are "decorated" by these torsions).

Construction of $B^{\nu,d}$

From $B^\nu =< \Sigma^\nu, \Delta^\nu, Q^\nu, F^\nu, R^\nu >$, we construct $B^{\nu,d} =< \Sigma^\nu, \Delta^{\nu,d}, Q^\nu, F^\nu, R^{\nu,d} >$ where $\Delta^{\nu,d}$ and $R^{\nu,d}$ are defined by:

$\sigma(q_1(x_1), .., q_n(x_n)) \to q(\delta_\theta(x_{\theta(1)}, .., x_{\theta(m)})) \in R^{\nu,d}$ and $\delta_\theta \in \Delta^{\nu,d}$ if $\sigma(q_1(x_1), .., q_n(x_n)) \to q(\delta(x_{\theta(1)}, .., x_{\theta(m)})) \in R^\nu$, and any ground rule $\sigma(q_1(x_1), .., q_n(x_n)) \to q^\diamond(\delta)$ of R^ν is a rule of $R^{\nu,d}$.

In the following, for any couple (t, u) of $\widehat{B}^\nu$, we will denote by (t, u^d) the corresponding couple of $\widehat{B}^{\nu,d}$.

To establish the fact that, when ν is large enough, we have $\widehat{B}_E = \widehat{B}_F \Leftrightarrow \widehat{B}_E^{\nu,d} = \widehat{B}_F^{\nu,d}$ we will use the following technical lemma:

Lemma 3. *Let E and F be two sets of globally equivalent states of the ν-semi-normalized form B^ν of a transducer B. When ν is large enough, for any couple (t, u) of $\widehat{B}_E^\nu$ ($= \widehat{B}_F^\nu$), for any prefix u_0 of u, for any state q of E, for any computation*

$$t_0(t_1, .., t_n) \overset{*}{\longmapsto}_{B^\nu} t_0(q_1(u_1), .., q_n(u_n)) \overset{*}{\longmapsto}_{B^{\nu,d}} q(u_0^d(u_{\theta(1)}, .., u_{\theta(m)}))$$

there exists $k \in F$ such that

$$t_0(t_1, .., t_n) \overset{*}{\longmapsto}_{B^\nu} t_0(k_1(u_1), .., k_n(u_n)) \overset{*}{\longmapsto}_{B^{\nu,d}} k(u_0^d(u_{\theta(1)}, .., u_{\theta(m)})).$$

PROOF: By induction on the prefix u_0 of u. Let $\nu = \Lambda$ as defined in corollary 1.

– From the construction of B^Λ and by means of lemma 2 the property is true when the prefix of u is reduced to a letter of Δ^Λ.

– Assume now that property is true for a prefix u_o of u , that is to say for couples of the form $(t, u_0(u_1, .., u_m))$ of $\widehat{B}_E^\Lambda$ and let us show that it is true again for a larger prefix.

For any $j \in [m]$ we consider the sets

$$Q_j = \{q_r \mid t_0(q_1(x_1), .., q_r(x_r), .., q_n(x_n)) \overset{*}{\longmapsto}_{B^{\Lambda,d}} q(u_0^d(x_{\theta(1)}, .., x_r, .., x_{\theta(m)})), \text{ with } q \in E \text{ and } r = \theta(j)\} \text{ and}$$

$$K_j = \{k_r \mid t_0(k_1(x_1), .., k_r(x_r), .., k_n(x_n)) \overset{*}{\longmapsto}_{B^{\Lambda,d}} k(u_0^d(x_{\theta(1)}, .., x_r, .., x_{\theta(m)})), \text{ with } k \in F \text{ and } r = \theta(j)\}.$$

First, let us show that for any $j \in [m]$, Q_j and K_j are globally equivalent sets of states. Assume that there exists $j \in [m]$ such that Q_j and K_j are not globally equivalent. There would exist at least one couple $(\bar{\tau}, \bar{\mu})$ in $\widehat{B}_{Q_j} - \widehat{B}_{K_j}$ such that $t_0(\bar{t}_1, .., \bar{\tau}, .., \bar{t}_n) \overset{*}{\longmapsto}_{B^\Lambda} t_0(q_1(\bar{u}_1), .., q_{\theta(j)}(\bar{\mu}), .., q_n(\bar{u}_n)) \overset{*}{\longmapsto}_{B^{\Lambda,d}} q(u_0^d(\bar{u}_{\theta(1)}, .., \bar{\mu}, .., 6\bar{u}_{\theta(m)})))$ when, because $(\bar{\tau}, \bar{\mu}) \notin \widehat{B}_{K_j}$, there does not exist any computation from

$t_0(\bar{t}_1, .., \bar{\tau}, .., \bar{t}_n)$ which leads to $k(u_0^d(\bar{u}_{\theta(1)}, .., \bar{\mu}, .., \bar{u}_{\theta(m)})))$.
It would contradict the assumption that property holds for u_0 and so for any $j \in [m]$ the sets of states Q_j and K_j are globally equivalent.
Thus, for any $j \in [m]$, for any state $q' \in Q_j$, there exists at least one state $k' \in K_j$ such that the computations $t_{\theta(j)} \overset{*}{\longmapsto} q'(u_{\theta(j)})$ and $t_{\theta(j)} \overset{*}{\longmapsto} k'(u_{\theta(j)})$ are realized with the same final torsions (first point of this proof). Consequently the property is also satisfied for a larger prefix $(u_0(x_1, .., v_j, .., x_m)$ with v_j root of u_j). □

Proposition 1. *Let B be a bottom-up transducer. When ν is large enough, for any couple (E, F) of sets of states, $\widehat{B}_E^{\nu,d} = \widehat{B}_F^{\nu,d} \Leftrightarrow \widehat{B}_E = \widehat{B}_F$.*

Hint of Proof: We have obviously $\widehat{B}_E^{\nu,d} = \widehat{B}_F^{\nu,d} \Rightarrow \widehat{B}_E = \widehat{B}_F$. Conversely, we use the previous lemma (using as prefix of a tree the tree itself). □

3.3 ν-normalized forms

In the previous section proposition 1 established the fact that, when ν is large enough, for any transducer B, for globally equivalent sets of states E and F, all computations can be realized with the same torsions in the Λ-semi-normalized form $B^{\nu,d}$. So if some subtrees are deleted or duplicated in a computation of a couple (t, u) of $B_E^{\nu,d}$, we claim that there exists a computation of (t, u) in $B_F^{\nu,d}$ which delete or duplicate the same subtrees. Because torsions have been encoded in the nodes of the output trees, it is not significant to apply them effectively. These facts lead us to define a ν-*n*ormalized form $B^{\nu,n}$ which is a torsion-free transducer.

For the sake of comprehension, we describe the construction by means of examples where only one kind of torsion occurs:

- *Permutation:* from any rule of the form $\sigma(q_1(x_1), q_2(x_2)) \rightarrow q(\delta_\theta(x_2, x_1))$, we construct the rule $\sigma(q_1(x_1), q_2(x_2)) \rightarrow q(\delta_\theta(x_1, x_2))$.
- *Non-linearity:* by using a non-linear rule, a bottom-up transducer can only generate identical copies and so we will only keep one of them. So, from the rule $\sigma(q_1(x)) \rightarrow q(\delta_\theta(x, x))$ we construct $\sigma(q_1(x)) \rightarrow q(\delta_\theta'(x))$.
- *Deletion:* A bottom-up transducer has the ability of inspecting a subtree before deleting it. So, for instance, to any rule of the form $\sigma(q_1(x_1), q_2(x_2)) \rightarrow q(\delta_\theta(x_1))$ we substitute the non-deleting rule $\sigma(q_1(x_1), \bar{q}_2(x_2)) \rightarrow q(\delta_\theta'(x_1, x_2))$ where the transformation associated with this new state $\bar{q}_2$ is the identity that is to say the set $\{(t,t) \mid t \in dom(\widehat{B}_{q_2}^{\nu,d})\}$. Note that, in particular, we have $dom(\widehat{B}_{q_2}^{\nu,d}) = dom(\widehat{B}_{\bar{q}_2}^{\nu,d})$.
  Moreover, for any state q, in order to realize the identity transformation on $dom(\widehat{B}_q)$, from any rule $\sigma(q_1(x_1), .., q_n(x_n)) \rightarrow q(\delta_\theta(x_{\theta(1)}, .., x_{\theta(m)}))$ of $B^{\nu,d}$, we construct the rule $\sigma(\bar{q}_1(x_1), .., \bar{q}_n(x_n)) \rightarrow \bar{q}(\sigma(x_1, .., x_n))$.

As these phenomena can be mixed in a same rule, the construction in the general case is a combinaison of the previous ones.

Example 2 *(continued)* We only give here the usable rules of the 1-normalized form of B_1. States have been renamed.

$$\boxed{\sigma(.,\bar{a})}\,r_1(x) \to q(\boxed{\delta(e,e)}_1(x)) \qquad \boxed{\sigma(\bar{a},.)}\,r_2(x) \to q(\boxed{\delta(e,e)}_1(x))$$

$$\boxed{\sigma(\bar{a},\bar{a})} \to q(\boxed{\delta(e,e)}) \qquad \sigma(r_1(x), r_2(y)) \to q(\boxed{\delta(e,e)}_2(x,y))$$

$$\bar{a} \to r_1(\bar{a}) \qquad \boxed{a(\bar{a})} \to r_3(\boxed{a(\bar{a})}) \qquad a(r_3(x)) \to r_1(a(x))$$

$$a(r_3(x)) \to r_5(a(x)) \qquad a(r_5(x)) \to r_3(a(x))$$

$$\bar{a} \to r_2(\bar{a}) \qquad \boxed{a(\bar{a})} \to r_2(\boxed{a(\bar{a})}) \qquad \boxed{a(\bar{a})} \to r_4(\boxed{a(\bar{a})})$$

$$a(r_4(x)) \to r_4(a(x)) \qquad a(r_4(x)) \to r_2(a(x))$$

Note that $\boxed{\delta(e,e)}_1$ is a new letter of rank 1 and $\boxed{\delta(e,e)}_2$ is of rank 2. Moreover, due to the deleting rules of B_1, many rules of this normalized form are automaton rules like. □

By means of proposition 1 we know that, when ν is large enough, for any couple (E,F) of sets of states, $\widehat{B}_E^{\nu,d} = \widehat{B}_F^{\nu,d} \Leftrightarrow \widehat{B}_E = \widehat{B}_F$. Now, by the previous construction, equivalence of states is obviously preserved and so we obtain:

Proposition 2. *Let B be a letter-to-letter bottom-up transducer. When ν is large enough, for any couple of sets of states (E,F), $\widehat{B}_E = \widehat{B}_F \Leftrightarrow \widehat{B}_E^{\nu,n} = \widehat{B}_F^{\nu,n}$.*

3.4 Decidability of equivalence

Using the previous result, we can now prove:

Theorem 1. *Equivalence of letter-to-letter bottom-up transducers is decidable.*

PROOF: Let $B =< \Sigma, \Delta, Q, F, R >$ and $B' =< \Sigma, \Delta, Q', F', R' >$ with $Q \cap Q' \neq \emptyset$ (otherwise, we can relabel them). As equivalence is decidable for bottom-up relabelings [4], from proposition 2 applied to the sets of states F and F' (of $B \cup B'$) we obtain that equivalence of B and B' is semi-decidable. Because non-equivalence is obviously semi-decidable, we conclude. □

4 Compositions of letter-to-letter tree transducers

Following the Engelfriet's works [7], we consider the tree transformations realized by compositions of two letter-to-letter tree transducers: a first phase accomplished by a bottom-up transducer followed by a second one realized by a top-down transducer. These compositions can, for instance perform some optimizations on relational databases as it is illustrated in the following example.

Example 3 We assume the reader is familiar with the relational data model. We consider here the set-of-mappings viewpoint in which columns of all relations have attributes names and tuples are regarded as mapping from attributes to values. Let us consider a relational scheme $\mathcal{R}$ constituted of the relations $R_1, R_2, ..., R_n$. Let be $\mathcal{A} = \{a_1, a_2, ..., a_p\}$ the set of the attributes of these relations. We only consider here the following operators of the relational algebra:
Selection: $Select_F$ where F is a formula involving attributes referred by their name. Let us denote by $\nu(F)$ the set of attributes that appear in formula F.
Natural join: $\bowtie$. $R \bowtie S$ denotes the join of R and S on each attribute that is both in R and S.
Projection: the projection of relation R on x will be denoted by $R[x]$.
"Selection" and "Join" can be composed sequentially with a projection on a subset x of attributes. We will use the shorthands $Select_F[x], \bowtie [x]$ for these compositions.
With any relational expression, we can associate its parse tree, so query optimization by algebraic manipulation can be seen as tree transformation. We show that the move of the projections as far down the tree as possible can be obtained by such a composition of transducers.

Letter to letter bottom-up transducer
This first transformation labels the natural join operators with the couple of sets of attributes of the joined relations.The rules of this transducer correspond also to validity checks.
Let $T_\uparrow =< Q, \Sigma, \Delta, F, \mathcal{R} >$ where

- the states of Q are the subsets of $\mathcal{A}$; $F = Q$
- $\Sigma_0 = \{R_i, R_i[x]/i \in [n], x \subset \mathcal{A}\}$;
  $\Sigma_1 = \{Select_x, Select_x[y]/x, y \subset \mathcal{A}\}$; the label $Select_x$ is associated with any operator $Select_F$ where $\nu(F) = x$; $\Sigma_2 = \{\bowtie\} \cup \{\bowtie [x]/x \subset \mathcal{A}\}$
- $\Delta_0 = \{R_i/i \in [n]\}; \Delta_1 = \{Select_x/x \subset \mathcal{A}\}; \Delta_2 = \{\bowtie_{(y,z)} /y, z \subset \mathcal{A}\}$
- rules of $\mathcal{R}$ are constructed as follows:
  - Let s be the set of attributes of R. $R \rightarrow s(R), R[x] \rightarrow x(R)$ iff $x \subset s$
  - $Select_x(s) \rightarrow s(Select_x)$ iff $x \subset s$, $Select_x[r](s) \rightarrow r(Select_x)$ iff $(x \cup r) \subset s$
  - $\bowtie (s, s') \rightarrow s''(\bowtie_{(s,s')})$ with $s'' = s \cup s'$, $\bowtie [r](s, s') \rightarrow r(\bowtie_{(s,s')})$ iff $r \subset (s \cup s')$

Letter to letter top-down transducer
This transducer associates with each operator which occurs in the expression, the projection onto the minimal set of attributes that is useful to evaluate the expression. Its input alphabet is Δ and its output alphabet Σ. The initial state of a top-down computation will be the state reached at the end of the bottom-up computation. So its rules have the following forms:
$s(R) \rightarrow R[s]$, $s(Select_x) \rightarrow Select_x[s](x \cup s)$,
$s(\bowtie_{(r_1,r_2)}) \rightarrow \bowtie [s](r_1 \cap (r_2 \cup s), r_2 \cap (r_1 \cup s))$ for $s \subset \mathcal{A}$ and $s \neq \emptyset$

Application
Let us consider the relational database scheme:
Customer(C#,C_name,C_adress), Order(O#,C#,O_date), Include(O#, A#, quantity), Article(A#, A_description, A_price, S#), Supplier(S#, S_name, S_adress). C#, O#, A#, S# refer primary keys on relations *Customer, Order, Article, Supplier.*
Let us now consider the query: `Which customers have given orders for articles supplied by a given supplier ?`
This query is turned into a relational expression. The following figure presents the parse

tree of this expression versus its optimized tree obtained by the considered two-way transducer.

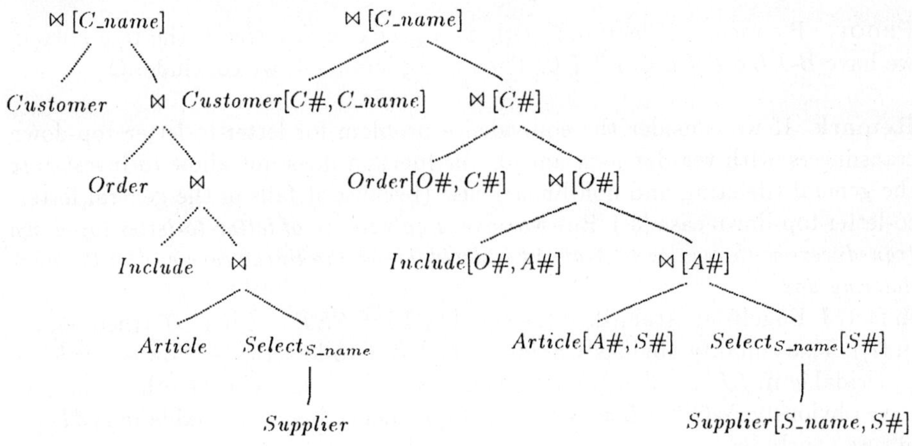

□

We show that compositions correspond closely to transformations realized by letter-to-letter top-down tree transducers with regular look-ahead. In [7], J. Engelfriet proved that T^R-$FST \subseteq DB$-$LAB \circ T$-FST. Here, we have

Lemma 4. T^R-$LL \subseteq B$-$LL \circ T$-LL.

PROOF: By applying the construction described in the proof of theorem 2.6 of [7] to the letter-to-letter case, we immediately obtain that T^R-$LL \subseteq DB$-$LAB \circ T$-LL. Now DB-$LAB \subseteq B$-LL and so T^R-$LL \subseteq B$-$LL \circ T$-LL. □

In order to obtain the reverse property (B-$LL \circ T$-$LL \subseteq T^R$-LL), with any couple (B, T) of letter-to-letter transducers (where B is a bottom-up transducer and T is a top-down one), we associate the letter-to-letter top-down tree transducer with regular look-ahead T^R the rules of which are constructed as follows:
$(q,k)(\sigma(x_1,..,x_n)) \rightarrow \gamma((q_{\theta(\mu(1))},k_1)(x_{\theta(\mu(1))}),..,(q_{\theta(\mu(p))},k_p)(x_{\theta(\mu(p))})), < L_1,.., L_n > \in T^R$ if and only if
$\sigma(q_1(x_1),..,q_n(x_n)) \rightarrow q(\delta(x_{\theta(1)},..,x_{\theta(m)}))$ is a rule of B, with for any $i \in [n]$, $dom(\widehat{B}_{q_i}) = L_i$ and $k(\delta(x_1,..,x_m)) \rightarrow \gamma(k_1(x_{\mu(1)}),..,k_p(x_{\mu(p)}))$ is a rule of T.

The so constructed transducer with look-ahead verifies the following property:

Lemma 5. *For any tree t, for any prefix t_0 of t,*

$$t_0(t_1,..,t_n) \overset{*}{\longmapsto}_B t_0(q_1(u_1),..,q_n(u_n)) \overset{*}{\longmapsto}_B q(u_0(u_{\theta(1)},..,u_{\theta(m)}))$$
and $k(u_0(u_{\theta(1)},..,u_{\theta(m)})) \overset{*}{\longmapsto}_T v_0(k_1(u_{\theta(\mu(1))}),..,k_p(u_{\theta(\mu(p))}))$

if and only if

$$(q,k)(t_0(t_1,..,t_n)) \overset{*}{\longmapsto}_{T^R} v_0((q_{\theta(\mu(1))},k_1)(t_{\theta(\mu(1))}),..,(q_{\theta(\mu(p))},k_p)(t_{\theta(\mu(p))}))$$
with, for any $i \in [n]$, $t_i \in dom(\widehat{B}_{q_i})$.

The proof, by induction on t, is given in the appendix.

Theorem 2. T^R-$LL = B$-$LL \circ T$-LL.

PROOF: By means of lemma 5 with as a prefix of any tree t, the tree t itself, we have B-$LL \circ T$-$LL \subseteq T^R$-LL. Then using lemma 4, we conclude. □

Remark If we consider the equivalence problem for letter-to-letter top-down transducers with regular look-ahead, our method does not allow to investigate the general (deleting and non-linear) case (because it fails in the general letter-to-letter top-down case [3]). But we have: *Equivalence of letter-to-letter top-down transducers with regular look-ahead is decidable in the linear case and in the non-deleting one.*
In fact, J. Engelfriet established the equality LT^R-$FST = LB$-FST (theorem 2.8 in [7]). This equality obviously holds in the letter-to-letter case. Now equivalence is decidable in LB-LL (theorem 1) then it is in LT^R-LL. On the other hand, we have obviously NdT^R-$LL = NdT$-LL. Equivalence being decidable in NdT-LL [3], we conclude. □

5 Extensions

Non-linearity is an important phenomenon which often appears in trees, for instance in the rewrite rules $-(x, x) \rightarrow 0$ and $*(x, x) \rightarrow sqr(x)$. So a natural extension of our work would be to investigate letter-to-letter bottom-up transducers the rules of which can have non-linear left-hand sides. In this section, we only consider a restricted case.

5.1 Definitions

A *generalized letter-to letter bottom-up tree transducer* is a 5-tuple $B =< \Sigma, \Delta, Q, F, R >$ where Σ, Δ, Q and F are defined as for "classical" bottom-up tree transducer and R is a finite set of rules of the form $\sigma(q_1(x_{\theta(1)}), .., q_n(x_{\theta(n)})) \mapsto q(\delta(x_{\mu(1)}, .., x_{\mu(m)}))$ where θ is a surjective mapping from $[n]$ to $[p]$ (with $p \leq n$) and μ is a mapping from $[m]$ to $[p]$. By **gB-LL**, we denote the class of all generalized Letter-to Letter Bottom-up tree transducer.
In the following, we restrict ourselves to generalized letter-to letter, called *one-state* transducers, for which Q is reduced to one state.
We first define an order relation on the set of rules of any transducer such that a rule r is said to be "more general" than a rule r' if everywhere the rule r' is applied, the rule r can be used with the same result.
Formally, let $r : \sigma(q(x_{\theta(1)}), .., q(x_{\theta(n)})) \rightarrow q(\delta(x_{\mu(1)}, .., x_{\mu(m)}))$ and $r' : \sigma(q(x_{\theta'(1)}), .., q(x_{\theta'(n)})) \rightarrow q(\delta(x_{\mu'(1)}, .., x_{\mu'(m)}))$ be two rules of a one-state transducer. r is *more general* than r' if there exists a mapping ϕ such that $\phi \circ \theta = \theta'$ and $\phi \circ \mu = \mu'$. We write $r \succeq r'$ (or $r' \preceq r$).

Example Let $r_1 : \sigma(q(x_1), q(x_2), q(x_1), q(x_3)) \to q(\delta(x_1, x_1, x_2, x_3))$, $r_2 : \sigma(q(x_1), q(x_2), q(x_1), q(x_2)) \to q(\delta(x_1, x_1, x_2, x_2))$, $r_3 : \sigma(q(x_1), q(x_2), q(x_3), q(x_1)) \to q(\delta(x_1, x_1, x_2, x_3))$; we have $r_1 \succeq r_2$ but neither $r_1 \succeq r_3$ nor $r_3 \succeq r_1$.

A one-state generalized transducer is said to be *cleaned* if for any rule r there does not exist any rule r' such that $r \succeq r'$.

Property 2. *With any one-state transducer B of* **gB-LL** *we can associate a cleaned one-state transducer B^c which is equivalent to B.*

PROOF: If r and r' are two rules of a transducer B such that $r \succeq r'$ then anywhere r' is applied, we can apply r without difference in the transformation and so r' is not useful. By suppressing such rules, we obtain a cleaned transducer which is equivalent to B. □

5.2 Equivalence of one-state transducers

Theorem 3. *Two one-state transducers of* **gB-LL** *are equivalent if and only if their cleaned forms are equal, and so their equivalence is decidable.*

PROOF: Let B_1 and B_2 be two equivalent one-state transducers and let B_1^c and B_2^c be their cleaned forms. To establish the equality $B_1^c = B_2^c$, we show that, for any rule $r : \sigma(q_1(x_{\theta(1)}), .., q_1(x_{\theta(n)})) \mapsto q_1(\delta(x_{\mu(1)}, .., x_{\mu(m)}))$ of B_1^c, with θ and μ mapping into $[p]$, there exists the same rule $\sigma(q_2(x_{\theta(1)}), .., q_2(x_{\theta(n)})) \mapsto q_2(\delta(x_{\mu(1)}, .., x_{\mu(m)}))$ in B_2^c.
Let us consider the couples of trees (t_1, u_1), .., (t_p, u_p) with, for any i and j in $[p]$, $\pi(u_i) \neq \pi(u_j)$ (it is possible if there exists at least a rule producing a letter of rank greater than 0 [1]) and such that $\sigma(t_{\theta(1)}, .., t_{\theta(n)}) \overset{*}{\longmapsto}_{B_1^c} \sigma(q_1(u_{\theta(1)}), .., q_n(u_{\theta(n)})) \mapsto_{B_1^c} q_1(\delta(u_{\mu(1)}, .., u_{\mu(m)}))$.
B_1 and B_2 being equivalent there would exist in B_2^c a rule r' such that $r' \succeq r$.
Let $r' : \sigma(q_2(x_{\theta'(1)}), .., q_2(x_{\theta'(n)})) \mapsto q_2(\delta(x_{\mu'(1)}, .., x_{\mu'(m)}))$ (θ' mapping from $[n]$ to $[s]$) such that and let us consider the couples of trees (t'_1, u'_1), .., (t'_s, u'_s) with, for any i and j in $[s]$, $\pi(u'_i) \neq \pi(u'_j)$ and such that $\sigma(t_{\theta'(1)}, .., t_{\theta'(n)}) \overset{*}{\longmapsto}_{B_2^c} \sigma(q_2(u_{\theta'(1)}), .., q_2(u_{\theta'(n)})) \mapsto_{B_2^c} q_2(\delta(u_{\mu'(1)}, .., u_{\mu'(m)}))$.
B_1^c and B_2^c being equivalent we would find in B_1^c a rule r'' with $r'' \succeq r'$. Now B_1^c is cleaned then $r = r' = r''$.
Thus, if two one-state transducers are equivalent, their cleaned forms are equal. The converse is obviously true and so we conclude. □

References

[1] Y. André and M. Dauchet. Decidability of equivalence for a class of non-deterministic tree transducers. *RAIRO, Theoretical Informatics and Applications.* Vol 28, n°5, 1994, pp 447-463.

[1] the result is valid as soon as the output alphabet Δ contains two letters. On the contrary, it is not true if Δ is a singleton. That is the case, for instance, for the two transducers $\{\sigma(x, y) \to a, a \to a\}$ and $\{\sigma(x, x) \to a, a \to a\}$. In such situations, two transducers are equivalent if the same couples of letters appear in the rules.

[2] Y. André and F. Bossut. Decidability of equivalence for linear letter-to-letter top-down tree transducers. *Proceedings of FCT'93.* LNCS 710, pp 142-151.

[3] Y. André and F. Bossut. On the equivalence problem for letter-to-letter top-down tree transducers. Submitted to publication.

[4] S. Bozapalidis. Alphabetic tree relations. *T.C.S. 99*, pp 177-211. 1992.

[5] J.L. Coquidé, M. Dauchet, R. Gilleron and S. Vágvölgyi. Bottom-up tree pushdown automata: classification and connection with rewrite systems. *T.C.S. 127*, pp 69-98. 1994.

[6] J. Engelfriet. Bottom-up and top-down tree transformations: a comparison. *Mathematical system theory.* Vol 9. pp 198-231. 1975.

[7] J. Engelfriet. Top-down Tree Transducers with Regular Look-ahead. *Mathematical system theory.* Vol 10. pp 289-303. 1977.

[8] J. Engelfriet and H. Vogler. Macro Tree Transducers. *J.C.S.S. 31*, pp 71-146. 1985.

[9] J. Engelfriet and H. Vogler. Modular Tree Transducers. *T.C.S. 78*, pp 267-303. 1991.

[10] Z. Esik. Decidability results concerning tree transducers I. *Acta Cybernetica*,Tom.5, Fasc.1, pp 1-20, Szeged, 1980.

[11] Z. Fülöp and S. Vágvölgyi. Variants of top-down tree transducers with look-ahead. *Mathematical Systems Theory 21.* pp125-145. 1989.

[12] F. Gecseg and M. Steinby. Tree automata. Akademiai Kiado, Budapest. 1984.

[13] W.C. Rounds. Trees, transducers and transformations. *Ph.D. Thesis.* Standford University. 1968.

[14] H. Seidl. Equivalence of finite-valued bottom-up finite state tree transducers is decidable. *Proceedings of CAAP'90.* LNCS 431, pp 269-284.

[15] J.W. Thatcher. Generalized sequential machine maps. *J.C.S.S. 4.* 1970.

[16] Z. Zachar. The solvability of the equivalence problem for deterministic frontier-to-root tree transducers. *Acta Cybernetica*, v.4, 1978, pp 167-177.

6 Appendix

Proof of lemma 5 It is by induction on the prefix of any tree t.

Induction base According to the construction, the property is true when t_0 is reduced to a letter.

Induction step Assume that property is true for a prefix t_0 of t and let us show that it is true again for a larger prefix. Let $t = t_0(t_1, .., t_i, .., t_n)$ with $t_i = a(t'_1, .., t'_r)$. So, we have:

$$\begin{aligned} t_0(t_1, .., a(t'_1, .., t'_r), .., t_n) &\overset{*}{\longmapsto}_B t_0(q_1(u_1), .., a(q'_1(u'_1), .., q'_r(u'_r)), .., q_n(u_n)) \\ &\overset{*}{\longmapsto}_B t_0(q_1(u_1), .., q_i(b(u'_{\alpha(1)}, .., u'_{\alpha(s)})), .., q_n(u_n)) \\ &\longmapsto_B \quad q(u_0(u_{\theta(1)}, .., u_{\theta(m)})) \end{aligned}$$

(so, for any $j \in [m]$ such that $\theta(j) = i\; u_{\theta(j)} = b(u'_{\alpha(1)}, .., u'_{\alpha(s)})$, for any $i \in [n]$ $t_i \in dom(\widehat{B}_{q_i})$, and for any $i \in [r]$ $t'_i \in dom(\widehat{B}_{q'_i})$)
and $k(u_0(u_{\theta(1)}, .., u_{\theta(m)})) \overset{*}{\longmapsto}_T v_0(k_1(u_{\theta(\mu(1))}), .., k_p(u_{\theta(\mu(p))}))$.

Let $\theta \circ \mu = \phi$ and assume that there exists at least l such that $\phi(l) = i$. Thus
$v_0(k_1(u_{\phi(1)}), .., k_l(u_{\phi(l)}), .., k_p(u_{\phi(p)})) \mapsto_B$
$v_0(k_1(u_{\phi(1)}), .., c(k'_1(u'_{\alpha(\beta(1))}), .., k'_w(u'_{\alpha(\beta(w))})), .., k_p(u_{\phi(p)}))$
$= v_0(k_1(u_{\phi(1)}), .., c(k'_1(u'_{\gamma(1)}), .., k'_w(u'_{\gamma(w)})), .., k_p(u_{\phi(p)}))$ where $\gamma = \alpha \circ \beta$.
Note that if there does not exist any l such that $\phi(l) = i$ for

i) there does not exist i' such that $\theta(i') = i$

ii) for any i' such that $\theta(i') = i$, there does not exist i'' such that $\mu(i'') = i$,

we have a weaker form of the previous case. Let us point out that these cases justify the introduction of a regular look-ahead check.

These computations are equivalent to

i) *by the induction hypothesis:*

$(q_{\phi(l)}, k_l)(t_{\phi(l)}) = (q_{\phi(l)}, k_l)(a(t'_1, .., t'_r)) \overset{*}{\longmapsto} c((q'_{\gamma(1)}, k'_1)(u'_{\gamma(1)}), .., (q'_{\gamma(w)}, k'_w)(u'_{\gamma(w)}))$

ii) *by the induction base:*

$(q_{\phi(l)}, k_l)(t_{\phi(l)}) = (q_{\phi(l)}, k_l)(a(t'_1, .., t'_r)) \overset{*}{\longmapsto} c((q'_{\gamma(1)}, k'_1)(u'_{\gamma(1)}), .., (q'_{\gamma(w)}, k'_w)(u'_{\gamma(w)}))$

That is to say
$(q, k)(t_0(t_1, .., a(t'_1, .., t'_r), .., t_n)) \overset{*}{\longmapsto}_{TR}$
$v_0((q_{\phi(1)}, k_1)(t_{\phi(1)}), .., c((q'_{\gamma(1)}, k'_1)(u'_{\gamma(1)}), .., (q'_{\gamma(w)}, k'_w)(u'_{\gamma(w)})), .., (q_{\phi(p)}, k_p)(t_{\phi(p)}))$
with for any $i \in [n]$ $t_i \in dom(\widehat{B}_{q_i})$ and for any $i \in [r]$ $t'_i \in dom(\widehat{B}_{q'_i})$. So the property is true for the larger prefix $t_0(x_1, .., a(x'_1, .., x'_r), .., x_n)$ of t (modulo a renaming of the variable $x_1, .., x_{i-1}, x'_1, .., x'_r, x_{i+1}, .., x_n$) .

Conversely, an analogous proof is developed.

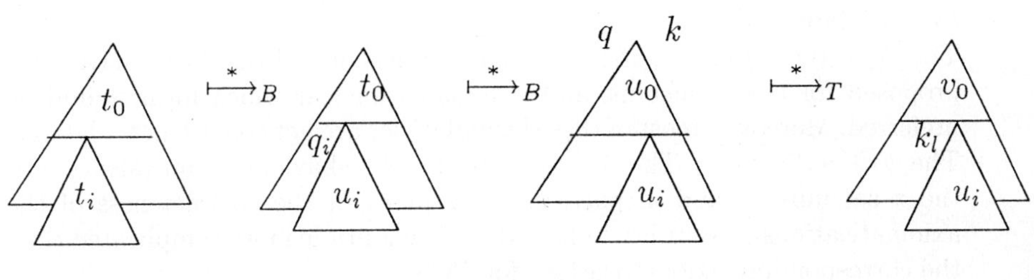

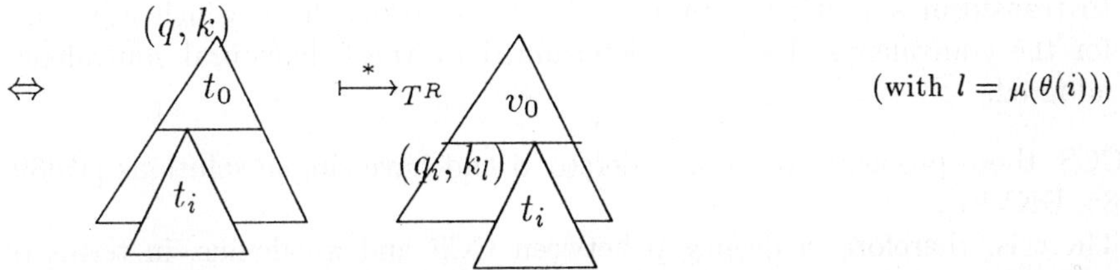

□

πI: a symmetric calculus based on internal mobility

Davide Sangiorgi

INRIA- Sophia Antipolis, France. Email: davide@cma.cma.fr.

1 Motivations

The π-calculus is a development of CCS where names (a synonymous for "channels") can be passed around. This permits the description of mobile systems, i.e., systems whose communication topology can change dynamically.

Name communication gives π-calculus a much greater expressiveness than CCS. For instance, in the π-calculus there are simple and intuitive encodings for: *Data values* [MPW92, Mil91], *agent-passing* process calculi [Tho90, San92] (i.e., calculi where terms of the language can be exchanged), the λ*-calculus* [Mil92], certain *concurrent object-oriented languages* [Jon93, Wal95], the locality and causality relations among the activities of a system, typical of *true-concurrent behavioural equivalences* [BS95]. In CCS, the modelling of such objects is possible, at best, in a clumsy and unnatural way — for instance making heavy use of infinite summations.

But research has also showed that the π-calculus has a much more complex mathematical theory than CCS. This shows up in:

- The *operational semantics.* Certain transition rules of the π-calculus are hard to assimilate.
- The *definition of bisimulation.* Various definitions of bisimilarity have been proposed for the π-calculus, and it remains unclear which form should be preferred. Moreover, most of these bisimilarities are not congruence relations.
- The *axiomatisations.* The axiomatisations of behavioural equivalences for the π-calculus — and in particular the proof of the completeness of the axiomatisations — is at least one order of magnitude more complicated than the corresponding axiomatisations for CCS.
- The *construction of canonical normal forms.* In general we do not know how to transform a π-calculus process P into a normal form which is unique for the equivalence class of P determined by the behavioural equivalence adopted.

In CCS, these problems are well-understood and have simple solutions [Mil89, BK85, DKV91].

There is, therefore, a deep gap between CCS and π-calculus, in terms of expressiveness and mathematical theory. The main goal of the paper is to explain this gap and to examine whether there are interesting intermediate calculi. For instance, are the complications of the theory of the π-calculus w.r.t. that of CCS an inevitable price to pay for the increase in expressiveness?

We shall isolate and analyse one such intermediate calculus, called πI. This calculus appears to have considerable expressiveness: Data values, the lambda calculus, agent-passing calculi, the locality and causality relations of true-concurrent behavioural equivalences can be modelled in πI much in the same way as they are in the π-calculus. But, nevertheless, the theory of πI remains very close to the theory of CCS: Alpha conversion is, essentially, the new ingredient. To obtain πI, we separate the mobility mechanisms of the π-calculus into two, namely *internal* mobility and *external* mobility. The former arises when an input meets a bound output, i.e., the output of a private name; the latter arises when an input meets a free output, i.e., the output of a known name. In πI only internal mobility is retained — the free output construct is disallowed. A pleasant property of πI is the full symmetry between input and output constructs. The operators of matching and mismatching, that in the π-calculus implement a form of case analysis on names and are important in the algebraic reasoning, are not needed in the theory of πI.

Sections 2-4 are devoted to introducing πI and its basic theory. The encoding of the λ-calculus into πI is studied in Section 5: It is challenging because all known encodings of the λ-calculus into π-calculus exploit, in an important way, the free-output construct, disallowed in πI. We sketch the comparison between πI and agent-passing calculi in Section 6. There is an exact correspondence, in terms of expressiveness, between a hierarchy of subcalculi of πI and a hierarchy of agent-passing calculi obtained from the Higher-Order π-calculus [San92]. The definitions of two hierarchies rely on the order of the typing systems of πI and of the Higher-Order π-calculus.

In this short version of the paper, the presentation is kept rather informal; for technical details and proofs, we refer to the full version [San95].

Acknowledgements. I have benefited from discussions with Gerard Boudol, Claudio Calvelli, Robin Milner, David Turner and David Walker, and from the comments of the anonymous referees. This research has been supported by the Esprit BRA project 6454 "CONFER".

2 The calculus πI

In this section we introduce (the finite part of) πI. We examine the move from π-calculus to πI from three different angles: First, our guiding criterion is symmetry; then we take into account the mobility mechanisms; finally, we focus on the algebraic theory. There are not compelling reasons for wanting symmetry: Our major motivation is elegance, which will show up in the presentation of the calculus and of its properties.

Throughout the paper we use a tilde ($\tilde{}$) to denote a finite and possibly empty tuple. All notations are extended to tuples componentwise.

2.1. Looking for symmetry: From π-calculus to πI We shall derive the grammar for πI from the one below, which collects the principal operators of the π-calculus, namely guarded sum, parallel composition and restriction.

Symbols $x, y, z, \ldots$ will range over the infinite set of names; P, Q and R will be metavariables over processes; prefixes, ranged over by α, can be of the form τ (*silent prefix*), $x(y)$ (*input prefix*), or $\overline{x}y$ (*free-output prefix*):

$$P ::= \sum_{i\in I} \alpha_i.\, P_i \;\mid\; P \,|\, P \;\mid\; \boldsymbol{\nu}\, x\, P$$

$$\alpha ::= \tau \mid x(y) \mid \overline{x}y$$

I is a finite indexing set; if I is empty, we abbreviate the sum as $\mathbf{0}$. As usual, $+$ is binary sum. Sometimes, we shall write $\alpha_1.\, P_1 + \ldots + \alpha_n.\, P_n$ for $\sum_{1\leq i\leq n} \alpha_i.\, P_i$.

An input prefix $x(y).\, P$ and a restriction $\boldsymbol{\nu}\, y\, P$ bind all free occurrences of name y in P. *Free* and *bound* names of processes and of prefixes, and *alpha conversion* are defined as expected. $P\{x/y\}$ denotes the substitution of x for y in P, with renaming possibly involved to avoid capture of free names. In examples, the object part of prefixes will be omitted if not important. A process $\alpha.\,\mathbf{0}$ will often be abbreviated as α, and $\boldsymbol{\nu}\, x_1 \ldots \boldsymbol{\nu}\, x_n\, P$ as $\boldsymbol{\nu}\, x_1, \ldots, x_n\, P$. Sum and parallel composition will have the lowest syntactic precedence; substitution the highest.

The grammar above does not mention the match and mismatch operators, written $[x = y]P$ and $[x \neq y]P$, respectively. The former means: "if x equal to y, then P"; the latter means "if x different from y, then P". Match and mismatch are often included in the π-calculus, mainly because very useful in the algebraic theory. But they will not be needed in the algebraic theory of πI, as shown in Section 3.

We wish to make two remarks about the π-calculus language above presented. The first regards the asymmetry between the input and output constructs, namely $x(y).-$ and $\overline{x}y.-$. The asymmetry is both syntactic — the input is a binder whereas the output is not — and semantic — in an input *any* name can be received, whereas in an output a *fixed* name is emitted. The second remark regards a derived form of prefix, called *bound output*, written $\overline{x}(y)$ as an abbreviation for $\boldsymbol{\nu}\, y\, \overline{x}y$. Bound output plays a central role in π-calculus theory, for instance in the operational semantics and in the axiomatisation. In the operational semantics, bound output is introduced in the OPEN rule, one of the of the two rules for restriction:

$$\texttt{OPEN}: \quad \frac{P \xrightarrow{\overline{x}y} P'}{\boldsymbol{\nu}\, y\, P \xrightarrow{\overline{x}(y)} P'} \quad x \neq y\,.$$

(We can make an analogy between bound output and silent prefix: Both can be viewed as derived operators — $\tau.P$ as abbreviation for $\boldsymbol{\nu}\, x\, (x.\, P \mid \overline{x})$, for some x not free in P; and both are needed in the operational semantics and axiomatisations.)

Having noticed the importance of bound output, we can reasonably add it to the grammar of prefixes:

$$\alpha ::= \tau \mid x(y) \mid \overline{x}y \mid \overline{x}(y)\,.$$

The new syntax still contains asymmetries: First, the free-output construct has no input counterpart. Second, input and bound output, although syntactically similar — both are binders — are semantically very far apart, as revealed by the interactions they can participate in: *Any* name can be received through an input, whereas only a *fresh* name can be emitted through a bound output.

We move to πI by eliminating the free output construct.

Definition 1 (finite πI). The class of finite πI processes is described by the following grammar:

$$P ::= \sum_{i \in I} \alpha_i . P_i \mid P \mid P \mid \nu x\, P$$

$$\alpha ::= \tau \mid x(y) \mid \overline{x}(y) .$$

In πI, the input and output constructs are truly symmetric: Since only outputs of private names are possible, an input $x(y). P$ means "receive a fresh name at x", which is precisely the dual of the output $\overline{x}(y). P$. Indeed, we can define an operation "`dual`" which transforms every output into an input and vice versa: The symmetry of the calculus is then manifested by the fact that `dual` commutes with the transition relation (Lemma 2).

2.2. Internal and external mobility Above, the motivation to the introduction of πI was symmetry. A more pragmatic motivation is given here.

What distinguishes π-calculus from CCS is *mobility*, that is, the possibility that the communication linkage among processes changes at run-time. In the π-calculus there are two mechanisms to achieve mobility, which are embodied in the two communication rules of the calculus (usually called COM and CLOSE). Accordingly, we can distinguish between two forms of mobility, *internal mobility* and *external mobility*. Internal mobility shows up when a bound output meets an input, for instance thus:

$$\overline{x}(y). P \mid x(y). Q \xrightarrow{\tau} \nu y\, (P \mid Q) .$$

Two separate local (i.e., internal) names are identified and become a single local name. The two participants in the interaction, $\overline{x}(y). P$ and $x(y). Q$, agree on the bound name; for this, some alpha conversion might have to be used. The interaction consumes the two prefixes but leave unchanged the derivatives underneath. With internal mobility, alpha conversion is the only form of name substitution involved.

External mobility shows up when a free output meets an input, for instance thus:

$$\overline{x}y. P \mid x(z). Q \xrightarrow{\tau} P \mid Q\{y/z\} .$$

Here, a local name gets identified with a free (i.e., external) name. In this case, alpha conversion is not enough: Name y is free, and might occur in Q; hence in general z cannot be alpha converted to y. Instead, a substitution must be imposed on the derivatives so to force the equality between y and z.

In πI, only internal mobility is present. Studying πI means examining internal mobility in isolation, and investigating its impact on expressiveness and mathematical theory. From the experimentation that we have conducted so far, it appears that internal mobility is responsible for much of the expressiveness of the π-calculus, whereas external mobility is responsible for much of the semantic complications. Some evidence to this will be given in the remaining sections.

2.3. Some advantages of the theory of πI Through examples, we show a few weaknesses of the theory of the π-calculus, and we show why they do not arise in πI.

Below, $\sim_\pi$ denotes π-calculus original bisimilarity, as in [MPW92]; it is sometimes called *late bisimilarity.* (The examples we use are rather simple, so we do not need to recall the definition of $\sim_\pi$.) Consider the π-calculus process $x \mid \overline{y}$, where x and y are different names. We can rewrite it as follows, using expansion:

$$x \mid \overline{y} \sim_\pi x.\overline{y} + \overline{y}.x\,. \tag{1}$$

However, this equality can break down underneath an input prefix:

$$z(x).(x \mid \overline{y}) \not\sim_\pi z(x).(x.\overline{y} + \overline{y}.x)\,. \tag{2}$$

The process on the left-hand side can receive y in the input and become $y \mid \overline{y}$, which then can terminate after a silent step. This behaviour is not matched by the process $z(x).(x.\overline{y} + \overline{y}.x)$, which, upon receiving y, can only terminate after two visible actions.

To have a fully-substitutive equality, some case analysis has to be added to the expansion (1), by means of the *match* operator:

$$x \mid \overline{y} \sim_\pi x.\overline{y} + \overline{y}.x + [x = y]\tau\,.$$

The third summand allows a τ if x and y are the same name. This equality can now be used underneath a prefix:

$$z(x).(x \mid \overline{y}) \sim_\pi z(x).(x.\overline{y} + \overline{y}.x + [x = y]\tau)\,.$$

The above discussion outlines two important points: First, π-calculus bisimilarity is not preserved by input prefix; second, to get congruence equalities some case analysis on names might be needed. In the above example, one level of case analysis was enough, but for more complex processes it can be heavier; the mismatch operator might be needed too. In general, if in the π-calculus we wish to manipulate a subcomponent P of a given process algebraically, then we cannot assume that the free names of P will always be different with each other: By the time the computation point has reached P, some of these names might have become equal. Therefore we have to take into account all possible equalities and inequalities among these names; if they are n, then there are 2^n cases to consider.

These inconvenients do not arise in πI. Bisimilarity is naturally a full congruence, and no case analysis on names is required. For instance, consider processes $x \mid \overline{y}$ and $x.\overline{y} + \overline{y}.x$ in (1), and let $\sim$ be πI bisimilarity. As in the π-calculus, so in πI the two processes are bisimilar; but, unlike the π-calculus, their bisimilarity is preserved by input prefix:

$$z(x).(x \mid \overline{y}) \sim z(x).(x.\overline{y} + \overline{y}.x)\,.$$

This because in πI only fresh names are communicated, hence the free name y can never be received in an input at z. The absence of case analysis explains why match has not been included among the πI operators.

Besides late bisimilarity, other formulations of bisimilarity for the π-calculus have appeared in the literature (see [FMQ94]), and it is far from clear which one should be preferred. (Some of these relations are full congruences, but all require the case analysis on names mentioned before.) The differences among these bisimilarities are due to the different interpretation of name substitution in an input action. The choice is about *when* should such a substitution be made: For instance immediately, in the input rule, or later, in the communication rule, or only when the name received is needed. The choice affects the resulting behavioural equivalence, since a substitution can change the relationships of equality or inequality among names. In πI, alpha conversion is the only form of name substitution needed. Alpha conversion is semantically harmless, because it does not change the equalities and inequalities among names; hence in πI the bisimilarity relation is unique.

3 Basic theory of πI

We consider the basic theory of πI: Operational semantics, bisimilarity, axiomatisation, construction of canonical normal forms. In all these cases, a clause for alpha conversion represents the only difference w.r.t. the theory of CCS. An exception to this is the appearance of a restriction in the communication rule for πI.

3.1. Operational semantics and bisimilarity We write $\overline{\alpha}$ for the complementary of α; that is, if $\alpha = x(y)$ then $\overline{\alpha} = \overline{x}(y)$, if $\alpha = \overline{x}(y)$ then $\overline{\alpha} = x(y)$, and if $\overline{\alpha} = \tau$, then $\overline{\alpha} = \alpha$. We write $P \equiv_\alpha Q$ if P and Q are alpha convertible. We write $\mathrm{fn}(P), \mathrm{bn}(P)$ (resp. $\mathrm{fn}(\alpha), \mathrm{bn}(\alpha)$) for the *free names* and the *bound names* of P (resp. α). The *names* of P or α, written $\mathrm{n}(P)$ and $\mathrm{n}(\alpha)$, are the union of their free and bound names. Table 1 contains the set of the transition rules for πI. We have omitted the symmetric of rule PAR. The only formal difference w.r.t. the set of rules for CCS is the presence of the alpha conversion rule and the generation of a restriction in the communication rule. Unlike the π-calculus, there is only one rule for communication and one rule for the restriction operator. Note that the alphabet of actions is the same as the alphabet of prefixes. We call a transition $P \stackrel{\tau}{\longrightarrow} P'$ a *reduction*.

We define an operation `dual` which complements all visible prefixes of a πI process: If $P \in \pi$I, then $\overline{P}$ is obtained from P by transforming every prefix α into the prefix $\overline{\alpha}$. Operation `dual` can be defined on πI because of its *syntactic* symmetry. The following lemma shows that the symmetry is also *semantic*.

Lemma 2. *If $P \stackrel{\alpha}{\longrightarrow} P'$, then $\overline{P} \stackrel{\overline{\alpha}}{\longrightarrow} \overline{P'}$.* □

Note that since $\overline{\overline{P}} = P$, the converse of Lemma 2 holds too.

$$\text{ALPHA: } \frac{P \equiv_\alpha P' \qquad P' \xrightarrow{\alpha} P''}{P \xrightarrow{\alpha} P''} \qquad \text{PRE: } \alpha.\, P \xrightarrow{\alpha} P$$

$$\text{PAR: } \frac{P \xrightarrow{\alpha} P'}{P \mid Q \xrightarrow{\alpha} P' \mid Q} \text{ if } \mathrm{bn}(\alpha) \cap \mathrm{fn}(Q) = \emptyset \qquad \text{RES: } \frac{P \xrightarrow{\alpha} P'}{\boldsymbol{\nu}\, x\, P \xrightarrow{\alpha} \boldsymbol{\nu}\, x\, P'} \text{ if } x \notin \mathrm{n}(\alpha)$$

$$\text{COM: } \frac{P \xrightarrow{\alpha} P' \qquad Q \xrightarrow{\overline{\alpha}} Q'}{P \mid Q \xrightarrow{\tau} \boldsymbol{\nu}\, x\, (P' \mid Q')} \text{ for } \alpha \neq \tau,\, x = \mathrm{bn}(\alpha) \quad \text{SUM: } \frac{P_i \xrightarrow{\alpha} P_i',\ i \in I}{\sum_{i \in I} P_i \xrightarrow{\alpha} P_i'}$$

Table 1. The transition system for πI

Definition 3 (πI strong bisimilarity). *Strong bisimilarity* is the largest symmetric relation $\sim$ on πI processes s.t. $P \sim Q$ and $P \xrightarrow{\alpha} P'$, with $\mathrm{bn}(\alpha) \cap \mathrm{fn}(Q) = \emptyset$, imply that there is Q' s.t. $Q \xrightarrow{\alpha} Q'$ and $P' \sim Q'$.

By contrast with πI bisimilarity, in π-calculus bisimilarity [MPW92] the clauses for input and output must be distinguished, the reason being that input and output are not symmetric.

Lemmas 4 and 5 are technical results useful to deal with the alpha convertibility clause on processes and transitions. Lemma 5 shows that bisimilarity is preserved by injective substitutions on names.

Lemma 4. If $P \equiv_\alpha Q$, then $P \sim Q$. □

Lemma 5. If $y \notin fn(P)$, then for all x, $P \sim Q$ implies $P\{y/x\} \sim Q\{y/x\}$. □

Proposition 6 (congruence for $\sim$). *Strong bisimilarity is a congruence.*

PROOF: By showing that it is preserved by all operators of the language. Each case is simple. For instance, for prefixes, one shows that $\{(\alpha.\, P, \alpha.\, Q)\} \cup \sim$ is a strong bisimulation. The move $\alpha.\, P \xrightarrow{\alpha} P$ is matched by $\alpha.\, Q \xrightarrow{\alpha} Q$; this is enough even if α is an input prefix, since no instantiation of the bound name is required. □

Weak transitions and weak bisimilarity, written $\approx$, are defined in the expected way. As strong bisimilarity, so weak bisimilarity is preserved by all operators of the language.[1]

3.2. Axiomatisation We show a sound and complete axiomatisation for strong bisimilarity over finite πI processes.

To have more readable axioms, it is convenient to decompose sums $\sum_{i \in I} \alpha_i.\, P_i$ into binary sums. Thus we assume that sums are generated by the grammar

$$M := M + N \mid \alpha.\, P \mid \mathbf{0}\,.$$

[1] The congruence is not broken by sum because of the guarded form of our sums.

We let M, N, L range over such terms. The axiom system is reported in Table 2; we call it $\mathcal{A}$. We write $\mathcal{A} \vdash P = Q$ if $P = Q$ can be inferred from the axioms in $\mathcal{A}$ using equational reasoning.

Alpha-conversion:	If P and Q alpha-convertible then	$P = Q$
Summation:	$M + \mathbf{0} = M$	$M + N = N + M$
	$M + (N + L) = (M + N) + L$	$M + M = M$
Restriction:	if, for all $i \in I$, $x \notin \mathrm{n}(\alpha_i)$ then	$\boldsymbol{\nu} x\,(\sum_i \alpha_i.\, P_i) = \sum_i \alpha_i.\, \boldsymbol{\nu} x\, P_i$
	if x is the subject of α then	$\boldsymbol{\nu} x\,(M + \alpha.\, P) = \boldsymbol{\nu} x\, M$

Expansion:

Assume that $P = \sum_i \alpha_i.\, P_i$ and $Q = \sum_j \beta_j.\, Q_j$, and that for all i and j with $\alpha_i, \beta_j \neq \tau$, it holds that $\mathrm{bn}(\alpha_i) = \mathrm{bn}(\beta_j) = x \notin \mathrm{fn}(P, Q)$. Then infer

$$P \mid Q = \sum_i \alpha_i.\, (P_i \mid Q) + \sum_j \beta_j.\, (P \mid Q_j) + \sum_{\alpha_i \; opp \; \beta_j} \tau.\, \boldsymbol{\nu} x\, (P_i \mid Q_j)$$

where α_i *opp* β_j holds if $\alpha_i = \overline{\beta_j}$.

Table 2. The axiom system for finite πI processes

Theorem 7 (soundness and completeness). $P \sim Q$ iff $\mathcal{A} \vdash P = Q$. □

Omitting the axiom for alpha conversion and the bound name x in the expansion scheme, the axioms of Table 2 form a standard axiom system for strong bisimilarity of CCS. Also the proofs of soundness and completeness for the πI axiomatisation are very similar to those for CCS [Mil89]. For instance, as in CCS, so in the completeness proof for πI a restriction can be pushed down into the tree structure of a process until either a $\mathbf{0}$ process is reached, or a $\mathbf{0}$ process is introduced by cutting branches of the tree, and then the restriction disappears.

The proof of completeness of the axiomatisation [San95] exploits a transformation of processes to normal forms, that is tree-like structures built from the operators of sum, prefixing and $\mathbf{0}$. Then the axioms for commutativity, associativity and idempotence of sum, and alpha conversion can be used to obtain canonical and minimal representatives for the equivalence classes of $\sim$. Again, this mimics a well-known procedure for CCS.

4 Extending the signature of the finite and monadic πI

4.1. Infinite processes To express processes with an infinite behaviour, we add recursive agent definitions to the language of finite πI processes. We assume a set of constants, ranged over by D, each of which has a non-negative *arity*, and add the production

$$P ::= D\langle\widetilde{x}\rangle$$

to the grammar of Definition 1. It is assumed that each constant D has a unique defining equation of the form $D \stackrel{\text{def}}{=} (\widetilde{x})\, P$. Both in a constant definition $D \stackrel{\text{def}}{=} (\widetilde{x})\, P$ and in a constant application $D\langle\widetilde{x}\rangle$, the parameter $\widetilde{x}$ is a tuple of all distinct names whose length equals the arity of D.

The constraint that the actual parameters $\widetilde{x}$ in a constant application should be distinct — normally not required in the π-calculus — ensures that alpha conversion remains the only relevant form of name substitution in πI. The transition rule for constants is:

$$\frac{P \stackrel{\alpha}{\longrightarrow} P'}{D\langle\widetilde{x}\rangle \stackrel{\alpha}{\longrightarrow} P'} \text{if } D \stackrel{\text{def}}{=} (\widetilde{y})\, Q \text{ and } (\widetilde{y})\, Q \equiv_\alpha (\widetilde{x})\, P\,.$$

4.2. Polyadicity The calculi seen so far are *monadic*, in that precisely *one* name is exchanged in any communication. We extend these calculi with polyadic communications following existing polyadic formulations of the π-calculus [Mil91]. The operational semantics and the algebraic theory of the polyadic πI are straightforward generalisations of those of the monadic πI, and will be omitted.

The syntax of the polyadic πI only differs from that of the monadic calculus because the object part of prefixes is a tuple of names:

$$\alpha ::= \tau \;\mid\; x(\widetilde{y}) \;\mid\; \overline{x}(\widetilde{y})\,.$$

Names in $\widetilde{y}$ are all pairwise different. When $\widetilde{y}$ is empty, we omit the surrounding parenthesis.

As in the π-calculus [Mil91, section 3.1], so in πI the move to polyadicity does not increase expressiveness: A polyadic interaction can be simulated using monadic interactions and auxiliary fresh names.

4.3. Typing Having polyadicity, one needs to impose some discipline on names so to avoid run-time arity mismatchings in interactions, as for $x(y).\,P\,|\,\overline{x}(y,z).\,Q$. In the π-calculus, this discipline is achieved by means of a *typing system* (in the literature it is sometimes called *sorting system*; in this paper we shall prefer the word "type" to "sort"). A typing allows us to specify the arity of a name and, recursively, of the names carried by that name. The same formal systems can be used for the typing of πI. (However, the typed πI enjoys a few properties which are not true in the typed π-calculus; one such property is that the *by-structure* and *by-name* definitons of equality between types [PS93] coincide.) We shall not present the type system here; an extensive treatment is in [San95].

4.4. Recursion versus replication Some presentations of the π-calculus have the replication operator in place of recursion. A replication $!P$ stands for an infinite number of copies of P in parallel, and is easily definable in terms of recursion. The typing system of πI, as well as that of the π-calculus, allows recursive types. However, if in πI recursion is replaced by replication, then all processes can be typed without the use of recursive types. Starting from this observation, in [San95] we show that recursion cannot be encoded in terms of replication. This contrasts with the π-calculus, where recursion and replication are interdefinable [Mil91].

5 The encoding of the λ-calculus

πI appears to have considerable expressiveness. We have examined various non-trivial applications, which include the encodings of values and data structures, the λ-calculus, agent-passing calculi, and the locality and causality relations among actions of processes. Values and data structures can be modelled in πI in the same way as they are in π-calculus: The π-calculus representations given by Milner [Mil91, Sections 3.3., 6.2 and 6.3] only utilise the πI operators. Also, the encodings of locality and causality into π-calculus in (see [BS95]) can be easily adapted to πI. More interesting is the encoding of the λ-calculus and of agent-passing calculi. We look at the λ-calculus here, and sketch the study of agent-passing calculi in Section 6.

In this section, $M, N, \ldots$ are λ-calculus terms, whose syntax is given by

$$M := x \mid \lambda x.M \mid MM$$

where x and y range over λ-calculus variables. In Abramsky's *lazy lambda calculus* [Abr89], the redex is always at the extreme left of a term. There are two reduction rules:

$$\texttt{beta:}\quad (\lambda x.M)N \Longrightarrow M\{N/x\}\,, \qquad\qquad \texttt{app-L:}\quad \frac{M \Longrightarrow M'}{MN \Longrightarrow M'N}\,.$$

We first encode the *linear* lazy λ-calculus, in which no subterm of a term may contain more than one occurrence of x, for any variable x. We begin by recalling Milner's encoding $\mathcal{C}$ into the π-calculus. Then we describe the changings to be made to obtain an encoding $\mathcal{P}$ into πI. Both encodings are presented in Table 3. The core of any encoding of the λ-calculus into a process calculus is the translation of function application. This normally becomes a particular form of parallel combination of two agents, the function and its argument; beta-reduction is then modeled as process reduction.

Let us examine $\mathcal{C}$. In the pure λ-calculus, every term denotes a function. When supplied with an argument, it yields another function. Analogously, the translation of a λ-term M is a process with a location p. It rests dormant until it receives along p two names: The first is a trigger x for its argument and the second is the location to be used for the next interaction. The location of a term M is the unique port along which M interacts with its environment. Two types of names are used in the encoding: *Location names*, ranged over by p, q and r, and *trigger names*, ranger over by x, y and z. For simplicity, we have assumed that the set of trigger names is the same as the set of λ-variables. More details on this encoding and a study of its correctness can be found in [Mil91, San92].

The encoding into π-calculus; $\overline{r}(x)p.-$ is an output prefix at r in which the private name x and the free name p are emitted.

$$\mathcal{C}[\![\lambda x.M]\!]_p \stackrel{\text{def}}{=} p(x,q).\,\mathcal{C}[\![M]\!]_q$$

$$\mathcal{C}[\![x]\!]_p \stackrel{\text{def}}{=} \overline{x}p$$

$$\mathcal{C}[\![MN]\!]_p \stackrel{\text{def}}{=} \boldsymbol{\nu}\, r\,(\mathcal{C}[\![M]\!]_r \mid \overline{r}(x)p.\,x(q).\,\mathcal{C}[\![N]\!]_q) \qquad x \text{ fresh}$$

....

The encoding into πI:

$$\mathcal{P}[\![\lambda x.M]\!]_p \stackrel{\text{def}}{=} \overline{p}(w).\,w(x,q).\,\mathcal{P}[\![M]\!]_q$$

$$\mathcal{P}[\![x]\!]_p \stackrel{\text{def}}{=} \overline{x}(r).\,r \rightarrow p$$

$$\mathcal{P}[\![MN]\!]_p \stackrel{\text{def}}{=} \boldsymbol{\nu}\, r\,(\mathcal{P}[\![M]\!]_r \mid r(w).\,\overline{w}(x,q').\,(q' \rightarrow p \mid x(q).\,\mathcal{P}[\![N]\!]_q) \qquad x \text{ fresh}$$

Table 3. The encodings of the linear lazy λ-calculus

Encoding $\mathcal{C}$ is not an encoding into πI because there are outputs of free names, one in the rule for variables, and one in the rule for applications. Indeed, the free output construct plays an important role in $\mathcal{C}$: It is used to redirect location names which, in this way, can bounce an unbounded number of times before arresting as subject of a prefix.

Encoding $\mathcal{P}$ is obtained from $\mathcal{C}$ with two modifications. First, the output of a free name b is replaced by the output of a bound name c plus a *link* from c to b, written $c \rightarrow b$. Names b and c are "connected" by the link, in the sense that a process performing an output at c and a process performing an input at b can interact, asynchronously, through the link. In other words, a link behaves a little like a name buffer: It receives names at one end-point and transmit names at the other end-point. However, the latter names are not the same as the former names — as it would be in a real buffer — but, instead, are *linked* to them: This accounts for the recursion in the definition of links below. For tuples of names $\widetilde{u} = u_1, \ldots, u_n$ and $\widetilde{v} = v_1, \ldots, v_n$ we write $\widetilde{u} \rightarrow \widetilde{v}$ to abbreviate $u_1 \rightarrow v_1 \mid \ldots \mid u_n \rightarrow v_n$.

If a and b have the same type, then we define: $\quad a \rightarrow b \stackrel{\text{def}}{=} a(\widetilde{u}).\,\overline{b}(\widetilde{v}).\,\widetilde{v} \rightarrow \widetilde{u}$

(for convenience, we have left the parameters a and b of the link on the left-hand side of the definition). Note that the link is ephemeral for a and b — they can only be used once — and that it inverts its direction at each cycle — the recursive call creates links from the objects of b to the objects of a. Both these features are tailored to the specific application in exam, namely the encoding of the lazy λ-calculus.

The other difference between encodings $\mathcal{C}$ and $\mathcal{P}$ is that the latter has a level of indirection in the rule for abstraction. A term signals to be an abstraction before receiving the actual arguments. This is implemented using a new type of names, ranged over by w. This modification could be avoided using more sophisticated links, but they would complicate the proofs in Lemma 8.

When reasoning about encoding $\mathcal{P}$, one does not have to remember the definition of links; the algebraic properties of links in Lemma 8 are enough. Assertion (1) of this lemma shows that two links with a common hidden end-point behave like a single link; assertions (2) and (3) show that a link with a hidden end-point acts as a substitution on the encoding of a λ-term.

Lemma 8. *Let M be a linear λ-term.*

1. *If a, b and c are distinct names of the same type, then* $\nu\, b\,(a \to b \mid b \to c) \approx a \to c$.
2. *If x and y are distinct trigger names and y is not free in M, then* $\nu\, x\,(x \to y \mid \mathcal{P}[\![M]\!]_r) \approx \mathcal{P}[\![M\{y/x\}]\!]_p$.
3. *If p and r are distinct location names, then* $\nu\, r\,(r \to p \mid \mathcal{P}[\![M]\!]_r) \approx \mathcal{P}[\![M]\!]_p$.

The main result needed to convince ourselves of the correctness of $\mathcal{P}$ is the validity of beta-reduction. The proof is conceptually the same as the proof of validity of beta-reduction for Milner's encoding into π-calculus; in addition, one has to use Lemma 8(3).

Theorem 9. *For all M, N, p it holds that* $\mathcal{P}[\![(\lambda.xM)N]\!]_p \approx \mathcal{P}[\![M\{N/x\}]\!]_p$. □

To encode the full lazy λ-calculus, where a variable may occur free in a term more than once, the argument of an application must be made persistent. This is achieved by adding, in both encodings $\mathcal{C}$ and $\mathcal{P}$, a replication in front of the prefix $x(q).-$, in the rule for application (recall that replication is a derived operator in a calculus with recursion). In addition, for $\mathcal{P}$ also the link for trigger names must be made persistent, so that it can serve the possible multiple occurrences of a trigger in a term. Thus

if x and y are trigger names, then we define: $\quad x \to y \stackrel{\text{def}}{=} !\, x(\tilde{u}).\, \overline{y}(\tilde{v}).\, \tilde{v} \to \tilde{u}\,.$

In this way, Lemma 8 and Theorem 9 remain true for the full lazy λ-calculus.

Links — as defined here, or variants of them — can be used to increase the parallelism of processes. For instance, adding links in the encoding of λ-abstractions, as below, gives an encoding of a *strong lazy* strategy, where reductions can also occur underneath an abstraction (i.e., the `Xi` rule, saying that if $M \longrightarrow M'$ then $\lambda x.\, M \longrightarrow \lambda x.\, M'$, is now allowed):

$$\mathcal{P}[\![\lambda x.M]\!]_p \stackrel{\text{def}}{=} \nu\, q, x\, \big(\overline{p}(w).\, w(y, r).\, (q \to r \mid x \to y) \mid \mathcal{P}[\![M]\!]_q\big)\,.$$

In the lazy λ-calculus encoding, there is a rigid sequentialisation between the behaviour of (the encodings of) the head $\lambda x.-$ and of the body M of the abstraction: The latter cannot do anything until the former has supplied it with its arguments x and q. In the strong-lazy encoding, the *only* dependencies of the body from the head are given by the actions in which these arguments appear; any other activity of the body can proceed independently from the activity of the head.

6 Relationship with agent-passing process calculi

We have used πI and subcalculi of it, to study the expressiveness of *agent-passing process calculi* (they are sometimes called *higher-order* process calculi in the literature). In these calculi, agents, i.e., terms of the language, can be passed as values in communications. The agent-passing paradigm is often presented in opposition to the *name-passing* paradigm, followed by π-calculus and related calculi, where mobility is modelled using communication of names, rather than of agents. An important criterion for assessing the value of the two paradigms is the expressiveness which can be achieved. Below, we briefly summarise work reported in [San95].

6.1. A hierarchy of πI subcalculi Using the typing system of πI and imposing constraints on it, we have defined a hierarchy of calculi $\{\pi\mathrm{I}^n\}_{n\leq\omega}$. A calculus $\pi\mathrm{I}^n$ includes those πI processes which can be typed using types of order n or less than n, and $\pi\mathrm{I}^\omega$ is the union of the $\pi\mathrm{I}^n$'s. Instead of giving the formal definition of the order of a type, we explain — very informally — what syntactic constraints the orders of types impose on processes. Take a process in which the bound names are all distinct from each other and from the free names; we say that a name of this process *depends on* another name if the latter carries the former. For instance, in process $x(y).\,\overline{y}(z).\,z.\,\mathbf{0}$, name y depends on x and z depends on y. A *dependency chain* is a sequence $x_1, \ldots, x_n$ of names s.t. x_{i+1} depends on x_i, for all $1 < i \leq n$. Thus the processes in $\pi\mathrm{I}^n$ are those which have *dependency chains* among names of length at most n. For instance, process $x(y).\,\overline{y}(z).\,z.\,\mathbf{0}$ is in $\pi\mathrm{I}^n$, for all $n \geq 3$, since its maximal dependency chain has length 3, involving names x, y and z. Calculus $\pi\mathrm{I}^1$ includes processes like $a.\,b\,|\,\overline{a}.\,\overline{b}$ in which names are only used for pure synchronisation; $\pi\mathrm{I}^1$ represents the core of CCS. $\pi\mathrm{I}^2$ includes processes like

$$x(y,z).\,(\overline{y}\mid z) \qquad \text{and} \qquad y.\,x(z).\,\overline{y}.\,z$$

where if a name carries another name, then the latter can only be used for pure synchronisation. A technical remark: The syntax of the calculi $\{\pi\mathrm{I}^n\}_{n\leq\omega}$, in [San95], uses the replication operator in place of recursion; this makes sense because, as mentioned at the end of Section 4, the typability of the processes which use replication does not require recursive types (i.e, all types have a bounded order).

Intuitively, the calculi $\pi\mathrm{I}^1, \pi\mathrm{I}^2, \ldots, \pi\mathrm{I}^n, \ldots \pi\mathrm{I}^\omega, \pi\mathrm{I}$ are distinguished by the "degree" of mobility allowed; indeed, if mobility is taken into account, then they form a hierarchy of calculi of strictly increasing expressiveness.

6.2. Correspondence with a hierarchy of agent-passing process calculi Agent-passing developments of CCS are the calculi *Plain CHOCS* [Tho90], and *Strictly-Higher-Order π-calculus*; the latter, abbreviated HOπ^ω, is the fragment of the Higher-Order π-calculus [San92] which is purely higher order, i.e., no name-passing feature is present. In Plain CHOCS processes only can be exchanged. In HOπ^ω besides processes also abstractions, i.e., functions from agents to agents, of arbitrary high order can be exchanged. Roughly, $\mathrm{HO}\pi^\omega$ is as an extension of CCS with the constructs of the simply-typed λ-calculus, namely variable X, abstraction $(X)\,A$ (it would be written $\lambda X.\,A$ in a λ-calculus notation) and application $A\langle B\rangle$ (where B is the argument of the application). An example of abstraction is $F \stackrel{\mathrm{def}}{=} (X)\,(P \mid X)$: It represents a function from processes to processes, where the process-argument is run in parallel with P in the process-result; for instance, $F\langle Q\rangle$ beta-reduces to $P|Q$. An abstraction one order higher than F is $G \stackrel{\mathrm{def}}{=} (Y)\,(P \,|\, Y\langle Q\rangle)$, which takes abstractions of the same type as F as argument. The application $G\langle F\rangle$ beta-reduces to $P \mid P \mid Q$. The types used in $\mathrm{HO}\pi^\omega$ are those of the simply-typed λ-calculus with the process type $\bullet$ as the only first-order (i.e., basic) type. For instance, the abstractions F and G above have types $\bullet \longrightarrow \bullet$ and $(\bullet \longrightarrow \bullet) \longrightarrow \bullet$, respectively. The order of a type is determined by the level of arrow-nesting in its definition.

As in πI, so in $\mathrm{HO}\pi^\omega$ we can discriminate processes according to order of the types needed in the typing. This yields a hierarchy of agent-passing calculi $\{\mathrm{HO}\pi^n\}_{n<\omega}$, where $\mathrm{HO}\pi^1$ coincides with $\pi\mathrm{I}^1$ — hence with the core of CCS — and $\mathrm{HO}\pi^2$ is the core of Plain CHOCS. For each $n \le \omega$, we have compared the agent-passing calculus $\mathrm{HO}\pi^n$ with the name-passing calculus $\pi\mathrm{I}^{n-}$; the latter is a subcalculus of $\pi\mathrm{I}^n$ whose processes respect a discipline on the input and output usage of names similar to those studied in [PS93]. We have showed that $\mathrm{HO}\pi^n$ and $\pi\mathrm{I}^{n-}$ have the same expressiveness, by exhibiting faithful encodings of $\mathrm{HO}\pi^n$ into $\pi\mathrm{I}^{n-}$ and of $\pi\mathrm{I}^{n-}$ into $\mathrm{HO}\pi^n$. The encodings are fully abstract w.r.t. the reduction relations of the two calculi. (The encoding from $\mathrm{HO}\pi^n$ to $\pi\mathrm{I}^{n-}$ is a special case of the compilation of the full Higher-Order π-calculus into π-calculus studied in [San92]; the communication of an agent is translated as the communication of a private name with which the recipient can activate a copy of the agent.) Note in particular the correspondence between $\mathrm{HO}\pi^2$ and $\pi\mathrm{I}^{2-}$: Process passing only gives little expressiveness more than CCS.

These results establish an exact connection between agent-passing calculi and name-passing calculi based on internal mobility, and strengthen the relevance of the latter calculi.

7 Future work

We wish to develop the study of the expressiveness of πI, which we expect to be rather close to that of the π-calculus. The translation of the λ-calculus presented is obtained by refining Milner's encoding into the π-calculus, which makes non-trivial use of the free-output construct — disallowed in πI. We hope that the encoding might also give insights into the comparison between πI and π-calculus.

For the translation of the λ-calculus, we first adopted Abramsky's *lazy* reduction strategy. Our encoding of it uses special πI processes called *links*. We believe that understanding the algebraic properties of links can be helpful to justify transformations of processes aimed at augmenting their parallelism. For instance, in Section 5 by manipulating links we have modified the encoding of the lazy strategy into an encoding of a *strong-lazy* strategy which is more permissive (i.e., more parallel) because it also allows reductions inside abstractions (the `Xi` rule). At present we are studying the properties of this encoding. We are not aware of other encodings, into a process algebra, of λ-calculus strategies encompassing the `Xi` rule.

We have showed that name-passing process calculi based on internal mobility have a simple algebraic theory, in which the main difference from the theory of CCS is the use of alpha conversion. These calculi also possess a pleasant symmetry in their communication constructs. These features might become useful in the development of denotational models.

References

[Abr89] S. Abramsky. The lazy lambda calculus. In D. Turner, editor, *Research Topics in Functional Programming*, pages 65–116. Addison-Wesley, 1989.

[BK85] J.A. Bergstra and J.W. Klop. Algebra for communicating processes with abstraction. *Theoretical Computer Science*, 37(1):77–121, 1985.

[BS95] M. Boreale and D. Sangiorgi. A fully abstract semantics for causality in the π-calculus. *Proc. STACS'95*, To appear.

[DKV91] P. Degano, S. Kasangian, and S. Vigna. Applications of the calculus of trees to process description languages. *Proc. CTCS '91*, LNCS 530, 1991.

[FMQ94] G. Ferrari, U. Montanari, and P. Quaglia. A π-calculus with explicit substitutions: the late semantics. *Proc. MFCS'94*, LNCS, 1994.

[Jon93] C.B. Jones. A π-calculus semantics for an object-based design notation. In E. Best, editor, *Proceedings of CONCUR '93*, LNCS 715, 1993.

[Mil89] R. Milner. *Communication and Concurrency*. Prentice Hall, 1989.

[Mil91] R. Milner. The polyadic π-calculus: a tutorial. Technical Report ECS–LFCS–91–180, LFCS, Dept. of Comp. Sci., Edinburgh Univ., October 1991.

[Mil92] R. Milner. Functions as processes. *Journal of Mathematical Structures in Computer Science*, 2(2):119–141, 1992.

[MPW92] R. Milner, J. Parrow, and D. Walker. A calculus of mobile processes, (Parts I and II). *Information and Computation*, 100:1–77, 1992.

[PS93] B. Pierce and D. Sangiorgi. Typing and subtyping for mobile processes. In *8th LICS Conf.*, pages 376–385. IEEE Computer Society Press, 1993.

[San92] D. Sangiorgi. *Expressing Mobility in Process Algebras: First-Order and Higher-Order Paradigms*. PhD thesis CST–99–93, Department of Computer Science, University of Edinburgh, 1992.

[San95] D. Sangiorgi. Full version of this paper. To Appear as Technical Report, INRIA-Sophia Antipolis, 1995.

[Tho90] B. Thomsen. *Calculi for Higher Order Communicating Systems*. PhD thesis, Department of Computing, Imperial College, 1990.

[Wal95] D. Walker. Objects in the π-calculus. *Information and Computation*, 1995. To appear.

Complete Inference Systems for Weak Bisimulation Equivalences in the π-Calculus

Huimin Lin*

Institute of Software, Chinese Academy of Sciences
P.O.Box 8718, Beijing 100080
E-mail: lhm@ios.ac.cn

Abstract

Proof systems for weak bisimulation equivalences in the π-calculus are presented, and their soundness and completeness are shown. The proofs of the completeness results rely on the notion of *symbolic bisimulation*. Two versions of π-calculus are investigated, one without and the other with the *mismatch* construction. For each version of the calculus proof systems for both *late* and *early* weak bisimulation equivalences are studied. Thus there are four proof systems in all. These proof systems are related in a natural way: the proof systems for early and late equivalences differ only in the inference rule for the input prefix, while the proof system for the version of π-calculus with mismatch is obtained by adding a single inference rule for the version without it.

1 Introduction

This paper aims to provide complete proof systems for weak bisimulation equivalences in the π-calculus. *Bisimulation equivalences* are among the most well-developed semantic theories for process calculi. The π-calculus inherits from *CCS* the invisible τ action, so the usual distinction between *strong* and *weak* bisimulations applies: the strong version gives the τ action the same weight as any other normal, or visible, actions, while the weak version ignores τ moves. As τ action is used to represent internal communication and as such is not observable, the weak equivalence is what used for practical applications. On the other hand, for message-passing process calculi, of which the π-calculus is a special instance, another distinction can be made, namely *late* and *early* bisimulations [MPW92, HL92], according to when input variables are instantiated. Thus for the π-calculus we have at least four bisimulation equivalences to study.

The original π-calculus paper [MPW92] only gave an axiomatisation for the *late* version of *strong* ground bisimulation. Subsequently, efforts have been made to formulate complete proof systems for other equivalences for this calculus: [PS93, BD94] for both early and late strong bisimulation congruences,

*This work has been supported by research grants from the President Fund of the Chinese Academy of Sciences and the Natural Science Foundation of China

[Hen91, BD92] for *testing* equivalence, and [San93] for (strong) *open bisimulation*. Axiomatisations for weak bisimulations are still missing, though it has been widely conjectured that they can be obtained by adding Milner's τ-laws to proof systems for strong equivalences.

In [Lin94b] we presented proof systems for strong bisimulation equivalences in the π-calculus. These proof systems consist of a set of inference rules together with some standard equations. The judgements of the inference systems are of the form

$$C \triangleright t = u$$

where t, u are π-calculus terms and C, called a *condition*, is a set of equality or inequality tests between names. It is important to note that C is *not* a construction in the π-calculus; it is a construction used in our meta language in order to reason about bisimulation equivalences for the calculus. To give a taste of the proof system, here is the inference rule for match:

$$\text{MATCH} \quad \frac{C \cup \{x = y\} \triangleright t = u \qquad C \cup \{x \neq y\} \triangleright \mathbf{0} = u}{C \triangleright [x = y]t = u}$$

It involves a case analysis: if we can establish $t = u$ under the condition $x = y$, and $\mathbf{0} = u$ under the condition $x \neq y$, then we can conclude $[x = y]t = u$. Here it can be seen clearly how the inequalities *in the meta-language* help to characterise constructions *in the calculus*. For the extension of the π-calculus with the *mismatch* operator, only a single inference rule, which is dual to the above rule for match, has to be added to the proof systems.

In this paper we shall extend these results to weak bisimulation equivalences. It turns out that, as in *CCS*, the three τ-laws ([Mil89]) are sufficient for this purpose. We shall demonstrate how, by exploiting the notion of *maximally consistent extensions* of a condition, the standard techniques used to prove the completeness results in *CCS* can be re-cast for the π-calculus.

As in *CCS*, weak bisimulations in the π-calculus are defined in terms of double arrows that abstract away τ-moves. But care must be taken in dealing with late equivalence: in this case input moves should not be allowed to absorb the τ-moves *after* them, for otherwise the resulted relation would not be transitive. Also as in *CCS*, weak bisimulations are not preserved by the choice operator, so we have to work with observation equivalences.

The proofs of the completeness results for our inference systems rely on the notion of *symbolic bisimulations* [HL92, HL93]. In [MPW92] a general notion of bisimulation, $\sim^D$, called *distinction indexed bisimulation*, is introduced, where the index D is a set of inequations on names such that $t \sim^D u$ *iff* $t\sigma \dot\sim u\sigma$ for every substitution σ that satisfies D. In the setting of the π-calculus, symbolic bisimulation is a mild generalisation of distinction indexed bisimulation, it is indexed by *conditions* consisting of name inequations *as well as* name equations. This generalisation makes it possible to give a direct definition of symbolic bisimulation (in terms of *symbolic transitional semantics*) instead of as substitution closure on top of ground bisimulation, which facilitates the proofs of the completeness results for the inference systems.

The main advantage of working with π-calculus over general message-passing calculi is that the language for the message domain is known: it is simply a set of *port names* upon which the only allowed operations are tests for equality and inequality. To define the notion of symbolic bisimulation for the π-calculus, we first develop a simple theory of *conditions* which are sets of equalities and inequalities over names. A *maximally consistent* condition is a *complete*, or *saturated*, condition, in the sense that adding to it anything not implied by it will result in inconsistency. This notion plays an important rôle in the definition of symbolic bisimulation and in the proofs of the completeness results.

The rest of this paper is organised as follows: The calculus and its semantics are introduced in the next section. The inference system is presented in Section 3, along with the completeness proof. Section 4 demonstrates how the theory developed for the late equivalence in the previous sections can be carried over to the early case. Section 5 discusses extensions to the calculus. The paper is concluded with Section 6, where related work is also discussed.

Due to space limitation, most of the proofs have been omitted. They can be found in the full version of this paper [Lin94a].

2 The π-Calculus And Bisimulations

2.1 Names and Conditions

The basic entities of the π-calculus are *names*, *i.e.* identifiers for communication channels. Let $\mathcal{N}$, ranged over by x, y, z, ... be a countably infinite set of names.

Conditions, ranged over by C, D, are finite sets of equality or inequality tests on names. We will write $n(C)$ for the set of names appearing in C. We say C is a condition on a name set V if $n(C) \subseteq V$. The empty condition will sometimes be denoted by *true*. *Matches*, ranged over by M, N, L, are special conditions which consist of only name equalities. Matches are part of the π-calculus, while conditions are only used in our meta-theory about the π-calculus, namely in the definition of symbolic bisimulations and in the formulation of inference rules.

Substitutions, ranged over by σ and δ, are mappings from $\mathcal{N}$ to $\mathcal{N}$, and $[\overline{y}/\overline{x}]$ is the substitution sending $\overline{x}$ to $\overline{y}$ and is identity otherwise. Substitutions are postfix operators, and have higher precedence than the operators in the language. If $\sigma = [\overline{y}/\overline{x}]$ then $n(\sigma) = \{\overline{y}\} \cup \{\overline{x}\}$. So for any $x \notin n(\sigma)$, $y\sigma = x$ *iff* $y = x$.

A substitution σ satisfies a condition C, written $\sigma \models C$, if $x\sigma = y\sigma$ for any $x = y \in C$ and $x\sigma \neq y\sigma$ for any $x \neq y \in C$. We write $C \Rightarrow D$ to mean that $\sigma \models C$ implies $\sigma \models D$ for any substitution σ.

The elements in a condition are treated as conjuncts. We avoid introducing disjunction into the theory of conditions. The major advantage is that the relation $C \Rightarrow D$ can be tested in linear time w.r.t the size of C and D:

Proposition 2.1 *The relation $C \Rightarrow D$ is linear time decidable.*

Allowing disjunction does not affect our theoretical results. The only consequence is that the above implication relation would in general take exponential time to decide.

Two substitutions σ and σ' are equal on V, written $\sigma =^V \sigma'$, if $x\sigma = x\sigma'$ for all $x \in V$. A condition C is *consistent* if there are no $x, y \in \mathcal{N}$ such that $C \Rightarrow x = y$ and $C \Rightarrow x \neq y$. C is *maximally consistent* on $V \subset \mathcal{N}$ if for any $x, y \in V$ either $C \Rightarrow x = y$ or $C \Rightarrow x \neq y$.

C' is a *maximally consistent extension* of C on V, written $C' \in MCE_V(C)$, if $C \subseteq C'$ and C' is maximally consistent on V. The set of maximally consistent extensions of a given condition on a finite set of names V is finite. We will abbreviate $MCE_V(true)$ as MC_V.

Lemma 2.2 $\bigvee MCE_V(C) = C$

Lemma 2.2 shows that the set of all consistent extensions of a condition (on a given name set) constitutes a boolean *partition* ([HL92, HL93]) of the condition.

Proposition 2.3 *Suppose C is maximally consistent on V. If σ and σ' both satisfy C, then $\sigma =^V \sigma'\delta$ for some injective substitution δ.*

2.2 The Language And Operational Semantics

The language of π-calculus can be given by the following BNF grammar

$$\begin{array}{lcl} t & ::= & \mathbf{0} \mid \alpha.t \mid t+t \mid [x=y]t \mid (x)t \mid t\,|\,t \mid A(y_1,...,y_n) \\ \alpha & ::= & \tau \mid a(x) \mid \overline{a}x \end{array}$$

We refer to [MPW92] for intended meanings of these operators.

In $a(x).t$ and $(x)t$ x is a bound name with scope t. We use $bn(t)$ and $fn(t)$ for the set of bound and free names in t, respectively. Bound names induce the notion of α-equivalence as usual. In the sequel we will not distinguish between α-equivalent terms, using $\equiv$ for both syntactical equality and α-equivalence. In the π-calculus no clear distinction is made between constants and variables, and we will call "processes" those terms whose free names are not to be instantiated.

The operational semantics of the language is reported in Figure 1, where a transition is of the form $t \xrightarrow{\alpha} u$ with α ranging over four kinds of actions: τ, $a(x)$, $\overline{a}x$ and $\overline{a}(x)$. We have omitted the symmetric rules for sum and par. Transitions are defined upto α-equivalence, i.e. α-equivalent terms are deemed to have the same transitions. Bound names for actions are defined by: $bn(a(x)) = bn(\overline{a}(x)) = \{x\}$ and $bn(\tau) = bn(\overline{a}x) = \emptyset$.

We write $\alpha =^C \beta$ to mean

$$\begin{array}{l} \text{if } \alpha \equiv \tau \text{ then } \beta \equiv \tau \\ \text{if } \alpha \equiv \overline{a}x \text{ then } \beta \equiv \overline{b}y \text{ and } C \Rightarrow a = b,\ C \Rightarrow x = y \\ \text{if } \alpha \equiv \overline{a}(x) \text{ then } \beta \equiv \overline{b}(x) \text{ and } C \Rightarrow a = b \\ \text{if } \alpha \equiv a(x) \text{ then } \beta \equiv b(x) \text{ and } C \Rightarrow a = b \end{array}$$

The transitions defined in Figure 1 are *concrete* in the sense that they will always be fired regardless the contexts in which terms are placed. In our work

$$\text{pre}\ \frac{}{\alpha.t \xrightarrow{\alpha} t} \qquad \text{match}\ \frac{t \xrightarrow{\alpha} t'}{[x=x]t \xrightarrow{\alpha} t'}$$

$$\text{sum}\ \frac{t \xrightarrow{\alpha} t'}{t+u \xrightarrow{\alpha} t'} \qquad \text{par}\ \frac{t \xrightarrow{\alpha} t'}{t \mid u \xrightarrow{\alpha} t' \mid u}\ bn(\alpha) \cap fn(u) = \emptyset$$

$$\text{res}\ \frac{t \xrightarrow{\alpha} t'}{(x)t \xrightarrow{\alpha} (x)t'}\ x \notin n(\alpha) \qquad \text{com}\ \frac{t \xrightarrow{a(x)} t' \quad u \xrightarrow{\overline{a}y} u'}{t \mid u \xrightarrow{\tau} t'[y/x] \mid u'}$$

$$\text{open}\ \frac{t \xrightarrow{\overline{a}x} t'}{(x)t \xrightarrow{\overline{a}(x)} t'}\ a \neq x \qquad \text{close}\ \frac{t \xrightarrow{a(x)} t' \quad u \xrightarrow{\overline{a}(x)} u'}{t \mid u \xrightarrow{\tau} (x)(t' \mid u')}$$

$$\text{id}\ \frac{t[y_1,...,y_n/x_1,...,x_n] \xrightarrow{\alpha} t'}{A(y_1,...,y_n) \xrightarrow{\alpha} t'}\ A(x_1,...,x_n) \stackrel{def}{=} t$$

Figure 1: π-Calculus Transitional Semantics

on general message-passing processes [HL92, HL93] we use a more abstract form of transitions called *symbolic transitions*. A symbolic transition takes the form $t \xrightarrow{b,\alpha} u$, where b is a boolean condition. Intuitively b represents the context under which action α can actually be fired from t. In the setting of the π-calculus b will be a set of *matches*, i.e. equality tests on names. This kind of transition has also been used in the work of open bisimulation by Sangiorgi [San93].

The symbolic transitional semantics of the π-calculus is given in Figure 2. For notational convenience we write MN for the union of M and N. Again the symmetric rules for Sum and Par have been omitted.

2.3 Weak Bisimulations

Strong bisimulations for the π-calculus and their proof systems have been studied in [Lin94b], so here we only consider weak equivalences. For the bulk of this paper we will concentrate on *late* bisimulation, and we will sketch in a later section how these results can be carried over to *early* bisimulation in a systematic manner. So until Section 4, the word "bisimulation" means "late bisimulation".

As in *CCS*, weak bisimulation is defined in terms of double arrows which ignore τ-moves. But late bisimulation insists that an input move from one process be matched by a *single* input move from the other. As a consequence, in defining late double arrows input moves should *not* be allowed to absorb τ moves *after* them.

The (concrete) late double arrow relation is generated by the following rules

- $p \stackrel{\varepsilon}{\Longrightarrow}_l p$.
- $p \xrightarrow{\alpha}_l q$ implies $p \stackrel{\alpha}{\Longrightarrow}_l q$.

$$\text{Pre}\ \frac{}{\alpha.t \xrightarrow{true,\alpha} t} \qquad \text{Match}\ \frac{t \xrightarrow{M,\alpha} t'}{[x=y]t \xrightarrow{ML,\alpha} t'}\ L = \left\{ \begin{array}{ll} x=y & \textit{if } x \neq y \\ \emptyset & \textit{otherwise} \end{array} \right.$$

$$\text{Sum}\ \frac{t \xrightarrow{M,\alpha} t'}{t+u \xrightarrow{M,\alpha} t'} \qquad \text{Par}\ \frac{t \xrightarrow{M,\alpha} t'}{t \mid u \xrightarrow{M,\alpha} t' \mid u}\ bn(\alpha) \cap fn(u) = \emptyset$$

$$\text{Res}\ \frac{t \xrightarrow{M,\alpha} t'}{(x)t \xrightarrow{M,\alpha} (x)t'}\ x \notin n(M,\alpha) \quad \text{Open}\ \frac{t \xrightarrow{M,\bar{a}x} t'}{(x)t \xrightarrow{M,\bar{a}(x)} t'}\ x \notin n(M,a)$$

$$\text{Com}\ \frac{t \xrightarrow{M,a(x)} t' \quad u \xrightarrow{N,\bar{b}y} u'}{t \mid u \xrightarrow{MNL,\tau} t'[y/x] \mid u'}\ L = \left\{ \begin{array}{ll} a=b & \textit{if } a \neq b \\ \emptyset & \textit{otherwise} \end{array} \right.$$

$$\text{Close}\ \frac{t \xrightarrow{M,a(x)} t' \quad u \xrightarrow{N,\bar{b}(x)} u'}{t \mid u \xrightarrow{MNL,\tau} (x)(t' \mid u')}\ L = \left\{ \begin{array}{ll} a=b & \textit{if } a \neq b \\ \emptyset & \textit{otherwise} \end{array} \right.$$

$$\text{Id}\ \frac{t[y_1,...,y_n/x_1,...,x_n] \xrightarrow{M,\alpha} t'}{A(y_1,...,y_n) \xrightarrow{M,\alpha} t'}\ A(x_1,...,x_n) \stackrel{def}{=} t$$

Figure 2: π-Calculus Symbolic Transitional Semantics

- $p \xrightarrow{\tau}_l \stackrel{\alpha}{\Longrightarrow}_l q$ implies $p \stackrel{\alpha}{\Longrightarrow}_l q$.
- If α does not have the form $a(x)$ then $p \stackrel{\alpha}{\Longrightarrow}_l \xrightarrow{\tau}_l q$ implies $p \stackrel{\alpha}{\Longrightarrow}_l q$.

Let $\stackrel{\hat{\tau}}{\Longrightarrow}_l$ be $\stackrel{\varepsilon}{\Longrightarrow}_l$, and $\stackrel{\hat{\alpha}}{\Longrightarrow}_l$ be $\stackrel{\alpha}{\Longrightarrow}_l$ for $\alpha \not\equiv \tau$.

Definition 2.4 A symmetric relation R is a late weak ground bisimulation if $(p,q) \in R$ implies:

- whenever $p \xrightarrow{a(x)} p'$ with $x \notin fn(p,q)$ then $q \stackrel{a(x)}{\Longrightarrow}_l q''$ for some q'' s.t for any y there is $q''[y/x] \stackrel{\hat{\tau}}{\Longrightarrow}_l q'$ and $(p'[y/x], q') \in R$.
- whenever $p \xrightarrow{\alpha} p'$ for any other action α with $bn(\alpha) \cap fn(p,q) = \emptyset$ then $q \stackrel{\hat{\alpha}}{\Longrightarrow}_l q'$ for some q' and $(p',q') \in R$.

Write $p \dot{\approx}_l q$ if there exists a late weak ground bisimulation R s.t. $(p,q) \in R$. t is late weak bisimular to u, written $t \approx_l u$, if $t\sigma \dot{\approx}_l u\sigma$ for every substitution σ. □

Similar to *CCS*, $\approx_l$ is not preserved by $+$. So we have to work with the modified relation:

Definition 2.5 p and q are late ground observation equivalent, written $p \dot{\simeq}_l q$, if

- whenever $p \xrightarrow{a(x)} p'$ with $x \notin fn(p,q)$ then $q \overset{a(x)}{\Longrightarrow}_l q''$ for some q'' s.t for any y there is $q''[y/x] \overset{\hat{\tau}}{\Longrightarrow}_l q'$ and $p'[y/x] \approx_l q'$.
- whenever $p \xrightarrow{\alpha} p'$ for any other action α with $bn(\alpha) \cap fn(p,q) = \emptyset$ then $q \overset{\alpha}{\Longrightarrow}_l q'$ for some q' and $p' \approx_l q'$.

And similarly for u.
t is late observation congruent to u, written $t \simeq_l u$, if $t\sigma \simeq_l u\sigma$ for every substitution σ. □

The late symbolic double arrows are defined as the least relations satisfying the following rules:

- $t \overset{true,\varepsilon}{\Longrightarrow}_L t$.
- $t \xrightarrow{M,\alpha}_L u$ implies $t \overset{M,\alpha}{\Longrightarrow}_L u$.
- $t \xrightarrow{M,\tau}_L \overset{N,\alpha}{\Longrightarrow}_L u$ implies $t \overset{MN,\alpha}{\Longrightarrow}_L u$.
- If α does not have the form $a(x)$ then $t \overset{M,\alpha}{\Longrightarrow}_L \xrightarrow{N,\tau}_L u$ implies $t \overset{MN,\alpha}{\Longrightarrow}_L u$.

Let $\overset{M,\hat{\tau}}{\Longrightarrow}_L$ be $\overset{M,\varepsilon}{\Longrightarrow}_L$, and $\overset{M,\hat{\alpha}}{\Longrightarrow}_L$ be $\overset{M,\alpha}{\Longrightarrow}_L$ for $\alpha \not\equiv \tau$.

Definition 2.6 A condition indexed family of symmetric relations $\mathcal{S} = \{S^C\}$ is a late weak symbolic bisimulation if $(t,u) \in S^C$ implies whenever $t \xrightarrow{M,\alpha} t'$ with $bn(\alpha) \cap fn(t,u) = \emptyset$, then for each $D \in MCE_{fn(t,u)}(C \cup M)$ there is a $u \overset{N,\hat{\beta}}{\Longrightarrow}_L u'$ such that $D \Rightarrow N$, $\alpha =^D \beta$, and

- If $\alpha \equiv a(x)$ then for each $D' \in MCE_{fn(t,u)\cup\{x\}}(D)$ there is $u' \overset{N',\hat{\tau}}{\Longrightarrow}_L u''$ s.t. $D' \Rightarrow N'$ and $(t',u'') \in S^{D'}$.
- If $\alpha \equiv \overline{a}(x)$ then $(t',u') \in S^{D\cup\{x\neq y \mid y \in fn(\alpha.t',\beta.u')\}}$.
- Otherwise $(t',u') \in S^D$.

Let $\approx_L$ be the largest late weak symbolic bisimulation. □

Proposition 2.7 *$t \approx_L^C u$ iff $t\sigma \approx_l u\sigma$ for every $\sigma \models C$.*

Late symbolic observation equivalence is defined in terms of $\approx_L$ as usual:

Definition 2.8 Two terms t, u are *late symbolic observation equivalent* over C, written $t \simeq_L^C u$, if whenever $t \xrightarrow{M,\alpha} t'$ with $bn(\alpha) \cap fn(t,u) = \emptyset$, then for each $D \in MCE_{fn(t,u)}(C \cup M)$ there is a $u \overset{N,\beta}{\Longrightarrow}_L u'$ such that $D \Rightarrow N$, $\alpha =^D \beta$, and

- If $\alpha \equiv a(x)$ then for each $D' \in MCE_{fn(t,u)\cup\{x\}}(D)$ there is $u' \overset{M',\hat{\tau}}{\Longrightarrow}_L u''$ s.t. $D' \Rightarrow M'$ and $t' \approx_L^{D'} u''$.

$$\text{ALPHA}\quad \frac{}{true \rhd t = u}\; t \equiv u$$

$$\text{AXIOM}\quad \frac{}{true \rhd t = u}\; t = u \text{ an axiom instance}$$

$$\text{CHOICE}\quad \frac{C \rhd t_i = u_i}{C \rhd t_1 + t_2 = u_1 + u_2} \qquad \text{TAU}\quad \frac{C \rhd t = u}{C \rhd \tau.t = \tau.u}$$

$$\text{L-INPUT}\quad \frac{C \rhd t = u}{C \rhd a(x).t = b(x).u}\; C \Rightarrow a = b,\ x \notin n(C)$$

$$\text{OUTPUT}\quad \frac{C \rhd t = u}{C \rhd \overline{a}x.t = \overline{b}y.u}\; C \Rightarrow a = b,\ C \Rightarrow x = y$$

$$\text{MATCH}\quad \frac{C \cup \{x = y\} \rhd t = u \qquad C \cup \{x \neq y\} \rhd \mathbf{0} = u}{C \rhd [x = y]t = u}$$

$$\text{RES}\quad \frac{C \cup \{\, x \neq y \mid y \in fn((x)t, (x)u) \,\} \rhd t = u}{C \rhd (x)t = (x)u}\; x \notin n(C)$$

$$\text{CUT}\quad \frac{C \cup \{x = y\} \rhd t = u \qquad C \cup \{x \neq y\} \rhd t = u}{C \rhd t = u}$$

$$\text{CONSEQ}\quad \frac{C \rhd t = u}{C' \rhd t = u}\; C' \Rightarrow C \qquad \text{ABSURD}\quad \frac{}{false \rhd t = u}$$

Figure 3: The Inference Rules for Late Symbolic Bisimulation

- If $\alpha \equiv \overline{a}(x)$ then $t' \approx_L^{D \cup \{\, x \neq y | y \in fn(\alpha.t', \beta.u') \,\}} u'$.
- Otherwise $t' \approx_L^D u'$.

And similarly for u. □

Proposition 2.9 *$t \simeq_L^C u$ iff $t\sigma \dot{\simeq}_l u\sigma$ for every $\sigma \models C$.*

3 The Inference System

In this section we will concentrate on a sublanguage without the parallel composition operator $|$. Later we will see that this operator can be axiomatised easily.

The inference system for late symbolic bisimulation is reported in Figure 3. The judgements are *conditional equations* of the form

$$C \rhd t = u$$

where $t = u$ is an equation in the π-calculus and C is a condition.

S1	$X + 0 = X$	R1	$(x)0 = 0$
S2	$X + X = X$	R2	$(x)\alpha.X = \alpha.(x)X$ if $x \notin n(\alpha)$
S3	$X + Y = Y + X$	R3	$(x)\alpha.X = 0$ if x is the port of α
S4	$(X + Y) + Z = X + (Y + Z)$	R4	$(x)(y)X = (y)(x)X$
		R5	$(x)(X + Y) = (x)X + (x)Y$
T1	$\alpha.\tau.X = \alpha.X$	T2	$X + \tau.X = \tau.X$
T3	$\alpha.(X + \tau.Y) + \alpha.Y = \alpha.(X + \tau.Y)$		

Figure 4: The Axioms for Choice, Restriction and τ

In order to derive interesting equations from this inference system we need some standard axioms. These include the axioms for the choice operator (S1 – S4), the axioms for the restriction operator (R1 – R5), and the τ-laws (T1 – T3) in Figure 4. Let $\mathcal{A}_s = \{S1, S2, S3, S4, R1, R2, R3, R4, R5\}$ and $\mathcal{A}_w = \mathcal{A}_s \cup \{T1, T2, T3\}$.

We write $\vdash C \rhd t = u$ and $\vdash_{wL} C \rhd t = u$ to mean that $C \rhd t = u$ can be derived from $\mathcal{A}_s$ and $\mathcal{A}_w$, respectively, using the above inference rules. It is immediate from the definition that $\vdash C \rhd t = u$ implies $\vdash_{wL} C \rhd t = u$. Some properties of these proof systems are listed bellow.

Proposition 3.1 *1. If $C \Rightarrow M$ and $\vdash C \rhd t = u$ then $\vdash C \rhd Mt = u$.*

2. If $C \cup M \Rightarrow false$ then $\vdash C \rhd Mt = 0$.

3. $\vdash t = t + Mt$.

Proposition 3.2 *If $\vdash D \rhd t = u$ for each $D \in MCE_V(C)$ then $\vdash C \rhd t = u$.*

Proposition 3.3 *1. $\vdash (x)[x = x]t = (x)t$.*

2. $\vdash (x)[x = y]t = 0$.

3. $\vdash (x)[y = z]t = [y = z](x)t$.

The soundness and completeness of $\vdash$ w.r.t $\sim_L$ (hence $\sim_l$) have been proved in [Lin94b]. The rest of this section is devoted to the proof of completeness result for $\vdash_{wL}$.

If $a \neq x$ then we abbreviate $(x)\overline{a}x.t$ as $\overline{a}(x).t$. $\overline{a}(x)$ is a derived action called *bound output*. Using RES the following two equations can be easily derived from T1 and T3:

$$\overline{a}(x).\tau.X = \overline{a}(x).X$$

$$\overline{a}(x).(X + \tau.Y) + \overline{a}(x).Y = \overline{a}(x).(X + \tau.Y)$$

So from now on we will allow the action α in T1 and T3 to range over bound output as well.

We also have the following derived inference rule for bound output:

Proposition 3.4 *Suppose* $C \Rightarrow a = b$, $x \notin n(C)$. *If* $\vdash C \cup \{x \neq y \mid y \in fn(\overline{a}(x).t, \overline{b}(x).u)\} \rhd t = u$ *then* $\vdash C \rhd \overline{a}(x).t = \overline{b}(x).u$.

A term is restriction-free if, using the above abbreviation, it does not explicitly contain any occurrences of the restriction operator.

A restriction-free term is a *standard form* if it has the form $\sum_i M_i\alpha_i.t_i$ and each t_i is a standard form. A standard form $\sum_i M_i\alpha_i.t_i$ is a *full standard form* if

- $t \overset{M,\alpha}{\Longrightarrow}_L t'$, where $bn(\alpha) \cap n(M) = \emptyset$, implies $t \overset{M,\alpha}{\longrightarrow} t'$;
- Each t_i is in full standard form.

The following two crucial lemmas hold:

Lemma 3.5 *(Absorption) If* $t \overset{M,\alpha}{\Longrightarrow}_L t'$ *with* $bn(\alpha) \cap n(M) = \emptyset$ *then* $\vdash_{wL} t = t + M\alpha.t'$.

Lemma 3.6 *If* $t \overset{M,\hat{\tau}}{\Longrightarrow}_L t'$, $C \Rightarrow M$ *and* $\vdash_{wL} C \rhd \tau.t' = \tau.u$, *then* $\vdash_{wL} C \rhd \tau.t = \tau.t + \tau.u$.

Let the *height* of a term t, $|\, t\,|$, be defined as the maximum depth of action nesting in t.

Lemma 3.7 *For any term* t *there is a full standard form* t' *such that* $\vdash_{wL} t = t'$ *and* $|\, t'\,| \leq |\, t\,|$.

The following proposition relates observation equivalence to weak bisimulation. It will play an important rôle in the proof of the completeness theorem.

Proposition 3.8 *Suppose* $D \in MC_{fn(t,u)}$. *Then* $t \approx_L^D u$ *if and only if either* $t \simeq_L^D u$, *or* $\tau.t \simeq_L^D u$, *or* $t \simeq_L^D \tau.u$.

Using Lemmas 3.7, 3.6 and 3.8 we can prove the main theorem of this paper:

Theorem 3.9 *(Completeness of* $\vdash_{wL}$*) If* $t \simeq_L^C u$ *then* $\vdash_{wL} C \rhd t = u$.

Proof: By Lemma 3.7 we may assume t, u are standard forms: $t \equiv \sum_i M_i\alpha_i.t_i$, $u \equiv \sum_j N_j\beta_j.u_j$. We may further assume that bound actions in α_i, β_j use the same bound name $z \notin fn(t, u, C)$. The proof is by induction on the joint height of t and u. By Proposition 3.2 we need only to show $\vdash_{wL} D \rhd t = u$ for each $D \in MCE_{fn(t,u,C)}(C)$, and for this it is sufficient to show $\vdash_{wL} D \rhd t = t + N_j\beta_j.u_j$ for each j.

If $D \not\Rightarrow N_j$ then, since D is maximally consistent, $D \cup N_j \Rightarrow false$. So by Proposition 3.1, $\vdash_{wL} D \rhd N_j\beta_j.u_j = \mathbf{0}$. Hence $\vdash_{wL} D \rhd t = t + N_j\beta_j.u_j$ by S1.

Now assume $D \Rightarrow N_j$ (then $D \in MCE_{fn(t,u,C)}(C \cup N_j)$), and consider four cases according to the type of β_j.

- $\beta_j \equiv \tau$. Then $u \overset{N_j,\tau}{\longrightarrow} u_j$. Since $t \simeq_L^C u$ and t is a full normal from, $t \overset{M_i,\tau}{\Longrightarrow}_L t_i$ for some i s.t. $D \Rightarrow M_i$ and $t_i \approx_L^D u_j$. By Proposition 3.8 we have either $t_i \simeq_L^D u_j$, or $\tau.t_i \simeq_L^D u_j$, or $t_i \simeq_L^D \tau.u_j$. In the first case we can apply induction to get $\vdash_{wL} D \rhd t_i = u_j$, and by TAU, $\vdash_{wL} D \rhd \tau.t_i = \tau.u_j$. In the second case, by Lemma 3.7 there is a full normal form t' with height no greater than t s.t. $\vdash_{wL} \tau.t_i = t'$. By the soundness of $\vdash_{wL}$, $t' \simeq_L^{true} \tau.t_i$, hence $t' \simeq_L^D u_j$. By induction $\vdash_{wL} D \rhd t' = u_j$, so $\vdash_{wL} D \rhd \tau.t_i = u_j$. Apply TAU and T1 we get $\vdash_{wL} D \rhd \tau.t_i = \tau.u_j$. In the third case we can similarly get $\vdash_{wL} D \rhd \tau.t_i = \tau.u_j$. Since $D \Rightarrow M_i$ and $D \Rightarrow N_j$, by Proposition 3.1 $\vdash_{wL} D \rhd M_i\tau.t_i = N_j\tau.u_j$. Finally by S2, $\vdash_{wL} D \rhd t = t + N_j\tau.u_j$.

- $\beta_j \equiv \overline{b}(z)$. Then $u \overset{N_j,\overline{b}(z)}{\longrightarrow} u_j$, so $t \overset{M_i,\overline{a_i}(z)}{\Longrightarrow}_L t_i \overset{M',\hat{\tau}}{\Longrightarrow}_L t'$ for some i s.t. $D \Rightarrow M_iM'$, $D \Rightarrow a_i = b$ and $t' \approx_L^{D\cup\{\, z\neq y \mid y\in fn(\overline{a_i}(z).t_i,\overline{b}(z).u_j)\,\}} u_j$. Note that $D \cup \{\, z \neq y \mid y \in fn(\overline{a_i}(z).t_i, \overline{b}(z).u_j)\,\} \in MC_{fn(t_i,u_j)}$, so by the same argument as in the τ case, $\vdash_{wL} D \cup \{\, z \neq y \mid y \in fn(\overline{a_i}(z).t_i, \overline{b}(z).u_j)\,\} \rhd \tau.t' = \tau.u_j$. By Lemma 3.6, $\vdash_{wL} D' \rhd \tau.t_i = \tau.t_i + \tau.u_j$. By Proposition 3.4, $\vdash_{wL} D \rhd \overline{a_i}(z).\tau.t_i = \overline{a_i}(z).(\tau.t_i + \tau.u_j)$. Hence

$$\begin{aligned}
\vdash_{wL} D \rhd \overline{a_i}(z).t_i &\overset{T1}{=} \overline{a_i}(z).\tau.t_i \\
&= \overline{a_i}(z).(\tau.t_i + \tau.u_j) \\
&\overset{T3}{=} \overline{a_i}(z).(\tau.t_i + \tau.u_j) + \overline{a_i}(z).u_j \\
&= \overline{a_i}(z).t_i + \overline{a_i}(z).u_j \\
&= \overline{a_i}(z).t_i + \overline{b}(z).u_j
\end{aligned}$$

  Since $D \Rightarrow M_i$ and $D \Rightarrow N_j$, by Proposition 3.1, $\vdash_{wL} D \rhd M_i\overline{a_i}(z).t_i = M_i\overline{a_i}(z).t_i + N_j\overline{b}(z).u_j$. Hence $\vdash_{wL} D \rhd t = t + N_j\overline{b}(z).u_j$ by S2.

- The other two cases are similar. □

4 The Early Case

Early weak (concrete) bisimulation and congruence have been discussed in [Wal94], here we only give the definitions for thier symbolic counterpart.

To define early symbolic double arrow, $\Longrightarrow_E$, we simply remove the "non-input action" restriction to the last rule in the definition of late double arrow in Section 2.3, with the other rules unchanged.

Definition 4.1 A condition indexed family of symmetric relations $\mathcal{S} = \{S^C\}$ is an early weak symbolic bisimulation if $(t, u) \in S^C$ implies

whenever $t \overset{M,\alpha}{\longrightarrow} t'$ with $bn(\alpha) \cap fn(t,u) = \emptyset$, then for each $D \in MCE_V(C \cup M)$ there is a $u \overset{N,\hat{\beta}}{\Longrightarrow}_E u'$ such that $D \Rightarrow N$, $\alpha =^D \beta$, and $(t', u') \in S^{D'}$, where

$$V = \begin{cases} fn(t,u) \cup \{x\} & \textit{if } \alpha \equiv a(x) \\ fn(t,u) & \textit{otherwise} \end{cases}$$

$$D' = \begin{cases} D \cup \{ x \neq y \mid y \in fn(\alpha.t', \beta.u') \} & \textit{if } \alpha \equiv \overline{a}(x) \\ D & \textit{otherwise} \end{cases}$$

Let $\approx_E$ be the largest early weak symbolic bisimulation. □

Early symbolic observation equivalence $\simeq_E$ can then be defined in terms of $\approx_E$ as usual.

Proposition 4.2 *$t \simeq_E^C u$ iff $t\sigma \simeq_e u\sigma$ for every $\sigma \models C$.*

The proof systems for early weak equivalence can be obtained by replacing the L-INPUT rule in Figure 3 with the following one

$$\text{E-INPUT} \quad \frac{C \rhd \sum_{i \in I} \tau.t_i = \sum_{j \in J} \tau.u_j}{C \rhd \sum_{i \in I} a_i(x).t_i = \sum_{j \in J} b_j(x).u_j} \quad \begin{array}{l} C \Rightarrow a_i = b_j,\ i \in I,\ j \in J \\ x \notin n(C) \end{array}$$

Let us write $\vdash_{wE} C \rhd t = u$ to mean $C \rhd t = u$ can be derived from this new proof system. It is easy to see that, in the presence of the TAU rule, L-INPUT can be derived from E-INPUT, but not the other way round. So $\vdash_{wE}$ is strictly stronger than $\vdash_{wL}$.

All the lemmas in the previous section hold for $\vdash_{wE}$ as well. And we have the following counterpart of Theorem 3.9:

Theorem 4.3 *(Completeness of $\vdash_{wE}$) If $t \simeq_E^C u$ then $\vdash_{wE} C \rhd t = u$.*

5 Other Operators

5.1 Parallel Composition

To deal with parallel composition all we need is a suitable form of expansion law which is presented in Figure 5. With this law it is standard that any term containing parallel operator can be reduced to a term without it, hence the normal form lemma still holds, as does the completeness theorem.

5.2 Mismatch

To include mismatch, *i.e.* testing inequality between names, into the language we first extend the operational semantics by including the following two rules: "mismatch" and "Mismatch" in Figure 1 and Figure 2, respectively (now M ranges over conditions)

$$\text{mismatch} \quad \frac{t \xrightarrow{\alpha} t'}{[x \neq y]t \xrightarrow{\alpha} t'} \quad x \neq y \qquad\qquad \text{Mismatch} \quad \frac{t \xrightarrow{M,\alpha} t'}{[x \neq y]t \xrightarrow{M[x \neq y],\alpha} t'}$$

Let $t \equiv \sum_i M_i\alpha_i.t_i$ and $u \equiv \sum_j N_j\beta_j.u_j$ with $bn(\alpha_i) \cap fn(u) = bn(\beta_j) \cap fn(t) = \emptyset$. Then

$$t \mid u = \sum_i M_i\alpha_i.(t_i \mid u) \; + \; \sum_j N_j\beta_j.(t \mid u_j) \; + \sum_{\alpha_i \; opp \; \beta_j} M_iN_j[a_i = b_j]\tau.v_{ij}$$

where α_i *opp* β_j and v_{ij} are defined as follows

1. $\alpha_i \equiv a(x), \beta_j \equiv \bar{b}y$; then $v_{ij} \equiv t_i[y/x] \mid u_j$;
2. The converse of the above clause;
3. $\alpha_i \equiv a(x), \beta_j \equiv \bar{b}(y)$; then $v_{ij} \equiv (z)(t_i[z/x] \mid u_j[z/y])$ with $z \notin fn(t, u)$;
4. The converse of the above clause.

Figure 5: The Expansion Law

The inference rule for mismatch is dual to that for match:

$$\text{MISMATCH} \quad \frac{C \cup \{x \neq y\} \rhd t = u \qquad C \cup \{x = y\} \rhd \mathbf{0} = u}{C \rhd [x \neq y]t = u}$$

With this rule Proposition 3.1 can be generalised to allow M to be an arbitrary condition, not just a match.

Now, in a normal form $\sum_i M_i\alpha_i.t_i$, M_i may contain inequality tests as well as equality tests. This does not affect the proofs of the normal form lemma and the completeness theorem.

6 Conclusions And Related Work

We have presented complete proof systems for late and early weak observation equivalences for the π-calculus. The inference system for the early equivalence is obtained by adding the E-INPUT rule to the inference system for the late equivalence. To enrich the language with the *mismatch* construction we only need to extend the inference systems with a single rule, namely MISMATCH. In each case the proof system for weak equivalence is obtained by adding the standard τ-laws to the one for the strong equivalence. Thus in all we have eight proof systems. The relationship between them are pictured in Figure 6, where arrows stand for "extension" and $\pi^{\neq}$ is the version of π-calculus enriched with mismatch.

Our results verify a conjecture posed in [MPW92, PS93, BD94]: the three τ-laws are sufficient for the transition from strong to weak bisimulation equivalences for the π-calculus, as in the case of *CCS*.

The current work inherits the main ideas from our previous work on general message-passing process calculi [HL92, HL93]. As the process calculi considered

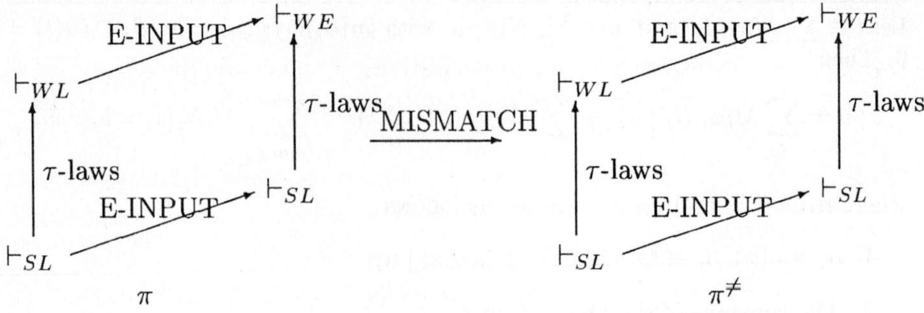

Figure 6: The Relationship between Proof Systems

there take the languages for data and boolean expressions as parameters, the completeness results in those papers are relative to data reasoning. Here, by exploiting the specific features presented in the π-calculus, there is no need to refer to an "oracle" for the data domain and the completeness results are no longer relative to reasoning about data.

Parrow and Sangiorgi ([PS93]) provided complete equational theories for both late and early strong congruences for name-passing calculi, *i.e.* extensions of the π-calculus with the mismatch construction. Mismatch plays an essential rôle in at least two places: the definition of normal form and the axiom for early equivalence. The equational characterisation of the restriction operator also relies on mismatch.

In [BD94] Moreale and De Nicola proposed "symbolic" semantics and proof systems very similar to [Lin94b]. Again they work with the extension of the π-calculus with mismatch instead of the π-calculus proper, and only strong equivalences were treated.

[Liu94] gives a symbolic version of distinction-indexed bisimulation for a sublanguage of the π-calculus (without the *match* operator) and shows that this notion of bisimulation captures the conventional bisimulation equivalences. But no proof system is considered there.

In [San93] another notion of bisimulation, called *open bisimulation*, for the π-calculus is proposed, along with an equational axiomatisation. A "symbolic" characterisation of open bisimulation is also given. To deal with the restriction operator, distinctions have to be exploited as indices in the definition of open bisimulation as well as in the axiomatisation. Open bisimulation has been further studied in [Wal94].

We are not aware any other published work on axiomatising weak bisimulation equivalences in the π-calculus.

Acknowledgment Thanks to Matthew Hennessy for reading a draft of this paper and suggesting many improvements.

References

[BD92] M. Boreale and R. DeNicola. Testing equivalence for mobile processes. In *CONCUR'92*, number 630 in Lecture Notes in Computer Science, pages 2 – 16. Springer–Verlag, 1992.

[BD94] M. Boreale and R. DeNicola. A symbolic semantics for the π-calculus. In *CONCUR'94*, Lecture Notes in Computer Science. Springer–Verlag, 1994.

[Hen91] M. Hennessy. A model for the π-calculus. Technical Report 8/91, CSAI, University of Sussex, 1991.

[HL92] M. Hennessy and H. Lin. Symbolic bisimulations. Technical Report 1/92, CSAI, University of Sussex, 1992. to appear in *Theoretical Computer Science*.

[HL93] M. Hennessy and H. Lin. Proof systems for message-passing process algebras. In *CONCUR'93*, number 715 in Lecture Notes in Computer Science, pages 202–216, 1993.

[Lin94a] H. Lin. Complete inference systems for weak bisimulation equivalences in the π-calculus. Report ISCAS-LCS-94-11, Laboratory for Computer Science, Institute of Software, Chinese Academy of Science, 1994.

[Lin94b] H. Lin. Symbolic bisimulations and proof systems for the π-calculus. Report 7/94, Computer Science, University of Sussex, 1994.

[Liu94] X. Liu. Characterizing bisimulation congruence in the π-calculus. In *CONCUR'94*, Lecture Notes in Computer Science. Springer–Verlag, 1994.

[Mil89] R. Milner. *Communication and Concurrency*. Prentice-Hall, 1989.

[MPW92] R. Milner, J. Parrow, and D. Walker. A calculus of mobile proceses, part I,II. *Information and Computation*, 100:1–77, 1992.

[PS93] J. Parrow and D. Sangiorgi. Algebraic theories for name-passing calculi. Report ECS-LFCS-93-262, LFCS, University of Edinburgh, 1993.

[San93] D. Sangiorgi. A theory of bisimulation for the π-calculus. In *CONCUR'93*, number 715 in Lecture Notes in Computer Science, 1993.

[Wal94] D. Walker. On bisimulation in the π-calculus. In *CONCUR'94*, Lecture Notes in Computer Science. Springer–Verlag, 1994.

Reasoning about Higher-Order Processes

Roberto M. Amadio[1]* and Mads Dam[2]**

[1] CNRS, BP 145, Sophia-Antipolis, F-06903, France, e-mail: amadio@cma.cma.fr
[2] SICS, Box 1263, S-164 28, Kista, Sweden, e-mail: mfd@sics.se

Abstract. We address the specification and verification problem for process calculi such as Chocs, CML and Facile where processes or functions are transmissible values. Our work takes place in the context of a static treatment of restriction and of a bisimulation-based semantics. As a paradigmatic and simple case we concentrate on (Plain) Chocs. We show that Chocs bisimulation can be characterized by an extension of Hennessy-Milner logic including a constructive implication, or function space constructor. This result is a non-trivial extension of the classical characterization result for labelled transition systems. In the second part of the paper we address the problem of developing a proof system for the verification of process specifications. Building on previous work for CCS we present a sound proof system for a Chocs sub-calculus not including restriction. We present two completeness results: one for the full specification language using an infinitary system, and one for a special class of so-called *well-described* specifications using a finitary system.

1 Introduction

In the last years there has been a rising interest in calculi and programming languages where *complex* data such as processes and functions are transmissible values [3, 5, 11, 13, 18]. At least two main motivations for these studies can be identified: (i) to generalize the functional model of computation to a parallel and/or concurrent framework, and (ii) to model the notion of code transmission which is relevant to the programming of distributed systems.

A key issue in these languages is the interaction between process transmission and the *static* scoping discipline for communication channels. Here we consider Thomsen's Plain Chocs. This is an extension of CCS where processes are transmissible values and the restriction operator is subject to a static scoping discipline.

A considerable effort has been put into the development of a bisimulation based semantics for this calculus (c.f. [18, 2, 14]). The *specification* of Plain Chocs processes (and processes in related calculi) is a much less developed topic. Two notable attempts in this direction are described in [17, 6]. These works are based on logics extracted from a domain theoretic interpretation of the calculus,

* Partially supported by ESPRIT BRA 6454 CONFER. Part of the work was done while visiting SICS.

** Partially supported by ESPRIT BRA 8130 LOMAPS.

following general ideas described in, e.g., [1]. This approach has been rather successful in the case of *dynamic* scoping. On the other hand it is not clear how to obtain a fully abstract denotational semantics of restriction in the case of *static* scoping (c.f. [12] for some typical problems). This motivates our shift towards an operational approach to the problem, along the lines of Hennessy and Milner [8].

What to specify? First, let us fix some notation for a process calculus of higher-order processes: $c!P.P'$ is the process which sends P along the channel c and then becomes P', $c?x.P$ is the process which performs an input along the channel c, and upon reception of some process Q becomes $[Q/x]P$. In $\nu c.P$ the restriction operator ν creates a new channel which will be local to the process P. Finally $+$ is the non-deterministic choice, $|$ is the parallel composition, and 0 is the nil process, with the usual CCS semantics [9]. We briefly refer to this calculus as Chocs, after [17].

Second, we should determine some requirements for our candidate specification logic. Roughly, we expect it to be an extension of Hennessy-Milner logic which characterizes some standard Chocs bisimulation.

Previous work on extending Hennessy-Milner logic to calculi including value and channel transmission (c.f. [4, 7, 10]) relies on the recurrent idea of introducing modalities that state properties of the transmitted values. For instance, one can specify that a process P can output the value 3 on channel c and then satisfy property ϕ by writing: $P : \langle c!3\rangle.\phi$.

This approach does not seem to scale up to process transmission. The naive idea of writing:

$$P : \langle c!\phi'\rangle.\phi \text{ if } P \stackrel{c!P'}{\rightarrow} Q \text{ and } P' : \phi' \text{ and } Q : \phi$$

does not take into account the fact that P' and Q might share local channels. For instance, consider the process $P = \nu a.c!(a?x.x).a!0.Q$. In this example the actions of the process transmitted on channel c and of the relative continuation are clearly inter-dependent. We did not find any satisfying way to express this dependency. An alternative is to express properties of processes like P above in terms of the effect the output has when P is put in a receiving environment. Since receiving environments are just abstractions this suggests a simple extension of Hennessy-Milner logic by means of a constructive implication, say $\Rightarrow$. We can now write specifications such as:

$$P : [c?](\phi \Rightarrow \psi) \qquad Q : \langle c!\rangle((\phi \Rightarrow \psi) \Rightarrow \gamma)$$

For inputs the interpretation is the expected one: P satisfies $[c?](\phi \Rightarrow \psi)$ if whenever P makes an input action on channel c and receives an input satisfying ϕ then the continuation will satisfy ψ. In a first approximation, the intuition for output is the following: Q satisfies $\langle c!\rangle((\phi \Rightarrow \psi) \Rightarrow \gamma)$ if it is possible for Q to output a process, say Q_1, along c such that in any receiving context, say $\lambda x.Q_2$, if $\lambda x.Q_2$ satisfies $\phi \Rightarrow \psi$, and if Q_3 is the continuation of Q after performing its output, then $([Q_1/x]Q_2) \mid Q_3$ satisfies γ. In general Q_1 and Q_3

may share channels local to Q, say $c_1, ..., c_n$, whose scope is *extruded* by the output communication. Note that in the specification we never need to speak about these extruded channels.

Operational Semantics. Reflecting this intuition, a labelled transition system is given to Plain Chocs that maps (closed) processes to (closed) process functionals, depending on the action performed. More precisely, a process Q rewrites by an input action to a process function $\lambda x.Q_2$ and by an output action to a process functional $\lambda f.\nu c_1...c_n.(fQ_1 \mid Q_3)$, where, as above, Q_1 is the transmitted process, Q_3 is the continuation, and $c_1, ..., c_n$ are shared local channels. The result of a communication is simply computed by applying the process functional to the process function:

$$(\lambda f.\nu c_1...c_n.(fQ_1 \mid Q_3))(\lambda x.Q_2) \equiv \nu c_1...c_n.([Q_1/x]Q_2 \mid Q_3)$$

The standard rules for substitution avoid clashes between local channels. Also note that in this formulation Plain Chocs actions coincide with standard CCS actions. Of course one has to pay a price for this, namely one has to lift the notion of bisimulation higher-order by introducing a suitable notion of exponentiation. Section 2 will show that this can be achieved in an elegant and simple way. It should be remarked that the resulting bisimulation coincides with the one considered in [2, 14], which in turn has been shown to be compatible with the π-calculus semantics.

Logical Characterization. Having found a suitable way to specify properties of Chocs processes we pursue our programme of relating logical equivalence to bisimulation equivalence. In the CCS case, this is achieved by means of a co-inductive view of bisimulation. Roughly, the bisimulation relation, say $\sim$, can be seen as the limit of a descending sequence of equivalence relations $\sim^k$. Equivalence in $\sim^k$ is then related to logical equivalence w.r.t. formulas having modal depth bound by k. In the higher-order case the task is complicated by the *contravariance* of the constructive implication in its first argument. This is discussed in more detail in section 2 once some notation has been introduced. We obtain a logical characterization of Chocs bisimulation modulo a technical lemma that relates the approximation $\sim^k$ to a *sharpened* approximation $\sim^k_\sharp$.

Towards a Proof System. As a second contribution, we address the problem of developing a sound and complete proof system to verify that a process meets (or realizes) a specification. We found a simple and clean solution for the restriction-free fragment of the calculus. The basic judgment $\Gamma \vdash P : \psi$ states that the process P realizes the specification ψ under the hypothesis Γ. Hypotheses state assumptions on the parameters of P. The system thus allows for reasoning about open processes. A rather rough completeness result for the system can be achieved by the introduction of an ω-rule and by the hypothesis that there is only a finite number of channels. To give a more accurate picture of the power of our logical system we also exhibit a finitary system which is complete on a particular collection of *well-described* specifications. Concerning the restriction operator it appears this may require considerable complication of the proof system as one has to represent the dependencies among functional variables and dynamically generated channels. We leave this problem for further investigation.

2 The Calculus and its Bisimulation Based Semantics

Language. The expressions of the language are classified in two kinds: channels and processes. Channels are variables and ranged over by $c, d, \ldots$. Actions have one of the forms τ, $c?$ or $c!$ and they are ranged over by $\alpha, \alpha', \ldots$. To each process is associated a unique order among the orders: 0 (processes), 1 (process functions), and 2 (process functionals). We use $x, x', \ldots, f, f' \ldots$, and $F, F' \ldots$, for variables of order $0, 1, 2$, respectively. We use $z, z' \ldots$ as generic variables. Open processes of order 0 are then generated by the following grammar:

$$P ::= 0 \,\big|\, x \,\big|\, fP \,\big|\, P + P \,\big|\, P \mid P \,\big|\, \nu c.P \,\big|\, c!P.P \,\big|\, c?x.P$$

Whenever we write $P[z]$ we intend that z is the only variable that can be free in P and moreover we identify P with the function $\lambda z.P$. Thus alpha-conversion applies to identify $P[z]$ with $([z'/z]P)[z']$ whenever z' does not occur freely in $\lambda z.P$, and to identify, e.g., $\nu c.(P[z])$ with $(\nu c.P)[z]$. We also write $P(z)$ for an open process in which z is the only variable that can occur free. If z is free then $P(z)$ is identified with $P[z]$. If z is not free then $P(z)$ can ambiguously represent either a closed process or the constant function $\lambda z.P$. The context will allow us to disambiguate this situation.

Operational semantics. The labelled transition system is based on three kinds of judgments: $P \xrightarrow{\tau} Q$, $P \xrightarrow{c?} Q'[x]$, and $P \xrightarrow{c!} Q''[f]$, where P, Q are closed processes. We assume that sum and parallel composition are associative and commutative operators, and that restriction commutes with parallel composition according to the standard law $(\nu c.P) \mid P' = \nu c.(P \mid P')$ whenever c is not free in P'. Then it can be showed that whenever $P \xrightarrow{c!} Q''[f]$ in the transition system specified below then $Q''[f]$ has the form $\nu c_1. \cdots \nu c_n.(fP' \mid P'')[f]$. Finally, note that in the rule (!?) a *second-order substitution* is employed. That is, one replaces first $Q'[x]$ for f, and then the argument of f for x.

(!) $c!P'.P \xrightarrow{c!} (fP' \mid P)[f]$ (?) $c?x.P \xrightarrow{c?} P[x]$

(!?) if $P \xrightarrow{c!} P'[f]$ and $Q \xrightarrow{c?} Q'[x]$ then $P \mid Q \xrightarrow{\tau} [Q'[x]/f]P'[f]$

(+) if $P \xrightarrow{\alpha} P'$ then $P + Q \xrightarrow{\alpha} P'$ (|) if $P \xrightarrow{\alpha} P'$ then $P \mid Q \xrightarrow{\alpha} P' \mid Q$

(ν) if $P \xrightarrow{\alpha} P'$ and $\alpha \neq c!, c?$ then $\nu c.P \xrightarrow{\alpha} \nu c.P'$

Bisimulation. Let Pr_0 be the collection of closed processes, Pr_1 be the collection of $P[x]$ processes, and Pr_2 be the collection of $P[f]$ processes. Because of the input-output actions a notion of bisimulation over Pr_0 needs to be lifted to

Pr_1 and Pr_2. For this purpose the following general notion of *exponentiation* is introduced:

$$P[z]\ [S \Rightarrow S']\ P'[z] \text{ if } Q(w)\ S\ Q'(w) \text{ implies } [Q(w)/z]P\ S'\ [Q'(w)/z]P'$$

Given a relation S over Pr_0^2 and an action α we define the relations $S[\alpha]$ as follows, where $Id_0 = \{(P,P) \mid P \in Pr_0\}$, and $Id_1 = \{(P[x],P[x]) \mid P[x] \in Pr_1\}$:

$$S[\tau] = S \qquad S[c?] = [Id_0 \Rightarrow S] \qquad S[c!] = [Id_1 \Rightarrow S]$$

Definition 1 Bisimulation. A *bisimulation* S is a relation over Pr_0 such that whenever PSQ and $P \xrightarrow{\alpha} P'(z)$ then for some $Q'(z)$, $Q \xrightarrow{\alpha} Q'(z)$ and $P'(z)S[\alpha]Q'(z)$; and symmetrically. We denote with $\sim$ the largest bisimulation.

Up to some notational conventions $\sim$ is the bisimulation studied in [2, 14]. The relation $\sim$ is extended to process functionals by considering their equivalence on all closed instances, e.g. $P[f] \sim Q[f]$ if any $R[x]$, $[R[x]/f]P \sim [R[x]/f]Q$. Define now the function $F : Pr_0^2 \to Pr_0^2$ by $P\ F(S)\ Q$ if whenever $P \xrightarrow{\alpha} P'(z)$ then $Q \xrightarrow{\alpha} Q'(z)$ for some $Q'(z)$ and $P'(z)\ S[\alpha]\ Q'(z)$; and symmetrically. Also, let $\sim^0 = Pr_0^2$, $\sim^{\kappa+1} = F(\sim^\kappa)$, and $\sim^\lambda = \bigcap_{\kappa<\lambda} \sim^\kappa$. The relations $\sim^\kappa$ are extended to functionals following the convention for $\sim$. We obtain the following standard properties:

Proposition 2 Properties of F. *The set $2^{Pr_0^2}$ is a complete lattice when ordered by set inclusion. Then:*
(1) F is monotone.
(2) S is a bisimulation iff $S \subseteq F(S)$.
(3) If $\{X_i\}_{i\in I}$ is a codirected set, then $F(\bigcap_{i\in I} X_i) = \bigcap_{i\in I} F(X_i)$.
(4) The greatest bisimulation $\sim$ exists and coincides with $\sim^\omega$. □

Proposition 3 Congruence. *The relations $\sim^k$, for $k \leq \omega$, are congruences with respect to all the calculus operators. That is,*

$$\begin{array}{ll} P_i \sim^k Q_i,\ i=1,2 & \Rightarrow P_1+P_2 \sim^k Q_1+Q_2,\ P_1 \mid P_2 \sim^k Q_1 \mid Q_2,\ c!P_1.P_2 \sim^k c!Q_1.Q_2 \\ P \sim^k Q & \Rightarrow \nu c.P \sim^k \nu c.Q \\ P[x] \sim^k Q[x] & \Rightarrow c?x.P \sim^k c?x.Q \end{array}$$

Proof. The only difficulty arises with parallel composition. For instance, in the case $k = \omega$ one shows that $\{(\nu c_1.\cdots\nu c_n.(P \mid Q), \nu c_1.\cdots\nu c_n.(P' \mid Q)) \mid P \sim P'\}$ is a bisimulation. □

We give an alternative characterisation of the $\sim^k$ relations in terms of "sharpened" approximations, $\sim_\sharp^k$. These will be important when it comes to relating the logical and bisimulation based equivalences. These sharpened relations $\sim_\sharp^k$ are defined as follows:

$$\begin{array}{ll} P \sim_\sharp^0 Q & \text{always} \\ P \sim_\sharp^{k+1} Q & \text{if } P \xrightarrow{\alpha} P'(z) \text{ then } Q \xrightarrow{\alpha} Q'(z) \text{ for some } Q'(z) \\ & \text{such that } P'(z) \sim_\sharp^k Q'(z)\text{; and symmetrically} \\ P[x] \sim_\sharp^k Q[x] & \text{if } P[x]\ [\sim_\sharp^k \Rightarrow \sim_\sharp^k]\ Q[x] \\ P[f] \sim_\sharp^k Q[f] & \text{if } P[f]\ [[\sim_\sharp^k \Rightarrow \sim_\sharp^k] \Rightarrow \sim_\sharp^k]\ Q[f] \end{array}$$

We can now show that the sharpened approximation relations coincide with the approximations $\sim^k$. This result relies on the congruence properties of $\sim^k$.

Proposition 4. *For any $k < \omega$, $\sim^k$ coincides with $\sim^k_\sharp$.*

Proof. By induction on k and the order. □

3 Logical Characterization

Modal Formulas. Process properties are specified by the modal formulas which are generated by the following grammar, where X is a countable set. As in the case of processes, specifications also have an order. A specification of a certain order can only be predicated of a process of the same order. Conjunction and disjunction apply to formulas of the same order.

$$\phi ::= \bigwedge_{x \in X} \phi_x \Bigm| \bigvee_{x \in X} \phi_x \Bigm| \langle\alpha\rangle\phi \Bigm| [\alpha]\phi \Bigm| \phi \Rightarrow \phi$$

The truth- and falsehood constants $\top$ and $\bot$ are defined as usual: $\top = \bigwedge \emptyset$ and $\bot = \bigvee \emptyset$. These formulas are overloaded as they may have order 0, 1, and 2. We sometimes use $(\cdot)$ as a meta-connective ranging over $\{\langle\cdot\rangle, [\cdot]\}$.

Realizability. We specify when a process $P(z)$ realizes a formula ϕ, written as $\models P(z) : \phi$, by induction on the structure of ϕ. Note that a realizer of a formula $\phi \Rightarrow \psi$ is always a function, and a realizer of a modality is always a ground process.

$\models P(z) : \bigwedge_{x \in X} \phi_x$	if for all $x \in X \models P(z) : \phi_x$
$\models P(z) : \bigvee_{x \in X} \phi_x$	if for some $x \in X \models P(z) : \phi_x$
$\models P[z] : \phi \Rightarrow \psi$	if for all $Q(z')$, $\models Q(z') : \phi$ implies $\models [Q(z')/z]P : \psi$
$\models P : \langle\alpha\rangle\phi$	if for some $P'(z)$, $P \stackrel{\alpha}{\rightarrow} P'(z)$ and $\models P'(z) : \phi$
$\models P : [\alpha]\phi$	if whenever $P \stackrel{\alpha}{\rightarrow} P'(z)$, $\models P'(z) : \phi$

The *modal depth* $|\phi|$ of a formula ϕ is defined as follows:

$$|\bigwedge_{x \in X} \phi_x| = |\bigvee_{x \in X} \phi_x| = sup_{x \in X}|\phi_x|$$
$$|\phi \Rightarrow \psi| = |\psi| \qquad |\langle\alpha\rangle\phi| = |[\alpha]\phi| = 1 + |\phi|$$

Definition 5 Logical equivalences. We define the family of equivalence relations on process (functionals) $\sim^\kappa_L$ by $P(z) \sim^\kappa_L Q(z')$ if for all ϕ such that $|\phi| \leq \kappa$, $\models P(z) : \phi$ if and only if $\models Q(z') : \phi$. Also set: $P(z) \sim_L Q(z')$ if $P(z) \sim^\kappa_L Q(z')$, for any κ.

Proposition 6. *(1) For any κ, if $P(z) \sim^\kappa Q(z')$ then $P(z) \sim^\kappa_L Q(z')$. (2) If $P(z) \sim Q(z')$ then $P(z) \sim_L Q(z')$.*

Proof. (1) We show that if $P(z) \sim^{\kappa} Q(z')$, $|\phi| \leq \kappa$, and $\models P(z) : \phi$ then $\models Q(z') : \phi$ by induction on the structure of ϕ. The only non-standard case is when ϕ has the form $\phi_1 \Rightarrow \phi_2$. Suppose $\models P_1(z_1) : \phi_1$. Then $\models [P_1(z_1)/z]P : \phi_2$. By congruence of $\sim^{\kappa}$, $[P_1(z_1)/z]P \sim^{\kappa} [P_1(z_1)/z']Q$. By the induction hypothesis, $\models [P_1(z_1)/z']Q : \phi_2$ as desired.
(2) Immediate from (1). □

Definition 7 Characteristic formula. For any process functional $P(z)$, and ordinal $k \leq \omega$ we inductively define a formula $C^k(P(z))$:

$$C^0(P(z)) = \top$$

$$C^{k+1}(P) = \bigwedge_{P \xrightarrow{\alpha} P'(z)} (\langle\alpha\rangle . C^k(P'(z))) \wedge \bigwedge_{\alpha \in Act} ([\alpha]. \bigvee_{P \xrightarrow{\alpha} P'(z)} C^k(P'(z)))$$

$$C^{k+1}(P[z]) = \bigwedge_{R(z')} C^{k+1}(R(z')) \Rightarrow C^{k+1}([R(z')/z]P)$$

$$C^{\omega}(P(z)) = \bigwedge_{k<\omega} C^k(P(z))$$

Observe that for any $k \leq \omega$, $|C^k(P(z))| \leq k$.

Proposition 8. *For any $k < \omega$,*
(1) For all $P(z)$, $\models P(z) : C^k(P(z))$.
(2) For all $P(z), Q(z')$, $\models P(z) : C^k(Q(z'))$ iff $P(z) \sim^k Q(z')$.

Proof. One proves (1) and (2) at the same time, by induction on k and the order. We present the function case.
(1) We have to show: $\models P[x] : \bigwedge_R C^{k+1}(R) \Rightarrow C^{k+1}([R/x]P)$. Suppose that $\models R' : C^{k+1}(R)$. By the induction hypothesis and (2): $R' \sim_{k+1} R$. By congruence: $[R'/x]P \sim_{k+1} [R/x]P$. By ind. hyp. and (2): $\models [R'/x]P : C^{k+1}([R/x]P)$.
(2) Suppose $\models P[x] : C^{k+1}(Q[x])$. That is, $\models P[x] : C^{k+1}(R) \Rightarrow C^{k+1}([R/x]Q)$, any R. By ind. hyp and (1): $\models R : C^{k+1}(R)$. Hence: $\models [R/x]P : C^{k+1}([R/x]Q)$. That is: $[R/x]P \sim_{k+1} [R/x]Q$. Vice versa, suppose $P[x] \sim_{k+1} Q[x]$. Given any R, let $\models R' : C^{k+1}(R)$. Then $R' \sim_{k+1} R$, so $[R'/x]P \sim_{k+1} [R/x]P \sim_{k+1} [R/x]Q$ as desired. □

Theorem 9 Logical characterization. *For any processes P, Q,*

$$P \sim Q \text{ iff } P \sim_L Q.$$

Proof. Follows immediately from previous results. □

A Characterization of Chocs Bisimulation. There is an alternative and natural definition of bisimulation, which resembles the definition of sharpened approximation. Given a relation S over Pr_0^2 and an action α we define the relations $S\{\alpha\}$ as follows:

$$S\{\tau\} = S \qquad S\{c?\} = [S \Rightarrow S] \qquad S\{c!\} = [[S \Rightarrow S] \Rightarrow S]$$

Definition 10 Modified bisimulation. A modified bisimulation S is a relation over Pr_0 such that whenever PSQ and $P \overset{\alpha}{\to} P'(z)$ then for some $Q'(z)$, $Q \overset{\alpha}{\to} Q'(z)$ and $P'(z)S\{\alpha\}Q'(z)$; and symmetrically.

Proposition 11. *Among the modified bisimulations S such that $Id_0 \subseteq S$ and $[S \Rightarrow S] \subseteq Id_1$ there is a largest one and it coincides with the largest bisimulation.*

4 Towards a Proof System

As a second contribution we present a *sound* proof system to prove properties of processes stated in the *finitary fragment* of the Hennessy-Milner logic previously introduced. The following results are of a preliminary nature as they are obtained under the following strong assumptions: (1) We drop *restriction.* (2) We suppose that the calculus has a *finite number of channels.*

The restriction to finite label alphabets has two important corollaries. First, the rule PAR-BOX-τ for introducing the $[\tau]$-operator for parallel compositions becomes finitary. This condition could be lifted if, for instance, a channel quantifier was introduced into the specification language. Indeed this appears to be a natural extension. Note for example that the property that a process can perform no actions could be stated as: $\forall c.([c!]\bot \wedge [\tau]\bot \wedge [c?]\bot)$. Second, the k-th characteristic formula of any process becomes finite, for $k < \omega$. This is quite useful in arguing about the completeness of the system. We regard (1) as the main limitation of our system as in most applications one may assume a finite number of global channels.

4.1 Syntactic Conventions

Judgments. A context Γ is a set $z_1 : \psi_1, ..., z_n : \psi_n$ where all z_i are pairwise distinct. The basic judgments are sequents of the following shape: $\Gamma \vdash P : \psi$. The process P and the context Γ might contain variables of order $0, 1, 2$. There can be at most one variable which is free in P and does not occur in Γ. Following our conventions this variable should be intended as λ-abstracted (note that in our specific case this variable can be of order $0, 1$). The grammars of processes P_0, P_1, P_2 of orders $0, 1, 2$, respectively, in a context Γ can be given as follows:

$$P_0 ::= 0 \,\big|\, x \,\big|\, P_0 + P_0 \,\big|\, c!P_0.P_0 \,\big|\, c?x.P_0 \,\big|\, fP_0 \,\big|\, FP_1 \,\big|\, P_0 \mid P_0$$

$$P_1 ::= P_0[x] \qquad P_2 ::= P_0[f]$$

In the following P will denote a generic process and ψ a generic formula.

Eta-expansions. By convention we eta-expand functional variables so that: $f = fx[x], F = Ff[f]$. This allows to fit functional variables in the grammar for P_1 and P_2. In the following we will write $z_1 \mid P_0$. If $z_1 \equiv f_1$ then $z_1 \mid P_0 \equiv (f_1 x \mid P_0)[x]$, and, similarly, if $z_1 \equiv F_1$ then $z_1 \mid P_0 \equiv (F_1 f \mid P_0)[f]$ (x, f fresh variables).

Interpretation. We write $z_1 : \psi_1, ..., z_n : \psi_n \models P : \psi$ if for all closed P_i such that $\models P_i : \psi_i$ $(i = 1, ..., n)$ we have $\models [P_1/z_1, ..., P_n/z_n]P : \psi$.

4.2 Proof System

We divide the rules of the proof system (fig. 1) into *three groups*: general rules for the manipulation of the sequents, sequent calculus rules which allow for the (right and left) introduction of logical operators, and, finally, rules which exploit the process structure. Note that we have omitted the rules symmetric to AND-L, OR-R, SUM-DIA, PAR-DIA, and PAR-DIA-τ. Really, $\wedge, \vee, +$, and $\mid$ should be understood as commutative operators.

Most rules should be self-explanatory. The essential idea is that in general the holding of $\Gamma \vdash P : \phi$ depends on the structure of both P and ϕ. In all cases, but for the modal operators, P can be dealt with uniformly — these are the logical rules, and they can be seen as coming straight from proof theory. For the modal operators, however, the structure of P is essential, and its transition behaviour is exposed by the operational semantics from which the rules for the modal operators are derived in a quite systematic fashion. In formulating this last set of rules we follow to some extent previous work by Colin Stirling [15] on proof systems for CCS. The rules for parallel composition are, however, somewhat different. The rules reflect very closely the operational semantics. The most involved rules are those for parallel composition. To prove a property ϕ of a parallel composition, say, $P \mid Q$, one needs in general to: (1) *guess* properties of the parallel constituents P and Q, (2) show that they hold, and (3) show that the holding of these properties for the constituents entails the holding of ϕ for their parallel composition. We regard this as quite natural and reflecting closely the *compositional* nature of the proof system.

Example. In fig. 2 we give an example proof of the judgment $\vdash a!(b!0).b?y.c!0 \mid a?x.x : \langle\tau\rangle\langle\tau\rangle\langle c!\rangle\top$ where we have adopted the abbreviations $\phi_0 = \phi_1 \Rightarrow \phi_1$, $\phi_1 = \langle b!\rangle(\phi_2 \Rightarrow \langle c!\rangle\top)$, and $\phi_2 = \top \Rightarrow \langle c!\rangle\top$. Typically, proofs are constructed bottom up. It is useful to consider successive refinements of the formulas involved in the PAR-DIA-τ rule in fig. 2. In practice one introduces formula variables which are incrementally resolved as the proof goes on. For instance the instantiations of ϕ_0, ϕ_1 and ϕ_2 in fig. 2 have been arrived at in this way.

5 Soundness and (Infinitary) Completeness

In this section we *extend* the system (fig. 3) by an *infinitary* ω*-rule* which reduces the provability of open terms to the provability of their closed instances, and by

Sequent Structure Rules.

$$\textsc{Hyp}\ \frac{}{\Gamma, z:\psi \vdash z:\psi} \qquad \textsc{Cut}\ \frac{\Gamma \vdash P':\psi' \quad \Gamma, z:\psi' \vdash P:\psi}{\Gamma \vdash [P'/z]P:\psi}$$

Logical Rules.

$$\textsc{Bot-L}\ \frac{}{\Gamma, z:\bot \vdash P:\psi} \qquad \textsc{Top-R}\ \frac{}{\Gamma \vdash P:\top}$$

$$\textsc{And-L}\ \frac{\Gamma, z:\psi_1 \vdash P:\psi}{\Gamma, z:\psi_1 \wedge \psi_2 \vdash P:\psi} \qquad \textsc{And-R}\ \frac{\Gamma \vdash P:\psi_1 \quad \Gamma \vdash P:\psi_2}{\Gamma \vdash P:\psi_1 \wedge \psi_2}$$

$$\textsc{Or-L}\ \frac{\Gamma, z:\psi_1 \vdash P:\psi \quad \Gamma, z:\psi_2 \vdash P:\psi}{\Gamma, z:\psi_1 \vee \psi_2 \vdash P:\psi} \qquad \textsc{Or-R}\ \frac{\Gamma \vdash P:\psi_1}{\Gamma \vdash P:\psi_1 \vee \psi_2}$$

$$\Rightarrow\text{-L}\ \frac{\Gamma \vdash P':\psi_1 \quad \Gamma, x:\psi_2 \vdash P:\psi}{\Gamma, z:\psi_1 \Rightarrow \psi_2 \vdash [zP'/x]P:\psi} \qquad \Rightarrow\text{-R}\ \frac{\Gamma, z:\psi' \vdash P:\psi}{\Gamma \vdash P[z]:\psi' \Rightarrow \psi}$$

Process Structure Rules.

$$\textsc{Out-1}\ \frac{\Gamma \vdash (fP' \mid P)[f]:\psi}{\Gamma \vdash c!P'.P:(c!)\psi} \qquad \textsc{Out-2}\ \frac{\cdot}{\Gamma \vdash c!P'.P:[\alpha]\psi}\ (c! \neq \alpha)$$

$$\textsc{In-1}\ \frac{\Gamma \vdash P[x]:\psi}{\Gamma \vdash c?x.P:(c?)\psi} \qquad \textsc{In-2}\ \frac{\cdot}{\Gamma \vdash c?x.P:[\alpha]\psi}\ (c? \neq \alpha)$$

$$\textsc{Sum-dia}\ \frac{\Gamma \vdash P:\langle\alpha\rangle\psi}{\Gamma \vdash P+P':\langle\alpha\rangle\psi} \qquad \textsc{Sum-box}\ \frac{\Gamma \vdash P:[\alpha]\psi \quad \Gamma \vdash P':[\alpha]\psi}{\Gamma \vdash P+P':[\alpha]\psi}$$

$$\textsc{Nil}\ \frac{\cdot}{\Gamma \vdash 0:[\alpha]\psi} \qquad \textsc{Par-dia}\ \frac{\Gamma \vdash P_1:\langle\alpha\rangle\psi_1 \quad \Gamma, z_1:\psi_1 \vdash z_1 \mid P_2:\psi}{\Gamma \vdash P_1 \mid P_2:\langle\alpha\rangle\psi}$$

$$\textsc{Par-dia-}\tau\ \frac{\Gamma \vdash P_1:\langle d!\rangle\psi_1 \quad \Gamma \vdash P_2:\langle d?\rangle\psi_2 \quad z_1:\psi_1, z_2:\psi_2 \vdash z_1 z_2:\psi}{\Gamma \vdash P_1 \mid P_2:\langle\tau\rangle\psi}$$

$$\textsc{Par-box}\ \frac{\begin{array}{cc}\Gamma \vdash P_1:[\alpha]\psi_1 & \Gamma \vdash P_2:[\alpha]\psi_2 \\ \Gamma, z_1:\psi_1 \vdash z_1 \mid P_2:\psi & \Gamma, z_2:\psi_2 \vdash P_1 \mid z_2:\psi\end{array}}{\Gamma \vdash P_1 \mid P_2:[\alpha]\psi}\ (\alpha \neq \tau)$$

$$\textsc{Par-box-}\tau\ \frac{\begin{array}{cc}\Gamma \vdash P_1:[\tau]\psi_1 & \Gamma \vdash P_2:[\tau]\psi_2 \\ \Gamma, x_1:\psi_1 \vdash x_1 \mid P_2:\psi & \Gamma, x_2:\psi_2 \vdash P_1 \mid x_2:\psi \\ \Gamma \vdash P_1:[d?]\psi_{1,d?} \wedge [d!]\psi_{1,d!}\ (\text{all } d) & \Gamma \vdash P_2:[d?]\psi_{2,d?} \wedge [d!]\psi_{2,d!}\ (\text{all } d) \\ z_1:\psi_{1,d?}, z_2:\psi_{2,d!} \vdash z_2 z_1:\psi\ (\text{all } d) & z_1:\psi_{1,d!}, z_2:\psi_{2,d?} \vdash z_1 z_2:\psi\ (\text{all } d)\end{array}}{\Gamma \vdash P_1 \mid P_2:[\tau]\psi}$$

Fig. 1. Basic Proof System

$$
\dfrac{
\dfrac{
\dfrac{
\dfrac{
\dfrac{
\dfrac{\vdash 0 : \top \quad x : \langle c!\rangle\top \vdash x : \langle c!\rangle\top}{g : \phi_2 \vdash g0 : \langle c!\rangle\top}
}{\vdash g0[g] : \phi_2 \Rightarrow \langle c!\rangle\top}
}{\vdash b!0 : \phi_1}
\quad x : \phi_1 \vdash x : \phi_1
}{f : \phi_0 \vdash f(b!0) : \phi_1}
\quad
\dfrac{
\dfrac{
\dfrac{\vdash g0[g] : \top}{y : \top \vdash c!0 : \langle c!\rangle\top}
}{\vdash c!0[y] : \phi_2}
}{\vdash b?y.c!0 : \langle b?\rangle\phi_2}
}{f : \phi_0 \vdash f(b!0) \mid b?y.c!0 : \langle\tau\rangle\langle c!\rangle\top}
}{\vdash a!(b!0).b?y.c!0 : \langle a!\rangle(\phi_0 \Rightarrow \langle\tau\rangle\langle c!\rangle\top)}
\quad
\dfrac{
\dfrac{\vdash x : \phi_1 \vdash x : \phi_1}{\vdash x[x] : \phi_0}
}{\vdash a?x.x : \langle a?\rangle\phi_0}
}{\vdash a!(b!0).b?y.c!0 \mid a?x.x : \langle\tau\rangle\langle\tau\rangle\langle c!\rangle\top}
$$

Fig. 2. Proof example

a rule stating the monotonicity of the modal operators. [3] The OMEGA rule is needed to establish a completeness result for the full specification language whereas the MON rule is needed to prove the completeness of the finitary system for a special class of so-called *well-described* specifications (to be described in the next section). First, however, we prove the soundness of the extended system.

$$\text{OMEGA}\ \dfrac{\text{For all } P' \text{ such that} \models P' : \psi',\ \Gamma \vdash [P'/z]P : \psi}{\Gamma, z : \psi' \vdash P : \psi}$$

$$\text{MON}\ \dfrac{\Gamma, z : \phi \vdash z : \psi}{\Gamma, x : (\alpha)\phi \vdash x : (\alpha)\psi}$$

Fig. 3. Additional Rules for Completeness Results.

Proposition 12 Soundness. *If* $\Gamma \vdash P : \psi$ *then* $\Gamma \models P : \psi$.

Proof. Proofs are well-founded, countably branching trees. To every proof one can associate a (transfinite) ordinal which measures its depth. Proceed by transfinite induction on the proof depth. □

Proposition 13. *Suppose that there are a finite number of channels. Then, for any process* P *and number* $k < \omega$*: (1)* $C^k(P)$ *is a finite formula, (2)* $\{C^k(P) \mid P \text{ process}\}$ *is a finite set (up to identification of* ψ *with* $\psi \wedge \psi$*).*

Proof. Prove 1 and 2 together by induction on k and P order. □

Theorem 14 Completeness for closed processes. *If* $\models P : \psi$ *then* $\vdash P : \psi$.

[3] Note that in fact HYP is derivable using MON. This can be seen using a little structural induction.

Proof. Induction on the lexicographic order $(|\psi|, order(\psi), struct(P), struct(\psi))$. One proceeds by case analysis on the structure of P and ψ.

1. $\psi ::= \top \mid \bot$: Direct.
2. $\psi ::= \psi_1 \wedge \psi_2 \mid \psi_1 \vee \psi_2$: $struct(\psi)$ decreases.
3. $\psi ::= \psi_1 \Rightarrow \psi_2$: $order(\psi)$ decreases, use ω-rule.
4. $\psi ::= (\alpha)\psi$: We analyse the structure of the process P (which has order 0).
   (a) $P ::= 0$: Direct.
   (b) $P ::= c!P.P \mid c?x.P$: $|\psi|$ decreases.
   (c) $P ::= P + P$: $struct(P)$ decreases.
   (d) $P ::= P \mid P$: There are two subcases.
      i. $\psi ::= \langle\alpha\rangle\psi$: We give this case in some detail.
         • Suppose $\models P_1 \mid P_2 : \langle\alpha\rangle\psi$ because $P_1 \overset{\alpha}{\to} P_1'$ and $\models P_1' \mid P_2 : \psi$. Let $k = |\psi|$ and $\psi_1 = C^k(P_1')$. We know: $\models P_1' : \psi_1$. Hence: $\models P_1 : \langle\alpha\rangle\psi_1$. We can conclude $\vdash P_1 : \langle\alpha\rangle\psi_1$, by ind. hyp. on P.
         Next we show: $z_1 : \psi_1 \models z_1 \mid P_2 : \psi$. Suppose $\models P_1'' : \psi_1$, then $P_1'' \sim_k P_1'$, which implies $P_1'' \mid P_2 \sim_k P_1' \mid P_2$. Conclude: $\models P_1'' \mid P_2 : \psi$. By induction on $|\psi|$ we have: $\vdash P_1'' \mid P_2 : \psi$. By the ω-rule and PAR-DIA we prove: $\vdash P_1 \mid P_2 : \langle\alpha\rangle\psi$.
         • Otherwise suppose $\alpha \equiv \tau$ and $\models P_1 \mid P_2 : \langle\tau\rangle\psi$ because $P_1 \overset{d!}{\to} P_1'[f]$, $P_2 \overset{d?}{\to} P_2'[x]$, and $\models [P_2'[x]/f]P_1' : \psi$. Let $k = |\psi|$, $\psi_1 = C^k(P_1'[f])$, and $\psi_2 = C^k(P_2'[x])$, Clearly: $\models P_1 : \langle d!\rangle\psi_1$ and $\models P_2 : \langle d?\rangle\psi_2$. Conclude: $\vdash P_1 : \langle d!\rangle\psi_1$ and $\vdash P_2 : \langle d?\rangle\psi_2$, by ind. hyp. on P.
         It remains to show $z_1 : \psi_1, z_2 : \psi_2 \models z_1 z_2 : \psi$. Apply again the logical characterization of the $\sim_k$ relation. Then apply twice the ω rule to get: $z_1 : \psi_1, z_2 : \psi_2 \vdash z_1 z_2 : \psi$. Conclude $\vdash P_1 \mid P_2 : \langle\tau\rangle\psi$, by PAR-DIA-$\tau$.
      ii. $\psi ::= [\alpha]\psi$: This behaves as the previous case w.r.t. the induction hypothesis. □

Remark. Note that this proof never uses the left introduction rules (as hypotheses on the left of the sequent are eliminated by means of the ω-rule). Of course a *finitary* system makes essential use of the left introduction rules, as in fig. 2.

Corollary 15 Completeness. *If $\Gamma \models P : \psi$ then $\Gamma \vdash P : \psi$.* □

6 Finitary Completeness for Well-described Specifications

In this section we seek a finer evaluation of the power and weakness of the finitary system, i.e. the basic proof system in fig. 1 plus the MON rule. The guiding idea is that the system is complete provided specifications are presented in an "explicit" way. We intend to capture this idea by the concepts of k-determinedness, and well-describedness.

Definition 16. A formula ψ is *k-determined* ($k < \omega$) if there are $P_1(z), ..., P_n(z)$, $n \geq 1$, such that $\psi \equiv C^k(P_1(z)) \vee ... \vee C^k(P_n(z))$.

Definition 17. The class of *well-described* formulas is determined as follows:

$\top, \bot$ are well-described.
$\psi_1 \vee \psi_2, \psi_1 \wedge \psi_2$ are well-described if ψ_1, ψ_2 are.
$(\alpha)\psi$ is well-described if ψ is well-described.
$\psi_1 \Rightarrow \psi_2$ is well-described if ψ_2 is well-described and ψ_1 is k-determined, $|\psi_2| \leq k$.

Remarks.

1. The intention is to show that the proof system is complete on all well-formed judgments $z_1 : \psi_1, ..., z_n : \psi_n \vdash P : \psi$ such that $\psi_1 \Rightarrow ... \Rightarrow \psi_n \Rightarrow \psi$ is well-described. By convention we will call these judgments well-described.
2. Every k-determined formula is well-described (easy induction). However, there are well-described formulas which are not k-determined, for instance: $\langle \tau \rangle \top$.
3. The notion of k-determined formula (and therefore also the notion of well-described formula) is not invariant under interpretation equivalent formulas. For instance, $\top$ and $\bigvee_p C^1(p)$ are equivalent formulas but in general the former is not 1-determined (note that the second formula is finite modulo identification of $\psi \vee \psi$ with ψ).
4. Note that a k-determined formula is always realizable.

On well-described judgments the validity of a disjunction of formulas can always be reduced to the validity of one of the formulas. This property plays an important role in the following completeness proof.

Proposition 18. *If* $\Gamma \models P : \psi_1 \vee \psi_2$ *then* $\Gamma \models P : \psi_1$ *or* $\Gamma \models P : \psi_2$.

Proof. Suppose $|\psi_1 \vee \psi_2| = k$. W.l.o.g we may assume (the disjunction on the left can be eliminated): $z_1 : C^k(P_1(z)), ..., z_n : C^k(P_n(z)) \models P : \psi_1 \vee \psi_2$.
This implies: $\models [\mathbf{P_i(z)/z_i}]P : \psi_j$ for $j = 1$ or $j = 2$. Say $j = 1$, then:
$z_1 : C^k(P_1(z)), ..., z_n : C^k(P_n(z)) \models P : \psi_1$ as if $\models Q_i(z) : C^k(P_1(z))$, $i = 1, ..., n$ then $[\mathbf{Q_i(z)/z_i}]P \sim^k [\mathbf{P_i(z)/z_i}]P$ and therefore $\models [\mathbf{Q_i(z)/z_i}]P : \psi_1$. □

Theorem 19 Completeness on well-described judgments. *Suppose* $\Gamma \models P : \psi$ *and the judgment is well-described. Then* $\Gamma \vdash P : \psi$ *is provable without the* ω*-rule.*

Proof. Suppose $z_1 : \psi_1, ..., z_n : \psi_n \models P : \psi$. As in Theorem 14 proceed by induction on the lexicographic order: $(|\psi|, order(\psi), struct(P), struct(\psi))$ and by case analysis on the structure of P and ψ. We only discuss cases which differ in some important way from the corresponding case in the proof of Theorem 14.

1. $\psi ::= \psi_1 \vee \psi_2$: $struct(\psi)$ decreases. By the disjunctive property follows $\Gamma \models P : \psi_i$, say for $i = 1$. By ind. hyp. $\Gamma \vdash P : \psi_1$. Conclude by OR-R.

2. $\psi ::= \psi \Rightarrow \psi'$: $\Gamma \models P[z] : \psi \Rightarrow \psi'$ iff $\Gamma, z : \psi \models P : \psi'$, and $order(\psi)$ decreases.
3. $\psi ::= (\alpha)\psi$: We analyse the structure of the process P (which has order 0).
   (a) $P ::= x$: This case and the next one do not arise in the completeness proof for the infinitary system. W.l.o.g suppose $x : C^k(q) \models x : (\alpha)\psi$. Then $\models q : (\alpha)\psi$. Distinguish two cases:
      i. $(\alpha) \equiv \langle\alpha\rangle$. Then $q \xrightarrow{\alpha} q'$ and $\models q' : \psi$. Hence $C^k(q) \equiv \langle\alpha\rangle C^{k-1}(q') \wedge \psi'$, for some ψ'. It follows: $x : C^{k-1}(q') \models x : \psi$. By ind. hyp. $x : C^{k-1}(q') \vdash x : \psi$. Conclude by MON plus AND-R .
      ii. $(\alpha) \equiv [\alpha]$. If q can make no α transition then $C^k(q) \equiv [\alpha]\bot \wedge \psi'$, for some ψ'. Conclude from $z : \bot \vdash z : \psi$. Otherwise, suppose $q \xrightarrow{\alpha} q'$ then $x : C^{k-1}(q') \models x : \psi$. Conclude as in the previous case.
   (b) $P ::= zP$: W.l.o.g. suppose $\Gamma, z : C^k(q[z']) \models zP : (\alpha)\psi$, where $\Gamma \equiv z_1 : C^k(q_1(z')), \ldots, z_n : C^k(q_n(z'))$. Note that z does not occur in P. Let $r \equiv [\mathbf{q}/\mathbf{z}]P$. Then $\models q[r] : (\alpha)\psi$. Hence: $x : C^k(q[r]) \models x : (\alpha)\psi$ and $\Gamma \models P : C^k(r)$. By ind. hyp. ($struct(P)$ decreases) $x : C^k(q[r]) \vdash x : (\alpha)\psi$ and $\Gamma \vdash P : C^k(r)$. By $\Rightarrow$-L $\Gamma, z : C^k(r) \Rightarrow C^k(q[r]) \vdash zP : (\alpha)\psi$. By AND-L $\Gamma, z : C^k(q[z']) \vdash zP : (\alpha)\psi$. □

7 Research Directions

The issue of finitary completeness, and the attempt to expand the finitary completeness result to richer types of sequent is worth further investigation. We discuss this through a couple of examples.

Example 1. Consider the following valid judgment:

$$x : \top \vdash x : \langle\tau\rangle\top \vee [\tau]\bot$$

It is easy to see that this judgment cannot be proved in the finitary proof system as it stands. One solution could be the inclusion of a rule of consequence allowing the inference of $\Gamma, x : \phi \vdash x : \psi$ whenever $\phi \supset \psi$ is a a theorem of the modal logic K (c.f. [16]). Note that K-theoremhood is decidable. This would allow inference of a number of distribution-like properties such as $\wedge$-$\vee$ distribution and distribution of $\vee$ through $\langle\alpha\rangle$ which are not presently derivable. However we have currently no completeness result for this inference system.

Example 2. Next let us consider a more subtle valid judgment:

$$f : (1_\tau \Rightarrow 2_\tau) \wedge (2_\tau \Rightarrow 1_\tau) \vdash f : \bot$$

where $1_\tau \equiv C(\tau)$ and $2_\tau \equiv C(\tau.\tau)$ (C is the characteristic formula). Proving this judgment amounts to realise that there is no process function $p[x]$ which can separate the processes τ and $\tau.\tau$ without trying to execute them. A proof of this fact should rely on the structure of closed processes. For instance, one may consider adding an induction principle which analyses the structure of process (functionals).

Finally, yet another interesting problem which remains to be settled is that of developing a proof system which can handle restriction. In order to appreciate the difficulties, one may try to develop rules to prove the following valid fact, where Nil is a formula stating that a process can do no action:

$$\nu a.(b!(a?x.0).a?x.0) : \langle a! \rangle (Nil \Rightarrow Nil) \Rightarrow Nil.$$

Acknowledgments. We are indebted to L. Leth, S. Prasad, and B. Thomsen for several discussions on the topics presented here.

References

1. S. Abramsky. A domain equation for bisimulation. *Information and Computation*, 92:161–218, 1991.
2. R. Amadio. On the reduction of chocs bisimulation to π-calculus bisimulation. In *Proc. CONCUR 93, Hildesheim*, pages 112–126. SLNCS 715, 1993. Also appeared as Research Report Inria-Lorraine 1786, October 1992.
3. G. Boudol. Towards a lambda calculus for concurrent and communicating systems. *SLNCS*, 351, 1989. In Proc. TAPSOFT.
4. M. Dam. Model checking mobile processes. In *Proc. CONCUR'93,* Lecture Notes in Computer Science, 715:22–36, 1993. Full version in SICS report RR94:1, 1994.
5. A. Giacalone, P. Mishra, and S. Prasad. Facile: A symmetric integration of concurrent and functional programming. *International Journal of Parallel Programming*, 18(2):121–160, 1989.
6. M. Hennessy. A denotational model for higher-order processes. In *Proc. IEEE-LICS*, 1993.
7. M. Hennessy and X. Liu. A modal logic for message passing processes. Dept. of Computer Science, University of Sussex, Report 3/93, 1993.
8. M. Hennessy and R. Milner. Algebraic laws for nondeterminism and concurrency. *Journal of the ACM*, **32**:137–162, 1985.
9. R. Milner. *Communication and Concurrency.* Prentice Hall, 1989.
10. R. Milner, J. Parrow, and D. Walker. Modal logics for mobile processes. *TCS*, 114:149–171, 1993.
11. F. Nielsen. The typed lambda calculus with first class processes. *Springer Lecture Notes in Computer Science*, 366, 1989. In Proc. PARLE.
12. A. Pitts and I. Stark. What's new? In *Proc. Mathematical Foundations of Computer Science, Gdańsk, Poland.* SLNCS 711, 1993.
13. J. Reppy. Cml: A higher-order concurrent language. In *Proc. ACM-SIGPLAN 91, Conf. on Prog. Lang. Design and Impl.*, 1991.
14. D. Sangiorgi. *Expressing mobility in process algebras: first-order and higher order paradigms.* PhD thesis, University of Edinburgh, September 1992.
15. C. Stirling. Modal logics for communicating systems. *Theoretical Computer Science*, 49:311–347, 1987.
16. C. Stirling. Modal and temporal logics. In *Handbook of Logic in Computer Science* Vol. 2, Oxford University Press, 1992.
17. B. Thomsen. *A calculus of higher order communicating systems.* PhD thesis, Imperial College, London, 1990.
18. B. Thomsen. Plain chocs. *Acta Informatica*, 30:1–59, 1993. Also appeared as TR 89/4, Imperial College, London.

Confluence of Processes and Systems of Objects

Xinxin Liu* and David Walker

Department of Computer Science
University of Warwick
Coventry CV4 7AL, U.K.

Abstract

An extension to the theory of confluence in the process calculus CCS is presented. The theory is generalized to an extension of the π-calculus. This calculus is used to provide semantics by translation for a parallel object-oriented programming language. The confluence theory is applied to prove the indistinguishability in an arbitrary program context of two class definitions which generate binary tree data structures one of which allows concurrent operations.

1 Introduction

The aims of this paper are to present an extension to the theory of confluence in process calculus and to illustrate the new theory by applying it to a problem concerning concurrent operations on binary tree data structures expressed in a parallel object-oriented programming language. In fact, the development of the theory was stimulated by the problem. We begin by describing it.

Characteristic of the object-oriented style of programming is the description of a computational system as a collection of *objects* each of which is a self-contained entity possessing data (references to objects and simple values) and procedures (*methods*) for acting on those data. A program of a parallel object-oriented language typically consists of a collection of class definitions, each of which provides a template for its object *instances*, together with an indication of how a computation should be initiated. Such a program often describes a highly mobile concurrent system in which new objects are created as computation proceeds and references to objects are passed in communications. Parallel object-oriented languages differ from one another in the ways in which they integrate parallelism with object-oriented features; see e.g. [1, 8].

In [4] a development method for concurrent programs is proposed. Central to it are the application of program transformations to control the introduction of concurrency into designs and the use of ideas from object-oriented programming to control

*Supported by a grant from the U.K. Engineering and Physical Sciences Research Council

interference. The problem we consider concerns two classes taken, with minor modifications, from [4] whose instances may be used to construct binary tree-structured symbol tables. The first of these is as follows.

```
class T
var K:NAT, V:ref(A), L:ref(T), R:ref(T)
method Insert(X:NAT, W:ref(A))
    if K=nil then (K:=X ; V:=W ; L:=new(T) ; R:=new(T))
    else if X=K then V:=W
         else if X<K then L!Insert(X,W)
              else R!Insert(X,W) ;
    return
method Search(X:NAT):ref(A)
    if K=nil then return nil
    else if X=K then return V
         else if X<K then return L!Search(X)
              else return R!Search(X)
```

An object of this class represents a node which stores in its variables K, V, L, R an integer key, a value (a reference to an object of some class A) and references to two instances of the class (its left and right children in the tree structure of which it is a component). It has two actions: the method Insert which allows a key-value pair to be inserted, and the method Search which returns the value associated with its key parameter (or nil if there is none). When the expression new(T) is evaluated a new instance of the class is created; the value of the expression is a reference to that object. When an object is created all its variables have nil values and it assumes a quiescent state in which any of its methods may be invoked. On completing a method invocation an object returns to its quiescent state; another method may then be invoked. Execution of the statement L!Insert(X,W) involves left-to-right evaluation of L, X, W and then the invocation in the object to which the value of L is a reference of the Insert method with the values of X, W as parameters. The activity of the invoking object is suspended until it is released from the rendezvous by execution of a return statement by the object in which the method was activated. Note that new (empty) leaf nodes are created when an insertion with a fresh key is made; thus the data structures are full binary trees. The value of the expression L!Search(X) is the value returned to the object by the execution of a return statement in the child node to which the value of L is a reference.

A tree-structured symbol table is accessible to other objects in a system only through its root. Moreover when a method is invoked in the root the entire tree becomes inaccessible until the invocation has been passed down through the structure to the node which should handle it, the appropriate activity has taken place, a sequence of return statements has rippled back along the relevant path, and the root has released from the rendezvous the object which made the initial invocation. The second class definition is as follows.

```
class T
var K:NAT, V:ref(A), L:ref(T), R:ref(T)
method Insert(X:NAT, W:ref(A))
    return ;
    if K=nil then (K:=X ; V:=W ; L:=new(T) ; R:=new(T))
    else if X=K then V:=W
         else if X<K then L!Insert(X,W)
              else R!Insert(X,W)
method Search(X:NAT):ref(A)
    if K=nil then return nil
    else if X=K then return V
         else if X<K then commit L!Search(X)
              else commit R!Search(X)
```

Referring now to the first class as $\mathtt{T_0}$, the new class T can be obtained from it by applying two transformations: firstly, moving the `return` statements in the `Insert` method to the beginning of the body; and second, in the `Search` method, replacing the `return` statements invoking `Search` methods in the children by `commit` statements. The effect of moving the `return` statement in the `Insert` method is to free the invoking object from the rendezvous thus allowing it to proceed in parallel with the node which then proceeds to carry out the insertion. When an object α executes a `commit` statement by invoking a method in an object β, it is implicit (i) that β should return its result not to α but to the object γ to which α should return a result, and (ii) that α is freed from the task of returning a result to γ. In particular, execution of α may proceed in parallel with that of β. Thus if the `Search` method is invoked in a node with a key smaller (resp. larger) than that stored there, the node will commit that search to its left (resp. right) child, and we may think of the node as passing to the child the return address to which the result of the search should be sent. This address will have been received by the node either directly from the initiator of the search (if the node is the root) or from its parent in the tree.

The problem which stimulated the work of this paper was to determine whether the two classes above are interchangeable in an arbitrary program context, that is whether or not the observable behaviour of a program could be altered by replacing one of the classes by the other. A more difficult problem is to determine general conditions under which transformations such as the movement of `return` statements and the replacement of `return` statements by `commit` statements illustrated in the `Insert` and `Search` methods respectively are sound. Such general transformation rules are proposed in [4]. One point of the present work is to bring to the surface some difficulties concerning tractable, general transformation rules. This issue is discussed in the concluding section.

In previous work [22] it has been argued that process calculus provides a good framework for studying the behaviour of systems of concurrent objects. It has been shown [21, 23, 24, 22, 5, 7] that one may give quite natural semantics for parallel object-oriented languages by translation to calculi based on the π-calculus [13] in which agents may pass names of communication links to one another. In particular one may give precise, abstract descriptions of the behaviours of systems and employ the apparatus of process theory to reason about them. The present work gives further evidence of the utility of this kind of framework. To solve the problem stated above we isolate a class of agent contexts which contains all encodings of program contexts of the language in question and show that the agents representing the symbol table classes can not be distinguished by any context in this class.

An intuition which suggests that the symbol tables classes are interchangeable is that the behaviours which they generate are determinate. That is, if requested to execute any sequence of method invocations a table would reach a uniquely determined abstract state having returned a uniquely determined value for each call. That is not to say, however, that tables of the two classes would not be distinguishable in some environments. For example, a table of class T might accept several Search requests before returning the results of the searches in an order different from that in which they were initiated. By contrast, a $\mathtt{T}_0$-table imposes a strict invoke-release discipline on its environment.

A precise definition of *determinacy* is introduced and studied in the setting of the process calculus CCS in [11]. It is shown, among other things, that determinacy is not in general preserved by the CCS composition and restriction operators. With the aim of providing a theoretical framework within which one may build from determinate components systems which are guaranteed, by construction, to be determinate, a refined notion of determinacy, *confluence*, is then introduced. This notion arises in a variety of forms in the theory of computation. Its essence, to quote Milner [11], is that "of any two possible actions, the occurrence of one will never preclude the other". Its pertinence in the present setting is clear. To tackle the problem of the symbol table classes it is necessary to make a significant extension to the theory of confluence as an agent representing a program context may be highly non-confluent. (Incidentally, the generalization of the theory of confluence in CCS to the π-calculus raises interesting questions; a study of this topic will appear in [17].) We introduce a new notion of *partial confluence* which requires of an agent that it be "well-behaved" with respect to a distinguished class of actions. The precise definition is somewhat delicate and uses the branching bisimilarity introduced in [20]. It is chosen to be generous enough to encompass many systems but restrictive enough that it enjoys a strong theory. The main result states, roughly, that in certain contexts a partially-confluent agent may be replaced by a simpler "pruned" version of itself without altering the observable behaviour of the system. Confluence in value-passing CCS has been studied in [18, 19]. In the latter work the definition, from an unpublished note by Milner, of a notion called "partial confluence" for pure CCS agents is stated. Although the same name is used, the version of confluence studied here differs from it. The relationship between the two is explained in the text.

In the following section we collect background material. In section 3 we introduce the theory of partial confluence in the CCS setting and in section 4 generalize it to the process calculus, essentially an amalgamation of value-passing CCS and the π-calculus, which we use as semantic basis. In section 5 we use the theory developed to prove the interchangeability of the two symbol table classes in an arbitrary program context. The paper ends with some concluding remarks. To meet the space requirement most proofs are omitted.

Acknowledgment We thank Cliff Jones whose related research provided an important stimulus for the present work and with whom the second author has enjoyed helpful conversations.

2 Preliminaries

In this section we collect necessary background material on the parallel object-oriented programming language which is the setting for the problem described in the Introduction and on its semantics by translation to the π_v-calculus described in [22].

2.1 The programming language

The programming language is a variant of the $\pi o\beta\lambda$-language [4] which in turn derives from the POOL family [1]. The language has types NAT (natural numbers), BOOL (booleans), UNIT and ref(A) for A a class name. The UNIT type plays a rôle similar to that of the type of that name in the language Standard ML and a mode in ALGOL 68; it has a single value. A value of type ref(A) is a reference to an object of class A; class definitions are explained below. The principal syntactic entities are *statements* each of which is assigned a type in a standard way; we omit the details. The language has constant symbols 0, 1, ... and nil, the last of which is overloaded and is used to represent a reference to no object, the "undefined" value of type NAT and the value of type UNIT. In the abstract syntax definitions below we use K to range over constants, M over method names, A over class names, T over types, X, Y, Z over variables, and S over statements, and we write $\tilde{Z}$ for a tuple $Z_1, \ldots, Z_n$ of syntactic entities. Statements are the well-typed phrases given as follows:

$$\begin{array}{lll} S & ::= & K \mid X \mid \mathsf{new}(A) \mid S!M(\tilde{S}) \mid \mathsf{op}(\tilde{S}) \mid \\ & & X := S \mid S_1; S_2 \mid \mathsf{if}\ S\ \mathsf{then}\ S_1\ \mathsf{else}\ S_2 \mid \\ & & \mathsf{output}\ S \mid \mathsf{return}\ S \mid \mathsf{commit}\ S!M(\tilde{S}). \end{array}$$

The value of new(A) is a reference to a newly-created object of class A. The evaluation of $S!M(\tilde{S})$ involves the left-to-right evaluation of S and the statements in the tuple $\tilde{S}$ followed by the invocation in the object to which the value of S is a reference of the method M of the class of that object with parameters the values of $\tilde{S}$. The value of the statement is the simple value or reference returned to the object as the result of the method invocation. We assume that the basic operation symbols op are $=$, $<$ on NAT and not, and on BOOL. The assignment, sequence and conditional statements are standard. In output S, the statement S of type NAT is evaluated and its value output. The return and commit statements are explained in the Introduction.

Declarations are given as follows. Firstly, variable declarations are given by

$$Vdec \ ::= \ \mathsf{var}\ X_1 : T_1\,, \ldots,\ X_n : T_n$$

Then method declarations are given by

$$Mdec \ ::= \ \mathsf{method}\ M(\widetilde{Y} : \widetilde{T}) : T,\ Vdec,\ S$$

where $\widetilde{T}$ are the types of the formal parameters $\widetilde{Y}$, T is the result type and S is the body of the method with $Vdec$ declaring variables local to it. In the examples in the Introduction, we omit UNIT as result type and abbreviate return nil to return. Sequences of method declarations are given by

$$Mdecs \ ::= \ Mdec_1\,, \ldots,\ Mdec_q$$

class declarations by

$$Cdec \ ::= \ \mathsf{class}\ A,\ Vdec,\ Mdecs$$

and finally program declarations by

$$Pdec \ ::= \ Cdec_1\,, \ldots,\ Cdec_r,\ \ \mathsf{trigger}\ S$$

where S is of the form $\mathsf{new}(A)!M(\widetilde{K})$. The statement S acts as a trigger to initiate the computation by creating and activating a *root object* of one of the classes A.

2.2 The translational semantics

This paper is based on the translational semantics given in [22] which uses the π_v-calculus. To illustrate the sort discipline employed, consider the symbol table classes. As we will see below the class T is encoded as an abstraction of sort (LINK[T]). The sorting decrees that a name of sort LINK[T] carries a pair

$$m_1, m_2 : \mathsf{METH}^I_\mathsf{T}[\mathsf{NAT}, \mathsf{ref(A)}; \mathsf{UNIT}], \mathsf{METH}^S_\mathsf{T}[\mathsf{NAT}; \mathsf{ref(A)}]$$

of names, one for each method of the class (I for Insert, S for Search). A name $m_1 : \mathsf{METH}^I_\mathsf{T}[\mathsf{NAT}, \mathsf{ref(A)}; \mathsf{UNIT}]$ in turn carries an integer, an object identifier of class ref(A), and a return link of sort $\mathsf{RES}^I_\mathsf{T}[\mathsf{UNIT}]$, and similarly $m_2 : \mathsf{METH}^S_\mathsf{T}[\mathsf{NAT}; \mathsf{ref(A)}]$ carries an integer and a return link of sort $\mathsf{RES}^S_\mathsf{T}[\mathsf{ref}(A)]$. We write $\mathsf{OBJECT[T]} \equiv \mathsf{METH}^I_\mathsf{T}[\mathsf{NAT}, \mathsf{ref(A)}; \mathsf{UNIT}], \mathsf{METH}^S_\mathsf{T}[\mathsf{NAT}; \mathsf{ref(A)}]$.

A program $Pdec \equiv Cdec_1, \ldots, Cdec_r$, $\mathsf{trigger}\, S$ is encoded as a restricted composition of the translations of the class definitions and the trigger S:

$$[\![Pdec]\!] \stackrel{\mathrm{def}}{=} (\nu \ldots)([\![Cdec_1]\!]\langle\ldots\rangle \mid \ldots \mid [\![Cdec_r]\!]\langle\ldots\rangle \mid [\![S]\!]\langle\ldots\rangle).$$

It has at most one free name, namely out of sort LINK[NAT] at which integer values may be emitted; it is used in the translation of statements of the form output S. A class definition is translated as a replication with a *link* name to pass out an *object identifier* each time a new object is required. For example the encoding of the table class T has the following form:

$$[\![\mathtt{T}]\!] \stackrel{\text{def}}{=} (new)\,!\,(\nu ins, srch)\,\overline{new}(ins, srch).\,\mathrm{Obj}_{\mathtt{T}}\langle new, ins, srch\rangle$$

where new is the link name, $(ins, srch)$ is the object identifier, and $\mathrm{Obj}_{\mathtt{T}}\langle new, ins, srch\rangle$ represents the object. Note that $ins, srch$ are private names since each new instance of the class has a fresh identifier. Also, (!) is the replication operator from [12] which may be eliminated in favour of an agent constant. We can think of $!P$ as $P|P|P|\ldots$.

We do not repeat here the definition of $[\![\cdot]\!]$; see the papers cited above. Instead, we present two π_v-calculus agents T_0 and T which are simplifications of $[\![\mathtt{class\ T_0}]\!]$ and $[\![\mathtt{class\ T}]\!]$ respectively and explain some ideas of the translation using them. Thus:

$$\begin{array}{lcl} T_0 & \equiv & (new)\,!\,(\nu ins, srch)\,\overline{new}(ins,\ srch).\,E_0\langle new, ins, srch\rangle \\ T & \equiv & (new)\,!\,(\nu ins, srch)\,\overline{new}(ins,\ srch).\,E\langle new, ins, srch\rangle \end{array}$$

where $E_0, E : (\mathsf{LINK[T]}, \mathsf{OBJECT[T]})$, $C_0, C : (\mathsf{LINK[T]}, \mathsf{OBJECT[T]}, \mathsf{N}, \mathsf{OBJECT[A]}, \mathsf{OBJECT[T]}^2)$ are the abstractions defined as follows (where cond is a nested conditional):

$$\begin{array}{l} E_0 \stackrel{\text{def}}{=} (new,\ ins,\ srch) \\ \quad ins(x,w,r).\,new(insl,\ srchl).\,new(insr,\ srchr).\,\overline{r}.\,C_0\langle\ldots,\ x,\ w,\ \ldots\rangle \\ \quad +\,srch(x,r).\,\overline{r}(\mathsf{nil}).\,E_0\langle new,\ ins,\ srch\rangle \end{array}$$

$$\begin{array}{l} C_0 \stackrel{\text{def}}{=} (new,\ ins,\ srch,\ k,\ v,\ insl,\ srchl,\ insr,\ srchr) \\ \quad ins(x,w,r).\ \underline{\mathsf{cond}}\,(\ x = k\ :\overline{r}.\,C_0\langle\ldots,k,w,\ldots\rangle, \\ \qquad\qquad\qquad\qquad x < k\ :\overline{insl}(x,w,\nu r').\,r'.\,\overline{r}.\,C_0\langle\ldots,k,v,\ldots\rangle, \\ \qquad\qquad\qquad\qquad \mathsf{else}\ \ :\overline{insr}(x,w,\nu r').\,r'.\,\overline{r}.\,C_0\langle\ldots,k,v,\ldots\rangle) \\ \quad +\,srch(x,r).\ \underline{\mathsf{cond}}\,(\ x = k : \overline{r}v.\,C_0\langle\ldots,k,v,\ldots\rangle, \\ \qquad\qquad\qquad\qquad x < k : \overline{srchl}(x,\nu r').\,r'(y).\,\overline{r}y.\,C_0\langle\ldots,k,v,\ldots\rangle, \\ \qquad\qquad\qquad\qquad \mathsf{else}\ \ : \overline{srchr}(x,\nu r').\,r'(y).\,\overline{r}y.\,C_0\langle\ldots,k,v,\ldots\rangle) \end{array}$$

$$\begin{array}{l} E \stackrel{\text{def}}{=} (new,\ ins,\ srch) \\ \quad ins(x,w,r).\,\overline{r}.\,new(insl,\ srchl).\,new(insr,\ srchr).\,C\langle\ldots,x,w,\ldots\rangle \\ \quad +\,srch(x,r).\,\overline{r}(\mathsf{nil}).\,E\langle new,\ ins,\ srch\rangle \end{array}$$

$$\begin{array}{l} C \stackrel{\text{def}}{=} (new,\ ins,\ srch,\ x,\ w,\ insl,\ srchl,\ insr,\ srchr) \\ \quad ins(x,w,r).\,\overline{r}.\ \underline{\mathsf{cond}}\,(\ x = k : C\langle\ldots,k,w,\ldots\rangle, \\ \qquad\qquad\qquad\qquad x < k : \overline{insl}(x,w,\nu r').\,r'.\,C\langle\ldots,k,v,\ldots\rangle, \\ \qquad\qquad\qquad\qquad \mathsf{else}\ \ : \overline{insr}(x,w,\nu r').\,r'.\,C\langle\ldots,k,v,\ldots\rangle) \\ \quad +\,srch(x,r).\ \underline{\mathsf{cond}}\,(\ x = k : \overline{r}v.\,C\langle\ldots,k,v,\ldots\rangle, \\ \qquad\qquad\qquad\qquad x < k : \overline{srchl}(x,r).\,C\langle\ldots,k,v,\ldots\rangle, \\ \qquad\qquad\qquad\qquad \mathsf{else}\ \ : \overline{srchr}(x,r).\,C\langle\ldots,k,v,\ldots\rangle). \end{array}$$

Note that we write e.g. $\overline{insl}(x,w,\nu r')$ as an abbreviation for $(\nu r')\overline{insl}(x,w,r')$. From the expressions defining C_0 and C it is not hard to convince oneself (and it can be proved) that T_0 and T are branching bisimilar to $[\![\mathtt{class\ T_0}]\!]$ and $[\![\mathtt{class\ T}]\!]$ respectively.

3 Partial confluence in CCS

In [19], a notion called "R-partial confluence" due to Milner is defined in the setting of pure CCS, where R is a set of labels. It is a generalization of the notion of confluence in that a process is confluent just in case it is R-partially confluent when R is the set of all labels. However, a partially confluent process, like a confluent one, must be determinate with respect to internal moves. So this notion cannot be applied in a situation where internal moves may change an agent's state. In this section we introduce and study a more general version of confluence. Before defining it we introduce a convenient abbreviation: we write $P \Longrightarrow\stackrel{\alpha}{\longrightarrow} P'$ to mean that $P \Longrightarrow P'' \stackrel{\alpha}{\longrightarrow} P'$ for some P'' with $P'' \approx_b P$ and moreover if $\alpha = \tau$ then $P' \not\approx_b P$.

Definition 3.1 Let $R \subseteq \mathcal{L}$ be a set of labels. An agent P is *R-confluent* if for every derivative Q_0 of P, whenever $Q_0 \stackrel{r}{\longrightarrow} Q_1$ and $Q_0 \Longrightarrow\stackrel{\alpha}{\longrightarrow} Q_2$ with $r \in R$ and $\alpha \in Act$, then either $\alpha = r$ and $Q_1 \approx_b Q_2$, or $\alpha \neq r$ and agents Q_1', Q_2' can be found so that $Q_1 \Longrightarrow\stackrel{\alpha}{\longrightarrow} Q_1'$, $Q_2 \Longrightarrow\stackrel{r}{\longrightarrow} Q_2'$ and $Q_1' \approx_b Q_2'$.

It is easy to see that confluence implies R-confluence (for any R). However the converse fails as e.g. $(\tau.a + \tau.b) \mid r$ is $\{r\}$-confluent but not confluent. Although for convienience we have dropped the word "partial", the definition of "R-confluence" generalizes that of "R-partial confluence" stated in [19]. In fact, a process P is R-partially confluent if and only if P is R-confluent and for every derivative Q of P, whenever $Q \stackrel{\tau}{\longrightarrow} Q'$ then $Q \approx_b Q'$. This follows from the fact that if P is determinate with respect to internal moves, i.e. for every derivative P' of P, whenever $P' \stackrel{\tau}{\longrightarrow} P''$ then $P' \approx P''$, then $P \approx Q$ just in case $P \approx_b Q$. It is necessary to use $\approx_b$ instead of $\approx$ in the generalized theory of partial confluence. Roughly speaking, the reason is that since we no longer require processes to be determinate with respect to internal moves, $\approx$ cannot guarantee that R-confluence is a property of equivalence classes. It is straightforward to show that R-confluence is preserved by $\approx_b$.

It is convenient to introduce a further abbreviation. For $s = \alpha_1 \ldots \alpha_n \in Act^*$ we write $\stackrel{s}{\longrightarrow}_\approx$ for the composite relation $\approx_b\stackrel{\alpha_1}{\longrightarrow}\approx_b \ldots \approx_b\stackrel{\alpha_n}{\longrightarrow}\approx_b$. The following result enunciates a simple but useful property of R-confluent agents. Recall from the Preliminaries that s/α is the excess of s over α.

Lemma 3.2 If P is R-confluent then for any $s \in R^*$ and $\alpha \in Act$, whenever $P \stackrel{s}{\longrightarrow}_\approx P_1$ and $P \Longrightarrow\stackrel{\alpha}{\longrightarrow} P_2$, either α occurs in s and $P_2 \stackrel{s/\alpha}{\longrightarrow}_\approx P_1$, or α does not occur in s and there is P_0 such that $P_1 \Longrightarrow\stackrel{\alpha}{\longrightarrow} P_0$ and $P_2 \stackrel{s}{\longrightarrow}_\approx P_0$. □

Using this lemma we can establish the first significant result. It implies that the state of a restricted composition of R-confluent agents is not changed up to $\approx_b$ by an interaction between components via a name and a co-name in R, provided all names in R are restricted.

Lemma 3.3 If P, T are R-confluent, $P \stackrel{s}{\longrightarrow}_\approx P'$ and $T \stackrel{\bar{s}}{\longrightarrow}_\approx T'$ with $s, \bar{s} \in R^*$, $s = r_1 \ldots r_n$, $\bar{s} = \overline{r_1} \ldots \overline{r_n}$, and $R \subseteq L$ then $(P|T)\backslash L \approx_b (P'|T')\backslash L$. □

We now have a rather long definition.

Definition 3.4 Suppose M, R are disjoint sets of names and $\psi : M \rightarrow R$ a function. A derivation-closed set $\mathcal{S}$ of R-confluent agents is (M, R, ψ)-*tidy* if there is a partition $\{\mathcal{S}^{\tilde{r}} \mid \tilde{r}$ a finite submultiset of R$\}$ of $\mathcal{S}$ (an (M, R, ψ)-*tidy partition*) such that:

1. if $P \in \mathcal{S}^{\tilde{r}}$ and $P \xrightarrow{\alpha} P'$ where $\alpha \notin M \cup R$ then $P' \in \mathcal{S}^{\tilde{r}}$;
2. if $P \in \mathcal{S}^{\tilde{r}}$ and $P \xrightarrow{m} P'$ where $m \in M$ then $P' \in \mathcal{S}^{\tilde{r}, \psi(m)}$;
3. if $P \in \mathcal{S}^{\tilde{r}}$ and $P \xrightarrow{r} P'$ where $r \in R$ then $r \in \tilde{r}$ and $P' \in \mathcal{S}^{\tilde{r}-r}$.

Further, $\mathcal{S}$ is (M, R, ψ)-*disciplined* if it is (M, R, ψ)-tidy and

4a. if $P \in \mathcal{S}^{r}$ (where r is a singleton multiset) and $P \xrightarrow{m}$ where $m \in M$ then $P \Longrightarrow\xrightarrow{r}$;

and $\mathcal{S}$ is (M, R, ψ)-*ready* if it is (M, R, ψ)-tidy and

4b. if $P \in \mathcal{S}^{\tilde{r}}$ and $r \in \tilde{r}$ then $P \xrightarrow{r}$.

To grasp the motivation for this definition consider the agent T from the Preliminaries. An (M, R, ψ)-tidy partition is to capture the relationship between method invocations and the corresponding returns. One can view each derivative T' of T as a tree-structured collection of agents each of which represents a tree node. Each time a method is invoked, via $ins(x, w, r)$ or $srch(x, r)$, a return link (r) which does not occur free in T' is received. This name will occur free in each derivative of T' until the result of the call is returned. Now the notion of (M, R, ψ)-tidy partition express the relationship between $ins(x, w, r), r$ and $srch(x, r), r$ by setting $\psi(ins(x, w, r)) = \overline{r}$ and $\psi(srch(x, r)) = \overline{r}$. In more general terms, we can view ψ as an association between names of the distinguished sets M and R such that $\psi(m) \in R$ is the companion action, in some sense, of $m \in M$. An (M, R, ψ)-tidy partition of $\mathcal{S}$ divides its agents, all of which are required to be R-confluent, into classes whose indices record the outstanding companion actions of their elements; conditions 1–3 ensure that this interpretation is accurate. Condition 4b stipulates that an agent must be able to engage immediately in any of its outstanding companion actions. (In the case of the object example this corresponds to the property that when an object invokes a method, its activity is suspended as it awaits the return of the result of that invocation.) Finally, condition 4a requires that if an agent has one outstanding companion action r and it may initiate another activity via an action in M, then it may also perform r, possibly after some τ-actions which, however, do not change its $\approx_b$-state. The purpose of this condition is to ensure, in conjunction with the others, that in certain contexts the behaviour of the agent is indistinguishable from that of an agent obtained by pruning parts of its state space. This is explained in detail in the theorem which follows the definition of the pruning operation.

Definition 3.5 Given a labelled transition system $\mathcal{T}$ and a subset W of its set of points, $\mathcal{T}\lceil W$ is the system obtained by removing all points not in W and all arrows incident on such points. If $P \in W$ we write $\widehat{P}$ for the corresponding point of $\mathcal{T}\lceil W$.

We now have the main result in the CCS case.

Theorem 3.6 Suppose M, R are disjoint sets of names and $\psi : M \to R$, and define $\overline{\psi} : \overline{M} \to \overline{R}$ by setting $\overline{\psi}(\overline{m}) = \overline{\psi(m)}$. Suppose $\mathcal{P}$ is an (M, R, ψ)-ready system with (M, R, ψ)-tidy partition $\{\mathcal{P}^{\bar{r}}\}_{\bar{r}}$, and $\mathcal{T}$ an $(\overline{M}, \overline{R}, \overline{\psi})$-disciplined system with $(\overline{M}, \overline{R}, \overline{\psi})$-tidy partition $\{\mathcal{T}^{\bar{r}}\}_{\bar{r}}$. Suppose $P \in \mathcal{P}^{\emptyset}$, $T \in \mathcal{T}^{\emptyset}$ and $M \cup R \subseteq L$. Let $\widehat{T}$ be the agent corresponding to T in $\mathcal{T}\lceil(\mathcal{T}^{\emptyset} \cup \bigcup\{\mathcal{T}^{r} \mid r \text{ a singleton multiset}\})$. Then $(P|T)\backslash L \approx_b (P|\widehat{T})\backslash L$.

PROOF: Let $(S_1, S_2) \in \mathcal{B}^0$ if $S_1 = (P_1|T_1)\backslash L$ and $S_2 = (P_2|\widehat{T_2})\backslash L$ where $P_2 \in \mathcal{P}^{\emptyset}$, $T_2 \in \mathcal{T}^{\emptyset}$, $P_1 \stackrel{s}{\longrightarrow}_{\approx} P_2$, $T_1 \stackrel{\overline{s}}{\longrightarrow}_{\approx} T_2$ with $s, \overline{s} \in R^*$, $s = r_1 \ldots r_n$, $\overline{s} = \overline{r_1} \ldots \overline{r_n}$, and $M \cup R \subseteq L$. Let also $(S_1, S_2) \in \mathcal{B}^1$ if $S_1 = (P_1|T_1)\backslash L$ and $S_2 = (P_2|\widehat{T_2})\backslash L$ where $P_2 \in \mathcal{P}^r$, $T_2 \in \mathcal{T}^{\overline{r}}$, $P_1 \stackrel{s}{\longrightarrow}_{\approx} P_2$, $T_1 \stackrel{\overline{s}}{\longrightarrow}_{\approx} T_2$ with $s, \overline{s} \in R^*$, $s = r_1 \ldots r_n$, $\overline{s} = \overline{r_1} \ldots \overline{r_n}$, and $M \cup R \subseteq L$. Then $\mathcal{B}^0 \cup \mathcal{B}^1 \cup \approx_b$ is a branching bisimulation. The most interesting part of the proof is as follows.

Suppose $(S_1, S_2) \in \mathcal{B}^1$ where $S_1 = (P_1|T_1)\backslash L$ and $S_2 = (P_2|\widehat{T_2})\backslash L$ are as in the definition with $P_2 \in \mathcal{P}^r$ and $T_2 \in \mathcal{T}^{\overline{r}}$. Suppose $S_1 \stackrel{\tau}{\longrightarrow} Q_1$, and $Q_1 \equiv (P_1' \mid T_1')\backslash L$ where $P_1 \stackrel{m}{\longrightarrow} P_1'$ and $T_1 \stackrel{\overline{m}}{\longrightarrow} T_1'$ where $m \in M$. Let $\mathcal{T}^1$ be $\mathcal{T}^{\emptyset} \cup \bigcup\{\mathcal{T}^{\overline{r}}\}_r$.

Since $T_1 \stackrel{\overline{s}}{\longrightarrow}_{\approx} T_2$, by Lemma 3.2 there are T_0, T_2' such that $T_2 \Longrightarrow T_0 \stackrel{\overline{m}}{\longrightarrow} T_2'$ and $T_1' \stackrel{\overline{s}}{\longrightarrow}_{\approx} T_2'$ with $T_0 \approx_b T_2$. Since $\mathcal{T}$ is $(\overline{M}, \overline{R}, \overline{\psi})$-disciplined, $T_0 \in \mathcal{T}^{\overline{r}}$ and $m \in M$, $T_0 \Longrightarrow\stackrel{\overline{r}}{\longrightarrow}$. Hence $T_2 \Longrightarrow\stackrel{\overline{r}}{\longrightarrow} T_3$ for some T_3. Hence as T_2 is R-confluent, $T_3 \Longrightarrow T_4 \stackrel{\overline{m}}{\longrightarrow} T_5$ and $T_2' \stackrel{\overline{r}}{\longrightarrow}_{\approx} T_5$ for some T_4 and T_5 with $T_4 \approx_b T_3$. Now $T_3, T_4 \in \mathcal{T}^{\emptyset}$ and $T_5 \in \mathcal{T}^{\overline{r'}}$ where $r' = \psi(m)$, so the transitions $\widehat{T_2} \Longrightarrow\stackrel{\overline{r}}{\longrightarrow} \widehat{T_3} \Longrightarrow \widehat{T_4} \stackrel{\overline{m}}{\longrightarrow} \widehat{T_5}$ exist in $\mathcal{T}\lceil\mathcal{T}^1$.

Now since $P_1 \stackrel{s}{\longrightarrow}_{\approx} P_2$, by Lemma 3.2 there are P_0 and P_2' such that $P_2 \Longrightarrow P_0 \stackrel{m}{\longrightarrow} P_2'$, $P_0 \approx_b P_2$ and $P_1' \stackrel{s}{\longrightarrow}_{\approx} P_2'$. Because $\mathcal{P}$ is (M, R, ψ)-ready and $P_2 \in \mathcal{P}^r$, $P_2 \stackrel{r}{\longrightarrow} P_3$ for some P_3. Since P_2 is R-confluent, $P_3 \Longrightarrow P_4 \stackrel{m}{\longrightarrow} P_5$ and $P_2' \stackrel{r}{\longrightarrow}_{\approx} P_5$ for some P_4 and P_5 with $P_4 \approx_b P_3$. Thus $(P_2|\widehat{T_2})\backslash L \Longrightarrow\stackrel{\tau}{\longrightarrow} (P_3|\widehat{T_3})\backslash L \Longrightarrow (P_4|\widehat{T_4})\backslash L \stackrel{\tau}{\longrightarrow} (P_5|\widehat{T_5})\backslash L$.

It remains to note that by the construction $(S_1, (P_4 \mid \widehat{T_4})\backslash L) \in \mathcal{B}^0$ and $(Q_1, (P_5 \mid \widehat{T_5})\backslash L) \in \mathcal{B}^1$. These claims follow from Lemma 3.2. □

4 Partial confluence in the π_v-calculus

We now generalize the theory presented in the previous section.

Notation 4.1 (a) We write $\mathsf{subj}(\alpha)$ for the subject of the action α. If $s = \alpha_1 \ldots \alpha_n$ is a sequence of actions then $\mathsf{subj}(s) = \mathsf{subj}(\alpha_1) \ldots \mathsf{subj}(\alpha_n)$.

(b) Let R be a sort. We write R^+ (resp. R^-) for the set of actions with a positive (resp. negative) subject whose name is in R, and $R^\pm$ for $R^+ \cup R^-$.

Definition 4.2 Let R be a sort. A process P is *R-confluent* if for every derivative Q of P:

1. if $\rho \in R^{\pm}$, $\mathsf{subj}(\alpha) \neq \mathsf{subj}(\rho)$, $Q \stackrel{\rho}{\longrightarrow} Q_1$ and $Q \Longrightarrow\stackrel{\alpha}{\longrightarrow} Q_2$ then for some Q', $Q_1 \Longrightarrow\stackrel{\alpha}{\longrightarrow} Q'$ and $Q_2 \Longrightarrow\stackrel{\rho}{\longrightarrow}\dot{\approx}_b Q'$;
2. if $\rho_1, \rho_2 \in R^-$, $\mathsf{subj}(\rho_1) = \mathsf{subj}(\rho_2)$, $Q \stackrel{\rho_1}{\longrightarrow} Q_1$ and $Q \Longrightarrow\stackrel{\rho_2}{\longrightarrow} Q_2$ then $\rho_1 = \rho_2$ and $Q_1 \approx_b Q_2$;
3. if $\rho \in R^+$, $Q \stackrel{\rho}{\longrightarrow} Q_1$ and $Q \Longrightarrow\stackrel{\rho}{\longrightarrow} Q_2$ then $Q_1 \dot{\approx}_b Q_2$.

The theory presented in the previous section can be generalized, with some changes, to the new setting. In the space available, however, we can only state the main definition and theorem.

We first formulate analogues of the notions "(M, R, ψ)-tidy" etc. In the CCS case the purpose of the function ψ was to record an association between names in M and names in R. In the present setting this is achieved in a different way, namely via a sorting which associates with the sort M a tuple of sorts of the form $(\widetilde{S}, R, \widetilde{S'})$ where R does not occur in the tuples $\widetilde{S}$ and $\widetilde{S'}$. Then if $\alpha \in M^{\pm}$, the name of the subject of α is m and the component, $\mathsf{obj}_R(\alpha)$, of the object of α of sort R is r, then m and r are associated. It is appropriate also to reflect in the following definition the asymmetric nature of communication in the π_v-calculus. Thus we define "(M^-, R^+)-tidy" (with requirements on output actions whose subjects have names in M and input actions with subjects in R) rather than "(M, R)-tidy" etc.

Definition 4.3 Suppose M and R are distinct sorts and the sorting Σ is such that $\Sigma(M) = (\widetilde{S}, R, \widetilde{S'})$ for some tuples of sorts $\widetilde{S}$ and $\widetilde{S'}$ not containing R and R occurs in no other object sort. A derivation-closed set $\mathcal{S}$ of R-confluent processes is (M^-, R^+)*-tidy* if there is a partition $\{\mathcal{S}^{\tilde{r}} \mid \tilde{r}$ a finite subset of R$\}$ of $\mathcal{S}$ (an (M^-, R^+)*-tidy partition*) such that:

1. if $P \in \mathcal{S}^{\tilde{r}}$ and $P \stackrel{\alpha}{\longrightarrow} P'$ where $\alpha \notin M^- \cup R^+$ then $P' \in \mathcal{S}^{\tilde{r}}$;
2. if $P \in \mathcal{S}^{\tilde{r}}$ and $P \stackrel{\alpha}{\longrightarrow} P'$ where $\alpha \in M^-$ and $r \notin \tilde{r}$ where $r = \mathsf{obj}_R(\alpha)$ then $P' \in \mathcal{S}^{\tilde{r},r}$;
3. if $P \in \mathcal{S}^{\tilde{r}}$ and $P \stackrel{\alpha}{\longrightarrow} P'$ where $\alpha \in R^+$ then $\mathsf{subj}(\alpha) = r \in \tilde{r}$ and $P' \in \mathcal{S}^{\tilde{r}-r}$.

Further, $\mathcal{S}$ is (M^-, R^+)*-ready* if it is (M^-, R^+)-tidy and

4a. if $P \in \mathcal{S}^{\tilde{r}}$ and $r \in \tilde{r}$ then $P \stackrel{\alpha}{\longrightarrow}$ for any $\alpha \in R^+$ with $\mathsf{subj}(\alpha) = r$.

Similarly, we define (M^+, R^-)*-tidy (partition)* and say $\mathcal{S}$ is (M^+, R^-)*-disciplined* if it is (M^+, R^-)-tidy with (M^+, R^-)-tidy partition $\{\mathcal{S}^{\tilde{r}}\}_{\tilde{r}}$ and

4b. if $P \in \mathcal{S}^r$ (where r is a singleton multiset) and $P \stackrel{\alpha}{\longrightarrow}$ where $\alpha \in M^+$ then $P \Longrightarrow\stackrel{\beta}{\longrightarrow}$ for some $\beta \in R^-$ with $\mathsf{subj}(\beta) = \overline{r}$.

Theorem 4.4 Suppose M and R are distinct sorts and the sorting Σ is such that $\Sigma(M) = (\widetilde{S}, R, \widetilde{S'})$ for some tuples of sorts $\widetilde{S}$ and $\widetilde{S'}$ not containing R and R occurs in no other object sort. Suppose $\mathcal{P}$ is an (M^-, R^+)-ready set with (M^-, R^+)-tidy partition $\{\mathcal{P}^{\tilde{r}}\}_{\tilde{r}}$, and $\mathcal{T}$ an (M^+, R^-)-disciplined set with (M^+, R^-)-tidy partition $\{\mathcal{T}^{\tilde{r}}\}_{\tilde{r}}$. Suppose $P \in \mathcal{P}^{\emptyset}$, $T \in \mathcal{T}^{\emptyset}$ and no derivative of $(\nu\tilde{z})(P \mid T)$ contains a free occurrence in subject position of a name of sort R or of sort M. Let $\widehat{T}$ be the process corresponding to T in $\mathcal{T}\lceil(\mathcal{T}^{\emptyset} \cup \bigcup\{\mathcal{T}^r \mid r \text{ a singleton multiset}\})$. Then $(\nu\tilde{z})(P|T) \approx_b (\nu\tilde{z})(P|\widehat{T})$.

5 An example

In Section 2.4 we defined agents T_0 and T which are simplified encodings of the symbol table classes $\mathsf{T_0}$ and T respectively. To illustrate the theory of partial confluence we now use it to establish the equivalence of T_0 and T in the encoding of an arbitrary program context, thus proving the interchangeability of the symbol table classes $\mathsf{T_0}$ and T as discussed in the Introduction.

Suppose $\mathcal{C}[\cdot]$ is the encoding of a program context into which an abstraction of sort $(\mathsf{LINK[T]})$, the sort of the agents encoding the classes, may be placed. Then $\mathcal{C}[\cdot]$ is of the form $(\nu new)(P \mid \cdot\langle new\rangle)$ where P is the encoding of the other classes and the trigger of the program. Since the classes have more than one method, it is necessary to generalize the definitions of "(M^-, R^+)-tidy" etc. to the case when instead of single sorts M and R we have tuples $M = M_1 \ldots M_n$ and $R = R_1 \ldots R_n$ of distinct sorts where the sorting Σ is such that for each i, $\Sigma(M_i) = (\widetilde{S_i}, R_i, \widetilde{S'_i})$ for some tuples $\widetilde{S_i}$ and $\widetilde{S'_i}$. This is straightforward. The following theorem expresses the equivalence of the class definitions.

Theorem 5.1 Let $\mathcal{C}[\cdot] = (\nu new)(P \mid \cdot\langle new\rangle)$ be the translation of an arbitrary program context and T_0, T as in the Preliminaries. Then $\mathcal{C}[T] \approx_b \mathcal{C}[T_0]$.

PROOF: We want to show that $(\nu new)(P \mid T_0\langle new\rangle) \approx_b (\nu new)(P \mid T\langle new\rangle)$. Let $\mathcal{T}$ be the process system generated by $T_0\langle new\rangle$ and $T\langle new\rangle$, and $\mathcal{P}$ the process system generated by P. Let M be the pair of sorts $\mathsf{METH^I_T[NAT, ref(A); UNIT]}$, $\mathsf{METH^S_T[NAT; ref(A)]}$ and R the pair $\mathsf{RES^I_T[UNIT]}$, $\mathsf{RES^S_T[ref(A)]}$ and consider the generalized definitions of "(M^+, R^-)-tidy" etc. The proof involves showing:

1. $\mathcal{P}$ is (M^-, R^+)-ready.
2. $\mathcal{T}$ is (M^+, R^-)-disciplined.
3. $T_0\widehat{\langle new\rangle} \approx_b T\widehat{\langle new\rangle}$, where $T_0\widehat{\langle new\rangle}$ and $T\widehat{\langle new\rangle}$ are the states corresponding to $T_0\langle new\rangle$ and $T\langle new\rangle$ respectively in $\mathcal{T}\lceil(\mathcal{T}^{\emptyset} \cup \bigcup\{\mathcal{T}^r \mid r \text{ a singleton multiset}\})$.

By 1 and 2 above, applying the main theorem in the previous section we have

$$(\nu new)(P \mid T_0\langle new\rangle) \approx_b (\nu new)(P \mid T_0\widehat{\langle new\rangle}) \quad \text{and}$$
$$(\nu new)(P \mid T\langle new\rangle) \approx_b (\nu new)(P \mid T\widehat{\langle new\rangle}).$$

Together with 3 and the observation that by the nature of the translation the theorem's condition on names of sort M or R is met, these facts complete the proof.

In the space available we can only sketch the proof. We consider first 1. The names of sort R are return links for invocations via names of sort M. In the translation the use of these names has a very strict pattern: $\overline{m}(\tilde{p}, \nu r)$ where $m : M$ is always followed by an action with subject $r : R$, and an action with subject $r : R$ is always preceded by $\overline{m}(\tilde{p}, \nu r)$ where $m : M$. As illustrated in the Preliminaries, P is a restricted composition and it follows that any derivative of it must (up to structural congruence) have the form

$$Q \equiv (\nu\tilde{p})\,(r_1(x_1).P_1 \mid \ldots \mid r_n(x_n).P_n \mid r'_1.P'_1 \mid \ldots \mid r'_m.P'_m \mid Q') \tag{1}$$

where $r_1, \ldots, r_n$: $\mathsf{RES}^S_\mathsf{T}[\mathtt{ref(A)}]$ and $r'_1, \ldots, r'_m$: $\mathsf{RES}^I_\mathsf{T}[\mathsf{UNIT}]$ are pairwise distinct (as private names are used for returning results), and for any action $\alpha \in R^+$, $Q' \not\xrightarrow{\alpha}$, $P_i \not\xrightarrow{\alpha}$, $P'_i \not\xrightarrow{\alpha}$. As each of its elements has this form, $\mathcal{P}$ is an R-confluent process system. Now let $\{\mathcal{P}^{\tilde{r}} \mid \tilde{r}$ a finite subset of $R\}$ be the partition of $\mathcal{P}$ defined by setting $Q \in \mathcal{P}^{\tilde{r}}$ for Q of form (1) if $\tilde{r} = \{r_1, \ldots, r_n, r'_1, \ldots, r'_m\}$. It may be checked that this partition is (M^-, R^+)-tidy. It is clear that $\mathcal{P}$ is (M^-, R^+)-ready.

For $T_0\langle new\rangle$ and $T\langle new\rangle$ we can obtain the general form of the derivatives by analyzing their syntax. We may then apply the technique of unique solution of process equations to prove that $T_0\langle new\rangle \approx_b \widehat{T\langle new\rangle}$. Now by the translation no derivative of $\mathcal{C}[T] \equiv (\nu new)(P \mid T\langle new\rangle)$ contains a free occurrence in subject position of a name of sort M or R. Hence from 1, 2 and 3 above it follows by the generalized version of the main theorem of the preceding section that $\mathcal{C}[T_0] \stackrel{.}{\approx}_b \mathcal{C}[\widehat{T_0}]$ and $\mathcal{C}[T] \stackrel{.}{\approx}_b \mathcal{C}[\widehat{T}]$ and hence $\mathcal{C}[T] \stackrel{.}{\approx}_b \mathcal{C}[T_0]$. Moreover since out is the only free name it follows that $\mathcal{C}[T] \approx_b \mathcal{C}[T_0]$. □

6 Conclusion

The notion of partial confluence introduced here is worthy of further investigation. In addition to the intrinsic interest of the theory it may be useful in e.g. the study of concurrency control in databases [15]. As a further example we intend to study concurrent operations on binary search trees and B-trees as presented in e.g. [9, 10]. Also of interest are connections with non-interleaving semantics of concurrent systems and action/process refinement as in e.g. [3].

The proof presented in Section 5 can be viewed, as mentioned in the Introduction, as establishing the soundness of particular instances of general transformation rules such as those proposed in [6]. Those rules stipulate conditions under which (in the notation of the present paper) a statement of the form S; **return** S' may be replaced by **return** $S'; S$, and a statement of the form **return** $X!M(Y)$ by **commit** $X!M(Y)$. These conditions refer to termination of (executions of) statements and to properties of a distinguished class of program variables called "private references". No semantic account of "private references" if given in [6], nor is it stipulated how they may be used in programs. It appears that to satisfy the side conditions of the rules in question, quite severe syntactic restrictions may be necessary. Moreover the requirement to establish termination of (executions of) statements which may invoke methods in systems of objects with dynamically-evolving structure may be very demanding. The theory developed in this paper provides a framework, at an appropriate level of abstraction, for reasoning rigorously about the behaviours of systems of objects whose reference structures are (forests of) trees. It remains a tough challenge to provide a comparable framework on which to base a proof of the soundness of general transformation rules whose side conditions are not unduly restrictive or intractable.

References

[1] P. America. Issues in the design of a parallel object-oriented language. *Formal Aspects of Computing*, 1:366–411, 1989.

[2] U. Engberg and M. Nielsen. A calculus of communicating systems with label passing. Technical report, University of Aarhus, 1986.

[3] W. Janssen, M. Poel, and J. Zwiers. Action systems and action refinement in the development of parallel systems. In *CONCUR'91*, pages 298–316. Springer, 1991.

[4] C. Jones. Constraining interference in an object-based design method. In *Proceedings of TAPSOFT'93*, pages 136–150, 1993.

[5] C. Jones. A pi-calculus semantics for an object-based design notation. In *Proceedings of CONCUR'93*, pages 158–172, 1993.

[6] C. Jones. Process-algebraic foundations for an object-based design notation. Technical report, University of Manchester, 1993.

[7] C. Jones. Process algebra arguments about an object-based design method. In *Essays in Honour of C. A. R. Hoare*. Prentice-Hall, 1994.

[8] D. Kafura and R. G. Lavender. Concurrent object-oriented languages and the inheritance anomoly. In T. Casavant, editor, *Parallel Computers: Theory and Practice*. Computer Society Press, to appear.

[9] H. Kung and P. Lehman. Concurrent manipulation of binary search trees. *ACM Transactions on Database Systems*, 5:354–382, 1980.

[10] P. Lehman and S. B. Yao. Efficient locking for concurrent operations on B-trees. *ACM Transactions on Database Systems*, 6:650–670, 1981.

[11] R. Milner. *Communication and Concurrency*. Prentice-Hall, 1989.

[12] R. Milner. The polyadic π-calculus: a tutorial. In *Logic and Algebra of Specification.* Springer, 1992.

[13] R. Milner, J. Parrow, and D. Walker. A calculus of mobile processes, parts 1 and 2. *Information and Computation*, 100:1–77, 1992.

[14] R. Milner, J. Parrow, and D. Walker. Modal logics for mobile processes. *Theoretical Computer Science*, 114:149–171, 1993.

[15] C. Papadimitriou. *The Theory of Database Concurrency Control.* Computer Society Press, 1986.

[16] M. Papathomas. *Language Design Rationale and Semantic Framework for Concurrent Object-Oriented Programming.* PhD thesis, University of Geneva, 1992.

[17] A. Philippou. PhD thesis, University of Warwick, forthcoming.

[18] M. Sanderson. *Proof techniques for CCS.* PhD thesis, University of Edinburgh, 1982.

[19] C. Tofts. *Proof methods and pragmatics for parallel programming.* PhD thesis, University of Edinburgh, 1990.

[20] R. van Glabbeek and P. Weijland. Branching time and abstraction in bisimulation semantics. In *Information Processing '89*, pages 613–618, 1989.

[21] D. Walker. π-calculus semantics for object-oriented programming languages. In *Proceedings of TACS'91*, pages 532–547. Springer, 1991.

[22] D. Walker. Algebraic proofs of properties of objects. In *Proceedings of ESOP'94*, pages 501–516. Springer, 1994.

[23] D. Walker. Objects in the π-calculus. *Information and Computation*, to appear.

[24] D. Walker. Process calculus and parallel object-oriented programming lanaguages. In T. Casavant, editor, *Parallel Computers: Theory and Practice.* Computer Society Press, to appear.

An Algebraic Approach to Temporal Logic

Burghard von Karger*

Institut für Informatik 2, Christian-Albrechts-Universität, Preusserstr. 1-9, D-24105 Kiel, Germany. email: bvk@informatik.uni-kiel.d400.de

Abstract. The sequential calculus is an algebraic calculus, intended for reasoning about phenomena with a duration and their sequencing. It can be specialized to various domains used for reasoning about programs and systems, including Tarski's calculus of binary relations, Kleene's regular expressions, Hoare's CSP and Dijkstra's regularity calculus.

In this paper we use the sequential calculus as a tool for algebraizing temporal logics. We show that temporal operators are definable in terms of sequencing and we show how a specific logic may be selected by introducing additional axioms. All axioms of the complete proof system for discrete linear temporal logic (given in [9]) are obtained as theorems of sequential algebra.

Our work embeds temporal logic into an algebra naturally equipped with sequencing constructs, and in which recursion is definable. This could be a first step towards a design calculus for transforming temporal specifications by stepwise refinement into executable programs.

This paper is an extended abstract of a technical report [5] containing full proofs (available by ftp). Most proofs have been omitted and simplifying assumptions were made to make the presentation easier.

1 Introduction

The nature and purpose of abstraction has been described by Dijkstra in [4].

> We now take what is a standard step in mathematical theory building. The step is taken after the introduction of a notational novelty — such as a new abbreviation or a "mathematical macro" — for formulae that were interpreted in a familiar domain of discourse. The step consists of starting with a clean slate and axiomatising afresh the manipulations of the new formulae. In doing so, one creates a new domain of discourse; the rôle of the old, familiar domain of discourse, that used to constitute the subject matter, is thereby reduced to that of providing a possible model for the newly postulated theory. It is essential that the axioms of the new theory — which can be interpreted as theorems in the old universe of discourse — are clearly postulated as such and that the new theory is derived from them without any reference to the model of the

* This research has been funded by the Deutsche Forschungsgemeinschaft under grant KA 1052/1-1

old universe of discourse. This is the only way to assure that the axioms of the new theory provide an interface that is independent of the old universe of discourse and that, hence, the new theory is safely applicable to alternative models.

Temporal logic is a perfect example. The "old domain of discourse" consists of sequences of states inside some computer and the notational novelty is a collection of temporal operators like $\bigcirc$ (next) and $\diamond$ (eventually). Abstraction is achieved by singling out a set of axioms from the set of laws governing the manipulation of temporal formulae.

Mathematics derives its power from the nesting of abstractions. Here is an example of such nesting. Peano's axioms abstract away from any particular representation of the set **N** of natural numbers. Further abstraction yields the concept of a semigroup. Semigroups are more general, and **N** is a very specific semigroup, namely it is infinite and cyclic. Conversely, every infinite and cyclic semigroup satisfies the Peano axioms.

Similarly, sequential algebra is an abstraction of temporal logic which is itself an abstraction of a concrete computational model. Sequential algebra is more general than temporal logic, and temporal logic can be characterized as a sequential algebra with specific properties.

The increase in abstraction is not of the trivial kind, like in "groups are more general than rings" which results from simply dropping some of the given structure. It is interesting because it is based on a radically different approach. As in the example, a logical characterisation (the Peano axioms) is replaced by algebraic structure (semigroups).

Abstractions usually enjoy the advantage of greater simplicity (semigroups are specified by just one axiom). A sequential algebra is just a complete boolean algebra with a semigroup structure and a few axioms giving the interaction between composition and the boolean connectives (whereas Manna and Pnueli's axiomatization of linear temporal logic has 17 axioms, not counting the boolean ones). Semigroups and boolean algebras with operators are thoroughly investigated subjects of algebra and the connection to temporal logic might enable valuable cross fertilization.

Abstraction frequently offers opportunities of building additional algebraic structure. Semigroups can, under certain conditions, be embedded into groups; in our example this yields a construction of the integers. Our work embeds temporal logic into an algebra that is naturally equipped with programming constructs like sequential composition, nondeterministic choice and conditionals, and in which recursion is definable.

It is hard to foresee all possible uses of a new abstraction, but let us list some objectives worth striving for.

- *Power*: The embedding mentioned in the previous paragraph could be a first step towards a design calculus for transforming temporal specification by stepwise refinement, where each step replaces some abstract subterm by a more concrete one, until an executable program is reached.

- *Taxonomy*: Various temporal logics can be identified as subtheories of sequential algebra and large parts of sequential algebra theory can be developed before specialising to any particular of them. We should aim at a general theory, which can be specialised to interesting and/or well-known calculi or logics by adding axioms in an incremental fashion.
- *Applications*: In a pragmatic sense, the abstract approach may also help to discover new applications of temporal logic. The existing axiomatisation of temporal logic has been guided by a specific computational model, and the sheer number of axioms makes it hard to think of alternative models satisfying them. Showing that all of these axioms are consequences of a small number of assumptions expressible in a more abstract universe may make it easier to think of new situations where these assumptions also hold.

It is important to understand that sequential algebra is not proposed as an alternative to, or replacement of, temporal logic, in the same sense that semigroup theory cannot make Peano's axioms obsolete. Sequential algebra provides a very roundabout way of arriving at the simple and elegant set of operators of temporal logic. Their original discovery was a great intellectual achievement, and the value of temporal logic has been demonstrated abundantly in practical applications. Sequential algebra, on the other hand, aims at abstraction, integration, and classification, rather than direct usefulness for engineering problems. It is not decidable, and it is not complete. It cannot be, or else it could not encompass any theory that lacks these properties.

The rest of this paper is structured as follows. In the next section we gently introduce the sequential calculus. Section 3 collects basic concepts and laws, most of them familiar from the calculus of relations. Building on this, section 4 introduces the operators of temporal logic. In section 5 we come to the algebraic laws of temporal expressions, adding new axioms as needed on the way, until we obtain as theorems precisely the axioms listed in [9]. In the final section we discuss what progress we have achieved towards the three objectives set out above.

Except for a few examples, to show the style, we have to omit all proofs. They can be found in [5] (some also in [6]). But we do provide all the necessary lemmas, and the reader who was worked in the relational or a similar calculus should not find it too hard to fill the proofs in.

2 The Sequential Calculus

The relational calculus has been remarkably successful in reasoning about possibly non-deterministic systems, provided that their behaviour can be fully characterised by observation of just their initial and final states [1, 8, 12]. Many alternative models have been proposed for reactive systems, whose behaviour between initiation and termination is also of significance. A common feature of these calculi is that past observations cannot be cancelled or undone by what comes after.

The general modelling technique is to represent each possible system as a set, whose elements represent single *observations* of a single experiment on the system described. In the relational calculus [13], the observations are pairs (s, t), where s and t are drawn from the same set of states. In the calculus of intervals [3], these are required to be related by a total ordering $(s \leq t)$. In regular expressions [7] the observations are finite sequences of letters drawn from an alphabet A. In the regularity calculus [4], the sequences are given the structure of a free group. Another example is interval-based temporal logic (which is not to be confused with the point-based temporal logic studied in this paper), where observations are functions from time intervals to states, where time is a total ordering and may be discrete or continuous, finite or infinite [10, 14].

Any calculus for sets should start from consideration of the properties of their members; and sequential algebra relies only on qualities shared by *all* the observation spaces in question. The most basic common property is the existence of an associative composition operator $(x; y)$, which makes a possibly longer observation from subobservations x and y. For regular expressions, this is just concatenation of strings, and for free groups it is the group multiplication. In other cases, composition is a partial operator: in the relational calculus, the pair (r, s) can be composed with (s', t) only if $s = s'$; and when this equality holds, the intermediate state is omitted:

$$(r, s); (s, t) \;=\; (r, t). \tag{1}$$

Similarly, in interval temporal logic, composition is defined only when the end time and final state of the first operand are the same as the start time and initial state of the second operand. Then the two functions are compatible, so that their union is a function and can be taken as the result of the composition.

To help reasoning about the definedness of composition, we introduce two functions between observations. Each observation x has a left unit $\overleftarrow{x}$ and a right unit $\overrightarrow{x}$, which satisfy the unit properties for composition:

$$\overleftarrow{x}; x \;=\; x \;=\; x; \overrightarrow{x}.$$

For example, in the relational and interval calculi

$$\overleftarrow{(s,t)} = (s,s) \quad \text{and} \quad \overrightarrow{(s,t)} = (t,t).$$

In interval temporal logic $\overleftarrow{x}$ is the initial state and time, whereas $\overrightarrow{x}$ is the final state and time. In both cases, composition is defined just when the right unit of the left operand is the same as the left unit of the right operand:

$$x; y \text{ is defined iff } \overrightarrow{x} = \overleftarrow{y}.$$

In regular expressions (as in free groups) there is just a single unit for composition, the empty sequence. As a consequence $\rightarrow$ and $\leftarrow$ are constant functions, and composition is everywhere defined.

The unit functions have two additional properties[2]: they map units to themselves, and they depend only on the left or right operands of composition:

$$\overleftarrow{\overleftarrow{x}} = \overleftarrow{\overrightarrow{x}} = \overleftarrow{x} \quad \text{and} \quad \overrightarrow{\overleftarrow{x}} = \overrightarrow{\overrightarrow{x}} = \overrightarrow{x}$$

$$\overleftarrow{x;y} = \overleftarrow{x} \quad \text{and} \quad \overrightarrow{x;y} = \overrightarrow{y}.$$

Another property shared by all our models of reactive systems is *cancellativity*:

$$\text{If } x;y = x';y' \text{ then } (x = x') \equiv (y = y').$$

To formalize the idea that time can only progress in a single dimension we introduce a prefix ordering on observations. If $x = y;z$ then y is said to be a prefix of x (and z a postfix). We postulate

If x and y are prefixes of z then x is a prefix of y, or y is a prefix of x.

In reactive systems, it is not possible to backtrack or rewrite history by an inverting operation. The only action that can be undone is the trivial action that has not actually done anything, i.e. a unit $\overleftarrow{z}$. So we require that units are *indivisible*

$$x;y = \overleftarrow{z} \quad \text{implies} \quad x = y = \overleftarrow{z}.$$

The last assumption seems reasonable and it considerably simplifies the presentation of temporal logic through sequential algebra. However, we make it only for pedagogical reasons; the entire development is possible without it. It is given in full in [5].

Recall that the domain of temporal logic is given by

$$I \stackrel{def}{=} \Sigma^{\omega} \times \mathrm{N}$$

where Σ is some given set of states. Every observation $(\sigma, n) \in I$ consists of an infinite sequence of states and one position in that sequence, and a temporal formula P may be seen as denoting a set of them, namely

$$\{(\sigma, n) \in I \mid (\sigma, n) \models P\}.$$

But the observations (σ, n) have no duration. The only natural way to impose an observation space structure on I is by defining a trivial composition operator, namely $i;i = i$ and $i;j$ undefined for all distinct $i, j \in I$.

To make composition useful, we embed I into a larger space L in such a way that I is precisely the set of all units of L. Instead of a single index n into the sequence σ, we allow a pair $m \leq n$ of indices, specifying a (finite) interval, rather than a point. Composition of (σ, m, n) and (σ', m', n') is defined only when $\sigma = \sigma'$ and $n = m'$; and then we put

$$(\sigma, m, n); (\sigma, n, n') = (\sigma, m, n').$$

[2] These properties endow the observation space with the structure of a small category

Identifying (σ, n) with (σ, n, n) we are lead to define the projection operators by

$$\overleftarrow{(\sigma, m, n)} = (\sigma, m) \quad \text{and} \quad \overrightarrow{(\sigma, m, n)} = (\sigma, n).$$

A characteristic of this observation space is that each observation carries within it a knowledge of the entire past and future. Consequently, two observations with the same, say, left unit can only be distinguished by their duration, and the longer one must be an extension of the shorter. Formally

$$\overleftarrow{x} = \overleftarrow{y} \quad \Rightarrow \quad x \text{ is a prefix of } y \text{ or } y \text{ is a prefix of } x$$
$$\overrightarrow{x} = \overrightarrow{y} \quad \Rightarrow \quad x \text{ is a postfix of } y \text{ or } y \text{ is a postfix of } x.$$

An observation space with these properties is called *deterministic*, because each state determines the entire past and future.

Now let L be some fixed observation space. The objective of sequential algebra is to formalise a calculus of subsets of L. These obviously form a complete boolean algebra with join $\cup$, meet $\cap$, complement $\overline{\cdot}$, least element O and greatest element L. Just as relational composition is a lifted form of the composition of pairs (1), our more general sequential composition is obtained by lifting the composition defined for single observations.

$$PQ \stackrel{def}{=} \{z \mid \exists x \in P, y \in Q \,.\, x;y = z\}.$$

The identity element of composition is

$$I \stackrel{def}{=} \{x \mid \overleftarrow{x} = x = \overrightarrow{x}\}.$$

The absence of a general converse forces us to define a *relative* converse P/Q, to play the same role that $P\breve{Q}$ plays in the relational calculus. Each observation of P/Q is obtained from an observation of P by cutting from the end something that is an observation of Q:

$$P/Q \stackrel{def}{=} \{x \mid \exists\, z \in P\,,\, y \in Q \,.\, x;y = z\}.$$

and, symmetrically,

$$Q \backslash P \stackrel{def}{=} \{y \mid \exists\, x \in Q\,,\, z \in P \,.\, x;y = z\}.$$

We rule that composition binds more strongly than / and \, and, in turn, these bind more strongly than $\cup$ and $\cap$.

We now perform the abstraction step described by Dijkstra by listing a number of theorems valid in the power set algebra over an observation space and taking these as the axioms of a new algebraic structure, called a sequential algebra.

2.1 Definition A sequential algebra is a complete boolean algebra equipped with a constant I and three binary operators PQ, $P \backslash Q$, and P/Q satisfying axioms 2.2 – 2.5.

2.2 Monoid axiom Composition is associative and has I as its identity.

The second axiom is the Schröder law from the relational calculus, except that $P\breve{Q}$ and $\breve{P}Q$ are replaced by P/Q and $P\backslash Q$. The term 'exchange' is due to Dijkstra.

2.3 Exchange axiom $PQ \subseteq \overline{R}$ iff $P\backslash R \subseteq \overline{Q}$ iff $R/Q \subseteq \overline{P}$.

Not all laws of relational algebra translate into laws of sequential algebra. For example,

$$(PQ)\breve{R} = P(Q\breve{R}) = P(R\breve{Q})^{\cup}$$

holds in relational algebra, whereas in sequential algebra no two of the expressions $(PQ)/R$, $P(Q/R)$ and $P/(R/Q)$ are equal. In fact, PQ/R describes observations obtained from PQ by cutting off the right something in R. So do the other two terms, but in a more specific way. In $P(Q/R)$ the cut has to be placed *after* the transition from P to Q, whereas in $P/(R/Q)$ it must be *before*.

2.4 Split axiom $PQ/R = P(Q/R) \cup P/(R/Q)$.

The last axiom of sequential algebra is the following

2.5 Converse Axiom $I/P = P\backslash I$.

We do not explain this axiom here (but see [5]), because we will not use it. Our assumption that units are indivisible permits a much stronger axiom

2.6 Indivisibility Axiom $I/L = I$.

We need not postulate the symmetric counterpart of the last axioms, because they can be proved as theorems. The sequential calculus enjoys a perfect symmetry between past and future and with every theorem we prove we get for free its time-wise dual.

An observation space is deterministic iff its power set algebra satisfies the following law

2.7 Determinacy axiom $(P/L)L = PL \cup P/L$,

To understand this, note that P/L is the prefix closure of P. This axiom does not seem to imply its time-wise dual, so we postulate that also. Most of our theory can be developed without the determinacy axiom, and we will draw special attention to the place where it is needed.

This concludes the abstraction step. From now on observations must not be mentioned anymore (except for motivating definitions). Additional operators may only be defined in terms of the basic ones, and proofs must solely rely on the axioms of sequential algebra.

3 Basics of Sequential Algebra

In this section we define the analogues of some basic concepts of the relational calculus, and list relevant algebraic laws. — The composition and both of the partial converse operators are universally disjunctive. In particular, they have O as left and right zero. Moreover, the following laws hold

$$\begin{array}{ccc} P\backslash(Q/R)=(P\backslash Q)/R & P/QR=(P/R)/Q & P/I=P \\ \overline{PQ}/Q \subseteq \overline{P} & \overline{P/Q}\,Q \subseteq \overline{P} & \\ (R\cap P/S)S \supseteq RS\cap P & (R\cap PS)/S \supseteq R/S\cap P & \end{array} \tag{2}$$

Iteration is defined by $P^0 = I$, $P^{i+1} = PP^i$, and $P^* = \bigcup_{i\geq 0} P^i$.

3.1 Predicates

In the relational calculus, a state s can be represented by the observation (s, s). So, a *predicate* on states may be represented as a set of observations x with $\overleftarrow{x} = x = \overrightarrow{x}$. Generalising this idea to the sequential calculus, we call P a predicate iff $P \subseteq I$. By convention, B and C always denote predicates. Let us define a negation operator by

$$\neg P \overset{def}{=} \overline{P} \cap I.$$

We allow logical notation for predicates

$$\begin{array}{ccc} B \vee C \overset{def}{=} B \cup C & B \wedge C \overset{def}{=} B \cap C & B \rightarrow C \overset{def}{=} \neg B \vee C \\ \mathbf{T} \overset{def}{=} I & \mathbf{F} \overset{def}{=} O & \end{array}$$

Clearly, the set of all predicates forms a boolean algebra. Here are some laws:

$$\begin{array}{ccc} B(P\cap Q) = BP\cap Q & BC = B\cap C & (B\cap C)P = BP\cap CP \\ (\neg B)L = \overline{BL} & BP = B\backslash P & \\ PB/Q = P/QB & BP/Q = B(P/Q) & P/BQ = (P/Q)B \end{array} \tag{3}$$

3.2 Domain and Codomain

As in the relational calculus, every P can be projected to its domain or codomain

$$\overleftarrow{P} = \{\overleftarrow{x} \mid x \in P\} \quad \text{and} \quad \overrightarrow{P} = \{\overrightarrow{x} \mid x \in P\}. \tag{4}$$

These definitions can be given at the calculus level by

$$\overleftarrow{P} \overset{def}{=} I \cap P/P \quad \text{and} \quad \overrightarrow{P} \overset{def}{=} I \cap P\backslash P. \tag{5}$$

They satisfy a couple of useful Galois connections.

$$(\overleftarrow{P} \subseteq B) \equiv (P \subseteq BL) \tag{6}$$

$$(\overleftarrow{PB} \subseteq \neg C) \equiv (\overrightarrow{CP} \subseteq \neg B). \tag{7}$$

Here are some more laws

$$\begin{array}{lll} \overleftarrow{P}P = P & \overleftarrow{B} = B & L/P = L\overleftarrow{P} \\ \overleftarrow{BP} = B\overleftarrow{P} & \overleftarrow{P\overleftarrow{Q}} = \overleftarrow{PQ} & \overleftarrow{P}L = (P/L)L \end{array} \tag{8}$$

The next law depends on the determinacy axiom. It is crucial for establishing that the next and previous operators cancel each other out.

$$\overrightarrow{\overleftarrow{P}Q} \;=\; \overrightarrow{P\backslash Q} \cup \overleftarrow{Q\backslash P}. \tag{9}$$

The proof proceeds by indirect equality:

$$\begin{array}{ll}
\overrightarrow{\overleftarrow{P}Q} \subseteq \neg C & \\
\equiv \overleftarrow{QC} \subseteq \neg \overleftarrow{P} & \text{(by the Galois connection (6))} \\
\equiv QC \subseteq (\neg \overleftarrow{P})L & \text{(by the Galois connection (7))} \\
\equiv QC \subseteq \overline{\overleftarrow{P}L} & \text{(since } (\neg B)L = \overline{BL}\text{)} \\
\equiv QC \subseteq \overline{PL \cup P/L} & (\overleftarrow{P}L = (P/L)L\text{, determinacy axiom)} \\
\equiv (Q/C \subseteq \overline{PL}) \wedge (P/L \subseteq \overline{QC}) & (QC = Q/C\text{, boolean algebra)} \\
\equiv (PLC \subseteq \overline{Q}) \wedge (QCL \subseteq \overline{P}) & \text{(exchange axiom)} \\
\equiv (P\backslash Q \subseteq \overline{LC}) \wedge (Q\backslash P \subseteq \overline{CL}) & \text{(exchange axiom)} \\
\equiv (P\backslash Q \subseteq L(\neg C)) \wedge (Q\backslash P \subseteq (\neg C)L) & \text{(since } (\neg B)L = \overline{BL}\text{)} \\
\equiv \overrightarrow{P\backslash Q} \cup \overleftarrow{Q\backslash P} \subseteq \neg C & \text{(by the Galois connection (6))} \quad \blacksquare
\end{array}$$

3.3 The All-the-Time Operator

Suppose x is an observation with the following property: Whereever you cut x in two, you find a state at which the predicate B holds:

$$x = y; z \quad \Rightarrow \quad \overrightarrow{y} \in B.$$

Then B is said to hold *all the time* in x. The set $[B]$ of all observations x with this property can be defined as follows:

$$[B] \;\stackrel{def}{=}\; \overline{L(\neg B)\, L}.$$

The all-the-time operator is conjunctive and distributes over composition

$$\begin{array}{rcl} [B \cap C] & = & [B] \cap [C] \\ {[B]} \cap PQ & = & ([B] \cap P)([B] \cap Q). \end{array}$$

Moreover, B can be retrieved from $[B]$ by applying the domain (or codomain) operator

$$\overleftarrow{[B]} \;=\; B \;=\; \overrightarrow{[B]}.$$

4 The Operators of Temporal Logic

The smallest measurements of progress are non-unit observations that cannot be further decomposed into non-unit subobservations. Such observations correspond to single transitions of the observed system. The set of all transitions is described by

$$\mathit{step} \stackrel{\mathit{def}}{=} \overline{I} \cap \overline{\overline{I}\,\overline{I}}.$$

$\bigcirc B$ holds at some state s iff there is a transition x with $\overleftarrow{x} = s$ and B holds at $\overrightarrow{x}$. The time-wise dual of the 'next' operator is the 'previous' operator $\ominus$.

$$\bigcirc B \stackrel{\mathit{def}}{=} \overleftarrow{\mathit{step}\, B} \qquad \ominus B \stackrel{\mathit{def}}{=} \overrightarrow{B\, \mathit{step}}.$$

B 'until' C holds at a state s if there is an observation x with $\overleftarrow{x} = s$ such that $B \vee C$ holds all the time in x and C holds at the end. The time-wise dual is 'since':

$$B\, \mathcal{U}\, C \stackrel{\mathit{def}}{=} \overleftarrow{[B \vee C]C} \qquad B\, \mathcal{S}\, C \stackrel{\mathit{def}}{=} \overrightarrow{C[B \vee C]}.$$

The remaining operators are defined in terms of the four basic ones

$$\begin{array}{lll}
\Diamond B \stackrel{\mathit{def}}{=} \mathbf{T}\, \mathcal{U}\, B & \Box B \stackrel{\mathit{def}}{=} \neg\Diamond\neg B & B\, \mathcal{W}\, C \stackrel{\mathit{def}}{=} \Box B \vee B\, \mathcal{U}\, C \\
\ominus\!\!\!\!\Diamond B \stackrel{\mathit{def}}{=} \mathbf{T}\, \mathcal{S}\, B & \boxminus B \stackrel{\mathit{def}}{=} \neg\ominus\!\!\!\!\Diamond\neg B & B\, \mathcal{B}\, C \stackrel{\mathit{def}}{=} \boxminus B \vee B\, \mathcal{S}\, C \\
\tilde{\bigcirc} B \stackrel{\mathit{def}}{=} \neg\bigcirc\neg B & \tilde{\ominus} B \stackrel{\mathit{def}}{=} \neg\ominus\neg B & \\
\mathit{first} \stackrel{\mathit{def}}{=} \neg\ominus\mathbf{T} & \mathit{last} \stackrel{\mathit{def}}{=} \neg\bigcirc\mathbf{T} &
\end{array}$$

5 The Algebra of Temporal Logic

In this section we sketch how the axioms of a temporal logic may be proved as theorems of sequential algebra. The first task is to establish the (almost-Galois) connection between 'next' and 'previous':

$$(B \subseteq \bigcirc C) \quad \text{iff} \quad (B \subseteq \neg \mathit{last}) \wedge (\ominus B \subseteq C).$$

We prove the direction from right to left.

$$\begin{array}{lllll}
\bigcirc C & \stackrel{\text{premise}}{\supseteq} \bigcirc\ominus B & = \overleftarrow{\mathit{step}\, \overrightarrow{B\, \mathit{step}}} & \stackrel{(9)}{=} & \overrightarrow{(B\, \mathit{step})/\mathit{step}} \cup \overleftarrow{\mathit{step}/(B\, \mathit{step})} \\
\stackrel{(3)}{=} & \overrightarrow{B(\mathit{step}/\mathit{step})} \cup \overleftarrow{(\mathit{step}/\mathit{step})B} & & \stackrel{(5)}{\supseteq} & \overrightarrow{B\, \overleftarrow{\mathit{step}}} \cup \overleftarrow{\overleftarrow{\mathit{step}}\, B} \\
\stackrel{(3)}{=} & \overrightarrow{B \wedge \overleftarrow{\mathit{step}}} \cup \overleftarrow{\overleftarrow{\mathit{step}} \wedge B} & \stackrel{(8)}{=} B \wedge \overleftarrow{\mathit{step}} & = & B \wedge \bigcirc\mathbf{T} \; = \; B \wedge \neg\mathit{last} \\
\stackrel{\text{premise}}{\supseteq} & B. & & &
\end{array}$$

■

The definitions of the last section make also sense for continuous time (i.e. $step = O$), except that, of course, 'next' and 'previous' map everything to **F**. We will now restrict ourselves to the discrete case. We postulate[3].

5.1 Discreteness axiom $\quad L = step^*.$

Under the assumption of discreteness, 'until' can also be defined in terms of iteration

$$B \,\mathcal{U}\, C = \overleftarrow{(B\; step)^* C}.$$

which, in turn, gives a more intuitive definition of 'eventually'

$$\Diamond B = \bigcup_{i \geq 0} \bigcirc^i B. \tag{10}$$

It is now easy to prove that the temporal operators satisfy the following algebraic laws

$$\begin{aligned}
\tilde{\bigcirc} B &= last \vee \bigcirc B \\
\Box B &\subseteq B \\
\bigcirc \neg B &\subseteq \neg \bigcirc B \\
\tilde{\bigcirc}(B \to C) &= \tilde{\bigcirc} B \to \tilde{\bigcirc} C \\
\Box(B \to C) &\subseteq \Box B \to \Box C \\
\Box B &\subseteq \Box \tilde{\bigcirc} B \\
first \wedge \Box B &\subseteq \Box \widetilde{\ominus} B \\
\Box(B \to \tilde{\bigcirc} B) &\subseteq \Box(B \to \Box B) \\
first \wedge \Box(B \to \widetilde{\ominus} B) &\subseteq \Box(B \to \boxminus B) \\
B \,\mathcal{W}\, C &= C \vee (B \wedge \tilde{\bigcirc}(B \,\mathcal{W}\, C)) \\
\Box B &\subseteq B \,\mathcal{W}\, C \\
first &\subseteq \widetilde{\ominus} \mathbf{F} \\
B &\subseteq \tilde{\bigcirc} \ominus B
\end{aligned} \tag{11}$$

We have not, so far, made any assumptions violating time-wise symmetry, so the temporal duals of the above laws also hold. But Manna and Pnueli's logic applies to computations that continue forever: no computation can ever reach a last state. So we postulate

---

[3] The discreteness axiom can be weakened so as to allow infinite sequences of discrete transitions. A full treatment is given in [5]. This is not needed for the observation space suggested as domain for temporal logic on page 2, but is useful for dealing with recursion.

5.2 Progress axiom $\quad last = \mathbf{F}.$

Since $\widetilde{\bigcirc}B = last \vee \bigcirc B$, this implies that $\bigcirc$ coincides with its de Morgan dual $\widetilde{\bigcirc}$.

Our declared objective is to prove the axioms of temporal logic as theorems in sequential algebra. Since the conventions of algebra differ from those of logic we need to explain the correspondence.

In logic, temporal expressions achieve meaning through a validity relation, whereas in our approach they denote elements of a sequential algebra. Fortunately all we need to relate the two is a slight change of perspective.

Recall that a state corresponds to a pair (σ, n) where n is an index into the computation sequence σ; such a state is initial iff $n = 0$. In the logic we aim at, a formula is said to be valid if it holds at all initial states. Translating to algebra, we define a predicate B to be *valid* iff

$$first \subseteq B.$$

Temporal logic has stronger versions of implication and equivalence, denoted by $\Rightarrow$ and $\Leftrightarrow$. They are defined by

$$(B \Rightarrow C) \stackrel{def}{=} \Box(B \rightarrow C)$$

and

$$(B \Leftrightarrow C) \stackrel{def}{=} (B \Rightarrow C) \wedge (C \Rightarrow B).$$

B is said to *entail* C iff $B \Rightarrow C$ is valid. Two predicates B and C that entail each other are *congruent*.

5.3 Lemma $\quad$ Assume $B \subseteq C$. Then B entails C.

Using this lemma, and the equality of $\bigcirc$ and $\widetilde{\bigcirc}$, we can translate the laws (11) into temporal validities.

5.4 Theorem All of the following predicates are valid

$$\Box B \rightarrow B$$
$$\bigcirc\neg B \Leftrightarrow \neg\bigcirc B$$
$$\bigcirc(B \rightarrow C) \Leftrightarrow (\bigcirc B \rightarrow \bigcirc C)$$
$$\Box(B \rightarrow C) \Rightarrow (\Box B \rightarrow \Box C)$$
$$\Box B \rightarrow \Box\bigcirc B$$
$$(B \Rightarrow \bigcirc B) \rightarrow (B \Rightarrow \Box B)$$
$$(B \mathcal{W} C) \Leftrightarrow (C \vee (B \wedge \bigcirc(B \mathcal{W} C)))$$
$$\Box B \Rightarrow (B \mathcal{W} C)$$
$$B \Rightarrow \bigcirc\ominus B$$

$$\ominus B \Rightarrow \widetilde{\ominus} B$$
$$\widetilde{\ominus}(B \rightarrow C) \Leftrightarrow (\widetilde{\ominus} B \rightarrow \widetilde{\ominus} C)$$
$$\boxminus(B \rightarrow C) \Rightarrow (\boxminus B \rightarrow \boxminus C)$$
$$\Box B \rightarrow \Box\ominus B$$
$$(B \Rightarrow \widetilde{\ominus} B) \rightarrow (B \Rightarrow \boxminus B)$$
$$(B \mathcal{B} C) \Leftrightarrow (C \vee (B \wedge \bigcirc(B \mathcal{B} C)))$$
$$\widetilde{\ominus}\mathbf{F}$$
$$B \Rightarrow \widetilde{\ominus}\bigcirc B.$$

This is precisely the set of axioms given in [9]. — Manna and Pnueli define $\mathcal{U}$ and $\mathcal{S}$ in terms of $\mathcal{W}$ and $\mathcal{B}$, whereas we had to do it the other way round. This is not a problem, because their definitions come out as theorems

$$B\,\mathcal{U}\,C = B\,\mathcal{W}\,C \wedge \Diamond C \quad \text{and} \quad B\,\mathcal{S}\,C = B\,\mathcal{B}\,C \wedge \diamondminus C.$$

Manna and Pnueli assume that computations do not extend infinitely into the past: every computation sequence σ must have a first element. This is expressed by the following postulate:

5.5 Well-foundedness axiom $\diamondminus \mathit{first} \ = \ \mathbf{T}$.

It is a curious fact that all axioms of temporal logic can be proved without invoking well-foundedness. Its only use is in proving the entailment theorem, which states that congruence in logic corresponds precisely to equality in algebra.

5.6 Entailment Theorem B entails C if and only if $B \subseteq C$.

Proof. B entails C

$$\begin{array}{lr}
\equiv \mathit{first} \subseteq \Box(B \to C) & \text{(by def. of entailment and validity)} \\
\equiv \Diamond\neg(B \to C) \subseteq \neg\mathit{first} & \text{(by def. of } \Box) \\
\equiv \forall i \geq 0 : \bigcirc^i \neg(B \to C) \subseteq \neg\mathit{first} & \text{(by (10))} \\
\equiv \forall i \geq 0 : \overleftarrow{\mathit{step}^i \neg(B \to C)} \subseteq \neg\mathit{first} & \text{(by def. of } \bigcirc \text{ and } \overleftarrow{P\overleftarrow{Q}} = \overleftarrow{PQ}) \\
\equiv \forall i \geq 0 : \overrightarrow{\mathit{first}\ \mathit{step}^i} \subseteq (B \to C) & \text{(since } (\overleftarrow{PB} \subseteq \neg C) \equiv (\overrightarrow{CP} \subseteq \neg B)) \\
\equiv \forall i \geq 0 : \ominus^i \mathit{first} \subseteq (B \to C) & \text{(see two steps above)} \\
\equiv \diamondminus \mathit{first} \subseteq (B \to C) & \text{(see four steps above)} \\
\equiv B \subseteq C & \text{(by well-foundedness)} \ \blacksquare
\end{array}$$

6 Conclusion

We showed that all axioms of Manna and Pnueli's logic correspond to theorems of deterministic sequential algebra. Conversely, as we have explained in section 2, the domain $\Sigma^\omega \times \mathbf{N}$ of this logic can be embedded into an observation space, and then our definitions of $\bigcirc$ etc. coincides with the standard one. From this it follows that every equation between temporal expressions that can be proved in sequential algebra gives a valid congruence of temporal logic.

To summarise, we have modelled Manna and Pnueli's logic precisely. We have proved all the axioms as theorems, and we have shown that no theorem can be derived that would correspond to an invalid formula.

In the introduction we suggested three aims of an algebraic approach to temporal logic. Let us now review how much progress has been made towards these objectives.

Power. We have not attempted to outline a design calculus here, but a first attempt has been made in a companion paper [2]. But the proofs we have given (and those we had to omit) illustrate the interplay between the temporal expressions that pertain to single points and the sequential constructs which enable us to calculate with longer sections of a computation. They are also very similar in flavour to the relational calculus, which has been so successful for design and correctness proofs of conventional programs. This makes us hope that the sequential calculus may be similarly efficacious for the construction of reactive processes.

There is another interesting possibility. We considered the temporal operators as operators on predicates only, but nothing in their definitions prevents us from applying them to arbitrary arguments. For example, the predicate $\bigcirc(x := x+1)$ holds at some point iff the next but one transition increments x by one.

In another paper [6], we developed a fragment of interval temporal logic from sequential algebra (without needing any additional axioms). So we have also integrated point-based and interval-based temporal logic in a single framework, simpler and more general than either.

Taxonomy. We developed one variety of temporal logic from sequential algebra by adding four axioms to sequential algebra, each of which corresponds to one of four orthogonal design decisions (of Manna and Pnueli): The determinacy axiom for linearity of time, the discreteness axiom, the progress axiom for allowing only infinite computation sequences, and the well-foundedness axiom for requiring that every computation sequence must have a first element. Other choices lead to different points in temporal logic country, but it will need someone more widely travelled than this author to attempt a complete mapping.

We have also seen that definitions can be taken and many theorems can be proved before additional axioms are introduced. In particular, practically all work can be done before breaking time-wise symmetry. Late commitments are the key to avoiding painful duplication and backtracking.

Applications. Observation spaces provide models for sequential algebra, thereby providing a way of finding new uses for temporal logic. A promising candidate is Hoare's theory of Communicating Sequential Processes. Observation spaces for CSP are well explored [11] and all we need is to add a little twist to make them deterministic. It remains to be seen if this integration of CSP with relational calculus and temporal logic can lead to improved design methods for concurrent programs.

7 Acknowledgements

Thanks to Tony Hoare for supervising and encouraging the emergence of the sequential calculus, and for many helpful comments on an earlier version of this paper.

References

1. R. Berghammer, P. Kempf, G. Schmidt, and T. Ströhlein. Relation algebra and logic of programs. In *Algebraic Logic*, volume 54 of *Colloquia Mathematica Societatis János Bolyai*. Budapest University, 1988.
2. R. Berghammer and B. von Karger. Formal derivation of CSP programs from formal specifications. submitted to MPC 95, 1995.
3. S. M. Brien. A time-interval calculus. In R. Bird, C. Morgan, and J. Woodcock, editors, *Mathematics of Program Construction*, LNCS 669. Springer-Verlag, 1992.
4. E. W. Dijkstra. The unification of three calculi. In M. Broy, editor, *Program Design Calculi*, pages 197–231. Springer Verlag, 1993.
5. B. v. Karger. Temporal logic as a sequential calculus. Procos technical report [kiel bvk 17], Christian-Albrechts-Univ., Inst. f. Inf. und Prakt. Math., Kiel, 1994. available via WWW, `http://www.informatik.uni-kiel.de/~procos/kiel.html`.
6. B. v. Karger and C.A.R. Hoare. Sequential calculus. To appear in Information Processing Letters, 1995.
7. S. Kleene. Representation of events in nerve nets and finite automata. In Shannon and McCarthy, editors, *Automata Studies*, pages 3–42. Princeton University Press, 1956.
8. R. Maddux. A working relational model: The derivation of the Dijkstra-Scholten predicate transformer semantics from Tarski's axioms of the Peirce-Schröder calculus of relations. Manuscript, 1992.
9. Z. Manna and A. Pnueli. *The Temporal logic of Reactive and Concurrent Systems—Specification.* Springer-Verlag, 1991.
10. B. Moszkowski. Some very compositional temporal properties. Technical Report TR-466, University of Newcastle, 1993. Accepted for Procomet 1994, San Miniato.
11. E. Olderog and C. Hoare. Specification oriented semantics for communicating processes. *Acta Inf.*, 23:9–66, 1986.
12. G. Schmidt and T. Ströhlein. *Relations and Graphs.* EATCS Monographs on Theoretical Computer Science. Springer, 1991.
13. A. Tarski. On the calculus of relations. *Journal of Symbolic Logic*, 6(3):73–89, 1941.
14. C. Zhou, C.A.R. Hoare, and A. P. Ravn. A calculus of durations. *Information Processing Letters*, 40:269–276, 1992.

On behavioural abstraction and behavioural satisfaction in higher-order logic*

Martin Hofmann** and Donald Sannella***

Laboratory for Foundations of Computer Science
University of Edinburgh, Edinburgh EH9 3JZ

Abstract. The behavioural semantics of specifications with higher-order formulae as axioms is analyzed. A characterization of behavioural abstraction via behavioural satisfaction of formulae in which the equality symbol is interpreted as indistinguishability, due to Reichel and recently generalized to the case of first-order logic by Bidoit *et al*, is further generalized to this case. The fact that higher-order logic is powerful enough to express the indistinguishability relation is used to characterize behavioural satisfaction in terms of ordinary satisfaction, and to develop new methods for reasoning about specifications under behavioural semantics.

1 Introduction

An important ingredient in the use of algebraic specifications to describe data abstractions is the concept of *behavioural equivalence*, which seems to appropriately capture the "black box" character of data abstractions, see e.g. [GM82], [ST87]. Roughly speaking, two Σ-algebras A, B are behaviourally equivalent with respect to a set OBS of *observable types* if all computations that can be expressed in Σ and that yield a result in OBS produce the same result in both A and B. A specification of a data abstraction should characterize a class of algebras that is closed under behavioural equivalence; otherwise it forbids some realizations that are indistinguishable from acceptable ones. Closure can be ensured by means of a specification-building operation known as *behavioural abstraction* [SW83], [ST87]. The term "behavioural semantics" is used to characterize approaches that take the need for behavioural closure into account.

One issue in behavioural semantics is the relationship between the class of algebras produced by applying behavioural abstraction to a specification $\langle \Sigma, \Phi \rangle$, and that obtained by simply interpreting equality in Φ as *indistinguishability* rather than as identity. The latter approach, sometimes known as *behavioural satisfaction*, is due to Reichel [Rei85] who showed that these two classes coincide when the axioms involved are conditional equations, provided that the

---

* This is a condensed version of [HS95].

** E-mail mxh@dcs.ed.ac.uk. Supported by a Human Capital and Mobility fellowship, contract number ERBCHBICT930420.

*** E-mail dts@dcs.ed.ac.uk. Supported by an EPSRC Advanced Fellowship and EPSRC grants GR/H73103 and GR/J07303.

conditions used are equations between terms of types in OBS. Bidoit *et al* have recently generalized this to the case of specifications with first-order equational formulae and reachability constraints as axioms, and to arbitrary relations of behavioural equivalence and indistinguishability. In [BHW94] they show that the coincidence holds in this context as well, whenever the class of models of $\langle\Sigma,\Phi\rangle$ (under ordinary satisfaction) is closed under quotienting w.r.t. indistinguishability, provided that indistinguishability is *regular* and that behavioural equivalence is *factorizable* by indistinguishability.

We examine these issues for the case of (flat) specifications with higher-order logical formulae as axioms, generalizing the framework and results of [BHW94]. Although it is not made explicit there, the main results in [BHW94] including the characterization theorem do not strongly depend on the form of axioms. We give syntax and semantics for higher-order formulae and show that they have the required properties. We then define behavioural equivalence and indistinguishability and prove regularity and factorizability, which leads directly to a characterization result analogous to the one in [BHW94].

Higher-order logic provides sufficient power to express the indistinguishability relation as a predicate. We apply this fact to develop methods for reasoning about specifications under behavioural semantics. We characterize behavioural satisfaction in terms of ordinary satisfaction, by giving a translation that takes any formula φ to a "relativized" formula $\ulcorner\varphi\urcorner$ such that $\ulcorner\varphi\urcorner$ is satisfied exactly when φ is behaviourally satisfied. This, together with the characterization theorem, leads directly to various proof methods.

For reasons of space, proofs are omitted in this paper. See [HS95] for these and for additional material.

2 The language of higher-order logic

The syntax of the typed variant of higher-order logic we will use is described below. The logic is higher-order because quantification over predicates (i.e. sets) is allowed in addition to the usual quantification over individuals.

Definition 2.1 *A* signature Σ *consists of a set B of* base types *and a set C of* constants *such that each $c \in C$ has an arity $n \geq 0$, an n-tuple of argument types $b_1,\ldots,b_n \in B$ and a result type $b \in B$, which we abbreviate $c : b_1 \times \cdots \times b_n \to b$.*

Let $\Sigma = \langle B, C\rangle$ be a signature.

Definition 2.2 *The* types *over Σ are given by the grammar $\tau ::= b \mid [\tau_1,\ldots,\tau_n]$, where $b \in B$ and $n \geq 0$. $Types(\Sigma)$ denotes the set of all types over Σ.*

A type $[\tau_1,\ldots,\tau_n]$ is the type of n-ary predicates taking arguments of types $\tau_1,\ldots,\tau_n$. The type $[]$ may be thought of as **Prop**, the type of propositions. Let X be a fixed infinite set of variables, ranged over by x.

Definition 2.3 *The* terms *over Σ are given by the following grammar:*

$$t ::= x \mid c(t_1,\ldots,t_n) \mid \lambda(x_1{:}\tau_1,\ldots,x_n{:}\tau_n).t \mid t(t_1,\ldots,t_n) \mid t \Rightarrow t' \mid \forall x{:}\tau.t$$

where $c \in C$ *and* $n \geq 0$. *As usual, we regard* α*-convertible terms as equal.*

Function application $c(t_1, \ldots, t_n)$ is distinguished from predicate application $t(t_1, \ldots, t_n)$. λ-abstraction is for forming predicates; implication ($\Rightarrow$) and universal quantification are for forming propositions. There is just one syntax class for terms: terms that denote individuals are not distinguished syntactically from terms denoting predicates or propositions. But in order for a term to denote anything at all, it has to be typable according to the following definitions.

Definition 2.4 *A context* Γ *is a sequence* $x_1 : \tau_1, \ldots, x_n : \tau_n$ *where* $x_i \neq x_j$ *for all* $i \neq j$. *We write* $\Gamma(x_j)$ *for* τ_j *and* $Vars(\Gamma)$ *for* $\{x_1, \ldots, x_n\}$, *and we identify* Γ *with the* $Types(\Sigma)$*-sorted set of variables such that* $\Gamma_\tau = \{x \in Vars(\Gamma) \mid \Gamma(x) = \tau\}$ *for all* $\tau \in Types(\Sigma)$. *Let* $T \subseteq Types(\Sigma)$ *be a subset of the set of types over* Σ; *then* Γ *is called a* T-context *if* $\Gamma(x) \in T$ *for all* $x \in Vars(\Gamma)$.

Definition 2.5 *We write* $\Gamma \vdash t : \tau$ *if this judgement is derivable using the six rules below, and then we call* t *a* term in context Γ. *A term* t *is* closed *if* $\vdash t : \tau$. *A* predicate (in context Γ) *is a term* t *such that* $\Gamma \vdash t : [\tau_1, \ldots, \tau_n]$. *A* formula (in context Γ) *is a term* φ *such that* $\Gamma \vdash \varphi : []$.

$$\frac{}{\Gamma \vdash x : \Gamma(x)} \qquad \frac{\Gamma \vdash t : [\tau_1, \ldots, \tau_n] \quad \Gamma \vdash t_1 : \tau_1 \quad \cdots \quad \Gamma \vdash t_n : \tau_n}{\Gamma \vdash t(t_1, \ldots, t_n) : []}$$

$$\frac{\Gamma, x_1 : \tau_1, \ldots, x_n : \tau_n \vdash t : []}{\Gamma \vdash \lambda(x_1{:}\tau_1, \ldots, x_n{:}\tau_n).t : [\tau_1, \ldots, \tau_n]} \qquad \frac{\Gamma \vdash t : [] \quad \Gamma \vdash t' : []}{\Gamma \vdash t \Rightarrow t' : []}$$

$$\frac{c : b_1 \times \cdots \times b_n \to b \quad \Gamma \vdash t_1 : b_1 \quad \cdots \quad \Gamma \vdash t_n : b_n}{\Gamma \vdash c(t_1, \ldots, t_n) : b} \qquad \frac{\Gamma, x : \tau \vdash t : []}{\Gamma \vdash \forall x{:}\tau.t : []}$$

Equality is expressible using higher-order quantification. That is, suppose $\Gamma \vdash t : \tau$ and $\Gamma \vdash t' : \tau$; then

$$t =_\tau t' \text{ abbreviates } \forall P{:}[\tau].P(t) \Rightarrow P(t')$$

where $P \notin Vars(\Gamma)$. Existential quantification and the missing connectives are expressible as usual in terms of $\forall$ and $\Rightarrow$:

$true$ abbreviates $\forall P{:}[].P \Rightarrow P$
$false$ abbreviates $\forall P{:}[].P$
$\neg\varphi$ abbreviates $\varphi \Rightarrow false$

$\varphi \vee \varphi'$ abbreviates $(\neg\varphi) \Rightarrow \varphi'$
$\varphi \wedge \varphi'$ abbreviates $\neg(\neg\varphi \vee \neg\varphi')$
$\exists x{:}\tau.\varphi$ abbreviates $\neg\forall x{:}\tau.\neg\varphi$

Finally, there is no need to treat reachability constraints as a special case, since induction principles are expressible. For example, the following formula (call it $GENNAT$) asserts that nat is generated by 0 and $succ$:

$$\forall P{:}[nat].(\ P(0) \wedge \forall n{:}nat.(P(n) \Rightarrow P(succ(n)))\ ) \Rightarrow \forall n{:}nat.P(n)$$

See [HS95] for an example which gives a taste of the expressive power of the language thus defined.

3 Semantics of higher-order logic

Let $\Sigma = \langle B, C\rangle$ be a signature. Terms over Σ are interpreted in the context of a Σ-algebra which gives meaning to the base types and the constants in Σ.

Definition 3.1 *A Σ-algebra A consists of a* carrier set $[\![b]\!]_A$ *for every $b \in B$, and interpretations of constants $[\![c]\!]_A \in ([\![b_1]\!]_A \times \cdots \times [\![b_n]\!]_A \rightarrow [\![b]\!]_A)$ for every $c : b_1 \times \cdots \times b_n \rightarrow b$ in C. The class of all Σ-algebras is denoted $Alg(\Sigma)$.* Σ-homomorphisms *and* Σ-isomorphisms *are as usual.*

Let A be a Σ-algebra. We define two interpretations for terms. The first is the obvious "standard" interpretation and the second is modulo a partial congruence relation on A. In the latter interpretation, quantification is over only those elements of types that respect the congruence; as a result, equality in formulae refers to the congruence rather than to identity of values. The particular partial congruence of interest will be a relation of indistinguishability to be defined in Sect. 4. Theorem 3.19 demonstrates a relationship between the two interpretations that will be crucial in the sequel. Our use of *partial* congruences stems from the need to establish an appropriate relationship between indistinguishability and behavioural equivalence, see Theorem 5.12, in order to apply the characterization theorems in Sect. 6.

3.1 Standard interpretation

Definition 3.2 *Types of the form $[\tau_1, \ldots, \tau_n]$ are interpreted as follows:*

$$[\![[\tau_1, \ldots, \tau_n]]\!]_A = Pow([\![\tau_1]\!]_A \times \cdots \times [\![\tau_n]\!]_A).$$

Thus, $[\![[]]\!]_A$ is $\{\{\}, \{*\}\}$ where $*$ is the empty tuple. Recalling that $[]$ means **Prop**, $\{\}$ may be thought of as denoting **false** and $\{*\}$ as denoting **true**, so we will use the abbreviation *ff* for $\{\}$ and *tt* for $\{*\}$. Let Γ be a context.

Definition 3.3 *A* Γ-environment *(on A) is a $Types(\Sigma)$-sorted function $\rho = \langle \rho_\tau : \Gamma_\tau \rightarrow [\![\tau]\!]_A\rangle_{\tau \in Types(\Sigma)}$. The notation $\rho[x_1 \mapsto v_1, \ldots, x_n \mapsto v_n]$ denotes the environment ρ superseded at $x_1, \ldots, x_n$ by $v_1, \ldots, v_n$ respectively. When $x \in Vars(\Gamma)$ we write $\rho(x)$ for $\rho_{\Gamma(x)}(x)$. Let $T \subseteq Types(\Sigma)$; a Γ-environment ρ is* T-surjective *if $\rho_\tau : \Gamma_\tau \rightarrow [\![\tau]\!]_A$ is surjective for each $\tau \in T$.*

Definition 3.4 *Let ρ be a Γ-environment. The interpretation of constants is extended to terms in context Γ as follows:*

$$\begin{aligned}
[\![x]\!]_{\rho,A} &= \rho(x) \\
[\![c(t_1, \ldots, t_n)]\!]_{\rho,A} &= [\![c]\!]_A([\![t_1]\!]_{\rho,A}, \ldots, [\![t_n]\!]_{\rho,A}) \\
[\![\lambda(x_1{:}\tau_1, \ldots, x_n{:}\tau_n).t]\!]_{\rho,A} &= \{(v_1, \ldots, v_n) \mid v_1 \in [\![\tau_1]\!]_A \textit{ and } \cdots \textit{ and } v_n \in [\![\tau_n]\!]_A \\
&\qquad \textit{and } [\![t]\!]_{\rho[x_1 \mapsto v_1, \ldots, x_n \mapsto v_n],A} = tt\} \\
[\![t(t_1, \ldots, t_n)]\!]_{\rho,A} &= \textit{if } ([\![t_1]\!]_{\rho,A}, \ldots, [\![t_n]\!]_{\rho,A}) \in [\![t]\!]_{\rho,A} \textit{ then } tt \textit{ else } ff \\
[\![t \Rightarrow t']\!]_{\rho,A} &= \textit{if } [\![t]\!]_{\rho,A} = tt \textit{ then } [\![t']\!]_{\rho,A} \textit{ else } tt \\
[\![\forall x{:}\tau.t]\!]_{\rho,A} &= \textit{if } [\![t]\!]_{\rho[x \mapsto v],A} = tt \textit{ for all } v \in [\![\tau]\!]_A \textit{ then } tt \textit{ else } ff
\end{aligned}$$

Proposition 3.5 *If $\Gamma \vdash t : \tau$ and ρ is a Γ-environment then $[\![t]\!]_{\rho,A} \in [\![\tau]\!]_A$.* □

The following proposition demonstrates that $=_\tau$ really is equality.

Proposition 3.6 *Suppose $v, v' \in [\![\tau]\!]_A$ for some type τ. Then for any environment ρ, $[\![x =_\tau y]\!]_{\rho[x \mapsto v, y \mapsto v'],A} = tt$ iff $v = v'$.* □

Definition 3.7 *Let $B' \subseteq B$. A value $v \in [\![b]\!]_A$ is* B'-reachable *if there is a B'-context Γ, a term t with $\Gamma \vdash t : b$, and a Γ-environment ρ, such that $[\![t]\!]_{\rho,A} = v$.*

Intuitively, v is B'-reachable if v can be obtained by application of constants to values of types in B'. Recall that the formula $GENNAT$ asserts that nat is generated by 0 and $succ$. Indeed, for any algebra A over the relevant signature, $[\![GENNAT]\!]_{[],A} = tt$ iff every value of type nat in A is $\emptyset$-reachable.

Definition 3.8 *Let φ, φ' be formulae in context Γ. Let ρ be a Γ-environment; we write $A \models_\rho \varphi$ if $[\![\varphi]\!]_{\rho,A} = tt$. We write $A \models \varphi$ (A* satisfies *φ) if $A \models_\rho \varphi$ for all Γ-environments ρ. We write $\varphi \models\!\mid \varphi'$ (φ is* equivalent *to φ') if for all $A \in Alg(\Sigma)$ and all Γ-environments ρ, $A \models_\rho \varphi$ iff $A \models_\rho \varphi'$. Finally, if Φ is a set of formulae in context Γ then we write $A \models \Phi$ if $A \models \varphi$ for all $\varphi \in \Phi$.*

Proposition 3.9 *If $A \cong A'$ then $A \models \varphi$ iff $A' \models \varphi$.* □

3.2 Interpretation w.r.t. a partial congruence

Definition 3.10 *A* partial congruence *$\approx$ on A is a family of* partial equivalence relations *$\langle \approx_b \subseteq [\![b]\!]_A \times [\![b]\!]_A \rangle_{b \in B}$ such that for all $c : b_1 \times \cdots \times b_n \to b$ in C and all $v_j, v_j' \in [\![b_j]\!]_A$ such that $v_j \approx_{b_j} v_j'$ for $1 \leq j \leq n$, $[\![c]\!]_A(v_1, \ldots, v_n) \approx_b [\![c]\!]_A(v_1', \ldots, v_n')$. A (*total*)* congruence *is a reflexive partial congruence.*

Let $\approx$ be a partial congruence on A. We now generalise the definition of satisfaction up to $\approx$ in first-order equational logic to higher-order logic. Whereas in the first-order case it is enough to interpret the equality symbol as the partial congruence and to restrict all quantifiers to the domain of the partial congruence, the situation is more complicated here. We must make sure that the predicate variables only range over predicates which "respect" $\approx$. That our definition is the right generalisation is shown by Prop. 3.16 and Theorem 3.19.

The following definition extends the partial congruence $\approx$ to a so-called *logical relation* over all types. The resulting relation will be used below to interpret bracket types.

Definition 3.11 *We extend $\approx$ to "bracket" types by taking $p \approx_{[\tau_1,\ldots,\tau_n]} p'$ for $p, p' \in [\![[\tau_1, \ldots, \tau_n]]\!]_A$ iff for all $v_j, v_j' \in [\![\tau_j]\!]_A$ such that $v_j \approx_{\tau_j} v_j'$ for $1 \leq j \leq n$, $(v_1, \ldots, v_n) \in p$ iff $(v_1', \ldots, v_n') \in p'$. We say that $v \in [\![\tau]\!]_A$* respects *$\approx$ if $v \approx_\tau v$.*

A predicate $p \in [\![[\tau_1, \ldots, \tau_n]]\!]_A$ respects $\approx$ if it does not differentiate between values that are related by $\approx$. Note that $v \approx_{[]} v'$ iff $v = v'$.

The difference between the standard interpretation of terms and their interpretation with respect to a partial congruence stems from the following.

Definition 3.12 *Interpretation of types w.r.t.* $\approx$ *is defined as follows:*

$$[\![b]\!]^{\approx}_A = \{v \in [\![b]\!]_A \mid v \textit{ respects} \approx\}$$
$$[\![[\tau_1,\ldots,\tau_n]]\!]^{\approx}_A = \{p \in Pow([\![\tau_1]\!]^{\approx}_A \times \cdots \times [\![\tau_n]\!]^{\approx}_A) \mid p \textit{ respects} \approx\}$$

We have $[\![[\,]]\!]^{\approx}_A = [\![[\,]]\!]_A = \{\mathit{ff}, \mathit{tt}\}$. The second clause of the above definition is well-formed because $[\![\tau]\!]^{\approx}_A \subseteq [\![\tau]\!]_A$ for any type τ. Let Γ be a context.

Definition 3.13 *A* Γ-environment (w.r.t. $\approx$, on A) *is a* $Types(\Sigma)$*-sorted function* $\rho = \langle \rho_\tau : \Gamma_\tau \to [\![\tau]\!]^{\approx}_A \rangle_{\tau \in Types(\Sigma)}$.

Definition 3.14 *Let* ρ *be a* Γ*-environment w.r.t.* $\approx$*. The interpretation w.r.t.* $\approx$ *of terms in context* Γ *is defined as follows:*

$$[\![x]\!]^{\approx}_{\rho,A} = \rho(x)$$
$$[\![c(t_1,\ldots,t_n)]\!]^{\approx}_{\rho,A} = [\![c]\!]_A([\![t_1]\!]^{\approx}_{\rho,A},\ldots,[\![t_n]\!]^{\approx}_{\rho,A})$$
$$[\![\lambda(x_1{:}\tau_1,\ldots,x_n{:}\tau_n).t]\!]^{\approx}_{\rho,A} = \{(v_1,\ldots,v_n) \mid v_1 \in [\![\tau_1]\!]^{\approx}_A \textit{ and } \cdots \textit{ and } v_n \in [\![\tau_n]\!]^{\approx}_A \textit{ and } [\![t]\!]^{\approx}_{\rho[x_1\mapsto v_1,\ldots,x_n\mapsto v_n],A} = tt\}$$
$$[\![t(t_1,\ldots,t_n)]\!]^{\approx}_{\rho,A} = \textit{if } ([\![t_1]\!]^{\approx}_{\rho,A},\ldots,[\![t_n]\!]^{\approx}_{\rho,A}) \in [\![t]\!]^{\approx}_{\rho,A} \textit{ then } tt \textit{ else } \mathit{ff}$$
$$[\![t \Rightarrow t']\!]^{\approx}_{\rho,A} = \textit{if } [\![t]\!]^{\approx}_{\rho,A} = tt \textit{ then } [\![t']\!]^{\approx}_{\rho,A} \textit{ else } tt$$
$$[\![\forall x{:}\tau.t]\!]^{\approx}_{\rho,A} = \textit{if } [\![t]\!]^{\approx}_{\rho[x\mapsto v],A} = tt \textit{ for all } v \in [\![\tau]\!]^{\approx}_A \textit{ then } tt \textit{ else } \mathit{ff}$$

Proposition 3.15 *If* $\Gamma \vdash t : \tau$ *and* ρ *is a* Γ*-environment w.r.t.* $\approx$ *then* $[\![t]\!]^{\approx}_{\rho,A} \in [\![\tau]\!]^{\approx}_A$. □

The following shows that $=_\tau$ refers to $\approx$ under the interpretation w.r.t. $\approx$. This is because P in $\forall P{:}[\tau].P(t) \Rightarrow P(t')$ ranges over predicates that respect $\approx$.

Proposition 3.16 *Suppose* $v, v' \in [\![\tau]\!]^{\approx}_A$ *for some type* τ*. Then for any environment* ρ *w.r.t.* $\approx$, $[\![x =_\tau y]\!]^{\approx}_{\rho[x\mapsto v, y\mapsto v'],A} = tt$ *iff* $v \approx_\tau v'$. □

The interpretation of $GENNAT$ with respect to $\approx$ is also different from what it was under the standard interpretation. For any algebra A, $[\![GENNAT]\!]^{\approx}_{[\,],A} = tt$ iff every value in $[\![nat]\!]^{\approx}_A$ is congruent to a $\emptyset$-reachable value.

Definition 3.17 *Let* φ *be a formula in context* Γ*. Suppose* ρ *is a* Γ*-environment w.r.t.* $\approx$*; then we write* $A \models^{\approx}_\rho \varphi$ *if* $[\![\varphi]\!]^{\approx}_{\rho,A} = tt$*. We write* $A \models^{\approx} \varphi$ *(*A satisfies φ w.r.t. $\approx$*) if* $A \models^{\approx}_\rho \varphi$ *for all* Γ*-environments* ρ *w.r.t.* $\approx$*. If* Φ *is a set of formulae in context* Γ *then we write* $A \models^{\approx} \Phi$ *if* $A \models^{\approx} \varphi$ *for all* $\varphi \in \Phi$.

When $\approx$ is the indistinguishability relation (see Definition 4.1 below), $\models^{\approx}$ is known as *behavioural satisfaction*.

3.3 Relating $\models$ and $\models^{\approx}$

Let $\approx$ be a partial congruence on A.

Definition 3.18 *Suppose $v \in [\![b]\!]_A$ for $b \in B$ such that $v \approx_b v$; then the* congruence class *of v w.r.t. $\approx$ is defined as $[v]_{\approx_b} = \{v' \in [\![b]\!]_A \mid v \approx_b v'\}$. The* quotient *of A by $\approx$, written $A/\!\approx$, is then defined as follows:*

$$[\![b]\!]_{A/\approx} = \{[v]_{\approx_b} \mid v \in [\![b]\!]_A \text{ and } v \approx_b v\}$$

$$[\![c]\!]_{A/\approx}([v_1]_{\approx_{b_1}}, \ldots, [v_n]_{\approx_{b_n}}) = [[\![c]\!]_A(v_1, \ldots, v_n)]_{\approx_b}$$

The following demonstrates a fundamental relationship between $\models$ and $\models^{\approx}$. In the first-order case, it says that standard satisfaction of a formula φ in $A/\!\approx$ is equivalent to satisfaction of φ, with the symbol $=$ interpreted as $\approx$, in A itself.

Theorem 3.19 *$A/\!\approx \models \varphi$ iff $A \models^{\approx} \varphi$.* □

A trivial consequence of this is the fact that $\models^{=}$ coincides with $\models$.

4 Behavioural equivalence and indistinguishability

Let $\Sigma = \langle B, C\rangle$ be a signature, and let OBS, the *observable base types* of Σ, be a subset of B. The intention is that OBS includes just those base types that are directly visible to clients. All other types, including bracket types, are *hidden* in the sense that their values may only be inspected indirectly by performing experiments (i.e. evaluating terms) that yield a result of a type in OBS.

The following defines indistinguishability as in [NO88]; $v \approx_{OBS} v'$ if no experiment of observable type with observable inputs can distinguish between them.

Definition 4.1 *Let the family of partial congruences $\approx_{OBS} = \langle \approx_{OBS,A}\rangle_{A \in Alg(\Sigma)}$ be such that $v \approx_{OBS,A,b} v'$ ($v, v' \in [\![b]\!]_A$ are* indistinguishable*) iff v and v' are OBS-reachable, and for any OBS-context Γ, variable $x \notin Vars(\Gamma)$, term t with $\Gamma, x : b \vdash t : b'$ for $b' \in OBS$, and Γ-environment ρ, $[\![t]\!]_{\rho[x\mapsto v],A} = [\![t]\!]_{\rho[x\mapsto v'],A}$.*

By analogy with the terminology of denotational semantics, a Σ-algebra A is called *fully abstract* when the indistinguishability relation on A is equality. Such an A is called an *algebra of minimal redundancy* in [Rei85].

Definition 4.2 ([BHW94]) *Let $\approx = \langle \approx_A\rangle_{A \in Alg(\Sigma)}$ be a family of partial congruences. A Σ-algebra A is* $\approx$-fully abstract *when for all $v, v' \in [\![b]\!]_A$, $v \approx_A v'$ iff $v = v'$. For any $\mathcal{A} \subseteq Alg(\Sigma)$, define*

$$FA_{\approx}(\mathcal{A}) = \{A \in \mathcal{A} \mid A \text{ is } \approx\text{-fully abstract}\}.$$

The family $\approx$ is regular *if $A/\!\approx_A$ is $\approx$-fully abstract for every $A \in Alg(\Sigma)$.*

Proposition 4.3 *$\approx_{OBS}$ is regular.* □

We now define what it means for two Σ-algebras to be behaviourally equivalent. The definition resembles that of indistinguishability in that it is based on the idea of experiments. But in this case performing an experiment means testing satisfaction of a formula rather than evaluating a term of base type.

Definition 4.4 *An* observable equation *is a formula* $t =_b t'$ *in* OBS*-context* Γ *where* $b \in OBS$. $ObsEq_\Gamma(\Sigma)$ *is the set of observable equations in* Γ.

Definition 4.5 *A is* behaviourally equivalent *to* A', *written* $A \equiv_{OBS} A'$, *if there is an* OBS*-context* Γ *and* OBS*-surjective* Γ*-environments* ρ_A *on* A *and* $\rho_{A'}$ *on* A' *such that for any* $\varphi \in ObsEq_\Gamma(\Sigma)$, $A \models_{\rho_A} \varphi$ *iff* $A' \models_{\rho_{A'}} \varphi$.

Note that the definition of $\equiv_{OBS}$ does not make use of higher-order features, except as a result of the way that equality is expressed via quantification over predicates. So $\equiv_{OBS}$ is just the same as in e.g. [SW83], [MG85], [NO88]. But the natural modification of the definition of $\equiv_{OBS}$ to make use of higher-order formulae gives exactly the same relation, see Corollary 5.13.

The following definition is the key to understanding the relationship between indistinguishability and behavioural equivalence. The idea is that a family of partial congruences naturally induces an equivalence on $Alg(\Sigma)$. Since behavioural equivalence is the relation induced by indistinguishability (Theorem 5.12), we can translate constructions phrased in terms of behavioural equivalence into constructions phrased in terms of indistinguishability, and vice versa. There is a close analogy with the case of finite state machines, where two machines M, M' are equivalent if quotienting M and M' by the so-called *Nerode equivalence* on states yields isomorphic machines.

Definition 4.6 ([BHW94]) *Let* $\approx = \langle \approx_A \rangle_{A \in Alg(\Sigma)}$ *be a family of partial congruences, and let* $\equiv \subseteq Alg(\Sigma) \times Alg(\Sigma)$ *be an equivalence relation. Then* $\equiv$ *is* factorizable *by* $\approx$ *if for any* $A, A' \in Alg(\Sigma)$, $A \equiv A'$ *iff* $A/{\approx_A} \cong A'/{\approx_{A'}}$.

The following proposition gives half of factorizability of $\equiv_{OBS}$ by $\approx_{OBS}$. The other half is a consequence of a more general result, see Corollary 5.8 below.

Proposition 4.7 *If* $A \equiv_{OBS} A'$ *then* $A/{\approx_{OBS,A}} \cong A'/{\approx_{OBS,A'}}$. □

In this paper, we consider only the definitions of indistinguishability and behavioural equivalence given above. There are two other candidates for each of these, as described in [BHW94]. These alternatives are not studied here, although the results given here should hold for them as well.

5 Expressible congruences and relativization

Higher-order logic is powerful enough to express directly the indistinguishability relation $\approx_{OBS}$. Let $\Sigma = \langle B, C \rangle$ be such that B and C are finite.

Definition 5.1 *Let* $\approx = \langle \approx_A \rangle_{A \in Alg(\Sigma)}$ *be a family of partial congruences, and let* $\sim = \langle \sim_b \rangle_{b \in B}$ *be a family of closed predicates such that* $\vdash \sim_b : [b, b]$ *for every base type* $b \in B$. *Then* $\approx$ *is* expressible by $\sim$ *if* $[\![\sim_b]\!]_{[],A} = \approx_{A,b}$ *for every* $b \in B$.

Theorem 5.2 *The indistinguishability relation* $\approx_{OBS}$ *is expressible by a family of predicates* $\langle INDIST_b\rangle_{b\in B}$. □

In [Sch94] an analogous expressibility result for the indistinguishability relation used in [Rei85] is given for a language of second-order logic.

Let $\approx = \langle \approx_A \rangle_{A\in Alg(\Sigma)}$ be expressible by $\sim = \langle \sim_b \rangle_{b\in B}$. We can use $\sim$ to give predicates characterizing the values in the interpretation of types w.r.t. $\approx$.

Proposition 5.3 *For any type* τ *there is a closed predicate* DOM_τ *such that* $\vdash DOM_\tau : [\tau]$ *and* $[\![DOM_\tau]\!]_{[],A} = [\![\tau]\!]_A^{\approx_A}$. □

We can use the predicates DOM_τ thus defined to transform any formula φ into a formula $\ulcorner\varphi\urcorner$ such that $\ulcorner\varphi\urcorner$ is satisfied exactly when φ is satisfied w.r.t. $\approx$. We simply "relativize" each bound variable by attaching a requirement that its value is in the interpretation of its type w.r.t. $\approx$.

Definition 5.4 *Let* t *be a term in context* Γ. *The* $\sim$-relativization *of* t *is the term* $\ulcorner t\urcorner$ *(in context* Γ*) defined as follows:*

$$\begin{aligned}
\ulcorner x\urcorner &= x\\
\ulcorner c(t_1,\ldots,t_n)\urcorner &= c(\ulcorner t_1\urcorner,\ldots,\ulcorner t_n\urcorner)\\
\ulcorner \lambda(x_1{:}\tau_1,\ldots,x_n{:}\tau_n).t\urcorner &= \lambda(x_1{:}\tau_1,\ldots,x_n{:}\tau_n).DOM_{\tau_1}(x_1)\wedge\cdots\wedge DOM_{\tau_n}(x_n)\wedge\ulcorner t\urcorner\\
\ulcorner t(t_1,\ldots,t_n)\urcorner &= \ulcorner t\urcorner(\ulcorner t_1\urcorner,\ldots,\ulcorner t_n\urcorner)\\
\ulcorner t\Rightarrow t'\urcorner &= \ulcorner t\urcorner\Rightarrow\ulcorner t'\urcorner\\
\ulcorner \forall x{:}\tau.t\urcorner &= \forall x{:}\tau.DOM_\tau(x)\Rightarrow\ulcorner t\urcorner
\end{aligned}$$

Theorem 5.5 *Let* A *be a* Σ*-algebra, let* φ *be a formula in context* Γ *and let* ρ *be a* Γ*-environment w.r.t.* $\approx_A$. *Then* $A \models_\rho^{\approx_A} \varphi$ *iff* $A \models_\rho \ulcorner\varphi\urcorner$. □

The $\sim$-relativization of a formula is similar to the notion of "lifted" formula in [BH95], and Theorem 5.5 is a higher-order version of Theorem 15 there.

The relativization construction may be used to define another behavioural equivalence relation, in which two algebras are regarded as behaviourally equivalent provided they cannot be distinguished by relativized formulae. It will turn out (Corollary 5.13) that this "new" relation coincides with $\equiv_{OBS}$.

Definition 5.6 A *is* behaviourally equivalent *to* A' via relativized formulae, *written* $A \equiv_{RelForm} A'$, *if there is an* OBS*-context* Γ *and* OBS*-surjective* Γ*-environments* ρ_A *on* A *and* $\rho_{A'}$ *on* A' *such that for any formula* φ *in context* Γ, $A \models_{\rho_A} \ulcorner\varphi\urcorner$ *iff* $A' \models_{\rho_{A'}} \ulcorner\varphi\urcorner$, *where* $\ulcorner\varphi\urcorner$ *is the* $\langle INDIST_b\rangle_{b\in B}$*-relativization of* φ.

Theorem 5.7 *If* $A/{\approx_{OBS,A}} \cong A'/{\approx_{OBS,A'}}$ *then* $A \equiv_{RelForm} A'$. □

Corollary 5.8 *If* $A/{\approx_{OBS,A}} \cong A'/{\approx_{OBS,A'}}$ *then* $A \equiv_{OBS} A'$. □

Yet another definition of behavioural equivalence is obtained by extending the definition of $\equiv_{OBS}$ to use higher-order formulae to perform experiments.

Definition 5.9 *A type* τ *is* observable *if either:*

– τ *is a base type that is in OBS; or*
– $\tau = [\tau_1, \ldots, \tau_n]$ *and* τ_i *is observable for all* $1 \leq i \leq n$.

A formula φ *in OBS-context* Γ *is* observable *if all types occurring in* φ *(i.e. as types of bound variables) are observable. Let* $ObsForm_\Gamma(\Sigma)$ *be the set of observable formulae in context* Γ.

The restrictions on observable formulae ensure that predicates in such formulae always have observable type. Note that $ObsEq_\Gamma(\Sigma) \subset ObsForm_\Gamma(\Sigma)$.

Definition 5.10 *A is* behaviourally equivalent *to* A' via formulae, *written* $A \equiv_{OBSForm} A'$, *if there is an OBS-context* Γ *and OBS-surjective* Γ*-environments* ρ_A *on* A *and* $\rho_{A'}$ *on* A' *such that for any* $\varphi \in ObsForm_\Gamma(\Sigma)$, $A \models_{\rho_A} \varphi$ *iff* $A' \models_{\rho_{A'}} \varphi$.

Corollary 5.11 *If* $A/{\approx_{OBS,A}} \cong A'/{\approx_{OBS,A'}}$ *then* $A \equiv_{OBSForm} A'$. □

Theorem 5.12 $\equiv_{RelForm}$, $\equiv_{OBS}$ *and* $\equiv_{OBSForm}$ *are factorizable by* $\approx_{OBS}$. □

Corollary 5.13 $\equiv_{RelForm} = \equiv_{OBS} = \equiv_{OBSForm}$. □

This demonstrates that using formulae more complex than equations as experiments does not allow finer distinctions between algebras to be made. This is not necessarily what one would expect: in the case of non-deterministic algebras, the use of more complex formulae does yield a different relation, see [Nip88].

6 Relating abstractor and behavioural specifications

Definition 6.1 *A (*flat*)* specification *consists of a signature* Σ *and a set* Φ *of closed* Σ*-formulae, called* axioms. *The* models *of a specification* $\langle \Sigma, \Phi \rangle$ *are all the algebras in the class*

$$Mod(\langle \Sigma, \Phi \rangle) = \{A \in Alg(\Sigma) \mid A \models \Phi\}.$$

Let $\langle \Sigma, \Phi \rangle$ be a specification. Let $\approx\, = \langle \approx_A \rangle_{A \in Alg(\Sigma)}$ be a family of partial congruences, and let $\equiv\, \subseteq Alg(\Sigma) \times Alg(\Sigma)$ be an equivalence relation.

Definition 6.2 *For any* $\mathcal{A} \subseteq Alg(\Sigma)$, *the* closure *of* $\mathcal{A}$ *under* $\equiv$ *is*

$$Abs_\equiv(\mathcal{A}) = \{A \in Alg(\Sigma) \mid A \equiv A' \text{ for some } A' \in \mathcal{A}\}.$$

When $\equiv$ *is the relation* $\equiv_{OBS}$ *for some OBS,* $Abs_\equiv$ *is known as* behavioural abstraction. *An* abstractor specification, *written* abstract $\langle \Sigma, \Phi \rangle$ w.r.t. $\equiv$, *has as models all those* Σ*-algebras that are equivalent to models of* $\langle \Sigma, \Phi \rangle$:

$$Mod(\text{abstract } \langle \Sigma, \Phi \rangle \text{ w.r.t. } \equiv) = Abs_\equiv(Mod(\langle \Sigma, \Phi \rangle)).$$

Definition 6.3 *A* behavioural specification, *written* behaviour $\langle \Sigma, \Phi \rangle$ w.r.t. $\approx$, *has as models all those* Σ*-algebras that satisfy the axioms* Φ *w.r.t.* $\approx$:

$$Mod(\text{behaviour } \langle \Sigma, \Phi \rangle \text{ w.r.t. } \approx) = \{A \in Alg(\Sigma) \mid A \models^{\approx_A} \Phi\}.$$

We have now built up enough machinery to redo the development in [BHW94] for higher-order logic. Although it is not explicit there, their results are independent of the logic used in axioms, provided properties corresponding to Prop. 3.9 and Theorem 3.19 hold. We merely state the theorems; for proofs and discussion, see [BHW94].

Assumption *$\approx$ is regular and $\equiv$ is factorizable by $\approx$.*

The particular case of interest is where $\approx$ and $\equiv$ are $\approx_{OBS}$ and $\equiv_{OBS}$ respectively, for an arbitrary choice OBS of observable base types. These satisfy the assumption by Prop. 4.3 and Theorem 5.12.

Theorem 6.4 ([BHW94])
$Mod(\textsf{behaviour } \langle \Sigma, \Phi \rangle \textsf{ w.r.t. } \approx) = Abs_{\equiv}(FA_{\approx}(Mod(\langle \Sigma, \Phi \rangle)))$. □

Definition 6.5 ([BHW94]) *For any $\mathcal{A} \subseteq Alg(\Sigma)$, define the classes $Beh_{\approx}(\mathcal{A}) = Abs_{\equiv}(FA_{\approx}(\mathcal{A}))$ and $\mathcal{A}/{\approx} = \{A/{\approx_A} \mid A \in \mathcal{A}\}$.*

Theorem 6.6 ([BHW94])
$Mod(\textsf{abstract } \langle \Sigma, \Phi \rangle \textsf{ w.r.t. } \equiv) = Beh_{\approx}(Mod(\langle \Sigma, \Phi \rangle)/{\approx})$. □

The main characterization theorem is the following:

Theorem 6.7 ([BHW94]) *The following conditions are equivalent:*

1. $Mod(\textsf{behaviour } \langle \Sigma, \Phi \rangle \textsf{ w.r.t. } \approx) = Mod(\textsf{abstract } \langle \Sigma, \Phi \rangle \textsf{ w.r.t. } \equiv)$
2. $Mod(\langle \Sigma, \Phi \rangle) \subseteq Mod(\textsf{behaviour } \langle \Sigma, \Phi \rangle \textsf{ w.r.t. } \approx)$
3. $Mod(\langle \Sigma, \Phi \rangle)/{\approx} \subseteq Mod(\langle \Sigma, \Phi \rangle)$ □

7 Reasoning about specifications

A concrete benefit of the results above is a number of methods for reasoning about specifications. Let $\Sigma = \langle B, C \rangle$ be a signature. Let $\approx = \langle \approx_A \rangle_{A \in Alg(\Sigma)}$ be a family of partial congruences that is expressible by $\sim = \langle \sim_b \rangle_{b \in B}$, and let $\equiv \subseteq Alg(\Sigma) \times Alg(\Sigma)$ be an equivalence relation. We restrict attention to closed formulae.

Definition 7.1 *A formula φ is a* consequence *of a set Φ of formulae, written $\Phi \models \varphi$, if for any Σ-algebra A, $A \models \Phi$ implies $A \models \varphi$.*

Definition 7.2 *Let $\mathcal{A} \subseteq Alg(\Sigma)$. The* theory w.r.t. $\approx$ *of $\mathcal{A}$ is $Th_{\approx}(\mathcal{A}) = \{\varphi \mid A \models^{\approx_A} \varphi$ for every $A \in \mathcal{A}\}$. The* (ordinary) theory *of $\mathcal{A}$ is $Th(\mathcal{A}) = Th_{=}(\mathcal{A})$. We write $Th(SP)$ for $Th(Mod(SP))$ and $Th_{\approx}(SP)$ for $Th_{\approx}(Mod(SP))$.*

The essence of reasoning about specifications is to find a way of reducing the problems $\varphi \in Th(SP)$ and $\varphi \in Th_{\approx}(SP)$ to that of consequence ($\Phi \models \psi$ for appropriate Φ and ψ); then any proof system that is sound for $\models$ may be used to finish the job. We consider the most important cases below, giving proof methods that provide such reductions. See [HS95] for the remaining cases.

7.1 $\varphi \in Th_{\approx}(\langle\Sigma, \Phi\rangle)$

It is argued in [BH95] that a solution to this problem can be used to prove correctness of implementation steps in stepwise refinement.

The following proof method follows immediately from Theorem 5.5:

Proof Method 7.3 $\varphi \in Th_{\approx}(\langle\Sigma, \Phi\rangle)$ *iff* $\Phi \models \ulcorner\varphi\urcorner$. □

This is essentially the solution proposed in [BH95], except that because the analogue of our Corollary 5.5 there involves infinitary formulae, more work is required to reduce the problem to one of consequence for finitary formulae.

Alternatively, if Theorem 6.7 applies, then this problem is equivalent to the problem treated in Sect. 7.2 below according to the following result:

Proposition 7.4 ([BHW94]) *If* $\equiv$ *is factorizable by* $\approx$ *then* $Th_{\approx}(Abs_{\equiv}(\mathcal{A})) = Th_{\approx}(\mathcal{A})$. □

7.2 $\varphi \in Th_{\approx}$(behaviour $\langle\Sigma, \Phi\rangle$ w.r.t. $\approx$)

This problem is studied in [BH94], for the indistinguishability relation of [Rei85].

Theorem 5.5 yields the following proof method:

Proof Method 7.5 $\varphi \in Th_{\approx}$(behaviour $\langle\Sigma, \Phi\rangle$ w.r.t. $\approx$) *iff* $\ulcorner\Phi\urcorner \models \ulcorner\varphi\urcorner$. □

A more powerful approach is obtained via the following results:

Proposition 7.6 ([BHW94]) $Th_{\approx}(Abs_{\equiv}(FA_{\approx}(\mathcal{A}))) = Th(FA_{\approx}(\mathcal{A}))$ *if* $\equiv$ *is factorizable by* $\approx$. □

Proposition 7.7 ([BH95]) $Mod(\langle\Sigma, \Phi \cup \{\forall x, y{:}b.(x \sim_b y \Leftrightarrow x =_b y) \mid b \in B\}\rangle) = FA_{\approx}(Mod(\langle\Sigma, \Phi\rangle))$. □

These together with Theorem 6.4 yield the following:

Proof Method 7.8 *Suppose that* $\approx$ *is regular and* $\equiv$ *is factorizable by* $\approx$. *Then* $\varphi \in Th_{\approx}$(behaviour $\langle\Sigma, \Phi\rangle$ w.r.t. $\approx$) *iff* $\Phi \cup \{\forall x, y{:}b.(x \sim_b y \Leftrightarrow x =_b y) \mid b \in B\} \models \varphi$. □

This is essentially the method proposed in [BH95], with the proviso concerning infinitary formulae mentioned earlier.

Finally, a more direct approach to this problem is to reduce it trivially to consequence w.r.t. $\approx$:

Definition 7.9 *A formula* φ *is a* consequence *of a set* Φ *of formulae* w.r.t. $\approx$, *written* $\Phi \models^{\approx} \varphi$, *if for any* Σ*-algebra* A, $A \models^{\approx_A} \Phi$ *implies* $A \models^{\approx_A} \varphi$.

Proof Method 7.10 $\varphi \in Th_{\approx}$(behaviour $\langle\Sigma, \Phi\rangle$ w.r.t. $\approx$) *iff* $\Phi \models^{\approx} \varphi$. □

Then what is required to finish the job is a proof system that is sound for $\models^{\approx}$.

7.3 $\varphi \in Th(\mathsf{abstract}\ \langle \Sigma, \Phi \rangle\ \mathsf{w.r.t.}\ \equiv)$

This problem arises in reasoning about specifications in ASL [SW83] which includes a specification-building operation corresponding to abstract; cf. [Far92].

Theorems 5.5 and 6.7 yield the following:

Proof Method 7.11 *Suppose that* $\approx$ *is regular and* $\equiv$ *is factorizable by* $\approx$, *and the conditions in Theorem 6.7 hold for the specification* $\langle \Sigma, \Phi \rangle$. *Then* $\varphi \in Th(\mathsf{abstract}\ \langle \Sigma, \Phi \rangle\ \mathsf{w.r.t.}\ \equiv)$ *iff* $\ulcorner \Phi \urcorner \models \varphi$. □

Alternatively, if the formula to be proved is a relativized formula or is logically equivalent to such a formula, we obtain the following reduction.

Proof Method 7.12 *Suppose that* $\equiv$ *is factorizable by* $\approx$ *and* $\varphi \models\!\!\mid \ulcorner \psi \urcorner$ *for some* ψ. *Then* $\Phi \models \varphi$ *implies* $\varphi \in Th(\mathsf{abstract}\ \langle \Sigma, \Phi \rangle\ \mathsf{w.r.t.}\ \equiv)$. □

This is a direct extension of the method for reasoning about abstractor specifications presented in Sect. 4 of [ST87], which applies only to formulae built in certain ways from observable equations. A formula that is equivalent to a relativized formula is called a "$\approx$-invariant" formula in [BH95], but this concept is not used as the basis of a reasoning method there.

A useful special case of Proof Method 7.12 can be obtained by adding "respectful" abstraction λ^{r} and quantification $\forall^{\mathrm{r}}$ to the syntax, where:

$$\lambda^{\mathrm{r}}(x_1{:}\tau_1, \ldots, x_n{:}\tau_n).t \text{ abbreviates } \lambda(x_1{:}\tau_1, \ldots, x_n{:}\tau_n). \; DOM_{\tau_1}(x_1) \wedge \cdots \wedge DOM_{\tau_n}(x_n) \wedge t$$

$$\forall^{\mathrm{r}} x{:}\tau.t \text{ abbreviates } \forall x{:}\tau.DOM_{\tau}(x) \Rightarrow t$$

Definition 7.13 *A* respectful formula *is a formula that may contain* λ^{r} *and/or* $\forall^{\mathrm{r}}$ *but does not contain* λ *or* $\forall$.

It is easy to see that $\varphi \models\!\!\mid \ulcorner \varphi \urcorner$ for any respectful formula φ. This gives:

Proof Method 7.14 *Suppose that* $\equiv$ *is factorizable by* $\approx$ *and* φ *is a respectful formula. Then* $\Phi \models \varphi$ *implies* $\varphi \in Th(\mathsf{abstract}\ \langle \Sigma, \Phi \rangle\ \mathsf{w.r.t.}\ \equiv)$. □

In the case of behavioural abstraction, $\forall^{\mathrm{r}}$ on base types corresponds exactly to reachable quantification as in [Sch92]. Also, since every observable formula is equivalent to a respectful formulae, we have:

Proof Method 7.15 *Suppose that* φ *is an observable formula. Then* $\Phi \models \varphi$ *implies* $\varphi \in Th(\mathsf{abstract}\ \langle \Sigma, \Phi \rangle\ \mathsf{w.r.t.}\ \equiv_{OBS})$. □

In Section 5 of [Sch92], Schoett highlights an inadequacy in the method for reasoning about abstractor specifications presented in [ST87]. He gives a simple abstractor specification with axioms in first-order equational logic and a property that it satisfies, and shows that an infinite number of applications of the proof method in [ST87] would be required in a proof of that property. This example is easily dealt with using Proof Method 7.14: the required property can be expressed using higher-order respectful quantifiers and proved in the unabstracted specification, whereupon a single application of the proof method completes the proof.

8 Further work

One reason for studying behavioural semantics in higher-order logic was the desire to apply the results in the Extended ML framework for the formal development of ML programs [KST94]. The results are of direct relevance in this context: the interpretation of interfaces involves abstractor specifications, and axioms are written in (a form of) higher-order logic. However, the framework here needs to be extended in two ways to make the match perfect.

First, the framework needs to be generalized to allow functions of higher type, in addition to the predicates of higher type that are already present. This would involve adding constants of higher type to signatures and allowing λ-abstraction to be used for forming functions. This can be done, as we will describe in a future paper; it is not straightforward because $[\![\tau]\!]^{\approx}_{A} \not\subseteq [\![\tau]\!]_{A}$ if we extend Definition 3.12 with obvious choices for function types. But note that n-ary functions may already be coded as $(n+1)$-ary predicates in the usual way.

Second, the use of behaviour and abstract in the context of structured specifications needs to be studied. An attempt appears in [BHW94], where they define $Mod(\textsf{behaviour } SP \textsf{ w.r.t. } \approx) = Beh_{\approx}(Mod(SP))$. Unless SP is a flat specification, the result is different from what is obtained when the specification-building operations in SP are interpreted as usual but with axioms in SP satisfied according to $\models^{\approx}$ rather than $\models$. Further work is required to clarify the relationship between abstractor specifications (which generalize easily to structured specifications) and this alternative interpretation of behavioural specifications.

Applying the results and proof methods to concrete examples should shed considerable light. Without having attempted such examples, we are not yet in a position to understand the tradeoffs between the various proof methods. But in view of the complexity of the predicates $INDIST_b$ (see [HS95]), it seems clear that proof methods involving the manipulation of relativized formulae will not be convenient for use in practice when $\approx$ is $\approx_{OBS}$. Here, a promising avenue is the search for more tractable predicates which correctly express $\approx_{OBS}$ in restricted circumstances (cf. the notion of "conditional axiomatization" in [BH95]). Proof methods which make no use of the predicates $INDIST_b$ (e.g. Proof Methods 7.10 and 7.15) do not suffer from this problem.

Acknowledgements: Thanks to Michel Bidoit and Rolf Hennicker for many very useful comments. Proof Method 7.8 is due to them, and they pointed out that a previous version of Proof Methods 7.12 and 7.14 were unnecessarily restrictive. Thanks to Andrzej Tarlecki for many discussions on related topics and for drawing our attention to the idea behind $INDIST_b$ in Theorem 5.2. Thanks to David Aspinall and Wolfgang Degen for helpful suggestions.

References

[BH94] M. Bidoit and R. Hennicker. Proving behavioural theorems with standard first-order logic. *Proc. 4th Intl. Conf. on Algebraic and Logic Programming*, Madrid. Springer LNCS 850 (1994).

[BH95] M. Bidoit and R. Hennicker. Behavioural theories. *Selected Papers from the 10th Workshop on Specification of Abstract Data Types*, Santa Margherita Ligure. Springer LNCS, to appear (1995).

[BHW94] M. Bidoit, R. Hennicker and M. Wirsing. Behavioural and abstractor specifications. Report LIENS-94-10, Ecole Normale Supérieure (1994). To appear in *Science of Computer Programming.* A short version appeared as: Characterizing behavioural semantics and abstractor semantics. *Proc. 5th European Symp. on Programming*, Edinburgh. Springer LNCS 788, 105–119 (1994).

[Far92] J. Farrés-Casals. Verification in ASL and Related Specification Languages. Ph.D. thesis, Report CSR-92-92, Univ. of Edinburgh (1992).

[GM82] J. Goguen and J. Meseguer. Universal realization, persistent interconnection and implementation of abstract modules. *Proc. 9th Intl. Colloq. on Automata, Languages and Programming*, Aarhus. Springer LNCS 140, 265–281 (1982).

[HS95] M. Hofmann and D. Sannella. On behavioural abstraction and behavioural satisfaction in higher-order logic. Report ECS-LFCS-95-318, Univ. of Edinburgh (1995). Available on WWW in `http://www.dcs.ed.ac.uk/lfcsreps/EXPORT/95/ECS-LFCS-95-318`.

[KST94] S. Kahrs, D. Sannella and A. Tarlecki. The semantics of Extended ML: a gentle introduction. *Proc. Intl. Workshop on Semantics of Specification Languages*, Utrecht, 1993. Springer Workshops in Computing, 186–215 (1994).

[MG85] J. Meseguer and J. Goguen. Initiality, induction and computability. In: *Algebraic Methods in Semantics* (M. Nivat and J. Reynolds, eds.). Cambridge Univ. Press, 459–540 (1985).

[Nip88] T. Nipkow. Observing nondeterministic data types. *Selected Papers from the 5th Workshop on Specification of Abstract Data Types*, Gullane. Springer LNCS 332, 170–183 (1988).

[NO88] P. Nivela and F. Orejas. Initial behaviour semantics for algebraic specifications. *Selected Papers from the 5th Workshop on Specification of Abstract Data Types*, Gullane. Springer LNCS 332, 184–207 (1988).

[Rei85] H. Reichel. Behavioural validity of conditional equations in abstract data types. *Proc. of the Vienna Conf. on Contributions to General Algebra*, 1984. Teubner-Verlag, 301–324 (1985).

[ST87] D. Sannella and A. Tarlecki. On observational equivalence and algebraic specification. *Journal of Computer and System Sciences* 34:150–178 (1987).

[SW83] D. Sannella and M. Wirsing. A kernel language for algebraic specification and implementation. *Proc. 1983 Intl. Conf. on Foundations of Computation Theory*, Borgholm. Springer LNCS 158, 413–427 (1983).

[Sch92] O. Schoett. Two impossibility theorems on behavioural specification of abstract data types. *Acta Informatica* 29:595–621 (1992).

[Sch94] P.-Y. Schobbens. Second-order proof systems for algebraic specification languages. *Selected Papers from the 9th Workshop on Specification of Abstract Data Types*, Caldes de Malavella. Springer LNCS 785, 321–336 (1994).

Assumption/Guarantee Specifications in Linear-Time Temporal Logic* (Extended Abstract)**

Bengt Jonsson and Yih-Kuen Tsay

Department of Computer Systems, Uppsala University, Sweden

Abstract. Previous works on assumption/guarantee specifications typically reason about relevant properties at the semantic level or define a special-purpose logic. We feel it is beneficial to formulate such specifications in a more widely used formalism. Specifically, we adopt the linear-time temporal logic (LTL) of Manna and Pnueli. We find that, with past temporal operators, LTL admits a succinct *syntactic* formulation of assumption/guarantee specifications. This contrasts, in particular, with the work by Abadi and Lamport using TLA, where working at the syntactic level is more complicated. Our composition rules are derived entirely within LTL and can also handle internal variables. We had to overcome a number of technical problems in this pursuit, in particular, the problem of extracting the safety closure of a temporal formula. As a by-product, we identify general conditions under which the safety closure can be expressed in a succinct way that facilitates syntactic manipulation.

1 Introduction

An open system executes in parallel and interacts with its environment. Such a system is best described by an assumption/guarantee (A/G for brevity) specification, which gives the assumptions on the behavior of the environment and the properties guaranteed by the system if the environment obeys the assumptions. In this paper, we explore the use of linear-time temporal logic in writing and reasoning about A/G specifications.

The idea of representing concurrent systems (programs) and their specifications as formulae in temporal logic was first proposed by Pnueli [16]. Lamport later observed that if specifications are invariant under stuttering, then refinement between specifications can be represented by the usual implication in temporal logic [12]. A further advance towards the effective use of temporal logic for the specification of concurrent systems was to notice that hidden, or internal, variables can be represented by existential quantification over program variables [13, 17]. We intend to make a further contribution in the same vein by showing

* This work was supported in part by the Swedish Board for Industrial and Technical Development (NUTEK) as part of ESPRIT BRA project No. 6021 (REACT) and by the Swedish Research Council for Engineering Sciences (TFR).

** The full paper is available as [11]; direct requests to {bengt,tsay}@docs.uu.se.

that A/G specifications can be formulated entirely within linear-time temporal logic. Barringer and Kuiper [6] are, to our knowledge, the first to formulate A/G specifications in temporal logic; however, their formulation does not allow quantification over program variables.

Suppose we wish to specify that the behavior of a system satisfies a guarantee property M if the behavior of its environment satisfies an assumption property E. An obvious formulation would be the usual implication $E \Rightarrow M$. But, this formulation has a problem, for example, when we compose two systems — one satisfying $E \Rightarrow M$ and the other satisfying $M \Rightarrow E$. If E and M are safety properties (stating that "bad things" do not happen [5]), we naturally would expect that the composed system satisfies both E and M. However, we cannot come to this conclusion, since it is not possible to discharge any of the antecedents in the implications.

A solution to the preceding problem was originally proposed by Misra and Chandy [15]. The basic idea is that a system satisfies an A/G specification with assumption E and guarantee M if, in every state of an execution, the system guarantees M up to the current state provided that its environment has respected E up to the preceding state; the definition implies that M is satisfied in the first (initial) state. If both E and M are safety properties, then the circular reasoning encountered when composing two systems can be broken by induction on the length of executions. Misra and Chandy's formulation has been elaborated and extended in various contexts, e.g., [6, 9, 2, 4, 3, 8]. In particular, Abadi and Lamport [3] combine the formulation with the usual implication so that the guarantee part may contain liveness properties (stating that "good things" eventually happen [5]).[3]

We propose to formulate A/G specifications using the linear-time temporal logic (LTL for brevity) of Manna and Pnueli [14] that conform to the aforementioned interpretation. Previous works on A/G specifications, including [15, 10, 9, 2, 4, 3, 7, 8, 18], typically reason about relevant properties at the semantic level or define a special-purpose logic. In contrast, our definition of an A/G specification is syntactic and entirely within LTL, which is relatively well understood and widely applied. We derive inference rules for composing A/G specifications as the main results of the paper.

One important aspect of our formulation is being able to handle assumptions and guarantees with internal variables, which simply are existentially quantified variables in LTL. Internal variables can be very useful in shortening a specification, e.g., the specification of a queue. Abadi and Lamport's work [3] is most closely related to ours. Grønning et al. [9] have also considered internal variables, but in a semantic framework. In addition, their proof rules seem unnecessarily strong and are formulated indirectly in terms of simulations rather than directly in terms of computations. Recently, Collette [8] designed a UNITY-like logic for A/G specifications (with restricted forms of assumptions and guarantees) that can handle hiding.

[3] Abadi and Lamport's formulation of an A/G specification also allows liveness properties in the assumption part. However, their composition rule only works for safety assumptions.

The work of Abadi and Lamport [3] in using TLA [13] for A/G specifications has been one inspiration of our work. Although they have also used temporal logic as the basis, their approach is different from ours. Whereas we try to express and reason about A/G specifications *syntactically*, they work mostly at the *semantic* level (because, for A/G specifications, working at the syntactic level of TLA would be very complicated). In particular, they introduce an operator $\stackrel{+}{\rhd}$, which is defined semantically (though a syntactic definition is possible), to formulate A/G specifications; inference rules are then derived by semantic arguments. This in effect is introducing a new operator to the logic.

There are two main technical problems that arise in using linear-time temporal logic for A/G specifications: The first problem is to be able to talk about the satisfaction of (the safety part of) a formula with respect to a finite prefix of an infinite sequence (temporal formulae in LTL are interpreted over *infinite* sequences of states). Barringer and Kuiper [6] have pioneered the use of past temporal operators in overcoming the problem, while considering particular forms of assumptions and guarantees. Their idea intuitively is to regard the end of the prefix as the present and look at the past. We observe that Barringer and Kuiper's idea can be applied to any safety formulae of the form $\Box H$, where the truth value of H depends only on the present and the past states. This brings us to the second problem, which is to extract the safety part, or safety closure, of the guarantee part (i.e., the strongest safety property implied by the guarantee) in the form of $\Box H$. Although this is always possible, the obtained formula may be too complicated to reason about. We give a result showing that, if the guarantee is specified by a formula in a canonical form that satisfies certain general conditions, then its safety closure can be expressed in the desired form and in a more succinct way, which greatly facilitates syntactic manipulation. We actually could avoid calculating the safety closure, since our formulation of A/G specifications is applicable as long as the guarantee is given in the form of $\exists x : \Box H \wedge L$ with H depending only on the present and the past states (no other conditions on H or L are required). This would be similar to the approach of considering the guarantee as a pair of a safety property and an arbitrary supplementary property, e.g., [6, 18].

We give a brief, informal review of LTL in Section 2, where a canonical form of formulae is defined for expressing the assumption and the guarantee of an A/G specification. In Section 3, we show how the safety closure of a canonical formula can be expressed in a succinct way. Section 4 describes our formulation of A/G specifications in LTL. A general composition rule is derived and compared with that of Abadi and Lamport. An example is elaborated in Section 5. Section 6 is the conclusion.

2 Preliminaries

This section gives a brief and informal introduction to linear-time temporal logic (LTL) as defined in [14]. The use of the logic in specifying closed systems is explained, leading to the definition of canonical formulae. Canonical formulae are also suitable for expressing the assumption and the guarantee of an A/G specification, each of which, when standing alone, is a specification of some closed system.

2.1 LTL

LTL is a logic for expressing properties of infinite sequences of states, where each state is an assignment to a predefined universe of variables. An LTL formula is interpreted with respect to a position $i \geq 0$ in a sequence of states. We assume a set of constant, function, and predicate symbols with fixed interpretations. A *state formula* is a particular LTL formula built only from variables, constants, functions, and predicates using the usual first-order logic connectives. The interpretation of a state formula (such as "$y > 5 \wedge (\exists n : y = n^2)$") in position i is performed as usual using the particular interpretation of variables in state i (plus the fixed interpretations of constants, functions, and predicates). LTL also contains extra temporal operators; in this paper, we will use the following:

- $\bigcirc$ means "in the next state". The formula $\bigcirc\varphi$ is true in position i of a sequence σ (denoted $(\sigma, i) \models \bigcirc\varphi$) iff φ is true in position $i+1$ of σ (i.e., $(\sigma, i+1) \models \varphi$).
- $\Box$ means "always in the future (including the present)"; $(\sigma, i) \models \Box\varphi$ iff $\forall k \geq i : (\sigma, k) \models \varphi$.
- $\Diamond$ means "sometime in the future"; $(\sigma, i) \models \Diamond\varphi$ iff $\exists k \geq i : (\sigma, k) \models \varphi$.
- $\tilde{\ominus}$ means "in the previous state, if there is any"; $(\sigma, i) \models \tilde{\ominus}\varphi$ iff $(i > 0) \Rightarrow ((\sigma, i-1) \models \varphi)$.
- $\boxminus$ means "always in the past (including the present)"; $(\sigma, i) \models \boxminus\varphi$ iff $\forall k : 0 \leq k \leq i : (\sigma, k) \models \varphi$.
- $\Diamond\!\!\!-$ means "sometime in the past"; $(\sigma, i) \models \Diamond\!\!\!-\varphi$ iff $\exists k : 0 \leq k \leq i : (\sigma, k) \models \varphi$.
- For a variable u, the interpretation of u^- (the previous value of u) in position i is the same as the interpretation of variable u in position $i-1$; by convention, the interpretation of u^- in position 0 is the same as the interpretation of u in position 0.[4]
- *first* is an abbreviation for $\tilde{\ominus}$*false* which is true only in position 0.

We say that a sequence σ satisfies a formula φ (or φ is true for σ) if $(\sigma, 0) \models \varphi$, which will be abbreviated as $\sigma \models \varphi$. A formula φ is *valid*, denoted $\models \varphi$ (or simply φ when it is clear that validity is intended), if φ is satisfied by every sequence.

Quantification deserves special attention. Each variable is either *rigid* (having the same interpretation in all states of a sequence) or *flexible* (with no restrictions

[4] In contrast to Lamport and others who use "+"-superscribed (or primed) variables to denote their values in the next state, we use "−"-superscribed variables to denote their values in the previous state. The reason is that (for conformity) we wish to use only past operators in the safety part of a specification. The introduction of "−"-superscribed variables is convenient but not essential, since they can be encoded by the $\tilde{\ominus}$ operator.

on interpretation in different states). When specifying a system, flexible variables can represent program or control variables, whose value may change over time. For a formula $\exists u : \varphi$ we have $(\sigma, i) \models \exists u : \varphi$ iff there is another sequence σ', which differs from σ in at most the interpretation given in each state to u, such that $(\sigma', i) \models \varphi$;[5] note that the restrictions of rigid variables must be observed. Intuitively, this means that the truth of $\exists u : \varphi$ for a flexible variable u depends on the existence of an infinite sequence of u-values (one for each state), rather than just a single value, such that φ can be satisfied.

A formula without temporal operators but possibly with "$^-$"-superscribed variables is called a *transition formula* (the definition is slightly different from that in [14]). A formula without any future operator $\bigcirc$, $\square$, or $\diamond$ is called a *past formula*; in particular, a transition formula is a past formula. A property is said to be a safety property if the following condition holds: for any sequence σ, if each prefix of σ is a prefix of some sequence that satisfies the property, then σ also satisfies the property. A property is said to be a liveness property if every finite sequence is a prefix of some sequence that satisfies the property. A *safety formula* is one that specifies a safety property and a *liveness formula* is one that specifies a liveness property. Of particular importance, formulae of the form $\square H$ are safety formulae if the truth value of H depends only on the present and the past states, e.g., if H is a past formula. The form of a liveness formula is not important for our purposes. The *safety closure* of a given property is the strongest safety property implied by the given property, i.e., a safety property satisfied by exactly those sequences σ such that each prefix of σ is a prefix of some sequence that satisfies the given property. The safety closure of a property specified by an arbitrary temporal formula can also be specified by a temporal formula (see the next paragraph), making it meaningful to talk about the safety closure of a formula.

Notations We use $\Rightarrow$ (instead of $\rightarrow$) for implication. Square brackets "[" and "]" are sometimes used in place of parentheses "(" and ")" for readability. A formula φ is sometimes written as $\varphi(x)$ to indicate that the free variables of φ are among the tuple of variables x. We write $\varphi[t/u]$, where t is a state formula and u a variable, to denote the formula obtained from φ by simultaneously substituting t for every free occurrence of u, assuming no free variables in t become bound in φ; when no confusion may arise, we also use the same notation for changing the name of a bound variable or the value of a constant. $\varphi[t/u]$ is simply written as $\varphi[t]$ if the intended substitution is clear from context. The notation for substitutions generalizes to tuples in the obvious way. To avoid ambiguity (since there are different but equivalent formulae), the safety closure $\mathcal{C}(\varphi)$ of a formula $\varphi(x)$ is defined as $\square[\exists \bar{x} : \boxminus(\bar{x} = x) \wedge \diamondminus(\mathit{first} \wedge \varphi[\bar{x}/x])]$ (which

[5] We note that, in contrast to TLA advocated by Lamport, the semantics of existential quantification in LTL does not preserve invariance under stuttering, i.e., $\exists u : \varphi$ is not necessarily invariant under stuttering even if φ is. However, the composition rules derived in this paper will still be valid if we adopt the semantics of TLA for existential quantification.

is satisfied by exactly those sequences σ such that each prefix of σ is a prefix of some sequence that satisfies φ).

2.2 Canonical Formulae

Using LTL, we can specify the behavior of a closed system ([13, 17]). Each variable of the system is represented by a flexible variable in LTL. Each execution of the system is represented by an infinite sequence of states. The system can thus be specified by an LTL formula in the sense that the executions of the system are exactly those satisfying the formula.

In general, a closed system can be specified by the conjunction of a safety formula and a liveness formula. The safety formula can be put in the form of $\Box H$ with H being a past formula, particularly $\Box((\mathit{first} \Rightarrow \mathit{Init}) \wedge (\neg \mathit{first} \Rightarrow N))$, where *Init* is a state formula and N a transition formula. The exact form of the liveness formula is not important for our purposes. Existential quantifications may be introduced to hide internal variables. Thus, a complete specification can be put into the form

$$\exists x : \Box H \wedge L$$

where x is a tuple of flexible variables, H is a past formula (so that $\Box H$ is a safety formula), and L is a liveness formula. Formulae of this form are called *canonical formulae*; the condition that H is a past formula will be further relaxed.

As we will show in Section 3, it is desirable that the pair of $\Box H$ and L be "*machine-closed*" [1], i.e., $\mathcal{C}(\Box H \wedge L) \Leftrightarrow \Box H$; this condition can always be enforced as shown in the following paragraphs. One way of understanding machine-closedness is that L does not rule out safety properties that are allowed by $\Box H$. For example, "$\Box[\boxminus(x = 0) \vee \boxminus(x = 1)]$" (which equals "$\Box(x = 0) \vee \Box(x = 1)$") and "$\Box\Diamond(x = 1)$" is not machine-closed, since $\Box\Diamond(x = 1)$ rules out the possibility of $\Box(x = 0)$.

We have required H in a canonical formula "$\exists x : \Box H \wedge L$" to be a past formula so that the truth value of H depends only on the present and the past states and thus $\Box H$ is a safety formula. The requirement can be replaced by a more general but less practical one, since the fact that "the truth value of a formula φ depends only on the present and the past states" can be precisely expressed as "$\Box[\boxminus(x = y) \Rightarrow (\varphi[x] \Leftrightarrow \varphi[y])]$ is valid". A formula that meets the more general requirement is called a *historical* (or semantically past) formula.[6] Obviously, every past formula is historical. From the definition of a historical formula it follows that, if H is historical, then $\Box H$ specifies a safety property and thus is a safety formula. The defining formula for $\mathcal{C}(\varphi)$, for instance, is in this form.

Once H is generalized to be historical, the desirable condition of machine-closedness — $\mathcal{C}(\Box H \wedge L) \Leftrightarrow \Box H$, can always be enforced (at least in theory). In fact, any formula φ is equivalent to the formula $\mathcal{C}(\varphi) \wedge (\neg\mathcal{C}(\varphi) \vee \varphi)$, which is in the form of $\Box H_\varphi \wedge L_\varphi$ with H_φ being a historical formula and L_φ a liveness formula such that $\mathcal{C}(\Box H_\varphi \wedge L_\varphi) \Leftrightarrow \Box H_\varphi$. (This is analogous to the well-known

[6] The definition of historical formulae is due to Amir Pnueli.

result that every property is the conjunction of a safety property and a liveness property [5].) We may also apply the result to φ in the context of a specification of a closed system $\exists x : \varphi$, translating the specification into another canonical formula that satisfies the machine-closedness condition.

3 Calculating Safety Closures

We define the *stuttering-extensibility* of a safety formula and show that, under machine-closedness and stuttering-extensibility, the safety closure of a canonical formula can be expressed in a succinct way and in the desired form.

First, we invoke a result in [3]:

Lemma 1. *If $\exists x : \Box H \wedge L$ is a canonical formula such that $\mathcal{C}(\Box H \wedge L) \Leftrightarrow \Box H$, then $\mathcal{C}(\exists x : \Box H \wedge L) \Leftrightarrow \mathcal{C}(\exists x : \Box H)$.*

Note that $\exists x : \Box H$ may or may not be a safety formula; even if it is, the formula is not in the desired form of $\Box H'$ such that H' is past or historical.

Let $\sigma|_i$ denote the prefix of σ ($\equiv s_0, s_1, s_2, \ldots$) of length i, i.e., the finite sequence $s_0, s_1, \ldots, s_i$ (which contains $i{+}1$ states and i transitions). The *stuttering-extension* of $\sigma|_i$ is the infinite sequence obtained from $\sigma|_i$ by indefinitely repeating its last state s_i, i.e., the infinite sequence $s_0, s_1, \ldots, s_{i-1}, s_i, s_i, s_i, \ldots$. We say that a safety formula $\Box H$ (with H being a past or historical formula) is *stuttering-extensible* if the following condition holds: for every σ and every $i \geq 0$, if $\boxminus H$ is true at position i of σ, then $\Box H$ is true for the stuttering-extension of $\sigma|_i$. Equivalently, $\Box H$ is stuttering-extensible if $\Box[\boxminus H(w) \Rightarrow \exists \bar{w} : \boxminus(\bar{w} = w) \wedge \bigcirc\Box(\bar{w} = \bar{w}^-) \wedge \diamondminus(\mathit{first} \wedge \Box H[\bar{w}/w])$ is valid. The intuition is that, if a system has satisfied a stuttering-extensible safety property so far, then it will continue to satisfy the safety property simply by doing nothing. We note that stuttering-extensibility is conjunctive in the sense that the conjunction of two stuttering-extensible formulae is also stuttering-extensible.

Lemma 2. *If $\exists x : \Box H$ is a canonical formula such that $\Box H$ is stuttering-extensible, then $\mathcal{C}(\exists x : \Box H) \Leftrightarrow \Box(\exists x : \boxminus H)$.*

A weaker condition than stuttering-extensibility is sufficient for the above lemma to hold. However, the weaker condition lacks the conjunctivity property enjoyed by stuttering-extensibility. From Lemmas 1 and 2, it follows:

Theorem 3. *If $\exists x : \Box H \wedge L$ is a canonical formula such that $\mathcal{C}(\Box H \wedge L) \Leftrightarrow \Box H$ and $\Box H$ is stuttering-extensible, then $\mathcal{C}(\exists x : \Box H \wedge L) \Leftrightarrow \Box(\exists x : \boxminus H)$.*

4 Assumption/Guarantee Specifications

In this section, we describe our formulation of A/G specifications in LTL and derive inference rules for composing such specifications. In light of the results in Section 3, we consider A/G specifications where the assumption and the guarantee parts are expressed in the canonical form with the additional conditions of machine-closedness and stuttering-extensibility:

1. The assumption E is expressed as $\Box(\exists x : \boxminus H_E)$. Given that $\Box H_E$ is stuttering-extensible, $\Box(\exists x : \boxminus H_E)$ equals the safety closure of $\exists x : \Box H_E$, which is a specification of the safety properties of a system with the tuple x of internal variables hidden.
2. The guarantee M is expressed as $\exists y : \Box H_M \wedge L_M$ where $\mathcal{C}(\Box H_M \wedge L_M) \Leftrightarrow \Box H_M$ and $\Box H_M$ is stuttering-extensible so that the safety closure of M is equivalent to $\Box(\exists y : \boxminus H_M)$.

In fact, the conditions of machine-closedness and stuttering-extensibility are not absolutely necessary. The derived composition rules will still be valid without the two conditions if we regard M as a pair of the safety formula $\Box(\exists y : \boxminus H_M)$ and some supplementary formula and interpret the definition of $\rhd$ (Section 4.2) as a purely syntactical expansion.

4.1 Basic Formulation

Following Misra and Chandy [15], an A/G specification of a system should capture the following property: For every execution of the system, the guarantee M is satisfied initially and, for every $i \geq 1$, if the assumption E has been satisfied by the prefix of length $i-1$, then M is satisfied by the prefix of length i (recall that the length of an execution is the number of transitions, which is one less than the number of states in the execution). The satisfaction of a formula with respect to prefixes of an execution depends only the safety part of the formula (since each of the prefixes is finite and therefore, by definition, can be extended to an infinite execution satisfying the liveness part of the formula). Therefore, we first concentrate on the safety closure of E (which is E itself) and that of M; the liveness part of M will be taken into account in the next subsection. In other words, we consider the formulation of an A/G specification with assumption $\Box(\exists x : \boxminus H_E)$ and guarantee $\Box(\exists y : \boxminus H_M)$.

Since H_E and H_M (and hence $\exists x : \boxminus H_E$ and $\exists y : \boxminus H_M$) are historical, "$\Box(\exists x : \boxminus H_E)$ is satisfied by the prefix of length $i-1$ of σ" can be formally stated as "$(\sigma, i) \models \tilde{\ominus}\boxminus(\exists x : \boxminus H_E)$" or equivalently "$(\sigma, i) \models \tilde{\ominus}(\exists x : \boxminus H_E)$" (recall that the states of σ are numbered from 0) and "$\Box(\exists y : \boxminus H_M)$ is satisfied by the prefix of length i of σ" as "$(\sigma, i) \models (\exists y : \boxminus H_M)$". The property that we intended to capture can, therefore, be expressed as $\Box[\tilde{\ominus}(\exists x : \boxminus H_E) \Rightarrow (\exists y : \boxminus H_M)]$. This formula also implies that $(\exists y : \boxminus H_M)$, or simply $(\exists y : H_M)$, has to be satisfied initially, since $\tilde{\ominus}(\exists x : \boxminus H_E)$ always holds in the initial state.

In summary, we take $\Box[\tilde{\ominus}(\exists x : \boxminus H_E) \Rightarrow (\exists y : \boxminus H_M)]$ to be the A/G specification with assumption $\Box(\exists x : \boxminus H_E)$ and guarantee $\Box(\exists y : \boxminus H_M)$. The following lemma states that A/G specifications can be composed in a straightforward way:

Lemma 4. *Assuming that $x_1, \ldots, x_n$, $y_1, \ldots, y_n$ are pairwise disjoint,*

$$\bigwedge_{i=1}^{n} \Box[\tilde{\ominus}(\exists x_i : \boxminus H_{E_i}) \Rightarrow (\exists y_i : \boxminus H_{M_i})]$$
$$\Rightarrow \Box[\tilde{\ominus}(\exists x_1 \ldots x_n : \boxminus \bigwedge_{i=1}^{n} H_{E_i}) \Rightarrow (\exists y_1 \ldots y_n : \boxminus \bigwedge_{i=1}^{n} H_{M_i})].$$

From Lemma 4 and a simple induction, we obtain

Theorem 5.

$$\Box[\tilde{\ominus}(\exists y_1 : \boxminus H_{M_1}) \Rightarrow (\exists y_2 : \boxminus H_{M_2})] \wedge \Box[\tilde{\ominus}(\exists y_2 : \boxminus H_{M_2}) \Rightarrow (\exists y_1 : \boxminus H_{M_1})]$$
$$\Rightarrow \Box(\exists y_1 : \boxminus H_{M_1}) \wedge \Box(\exists y_2 : \boxminus H_{M_2}).$$

A special case of the theorem is the composition principle essentially formulated by Misra and Chandy:

$$\Box(\tilde{\ominus}\boxminus H_{M_1} \Rightarrow \boxminus H_{M_2}) \wedge \Box(\tilde{\ominus}\boxminus H_{M_2} \Rightarrow \boxminus H_{M_1}) \;\Rightarrow\; \Box H_{M_1} \wedge \Box H_{M_2}.$$

4.2 Adding Liveness

To allow liveness properties in the guarantee, we simply strengthen the specification by conjoining it with the usual implication between the assumption and the entire guarantee. As the complete formulation of an A/G specification with assumption $E \equiv \Box(\exists x : \boxminus H_E)$ and guarantee $M \equiv \exists y : \Box H_M \wedge L_M$, we define $E \rhd M$ as follows:

$$E \rhd M \triangleq \Box[\tilde{\ominus}(\exists x : \boxminus H_E) \Rightarrow (\exists y : \boxminus H_M)] \wedge [E \Rightarrow M]$$

This is consistent with our taking "$\Box[\tilde{\ominus}(\exists x : \boxminus H_E) \Rightarrow (\exists y : \boxminus H_M)]$" to be the A/G specification with assumption $\Box(\exists x : \boxminus H_E)$ and guarantee $\Box(\exists y : \boxminus H_M)$ in the previous subsection, since if M is a safety formula, the implication $E \Rightarrow M$ is subsumed by $\Box[\tilde{\ominus}(\exists x : \boxminus H_E) \Rightarrow (\exists y : \boxminus H_M)]$. Therefore, $[\Box(\exists x : \boxminus H_E) \rhd \Box(\exists y : \boxminus H_M)] \Leftrightarrow \Box[\tilde{\ominus}(\exists x : \boxminus H_E) \Rightarrow (\exists y : \boxminus H_M)]$.

The general composition rule is as follows (assuming that x, y, $x_1, \ldots, x_n$, $y_1, \ldots, y_n$ are pairwise disjoint); when M is a safety formula, Premise 2(b) can be dropped.

Theorem 6.

$$1. \quad \Box\Big[(\exists x : \boxminus H_E) \wedge (\exists y_1 \ldots y_n : \boxminus \bigwedge_{i=1}^{n} H_{M_i}) \Rightarrow (\exists x_1 \ldots x_n : \boxminus \bigwedge_{i=1}^{n} H_{E_i})\Big]$$

$$2.\ (a)\ \Box\Big[\tilde{\ominus}(\exists x : \boxminus H_E) \wedge (\exists y_1 \ldots y_n : \boxminus \bigwedge_{i=1}^{n} H_{M_i}) \Rightarrow (\exists y : \boxminus H_M)\Big]$$

$$(b)\ E \wedge \bigwedge_{i=1}^{n} M_i \Rightarrow M$$

$$\overline{\bigwedge_{i=1}^{n} (E_i \rhd M_i) \;\Rightarrow\; (E \rhd M)}$$

We now show how one goes about establishing the premises of the composition rule. Premise 2(b) is in the usual form of refinement between two canonical formulae, which can be proven by standard "refinement mapping" techniques [13, 17]. Premises 1 and 2(a) can respectively be rewritten as follows:

$$1.\ \Box\Big[\boxminus H_E \wedge \boxminus \bigwedge_{i=1}^{n} H_{M_i} \Rightarrow \exists x_1 \ldots x_n : \boxminus \bigwedge_{i=1}^{n} H_{E_i}\Big]$$

2. $\Box\left[\tilde{\ominus}\boxminus H_E \wedge \boxminus \bigwedge_{i=1}^{n} H_{M_i} \Rightarrow \exists y\colon \boxminus H_M\right]$

Both formulae are in a weaker form than the usual refinement between two canonical formulae, because the existential quantifications occur inside the $\Box$ operator. Like in the usual case, we may find appropriate functions $f_1, \ldots, f_n, g$ that map from the free variables of $H_E, H_{M_1}, \ldots, H_{M_n}$ to the domains of $x_1, \ldots, x_n, y$ respectively, and prove the following:

1. $\Box\left[\boxminus H_E \wedge \boxminus \bigwedge_{i=1}^{n} H_{M_i} \Rightarrow \boxminus \bigwedge_{i=1}^{n} H_{E_i}[f_i/x_i]\right]$
2. $\Box\left[\tilde{\ominus}\boxminus H_E \wedge \boxminus \bigwedge_{i=1}^{n} H_{M_i} \Rightarrow \boxminus H_M[g/y]\right]$

The first premise can be proven by showing

$$\Box\left[H_E \wedge \bigwedge_{i=1}^{n} H_{M_i} \Rightarrow \bigwedge_{i=1}^{n} H_{E_i}[f_i/x_i]\right].$$

The second premise needs more work. It can be shown that $\Box(\tilde{\ominus}\boxminus H_E \wedge \boxminus \bigwedge_{i=1}^{n} H_{M_i} \Rightarrow \boxminus H_M[g/y])$ is implied by $\Box(\tilde{\ominus} I_E \wedge \bigwedge_{i=1}^{n} H_{M_i} \Rightarrow H_M[g/y])$, where I_E is a state formula such that $\Box(\boxminus H_E \Rightarrow I_E)$. The validity of $\Box(\boxminus H_E \Rightarrow I_E)$ can be established by the usual proof of an invariant. Let I_E^- denote the transition formula obtained from I_E by superscribing every flexible variable with "$-$". It follows that the second premise can be proven by showing

$$\Box\left[(\neg \mathit{first} \Rightarrow I_E^-) \wedge \bigwedge_{i=1}^{n} H_{M_i} \Rightarrow H_M[g/y]\right].$$

It is sometimes possible, e.g., in the example of Section 5, to prove a stronger and simpler formula $\Box(\bigwedge_{i=1}^{n} H_{M_i} \Rightarrow H_M[g/y])$.

4.3 Comparison with Abadi and Lamport's Work

In [3], Abadi and Lamport further develop their earlier work on A/G specifications [2] using the framework of TLA [13]. Although they have also used temporal logic as the basis, their approach is different from ours. Whereas we express and reason about A/G specifications *syntactically*, they work mostly at the *semantic* level. Technically, due to the absence of past operators in TLA, they extend the semantic model for TLA formulae to include *finite* sequences so that the assertion "a finite prefix of an execution satisfies a formula" (which plays a central role in A/G specifications) can be stated directly, which otherwise would require extensive usage of auxiliary variables that result in long and complicated formulae.

Abadi and Lamport formulate an A/G specification by means of the operator $\overset{+}{\rhd}$. They define the formula $E \overset{+}{\rhd} M$ to be true of a behavior σ iff (a) $E \Rightarrow M$

is true of σ, (b) M holds initially, and (c) for every $n \geq 0$, if E holds for the prefix of σ of length n, then M holds for the prefix of σ of length $n+1$. Part (a) is also present in our formulation of $E \rhd M$. Parts (b) and (c) presuppose a definition of when a formula is satisfied by a prefix of a behavior; the definition of satisfaction by Abadi and Lamport depends only on the safety closure of a formula (i.e., parts (b) and (c) can be equivalently formulated using the safety closures $\mathcal{C}(E)$ and $\mathcal{C}(M)$ of E and M). Consequently, their general composition theorem, shown below, makes extensive use of safety closures.

$$\frac{\begin{array}{l} 1. \quad \mathcal{C}(E) \wedge \bigwedge_{i=1}^{n} \mathcal{C}(M_i) \Rightarrow \bigwedge_{i=1}^{n} E_i \\ 2. \; (a) \; \mathcal{C}(E)_{+v} \wedge \bigwedge_{i=1}^{n} \mathcal{C}(M_i) \Rightarrow \mathcal{C}(M) \\ \quad\; (b) \; E \wedge \bigwedge_{i=1}^{n} M_i \Rightarrow M \end{array}}{\bigwedge_{i=1}^{n} (E_i \overset{+}{\rhd} M_i) \Rightarrow (E \overset{+}{\rhd} M)}$$

where $\mathcal{C}(E)_{+v}$, for some tuple v of variables, intuitively means that the values of v may change in a state transition only if the prefix up to the current state satisfies $\mathcal{C}(E)$.

Aside from using the novel (and not very easy to reason about) operator "$_{+v}$", the theorem explicitly uses safety closures, which are a semantic notion. In contrast, our composition theorem is presented purely syntactically within LTL. It can be shown [11] that, under some general assumptions, the definitions of $\overset{+}{\rhd}$ and $\rhd$ are equivalent and the composition theorem of Abadi and Lamport can be derived from Theorem 6.

5 An Example

To illustrate the application of our formulation of A/G specifications, we consider the same example as used by Abadi and Lamport [3] and others, e.g., [6, 7], where two queues for storing natural numbers are composed in series to obtain a larger one. A queue is an open system whose environment is the user of the queue. In the most straightforward A/G specification of a queue, the guarantee part contains an internal variable that is used to store a finite sequence of natural numbers. To make the example more interesting, we stipulate that numbers are sent by the environment in ascending order. We deliberately introduce an internal variable (which could have been avoided) in the assumption part that stores the next number to be sent by the environment to the queue and we specify that the next number be greater than the previous one sent. It should be noted that internal variables are often introduced for the ease of writing specifications and need not correspond to actual program variables in an implementation. We take the liberty to borrow notions from [3] for our exposition of the example. We shall concentrate only on safety properties; liveness properties can be handled in a similar way as in [3]. Moreover, we shall adopt a noninterleaving representation of the queue, permitting the addition of a number to and the removal of another from the queue to occur simultaneously; an interleaving representation can also be treated in a similar way as in [3].

A queue interacts with its environment via two single-buffered channels: an input channel for receiving a number from the environment and an output channel for sending a number to the environment, as depicted in Figure 1. A channel c consists of two variables $c.sig$ and $c.ack$ of type boolean and a third variable (the single buffer) $c.val$ of type natural number. Boolean variables $c.sig$ and $c.ack$ are used for the synchronization between the sender and the receiver of channel c. The channel is ready for sending iff $c.sig = c.ack$. When $c.sig = c.ack$, the sender may deposit a number in $c.val$ and at the same time negate the value of $c.sig$ so that $c.sig \neq c.ack$, indicating that a value has been sent. Subsequently, the receiver may read the value of $c.val$ and negate $c.ack$, which makes $c.sig$ and $c.ack$ equal indicating that the channel is ready for sending again. This synchronization mechanism is usually referred to as the (two-phase) handshake protocol. We write c to denote $\langle c.sig, c.ack, c.val\rangle$ and $c.snd$ to denote $\langle c.sig, c.val\rangle$.

Fig. 1. A queue as an open system.

We introduce abbreviations for the initial condition and two relevant transition formulae on a channel:

$$\begin{aligned}
CInit(c) &\triangleq \neg c.sig \wedge \neg c.ack \wedge c.val = 0\\
Send(v,c) &\triangleq c.sig^- = c.ack^- \wedge c.ack = c.ack^- \wedge c.snd = \langle \neg c.sig^-, v\rangle\\
Ack(c) &\triangleq c.sig^- \neq c.ack^- \wedge c.ack = \neg c.ack^- \wedge c.snd = c.snd^-
\end{aligned}$$

In accordance with the handshake protocol, the environment of a queue with input channel i and output channel o is expected to obey the following assumption:

$$\begin{aligned}
E(i,o,x) &\triangleq \Box(\exists x : \boxdot H_E(i,o,x))\\
H_E(i,o,x) &\triangleq (first \Rightarrow Init_E) \wedge (\neg first \Rightarrow (Put \vee Get \vee GetPut \vee Skip_E))
\end{aligned}$$

where the initial condition and relevant transition formulae are defined as follows.

$$\begin{aligned}
Init_E &\triangleq CInit(i)\\
Put &\triangleq Send(x^-, i) \wedge x > x^- \wedge o.ack = o.ack^-\\
Get &\triangleq Ack(o) \wedge i.snd = i.snd^-\\
GetPut &\triangleq Ack(o) \wedge Send(x^-, i) \wedge x > x^-\\
Skip_E &\triangleq i.snd = i.snd^- \wedge o.ack = o.ack^- \wedge x = x^-
\end{aligned}$$

The queue in return should guarantee M as defined below:

$$M(i,o,q,max) \triangleq \Box(\exists q : \boxminus H_M(i,o,q,max))$$
$$H_M(i,o,q,max) \triangleq (first \Rightarrow Init_M) \wedge (\neg first \Rightarrow (Enq \vee Deq \vee DeqEnq \vee Skip_M))$$

where the relevant formulae are defined as follows.

$$\begin{aligned}
Init_M &\triangleq CInit(o) \wedge q = \langle\rangle \\
Enq &\triangleq |q^-| < max \wedge Ack(i) \wedge (q = q^- \circ \langle i.val^- \rangle) \wedge o.snd = o.snd^- \\
Deq &\triangleq |q^-| > 0 \wedge Send(head(q^-), o) \wedge q = tail(q^-) \wedge i.ack = i.ack^- \\
DeqEnq &\triangleq |q^-| > 0 \wedge Send(head(q^-), o) \wedge Ack(i) \wedge (q = tail(q^-) \circ \langle i.val^- \rangle) \\
Skip_M &\triangleq o.snd = o.snd^- \wedge i.ack = i.ack^- \wedge q = q^-
\end{aligned}$$

Note that H_E and H_M are indeed past and hence historical formulae as required. Both $\Box H_E$ and $\Box H_M$ are apparently stuttering-extensible. From Theorem 3, $\Box(\exists x : \boxminus H_E(i,o,x))$ and $\Box(\exists q : \boxminus H_M(i,o,q,max))$ express the safety closures of $\exists x : \Box H_E(i,o,x)$ and $\exists q : \Box H_M(i,o,q,max)$, respectively.

The assertion that the composition of two queues in series results in a larger one can be expressed by the following formula.

$$\begin{aligned}
&(E[i,m,x_1] \;\triangleright\; M[i,m,q_1,N_1]) \wedge (E[m,o,x_2] \;\triangleright\; M[m,o,q_2,N_2]) \\
&\Rightarrow\; (E[i,o,x] \;\triangleright\; M[i,o,q,(N_1+N_2+1)])
\end{aligned}$$

Figure 2 shows the statement in picture.

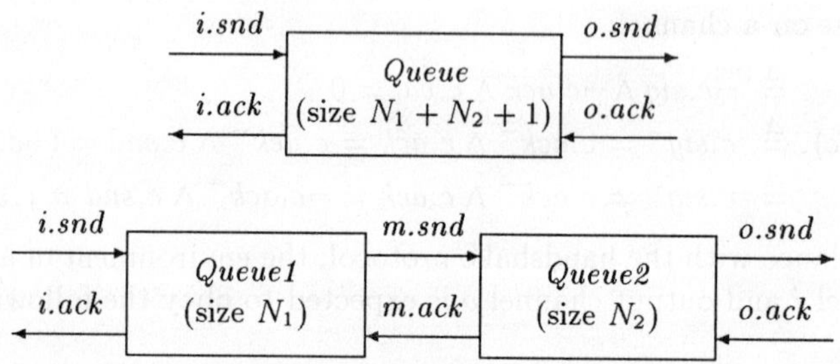

Fig. 2. Implementation of a queue by two composed in series.

We now apply Theorem 6 to show the validity of the above statement. Following the discussion in Section 4.2, the premises of the theorem translate into the following two formulae:

1. $\Box\Big[\boxminus H_E[i,o,x] \wedge \boxminus(H_M[i,m,q_1,N_1] \wedge H_M[m,o,q_2,N_2])$
$\Rightarrow \exists x_1 x_2 : \boxminus(H_E[i,m,x_1] \wedge H_E[m,o,x_2])\Big]$

2. $\Box\Big[\tilde{\ominus}\boxminus H_E[i,o,x] \land \boxminus(H_M[i,m,q_1,N_1] \land H_M[m,o,q_2,N_2])$
$\quad \Rightarrow \exists q : \boxminus H_M[i,o,q,(N_1+N_2+1)]\Big]$

The required mappings can be defined as follows:

1. For variable x_1, the required mapping $\bar{x}_1$ is simply $\bar{x}_1(x) = x$. For variable x_2, we define the mapping $\bar{x}_2$ as follows:

$$\bar{x}_2(x,i,q_1) \triangleq \begin{cases} head(q_1) & \text{if } q_1 \neq \langle\rangle \\ i.val & \text{if } q_1 = \langle\rangle \land i.sig \neq i.ack \\ x & \text{otherwise} \end{cases}$$

Intuitively, for the second queue, the next number to be sent by its environment is either the value at the head of q_1 (if not empty), $i.val$ (if q_1 is empty and channel i not empty), or x.

2. The mapping from q_1, m, and q_2 to q is the same as in [3]:

$$\bar{q}(q_1,m,q_2) \triangleq \begin{cases} q_2 \circ q_1 & \text{if } m.sig = m.ack \\ q_2 \circ \langle m.val\rangle \circ q_1 & \text{otherwise} \end{cases}$$

Using these mappings, it is straightforward to prove

1. $\Box\Big[H_E[i,o,x] \land (H_M[i,m,q_1,N_1] \land H_M[m,o,q_2,N_2])$
$\quad \Rightarrow H_E[i,m,\bar{x}_1] \land H_E[m,o,\bar{x}_2]\Big]$
2. $\Box\Big[H_M[i,m,q_1,N_1] \land H_M[m,o,q_2,N_2] \Rightarrow H_M[i,o,\bar{q},(N_1+N_2+1)]\Big]$

which implies the needed premises.

6 Conclusion

We have developed a formulation of A/G specifications within linear-time temporal logic. We have shown that, by using past temporal operators, it is possible to give a natural and general formulation of A/G specifications and to derive needed inference rules in a simple and straightforward way. We have also shown how internal variables can be handled. It is our intention that the results will further advance the use and applicability of temporal logic in specifying concurrent systems.

Acknowledgment

We thank Amir Pnueli for suggesting the notion of historical formulae. We also thank Martín Abadi, Pierre Collette, Leslie Lamport, and Qiwen Xu for comments and suggestions on earlier drafts of the paper.

References

1. M. Abadi and L. Lamport. The existence of refinement mappings. *Theoretical Computer Science*, 82:253–284, 1991.
2. M. Abadi and L. Lamport. Composing specifications. *ACM Transactions on Programming Languages and Systems*, 15(1):73–132, January 1993.
3. M. Abadi and L. Lamport. Conjoining specifications. Technical Report 118, SRC DEC, 1993. Part of the paper appears in PODC '94 as "Open Systems in TLA".
4. M. Abadi and G.D. Plotkin. A logical view of composition. *Theoretical Computer Science*, 114(1):3–30, June 1993.
5. B. Alpern and F.B. Schneider. Defining liveness. *Information Processing Letters*, 24(4):181–185, October 1985.
6. H. Barringer and R. Kuiper. Hierarchical development of concurrent systems in a temporal logic framework. In *Seminar on Concurrency, LNCS 197*, pages 35–61. Springer-Verlag, 1984.
7. P. Collette. Application of the composition principle to Unity-like specifications. In *TAPSOFT '93, LNCS 668*, pages 230–242. Springer-Verlag, 1993.
8. P. Collette. *Design of Compositional Proof Systems Based on Assumption-Guarantee Specifications — Application to UNITY*. PhD thesis, Université Catholique de Louvain, June 1994.
9. P. Grønning, T.Q. Nielsen, and H.H. Løvengreen. Refinement and composition of transition-based rely-guarantee specifications with auxiliary variables. In *FST&TCS, LNCS 472*, pages 332–348. Springer-Verlag, 1991.
10. C.B. Jones. Tentative steps towards a development method for interfering programs. *ACM Transactions on Programming Languages and Systems*, 5(4):596–619, October 1983.
11. B. Jonsson and Y.-K. Tsay. Assumption/guarantee specifications in linear-time temporal logic. Technical Report DoCS 95/58, Department of Computer Systems, Uppsala University, January 1995.
12. L. Lamport. What good is temporal logic? In R.E.A. Mason, editor, *Information Processing 83*, pages 657–668. IFIP, North-Holland, 1983.
13. L. Lamport. The temporal logic of actions. *ACM Transactions on Programming Languages and Systems*, 16(3):872–923, May 1994.
14. Z. Manna and A. Pnueli. *The Temporal Logic of Reactive and Concurrent Systems: Specification*. Springer-Verlag, 1992.
15. J. Misra and K.M. Chandy. Proofs of networks of processes. *IEEE Transactions on Software Engineering*, 7(4):417–426, July 1981.
16. A. Pnueli. The temporal semantics of concurrent programs. *Theoretical Computer Science*, 13:45–60, 1982.
17. A. Pnueli. System specification and refinement in temporal logic. In *FST&TCS, LNCS 652*, pages 1–38. Springer-Verlag, 1992.
18. Q. Xu, A. Cau, and P. Collette. On unifying assumption-commitment style proof rules for concurrency. In *CONCUR '94, LNCS 836*, pages 267–282. Springer-Verlag, 1994.

Fine Hierarchy of Regular ω-Languages

Victor Selivanov *
Novosibirsk Pedagogical University
Novosibirsk 630126 Russia

Abstract

By applying descriptive set theory we get several facts on the fine structure of regular ω-languages considered by K.Wagner. We present quite different, shorter proofs for main his results and get new results. Our description of the fine structure is new, very clear and automata–free. We prove also a closure property of the fine structure under Boolean operations. Our results demonstrate deep interconnections between descriptive set theory and theory of ω-languages.

1 Introduction

Regular ω-languages were introduced by J.R.Büchi in the sixties and studied by many people including B.A.Trakhtenbrot, R.McNaughton and M.O.Rabin. The subject quickly developed into a rich topic with several deep applications. For the history and references on the subject see e.g. [Th90,St87,Wa79]. We assume acquaintance with some basic concepts, notation and results in this field, all of them may be found in the cited papers.

One of branches of the discussed topic deals with the classifications of regular ω-languages by means of topology, hierarchies and reducibilities. A series of papers culminated with the paper [Wa79] giving in a sense the finest possible classification. Its formulation needs some notions.

Let X be a finite nontrivial alphabet (for simplicity assume that $X = \{x|x < k\}$ for a natural number $k > 1$). Let X^* and X^ω denote respectively the sets of all words and of all ω-words (i.e. sequences $\nu : \omega \to X$) over X. For $B, C \subseteq X^\omega$, B is said to be *DA-reducible* to C (in symbols $B \leq_{DA} C$), if $B = f^{-1}(C)$ for some function $f : X^\omega \to X^\omega$ computed by a deterministic asynchronous finite transducer (this relation was studied in [Wa79]). The relation $\leq_{DA}$ is clearly a preordering, and the join $B \oplus C$ gives as usual the supremum of B and C under this relation. By $\equiv_{DA}$ we denote the induced equivalence relation which gives rise to the structure of DA-degrees. Our notation and terminology on

***This work was done at the University of Heidelberg supported by the Alexander von Humboldt Foundation.**

reducibilities are standard and applicable to several modifications of the introduced notions which will be studied further on. Let ω^ω be the supremum of ordinals $\omega^k, k < \omega$. One of the main results from [Wa79] may be now reformulated as follows.

1.1. Theorem ([Wa79]). *There are regular ω-languages $A_\alpha (\alpha < \omega^\omega)$ such that $A_\alpha \not\leq_{DA} \bar{A}_\alpha$ and $A_\alpha \oplus \bar{A}_\alpha <_{DA} A_\beta$ for all $\alpha < \beta < \omega^\omega$, and any regular ω-language is DA-equivalent to one of $A_\alpha, A_\alpha \oplus \bar{A}_\alpha (\alpha < \omega^\omega)$.*

Note that we denote ordinals by $\alpha, \beta, \gamma, \ldots$ while ω-words—by $\mu, \nu, \xi, \ldots$.

An immediate corollary of Theorem 1.1 is the following assertion in which $\mathcal{R}$ denotes the class of all regular ω-languages. For a class $\mathcal{A}$ of ω-languages (i.e. of subsets of X^ω), the structure $(\mathcal{A}; \leq_{DA})$ is said to be *almost well-ordered*, if it is well founded and for all $B, C \in \mathcal{A}$ either $B \leq_{DA} C$ or $\bar{C} \leq_{DA} B$. To any such a structure an ordinal may be related in the usual way.

1.2. Corollary ([Wa79]). *The structure $(\mathcal{R}; \leq_{DA})$ is almost well-ordered with the corresponding ordinal ω^ω.*

The next fact follows from the constructiveness of the proof in [Wa79].

1.3. Corollary ([Wa79]). (i) *There is an algorithm computing from (a Muller automaton for) a regular ω-language B the (notation of the) language from 1.1 DA-equivalent to B.*

(ii) *The DA-reducibility on $\mathcal{R}$ coincides with the Wadge reducibility (i.e. with the reducibility $\leq_{CA}$ by functions continuous in the Cantor topology on the set X^ω).*

Our paper presents an alternative proof of the results stated above which are shorter than the quite complicated proofs from [Wa79]. The reason why it is possible is the fact that we use some nontrivial facts on Wadge degrees, on determinateness of games from [BL69] and on the so called fine hierarchy introduced by me in [Se83] in the context of recursion theory and then applied to some other fields in several subsequent publications. Our paper contains also alternative proofs of some other results from [Wa79] as well as several new results, e.g. an interesting closure property of the hierarchy in 1.1 under the Boolean operations.

Our proof of 1.1 (as well as of other facts from [Wa79]) gives additional information as compared with the proof of K.Wagner, namely:

(i) it gives the estimation of sets from 1.1 in the structure of Wadge degrees of Borel sets (which is known to be almost well–ordered under $\leq_{CA}$);

(ii) it gives a very clear algebraic description of the hierarchy from 1.1;

(iii) our description of the hierarchy in 1.1 is automata–free (as far as we see, the paper [Wa79] does not provide an automata–free description).

So our revision of [Wa79] is not just a simplification. It uses different methodology and is an automata–free supplement to [Wa79].

Though our paper implies most of the results from [Wa79], it by no means covers the paper [Wa79] completely. That paper contains e.g. sophisticated constructions on automata which are interesting in their own right.

The rest of the paper is organized as follows: in Sections 2—5 we formulate some auxiliary facts most of which are known, and in Section 6 we prove our main results.

2 Wadge Hierarchy of Borel Sets

Here we summarize some notation and well–known facts on Borel hierarchy and Wadge reducibility which are useful further on.

Let $\mathcal{B}$ denote the class of Borel subsets of X^ω, i.e. the least class containing the open sets and closed under complementation and countable union. These sets can be classified in a hierarchy the lowest levels of which are as follows: G and F are the classes of open and closed sets, respectively; G_δ (F_σ) is the class of countable intersections (unions) of open (resp. closed) sets; $G_{\delta\sigma}$ ($F_{\sigma\delta}$) is the class of countable unions (intersections) of G_δ- (resp. of F_σ-) sets, and so on.

In notation of hierarchy theory, $\mathbf{\Sigma}_0^0 = G \cap F$ is the class of clopen sets, $\mathbf{\Sigma}_1^0 = G$, $\mathbf{\Sigma}_2^0 = F_\sigma$, $\mathbf{\Sigma}_3^0 = G_{\delta\sigma}$, $\mathbf{\Sigma}_4^0 = F_{\sigma\delta\sigma}$ and so on, $\mathbf{\Pi}_n^0 = \{\bar{B} | B \in \mathbf{\Sigma}_n^0\}$ is the dual class for $\mathbf{\Sigma}_n^0$, and $\mathbf{\Delta}_n^0 = \mathbf{\Sigma}_n^0 \cap \mathbf{\Pi}_n^0$. The sequence $\{\mathbf{\Sigma}_n^0\}_{n<\omega}$ is known as *the finite Borel hierarchy*. It may be in a natural way extended on all countable ordinals; the resulting sequence, called *the Borel hierarchy,* exhausts the class $\mathcal{B}$.

Recall that a class $\mathcal{A}$ of sets is said to have *the reduction property,* if for all $B_0, B_1 \in \mathcal{A}$ there are disjoint $B_0', B_1' \in \mathcal{A}$ such that $B_i' \subseteq B_i$ and $B_0 \cup B_1 = B_0' \cup B_1'$. For $B, C \subseteq X^\omega$, let $B \oplus C = \{0 \cdot \mu, i \cdot \nu | 0 < i < k, \mu \in B, \nu \in C\}$ (recall that we assume $X = \{x | x < k\}, 1 < k < \omega$, and use some almost standard notation on words and ω-words). A set B is called *selfdual,* if $B \leq_{CA} \bar{B}$. A set B be is called *$\mathbf{\Sigma}_n^0$-complete,* if $B \in \mathbf{\Sigma}_n^0$ and any $\mathbf{\Sigma}_n^0$-set is CA-reducible to B; similarly one can define completeness for other classes of sets and other redicibilities. Let us state some well–known properties of the introduced notions. Proofs may be found e.g. in [Mo80].

2.1. Properties. (i) *For any n, the class $\mathbf{\Sigma}_n^0$ contains $\emptyset, X^\omega$, is closed under $\cup, \cap$, is closed downwards under $\leq_{CA}$ and has the reduction property.*

(ii) *Any level $\mathbf{\Sigma}_{n+1}^0$ has a universal set which is $\mathbf{\Sigma}_{n+1}^0$-complete and not selfdual.*

(iii) *For any n, $\mathbf{\Sigma}_n^0 \cup \mathbf{\Pi}_n^0 \subseteq \mathbf{\Delta}_{n+1}^0$, and for $n > 0$ the inclusion is strict.*

(iv) *For all $B, C \subseteq X^\omega$, $B \oplus C$ is the supremum of B and C under $\leq_{CA}$.*

(v) *For any $B \subseteq X^\omega$, the set $B \oplus \bar{B}$ is selfdual.*

Now let us formulate some more sophisticated properties of Wadge reducibility and of one of its modifications defined as follows. A set B is called *Lipschitz reducible* to a set C (in symbols $B \leq_{CS} C$), if $B = f^{-1}(C)$ for a synchronous continuous function $f : X^\omega \to X^\omega$ (i.e. a function satisfying $f(\xi)(n) = \varphi(\xi[n+1])$, where $\varphi : X^* \to X$ and $\xi[n+1]$ is the initial segment of ξ of length $n+1$). Note that for uniformity we use notation for Wadge and Lipschitz reducibilities from [Wa79] which is different from notation in descriptive set theory. Of course,

$\leq_{CS}$ implies $\leq_{CA}$. By $(B_0, B_1) \leq_{CA} (A_0, A_1)$ we denote the fact that for some continuous function f it holds $B_i = f^{-1}(C_i), i < 2$. Define the sets U_0, U_1 by $U_i = \bigcup_{n<\omega} 0^{2n+i} \cdot 1 \cdot X^\omega, i < 2$. For the proofs of the next assertions see e.g. [VW76].

2.2. Properties. (i) *For any $B \in \mathcal{B}$, $B \leq_{CS} \bar{B}$ iff $B \leq_{CA} \bar{B}$.*

(ii) *The structures $(\mathcal{B}; \leq_{CS})$ and $(\mathcal{B}; \leq_{CA})$ are almost well-ordered.*

(iii) *The sets U_0, U_1 are open and disjoint, and for all open disjoint sets V_0, V_1 it holds $(V_0, V_1) \leq_{CA} (U_0, U_1)$.*

3 Regular ω-Languages

Here we summarize some facts on regular sets most of which are known. Let $\xi = \langle \nu_0, \nu_1 \rangle$ be the code of the pair of ω-words defined by $\xi(2n+i) = \nu_i(n), i < 2$; in the same way one can code longer tuples of ω-words. Note that this coding provides a homeomorphism between $X^\omega \times X^\omega$ and X^ω. Along with the reducibility $\leq_{DA}$ from Introduction we consider the reducibility $\leq_{DS}$ by deterministic synchronous finite transducers which is defined in the obvious way and which was also studied in [Wa79]. Note that $\leq_{DS}$ implies $\leq_{DA}$, and these relations are effective versions of $\leq_{CS}$ and $\leq_{CA}$, respectively. Recall that $\mathcal{R}$ denotes the class of all regular ω-languages.

The assertions (i)—(vii) below are well-known (see [Th90,Wa79,SW74]) while the assertion (viii) is evident.

3.1. Properties. (i) *The class $\mathcal{R}$ is closed under Boolean operations.*

(ii) *Any regular set is a Boolean combination of regular F_σ-sets.*

(iii) *The classes of regular open and of regular F_σ-sets are closed under $\cup, \cap$ and are downward closed under $\leq_{DA}$.*

(iv) *There are regular sets in $G \setminus F$ and $F_\sigma \setminus G_\delta$.*

(v) *The relations $\leq_{DS}$ and $\leq_{CS}$ on $\mathcal{R}$ coincide.*

(vi) *The class of regular sets in $F_\sigma \cap G_\delta$ coincides with the class of Boolean combinations of regular open sets.*

(vii) *A regular set B is F_σ iff $B = \{\xi : I_{\mathcal{A}}(\xi) \subseteq T\}$ for a deterministic finite automaton $\mathcal{A} = [X, Z, f, z_0]$ and a set of states $T \subseteq Z$, where $I_{\mathcal{A}}(\xi)$ is the set of states which occur infinitely often when $\mathcal{A}$ runs along ξ starting from the initial state $z_0 \in Z$.*

(viii) *The "projections" $\langle \nu_0, \ldots, \nu_k \rangle \mapsto \nu_i$ are computable by deterministic asynchronous finite transducers.*

Note that the proofs of these facts were given before [Wa79] and do not use that paper (the assertion (v) was indeed proved in [Wa79] but it follows also from [BL69], see Remark 3 at the end of [Wa79]).

The next assertion seems formally new but it follows from the known proofs and constructions.

3.2. Proposition. (i) *The classes of regular open and of regular F_σ-sets have the reduction property.*

(ii) *Every two disjoint regular G_δ-sets A_0 and A_1 are separable by a Boolean combination of regular open sets (i.e. $A_0 \subseteq F \subseteq \bar{A}_1$ for a Boolean combination F of regular open sets).*

Proof. (i) Let $B_i, i < 2$, be regular open sets. By a result of L.Staiger (see [Wa79]), $B_i = W_i \cdot X^\omega$ for some regular sets of words $W_i \subseteq X^*$. Let

$$W_0' = \{a \in W_0 | \forall b \sqsubset a(b \notin W_1)\},\ W_1' = \{a \in W_1 | \forall b \sqsubseteq a(b \notin W_0)\}$$

and $B_i' = W_i' \cdot X^\omega$. Then the sets B_0', B_1' clearly reduce B_0, B_1 and are open. By considering the product of the automata recognizing the sets W_0 and W_1 one easily sees that the sets W_0', W_1' are regular, hence B_0', B_1' are regular too.

For the case of regular F_σ-sets $B_0, B_1 \subseteq X^\omega$, choose an automaton $\mathcal{A} = [X, Z, f, z_0]$ such that there are sets $T_0, T_1 \subseteq Z$ satisfying $B_i = \{\xi : I_\mathcal{A}(\xi) \subseteq T_i\}$. Then $B_0 \cap B_1 = \{\xi : I_\mathcal{A}(\xi) \subseteq T_0 \cap T_1\}$.

Let $\mathcal{A}' = [X, Z \times \{0,1\}, f', (z_0, 1)]$ where

$$f'((z,k),x) = \begin{cases} (f(z,x), 2-k) & \text{, if } k = 0 \wedge f(z,x) \notin T_0, \\ (f(z,x), 2-k) & \text{, if } k = 1 \wedge f(z,x) \notin T_1, \\ (f(z,x), k) & \text{, otherwise.} \end{cases}$$

By cases one easily checks that the sets $B_i' = \{\xi : I_{\mathcal{A}'}(\xi) \subseteq (T_i \times \{i\})\}, i \leq 1$, reduce the sets B_0, B_1.

(ii) The sets $B_i = \bar{A}_i$ are F_σ, so they are reduced by some regular F_σ-sets $B_i', i \leq 1$. We have $B_0' \cap B_1' = \emptyset$ and $B_0' \cup B_1' = X^\omega$ (because $B_0 \cup B_1 = X^\omega$). So the sets B_i' are in $F_\sigma \cap G_\delta$. By 3.1.(vi), both these sets are Boolean combinations of regular open sets, hence the set $F = B_1'$ has the desired property. This completes the proof.

4 Fine Hierarchy

Here we summarize some facts on the abstract version of the fine hierarchy considered in a series of my papers. The proofs are elementary but some of them are not at all trivial.

Let $(B; \cup, \cap, \bar{\ }, 0, 1)$ be a Boolean algebra. By *a base* (in B) we mean any sequence $\{L_n\}_{n<\omega}$ of sublattices of $(B; \cup, \cap, 0, 1)$ satisfying $L_n \cup \check{L}_n \subseteq L_{n+1}$, where $\check{L}_n = \{\bar{a} | a \in L_n\}$. Note that by Stone Representation Theorem we may think of the L_n's as of classes of sets.

4.1. Definition. (i) *A base L is* interpolable, *if for all $n < \omega$ any two disjoint elements $a, b \in \check{L}_{n+1}$ are separable by a Boolean combination c of elements of L_n (i.e. $a \subseteq c \subseteq \bar{b}$).*

(ii) *A base L is* reducible, *if any L_n has the reduction property.*

We need an operation *Bisep* on subsets of B defined by

$$Bisep(X, Y_0, Y_1, Y_2) = \{x_0 y_0 \cup x_1 y_1 \cup \bar{x}_0 \bar{x}_1 y_2 | x_i \in X, y_j \in Y_j, x_0 x_1 y_0 = x_0 x_1 y_1\},$$

where x_0y_0 stand for $x_0 \cap y_0$. This operation generilizes the following operation from [Lo83] used for a description of some levels of the Wadge hierarchy:

$$bisep(X, Y_0, Y_1, Y_2) = \{x_0y_0 \cup x_1y_1 \cup \bar{x}_0\bar{x}_1y_2 | x_i \in X, y_j \in Y_j, x_0x_1 = \emptyset\}.$$

Now we define a notion which will be the main technical instrument in further considerations. It uses the ordinal $\varepsilon_0 = sup\{\omega, \omega^\omega, \omega^{\omega^\omega}, \ldots\}$.

4.2. Definition. *By the fine hierarchy over L we mean the sequence* $\{S_\alpha\}_{\alpha<\varepsilon_0}$*, where* $S_\alpha = S^0_\alpha$ *and the classes* $S^n_\alpha (n < \omega)$ *are defined by induction on* α*:* $S^n_0 = \{0\}$*;* $S^n_{\omega^\gamma} = S^{n+1}_\gamma$ *for* $\gamma > 0$*;* $S^n_{\beta+1} = Bisep(L_n, S^n_\beta, \check{S}^n_\beta, S^n_0)$ *for all* $\beta < \varepsilon_0$*, and* $S^n_{\beta+\omega^\gamma} = Bisep(L_n, S^n_\beta, \check{S}^n_\beta, S^n_{\omega^\gamma})$ *for* $\gamma > 0$ *and* β *of the form* $\beta = \omega^\gamma \cdot \beta_1 > 0$.

Definition uses some ordinal arithmetic as described e.g. in [KM67]. To see that this definition is correct note that every nonzero ordinal $\alpha < \varepsilon_0$ is uniquely representable in the form $\alpha = \omega^{\gamma_0} + \cdots + \omega^{\gamma_k}$ for a finite sequence $\gamma_0 \geq \cdots \geq \gamma_k$ of ordinals $< \alpha$. Applying 4.2 we subsequently get $S^n_{\omega^{\gamma_0}}, S^n_{\omega^{\gamma_0}+\omega^{\gamma_1}}, \ldots, S^n_\alpha$. The classes S^n_γ for $n > 0$ play a technical role, they are among the classes S_α.

Let us formulate some technical properties of the introduced notions. The proofs may be found in [Se89,Se91] and, in a systematized form, in [Se9?].

4.3. Properties. (i) *If* $\alpha < \beta < \varepsilon_0$ *then* $S_\alpha \subseteq S_\beta \cap \check{S}_\beta$.

(ii) *For any* $n < \omega$, $\{S^n_k\}_{k<\omega}$ *is the difference hierarchy over* L_n*, i.e.* $S^n_0 = \{0\}$ *and* $S^n_{k+1} = \{\bar{a}u | a \in S^n_k, u \in L_n\}$.

(iii) *Classes of the fine hierarchy over a reducible base L coincide with the corresponding classes obtained by using the operation bisep in place of Bisep.*

(iv) *If L is interpolable then* $S_\alpha \cap \check{S}_\alpha = \cup_{\beta<\alpha}(S_\beta \cup \check{S}_\beta)$ *for all limit ordinals* $\alpha < \varepsilon_0$.

(v) *If L is reducible then, for all* $\beta < \varepsilon_0$, $S_{\beta+1} \cap \check{S}_{\beta+1}$ *is the class of elements* $a_0u_0 \cup a_1u_1$*, where* $a_0, \bar{a}_1 \in S_\beta$, $u_0, u_1 \in L_0$ *and* $u_0u_1 = 0, u_0 \cup u_1 = 1$.

The fine hierarchy as defined above may seem at first glance ad hoc. In [Se9?] we have given an especially natural and clear description of it in terms of the Boolean operations. Let T be the set of terms in the language $\{\cup, \cap, \bar{}, 0, 1\}$ with variables $v^n_k (k, n < \omega)$. Relate to any $t \in T$ the set $t(L)$ of all values of t when the variables $v^n_k (k < \omega)$ range over L_n for all $n < \omega$. The next result from [Se94,Se9?] relates these classes to the levels of the fine hierarchy over L. The proof is elementary, though rather technical.

4.4. Theorem. *For any reducible base L,* $\{S_\alpha, \check{S}_\alpha | \alpha < \varepsilon_0\} = \{t(L) | t \in T\}$. *There are algorithms computing from any ordinal* $\alpha < \varepsilon_0$ *a corresponding term* $t \in T$ *and vice versa.*

5 Examples of Fine Hierarchy

In our publications one could find several examples of the fine hierarchy with applications. Here we consider two concrete examples of the fine hierarchy relevant to the topic of this paper. By 2.1, $L = \{\Sigma^0_{n+1}\}_{n<\omega}$ is a reducible base. Let $\{\mathcal{S}_\alpha\}$ be the fine hierarchy over this base. The hierarchy $\{\mathcal{S}_\alpha\}$ is clearly a fragment of the Wadge hierarchy of Borel sets; in [Se9?] we proved that the hierarchy $\{\mathcal{S}_\alpha\}$ is just the finite version of the Wadge hierarchy of Borel sets.

Let B_n be a Σ^0_{n+1}-complete set for any $n < \omega$. Relate to the sequence $\{B_n\}$ the sets $A^n_\alpha (n < \omega)$ by induction on $\alpha < \varepsilon_0$ as follows: $A^n_0 = \emptyset$, $A^n_{\omega^\gamma} = A^{n+1}_\gamma$, $A^n_{\beta+1} = \{\langle\mu,\nu,\xi\rangle | (\mu \in U_0 \wedge \nu \in A^n_\beta) \vee (\mu \in U_1 \wedge \xi \notin A^n_\beta)\}$, and $A^n_{\beta+\omega^\gamma} = \{\langle\mu,\nu,\xi,\rho\rangle | (\mu \in U_0 \wedge \nu \in A^n_\beta) \vee (\mu \in U_1 \wedge \xi \notin A^n_\beta) \vee (\mu \notin (U_0 \cup U_1) \wedge \rho \in C^n_{\omega^\gamma})\}$, where the ordinals satisfy the same conditions as in Definition 4.2 and U_0, U_1 are the sets from 2.2.

Let us state some properties of the introduced objects.

5.1. Proposition. (i) *For any $\alpha < \varepsilon_0$, the class $\mathcal{S}_\alpha$ is downward closed under $\leq_{CA}$ and has a universal set.*

(ii) *For any $\alpha < \varepsilon_0$, the set A^0_α is $\mathcal{S}_\alpha$-complete with respect to $\leq_{CA}$ and is not selfdual.*

Proof. By induction on α one easily checks the assertion (i) for $\mathcal{S}^n_\alpha (n < \omega)$, so (i) is true. As is well–known from descriptive set theory, (i) implies that the universal set is not selfdual.

The evident induction shows that $A^n_\alpha \in \mathcal{S}^n_\alpha$ for all n, α, so it remains to reduce any $D \in \mathcal{S}^n_\alpha$ to A^n_α. This is also by induction. The cases $\alpha = 0, \omega^\gamma$ are trivial. The remaining cases are considered similarly to one another, so consider only the case $\alpha = \beta + 1$. By 4.3.(iii), $D = D_0 V_0 \cup D_1 V_1$ for some $D_0, \bar{D}_1 \in \mathcal{S}^n_\beta$ and disjoint open sets V_0, V_1. By 2.2 and induction hypothesis, $(V_0, V_1) \leq_{CA} (U_0, U_1)$, $D_0 \leq_{CA} A^n_\beta$ and $\bar{D}_1 \leq_{CA} A^n_\beta$. Let f, g_0 and g_1 be continuous functions witnessing these reductions. Then the function $\mu \mapsto \langle f(\mu), g_0(\mu), g_1(\mu)\rangle$ CA-reduces D to A^n_α. The set universal in $\mathcal{S}^n_\alpha$ is clearly $\mathcal{S}^n_\alpha$-complete, so it is CA-equivalent to A^n_α, hence A^n_α is not selfdual. This completes the proof.

Now consider our second example. Let $\mathcal{L}_0 = \mathcal{R} \cap G, \mathcal{L}_1 = \mathcal{R} \cap F_\sigma$ and $\mathcal{L}_{n+2} = \mathcal{R}$. By 3.1, $\mathcal{L} = \{\mathcal{L}_n\}_{n<\omega}$ is a reducible base, so we can construct the fine hierarchy $\{\mathcal{R}_\alpha\}$ over $\mathcal{L}$. Note that $\mathcal{R}_\alpha = \mathcal{R}$ for $\alpha \geq \omega^\omega$, hence the classes $\mathcal{R}_\alpha$ are interesting only for $\alpha < \omega^\omega$. By 3.1.(ii) and 4.3.(ii), $\cup_{\alpha<\omega^\omega}\mathcal{R}_\alpha = \mathcal{R}$. It is clear also that $\mathcal{R}_\alpha \subseteq \mathcal{S}_\alpha$ for all $\alpha < \varepsilon_0$.

Let B_0, B_1 be regular sets respectively from $G \backslash F$ and $F_\sigma \backslash G_\delta$, see Properties 3.1. Let $A_\alpha = A^0_\alpha, \alpha < \omega^\omega$, be sets constructed from B_0, B_1 as described above (note that the construction for $\alpha < \omega^\omega$ needs only the sets B_0, B_1). By 5.1, any A_α is $\mathcal{S}_\alpha$-complete and not selfdual. Repeating the proof of 5.1 we get the following "effective" version of this assertion.

5.2. Proposition. (i) *For any $\alpha < \omega^\omega$, the class $\mathcal{R}_\alpha$ is downward closed under $\leq_{DA}$.*

(ii) *For any $\alpha < \omega^\omega$, the set A_α is $\mathcal{R}_\alpha$-complete with respect to $\leq_{DA}$ and $A_\alpha \not\leq_{DA} \bar{A}_\alpha$.*

The introduced fine hierarchy of regular sets has several other interesting properties. We consider them in the next Section.

6 Main Results

Now we are able to prove our main results.

Proof of 1.1. By 5.2, the sets in 1.1 (defined as in 5.2) are ordered as stated in 1.1. It remains to show that any $E \in \mathcal{R}$ is DA-equivalent to one of $A_\alpha, \bar{A}_\alpha, A_\alpha \oplus \bar{A}_\alpha (\alpha < \omega^\omega)$. By 3.1.(ii) and 4.3.(ii), $E \in \mathcal{R}_\alpha \cup \check{\mathcal{R}}_\alpha$ for some $\alpha < \omega^\omega$. Choose the least such α. By 4.3.(i), one of the following alternatives holds:

$$E \in \mathcal{R}_\alpha \setminus \check{\mathcal{R}}_\alpha,\ E \in \check{\mathcal{R}}_\alpha \setminus \mathcal{R}_\alpha,\ E \in (\mathcal{R}_\alpha \cap \check{\mathcal{R}}_\alpha) \setminus \cup_{\beta<\alpha}(\mathcal{R}_\beta \cup \check{\mathcal{R}}_\beta). \qquad (1)$$

By 3.2.(ii), the base L from the end of Section 5 is interpolable. By 4.3.(iv), in the third alternative the ordinal α must be a successor, say $\alpha = \beta + 1$. It suffices to show that for the alternatives in (1) we respectively have $E \equiv_{DA} A_\alpha$, $E \equiv_{DA} \bar{A}_\alpha$ and $E \equiv_{DA} A_\beta \oplus \bar{A}_\beta$.

Assume first that $E \in \mathcal{R}_\alpha \setminus \check{\mathcal{R}}_\alpha$. By 5.2, $E \leq_{DA} A_\alpha$, so it remains to show $A_\alpha \leq_{DA} E$. Suppose the contrary, then $A_\alpha \not\leq_{DS} E$ and (by 3.1.(v)) $A_\alpha \not\leq_{CS} E$. By 2.2.(ii), $\bar{E} \leq_{CS} A_\alpha$, hence $\bar{E} \leq_{DS} A_\alpha$, $\bar{E} \leq_{DA} A_\alpha$ and (by 5.2) $E \in \check{\mathcal{R}}_\alpha$. A contradiction.

The second alternative is dual to the first one, so it remains to consider the third alternative. By the argument from preceding paragraph, $A_\beta, \bar{A}_\beta \leq_{DA} E$, so $A_\beta \oplus \bar{A}_\beta \leq_{DA} E$ and it remains to show that $E \leq_{DA} A_\beta \oplus \bar{A}_\beta$. By 4.3.(v), $E = E_0 V_0 \cup E_1 V_1$ for some $E_0, E_1 \in \mathcal{R}_\beta$ and $V_0, V_1 \in L_0$ with $V_0 V_1 = \emptyset$, $V_0 \cup V_1 = X^\omega$. Then $V_0 = \bar{V}_1$ and V_0 is clopen, so $V_0 = W \cdot X^\omega$ for a finite set $W \subseteq X^*$. By 5.2, there are deterministic asynchronous finite automata $\mathcal{A}_0, \mathcal{A}_1$ reducing respectively E_0 to A_β and E_1 to $\bar{A}_\beta$. It is an easy exercise to construct a deterministic asynchronous finite automaton reducing E to $A_\beta \oplus \bar{A}_\beta$. This completes the proof.

The proof shows that the hierarchy $\{\mathcal{R}_\alpha\}_{\alpha<\omega^\omega}$ coincides with the hierarchy from the end of [Wa79] for DA-reducibility. This gives very clear, purely algebraic and automata–free description of this hierarchy.

Proof of 1.3. (i) By 3.1.(v) and 2.2.(ii), for all regular ω-languages B, C, one of the conditions $B \leq_{DS} C$, $\bar{C} \leq_{DS} B$ holds. By a result in [BL69], there is an algorithm computing which one of the conditions holds (because the condition $B \leq_{DS} C$ may be written as a sequential finite–state condition, see Remark 3 at the end of [Wa79]). This algorithm together with the proof of 1.1 yields a desired algorithm.

(ii) By 1.1, it suffices to show that the relations $\leq_{CA}$ and $\leq_{DA}$ coincide on the class $\{A_\alpha, \bar{A}_\alpha, A_\alpha \oplus \bar{A}_\alpha | \alpha < \omega\}$. But this follows from 5.1 and 5.2 completing the proof.

The next result states close relationship between hierarchies from Section 5. This is an interesting fact because its analogs for other examples of the fine hierarchy usually fail.

6.1. Theorem. *For any* $\alpha < \omega^\omega$, $\mathcal{R}_\alpha = \mathcal{R} \cap \mathcal{S}_\alpha$.

Proof. The inclusion from left to right is trivial, so consider the converse inclusion. By 1.1, it suffices to show that if one of the sets $A_\beta, \bar{A}_\beta, A_\beta \oplus \bar{A}_\beta (\beta < \omega)$ is in $\mathcal{S}_\alpha$ then it is in $\mathcal{R}_\alpha$. But this follows from 1.3.(ii), 5.1 and 5.2 completing the proof.

Theorem 1.1 describes the structure $(\mathcal{R}; \leq_{DA})$. In [Wa79] there is also a similar description of the structure $(\mathcal{R}; \leq_{DS})$. We can give an equivalent shorter description. For all $\alpha < \omega^\omega$ and $k < \omega$, let $B^k_\alpha = \{0^{k+1} \cdot A_\alpha, a \cdot \bar{A}_\alpha | a \in X^{k+1}, a \neq 0^{k+1}\}$, where X^{k+1} is the set of words from X^* of length $k+1$.

6.2. Theorem. (i) *For all $\alpha < \beta < \omega^\omega$ and $k < \omega$, $A_\alpha \not\leq_{DS} \bar{A}_\alpha$ and $A_\alpha, \bar{A}_\alpha <_{DS} B^k_\alpha <_{DS} B^{k+1}_\alpha <_{DS} A_\beta, \bar{A}_\beta$.*

(ii) *Any $E \in \mathcal{R}$ is DS-equivalent to one of $A_\alpha, \bar{A}_\alpha, B^k_\alpha (\alpha < \omega^\omega, k < \omega)$.*

Proof. First we check that for any $F \in \mathcal{R}$, $F \leq_{DA} A_\alpha$ iff $F \leq_{DS} A_\alpha$. Nontrivial is only the implication from left to right. Suppose it is false, so $F \leq_{DA} A_\alpha$ and $F \not\leq_{DS} A_\alpha$. By 3.1.(v) and 2.2.(ii), $\bar{A}_\alpha \leq_{DS} F$, hence $\bar{A}_\alpha \leq_{DA} A_\alpha$. A contradiction. Note that the same argument proves also the equivalence $A_\alpha \leq_{DA} F$ iff $A_\alpha \leq_{DS} F$, as well as the analogs of the both equivalences with $\bar{A}_\alpha$ in place of A_α.

Now we prove (i). The condition $A_\alpha \not\leq_{DS} \bar{A}_\alpha$ follows from 5.2. For any $k < \omega$, $A_\alpha \oplus \bar{A}_\alpha \equiv_{DA} B^k_\alpha$, hence, by the preceding paragraph, $A_\alpha, \bar{A}_\alpha <_{DS} B^k_\alpha <_{DS} A_\beta, \bar{A}_\beta$. It remains to prove that $B^k_\alpha <_{DS} B^{k+1}_\alpha$. The condition $B^k_\alpha \leq_{DS} B^{k+1}_\alpha$ is clear while the condition $B^{k+1}_\alpha \not\leq_{DS} B^k_\alpha$ follows from Lemma 1 in [BL69] (consider the finite–state condition $\{(\mu, \nu) | \mu \in B^k_\alpha \leftrightarrow \nu \in B^{k+1}_\alpha\}$).

The assertion (ii) is proved as in the proof of 1.1. For the first two alternatives in (1) we have respectively $E \equiv_{DS} A_\alpha$ and $E \equiv_{DS} \bar{A}_\alpha$, by the remarks trom the beginning of this proof. For the third alternative, consider representations for E and V_0 from the proof of 1.1. Let $k < \omega$ satisfies $W \subseteq X^{k+1}$. The class $\{(a \cdot X^\omega) \cap E | a \in X^{k+1}\}$ coincides, modulo *DS*-equivalence, with $\{A_\beta, \bar{A}_\beta\}$ (otherwise $S \in \mathcal{R}_\beta \cup \check{\mathcal{R}}_\beta$). From this one easily deduces that $E \equiv_{DS} B^k_\beta$. This completes the proof.

6.3. Corollary. *The structure $(\mathcal{R}; \leq_{DS})$ is almost well-ordered with the corresponding ordinal ω^ω, but it is not isomorphic to the structure $(\mathcal{R}; \leq_{DA})$.*

Note that the argument above is very similar to that in the proof of properties of the Lipschitz reducibility in [VW76].

A good deal of [Wa79] treats the so called coarse structure $\{\widehat{C}^k_n, \widehat{D}^k_n\}$. It turns out that the coarse structure is a fragment of the hierarchy $\{\mathcal{R}_\alpha\}$ having especially nice and easy description in terms of Boolean operations. For classes of sets $\mathcal{A}$ and $\mathcal{B}$, let $\mathcal{A} + \mathcal{B} = \{A \,\Delta\, B | A \in \mathcal{A}, B \in \mathcal{B}\}$, where Δ is the symmetric difference. Define classes $\mathcal{P}_\alpha (\alpha < \omega^2)$ as follows: $\mathcal{P}_0 = \{\emptyset\}$, $\mathcal{P}_{k+1} = \mathcal{L}_0 + \cdots + \mathcal{L}_0$ ($k+1 < \omega$ members in the sum), $\mathcal{P}_{\omega \cdot (k+1)} = \mathcal{L}_1 + \cdots + \mathcal{L}_1$ ($k+1 < \omega$ members in the sum), and $\mathcal{P}_{\omega \cdot (k+1)+l+1} = \mathcal{P}_{\omega \cdot (k+1)} + \mathcal{P}_{l+1}$ for $k, l < \omega$, where $\mathcal{L}_0, \mathcal{L}_1$ are the classes from 5.2. The next result follows from [Wa79, Theorem 15], and results from [Se94].

6.4. Theorem. *For all $n, k < \omega$, $\widehat{C}^{k+1}_{2n+1} = \mathcal{P}_{\omega \cdot 2n+k}$, $\widehat{D}^{k+1}_{2n+2} = \mathcal{P}_{\omega \cdot (2n+1)+k}$, $\mathcal{P}_k = \mathcal{R}_k$ and $\mathcal{P}_{\omega \cdot (n+1)+k} = \mathcal{R}_{\omega^{n+1} \cdot (k+1)}$.*

We conclude the paper by the following corollary of 4.4 and 3.2.(i). This result gives probably the clearest possible description of the classes $\mathcal{R}_\alpha$ in terms of $\mathcal{L}_0, \mathcal{L}_1$. Let T_1 be the set of Boolean terms with variables $v_k^0, v_k^1 (k < \omega)$.

6.5. Theorem. *It holds* $\{\mathcal{R}_\alpha, \check{\mathcal{R}}_\alpha | \alpha < \omega^\omega\} = \{t(\mathcal{L}) | t \in T_1\}$.

The next corollary of 6.5 (for details see [Se9?]) states a natural closure property of the collection $\{\mathcal{R}_\alpha, \check{\mathcal{R}}_\alpha | \alpha < \omega^\omega\}$. Relate to any term $s = s(x_0, \ldots, x_{n-1})$ in the language $\{\cup, \cap, ^-, 0, 1\}$ an n-ary operation F_s on classes of sets as follows:

$$F_s(A_0, \ldots, A_{n-1}) = \{s(a_0, \ldots, a_{n-1}) | a_i \in A_i\}.$$

E.g., for $s = x_0 \cap x_1$ we have $F_s(A_0, A_1) = \{a_0 \cap a_1 | a_i \in A_i\}$.

6.6. Corollary. *The collection* $\{\mathcal{R}_\alpha, \check{\mathcal{R}}_\alpha | \alpha < \omega^\omega\}$ *is closed under the operations* F_s*, and the structure formed by this collection and these operations is recursive.*

6.7. Remark. In [Wa79] conditions on Muller automaton were found equivalent to the condition that the corresponding regular ω-language belongs to a given level of the coarse structure. Recently, we found similar conditions for all levels of the fine hierarchy, as well as for the hierarchy generated by DS-reducibility. Proofs of these results should appear somewhere else.

7 Acknowlegements

L.Staiger, W.Thomas and K.Wagner have given to me some papers turned out to be useful for this investigation. L.Staiger and W.Thomas in an e–mail correspondence confirmed my conjecture 3.2.(i) sketched the corresponding proof. I am grateful to these people for their help. Special thanks go to K.Wagner for his impressive work resulted in the paper [Wa79].

References

[BL69] J.R.Büchi and L.H.Landweber. Solving sequential conditions by finite–state strategies. *Trans. Amer. Math. Soc.*, 138 (1969), p.295—311.

[KM67] K.Kuratowski and A.Mostowski. *Set Theory*. North Holland, 1967.

[Lo83] A.Louveau. Some results in the Wadge hierarchy of Borel sets. In: Cabal Seminar 79—81, Proceedings, *Lec. Notes in Math.*, v. 1019 (1983), p.28—55.

[Mo80] Y.N.Moschovakis. *Descriptive set theory.* Amsterdam, North Holland, 1980.

[Se83] V.L.Selivanov. Hierarchies of hyperarithmetical sets and functions. *Algebra i Logika*, 22 (1983), p.666—692 (In Russian, English translation: *Algebra and Logic*, 22 (1983), p.473—491).

[Se89] V.L.Selivanov. Fine hierarchies of arithmetical sets and definable index sets. *Trudy Mat. Inst., Novosibirsk*, v.12 (1989), p.165—185 (in Russian).

[Se91] V.L.Selivanov. Fine hierarchy and definable index sets. *Algebra i logika*, 30 (1991), p.705—725 (in Russian, English translation: *Algebra and logic*, 30 (1991), p.463—475).

[Se94] V.L.Selivanov. Two refinements of the polynomial hierarchy, in: Proc. of Symposium on Theor. Aspects of Computer Science STACS–94, *Lecture Notes in Computer Science*, v. 775. Berlin, Springer, 1994, 439—448 (a complete version is available as Preprint No 9, University of Heidelberg, Chair of Math. Logic).

[Se9?] V.L.Selivanov. Fine hierarchies and Boolean terms. To appear in the *Journal of Symbolic Logic* (a previous version is available as the Preprint No 5, the University of Heidelberg, Chair of Math. Logic).

[St87] L.Staiger. Research in the theory of ω-languages. *J. Inform. Process. Cybernet.*, 23 (1987), p.415—439.

[SW74] L.Staiger and K.Wagner. Automatentheoretische und automatenfreie Characterisierungen topologischer klassen regulärer Folgenmengen. EIK 10 No 7 (1974), p.379—392.

[Th90] W.Thomas. Automata on Infinite Objects. *Handbook of Theor. Computer Science*, v. B (1990), p.133—191.

[VW76] Van Wesep. Wadge degrees and descriptive set theory. In: Cabal Seminar 76—77, Proceedings, *Lec. Notes in Math.*, v. 689, Berlin, Springer, 1976, p. 151—170.

[Wa79] K.Wagner. On ω-regular sets. *Inform. and Control*, 43 (1979), p.123—177.

Computing the Wadge Degree, the Lifschitz Degree, and the Rabin Index of a Regular Language of Infinite Words in Polynomial Time

Thomas Wilke* and Haiseung Yoo

Institut für Informatik und Prakt. Math., Christian-Albrechts-Universität zu Kiel, 24098 Kiel, Germany, E-mail: tw@informatik.uni-kiel.d400.de

Abstract. Based on a detailed graph theoretical analysis, Wagner's fundamental results of 1979 are turned into efficient algorithms to compute the Wadge degree, the Lifschitz degree, and the Rabin index of a regular ω-language: the two former can be computed in time $\mathcal{O}(f^2qb + k\log k)$ and the latter in time $\mathcal{O}(f^2qb)$ if the language is represented by a deterministic Muller automaton over an alphabet of cardinality b, with f accepting sets, q states, and k strongly connected components.

Formal languages are often compared via reductions: in recursion theory one compares formal languages using, e. g., truth-table reductions, in complexity theory formal languages are compared by, e. g., polynomial or log-space reductions, and in descriptive set theory continuous functions are used for the comparison of ω-languages.

In all these cases, given a formalism describing formal languages (such as Turing machines, grammars, automata, etc.), one can ask whether the reduction relation is decidable in the following sense: is there an algorithm that, on input of representations of languages X and Y, determines whether X is reducible to Y.

For ω-languages represented by Muller automata, in [9] Wagner answered this question affirmatively in case of continuous reductions and so-called 'synchronous' continuous reductions. Our main objective is to strengthen this by showing that the corresponding restrictions of the reduction relations are in fact decidable in polynomial time. This requires another thorough graph theoretical analysis of the loop structure of Muller automata, carried out below. We treat here only the asynchronous case; a glimpse at Wagner's paper [9] will suffice to realize the modifications necessary for the synchronous case.

A maximal class of formal languages that are pairwise reducible to each other is usually called degree. The degrees with respect to continuous and synchronous continuous reductions are called Wadge and Lifschitz degrees, respectively, see [7]. A such degree is called regular if it contains a regular ω-language.

In [9], K. W. Wagner introduced a naming system for regular Wadge and Lifschitz degrees. One important property of this system is that, given names α

* Supported by the ESPRIT BRA Working Group No. 6317, ASMICS 2.

and β for degrees D and E, respectively, one can determine in quadratic time whether the languages in D are reducible to the languages in E. Therefore, it is sufficient to establish a polynomial time algorithm that computes the name of the Wadge or Lifschitz degree of a regular ω-language given by a Muller automaton in order to prove that the respective restricted reduction relations are decidable in polynomial time.

We present an algorithm that, given a language L by a Muller automaton over an alphabet of cardinality b, with f accepting sets, q states, and k strongly connected components, computes the name of the Wadge degree of L in time $\mathcal{O}(f^2qb + k \log k)$. (Observe that always $k \leq q$ but f may be exponential in q.)

The algorithm is based on Wagner's discovery that the Wadge degree of a regular ω-language is determined by the loop structure—i. e., on the reachability relations and the inclusion relations between the accepting and rejecting loops—of any determinstic Muller automaton recognizing L. In other words, all Muller automata that recognize languages of one degree have the same loop structure.

As Wagner also discovered, all regular ω-languages with the same Rabin index (the least possible number of accepting pairs used in a Rabin automaton recognizing a language) form a set that is a union of Wadge degrees. Therefore our methods to analyse the loop structure of a Muller automaton can also be used to design an effecient algorithm computing the Rabin index of a regular ω-language. We present an algorithm running in time $\mathcal{O}(f^2qb)$, where f, q, and b are as above. This result contrasts with a recent result, see [3], that the problem of computing the Rabin index of a regular ω-language given by a deterministic Rabin or Streett automaton is $\mathcal{NP}$-complete. The reason for this is that the encoding of accepting loops using Rabin or Streett conditions may turn out more succinct than a mere enumeration (as in an equivalent Muller automaton on the same transition graph).

The paper is organized in six sections. In the first three sections we develop our algorithm computing the Rabin index of a regular ω-language, in the other three sections this algorithm is extended to our algorithm computing the Wadge degree. Sect. 1 introduces basic notions, in Sect. 2 the key lemma (Lemma 4) about the loop structure of a Muller automaton is stated and proved and the key procedure of all our algorithms is presented, and in Sect. 3 Wagner's result about the Rabin index and the results of Sect. 2 are combined to the desired algorithm. Sect. 4 and Sect. 5 review Wagner's results on the regular Wadge degrees, and in Sect. 6 we present our algorithm to compute the Wadge degree of a regular ω-language.

For Wagner's result concerning the Rabin index the reader is also referred to [8]. Wagner's approach to regular Wadge and Lifschitz degrees is automata theoretic,[2] a topological approach can be found in [4], an algebraic interpretation

---

[2] In [9], Wagner is mainly interested in (synchronous) reductions via functions definable by finite state machines. Yet in the last section of that paper he shows that, restricted to regular ω-languages, (synchronous) continuous reductions and (synchronous) finite-state machine definable reductions give rise to the same reduction relations.

is given in [1]. The article [6] is a general reference for ω-languages.

We would like to thank one of the referees for his or her comments which improved the paper significantly.

1 Alternating Chains and the Rabin Index

Throughout this paper, $\mathfrak{A}$ stands for a Muller automaton $(Q, q_0, \delta, \mathcal{F})$ over an alphabet denoted by B, and $\mathrm{L}(\mathfrak{A})$ stands for the language recognized by $\mathfrak{A}$.

The set V of nodes of the *transition graph* $\mathcal{G}_{\mathfrak{A}} = (V, E)$ of $\mathfrak{A}$ consists of the states of Q reachable from q_0, and an edge (q, q') belongs to the set E of edges of $\mathcal{G}_{\mathfrak{A}}$ if there exists a letter b such that $\delta(q, b) = q'$ and q is reachable from q_0. (Observe that the number of edges of $\mathcal{G}_{\mathfrak{A}}$ is bounded by $|Q||B|$.)

A *loop* in $\mathfrak{A}$ is a set $C \subseteq V$ such that the subgraph of $\mathcal{G}_{\mathfrak{A}}$ induced by C is strongly connected. The set $\mathcal{C}$ of all loops in $\mathfrak{A}$ is partitioned into the set $\mathcal{P} = \mathcal{C} \cap \mathcal{F}$ of *positive loops* and the set $\mathcal{N}$ of *negative loops*. The set of all maximal loops (with respect to set inclusion) is denoted by $\mathcal{M}$. (Notice that a maximal loop in $\mathfrak{A}$ is the same as a 'strongly connected component' of $\mathcal{G}_{\mathfrak{A}}$.) We shall use C, C_1, C', ... for loops, P, P_1, P', ... for positive loops, N, N_1, N', ... for negative loops, and M, M_1, M', ... for maximal loops.

An *alternating chain of length n* is of the form

$$C_1 \subset C_2 \subset C_3 \subset \ldots \subset C_n ,$$

where ($C_i \in \mathcal{C}$ for every i with $1 \leq i \leq n$ and) $C_i \in \mathcal{P}$ iff $C_{i+1} \notin \mathcal{P}$ for every i with $1 \leq i < n$. A *positive alternating chain* starts with a positive loop, i.e. $C_1 \in \mathcal{P}$, and a *negative alternating chain* starts with a negative loop. If we say that an alternating chain is 'positive' or 'negative' we speak of the *sign* of the alternating chain, and sign stands for the set $\{+, -\}$.

The function $c_{\mathfrak{A}} \colon \mathcal{P} \to \mathbf{N}$ is defined as to map every positive loop P onto the length of a longest alternating chain starting with P.

Wagner proved in [8] (see also [9]) the following about the Rabin index of a regular ω-language.

Theorem 1 (Wagner). *The Rabin index of a regular ω-language recognized by a Muller automaton $\mathfrak{A}$ is given by the term*

$$\lfloor(\max\{c_{\mathfrak{A}}(P) \mid P \in \mathcal{P}\} + 1)/2\rfloor . \qquad (1)$$

Term (1) was the starting point of our search for an efficient algorithm computing the Rabin index of a regular ω-language. After a graph theoretical analysis of the loop structure of Muller automata we found an efficient way to compute $c_{\mathfrak{A}}$, and thus could establish an efficient algorithm for computing the Rabin index. The graph theoretical analysis is subject of the next section, while the algorithms computing $c_{\mathfrak{A}}$ and the Rabin index are presented in the next but one section.

2 Negative Loops In Between?

In this section we develop an efficient procedure that checks whether for two positive loops P_* and P^* with $P_* \subset P^*$ there is a negative loop N with $P_* \subset N \subset P^*$. This will be the key subroutine in the algorithms searching for long(est) alternating chains.

The problem with finding alternating chains is that sometimes the number of negative loops in an automaton happens to be exponential in the number of states and the number of positive loops (i.e. in the size of the automaton). Therefore one cannot simply compute all negative loops and search for alternating chains in the obvious way.

Let $\mathfrak{A}$ and $\mathcal{G}_{\mathfrak{A}}$ be as above. We say that a loop C_1 is *between* the loops C_0 and C_2 if $C_0 \subset C_1 \subset C_2$ holds.

If there is a loop N between P_* and P^* that is comparable with some positive loop P between P_* and P^* then either $P_* \subset N \subset P \subset P^*$ or $P_* \subset P \subset N \subset P^*$ holds. In this case the test whether there is a negative loop between P_* and P^* can be reduced to a 'smaller' one: is there a negative loop between P_* and P or between P and P^*, respectively? But what if there is no negative loop between P_* and P^* that is comparable with some positive loop in between?— This is what we examine first.

Let (*) be the following condition:

$C_* \subset C^*$ are two loops and neither (2) nor (3) below hold for any $P \in \mathcal{P}$ and $N \in \mathcal{N}$. (*)

$$C_* \subset N \subset P \subset C^* \quad (2) \qquad C_* \subset P \subset N \subset C^* \quad (3)$$

Remark (complementation property). Assume (*). If $C_* \subset N \subset C^*$ and $C_* \subset P \subset C^*$, then $P \cup N = C^*$.

Proof. Assume $C = P \cup N$ is not C^*. If $C \in \mathcal{P}$, then $C_* \subset N \subset C \subset C^*$ contradicts (2). Otherwise $C_* \subset P \subset C \subset C^*$ contradicts (3). □

That is, two loops with complementary signs complement each other.

Let

$$D = \begin{cases} \bigcap\{P \mid C_* \subset P \subset C^*\}, & \text{if there is some } P \text{ with } C_* \subset P \subset C^*, \\ C^*, & \text{otherwise.} \end{cases} \quad (4)$$

Lemma 2. *Assume (*) and $C_* \subset C \subset C^*$. Then $C \in \mathcal{P}$ iff $D \subseteq C$.*

Proof. For the non-trivial direction let $C \in \mathcal{N}$. If there is no P with $C_* \subset P \subset C^*$, we have $D \not\subseteq C$, since $D = C^*$ by definition. Otherwise, $P \cup C = C^*$ for every P with $C_* \subset P \subset C^*$ by the complementation property; hence $C^* \setminus C \subseteq P$ for every such P, whence

$$C^* \setminus C \subseteq D. \quad (5)$$

If we had $D \subseteq C$, then (5) would imply $C^* \setminus C \subseteq C$, which, in turn, implies $C^* \subseteq C$. This is a contradiction to $C \subset C^*$, thus (5) cannot hold. Therefore $D \not\subseteq C$. □

If $\pi = q_1 \ldots q_m$ is a path in $\mathcal{G}_{\mathfrak{A}}$, we write $||\pi||$ for the set $\{q_1, \ldots, q_m\}$ and $|\pi|$ for m.

Definition 3. Let $C_* \subset C^*$. A *handle* is a non-empty path π satisfying the following conditions: $||\pi|| \subseteq C^* \setminus C_*$, and there exist $q, q' \in C_*$ such that $q\pi q'$ is also a path.

A handle is called *simple* if it is simple as a path.

Obviously, every minimal loop C with $C_* \subset C \subseteq C^*$ can be written as $C_* \cup ||\pi||$ where π is a simple handle. In presence of (*), this is true for negative and positive loops separately:

Remark. Assume (*).

1. If N is a minimal negative loop with $C_* \subset N \subseteq C^*$, then $N = C_* \cup ||\pi||$ for a suitable simple handle π. (A 'minimal negative loop N with $C_* \subset N \subseteq C^*$' is a minimal element of $\{N' \mid C_* \subset N \subseteq C^*\}$.)
2. If P is a minimal positive loop with $C_* \subset P \subseteq C^*$, then $N = C_* \cup ||\pi||$ for a suitable simple handle π.

Proof. 1) Consider a minimal loop C with $C_* \subset C \subseteq N$. This can be written as $C_* \cup ||\pi||$ for a suitable simple handle π. By (3), C is a negative loop, thus, by the minimality of N, $C = N$.

2) A dual argument applies. □

Lemma 4. *Assume (*) and the existence of a negative loop N between C_* and C^*. Then there is at most one minimal positive loop P between C_* and C^*.*

Proof. Assume for contradiction that there are two minimal positive loops P and P' of minimal cardinality between C_* and C^*. W.l.o.g. assume furthermore that N is minimal. Let P, P', and N be given by simple handles ϕ, ϕ', and ρ, respectively (see the above remark).

Since P and P' are distinct and minimal, there exist states q and q' with $q \in ||\phi|| \setminus ||\phi'||$ and $q' \in ||\phi'|| \setminus ||\phi||$. By Lemma 2, there exists a state $d \in D \setminus N$. This state is distinct from q and q', because otherwise $D \subseteq P$ or $D \subseteq P'$ would not hold (Lemma 2). Since $N \cup P = C^*$ and $N \cup P' = C^*$ (complementation property) we also have $q' \in N$ and $q \in N$.

According to the order in which q, q', and d occur in ϕ, ϕ', and ρ, we can write ϕ, ϕ', and ρ, respectively, as follows, where in each line the respective two possible choices are listed.

$$\phi = \phi_0 d \phi_1 q \phi_2 \quad (6) \qquad \phi = \phi_0 q \phi_1 d \phi_2 \quad (9)$$

$$\phi' = \phi'_0 d \phi'_1 q' \phi'_2 \quad (7) \qquad \phi' = \phi'_0 q' \phi'_1 d \phi'_2 \quad (10)$$

$$\rho = \rho_0 q \rho_1 q' \rho_2 \quad (8) \qquad \rho = \rho_0 q' \rho_1 q \rho_2 \quad (11)$$

(Observe that $\{d, q, q'\} \cap (\bigcup_{i=0}^{2} ||\phi_i|| \cup \bigcup_{i=0}^{2} ||\phi'_i|| \cup \bigcup_{i=0}^{2} ||\rho_i||) = \emptyset$ because of the minimality of P, P', and N.) We will see that every of the eight possible combinations leads to a contradiction.

Two arguments will be used again and again in what follows. For reference, we state them before carrying on with the proof.

Let C be a loop such that $C_* \subset C \subseteq C^*$ holds.

(i) If $d \notin C$, then $C \notin \mathcal{P}$.
(ii) If $q \notin C$ or $q' \notin C$, then $C \notin \mathcal{N}$.

The first claim is true, because d belongs to the intersection defined in (4). The second claim is true because of the complementation property: if $q \notin C$, then $q \notin C \cup P'$, thus $C \cup P \subset C^*$, hence $C \notin \mathcal{N}$ by the complementation property. A symmetric argument applies if $q' \notin C$.

Since the paths ϕ, ϕ', and ρ have points in common, it is possible to compose new paths (and handles) from suitable segments. Which paths can be built depends on the equations that hold. For instance, if we have (9) and (11), then $\phi_0 q \rho_2$ is a path, even a handle.

If one of

$$\phi_0 q \rho_2,\ \phi_0' q' \rho_2,\ \rho_0 q \phi_2, \text{ or } \rho_0 q' \phi_2' \tag{12}$$

is a path, the desired contradiction is easy to obtain. We demonstrate this for $\phi_0 q \rho_2$, the other cases are similar.

Consider $\pi = \phi_0 q \rho_2$, which is a handle. On the one hand, the loop $C_* \cup ||\pi||$ is not positive, because d does not belong to it (cf. (i)). On the other hand, q' does not belong to $C_* \cup ||\pi||$, hence $C_* \cup ||\pi||$ is no negative loop (cf. (ii)).

Only if

1. (9), (7), and (8) hold, or if
2. (6), (10), and (11) hold,

one cannot immediately construct one of the paths enumerated in (12). The two cases are symmetric, so we deal only with the first case.

Consider the handle $\pi = \phi_0' d \phi_2$. Since q does not belong to $C_* \cup ||\pi||$, this loop is positive (cf. (ii)). From the minimality of P' we know $|\phi_2| \geq |\phi_1' q' \phi_2'|$. (Otherwise the cardinality of $C_* \cup ||\pi||$ would be strictly smaller than the cardinality of P'.) Since q' does not belong to $||\phi_2||$, there exists a state $p \in ||\phi_2|| \setminus ||\phi_1' q' \phi_2'||$, say $\phi_2 = \psi_0 p \psi_1$.

We claim that p does not occur in ϕ_0' (which implies $p \notin ||\phi'||$ since $p \notin ||\phi_1' q' \phi_2'||$ by definition). For contradiction, assume p occurs in ϕ_0', say $\phi_0' = \delta_0 p \delta_1$. Then $\pi' = \delta_0 p \psi_1$ is a handle. But the loop $C_* \cup ||\pi'||$ is neither positive, since it does not contain d (cf. (i)), nor negative, since it does not contain q (cf. (ii)).

We have $p \notin ||\phi'||$, and $C_* \cup ||\phi_0' d \psi_0 p \psi_1||$ is a positive loop, since q does not belong to it (cf. (ii)). Therefore P and $\phi = \phi_0 q \phi_1 d \phi_2$ can be replaced by $C_* \cup ||\phi_0' d \psi_0 p \psi_1||$ and $\phi_0' d \psi_0 p \psi_1$, respectively. We encounter a case that leads immediately to a contradiction as above. □

By symmetry, we have:

Corollary 5. *Assume (*). If there are positive and negative loops between C_* and C^*, then there is a unique minimal (i. e. smallest) positive loop and a unique minimal (i. e. smallest) negative loop between C_* and C^*.*

We now can design an efficient procedure that takes loops $P_* \subset P^*$ as arguments and gives back TRUE if there exists N such that $P_* \subset N \subset P^*$ and FALSE otherwise, provided (*) holds (with $C_* = P_*$ and $C^* = P^*$):

1. Find a minimal loop C with $P_* \subset C \subseteq P^*$.
2. If $C \notin \mathcal{P}$, then return TRUE. (C is negative and between P_* and P^*.)
3. If $C = P^*$, then return FALSE. (There is no loop between P_* and P^*, in particular, no negative one.)
4. Search for a minimal loop C' with $P_* \subset C' \subseteq P^*$ and $C \neq C'$.
5. If there exists no such C', then return FALSE. (There is only one minimal loop between P_* and P^*, namely C, and this is positive. Thus, by (*), there is no negative loop between P_* and P^*.)
6. If there exists such a C' and
   (a) if $C' \notin \mathcal{P}$, then return TRUE (C' is negative and between P_* and P^*),
   (b) if $C' \in \mathcal{P}$, then return FALSE. (There is no unique minimal positive loop between P_* and P^*, thus there exists no negative loop between P_* and P^* by Lemma 4.)

To complete the description of the procedure we have to explain how steps 1 and 4 can be implemented.

Step 1. Since at least one minimal loop C with $P_* \subset C \subseteq P^*$ is given by a shortest handle, it is sufficient to search for a shortest handle π, and to set $C = P_* \cup ||\pi||$. We find such a handle using a breadth-first strategy in the subgraph of $\mathcal{G}_\mathfrak{A}$ induced by P^*: we search for a shortest non-empty path from P_* to P_* and leaving P_*. This takes time $\mathcal{O}(|P^*||B|)$.

Step 4. The situation is a bit more involved but essentially the same idea works; we search for simple paths satisfying certain conditions.

We obtain the following upper bound for the running time of the entire test.

Lemma 6. *Given a Muller automaton $\mathfrak{A}$ and two positive loops $P_* \subset P^*$ such that (*) holds (with $C_* = P_*$ and $C^* = P^*$), the above procedure checks in time $\mathcal{O}(|Q|(|B| + |\mathcal{F}|))$ whether there exists a negative loop between P_* and P^*.*

This bound takes also into account that we have to construct $\mathcal{G}_\mathfrak{A}$ and a search tree for the elements of $\mathcal{P}$ (in order to be able to perform a test as in step 2 in time $|Q|$).

3 Computing the Rabin Index

As pointed out at the end of Sect. 1, in order to compute the Rabin index we need to compute (the maximum value of) the function $c_\mathfrak{A}$. The rules that allow us to determine $c_\mathfrak{A}$ inductively are summed up in the following remark.

Remark. 1. If P is a maximal positive loop, then $c_\mathfrak{A}(P) = \begin{cases} 2, & \text{if } P \notin \mathcal{M}, \\ 1, & \text{otherwise.} \end{cases}$

2. If P is not a maximal positive loop, if $k = \max\{c_{\mathfrak{A}}(P') \mid P \subset P'\}$, and if $\mathcal{P}' = \{P' \mid P \subset P' \wedge c_{\mathfrak{A}}(P') = k\}$, then

$$c_{\mathfrak{A}}(P) = \begin{cases} k+2\,, & \text{if there are } N \text{ and } P' \in \mathcal{P}' \text{ such that } P \subset N \subset P', \\ k\,, & \text{otherwise.} \end{cases}$$

This remark motivates and proofs the correctness of the following procedure computing $c_{\mathfrak{A}}$:

1. For every maximal $P \in \mathcal{P}$, if $P \in \mathcal{M}$, then let $c_{\mathfrak{A}}(P) = 1$, else $c_{\mathfrak{A}}(P) = 2$.
2. For every non-maximal $P \in \mathcal{P}$ in non-increasing order:
   (a) Let $k = \max\{c_{\mathfrak{A}}(P') \mid P \subset P'\}$, $\mathcal{P}' = \{P' \mid P \subset P' \wedge c_{\mathfrak{A}}(P') = k\}$, and $c_{\mathfrak{A}}(P) = k$.
   (b) For every $P' \in \mathcal{P}'$ in non-decreasing order, if there is a negative loop between P and P', then let $c_{\mathfrak{A}}(P) = k + 2$ and exit this for-loop.

In step 2(b), it is essential to test the elements of $\mathcal{P}'$ in non-decreasing order because otherwise (*) could not be guaranteed (with $C_* = P$ and $C^* = P'$) when launching the test whether there exists a negative loop between P and P'.

Taking Lemma 6 into account we get:

Lemma 7. *Given a Muller automaton $\mathfrak{A} = (Q, q_0, \delta, \mathcal{F})$ over an alphabet B, the above procedure computes in time $\mathcal{O}(|\mathcal{F}|^2|Q||B|)$ the function $c_{\mathfrak{A}}$.*

The upper bound for the running time also takes into account the time we need to compute the set $\mathcal{M}$ (which is $\mathcal{O}(|Q||B|)$ by Tarjan's algorithm, see [5]) and the inclusion relation on $\mathcal{P}$ (which is $\mathcal{O}(|\mathcal{F}|^2|Q|)$).

As a consequence of Lemma 7 and Theorem 1, we obtain our first theorem:

Theorem 8. *The Rabin index of a regular ω-language given by a Muller automaton $\mathfrak{A} = (Q, q_0, \delta, \mathcal{F})$ over an alphabet B can be computed in time $\mathcal{O}(|\mathcal{F}|^2|Q||B|)$.*

4 Regular Wadge Degrees and Wagner's Naming System

The set B^ω of all ω-words over an alphabet B is turned into a metric space by introducing the distance function d with $d(\alpha, \beta) = 2^{-\min\{i \mid \alpha(i) \neq \beta(i)\}}$ for distinct ω-words α and β. A set $L \subset B^\omega$ is *Wadge reducible* to a set $M \subseteq B^\omega$, in symbols $L \leq_W M$, if L is the inverse image of M under a continuous function $B^\omega \to B^\omega$. The $\leq_W$-relation is an equivalence relation, and each equivalence class is called a *Wadge degree.* The relation $\leq_W$ extends in a natural way to the degrees. A Wadge degree is called *regular* if it contains a regular ω-language.

As mentioned in the introduction in [9] Wagner investigated the structure of the set of all regular Wadge degrees (ordered by $\leq_W$). In a unique way he denoted each degree by an expression, henceforth called *name,* of the form $E_{i_1}^{j_1} \ldots E_{i_{s-1}}^{j_{s-1}} x_{i_s}^{j_s}$, where x is either of the symbols C, D, or E, $s \geq 1$ and $i_1 > \ldots > i_s$ and, in case $x = E$, $i_s = 1$. In this paper, the name of the Wadge degree of a regular ω-language L is denoted by $W(L)$.

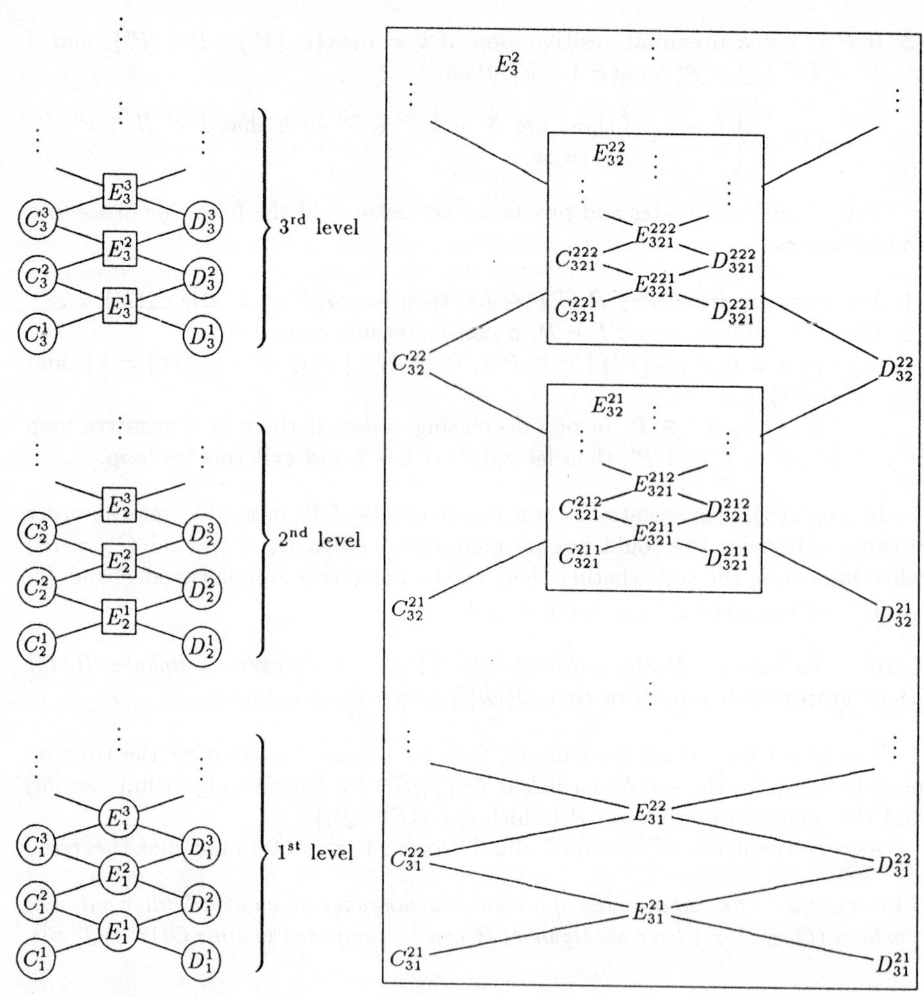

Fig. 1. The structure of the ordering of the regular Wadge degrees

Wagner's naming system is chosen in such a way that the $\leq_W$-relation can easily be read off: for regular degrees S and T with names $E_{i_1}^{j_1} \dots E_{i_{s-1}}^{j_{s-1}} x_{i_s}^{j_s}$ and $E_{k_1}^{l_1} \dots E_{k_{t-1}}^{l_{t-1}} y_{k_t}^{l_t}$, the relation $S \leq_W T$ holds iff there is an index u such that $i_v = k_v$ and $j_v = l_v$ for v with $1 \leq v \leq u$, and either (a) $s = u \leq t$, and $y = E$ or $x = y$, or (b) $u < s$ and $u < t$ and $i_{u+1} < k_{u+1}$.

The coarse structure of the set of all regular Wadge degrees can be presented graphically as in the left part of Fig. 1. For notational convenience we write $x_{i_1 i_2 \dots i_s}^{j_1 j_2 \dots j_s}$ for $E_{i_1}^{j_1} \dots E_{i_{s-1}}^{j_{s-1}} x_{i_s}^{j_s}$, and if $i_s > 1$ the union of all degrees whose names have $E_{i_1}^{j_1} \dots E_{i_s}^{j_s}$ as prefix is denoted by $E_{i_1 i_2 \dots i_s}^{j_1 j_2 \dots j_s}$. Circles represent one and only one degree, boxes stand for a union of several degrees. The first lower index of a name of a degree divides the entire hierarchy into an infinite number of levels. Every box E_m^n of the mth level ($m > 1$) is structured exactly as the part of the hierarchy that consists of the levels $1, \dots, m-1$. The corresponding circles and boxes in E_m^n are denoted by C_{mi}^{nj}, D_{mi}^{nj}, E_{mi}^{nj}, respectively. Again, if $i > 1$, then E_{mi}^{nj} is divided into further degrees by the same procedure. This gives a 'recursive' structure (but leading only to finite descending chains). For instance, the structure of E_3^2 is as depicted in the right part of Fig. 1.

5 Wagner's Naming Procedure

In the previous section, we presented and explained the structure of the regular Wadge degrees and how Wagner named them. In this section, we will explain how, given a Muller automaton $\mathfrak{A}$, one can determine the name of the degree of $L(\mathfrak{A})$. In principle, we follow [9]. By introducing the notion of 'condensed graph', we slightly change the style of presentation. This is useful from an algorithmic point of view.

We first come back to alternating chains, and assume a Muller automaton $\mathfrak{A} = (Q, q_0, \delta, \mathcal{F})$ over an alphabet B to be given. If $C_1 \subseteq \dots \subseteq C_n$ is an alternating chain in $\mathfrak{A}$, then all the loops C_i with $1 \leq i \leq n$ belong to the same maximal loop. If this loop is M then we say that *the chain is in M*.

With $\mathfrak{A}$, we associate the *length function* $l_{\mathfrak{A}}: \mathcal{M} \longrightarrow \mathbf{N}$ that maps every maximal loop M onto the length of a longest alternating chain in M.

Let M be a fixed maximal loop of $\mathfrak{A}$. In every longest alternating chain in M one can replace the last element by M itself. Therefore the signs of all longest alternating chains in M are the same, and the *sign function* $s_{\mathfrak{A}}: \mathcal{M} \longrightarrow$ sign that maps every maximal loop M on the sign of the longest alternating chain in M is well-defined.

A *condensed graph* is a quintuple (V, E, l, s) such that (V, E) is a directed acyclic graph and $l: V \longrightarrow \mathbf{N}$ and $s: V \longrightarrow$ sign are labellings of vertices. We say that a node v is positive if $s(v) = +$ and negative otherwise.

The *condensed graph associated with the Muller automaton* $\mathfrak{A}$ is the condensed graph $\mathcal{K}_{\mathfrak{A}} = (\mathcal{M}, E, l_{\mathfrak{A}}, s_{\mathfrak{A}})$, where E contains an edge from M to M' iff there is a path from M to M' in $\mathcal{G}_{\mathfrak{A}}$ that does not contain any state belonging to one of the other maximal loops (i.e. when M' is an immediate successor of M).

In the following, let $G = (V, E, l, s)$ be a condensed graph. We define m_G^+ to be the maximum of $\{l(M) \mid s(M) = +\} \cup \{0\}$, and m_G^- analogously. That is, if $G = \mathcal{K}_{\mathfrak{A}}$ then m_G^+ is the length of a longest positive alternating chain in $\mathfrak{A}$, and m_G^- stands for the length of a longest negative alternating chain in $\mathfrak{A}$. We write m_G for the maximum of m_G^+ and m_G^-.

A *top node* in G is a node M such that $l(M) = m_G$. An *alternating superchain* is a sequence $C_1, \dots, C_n$ of top nodes where for every i with $1 \leq i < n$ the node C_{i+1} is reachable from C_i and C_i is a positive top node iff C_{i+1} is not. The alternating superchain is called positive if C_1 is a positive top node and negative otherwise.

We define n_G^+ to be the maximum length of a positive superchain if there is some and 0 otherwise. The number n_G^- is defined correspondingly. The maximum of both numbers is denoted by n_G. A *longest superchain* is an alternating superchain of length n_G. The first node in a positive longest superchain is called a *positive base node* and the notion of a *negative base node* is defined similarly.

The condensed graph G is called *non-prime* if $n_G = n_G^- = n_G^+$ and *prime* otherwise.

For every condensed graph G with $m = m_G$ and $n = n_G$, we define its *type*, denoted by t_G. If G is non-prime, then $t_G = E_m^n$, if G is prime and $n_G^+ > n_G^-$, then $t_G = C_m^n$, else, if G is prime and $n_G^- > n_G^+$, then $t_G = D_m^n$. The set type is defined to be the set $\{x_m^n \mid x \in \{C, D, E\} \wedge m, n \in \mathrm{N}\}$. (So every name of a Wadge degree can be viewed as a string over type satisfying certain conditions.)

For a non-prime condensed graph $G = (V, E, l, s)$ we define its *derivative* ∂G. It is the condensed graph (V', E', l', s'), where V' is the set of nodes from which both a positive and a negative base node are reachable, $E' = E \cap (V' \times V')$, and l' and s' are the restrictions of l and s to V'.

With every condensed graph G, we associate a name $W(G)$. If $G = \mathcal{K}_{\mathfrak{A}}$ is the condensed graph of a Muller automaton $\mathfrak{A}$ recognizing the ω-language L, then $W(G)$ will be equal to $W(L)$.

The name $\alpha = W(G)$ is defined by the following procedure, also called *Wagner's naming procedure*, which iteratively constructs $W(G)$ by essentially concatenating the types of G, ∂G, $\partial^2 G$, ... :

1. Let $\alpha = \epsilon$, $i = 0$.
2. Do forever:
   (a) Let $i = i + 1$.
   (b) If G is empty then return αE_1^1.
   (c) If G is prime then return αt_G.
   (d) If G is non-prime, $m_G = 1$, and $i = 1$ then return t_G.
   (e) If G is non-prime, $m_G = 1$, and $i > 1$ then return $\alpha E_{m_G}^{n_G+1}$.
   (f) If G is non-prime and $m_G > 1$ then let $\alpha = \alpha t_G$ and $G = \partial G$.

Observe that only step 2(f) leads to a new iteration of the for loop.

The correctness of the naming procedure is stated in the following theorem.

Theorem 9 (Wagner). *For every Muller automaton $\mathfrak{A}$, $W(\mathrm{L}(\mathfrak{A})) = W(\mathcal{K}_{\mathfrak{A}})$.*

In particular, since the above naming procedure is effective, it follows that the name of the Wadge degree of a regular ω-language can be computed effectively.

In the next section, we will describe how the above procedure can be implemented efficiently.

6 Computing the Wadge degree

Following Theorem 9 our algorithm that, given a Muller automaton $\mathfrak{A}$, computes the name of the Wadge degree of $\mathrm{L}(\mathfrak{A})$ consists of three steps:

1. Build $G = \mathcal{K}_{\mathfrak{A}}$.
2. Determine $\alpha = W(G)$.
3. Output α.

Step 3 is straightforward. The other two steps are treated in the following two subsections.

6.1 Step 1

We first compute the transition graph $\mathcal{G}_{\mathfrak{A}}$ in an obvious way. Next, using Tarjan's algorithm, we compute the vertex set of $\mathcal{K}_{\mathfrak{A}}$ (i.e. the set $\mathcal{M}$ of all maximal loops of $\mathcal{G}_{\mathfrak{A}}$) and the edge relation.

In order to determine $l_{\mathfrak{A}}$ and $s_{\mathfrak{A}}$ we first compute $c_{\mathfrak{A}}$ as described in Sect. 3. After that, for each $M \in \mathcal{M}$, we partition the set $\mathcal{R}$ of all minimal positive loops in M into the sets $\mathcal{S}$ and $\mathcal{T}$ according to whether a loop is a superset of a negative loop or not. Using the following expressions we then determine $l_{\mathfrak{A}}(M)$ and $s_{\mathfrak{A}}(M)$.

$$l_{\mathfrak{A}}(M) = \max(\{c_{\mathfrak{A}}(P) + 1 \mid P \in \mathcal{S}\} \cup \{c_{\mathfrak{A}}(P) \mid P \in \mathcal{T}\}) \tag{13}$$

$$s_{\mathfrak{A}}(M) = \begin{cases} +, & \text{if } l_{\mathfrak{A}}(M) \equiv 1 \pmod 2 \text{ and } M \in P, \text{ or} \\ & \text{if } l_{\mathfrak{A}}(M) \equiv 0 \pmod 2 \text{ and } M \notin P, \\ -, & \text{otherwise} \end{cases} \tag{14}$$

To compute the sets $\mathcal{R}$, we need time $\mathcal{O}(|\mathcal{F}|^2)$. To partition one set $\mathcal{R}$ we need to check whether in a given connected subset of a graph there exists a smaller connected set. This can be done using a breadth-first search. (There exists no smaller connected subset iff the breadth-first search tree is a path and there are no back edges except for a back edge from the last point of the path to its beginning.)

The upper bound for the computation of $c_{\mathfrak{A}}$ (see Lemma 7) is $\mathcal{O}(|\mathcal{F}|^2|Q||B|)$ and dominates the time needed to compute $l_{\mathfrak{A}}$ and $s_{\mathfrak{A}}$, starting from $c_{\mathfrak{A}}$ as just described, and to perform Tarjan's algorithm.

Remark. Step 1 is performed in time $\mathcal{O}(|\mathcal{F}|^2|Q||B|)$.

6.2 Step 2

The execution of step 2 follows Wagner's naming procedure (see Sect. 5). To avoid misunderstanding, the two steps of that procedure are called *phases* hereafter. Apart from α and i, variables LEVEL, TYPE, TO-VISIT, and MAX-NODES are initialized in phase 1. These additional variables are used and updated in phase 2.

The current derivative (i.e. G) is represented by the array LEVEL: $\mathcal{M} \to \mathbf{N}$ according to the following convention (invariant).

($^*_*$) Before each execution of the for loop (i.e. at the beginning of 2(a)) G contains the nodes M with LEVEL[M] $\geq i$. The variable MAX-NODES contains a list of all maximal nodes of G (viewed as a partial order).

Recall that a derivative of a condensed graph is a subgraph induced by a certain set of nodes. Therefore the current derivative is fully determined by its set of nodes.

Phase 1: Initialization. The array TO-VISIT is initialized to PERHAPS, and LEVEL to the number of nodes of G. (The latter is in accordance with ($\overset{*}{*}$).)

Each vertex M of the condensed graph G is labelled with the type of the graph which is obtained from G by removing all vertices which M is not reachable from (see below). The labels are stored in the array TYPE. Furthermore, a list of the maximal nodes in G is produced and stored in MAX-NODES.

For the computation of TYPE we introduce two functions:

$$\sqcup\colon \text{type} \times \text{type} \to \text{type} \qquad \text{and} \qquad \lambda\colon \text{type} \times \mathbf{N} \times \text{sign} \to \text{type}.$$

The function $\sqcup$ is defined in such a way that if G_0 and G_1 are condensed graphs then $t_{G_0} \sqcup t_{G_1}$ is the type of the disjoint union of G_0 and G_1:

$$x^n_m \sqcup y^l_k = y^l_k \sqcup x^n_m = \begin{cases} x^n_m\,, & \text{if } m > k, \text{ or} \\ & \text{if } m = k \text{ and } n > l, \text{ or} \\ & \text{if } m = k \text{ and } n = l \text{ and } x = y, \\ E^n_m\,, & \text{otherwise.} \end{cases}$$

Obviously, $\sqcup$ is an associative and commutative operation.

The function λ is defined such that if $G_0 = (V, E, l, s)$ is a condensed graph with one unique maximal node v and if G_0 is obtained from a graph G_1 by adding v then $\lambda(t_{G_1}, l(v), s(v)) = t_{G_0}$. If $m' > m$ then

$$\lambda(x^n_m, m', s) = \begin{cases} C^1_{m'}\,, & \text{if } s = +, \\ D^1_{m'}\,, & \text{if } s = -. \end{cases}$$

If $m' < m$ then $\lambda(x^n_m, m', s) = x^n_m$. Furthermore

$$\lambda(x^n_m, m, s) = \begin{cases} x^{n+1}_m\,, & \text{if } s = -,\ x = C, \text{ and } n \equiv 1 \pmod 2, \text{ or} \\ & \text{if } s = +,\ x = D, \text{ and } n \equiv 1 \pmod 2, \\ C^{n+1}_m\,, & \text{if } s = +,\ x = E, \text{ and } n \equiv 0 \pmod 2, \text{ or} \\ & \text{if } s = -,\ x = E, \text{ and } n \equiv 1 \pmod 2, \\ D^{n+1}_m\,, & \text{if } s = +,\ x = E, \text{ and } n \equiv 1 \pmod 2, \text{ or} \\ & \text{if } s = -,\ x = E, \text{ and } n \equiv 0 \pmod 2, \\ x^n_m\,, & \text{otherwise,} \end{cases}$$

for every possible choice of x, m, s, and n.

Since both $\sqcup$ and λ are defined by simple case distinctions, each application of them in a procedure will take constant time.

Now, using $\sqcup$ and λ we can describe a rule that allows us to compute the values of the array TYPE: If $M_1, \ldots, M_r$ is the list of predecessors of node M, then

$$\text{TYPE}(M) = \lambda(\text{TYPE}(M_1) \sqcup \ldots \sqcup \text{TYPE}(M_r), l(M), s(M))\,.$$

Therefore, the types of all nodes can be computed using a simple for loop treating the nodes in a topological ordering (to make sure that the values of the predecessors are already known). For a minimal node M, we have TYPE$(M) = C^1_{l_{\mathfrak{A}}(M)}$ if $s(M) = +$ and TYPE$(M) = D^1_{l_{\mathfrak{A}}(M)}$ otherwise. In the same for loop one can also compute the list MAX-NODES for the entire graph. A topological ordering of the nodes of G can be computed in linear time (see [2]).

So we get the following for the complexity of phase 1.

Remark. Phase 1 is performed in time $\mathcal{O}(|\mathcal{M}| + |E|)$, where E is the number of edges in $\mathcal{K}_{\mathfrak{A}}$.

Phase 2: Execution of the For Loop. There are two points to be discussed here: I) how t_G (needed in 2(c), (d), and (f)) is determined, and II) how ∂G (needed in 2(f)) can be computed, if G is non-prime—the other parts of phase 2 are simple tests or assignments.

ad I). The type of G is determined by combining the TYPE values of the nodes in MAX-NODES using $\sqcup$; this takes time linear in the length of MAX-NODES.

ad II). We are in 2(f). So LEVEL and MAX-NODES have to be updated to represent the derivative of $G = (V, E, l, s)$ in the sense of $(\substack{*\\*})$. We use two additional arrays POS-S-CHAIN and NEG-S-CHAIN, and a heap H. The arrays POS-S-CHAIN and NEG-S-CHAIN store for every $M \in V$ the length of the longest positive and negative superchain, respectively, that is reachable from M in G. This information is used to determine the nodes that have to be deleted in order to obtain the desired derivative, i.e., the nodes from which no positive or no negative base loop is reachable. On the heap H, the candidates for deletion are stored, the node being the greatest in a topological ordering of $\mathcal{K}_{\mathfrak{A}}$ on top of H. The array TO-VISIT records which nodes are already on the heap and which of them are to be disregarded (although they are on the heap).

For every element M of MAX-NODES, we set LEVEL$[M]$ to $i - 1$, put all its predecessors on the heap H, and set TO-VISIT$[M']$ to YES for each such predecessor. If $l(M) = m_G$ and $s(M) = +$, the variable POS-S-CHAIN$[M]$ is set to 1 and POS-S-CHAIN$[M]$ to 0. If $l(M) = m_G$ and $s(M) = -$, the variable NEG-S-CHAIN$[M]$ is set to 1 and POS-S-CHAIN$[M]$ to 0. In all other cases, 0 is assigned to POS-S-CHAIN$[M]$ and NEG-S-CHAIN$[M]$. The list MAX-NODES is emptied.

In a while loop we proceed until the heap H is empty. In every iteration, a node M is extracted from H and processed as follows. If TO-VISIT$[M]$ is not YES, nothing happens. Otherwise, POS-S-CHAIN$[M]$ and NEG-S-CHAIN$[M]$ are determined. This is done by combining the corresponding values of the successors of M in G, the value $l(M)$, and the value $s(M)$. If POS-S-CHAIN$[M] < n_G$ or NEG-S-CHAIN$[M] < n_G$, LEVEL$[M]$ is set to $i - 1$, i.e., M is deleted, and every predecessor M' of M is added to the heap, provided TO-VISIT$[M'] =$ PERHAPS. In the other case, if POS-S-CHAIN$[M] =$ NEG-S-CHAIN$[M] = n_G$, M is put into MAX-NODES and TO-VISIT$[M']$ is set to NO for every predecessor M' of M. After exit of the while loop, TO-VISIT is reset to PERHAPS and H is emptied.

Remark. Phase 2 is performed in time $\mathcal{O}(|E| + |\mathcal{M}| \log |\mathcal{M}|)$, where E is the number of edges in $\mathcal{K}_{\mathfrak{A}}$.

The factor of $\log |\mathcal{M}|$ reflects the time that is needed to maintain the heap H.

Adding up the running times for step 1, phase 1, and phase 2, we finally obtain:

Theorem 10. *The name of the Wadge degree of a regular ω-language given by a Muller automaton $\mathfrak{A} = (Q, q_0, \delta, \mathcal{F})$ can be computed in time $\mathcal{O}(|\mathcal{F}|^2|Q||B| + |\mathcal{M}| \log |\mathcal{M}|)$, where $\mathcal{M}$ is the set of all maximal loops in $\mathfrak{A}$.*

References

1. O. CARTON. "Mots Infinis, ω-Semigroupes et Topologie". PhD thesis, Université Paris 7, France (1993).
2. D. E. KNUTH. "Fundamental Algorithms", vol. 1. Addison-Wesley (1968). Second edition 1973.
3. S. C. KRISHNAN, A. PURI, AND R. K. BRAYTON. Structural complexity of ω-automata. In "STACS 95: 12th Annual Symposium on Theoretical Aspects of Computer Science", München (1995), Lecture Notes in Computer Science. Springer-Verlag. To appear.
4. V. SELIVANOV. Fine hierarchy of regular ω-languages. This volume.
5. R. E. TARJAN. Depth first search and linear graphs. *SIAM J. Comput.* **1**(2), 146–160 (1972).
6. W. THOMAS. Automata on infinite objects. In J. VAN LEEUWEN, editor, "Handbook of Theoretical Computer Science", vol. B: Formal Methods and Semantics, pp. 134–191. Elsevier Science Publishers B. V. (1990).
7. R. VAN WESEP. Wadge degrees and descriptive set theory. In A. S. KECHRIS AND Y. N. MOSCHOVAKIS, editors, "Cabal Seminar 76–77", vol. 689 of "Lecture Notes in Mathematics", pp. 151–170 (1978). Springer-Verlag.
8. K. W. WAGNER. Eine topologische Charakterisierung einiger Klassen regulärer Folgenmengen. *Elektron. Informationsverarb. Kybernet.* **13**(9), 473–487 (1977).
9. K. W. WAGNER. On ω-regular sets. *Information and Control* **43**(2), 123–177 (1979).
10. H. YOO. Ein effizienter Algorithmus zur Bestimmung des Rabin-Index in Muller-Automaten. Diploma thesis, Inst. f. Inform. u. Prakt. Math, CAU Kiel, Germany (1994). 59 pages.

Semi-Trace Morphisms* and Rational Transductions

Pierre-André Wacrenier

LaBRI, Université Bordeaux I
351, cours de la Libération
33405 Talence cedex, France
wacren@labri.u-bordeaux.fr

Abstract. We investigate trace and semi-trace morphisms from an algebraic point of view thanks to rational transductions. The main result is a characterization of (semi-) trace morphisms which are equivalent to some rational transduction. Within this result we easily characterize context-free trace morphisms.

Introduction

The free partially commutative monoids study was initiated by Cartier and Foata [CF69] whose aim was to solve some combinatorial problems. Trace languages, which are subsets of a free partially commutative monoid, were proposed by Mazurkiewicz [Maz77] as tools for the description of concurrent program behaviour. Since then a lot of work has been done in this theory, the major contributions to this theory are presented in the *Book of Traces* [DR95].
A partially commutative alphabet is a couple (A, θ) in which A is an alphabet, and θ, the independence relation, is a symmetric and irreflexive binary relation over A. Associated with the independence relation θ, an application $f_\theta : 2^{A^*} \longrightarrow 2^{A^*}$ is defined as follows: $f_\theta(L)$ *is the set of the words which are equivalent to some word of* L *for the congruence generated by* θ. Thus f_θ is a unary operation over languages which is named *partial commutation function associated with* θ.
M. Clerbout and M. Latteux [CL87] introduced the notion of semi-commutation which generalizes the notion of commutation: a semi-commutation is an irreflexive independence relation over A. Thanks to non symmetric rules it is easy to model a program behaviour on a shared memory machine as, for instance, the producer/consumer system: let p and c denote respectively the producer and the consumer, the non-symmetric rule $cp \longrightarrow pc$ means that for all program $A = ucpv$, the program $B = upcv$ has got the same result.
Since the well known model of concurrent systems, the Petri-nets, are just collections of appropriately integrated producer/consumer systems, semi-commutations are useful for modelling behaviours of Petri-nets [HK89, Och90, Och92].

* This work has been supported by Esprit Basic Research Actions ASMICS II and the inter-PRC project “Modèles et Preuves de Systèmes Parallèles et Répartis”.

There is no need to prove the importance of morphisms within mathematics. There is, moreover, an important reason for investigations of morphisms on semi-commutations. Given a machine M_A with an instruction set A and a machine M_B with an instruction set B, the instruction set A may represent high level operations and B may represent basic operations. Such a correspondence between A and B is called the refinement of actions.
Trace morphisms were already investigated, in particular injective trace morphisms were studied by Chrobak et al., Ochmański [CR87, Och88] and more recently by Bruyère et al. and Diekert et al. [BDFG94, DMR94]. Recognizable trace morphisms (i.e. for which the image of any recognizable trace language is recognizable) were characterized by Duboc [Dub86a] and conditions were given for recognizable semi-commutation morphisms [CGL+92, OW93].
This paper deals with semi-trace morphisms which are equivalent to some rational transduction. We are not going to introduce special rational transductions for semi-traces. Our goal is just to use rational transductions as a tool to examine semi-trace morphisms from an algebraic point of view. Therefore we work in the free monoid: a semi-trace $[t\rangle_\theta$ is associated with a set of word $f_\theta(t)$ and a semi-trace morphism $\vec{\varphi} : \mathbb{M}(A,\theta) \mapsto \mathbb{M}(B,\gamma)$ is associated with a word morphism $\varphi : A^* \mapsto B^*$ and $\vec{\varphi}$ is equivatent to $\bar{\varphi} = f_\gamma \circ \varphi$.
The question to decide whether a semi-trace morphism is equivalent to some rational transduction can be reduced to the following one: given a semi-trace morphism $\vec{\varphi} : \mathbb{M}(A,\theta) \mapsto \mathbb{M}(B,\gamma)$, does there exist a rational transduction $\tau : A^* \mapsto 2^{B^*}$ such that for any word $u \in A^*$ we have $\bar{\varphi}(u) = f_\gamma \circ \varphi(u) = \tau \circ f_\theta(u)$?
In this paper we characterize semi-trace morphisms which are equivalent to some rational transduction. Thanks to this characterization we are able to decide whether or not a trace morphism is a context-free trace morphism, that is, given a trace morphism $\vec{\varphi} : \mathbb{M}(A,\theta) \mapsto \mathbb{M}(B,\gamma)$, is the image of any context-free language of $\mathbb{M}(A,\theta)$ by $\vec{\varphi}$ equal a context-free language of $\mathbb{M}(B,\gamma)$?
After recalling basic notions, we precise the notion of semi-trace morphisms. In Section 3, we introduce a model of rational transduction and show the limits of the model. In Section 4, within this model we characterize semi-trace morphisms which are equivalent to some rational transduction. Then, thanks to this result we characterize context-free trace morphisms and give a new proof of a result of Clerbout and Roos [CR90].

1 Background

We assume that the reader is familiar with the formal language theory.
For $w \in A^*$, alph(w) is the set of letters which occur in the word w, $|w|$ means the length of w.
We recall some basic notions about directed graphs: a *digraph* G is a pair (V_G, A_G) where V_G is a finite set of *vertices* and $A_G \subseteq V_G \times V_G$ is a finite set of *arcs*. There exists a *path* from a vertex u to a vertex v if there are arcs $(u_0,u_1),(u_1,u_2)...(u_n,u_{n+1})$ in A_G with $u_0 = u$ and $u_{n+1} = v$. A digraph G is *strongly connected* if, for each pair of vertices v, w there is a path in G from

v to w. A digraph G is *connected* if, for each pair of vertices v, w there is an undirected path in G from v to w.

Morphisms and rational transductions (from [Ber79])
Let A and B be two alphabets. Any mapping $\varphi : A \mapsto B^*$ extended to $\varphi : A^* \mapsto B^*$ with $\varphi(uv) = \varphi(u)\varphi(v)$ is said to be a *morphism.*
The mapping $\varphi^{-1} : B^* \mapsto 2^{A^*}$ defined by $\varphi^{-1}(u) = \{w \in A^* \mid \varphi(w) = u\}$ is named the *inverse morphism* associated with φ.
A morphism $\psi : A^* \mapsto 2^{B^*}$ is said to be a *substitution.*
The *projection* $\Pi_B(w) : A^* \mapsto B^*$, for $B \subset A$ is the morphism defined by: $\Pi_B(a) = a$ if $a \in B$ else $\Pi_B(a) = \varepsilon$.
Let A and B be alphabets. A *rational relation* R defined over $A^* \times B^*$ is a rational subset of $A^* \times B^*$.
A *transduction* τ from A^* into B^* is a function from A^* into 2^{B^*}, the *graph* of τ is the relation R defined by $R = \{(u, v) \mid v \in \tau(u)\}$.
A transduction $\tau : A^* \mapsto B^*$ is rational iff its graph R is a rational relation over A and B.
The next theorem, due to Nivat, characterized rational transduction:

Theorem 1 [Niv68]. *The following assertions are equivalent:*

- *τ is a rational transduction.*
- *There exist an alphabet Z, a rational language $K \subseteq Z^*$ and a couple (φ, ψ) of morphisms (a bimorphism) $\varphi : Z^* \mapsto A^*$ and $\psi : Z^* \mapsto B^*$ such that $\tau(u) = \psi(\varphi^{-1}(u) \cap K)$.*

As a corollary we have: the families of recognizable languages and context-free languages are closed under rational transductions.
An other important theorem, due to Elgot and Mezei, is that the composition of two rational transductions is again a rational transduction.

Semi-commutations
A *semi-commutation* (A, θ) is a finite alphabet A equipped with an *irreflexive semi-commutation relation* $\theta \subseteq A \times A - \{(x, x) \mid x \in A\}$.
The *converse* of θ is the relation $\theta^{-1} = \{(b, a) \mid (a, b) \in \theta\}$. A symmetrical semi-commutation (i.e. such that $\theta^{-1} = \theta$) is named a *partial commutation.*
The *non-commutation graph* of (A, θ) is the pair $(A, \bar{\theta})$, where $\bar{\theta} = A \times A - \theta$ is the *non-commutation relation* associated with θ.
We say that a word $w \in A^*$ is *(strongly) connected* iff the subgraph $(\text{alph}(w), \bar{\theta})$ is (strongly) connected.
With each semi-commutation (A, θ) is associated a rewriting system $S = < A, P >$ named *semi-commutation system* in which P is the set $\{xy \to yx \mid (x, y) \in \theta\}$. We write $u \underset{\theta}{\longrightarrow} v$ if there is a rule $xy \to yx$ in P and two words w and w' such that $u = wxyw'$ and $v = wyxw'$. We write $\overset{*}{\underset{\theta}{\longrightarrow}}$ for the reflexive and transitive closure of $\underset{\theta}{\longrightarrow}$.

Each semi-commutation (A,θ) induces a *semi-commutation function* $f_\theta : 2^{A^*} \mapsto 2^{A^*}$ as follows: $f_\theta(L) = \{u \in A^* \mid \exists w \in L, w \xrightarrow[\theta]{*} u\}$.
We say that a language $L \subseteq A^*$ is θ-closed iff $f_\theta(L) = L$. A word m in A^* is *rigid* for θ if $f_\theta(m) = \{m\}$.
We will use the following theorem proved by Clerbout and Latteux (see also [CLRZ92]):

Theorem 2 [CL87]. *If R_1 and R_2 are two recognizable θ-closed languages, then $R_1 \cup R_2$, $f_\theta(R_1R_2)$ are recognizable. Moreover, if any word in R_1 is strongly connected w.r.t. $\bar{\theta}$ then $f_\theta(R_1^*)$ is recognizable.*

Corollary 3 [CL87]. *Let $w \in A^*$. The language $f_\theta(w^*)$ is recognizable iff w is strongly connected w.r.t. $\bar{\theta}$.*

2 Semi-trace morphisms

Let (A,θ) be a semi-commutation. A semi-trace monoid is the 3-tuple $\mathbb{M}(A,\theta) = (\mathbb{M}, ., 1)$ where $\mathbb{M} = \{[u\rangle_\theta \mid u \in A^*\}$, the concatenation is defined $[u\rangle_\theta.[v\rangle_\theta = [uv\rangle_\theta$ and the neutral element $1 = [\varepsilon\rangle_\theta$. An element $[u\rangle_\theta$ in $\mathbb{M}(A,\theta)$ is called a *semi-trace*, it is equal to the set of words $f_\theta(u)$.
When (A,θ) is a partial commutation, $\mathbb{M}(A,\theta)$ is a trace monoid and an element of $\mathbb{M}(A,\theta)$ is called a trace.
Let (A,θ) and (B,γ) be semi-commutations. A word morphism $\varphi : A^* \mapsto B^*$ defines a *semi-trace morphism* $\vec{\varphi} : \mathbb{M}(A,\theta) \mapsto \mathbb{M}(B,\gamma)$ if *the image of a semi-trace is a semi-trace*: we must have $[\vec{\varphi}([u.v\rangle_\theta)\rangle_\gamma = [\vec{\varphi}([u\rangle_\theta).\vec{\varphi}([v\rangle_\theta)\rangle_\gamma$. They are such that $ab \xrightarrow[\theta]{} ba \Rightarrow \varphi(ab) \xrightarrow[\gamma]{*} \varphi(ba)$.
For instance, let $A = \{a,b\}$ and $\varphi : A^* \mapsto A^*$ be the idendity morphism, $\vec{\varphi} : \mathbb{M}(A, \{(a,b)\}) \mapsto \mathbb{M}(A,\emptyset)$ is not a semi-trace morphism: indeed $\vec{\varphi}([ab\rangle_\theta) = [ab\rangle_\emptyset + [ba\rangle_\emptyset = ab + ba$ and $\vec{\varphi}([a\rangle_\theta).\vec{\varphi}([b\rangle_\theta) = [ab\rangle_\emptyset = ab$.
Since rational transductions are defined over free monoids, we are not going to work directly with semi-traces: we consider that a semi-trace is a set of words. From this point of view $\vec{\varphi}$ is equivalent to $\bar{\varphi} : A^* \mapsto 2^{B^*}$ defined by $\bar{\varphi} = f_\gamma \circ \varphi$.

2.1 Recognizable trace morphisms

In [Dub86a] Duboc characterized recognizable trace morphisms i.e. such that the image of any recognizable trace language by the morphism is a recognizable trace language. For this purpose she defined the notion of connected trace morphism: *a trace morphism is connected iff the image of any connected trace (w.r.t. $\bar{\theta}$) is a connected trace (w.r.t. $\bar{\gamma}$).*

Proposition 4 [Dub86a]. *A trace morphism is recognizable iff it is connected.*

The next proposition characterizes trace morphisms which are connected, it is based on the characterization of the solutions of the equation $f_\theta(xy) = f_\theta(yx)$ obtained by Cori, Métivier [CM85] and generalized by Duboc [Dub86b].

Fact 5 [Och88]. *Let* (A,θ) *and* (B,γ) *be partial commutations. A connected word morphism* $\varphi : A^* \mapsto B^*$ *defines a trace morphism* $\vec{\varphi} : \mathbb{M}(A,\theta) \mapsto \mathbb{M}(B,\gamma)$ *iff* $\forall (a,b) \in \theta$*:*

- *either* $\mathrm{alph}(\varphi(a)) \times \mathrm{alph}(\varphi(b)) \subseteq \gamma$
- *or there exist two integers* α *and* β*, and a word* t *such that*
$$\bar{\varphi}(a) = f_\gamma(t^\alpha) \quad \text{and} \quad \bar{\varphi}(b) = f_\gamma(t^\beta)$$

2.2 Recognizable semi-trace morphisms

Definition 6. *A semi-trace morphism* $\vec{\varphi} : \mathbb{M}(A,\theta) \mapsto \mathbb{M}(B,\gamma)$ *is recognizable if for any* θ*-closed recognizable language* $L \subseteq A^*$ *the language* $\bar{\varphi}(L) \subseteq B^*$ *is recognizable.*

As we have already seen, when we speak about semi-commutations we deal with strongly connectivity rather than connectivity. We say that a semi-trace morphism is strongly connected iff the image of any strongly connected semi-trace (w.r.t. $\bar{\theta}$) is a strongly connected semi-trace (w.r.t. $\bar{\gamma}$). It is easy to see that a recognizable semi-trace morphism is strongly connected, but the converse is false. The problem of characterizing recognizable semi-trace morphism is still open ([CGL+92, OW93]).
In order to characterize strongly connected semi-trace morphisms we have to check for any $(x,y) \in \theta$ if the inclusion $\vec{\varphi}(yx) \subseteq \vec{\varphi}(xy)$ (i.e. $\bar{\varphi}(yx) \subseteq \bar{\varphi}(xy)$) holds. We will use the following lemma:

Lemma 7 [Roo89]. *Let* (A,θ) *be a semi-commutation and* u *be a strongly connected word of* A^**. If* $m_1 w m_2 \in f_\theta(u^*)$ *with* $|w|_y > 2|u|_y * \mathrm{Card}(\mathrm{alph}(u))$ *for some letter* y*, then* $\mathrm{alph}(w) = \mathrm{alph}(u)$*.*

Fact 8. *Let* (A,θ) *and* (B,γ) *be semi-commutations. A strongly connected word morphism* $\varphi : A^* \mapsto B^*$ *defines a strongly connected semi-trace morphism* $\vec{\varphi}$: $\mathbb{M}(A,\theta), \mapsto \mathbb{M}(B,\gamma)$ *iff* $\forall (x,y) \in \theta$ *we have* $\vec{\varphi}(yx) \subseteq \vec{\varphi}(xy)$ *that is:*

- *either* $\mathrm{alph}(\varphi(x)) \times \mathrm{alph}(\varphi(y)) \subseteq \gamma$
- *or there exist two integers* α *and* β*, and a word* t *such that*
$$\bar{\varphi}(x) = f_\gamma(t^\alpha) \quad \text{and} \quad \bar{\varphi}(y) = f_\gamma(t^\beta)$$

Proof. We focus on the case $(x,y) \in \theta$ and $\mathrm{alph}(\varphi(x)) \times \mathrm{alph}(\varphi(y)) \nsubseteq \gamma$. We are going to show that if $\vec{\varphi}$ is a strongly connected semi-trace morphism then there exist two positive integer p and q such that $\bar{\varphi}(x^p)) = \bar{\varphi}(y^q)$.
Set $u = \varphi(x)$ and $v = \varphi(y)$, let $a \in \mathrm{alph}(u)$ and $b \in \mathrm{alph}(b)$ be such that $(a,b) \in \bar{\gamma}$. If $\mathrm{alph}(u) \cap \mathrm{alph}(v) = \emptyset$ then $f_\gamma(\Pi_{ab}(uv)) = a^i b^j$ and $\Pi_{ab}(vu) = b^j a^i$ therefore $\bar{\varphi}(yx) \nsubseteq \bar{\varphi}(xy)$ i.e. $\vec{\varphi}$ is not a semi-trace morphism.
Let $a \in \mathrm{alph}(u) \cap \mathrm{alph}(v)$, and choose $p > 0$ and q such that $|u^p|_a = |v^q|_a$.
As $vu \in f_\gamma(uv)$ we get $v^q u^p \in f_\gamma(u^p v^q)$, and from Levi's Lemma for semi-trace there exist words u_1, u_2, v_1, v_2 such that: $u_1 u_2 \in f_\gamma(u^p)$, $v_1 v_2 \in f_\gamma(v^q)$, $\mathrm{alph}(u_2) \times \mathrm{alph}(v_1) \subseteq \gamma$, $v^q \in f_\gamma(u_1 v_1)$ and $u^p \in f_\gamma(u_2 v_2)$.

Since $|u^p|_a = |v^q|_a$ we must have $|u_2v_1|_a = 0$.
Suppose that $u_2 \neq \varepsilon$: observe that for any z in $\mathrm{alph}(u_2)$ we have $|u^p|_z > |v^q|_z$.
Let $N = |u_2|_b = |u^p|_b - |v^q|_b$ with $b \in \mathrm{alph}(u_2)$.
For every $k \in \mathbb{N}$ we have $v^{qk}u^{pk} \in f_\gamma(u^{pk}v^{qk})$ and there exist words $u_{1_k}, u_{2_k}, v_{1_k}, v_{2_k}$ such that: $u_{1_k}u_{2_k} \in f_\gamma(u^{kp})$, $v_{1_k}v_{2_k} \in f_\gamma(v^{kq})$, $\mathrm{alph}(u_{2_k}) \times \mathrm{alph}(v_{1_k}) \subseteq \gamma$, $v^{kq} \in f_\gamma(u_{1_k}v_{1_k})$ and $u^{kp} \in f_\gamma(u_{2_k}v_{2_k})$.
Clearly we have $|u_{2_k}v_{1_k}|_a = 0$ and $|u_{2_k}|_b = k.N$. Taking $k > 2|u|_b * \mathrm{Card}(\mathrm{alph}(u))$ we obtain a contradiction with Lemma 7 : we cannot have $u_{1_k}u_{2_k} \in f_\gamma(u^{pk})$ with $|u_{2_k}|_b > 2|u|_b * \mathrm{Card}(\mathrm{alph}(u))$ and $|u_{2_k}|_a = 0$ since u is strongly connected.
Thus $u_2 = \varepsilon$ and, by symmetry, $v_1 = \varepsilon$ and then we get $v^q \in f_\gamma(u^p)$ and $u^p \in f_\gamma(v^q)$ that is $vu \in f_{\gamma\cap\gamma^{-1}}(uv)$. So the inclusion $f_\gamma(vu) \subseteq f_\gamma(uv)$ is equivalent to the trace equation $f_{\gamma\cap\gamma^{-1}}(vu) = f_{\gamma\cap\gamma^{-1}}(uv)$. □

3 From words into semi-traces – $\vec{\varphi} \equiv \tau$

This section is devoted to a particular case: we want the transduction to do all the work... Since rational transductions have a lot of good properties, they are sometimes powerless, so the class of semi-trace morphisms which are equivalent to rational transductions is poor.
For instance, consider the following identity morphism $\vec{\varphi} : \mathbb{M}(\{a,b\},\{(a,b)\}) \mapsto \mathbb{M}(\{a,b\},\{(a,b)\})$. The morphism $\vec{\varphi}$ is not a rational transduction:
$\bar{\varphi}((ab)^*) \cap b^*a^* = \{b^na^n \mid n \in \mathbb{N}\}$ this is not a rational function.
The goal of this section is, in fact, to introduce a model of rational transduction which will be helpful for the general case. But first let us characterize semi-trace morphisms which are rational transductions.

Proposition 9. *A semi-trace morphism* $\vec{\varphi} : \mathbb{M}(A,\theta) \mapsto \mathbb{M}(B,\gamma)$ *is equivalent to a rational transduction iff*

- $\vec{\varphi}$ *is strongly connected.*
- $\forall (x,y) \in \theta$ *there exist two integers* α *and* β *and a word* $t \in B^*$ *such that* $\bar{\varphi}(x) = f_\gamma(t^\alpha)$ *and* $\bar{\varphi}(y) = f_\gamma(t^\beta)$.

Proof. If there exists a word w in A^* such that $\varphi(w)$ is not strongly connected for $\bar{\gamma}$ then from Corollary 3 the language $\bar{\varphi}(w^*)$ is not recognizable.
The second condition is necessary: since $\vec{\varphi}$ is a strongly connected semi-trace morphism we must have $\vec{\varphi}(xy) = \vec{\varphi}(yx)$, now if the second condition is not fullfilled (i.e. $\mathrm{alph}(\varphi(x)) \times \mathrm{alph}(\varphi(y)) \subseteq \gamma$, $\varphi(x) \neq \varepsilon$ and $\varphi(y) \neq \varepsilon$) it is not difficult to prove that $\bar{\varphi}((xy)^*)$ is not a recognizable language.
For the converse we construct a rational transduction τ:

3.1 The transduction

We are going to use a bimorphism to define the transduction – assume that $A \cap B = \emptyset$ – the first idea is to define the following transduction $\tau = \Pi_B \circ (\cap L) \circ \Pi_A^{-1}$,

where $L = f_\lambda\left((\bigcup_{a\in A} a\varphi(a))^*\right)$ with $(A\cup B,\lambda) = (A\cup B, \gamma\cup(A\times B)\cup(B\times A))$; and Π_A and Π_B are the projections over the alphabets A and B.
But generally this is not a rational function: the language L is not recognizable since $a\varphi(a)$ is not a strongly connected word as soon as $\varphi(a)$ is not ε. Hence we have to add a symmetric dependency between a and $\varphi(a)$, a good solution seems to connect the letter a with the last letter of $\varphi(a)$ but then, in general, there exist words such that $\tau(w) \subset \bar{\varphi}(w)$. It is impossible to define a general rational transduction over the alphabet $(A\cup B)$ with a semi-commutation. For this purpose we use a new alphabet B_ψ and a finite substitution ψ which allows to distinguish the position of any letter of each element of $\bar{\varphi}(a)$; then for any a in A we connect the letter a with the first letter and the last letter of each word in $\psi(a)$.
Let B_ψ be the following alphabet

$$B_\psi = \bigcup_{a\in A} \{a_{n,l} \mid 0 < n \leq \mathrm{Card}(\bar{\varphi}(a)) \text{ and } 0 < l < |\varphi(a)|\}$$

Let $\psi : A^* \mapsto 2^{B_\psi^*}$ be the following finite substitution:

$$\psi(a) = \begin{cases} \displaystyle\bigcup_{n=1}^{\mathrm{Card}(\bar{\varphi}(a))} \{a_{n,1}a_{n,2}\ldots a_{n,|\varphi(a)|}\} \text{ if } \varphi(a) \neq \varepsilon \\ \{\varepsilon\} \text{ if } \varphi(a) = \varepsilon \end{cases}$$

By definition, for each letter $a \in A$, there exists a bijection between $\psi(a)$ and $\bar{\varphi}(a)$: we associate $a_{n,1}a_{n,2}\ldots a_{n,|\varphi(a)|}$ with the nth element of $\bar{\varphi}(a)$, with respect to the lexicographic order.
The morphism $H_B : (A+B_\psi)^* \mapsto B^*$ erases letters of A and transforms a letter in B_ψ into a letter of B with respect to the bijection between $\psi(a)$ and $\bar{\varphi}(a)$:

$$H_B(x) = \begin{cases} \varepsilon \text{ if } x \in A \\ b \text{ if } x = a_{n,k} \text{ where } b \text{ is the } k^{\text{th}} \text{ letter of the } n^{\text{th}} \text{ element} \\ \qquad \text{of } \bar{\varphi}(a) \text{ with respect to the lexicographic order.} \end{cases}$$

Let us define the morphism $\Pi_A : (A+B_\psi)^* \mapsto A^*$ which erases letters of B_ψ: $\Pi_A(x) = x$ if $x \in A$, ε otherwise.
The rational transduction works on the alphabet $(A + B_\psi)$:

$$\tau = H_B \circ (\cap L) \circ \Pi_A^{-1} \quad \text{with} \quad L = f_\lambda\left((\bigcup_{a\in A} a\psi(a))^* \right)$$

where f_λ is the semi-commutation function associated with the semi-commutation $(A \cup B_\psi, \lambda)$:

$$\begin{aligned} \lambda = \{&(a_{n,k}, b_{n',k'}) \in B_\psi \times B_\psi \mid (H_B(a_{n,k}), H_B(b_{n',k'})) \in \gamma\} \\ &- \{(a_{n,1}, b_{n',|\varphi(b)|}) \in B_\psi \times B_\psi\} \\ &+ A \times B_\psi - \{(a, a_{n,|\varphi(a)|}) \in A \times B_\psi\} \\ &+ B_\psi \times A - \{(a_{n,1}, a) \in B_\psi \times A\} \end{aligned}$$

Actually the semi-commutation $(A \cup B_\psi, \lambda)$

- simulates f_γ over B_ψ^* but any first letter of any element of $\psi(a)$ cannot commute to the right with the last letter of any element of $\psi(b)$ – this is important to simplify proofs and definitions but not necessary.
- forbids any commutation between letters of A – there is no need to change the input word.
- forbids any letter a in A to commute to the right with the last letter of any element of $\psi(a)$ and to the left with the first letter of any word in $\psi(a)$. Thus any word in $a\psi(a)$ is strongly connected w.r.t. $\bar{\lambda}$ and consequently the language L is recognizable.

3.2 The power of τ

First it is easy to see that the set $H_B \circ f_\lambda \circ \psi(u)$ is included in $\bar{\varphi}(u)$: remind that λ is very close to γ – the main difference is that the complete commutation of the images of any two letters is forbidden in λ:

Lemma 10. *Let $u \in A^*$ and $w \in B^*$. If $w \in \bar{\varphi}(u)$ and if the images of any two letters of u have not commuted completely in w w.r.t. u then $w \in H_B \circ f_\lambda \circ \psi(u)$.*

The next lemma shows that letters of A do not make troubles. Indeed, if we have $a_{r,s} \xrightarrow{\bar{\lambda}} a \xrightarrow{\bar{\lambda}} b \xrightarrow{\bar{\lambda}} b_{p,q}$ or $a_{r,s} \xrightarrow{\bar{\lambda}} a \xrightarrow{\bar{\lambda}} a_{p,q}$ then $a_{r,s}$ is the first letter of an element of $\psi(a)$ and $b_{p,q}$ (resp. $a_{p,q}$) is the last letter of an element of $\psi(b)$ (resp. $\psi(a)$). Thus we have

Lemma 11. *Let $u \in A^*$ and $w \in B^*$. If $w \in H_B \circ f_\lambda \circ \psi(u)$ then $w \in \tau(u)$.*

To establish Proposition 9 we prove that the rational transduction τ is equal to $\bar{\varphi}$: observe that from the necessary conditions we have $\mathrm{alph}(\varphi(a)) \times \mathrm{alph}(\varphi(b)) \not\subseteq \gamma$ for any non erased letters a and b in A: on one hand we know that for any $(a, b) \in \theta$ we have $\mathrm{alph}(\varphi(a)) = \mathrm{alph}(\varphi(b))$; on the other hand φ is strongly connected.
Therefore the images of two letters cannot totally commute with γ. Thus, due to Lemma 10, for any u we have $H_B \circ f_\lambda \circ \psi(u) = \bar{\varphi}(u)$, and thanks to Lemma 11, we conclude that $\tau = \bar{\varphi}$.

4 The general case – $\vec{\varphi} \equiv \tau \circ f_\theta$

In this part we apply first f_θ and then the transduction τ i.e. we first compute a set of words equivalent to a semi-trace and then we apply to this set a transduction. We will show $\vec{\varphi}$ is equivalent to $\tau \circ f_\theta$ iff the the transduction defined in the previous section fits.

Example 12. *Let $A = \{a,b,c\}$, $B = \{x, y_1, y_2, y_3, z\}$, $\varphi(a) = x$, $\varphi(b) = y_1y_2y_3$, $\varphi(c) = z$ and the semi-commutations defined by the following non-commutation graphs:*

$$a \rightarrow b \rightarrow c \qquad\qquad \begin{matrix} & y_1 & \\ & \updownarrow & \\ x \rightarrow & y_2 & \rightarrow z \\ & \updownarrow & \\ & y_3 & \end{matrix}$$

$$\bar{\theta} \qquad\qquad\qquad\qquad \bar{\gamma}$$

we give two different transductions such that $\vec{\varphi} = \tau \circ f_\theta$.

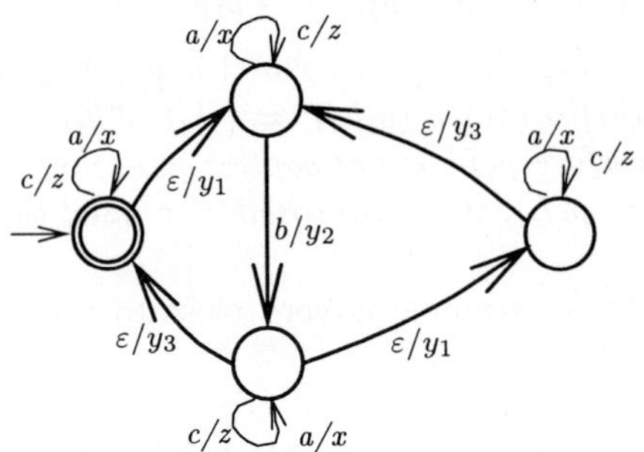

First Solution: a transducer

Second solution: $\tau = \Pi_B \circ (\cap f_\lambda((ax + by_1y_2y_3 + cz)^*)) \circ \Pi_A^{-1}$ *with* $\lambda = \{a\} \times \{y_1, y_3, z\} \cup \{b\} \times \{x, y_1, y_3, z\} \cup \{c\} \times \{x, y_1, y_2, y_3\} \cup \{x\} \times \{b, c, y_1, y_3, z\} \cup \{y_1\} \times \{a, b, c, x, z, y_3\} \cup \{y_2\} \times \{a, c, x\} \cup \{y_3\} \times \{a, b, c, x, y_1, z\} \cup \{z\} \times \{a, b, x, y_1, y_2, y_3\}$

In the previous section we saw that φ must be strongly connected. Of course this condition is still necessary. First observe that the equation $\bar{\varphi} = \tau \circ f_\theta$ concerns only semi-trace morphisms: $\bar{\varphi}$ must be *as powerful* as the function $\bar{\varphi} \circ f_\theta$.

Fact 13. *Let (A, θ) and (B, γ) be two semi-commutations and $\varphi : A^* \mapsto B^*$ be a morphism. If $\vec{\varphi} : \mathbb{M}(A, \theta) \mapsto \mathbb{M}(B, \gamma)$ is not a semi-trace morphism then there does not exist a rational transduction τ such that $\bar{\varphi} = \tau \circ f_\theta$.*

Proof. Suppose that $(a, b) \in \theta$. If $\bar{\varphi} = \tau \circ f_\theta$ then we have $\varphi(ba) \in \tau \circ f_\theta(ba)$. On the other hand we have $\tau \circ f_\theta(ba) \subseteq \tau \circ f_\theta(ab)$ hence $\bar{\varphi}(ba) \subseteq \bar{\varphi}(ab)$ therefore $\varphi(ba) \in \bar{\varphi}(ab)$. □

Let us define the notion of local semi-trace morphisms: intuitively φ is local iff for every couple (u, v), such that $v \in \bar{\varphi}(u)$, there exists a word in $f_\theta(u)$ *near* v such that f_γ does not need to commute the images of any two letters in u in order to reach v. More formally we have:

Definition 14. *Let $\vec{\varphi} : \mathbb{M}(A, \theta) \mapsto \mathbb{M}(B, \gamma)$ be a semi-trace morphism. The morphism φ is local iff for any u in A^* and for each v in $\bar{\varphi}(u)$ there exists a word $w \in f_\theta(u)$ such that $v \in \Pi_B \circ f_\lambda \circ \psi(w)$.*

Clearly if φ is strongly connected and local then the transduction τ defined in the previous section is convenient: we have, from Lemma 10, $H_B \circ f_\lambda \circ \psi \circ f_\theta(m) = \bar{\varphi}(m)$ hence, due to Lemma 11, $\tau \circ f_\theta = \bar{\varphi}$.
What about the converse ? Let us give some examples of non-local semi-trace morphisms – the first one deals with partial commutations:

Example 15. *Let (A, θ) with $A = \{a, b, c\}$ and $\theta = \{(a, c), (c, a)\}$, (B, γ) with $B = \{a, b_1, b_2, c\}$ and $\gamma = \{(a, c), (c, a), (a, b_1), (b_1, a), (b_2, c), (c, b_2)\}$.
Let the semi-trace morphism $\vec{\varphi} : \mathbb{M}(A, \theta) \mapsto \mathbb{M}(B, \gamma)$ with $\varphi(a) = a$ $\varphi(b) = b_1 b_2$ $\varphi(c) = c$. Notice that $\vec{\varphi}$ is connected. The word abc is* rigid *for $\bar{\theta}$: $f_\theta(abc) = \{abc\}$. Moreover $\varphi(a^n bc^n) = a^n b_1 b_2 c^n \xrightarrow[\gamma]{*} b_1 a^n c^n b_2 \xrightarrow[\gamma]{*} b_1 (ac)^n b_2$.
Observe that the language $L = \{b^p a^p bc^n b^n \mid n, p \in \mathbb{N}\}$ is θ-closed and context-free. But $\bar{\varphi}(L) \cap (b_1 b_2)^* b_1 (ac)^* b_2 (b_1 b_2)^* = \{(b_1 b_2)^n b_1 (ac)^n b_2 (b_1 b_2)^n \mid n \in \mathbb{N}\}$ is not context-free, therefore $\bar{\varphi}(L)$ is not context-free. Since any word in L is rigid, we must have $\tau(L) = \bar{\varphi}(L)$, this is impossible: τ must be a rational function.*

As a matter of fact this example is very close to the general case for partial commutations:

Definition 16. *A trace morphism $\vec{\varphi} : \mathbb{M}(A, \theta) \mapsto \mathbb{M}(B, \gamma)$ is rigid if for each word $w = x_1 \ldots x_n$ in A^* rigid for θ there exists a subword $y_1 \ldots y_k$ of $\varphi(w)$ which is rigid for γ and such that $y_1 \in \mathrm{alph}(\varphi(x_1))$ and $y_k \in \mathrm{alph}(\varphi(x_n))$.*

Theorem 17. *Let $\vec{\varphi} : \mathbb{M}(A, \theta) \mapsto \mathbb{M}(B, \gamma)$ be a trace morphism. There exists a rational transduction τ such that $\bar{\varphi} = \tau \circ f_\theta$ iff φ is connected and rigid.*

The condition is sufficient since if φ is rigid then it is local. The proof of the necessary condition is only a generalization of Example 15.
For semi-trace morphisms the situation is more complex: let us start with an example.

Example 18. *Let (A, θ) with $A = \{a, b, c\}$, $\theta = \{(a, c), (a, b)\}$,
(B, γ) with $B = \{a, b_1, b_2, c\}$ and $\gamma = \{(a, c), (a, b_1), (b_1, a), (a, b_2), (b_2, c)\}$.
The semi-trace morphism $\vec{\varphi} : \mathbb{M}(A, \theta) \mapsto \mathbb{M}(B, \gamma)$ is defined by
$\varphi(a) = a$ $\varphi(b) = b_1 b_2$ $\varphi(c) = c$. Notice that φ is strongly connected. Unlike the previous example the word abc is not rigid for θ: $f_\theta(abc) = \{abc\ ,\ bac\ ,\ bca\}$.
Nevertheless we have $\varphi(abc) = ab_1 b_2 c \xrightarrow[\gamma]{2} b_1 acb_2 \xrightarrow[\gamma]{} b_1 cab_2$.
But $b_1 cab_2$ belongs neither to $\bar{\varphi}(bac)$, nor to $\bar{\varphi}(bca)$: the couple (b_2, a) does not belong to γ. Thus, as in the previous example, we have for all integers p, q: $b_1 c^q a^p b_2 \in \tau(a^p bc^q)$. The function $(\cap b_1 c^* a^* b_2) \circ \tau$, defined by the graph $\{(a^p bc^q, b_1 c^q a^p b_2) \mid p, q \in \mathbb{N}\}$, is not a rational subset of $A^* \times B^*$. There does not exist a rational transduction τ such that $\bar{\varphi} = \tau \circ f_\theta$.*

This is the characterization of local semi-trace morphisms:

Proposition 19. *Let $\bar{\varphi} : \mathbb{M}(A,\theta) \mapsto \mathbb{M}(B,\gamma)$ be a semi-trace morphism. The morphism φ is local iff there does not exist a word $w = x_0 \ldots x_n$ in A^* which does not contain two occurrences of the same letter and a word v in $\bar{\varphi}(w)$ such that:*

1. $\varphi(x_0) \neq \varepsilon$, $\varphi(x_n) \neq \varepsilon$ *and* $\text{alph}(\varphi(x_0)) \cap \text{alph}(\varphi(x_n)) = \emptyset$.
2. *for any index i in $[0, n-1]$ the couple (x_i, x_{i+1}) belongs to $\bar{\theta} \cup \bar{\theta}^{-1}$ and moreover if $(x_i, x_{i+1}) \in \theta$ then there exist two letters $\alpha \in \text{alph}(\varphi(x_i))$ and $\beta \in \text{alph}(\varphi(x_{i+1}))$ such that:*
   - $\Pi_\alpha(\varphi(w)) = \Pi_\alpha(\varphi(x_i))$.
   - $\Pi_\beta(\varphi(w)) = \Pi_\beta(\varphi(x_{i+1}))$.
   - $\Pi_{\alpha\beta}(v) \notin f_\gamma \circ \Pi_{\alpha\beta} \circ \varphi(x_{i+1} x_i)$.
3. $v = v_1 \varphi(x_n) \varphi(x_0) v_2$ *with*
   $\text{alph}(\varphi(x_0)) \times \text{alph}(v_1) \subseteq \gamma$ *and* $\text{alph}(v_2) \times \text{alph}(\varphi(x_n)) \subseteq \gamma$.

Observe that if a morphism is strongly connected on letters and local then it is strongly connected. With this characterization it is easy to show that being local is a necessary condition – the proof of the following lemma is based on a generalization of Example 18:

Lemma 20. *Let $\bar{\varphi} : \mathbb{M}(A,\theta) \mapsto \mathbb{M}(B,\gamma)$ be a semi-trace morphism. If φ is not local then there does not exist a rational transduction τ such that $\bar{\varphi} = \tau \circ f_\theta$.*

Now we are able to conclude this section:

Theorem 21. *Let $\bar{\varphi} : \mathbb{M}(A,\theta) \mapsto \mathbb{M}(B,\gamma)$ be a semi-trace morphism. There exists a rational transduction τ such that $\bar{\varphi} = \tau \circ f_\theta$ iff φ is strongly connected and local.*

5 Context-free trace morphisms

First let us define the notion of context-free trace morphisms:

Definition 22. *A trace morphism $\bar{\varphi} : \mathbb{M}(A,\theta) \mapsto \mathbb{M}(B,\gamma)$ is a context-free trace morphism if for any θ-closed context-free language L the language $\bar{\varphi}(L)$ is context-free.*

We have seen that a trace morphism is recognizable iff it is connected, this condition is not necessary for context-free trace morphisms: consider the trace morphism $\bar{\varphi} : \mathbb{M}(\{a\},\emptyset) \mapsto \mathbb{M}(\{a,b\},\{(a,b),(b,a)\})$ with $\varphi(a) = ab$.
It is well known that on a one letter alphabet the family of recognizable languages and context-free languages are equal. For any recognizable language L we have $\bar{\varphi}(L) = (L \sqcup b^*) \cap D_1^*$, where $D_1^* = \{m \in (a+b)^* \mid |m|_a = |m|_b\}$ is the Dyck language, a famous context-free language. Since $L \sqcup b^*$ is recognizable, $\bar{\varphi}(L)$ is context-free, therefore $\bar{\varphi}$ is a context-free trace morphism.
The following proposition characterizes context-free trace morphisms when the alphabet B contains only two letters. Then we generalize this result for non connected morphisms.

Proposition 23 [Lat79]. *Let $(B,\gamma) = (\{a,b\},\{(a,b),(b,a)\})$ be a partial commutation. If the language $L \subseteq B^*$ is context-free then $f_\gamma(L)$ is context-free.*

Thanks to rational transductions we have:

Lemma 24. *A trace morphism $\vec{\varphi} : \mathbb{M}(A,\theta) \mapsto \mathbb{M}(B,\gamma)$ is a context-free trace morphism if there exist two words t_1 and t_2 connected w.r.t. $\bar{\gamma}$ such that for each $x \in A$ we have $\bar{\varphi}(x) \subseteq f_\gamma(t_1^* t_2^*)$.*

Proof. Let $A = \{a_1, \ldots, a_n\}$; for all a_i we have $\bar{\varphi}(a_i) = f_\gamma(t_1^{\alpha_i} t_2^{\beta_i})$.
Let $X = \{x, y\}$, and the morphism $\psi : A^* \mapsto X^*$ defined by $\psi(a_i) = x^{\alpha_i} y^{\beta_i}$ for all $a_i \in A$.
Let (X, λ) be the total commutation. Let $\vec{\delta} : \mathbb{M}(X,\lambda) \mapsto \mathbb{M}(B,\gamma)$ be the trace morphism defined by $\delta(x) = t_1$ and $\delta(y) = t_2$.
Clearly we have for all word u in A^* $\bar{\varphi}(u) = \bar{\delta}\circ\psi(u)$; the trace morphism $\vec{\delta}$ is connected and rigid. Thus there exists a rational transduction τ such that $f_\gamma\circ\delta = \tau\circ f_\lambda$. From Proposition 23, for all context-free language $L \subseteq A^*$, $f_\lambda\circ\psi(L)$ is context-free thus the language $\tau\circ f_\lambda\circ\psi(L) = \bar{\varphi}(L)$ is context-free too. □

When the morphism $\vec{\varphi}$ is not connected this condition becomes necessary:

Lemma 25. *A non-connected trace morphism $\vec{\varphi} : \mathbb{M}(A,\theta) \mapsto \mathbb{M}(B,\gamma)$ is a context-free trace morphism iff there exist two words t_1 and t_2 connected for $\bar{\gamma}$ such that for each $x \in A$ we have $\bar{\varphi}(x) \subseteq f_\gamma(t_1^* t_2^*)$.*

If a connected trace morphism $\vec{\varphi}$ is rigid, then there exists a rational transduction τ such that $\bar{\varphi} = \tau\circ f_\theta$ and therefore $\vec{\varphi}$ is a context-free morphism. The converse is true: Example 15 is closed to the general case.

Lemma 26. *A connected trace morphism $\vec{\varphi} : \mathbb{M}(A,\theta) \mapsto \mathbb{M}(B,\gamma)$ is a context-free trace morphism iff it is rigid.*

Thanks to the three previous lemmas we obtain

Proposition 27. *A trace morphism $\vec{\varphi} : \mathbb{M}(A,\theta) \mapsto \mathbb{M}(B,\gamma)$ is a context-free trace morphism iff*

- *Either there exist two words t_1 and t_2 connected for $\bar{\gamma}$ such that for each $x \in A$ we have $\bar{\varphi}(x) \subseteq f_\gamma(t_1^* t_2^*)$.*
- *Or φ is connected and rigid.*

We have seen that trace morphisms which are equivalent to some rational transduction form a proper subclass of recognizable trace morphisms. Since a context-free trace morphism may be not connected, the class of recognizable trace morphisms and the class of context-free trace morphisms are incomparable. At the first glance this is quite surprising, but observe that, unlike the family of recognizable trace languages, the family of context-free trace languages is not closed under concatenation.
Notice that we are not able to characterize context-free semi-trace morphisms: as usually the introduction of non-symmetric dependences modifies considerably the problem.

6 Deciding whether $f_\gamma(u^*)$ is context-free

Clerbout and Roos [CR90] have proved that, given a semi-commutation (A,θ) and word u, the language $f_\theta(u^*)$ is context-free iff the graph $(\text{alph}(u),\bar{\theta})$ contains at most two strongly connected components. Thanks to rational transductions we are able to give a new proof of this characterization.

Proposition 28 [CR90]. *Let (B,γ) be a semi-commutation and u be a word in B^*. The language $f_\gamma(u^*)$ is context-free iff the graph $(\text{alph}(u),\bar{\gamma})$ contains at most two strongly connected components.*

This condition is clearly necessary: for instance consider $\gamma = \{(a,b),(c,b),(c,a)\}$ we have $f_\gamma((abc)*) \cap b^*a^*c^* = \{b^n a^n c^n \mid n \in \mathbb{N}\}$.
Here we focus on the converse. Of course if $(\text{alph}(u),\bar{\gamma})$ strongly connected we know that (Corollary 3) the language $f_\gamma(u^*)$ is recognizable. We have to deal with the case "$(\text{alph}(u),\bar{\gamma})$ *contains two strongly connected components*".
We may assume that u does not contain twice a same letter (otherwise we numbered the different occurrences of the letters of u). We will denote m and w the projections of u over the two components.

6.1 The case $f_\gamma(u) = f_\gamma(mw)$

Here we assume that $f_\gamma(u) = f_\gamma(mw)$ i.e. $u \xrightarrow[\gamma\cap\gamma^{-1}]{*} mw$.
Let $A = \{a,b\}$ and let $\varphi : A^* \mapsto B^*$ be the morphism defined by

$$\varphi(a) = m \quad \textit{and} \quad \varphi(b) = w$$

Let (A,θ) be semi-commutation defined by:
$(a,b) \in \theta$ if $\text{alph}(m) \times \text{alph}(w) \subseteq \gamma$
$(b,a) \in \theta$ if $\text{alph}(w) \times \text{alph}(m) \subseteq \gamma$
Remark that $f_\gamma(u^*) = f_\gamma((mw)^*) = f_\gamma{\circ}\varphi((ab)^*) = \bar{\varphi}((ab)^*)$.
Note that the morphism φ is strongly connected and, due to the definition of θ, it is a semi-trace morphism and local. Thus there exists a rational transduction τ such that $\bar{\varphi} = \tau{\circ}f_\theta$. So $\bar{\varphi}((ab)^*)$ is context-free iff $f_\theta((ab)^*)$ is context-free, this is obvious:

$$f_\theta((ab)^*) = \begin{cases} D_1^*(a,b) \text{ if } (a,b) \in \theta \cap \theta^{-1} \\ D_1'^*(a,b) \text{ if } (b,a) \in \theta \cap \bar{\theta}^{-1} \\ (D_1'^*(b,a) + ab)^* \text{ if } (a,b) \in \theta \cap \bar{\theta}^{-1} \end{cases}$$

Thus when $f_\gamma(u) = f_\gamma(mw)$, $f_\gamma(u^*)$ is context-free.

6.2 The case $f_\gamma(u) \neq f_\gamma(mw)$

Here we assume that we have neither $u \xrightarrow[\gamma\cap\gamma^{-1}]{*} mw$, nor $u \xrightarrow[\gamma\cap\gamma^{-1}]{*} wm$. Note that it is impossible to use the same construction as above.
Set $u \xrightarrow[\gamma]{*} mw$ with $wm \xrightarrow[\gamma]{+} mw$.
Let B_{12} be the alphabet $B_1 \cup B_2$ with $B_i = \{x_i \mid x \in B\}$.
We denote by $H_B : B_{12}^* \mapsto B^*$ the morphism defined by $H_B(x_i) = x, \forall x \in B_{12}$.
Let (B_{12}, λ) be the following semi-commutation:

$$\lambda = \{(x_i, y_j) \in B_{12}\times B_{12} \mid (x,y) \in \gamma\}\cup\{(x_i, y_i) \in \text{alph}(m_i)\times\text{alph}(w_i) \mid \Pi_{xy}(u) = yx\}$$

Remark that $f_\gamma(u) = H_B{\circ}f_\lambda(m_1w_1) = H_B{\circ}f_\lambda(m_2w_2)$, moreover we have

$$f_\gamma(u^*) = H_B{\circ}f_\lambda((m_1w_1m_2w_2)^*(\varepsilon + m_1w_1))$$

Let A_{12} be the alphabet $\{a_1, a_2, b_1, b_2\}$ and $\varphi : A_{12}^* \mapsto B_{12}^*$ be the morphism defined by $\varphi(a_i) = m_i$ and $\varphi(b_i) = w_i$, where $m_i \in B_i^*$, $H_B(m_i) = m$ and $w_i \in B_i^*$, $H_B(w_i) = w$. We have

$$f_\gamma(u^*) = H_B{\circ}f_\lambda((m_1w_1m_2w_2)^*(\varepsilon{+}m_1w_1)) = H_B{\circ}f_\lambda{\circ}\varphi((a_1b_1a_2b_2)^*(\varepsilon{+}a_1b_1)) \ .$$

Let $\theta_{12} = \{(b_1, a_1)\ , (b_1, a_2)\ , (b_2, a_1)\ ,\ (b_2, a_2)\}$.

It is not difficult to see that $\varphi : \mathbb{M}(A_{12}, \theta_{12}) \mapsto \mathbb{M}(B_{12}, \lambda)$ is a semi-trace morphism, strongly connected and local: therefore there exists a rational transduction τ such that $f_\lambda{\circ}\varphi = \bar{\varphi} = \tau{\circ}f_{\theta_{12}}$. Thus $H_B{\circ}\bar{\varphi} = H_B{\circ}\tau{\circ}f_{\theta_{12}}$ and we get

$$f_\gamma(u^*) = H_B{\circ}\bar{\varphi}((a_1b_1a_2b_2)^*(\varepsilon + a_1b_1)) = H_B{\circ}\tau{\circ}f_{\theta_{12}}((a_1b_1a_2b_2)^*(\varepsilon + a_1b_1))$$

To conclude we have to check that $f_{\theta_{12}}((a_1b_1a_2b_2)^*(\varepsilon + a_1b_1))$ is context-free:
Let $(A, \theta) = (\{a, b\}, \{(b, a)\}$ and alt : $A^* \mapsto 2^{A_{12}^*}$ be the following rational transduction:

$$\text{alt}(vx) = \text{alt}(v)x_i \text{ with} \left| \begin{array}{l} i = 1 \text{ if } |v|_x = 2p \\ i = 2 \text{ if } |v|_x = 2p+1 \end{array} \right. \forall v \in A^*\forall x \in A \ .$$

Clearly alt$\circ f_\theta((ab)^*) = f_{\theta_{12}}((a_1b_1a_2b_2)^*(\varepsilon + a_1b_1))$. As $f_\theta((ab)^*) = D_1'^*(a, b)$ is context-free, the language $f_{\theta_{12}}((a_1b_1a_2b_2)^*(\varepsilon + a_1b_1))$ is context-free too.

Acknowledgments: I thanks the referees and Les Chtimis for their comments and remarks.

References

[BDFG94] V Bruyère, C De Felice, and G Guaiana. Coding with traces. In P Enjalbert, editor, *Proceedings of STACS'94*, L.N.C.S. Springer, 1994.

[Ber79] J. Berstel. *Transductions and Context Free Languages.* Teubner Studienbucher Informatik, 1979.

[CF69] P. Cartier and D. Foata. *Problèmes combinatoires de commutation et réarrangements.* L.N.C.S. Springer, 1969.

[CGL+92] M. Clerbout, D. Gonzalez, M. Latteux, E. Ochmański, Y. Roos, and P.A. Wacrenier. Recognizable morphisms on semi commutations. Technical report i.t. 238, Université des Sciences et Technologies de Lille, 1992.

[CL87] M. Clerbout and M. Latteux. Semi-Commutations. *Information and Computation*, 73:59–74, 1987.

[CLRZ92] M. Clerbout, M. Latteux, Y. Roos, and W. Zielonka. Semi-commutations and rational expressions. In W. Kuich, editor, *Proceedings of ICALP'92, Vienna 1992*, number 623 in L.N.C.S., pages 113–125. Springer, 1992.

[CM85] R. Cori and Y. Métivier. Recognizable subsets of some partially abelian monoids. *Theoretical Computer Science*, 35:241–254, 1985.

[CR87] M. Chrobak and W. Rytter. Unique decipherability for partially commutative alphabets. *Fundamenta Informaticae*, X:323–336, 1987.

[CR90] M. Clerbout and Y. Roos. Semi-commutations and algebraic languages. In C. Choffrut et al., editors, *Proceedings of the STACS'90, Rouen (France) 1990*, number 415 in L.N.C.S., pages 82–93. Springer, 1990.

[DMR94] V Diekert, A Muscholl, and K Reinhardt. Trace coding. STACS'95, 1994.

[DR95] V. Diekert and G. Rozenberg, editors. *Book on Traces.* World Scientific, 1995.

[Dub86a] C. Duboc. Mixed product and asynchronous automata. *Theoretical Computer Science*, 48:183–199, 1986.

[Dub86b] C. Duboc. On some equations in free partially commutative monoids. *Theoretical Computer Science*, 46:159–174, 1986.

[HK89] D. V. Hung and E. Knuth. Semi-commutations and Petri-nets. *Theoretical Computer Science*, 34:67–81, 1989.

[Lat79] M. Latteux. Cônes rationnels commutatifs. *Journal of Computer and System Sciences*, 18:307–333, 1979.

[Maz77] A. Mazurkiewicz. Concurrent program schemes and their interpretations. DAIMI Rep. PB 78, Aarhus University, Aarhus, 1977.

[Niv68] M. Nivat. Transductions des langages de chomsky. *Annuaire de l'Institut Fourier*, 18:339–456, 1968.

[Och88] E. Ochmański. On morphisms of trace monoids. In R. Cori and M. Wirsing, editors, *Proceedings of STACS'88, Bordeaux (Fr) 1988*, number 294 in L.N.C.S., pages 346–355. Springer, 1988.

[Och90] Ochmański. Semi-commutation and deterministic Petri-nets. In B. Rovan, editor, *Proceedings of MFCS'90, Banská Bystrica 1990*, number 452 in L.N.C.S., pages 430–438, 1990.

[Och92] E. Ochmański. Modelling concurrency with semi-commutations. In I. M. Havel and V. Koubek, editors, *Proceedings of MFCS'92, Prague, 1992*, number 629 in L.N.C.S., pages 412–420. Springer, 1992.

[OW93] E. Ochmański and P.A. Wacrenier. On regular compatibility of semi-commutations. In A. Lingas, editor, *Proceedings of ICALP'93, Lund (Sweden)*, L.N.C.S., pages 445–456. Springer, 1993.

[Roo89] Y. Roos. *Contribution à l'Etude des Fonctions de Commutation Partielle.* Thèse, Université des Sciences et Technologies de Lille, 1989.

Nonfinite Axiomatizability of Shuffle Inequalities

Stephen L. Bloom* and Zoltán Ésik**

Stevens Institute of Technology
Department of Computer Science
Hoboken, NJ 07030
bloom@gauss.stevens-tech.edu

A. József University
Department of Computer Science
Szeged, Hungary
esik@inf.u-szeged.hu

Abstract. There is some set of inequations $t \leq t'$ whose models are the algebras in the variety of ordered algebras generated by the algebras $\mathcal{L}_\Sigma = (P_\Sigma, \cdot, \otimes, 1)$, where P_Σ consists of all subsets of the free monoid Σ^*, $B \cdot C = \{uv : u \in B, v \in C\}$, and $B \otimes C$ is the shuffle product of the two languages. We show that there is no finite set of such inequations.

1 Introduction

In a previous paper [4], the authors found concrete descriptions of the free algebras in varieties generated by languages equipped with various sets of operations all involving the shuffle operation. For example, we considered the variety generated by the structures $\mathcal{L}_\Sigma = (P_\Sigma, \cdot, \otimes, 1)$, where P_Σ consists of all subsets of the free monoid Σ^*, $B \cdot C = \{uv : u \in B, v \in C\}$, and $B \otimes C$ is the shuffle product of the two languages. The free algebras in this variety are labeled series-parallel posets. The free algebras in the variety of *ordered* algebras generated by the structures $(\mathcal{L}_\Sigma, \subseteq)$ are again the labeled series-parallel posets equipped with an ordering we call the trace ordering. (In [7], labeled posets with the "subsumption order" were shown to be the free ordered algebras in a finitely axiomatizable variety.) "Closed subsets" of the labeled posets are the free algebras in the variety generated by the structures $(P_\Sigma, \cdot, \otimes, +, ^*, 0, 1)$, where $+$ is binary union and * is the Kleene star operation. These results seem to show that two different models of parallelism are equivalent: the so-called language or interleaving model, and a pomset model.

What the result in [4] does not establish is precisely what the valid inequations or equations are in each of the varieties considered. One would like to have an

* Partially supported by the US-Hungarian Joint Fund under grant number 351.

** Partially supported by a grant of the National Foundation for Scientific Research of Hungary, the Alexander von Humboldt Foundation, and by the US-Hungarian Joint Fund under grant number 351.

axiomatic description of the set of valid equations and inequations, preferably via a simple finite set of axioms. In this paper, we consider the variety $\mathbf{Lg}_{\leq}$ of ordered algebras generated by the language structures $(P_\Sigma, \cdot, \otimes, 1, \subseteq)$ and show that there is no finite set of inequations which axiomatize the inequations valid in $\mathbf{Lg}_{\leq}$.

The axiomatization of the varieties generated by the language structures $(P_\Sigma, \cdot, \otimes, +, 0, 1)$ and $(P_\Sigma, \cdot, \otimes, +, ^*, 0, 1)$ is considered in the paper [5].

2 Review

In this section, we review the necessary definitions and results from [4].

Definition 1. A **bimonoid** $\mathrm{M} = (M, \cdot, \otimes, 1)$ consists of a monoid $(M, \cdot, 1)$ and a commutative monoid $(M, \otimes, 1)$ with a common neutral element. A **bimonoid morphism** $\mathrm{M} \to \mathrm{M}'$ is a function $M \to M'$ which preserves the unit and the two binary operations.

Definition 2. An **ordered bimonoid** $(\mathrm{M}, \leq)$ is a bimonoid $(M, \cdot, \otimes, 1)$ whose underlying set M is equipped with a partial ordering $\leq$ such that for all $x, y, a, b \in M$,

$$x \leq a,\ y \leq b \Rightarrow x \cdot y \leq a \cdot b \text{ and } x \otimes y \leq a \otimes b.$$

A **morphism of ordered bimonoids** is an order preserving bimonoid morphism.

Three motivating examples of ordered bimonoids are the language structures $\mathcal{L}_\Sigma := (P_\Sigma, \cdot, \otimes, 1)$, $\mathcal{R}_\Sigma := (R_\Sigma, \cdot, \otimes, 1)$, $\mathcal{F}_\Sigma := (F_\Sigma, \cdot, \otimes, 1)$, where P_Σ is the collection of all subsets, R_Σ consists of the regular subsets, and F_Σ consists of the finite subsets of the free monoid Σ^*. The ordering on each bimonoid is that of set inclusion. The set $B \cdot C$ is $\{uv : u \in B, v \in C\}$, and $B \otimes C$ is the shuffle product of languages:

$$B \otimes C := \{u_1 v_1 \cdots u_n v_n : u_1 \cdots u_n \in B, v_1 \cdots v_n \in C, u_i, v_i \in \Sigma^*, n \geq 0\}$$

If $f : A \to B$ is a morphism of ordered bimonoids, we say f is **order-reflecting** if $xf \leq yf \Leftrightarrow x \leq y$. Note that an order-reflecting morphism is necessarily injective. Say that the ordered bimonoid A is an ordered subalgebra of the ordered bimonoid B if there is an order-reflecting morphism $A \to B$. A **variety** $\mathcal{V}$ **of ordered bimonoids** is a collection of ordered bimonoids closed under products (ordered componentwise), ordered subalgebras and order preserving morphic images. Equivalently, (see [3]), a variety of ordered bimonoids is the collection of all ordered bimonoids which satisfy a set of inequations $t \leq t'$, for certain bimonoid terms t, t'. Any collection of ordered bimonoids is contained in a least variety of ordered bimonoids.

One variety of interest is that generated by the language bimonoids.

Definition 3. **Lg** denotes the variety of bimonoids generated by the language bimonoids $\mathcal{L}_\Sigma$, and $\mathbf{Lg}_\leq$ denotes the variety of ordered bimonoids generated by the ordered bimonoids of languages $(\mathcal{L}_\Sigma, \subseteq)$.

Remark 4. The variety $\mathbf{Lg}_\leq$ is generated by the ordered bimonoids of finite languages $\mathcal{F}_\Sigma$ and thus by the the ordered bimonoids $\mathcal{R}_\Sigma$ of regular languages [4].

Labeled posets with serial and parallel product form another example of a bimonoid. An A-**labeled poset** $P = (P, \leq, \ell)$ consists of a poset $(P, \leq_P)$, sometimes written just $(P, \leq)$, and an assignment of an element $v\ell$ in A to each vertex v in P. (Here P denotes both the poset and the underlying set of elements or "vertices" of P. Thus the expression "$v \in P$" is meaningful.) When A is understood, we will say only "labeled poset". A **morphism** $f : P \to Q$ of A-labeled posets is a function $P \to Q$ which preserves the ordering and the labeling. We agree to identify isomorphic labeled posets, without further mention. (Many authors call an isomorphism class of a labeled poset a "pomset".) *To save space, we assume "poset" means "finite poset".* We denote the empty poset by **1**. Two operations on labeled posets are important here, sequential, or serial product $P \cdot Q$ and parallel or shuffle product $P \otimes Q$. Given labeled posets P, Q, with disjoint underlying sets,

$$P \cdot Q := (P \cup Q, \leq_{P \cdot Q})$$
$$P \otimes Q := (P \cup Q, \leq_{P \otimes Q}),$$

where for $v, v' \in P \cup Q$,

$$v \leq_{P \cdot Q} v' \Leftrightarrow v \leq_P v' \text{ or } v \leq_Q v' \text{ or }$$
$$v \in P \text{ and } v' \in Q.$$
$$v \leq_{P \otimes Q} v' \Leftrightarrow v \leq_P v' \text{ or } v \leq_Q v'.$$

The labeling is extended to $P \otimes Q$ and $P \cdot Q$ in the obvious way.

Definition 5. We let SP_A, for "series-parallel" or "shuffle product", denote the least class of posets containing the empty poset **1**, the singleton posets a, labeled a, for each $a \in A$, closed under the operations $P \cdot Q$, $P \otimes Q$. The posets in SP_A will be called "series-parallel" posets. We let $\mathbf{SP}(A)$ be the following bimonoid:

$$\mathbf{SP}(A) := (\mathrm{SP}_A, \cdot, \otimes, \mathbf{1}).$$

Remark 6. Grabowski [8] and Valdes [10] found the following "N-condition" to characterize the series-parallel posets. A poset P is series-parallel iff there is no four-element subset $\{a, b, c, d\} \subseteq P$ whose only nontrivial order relationships are given by

$$a < c, \quad a < d, \quad b < d.$$

A nice proof of this fact is given in [7]. It follows from this characterization that any subset of a series-parallel poset, ordered with the inherited order, is itself series-parallel. This fact will be used several times without mention.

Theorem 7. [7] $\mathbf{SP}(A)$ is freely generated in the variety of all bimonoids by the set A.

We will impose an ordering on $\mathbf{SP}(A)$ making use of the alphabet $\Sigma(A)$, defined below. Given the set A, let $\overline{A}$ be a set disjoint from A, and let

$$a \mapsto \overline{a}$$

be a bijection. Define the sets A_N and $\overline{A}_N$ by:

$$A_N := A \times \mathbf{N}$$
$$\overline{A}_N := \overline{A} \times \mathbf{N}$$

where $\mathbf{N} = \{0, 1, \ldots\}$. We denote elements in A_N as a_i, b_j, etc., and elements in $\overline{A}_N$ as $\overline{a}_i, \overline{b}_j$. Let $\Sigma(A)$ be the infinite alphabet

$$\Sigma(A) := A_N \cup \overline{A}_N.$$

Let $h_0 : \mathbf{SP}(A) \to \mathcal{L}_{\Sigma(A)}$ be the unique bimonoid morphism satisfying

$$ah_0 := \{a_1\overline{a}_1, a_2\overline{a}_2 \ldots, a_n\overline{a}_n, \ldots\},$$

each $a \in A$.

Remark 8. An *expansion* of a poset $P \in \mathbf{SP}(A)$ is a poset P' in $\mathbf{SP}(\Sigma(A))$ obtained from P by replacing each vertex v of P by a two element chain $v(1) < v(2)$. The ordering in P' is defined as follows:

$$v(i) \leq v'(j) \Leftrightarrow v < v' \text{ in } P \text{ or } v = v' \text{ and } i \leq j \in [2].$$

If v is labeled a in P, then for some $i \geq 1$, $v(1)$ is labeled a_i and $v(2)$ is labeled $\overline{a}_i$. Suppose that

$$v_1 v_2 \ldots v_m$$

is a topological run of P' (i.e., a surjection $v : [m] \to P$ such that $v_i \leq_P v_j \Rightarrow i \leq j$). The *trace* of this run is the word in $\Sigma(A)^*$ formed by concatenating the labels of the vertices in the run. In [4] it is shown that for any poset $P \in \mathbf{SP}(A)$, a word u belongs to Ph_0 iff u is a trace of an expansion of P.

One of the main results of [4] is the following.

Theorem 9. The morphism h_0 is injective. It follows that $\mathbf{Lg}$ is the variety of *all* bimonoids. □

For any labeled poset P, the words u in Ph_0 satisfy at least the following conditions:

(i) $|u|_a = |u|_{\overline{a}}$, for each $a \in A$. ($|u|_a$ is the number of occurrences of the letter a in the word u.)
(ii) If w is a prefix of u, $|w|_a \geq |w|_{\overline{a}}$, for each $a \in A$.

We say a word in $\Sigma(A)^*$ is balanced if it satisfies both conditions (i) and (ii).

Definition 10. A monoid endomorphism φ of $(A_N \cup \overline{A}_N)^*$ is **admissible** if, for each $a \in A$, $i \in \mathbf{N}$, there is some $j \in \mathbf{N}$ with

$$a_i\varphi = a_j, \quad \text{and}$$
$$\overline{a}_i\varphi = \overline{a}_j.$$

Thus, admissible morphisms only change subscripts on letters. For example, an admissible morphism may identify a_1 and a_2.

Definition 11. The preorder $\sqsubseteq$ on the set of (balanced) words in $\Sigma(A)^*$ is the least reflexive and transitive relation which satisfies the following conditions. $u \sqsubseteq u'$ if, for some words w, w' and distinct letters a_i, b_j,

$$u = wa_ib_jw' \text{ and } u' = wb_ja_iw'; \quad \text{or}$$
$$u = w\overline{a}_i\overline{b}_jw' \text{ and } u' = w\overline{b}_j\overline{a}_iw'; \quad \text{or}$$
$$u = w\overline{a}_ib_jw' \text{ and } u' = wb_j\overline{a}_iw'; \quad \text{or}$$
$$u = u'\varphi, \qquad \text{for some admissible } \varphi.$$

Definition 12. For A-labeled posets P, Q in $\mathbf{SP}(A)$, $P \leq Q$ iff for each word $u \in Ph_0$ there is a word $u' \in Qh_0$ with $u \sqsubseteq u'$. We call the order $\leq$ the **trace ordering** on $\mathbf{SP}(A)$ (see Remark 8).

We note some easy consequences of Definition 12.

Proposition 13. *For posets $P, Q \in \mathbf{SP}(A)$, the following are equivalent.*

1. $P \leq Q$
2. $Ph_0 \subseteq Qh_0$. □

Since h_0 is injective, the relation $\leq$ is a partial order on $\mathbf{SP}(A)$.

Remark 14. If u, v are words and $v \in Ph_0$, for some $P \in \mathbf{SP}(A)$, and if $u \sqsubseteq v$, then $u \in Ph_0$. It follows that for posets $P, Q \in \mathbf{SP}(A)$, $P \leq Q$ iff for each word u which is maximal in Ph_0 there is some word v which is maximal in Qh_0 with $u \sqsubseteq v$. Note that by the last clause in Definition 11, each letter occurs at most once in any maximal word.

Proposition 15. *Suppose that in $\mathbf{SP}(A)$, $P \leq P_1$ and $Q \leq Q_1$. Then*

$$P \cdot Q \leq P_1 \cdot Q_1 \quad \text{and} \quad P \otimes Q \leq P_1 \otimes Q_1.$$

Thus, $(\mathbf{SP}(A), \leq)$ is an ordered bimonoid in $\mathbf{Lg}_{\leq}$. □

Theorem 16. [4] For each set A, $(\mathbf{SP}(A), \leq)$ is the free ordered bimonoid in the variety of ordered bimonoids $\mathbf{Lg}_{\leq}$. □

For later use, we note several other properties of the trace order.

Lemma 17. *Suppose that $P \leq Q$ in $\mathbf{SP}(A)$. Then*

1. *For each $a \in A$, the number of vertices of P labeled a, $|P|_a$, is the same as $|Q|_a$;*
2. *The number of minimal elements in Q is at least the number of minimal elements in P;*
3. *The number of maximal elements in Q is at least the number of maximal elements in P;*
4. *The height of P is at least the height of Q;*
5. *The width of Q is at least the width of P.* □

3 A Metatheorem

In this section, we present a method to show that the variety $\mathbf{Lg}_{\leq}$ of ordered bimonoids defined above is not finitely axiomatizable. The method depends upon finding a sequence of posets P_n, P'_n satisfying certain properties.

Suppose that A is the singleton set $\{a\}$.

Theorem 18. Suppose that for each integer $n \geq 1$ there are posets P_n and P'_n in $\mathbf{SP}(A)$ with the following properties:

(P1) P'_n is a successor of P_n with respect to the trace ordering, so that $P_n < P'_n$ and for all P in $\mathbf{SP}(A)$, $P_n \leq P < P'_n$ implies $P = P_n$.

(P2) $|P_n| > n$.

(P3) P'_n does not have a nontrivial series decomposition.

(P4) There are no nonempty posets $U \leq U'$, $V \leq V'$ with $P_n = U \otimes V$ and $P'_n = U' \otimes V'$.

(P5) If

$$t(x_1, \ldots, x_k) \leq t'(x_1, \ldots, x_k)$$

is a valid inequation in $\mathbf{Lg}_{\leq}$ and

$$P_n = t(R_1, \ldots, R_k)$$
$$P'_n = t'(R_1, \ldots, R_k),$$

for some posets $R_1, \ldots, R_k$ in $\mathbf{SP}(A)$, then $|t| > n$.

Then the variety $\mathbf{Lg}_{\leq}$ is not finitely axiomatizable.

The number $|t|$ in condition (P5) denotes the number of occurrences of variables in t. Note that since $\mathbf{Lg}_{\leq} \models t \leq t'$, it follows that for each variable x_i, the number of occurrences of x_i in t is the same as the number of occurrences of x_i in t'. Thus $|t| = |t'|$. Note also that condition (P2) follows from (P5) and (P1): Let $t(x), t'(x)$ be terms such that $t(a) = P_n$ and $t'(a) = P_n'$.

The remainder of this section is devoted to the proof of Theorem 18.

Let E be a finite set of inequations between bimonoid terms with $\mathbf{Lg}_{\leq} \models E$. Let

$$n := \max\{|t|,\ |t'| : t \leq t' \in E\}$$

and $m := |P_n|$. Using the properties of the posets, we construct an ordered bimonoid B_E and terms $p(x)$ and $p'(x)$ such that:

1. $B_E \models E$;
2. $B_E \not\models p(x) \leq p'(x)$;
3. $\mathbf{Lg}_{\leq} \models p(x) \leq p'(x)$.

To construct B_E, consider the free bimonoid $\mathbf{SP}(A)$. The relation $\sim$ defined by

$$P \sim Q \Leftrightarrow |P|, |Q| > m \text{ or } P = Q,$$

is a bimonoid congruence relation on $\mathbf{SP}(A)$. The quotient $\mathbf{SP}(A)/\sim$ may be conveniently represented as the bimonoid whose elements are the labeled posets $P \in \mathbf{SP}(A)$ with $|P|$ at most m, and the element 0 which represents the congruence class of the posets P with $|P| > m$. The operations are defined in a straightforward manner.

Now we introduce a partial order on the bimonoid $\mathbf{SP}(A)/\sim$. For P, Q in $\mathbf{SP}(A)/\sim$, we define

$$P \sqsubseteq Q$$

iff $P = Q$, or $P, Q \neq 0$, $P \leq Q$, and either $P \neq P_n$ or $Q \neq P_n'$. Thus, for nonzero elements we keep the ordering in $\mathbf{SP}(A)$, except P_n and P_n' become unrelated. The element 0 is not comparable to any other element. Clearly, $\sqsubseteq$ is reflexive and antisymmetric.

Proposition 19. *If $P \sqsubset Q \sqsubset R$, then $P \sqsubset R$. Thus, $\sqsubseteq$ is a partial order.*

Proof. The only possible concern is $P = P_n$ and $R = P_n'$. But this is impossible, since P_n' is a successor of P_n in the trace ordering. □

The resulting structure, which we denote B_E, is an ordered bimonoid, since the fact that the operations are monotonic is immediate from (P3) and (P4).

Claim: B_E satisfies the inequations in E.

Suppose

$$t(x_1,\ldots,x_k) \leq t'(x_1,\ldots,x_k)$$

is in E. Since $\mathbf{Lg}_{\leq} \models E$, the variables which actually appear in t are the same as that appearing in t'. We may assume that these are the variables $x_1,\ldots,x_k$. Moreover, for each x_i, the number of occurrences of x_i in t is the same as the number of occurrences of x_i in t', in notation: $|t|_{x_i} = |t'|_{x_i}$. We need to show that

$$t(R_1,\ldots,R_k) \sqsubseteq t'(R_1,\ldots,R_k), \tag{1}$$

for all $R_1,\ldots,R_k$ in B_E. But the left hand side is 0 iff the right hand side is 0. If the two sides are nonzero, then the R_i's are nonzero, and the two sides are evaluated in B_E in the same way as in $\mathbf{SP}(A)$. Thus,

$$t(R_1,\ldots,R_k) \leq t'(R_1,\ldots,R_k).$$

But, by (P5) and the choice of the integer m, it is not possible that the left hand side is P_n and the right hand side is P_n', proving (1).

Claim: There is some inequation $p(x) \leq p'(x)$ which holds in $\mathbf{Lg}_{\leq}$ but not in B_E. Indeed, let $p(x)$ and $p'(x)$ be terms with $p(a) = P_n$ and $p'(a) = P_n'$ in $\mathbf{SP}(A)$. Since $P_n \leq P_n'$ in $\mathbf{SP}(A)$, $p(x) \leq p'(x)$ holds in $\mathbf{Lg}_{\leq}$, but fails in B_E, by construction.

Thus we have proved: If there are posets P_n, P_n' satisfying conditions (P1)–(P5), then for each finite set E of inequations which are valid in $\mathbf{Lg}_{\leq}$ there exists a finite ordered bimonoid B_E and a unary inequation $p(x) \leq p'(x)$ which holds in $\mathbf{Lg}_{\leq}$ but not in B_E.

Remark 20. It follows easily from the compactness theorem that there is no finite first order axiomatization of $\mathbf{Lg}_{\leq}$ either.

4 The Construction

In this section, we define the sequence of posets P_n and P_n' and prove a number of facts about the ordering of the posets in $\mathbf{SP}(A)$ in order to show the sequence has the properties (P1)–(P5) of Theorem 18. All posets are assumed to belong to $\mathbf{SP}(A)$, where A is a singleton set, say $A = \{a\}$.

The collection of posets in $\mathbf{SP}(B)$ with a unique maximal vertex and a unique minimal vertex is denoted $\mathbf{SP}_1(B)$.

For any poset $R \in \mathbf{SP}(B)$, where B contains the letter a, define the "top-bottom" of R, $tb(R)$ as follows:

$$tb(R) := a \cdot R \cdot a. \tag{2}$$

Thus, $tb(R)$ has a unique maximal and minimal element.

Definition 21. Define the following sequence of posets in $\mathbf{SP}(A)$.

$$P_1 = a \cdot a \tag{3}$$

$$P_1' = a \otimes a. \tag{4}$$

Assume P_n, P_n' defined so that P_n' is a successor of P_n.

$$P_{n+1} := (a \cdot tb(P_n)) \otimes (a \cdot tb(P_n)) \otimes (a \cdot tb(P_n')) \tag{5}$$

$$P_{n+1}' := a \cdot (tb(P_n) \otimes tb(P_n')) \otimes (a \otimes a) \cdot tb(P_n'). \tag{6}$$

The fact that the posets P_n, P_n' satisfy properties (P2),(P3) and (P4) of Theorem 18 is either immediate or follows easily from Lemma 17. Thus, it remains to establish properties (P1) and (P5).

It is clear that P_1' is the unique successor of P_1. ¿From Lemma 30 below, it follows that P_n' is a successor of P_n, for all $n \geq 1$.

Suppose that R is a poset in $\mathbf{SP}(A)$ having the minimal elements $x_1, x_2, \ldots$. Define the subposet R_i to consist of those vertices above only the one minimal vertex x_i:

$$R_i := \{v \in R : x_j \leq v \Rightarrow j = i\}. \tag{7}$$

Lemma 22. *The subposet R_i of R contains a maximal element of R iff*

$$R = R_i \otimes (R - R_i).$$

Proof. Clearly, if $R = R_i \otimes (R - R_i)$, then any vertex maximal in R_i is maximal in R. We prove the converse. Suppose that R_i contains the maximal vertex y_i. If $v \notin R_i$, then $v \geq x_j$ for some $j \neq i$. Thus for any $v' \in R_i$, it is impossible that $v' \geq v$. Conversely, if $v \geq v'$, the subposet of R consisting of y_i, x_i, v, x_j shows that R violates the "N-condition", and cannot belong to $\mathbf{SP}(A)$. (See Remark 6 for the "N-condition".) □

Lemma 23. *Suppose that the posets P_i, Q_i, $i \in [3]$, all belong to $\mathbf{SP}_1(A)$ and each has $N \geq 1$ vertices. Let $P := \otimes_{i=1}^3 P_i$, $Q := \otimes_{i=1}^3 Q_i$. If*

$$P \leq R \leq Q,$$

then there are posets $R_i, i \in [3]$ in $\mathbf{SP}_1(A)$ such that $R = \otimes_{i=1}^3 R_i$, and each R_i has size N.

Proof. We may assume $N > 1$ or else $P = R = Q$. Now by Lemma 17, R has 3 minimal and 3 maximal vertices. Suppose that $\{x_1, x_2, x_3\}$ are the minimal vertices and that $\{y_1, y_2, y_3\}$ are the maximal vertices in R. The poset R has no isolated vertex. (Indeed, if S, T are any posets in $\mathbf{SP}(A)$ such that $a \otimes S \leq T$ then $T = a \otimes T'$, for some $T' \in \mathbf{SP}(A)$.) Thus, the vertices x_i, y_j are all distinct. For an element $i \in [3]$, the set R_i was defined in (7).

Sublemma 24. – *Some set R_i has at least N vertices.*

– *No set R_i can have more than N vertices.*

– *One of the sets R_i which has exactly N vertices contains one of the maximal vertices y_j.*

– *None of the sets R_i can contain 2 maximal vertices.*

Proof. We show first that some set R_i has at least N vertices. Indeed, the word

$$u := a_1^3\bar{a}_1(a_2\bar{a}_2)^{N-1}\bar{a}_1(a_2\bar{a}_2)^{N-1}\bar{a}_1(a_2\bar{a}_2)^{N-1}$$

belongs to Ph_0 and hence to Rh_0. The vertices in R of any run with trace u (see Remark 8) corresponding to the first occurrence of $\bar{a}_1$ and the first $N-1$ a_2's belong to some set R_i. Hence this R_i has at least N vertices.

But no set R_i can have more than N vertices. Otherwise, there is a word

$$a_1^3\bar{a}_1(a_2\bar{a}_2)^k w$$

in Rh_0 where $k \geq N$, but there is no such word in Qh_0. Thus, some set R_i contains exactly N vertices.

One of the sets R_i which has exactly N vertices must contain one of the maximal vertices y_j. Indeed, otherwise, the word

$$a_1^3\bar{a}_1(a_2\bar{a}_2)^{N-2}a_3\bar{a}_1(a_2\bar{a}_2)^{N-2}a_3\bar{a}_1(a_2\bar{a}_2)^{N-2}a_3\bar{a}_3^3 \quad (8)$$

does not belong to Rh_0 even though it does belong to Ph_0.

Now we show none of the sets R_i can contain 2 maximal vertices. Indeed, if $|R_i| = k+3 \leq N$ and R_i contains two of the y_j, then there is a word

$$a_1^3\bar{a}_1(a_2\bar{a}_2)^k a_3a_3v\bar{a}_3\bar{a}_3$$

in Rh_0, where v does not contain $\bar{a}_3$. But there is no such word in Qh_0. □

Now suppose that R_1 has N vertices and contains the maximal element y_1, say. Then by Lemma 22,

$$R = R_1 \otimes (R - R_1).$$

Let $R' = (R - R_1)$. We now show $R' = R_2 \otimes R_3$. Note that $R_2 \cup R_3 \subseteq R'$. We know R' contains the two maximal vertices y_2, y_3 and the two minimal vertices x_2, x_3. Suppose, without loss of generality, that $y_2 > x_2$. Then it is impossible that $y_2 > x_3$. Otherwise, if $y_3 > x_2$ (or $y_3 > x_3$), the "N-condition" implies that both y_2 and y_3 are greater than both x_2 and x_3. But then, the word u of (8) is not in Rh_0 even though it belongs to Ph_0. Thus, $y_2 \in R_2$, showing that

$$R' = R_2 \otimes (R' - R_2),$$

by Lemma 22. But $R_3 = R' - R_2$, since R has only 3 minimal vertices. Thus,

$$R = R_1 \otimes R_2 \otimes R_3.$$

Since $|R_1| = N$, and $|R_2|, |R_3| \leq N$ and $|R| = 3N$, it follows that $|R_2| = |R_3| = N$, completing the proof of Lemma 23. □

Remark 25. Lemma 23 holds when 3 is replaced by any positive integer.

Lemma 26. *Suppose that Q is a successor of P, where $P, Q \in \mathbf{SP}_1(A)$, and that R_1, R_2, R_3 are posets in $\mathbf{SP}_1(A)$ with $|P| = |Q| = |R_1| = |R_2| = |R_3|$. If*

$$P \otimes P \otimes Q \ \leq\ R_1 \otimes R_2 \otimes R_3 \ \leq\ P \otimes Q \otimes Q,$$

then, for each $i \in [3]$, $R_i \in \{P, Q\}$ and either exactly one or exactly two of the R_i are equal to P.

Proof. First we show $P \leq R_i$, for each $i \in [3]$. Otherwise, there is a maximal word $a_1\overline{a}_1ua_2\overline{a}_2$ in Ph_0 which is not in R_ih_0. Then

$$a_1^3\overline{a}_1ua_2\overline{a}_2\overline{a}_1ua_2\overline{a}_2\overline{a}_1ua_2\overline{a}_2$$

is in $(P \otimes P \otimes Q)h_0$ but not in $(R_1 \otimes R_2 \otimes R_3)h_0$.

Now we show $R_i \leq Q$, for each $i \in [3]$. Otherwise, choose a word $a_1\overline{a}_1ua_2\overline{a}_2$ in R_ih_0 not in Qh_0 such that $a_1, \overline{a}_1$ do not occur in u. Since $P \leq Q$, this word does not occur in Ph_0 either. Then there is a word

$$a_1^3\overline{a}_1ua_2\overline{a}_2v$$

in $(R_1 \otimes R_2 \otimes R_3)h_0$ not in $(P \otimes Q \otimes Q)h_0$.

Since Q is a successor of P, it follows that either two of the R_i are P or exactly one R_i is P. □

Corollary 27. *Suppose that $P, Q \in \mathbf{SP}_1(A)$. If Q is a successor of P, then $P \otimes Q \otimes Q$ is a successor of $P \otimes P \otimes Q$.*

Proof. Suppose that

$$P \otimes P \otimes Q \ \leq\ R \ \leq\ P \otimes Q \otimes Q.$$

By Lemma 23, $R = R_1 \otimes R_2 \otimes R_3$, where P, Q and the R_i satisfy the hypotheses of Lemma 26. Hence, by that Lemma, $R = P \otimes Q \otimes Q$ or $R = P \otimes Q \otimes Q$. □

Lemma 28. *Suppose that P, Q belong to $\mathbf{SP}(A)$, and that Q is a successor of P. Then $tb(Q)$ is a successor of $tb(P)$, and both $tb(P)$ and $tb(Q)$ belong to $\mathbf{SP}_1(A)$.* □

Lemma 29. *Suppose that P, Q belong to $\mathbf{SP}(A)$ and that $P \leq Q$. Let P', Q' be defined by*

$$P' := (a \cdot P) \otimes (a \cdot P) \otimes (a \cdot Q)$$
$$Q' := (a \cdot (P \otimes Q)) \otimes ((a \otimes a) \cdot Q).$$

Then $P' \leq Q'$.

Proof. Up to an admissible bijection, each maximal word in $P'h_0$ is in either U_1 or U_2, where $K = Ph_0$ and $L = Qh_0$ and where

$$U_1 := a_1a_2a_3\overline{a}_1(K \otimes \overline{a}_2K \otimes \overline{a}_3L)$$
$$U_2 := a_1a_2a_3\overline{a}_1(L \otimes \overline{a}_2K \otimes \overline{a}_3K).$$

But, $K \subseteq L$, so that

$$(K \otimes \overline{a}_2K \otimes \overline{a}_3L) \subseteq (K \otimes \overline{a}_2L \otimes \overline{a}_3L).$$

The inequation

$$(x \cdot z) \otimes (y \cdot z) \leq z \otimes ((x \otimes y) \cdot z)$$

is valid in $\mathbf{SP}(A)$ (see [7]). Hence,

$$(K \otimes \overline{a}_2L \otimes \overline{a}_3L) \subseteq (K \otimes L \otimes (\overline{a}_2 \otimes \overline{a}_3)L).$$

Thus,

$$\begin{aligned} U_1 &\subseteq a_1a_2a_3\overline{a}_1(K \otimes L \otimes (\overline{a}_2 \otimes \overline{a}_3)L) \\ &\subseteq Q'h_0. \end{aligned}$$

Similarly,

$$\begin{aligned} L \otimes \overline{a}_2K \otimes \overline{a}_3K &\subseteq L \otimes K \otimes (\overline{a}_2 \otimes \overline{a}_3)K \\ &\subseteq K \otimes L \otimes (\overline{a}_2 \otimes \overline{a}_3)L, \end{aligned}$$

so that

$$\begin{aligned} U_2 &\subseteq a_1a_2a_3\overline{a}_1(K \otimes L \otimes (\overline{a}_2 \otimes \overline{a}_3)L) \\ &\subseteq Q'h_0. \quad \square \end{aligned}$$

Lemma 30. *Suppose that P, Q belong to $\mathbf{SP}_1(A)$ and that Q is a successor of P. Let P', Q' be defined by*

$$P' := (a \cdot P) \otimes (a \cdot P) \otimes (a \cdot Q)$$
$$Q' := (a \cdot (P \otimes Q)) \otimes ((a \otimes a) \cdot Q).$$

Then Q' is a successor of P'.

Proof. Lemma 29 showed that $P' \leq Q'$. Suppose that

$$P' \leq R \leq Q'.$$

R must have 3 minimal vertices. Let R_1 denote the poset in $\mathbf{SP}(A)$ obtained from R by deleting the minimal vertices. Let $P_1 := P \otimes P \otimes Q$ and $Q_1 := P \otimes Q \otimes Q$.

We claim that $P_1 \leq R_1 \leq Q_1$. Indeed, if $R_1 \not\leq Q_1$, there is a word $u \in R_1h_0 - Q_1h_0$. Then $a_1^3\overline{a}_1^3u \in Rh_0 - Q'h_0$, a contradiction. Similarly, $P_1 \leq R_1$. But, since Q_1 is a successor of P_1 by Lemma 27, it follows that $R_1 = P_1$ or $R_1 = Q_1$. Thus, R_1 has 3 connected components, each having a unique minimal element.

Suppose that the minimal elements of R_1 are y_1, y_2, y_3. But R itself has three minimal elements, say x_1, x_2, x_3. Each y_i is a successor of at least one x_j. Up to isomorphism, there are only two possible posets determined by the order relations among the x_i's and y_j's:

$$(x_1 \cdot y_1) \otimes (x_2 \cdot y_2) \otimes (x_3 \cdot y_3) \tag{9}$$

or

$$((x_1 \otimes x_2) \cdot y_1) \otimes (x_3 \cdot (y_2 \otimes y_3)). \tag{10}$$

Indeed, if, for example, the ordering were

$$((x_1 \otimes x_2) \cdot (y_1 \otimes y_2)) \otimes (x_3 \cdot y_3),$$

then the word

$$a_1^3 \overline{a}_1 (a_2 \overline{a}_2)^K \overline{a}_1 (a_2 \overline{a}_2)^K \overline{a}_1 (a_2 \overline{a}_2)^K$$

would be in $P'h_0 - Rh_0$, where $K = |P| \geq 2$.

Note that by the "N-condition" (see Remark 6), in case (9) it is impossible that x_i is below any vertex above x_j, when $i \neq j$. In case (10), x_3 is not below any vertex above both x_1 and x_2, and neither x_1 nor x_2 is below any vertex above x_3.

We now consider the two cases separately.

Case (9). In this case, either

$$R = (a \cdot P) \otimes (a \cdot P) \otimes (a \cdot Q) \; = \; P', \text{ or} \tag{11}$$

$$R = (a \cdot P) \otimes (a \cdot Q) \otimes (a \cdot Q). \tag{12}$$

We show that (12) is impossible. Indeed, if v is a word in $Qh_0 - Ph_0$ and u is a word in Ph_0, neither of which contain the letters $a_1, \overline{a}_1$, then

$$a_1^3 \overline{a}_1 v \overline{a}_1 v \overline{a}_1 u \in Rh_0 - Q'h_0.$$

Case (10). In this case, either

$$R = a \cdot (P \otimes Q) \otimes (a \otimes a) \cdot Q \; = \; Q', \;\text{ or} \tag{13}$$

$$R = a \cdot (Q \otimes Q) \otimes (a \otimes a) \cdot P, \;\text{ or,} \tag{14}$$

$$R = a \cdot (P \otimes Q) \otimes (a \otimes a) \cdot P, \;\text{ or,} \tag{15}$$

$$R = a \cdot (P \otimes P) \otimes (a \otimes a) \cdot Q. \tag{16}$$

We show each of the last three possibilities leads to a contradiction. Choose maximal words v in $Qh_0 - Ph_0$ and $u \in Ph_0$, neither of which contain the letters $a_1, \overline{a}_1$.

(15) and (16) are impossible. Otherwise $P' \not\leq R$. Indeed, if (15) holds,

$$a_1^3 \overline{a}_1 u \overline{a}_1 u \overline{a}_1 v \in P'h_0 - Rh_0.$$

And if (16) holds,

$$a_1^3 \overline{a}_1 v \overline{a}_1 u \overline{a}_1 u \in P'h_0 - Rh_0.$$

(14) is impossible: otherwise $R \not\leq Q'$. Indeed, writing $v = a_i \overline{a}_i v'$,

$$a_1^3 \overline{a}_1 a_i a_i \overline{a}_i v' \overline{a}_i v' \overline{a}_1 \overline{a}_1 u \in Rh_0 - Q'h_0.$$

The proof of Lemma 30 is complete. □

Corollary 31. *For each $n \geq 1$, P'_n is a successor of P_n. Thus property (P1) of Theorem 18 is established.* □

We now establish property (P5) in the following form.

Lemma 32. *Suppose that B is any set containing the letter 'a'. Suppose that $Q \leq Q' \in \mathbf{SP}(B)$ and $\varphi : \mathbf{SP}(B) \to \mathbf{SP}(A)$ is an ordered bimonoid morphism such that $Q\varphi = P_n$ and $Q'\varphi = P'_n$. Then $|Q| > n$.*

Proof. We may assume that $b\varphi \neq 1$, all $b \in B$, and that $b\varphi = a \Rightarrow b = a$. We use induction on n. The case $n = 1$ is clear. Suppose that $Q \leq Q'$ and that $Q\varphi = P_{n+1}$ and $Q'\varphi = P'_{n+1}$. It is easy to see that

$$Q = (a \cdot Q_1) \otimes (a \cdot Q_2) \otimes (a \otimes Q_3)$$
$$Q' = (a \cdot (Q'_1 \otimes Q'_2)) \otimes ((a \otimes a) \cdot Q'_3),$$

where

$$Q_i\varphi = tb(P_n), \quad i = 1, 2 \quad \text{and} \quad Q_3\varphi = tb(P'_n)$$
$$Q'_1\varphi = tb(P_n) \quad \text{and} \quad Q'_j\varphi = tb(P'_n), \quad j = 2, 3.$$

The posets Q_i, Q'_i, $i \in [3]$, have a unique maximal and minimal element.

Sublemma 33. *Suppose that R_i, R'_i, $i = 1, 2$, are posets in $\mathbf{SP}_1(B)$ such that*

$$R_1 \otimes R_2 \leq R'_1 \otimes R'_2.$$

Then either $R_1 \leq R'_2$ or $R_2 \leq R'_2$.

Proof. In order to obtain a contradiction, assume that u_i is a maximal word in $R_i ho - R'_2 ho$, $i = 1, 2$. We may assume that

$$u_1 = x\overline{x}v_1 y\overline{y}$$
$$u_2 = x'\overline{x'}v_2 y'\overline{y'}$$

where x, y, x', y' are distinct letters in $\Sigma(B)$ and where v_1 and v_2 have no letter in common and do not contain the symbols $x, y, x', y', \overline{x}, \overline{y}, \overline{x'}, \overline{y'}$. Then

$$xx'\overline{x}v_1 yx'v_2 y'\overline{y}\overline{y'} \in R_1 ho \otimes R_2 ho - (R'_1 ho \otimes R'_2 ho). \quad \square$$

Note that by symmetry, with the assumptions of Sublemma 33, also $R_1 \leq R'_1$ or $R_2 \leq R'_1$.

Sublemma 34. *Suppose that R_i, R'_i, $i \in [3]$, belong to $\mathbf{SP}_1(B)$. Let*

$$R := (a \cdot R_1) \otimes (a \cdot R_2) \otimes (a \cdot R_3)$$
$$R' := (a \cdot (R'_1 \otimes R'_2)) \otimes ((a \otimes a) \cdot R'_3).$$

Then if $R \leq R'$, then

$$R_1 \otimes R_2 \leq R'_1 \otimes R'_2$$
$$R_3 \leq R'_3, \quad \text{and}$$
$$|R_1| = |R_2| = |R_3|.$$

Of course, by symmetry, also many more relations hold, e.g.,

$$R_1 \otimes R_3 \leq R_1' \otimes R_2'$$
$$R_2 \leq R_3'.$$

Proof of Sublemma 34. First, we show $|R_1| + |R_2| = |R_1'| + |R_2'|$. Let $u_i \in R_i h_0$ be maximal, $i \in [3]$, and assume the three words have no letter in common and do not contain the letter a_1. Write

$$u_i = u_i' y_i \overline{y}_i,$$

where $y_i, i \in [3]$, are letters. Since the word

$$w := a_1^3 \overline{a}_1 u_1' y_1 \overline{a}_1 u_2' y_2 \overline{a}_1 u_3' y_3 \overline{y}_1 \overline{y}_2 \overline{y}_3$$

is in Rh_0 and since $R \leq R'$, we know $w \in R'h_0$. This is possible only if $|R_1| + |R_2| = |R_1'| + |R_2'|$. By symmetry, $|R_1| + |R_3| = |R_1'| + |R_2'|$ and $|R_2| + |R_3| = |R_1'| + |R_2'|$. Hence,

$$|R_1| = |R_2| = |R_3| = N, \text{ say.}$$

Then, $|R_1'| + |R_2'| = 2N$ and $|R_3'| = N$. But then

$$R_1 \otimes R_2 \leq R_1' \otimes R_2' \quad \text{and} \quad R_3 \leq R_3'.$$

Indeed, let $u \in (R_1 \otimes R_2)h_0$ be a word not containing the symbol a_1. Let $v \in R_3 h_0$ have no letter in common with u. Then

$$w := a_1^3 \overline{a}_1 \overline{a}_1 u \overline{a}_1 v \in Rh_0,$$

so that $w \in R'h_0$. But this can happen only if $u \in (R_1' \otimes R_2')h_0$ and $v \in R_3' h_0$. □

Proof of Lemma 32, completed. By Sublemmas 34 and 33, it follows that $Q_1 \leq Q_2'$ or $Q_2 \leq Q_2'$. Suppose that $Q_2 \leq Q_2'$. Since $Q_2\varphi = tb(P_n)$ and $Q_2'\varphi = tb(P_n')$, we have $Q_2 = tb(\overline{Q}_2)$ and $Q_2' = tb(\overline{Q_2'})$, where $\overline{Q}_2\varphi = P_n$ and $\overline{Q_2'}\varphi = P_n'$. By the induction assumption, $|\overline{Q}_2| > n$, so that $|Q_2| > n+2$, showing $|Q| > n+1$. □

Remark 35. With a different argument, we can show that the posets P_n and P_n' satisfy the following stronger version of (P5). For all terms $t(x_1, ..., x_k)$ and $t'(x_1, ..., x_k)$ such that each variable x_i occurs the same number of times in t as in t', if $P_n = t(Q_1, ..., Q_k)$ and $P_n' = t'(Q_1, ..., Q_k)$, for some posets Q_j in $\mathbf{SP}(A)$, then $|t| > n$.

5 Final Remarks

Although in the last section we formulated most of the lemmas only for the case that A is a singleton, several of them hold for larger alphabets. The assumption that A is a singleton made some proofs notationally simpler.

After proving the metatheorem Theorem 18, the nontrivial task was to find the actual posets P_n, P_n' satisfying (P1)–(P5). The difficulty was finding the balance among the various properties. According to (P1), P_n and P'_n should be close to one another. But, by (P4) and (P5), their structure should be very different. By (P4), they cannot have a parallel decomposition into nontrivial posets related by the trace ordering, again a property that says they are far from one another. The particular construction we used was not forced. In particular, we might have made the following definitions:

$$P_{n+1} := ((a \otimes a) \cdot tb(P_n)) \otimes ((a \otimes a) \cdot tb(P'_n))$$
$$P'_{n+1} := (a \cdot tb(P'_n)) \otimes ((a \otimes a \otimes a) \cdot tb(P'_n)).$$

The proof for this choice is similar.

The lemmas proved in Section 4 do not give a full account of the order structure of $\mathbf{SP}(A)$, but are sufficient for the present paper. We plan to give a systematic account of this topic, together with some other results, in a future paper.

6 Acknowledgments

The second author would like to thank Volker Diekert and the Theory Group at the Institute of Computer Science of the University of Stuttgart for their hospitality. We both thank László Bernátsky for his very careful proof reading.

References

1. L. Aceto. Full abstraction for series-parallel pomsets. In *Proceedings of TAPSOFT '91*, volume 493 of *Lecture Notes in Computer Science*, pages 1–40. Springer-Verlag, 1991.
2. L. Aceto and M. Hennessy. Towards action refinement in process algebras. *Information and Computation*, 103(2):204–269, 1993.
3. S. L. Bloom. Varieties of ordered algebras. *Journal of Computer and System Sciences*, 45:200–212, 1976.
4. S. L. Bloom and Z. Ésik. Free Shuffle Algebras in Language Varieties. To appear. Obtainable by anonymous ftp from `menger.eecs.stevens-tech.edu` in directory `pub/bloom/shuffle`.
5. Z. Ésik and M. Bertol. Nonfinite axiomatizability of the equational theory of shuffle. To appear.
6. Jay Loren Gischer. *Partial Orders and the Axiomatic Theory of Shuffle*. PhD thesis, Stanford University, Computer Science Dept., 1984.
7. Jay Loren Gischer. The equational theory of pomsets. *Theoretical Computer Science*, 61:199–224, 1988.
8. Jan Grabowski. On partial languages. *Fundamenta Informatica*, IV(2):427–498, 1981.
9. Vaughan Pratt. Modeling concurrency with partial orders. *International Journal of Parallel Processing*, 15(1):33–71, 1986.
10. J. Valdes, R. E. Tarjan, and E. L. Lawler. The recognition of series-parallel digraphs. *SIAM Journal of Computing*, 11(2):298–313, 1981.

On the Category of Petri Net Computations

In Memory and Dedication to my Beloved mother Liana

Vladimiro Sassone[◇]

BRICS* – Computer Science Dept., University of Aarhus

Abstract. We introduce the notion of *strongly concatenable process* as a refinement of concatenable processes [3] which can be expressed axiomatically via a *functor* $\mathcal{Q}[\_]$ from the category of Petri nets to an appropriate category of symmetric strict monoidal categories, in the precise sense that, for each net N, the strongly concatenable processes of N are isomorphic to the arrows of $\mathcal{Q}[N]$. In addition, we identify a *coreflection* right adjoint to $\mathcal{Q}[\_]$ and characterize its *replete image*, thus yielding an axiomatization of the category of net computations.

Introduction

Petri nets, introduced by C.A. Petri [8] (see also [10]), are unanimously considered among the most representative *models for concurrency*, since they are a fairly simple and natural model of *concurrent* and *distributed* computations. However, Petri nets are, in our opinion, not yet completely understood.

Among the semantics proposed for Petri nets, a relevant role is played by the various notions of *process* [9, 4, 1], whose merit is to provide a faithful account of computations involving many different transitions and of the *causal connections* between the events occurring in a computation. However, process models, at least in their standard forms, fail to bring to the foreground the *algebraic structure* of nets and their computations. Since such a structure is relevant to the understanding of nets, they fail, in our view, to give a comprehensive account of net behaviours.

The idea of looking at nets as *algebraic structures* [10, 7, 13, 14, 2] has been given an original interpretation by considering monoidal categories as a suitable framework [6]. In fact, in [6, 3] the authors have shown that the semantics of Petri nets can be understood in terms of *symmetric monoidal categories*—where objects are states, arrows processes, and the tensor product and the arrow composition model, respectively, the operations of parallel and sequential composition of processes. In particular, [3] introduced *concatenable processes*—the slightest variation of Goltz-Reisig processes [4] on which sequential composition can be defined—and structured the concatenable processes of a Petri net N as the arrows of the symmetric strict monoidal category $\mathcal{P}[N]$. This yields an axiomatization of the causal behaviour of a net as an *essentially algebraic theory* and thus provides a *unification* of the process and the algebraic view of net computations.

However, also this construction is somehow unsatisfactory, since it is not functorial. More strongly, given a morphism between two nets, i.e., a *simulation* between them, it may not be possible to identify a corresponding monoidal functor between the respective categories of computations. This fact, besides

* **Basic Research in Computer Science, Centre of the Danish National Research Foundation.**

◇ **Supported by EU Human Capital and Mobility grant ERBCHBGCT920005.**

showing that our understanding of the algebraic structure of Petri nets is still incomplete, prevents us from identifying the ***category*** (of the categories) ***of net computations***, i.e., from axiomatizing the behaviour of Petri nets 'in the large'.

This paper presents an analysis of this issue and a solution based on the new notion of ***strongly concatenable processes***, introduced in Section 4. These are a slight refinement of concatenable processes which are still rather close to the standard notion process: they are Goltz-Reisig processes whose minimal and maximal places are linearly ordered. In the paper we show that, similarly to concatenable processes, also this new notion can be axiomatized as an algebraic construction on N by providing an abstract symmetric strict monoidal category $\mathcal{Q}[N]$ whose arrows are in one-to-one correspondence with the strongly concatenable processes of N. The category $\mathcal{Q}[N]$ constitutes our proposed axiomatization of the behaviour of N in categorical terms.

Corresponding directly to the linear ordering of pre- and post-sets which characterizes strongly concatenable processes, the key feature of $\mathcal{Q}[\_]$ is that, differently from $\mathcal{P}[\_]$, it associates to the net N a monoidal category whose objects form a free ***non-commutative*** monoid. The reason for renouncing to commutativity when passing from $\mathcal{P}[\_]$ to $\mathcal{Q}[\_]$, a choice that at first may seem odd, is explained in Section 2, where the following negative result is proved: under very reasonable assumptions, ***no*** mapping from nets to symmetric strict monoidal categories whose monoids of objects are commutative can be lifted to a functor, since there exists a morphism of nets which *cannot* be extended to a ***monoidal*** functor between the appropriate categories. Thus, abandoning the commutativity of the monoids of objects and considering ***strings*** as representatives of multisets, i.e., considering strongly concatenable processes, seem to be a choice forced upon us by the aim of a functorial algebraic semantics of nets. As a consequence of this choice, any transition of N has many corresponding arrows in $\mathcal{Q}[N]$, actually one for each linearization of its pre-set and of its post-set. However, such arrows are 'related' to each other by a ***naturality*** condition, in the precise sense that, when collected together, they form a natural transformation between appropriate functors. This naturality axiom is the second relevant feature of $\mathcal{Q}[\_]$ and it is actually the key to keep the computational interpretation of the new category $\mathcal{Q}[N]$, i.e., the strongly concatenable processes, surprisingly close to that of $\mathcal{P}[N]$, i.e., the concatenable processes.

Concerning our main issue, *viz.* functoriality, in Section 3 we introduce a category $\underline{\mathsf{TSSMC}}^{\otimes}$ of symmetric strict monoidal categories with free non-commutative monoids of objects, called *symmetric Petri categories*, whose arrows are equivalence classes—accounting for our view of strings as representatives of multisets—of those symmetric strict monoidal functors which preserve some further structure related to nets, and we show that $\mathcal{Q}[\_]$ is a functor from $\underline{\mathsf{Petri}}$, a rich category of nets introduced in [6], to $\underline{\mathsf{TSSMC}}^{\otimes}$. In addition, we prove that $\mathcal{Q}[\_]$ has a ***coreflection*** right adjoint $\mathcal{N}[\_]\colon \underline{\mathsf{TSSMC}}^{\otimes} \to \underline{\mathsf{Petri}}$. This implies, by general reasons, that $\underline{\mathsf{Petri}}$ is ***equivalent*** to an easily identified coreflective subcategory of $\underline{\mathsf{TSSMC}}^{\otimes}$, namely the ***replete image*** of $\mathcal{Q}[\_]$. The category $\underline{\mathsf{TSSMC}}^{\otimes}$, together with the functors $\mathcal{Q}[\_]$ and $\mathcal{N}[\_]$, constitutes our proposed axiomatization ('in the large') of Petri net computations in categorical terms.

Although this contribution is a first attempt towards the aims of a functorial algebraic semantics for nets and of an axiomatization of net behaviours 'in the large', we think that the results given here help to deepen the understanding of the subject. We remark that the refinement of concatenable processes into strongly concatenable processes is similar and comparable to the one which brought from Goltz-Reisig processes to them, and that the result of Section 2 makes strongly concatenable processes 'unavoidable' if a functorial construction is desired. In addition, from the categorical viewpoint, our approach is quite natural, since it is the one which simply observes that multisets are equivalence classes of strings and then takes into account the categorical paradigm, following which one always prefers to add suitable isomorphisms between objects rather than considering explicitly equivalence classes of them. Finally, concerning the use of category theory in semantics, and in particular in this paper, it may be appropriate to observe here that the categorical framework made it possible to discover and amend a significant 'anomaly' of $\mathcal{P}[\_]$ which, although of general relevance, would have not been easily noticed in other frameworks.

Due to the extended abstract nature of this exposition, most of the proofs are omitted. Some preliminary related results appear also in [11].

Notation. When dealing with a category $\underline{\mathsf{C}}$ in which arrows are meant to represent computations, in order to stress their computational interpretation, we write arrow composition from left to right, i.e., in the diagrammatic order, and we denote it by $\_;\_$. The reader is referred to [5] for the categorical concepts used.

Acknowledgements. I wish to thank José Meseguer and Ugo Montanari to whom I am indebted for several discussions on the subject. Thanks to Mogens Nielsen, Claudio Hermida and Jaap van Oosten for their valuable comments on an early version of this paper.

1 Concatenable Processes

In this section we recall the notion of concatenable processes [3].

Notation. Given a set S, we denote by $S^\oplus$ the set of *finite multisets* of S, i.e., the set of all functions from S to the set ω of natural numbers which yield nonzero values only on finitely many $s \in S$. We recall that $S^\oplus$ is a *commutative monoid*, actually the *free* commutative monoid on S, under the operation of multiset union, in the following denoted by $\oplus$, with unit element the empty multiset 0.

Definition 1.1 *(Petri Nets)*
A Petri net is a structure $N = (\partial_N^0, \partial_N^1 : T_N \to S_N^\oplus)$, where T_N is a set of transitions, S_N is a set of places, and ∂_N^0 and ∂_N^1 are functions.
A morphism of Petri nets from N_0 to N_1 is a pair $\langle f, g\rangle$, where $f: T_{N_0} \to T_{N_1}$ is a function and $g: S_{N_0}^\oplus \to S_{N_1}^\oplus$ is a monoid homomorphism such that $\langle f, g\rangle$ respects source and target, i.e., $\partial_{N_1}^i \circ f = g \circ \partial_{N_0}^i$, for $i = 0, 1$.
This defines the category $\underline{\mathsf{Petri}}$ of Petri nets.

This describes a Petri net precisely as a graph whose set of nodes is a free commutative monoid, i.e., the set of *finite multisets* on a given set of *places*. The source and target of an arc, here called a *transition*, are meant to represent, respectively, the *markings* consumed and produced by the firing of the transition.

Definition 1.2 *(Process Nets and Processes)*
A process net is a finite, acyclic net Θ such that for all $t \in T_\Theta$, $\partial^0_\Theta(t)$ and $\partial^1_\Theta(t)$ are sets (as opposed to multisets), and for all $t_0 \neq t_1 \in T_\Theta$, $\partial^i_\Theta(t_0) \cap \partial^i_\Theta(t_1) = \varnothing$, for $i = 0, 1$. Given $N \in$ Petri, a process of N is a morphism $\pi\colon \Theta \to N$, where Θ is a process net and π is a net morphism which maps places to places (as opposed to morphisms which map places to markings).

We consider as identical process nets which are isomorphic. Consequently, we shall make no distinction between two processes $\pi\colon \Theta \to N$ and $\pi'\colon \Theta' \to N$ for which there exists an isomorphism $\varphi\colon \Theta \to \Theta'$ such that $\pi' \circ \varphi = \pi$.

The equivalence of the following definition of $\mathcal{P}[N]$ with the original one in [3] has been proved in [12]. The reader is referred to the cited works for a more explicit description of $\mathcal{P}[N]$, a wider discussion, and for related examples.

Definition 1.3 *(The Category $\mathcal{P}[N]$)*
The category $\mathcal{P}[N]$ is the monoidal quotient of $\mathfrak{F}(N)$, the symmetric strict monoidal category whose monoid of objects is $S_N^\oplus$ and whose arrows are freely generated from the transitions of N, modulo the axioms

$$\begin{aligned} \gamma_{a,b} &= id_{a\oplus b} && \text{if } a, b \in S_N \text{ and } a \neq b, \\ t\,;(id_u \otimes \gamma_{a,a} \otimes id_v) &= t && \text{if } t \in T_N \text{ and } a \in S_N, \\ (id_u \otimes \gamma_{a,a} \otimes id_v)\,;t &= t && \text{if } t \in T_N \text{ and } a \in S_N, \end{aligned}$$

where γ is the symmetry isomorphism of $\mathfrak{F}(N)$.

The arrows of $\mathcal{P}[N]$ have a nice computational interpretation as *concatenable processes*, a slight refinement of the classical notion of process consisting of a suitable labelling of the minimal and the maximal places of process nets which distinguishes among the different instances of a place in a process of N. The role of the *symmetries*—which in a symmetric monoidal category are the arrows generated via tensor and composition from the components of the symmetry isomorphism and the identities—is to *regulate the flow of causality* between subprocesses by permuting instances of places appropriately, i.e., by exchanging causes. In this view, the first axiom says that permuting different places does not change the causal relationships, and the remaining two that the same happens when permuting places in the pre- and in the post-set of a transition. Using the labels, it is then easy to define an operation of concatenation of concatenable processes and, thus, a category $\mathcal{CP}[N]$ whose objects are the multisets $S_N^\oplus$ and whose arrows are the concatenable processes of N. It has been proved in [3] that $\mathcal{CP}[N]$ is a symmetric strict monoidal category and that the following result holds.

Theorem 1.4 *(Concatenable Processes* vs. *$\mathcal{P}[\_]$)*
$\mathcal{CP}[N]$ and $\mathcal{P}[N]$ are isomorphic.

2 A Negative Result about Functoriality

Among the primary requirements usually imposed on constructions like $\mathcal{P}[\_]$ there is that of *functoriality*. One of the main reasons supporting the choice of a categorical treatment of semantics is the need of specifying further the structure of the systems under analysis by giving explicitly the morphisms or, in other words, by specifying how the given systems simulate each other. This, in turn, means to choose precisely what the relevant (behavioural) structure of the systems is. It is then clear that such morphisms should be preserved at the semantic level. In our case, the functoriality of $\mathcal{P}[\_]$ means that if N can be mapped to N' via a morphism $\langle f, g\rangle$, which by the very definition of net morphisms implies that N can be simulated by N', there must be a way, namely $\mathcal{P}[\langle f, g\rangle]$, to see the processes of N as processes of N'. However, this is not possible for $\mathcal{P}[\_]$. The problem, as illustrated by the following example, is due to the first axiom in Definition 1.3 which, on the other hand, is exactly what makes $\mathcal{P}[N]$ capture quite precisely the notion of processes of N.

EXAMPLE 2.1 *($\mathcal{P}[\_]$ cannot be a functor)*
Consider the nets N and $\bar{N}$ in the picture below, where we use the standard graphical representation of nets in which circles are places, boxes are transitions, and sources and targets are directed arcs. We have $S_N = \{a_0, a_1, b_0, b_1\}$ and T_N consisting of the transitions $t_0\colon a_0 \to b_0$ and $t_1\colon a_1 \to b_1$, while $S_{\bar{N}} = \{\bar{a}, \bar{b}_0, \bar{b}_1\}$ and $T_{\bar{N}}$ contains $\bar{t}_0\colon \bar{a} \to \bar{b}_0$ and $\bar{t}_1\colon \bar{a} \to \bar{b}_1$.

Consider now the net morphism $\langle f, g\rangle$ where $f(t_i) = \bar{t}_i$, $g(a_i) = \bar{a}$ and $g(b_i) = \bar{b}_i$, for $i = 0, 1$. We claim that $\langle f, g\rangle$ cannot be extended to a monoidal functor $\mathcal{P}[\langle f, g\rangle]$ from $\mathcal{P}[N]$ to $\mathcal{P}[\bar{N}]$. Suppose in fact that F is such an extension. Then, it must be $\mathsf{F}(t_0 \otimes t_1) = \mathsf{F}(t_0) \otimes \mathsf{F}(t_1) = \bar{t}_0 \otimes \bar{t}_1$. Moreover, since $t_0 \otimes t_1 = t_1 \otimes t_0$, we would have

$$\bar{t}_0 \otimes \bar{t}_1 = \mathsf{F}(t_1 \otimes t_0) = \bar{t}_1 \otimes \bar{t}_0,$$

which is impossible since the leftmost and the rightmost terms above are different processes in $\mathcal{P}[\bar{N}]$, as follows from Definition 1.3.

Formally speaking, the problem is that the category of symmetries sitting inside $\mathcal{P}[N]$, say Sym_N, is *not free* on N. Moreover, it is easy to verify that as soon as one imposes axioms on $\mathcal{P}[N]$ which guarantee to get a functor, one annihilates all the symmetries and, therefore, destroys the ability of $\mathcal{P}[N]$ of dealing with causality. It is important to observe that it would be definitely *meaningless* to try to overcome the problem simply by dropping from Petri the morphisms which 'behave badly': the morphism $\langle f, g\rangle$ of Example 2.1, for instance, is clearly a *simulation* and, as such, it should definitely be allowed by any serious attempt to formulate a definition of net morphisms. The following result shows that the problem illustrated in Example 2.1 is serious, actually deep enough to prevent any naive modification of $\mathcal{P}[\_]$ from being functorial.

THEOREM 2.2 *(No simple variation of $\mathcal{P}[\_]$ can be a functor)*
Let $\mathcal{X}[\_]$ be a function which assigns to each net N a symmetric strict monoidal category whose monoid of objects is commutative and contains the places of N. Suppose that the group of symmetries at any object of $\mathcal{X}[N]$ is finite and suppose that there exists a net N with a place $a \in N$ such that, for each $n > 1$, we have that the components at (na, na) of the symmetry isomorphism of $\mathcal{X}[N]$ is not an identity. Then, there exists a Petri net morphism $\langle f, g\rangle: N_0 \to N_1$ which cannot be extended to a symmetric strict monoidal functor from $\mathcal{X}[N_0]$ to $\mathcal{X}[N_1]$.

Proof. (Sketch.) Let N' be a net such that, for each n, we have $c'_{na,na} \neq id$, where c' is the symmetry natural isomorphism of $\mathcal{X}[N']$, and let N be a net with two distinct places a and b and with *no* transitions, and let c' be the symmetry natural isomorphism of $\mathcal{X}[N]$. Since the group of symmetries at ab is finite, there is a *cyclic* subgroup generated by $c_{a,b}$, i.e., there exists $k > 1$, the order of the subgroup, such that $(c_{a,b})^k = id$ and $(c_{a,b})^n \neq id$ for any $1 \leq n < k$. Let p be any prime number greater than k. Then, exploiting general properties of monoidal categories and reasoning as in Example 2.1, one sees that the Petri net morphism $\langle f, g\rangle: N \to N'$, where f is the function $\varnothing \to T_{N'}$ and g is the monoid homomorphism such that $g(b) = (p-1)a$ and g is the identity on the other places of N, cannot be extended to a symmetric strict monoidal functor $\mathsf{F}: \mathcal{X}[N] \to \mathcal{X}[N']$. ✓

The contents of the previous theorem can be restated in different terms by saying that in the *free* category of symmetries on a commutative monoid M there are *infinite* homsets. This means that dropping axiom $\gamma_{a,b} = id_{a\oplus b}$ in the definition of $\mathcal{P}[N]$ causes an 'explosion' of the structure of the symmetries. More precisely, if we omit that axiom we can find some object u such that the group of symmetries on u has infinite order. Of course, since symmetries represent causality, and as such they are integral parts of processes, this makes the category so obtained completely useless for the application we have in mind.

The hypotheses of Theorem 2.2 can be certainly weakened in several ways, at the expense of complicating the proof. However, we avoided such complications since the conditions stated above are *already* weak enough if one wants to regard $\mathcal{X}[N]$ as a category of processes of N. In fact, since places represent the atomic bricks of which states are built, one needs to consider them in $\mathcal{X}[N]$, since symmetries regulate the 'flow of causality', there will be $c_{na,na}$ different from the identity, and since in a computation we can have only finitely many 'causality streams', there will not be categories with infinite groups of symmetries. Therefore, the given result means that there is no chance to have a functorial construction along the lines of $\mathcal{P}[\_]$ for the categories of processes of Petri nets if their objects form commutative monoids.

3 The Category $\mathcal{Q}[N]$

In this section we introduce the symmetric strict monoidal category $\mathcal{Q}[N]$ which is meant to represent the processes of the Petri net N and which supports a functorial construction. This will allow us to characterize the category of the categories of net behaviours, i.e., to axiomatize net behaviours 'in the large'.

Theorem 2.2 shows that, necessarily, there is a price to be payed. Here, the idea is to renounce to the commutativity of the monoids of objects. More precisely, we build the arrows of $\mathcal{Q}[N]$ starting from the Sym^*_N, the 'free' category of symmetries over the set S_N of places of N. Similarly to Sym_N, Sym^*_N serves a double purpose: from the categorical point of view it provides the symmetry isomorphism of a symmetric monoidal category, while from a semantic perspective it regulates the flow of causal dependency. Generally speaking, a symmetry in $\mathcal{Q}[N]$ should be interpreted as a *'reorganization'* of the tokens in the global state of the net which, when reorganizing multiple instances of the same place, yields a exchange of causes exactly as Sym_N does for $\mathcal{P}[N]$.

Notation. In the following, we use $S^\otimes$ to indicate the set of (finite) strings on set S, more commonly denoted by S^*. In the same way, we use $\otimes$ to denote string concatenation, while 0 denotes the empty string. As usual, for $u \in S^\otimes$, we indicate by $|u|$ the length of u and by u_i its i-th element.

DEFINITION 3.1 *(The Category of Permutations)*
Let S be a set. The category Sym^*_S has for objects the strings $S^\otimes$ and an arrow $p\colon u \to v$ if and only if p is a permutation of $|u|$ elements, and v is the string obtained by applying the permutation p to u, i.e., $v_{p(i)} = u_i$.
Arrows composition in Sym^*_S is obviously given by the product of permutations, i.e., their composition as functions, here and in the following denoted by $\_;\_$.

Graphically, we represent an arrow $p\colon u \to v$ in Sym^*_S by drawing a line between u_i and $v_{p(i)}$, as for example in Figure 1. Of course, it is possible to define a tensor product on Sym^*_S together with interchange permutations which make it a symmetric monoidal category (see also Figure 1 where γ is the permutation $\{1 \to 2, 2 \to 1\}$).

DEFINITION 3.2 *(Operations on Permutations)*
Given the permutations $p\colon u \to v$ and $p'\colon u' \to v'$ in Sym^*_S their parallel composition $p \otimes p'\colon u \otimes u' \to v \otimes v'$ is the permutation such that

$$i \mapsto \begin{cases} p(i) & \text{if } 0 < i \leq |u| \\ p'(i - |u|) + |u| & \text{if } |u| < i \leq |u| + |u'| \end{cases}$$

Given a permutation π of m elements and the strings $u_i \in S^\otimes$, $i = 1, \ldots, m$, the interchange permutation $\pi(u_1, \ldots, u_m)$ is the permutation p such that

$$p(i) = i - \sum_{j=1}^{h-1} |u_j| + \sum_{\pi(j)<\pi(h)} |u_j| \quad \text{if } \sum_{j=1}^{h-1} |u_j| < i \leq \sum_{j=1}^{h} |u_j|.$$

It is easy to see that $\otimes$ extends to a functor $\otimes\colon Sym^*_S \times Sym^*_S \to Sym^*_S$ making Sym^*_S a strict monoidal category. Moreover, the family of interchange permutations $\gamma = \{\gamma(u,v)\}_{u,v \in Sym^*_S}$ provides the symmetry isomorphism which makes Sym^*_S a symmetric strict monoidal category.

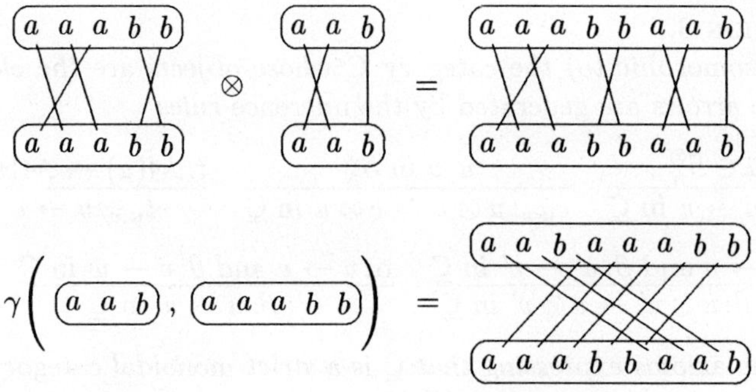

Figure 1: The monoidal structure of Sym_S^*

Theorem 3.3 *(Sym_S^* is free)*
Let S be a set, let $\underline{C}$ be a symmetric strict monoidal category and let F be a function from S to the set of objects of $\underline{C}$. Then, there exists a unique symmetric strict monoidal functor $\mathsf{F}\colon Sym_S^* \to \underline{C}$ extending F.

The preceding result proves that the mapping $S \mapsto Sym_S^*$ extends to a *left adjoint* functor from Set, the category of sets, to SSMC, the category of symmetric strict monoidal categories. Equivalently, Sym_S^* is the free symmetric strict monoidal category on the set S, which is the key point about Sym_S^*.

In the following, given a string $u \in S^{\otimes}$, let $\mathcal{M}(u)$ denote the multiset corresponding to u, and, given a net N, let Sym_N^* the category $Sym_{S_N}^*$.

Definition 3.4 *(The category $\mathcal{Q}[N]$)*
Let N be a net in Petri. Then $\mathcal{Q}[N]$ is the category which includes Sym_N^* as subcategory and has as additional arrows those defined by the following inference rules:

$$\frac{t\colon \mathcal{M}(u) \to \mathcal{M}(v) \text{ in } T_N}{t_{u,v}\colon u \to v \text{ in } \mathcal{Q}[N]}$$

$$\frac{\alpha\colon u \to v \text{ and } \beta\colon u' \to v' \text{ in } \mathcal{Q}[N]}{\alpha \otimes \beta\colon u \otimes u' \to v \otimes v' \text{ in } \mathcal{Q}[N]} \qquad \frac{\alpha\colon u \to v \text{ and } \beta\colon v \to w \text{ in } \mathcal{Q}[N]}{\alpha\,;\,\beta\colon u \to w \text{ in } \mathcal{Q}[N]}$$

plus the axioms expressing the fact that $\mathcal{Q}[N]$ is a symmetric strict monoidal category with symmetry isomorphism γ, and the following axiom ('naturality') involving (instances of) transitions and symmetries.

$$p\,;\,t_{u',v'} = t_{u,v}\,;\,q, \quad \text{where } p\colon u \to u' \text{ and } q\colon v \to v' \text{ in } Sym_N^*. \qquad (\Phi)$$

Exploiting the freeness of Sym_N^*, it is easy to prove the following completely axiomatic description of $\mathcal{Q}[N]$, which can be useful in many contexts.

Proposition 3.5
$\mathcal{Q}[N]$ is (isomorphic to) the category $\underline{\mathsf{C}}$ whose objects are the elements of $S_N^{\otimes}$ and whose arrows are generated by the inference rules

$$\frac{u \in S_N^{\otimes}}{id_u : u \to u \text{ in } \underline{\mathsf{C}}} \qquad \frac{u, v \text{ in } S_N^{\otimes}}{c_{u,v} : u \otimes v \to v \otimes u \text{ in } \underline{\mathsf{C}}} \qquad \frac{t : \mathcal{M}(u) \to \mathcal{M}(v) \text{ in } T_N}{t_{u,v} : u \to v \text{ in } \underline{\mathsf{C}}}$$

$$\frac{\alpha : u \to v \text{ and } \beta : u' \to v' \text{ in } \underline{\mathsf{C}}}{\alpha \otimes \beta : u \otimes u' \to v \otimes v' \text{ in } \underline{\mathsf{C}}} \qquad \frac{\alpha : u \to v \text{ and } \beta : v \to w \text{ in } \underline{\mathsf{C}}}{\alpha \,;\, \beta : u \to w \text{ in } \underline{\mathsf{C}}}$$

modulo the axioms expressing that $\underline{\mathsf{C}}$ is a strict monoidal category, namely,

$$\begin{array}{rcl} \alpha \,;\, id_v = \alpha = id_u \,;\, \alpha & \text{and} & (\alpha \,;\, \beta) \,;\, \delta = \alpha \,;\, (\beta \,;\, \delta), \\ (\alpha \otimes \beta) \otimes \delta = \alpha \otimes (\beta \otimes \delta) & \text{and} & id_0 \otimes \alpha = \alpha = \alpha \otimes id_0, \\ id_u \otimes id_v = id_{u \otimes v} & \text{and} & (\alpha \otimes \alpha') \,;\, (\beta \otimes \beta') = (\alpha \,;\, \beta) \otimes (\alpha' \,;\, \beta'), \end{array}$$

the latter whenever the right hand term is defined, the following axioms expressing that $\underline{\mathsf{C}}$ is symmetric with symmetry isomorphism $c = \{c_{u,v}\}_{u,v \in S_N^{\otimes}}$

$$\begin{array}{rcl} c_{u,v \otimes w} & = & (c_{u,v} \otimes id_w) \,;\, (id_v \otimes c_{u,w}), \\ c_{u,u'} \,;\, (\beta \otimes \alpha) & = & (\alpha \otimes \beta) \,;\, c_{v,v'} \quad \text{for } \alpha : u \to v,\ \beta : u' \to v' \text{ in } \underline{\mathsf{C}}, \\ c_{u,v} \,;\, c_{v,u} & = & id_{u \otimes v}, \end{array}$$

and the following axiom corresponding to axiom (Φ).

$$p \,;\, t_{u',v'} \,;\, q = t_{u,v}, \quad \text{where } p : u \to u' \text{ and } q : v' \to v \text{ are symmetries of } \underline{\mathsf{C}}.$$

We show next that $\mathcal{Q}[\_]$ can be lifted to a functor from the category of Petri nets to an appropriate category of symmetric strict monoidal categories and equivalence classes of symmetric strict monoidal functors. The role of such an equivalence is to take into account that we look at the strings of $S_N^{\otimes}$ as concrete representatives of the multisets of $S_N^{\oplus}$ and, therefore, we want to consider perfectly *equal* those functors which differ only by picking up different, yet compatible, linearizations of multisets.

Definition 3.6 *(Symmetric Petri Categories)*
A symmetric Petri category is a symmetric strict monoidal category $\underline{\mathsf{C}}$ in $\underline{\mathsf{SSMC}}$ whose monoid of objects is the free monoid $S^{\otimes}$ for some set S.

For any pair $\underline{\mathsf{C}}$ and $\underline{\mathsf{D}}$ of symmetric Petri categories, consider the binary relation $\mathcal{R}_{\underline{\mathsf{C}},\underline{\mathsf{D}}}$ on the symmetric strict monoidal functors from $\underline{\mathsf{C}}$ to $\underline{\mathsf{D}}$ defined as $\mathsf{F}\ \mathcal{R}_{\underline{\mathsf{C}},\underline{\mathsf{D}}}\ \mathsf{G}$ if and only if there exists a *monoidal natural isomorphism* $\sigma : \mathsf{F} \cong \mathsf{G}$ whose components are all *symmetries*. Clearly, $\mathcal{R}_{\underline{\mathsf{C}},\underline{\mathsf{D}}}$ is an equivalence relation and the family $\mathcal{R} = \{\mathcal{R}_{\underline{\mathsf{C}},\underline{\mathsf{D}}}\}_{\underline{\mathsf{C}},\underline{\mathsf{D}} \in \underline{\mathsf{SSMC}}}$ is a congruence with respect to functor composition. Therefore, the following definition makes sense.

Definition 3.7 *(The category $\underline{\mathsf{SSMC}}^{\otimes}$)*
Let $\underline{\mathsf{SSMC}}^{\otimes}$ be the quotient of the full subcategory of $\underline{\mathsf{SSMC}}$ consisting of the symmetric Petri categories modulo the congruence $\mathcal{R}$.

THEOREM 3.8 *($\mathcal{Q}[\_]$: $\underline{\mathsf{Petri}} \rightarrow \underline{\mathsf{SSMC}^{\otimes}}$)*
$\mathcal{Q}[\_]$ extends to a functor from $\underline{\mathsf{Petri}}$ to $\underline{\mathsf{SSMC}^{\otimes}}$.

Proof. (Sketch.) Let $\langle f, g\rangle: N_0 \rightarrow N_1$ be a morphism of Petri nets. In order define $\mathcal{Q}[\langle f, g\rangle]$ we need to be able to embed N in $\mathcal{Q}[N]$. To this end, consider any function $in_{N_1}: S^{\oplus}_{N_1} \rightarrow S^{\otimes}_{N_1}$ such that $\mathcal{M}(in_{N_1}(\nu)) = \nu$. Since g is a monoid homomorphism from the free monoid $S^{\oplus}_{N_0}$ to $S^{\oplus}_{N_1}$, it corresponds to a unique function g' from S_{N_0} to $S^{\oplus}_{N_1}$, whence we obtain $\hat{g} = in_{N_1} \circ g': S_{N_0} \rightarrow S^{\otimes}_{N_1}$, i.e., a function from S_{N_0} to the set of objects of $\mathcal{Q}[N_1]$. Then, from Theorem 3.3, we have the symmetric strict monoidal functor $\mathsf{F}': Sym_{S_{N_0}} \rightarrow \mathcal{Q}[N_1]$. Finally, we extend F' to a functor $\mathcal{Q}[\langle f, g\rangle]$ from $\mathcal{Q}[N_0]$ to $\mathcal{Q}[N_1]$ by considering the symmetric strict monoidal functor F which coincides with F' on Sym_{N_0} and maps $t_{u,v}: u \rightarrow v$ to $f(t)_{\mathsf{F}(u),\mathsf{F}(v)}: \mathsf{F}(u) \rightarrow \mathsf{F}(v)$. Since monoidal functors map symmetries to symmetries, and since $f(t)$ is transition of N_1, it follows immediately that F preserves axiom (Φ), i.e., that F is well defined. Moreover, since a different choice of in_{N_1} would clearly give a functor G such that $\mathsf{F}\ \mathfrak{R}\ \mathsf{G}$, we have that $\mathcal{Q}[\_]$ does not depend on in_{N_1}. It is easy to check that this definition makes $\mathcal{Q}[\_]$ into a functor. ✓

However, the category $\underline{\mathsf{SSMC}^{\otimes}}$ is still too general for our purpose. In particular, it is easily noticed that $\mathcal{Q}[\_]$ is not *full*. This signifies that $\underline{\mathsf{SSMC}^{\otimes}}$ has too little structure to represent net behaviours precisely enough; equivalently, since the structure of the objects of a category $\underline{\mathsf{C}}$ is 'encoded' in the morphisms of $\underline{\mathsf{C}}$, it signifies that the morphisms of $\underline{\mathsf{SSMC}^{\otimes}}$ do not capture the structure of symmetric Petri categories precisely enough. Specifically, the transitions, which are definitely primary components of nets, and as such are treated by the morphisms in $\underline{\mathsf{Petri}}$, have *no* corresponding notion in $\underline{\mathsf{SSMC}^{\otimes}}$: we need to identify such a notion and refine the choice of the category of net computations accordingly.

The key to accomplish our task is the following observation about axiom (Φ) in Definition 3.4: as already mentioned, it simply expresses that the collection of the arrows $t_{u,v}$ of $\mathcal{Q}[N]$, for $t \in T_N$ and $u, v \in S^{\otimes}_N$, is a natural transformation. Namely, for $\underline{\mathsf{C}}$ a symmetric Petri category with objects $S^{\otimes}$, and ν a multiset in $S^{\oplus}$, let $Sym_{\underline{\mathsf{C}},\nu}$ be the subcategory of $\underline{\mathsf{C}}$ consisting of those objects $u \in S^{\otimes}$ such that $\mathcal{M}(u) = \nu$ and the symmetries between them, and let $in_{\underline{\mathsf{C}},\nu}$ be the inclusion of $Sym_{\underline{\mathsf{C}},\nu}$ in $\underline{\mathsf{C}}$. Then, for $\nu, \nu' \in S^{\oplus}$, one obtains a pair of parallel functors $\pi_{\underline{\mathsf{C}},\nu}$ and $\pi_{\underline{\mathsf{C}},\nu'}$ by composing $in_{\underline{\mathsf{C}},\nu}$ and $in_{\underline{\mathsf{C}},\nu'}$ respectively with the first and with the second projection of $Sym_{\underline{\mathsf{C}},\nu} \times Sym_{\underline{\mathsf{C}},\nu'}$.

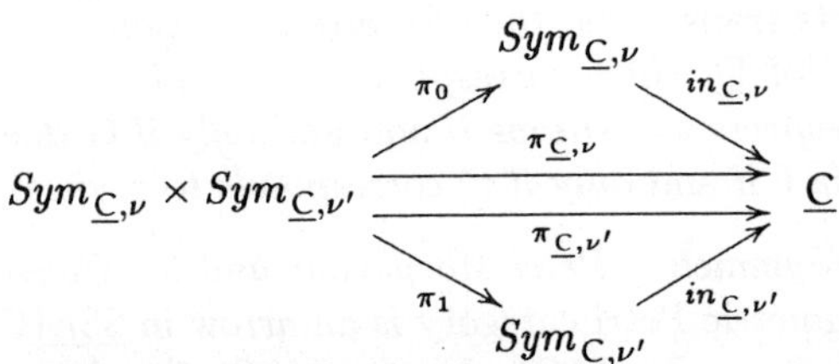

It follows directly from the definitions that, when $\underline{\mathsf{C}}$ is $\mathcal{Q}[N]$, axiom (Φ) states exactly that, for all $t: \nu \rightarrow \nu' \in T_N$, the set $\{t_{u,v} \mid \mathcal{M}(u) = \nu, \mathcal{M}(v) = \nu'\}$ is a natural transformation from $\pi_{\mathcal{Q}[N],\nu}$ to $\pi_{\mathcal{Q}[N],\nu'}$.

A further very relevant property of the transitions of N when considered as arrows of $\mathcal{Q}[N]$ is that of being decomposable as a tensor only trivially and as a composition only by means of symmetries. This is easily captured by the following notion of *primitive* arrow.

Definition 3.9 *(Primitive Arrows)*
Let $\underline{\mathsf{C}}$ be a symmetric Petri category. An arrow τ in $\underline{\mathsf{C}}$ is primitive if

i) τ is not a symmetry;

ii) $\tau = \alpha\,;\beta$ implies α is a symmetry and β is primitive, or vice versa;

iii) $\tau = \alpha \otimes \beta$ implies $\alpha = id_0$ and β is primitive, or vice versa.

A simple inspection of Definition 3.4 shows that the only primitive arrows in $\mathcal{Q}[N]$ are the arrows $t_{u,v}$, for $t: \mathcal{M}(u) \to \mathcal{M}(v)$ a transition of N. As a consequence, the natural transformations $\tau: \pi_{\mathcal{Q}[N],\nu} \dot{\to} \pi_{\mathcal{Q}[N],\nu'}$ whose components are primitive are in one-to-one correspondence with the transitions of N. Following the usual categorical paradigm, we then use the properties that characterize the transitions of N in $\mathcal{Q}[N]$, expressed in abstract categorical terms, to define the notion of transition in any symmetric Petri category.

Definition 3.10 *(Transitions of Symmetric Petri Categories)*
Let $\underline{\mathsf{C}}$ be a symmetric Petri category and let $S^{\otimes}$ be its monoid of objects. A transition of $\underline{\mathsf{C}}$ is a natural transformation $\tau: \pi_{\underline{\mathsf{C}},\nu} \dot{\to} \pi_{\underline{\mathsf{C}},\nu'}$, for ν, ν' in $S^{\oplus}$, whose components $\tau_{u,v}$ are primitive arrows of $\underline{\mathsf{C}}$.

It is clear now what the extra structure required in $\underline{\mathsf{SSMC}}^{\otimes}$ is: transitions must be preserved by morphisms of symmetric Petri categories. Formally, for $\underline{\mathsf{C}}$ and $\underline{\mathsf{D}}$ in $\underline{\mathsf{SSMC}}^{\otimes}$ and $\mathsf{F}: \underline{\mathsf{C}} \to \underline{\mathsf{D}}$ in $\underline{\mathsf{SSMC}}$, F *respects transitions* if, for each transition $\tau: \pi_{\underline{\mathsf{C}},\nu} \dot{\to} \pi_{\underline{\mathsf{C}},\nu'}$ of $\underline{\mathsf{C}}$, there exists a transition $\tau': \pi_{\underline{\mathsf{D}},\bar{\nu}} \dot{\to} \pi_{\underline{\mathsf{D}},\bar{\nu}'}$ of $\underline{\mathsf{D}}$ such that $\mathsf{F}(\tau_{u,v}) = \tau'_{\mathsf{F}(u),\mathsf{F}(v)}$ for all (u, v) in $Sym_{\underline{\mathsf{C}},\nu} \times Sym_{\underline{\mathsf{C}},\nu'}$; in this case, we say that τ' *corresponds to* τ *via* F.

The following lemma shows that a symmetric strict monoidal functor which respects transitions defines a mapping between sets of transitions and that, moreover, this property extends to the arrows of $\underline{\mathsf{SSMC}}^{\otimes}$. It follows immediately that Definition 3.12 is well given.

Lemma 3.11
If $\mathsf{F}: \underline{\mathsf{C}} \to \underline{\mathsf{D}}$ respects transitions, then for any transition τ of $\underline{\mathsf{C}}$, there exists a unique transition τ' of $\underline{\mathsf{D}}$ which corresponds to τ via F.
If $\mathsf{F}\,\mathfrak{R}\,\mathsf{G}$, then F respects transitions if and and only if G does so, and then τ' corresponds to τ via F if and only if τ' corresponds to τ via G.

Definition 3.12 *(Symmetric Petri Morphisms and the Category $\underline{\mathsf{TSSMC}}^{\otimes}$)*
A morphism of symmetric Petri category is an arrow in $\underline{\mathsf{SSMC}}^{\otimes}$ which respects transitions. We shall use $\underline{\mathsf{TSSMC}}^{\otimes}$ denote the (lluf) subcategory of $\underline{\mathsf{SSMC}}^{\otimes}$ whose arrows are the morphisms of symmetric Petri categories.

Finally, it is easy to prove that $\mathcal{Q}[\_]$ is actually a functor to $\underline{\mathsf{TSSMC}}^{\otimes}$.

PROPOSITION 3.13 *($\mathcal{Q}[\_]$: $\underline{\mathsf{Petri}} \to \underline{\mathsf{TSSMC}}^{\otimes}$)*
The functor $\mathcal{Q}[\_]$ restricts to a functor from $\underline{\mathsf{Petri}}$ to $\underline{\mathsf{TSSMC}}^{\otimes}$.

Proof. It is enough to verify that, for any morphism $\langle f, g\rangle: N_0 \to N_1$ in $\underline{\mathsf{Petri}}$, a representative F of $\mathcal{Q}[\langle f, g\rangle]$ respects transitions. This follows at once, since f is a function $T_{N_0} \to T_{N_1}$, $\mathsf{F}(t_{u,v}) = f(t)_{\mathsf{F}(u),\mathsf{F}(v)}$, and the transitions of $\mathcal{Q}[N_i]$ are exactly the natural transformations $\left\{t_{u,v} \mid \mathcal{M}(u) = \nu, \mathcal{M}(v) = \nu'\right\}$ for $t: \nu \to \nu' \in T_{N_i}$. ✓

Interestingly enough, we can identify a functor from $\underline{\mathsf{TSSMC}}^{\otimes}$ to $\underline{\mathsf{Petri}}$ which is a *coreflection* right adjoint to $\mathcal{Q}[\_]$. It is worth remarking that this answers to a possible legitimate doubt about the category $\underline{\mathsf{TSSMC}}^{\otimes}$: in principle, in fact, the functoriality of $\mathcal{Q}[\_]$ could be due to a very tight choice of the target category, e.g., the congruence $\mathcal{R}$ could induce too many isomorphisms of categories and $\mathcal{Q}[\_]$ make undesirable identifications of nets. The existence of a coreflection right adjoint to $\mathcal{Q}[\_]$ is, of course, the best possible proof of the adequacy of $\underline{\mathsf{TSSMC}}^{\otimes}$: it implies that $\underline{\mathsf{Petri}}$ is embedded in it *fully* and *faithfully* as a coreflective subcategory. This result supports our claim that $\underline{\mathsf{TSSMC}}^{\otimes}$ is an axiomatization of the category of net computations.

THEOREM 3.14 *($\mathcal{Q}[\_] \dashv \mathcal{N}[\_]$: $\underline{\mathsf{Petri}} \to \underline{\mathsf{TSSMC}}^{\otimes}$)*
Let $\underline{\mathsf{C}}$ be a symmetric Petri category, and let $S^{\otimes}$ be its monoid of objects. Define $\mathcal{N}[\underline{\mathsf{C}}]$ to be the Petri net $(\partial^0, \partial^1: T \to S^{\oplus})$, where

- *T is the set of transitions $\tau: \pi_{\underline{\mathsf{C}},\nu} \dot{\to} \pi_{\underline{\mathsf{C}},\nu'}$ of $\underline{\mathsf{C}}$;*
- *$\partial^0(\tau: \pi_{\underline{\mathsf{C}},\nu} \dot{\to} \pi_{\underline{\mathsf{C}},\nu'}) = \nu$ and $\partial^1(\tau: \pi_{\underline{\mathsf{C}},\nu} \dot{\to} \pi_{\underline{\mathsf{C}},\nu'}) = \nu'$.*

Then, $\mathcal{N}[\_]$ extends to a functor $\underline{\mathsf{TSSMC}}^{\otimes} \to \underline{\mathsf{Petri}}$ which is right adjoint to $\mathcal{Q}[\_]$. In addition, since the unit is an isomorphism, the adjunction is a coreflection.

Proof. For any symmetric Petri category $\underline{\mathsf{C}}$, there is a (unique) symmetric strict monoidal functor $\varepsilon_{\underline{\mathsf{C}}}: \mathcal{Q}\mathcal{N}[\underline{\mathsf{C}}] \to \underline{\mathsf{C}}$ which is the identity on the objects and which sends the component at (u, v) of the transition $\tau: \nu \to \nu'$ of $\mathcal{N}[\underline{\mathsf{C}}]$ to the component $\tau_{u,v}$ of the natural transformation $\tau: \pi_{\underline{\mathsf{C}},\nu} \dot{\to} \pi_{\underline{\mathsf{C}},\nu'}: Sym_{\underline{\mathsf{C}},\nu} \times Sym_{\underline{\mathsf{C}},\nu'} \to \underline{\mathsf{C}}$. Since it clearly preserves transitions, we have that $\varepsilon_{\underline{\mathsf{C}}}$ is a (representative of a) morphism of symmetric Petri categories. It is not difficult to prove that $\varepsilon_{\underline{\mathsf{C}}}$ enjoys the couniversal property making it the counit of the adjunction. The unit $\eta_N: N \to \mathcal{N}\mathcal{Q}[N]$ is the morphism $\langle f, id\rangle$, where f sends $t \in T_N$ to $\{t_{u,v}\} \in T_{\mathcal{N}\mathcal{Q}[N]}$, which is an iso. ✓

Finally, we can identify the replete image of $\mathcal{Q}[\_]$ in $\underline{\mathsf{TSSMC}}^{\otimes}$, i.e., identify those symmetric Petri categories which are isomorphic to $\mathcal{Q}[N]$, for some net N.

THEOREM 3.15 *($\underline{\mathsf{Petri}} \cong \underline{\mathsf{PSSMC}}$)*
Let $\underline{\mathsf{PSSMC}}$ be the full subcategory of $\underline{\mathsf{TSSMC}}^{\otimes}$ consisting of those symmetric Petri categories $\underline{\mathsf{C}}$ whose arrows can be generated by tensor and composition from symmetries, and components of transitions of $\underline{\mathsf{C}}$, uniquely up to the axioms of symmetric strict monoidal categories, i.e., the axioms in Proposition 3.5, and the naturality of transitions, i.e., axiom (Φ).
Then, $\underline{\mathsf{PSSMC}}$ and $\underline{\mathsf{Petri}}$ are equivalent via $\mathcal{N}[\_]$ and $\mathcal{Q}[\_]$.

Proof. By Theorem 3.14, it is enough to show that $\underline{\mathsf{C}}$ belongs to $\underline{\mathsf{PSSMC}}$ if and only if $\varepsilon_{\underline{\mathsf{C}}}: \mathcal{Q}\mathcal{N}[\underline{\mathsf{C}}] \to \underline{\mathsf{C}}$ is an isomorphism, which is easy. ✓

4 Strongly Concatenable Processes

In this section we introduce a slight refinement of concatenable processes and we show that they are abstractly represented by the arrows of the category $\mathcal{Q}[N]$. In other words, we find a process-like representation for the arrows of $\mathcal{Q}[N]$. This provides a functorial construction for the category of the processes of a net N.

DEFINITION 4.1 *(Strongly Concatenable Processes)*
Given a petri net N in Petri, a strongly concatenable process of N is a tuple (π, ℓ, L) where $\pi: \Theta \to N$ is a process of N, and $\ell: \min(\Theta) \to \{1, \ldots, |\min(\Theta)|\}$ and $L: \max(\Theta) \to \{1, \ldots, |\max(\Theta)|\}$ are isomorphisms, i.e., total orderings of, respectively, the minimal and the maximal places of Θ.
An isomorphism of strongly concatenable processes is an isomorphism of the underlying processes which, in addition, preserves the orderings ℓ and L. As usual, we identify isomorphic strongly concatenable processes.

As in the case of concatenable processes, it is easy to define an operation of concatenation of strongly concatenable processes. We associate a source and a target in $S_N^{\otimes}$ to each strongly concatenable process by taking the *string* corresponding to the linear ordering of, respectively, $\min(\Theta)$ and $\max(\Theta)$. Then, the concatenation of $(\pi_0: \Theta_0 \to N, \ell_0, L_0): u \to v$ and $(\pi_1: \Theta_1 \to N, \ell_1, L_1): v \to w$ is the strongly concatenable process $u \to w$ obtained by merging the maximal places of Θ_0 and the minimal of Θ_1 according to L_0 and ℓ_1. (See Figure 2, where we enrich the usual representation of non-sequential processes by labelling the minimal and the maximal places with the values of, respectively, ℓ and L.)

PROPOSITION 4.2 *(The Category $\mathcal{CQ}[N]$)*
Under the above defined operation of sequential composition, the strongly concatenable processes of N form a category $\mathcal{CQ}[N]$ whose identities are those processes consisting only of places, which therefore are both minimal and maximal, and such that $\ell = L$.

Strongly concatenable processes admit a tensor product $\otimes$ such that, given $SCP = (\pi_0: \Theta_0 \to N, \ell_0, L_0): u \to v$ and $SCP' = (\pi_1: \Theta_1 \to N, \ell_1, L_1): u' \to v'$, $SCP \otimes SCP'$ is the strongly concatenable process $(\pi: \Theta \to N, \ell, L): u \otimes u' \to v \otimes v'$ given below (see also Figure 2), where $+$, besides the usual sum of natural numbers, denotes also the disjoint union of sets and functions, and in_0 and in_1 the corresponding injections.

- $\Theta = (\partial^0_{\Theta_0} + \partial^0_{\Theta_1}, \partial^1_{\Theta_0} + \partial^1_{\Theta_1}: T_{\Theta_0} + T_{\Theta_1} \to (S_{\Theta_0} + S_{\Theta_1})^{\oplus})$;
- $\pi = \pi_0 + \pi_1$;
- $\ell(in_0(a)) = \ell_0(a)$ and $\ell(in_1(a)) = |\min(\Theta_0)| + \ell_1(a)$;
- $L(in_0(a)) = L_0(a)$ and $L(in_1(a)) = |\max(\Theta_1)| + L_1(a)$.

Observe that $\otimes$ is a functor $\otimes: \mathcal{CQ}[N] \times \mathcal{CQ}[N] \to \mathcal{CQ}[N]$. The strongly concatenable processes consisting only of places are analogous in $\mathcal{CQ}[N]$ of the permutations of $\mathcal{Q}[N]$. In particular, for any $u, v \in S^{\otimes}$, the strongly concatenable process $\bar{\gamma}(u, v)$ consisting of places in one-to-one correspondence with the

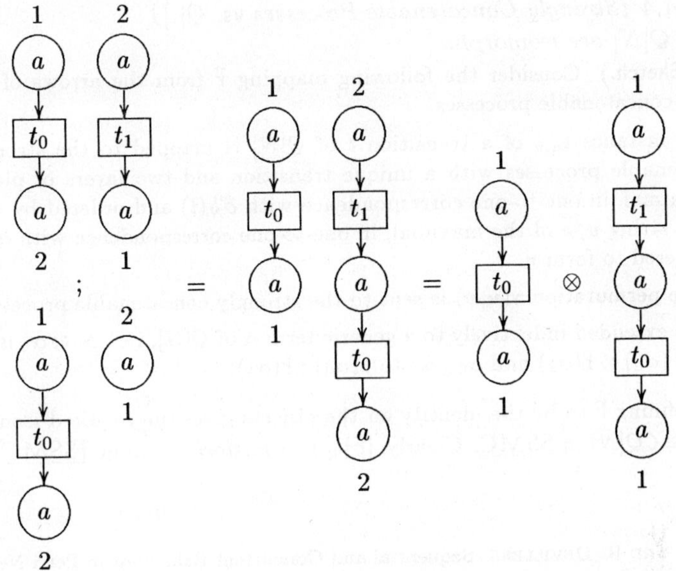

Figure 2: An example of the algebra of concatenable processes

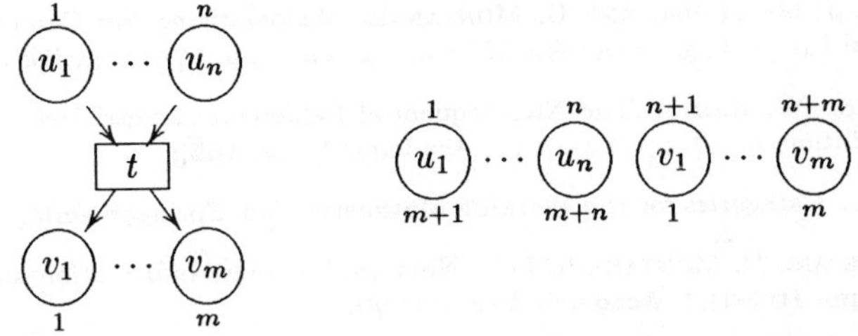

Figure 3: A transitions $t_{u,v}: u \to v$ and the symmetry $\gamma(u, v)$ in $\mathcal{CQ}[N]$

elements of the string $u \otimes v$ mapped by π to the corresponding places of N, and such that $\ell(u_i) = i$, $\ell(v_i) = |u| + i$, $L(u_i) = |v| + i$ and $L(v_i) = i$, plays in $\mathcal{CQ}[N]$ the role played by the permutation $\gamma(u, v)$ in $\mathcal{Q}[N]$ (see also Figure 3).

Proposition 4.3 *(The Symmetric Petri Category $\mathcal{CQ}[N]$)*
Under the above defined tensor product $\mathcal{CQ}[N]$ is a symmetric Petri category whose symmetry isomorphism is the family $\{\bar{\gamma}(u, v)\}_{u,v \in S_N^{\otimes}}$.

The transitions t of N are faithfully represented in the obvious way by processes with a unique transition which is in the post-set of any minimal place and in the pre-set of any maximal place, minimal and maximal places being in one-to-one correspondence, respectively, with $\partial_N^0(t)$ and $\partial_N^1(t)$. Thus, varying ℓ and L on the process corresponding to a transition we obtain a representative in $\mathcal{CQ}[N]$ of each instance $t_{u,v}$ of t in $\mathcal{Q}[N]$ (see also Figure 3).

THEOREM 4.4 *(Strongly Concatenable Processes* vs. $\mathcal{Q}[\_]$*)*
$\mathcal{CQ}[N]$ and $\mathcal{Q}[N]$ are isomorphic.

Proof. **(Sketch.)** Consider the following mapping F from the arrows of $\mathcal{Q}[N]$ to strongly concatenable processes.

- An instance $t_{u,v}$ of a transition t of $\mathcal{Q}[N]$ is mapped to the strongly concatenable processes with a unique transition and two layers of places: the minimal, in one-to-one correspondence with $\partial^0_N(t)$ and ordered by ℓ to form the string u, and the maximal, in one-to-one correspondence with $\partial^1_N(t)$ and ordered to form v.
- The permutation $\gamma(u, v)$ is sent to the strongly concatenable process $\bar{\gamma}(u, v)$.
- F is extended inductively to a generic term α of $\mathcal{Q}[N]$, i.e., $\alpha_0 \otimes \alpha_1$ is mapped to $\mathsf{F}(\alpha_0) \otimes \mathsf{F}(\alpha_1)$ and $\alpha_0 \, ; \alpha_1$ to $\mathsf{F}(\alpha_0) \, ; \mathsf{F}(\alpha_1)$.

Then, defining F to be the identity on the objects gives the required isomorphism $\mathsf{F}: \mathcal{Q}[N] \cong \mathcal{CQ}[N]$ in <u>SSMC</u>. Clearly, $[\mathsf{F}]_{\mathfrak{R}}$ is *a fortiori* an iso in <u>TSSMC</u>$^{\otimes}$. ✓

References

[1] E. BEST AND R. DEVILLERS. Sequential and Concurrent Behaviour in Petri Net Theory. *Theoretical Computer Science*, n. 55, pp. 87–136, Elsevier, 1987.

[2] C. BROWN, D. GURR, AND V. DE PAIVA. *A Linear Specification Language for Petri Nets.* Technical Report DAIMI PB-363, Computer Science Dept., Aarhus University, 1991.

[3] P. DEGANO, J. MESEGUER, AND U. MONTANARI. Axiomatizing Net Computations and Processes. In *Proceedings of the 4th LICS Symposium*, pp. 175–185, IEEE, 1989.

[4] U. GOLTZ AND W. REISIG. The Non-Sequential Behaviour of Petri Nets. *Information and Computation*, n. 57, pp. 125–147, Academic Press, 1983.

[5] S. MACLANE. *Categories for the Working Mathematician.* Springer-Verlag, 1971.

[6] J. MESEGUER AND U. MONTANARI. Petri Nets are Monoids. *Information and Computation*, n. 88, pp. 105–154, Academic Press, 1990.

[7] M. NIELSEN, G. PLOTKIN, AND G. WINSKEL. Petri Nets, Event Structures and Domains, Part 1. *Theoretical Computer Science*, n. 13, pp. 85–108, Elsevier, 1981.

[8] C.A. PETRI. *Kommunikation mit Automaten.* PhD thesis, Institut für Instrumentelle Mathematik, Bonn, Germany, 1962.

[9] C.A. PETRI. *Non-Sequential Processes.* Interner Bericht ISF–77–5, Gesellschaft für Mathematik und Datenverarbeitung, Bonn, Germany, 1977.

[10] W. REISIG. *Petri Nets.* Springer-Verlag, 1985.

[11] V. SASSONE. *On the Semantics of Petri Nets: Processes, Unfoldings, and Infinite Computations.* PhD Thesis TD 6/94, Dipartimento di Informatica, Università di Pisa, 1994.

[12] V. SASSONE. *Some Remarks on Concatenable Processes.* Technical Report TR 6/94, Dipartimento di Informatica, Università di Pisa, 1994.

[13] G. WINSKEL. A New Definition of Morphism on Petri Nets. In *Proceedings of STACS '84*, LNCS, n. 166, pp. 140–150, Springer-Verlag, 1984.

[14] G. WINSKEL. Petri Nets, Algebras, Morphisms and Compositionality. *Information and Computation*, n. 72, pp. 197–238, Academic Press, 1987.

High undecidability of weak bisimilarity for Petri nets

Petr Jančar *
Dept. of Computer Science, University of Ostrava
Dvořákova 7, 701 03 Ostrava, Czech Republic
e-mail: jancar@oudec.osu.cz

Abstract

It is shown that the problem whether two labelled place/transition Petri nets (with initial markings) are weakly bisimilar is highly undecidable – it resides at least at level ω of the hyperarithmetical hierarchy; on the other hand it belongs to Σ_1^1 (the first level of the analytical hierarchy). It contrasts with Π_1^0-completeness of the same problem for trace (language) equivalence. Relations to similar problems for the process algebra BPP (Basic Parallel Processes) are also discussed.

1 Introduction

In the theory of parallelism and concurrency, much effort is devoted to the decidability questions for various classes of (models of) processes and various notions of behavioural equivalences. For natural reasons, the question of algorithmic decidability is among the first ones to be asked when developing automatic verification techniques.

Although the main result here concerns Petri nets and high undecidability, an important source of motivation can be found in a decidability question for the process algebra BPP (Basic Parallel Processes, cf. e.g. [2]).

Recently, interesting results have been obtained for both BPP and Petri nets; the results concerned two of the central behavioural equivalences, namely the bisimulation equivalence (or bisimilarity) and the trace (or language) equivalence. In fact, BPP can be viewed as a subclass of Petri nets and the processes of obtaining the mentioned results for both models have been closely interconnected. A short survey is contained in the next paragraphs.

*Supported by the Grant Agency of Czech republic, Grant No. 201/93/2123

First we briefly recall a definition of BPP (the precise definition of Petri nets being given in Section 2).
The abstract syntax of a BPP-expression is

$$E ::= \mathbf{0} \mid X \mid a.E \mid E + E \mid E \| E$$

The operational semantics is standard – $\mathbf{0}$ is a nil-process, X is a process variable, $a.E$ performs the action a and then behaves like E, the operator $+$ means nondeterministic choice and $\|$ parallel merging (no communication between processes is allowed). A BPP-process is given by a family of equations $X_1 = E_1, \ldots, X_n = E_n$ where X_1 is the leading variable (the initial state).

It is easy to verify that, with respect to the "natural" corresponding transition systems, BPP can be viewed as a subclass of (labelled) Petri nets – every transition has exactly one input place in this case.

In [2] it is shown in an elegant way that (strong) bisimilarity is decidable for BPP.

Remark. In fact, the decidability was first established for a subclass – the normed processes – and later extended for all BPP. Recently, a polynomial algorithm for the normed BPP has been shown (the complexity for all BPP remaining open); cf. [9].
Although using different techniques, the results for BPP resemble very much those for BPA (Basic Process Algebra; cf. [3], [8]).

The decidability result for BPP still left unsolved the decidability question for the whole class of Petri nets which had been open for some time. Later the question was answered negatively in [12] – bisimilarity is undecidable for Petri nets. As for the trace equivalence, its undecidability for Petri nets has been known from [6]; in fact, [12] also provides a more direct proof of this undecidability. It is interesting that the trace equivalence is undecidable even for BPP; it is shown in [7] by a clever modification of the technique of [12].

Remark. In [11], another modification was added – to show undecidability for other equivalences in the linear time – branching time spectrum of [5] on BPP. On the other hand, decidability results for some finer versions of bisimilarity on BPP have been obtained in [14].

Allowing nonobservable, internal, actions (commonly denoted by τ), weak versions of the considered equivalences can be defined. For practice, these are more important, unfortunately the decidability is often affected; instead of finitely branching transition systems we can get infinitely branching ones and it surely makes things less feasible.

Of course, undecidability for a (strong) equivalence immediately implies undecidability for the relevant weak version. Therefore when being interested strictly in decidability/undecidability questions, the most important question emerging from the above discussion is that of decidability of weak bisimilarity for BPP.

It nicely demonstrates a difference between finite branching and infinite branching.
In finitely branching systems, the problem of non-bisimilarity (non-equivalence) of two states s, s' is usually easier than that of bisimilarity (equivalence). There is a natural systematic method exploring all possibilities of constructing a minimal bisimulation relation containing the pair (s, s'). The method resembles constructing a (finitely branching) tree in the breadth-first manner (any node corresponds to a finite set of pairs). If s,s' are non-bisimilar, it will be revealed eventually – any leaf of the so far constructed tree will correspond to a (finite) relation containing an (obviously) non-bisimilar pair. Thus we get, in fact, a finite witness of the non-bisimilarity. Therefore semi-decidability of the negative case is clear.
In the positive case, a similar finite witness of equivalence often does not exist. If it does exist, it is then much more demanding to show it; cf. [2] for the case of bisimilarity on BPP or [3] for BPA.
For the weak bisimilarity on BPP, [4] shows that a finite witness of the *positive* case exists and it is the *negative* case for which semi-decidability is not clear (leaving the decidability question open). In other words, the task to show the existence of a finite witness of weak non-bisimilarity for BPP-processes has not been accomplished yet.

Remark. One thing is clear: if the problem should be undecidable (i.e. the negative case being non-semidecidable), it can not be shown by reducing the halting problem to the negative case, which was, in principle, the method of showing the undecidability results mentioned above.
We should also mention that some decidability results for weak versions of some finer equivalences on a *subclass* of BPP are shown in [14].

It brings us back to a closer look at the whole class of Petri nets. In fact, we have indicated that the (strong) bisimulation equivalence problem is Π^0_1-complete – the non-equivalence (the negative case) being recursively equivalent to the halting problem (hence Σ^0_1-complete). Therefore it still could be the case that the weak non-bisimilarity is semi-decidable for the whole class of Petri nets, which would imply decidability for BPP. It is not unimaginable at first sight that non-bisimilarity could be demonstrated in some reasonable sense (by a finite witness). Unfortunately, we show here that it is not the case. It turns out that the weak non-bisimilarity on Petri nets is not only non-semidecidable but is beyond the arithmetical hierarchy (!). It might explain a bit why the semi-decidability of weak non-bisimilarity for BPP (which hopefully is the case) is not so easy to prove.

Although the result does not imply the desired decidability for BPP and has therefore no direct "practical" consequence, it has some value (as the author hopes) at least from the theoretical viewpoint. Having estimated the degree of undecidability for the weak version of bisimilarity for Petri nets, it is natural to ask a similar question for the (weak) trace equivalence. Using some well-known results concerning Petri nets, we show here that this problem remains

Π_1^0-complete. In this sense, the result highlights an aspect of the difference between the bisimilarity and the trace equivalence. On the other hand, in case of BPP the trace equivalence (in both versions) is Π_1^0-complete but it seems very probable that the weak bisimilarity is decidable (at least it is in Σ_1^0), which shows an interesting difference with the situation at Petri nets. It might illustrate the power of internal communication in some sense.

The main result is also completed by an upper bound, which is natural to be looked for when having a lower bound. The problem of weak bisimilarity for Petri nets is easily shown to be in Σ_1^1 (the first level of the analytical hierarchy); hence the negative formulation is in Π_1^1. Whether the problem belongs to the intersection Δ_1^1 (i.e. whether it is hyperarithmetical) is left open.

The paper is organized as follows. Section 2 gives basic definitions and claims the results. The relevant proofs are given in Section 3.

A preliminary version of the paper appeared as the report [13]. The report is self-contained since it includes an appendix describing a needed construction of [12]. Here we only refer to [12] omitting the appendix.

2 Definitions and results

$\mathcal{N}$ denotes the set of nonnegative integers, A^* the set of finite sequences of elements of A.

A labelled net is a tuple $\Sigma = (P, T, F, L)$ where P and T are finite disjoint sets of *places* and *transitions* respectively, $F : (P \times T) \cup (T \times P) \longrightarrow \{0, 1\}$ is a *flow function* (for $F(x, y) = 1$, there is an *arc* from x to y; we do not use multiple arcs in the paper) and $L : T \longrightarrow A$ is a *labelling* (attaches an action name – from a set A – to each transition). We can suppose a fixed (countable) A containing a special, *unobservable*, action τ, the other actions being *observable*.

By *a Petri net* we mean a tuple $N = (\Sigma, M_0)$, where Σ is a labelled net and M_0 the *initial marking*; a *marking* M being a function $M : P \longrightarrow \mathcal{N}$. (A marking gives the number of *tokens* for each place). A transition t is *enabled* at a marking M, $M \xrightarrow{t}_\Sigma$, if $M(p) \geq F(p, t)$ for every $p \in P$. An enabled transition t may *fire* at a marking M yielding marking M', $M \xrightarrow{t}_\Sigma M'$, where $M'(p) = M(p) - F(p, t) + F(t, p)$ for all $p \in P$.
In the natural way, the definitions can be extended for finite sequences of transitions $\sigma \in T^*$.

For any $a \in A$ (including τ), by $M \xrightarrow{a}_\Sigma M'$ we mean that $M \xrightarrow{t}_\Sigma M'$ for some t with $L(t) = a$; by $M \overset{a}{\Longrightarrow}_\Sigma M'$ we mean that $M \xrightarrow{\sigma}_\Sigma M'$ for some sequence σ of transitions, one of them being labelled by a, the others by τ (in case $a = \tau$, the sequence can be empty; i.e. $M \overset{\tau}{\Longrightarrow}_\Sigma M$ for all markings M). In the natural way, we define the relations $M \overset{w}{\Longrightarrow}_\Sigma$ and $M \overset{w}{\Longrightarrow}_\Sigma M'$ for finite sequences $w \in A^*$.

The *set of (observable) traces* (or the *language*) of a Petri net $N = (\Sigma, M_0)$ is defined as $\mathcal{T}(N) = \{w \in (A \setminus \{\tau\})^* \mid M_0 \stackrel{w}{\Longrightarrow}_\Sigma\}$. Two Petri nets N_1, N_2 are *(weakly) trace equivalent* if $\mathcal{T}(N_1) = \mathcal{T}(N_2)$.

Given two labelled nets $\Sigma_1 = (P_1, T_1, F_1, L_1)$, $\Sigma_2 = (P_2, T_2, F_2, L_2)$, a binary relation $R \subseteq \mathcal{N}^{P_1} \times \mathcal{N}^{P_2}$ is a *weak bisimulation* (cf. [16]) if the following conditions hold for all $(M_1, M_2) \in R$:
– for every a and M_1' s.t. $M_1 \stackrel{a}{\Longrightarrow}_{\Sigma_1} M_1'$, there is M_2' s.t. $M_2 \stackrel{a}{\Longrightarrow}_{\Sigma_2} M_2'$, where $(M_1', M_2') \in R$
and conversely
– for every a and M_2' s.t. $M_2 \stackrel{a}{\Longrightarrow}_{\Sigma_2} M_2'$, there is M_1' s.t. $M_1 \stackrel{a}{\Longrightarrow}_{\Sigma_1} M_1'$, where $(M_1', M_2') \in R$.

Two Petri nets N_1, N_2 are *weakly bisimilar* if there is a weak bisimulation relating their initial markings.

(If the relation $\stackrel{a}{\Longrightarrow}$ is replaced by $\stackrel{a}{\longrightarrow}$, we get the notion of strong bisimilarity.)

Let TE denote the set of (Gödel numbers, codes or notations of) all pairs of Petri nets (N_1, N_2) which are (weakly) trace equivalent. NTE will denote the set of all (weakly) trace non-equivalent pairs.
Similarly, let WB denote the set of all pairs of Petri nets (N_1, N_2) which are weakly bisimilar and NWB the set of all weakly non-bisimilar pairs.

The next theorems show the position of the defined sets in the (hyper)arithmetical and analytical hierarchies, the details of which can be found e.g. in [1].

Theorem 1.

NTE is Σ_1^0-complete (i.e. complete among the recursively enumerable sets); hence TE is Π_1^0-complete.

Theorem 2.

WB is in Σ_1^1 (the 1st level of the analytical hierarchy); hence NWB is in Π_1^1.

Theorem 3.

WB and NWB reside at least at the level ω in the hyperarithmetical hierarchy.

Theorem 1 is established using some well-known results regarding (un)decidability in Petri nets.

The upper bound of Theorem 2 is established by using directly the definition of weak bisimilarity.

The proof of the lower bound in Theorem 3 is more involved. It shows an algorithm which, given a 1st order formula ϕ of the standard arithmetic structure $(\mathcal{N}, 0, S, +, \cdot)$, constructs two Petri nets which are weakly bisimilar iff ϕ is true. This yields the result since the set of true 1st order sentences of arithmetics lies at level ω in the hyperarithmetical hierarchy (cf. e.g. [1], p. 560).

3 Proofs

We start with the proof concerning the trace equivalence.

Proof of Theorem 1.

It is well-known that the halting problem is Σ_1^0-complete. Since it is recursively reducible to *NTE* (via Hilbert's 10th problem as in [6] or directly as in [12]), it suffices to show that it is semi-decidable, given two Petri nets N_1, N_2, whether $\mathcal{T}(N_1) \neq \mathcal{T}(N_2)$.

The semi-decidability follows immediately from the decidability of the problem $\mathcal{P}$:

Instance: a Petri net N and an (observable) sequence w.

Question: Is $w \in \mathcal{T}(N)$?

We can then generate all finite (observable) traces and stop when reaching a sequence belonging to one of the sets $\mathcal{T}(N_1)$, $\mathcal{T}(N_2)$ and not belonging to the other.

The decidability of the problem $\mathcal{P}$ can be shown by various ways using some well-known results from Petri net theory. We outline one of these ways.

To the net N we can add a finite control unit whose states determine which transitions are allowed to fire next; it simplifies our considerations but, of course, it could be modelled by a modification directly in the net N (cf. e.g. [10]). In our case, for $w = a_1 a_2 \ldots a_n$, the control unit will have states $q_1, q_2, \ldots, q_{n+1}$, where q_1 is the initial one. Each q_i ($i = 1, 2, \ldots, n$) only allows transitions labelled by τ or a_i; any τ-transition leaves the control unit in the (current) state q_i whereas any a_i-transition moves it into the (next) state q_{i+1}. Then it suffices to ask whether q_{n+1} is reachable, which is decidable (cf. [15]).

(In fact, we do not need the decidability of reachability. A technique using the Karp, Miller reachability tree, related to the coverability problem, would suffice; cf. e.g. [18] for definitions.)

□

We continue with a short proof of the upper bound for *WB*.

Proof of Theorem 2.

By definition,

(the code of) a pair (Σ_1, M_1), (Σ_2, M_2) is in *WB*

iff

there is a set $X \subseteq \mathcal{N}^{r_1} \times \mathcal{N}^{r_2}$ (where r_i is the number of places in Σ_i) such that

$$(M_1, M_2) \in X \;\wedge$$

$$\wedge\; \forall (x,y) \in X\; [\; \forall a \forall x'\; (\; (x \overset{a}{\Longrightarrow}_{\Sigma_1} x') \longrightarrow \exists y' (y \overset{a}{\Longrightarrow}_{\Sigma_2} y' \wedge (x',y') \in X)\;)\;] \;\wedge$$

$$\wedge\; \forall (x,y) \in X\; [\; \forall a \forall y'\; (\; (y \overset{a}{\Longrightarrow}_{\Sigma_2} y') \longrightarrow \exists x' (x \overset{a}{\Longrightarrow}_{\Sigma_1} x' \wedge (x',y') \in X)\;)\;]$$

where $\forall a$ means for all a which occur in Σ_1 and/or Σ_2.

Because the relation $\overset{a}{\Longrightarrow}$ surely is arithmetical (it is even recursive due to the decidability of the reachability problem), it can be easily verified that there is a 2nd order formula $\phi(x, X)$ with one free individuum variable x, one free set variable X and with no set quantifiers such that for all (codes) $c \in \mathcal{N}$:

$$c \in WB \Longleftrightarrow \exists X \phi(c, X)$$

Thus the desired upper bound is established. □

Now we prove Theorem 3.

The main idea lies in showing a certain (algorithmic) construction $\mathcal{CONS}$ which can be used for any Minsky counter machine C ([17]) with an even (for convenience) number of (nonnegative) counters $c_1, c_2, \ldots, c_{2n}$; the construction yields a pair of Petri nets N_1, N_2 such that

$$\begin{gathered} N_1,\ N_2 \text{ are weakly bisimilar} \\ \text{iff} \\ \text{it is true that } \exists x_1 \forall x_2 \ldots \exists x_{2n-1} \forall x_{2n} \neg ! C(x_1, x_2, \ldots, x_{2n}) \end{gathered}$$

By the notation $\neg ! C(x_1, x_2, \ldots, x_{2n})$ we mean that C does not halt for the input counter values $x_1, x_2, \ldots, x_{2n}$.

When we show the construction $\mathcal{CONS}$, the claim is obvious:

Proof of Theorem 3. (supposing the construction $\mathcal{CONS}$)

Given any 1st order formula ϕ of the standard arithmetic structure $(\mathcal{N}, 0, S, +, \cdot)$, we can transform it into an equivalent formula in the form $\exists x_1 \forall x_2 \ldots \exists x_{2n-1} \forall x_{2n} \phi'(x_1, x_2, \ldots, x_{2n})$ for some n, ϕ' being quantifier-free. (It can be accomplished by a standard transformation into the prenex normal form and by using dummy variables.)

Formula ϕ' is, in fact, a recursive predicate and it is a technical routine to construct a counter machine C with $2n$ counters such that for all $x_1, x_2, \ldots, x_{2n}$

$$\neg ! C(x_1, x_2, \ldots, x_{2n}) \quad \text{iff} \quad \phi'(x_1, x_2, \ldots, x_{2n}) \text{ is true}$$

(in fact, C could need some additional counter(s); in this case we could use more dummy variables and then use the respective counters as the additional ones).

For C, we can construct N_1, N_2 by our (promised) construction $\mathcal{CONS}$ and we have

$$\begin{gathered} \phi \text{ is true in } (\mathcal{N}, 0, S, +, \cdot) \\ \text{iff} \\ \exists x_1 \forall x_2 \ldots \exists x_{2n-1} \forall x_{2n} \phi'(x_1, x_2, \ldots, x_{2n}) \text{ is true in } (\mathcal{N}, 0, S, +, \cdot) \\ \text{iff} \\ \exists x_1 \forall x_2 \ldots \exists x_{2n-1} \forall x_{2n} \neg ! C(x_1, x_2, \ldots, x_{2n}) \text{ is true} \\ \text{iff} \\ N_1,\ N_2 \text{ are weakly bisimilar} \end{gathered}$$

by which the proof is finished.

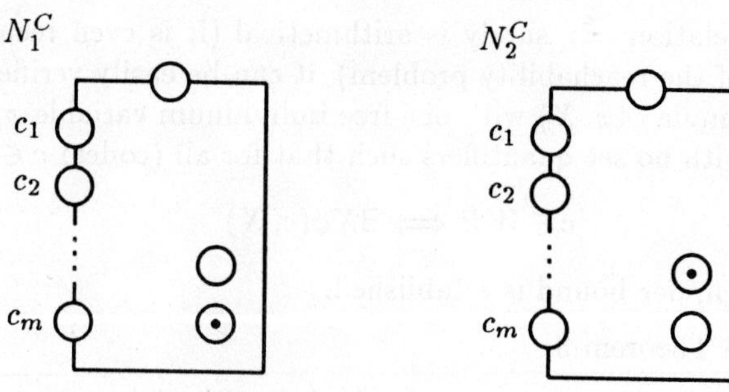

Figure 1:

□

Now we have to describe the construction $\mathcal{CONS}$.

As a basis, we use a result from [12]. It shows a construction which, given a counter machine C with m counters, yields two Petri nets N_1^C and N_2^C (cf. Fig.1). The nets have the same static structure; places $c_1, c_2, \ldots, c_m$ for counters, a "start" place (the upper one in Fig.1), two special places (drawn inside the box) and some other places (and transitions, of course). They only differ in the (predefined) initial marking which is zero except for the two special places (as shown in Fig.1).

Remark. By labelling the transitions in N_1^C (and hence also in N_2^C) no τ-labels are used; therefore weak and strong bisimilarity coincide in this case.

We do not describe details of the construction, which can be found in [12] or in the appendix of [13]. They are only necessary for checking the proof of the following (basic) proposition.

Proposition BP

There is an algorithm which, given any counter machine C, constructs two Petri nets N_1^C, N_2^C, each containing a designated start place and places $c_1, c_2, \ldots, c_m$ where m is the number of counters of C, such that: for any $x_1, \ldots, x_m$ and $x'_1, \ldots, x'_m$, if we put a token in the start place of both N_1^C and N_2^C, $x_1, \ldots, x_m$ tokens in places $c_1, \ldots, c_m$ of N_1^C and $x'_1, \ldots, x'_m$ tokens in $c_1, \ldots, c_m$ of N_2^C respectively then the resulting nets are (weakly) bisimilar iff $x_i = x'_i$ for all i, $1 \le i \le m$, and $\neg !C(x_1, \ldots, x_m)$.

Proof.

If we considered the case with the same input counter values only ($x_i = x'_i$ for all i), the construction from [12] would be the desired algorithm, in fact.

When a counter machine C has different computations for any different inputs $x_1, \ldots, x_m$ and $x'_1, \ldots, x'_m$ then an easy inspection of the construction of [12] shows that N_1^C and N_2^C are nonbisimilar when starting with different counter values (Player 1 in the below described bisimulation game forces the situation, when the counter to be tested is zero in one net and nonzero in the other; i.e. in one net a transition, with its unique label, is enabled while in the other net not). Therefore for such a machine C, the construction of [12] is sufficient again.

To prove the proposition completely, it suffices to realize that for any C we can construct the following C' with an additional auxiliary counter: C' starts with "moving" the value of each counter, successively, into the auxiliary counter and back and then computes like C. Therefore C' really has different computations for any different inputs (and is equivalent to C w.r.t. halting). Hence the nets $N_1^{C'}$ and $N_2^{C'}$ in the "original" sense of [12], with the place for the auxiliary counter viewed as "internal", can be taken as N_1^C, N_2^C in our proposition. □

For describing and verifying $\mathcal{CONS}$, some game terminology will be useful. First we recall a natural definition of a bisimulation game (cf. e.g. [19]).

(Weak) Bisimulation Game

1. *Prerequisities*
   There are two players, Player 1 and Player 2, and a pair of Petri nets N_1, N_2 (as the "playboard").

2. *Rules*
   Player 1 chooses one of the nets and changes the marking (by firing a sequence of transitions) according to the relation $\stackrel{a}{\Longrightarrow}$ for some a.
   Then Player 2 replies by changing the marking in *the other* net according to $\stackrel{a}{\Longrightarrow}$ for the same a (if it is possible).
   Again, Player 1 chooses one of the nets ..., Player 2 replies ... etc.

3. *Result*
   The player who has no possible move (being his turn) loses; the other player wins. The case of an infinite run of the game is considered as successful for Player 2 (he defends successfully).

It is not difficult to see that Player 1 has a winning strategy if and only if N_1, N_2 are not weakly bisimilar.

In the rest of this section, we suppose a fixed counter machine C with $2n$ counters $c_1, c_2, \ldots, c_{2n}$. Let us now consider another game.

Game G (for Player 1 and Player 2)

a/ *Board:* Petri nets N_1^C and N_2^C (cf. Fig.1)

b/ *Rules:*

1. First, there are $2n$ special moves:
   – Player 2 begins and puts an arbitrary number of tokens x_1 in the

places c_1 in both nets (the same value in both nets),
– Player 1 continues and puts an arbitrary number of tokens x_2 in the places c_2,
– Player 2 continues setting the value of c_3,
...
– Player 1 sets the value of c_{2n}.

2. After these $2n$ moves, a token is put in the start place of N_1^C as well as in the start place of N_2^C and the bisimulation game starts (Player 1 chooses ...).

Proposition BP ensures that Player 1 has no winning strategy in the game G (in other words: Player 2 has a defending strategy) iff it is true that $\exists x_1 \forall x_2 \ldots \exists x_{2n-1} \forall x_{2n} \neg ! C(x_1, x_2, \ldots, x_{2n})$.

In fact, $\mathcal{CONS}$ will yield Petri nets N_1, N_2 such that the game G on N_1^C, N_2^C can be simulated by playing the bisimulation game on N_1, N_2. These Petri nets will be based on (more copies of) N_1^C, N_2^C. Any concrete run of the game G on N_1^C, N_2^C will correspond to a run of the bisimulation game on N_1, N_2. There will be runs on N_1, N_2 which do not correspond to runs on N_1^C, N_2^C but it will be shown that neither of the Players can get any advantage by causing such runs. In this sense, the "external" rules of G for the first $2n$ moves on N_1^C, N_2^C are inherently present in the bisimulation game on N_1, N_2. Let us remark that setting a counter value will be accomplished by τ-transitions, which is their "only" use.

Now we show an inductive construction, for $j = 2n, 2n-1, \ldots, 1, 0$, of Petri nets N_j^L, N_j^R (L for "left", R for "right"). N_0^L, N_0^R will be the desired N_1, N_2 (the output of $\mathcal{CONS}$). Intuitively, (starting) the pair N_j^L, N_j^R corresponds to the situation in the game G where j counters have been set.

We illustrate the construction in figures where we use broken arrows leading from a place to a (sub)net; the meaning is explained in Fig.2. Such an arrow leading from a place r to a (sub)net Σ and being labelled by a subset of places of Σ denotes the fact that there are special τ-labelled transitions; r is a "run-place" for these transitions and firing a sequence of them allows to add (or to subtract) an arbitrary – but the same for all – number to (or from) all places in the subset. Fig.2 illustrates it for a 2-element subset.

N_j^L and N_j^R will contain more "copies" of (places corresponding to) counters. By labelling a broken arrow by c_{2k+1}, for example, we understand that the label c_{2k+1} stands for the set of all copies of the counter c_{2k+1} in the target subnet.

The (inductive) construction of N_j^L and N_j^R

1. Let N_{2n}^L be N_1^C and let N_{2n}^R be N_2^C.

2. For an odd $j = 2k+1$, N_{2k+1}^L, N_{2k+1}^R are shown in Fig.3. (N_{2k+1}^L contains N_{2k+1}^R as a subnet).

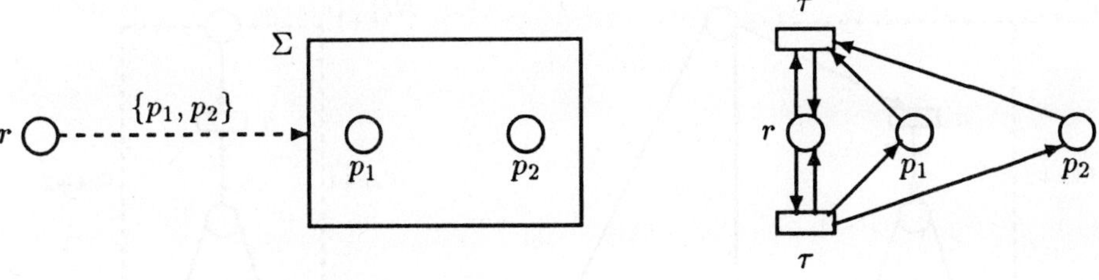

Figure 2: Meaning of broken arrows

3. For an even $j = 2k$, N_{2k}^L, N_{2k}^R are shown in Fig.4. (N_{2k}^R contains N_{2k}^L as a subnet).

The action a in the figures is observable (not τ). By the "start place" of N_j^L (or N_j^R) we mean the upper place in the figure.

Consider now the bisimulation game on the nets N_0^L and N_0^R with a token in the start place of both – and zero elsewhere with the exception of the special (internal) places of copies of N_1^C, N_2^C (recall Fig.1), which are subnets of the nets being considered.

Notice that, within any move, none of the Players has any reason for firing a τ-sequence only or for adding some τ-sequence after firing an a – the results with and without such a τ-sequence are obviously weakly bisimilar (the effect of such a sequence can be achieved or "undone" freely by a τ-sequence starting the next move). Therefore we can suppose the beginning of the game as follows: Player 1 fires some τ-sequence and an a-transition in one net, Player 2 replies with firing a τ-sequence and an a-transition in the other net etc. – after $2n$ such moves of Player 1 (and $2n$ answers of Player 2), two from the copies of N_1^C, N_2^C are "started" (with some input values determined by previous τ-sequences).

Now it suffices to prove the following propositions $\mathcal{P}_j$, $j = 2n, 2n-1, \ldots, 1, 0$. $\mathcal{P}_0$ shows that N_0^L, N_0^R are really our "desired" N_1, N_2 (the output of $\mathcal{CONS}$ relevant to our fixed counter machine C). We again deal with the cases "j even" and "j odd" separately.

Proposition $\mathcal{P}_{2k}$

For any $x_1, x_2, \ldots, x_{2k}$ and $x'_1, x'_2, \ldots, x'_{2k}$, when we put a token in the start place of both N_{2k}^L and N_{2k}^R, $x_1, x_2, \ldots, x_{2k}$ tokens in all copies of $c_1, c_2, \ldots, c_{2k}$ in N_{2k}^L and $x'_1, x'_2, \ldots, x'_{2k}$ tokens in all copies of $c_1, c_2, \ldots, c_{2k}$ in N_{2k}^R respectively then the resulting nets are weakly bisimilar iff $x_i = x'_i$ for all $i = 1, 2, \ldots, 2k$ and $\exists x_{2k+1} \forall x_{2k+2} \ldots \exists x_{2n-1} \forall x_{2n} \neg ! C(x_1, x_2, \ldots, x_{2n})$.

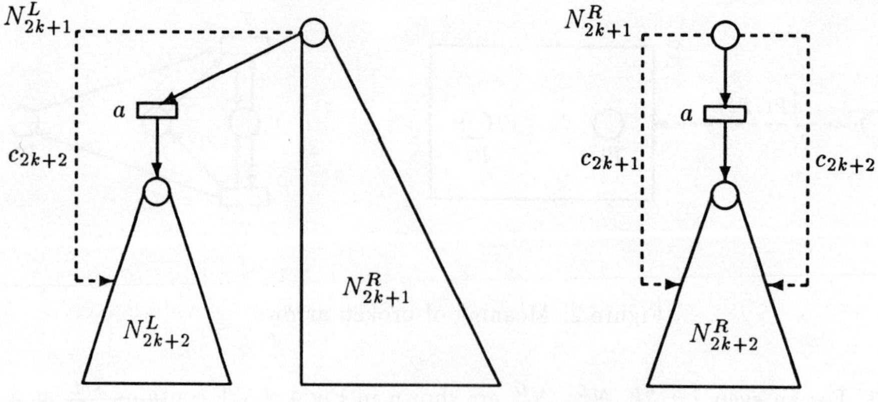

Figure 3: N^L_j and N^R_j for ODD $j = 2k+1$

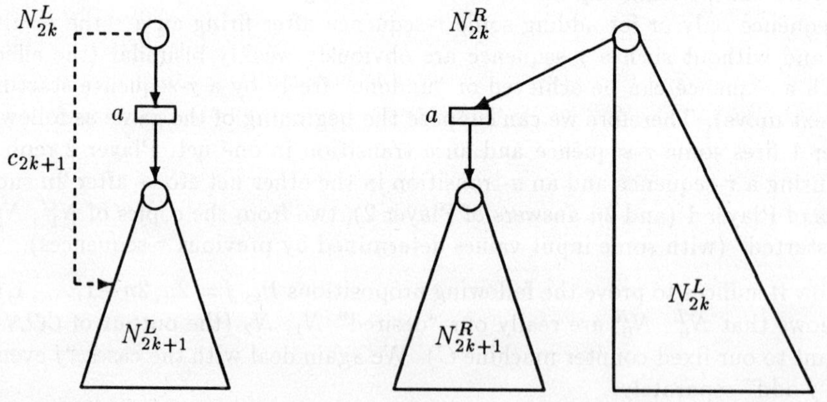

Figure 4: N^L_j and N^R_j for EVEN $j = 2k$

Proposition $\mathcal{P}_{2k+1}$

For any $x_1, x_2, \ldots, x_{2k}$, any $x'_1, x'_2, \ldots, x'_{2k}$ and any x_{2k+1}, when we put a token in the start place of both N^L_{2k+1} and N^R_{2k+1}, $x_1, x_2, \ldots, x_{2k}$ tokens in all copies of $c_1, c_2, \ldots, c_{2k}$ in N^L_{2k+1}, $x'_1, x'_2, \ldots, x'_{2k}$ tokens in all copies of $c_1, c_2, \ldots, c_{2k}$ in N^R_{2k+1} respectively and x_{2k+1} tokens in all copies of c_{2k+1} in N^L_{2k+1} then the resulting nets are weakly bisimilar iff $x_i = x'_i$ for all $i = 1, 2, \ldots, 2k$ and $\forall x_{2k+2} \exists x_{2k+3} \forall x_{2k+4} \ldots \exists x_{2n-1} \forall x_{2n} \neg ! C(x_1, x_2, \ldots, x_{2n})$.

First note that the base case, Proposition $\mathcal{P}_{2n}$, follows immediately from Proposition BP. (Recall that N^L_{2n} is N^C_1 and N^R_{2n} is N^C_2.) Therefore to prove $\mathcal{P}_{2k}$ ($\mathcal{P}_{2k+1}$), we can suppose that $\mathcal{P}_{2k+1}$ ($\mathcal{P}_{2k+2}$) holds. We start with Proposition $\mathcal{P}_{2k}$ since it is a bit easier.

Proof of Proposition $\mathcal{P}_{2k}$

Consider N^L_{2k} and N^R_{2k}, $k < n$, (cf. Fig.4) with a token in the start place of both and $x_1, x_2, \ldots, x_{2k}$ tokens in all copies of $c_1, c_2, \ldots, c_{2k}$ in N^L_{2k} and $x'_1, x'_2, \ldots, x'_{2k}$ tokens in all copies of $c_1, c_2, \ldots, c_{2k}$ in N^R_{2k} respectively.

If $x_i \neq x'_i$ for some $i, 1 \leq i \leq 2k$, then Player 1 can "start" N^R_{2k+1} firing the "left" a-transition in N^R_{2k} after which Player 2 is forced to start N^L_{2k+1} – but not having the possibility to change the inequality $x_i \neq x'_i$, he reaches a "situation" which is non-bisimilar due to Proposition $\mathcal{P}_{2k+1}$.

Now suppose $x_i = x'_i$ for all $i, 1 \leq i \leq 2k$. If Player 1 wants to win, he has to choose the left a in N^R_{2k} – by choosing another a, Player 2 could obviously reach the identical situation in both nets (the same "active" subnets). Recall that it has no sense for Player 1 to add a τ-sequence and note that values of $c_1, c_2, \ldots, c_{2k}$ remain unchanged in (now active) N^R_{2k+1}. Player 2 answers by firing a in N^L_{2k} preceeded by setting an arbitrary value x_{2k+1} in (all copies of) c_{2k+1} in N^L_{2k+1} (which now becomes active). If there is some x_{2k+1} such that $\forall x_{2k+2} \exists x_{2k+3} \forall x_{2k+4} \ldots \exists x_{2n-1} \forall x_{2n} \neg ! C(x_1, x_2, \ldots, x_{2n})$ then Player 2 could choose such x_{2k+1} and reach a bisimilar situation; otherwise, no matter what he sets in c_{2k+1}, the resulting situation is non-bisimilar (both variants follow from Proposition $\mathcal{P}_{2k+1}$). □

Proof of Proposition $\mathcal{P}_{2k+1}$

Consider N^L_{2k+1} and N^R_{2k+1}, (cf. Fig.3) with a token in the start place of both, $x_1, x_2, \ldots, x_{2k}$ tokens in all copies of $c_1, c_2, \ldots, c_{2k}$ in N^L_{2k+1}, $x'_1, x'_2, \ldots, x'_{2k}$ tokens in all copies of $c_1, c_2, \ldots, c_{2k}$ in N^R_{2k+1} respectively and x_{2k+1} tokens in all copies of c_{2k+1} in N^L_{2k+1}.

The case with $x_i \neq x'_i$ for some $i, 1 \leq i \leq 2k$ is similar to that in the proof for $\mathcal{P}_{2k}$.

Now suppose $x_i = x'_i$ for all $i, 1 \leq i \leq 2k$. It is clear that if Player 1 wants to win, he has to choose the left a – now in N^L_{2k+1}, thus starting N^L_{2k+2}. But before this starting he can set any value x_{2k+2} in (all copies of) c_{2k+2} in N^L_{2k+2}. Player

2 answers in N^R_{2k+1} by setting the same values of (all copies of) c_{2k+1} and c_{2k+2} in N^R_{2k+2} as are set in N^L_{2k+2} (in fact, Player 2 sets the same value of c_{2k+1} as he chose in the "left" net in the previous move and sets the same value of c_{2k+2} as Player 1 has just chosen); note that if he had not set the same values, he would have reached a nonbisimilar situation due to Proposition $\mathcal{P}_{2k+2}$. If now for all x_{2k+2} it holds that $\exists x_{2k+3} \forall x_{2k+4} \ldots \exists x_{2n-1} \forall x_{2n} \neg! C(x_1, x_2, \ldots, x_{2n})$ we have surely arrived at a bisimilar situation; otherwise Player 1 could choose some x_{2k+2} which ensures arriving at a nonbisimilar situation (again due to induction hypothesis $\mathcal{P}_{2k+2}$). □

Thus we have finished the description and the correctness proof for the construction $\mathcal{CONS}$ and we are done.

Acknowledgements

I would like to thank J.Bradfield and J.Esparza for discussions and comments on the first version of this paper.

References

[1] J. Barwise (ed.), *Handbook of Mathematical Logic* (North Holland, 5th printing 1989).

[2] S. Christensen, Y. Hirshfeld and F. Moller, Bisimulation equivalence is decidable for all Basic Parallel Processes, in: *Proc. CONCUR'93*, Lecture Notes in Computer Science, Vol. 715 (Springer, Berlin, 1993) 143–157.

[3] S. Christensen, H. Hüttel and C. Stirling, Bisimulation equivalence is decidable for all context-free processes, in: *Proc. CONCUR'92*, Lecture Notes in Computer Science, Vol. 630 (Springer, Berlin, 1992) 138–147.

[4] J. Esparza, On the uniform word problem for commutative context-free grammars, unpublished.

[5] R.J. van Glabbeek, The linear time – branching time spectrum, in: *Proc. CONCUR'90*, Lecture Notes in Computer Science, Vol. 458 (Springer, Berlin, 1990) 278–297.

[6] M. Hack, Decision problems for Petri nets and vector addition systems, MAC Tech. Memo 53, MIT, 1975.

[7] Y. Hirshfeld, Petri nets and the equivalence problem, in: *Proc. Computer Science Logic '93*, Lecture Notes in Computer Science, Vol. 832 (Springer-Verlag, 1994) 165–174.

[8] Y. Hirshfeld, M. Jerrum and F. Moller, A polynomial algorithm for deciding bisimilarity of normed context-free processes, Tech.rep. ECS-LFCS-94-286, Dept. of comp. sci., Univ. of Edinburgh, UK, March 1994 (to appear in *Theor. Comp. Sci.*).

[9] Y. Hirshfeld, M. Jerrum and F. Moller, A polynomial-time algorithm for deciding bisimulation equivalence of normed Basic Parallel Processes, Tech.rep. ECS-LFCS-94-288, Dept. of comp. sci., Univ. of Edinburgh, UK, April 1994.

[10] J. Hopcroft and J. Pansiot, On the reachability problem for 5-dimensional vector addition systems, *Theoret. Comput. Sci.* **8** (1979) 135–159.

[11] H. Hüttel, Undecidable equivalences for Basic Parallel processes, 13th Conf. on Foundations of Software Technology and Theoretical Computer Science, Bombay, India, 1993
(also Tech.rep. ECS-LFCS-93-276, Dept. of comp. sci., Univ. of Edinburgh, UK, August 1993).

[12] P. Jančar, Decidability questions for bisimilarity of Petri nets and some related problems, in *Proc. STACS'94*, Lecture Notes in Computer Science, Vol. 775 (Springer, Berlin, 1994) 581–592
(an extended version should appear in *Theor. Comp. Sci.*)

[13] P. Jančar, High undecidability of weak bisimilarity for Petri nets, Tech.rep. ECS-LFCS-94-298, Dept. of comp. sci., Univ. of Edinburgh, UK, August 1994.

[14] A. Kiehn and M. Hennessy, On the decidability of non-interleaving process equivalences, in *Proc. CONCUR'94*, Lecture Notes in Computer Science, Vol. 836 (Springer-Verlag, 1994).

[15] E. Mayr, An algorithm for the general Petri net reachability problem, *SIAM J. Comput.* **13** (1984) 441–460.

[16] R. Milner, *Communication and Concurrency* (Prentice Hall, 1989).

[17] M. Minsky, *Computation: Finite and Infinite Machines* (Prentice Hall, 1967).

[18] J.L. Peterson, *Petri Net Theory and the Modelling of Systems* (Prentice Hall, 1981).

[19] C. Stirling, Modal and temporal logics for processes, Lecture notes to the Summerschool in logical methods in concurrency, Aarhus University, Denmark, 1993.

Polynomial Algorithms for the Synthesis of Bounded Nets *

Eric Badouel, Luca Bernardinello, and Philippe Darondeau

Irisa, Campus de Beaulieu, F-35042 Rennes Cedex, France
E-mail : {Eric.Badouel, Luca.Bernardinello, Philippe.Darondeau}@irisa.fr

Abstract. The so-called synthesis problem for nets, which consists in deciding whether a given graph is isomorphic to the case graph of some net, and then constructing the net, has been solved in the litterature for various types of nets, ranging from elementary nets to Petri nets. The common principle for the synthesis is the idea of regions in graphs, representing possible extensions of places in nets. However, no practical algorithm has been defined so far for the synthesis. We give here explicit algorithms solving in polynomial time the synthesis problem for bounded nets from regular languages or from finite automata.

1 Introduction

The so-called synthesis problem for nets consists in deciding whether a given graph is isomorphic to the case graph of some net, and then constructing the net. This problem has been solved for various types of nets, ranging from elementary nets to Petri nets. However, no practical algorithm has been defined so far for the synthesis. In this paper we give an explicit algorithm for the synthesis of bounded nets from finite automata. This algorithm is polynomial in time (and space) in the size of the automata. We also consider a variant of the synthesis problem which consists in deciding whether a given regular language is the language accepted by some bounded net, and then constructing the net. We give an independent algorithm solving this problem. This algorithm is polynomial in time (and space) in the size of regular expressions in "failure tree form". Any regular language can be described by such an expression, that can be derived (in exponential time) from a finite automaton recognizing the language.

Ehrenfeucht and Rozenberg addressed in [ER90] the problem of characterizing axiomatically the class of simple directed graphs labeled on arcs which may be represented unambiguously by a set of subsets of an overall coding set together with a set of mutual differences between them. Central to that work is the concept of *region* in a graph, defined as a set of vertices which are entered, exited, or left invariant by all arcs with an identical label. The overall coding set for a graph may always be chosen as its set of regions. A region is a property of the vertices it contains. Conversely, a vertex may be represented as the set of regions which it belongs to, and

* This work was partly supported by the French P.R.C. *Modèles et Preuves*, by the H.C.M. Network *Express*, and by the H.C.M. fellowship granted to Luca Bernardinello, on leave from the University of Milan.

that representation is unambiguous if and only if every pair of vertices is *separated* in the usual sense by some region. Since all arcs with an identical label carry the same change of properties, a label may be represented as the mutual difference between the respective sets of properties of the source and target vertices of any arc associated with that label in the graph, and that representation is unambiguous due to simpleness. The graph may be reconstructed from the set of mutual differences if each vertex which is not the origin of any arc with a given label is *separated* from that label by some region, which means that the region contains all the origins of the arcs carrying that label, but not the considered vertex. The so-called *regional axioms* specify those two different requirements of separation. Ehrenfeucht and Rozenberg applied the regional axioms to solve the synthesis problem for elementary nets in [ER90]. Given a simple directed graph labeled on arcs, they construct from that graph an elementary net with one place per region, one transition per label, and with flow relations between places and transitions laid down according to the mutual differences between vertices seen as sets of places, or markings. The case graph of the net assembled in this way is isomorphic to the given graph if and only if that graph is an *elementary transition system*, which implies essentially that the two regional axioms are satisfied. It is worth noting that in case the given graph is the case graph of an elementary net, the construction leads to a *saturated* version of that net, where extra places have been added without disturbing the behaviour but only copies of those places can still be added. Desel and Reisig observed in [DR92] that one may optimize the solution of the synthesis problem by computing any reduced set of regions sufficient to ensure satisfaction of the regional axioms in the graph. Along a similar line, Bernardinello proved in [Ber93] that the set of minimal regions (w.r.t. set inclusion) is adequate for that purpose. Unfortunately, this result does not seem to lead specially to practical algorithms with low complexity.

We will show that standard techniques of linear algebra lead to smooth algorithms for the synthesis of bounded nets in the extended framework of *general regions*, which were introduced under variant forms by Droste and Shortt [DS93], Mukund [Muk93], and Bernardinello, De Michelis and Petruni [BDP93]. General regions are multisets where regions are sets. A general region in a labeled graph is a multiset of vertices whose rank of membership is modified by a uniform translation along all arcs with an identical label. Since ranks of membership are whole numbers, uniform translations on ranks are defined by relative numbers. A general region is a property which may be satisfied at different degrees, measured by ranks of membership of vertices. In a dual way, a vertex may be represented as the multiset of properties which it satisfies at some positive rank. Given a simple directed graph labeled on arcs, one can construct an induced place transition net with one place per general region, one transition per label, and with arcs between places and transitions weighted by norms of uniform translations and directed according to the signs of their defining numbers. Here again, the place transition net assembled in this way is a saturated net and its case graph is isomorphic to the given graph if and only if that graph satisfies the two regional axioms, restated in terms of ranked membership.

The object of this paper is to provide practical algorithms for deciding satisfaction of the regional axioms in a *finite* graph and for computing in that case just enough general regions to induce a place transition net with an isomorphic case graph. We leave for further study possible extensions to particular classes of infinite graphs. For sure, a finite graph is never the case graph of an unbounded Net. We shall therefore deal exclusively with bounded nets, whose precise definition is given in section 2.

We tackle in a first stage a relaxation of the synthesis problem for bounded nets, which is addressed in section 3 for languages defined by regular expressions. A language closed under left factors may be identified with a deterministic labeled tree. Regions in a language may therefore be defined as general regions in the underlying tree. Of special interest since we deal with bounded nets are general regions with bounded rank of membership, which we call *bounded regions.* The synthesis problem for languages is not quite the same as for labeled graphs: the sole constraint on the net assembled from regions in a language is to behave according to that language, which is significantly weaker than having a case graph isomorphic to the underlying tree. This weaker requirement is met if and only if that tree satisfies the second regional axiom, which was observed by Hoogers, Kleijn and Thiagarajan in the context of trace languages [HKT92]. A region in a language is totally determined by an offset, which is the rank of membership of the empty word, and by a vector of displacements, which are relative numbers defining the uniform translations attached to labels. Abstracting a little more, one may forget about offsets and consider *abstract regions* defined as vectors of relative numbers, or yet equivalently as morphisms from the free monoid over the set of labels to the additive monoid of relative numbers. The abstract regions which are the projections of the bounded regions in a regular language form a module of finite dimension over $\mathbb{Z}$. We will show that deciding whether a regular language satisfies the second regional axiom and computing in that case a bounded net with equivalent behaviour may be reduced to solving finite linear systems over the integers, uniform in the regular expression. We evolve therefrom a practical method for the synthesis of bounded nets, based on *polynomial* algorithms discovered in the late seventies for linear programming over the rational field. Altogether, we obtain a polynomial algorithm for the synthesis of nets from regular expressions in the so-called failures tree form (which in particular means they are represented by trees labeled with action symbols and starred expressions).

We tackle in a second stage the general synthesis problem for bounded nets, which is addressed in section 4 for finite automata. Since we are back in the framework of labeled graphs, the first regional axiom is re-imposed. A general region in a finite automaton is determined by an offset, which is the rank of membership of the initial state, and by a vector of relative numbers which associate uniform translations to labels. A region in a finite automaton is always a region in the language of the automaton, but the converse is not true. The set of abstract regions in a finite automaton is a submodule of the module of abstract regions in the language of the automaton. The abstract regions which are projections of bounded regions are the solutions of a system of linear equations which express equality constraints relative to states, stronger in general than the boundedness constraints relative to the language of the automaton. Altogether, one retrieves the constraints set on *synchronic distances* in [BDP93], which shows that abstract regions are in a one-one correspondence with synchronic distances. The advantage of the more algebraic view taken here is to lead directly to algorithms. We will show that deciding whether a finite automaton satisfies the two regional axiom and then computing a bounded net with equivalent behaviour, reduce again to solving finite linear systems over the rational field, uniform in the automaton. Altogether, we obtain a polynomial algorithm for the synthesis of nets from finite automata.

2 Notations for Petri Nets

We adopt in this paper a notation for Place/Transition nets slightly different from the usual one; this should not cause confusion.

Definition 2.1 (Nets) *A* net *is a structure* $N = (P, T, W)$, *where* P *and* T *are disjoint sets, of* places *and* transitions *respectively, and* $W : P \times T \rightarrow \mathbb{Z}$ *is the* weight *function. The set of* input *(resp.* output*) places of a transition* t *is the set* ${}^\bullet t$ *(resp.* $t^\bullet$*) of places* p *such that* $W(p,t) < 0$ *(resp.* $W(p,t) > 0$*). A* marking *of* N *is a map* $m : P \rightarrow \mathbb{N}$.

Nets are usually equipped with a flow relation $F \subseteq (P \times T) \cup (T \times P)$ and a weight function $W : F \rightarrow \mathbb{N}^+$. We can adopt here a more compact notation because we consider exclusively *pure* nets, i.e. nets such that $\forall x, y \in P \cup T \quad (x,y) \in F \Rightarrow (y,x) \notin F$.

The overall behaviour of a Place/Transition net is determined by the so-called *firing rule* which tells that a transition is enabled at a marking if that marking supplies enough resources in each of its input places.

Definition 2.2 (Firing rule) *Let* $N = (P, T, W)$ *be a net and* M *a marking of* N*; a transition* $t \in T$ *is* enabled *at* m *if* $\forall p \in P \quad M(p) + W(p,t) \geq 0$. *If transition* t *is enabled at marking* M, *then it can fire; in doing so, it produces a new marking* M', *defined by* $\forall p \in P \quad M'(p) = M(p) + W(p,t)$. *This firing step is denoted* $M[t{>}M'$. *A sequence of transitions* $u = t_1 t_2 \cdots t_n$ *is enabled at a marking* M_0 *if* $\exists M_1, \ldots M_n$ *such that* $M_{i-1}[t_i{>}M_i$, *for all* $i = 1, \ldots, n$. *This firing sequence is denoted* $M_0[u{>}M_n$.

While the overall behaviour of a Place/Transition net reflects its whole structure, one is most often interested in restricted behaviours induced by initial markings.

Definition 2.3 (Marked net) *A* marked *net is a structure* $N = (P, T, W, M_0)$, *where* (P, T, W) *is a net and* $M_0 : P \rightarrow \mathbb{N}$ *is the* initial marking. *The set of* reachable markings *of* N *is the smallest set* $\mathcal{M}(N)$ *of markings such that*

1. $M_0 \in \mathcal{M}(N)$,
2. if $M \in \mathcal{M}(N)$ *and* $M[t{>}M'$ *then* $M' \in \mathcal{M}(N)$.

The marking graph *of* N *is the labeled transition system* $ng(N)$ *with set of states* $\mathcal{M}(N)$, *initial state* M_0, *set of labels* T, *and set of labeled transitions* $Tr(N) \subseteq \mathcal{M}(N) \times T \times \mathcal{M}(N)$ *defined by* $(M, t, M') \in Tr(N) \Leftrightarrow M[t{>}M'$. *The* language *of net* N, *or equivalently the language of the marking graph* $ng(N)$, *is the set of all sequences of transitions enabled at* M_0 *(thus this language is prefix closed).*

Of special interest in this paper are marked nets with finite sets of reachable markings. A relaxed form of finiteness may be defined as follows.

Definition 2.4 (Bounded net) *A place* p *of a marked net* $N = (P, T, W, M_0)$ *is* bounded *if the set* $\{M(p) | M \in \mathcal{M}(N)\}$ *is finite. A marked net with bounded places is called a* bounded *net.*

Droste and Shortt observed in [DS92] that a bounded net with finitely many transitions must have a finite set of reachable markings. Hence any bounded net with finite dimension may be transformed into a finite equivalent net.

3 Regions in Regular Languages

The goal of the section is to solve the following problem:

Problem 3.1 *Given a prefix-closed language $L \subseteq A^*$, decide whether there exists a marked net with language L and if so, construct such a net.*

We will present a polynomial algorithm which answers this problem for regular languages. The basic constituent of the proposed solution is the principle of abstract regions which may in fact be applied to arbitrary languages. We shall therefore cast the definition of regions in a general context, and subsequently focus on regular languages.

Throughout the section, let L denote a *prefix-closed* language over a finite alphabet $A = \{a_1, \ldots, a_n\}$, ranged over by a, and for any map $\rho : A \longrightarrow \mathbb{Z}$, let $\hat{\rho} : A^* \longrightarrow \mathbb{Z}$ denote the monoid morphism $\hat{\rho}(ua) = \hat{\rho}(u) + \rho(a)$. Thus in particular $0 \in \hat{\rho}(L)$, where $\hat{\rho}(L) = \{\hat{\rho}(u) \mid u \in L\}$.

3.1 Regions in Formal Languages

An abstract region in a prefix-closed language L over alphabet A is a morphism from A^* to $\mathbb{Z}$, satisfying the requirement that L should be mapped to an interval of $\mathbb{Z}$ bounded from below. If one imagines the morphic image of a word in L as the measure of variation of an abstract resource through a deterministic process, the requirement guarantees that starvation may be avoided globally by feeding in every process in L with a fixed amount of initial resource. Bounded abstract regions, which will play an essential role in our study of regular languages, satisfy the stronger requirement that L should be mapped to a finite interval of $\mathbb{Z}$, reflecting the intuition that a language considered as a non-deterministic process can only produce a bounded amount of resource.

Definition 3.2 (Regions of a language) *A region of L is a map $\rho : A \longrightarrow \mathbb{Z}$ such that the set $\{\hat{\rho}(w) \mid w \in L\}$ has an infimum. A* bounded *region of L is a region ρ of L such that the set $\{\hat{\rho}(w) \mid w \in L\}$ has also a supremum. Let R_L, resp. BR_L denote the set of regions, resp. bounded regions of L.*

The algebraic properties of abstract regions which follow immediately from the definition are gathered below.

Fact 3.3 *The sets R_L and BR_L are closed under pointwise sum of maps, and the null region ρ_0 with constant value $\rho_0(a) = 0$ is the neutral element for sum. Moreover, the set BR_L is closed under inverses. Thus R_L is a monoid, and BR_L is an abelian group.*

As already observed in [BDP93], the bounded regions of a language over alphabet A are a subgroup of the free abelian group of maps from A to $\mathbb{Z}$, which is finitely generated since A is finite. As a consequence, BR_L is also a free group with a finite set of generators, which is tantamount to a module of finite dimension over $\mathbb{Z}$. In order to recover *concrete* regions from *abstract* regions, it suffices to attach to each abstract region $\rho \in R_L$ the minimal *offset* $M_L(\rho)$ such that any possible displacement $\hat{\rho}(u)$ associated with some word $u \in L$ leads therefrom to a non negative value $M_L(\rho) + \hat{\rho}(u)$. The term *region* is used in all the sequel as an abbreviation for *abstract region.*

We are now in a position to derive marked nets from prefix-closed languages: the transitions are the symbols in the alphabet, the places are regions, and the weight functions are set in agreement with the values of regions.

Definition 3.4 (Nets derived from languages)

1. *The* saturated net $\mathcal{N}(L)$ *derived from L is the net* (R_L, A, W, M_L), *where* $W(\rho, a) = \rho(a)$ *for* $\rho \in R_L$, *and* $M_L(\rho) = -\inf\{\hat{\rho}(u) \mid u \in L\}$.
2. *For any set of regions* $R \subseteq R_L$, *the* R-net *derived from L is the sub-net of* $\mathcal{N}(L)$ *with set of places* R.
3. *In particular, the* saturated bounded net $\mathcal{BN}(L)$ *derived from L is the sub-net of* $\mathcal{N}(L)$ *with set of places* BR_L.

Notice that since L is prefix-closed $M_L(\rho) \geq 0$. We are mostly interested in determining the necessary and sufficient conditions under which the languages of the nets $\mathcal{N}(L)$ or $\mathcal{BN}(L)$ coincide with the language L. Those conditions may be stated in terms of the following properties of separation.

Definition 3.5 (Separation properties for languages) *Let* $R \subseteq R_L$ *be a subset of regions of L, then L is said to be* separated by R *if and only if for all word* u, $(u \notin L \Rightarrow \exists \rho \in R \quad M_L(\rho) + \hat{\rho}(u) < 0)$. *The language L is* separated *if it is separated by* R_L, *and* boundedly separated *if it is separated by* BR_L.

Remark 3.6 *We say that a region ρ of L kills the word ua whenever* $M_L(\rho) + \hat{\rho}(ua) < 0$ *whereas* $M_L(\rho) + \hat{\rho}(u) \geq 0$. *Thefore a prefix-closed language L is separated by R if and only if every* faulty word $u \cdot a \in (L \cdot A) \setminus L$ *is killed by some region of R.*

Example 3.7

1. *Let L be the (prefix-closed) regular language* $a^* + a^*b$ *then necessarily* $\rho(a) \geq 0$ *for every region ρ of L, thus no region* $\rho \in R_L$ *kills the word ba and L is not separated (since* $b \in L$ *and* $ba \notin L$).
2. *Let L be the (prefix-closed) regular language* $a^* + a(a^*)b(a^*)$ *then L is separated, but L is not boundedly separated, since any region ρ of L which kills the word* $b \notin L$ *satisfies* $\rho(a) > 0$ *(any region ρ of L must satisfy* $M_L(\rho) + \hat{\rho}(ab) \geq 0$).
3. *Let L be the prefix-closure of the language* $\{(a.\bar{a})^n b(c.\bar{c})^n | n \in \mathbb{N}\}$, *which is algebraic but not regular, then L is separated by a finite set of regions but it cannot be separated by any set of bounded regions (if it was, L would be regular according to the remark of Droste and Schortt).*

The places of a net may always be identified with regions in the language of that net, moreover the language of a net is separated by the set of regions associated with places in the net, even though $M_L(\rho)$ does not necessarily coincide with the value of the initial marking of the net at the place associated with ρ.

Proposition 3.8 *A prefix-closed language L coincides with the language of the R-net derived from L iff it is separated by R.*

Corollary 3.9

1. *A prefix-closed language L coincides with the language of the saturated net $\mathcal{N}(L)$ iff it is separated.*
2. *A prefix-closed language L coincides with the language of the saturated bounded net $\mathcal{BN}(L)$ iff it is boundedly separated.*

Observe that no place (except places obtained from existing places by possibly increasing their values at the initial marking) can be added to the saturated net $\mathcal{N}(L)$ derived from a separated language L without modifying its behaviour (and similarly for bounded places w.r.t saturated bounded nets and boundedly separated languages). In the rest of the section, we concentrate on the problem of synthesizing bounded nets from regular expressions.

3.2 Computing a Basis for Bounded Regions in a Regular Language

We already observed (see Fact. 3.3) that the bounded regions of a prefix-closed language form a module of finite dimension over $\mathbb{Z}$. Our purpose is now to design an algorithm which computes in polynomial time a basis of that module for any prefix-closed and regular language given by a regular expression. Let us fix the notation.

Definition 3.10 (Regular expressions) *A* regular expression *over alphabet A is an expression E in the B.N.F. syntax $E ::= \varepsilon \mid a \mid E{+}E \mid E \times E \mid E^*$, where $a \in A$.*

Regular expressions E are mapped to regular languages $|E|$ by the obvious morphism $|\cdot|$, which is onto. By abuse of notations, we shall often extend to regular expressions notations defined for their languages, for instance BR_E will stand for the module of bounded regions of the language $|E|$. From now on, E is a fixed regular expression denoting a prefix-closed language. We will show that the module of regions BR_E is the kernel of a linear system over $\mathbb{Z}$, obtained by decomposing E into so-called *cyclic factors*, next translated independently to equations whose unknowns are the values $\rho(a_1), \ldots, \rho(a_n)$ of an abstract region.

Definition 3.11 (Cyclic factors of a regular expression) *A* cyclic factor *of the regular expression E is the image of an* iterated *sub-expression F of E (i.e. such that F^* appears in E) by the* shortcut operator $\cdot^{@}$ *with inductive definition as follows: $(E^*)^{@} = \varepsilon$, $(E \times E')^{@} = (E)^{@} \times (E')^{@}$, $(E{+}E')^{@} = (E)^{@} + (E')^{@}$, $a^{@} = a$, $\varepsilon^{@} = \varepsilon$. Let $CF(E)$ denote the set of cyclic factors of E.*

Observation 3.12 *The sum of sizes of the cyclic factors of E is bounded from above by the size of E.*

Proposition 3.13 *A map $\rho : A \rightarrow \mathbb{Z}$ is a bounded region of the language defined by E iff $\hat{\rho}(E_i) = \{0\}$ for every cyclic factor E_i of E.*

Proposition 3.13 shows that the module BR_E of bounded regions of E is the kernel $Ker(M_E)$ of a linear map $M_E : \mathbb{Z}^n \rightarrow \mathbb{Z}^m$, operating on n-vectors $\rho = <\rho(a_1), \ldots, \rho(a_n)>$ which represent maps $\rho : A \rightarrow \mathbb{Z}$, where $A = \{a_1, \ldots, a_n\}$. For each cyclic factor E_i of E, the condition $\hat{\rho}(E_i) = \{0\}$ laid down by the proposition may in fact be translated in polynomial time to an equivalent condition $M_i(\rho) = 0$, where M_i is a linear map from $\mathbb{Z}^n$ to $\mathbb{Z}^{m_i}$ for some finite dimension m_i bounded from above by the size of E_i. The overall dimension $m = \sum\{m_i | E_i \in CF(E)\}$ is then bounded from above by the size of E.

We give here the sketch of a polynomial algorithm computing the integer matrix M_i from the cyclic factor E_i. Let $E_{i,j}$ be an enumeration of the regular subexpressions of E_i, where $E_i = E_{i,0}$ and $0 \leq j \leq p_i$, and let $\{x_j \mid 0 \leq j \leq p_i\}$ be a set of integer variables. Each variable x_j is aimed at representing the contents of the corresponding set $\hat{\rho}(E_{i,j})$, which must be a singleton set in order that condition $\hat{\rho}(E_i) = \{0\}$ may be satisfied. Let $\{y_k \mid 1 \leq k \leq n\}$ be another set of integer variables, aimed at representing the values $\rho(a_k)$. By iterating the following step indexed by j, one assembles a system of linear equations in variables x_j and y_k. For each $j \in \{0, \ldots, p_i\}$:

1. if $E_{i,j} = \varepsilon$, write the equation $x_j = 0$;
2. if $E_{i,j} = a_k$, write the equation $x_j = y_k$;
3. if $E_{i,j} = E_{i,j_1} \times E_{i,j_2}$, write the equation $x_j = x_{j_1} + x_{j_2}$;
4. if $E_{i,j} = E_{i,j_1} + E_{i,j_2}$, write the pair of equations $x_j = x_{j_1}$ and $x_j = x_{j_2}$

Let the equation $x_0 = 0$ be added to the system assembled in this way. The operator M_i is finally obtained by gaussian elimination of the variables x_j.

Once an $(m_i \times n)$ matrix M_i such that $M_i\ \rho = 0$ iff $\hat{\rho}(E_i) = \{0\}$ has been obtained for each cyclic factor E_i of E, it only remains to pile up all the matrices M_i in order to form an $(m \times n)$ matrix M_E satisfying $BR_E = \{\rho \mid M_E \rho = 0\}$. At this stage, the algorithm of von zur Gathen and Sieveking (see [Sch86] p.58) may be used to compute in polynomial time a family of vectors $\rho_1, \ldots, \rho_t$ of integers such that

$$\{\rho \mid M_E \rho = 0\} = \{\lambda_1\, \rho_1 + \ldots + \lambda_t\, \rho_t \mid \lambda_1, \ldots, \lambda_t \in \mathbb{Z}\}$$

with $\rho_1, \ldots, \rho_t$ linearly independent. In the sequel, $\{\rho_1 \ldots \rho_t\}$ is assumed to be a fixed basis of the module of bounded regions of the language defined by the expression E.

3.3 Deciding upon Separatedness of a Regular Language

Resting upon the availability of computable bases for modules of regions, we now intend to design an algorithm deciding whether a prefix-closed and regular language is boundedly separated or equivalently, whether it coincides with the language of a bounded net. We do not know how to solve this problem in polynomial time for arbitrary regular expressions. We shall therefore focus on a special form of regular expressions, allowing to decide on separatedness in polynomial time. These expressions may be seen as trees, labeled on arcs with action symbols or starred expressions, such that any restriction of a tree T to a particular branch induces a regular language where all words are failure equivalent in $|T|$.

Definition 3.14 (Regular expressions in tree form) *A regular expression in* tree form *is a regular expression* T *written according to the restricted syntax*

$$T ::= \varepsilon \mid a \times T \mid E^* \times T \mid T + T,$$

where E *is a regular expression. The* branches *of* T *are the regular expressions in the set* $br(T)$ *defined as*

$$br(\varepsilon) = \{\varepsilon\} \quad br(T_1 + T_2) = br(T_1) \cup br(T_2)$$
$$br(a \times T) = \{a \times B | B \in br(T)\} \quad br(E^* \times T) = \{E^* \times B \mid B \in br(T)\}$$

Clearly, every regular expression may be set in tree form, but that transformation may induce an exponential increase in size.

Consider for instance the indexed family of regular expressions $E_n = (\varepsilon + a + b) \times \dots \times (\varepsilon + a + b)$, where E_n contains n occurrences of the symbol a (or b). The language $|E_n|$ contains exactly the words of length less than or equal to n over the alphabet $\{a, b\}$. The tree-like expansion of E_n contains $2^n - 1$ occurrences of the symbol a (or b), and the minimal words on two letters which do not belong to $|E_n|$, i.e. the words of length $n + 1$, are 2^{n+1} in number. Our algorithm will take one step for each of these faulty words, and thus altogether 2^{n+1} steps, for deciding on separatedness, when the constant region $\rho(a) = \rho(b) = -1$ with offset $M_L(\rho) = n$ suffices to separate $|E_n|$!

Definition 3.15 (Regular expressions in failures tree form) *A regular expression in* failures tree *form is a regular expression* T *in tree form such that*

$$\forall B \in br(T) \ \forall u, u' \in |B| \ \forall a \in A \ \ u \cdot a \in |T| \Leftrightarrow u' \cdot a \in |T|$$

One can naturally decide whether a regular expression is in failures tree form, but the decision algorithm is exponential. In order to show that every regular expression may be set in failures tree form, we sketch below an (exponential) algorithm which produces such expressions from deterministic finite automata.

Let $\mathcal{A} = (Q, A, T, q_0, F)$ be a deterministic automaton, with initial state $q_0 \in Q$ and final states $F \subseteq Q$, recognizing a regular language L. For $q, q' \in Q$ and $R \subseteq Q$, let $L^R_{q,q'}$ denote the set of non-empty words $a_1 \dots a_n$ labeling sequences of transitions $q_0 \xrightarrow{a_1} q_1 \xrightarrow{a_2} q_2 \dots q_{n-1} \xrightarrow{a_n} q_n$ such that $q_0 = q$, $q_i \in R$ for $1 \le i \le n-1$, and $q_n = q'$. Similarly, let L^R_q denote the set which contains the empty word if $q \in F$, and in any case the non-empty words $a_1 \dots a_n$ labeling sequences of transitions $q_0 \xrightarrow{a_1} q_1 \xrightarrow{a_2} q_2 \dots q_{n-1} \xrightarrow{a_n} q_n$ such that $q_0 = q$, $q_i \in R$ for $1 \le i \le n-1$, and $q_n \in F \cap R$. Then the following equations

$$L = L^Q_{q_0}$$

$$L^R_q = (L^{R\setminus\{q\}}_{q,q})^* \cdot L^{R\setminus\{q\}}_q \qquad \text{if } q \in R$$

$$L^R_q = \begin{cases} \varepsilon + \sum_{q \xrightarrow{a} q',\ q' \in R} a \cdot L^R_{q'} & \text{if } q \in F \\ \sum_{q \xrightarrow{a} q',\ q' \in R} a \cdot L^R_{q'} & \text{otherwise} \end{cases} \qquad \text{if } q \notin R$$

produce a regular expression in failures tree form for language L, with branches

$$(L^{R_0}_{q_0,q_0})^* \cdot a_1 \cdot (L^{R_1}_{q_1,q_1})^* \cdot a_2 \ldots (L^{R_n}_{q_n,q_n})^* \varepsilon$$

such that $q_0 \xrightarrow{a_1} q_1 \xrightarrow{a_2} q_2 \ldots q_{n-1} \xrightarrow{a_n} q_n$, $q_{i+1} \in R_i = Q \setminus \{q_0, \ldots, q_{i-1}\}$, and $q_n \in F$.

The main interest of the failures tree form lies in the next two propositions. From now on, let T be a fixed regular expression in failures tree form, denoting a prefix-closed language over $A = \{a_1, \ldots, a_n\}$.

Proposition 3.16 $\{\hat{\rho}(w) \mid w \in T\} = \{\hat{\rho}(w) \mid w \in T^@\}$ *for every bounded region* ρ *of* T *(where* $\cdot^@$ *is the shortcut operator, see Def. 3.11).*

Proposition 3.17 T *is boundedly separated iff every* faulty word $w \in (T^@ A \setminus T)$ *is killed by some bounded region of* T.

Let $\{u_h \mid 1 \leq h \leq H_T\}$ be an enumeration of $T^@$, and let $\{v_k \mid 1 \leq k \leq K_T\}$ be an enumeration of $(T^@ A \setminus T)$. H_T and K_T are clearly bounded from above by linear functions of the size of T. In view of Def. 3.5, a bounded region $\rho \in BR_T$ kills a faulty word v_k iff $M_T(\rho) + \hat{\rho}(v_k) < 0$, with $M_T(\rho) = -\inf\{\hat{\rho}(w) \mid w \in T\}$. In view of Prop. 3.16, $M_T(\rho) = -\inf\{\hat{\rho}(u_h) \mid u_h \in T^@\}$. Thus, by Prop. 3.17, T is boundedly separated iff the following problem may be solved for every k (with $1 \leq k \leq K_T$):

Problem 3.18 *Find a linear combination* $\rho = \lambda_1\ \rho_1 + \ldots + \lambda_t\ \rho_t$ *of the base vectors of the module* BR_T *such that* $\hat{\rho}(v_k) - \hat{\rho}(u_h) < 0$ *for every* h *(with* $1 \leq h \leq H_T$*).*

We address now the above problem for a fixed word $v_k \in (T^@ A \setminus T)$. Let $\mathbf{x} =< x_1, \ldots, x_n >$ be the Parikh image of v_k, where x_i counts the occurrences of a_i. Similarly, let $\mathbf{y}_h$ be the Parikh image of u_h. Each condition $\hat{\rho}(v_k) - \hat{\rho}(u_h) < 0$ induces a corresponding constraint on the unknown $\boldsymbol{\Lambda} =< \lambda_1, \ldots, \lambda_t > (\in \mathbb{Z}^t)$, viz the inequation: $\lambda_1\ \rho_1\ (\mathbf{x} - \mathbf{y}_h) + \ldots + \lambda_t\ \rho_t\ (\mathbf{x} - \mathbf{y}_h) < \mathbf{0}$. Assembling the constraints for $1 \leq h \leq H_T$, one obtains a linear system

$$M_k \boldsymbol{\Lambda} \leq (-1)^{H_T} \tag{1}$$

where $\mathbf{M}_k$ is an integral matrix and $(-1)^{H_T} =< -1, \ldots, -1 > (\in \mathbb{Z}^{H_T})$. We claim that (1) has an integral solution iff it has a rational solution. A rational solution $\boldsymbol{\Lambda} =< z_1/n_1, \ldots, z_t/n_t >$ gives indeed rise to an integral solution $n\boldsymbol{\Lambda}$ for any common multiple n of the denominators n_i. At this stage, the method of Khachiyan (see [Sch86] p.170) may be used to decide the feasability of (1) and to compute an explicit solution, if it exists, in polynomial time. Thus, every instance of Prob. 3.18 is solved explicitly, or shown unfeasible, in polynomial time.

Now, deciding whether T is boundedly separated takes polynomial time, since it reduces to solving K_T instances of Prob. 3.18.

3.4 Computing a Finite Net from a Regular Language

Let T be a boundedly separated, prefix-closed, and regular language. Thus, every faulty word $v_k \in (T^@ A \setminus T)$ is killed by some region $\rho'_k \in BR_T$. Let $R = \{\rho'_k \mid 1 \leq k \leq K_T\}$, where ρ'_k kills v_k. In view of Prop. 3.8, T coincides with the language of the R-net derived from L, i.e. the finite net (R, A, W, M) with $W(\rho'_k, a) = \rho'_k(a)$ and $M(\rho'_k) = -\inf\{\hat{\rho}'_k(u_h) \mid 1 \leq h \leq H_T\}$. Hence the results of the section may be summarized as follows.

Theorem 3.19 *Let T be a prefix-closed language given by a regular expression in failures tree form, then one may decide whether $|T|$ coincides with the language of some finite net and construct that net in polynomial time.*

4 Regions in Finite Graphs

The goal of the section is to solve the following problem:

Problem 4.1 *Given an A-labeled graph G, decide whether there exists a marked net with marking graph isomorphic to G and if so, construct such a net.*

We will present a polynomial algorithm answering this problem for finite graphs. The basic constituent of the proposed solution is again the principle of abstract regions, but regions in graphs are more tightly constrained than regions in languages, as will appear soon. Since equality of languages is strictly weaker than isomorphism of graphs, the synthesis problem for languages is a weakening of the synthesis problem for graphs. Nevertheless, we do not know any polynomial reduction of one problem to the other. We propose therefore two variant but not directly related algorithms for solving the two different synthesis problems.

The principle of regions applies more generally to infinite graphs. We shall therefore introduce regions for general graphs, and then focus on finite graphs.

4.1 Some Graph Terminology

Definition 4.2 (Graphs) *A* graph $G = [S, T]$ *is given by a set S of* nodes, *a set T of transitions (or arcs), together with two maps $\partial^0, \partial^1 : T \to S$, indicating respectively the* source *and* target *of transitions. A* path *in G is a finite sequence of transitions $t_1 \ldots t_k$ where $\partial^1(t_i) = \partial^0(t_{i+1})$ for $i < k$. Nodes $\partial^0(t_1)$ and $\partial^1(t_k)$ are the* extremities, *or respectively the* initial *and* terminal *nodes of the path. A* chain *in G is a path in the graph $[S, T + T^{-1}]$, where $\partial^0(t^{-1}) = \partial^1(t)$ and $\partial^1(t^{-1}) = \partial^0(t)$ for $t \in T$. A* cycle *is a chain with identical extremities. A cycle which is a path is* directed. *A* rooted *graph is a graph with a distinguished node, called the* initial *node. Paths from the initial node are* initial *paths. An* accessible *graph is a rooted graph in which every node, to the possible exception of the initial node, is the terminal node of some initial path.*

Definition 4.3 (Labeled Graphs) *A* labeled graph $G = [S, T, A, l]$ *is a graph $[S, T]$ enriched with a* labeling *function $l : T \to A$, where A is the set of* actions. *A labeled graph is* deterministic *if $(\partial^0(t) = \partial^0(t') \wedge l(t) = l(t')) \Rightarrow \partial^1(t) = \partial^1(t')$. The* label *of chain c, denoted $l(c)$, is the sequence of actions a and* inverse *actions a^{-1} labeling arcs on that chain. The* Parikh image *of a chain c, denoted $\pi(c)$, is the evaluation of its label $l(c)$ in the commutative group $F_{CG}(A)$ freely generated by A. The* language *$L(G) \subseteq A^*$ of graph G is the set of labels of initial paths in G.*

Observe that $F_{CG}(A)$ can be identified with the set of maps $\rho : A \to \mathbb{Z}$ equipped with pointwise sum, which permits to represent the elements of the commutative group as A-indexed vectors of integers. Henceforth, for any map $\rho : A \to \mathbb{Z}$, let

$\tilde{\rho} : F_{CG}(A) \to \mathbb{Z}$ denote the group morphism $\tilde{\rho}(ua) = \tilde{\rho}(u) + \rho(a)$, where $u \in F_{CG}(A)$ and $a \in A \cup A^{-1}$ ($\subset F_{CG}(A)$). Thus in particular, $\tilde{\rho}(a^{-1}) = -\tilde{\rho}(a) = -\rho(a)$. The map $\tilde{(.)}$ is related to the map $\hat{(.)}$ used in the preceding section by the formula

Observation 4.4 *$\hat{\rho}(u) = \tilde{\rho}(ev(u))$, where ev (the evaluation map mentioned in Def.4.3) takes a word $u \in (A+A^{-1})^*$ (i.e. a sequence of actions and inverse actions) to the vector whose component in a is the difference between the respective numbers of occurrences of a and a^{-1} in u: $ev(u)(a) = \sharp_u(a) - \sharp_u(a^{-1})$.*

4.2 Regions in Accessible Graphs with Deterministic Labeling

An abstract region in an accessible graph represents a resource, measured at each node by a displacement (w.r.t. the initial amount) which must be the same through any initial path leading to that node.

Definition 4.5 (Regions in accessible graphs with deterministic labeling) *A* region *of G is a region of L(G) which gives identical value to all labels of initial paths having the same terminal node, i.e. $\rho \in R_{L(G)}$, and for every initial paths p_1, p_2, $[\partial^1(p_1) = \partial^1(p_2) \Rightarrow \hat{\rho}(l(p_1)) = \hat{\rho}(l(p_2))$. Let R_G, resp. BR_G denote the set of regions, resp. bounded regions of G.*

Again, R_G is a monoid, BR_G is an abelian group, and *concrete* regions $\rho : S \to \mathbb{N}$ may be derived from *abstract* regions $\rho : A \to \mathbb{Z}$, where $G = [S, T, A, l]$, by assigning to each node $s \in S$, reached by some initial path p_s, the value $M_G(\rho) + \tilde{\rho}(\pi(p_s))$ ($= M_G(\rho) + \hat{\rho}(l(p_s))$ by Obs. 4.4) where $M_G(\rho) = M_{L(G)}(\rho)$. Likewise, nets derived from graphs are defined by a straightforward adaptation of Def.3.4.

Definition 4.6 (Nets derived from graphs)

1. *The* saturated net *$\mathcal{N}(G)$ derived from G is the net (R_G, A, W, M_G), where $W(\rho, a) = \rho(a)$ for $\rho \in R_G$, and $M_G(\rho) = -\inf\{\hat{\rho}(u) \mid u \in L(G)\}$.*
2. *For any set of regions $R \subseteq R_G$, the R-*net *derived from G is the sub-net of $\mathcal{N}(G)$ with set of places R.*
3. *In particular, the* saturated bounded net *$\mathcal{BN}(G)$ derived from G is the sub-net of $\mathcal{N}(G)$ with set of places BR_G.*

However, it does *not* suffice, for obtaining the necessary and sufficient conditions under which the marking graphs of nets $\mathcal{N}(G)$ or $\mathcal{BN}(G)$ are isomorphic to the given graph G, to translate literally to graph terminology the properties of separation defined earlier for languages, because isomorphism of graphs is stronger than equality of languages. The adequate properties for graphs are the following.

Definition 4.7 (Separation properties for graphs) *Let $G = [S, T, A, l]$. Two nodes $s, s' \in S$ are* separated *by a region $\rho \in R_G$ if $\hat{\rho}(u) \neq \hat{\rho}(u')$ for some words u, u' labeling initial paths with terminal nodes s, s'. Let $R \subseteq R_G$ be a subset of regions of G. Graph G is* separated by *R if L(G) is separated by R and every non identical pair $s, s' \in S$ is separated by some $\rho \in R$. Graph G is* separated *if it is separated by R_G, and* boundedly separated *if it is separated by BR_G.*

Since the places of a net may always be identified with regions of its marking graph, the marking graph of a net is necessarily separated. The converse is stated in Prop. 4.8 and its corollary.

Proposition 4.8 *An accessible graph with deterministic labeling is isomorphic to the derived R-net if, and only if, it is separated by R.*

Corollary 4.9 *Given an accessible graph G with deterministic labeling:*

1. *G is isomorphic to the marking graph of the saturated net $N(G)$ iff it is separated;*
2. *G is isomorphic to the marking graph of the saturated bounded net $BN(G)$ iff it is boundedly separated.*

Observing that every region in a finite graph is finite, we concentrate in the rest of the section on the problem of synthesizing finite nets from finite graphs.

4.3 Regions in Finite Accessible Graphs with Deterministic Labeling

From now on, $G = [S, T, A, l]$ is a *finite* accessible graph with deterministic labeling on $A = \{a_1, \ldots, a_n\}$. Therefore, $R_G = BR_G$, and this module is a sub-module of the finite dimensional $\mathbb{Z}$-module $BR_{L(G)}$. In a first stage, we will provide an algorithm which computes in polynomial time a basis for the module of regionsR_G. Let us start with an algebraic characterization of regions.

Proposition 4.10

1. *A map $\rho : A \to \mathbb{Z}$ is a bounded region of the* language $L(G)$ *iff $\tilde{\rho}(\pi(c)) = 0$ for every directed cycle c in G.*
2. *A map $\rho : A \to \mathbb{Z}$ is a bounded region of graph G iff $\tilde{\rho}(\pi(c)) = 0$ for every cycle c in G.*

Proposition 4.10 tells us that R_G, the module of regions of G represented as n-vectors $< \rho(a_1), ..., \rho(a_n) >$, is the kernel of a linear transformation from $\mathbb{Z}^n$ to $\mathbb{Z}^\alpha$ for α equal to the cardinal of the set of cycles in G. Surely, α may be infinite, but there are at most n linearly independent constraints $\pi(c) \cdot \rho = 0$ imposed by cycles c on regions ρ. According to a usual practice in graph theory (see e.g. [Ber70]), let us represent a cycle c as a vector $\mathbf{c} \in (T \to \mathbb{Z})$. It is a well known fact that all vectors representing cycles in G may be generated from a basis of $\nu(G)$ linearly independent vectors, with $\nu(G) = |T| - |S| + 1$. Let us observe that π is a linear operator from $F_{CG}(T)$ $(= (T \to \mathbb{Z}))$ to $F_{CG}(A)$ $(= (A \to \mathbb{Z}))$. Therefore, $\nu(G)$ equations of the form $\pi(c) \cdot \rho = 0$ suffice to generate all of them! Summing up, the following proposition holds.

Proposition 4.11 *Let $\{\mathbf{c}_1, \ldots, \mathbf{c}_{\nu(G)}\}$ be a basis of cycles of $G = [S, T, A, l]$, where $T = \{t_1 \ldots t_m\}$ and $A = \{a_1, \ldots, a_n\}$, then R_G is the kernel of the linear transformation defined by the $(\nu(G) \times n)$ matrix $\mathbf{M}_G$ with integral elements:*

$$M_G(i,j) = \sum\{\mathbf{c}_i(t_k) \mid (1 \leq k \leq m) \wedge (l(t_k) = a_j)\}.$$

If we can compute the integral matrix M_G, the algorithm of von zur Gathen and Sieveking yields now in polynomial time a basis of linearly independent vectors $\{\rho_1, \ldots, \rho_l\}$ for the module of regions R_G.

4.4 Computing a Spanning Tree and a Basis of Cycles for G

We show here how to compute (in polynomial time) a basis of cycles for a finite and accessible graph $G = [S, T]$. In view of the following proposition, borrowed from [GM85], this task reduces to constructing a spanning tree in graph G.

Proposition 4.12 (Gondran and Minoux) *Let $G = [S, T]$ be a finite graph with p connected components. Let $\mathcal{F} = [S, U]$ be a maximal* forest *(i.e. graph without cycle) in G. For $t \in (T - U)$, let c^t be the cycle with set of arcs $U + \{t\}$ (this cycle is unique up to reversal). Cycles c^t, for t ranging over $(T - U)$, form a basis of cycles of G, with dimension $\nu(G) = |T| - |S| + p$.*

In case when G is an accessible graph, the maximal forest of the proposition may naturally be chosen among the spanning trees rooted at the initial node of the graph. Constructing a spanning tree takes polynomial time, hence computing a basis of cycles for G takes polynomial time.

4.5 Deciding upon Separatedness of a Finite Accessible Graph

Let $G = [S, T, A, l]$ be a finite accessible graph, and let $Span(G)$ be a spanning tree of G. By Def. 4.7, graph G is separated if and only if the following problems are solvable:

Problem 4.13 *For each non identical pair of initial paths p, p' in $Span(G)$, including the empty path ε, find a linear combination $\rho = \lambda_1\, \rho_1 + \ldots + \lambda_t\, \rho_t$ of the base vectors of the module R_G such that $\tilde{\rho}(\pi(p)) \neq \tilde{\rho}(\pi(p'))$.*

Problem 4.14 *For each action $a \in A$ and for each initial path p in $Span(G)$ such that $(l(p) \cdot a) \notin L(G)$, where possibly $p = \varepsilon$, find a linear combination $\rho = \lambda_1\, \rho_1 + \ldots + \lambda_t\, \rho_t$ of the base vectors of the module R_G such that $\tilde{\rho}(\pi(p)) + \rho(a) - \tilde{\rho}(\pi(p')) < 0$ for every path p' in $Span(G)$.*

Now Prob. 4.13 is trivial, whereas Prob. 4.14 may be solved in polynomial time following Khachiyan's method (along the same lines as in section 3.3). Hence, we can sum up the section as follows.

Theorem 4.15 *Let G be a finite and accessible graph with deterministic labeling, then one may decide whether G is isomorphic to the case graph of some finite (and irreducible) net, and construct that net, in polynomial time.*

5 Conclusion

In the introduction the notion of synchronic distance is briefly mentioned; it was introduced, in the context of net theory, by C.A. Petri as a tool to measure the relative degree of freedom between sets of transitions in a concurrent system. The close relation between synchronic distances and regions has been discussed in some detail in [BDP93] –where further references can be found–. In brief, to each region in a separated graph corresponds a finite synchronic distance and vice versa. Actually, the existence of a bounded abstract region in a language or in a graph implies a constraint on the relative frequence of execution of the transitions affecting the region itself. The range of variation of the region, that is, the difference between its minimum and maximum values, is a measure of the reciprocal independence: higher values mean looser constraints. This is in agreement with the interpretation of regions as abstract resources shared by transitions, given in this paper. Hence, the algorithms presented here can be seen as a way to compute efficiently synchronic distances.

The results presented in this paper should be contrasted with the one in [BBD95] where we prove that the synthesis problem for elementary net systems is NP-complete, thus extending complexity results by Hiraishi [Hir94].

References

[BBD95] Badouel, E., Bernardinello, L., and Darondeau, Ph., *The Synthesis Problem for Elementary Net Systems is NP-Complete.* Irisa/Inria research report to appear (1995).

[Ber70] Berge, C., *Graphes et hypergraphes.* Dunod, Paris (1970).

[Ber93] Bernardinello, L., *Synthesis of Net Systems.* Application and Theory of Petri Nets, Springer-Verlag Lecture Notes in Computer Science, vol. 691 (1993) 89–105.

[BDP93] Bernardinello, L., De Michelis, G., and Petruni, K., *Synchronic distances as Generalized Regions.* Rapporto Interno n. 107–93, Dipartimento di Scienze dell'Informazione, Università degli Studi di Milano (1993).

[DR92] Desel, J., and Reisig, W., *The Synthesis Problem of Petri Nets.* TUM research report, Munich (1992).

[DS92] Droste, M., and Shortt, R.M., *Bounded Petri Nets of Finite Dimension have only Finitely Many Reachable Markings.* Bulletin of the European Association for Computer Science, number 48, (1992) 172–174.

[DS93] Droste, M., and Shortt, R.M., *Petri Nets and Automata with Concurrency Relations – an Adjunction.* in "Semantics of Programming Languages and Model Theory", M. Droste and Y. Gurevich eds(1993) 69–87.

[ER90] Ehrenfeucht, A., and Rozenberg, G., *Partial 2-structures ;* Part I : *Basic Notions and the Representation Problem*, and Part II : *State Spaces of Concurrent Systems*, Acta Informatica, vol 27 (1990).

[GM85] Gondran, M., and Minoux, M., *Graphes et algorithmes.* Eyrolles, Paris (1985).

[Hir94] Hiraishi, K., *Some complexity results on transitions systems and elementary net systems.* Theoretical Computer Science 135 (1994) 361–376.

[HKT92] Hoogers, P.W., Kleijn, H.C.M., and Thiagarajan, P.S., *A trace semantics for Petri nets.* Springer-Verlag, Lecture Notes in Computer Science, vol. 623 (1992) 595–604.

[Muk93] Mukund, M., *Petri Nets and Step Transition Systems.* International Journal of Foundation of Computer Science, vol 3, n° 3 (1993).

[Sch86] Schrijver, A., *Theory of Linear and Integer Programming.* John Wiley (1986).

Semi-completeness of Hierarchical and Super-hierarchical Combinations of Term Rewriting Systems

M. R. K. Krishna Rao*

Computer Science Group
Tata Institute of Fundamental Research
Colaba, BOMBAY 400 005, INDIA
e-mail: **krishna@tifrvax.bitnet**

Abstract. In this paper, we study modular aspects of hierarchical and super hierarchical combinations of term rewriting systems. In particular, a sufficient condition for modularity of semi-completeness of hierarchical and super hierarchical combinations is proposed. We first establish modularity of weak normalization for this class (defined by the sufficient condition) and modularity of semi-completeness for a class of crosswise independent unions. From these results, we obtain modularity of semi-completeness for a class of hierarchical and super hierarchical combinations. Our results generalize the semi-completeness results of Ohlebusch [14] and Middeldorp and Toyama [13]. The notion of crosswise independent unions is a generalization of both constructor sharing unions as well as Plump's crosswise disjoint unions.

1 Introduction

In the last few decades, term rewriting systems (TRS, for short) have played a fundamental role in the analysis and implementation of abstract data type specifications, decidability of word problems, theorem proving, computability theory, design of functional programming languages (e.g. Miranda), integration of functional programming and logic programming paradigms, etc. The study of properties which are preserved under combinations of term rewriting systems (called modular properties) is of both theoretical and practical importance. In particular, the modularity results facilitate (i) incrementality in the synthesis of systems and (ii) divide-and-conquer approach in the analysis of systems. One of the important properties of TRSs is semi-completeness (confluence + weak normalization). This property is very useful in establishing consistency of equality theories. In this paper, we study modularity of semi-completeness.

Starting with a seminal paper [18] by Toyama, modularity has been receiving a lot of attention in the last ten years. Since none of the interesting properties are modular under arbitrary combinations, a start is made by considering unions of

* Some of the details were worked out during the author's stay at Max-Planck-Institut für Informatik, Saarbrücken.

TRSs with disjoint alphabets (such unions are called direct-sums). After a good number of results were obtained (in among others, [18, 16, 11, 9]), researchers (see a.o. [10, 13, 4, 14]) considered unions of systems sharing constructor symbols — a function symbol is a constructor in a given TRS if it does not occur at the outermost level in the left-hand side of any rewrite rule in the system; otherwise it is called a defined symbol. Very recently, more practical unions called hierarchical combinations — where one system is allowed to use defined symbols of the other system as constructors (or built-ins) — are considered in [6, 7, 2]. See [12] for a comprehensive study of modularity results for direct-sums and (extended version of) [6] for a brief survey of the very recent results.

The following diagram gives the pictorial view of direct-sums, constructor sharing systems and hierarchical combinations. The sets of defined and constructor symbols of $\mathcal{R}_i$ are denoteed by D_i and C_i respectively.

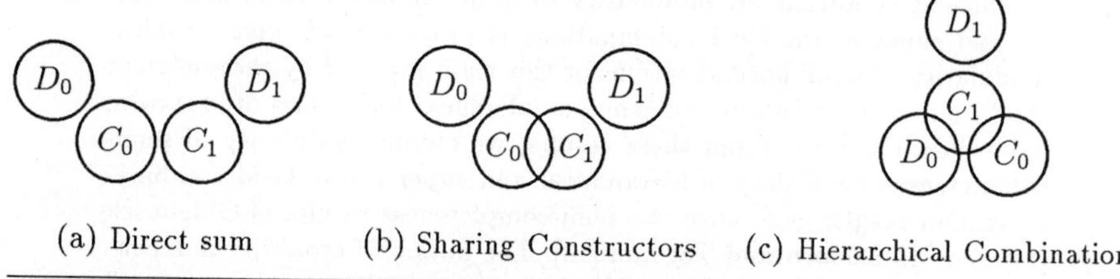

(a) Direct sum (b) Sharing Constructors (c) Hierarchical Combination

In this paper, we deal with modular aspects of hierarchical combinations (in fact, a larger class called super hierarchical combinations), in particular *semi-completeness.* A TRS is semi-complete if it is both weakly-normalizing and confluent. It's known that confluence is not modular even for constructor sharing systems. Recently, Ohlebusch [14] established that confluence is modular for constructor sharing systems provided the constituent systems are weakly-normalizing. Since weak-normalization is known to be modular for constructor sharing systems, this amounts to showing modularity of semi-completeness for constructor sharing systems. However, neither semi-completeness nor weak-normalization is modular for hierarchical combinations. In this paper, we propose a set of sufficient conditions for modularity of semi-completeness of hierarchical combinations. It may be noted that techniques of neither [14] nor [6, 7, 2] are applicable in establishing our results.

We first establish modularity of weak normalization for a class of super hierarchical combinations by giving an algorithm to find a normal form of a given term. This algorithm is described by a strongly normalizing relation, called $\rightarrow_a$. It is shown that $\rightarrow_a$ is confluent if the two component systems are semi-complete. Then, we establish modularity of semi-completeness for a class of crosswise independent unions. From these results, we obtain modularity of semi-completeness for a class of hierarchical and super hierarchical combinations using Staples' lemma.

The rest of the paper is organized as follows. The next section gives preliminary definitions and results needed later. In section 3, some classes of hierarchical and super hierarchical combinations (nice-extensions and nice-extensions*) are defined. Section 4 establishes modularity of weak normalization for nice extensions*. Using this result and Staples lemma, modularity of semi-completeness for a class of nice extensions* is established in section 5. Section 6 discusses some extensions of these results which are omitted due to space restrictions. Section 7 concludes with a summary.

2 Preliminaries

We assume that the reader is familiar with the basic terminology of term rewriting systems and give definitions only when they are required. The notations not defined in the paper can be found in Dershowitz and Jouannaud [1], Klop [5] or Middeldorp [12].

Definition 1 (critical pairs)
Let $l_1 \rightarrow r_1$ and $l_2 \rightarrow r_2$ be renamed versions of rewrite rules of a TRS $\mathcal{R}$ such that they have no variables in common. Suppose $l_{1|p}$ is not a variable for some position p and $l_{1|p}$ unifies with l_2 through a most general unifier σ. *The pair of terms* $\langle l_1[r_2]_p\sigma,\ r_1\sigma\rangle$ *is called a critical pair of* $\mathcal{R}$. If $l_1 \rightarrow r_1$ and $l_2 \rightarrow r_2$ are renamed versions of the same rewrite rule, we do not consider the case $p = \epsilon$. A critical pair $\langle l_1[r_2]_p\sigma,\ r_1\sigma\rangle$ with $p = \epsilon$ is called an overlay and a critical pair $\langle s,\ t\rangle$ is trivial if $s \equiv t$.

In the following, $\mathcal{T}(\mathcal{F}, \mathcal{X})$ denotes the set of terms constructed from set of function symbols $\mathcal{F}$ and set of variables $\mathcal{X}$, and $F(t)$ denotes the set of function symbols occurring in term t. $root(t) = f$ if $t \equiv f(s_1, \ldots, s_n)$, and $root(t) = t$ if $t \in \mathcal{X}$.

Definition 2 The set $D_\mathcal{R}$ of *defined* symbols of a TRS $\mathcal{R}(\mathcal{F}, R)$ is defined as $\{root(l) \mid l \rightarrow r \in R\}$ and the set $C_\mathcal{R}$ of *constructor* symbols of $\mathcal{R}(\mathcal{F}, R)$ is defined as $\mathcal{F} - D_\mathcal{R}$.

We need the following definitions and lemmas in the sequel.

Definition 3 The dependency relation of TRS $\mathcal{R}(D, C, R)$ is defined as:

1. We say that a defined symbol $f \in D$ *directly depends on* defined symbol $g \in D$ (denoted as $f \rightarrow_d g$) if there is a rewrite rule $l \rightarrow r \in R$ such that $f \equiv root(l)$ and $g \in F(r)$.
2. The dependency relation of $\mathcal{R}$ is the transitive reflexive closure of $\rightarrow_d$. We say that h depends on f if $h \rightarrow_d^* f$.
3. The set of symbols depending on a set of symbols S is defined as $\{f \mid f \rightarrow_d^* g$ and $g \in S\}$.

The following fundamental result due to Staples is very useful in establishing confluence (and hence semi-completeness) of relations.

Definition 4 (Staples [17])
Let S be a set and $\rightarrow_a$ and $\rightarrow_b$ be two binary relations on S. We say that the relation $\rightarrow_b$ is a *refinement of the relation* $\rightarrow_a$ *if* $\rightarrow_a \subseteq \rightarrow_b^*$. A refinement $\rightarrow_b$ of $\rightarrow_a$ is a *compatible refinement* of $\rightarrow_a$ if $\forall s,t,u \in S\ \exists v \in S\ (s \rightarrow_b t \rightarrow_a^* u \Longrightarrow u \rightarrow_a^* v \ \&\ s \rightarrow_a^* v)$.

Lemma 1 (Staples [17])
Let S be a set and $\rightarrow_a$ and $\rightarrow_b$ be two binary relations on S such that $\rightarrow_b$ is a *compatible refinement* of $\rightarrow_a$. *Then,* $\rightarrow_a$ *is confluent if and only if* $\rightarrow_b$ *is confluent.*

When $\rightarrow_a$ is confluent, the following lemma exploiting this fact is useful.

Lemma 2 Let S be a set and $\rightarrow_a$ and $\rightarrow_b$ be two binary relations on S such that $\rightarrow_b$ is a refinement of $\rightarrow_a$ and $\rightarrow_a$ is confluent. *Then,* $\rightarrow_b$ *is a* compatible refinement *of* $\rightarrow_a$ *if* $\forall s,t \in S\ \exists u \in S\ (s \rightarrow_b t \Longrightarrow s \rightarrow_a^* u \ \&\ t \rightarrow_a^* u)$.

3 Hierarchical and Super-hierarchical Combinations

In this section, we define a class (called, nice-extensions) of hierarchical combinations for which modularity of weak-normalization and semi-completeness properties is studied in later sections. The term nice-extension was first introduced by Krishna Rao [6] where modularity of completeness was established. In [7], Krishna Rao proved modularity of simple termination for a very similar (but slightly different) class of hierarchical combination using techniques very different from those of [6]. This lead to some confusion about nice-extensions. One of the contributions of this section is to clarify this confusion and give a definition of nice-extensions which includes both the classes considered in [6] and [7]. Before defining this class, we show that weak-normalization and semi-completeness are not modular for hierarchical combinations in general.

Example 1 It is easy to see that the following two systems $\mathcal{R}_0$ and $\mathcal{R}_1$ are *complete* and hence both weakly-normalizing and semi-complete.

$\mathcal{R}_0$: $\mathtt{f(x)} \rightarrow \mathtt{x}$

$\mathcal{R}_1$: $\mathtt{g(y)} \rightarrow \mathtt{f(y)}$
$\mathtt{h(a)} \rightarrow \mathtt{h(g(a))}$

To wit, the combined system is not weakly-normalizing (and hence not semi-complete). The term $\mathtt{h(a)}$ has no normal form with respect to the combined system — note the cyclic derivation:
$\mathtt{h(a)} \Rightarrow_{\mathcal{R}_1} \mathtt{h(g(a))} \Rightarrow_{\mathcal{R}_1} \mathtt{h(f(a))} \Rightarrow_{\mathcal{R}_0} \mathtt{h(a)} \cdots$ □

In the above example, the combined system is confluent. This might give an impression that confluence is modular for hierarchical combinations. However, it is not the case even for constructor sharing systems as pointed out by Kurihara and Ohuchi [10].

Example 2 The following two systems with a shared constructor, h, are confluent.

$$\mathcal{R}_0: \quad \mathtt{f(x,x)} \to \mathtt{a} \qquad\qquad \mathcal{R}_1: \quad \mathtt{g} \to \mathtt{h(g)}$$
$$\mathtt{f(x,h(x))} \to \mathtt{b}$$

But $\mathcal{R}_0 \cup \mathcal{R}_1$ is not confluent; $\mathtt{f(g,\ g)}$ has two different normal forms, a and b. □

For discussions in the sequel, it is convenient to classify defined symbols in D_1 into two sets (i) $D_1^0 = \{ f \mid f \in D_1 \text{ and } f \to_d^* D_0 \}$ consisting of function symbols depending on D_0 and (ii) $D_1^1 = D_1 - D_1^0$ consisting of function symbols not depending on D_0.

The following definition characterizes the class of hierarchical combinations we are interested in.

term rewriting system

Definition 5 A term rewriting system $\mathcal{R}_1(D_1, C_1, R_1)$ is a *nice-extension* of another system $\mathcal{R}_0(D_0, C_0, R_0)$ if the following conditions are satisfied:

1. $D_0 \cap D_1 = C_0 \cap D_1 = \phi$ (i.e., $\mathcal{R}_0 \cup \mathcal{R}_1$ is a hierarchical combination).
2. Each rewrite rule $l \to r \in \mathcal{R}_1$ satisfies the following condition:
(H1): For every subterm s of r, if $root(s) \in D_1^0$, then s contains no function symbol depending on D_0 except at the outermost level (of s).

The second (and the main) condition essentially says that nesting of defined symbols from D_1^0 is not allowed in the right-hand side terms of rules and no symbol from D_0 occurs below D_1^0-symbols.

Example 3 The following system $\mathcal{R}_1$ is a nice-extension of $\mathcal{R}_0$.

$$\mathcal{R}_0: \quad \mathtt{add(0,\ x)} \to \mathtt{x} \qquad\qquad \mathcal{R}_1: \quad \mathtt{mult(0,\ x)} \to \mathtt{0}$$
$$\mathtt{add(S(x),\ y)} \to \mathtt{S(add(x,\ y))} \qquad\qquad \mathtt{mult(S(x),\ y)} \to \mathtt{add(y,mult(x,\ y))}$$

3.1 Super-hierarchical Combinations

In hierarchical combinations, defined symbols of $\mathcal{R}_1$ are not allowed to occur in $\mathcal{R}_0$. In a few (very rare) situations, it may not be possible to divide a system into two subsystems $\mathcal{R}_0$ and $\mathcal{R}_1$ such that the combination is hierarchical, but it might be possible to divide that system into two subsystems $\mathcal{R}_0$ and $\mathcal{R}_1$ such that the defined symbols of $\mathcal{R}_0$ do not depend on the defined symbols of $\mathcal{R}_1$. Basically, the defined symbols of $\mathcal{R}_1$ are allowed to occur in the left-hand side (but not in the right-hand side) terms of $\mathcal{R}_0$ and defined symbols of $\mathcal{R}_0$ can occur in both the left and the right-hand side terms of $\mathcal{R}_1$. Such combinations are called super-hierarchical combinations. It may be noted that such a situation can occur with TRSs generated by completion procedures.

Definition 6 A term rewriting system $\mathcal{R}_1(D_1, C_1, R_1)$ is a *nice-extension** of another system $\mathcal{R}_0(D_0, C_0, R_0)$ if condition (H1) of definition 5 and the following condition are satisfied (here, $\rightarrow_d^*$ is the dependency relation of the combined system):

$$\forall f \in D_0,\ \forall g \in D_1,\ f \not\rightarrow_d^* g \text{ (i.e., } \mathcal{R}_0 \cup \mathcal{R}_1 \text{ is a super-hier. combination).}$$

Notation: Until further notice, we deal with nice-extensions*. We denote the set of constructors $(C_0 \cup C_1) - (D_0 \cup D_1)$ of the combined system by $Constr$. $\mathcal{T}_i$ denotes $\mathcal{T}(D_i \cup Constr, \mathcal{X})$ and $\mathcal{C}_i$ denotes the set of contexts of $D_i \cup Constr$, i.e., terms in $\mathcal{T}(D_i \cup Constr \cup \{\Box\}, \mathcal{X})$. By $\mathcal{C}_0^1$, we denote the set of contexts of $Constr \cup D_0 \cup D_1^1$.

The following lemma characterizes the rewrite rules in nice-extensions*.

Lemma 3 *If $\mathcal{R}_1$ is a nice-extension* of $\mathcal{R}_0$ then for each rule $l \rightarrow r \in \mathcal{R}_1$, r is of the form $C[t_1, \ldots, t_n]$, where $C \in \mathcal{C}_0^1$, $root(t_i) \in D_1^0$ and $t_i \in \mathcal{T}_1$, $1 \leq i \leq n$ $(n \geq 0)$. Further, no proper subterm of t_i contains any function symbol depending on D_0.*

Proof: Follows from the condition (H1) of Definition 5. □

4 Weak Normalization

In this section, we establish modularity of weak normalization (WN) property for nice-extensions*. We basically have to show that every term has a normal form with respect to the combined system. We do more than required by giving an algorithm to compute a normal form of any given term. This algorithm is described by the following relation $\rightarrow_a$ on terms. In the following, we assume that $\mathcal{R}_0$ and $\mathcal{R}_1$ are weakly normalizing (WN).

Definition 7 The relation $\rightarrow_a$ on terms is defined as follows:

$$C[s] \rightarrow_a C[t]$$

if (i) s is an innermost redex in $C[s]$ and (ii) t is a normal form of s w.r.t. $\mathcal{R}_i$ if $root(s) \in D_i$.

We show that this relation gives an effective algorithm by establishing strong normalization (termination) of $\rightarrow_a$. Towards this purpose, we need the following lemmas.

Lemma 4 If $\mathcal{R}_1$ is a nice-extension* of $\mathcal{R}_0$ and t is a term such that no subterm (say, s) of t with $root(s) \in D_1$ is reducible by $\mathcal{R}_0 \cup \mathcal{R}_1$, then *any normal form of t with respect to $\mathcal{R}_0$ is also a normal form of t with respect to $\mathcal{R}_0 \cup \mathcal{R}_1$.*

Proof: Follows from the fact that the defined symbols of $\mathcal{R}_1$ do not occur in the right-hand side terms of $\mathcal{R}_0$. □

The above lemma is useful in establishing that normalization of an innermost redex w.r.t. $\mathcal{R}_0$ decreases the depth of innermost redexes. The following two lemmas are useful in establishing that normalization of an innermost redex w.r.t. $\mathcal{R}_1$ decreases the depth of innermost reducible terms with root in D_1^0.

Lemma 5 If $\mathcal{R}_1$ is a nice-extension* of $\mathcal{R}_0$ and t is a term of the form $C[t_1,\ldots,t_n]$, $C \in \mathcal{C}_0^1$, $root(t_i) \in D_1^0$ such that no proper subterm (say, s) of t_i, $1 \leq i \leq n$ with $root(s) \in (D_0 \cup D_1^0)$ is reducible by $\mathcal{R}_0 \cup \mathcal{R}_1$ and $t \Rightarrow_{\mathcal{R}_1} t'$, then *$t'$ is of the form $C'[s_1,\ldots,s_m]$, $C' \in \mathcal{C}_0^1$, $root(s_i) \in D_1^0$ such that no proper subterm (say, s) of s_i, $1 \leq i \leq m$ with $root(s) \in (D_0 \cup D_1^0)$ is reducible by $\mathcal{R}_0 \cup \mathcal{R}_1$.*

Proof: Let $l \rightarrow r$ be the rewrite rule applied in $t \Rightarrow_{\mathcal{R}_1} t'$ and σ be the applied matching substitution. There are two cases.

Case (a): $root(l) \in D_1^1$. There are two subcases. (1) the reduction took place in C. By definition, no function symbol in D_1^0 occurs in r and hence, t' is of the form $C'[s_1,\ldots,s_m]$, $C' \in \mathcal{C}_0^1$, $root(s_i) \in D_1^0$ such that each s_i is a subterm of some t_j. The lemma holds. (2) the reduction took place in some t_i and $t' \equiv C[t_1,\cdots,t_{i-1},t_i',t_{i+1},\cdots,t_n]$. Let t_i be of the form $C_1[u_1,\ldots,u_m]$ such that $root(u_j) \in (D_0 \cup D_1^0)$ and no symbol from $(D_0 \cup D_1^0)$ occurs in C_1 except at the root. By hypothesis, each u_k is irreducible. Since no function symbol from $(D_0 \cup D_1^0)$ occurs in r, t_i' is of the form $C_1'[s_1,\ldots,s_{m'}]$ such that $root(s_j) \in (D_0 \cup D_1^0)$ and no symbol from $(D_0 \cup D_1^0)$ occurs in C_1' except at the root. Further, each s_j is a subterm of some u_k and hence irreducible and the lemma holds.

Case (b): $root(l) \in D_1^0$. In this case, the reduction should take place at the root of some t_i. It follows from lemma 3 and irreducibility of proper subterms (with root in $(D_0 \cup D_1^0)$) of t_i that $r\sigma$ is of the form $C'[u_1,\ldots,u_m]$, $C' \in \mathcal{C}_0^1$, $root(u_i) \in D_1^0$ such that no proper subterm (say, s) of u_i, $1 \leq i \leq m$ with $root(s) \in (D_0 \cup D_1^0)$ is reducible by $\mathcal{R}_0 \cup \mathcal{R}_1$. It is easy to see that $t' \equiv C[t_1,\cdots,t_{i-1},r\sigma,t_{i+1},\cdots,t_n]$ can be written as $C''[s_1,\ldots,s_{m+n-1}]$, $C'' \in \mathcal{C}_0^1$, $root(s_i) \in D_1^0$ such that no proper subterm (say, s) of s_i, $1 \leq i \leq m+n-1$ with $root(s) \in (D_0 \cup D_1^0)$ is reducible by $\mathcal{R}_0 \cup \mathcal{R}_1$. □

The following lemma about normal forms easily follows from this lemma.

Lemma 6 If $\mathcal{R}_1$ is a nice-extension* of $\mathcal{R}_0$ and t is a term of the form $C[t_1,\ldots,t_n]$, $C \in \mathcal{C}_0^1$, $root(t_i) \in D_1^0$ such that no proper subterm (say, s) of t_i, $1 \leq i \leq n$ with $root(s) \in (D_0 \cup D_1^0)$ is reducible by $\mathcal{R}_0 \cup \mathcal{R}_1$ and t' is a normal form of t with respect to $\mathcal{R}_1$, then t' *is of the form* $C'[s_1,\ldots,s_m]$, $C' \in \mathcal{C}_0^1$, $root(s_i) \in D_1^0$ *such that each s_i, $1 \leq i \leq m$ is irreducible by $\mathcal{R}_0 \cup \mathcal{R}_1$.*

Now, we are in a position to establish strong normalization of $\rightarrow_a$.

Theorem 1 *If $\mathcal{R}_1$ is a nice-extension* of $\mathcal{R}_0$ and $\rightarrow_a$ is the relation defined above, then $\rightarrow_a$ is strongly normalizing.*

Proof: We basically prove this using a terminating function f. For any given term t, $f(t)$ is an ordered pair $\langle f_1(t),\ f_2(t)\rangle$, where f_1 and f_2 are defined as follows: $f_1(t)$ is the set $\{p \mid root(t_{|p}) \in D_1^0,\ t_{|p}$ is reducible and no proper subterm s of $t_{|p}$ with $root(s) \in D_1^0$ is reducible$\}$ of deepest reducible D_1^0-positions in t and $f_2(t)$ is the set of innermost redex positions. It may be noted that p need not be a redex position but $t_{|p}$ is reducible.

We use the lexicographic ordering $\prec$ induced by two ordering $\prec_1$ and $\prec_2$ on the two components as the well-founded ordering. The orderings $\prec_1$ and $\prec_2$ are multiset orderings induced by the prefix ordering over positions.

To establish strong normalization of $\rightarrow_a$, it is enough to show that $f(t) \succ f(t')$ whenever $t \rightarrow_a t'$. Now consider $t \equiv C[u] \rightarrow_a C[v] \equiv t'$ such that u is the innermost redex normalized to v. There are two cases: (a) $root(u) \in D_0$ and (b) $root(u) \in D_1$.

In case (a), it's obvious that $f_2(t) \succ_2 f_2(t')$ as v is a normal form of the combined system by lemma 4. Let p be the nearest D_1^0 position above u in $C[u]$. By definition, p is in $f_1(t)$. It's easy to see that no position below p can occur in $f_1(t')$ and in fact p itself *may* not be there in $f_1(t')$ — $t'_{|p}$ may not be reducible. This clearly shows $f(t) \succ f(t')$.

In case (b) there are two subcases: (i) $root(u) \in D_1^0$ and (ii) $root(u) \in D_1^1$. In subcase (i) it's obvious that $f_1(t) \succ_1 f_1(t')$ by lemma 6. In subcase (ii), v is also a normal form of $\mathcal{R}_0$ as D_1^1 symbols do not depend on D_0 and hence $f_2(t) \succ_2 f_2(t')$. Further, $f_1(t) \succeq_1 f_1(t')$ as in case(a). Hence, $f(t) \succ f(t')$. □

From this lemma, it follows that weak normalization (WN) is modular for the class of nice-extensions*.

Theorem 2 *Let $\mathcal{R}_0$ and $\mathcal{R}_1$ be two* TRSs *such that $\mathcal{R}_1$ is a nice-extension* of $\mathcal{R}_0$. Then, the combined system $\mathcal{R}_0 \cup \mathcal{R}_1$ is weakly normalizing (WN) if $\mathcal{R}_0$ and $\mathcal{R}_1$ are weakly normalizing (WN).*

In general, weak normalization (WN) is not modular for hierarchical combinations as demonstrated by Example 1.

5 Semi-completeness

In this section, we study modularity of semi-completeness for nice-extensions*. Unlike weak normalization, semi-completeness is not modular for the whole class of nice-extensions* as shown by the following counterexample.

Example 4 The following systems are semi-complete and $\mathcal{R}_1$ is a nice-extension* of $\mathcal{R}_0$.

$\mathcal{R}_0$: `g(x, y)` $\rightarrow$ `y` $\qquad\qquad$ $\mathcal{R}_1$: `f(g(x, y))` $\rightarrow$ `x`

However, $\mathcal{R}_0 \cup \mathcal{R}_1$ is not semi-complete as the term `f(g(x, y))` has two different normal forms `x` and `f(y)`. □

In the following, we give a class of nice-extensions* for which semi-completeness is modular. Since weak normalization (WN) is shown to be modular for nice-extensions*, it is enough to show that the combined system is confluent whenever the two components are semi-complete. We establish this using Staples' lemma by establishing that the rewrite relation of the combined system is a compatible refinement of $\rightarrow_a$ and $\rightarrow_a$ is confluent. In the rest of this section, we assume that $\mathcal{R}_0$ and $\mathcal{R}_1$ are semi-complete.

The following theorem establishes that $\rightarrow_a$ is confluent for semi-complete systems.

Theorem 3 *The above relation $\rightarrow_a$ is confluent if $\mathcal{R}_0$ and $\mathcal{R}_1$ are semi-complete.*

Proof: Since $\rightarrow_a$ is strongly normalizing by theorem 1, it is enough to show that $\rightarrow_a$ is locally confluent. Let u, v, w be terms such that $u \rightarrow_a v$ and $u \rightarrow_a w$. We have to show that v and w are joinable by $\rightarrow_a$. By the definition of $\rightarrow_a$, the two reductions must take place either (i) at two disjoint positions or (ii) at one position. In case (i) joinability is obvious and in case (ii) semi-completeness of $\mathcal{R}_0$ and $\mathcal{R}_1$ implies that $v \equiv w$. Therefore, $\rightarrow_a$ is confluent. □

In establishing that the rewrite relation of the combined system is a compatible refinement of $\rightarrow_a$, it is useful to first establish modularity of semi-completeness for a smaller class of combinations.

5.1 Semi-completeness of crosswise independent unions

In this section, we study modularity of semi-completeness for crosswise independent unions. The notion of crosswise independent unions is a generalization of constructor sharing unions and Plump's crosswise disjoint unions [15].

Definition 8 We say that two TRSs $\mathcal{R}_0(D_0, C_0, R_0)$ and $\mathcal{R}_1(D_1, C_1, R_1)$ are *crosswise independent* if $f_i \not\rightarrow_d^* f_{1-i}$ *for each* $f_i \in D_i$ *and* $f_{1-i} \in D_{1-i}$, *where* $i \in \{0, 1\}$. We say that $\mathcal{R}_0 \cup \mathcal{R}_1$ is a crosswise independent union if $\mathcal{R}_0$ and $\mathcal{R}_1$ are crosswise independent.

Now, we establish that the rewrite relation of the crosswise independent union is a compatible refinement of $\rightarrow_a$ for the following class of systems.

Theorem 4 Let $\mathcal{R}_0$ and $\mathcal{R}_1$ be two crosswise independent semi-complete TRSs such that

> if $l \rightarrow r \in \mathcal{R}_i$ and s is a subterm of l with $root(s) \in D_{1-i}$ then no nonvariable subterm of s unifies with the left-hand side term of any rule in $\mathcal{R}_0 \cup \mathcal{R}_1$.

Then, *the rewrite relation $\Rightarrow_{\mathcal{R}_0} \cup \Rightarrow_{\mathcal{R}_1}$ (denoted by $\rightarrow_b$ henceforth) of the combined system is a compatible refinement of the relation $\rightarrow_a$ defined above.*

Proof: Consider a reduction $s \equiv C[l\sigma] \rightarrow_b C[r\sigma] \equiv t$. To prove that $\rightarrow_b$ is a *compatible* refinement of $\rightarrow_a$, we have to show that s and t are joinable by $\rightarrow_a$. That's, $\exists u\ (s \rightarrow_a^* u$ and $t \rightarrow_a^* u)$.

Let σ' be the irreducible substitution obtained from σ by reducing the terms in its range to normal forms with respect to $\rightarrow_a$. Since $\rightarrow_a$ is confluent and strongly normalizing, σ' is unique. It is obvious that $s \rightarrow_a^* s' \equiv C[l\sigma']$ and

$t \to_a^* t' \equiv C[r\sigma']$. Without any loss of generality assume that $l \to r \in \mathcal{R}_0$. Now, let v be the normal form of $r\sigma'$ with respect to $\mathcal{R}_0$. Since D_0-symbols do not depend on D_1, it follows that no rule from $\mathcal{R}_1$ is applicable on $r\sigma'$ or on any term derived from $r\sigma'$. Therefore, $r\sigma' \to_a^* v$ (every time we reduce an innermost redex to its normal form w.r.t. $\mathcal{R}_0$). By semi-completeness of $\mathcal{R}_0$ it follows that v is the normal form of $l\sigma'$ as well and hence $l\sigma' \Rightarrow_{\mathcal{R}_0}^* v$. Since $\mathcal{R}_0$ and $\mathcal{R}_1$ satisfy the above condition, each subterm s of $l\sigma'$ with $root(s) \in D_1$ is a normal form. Again due to crosswise independence, no rule of $\mathcal{R}_1$ is applicable on any term derived from $l\sigma'$ and hence $l\sigma' \to_a^* v$. Therefore, $\to_b$ is a compatible refinement of $\to_a$ as $s \to_a^* s' \equiv C[l\sigma'] \to_a^* C[v] \equiv u$ and $t \to_a^* t' \equiv C[r\sigma'] \to_a^* C[v] \equiv u$. □

The modularity of semi-completeness follows from the above theorem and Staples' lemma.

Theorem 5 Let $\mathcal{R}_0$ and $\mathcal{R}_1$ be two crosswise independent semi-complete TRSs such that

> if $l \to r \in \mathcal{R}_i$ and s is a subterm of l with $root(s) \in D_{1-i}$ then no nonvariable subterm of s unifies with the left-hand side of any rule in $\mathcal{R}_0 \cup \mathcal{R}_1$.

Then, *$\mathcal{R}_0 \cup \mathcal{R}_1$ is semi-complete too.*

Proof: Confluence of $\mathcal{R}_0 \cup \mathcal{R}_1$ follows from the above theorem and Staples' lemma. Weak normalization of $\mathcal{R}_0 \cup \mathcal{R}_1$ follows from theorem 1. □

This theorem is a generalization Ohlebusch's result (cf. [14]) on the modularity of semi-completeness for constructor sharing systems as the constructor sharing systems (i) are clearly crosswise independent and (ii) since D_i symbols do not occur in $\mathcal{R}_{1-i}$, the above condition is vacuously satisfied.

5.2 Semi-completeness of nice-extensions*

Theorem 6 Let $\mathcal{R}_0$ and $\mathcal{R}_1$ be two semi-complete TRS such that

1. $\mathcal{R}_1$ is a nice-extension* of $\mathcal{R}_0$,
2. if $l \to r \in \mathcal{R}_i$ and s is a subterm of l with $root(s) \in D_{1-i}$ then no nonvariable subterm of s unifies with the left-hand side of any rule in $\mathcal{R}_0 \cup \mathcal{R}_1$ and
3. if $l \to r \in \mathcal{R}_1$ and $root(l) \in D_1^0$ then all the critical pairs involving this rule are overlays.

Then, *the rewrite relation $\Rightarrow_{\mathcal{R}_0} \cup \Rightarrow_{\mathcal{R}_1}$ (denoted by $\to_b$ henceforth) of the combined system is a compatible refinement of the relation $\to_a$ defined in the previous section.*

Proof: Consider a reduction $s \equiv C[l\sigma] \to_b C[r\sigma] \equiv t$. We have to show that $\exists u\ (s \to_a^* u$ and $t \to_a^* u)$. Let σ' be the irreducible substitution obtained from σ by reducing the terms in its range to normal forms with respect to $\to_a$. Since $\to_a$ is confluent and strongly normalizing, σ' is unique. It is obvious that $s \to_a^*$

$s' \equiv C[l\sigma']$ and $t \to_a^* t' \equiv C[r\sigma']$. Now, we have two cases: (i) $l \to r \in \mathcal{R}_0$ and (ii) $l \to r \in \mathcal{R}_1$.

Case (i). Let v be the normal form of $l\sigma'$ with respect to $\mathcal{R}_0$. By semi-completeness of $\mathcal{R}_0$ it follows that v is the normal form of $r\sigma'$ as well. By condition 2, every subterm s of $l\sigma'$ with $root(s) \in D_1$ is irreducible. Further, since D_0-symbols do not depend on D_1, it follows that no rule from $\mathcal{R}_1$ is applicable on any term derived from $l\sigma'$. Therefore, $l\sigma' \to_a^* v$ and $r\sigma' \to_a^* v$. Hence, $s \to_a^* s' \equiv C[l\sigma'] \to_a^* C[v] \equiv u$ and $t \to_a^* t' \equiv C[r\sigma'] \to_a^* C[v] \equiv u$.

Case (ii). Let v be the normal form of $l\sigma'$ with respect to $\mathcal{R}_1$. By semi-completeness of $\mathcal{R}_1$ it follows that v is the normal form of $r\sigma'$ as well. There are two subcases: (a) $root(l) \in D_1^1$ and (b) $root(l) \in D_1^0$. By conditions 2 and 3 of the theorem, in case (a) it follows that no rule $l' \to r'$ with $root(l') \in (D_0 \cup D_1^0)$ is applicable on $l\sigma'$. Since D_1^1-symbols do not depend on $(D_0 \cup D_1^0)$ these rules are not applicable on any term derived from $l\sigma'$. Therefore, $l\sigma' \to_a^* v$ and $r\sigma' \to_a^* v$. Hence, $s \to_a^* s' \equiv C[l\sigma'] \to_a^* C[v] \equiv u$ and $t \to_a^* t' \equiv C[r\sigma'] \to_a^* C[v] \equiv u$.

In subcase (b), by conditions 2 and 3, it follows that $l\sigma'$ is an innermost redex and hence $l\sigma' \to_a v$. By lemma 3, r is of the form $C'[s_1, \cdots, s_n]$, $C' \in \mathcal{C}_0^1$, $root(s_i) \in D_1^0$ and no proper subterm of s_i has root in $(D_1^0 \cup D_0)$. Therefore, $\mathcal{R}_0$ is not applicable on any proper subterm of $s_i\sigma'$ or on any term derived from a proper subterm of $s_i\sigma'$. Hence it follows that $s_i\sigma' \to_a^* t_i$, where t_i is the normal form of $s_i\sigma'$ w.r.t. $\mathcal{R}_1$ (in $s_i\sigma' \to_a^* t_i$, every time we normalize an innermost redex w.r.t. $\mathcal{R}_1$). By lemma 6, t_i is of the form $C_i[t_{i_1}, \cdots, t_{i_{k_i}}]$, $C_i \in \mathcal{C}_0^1$, $root(t_{i_j}) \in D_1^0$ and t_{i_j} is a normal form of $\mathcal{R}_0 \cup \mathcal{R}_1$. By reducing each $s_i\sigma'$ to t_i, we get $r\sigma' \to_a^* C'[t_1, \cdots, t_n] \equiv v'$ and $r\sigma' \Rightarrow_{\mathcal{R}_1}^* v'$. By semi-completeness of $\mathcal{R}_1$, it follows that v is the normal form of v' w.r.t. $\mathcal{R}_1$ and $v' \Rightarrow_{\mathcal{R}_1}^* v$. The term v' can be written as $C''[t_{1_1}, \cdots, t_{1_{k_1}}, \cdots, t_{n_1}, \cdots, t_{n_{k_n}}]$ such that $C'' \in \mathcal{C}_0^1$, $root(t_{i_j}) \in D_1^0$, where $C'' \equiv C'[C_1, \cdots, C_n]$. Since each t_{i_j} is a normal form of $\mathcal{R}_0 \cup \mathcal{R}_1$, no rule $l' \to r'$ with $root(l') \in D_1^0$ is applicable on v' or on any term derived from v' (since $C'' \in \mathcal{C}_0^1$). By a similar reasoning it follows that no rule $l' \to r'$ with $root(l') \in D_1^0$ is applicable on v or on any term derived from v.

The situation can be paraphrased as follows: (i) $v' \Rightarrow_{\mathcal{R}_1'}^* v$ and (ii) the only rules applicable on v and v' and any term derived from them are from $\mathcal{R}_0 \cup \mathcal{R}_1'$, where $\mathcal{R}_1' = \{l \to r \in \mathcal{R}_1 \mid root(l) \in D_1^1\}$. The system $\mathcal{R}_1'$ is semi-complete since no symbol in D_1^1 depends on D_1^0. Since $\mathcal{R}_0$ and $\mathcal{R}_1'$ are crosswise independent, $\mathcal{R}_0 \cup \mathcal{R}_1'$ is semi-complete by theorem 5. Therefore, v and v' have the same normal form (say, u) w.r.t. $\mathcal{R}_0 \cup \mathcal{R}_1'$ and $v \to_a^* u$ and $v' \to_a^* u$ (every time we normalize an innermost redex w.r.t. $\mathcal{R}_0$ or $\mathcal{R}_1'$). Hence $s \to_a^* s' \equiv C[l\sigma'] \to_a C[v] \to_a^* C[u]$ and $t \to_a^* t' \equiv C[r\sigma'] \to_a^* C[v'] \to_a^* C[u]$. □

Remark: note that, $l\sigma' \to_a v$ need not be true in case (i) and subcase (a) of case (ii) in the proof of the above Theorem — in particular $l\sigma'$ may not be an innermost redex.

The modularity of semi-completeness follows from the above theorem and Staples' lemma.

Theorem 7 Let $\mathcal{R}_0$ and $\mathcal{R}_1$ be two semi-complete TRS such that

1. $\mathcal{R}_1$ is a nice-extension* of $\mathcal{R}_0$,
2. if $l \rightarrow r \in \mathcal{R}_i$ and s is a subterm of l with $root(s) \in D_{1-i}$ then no nonvariable subterm of s unifies with the left-hand side of any rule in $\mathcal{R}_0 \cup \mathcal{R}_1$ and
3. if $l \rightarrow r \in \mathcal{R}_1$ and $root(l) \in D_1^0$ then all the critical pairs involving this rule are overlays.

Then, *the combined system $\mathcal{R}_0 \cup \mathcal{R}_1$ is semi-complete as well.*

6 Extending the results

In this section, we discuss the extensions of the above results in two directions. These (extensions of the) results are established in the larger version of the paper, but omitted here to meet the space restrictions.

In the above, we assume that the two component systems do not share any rules and defined symbols, i.e., $D_0 \cap D_1 = \phi$. However, we can allow two systems to share defined symbols provided the rules defining these symbols are the same in both the systems, i.e., we can consider the following situation: two systems $\mathcal{R}_0(D_0 \cup D, C_1, R_1)$ and $\mathcal{R}_1(D_1 \cup D, C_1, R_1)$ sharing defined symbols D and rules $R_0 \cap R_1 = \{l \rightarrow r \mid root(l) \in D\}$. This generalization is in particular useful while studying properties like weak normalization, innermost normalization, confluence and semi-completeness, which do not have the following hereditary property: *if R has property* **P** *and R' is a subsystem of R then R' has property* **P**. Lack of this property forces us to allow two components to share some rules while studying (and proving) these properties in a modular way.

The notion of generalized nice-extension* allows such sharing. The notations of D_1^1 and D_1^0 need slight changes: $D_1^0 = \{ f \mid f \in (D_1 \cup D)$ and $f \rightarrow_d^* D_0 \}$ and $D_1^1 = (D_1 \cup D) - D_1^0$.

Definition 9 A TRS $\mathcal{R}_1(D_1 \cup D, C_1, R_1)$ is a *generalized nice-extension** of another TRS $\mathcal{R}_0(D_0 \cup D, C_0, R_0)$ if the following conditions are satisfied:

1. $D_0 \cap D_1 = \phi$ and $R_0 \cap R_1 = \{l \rightarrow r \mid root(l) \in D\}$.
2. $\forall f \in (D_0 \cup D)$, $\forall g \in D_1$, $f \not\rightarrow_d g$ (i.e., $\mathcal{R}_0 \cup \mathcal{R}_1$ is a super-hierarchical combination).
3. Each rewrite rule $l \rightarrow r \in R_1$ satisfies the following condition:
(H1'): For every subterm s of r, if $root(s) \in (D_1^0 - D)$, then s contains no function symbol depending on D_0 except at the outermost level (of s).

All theorems in the above sections can be established for generalized nice-extensions*. However, the definition of $\rightarrow_a$ needs a modification to handle the shared defined symbols (and rules). The proofs of all the above results can be done using just the techniques used above, but they need much more detailed case analysis. The reader is refered to [8] for the proofs of the generalized results. The main result for generalized nice-extensions* is the following.

Theorem 8 Let $\mathcal{R}_0$ and $\mathcal{R}_1$ be two semi-complete TRS such that

1. $\mathcal{R}_1$ is a generalized nice-extension* of $\mathcal{R}_0$,
2. if $l \to r \in \mathcal{R}_i$ and s is a subterm of l with $root(s) \in D_{1-i}$ then no nonvariable subterm of s unifies with the left-hand side of any rule in $\mathcal{R}_0 \cup \mathcal{R}_1$ and
3. if $l \to r \in \mathcal{R}_1$ and $root(l) \in D_1^0$ then all the critical pairs involving this rule are overlays.

Then, *the combined system $\mathcal{R}_0 \cup \mathcal{R}_1$ is semi-complete as well.*

Using this theorem, we can extend the results (as in [6, 7]) to the class of generalized proper-extensions*, where nesting of D_1^0 symbols is allowed in the right-hand side terms.

Definition 10 A TRS $\mathcal{R}_1(D_1 \cup D, C_1, R_1)$ is a *generalized proper-extension** of another TRS $\mathcal{R}_0(D_0 \cup D, C_0, R_0)$ if conditions 1 and 2 of the above definition and the following condition are satisfied:

3 Each rewrite rule $l \to r \in R_1$ satisfies the following condition:
(H2): For every subterm s of r, if $root(s) \in (D_1^0 - D)$ and $root(s) \to_d^* root(l)$, then s contains no function symbol depending on D_0 except at the outermost level (of s).

To relate the notion of generalized proper-extension* with generalized nice-extension*, we need the following definition.

Definition 11 From the dependency relation, $\to_d^*$ (see Def. 3) of $\mathcal{R}_1$, we define

1. Equivalence relation $\approx$ ($f \approx g$ if $f \to_d^* g$ and $g \to_d^* f$) on the set of defined symbols D_1^0. We denote the equivalence class containing f by $[f]$.
2. Partial ordering $\sqsupset$ ($[f] \sqsupset [g]$ if $f \to_d^* g$ and $g \not\to_d^* f$) on the set of equivalence classes.

Assumption: In the following we assume that the relation $\sqsupset$ on D_1^0 is noetherian.

Since signature of any TRS is a countable set, the equivalence relation $\approx$ partitions D_1^0 into a countable set E of equivalence classes. Since relation $\sqsupset$ is noetherian, one can easily extend it to a well-ordering of order type λ, where λ is a countable ordinal.

Notation: For any ordinal α, we denote the αth element in the above well-ordering by E_α (for all ordinals $\alpha > \lambda$, we let $E_\alpha = \phi$) and the TRS $\{l \to r \in \mathcal{R}_1 \mid root(l) \in D \cup D_1^1 \cup (\bigcup_{\beta \leq \alpha} E_\beta)\}$ by R_α and the combined system $(\bigcup_{\beta < \alpha} R_\beta) \cup \mathcal{R}_0$ by S_α. In particular, S_0 is $\mathcal{R}_0$ and S_κ is $\mathcal{R}_0 \cup \mathcal{R}_1$ for any ordinal κ above λ.

The following theorem relates generalized proper-extensions* and generalized nice-extensions*.

Theorem 9 Let $\mathcal{R}_0$ and $\mathcal{R}_1$ be two TRSs such that $\mathcal{R}_1$ is a generalized proper-extension* of $\mathcal{R}_0$ and $\sqsupset$ is noetherian. *Then, R_α is a generalized nice-extension* of S_α for every ordinal α, where R_α and S_α denote the objects explained in the above notation.*

It is easy to see that R_α is semi-complete and satisfies conditions 2 and 3 of Theorem 9 if $\mathcal{R}_1$ satisfies them. Therefore by induction, we have:

Theorem 10 Let $\mathcal{R}_0$ and $\mathcal{R}_1$ be two semi-complete TRS such that

1. $\mathcal{R}_1$ is a generalized proper-extension* of $\mathcal{R}_0$ and $\sqsupset$ is noetherian,
2. if $l \to r \in \mathcal{R}_i$ and s is a subterm of l with $root(s) \in D_{1-i}$ then no nonvariable subterm of s unifies with the left-hand side of any rule in $\mathcal{R}_0 \cup \mathcal{R}_1$ and
3. if $l \to r \in \mathcal{R}_1$ and $root(l) \in D_1^0$ then all the critical pairs involving this rule are overlays.

Then, *the combined system $\mathcal{R}_0 \cup \mathcal{R}_1$ is semi-complete as well.*

7 Conclusion

In this paper, the modular aspects of hierarchical and super hierarchical combinations are investigated. We identified some classes of hierarchical and super hierarchical combinations for which *semi-completeness* property is modular. It is also shown that *semi-completeness* property is modular for a class of crosswise independent unions. The crosswise independent unions are generalization of constructor sharing unions as well as Plump's crosswise disjoint unions.

References

1. N. Dershowitz and J.-P. Jouannaud (1990), *Rewrite Systems*, In J. van Leeuwen (ed.), *Handbook of Theoretical Computer Science*, Vol. **B**, pp. 243-320, North-Holland.
2. N. Dershowitz (1995), *Hierarchical termination*, to appear in Proc. of CTRS'94, forthcoming LNCS, Springer-Verlag.
3. B. Gramlich (1992), *Relating innermost, weak, uniform and modular termination of term rewrite systems*, Proc. of Logic Prog. and Automated Reasoning, LPAR'92, Lecture Notes in Computer Science **624**, pp. 285-296, Springer-Verlag.
4. B.Gramlich (1994), *Generalized sufficient conditions for modular termination of rewriting*, in AAECC (Applicable Algebra in Engineering, Communication and Computing) **5**, pp. 131-158.
5. J.W. Klop (1992), *Term Rewriting Systems*, tech rep. CS-R9073, CWI, Amsterdam. Also appears as a chapter in S. Abramsky, D. Gabbay and T. Maibaum (ed.), *Handbook of Logic in Computer Science*, Vol. **2**, Oxford University Press.

6. M.R.K. Krishna Rao (1993), *Completeness of hierarchical combinations of term rewriting systems*, Proc. of 13th conference on Foundations of Software Technology and Theoretical Computer Science, FST&TCS'93, Lecture Notes in Computer Science **761**, pp. 125-138, Springer-Verlag.

7. M.R.K. Krishna Rao (1994), *Simple termination of hierarchical combinations of term rewriting systems*, Proc. of Theoretical Aspects of Computer Science, TACS'94, Lecture Notes in Computer Science **789**, pp. 203-223, Springer-Verlag.

8. M.R.K. Krishna Rao (1994), *Semi-completeness of hierarchical and super hierarchical combinations of term rewriting systems*, Technical report, TIFR, Bombay, October.

9. M. Kurihara and A. Ohuchi (1990), *Modularity of simple termination of term rewriting systems*, Journal of IPS, Japan **34**, pp. 632-642.

10. M. Kurihara and A. Ohuchi (1992), *Modularity of simple termination of term rewriting systems with shared constructors*, Theoretical Computer Science **103**, pp. 273-282.

11. A. Middeldorp (1989), *A sufficient condition for the termination of the direct sum of term rewriting systems*, Proc. of LICS'89, pp. 396-401.

12. A. Middeldorp (1990), *Modular properties of term rewriting systems*, Ph.D. Thesis, Free University, Amsterdam.

13. A. Middeldorp and Y. Toyama (1991), *Completeness of combinations of constructor systems*, Proc. of RTA'91, Lecture Notes in Computer Science **488**, pp. 188-199, Springer-Verlag. Also appears in J. Symb. Comp. **15**, pp. 331-348.

14. E. Ohlebusch (1994), *On the modularity of confluence of constructor-sharing term rewriting systems*, Proc. of CAAP'94, Lecture Notes in Computer Science **787**, pp. 261-275, Springer-Verlag.

15. D. Plump (1993), *Evaluation of functional expressions by hypergraph rewriting*, Ph.D. Thesis, University of Bremen.

16. M. Rusinowitch (1987), *On termination of the direct sum of term rewriting systems*, Information Processing Letters, IPL **26**, pp. 65-70.

17. J. Staples (1975), *Church-Roser Theorems for Replacement Systems*, in J. Crosley (ed.), *Algebra and Logic*, Lecture Notes in Mathematics, Vol **450**, pp. 291-307, Springer-Verlag.

18. Y. Toyama (1987), *On the Church-Rosser property for the direct sum of term rewriting systems*, JACM **34**, pp. 128-143.

19. Y. Toyama (1987), *Counterexamples to termination for the direct sum of term rewriting systems*, Information Processing Letters, IPL **25**, pp. 141-143.

20. Y. Toyama, J.W. Klop and H.P. Barendrget (1989), *Termination for the direct sum of left-linear term rewriting systems*, Proc. of RTA'89, Lecture Notes in Computer Science **355**, pp. 477-491, Springer-Verlag.

Lazy Narrowing: Strong Completeness and Eager Variable Elimination (Extended Abstract)

Satoshi Okui Aart Middeldorp Tetsuo Ida

Institute of Information Sciences and Electronics

University of Tsukuba, Tsukuba 305, Japan

ABSTRACT

Narrowing is an important method for solving unification problems in equational theories that are presented by confluent term rewriting systems. Because narrowing is a rather complicated operation, several authors studied calculi in which narrowing is replaced by more simple inference rules. This paper is concerned with one such calculus. Contrary to what has been stated in the literature, we show that the calculus lacks strong completeness, so selection functions to cut down the search space are not applicable. We prove completeness of the calculus and we establish an interesting connection between its strong completeness and the completeness of basic narrowing. We also address the eager variable elimination problem. It is known that many redundant derivations can be avoided if the variable elimination rule, one of the inference rules of our calculus, is given precedence over the other inference rules. We prove the completeness of a restricted variant of eager variable elimination in the case of orthogonal term rewriting systems.

1. Introduction

E-unification—solving equations modulo some equational theory E—is a fundamental technique in automated reasoning. Narrowing ([19, 4, 11]) is a general E-unification procedure for equational theories that are presented by confluent term rewriting systems (TRSs for short). Narrowing is the computational mechanism of many functional-logic programming languages (see Hanus [7] for a recent survey on the integration of functional and logic programming). It is well-known that narrowing is complete with respect to normalizable solutions. Completeness means that for every solution to a given equation, a more general solution can be found by narrowing. If we extend narrowing to goals consisting of several equations, we obtain *strong* completeness. This means that we don't lose completeness when we restrict applications of the narrowing rule to a single equation in each goal.

Since narrowing is not easily implemented, several authors studied calculi consisting of a small number of more elementary inference rules that simulate narrowing (e.g. [15, 8, 9, 13, 20, 6]). In this paper we are concerned with a subset (actually the specialization to confluent TRSs) of the calculus TRANS proposed by Hölldobler [9]. We call this calculus *lazy narrowing calculus* (LNC for short). Because the purpose of LNC is to simulate narrowing by more elementary inference rules, it is natural to expect that LNC inherits strong completeness from narrowing, and indeed this is stated by Hölldobler (Corollary 7.3.9 in [9]). We show however that LNC lacks strong completeness.

An important improvement over narrowing is *basic* narrowing (Hullot [11]). In basic narrowing narrowing steps are never applied to (sub)terms introduced by previous narrowing substitutions, resulting in a significant reduction of the search space. In this paper we establish a interesting connection between LNC and basic narrowing: we show that LNC is strongly complete whenever basic narrowing is complete. The latter is known for complete (i.e., confluent and terminating) TRSs (Hullot [11]). Other sufficient conditions are right-linearity and orthogonality (Middeldorp and Hamoen [16]). So LNC is strongly complete for these three classes of TRSs. We prove completeness of LNC for the general case of confluent TRSs. In the literature completeness of LNC-like calculi is proved under the additional termination assumption. Without this assumption the completeness proof is significantly more involved.

It is known that LNC-like calculi generate many derivations which produce the same solutions (up to subsumption). Martelli *et al.* [15, 13] and Hölldobler [9], among others, pointed out that many of these redundant derivations can be avoided by giving the variable elimination rule, one of the inference rules of LNC-like calculi, precedence over the other inference rules. The problem whether this strategy is complete or not is called the *eager variable elimination* problem in [9, 20]. Martelli *et al.* stated in [13] that this is easily shown in the case of terminating (and confluent) TRSs, but Snyder questions the validity of this claim in his monograph [20] on E-unification. We address the eager variable elimination problem for non-terminating TRSs. We prove completeness of a slightly restricted version of eager variable elimination in the case of orthogonal TRSs. To this end we simplify and extend the main result of You [22] concerning the completeness of *outer* narrowing for orthogonal *constructor-based* TRSs.

The remainder of the paper is organized as follows. In a preliminary section we introduce narrowing and state the relevant completeness results. The narrowing calculus that we are interested in—LNC—is defined in Section 3. In that section we also show that LNC is not strongly complete. In Section 4 we establish the connection between the strong completeness of LNC and the completeness of basic narrowing. We prove the completeness of LNC for general confluent systems in Section 5. Section 6 is concerned with the eager variable elimination problem. In the final section we give suggestions for further research.

Due to lack of space, the present paper doesn't contain any proof details. All proofs can be found in the full version [18].

2. Preliminaries

We assume the reader's familiarity with the basic notions of term rewriting ([2, 12]). We use the position formalism to denote subterm occurrences. The set of positions in a term is denoted by $\mathcal{P}os(t)$. If $p \in \mathcal{P}os(t)$ then $t_{|p}$ denotes the subterm of t at position p and $t[s]_p$ denotes the term that is obtained from t by replacing the subterm at position p by the term s. The set $\mathcal{P}os(t)$ is partitioned into $\mathcal{P}os_{\mathcal{V}}(t)$ and $\mathcal{P}os_{\mathcal{F}}(t)$ as follows: $\mathcal{P}os_{\mathcal{V}}(t) = \{p \in \mathcal{P}os(t) \mid t_{|p} \in \mathcal{V}\}$ and $\mathcal{P}os_{\mathcal{F}}(t) = \mathcal{P}os(t) - \mathcal{P}os_{\mathcal{V}}(t)$. Positions are partially ordered by the prefix ordering $\leqslant$, i.e., $p \leqslant q$ if there exists a (necessarily unique) r such that $p{\cdot}r = q$. In that case we define $q\backslash p$ as the position r. We write $p < q$ if $p \leqslant q$ and $p \neq q$. If neither $p \leqslant q$ nor $q \leqslant p$, we write $p \perp q$. The domain $\mathcal{D}(\theta)$ of a substitution θ is the set $\{x \in \mathcal{V} \mid x\theta \neq x\}$. As usual, this set is required to be finite. We denote the set $\bigcup_{x \in \mathcal{D}(\theta)} \mathcal{V}(x\theta)$ by $\mathcal{I}(\theta)$. We distinguish a nullary function symbol `true` and a binary function symbol $\doteq$, written in infix notation. A term of the form $s \doteq t$, where neither s nor t contains any occurrences of $\doteq$ and `true`, is called an *equation*. The term `true` is also viewed as an equation. The extension of a TRS $\mathcal{R}$ with the rewrite rule $x \doteq x \to \mathtt{true}$ is denoted by $\mathcal{R}_+$. A *goal* is a sequence of equations. We use $\top$ as a generic notation for goals containing only equations `true`. Let G be a goal and θ a substitution. If there exists a rewrite sequence $G\theta \to^*_{\mathcal{R}_+} \top$, we write $\mathcal{R} \vdash G\theta$ and we say that θ is an ($\mathcal{R}$-)*solution* of G. Narrowing is formulated as the following inference rule:

$$\frac{G_1, e, G_2}{(G_1, e[r]_p, G_2)\theta}$$

if there exist a fresh variant $l \to r$ of a rewrite rule in $\mathcal{R}_+$, a position $p \in \mathcal{P}os_{\mathcal{F}}(e)$, and a most general unifier θ of $e_{|p}$ and l.

In the above situation we write $G_1, e, G_2 \rightsquigarrow_{\theta,p,l\to r,e} (G_1, e[r]_p, G_2)\theta$. This is called an NC-*step* (NC stands for narrowing calculus). Subscripts will be omitted when they are clear from the context or irrelevant. A sequence $G_1 \rightsquigarrow_{\theta_1} \cdots \rightsquigarrow_{\theta_{n-1}} G_n$ of NC-steps is called an NC-*derivation* and abbreviated to $G_1 \rightsquigarrow^*_{\theta} G_n$ where $\theta = \theta_1 \cdots \theta_{n-1}$. We use the symbol Π (and its derivatives) to denote NC-derivations. An NC-derivation which ends in $\top$ is called an NC-*refutation*. The following completeness result is essentially due to Hullot [11].

THEOREM 2.1. *Let $\mathcal{R}$ be a confluent TRS. If $\mathcal{R} \vdash G\theta$ and $\theta\restriction_{\mathcal{V}ar(G)}$ is normalized then there exists an* NC*-refutation $G \rightsquigarrow^*_{\theta'} \top$ such that $\theta' \leqslant \theta$ $[\mathcal{V}ar(G)]$.* □

There are three sources of non-determinism in NC: the choice of the equation e, the choice of the subterm $e_{|p}$, and the choice of the rewrite rule $l \to r$. The last two choices are *don't know* non-deterministic, meaning that in general all possible choices have to be considered in order to guarantee completeness. The choice of the equations e is *don't care* non-deterministic, because of the *strong completeness* of NC. Strong completeness means completeness independent of selection functions. A *selection function* is mapping that assigns to every goal G different from $\top$ an equation $e \in G$ different from `true`. An example of a selection function is $\mathcal{S}_{left}$ which always returns the leftmost equation different from **true**. We say that an NC-derivation Π *respects* a selection function $\mathcal{S}$ if the selected equation in every step $G_1 \rightsquigarrow G_2$ of Π coincides with $\mathcal{S}(G_1)$. Now strong completeness of NC is formulated as follows.

THEOREM 2.2. *Let $\mathcal{R}$ be a confluent TRS and $\mathcal{S}$ a selection function. If $\mathcal{R} \vdash G\theta$ and $\theta\lceil_{\mathcal{V}ar(G)}$ is normalized then there exists an* NC*-refutation $G \rightsquigarrow^*_{\theta'} \top$ respecting $\mathcal{S}$ such that $\theta' \leqslant \theta$ $[\mathcal{V}ar(G)]$.* □

3. Lazy Narrowing Calculus

Calculi in which the narrowing inference rule is replaced by a small number of more primitive operations are comprehensively examined by Hölldobler in his thesis [9] and Snyder in his monograph [20]. The calculus that we investigate in this paper is the specialization of Hölldobler's calculus TRANS, which is defined for general equational systems and based on paramodulation, to (confluent) TRSs and narrowing.

DEFINITION 3.1. Let $\mathcal{R}$ be a TRS. The *lazy narrowing calculus*, LNC for short, consists of the following five inference rules:

[*on*] *outermost narrowing*

$$\frac{G_1, f(s_1, \ldots, s_n) \simeq t, G_2}{G_1, s_1 \doteq l_1, \ldots, s_n \doteq l_n, r \doteq t, G_2}$$

if there exists a fresh variant $f(l_1, \ldots, l_n) \rightarrow r$ of a rewrite rule in $\mathcal{R}$,

[*im*] *imitation*

$$\frac{G_1, f(s_1, \ldots, s_n) \simeq x, G_2}{(G_1, s_1 \doteq x_1, \ldots, s_n \doteq x_n, G_2)\theta}$$

if $\theta = \{x \mapsto f(x_1, \ldots, x_n)\}$ with $x_1, \ldots, x_n$ fresh variables,

[*d*] *decomposition*

$$\frac{G_1, f(s_1, \ldots, s_n) \doteq f(t_1, \ldots, t_n), G_2}{G_1, s_1 \doteq t_1, \ldots, s_n \doteq t_n, G_2},$$

[*v*] *variable elimination*

$$\frac{G_1, x \simeq t, G_2}{(G_1, G_2)\theta}$$

if $x \notin \mathcal{V}ar(t)$ and $\theta = \{x \mapsto t\}$,

[*t*] *removal of trivial equations*

$$\frac{G_1, x \doteq x, G_2}{G_1, G_2}.$$

Here $s \simeq t$ stands for $s \doteq t$ or $t \doteq s$.

The variable elimination rule [*v*] is different from the one of Martelli *et al.* [15, 13] in that we don't keep the solved equation $x \simeq t$ around. The rules [*v*], [*d*], and [*t*] constitute the syntactic unification algorithm of Martelli and Montanari

[14]. We refer to these three rules as UC, which stands for *unification calculus*. Because syntactic unification is performed by UC, the rewrite rule $x \doteq x \to \mathtt{true}$ is no longer used in LNC. As a consequence, we may assume that the symbol **true** doesn't occur in LNC-goals.

Contrary to usual narrowing, the outermost narrowing rule $[on]$ generates new *parameter-passing* equations $s_1 \doteq l_1, \ldots, s_n \doteq l_n$ besides the *body* equation $r \doteq t$. These parameter-passing equations must eventually be solved in order to obtain a refutation, but we don't require that they are solved right away. That is the reason why we call the calculus *lazy*. We introduce some useful notations relating to the calculus LNC. If G and G' are the upper and lower goal in the inference rule $[\alpha]$ ($\alpha \in \{on, im, d, v, t\}$), we write $G \Rightarrow_{[\alpha]} G'$. This is called an LNC-step. The applied rewrite rule or substitution may be supplied as subscript, that is, we will write things like $G \Rightarrow_{[on], l \to r} G'$ and $G \Rightarrow_{[im], \theta} G'$. LNC-derivations are defined as in the case of NC. An LNC-refutation is an LNC-derivation ending in the empty goal $\square$. UC-steps, derivations, and refutations are defined in exactly the same way.

Because the purpose of LNC is to simulate narrowing, it is natural to expect that LNC inherits strong completeness from NC. Indeed, Hölldobler [9, Corollary 7.3.9] states the strong completeness of LNC for confluent TRSs with respect to normalizable solutions. However, this does not hold.

COUNTEREXAMPLE 3.2. Consider the TRS $\mathcal{R} = \{f(x) \to g(h(x), x), g(x, x) \to a, b \to h(b)\}$ and the goal $G = f(b) \doteq a$. Confluence of $\mathcal{R}$ can be proved by a routine induction argument on the structure of terms. The (normalized) empty substitution ε is a solution of G because $f(b) \doteq a \to_{\mathcal{R}} g(h(b), b) \doteq a \to_{\mathcal{R}} g(h(b), h(b)) \doteq a \to_{\mathcal{R}} a \doteq a \to_{\mathcal{R}_+} \mathtt{true}$. Consider the selection function $\mathcal{S}_{right}$ that selects the rightmost equation in every goal. There is essentially only one LNC-derivation issued from G respecting $\mathcal{S}_{right}$:

$$\begin{array}{lll}
f(b) \doteq a & \Rightarrow_{[on], f(x) \to g(h(x), x)} & b \doteq x, g(h(x), x) \doteq a \\
& \Rightarrow_{[on], g(x_1, x_1) \to a} & b \doteq x, h(x) \doteq x_1, x \doteq x_1, a \doteq a \\
& \Rightarrow_{[d]} & b \doteq x, h(x) \doteq x_1, x \doteq x_1 \\
& \Rightarrow_{[v], \{x_1 \mapsto x\}} & b \doteq x, h(x) \doteq x \\
& \Rightarrow_{[im], \{x \mapsto h(x_2)\}} & b \doteq h(x_2), h(x_2) \doteq x_2 \\
& \Rightarrow_{[im], \{x_2 \mapsto h(x_3)\}} & \cdots
\end{array}$$

This is clearly not a refutation. (The alternative binding $\{x \mapsto x_1\}$ in the $\Rightarrow_{[v]}$-step results in a renaming of the above LNC-derivation.) Hence LNC is *not* strongly complete.

This counterexample doesn't refute the completeness of LNC. The goal $f(b) \doteq a$ can be solved, for instance, by adopting the selection function $\mathcal{S}_{left}$.

In Section 5 we show that LNC is complete in the general case of confluent TRSs and normalized solutions. In the next section we present sufficient conditions for the strong completeness of LNC, which turns out to be a simpler than proving completeness.

4. Restoring Strong Completeness

In Middeldorp and Hamoen [16] it is shown that basic narrowing is not able to solve the goal $f(b) \doteq a$ with respect to the TRS $\mathcal{R}$ of Counterexample 3.2. This suggests a connection between strong completeness of LNC and completeness of basic NC. In this section we prove that LNC is strongly complete whenever basic NC is complete.

The basis of our proof is the specialization of the transformation process used by Hölldobler in his proof of the (strong) completeness of TRANS. First we formalize the intuitively clear propagation of equations along NC-derivations.

DEFINITION 4.1. Let $G \leadsto_{\theta,p,l\to r} G'$ be an NC-step and e an equation in G. If e is the selected equation in this step, then e is narrowed into the equation $e[r]_p\theta$ in G'. In this case we say that $e[r]_p\theta$ is the *descendant* of e in G'. Otherwise, e is simply instantiated to the equation $e\theta$ in G' and we call $e\theta$ the descendant of e. The notion of descendant extends to NC-derivations in the obvious way.

Observe that in an NC-refutation $G \leadsto^* \top$ every equation $e \in G$ has exactly one descendant **true** in $\top$. We now introduce four transformation steps on NC-refutations. The first one corresponds to Proposition 7.3.4 in Hölldobler [9].

LEMMA 4.2. *Let* $\Pi\colon G_1, s \doteq t, G_2 \leadsto^*_\theta \top$ *be an* NC*-refutation with the property that narrowing is applied to a descendant of* $s \doteq t$ *at position* 1. *Let* V *be a finite set of variables such that* $\mathcal{V}ar(G_1, s \doteq t, G_2) \subseteq V$. *If* $l \to r$ *is the applied rewrite rule in the first such step then there exists an* NC*-refutation* $\phi_{[on]}(\Pi)\colon G_1, s \doteq l, r \doteq t, G_2 \leadsto^*_{\theta'} \top$ *such that* $\theta = \theta'$ $[V]$. □

The second transformation step corresponds to Proposition 7.3.3 in [9].

LEMMA 4.3. *Let* e *be the equation* $f(s_1,\ldots,s_n) \doteq f(t_1,\ldots,t_n)$. *Let* $\Pi\colon G_1, e, G_2 \leadsto^*_\theta \top$ *be an* NC*-refutation with the property that narrowing is never applied to a descendant of* e *at position 1 or 2. Let* V *be a finite set of variables that includes* $\mathcal{V}ar(G_1, e, G_2)$. *There exists an* NC*-refutation* $\phi_{[d]}(\Pi)\colon G_1, s_1 \doteq t_1, \ldots, s_n \doteq t_n, G_2 \leadsto^*_{\theta'} \top$ *such that* $\theta = \theta'$ $[V]$. □

The third transformation step corresponds to Corollary 7.3.5 in Hölldobler [9]. This corollary is an immediate consequence of Hölldobler's lifting lemma for reflection, instantiation, and paramodulation (Lemma 6.2.6 in [9]). This easy proof does not work in our case since narrowing, unlike paramodulation, cannot be applied at variable positions. Nevertheless, we can repeat the proof of the lifting lemma (for NC) to obtain the validity of the third transformation step.

LEMMA 4.4. *Let* $\Pi\colon G \leadsto^*_\theta \top$ *be an* NC*-refutation with the property that* $x\theta = f(t_1,\ldots,t_n)$ *for some* $x \in \mathcal{V}ar(G)$ *and let* V *be a finite set of variables such that* $\mathcal{V}ar(G) \subseteq V$. *Let* $\gamma = \{x \mapsto f(x_1,\ldots,x_n)\}$ *with* $x_1,\ldots,x_n \notin V$. *There exists an* NC*-refutation* $\phi_{[im]}(\Pi)\colon G\gamma \leadsto^*_{\theta'} \top$ *which employs the same rewrite rules at the same positions in the corresponding equations of the goals in* Π *such that* $\gamma\theta' = \theta$ $[V]$. □

The fourth and final transformation step is presented in the following lemma.

LEMMA 4.5. *For every* NC*-refutation* $\Pi: G_1, s \doteq t, G_2 \rightsquigarrow_{\theta_1,\epsilon} (G_1, \mathtt{true}, G_2)\theta_1 \rightsquigarrow^*_{\theta_2} \top$ *there exists an* NC*-refutation* $\phi_{UC}(\Pi): (G_1, G_2)\theta_1 \rightsquigarrow^*_{\theta_2} \top$. □

The idea now is to repeatedly apply the above transformation steps to a given NC-refutation, connecting the initial goals of (some of) the resulting NC-refutations by LNC-steps, until we reach the empty goal. In order to guarantee termination of this process, we need a well-founded order on NC-refutations that is compatible with the four transformation steps.

DEFINITION 4.6. The *depth* $|t|$ of a term t is inductively defined as follows: $|t| = 1$ if t is a variable and $|t| = 1 + \max\{|t_1|, \ldots, |t_n| \mid 1 \leqslant i \leqslant n\}$ if $t = f(t_1, \ldots, t_n)$. The *complexity* $|\Pi|$ of an NC-refutation $\Pi: G \rightsquigarrow^*_\theta \top$ is defined as the triple (n, M, s) where n is the number of applications of narrowing in Π at non-root positions (so the number of steps that do not use the rewrite rule $x \doteq x \to \mathtt{true}$), M is the multiset $\{|x_1\theta|, \ldots, |x_m\theta| \mid \{x_1, \ldots, x_m\}$ is the *multiset* of variables occurring in $G\}$, and s is the number of occurrences of symbols different from $\doteq$ and $\mathtt{true}$ in G. We define a partial order $\gg$ on NC-refutations as follows: $\Pi_1 \gg \Pi_2$ if $|\Pi_1| \; lex(>, >_{mul}, >) \; |\Pi_2|$. Here $lex(>, >_{mul}, >)$ denotes the lexicographic product of $>$ (the standard order on $\mathbb{N}$), $>_{mul}$ (the multiset extension [3] of $>$), and $>$.

LEMMA 4.7. *The partial order* $\gg$ *is a well-founded order on* NC*-refutations.* □

Our complexity measure on NC-refutations is different from the one in Hölldobler [9, p. 188]. Since we are concerned with one-directional term rewriting and narrowing (as opposed to bi-directional equational reasoning and paramodulation in [9]), our simpler definition suffices. The next lemma states that $\gg$ is compatible with the transformation steps defined above.

LEMMA 4.8. *Let* Π *be an* NC*-refutation. We have* $\Pi \gg \phi_{[on]}(\Pi)$, $\phi_{[d]}(\Pi)$, $\phi_{[im]}(\Pi)$, $\phi_{UC}(\Pi)$ *whenever the latter are defined.* □

In the case of $\phi_{[on]}$ and $\phi_{[d]}$ this is easily verified. The validity of Lemma 4.8 for the transformation steps $\phi_{[im]}$ and ϕ_{UC} requires more effort. The following example illustrates how the above results are used to transform NC-refutations into LNC-refutations.

EXAMPLE 4.9. Consider the TRS $\mathcal{R} = \{f(g(y)) \to y\}$ and the NC-refutation

$$\Pi_1: g(f(x)) \doteq x \rightsquigarrow_{\{x \mapsto g(y)\}} g(y) \doteq g(y) \rightsquigarrow_\epsilon \mathtt{true}.$$

In Π_1 the variable x is bound to $g(y)$, so the complexity of Π_1 is $(1, \{2, 2\}, 4)$. Transformation steps $\phi_{[on]}$, $\phi_{[d]}$, and ϕ_{UC} are not applicable to Π_1. Hence we try $\phi_{[im]}$. This yields the NC-refutation

$$\Pi_2 = \phi_{[im]}(\Pi_1): g(f(g(x_1))) \doteq g(x_1) \rightsquigarrow_{\{x_1 \mapsto y\}} g(y) \doteq g(y) \rightsquigarrow_\epsilon \mathtt{true}$$

which has complexity $(1, \{1,1\}, 6)$. Next we apply $\phi_{[d]}$. This gives the NC-refutation

$$\Pi_3 = \phi_{[d]}(\Pi_2)\colon f(g(x_1)) \doteq x_1 \leadsto_{\{x_1 \mapsto y\}} y \doteq y \leadsto_{\epsilon} \mathtt{true}$$

with complexity $(1, \{1,1\}, 4)$. Observe that the initial goal of Π_1 is transformed into the initial goal of Π_3 by the single LNC-step $g(f(x)) \doteq x \Rightarrow_{[im],\{x \mapsto g(x_1)\}} f(g(x_1)) \doteq x_1$. In Π_3 narrowing is applied to the initial equation at position 1. This calls for the transformation step $\phi_{[on]}$:

$$\Pi_4 = \phi_{[on]}(\Pi_3)\colon f(g(x_1)) \doteq f(g(y)), y \doteq x_1 \leadsto_{\{x_1 \mapsto y\}} \mathtt{true}, y \doteq y \leadsto_{\epsilon} \top.$$

NC-refutation Π_4 has complexity $(0, \{1,1,1,1\}, 8)$. If we apply $\phi_{[d]}$ to Π_4, we obtain the NC-refutation

$$\Pi_5 = \phi_{[d]}(\Pi_4)\colon g(x_1) \doteq g(y), y \doteq x_1 \leadsto_{\{x_1 \mapsto y\}} \mathtt{true}, y \doteq y \leadsto_{\epsilon} \top$$

with complexity $(0, \{1,1,1,1\}, 6)$. The initial goals of Π_3 and Π_5 are connected by an $\Rightarrow_{[on]}$-step: $f(g(x_1)) \doteq x_1 \Rightarrow_{[on]} g(x_1) \doteq g(y), y \doteq x_1$. In the first step of Π_5 narrowing is applied at the root position of the selected equation $g(x_1) \doteq g(y)$. Hence we use ϕ_{UC}, yielding the NC-refutation

$$\Pi_6 = \phi_{UC}(\Pi_5)\colon y \doteq y \leadsto_{\epsilon} \mathtt{true}$$

with complexity $(0, \{1,1\}, 2)$. The initial goals of Π_5 and Π_6 are connected by the UC-derivation $g(x_1) \doteq g(y), y \doteq x_1 \Rightarrow_{[d]} x_1 \doteq y, y \doteq x_1 \Rightarrow_{[v],\{x_1 \mapsto y\}} y \doteq y$. Another application of ϕ_{UC} results in the empty NC-refutation

$$\Pi_7 = \phi_{UC}(\Pi_6)\colon \square$$

which has complexity $(0, \varnothing, 0)$. Clearly $y \doteq y \Rightarrow_{[t]} \square$. Concatenating the various LNC-sequences yields an LNC-refutation $g(f(x)) \doteq x \Rightarrow^*_{\theta} \square$ whose substitution θ satisfies $x\theta = g(y)$.

Unfortunately, the simulation of NC by LNC illustrated above doesn't always work, as shown in the following example.

EXAMPLE 4.10. Consider the TRS $\mathcal{R} = \{f(x) \to x, a \to b, b \to g(b)\}$ and the NC-refutation $\Pi_{fail}\colon f(a) \doteq g(a) \leadsto f(a) \doteq g(b) \leadsto a \doteq g(b) \leadsto b \doteq g(b) \leadsto g(b) \doteq g(b) \leadsto \mathtt{true}$. Because we apply narrowing at position 1 in the descendant $f(a) \doteq g(b)$ of the initial equation $f(a) \doteq g(a)$, using the rewrite rule $f(x) \to x$, we transform Π_{fail} using $\phi_{[on]}$ and $\phi_{[d]}$. This yields the NC-refutation $\phi_{[d]}(\phi_{[on]}(\Pi_{fail}))\colon a \doteq x, x \doteq g(a) \leadsto a \doteq x, x \doteq g(b) \leadsto a \doteq g(b) \leadsto b \doteq g(b) \leadsto g(b) \doteq g(b) \leadsto \mathtt{true}$. Observe that the initial goals of Π_{fail} and $\phi_{[d]}(\phi_{[on]}(\Pi_{fail}))$ are connected by $\Rightarrow_{[on]}$. Since in the refutation $\phi_{[d]}(\phi_{[on]}(\Pi_{fail}))$ narrowing is applied at position 1 in the descendant $a \doteq g(b)$ of the selected equation $x \doteq g(a)$ in the initial goal $a \doteq x, x \doteq g(a)$, we would like to use once more the transformation steps $\phi_{[on]}$ and $\phi_{[d]}$. This is however impossible since the subterm of $x \doteq g(a)$ at position 1 is a variable.

The reason why Π_{fail} cannot be transformed to an LNC-refutation by the transformation steps in this section is that in $\phi_{[d]}(\phi_{[on]}(\Pi_{fail}))$ narrowing is applied to a subterm introduced by a previous narrowing substitution. One might be tempted to think that this problem cannot occur if we restrict ourselves to normalized solutions. This is not true, however, because Π_{fail} computes the empty substitution ε, which is clearly normalized, but $\phi_{[d]}(\phi_{[on]}(\Pi_{fail}))$ computes the non-normalized solution $\{x \mapsto a\}$. So the transformation steps do not preserve *normalization* of the computed NC-solutions (restricted to the variables in the initial goal). However, it turns out that *basicness* ([11, 16]) is preserved. This is one of the two key observations to the connection between strong completeness of LNC and completeness of basic NC.

LEMMA 4.11. *Let Π be a basic* NC*-refutation. The* NC*-refutations $\phi_{[on]}(\Pi)$, $\phi_{[d]}(\Pi)$, $\phi_{[im]}(\Pi)$, and $\phi_{UC}(\Pi)$ are basic whenever they are defined.* □

The other key observation is that for basic NC, strong completeness and completeness coincide.

LEMMA 4.12. *Let $\mathcal{S}$ be a selection function. For every basic* NC*-refutation $\Pi: G \leadsto_\theta^* \top$ there exists a basic* NC*-refutation $\Pi_\mathcal{S}: G \leadsto_\theta^* \top$ respecting $\mathcal{S}$ with the same complexity.* □

We are now ready to present the main result of this section.

THEOREM 4.13. *Let $\mathcal{R}$ be a TRS and $G \leadsto_\theta^* \top$ a basic* NC*-refutation. For every selection function $\mathcal{S}$ there exists an* LNC*-refutation $G \Rightarrow_{\theta'}^* \Box$ respecting $\mathcal{S}$ such that $\theta' = \theta\ [\mathcal{V}ar(G)]$.* □

A related result for lazy paramodulation calculi is given by Moser [17]. He showed the completeness of his calculus $\mathcal{T}_{BP}$, a refined version of the calculus $\mathcal{T}$ of Gallier and Snyder [5], by a reduction to the basic superposition calculus $\mathcal{S}$ of [1]. Strong completeness (of $\mathcal{T}_{BP}$) follows because $\mathcal{T}_{BP}$ satisfies the so-called "switching lemma". Since from every $\mathcal{T}_{BP}$-refutation one easily extracts a $\mathcal{T}$-refutation respecting the same selection function, strong completeness of $\mathcal{T}$ is an immediate consequence.

Basic narrowing is known to be complete (with respect to normalized solutions) for confluent and terminating TRSs (Hullot [11]), orthogonal TRSs under the additional assumption that $G\theta$ is normalizable (Middeldorp and Hamoen [16]), and confluent and right-linear TRSs ([16]). Hence for these three classes of TRSs we obtain the strong completeness (with respect to normalized solutions) of LNC as a corollary of Theorem 4.13.

The converse of Theorem 4.13 does not hold, as witnessed by the confluent TRS $\mathcal{R} = \{f(x) \to g(x,x), a \to b, g(a,b) \to c, g(b,b) \to f(a)\}$ from Middeldorp and Hamoen [16]. They show that the goal $f(a) \doteq c$ cannot be solved by basic narrowing. Straightforward calculations reveal that for any selection function $\mathcal{S}$ there exists an LNC-refutation $f(a) \doteq c \Rightarrow^* \Box$ respecting $\mathcal{S}$.

5. Completeness

In this section we show the completeness of LNC for confluent TRSs with respect to normalized solutions. Actually we show a stronger result: all normalized solutions are subsumed by substitutions produced by LNC-refutations that respect $\mathcal{S}_{left}$. Basic narrowing is of no help because of its incompleteness [16] for this general case. If we are able to define a class of NC-refutations respecting $\mathcal{S}_{left}$ that (1) includes all NC-refutations respecting $\mathcal{S}_{left}$ that produce normalized solutions, and (2) which is closed under the transformation steps $\phi_{[on]}$, $\phi_{[d]}$, $\phi_{[im]}$, and ϕ_{UC}, then completeness with respect to $\mathcal{S}_{left}$ follows along the lines of the proof of Theorem 4.13. We didn't succeed in defining such a class, the main problem being the fact that an application of $\phi_{[on]}$ or $\phi_{[d]}$ to an NC-refutation that respects $\mathcal{S}_{left}$ may result in an NC-refutation that doesn't respect $\mathcal{S}_{left}$. We found however a class of NC-refutations respecting $\mathcal{S}_{left}$ that satisfies the first property and which is closed under $\phi_{[on]} \circ \phi_1$, $\phi_{[d]} \circ \phi_2$, $\phi_{[im]}$, and ϕ_{UC}. Here ϕ_1 and ϕ_2 are transformations that preprocess a given NC-refutation in such a way that a subsequent application of $\phi_{[on]}$ and $\phi_{[d]}$ results in an NC-refutation respecting $\mathcal{S}_{left}$. The following definition introduces our class of NC-refutations.

DEFINITION 5.1. An NC-refutation $\Pi\colon G \leadsto_\theta^* \top$ respecting $\mathcal{S}_{left}$ is called *normal* if it satisfies the following property: if narrowing is applied to the left-hand side (right-hand side) of a descendant of an equation $s \doteq t$ in G then $\theta_2\lceil_{\mathcal{V}ar(s\theta_1)}$ ($\theta_2\lceil_{\mathcal{V}ar(t\theta_1)}$) is normalized. Here θ_1 and θ_2 are defined by writing Π as $G = G_1, s \doteq t, G_2 \leadsto_{\theta_1}^* \top, (s \doteq t, G_2)\theta_1 \leadsto_{\theta_2}^* \top$.

The following result states that the class of normal NC-refutations satisfies property (1) mentioned above.

LEMMA 5.2. *Every* NC*-refutation respecting* $\mathcal{S}_{left}$ *that produces a normalized solution is normal.* □

The converse of this lemma is not true. The next two lemmata introduce the transformations ϕ_1 and ϕ_2. Both proofs rely on the same switching lemma.

LEMMA 5.3. *Let* e *be the equation* $s \doteq t$. *For every normal* NC*-refutation* $\Pi\colon e, G \leadsto_{\theta_1}^* s' \doteq t', G\theta_1 \leadsto_{\theta_2,1,l\to r} (r \doteq t', G\theta_1)\theta_2 \leadsto_{\theta_3}^* \top$ *with the property that narrowing is not applied to a descendant of* e *at position 1 in the subderivation that produces substitution* θ_1, *there exists a normal* NC*-refutation* $\phi_1(\Pi)\colon e, G \leadsto_{\sigma_1}^* s'' \doteq t\sigma_1, G\sigma_1 \leadsto_{\sigma_2,1,l\to r} (r \doteq t\sigma_1, G\sigma_1)\sigma_2 \leadsto_{\sigma_3}^* \top$ *with the same complexity such that* $\sigma_1\sigma_2\sigma_3 = \theta_1\theta_2\theta_3$ *and narrowing is neither applied at position 1 nor in the right-hand side of a descendant of* e *in the subderivation that produces the substitution* σ_1. □

LEMMA 5.4. *Let* e *be the equation* $f(s_1, \ldots, s_n) \doteq f(t_1, \ldots, t_n)$. *For every normal* NC*-refutation* $\Pi\colon e, G \leadsto_{\theta_1}^* \texttt{true}, G\theta_1 \leadsto_{\theta_2}^* \top$ *with the property that narrowing is never applied to a descendant of* e *at position 1 or 2, there exists a normal* NC*-refutation* $\phi_2(\Pi)\colon e, G \leadsto_{\theta_1}^* \texttt{true}, G\theta_1 \leadsto_{\theta_2}^* \top$ *with the same complexity such that in the subderivation producing substitution* θ_1 *narrowing is applied to the subterms* $s_1, \ldots, s_n, t_1, \ldots, t_n$ *in the order* $s_1, t_1, s_2, t_2, \ldots, s_n, t_n$. □

The next result states that the transformation steps $\phi_{[on]} \circ \phi_1$, $\phi_{[d]} \circ \phi_2$, $\phi_{[im]}$, and ϕ_{UC} preserve normality.

LEMMA 5.5. *Let Π be a normal* NC*-refutation. The* NC*-refutations $\phi_{[on]}(\phi_1(\Pi))$, $\phi_{[d]}(\phi_2(\Pi))$, $\phi_{[im]}(\Pi)$, and $\phi_{UC}(\Pi)$ are normal whenever they are defined.* $\square$

EXAMPLE 5.6. Consider again the NC-refutation Π_{fail} of Example 4.10. This refutation is easily seen to be normal. An application of $\phi_{[on]}$ results in the NC-refutation $\phi_{[on]}(\Pi_{fail})$: $f(a) \doteq f(x), x \doteq g(a) \leadsto f(a) \doteq f(x), x \doteq g(b) \leadsto a \doteq g(b) \leadsto b \doteq g(b) \leadsto g(b) \doteq g(b) \leadsto \mathtt{true}$. which doesn't respect $\mathcal{S}_{left}$. If we first apply ϕ_1 we obtain the NC-refutation $\phi_1(\Pi_{fail})$: $f(a) \doteq g(a) \leadsto a \doteq g(a) \leadsto a \doteq g(b) \leadsto b \doteq g(b) \leadsto g(b) \doteq g(b) \leadsto \mathtt{true}$. An application of $\phi_{[on]}$ to this normal NC-refutation yields $\phi_{[on]}(\phi_1(\Pi_{fail}))$: $f(a) \doteq f(x), x \doteq g(a) \leadsto a \doteq g(a) \leadsto a \doteq g(b) \leadsto b \doteq g(b) \leadsto g(b) \doteq g(b) \leadsto \mathtt{true}$. This NC-refutation is normal even though the produced substitution restricted to the variable in the initial goal is not normalized.

The following lemma is the counterpart of Lemma 4.12 for normal NC-refutations.

LEMMA 5.7. *For every* NC*-refutation $\Pi: G \leadsto_\theta^* \top$ with $\theta\lceil_{\mathcal{V}ar(G)}$ is normalized there exists a normal* NC*-refutation $\Pi_{\mathcal{S}_{left}}: G \leadsto_\theta^* \top$ of the same complexity.* $\square$

Putting all pieces together, the following result can be proved along the lines of the proof of Theorem 4.13.

THEOREM 5.8. *Let $\mathcal{R}$ be a TRS. For every* NC*-refutation $G \leadsto_\theta^* \top$ with the property that $\theta\lceil_{\mathcal{V}ar(G)}$ is normalized there exists an* LNC*-refutation $G \Rightarrow_{\theta'}^* \top$ respecting $\mathcal{S}_{left}$ such that $\theta' = \theta\ [\mathcal{V}ar(G)]$.* $\square$

COROLLARY 5.9. *Let $\mathcal{R}$ be a confluent TRS. If $\mathcal{R} \vdash G\theta$ and $\theta\lceil_{\mathcal{V}ar(G)}$ is normalized then there exists an* LNC*-refutation $G \Rightarrow_{\theta'}^* \square$ respecting $\mathcal{S}_{left}$ such that $\theta' \leqslant \theta\ [\mathcal{V}ar(G)]$.* $\square$

6. Eager Variable Elimination

LNC has three sources of non-determinism: the choice of the equation in the given goal, the choice of the inference rule, and the choice of the rewrite rule (in the case of [*on*]). In Section 4 we were concerned with the first kind of non-determinism. In this section we address the second kind of non-determinism. The non-deterministic application of the various inference rules to selected equations causes LNC to generate many redundant derivations. Consider for example the (orthogonal hence confluent) TRS $\{f(g(x)) \to a, b \to g(b)\}$. Figure 1 shows all LNC-refutations issued from the goal $f(b) \doteq a$ that respect the selection function $\mathcal{S}_{left}$. There are infinitely many such refutations. Because the initial goal is ground, one of them suffices for completeness. At several places in the literature

$$
\begin{array}{ccccccc}
f(b) \doteq a & & & & & & \\
\Downarrow_{[on]} & & & & & & \\
b \doteq g(x), a \doteq a & & & & & & \\
\Downarrow_{[on]} & & & & & & \\
g(b) \doteq g(x), a \doteq a & & & & & & \\
\Downarrow_{[d]} & & & & & & \\
b \doteq x, a \doteq a & \Rightarrow_{[on]} & g(b) \doteq x, a \doteq a & \Rightarrow_{[im]} & b \doteq x_1, a \doteq a & \Rightarrow_{[on]} & \cdots \\
\Downarrow_{[v]} & & \Downarrow_{[v]} & & \Downarrow_{[v]} & & \\
a \doteq a & & a \doteq a & & a \doteq a & & \\
\Downarrow_{[d]} & & \Downarrow_{[d]} & & \Downarrow_{[d]} & & \\
\square & & \square & & \square & &
\end{array}
$$

Fig. 1.

it is mentioned that this type of redundancy can be greatly reduced by applying the variable elimination rule $[v]$ prior to other applicable inference rules, although to the best of our knowledge there is no supporting proof of this so-called *eager variable elimination problem* for the general case of confluent systems.

In this section we show that a restricted version of the eager variable elimination strategy is complete with respect to $\mathcal{S}_{left}$ for orthogonal TRSs. Before we can define our strategy, we need to extend the concept of descendant to LNC-derivations. Descendants of non-selected equations are defined as in Definition 4.1. The selected equation $f(s_1, \ldots, s_n) \simeq t$ in the outermost narrowing rule $[on]$ has the body equation $r \doteq t$ as only (one-step) descendant. In the imitation rule $[im]$, all equations $s_i\theta \doteq x_i$ $(1 \leqslant i \leqslant n)$ are descendants of the selected equation $f(s_1, \ldots, s_n) \simeq x$. The selected equation $f(s_1, \ldots, s_n) \simeq f(t_1, \ldots, t_n)$ in the decomposition rule $[d]$ has all equations $s_1 \doteq t_1, \ldots, s_n \doteq t_n$ as (one-step) descendants. Finally, the selected equations in $[v]$ and $[t]$ have no descendants.

DEFINITION 6.1. An equation of the form $x \simeq t$, with $x \notin \mathcal{V}ar(t)$, is called *solved*. An LNC-derivation Π is called *eager* if the variable elimination rule $[v]$ is applied to all selected solved equations that are descendants of a parameter-passing equation in Π.

Of the infinitely many LNC-refutations in Figure 1 only the leftmost one is eager since all others apply the outermost narrowing rule $[on]$ to the solved descendant $b \doteq x$ of the parameter-passing equation $b \doteq g(x)$ introduced in the first $\Rightarrow_{[on]}$-step.

In this section we prove that eager LNC is complete with respect to $\mathcal{S}_{left}$ for orthogonal TRSs (with respect to normalized solutions). The outline of our proof is as follows.

(1) We define *outside-in* NC-derivations. These are the narrowing counterpart to the outside-in rewrite sequences of Huet and Lévy [10].
(2) We show that the completeness of outside-in NC for orthogonal TRSs with respect to normalized solutions is an easy consequence of Huet and Lévy's *standardization* theorem.

(3) We show that the translation steps ϕ_1, ϕ_2, $\phi_{[on]}$, $\phi_{[d]}$, $\phi_{[im]}$, and ϕ_{UC} preserve the outside-in property.
(4) We verify that the LNC-refutation obtained from an outside-in NC-refutation by means of the transformation described in the previous section is in fact eager.

Before defining outside-in NC-derivations, we introduce the concept of NC-*trace*. Let $\Pi : G \rightsquigarrow_\theta G'$ be an NC-step and e an equation in G different from $\mathtt{true}$. Let e' be the (unique) descendant of e in G'. The construct $e \rightarrowtail_\theta e'$ is called a one-step NC-trace. NC-traces are obtained by concatenating one-step NC-traces. An NC-trace $e_1 \rightarrowtail_{\theta_1} \cdots \rightarrowtail_{\theta_{n-1}} e_n$ may be rendered as $e_1 \rightarrowtail^*_\theta e_n$ where $\theta = \theta_1 \cdots \theta_{n-1}$. For every such NC-trace π there is a corresponding rewrite sequence $\mathcal{R}(\pi)$: $e_1\theta \rightarrow^*_{\mathcal{R}_+} e_n$. This rewrite sequence will be shorter than π if the latter contains one-step NC-traces of the form $e_i \rightarrowtail_{\theta_i} e_i\theta_i$—indicating that e_i was not selected in the underlying NC-step—which translate to identity at the rewrite level.

DEFINITION 6.2. Let $\mathcal{R}$ be an orthogonal TRS. A rewrite sequence $e_1 \rightarrow_{p_1, l_1 \rightarrow r_1} \cdots \rightarrow_{p_{n-1}, l_{n-1} \rightarrow r_{n-1}} e_n$ in $\mathcal{R}_+$ is called *outside-in* if the following condition is satisfied for all $1 \leqslant i < n-1$: if there exists a j with $i < j < n$ such that $\epsilon < p_j < p_i$ then $p_i \backslash p_j \in \mathcal{P}os_{\mathcal{F}}(l_j)$ for the least such j.

This definition is equivalent to the one given by Huet and Lévy in their seminal paper [10] on call-by-need computations in orthogonal TRSs. The following result is an immediate consequence of their standardization theorem (Theorem 3.19 in [10]).

THEOREM 6.3. *Let $\mathcal{R}$ be an orthogonal TRS. For every rewrite sequence $e \rightarrow^*_{\mathcal{R}_+}$ $\mathtt{true}$ there exists an outside-in rewrite sequence $e \rightarrow^*_{\mathcal{R}_+}$ $\mathtt{true}$.* □

DEFINITION 6.4. Let $\mathcal{R}$ be an orthogonal TRS. An NC-derivation Π issued from a goal G is called *outside-in* if $\mathcal{R}(\pi)$ is outside-in for all traces π of the equations $e \in G$.

The following result is an easy consequence of Theorem 6.3 and the lifting lemma for NC.

THEOREM 6.5. *Let $\mathcal{R}$ be an orthogonal TRS. For every NC-refutation $G \rightsquigarrow^*_\theta \top$ with $\theta\restriction_{\mathcal{V}ar(G)}$ normalized there exists an outside-in NC-refutation $G \rightsquigarrow^*_{\theta'} \top$ such that $\theta' \leqslant \theta$ $[\mathcal{V}ar(G)]$.* □

The above theorem extends and simplifies the main result of You [22]: the completeness of *outer* narrowing for orthogonal *constructor-based* TRSs with respect to *constructor-based* solutions. One easily verifies that outer narrowing coincides with outside-in narrowing in the case of orthogonal constructor-based TRSs and that constructor-based substitutions are a special case of normalized substitutions. Hence You's completeness result (Theorem 3.13 in [22]) is a consequence of Theorem 6.5. Since You doesn't use the powerful standardization theorem of Huet and Lévy, his completeness proof is (much) more complicated. Moreover, our result covers a larger class of TRSs.

A careful inspection of the transformation steps described in the preceding two sections reveals that ϕ_1, ϕ_2, $\phi_{[on]}$, $\phi_{[d]}$, $\phi_{[im]}$, and ϕ_{UC} preserve the outside-in property. Moreover, the LNC-refutation obtained from an outside-in NC-refutation can be shown to be eager, i.e., we obtain the following result.

THEOREM 6.6. *Let $\mathcal{R}$ be an orthogonal TRS. For every outside-in NC-refutation $G \rightsquigarrow_\theta^* \top$ with $\theta\lceil_{\mathcal{V}ar(G)}$ normalized there exists an eager LNC-refutation $G \Rightarrow_{\theta'}^* \top$ respecting $\mathcal{S}_{left}$ such that $\theta' \leqslant \theta$ $[\mathcal{V}ar(G)]$.* □

The combination of the last two results yields the final result of this paper.

THEOREM 6.7. *Let $\mathcal{R}$ be an orthogonal TRS. If $\mathcal{R} \vdash G\theta$ and $\theta\lceil_{\mathcal{V}ar(G)}$ is normalized then there exists an eager LNC-refutation $G \Rightarrow_{\theta'}^* \top$ respecting $\mathcal{S}_{left}$ such that $\theta' \leqslant \theta$ $[\mathcal{V}ar(G)]$.* □

7. Suggestions for Further Research

This paper leaves many questions unanswered. In the near future we would like to address the following two problems.

In Section 4 we have shown the strong completeness of LNC in the case of orthogonal TRSs, using the transformation steps $\phi_{[on]}$, $\phi_{[d]}$, $\phi_{[im]}$, and ϕ_{UC}. In Section 6 we showed the completeness of eager LNC with respect to $\mathcal{S}_{left}$ for orthogonal TRSs, using the transformation steps $\phi_{[on]} \circ \phi_1$, $\phi_{[d]} \circ \phi_2$, $\phi_{[im]}$, and ϕ_{UC}. A natural question is whether these two results can be combined, i.e., is eager LNC strongly complete for orthogonal TRSs. Recall the NC-refutation Π_{fail} in Example 4.10. It is easy to see that Π_{fail} is outside-in. Nevertheless, $\phi_{[on]}$, together with $\phi_{[d]}$, results in failure. Hence the use of ϕ_1 and ϕ_2 is essential for the completeness of eager LNC. This suggests that it is not obvious whether or not eager LNC is strongly complete for orthogonal TRSs.

The orthogonality assumption in our proof of the completeness of eager LNC is essential since we make use of Huet and Lévy's standardization theorem. We didn't succeed in finding a non-orthogonal TRS for which eager LNC is not complete. Hence it is an open problem whether our restricted variable elimination strategy is complete for arbitrary confluent TRSs with respect to normalized solutions. A more general question is of course whether the variable elimination rule can always be eagerly applied, i.e., is the restriction to solved descendants of parameter-passing equations essential? In a recent paper Socher-Ambrosius [21] reports that the eager variable elimination problem has a positive solution in case of lazy paramodulation for arbitrary equational theories. It remains to be seen whether his techniques can be lifted to the present setting.

Acknowledgements. We thank an anonymous referee for drawing our attention to the work of Moser.

References

1. L. Bachmair, H. Ganzinger, C. Lynch, and W. Snyder, *Basic Paramodulation and Superposition*, Proc. 11th CADE, LNCS **607**, pp. 462–476, 1992.
2. N. Dershowitz and J.-P. Jouannaud, *Rewrite Systems*, in: Handbook of Theoretical Computer Science, Vol. B, ed. J. van Leeuwen), North-Holland, pp. 243–320, 1990.
3. N. Dershowitz and Z. Manna, *Proving Termination with Multiset Orderings*, Communications of the ACM **22**(8), pp. 465–476, 1979.
4. M. Fay, *First-Order Unification in Equational Theories*, Proc. 4th CADE, Austin, pp. 161–167, 1979.
5. J. Gallier and W. Snyder, *Complete Sets of Transformations for General E-Unification*, TCS **67**, pp. 203–260, 1989.
6. M. Hanus, *Efficient Implementation of Narrowing and Rewriting*, Proc. PDK-91, LNAI **567**, pp. 344–365, 1991.
7. M. Hanus, *The Integration of Functions into Logic Programming: From Theory to Practice*, JLP **19 & 20**, pp. 583–628, 1994.
8. S. Hölldobler, *A Unification Algorithm for Confluent Theories*, Proc. 14th ICALP, LNCS **267**, pp. 31–41, 1987.
9. S. Hölldobler, *Foundations of Equational Logic Programming*, LNAI **353**, 1989.
10. G. Huet and J.-J. Lévy, *Computations in Orthogonal Rewriting Systems, I and II*, in: Computational Logic, Essays in Honor of Alan Robinson (eds. J.-L. Lassez and G. Plotkin), The MIT Press, pp. 396–443, 1991.
11. J.-M. Hullot, *Canonical Forms and Unification*, Proc. 5th CADE, LNCS **87**, pp. 318–334, 1980.
12. J.W. Klop, *Term Rewriting Systems*, in: Handbook of Logic in Computer Science, Vol. II (eds. S. Abramsky, D. Gabbay, and T. Maibaum), Oxford University Press, pp. 1–116, 1992.
13. A. Martelli, C. Moiso, and G.F. Rossi, *Lazy Unification Algortihms for Canonical Rewrite Systems*, in: Resolution of Equations in Algebraic Structures, Vol. II (eds. H. Aït-Kaci and M. Nivat), Academic Press, pp. 245–274, 1989.
14. A. Martelli and U. Montanari, *An Efficient Unification Algorithm*, ACM TOPLAS **4**(2), pp. 258–282, 1982.
15. A. Martelli, G.F. Rossi, and C. Moiso, *An Algortihm for Unification in Equational Theories*, Proc. 1986 Symposium on Logic Programming, pp. 180–186, 1986.
16. A. Middeldorp and E. Hamoen, *Completeness Results for Basic Narrowing*, AAECC **5**, pp. 213–253, 1994.
17. M. Moser, *Improving Transformation Systems for General E-Unification*, Proc. 5th RTA, LNCS **690**, pp. 92–105, 1993.
18. S. Okui, A. Middeldorp, and T. Ida, *Lazy Narrowing: Strong Completeness and Eager Variable Elimination*, Report ISE-TR-94-114, University of Tsukuba, 1994.
19. J.R. Slagle, *Automatic Theorem Proving in Theories with Simplifiers, Commutativity and Associativity*, Journal of the ACM **21**, pp. 622–642, 1974.
20. W. Snyder, *A Proof Theory for General Unification*, Birkhäuser, 1991.
21. R. Socher-Ambrosius, *A Refined Version of General E-Unification*, Proc. 12th CADE, LNAI **814**, pp. 665-677, 1994.
22. Y.H. You, *Enumerating Outer Narrowing Derivations for Constructor Based Term Rewriting Systems*, JSC **7**, pp. 319–343, 1989.

On the expressive power of algebraic graph grammars with application conditions

Annika Wagner

Technical University of Berlin
Computer Science Department
Sekr. FR 6 - 1, Franklinstr. 28/29, D-10587 Berlin
e-mail: aw@cs.tu-berlin.de

Abstract. In this paper we introduce positive, negative and conditional application conditions for the single and the double pushout approach to graph transformation. To give the reader some intuition how the formalism can be used for specification we consider consistency and an interesting representation for specific conditions, namely (conditional) equations. Using a graph grammar notion without nonterminal graphs, i.e. each derivation step leads to a graph of the generated language, we prove a hierarchy: graph grammars over rules with positive application conditions are as powerful as the ones over rules without any extra application condition. Introducing negative application conditions makes the formalism more powerful. Graph grammars over rules with conditional application conditions are on top of the hierarchy.

1 Introduction

Graph transformations are a good means for describing the development of structured states in elementary steps. Although the generative power of most of the known graph grammar approaches is sufficient to generate any recursively enumerable set of graphs, additional application conditions are a necessary part of every non-trivial specification. Often they are expressed informally by assuming some kind of control mechanism or they are coded into the graphs using flags and additional labels. Both possibilities make it hard to analyse the specification. In contrast to textual application conditions expressed in logical formulas (see e.g. [12], [13]) we propose a formalism where these additional and more complex application conditions are treated *formally and graphically*. In order to show that we can really express more with our new notion(s), i.e. that we extended the *expressive power* of the graph grammar approach, we consider specification aspects on one hand and the generative power one the other hand. The main result concerning specification is that specific positive (negative) application conditions can be characterized by (non-)equations while specific conditional application conditions correspond to conditional equations. As stated above the generative power of the pure algebraic approach is sufficient for every recursively enumerable set of graphs. Hence in order to achieve a new illustrative result we had to change the notion of a graph grammar not to contain non-terminal graphs, i.e. every derivation step leads to a graph of the generated language. This makes it nearly impossible to encode control structure into flags and labels of a graph. Using the formalism to formalize algorithms or to describe the operational semantics of complex systems hence leads to more abstract specifications.

The algebraic approach to graph transformation [1], i.e. the single and the double pushout approach ([11], [2]), provides a framework where because of its categorical nature a lot of different results (concerning parallelism and concurrency for example) have been achieved. The extensions presented in this paper are of the same nature. As presented in [6] additional algebraic application conditions are compatible with that theory. High-level replacement systems ([4], [5]) are a categorical generalization of the algebraic approach to graph grammars. In this context the same notions are formulated not only for graphs but for objects of arbitrary categories. Because of their nature all notions introduced in this paper can easily transfered to high-level replacement systems. Furthermore application conditions can close the gap between the pure single pushout approach and the more restrictive double pushout approach, allowing specific "gluing conditions" for arbitrary subgraphs of the left hand side of productions.

The paper is organized as follows: In section 2 we introduce all basic notions. Then we change over to the expressive power of the formalism. Section 3 is devoted to the specification aspects, while our notion of graph grammar and its generative power is presented in section 4. In the last section we conclude with a general discussion of the presented approach and possibilities for further development.

The reader is assumed to be familar with basic notions of category theory and universal algebra (see e.g. [9] or [1]).

2 Basic notions and definitions

In this section we first recover some basic notions of the single and the double pushout approach to graph transformation. Then we introduce positive, negative and conditional application conditions for rules and define their applicability.

Definition 1 (Graph, Morphism). A *graph* $G = (G_V, G_E, s^G, t^G)$ consists of a set of vertices G_V, a set of edges G_E and two mappings $s^G, t^G : G_E \rightarrow G_V$ which provide a source resp. target vertex for every edge. A *graph morphism* $f : G \rightarrow H$ is a pair of total mappings $(f_V : G_V \rightarrow H_V, f_E : G_E \rightarrow H_E)$ which are compatible with the source and target assignments, i.e. $f_V(s^G(e)) = s^H(f_E(e))$ for all $e \in G_E$ (and analogously for the target mapping). A *partial graph morphism* g from G to H is a total graph morphism from some subgraph $G(g)$ of G to H.

If we define composition of these morphisms by composition of the components and identities as pairs of component identities, the objects and (partial) morphisms w.r.t. definition 1 form a category denoted by $\underline{GRA}$ ($\underline{GRA^P}$) in the following. If we want to state a property of a morphism we often do not divide between vertices and edges. Hence we write $f(x)$ for all objects x instead of $f_V(v)$ for all vertices v and $f_E(e)$ for all edges e.

Generally, the rewriting of a graph G via some rule r is done by first deleting some part DEL (from G) and then adding a new part ADD finally resulting in a derived graph H. Often this shall only be done if G additionally contains some

---

1 Note that although "algebraic" is frequently used as synonymous of "context-free" in language theory, in this paper we use it in a different sense.

context K which is essentially to be kept. We additionally allow that the context is glued together. Thus rewriting means to replace some part $L = DEL \cup K_L$ by another one $R = K_R \cup ADD$, where K_R is constructed from K_L by gluing of vertices and edges.

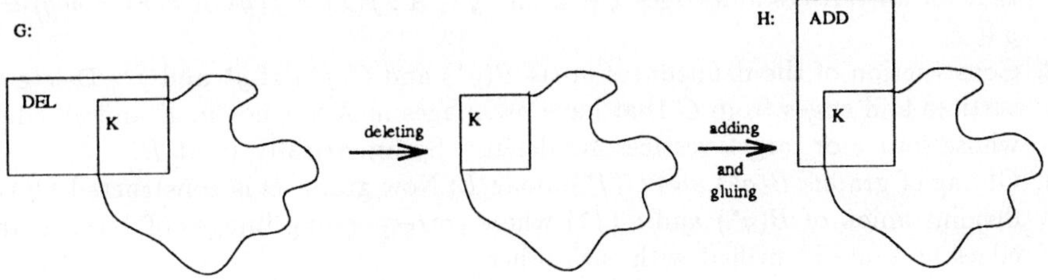

Fig. 1. How graph transformation works

Consequently a rule consists of two graphs L and R, called left and right hand side resp. (the square parts in figure 1), together with a partial graph morphism $r : L \to R$ which maps the context contained in the left hand side to the context of the right hand side of the rule. All vertices and edges for which r is not defined are intended to be deleted. Applying a rule means to match the left hand side with a subgraph of the mother graph (here we allow that different items from L are mapped onto the same item in G), then to remove it and finally to add the right hand side. The result is the daughter graph H.

Deleting is not always unproblematic. For example if a vertex shall be deleted by the rule but the mother graph G contains an edge pointing to that vertex. Another kind of conflict may arise if parts which shall be deleted and parts which shall be preserved are identified in G. In general we have two possibilities to handle these problems. First we can forbid the application of the rule in such cases and second we can solve all conflicts destructively by deleting the conflicting items. The first alternative is choosen in the 'classical' double-pushout approach, the second in the framework of single-pushout transformations.

Definition 2 (Simple rule, simple derivation). A *simple rule* $r : L \to R$ is a partial morphism from it's left hand side L to it's right hand side R. A *match* for r in some object G is a total morphism $m : L \to G$ from the left hand side of the rule to g. A match m is called *d - injective* if $m(x) = m(y)$ implies $x = y$ or $x, y \in L(r)$. It is called *d - complete* if for each edge $e \in G_E$ with $s^G(e), t^G(e) \in m_V(L_V - L(r)_V)$ we have $e \in m_E(L_E - L(r)_E)$. Given a simple rule r and a match m for r in a graph G the *simple direct derivation* from G with r at m, written $G \overset{r,m}{\Longrightarrow} H$, is the pushout of r and m in $\underline{GRA^P}$. If the match m is d-injective and d-complete we call a direct derivation *classical*. A sequence of direct derivations of the form $G_0 \overset{r_1,m_1}{\Longrightarrow} \ldots \overset{r_k,m_k}{\Longrightarrow} G_k$ constitutes a *derivation* from G_0 to G_k by $r_1, \ldots, r_k$. Such a derivation is denoted by $G_0 \overset{*}{\Longrightarrow} G_k$.

The following construction shows how the direct derivation of a graph can be achieved.

Construction 3 (Pushout in $\underline{GRA^P}$). If $f : A \to B$ and $g : A \to C$ is a pair of (partial) morphisms the pushout $(D, f^* : C \to D, g^* : B \to D)$ of f and g in $\underline{GRA^P}$ can be constructed in three steps:

1. Construction of the gluing graph: Let E be the largest subgraph of $A(f)$ such that for all vertices and edges $x \in E$ and $y \in A : f(x) = f(y)$ or $g(x) = g(y) \Longrightarrow y \in E$.
2. Construction of the definedness areas $B(g^*)$ and $C(f^*)$ of g^* and f^*: Delete all vertices and edges from C that have preimages in A but not in E and all edges whose source or target vertices are deleted. Symmetrically, treat B.
3. Gluing of graphs $B(g^*)$ and $C(f^*)$ along E: Now graph D is constructed by the disjoint union of $B(g^*)$ and $C(f^*)$ where corresponding images of vertices and edges in E are identified with each other.

The proof for the more general case of graph structures can be found in [11]. Some essential properties of the pushout diagram directly follow from the construction.

Lemma 4 (Properties of pushouts in $\underline{GRA^P}$). *Let $(D, f^* : C \to D, g^* : B \to D)$ be the pushout of $f : A \to B$ and $g : A \to C$ in $\underline{GS}$. Then the following properties are fulfilled:*

1. $v \notin C(f^*)_V \Longrightarrow v \in g(A(g)_V)$
2. $f^*(x) = g^*(y) \Longrightarrow x \in g(A)$ and $y \in f(A)$
3. f^* and g^* are together surjective

Proof. Property (1) is a direct consequence of step (2) of construction 3. The second and the third property follow from step (3) of the construction. □

The following technical lemma is used in later sections to show that the presented results can also be achieved if one is restricted to classical matches.

Lemma 5 (Embedding of derivations). *If $G \overset{r,m}{\Longrightarrow} H$ is a direct derivation with rule $r : L \to R$ it can be embedded into a bigger context G', i.e. every inclusion $i : G \to G'$ induces a match $i \circ m$ for the rule r. If m is classical and $\forall e \in (G'_E - i_E(G_E)) : s^{G'}(e), t^{G'}(e) \in i(G) \Longrightarrow s^{G'}(e), t^{G'}(e) \in i(G - m(L))$ or $s^{G'}(e), t^{G'}(e) \in i(m(L(r)))$ then $i \circ m$ is classical, too.*

Proof. $i \circ m$ is obviously a match for r. We only prove that it is classical under the stated condition. $i \circ m$ is d-injective because i is injective and m is d-injective. Now suppose that $s^{G'}(e') \in i_V(m_V(L_V - L(r)_V))$ for $e' \in G'_E$. With the above condition we get that $e' \in i_E(G_E)$. Because m is assumed to be d-complete $i \circ m$ is d-complete, too. □

Remark (Classical derivations). Rules in the double-pushout framework look quite different from those in the single pushout framework (definition 2) but they can be transformed into each other. Then for each transformation in the double-pushout approach there exists a transformation as defined in 2 in the single-pushout approach using the same match and achieving the same result. Conversely a single-pushout derivation has an equivalent one in the double-pushout framework if and only if it is classical. Hence the double-pushout framework is a very elegant formulation of graph transformation with a *special application condition*: the gluing condition, which corresponds to d-injectivity and d-completeness of the match in the sigle-pushout framework. This is formally proven in [11].

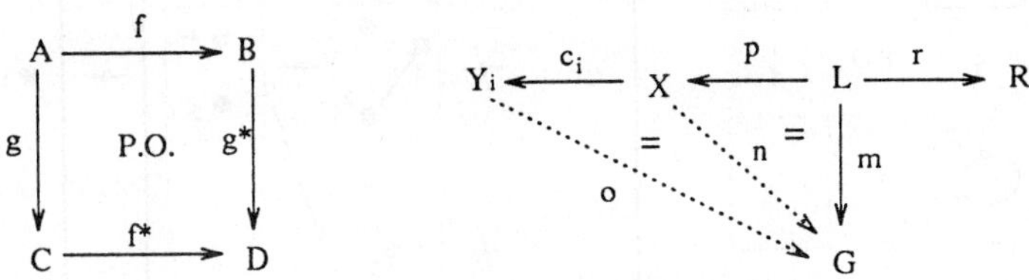

Fig. 2. Pushout diagram and satisfaction of conditional constraint

Now we want to consider more complex rules with application conditions. The general idea is to have a left hand side not only consisting of one graph but of several ones connected by morphisms. Positive and negative application conditions have already been investigated in [6] and [8]. Conditional application conditions consist of a premise and a conclusion which both are more or less simple positive application conditions.

Definition 6 (Application condition). Let $r : L \to R$ be a simple rule. A *simple constraint* s for r is total morphism $s : L \to X$. A *conditional constraint* for r $(p : L \to X, (c_i : X \to Y_i)_{i=1..n})$ is a pair consisting of a simple constraint p and a (possibly empty) family of total morphisms c_i. A *positive (negative)* resp. *conditional application condition* $A(r)$ for r consists of a finite set of simple resp. conditional constraints.

Definition 7 (Satisfaction of conditions). A total morphism $m : L \to G$ *p-satisfies* a simple constraint $s : L \to X$, written $m \models_p s$, if there exists a total morphism $n : X \to G$ such that $n \circ s = m$. m *n-satisfies* s if it does not p-satisfy s, i.e. $m \models_n s \iff m \not\models_p s$. Furthermore, we say that m *c-satisfies* a conditional constraint $cc = (p : L \to X, (c_i : X \to Y_i)_{i=1..n})$,written $m \models_c cc$, if for all total morphisms $n : X \to G$ with $n \circ p = m$ there exists a total morphism $o : Y_i \to G$ with $o \circ c_i = n$ for at least one $i \in \{1..n\}$. m *satisfies* a positive application condition if it p-satisfies at least one simple constraint of the condition. m *satisfies* a negative (conditional) application condition if it n-satisfies (c-satisfies) all negative (conditional) constraints the condition consists of.

Definition 8 (Conditional rule, derivation). A *p- (n-, c-) conditional rule* $\hat{r}$ is a pair $(r : L \to R, A(r))$ consisting of a simple rule r and a positive (negative, conditional) application condition. $\hat{r}$ is *applicable* to a graph G if there exists a match $m : L \to G$ for r that satisfies $A(r)$. If $\hat{r}$ is applicable to G via m the direct conditional derivation of G to H is the simple direct derivation.

Example 1 (Gluing condition). For each rule $r : L \to R$ the gluing condition of matches (d-injectivity and d-completeness) can be expressed using a conditional application condition. Because of a lack of space we do not show the general case,

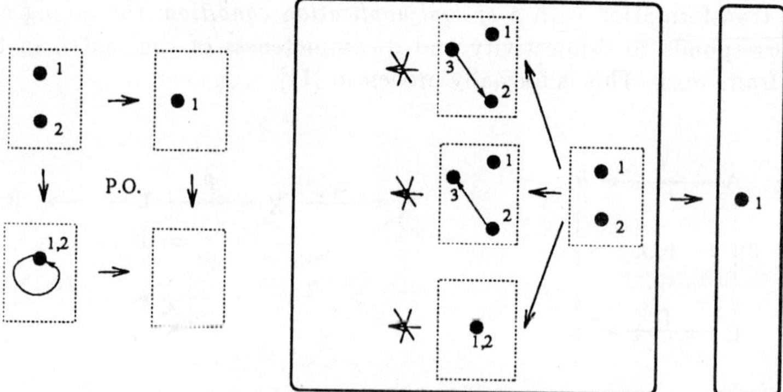

Fig. 3. Simulation of the gluing condition

but the very simple example in figure 3 demonstrates the idea. On the left hand side a single pushout derivation with a simple rule is shown where the match is not classical. On the right hand side the rule is equipped with three conditional application conditions. Hence it's left hand side is blown up. The arrows crossed out indicate an empty conclusion. The first two conditions make sure that the match is d-complete and the third one is dedicated to the d-injectivity of the match. If the rule contains edges the application conditions for the d-completeness have a non-empty conclusion.

3 Specification aspects

In this section we want to give the reader some intuition how application conditions can be used for specification. For this purpose we first show how different combinations of constraints can be put together in application conditions. Furthermore application conditions which contain surjective constraints only are characterized by (conditional) equations.

3.1 Combination of constraints

In definition 7 we define the satisfaction of a positive application condition to be a disjunction of constraints while we use a conjunction in the case of negative resp. conditional application conditions. This is motivated by the fact that the other combinations of constraints can be achieved by gluing the different constraints together as it is demonstrated in the following.

Definition 9 (Combination of constraints). If $s_i : L \to X_i$ $(c_i = (p_i : L \to X_i, (c_{ij} : X_i \to Y_{ij})_{j=1..k_i}))$ for $i = 1, 2$ are simple (conditional) constraints for a rule $r : L \to R$, their combination is given by single simple (conditional) constraint $s = s_2^* \circ s_1$ $(c = (p = p_2^* \circ p_1, (c_{ij}^* : X \to Y'_{ij})_{i=1,2;j=1..k_i}))$ s.t. (1) (1, (2) and (3)) in the left (right) diagram of figure 4 become(s) a pushout.

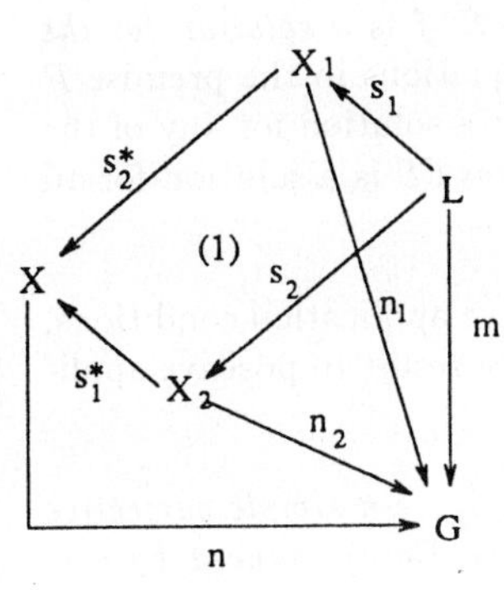

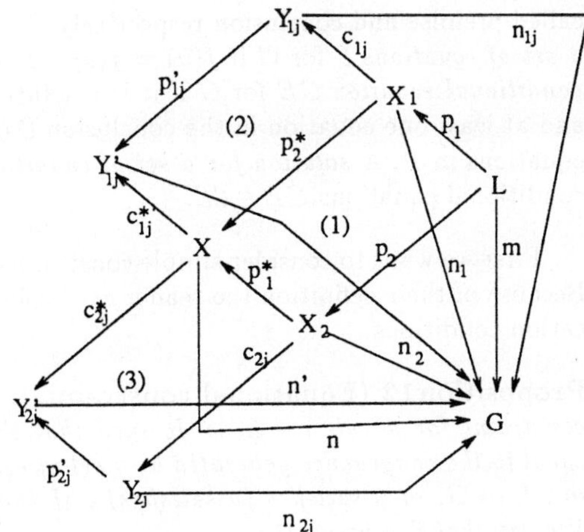

Fig. 4. Combination of constraints

Proposition 10 (Combination of constraints). *Let s (c) be the combination of two simple (conditional) constraints s_1 and s_2 resp. c_1 and c_2 as defined above. Then for all matches $m : L \to G$ we have*

1. $m \models_p s_1 \wedge m \models_p s_2 \Longleftrightarrow m \models_p s$,

2. $m \models_n s_1 \vee m \models_n s_2 \Longleftrightarrow m \models_n s$.

3. $m \models_c c_1 \vee m \models_c c_2 \Longleftrightarrow m \models_c c$.

Proof. 1./2. : We show that $\exists n : X \to G$ with $n \circ s = m \Longleftrightarrow \exists n_i : X_i \to G$ with $n_i \circ s_i = m$ for $i = 1, 2$. Then the assertion follows from definition 7. Given n as above we have $n_1 = n \circ s_2^*$ and $n_2 = n \circ s_1^*$, where $m = n \circ s = n \circ s_2^* \circ s_1 = n_1 \circ s_1$ (and similarily for s_2). Given n_1, n_2 as above, the left hand side of the equivalence follows from the universal property of X.

3. : Analogously to the above proof we get that $\exists n : X \to G$ with $n \circ p = m$ $\Longleftrightarrow \exists n_i : X_i \to G$ with $n_i \circ p_i = m$ for $i = 1, 2$. With the same arguments for the pushouts (2) and (3) we get $\exists n'_{ij} : Y'_{ij} \to G$ with $n'_{ij} \circ c^*_{ij} = n \Longleftrightarrow \exists n_{ij} : Y_{ij} \to G$ with $n_{ij} \circ c_{ij} = n_i$ for $i = 1, 2$ and $j = 1..k_i$. Then the proposition 10 3. follows from definition 7. □

3.2 Surjective constraints

In this section we show that special application conditions, namely those which contain surjective constraints only, can be characterized using (conditional) equations. This seems to be useful, because the graphical representation of complex application conditions is rather hard to understand, but nice if one wants to achieve theoretical results.

Definition 11 ((Conditional) Equations). An *equation* E for a graph G is a pair $(a = b)$ such that a and b are elements of the same domain of G. A *conditional equation* CE for G is a pair $(\mathcal{P}, \mathcal{C})$ consisting of two finite sets of equations $\mathcal{P}$ and $\mathcal{C}$

called premise and conclusion respectively. A morphism $f : G \to H$ is a *solution for a set of equations* $\mathcal{E}$ for G if $f(a) = f(b)$ for all $(a = b) \in \mathcal{E}$. f is a *solution for the conditional equation* CE for G if it is a solution for all equations in the premise $\mathcal{P}$ and at least one equation in the conclusion $\mathcal{C}$ or if it is not a solution for any of the equations in $\mathcal{P}$. A *solution for a set of conditional equations* $\mathcal{CE}$ is a solution for all conditional equations $CE \in \mathcal{CE}$.

First we want to consider simple constraints and negative application conditions. Because of their definition the reader can easily transfer the result to positive application conditions.

Proposition 12 (Equational constraints). *Let $c : L \to X$ be a simple surjective constraint for a rule $r : L \to R$ such that the congruence $Eq(c)$ induced by c is equal to the congruence generated by a set of equations $\mathcal{E}$ for L. Then, given a match $m : L \to G$, m p-satisfies (n-satisfies) c if and only if m is (not) a solution for $\mathcal{E}$. We say that $\mathcal{E}$ represents c.*

For the proof of this proposition we refer to [8].

Corollary 13 (Negative application condition). *Given an n-conditional rule $\hat{r} = (r : L \to R, A(r))$ and sets of equations $\mathcal{E}_c$ such that each $\mathcal{E}_c$ represents a simple constraint $c \in A(r)$. Then a match $m : L \to G$ for r satisfies $A(r)$ if and only if m is not a solution for any $\mathcal{E}_c$.*

The proof directly follows from the definitions 7 resp. 11 and proposition 12.

If negative application conditions correspond to non-equations it seems to be natural that conditional ones correspond to conditional equations.

Proposition 14 (Conditional constraints). *Let $c = (p : L \to X, c_i : X \to Y_i)_{i=1..n}$ be a conditional constraint for a rule $r : L \to R$ with p being surjective and c_i being total and surjective for $i = 1..n$ such that the congruence $Eq(p)$ $(Eq(c_i \circ p))$ induced by p $(c_i \circ p)$ is equal to the congruence generated by a set of equations $\mathcal{E}_p$ $(\mathcal{E}_{c_i op})$ for L. $\Pi\mathcal{E}$ denotes the cartesian product of $\mathcal{E}_{c_i op}$ for $i = 1..n$. $F : \Pi\mathcal{E} \to Set$ denotes the function assigning to each tuple $(E_1, .., E_n)$ the set $\{E_1, .., E_n\}$. Now, given a match $m : L \to G$, m c-satisfies c if and only if m is a solution for the set of conditional equations $\mathcal{CE} = \{(\mathcal{E}_p, F(E)) | E \in \Pi\mathcal{E}\}$. We say that $\mathcal{CE}$ represents c.*

Proof. If $m \models_c c$ and there is no morphism $n : X \to G$ with $n \circ p = m$ then by proposition 12 m is not a solution for $\mathcal{E}_p$ and hence m is a solution for $\mathcal{CE}$. Now assume that there is a morphism $n : X \to G$ with $n \circ p = m$ and m is a solution for $\mathcal{E}_p$. Then there exists $o : Y_i \to G$ with $o \circ c_i = n$ for at least one $i \in \{1..n\}$. By proposition 12 m is a solution for $\mathcal{E}_{c_i op}$. For each $CE \in \mathcal{CE}$ the conclusion contains one equation $E \in \mathcal{E}_{c_i op}$. Hence by definition 11 m is a solution for $\mathcal{CE}$.

Now assume that m is a solution for $\mathcal{CE}$. Again we only consider the case that m is a solution for $\mathcal{E}_p$. For the other case we refer to proposition 12. m must be a solution for all conclusions of conditional equations in $\mathcal{CE}$. This implies that m is a solution for at least one $\mathcal{E}_{c_i op}$. The existence of $o : Y_i \to G$ with $o \circ (c_i \circ p) = m$ follows from proposition 12. □

Corollary 15 (Conditional application condition). *Given a c-conditional rule $\hat{r} = (r : L \to R, A(r))$ and sets of conditional constraints $\mathcal{CE}_c$ such that each $\mathcal{CE}_c$ represents a conditional constraint $c \in A(r)$. Then a match $m : L \to G$ for r satisfies $A(r)$ if and only if m is a solution for $\bigcup_c \mathcal{CE}_c$.*

The proof directly follows from the definitions 11 resp. 7 and proposition 14.

4 Generative Power

The notion of a grammar as it is used in formal language theory deals with terminal and nonterminal objects. In the literature this is carried over to graph grammars leading to terminal and nonterminal graphs. Using graph transformations for system specification it makes sense to forbid nonterminal graphs in order to make it impossible to encode control structure into flags and additional labels. With this background we define graph grammars and their generated language.

Definition 16 (Graph grammar). A graph grammar $GG = (S, \mathcal{R})$ consists of a starting graph S and a finite set of rules $\mathcal{R}$. The language $L(GG)$ generated by the graph grammar GG is the set of all those graphs which can be derived from the starting graph S using rules of $\mathcal{R}$.

Note that the notion of graph grammars and their generated language is parametric over the notions of rules and derivations. We say $GG = (S, \mathcal{R})$ is a graph grammar over simple resp. p- (n-, c-) conditional rules if $\mathcal{R}$ contains simple resp. p- (n-, c-) conditional rules only. In this paper most of the results can be achieved for the single and the (classical) double pushout approach. Hence we denote the corresponding languages by $L^P(GG)$, $L^N(GG)$ and $L^C(GG)$ if no distinction is necessary whether the used matches are classical or not. Only if we want to indicate the match type we use additional subscripts c resp. $\not c$ (for classical resp. non-classical). $\mathcal{L}^S$, $\mathcal{L}^P$, $\mathcal{L}^N$ and $\mathcal{L}^C$ are the classes of all graph languages generated by graph grammars over simple, p-, n- resp. c-conditional rules.

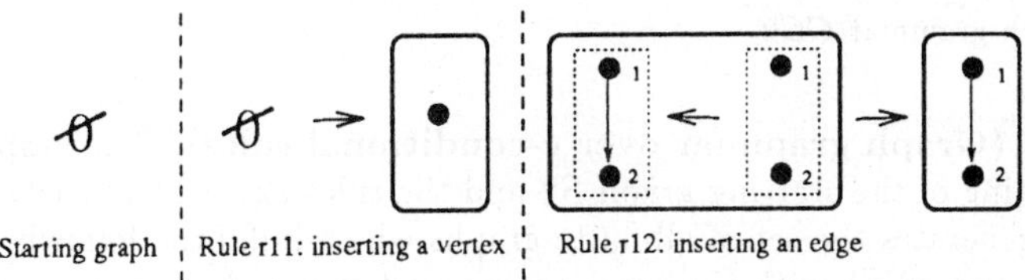

Fig. 5. Graph grammar $GG1$

Example 2 (Graph grammar over n-conditional rules). The graph grammar $GG1$ consisting of the starting graph $S1$ and the rules $r11$ and $r12$ as depicted in figure 5 generates the set of all finite graphs which have at most one edge between two vertices in each direction. We call this graph language $L1$ in the following. Rule $r11$ adds a new vertex in any situation. The negative application condition of rule $r12$ makes sure that there is not already an edge from $m(1)$ to $m(2)$ if a new edge with the same direction between these two vertices is inserted. Note that all matches for the rules $r11$ and $r12$ are classical due to the fact that the rule morphisms are total.

Proposition 17 (*GG*1 **generates** *L*1)**.** *The graph grammar GG1 from example 2 generates all and only those graphs in which for each pair of vertices (v1, v2) there is at most one edge with source vertex v1 and target vertex v2, i.e.* $L^N(GG1) = L1$.

Proofidea. $L^N(GG1) \subseteq L1$ can easily be shown by induction over the length of the derivation sequence and $L1 \subseteq L^N(GG1)$ analogously by induction. over the number of objects (vertices and edges) in a graph $G \in L1$. □

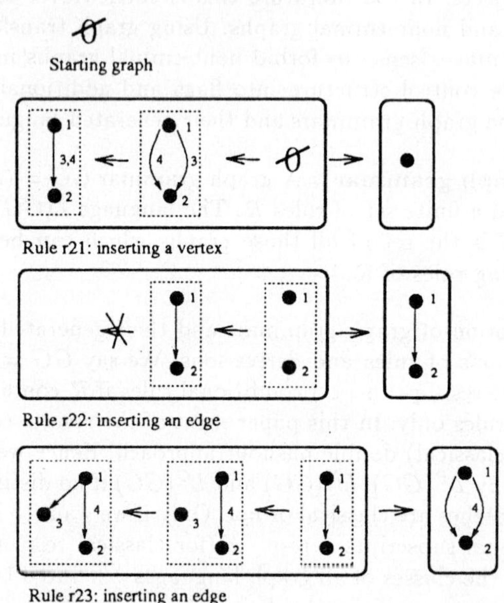

Fig. 6. Graph grammar *GG*2

Example 3 (Graph grammar over c-conditional rules). The graph grammar $GG2$ consisting of the starting graph $S2$ and the rules $r21$, $r22$ and $r23$ as depicted in figure 6 generates the set of all finite graphs which fulfill the following condition: If there are two edges with the same source vertex v and the same target vertex, there exists an edge from v to every vertex in the graph. We call this language $L2$ in the following.

Rule $r21$ adds a new vertex if there is no vertex with more than one outgoing edge to the same target vertex. Note that the edges in the application condition are identified. New edges are inserted by the rules $r22$ and $r23$ where $r23$ inserts an edge if the vertex becoming the source of this edge has an outgoing edge to every vertex in the graph. Rule $r22$ is applicable to vertices $m(1)$ and $m(2)$ if there is no edge from $m(1)$ to $m(2)$. Note that there is a certain application order for the rules of $GG2$: If rule $r23$ has been applied once rule $r21$ is not applicable any more. Note that all matches for the rules $r21$, $r22$ and $r23$ are classical due to the fact that the rule morphisms are total.

Proposition 18 (**$GG2$ generates $L2$**). *The graph grammar $GG2$ from example 3 generates all and only those graphs which have the following property: If there are two edges with the same source vertex v and the same target vertex, there exists an edge from v to every vertex in the graph.*

Proof. We prove $L^C(GG2) = L2$ showing $L2 \subseteq L^C(GG2)$ by induction over the number of objects (vertices and edges) of a graph. It is easy to show $L^C(GG2) \subseteq L2$ by induction over the length of the derivation sequence.

The basis is given by the starting graph which is the only graph within $L2$ having no objects. For the induction step we divide three cases: if $G \in L2$ contains at least two edges with the same source and target vertex, an application of rule $r23$ derives G from a graph with n objects. In the second case we consider graphs that contain edges but none of them have the same source and target vertex. These graphs may have an application of rule $r22$ in their last derivation step. If we have a graph without any edge, rule $r21$ inserts a vertex to the graph with one vertex less. □

4.1 Generative power of positive and negative application conditions

In this section we investigate which classes of graph languages can be generated with graph grammars over rules with positive resp. negative application conditions. It turns out that positive application conditions are just avoiding rule schemes, if one does not restrict the matches to be classical. In contrast rules with negative application conditions really extend the generative power of the graph grammar notion.

Proposition 19 (**Generative power of pos. appl. conditions**). *For every graph grammar GG over rules with positive application conditions there exists a graph grammar GG' over simple rules such that $L^P_\gamma(GG) = L^S_\gamma(GG')$.*

Proofidea. Let $\hat{r} = (r : L \to R, A(r))$ be a p-conditional rule. Applying the simple rule r to every constraint $c : L \to X$ of $A(r)$ leads to a set $\mathcal{R}$ of simple rules r^* where $(R', r^* : X \to R', c^* : R \to R')$ is the pushout of r and c. For every direct derivation of a graph G to H with the p-conditional rule $\hat{r}$ there exists a direct derivation of G to H with one rule $r^* \in \mathcal{R}$ and vice versa. Note that not every classical match for r which satisfies $A(r)$ induces a classical match for r^*. Induction over the length of the derivation sequence makes sure that $L^P_\gamma(GG) = L^S_\gamma(GG')$. □

A simular proof can be found in [6]. It is a bit more complicated because the notion of satisfaction of a positive application condition is different but the general idea of context enlargement is the same.

In the following we want to show that graph grammars over rules with negative application conditions are more powerful than graph grammars over simple rules. For this purpose we use the graph language $L1$ and the graph grammar $GG1$ introduced in example 2 by showing that $L1$ cannot be generated by any graph grammar over simple rules. The principle of the proof is to state a property of every graph grammar over simple rules generating $L1$ and show that a grammar with this property cannot generate $L1$.

Lemma 20 (Property of $L1$). *For any possible graph grammar (over simple rules) generating $L1$ there is no derivation sequence containing a single step $G \stackrel{r,m}{\Longrightarrow} H$ in which a new edge from an existing vertex $v1$ to an existing vertex $v2$ is inserted.*

Proof. Assume such a derivation would exist. Because $H \in L1$ G cannot contain an edge from $v1$ to $v2$. But there exists an inclusion morphism $i : G \to G'$ where G' is the graph G extended by one edge from $v1$ to $v2$. G' belongs to the language $L1$ and hence has a derivation sequence from the starting graph. $i \circ m$ is a match for r in G' by lemma 5. If m is classical then $i \circ m$ is classical, too, because $v1, v2$ are preserved by the application of rule r. Applying r to G' leads to a graph H' which has two edges with the same source and target vertex. Because there cannot be such a derivation sequence for H' the outdegree of an existing vertex can only be increased by inserting a new vertex. □

Proposition 21 ($L1 \notin \mathcal{L}^S$). *There exists no graph grammar over simple rules that generates the language $L1$, i.e. $L1 \notin \mathcal{L}^S$.*

Proof. Assume that there is a graph grammar (over simple rules) generating $L1$. This graph grammar must certainly fulfill the condition of lemma 20. Let n be the maximum outdegree of a vertex in the right hand side of a rule which has no preimage in the left hand side, i.e. it is inserted if the rule is applied. m is the number of vertices of the starting graph. The graph N with $m + n + 2$ vertices which has exactly one edge from each vertex to any other vertex belongs to $L1$. Note that the outdegree of each vertex is $m+n+1$ and that in order to derive N from the starting graph at least $n + 2$ vertices must be inserted. Within the derivation sequence of N there must be one step where the last time a vertex is inserted. This vertex has an outdegree less or equal to n which is less than $m+n+1$. But because no more vertices are added the outdegree cannot be increased (see the property of the graph grammar above). Hence there is no derivation sequence for N leading to a contradiction. □

Proposition 17 and 21 immediately lead to the following corollary.

Corollary 22 (Generative power of negative appl. conditions). *Graph grammars over rules with negative application conditions are more powerful than graph grammars over simple rules, i.e. $\mathcal{L}^S \subset \mathcal{L}^N$.*

4.2 Generative power of conditional application conditions

In this section we show that graph grammars over rules with conditional application conditions are more powerful than graph grammars over rules with negative application conditions. First we show that for each graph grammar over rules with negative application conditions there exists a graph grammar over rules with conditional application conditions which generates the same language. Furthermore we show that there exists a graph language which can be generated using rules with conditional application conditions but not with negative ones.

Proposition 23 (Simulating negative application conditions). *For every rule $\hat{r} = (r : L \to R, A(r))$ with a negative application condition $A(r)$ there exists a rule $\hat{r}' = (r : L \to R, A(r'))$ with a conditional application condition $A(r')$ such that $\hat{r}$ is applicable to a graph G if and only if $\hat{r}'$ is applicable to G.*

Proof. Choose $A(r') = \{(L \to X, \emptyset) | (L \to X) \in A(r)\}$. [2] Let $m : L \to R$ be a total morphism that satisfies $A(r)$, i.e. for each simple constraint $s : L \to X$ there exists no total morphism $n : X \to G$ with $n \circ s = m$. By definition 7 m c-satisfies each single conditional constraint in $A(r')$ and hence m satisfies $A(r')$. Now assume that m does not satisfy $A(r)$, i.e. there exists a simple constraint $s : L \to X$ and a morphism $n : X \to G$ such that $n \circ s = m$. But because of the empty conclusion of the constraint in $A(r')$ m does not satisfy $A(r')$. □

Now we use the graph language $L2$ and the graph grammar $GG2$ from example 3 to show that introducing conditional application conditions increases the generative power of algebraic graph transformations, i.e. we show that $L2$ cannot be generated by any graph grammar over rules with negative application conditions. Analogously to the previous section we first prove a property such a grammar would have and then show that this is not possible.

Lemma 24 (Property of $L2$). *Every graph grammar $GG = (S, \mathcal{R})$ over rules with negative application conditions that generates the language $L2$ must fullfill the following property for all graphs $G, H \in L2$: If the number of vertices of G is greater than x and $G \Longrightarrow H$ then $V(H) \leq V(G)$.*

Where x is the maximum number of vertices of a left hand side of a rule in $\mathcal{R}$ and $V(G)$ denotes the number of vertices of graph G which have at least two outgoing edges with the same target vertex.

Proof. The stated property holds due to the fact that if $G \overset{\hat{r},m}{\Longrightarrow} H$ and $V(G) < V(H)$ then m must be surjective on the vertices which is not possible if G contains more than x vertices. This fact is shown in the following: Let $r : L \to R$ be the simple rule of $\hat{r}$ and $m : L \to G$ be a match for r which satisfies the negative application condition of $\hat{r}$. $(H, r^* : G \to H, m^* : R \to H)$ is the pushout for the direct derivation of G to H with rule r at match m. If m is not surjective for the vertices there exists a vertex v of graph G which has no preimage under m in L. $V(G) < V(H)$ implies that there is $v' \in H$ with $i \geq 2$ outgoing edges pointing to the same target vertex, what is not true for a possible preimage of v' under r^* in G. By lemma 4 (1) r^* is defined for v. Because $H \in L2$ there exists an edge e from v' to $r^*(v)$. By lemma 4 (2) $r^*(v) \notin m^*(R)$. m^* is a morphism. Hence e has no preimage under m^*. With lemma 4 (3) e and v' have a preimage under r^*. Remember that $r^{*-1}(v')$ has at most one edge pointing to each vertex of graph G. Hence G' which is G without the edge(s) $r^{*-1}(e)$ is also a graph of language $L2$ and can be derived from the starting graph using rules of GG. m induces a match $m' : L \to G'$ for r, because $r^{*-1}(e)$ has no preimage under m. m' satisfies the negative application condition of r because it is satisfied by m. Note that if m is classical m' is classical, too. Applying r to G' at m' leads to a graph H' which is just H without the edge e. H' is not in $L2$, because

[2] Here $\emptyset$ denotes the empty family.

there is no edge from the vertex corresponding to v' to the vertex corresponding to $r^*(v)$. Hence we have a contradiction to the assumption that GG generates $L2$. □

Proposition 25 ($L2 \notin \mathcal{L}^N$). *There exists no graph grammar over rules with negative application conditions that generates the language L2, i.e.* $L2 \notin \mathcal{L}^N$.

Proof. Assume that there exists a graph grammar $GG = (S, \mathcal{R})$ over rules with negative application conditions generating $L2$. Furthermore we use the notation of lemma 24. Let o be the number of vertices of the starting graph S and n the maximum number of vertices which can be inserted in one derivation step, i.e. the maximum number of vertices in the right hand side of a rule which have no preimages under the rule morphism. Choose the graph M to have $o+n+1+x$ vertices where for each pair of vertices $v1, v2$ there are exactly two edges with source vertex $v1$ and target vertex $v2$, i.e. $V(M) = o+n+1+x$. $M \in L2$ because every vertex has an outgoing edge to every other vertex. Now consider a derivation sequence $S \overset{*}{\Longrightarrow} N \Longrightarrow M$. Within the last derivation step not more than n vertices can be added. Hence N has more than x vertices and we get $V(N) \leq V(M) = o+n+1+x$ by lemma 24. But $V(N)$ cannot be greater than the number of vertices of N and hence N has at least $o+n+1+x$ vertices. With the same argument we can follow backwards the derivation sequence. Because it is finite we sometimes arrive at the first derivation step. But here we know that S only has o vertices such that at least one must be added leading to a contradiction to the assumption. □

Proposition 18 and 25 immediately lead to the following corollary.

Corollary 26 (Generative power of condit. appl. conditions). *Graph grammars over rules with conditional application conditions are more powerful than graph grammars over rules with negative application conditions, i.e.* $\mathcal{L}^N \subset \mathcal{L}^C$.

5 Conclusions

In this paper the concept of positive and negative application conditions as introduced in [6] is extended to conditional application conditions. It is shown that from the specification point of view these additional features increase the expressive power. We presented a hierarchy of classes of graph languages $\mathcal{L}^S_{\not c} = \mathcal{L}^P_{\not c} \subset \mathcal{L}^N \subset \mathcal{L}^C$ for the single pushout approach which is not much different for the double pushout approach ($\mathcal{L}^S_c \subseteq \mathcal{L}^P_c$).

Furthermore we have shown that special application conditions can be represented using non-equations resp. conditional equations. In the general case additionally the existence of specific structures can be recommanded. It is left to future research to give a logical representation for all possible application conditions. Such a representation could be very useful if one wants to prove the consistency of a specification. In [3] also application conditions for the right hand side of the rule were presented. Consistency conditions based one equations were already introduced in [10]. It is an open question wether both can be brought together, i.e. it is possible to prove that the satisfaction of application conditions implies that consistency is preserved.

Another interesting task is to carry over theoretical results known for the pure single pushout approach to this extended one, for example concepts of independence and parallelism of graph transformations, embedding, concurrency etc. First results are present for graph grammars over rules with positive and negative application conditions in [6] and [7].

Acknowledgements

The author is grateful to H.Ehrig, R.Heckel and G.Taentzer for comments and fruitful discussions on the topics presented in this paper.

References

1. M. Arbib and E.G. Manes. *Arrows, Structures, and Functors: The Categorical Imperative.* Academic Press, New York, 1975.
2. H. Ehrig. Introduction to the algebraic theory of graph grammars. In V. Claus, H. Ehrig, and G. Rozenberg, editors, *1st Graph Grammar Workshop, Lecture Notes in Computer Science 73*, pages 1–69, 1979.
3. H. Ehrig and A. Habel. Graph grammars with application conditions. In G. Rozenberg and A. Salomaa, editors, *The Book of L*, pages 87–100. 1985.
4. H. Ehrig, A. Habel, H.-J. Kreowski, and F. Parisi-Presicce. From graph grammars to High Level Replacement Systems. pages 269–291, 1991. Lecture Notes in Computer Science 532.
5. H. Ehrig and M. Löwe. Categorical principles, techniques and results for high-level replacement systems in computer science. *Applied Categorical Structures*, 1(1):21–50, 1993.
6. A. Habel, R. Heckel, and G. Taentzer. Graph grammars with negative application conditions. accepted for special issue of Fundamenta Informaticae, 1994.
7. R. Heckel. Embedding of conditional graph transformations. unpublished, 1994.
8. R. Heckel, J. Müller, G. Taentzer, and A. Wagner. Attributed graph transformations with controlled application of rules. submitted to proceedings of Graphgrammar Mallorca Workshop 94, 1994.
9. H. Herrlich and G. Strecker. *Category Theory.* Allyn and Bacon, Rockleigh, New Jersey, 1973.
10. M. Korff. Single pushout transformations of equationally defined graph structures with applications to actor systems. In *Proc. Graph Grammar Workshop Dagstuhl 93*, pages 234–247, 1994. Lecture Notes in Computer Science 776.
11. M. Löwe. Algebraic approach to single-pushout graph transformation. *TCS*, 109:181–224, 1993.
12. U. Montanari. Separable graphs, planar graphs and web grammars. *Information and Control 16*, pages 243–267, 1970.
13. A. Schürr. Progress: A vhl-language based on graph grammars. In *LNCS532.* Springer, 1991.
14. A. Wagner. On the expressive power of graph grammars with application conditions. Technical Report 27, TU Berlin, 1994.

Generated models and the ω-rule: the nondeterministic case

Michal Walicki *)
michal@ii.uib.no

Sigurd Meldal
sigurd@ii.uib.no

University of Bergen
Department of Informatics
HiB, 5020 Bergen, NORWAY

Abstract. A language for specifying nondeterministic operations which generalizes the equational specification language is introduced. Then, various notions of generated multimodels are discussed and sufficient conditions for the existence of quasi-initial semantics of nondeterministic specifications are given. Two calculi are introduced: NEQ and NIP. The former is sound and complete with respect to the class of all multimodels. The latter is an extension of the former with the ω-rule. It is sound and complete with respect to one of the classes of the generated multimodels. The calculi reduce to the respective deterministic calculi whenever the specification involves only deterministic operations.

1. Introduction

The notion of *nondeterminism* arises naturally in describing concurrent systems. Various approaches to the theory and specification of such systems, for instance, CCS [23], CSP [16], process algebras [1], event structures [39], include the phenomenon of nondeterminism. But nondeterminism is also a natural concept in describing sequential programs, as witnessed for instance, by the powerdomain constructions of denotational semantics [28, 31, 29, 4] and by attempts to extend abstract data types with nondeterministic operations [3, 2, 25, 26].

As we argued elswhere [35, 38] the use of nondeterministic operators is an appropriate and useful abstraction tool, and more: nondeterminism is a *natural* abstraction concept whenever there is a hidden state or other components of a system description which are, methodologically, conceptually or technically, inaccessible at a particular level of abstraction. Whether the world really is nondeterministic or not we leave to the physicists and philosophers to ponder. A computer system in isolation certainly is deterministic: When started from a particular state (given in full detail) twice, both executions will demonstrate identical behavior. Possible sources of perceived nondeterminism lie only in the unpredictability of the environment such as hardware failures or human factors. Considering all such factors as parts of the total state given in full detail may obviate the perceived nondeterminism, but leads to undesirable complexity and is possible only in principle.

The primary argument in favor of accepting nondeterministic operators is instrumental, and identical to the credo of the abstract data type community: *One should specify a system only in such detail that any implementation satisfying the specification also satisfies the user, and no more.* It turns out that nondeterministic operators ease the process of specifying systems by allowing one to disregard irrelevant aspects – be they the external influ-

*) This work has been partially supported by the Architectural Abstraction project under NFR (Norway), by CEC under ESPRIT–II Basic Reearch Working Group No. 6112 COMPASS, by the US DARPA under ONR contract N00014-92-J-1928, N00014-93-1-1335 and by the US Air Force Office of Scientific Research under Grant AFOSR-91-0354.

ences or implementation details – and thus reducing the danger of overspecification resulting from technical rather than methodical reasons.

In recent years several authors have tried to provide algebraic specifications of nondeterminism with the semantics based on the notion of *multialgebras* [22, 15, 17, 24, 21]. It is also the approach we are taking here. Multialgebras seem to offer a natural generalization needed for the adequate treatment of nondeterminism. However, since a multialgebra models the nondeterministic terms as *sets* of individuals, the concept of reachability of such a model remains unclear. For instance, is an element which can be returned as one of the possible results of a nondeterministic operation, but which is not a unique interpretation of any (deterministic) term, to be considered reachable or not? The logical counterpart of the deterministic generated models is the induction principle. What form should it have if we want to apply it to multialgebras? And which multialgebraic models should we choose in order to obtain sound inductive reasoning? In this paper we intend to answer some of these questions.

Let SP denote an equational specification; Mod(SP) the class of its models, $Mod_{\Sigma}(SP)$ the generated models, T_{SP} an initial model; SP $\vdash_{CAL}$ *e* provability of an equation *e* from the axioms of SP with a calculus CAL. Among the fundamental results for the deterministic equational specifications there are the following theorems:

1. Mod(SP) $\models e$ iff SP $\vdash_{EQ} e$ – soundness and completeness of equational calculus
2. $Mod_{\Sigma}(SP) \models e$ iff SP $\vdash_{IP} e$ – soundness and completeness of induction principle
3. $T_{SP} \in Mod_{\Sigma}(SP)$ – initial models are generated

We present the analogous theorems for the specifications involving nondeterministic operations. Section 2 introduces the specification language $\mathcal{L}$ and discusses briefly its main features. Section 3 defines the multialgebraic semantics of specifications in $\mathcal{L}$. Then we discuss various notions of generated multimodels (section 4), suggest a generalization of the initial semantics to the nondeterministic context and give the sufficient condition for the existence of such semantics (section 5), and present the results analogous to 3. (section 5), 1. (section 6), and 2. (section 7). All the constructions and theorems are *non-intrusive* in the sense that, when restricted to the deterministic context, they specialize to the above (and other) standard results.

The present paper is a self-contained version of some of the results from [36]. The reader interested in the motivation for some unorthodox decisions we have made here, as well as the explanations of some technical details is referred to [36] where he can also find the proofs omitted here.

2. The specification language

A specification is a pair (Σ, Π), where the *signature* Σ is a pair of a sets (**S**, **F**) of sorts **S** and operation symbols **F** (with arguments and result sorts in **S**). There exists a denumerable set $\mathcal{V}$ of variables for every sort. For any syntactic entity (term, formula, set of formulae) χ, $\mathcal{V}[\chi]$ will denote the set of variables in χ. Letters from the end of the latin alphabet, *x,y,z* are used for variables. The set of terms over the signature Σ and a variable set X is denoted $W_{\Sigma,X}$. We always assume that, for every sort S, the set of ground terms of sort S, $(W_{\Sigma})_S$, is not empty. [1]

Formulae of the language $\mathcal{L}$ are *clauses* and Π is a set of such formulae. Each clause *C* is a set of atomic formulae (i.e., the ordering and multiplicity of the atomic formulae

[1] We do not address the problem of empty sorts here and will present calculi which work under the assumption that sorts are not empty. We will usually give signatures with at least one constant for every sort, but other means of restricting the signatures [19, 10] or ensuring nonemptiness [10, 12] can be used instead. It seems also that the most flexible approach which generalizes calculus by introducing explicit variables [10, 11, 7] can be adapted to our framework.

do not matter), written as $a_1,\ldots,a_n$ (possibly within "{ }"). To ease readability we will sometimes write disjunction explicitly as $a_1 \vee \ldots \vee a_n$. Comma indicates concatenation of clauses, and semicolon a collection. E.g., if C is $\{c_1,\ldots,c_n\}$, D is $\{d_1,\ldots,d_m\}$, then "C ; D" denotes the conjunction of the two clauses, while "C, D" denotes the clause $\{c_1,\ldots,c_n,d_1,\ldots,d_m\}$. Usually, we use uppercase Latin letters for single clauses, uppercase Greek letters for sets of clauses, and lowercase Latin letters c, t for terms.

An atomic formula (atomic clause) is either an *equation,* $t \doteq s$, an *inclusion,* $t \prec s$, or an *inequalities,* $t \# s$, of terms $t, s \in W_{\Sigma X}$. Equalities are understood to mean *necessary* equality (i.e. the two terms *always* return the same result). Inequalities are understood to mean *necessary* inequality (i.e. the two terms *never* return the same results). Equations and inclusions are called *positive* atoms, and inequalities *negative* atoms. This distinction expresses the fact that a clause $\{ t \# s, p \prec r \}$ is equivalent to the conditional formula $\neg(t \# s) \Rightarrow p \prec r$, stating that whenever t intersects s, p is included in r. A clause with exactly one positive atom is called a *Horn formula*, and a Horn formula with no negative atoms a *simple formula*.

All variables occurring in a clause are implicitly universally quantified over the whole clause. A clause is satisfied if, for every assignment to the variables, at least one of the atoms is true. For a specification SP=(Σ, Π), $\mathcal{L}$(SP) is the restriction of $\mathcal{L}$ to $W_{\Sigma,\mathcal{V}}$.

A specification SP is interpreted in a multialgebra where the (nondeterministic) operations correspond to *set-valued functions*. The main point concerning the interpretation of $\mathcal{L}$ is related to the meaning of equality. Since terms are interpreted in a multialgebra as sets of the possible results, the formula $t{=}s$ is usually interpreted as the equality of *the sets corresponding to all possible results* of the operations. This gives a model which is mathematically plausible but does not correspond to our operational intuition. The equality $t{=}s$ does not guarantee that the result returned by some particular application of t will actually be equal to the result returned by an application of s. It merely tells us that *in principle* (in all possible executions) any result produced by t can also be produced by s and vice versa.

Equality in our view, on the other hand, should be a *necessary* equality which must hold in every evaluation of a program (specification). *It does not correspond to set equality, but to identity of 1-element sets.* Thus the simple formula $t \doteq s$ should hold in a multistructure M iff both t and s are interpreted in M as one and the same set which, in addition, *has only one element*. (This is the reason for using the symbol $\doteq$ instead of usual =.) Equality is then a *partial equivalence relation* (not necessarily reflexive) and terms t for which $t \doteq t$ holds are exactly the deterministic terms, denoted by $\mathcal{D}_{\mathrm{SP,X}}$. More precisely, $t \in \mathcal{D}_{\mathrm{SP,X}}$ if $t \doteq t$ holds in every model of the specification. (In particular, variables will always be interpreted deterministically.)

If it is possible to produce a computation where t and s return different results – and this is possible whenever they are nondeterministic – then the terms are not equal but, at best, equivalent. They are equivalent if they are capable of returning the same results, i.e., if they are interpreted as the same set. This may be expressed using the inclusion relation: $s \prec t$ holds iff the set of possible results of s is included in the set of possible results of t, and $s \asymp t$ iff each is included in the other.

A nondeterministic operation may then be specified by a series of inclusions – each defining one of its possible results. Such a specification establishes only a "lower bound" on the admitted nondeterminism.

Example 2.1

S:	{ Nat },			
F:	0:		→ Nat	(zero)
	s_:	Nat	→ Nat	(successor)
	_⊔_:	Nat×Nat	→ Nat	(binary nondeterministic choice)

Π: 1. $0 \doteq 0$
2. $s(x) \doteq s(x)$
3. $1 \# 0$ (As usual, we abbreviate $s^n(0)$ as n.)
4. $0 \prec 0 \sqcup 1$ $1 \prec 0 \sqcup 1$ □

The first two axioms make zero and successor deterministic. A limited form of negation is present in $\mathcal{L}$ in the form of clauses with only negative atoms. Axiom 3. makes 0 distinct from 1. Axioms 4. make then ⊔ a nondeterministic choice with 0 and 1 among its possible results. This, however, ensures only that in every model both 0 and 1 can be returned by $0 \sqcup 1$. In most models all other kinds of elements may be among its possible results as well, since no extension of the result set of $0 \sqcup 1$ will violate the inclusions of 4. If we are satisfied with this degree of precision, we may stop here and use only Horn formula. All the results in the rest of the paper apply to this special case. But to specify an "upper bound" of nondeterministic operations we also need disjunction of positive atoms. Before we illustrate this we have to consider another feature of the language.

The fact that equality is not reflexive for the nondeterministic terms reflects the intended interpretation of terms as *applications* of the respective operations. Every two syntactic occurrences of a term t refer to *possibly distinct* applications of t. For nondeterministic t, the equality $t \doteq t$ does not hold because the first occurrence refers to an arbitrary application of t and the second one to an arbitrary, hence possibly distinct, application of the same operation t. The equality says that arbitrary two applications return the same result. Now, if we write the axiom:

5. $0 \sqcup 1 \doteq 0 \vee 0 \sqcup 1 \doteq 1$

the two occurrences of $0 \sqcup 1$ refer to two arbitrary applications and, consequently, we obtain that either any application of $0 \sqcup 1$ equals 0 or else it equals 1, i.e., that ⊔ is not really nondeterministic but merely underspecified. Since axioms 4. require that both 0 and 1 be among the results of t, addition of 5. will actually make the specification inconsistent.

What we are trying to say with the disjunction 5. is that *every application* of $0 \sqcup 1$ returns either 0 or 1, i.e., we need a means of identifying two occurrences of a nondeterministic term as referring to one and the same application. This can be done by *binding* both occurrences to a variable. We would write instead

5′. $x \# 0 \sqcup 1 \vee x \doteq 0 \vee x \doteq 1$

The axiom says: whenever $0 \sqcup 1$ returns x, then x equals 0 or x equals 1. Notice that such an interpretation presupposes that variables refer to unique, individual values. Variants of this interpretation are known as *call-time-choice* [14, 6], *singular* [30], *inside-out* or *IO* [8, 9] and correspond, roughly, to the call-by-value passing of deterministic parameters. This is the most common approach in the literature on the algebraic semantics of nondeterministic specification languages, in spite of the fact that it prohibits unrestricted substitution of terms for variables. Any substitution must now be guarded by the check that the substituted term yields a unique value, i.e., is deterministic. We return to this point in the section on reasoning where we introduce a calculus with the appropriately restricted substitution rules. (For a further discussion of the distinction between plural and singualr semantics of variables, see [33, 38].)

3. Multistructures and multimodels.

Definition 3.2 (Multistructures). For a signature Σ, M is a Σ-*multistructure* if

1. its carrier |M| is an **S**-sorted set, and
2. for every $f: S_1 \times \ldots \times S_n \to S$ in **F**, there is a corresponding function $f^M: S_1^M \times \ldots \times S_n^M \to \mathcal{P}^+(S^M)$.

A function Φ: A→B (i.e., a family of functions Φ_S: $S^A \to S^B$, for every S∈**S**) is a *multihomomorphism* from a Σ-multistructure A to B if

H1. for each constant symbol $c \in$ **F**, $\Phi(c^A) \subseteq c^B$ and

H2. for every $f: S_1 \times \ldots \times S_n \to S$ in **F** and $\underline{a}_1 \ldots \underline{a}_n \in S_1{}^A \times \ldots \times S_n{}^A$:
$\Phi(f^A(\underline{a}_1 \ldots \underline{a}_n)) \subseteq f^B(\Phi(\underline{a}_i) \ldots \Phi(\underline{a}_n))$

If all inclusions in H1 and H2 are (set) equalities the homomorphism is *tight*, otherwise it is strictly loose (or just *loose*). □

Operations applied to sets refer to their unique pointwise extensions; $\mathcal{P}^+(S)$ is the set of non-empty subsets of S. Notice that for a constant *c: →S*, 2. indicates that c^M can be a *set* of several elements of sort *S*.

If there exists a multihomomorphims Φ: A→B which is an inclusion we say that A is a *submultistructure* of B. (Optionally, we may only require that Φ is injective.) If, in addition, Φ is tight A is a *tight submultistructure* of B.

Since multihomomorphisms are defined on individuals and not sets they preserve singletons and are ⊆-monotonic. We denote the class of Σ-multistructures by MStr(Σ). It has the distinguished word structure:

Definition 3.3 (Word multistructure). The *word multistructure* MW_Σ for a specification SP over signature Σ=(S,F) is defined as:

1. for each S∈**S**, S^{MW_Σ} is the set of all 1-element sets containing ground words of sort S,
2. for each f: $S_1 \times \ldots \times S_n \to S$ in **F**, $\{t_i\} \in S_i{}^{MW_\Sigma}$: $f^{MW_\Sigma}(\{t_1\},\ldots,\{t_n\}) = \{f(t_1,\ldots,t_n)\}$

□

According to 2. every ground term is interpreted in MW_Σ as a singleton set. We will often treat such results as terms rather than 1-element sets (i.e., we do not take special pains to distinguish MW_Σ and W_Σ).

With this definition MW_Σ is not an initial Σ-structure since it is deterministic and there can exist several homomorphisms from it to a given multistructure. In [18] it is shown that it is (tightly) initial if we modify definition 3.2 by allowing a homomorphism Φ: $A \to B$ to send single elements of $|A|$ to (nonempty) sets of elements of $|B|$ (i.e., letting Φ: $|A| \to \mathcal{P}^+(|B|)$). We will retain the notion of homomorphism as in definition 3.2 because such a generalization is not needed. It merely "disguises" some strictly loose homomorphisms as tight ones since we may then have $c^A=\{\underline{c}\}$ and $\Phi(c^A)=\{\underline{c}_1,\ldots,\underline{c}_n\}=c^B$. (Underscored lower case letters, such as $\underline{a}$, $\underline{c}$, are used for the elements of a semantic domain.)

More importantly, it is a known fact [18, 24] that, in the general case, one should not expect the existence of initial multi*models*. In [18] Hußmann has shown that such multimodels may not exist even if the specification language is restricted to simple formulae. Therefore we allow general clauses in the specifications and will concentrate on the whole class of multimodels of a specification. For the discussion of the structure of this class and (the lack of) initiality results, the reader is referred to [18, 37, 36]. In the present context, the significance of the term structure is expressed in

Lemma 3.4. If M is a Σ-multistructure then, for every set of variables X and assignment β: X→|M|, there exists a unique function β[_]: $W_{\Sigma,X} \to \mathcal{P}^+(|M|)$ such that:

$\beta[x] = \{\beta(x)\}$ $\qquad \beta[c] = c^M$ $\qquad \beta[f(t_i,\ldots,t_n)] = \bigcup\{f^M(t1,\ldots tn) \mid ti \in \beta[t_i]\}$ □

In particular, for X=∅, there is a unique interpretation function (not a multihomomorphism) $\mathcal{I}$: $W_\Sigma \to \mathcal{P}^+(|M|)$ satisfying the last two points of this definition. Observe that, as a consequence of the definition of multistructures, operations in M are $\subseteq$-monotonic, i.e., $\beta[s]\subseteq\beta[t] \Rightarrow \beta[f(s)]\subseteq\beta[f(t)]$. Next we define the class of multimodels of a specification:

Definition 3.5 (Satisfiability). Let M be an Σ-multistructure, β: X$\rightarrow$|M| an assignment to a set of variables X. M satisfies an atom *a* under β iff

- *a* is $s\prec t$ and $\beta[s] \subseteq \beta[t]$
- *a* is $s\# t$ and $\beta[s] \cap \beta[t] = \emptyset$
- *a* is $s\doteq t$ and $\beta[s] = \beta[t] = \{x\}$, for some $x\in|M|$.

M *satisfies* a clause *C*, M$\models$*C*, iff for each β, M satisfies at least one atom of *C*.
An SP-*multimodel* is an SP-multistructure which satisfies all the axioms of SP.
MMod(SP) denotes the class of multimodels of SP. □

The reason for using empty intersection (and not set inequality) as the interpretation of the negative atomic formulae $s\# t$ is the same as for using "elementwise" equality as the interpretation of $\doteq$. Since we avoid set equality in the positive sense, the most natural negative form seems to be the one we have chosen. Under the chosen interpretation, $\doteq$ denotes *necessary* equality and # *necessary* inequality. For deterministic terms *t* and *s*, $s\# t$ is the same as $s\neq t$, i.e., deterministic negative atoms correspond exactly to equational (deterministic) conditions.

For nondeterministic terms the predicate # reflects our interest in *binding* such terms. According to the last definition variables may be assigned only single elements from the carrier |M| and so always denote individual values. This means that, for instance, the clause $s\# t$ is equivalent to $\{ x\# s, x\# t \}$. Considering x to be an individual and t a set, $x\# t$ may be seen as the more familiar $x\notin t$. Thus we may treat our notation as an abbreviation for more elaborate formulae with two negated membership relations and one new variable (not occurring in the rest of the clause).

4. Generated multimodels.

Consider a deterministic specification over signature Σ, and let *Str*(Σ) denote the class of Σ-structures, and W_Σ the word structure over signature Σ.

Definition 4.6. A$\in$Str(Σ) is *generated* iff the unique (interpretation) homomorphism $\mathcal{I}$: $W_\Sigma\rightarrow$A is surjective. □

It is convenient to use a more general notion of generatedness. For specifications with constructors, sufficient completeness corresponds to models being generated by the constructor operations. In the context of nondeterministic specifications we may want to say that a model is to be generated by the deterministic operations only. This motivates

Definition 4.7. Let $\mathcal{T}\subseteq W_\Sigma$. A$\in$Str($\Sigma$) is $\mathcal{T}$-*generated* iff the unique homomorphism $\mathcal{I}$: $W_\Sigma\rightarrow$A is surjective when restricted to $\mathcal{T}$, i.e., $\mathcal{I}[\mathcal{T}] = |A|$. □

In particular, "generated" will mean W_Σ-generated. We may allow $\mathcal{T}$ to comprise only terms of some (not all) sorts and speak about $\mathcal{T}$-generated structures meaning the structures where only the corresponding sorts are $\mathcal{T}$-generated.

The notion of generated structure does not generalize trivially to multistructures. As usual, there are several possibilities for extending the deterministic concepts to the nondeterministic context.

Since nondeterministic terms may be interpreted as sets of values rather than as individuals, the choices we are facing concern which of these values are to be considered as generated. The first definition comes from [17]:

Definition 4.8. A structure $M \in MStr(\Sigma)$ is *1-$\mathcal{T}$-generated* iff for every $\underline{m} \in |M|$ there exists a $t \in \mathcal{T}$: $\{\underline{m}\}=t^M$. □

According to this definition, every value in M must be denoted by some term t which, in addition, is interpreted in M deterministically even if $t \doteq t$ is not a consequence of SP.

The next definition is less restrictive in this respect:

Definition 4.9. $M \in MStr(\Sigma)$ is *2-$\mathcal{T}$-generated* iff there exists a multihomomorphism $\hbar$: $MW_\Sigma \to M$ which is surjective when restricted to $\mathcal{T}$. □

It implies that all elements of the carrier of M are denotable by some term – for every $\underline{m} \in |M|$ there exists a $t \in \mathcal{T}(\{t\} \in MW_\Sigma)$ such that $\hbar(t)=\underline{m}$. Here a nondeterministic term c can be used by the homomorphism $\hbar$ as a pre-image of some individual, even if its interpretation c^M may be a set of several values.

Both definitions focus on the elements of the structure and do not require that also all sets be denotable. The last definition, from [15], allows most freedom in the generated multistructures:

Definition 4.10. A structure $M \in MStr(\Sigma)$ is *3-$\mathcal{T}$-generated* iff for every $\underline{m} \in |M|$ there exists a $t \in \mathcal{T}$: $\underline{m} \in t^M$. □

Equality from the first definition has been replaced here by the membership relation. According to this definition a structure is generated if every element is a member of a set denoted by some term.

Definition 4.11. M is a *n-$\mathcal{T}$-generated multimodel* (for n=1,2,3), $M \in MMod_{n\text{-}\mathcal{T}}(SP)$, if it is a n-$\mathcal{T}$-generated multistructure and satisfies the axioms of the specification SP. □

The following example illustrates the relation between the three definitions:

Example 4.12

Let SP = (({S}, {a,c: →S}), { a≺c }):

	A1	A2	A3
a	$\{\underline{a}\}$	$\{\underline{a}\}$	$\{\underline{a}_1,\underline{a}_2,\ldots\}$
c	$\{\underline{a}\}$	$\{\underline{a},\underline{c}\}$	$\{\underline{a}_1,\underline{a}_2,\ldots,\underline{c}_1,\underline{c}_2,\ldots\}$

A1 is 1-, 2-, and 3-generated, A2 is 2- and 3-generated, and A3 is only 3-generated. A2 is not 1-generated because there is no term (among {a,c}) which can be interpreted deterministically as $\{\underline{c}\}$ (c cannot be such a term without violating the axiom). A3 is not 2-generated because there is no surjective homomorphism from {a,c} onto the elements of |A3|. □

1-generatedness is characterised by the non-existence of substructures: M is 1-generated (for $\mathcal{T}=W_\Sigma$) if and only if it has no proper submultistructure. This notion corresponds to the idea of deterministic constructors – only the values which can be reached by some deterministic operation are considered generated. It reflects the intuition that programs operate on some definite universe of values. 3-generatedness stands on the opposite side allowing constructors to be nondeterministic – anything such operations can return is taken to be generated. 3-generated models may be convenient when some axioms are given for nondeterministic terms without reference to any (intended or actual) deterministic basis. This concept corresponds to the non-existence of tight substructures: M is 3-generated if and only if it has no proper tight submultistructure. 2-generatedness may seem a bit strange but it too has a plausible interpretation. It restricts nondeterminism, but preserves the information about underspecified nondeterministic operations. The axiom $a \prec c$ indicates only that a must be a possible result of c. But nondeterminism of c is not exhausted by this information and so 2-generatedness allows the generated model A2 to have an additional element $\underline{c}$ representing the possibility of c returning something more than $\underline{a}$.

Obviously, 1-$\mathcal{T}$-generatedness is the smallest predicate and we have the trivial

Lemma 4.13. $\mathrm{MMod}_{1\text{-}\mathcal{T}}(\mathrm{SP}) \subseteq \mathrm{MMod}_{2\text{-}\mathcal{T}}(\mathrm{SP}) \subseteq \mathrm{MMod}_{3\text{-}\mathcal{T}}(\mathrm{SP})$. □

Which of the definitions one prefers may be a matter of taste, and we will not attempt to choose among them at this point. The choice will be suggested in section 7 on inductive reasoning. At the moment, we only observe that when $\mathcal{T} \subseteq \mathcal{D}_{\mathcal{SP}}$, they are all equivalent to the classical definition.

Definition 4.14. M∈MMod(SP) is *DET-generated* iff it is $\mathcal{T}$-generated, for some $\mathcal{T} \subseteq \mathcal{D}_{\mathcal{SP}}$. □

We have dropped the numbering of generatedness because all three definitions are equivalent for $\mathcal{T} \subseteq \mathcal{D}_{\mathcal{SP}}$.

Lemma 4.15. Let $\mathcal{T} \subseteq \mathcal{D}_{\mathcal{SP}}$. Then $\mathrm{MMod}_{1\text{-}\mathcal{T}}(\mathrm{SP}) = \mathrm{MMod}_{2\text{-}\mathcal{T}}(\mathrm{SP}) = \mathrm{MMod}_{3\text{-}\mathcal{T}}(\mathrm{SP})$. □

The difference between 1-$\mathcal{T}$-generated and DET-generated structures is that the former simply enforce the deterministic interpretation of (possibly nondeterministic) terms from $\mathcal{T}$ while the latter can only contain elements which are denoted by terms which have to be deterministic.

The DET-generated multialgebras have the important property that the homomorphisms from such structures are unique.

Example 4.16

Let SP contain only one operation c: →S. Any 1- or 2-generated multialgebra N1, N2 will have a 1-element S sort – $S^N = \{\underline{c}\}$. A 3-generated multialgebra N3 may have any number of elements in the sort S. Let N∈MStr(SP) interpret c nondeterministically, e.g. $c^N = \{\underline{c}_0, \underline{c}_1\}$. Obviously, there are two homomorphisms from the generated N1, N2 to N. Also, for any N3 there will be at least two homomorphisms to N.

Let SP1 contain, in addition, the operations a, b: →S, and the axioms

1. $a \prec c$ 2. $b \prec c$ 3. $a \doteq a$, 4. $b \doteq b$ 5. $a \# b$

and consider (1- and 2-)generated multimodels of SP1, M1 and M2, where

$S^{M1} = \{\underline{a}, \underline{b}\}$, $S^{M2} = \{\underline{a}, \underline{b}, \underline{c}\}$,
$c^{M1} = \{\underline{a}, \underline{b}\}$ $c^{M2} = \{\underline{a}, \underline{b}, \underline{c}\}$

Let N∈MMod(SP1). For M2 (and M3 with more than 2 elements of sort S), a homomorphism to N will not be unique. But if there is a homomorphism ϕ:M1→N then such a ϕ is unique since

$\phi(a^{M1}) = a^N$ $\phi(b^{M1}) = b^N$ $\phi(c^{M1}) = \phi(\{\underline{a}, \underline{b}\}) = \{\phi(a^{M1}), \phi(b^{M1})\} = \{a^N, b^N\} \subseteq c^N$

□

From the first part of this example we can see that 1-generatedness of N1 does not guarantee uniqueness of the homomorphisms from N1. Uniqueness of ϕ is a consequence not of M1 being 1-generated but of the fact that it is DET-generated.

Lemma 4.17. Let M,N$\in$MMod(SP) and let M be DET-generated. There exists at most one homomorphism ϕ: M$\rightarrow$N.

Proof idea:

Any homomorphism ϕ: M$\rightarrow$N must satisfy $\phi(t^M) \subseteq t^N$, which for deterministic t means identity. DET-generatedness of M implies then that the image of any homomorphism from M is uniquely determined by the image of the interpretations of the deterministic terms. □

5. Quasi-initial semantics.

The last lemma is important because it allows us to define quasi-initial semantics of nondeterministic specifications. Since we have allowed the use of disjunction in the specifications it should not be surprising that, in general, we do not have initial (multi)models. However, as shown for instance in [17, 18], even if we restrict the specifications to Horn formulae, or even to simple formulae, initial multimodels still need not exist.

Quasi-initial semantics assigns to a specification an initial covering of its model class. It is a natural generalization of initial semantics in that it effects a partition of the model class into components – each with an initial object which is the quasi initial object from the covering. It was used by several authors as the basis for the semantics of specifications using more expressive language than Horn formulae [20, 13, 32, 42].

The class MMod(SP) together with the multihomomorphisms is a pre-order, denoted (MMod(SP),$\rightarrow$), where N$\rightarrow$M iff there is a multihomomorphism from N to M.

Definition 5.18 (Minimal, Quasi-Initial). M$\in$MMod(SP) is

1. *minimal* in the pre-order (MMod(SP),$\rightarrow$) iff, for all N$\in$MMod(SP), N$\rightarrow$M implies M$\rightarrow$N,
2. *quasi-initial* iff it is minimal and for every N$\in$MMod(SP), there exists at most one homomorphism M$\rightarrow$N. □

Definition 5.19 (Covering).

1. A *covering* of a pre-order (MMod(SP),$\rightarrow$) is a subset **C**$\subseteq$MMod(SP) such that for each M$\in$MMod(SP) there is a C$\in$**C** with C$\rightarrow$M.
2. A covering is *minimal* if none of its proper subsets is a covering.
3. A covering **C** is *initial* iff it is minimal and contains only quasi-initial objects. □

The general result is

Theorem 5.20. If MMod(SP) is not empty then it has a minimal covering.

Proof idea:

Every non-empty chain in (MMod(SP),$\rightarrow$) has a lower bound. Zorn's lemma implies the conclusion. □

Unfortunately, we cannot ensure the existence of an initial covering in the general case. To obtain a sufficient condition for its existence we need an appropriate restriction on the form of the specifications. Lemma 4.17 indicates that if a minimal covering contains only DET-generated models then the covering is initial. To ensure the existence of DET-generated models we need

Definition 5.21. SP=(Σ,Π) is *DET-complete* iff for every $t\in W_\Sigma$ there exists an $s\in \mathcal{D}_{SP}$ such that $s\prec t$ is valid. □

The restriction to DET-complete specifications was introduced, for slightly different reasons, in [17]. DET-generated structures constitute the semantic counterpart of DET-completeness in the sense that only DET-complete specifications are guaranteed to possess DET-generated multimodels.

Lemma 5.22. Let SP be DET-complete. Every M∈MMod(SP) has a DET-generated subalgebra N, i.e., such that there is an injective homomorphism ι: N→M.

Proof idea:
For every $t\in W_\Sigma$ let $t^N = t^M \cap \mathcal{D}^M_{SP}$. DET-completeness of SP ensures that no such set is empty and the inclusion $|N| \subseteq |M|$ is the required homomorphism. □

Moreover, for DET-complete specifications, the DET-generated subalgebras of minimal models are exactly the quasi-initial models.

Lemma 5.23. Let SP be DET-complete, M∈MMod(SP) and N be DET-generated subalgebra of M. Then:

1. if M is quasi-initial then M is DET-generated,
2. if M is minimal then N is quasi-initial.

Proof idea:
1. Quasi-initiality of M forces the inclusion $|N| \subseteq |M|$ to be surjective.
2. Inclusion homomorphism $|N| \subseteq |M|$, minimality of M and lemma 4.17. □

Finally, for the DET-complete specifications we have:

Theorem 5.24. If SP is a DET-complete specification and MMod(SP)≠∅ then MMod(SP) has an initial covering.

Proof idea:
Take the DET-generated subalgebras of the elements of a minimal covering. □

6. The calculus for nondeterministic specifications.

In [36] we have introduced the calculus NEQ which is sound and complete with respect to the class MMod(SP). Its rules are given below:

R0: $\vdash C$ for any $C \in \Pi$

R1: a) $\vdash x\#y, x\doteq y$ b) $\vdash x\#t, x\prec t$ $x,y\in\mathcal{V}$

R2: $$\frac{\vdash C^x_t \quad ; \quad \vdash D, s\doteq t}{\vdash C^x_s, D}$$

R3: $$\frac{\vdash C^x_t \quad ; \quad \vdash D, s\prec t}{\vdash C^x_s, D}$$ x not in a right-hand side of $\prec$ in C

R4: $\dfrac{\vdash C, s \preceq t \quad ; \quad \vdash D, s \# t}{\vdash C, D}$ (CUT) ($\preceq$ being either $\doteq$ or $\prec$)

R5: $\dfrac{\vdash C}{\vdash C, e}$ (WEAK)

R6: $\dfrac{\vdash C, x \# t}{\vdash C^x_t}$ (ELIM) $x \in \mathcal{V} - \mathcal{V}[t]$, at most one x in C

C^x_t denotes C with t substituted for x. We will write $\Pi \vdash C$ to indicate that C is provable from Π with the calculus NEQ. Few comments regarding the rules may be in order.

R1 expresses the relation between # and equality and inclusion. Since variables x and y are individuals, the two rules correspond to, respectively, $x \neq y \vee x = y$, and $x \notin t \vee x \in t$. They also capture the fact that '$\doteq$' is a partial equivalence relation and is reflexive only for variables (see PER below).

R2 is a paramodulation rule allowing replacement of deterministic terms (in the case when $s \doteq t$ holds in the second assumption). In particular, it allows derivation of the standard substitution rule when the substituted terms are deterministic, and prevents substitution of nondeterministic terms for variables.

R3 allows "specialization" of a clause by substituting for a term t another term s which is included in t. The restriction that the occurrences of t which are substituted for don't occur in the right-hand side of $\prec$ in C is needed to prevent, for instance, the unsound conclusion $\vdash p \prec s$ from the premises $\vdash p \prec t$ and $\vdash s \prec t$.

$s \# t$ implies both negation of $s \doteq t$ and of $s \prec t$. R4 allows us to resolve these complementary atoms.

R6 eliminates redundant bindings, namely those that bind an application of a term occurring at most once in the rest of the clause.

The following derived rules illustrate some consequences of NEQ.

PER: $\vdash x \doteq x$ variables are guaranteed to be deterministic

NE: $\dfrac{\vdash x \# t}{\vdash \emptyset}$ R6 terms are interpreted as non-empty sets

SUB: $\dfrac{\vdash C \quad ; \quad \vdash t \doteq t}{\vdash C^x_t}$ variables can be substituted by deterministic terms

The counterpart of soundness/completeness of the equational calculus is the following:

Theorem 6.25. NEQ is sound and complete wrt. MMod(SP):

$$\text{MMod(SP)} \models C \text{ iff } \Pi \vdash C. \qquad \square$$

The proof of this theorem is a rather involved Henkin-style argument which we cannot even sketch here (see [34]). In the next section we consider extension of NEQ with an induction principle.

7. The nondeterministic ω-rule.

Let SP=(Σ,Π) be a deterministic specification, C be a formula in the associated specification language $\mathcal{K}$ with a free variable x of sort S. Let $\mathcal{T}\subseteq W_\Sigma$ and $\mathrm{Mod}_{\mathcal{T}}(\mathrm{SP})$ be the class of $\mathcal{T}$-generated models of SP. The *ω-rule* is a semi-formal proof rule [e.g., 40, 41]: [2]

$$\frac{\Pi \vdash C^x_t \qquad \forall t\in\mathcal{T}}{\Pi \vdash C} \tag{IP}$$

Then, for instance for the equational specification language $\mathcal{K}$, one can prove the metatheorem

$$\mathrm{Mod}_{\mathcal{T}}(\mathrm{SP}) \models C \text{ iff } \Pi\vdash C^x_t \text{ for all } t\in\mathcal{T} \qquad \text{(IP-completness)}$$

The *inductive proof schema* specifies, in addition, the strategy for proving the premise of IP by means of some enumeration of all terms in $\mathcal{T}$. For example, if $\mathcal{T}$ can be built from a set of constants C of sort S, and operations $F=\{f_1,\ldots,f_n: S\to S\}$ then the induction schema will be

$$\frac{\begin{array}{ll}\Pi\vdash C^x_c & \forall c\in C\\ \Pi\vdash C \Rightarrow \Pi\vdash C^x_{f(x)} & \forall f\in F\end{array}}{\Pi \vdash C} \tag{IS}$$

Obviously, soundness of IP implies soundness of IS but, in general, IS is not complete [27]. We will focus on the ω-rule – a particular induction schema must be constructed depending on the chosen set $\mathcal{T}$.

We first consider the question of which among the notions of generatedness we have introduced constitute a natural semantic counterpart of the possible nondeterministic induction. DET-generated models are certainly of special interest and we will consider them at the end of this section. 1- and 2-$\mathcal{T}$-generated models turn out to be ill-suited for the purpose. At least two reasons for this are that:

1. they are not guaranteed to exist, and inconsistency may be unprovable with the induction principle, and
2. even if they do exist, additional semantic and syntactic assumptions are needed in order to make the natural induction principle sound.

We elaborate on these two points with respect to 1-$\mathcal{T}$-generated models. The case of 2-$\mathcal{T}$-generated models is similar and merely involves even further complications.

Example 7.26

Let SP contain three constants $a, b, c\colon \to$ S, and the following three axioms:

Π: $\{ a\prec c \;;\; b\prec c \;;\; a\#b \}$

SP does not have a 1-$\{a,c\}$-generated model because in such a model both a and c must be interpreted deterministically, and then, due to the third axiom, $\underline{b}$ cannot be contained in the set $\{\underline{c}\}=\{\underline{a}\}$. □

1-$\{a,c\}$-generatedness is inconsistent with SP because it forces the elements a, c to be interpreted as deterministic operations while SP requires c to be nondeterministic. It might seem that we could prove inconsistency by adding the determinacy axiom for every term $t\in\mathcal{T}$. But this would lead to unsound reasoning because not *all* interpretations of the $\mathcal{T}$-terms have to be deterministic in a 1-$\mathcal{T}$-generated multimodel.

---

[2] We formulate the principle, as well as the theorems, for one variable x. The general formulations are obtained trivially by replacing the occurrences of single x and t by the tuples $x_1,\ldots,x_n$ and $t_1,\ldots,t_n$.

Example 7.27

Let SP1 contain three constants $a, b, c : \rightarrow S$, and no axioms. There are several 1-$\{a,b,c\}$-generated models of SP1:

	A1	A2	A3	A4	A5
a	$\{\underline{a}\}$	$\{\underline{a}\}$	$\{\underline{a}\}$	$\{\underline{b},\underline{c}\}$	$\{\bullet\}$
b	$\{\underline{b}\}$	$\{\underline{b}\}$	$\{\underline{a},\underline{c}\}$	$\{\underline{b}\}$	$\{\bullet\}$
c	$\{\underline{c}\}$	$\{\underline{a},\underline{b}\}$	$\{\underline{c}\}$	$\{\underline{c}\}$	$\{\bullet\}$

The suggested determinacy axioms, $a \doteq a$, $b \doteq b$, $c \doteq c$ hold only for A1 and A5.
□

Thus, on the one hand we need the additional determinacy axioms and, on the other hand, they are too strong for the whole class of 1-$\mathcal{T}$-generated models. To remove this contradiction several additional restrictions on the form of specifications as well as the model class are needed. Hußmann, who in [17] uses 1-generated models, introduced for a limited version of the language $\mathcal{L}$ restrictions to DET-complete, DET-additive specifications and *maximally deterministic* models (in the last example only A1 and A5 would be maximally deterministic) which allow only a reduced version of the induction principle.

We therefore turn to 3-$\mathcal{T}$-generated models as being more promising. For every M in the class $\text{MMod}_{3\text{-}\mathcal{T}}(\text{SP})$ of 3-$\mathcal{T}$-generated models, all elements are in the result set of some term $t \in \mathcal{T}$. However, we cannot base our induction on the assumption that C^x_t is provable for all $t \in \mathcal{T}$ since for nondeterministic t such a substitution does not correspond to the validity of the clause C for all elements of a generated domain. The correct formulation of the ω-rule is the following:

$$\text{If } \Pi \vdash \{x \# t, C\} \text{ for all } t \in \mathcal{T} \text{ then } \Pi \vdash C \qquad \text{(NIP)}$$

Let NIP denote the calculus NEQ+NIP. Our main result is

Theorem 7.28. Let C be an $\mathcal{L}(\text{SP})$ clause:

$$\text{SP} \vdash_{\text{NIP}} C \text{ iff } \text{MMod}_{3\text{-}\mathcal{T}}(\text{SP}) \models C \qquad \square$$

Soundness is an easy consequence of soundness of NEQ, the proof of completeness is a more elaborate application of the omitting type theorem from [5].

As a trivial consequence of lemma 4.15, the induction principle NIP can be used for the DET-generated models. In this case $\mathcal{T} \subseteq \mathcal{D}_{\text{SP}}$, so NIP reduces to IP, because binding a deterministic term t to x in a clause C is equivalent to the substitution C^x_t:

Lemma 7.29. Suppose that $\Pi \vdash t \doteq t$. Then:

$$\Pi \vdash C^x_t \text{ iff } \Pi \vdash \{x \# t, C\} \qquad \square$$

8. Conclusion.

We have defined four notions of generated multistructures for nondeterministic specifications. Three of them admit generated structures with respect to arbitrary terms, and the fourth – DET-generatedness – models generated by the deterministic terms only. We have shown that in the case of DET-generatedness all definitions are equivalent, and hence, correspond also to the classical definition of the generated structures.

We have also given the sufficient condition of DET-completeness for the existence of quasi-initial semantics for nondeterministic specifications and shown that quasi-initial models are DET-generated.

We have presented two calculi for reasoning about nondetermism. NEQ is sound and complete with respect to all multimodels of a nondeterministic specification. Furthermore, when all terms are deterministic, it is a generalization of the equational calculus to conditional disjunctive equations. NIP is NEQ extended with the induction principle. We have stated soundness and completeness of NIP with respect to the class of 3-generated multimodels, as well as the equivalence of the principle with the classical induction in the case when the generating terms are deterministic.

Thus we have generalized the results on induction in the deterministic specifications to the case of nondeterminism. This extension is non-intrusive in the sense that, whenever an $\mathcal{L}$-specification happens to be deterministic, the results and constructions provided by the classical theory coincide with those introduced in this paper.

Acknowledgment.

We thank an anonymous referee for useful suggestions, in particular, for drawing our attention to the equivalence of the definitions 4.8 and 4.10 to the respective notions of submultistructures.

REFERENCES

[1] Bergstra, J.A., Klop, J.W., "Algebra of communicating processes," *Proc. of CWI Symposium on Mathematics and CS*, 89 - 138, Oct. 6-7 1986.

[2] Broy, M., Gnatz, R., Wirsing, M., "Semantics of Nondeterministic and Noncontinuous Constructs," LNCS, vol. 69, Springer, 1980, pp. 553 - 392.

[3] Broy, M., Wirsing, M., "On the Algebraic Specification of Nondeterministic Programming Languages," in *CAAP'81*, LNCS, vol. 112, Springer, 1981, pp. 162 - 179.

[4] Broy, M., "On the Herbrand Kleene universe for nondeterministic computations," in *Proc. MFCS'84*, LNCS, vol. 176, Springer, 1984.

[5] Chang, C.C., Keisler, H.J., *Model Theory*, Amsterdam, North-Holand, 1977.

[6] Clinger, W., "Nondeterministic call by need is neither lazy nor by name," *Proc. ACM Symp. LISP and Functional Programming*, 226-234, 1982.

[7] Ehrig, H., Mahr, B., *Fundamentals of Algebraic Specification*, vol. 1, Springer, 1985.

[8] Engelfriet, J., Schmidt, E.M., "IO and OI. 1," *Journal of Computer and System Sciences*, vol. 15, 328-353, 1977.

[9] Engelfriet, J., Schmidt, E.M., "IO and OI. 2," *Journal of Computer and System Sciences*, vol. 16, 67-99, 1978.

[10] Goguen, J.A., Meseguer, J., "Completeness of Many-Sorted Equational Logic," *SIGPLAN Notices*, vol. 16, no. 7, 1981.

[11] Goguen, J.A., Meseguer, J., "Universal realization, persistent interconnection and implementation of abstract modules," in *Proc., 9th Int. Coll. on Automata, Languages and Programming*, LNCS, vol. 140, Springer, 1982.

[12] Goguen, J.A., Meseguer, J., "Remarks on Remarks on Many-Sorted Equational Logic," *SIGPLAN Notices*, vol. 22, no. 4, 41-48, April 1987.

[13] Goguen, J.A., *What is unification? A categorical view of substitution, equation, and solution*, Tech. Rep. CSLI-88-124, Center for Study of Languages and Information, 1988.

[14] Hennessy, M.C.B., "The semantics of call-by-value and call-by-name in a nondeterministic environment," *SIAM J. Comput.*, vol. 9, no. 1, 1980.

[15] Hesselink, W.H., "A Mathematical Approach to Nondeterminism in Data Types," *ACM Transactions on Programming Languages and Systems*, vol. 10, 1988.

[16] Hoare, C.A.R., *Communicating Sequential Processes*, Prentice-Hall International Ltd., 1985.

[17] Hußmann, H., *Nondeterministic Algebraic Specifications*, Ph.D. thesis, Fakultät für Mathematik und Informatik, Universität Passau, 1990.

[18] Hußmann, H., *Nondeterminism in Algebraic Specifications and Algebraic Programs*, Birkhäuser, 1993.

[19] Huet, G., Oppen, D., "Equations and Rewrite Rules: A Survey," in *Formal Language Theory: Perspectives and Open Problems*, Academic Press, 1980.

[20] Kaplan, S., "Conditional Rewriting," in *Conditional Term Rewriting Systems*, LNCS, vol. 308, Springer, 1987.

[21] Kaplan, S., "Rewriting with a Nondeterministic Choice Operator," *Theoretical Computer Science*, vol. 56, 37-57, 1988.

[22] Kapur, D., *Towards a theory of abstract data types*, Ph.D. thesis, Laboratory for CS, MIT, 1980.

[23] Milner, R., *Calculi for Communicating Systems*, LNCS vol 92, Springer, 1980.

[24] Mosses, P.D., "Unified Algebras and Institutions," in *Proc. of LICS'89, Fourth Annual Symposium on Logic in Computer Science*, 1989.

[25] Nipkow, T., "Non-deterministic Data Types: Models and Implementations," *Acta Informatica*, vol. 22, 629 - 661, 1986.

[26] Nipkow, T., "Observing nondeterministic data types," in *Recent Trends in Data Type Specification*, LNCS, vol. 332, Springer, 1987.

[27] Nourani, F., "On induction for program logic: Syntax, semantics, and inductive closure," *EATCS Bulletin*, vol. 13, 1981.

[28] Plotkin, G., "A power domain construction," *SIAM Jour. Comp.*, vol. 5, no. 3, 452 - 487, 1976.

[29] Plotkin, G., Apt, K.R., "Countable Nondeterminism and Random Assignment," *Tech. Rep. University of Edinburgh*, 1982.

[30] Søndergaard, H., Sestoft, P., *Non-Determinacy and Its Semantics*, Tech. Rep. 86/12, Datalogisk Institut, Københavns Universitet, January 1987.

[31] Smyth, M.B., "Power domains," *J. of Computer and System Sciences*, vol. 16, 1978.

[32] Volger, H., "The semantics of disjunctive deductive databases," in *CSL'89*, LNCS, vol. 440, Springer, 1989.

[33] Walicki, M.A., Meldal, S., "Singular and plural nondeterministic parameters," *SIAM Journ. of Computing (submitted)*, .

[34] Walicki, M.A., Meldal, S., "A complete calculus for the multialgebraic and functional semantics of nondeterminism," *ACM Transactions on Programming Languages and Systems (submitted)*, .

[35] Walicki, M., Meldal, S., "Sets and Nondeterminism," in *Proc. of the Workshop on Logic Programming with Sets: ICLP'93*, 1993.

[36] Walicki, M., *Algebraic Specifications of Nondeterminism*, Ph.D. thesis, University of Bergen, Department of Informatics, 1993.

[37] Walicki, M., Meldal, S., "Initiality + Nondeterminism Implies Junk," in *Proc. of NIK'93*, Haveraaen, M., Tapir, November 1993, pp. 129-138.

[38] Walicki, M., Meldal, S., "Multialgebras, Power Algebras and Complete Calculi of Identities and Inclusions," to be publsihed in *Recent Trends in Data Type Specifications*, LNCS 1995.

[39] Winskel, G., "An introduction to event structures," LNCS, vol. 354, Springer, 1988.

[40] Wirsing, M., *Algebraic Specification*, Tech. Rep. MIP-8914, Universität Passau, 1989.

[41] Wirsing, M., "Algebraic Specification," in *Handbook of Theoretical Computer Science*, vol. B, The MIT Press, 1990.

[42] Wolter, U., Löwe, M., "Beyond Conditional Equations," in *CAAP'92*, LNCS, vol. 581, Springer, 1992.

CPO Models for a Class of GSOS Languages

Luca Aceto ⋆ Anna Ingólfsdóttir ⋆⋆

BRICS⋆⋆⋆
Department of Mathematics and Computer Science
Aalborg University
Fredrik Bajersvej 7E
9220 Aalborg Ø, Denmark
Email: {luca,annai}@iesd.auc.dk

Abstract. In this paper, we present a general way of giving denotational semantics to a class of languages equipped with an operational semantics that fits the GSOS format of Bloom, Istrail and Meyer. The canonical model used for this purpose will be Abramsky's domain of synchronization trees, and the denotational semantics automatically generated by our methods will be guaranteed to be fully abstract with respect to the finitely observable part of the bisimulation preorder. In the process of establishing the full abstraction result, we also obtain several general results on the bisimulation preorder (including a complete axiomatization for it), and give a novel operational interpretation of GSOS languages.

1 Introduction

In this paper, we present a general way of giving denotational semantics to a class of languages equipped with an operational semantics that fits the GSOS format of Bloom, Istrail and Meyer [6]. The canonical model used for this purpose will be Abramsky's domain of synchronization trees $\mathcal{D}$ presented in [1], and the denotational semantics automatically generated by our methods will be guaranteed to be fully abstract with respect to the finitely observable part of the bisimulation preorder studied in, e.g., [9, 11]. Moreover, in the process of establishing the full abstraction result, we also give an algorithm, along the lines of those given in [2], to generate a complete axiomatization of the bisimulation preorder. As a byproduct of our denotational semantics, we shall be able to establish very general results about the bisimulation preorder that would be hard to prove using purely operational definitions. (For an example, cf. Thm 20.)

The class of GSOS systems we shall give denotational semantics to will have the structure of most standard process algebras (see, e.g., [12, 5]). They will consist of a set of operations to construct finite, acyclic process graphs, and a facility for the recursive definition of behaviours. Borrowing a terminology introduced in [10] in

⋆ On leave from School of Cognitive and Computing Sciences, University of Sussex, Brighton BN1 9QH, UK. Partially supported by HCM project EXPRESS.

⋆⋆ Partially supported by a grant from the Danish Research Council.

⋆⋆⋆ Basic Research in Computer Science, Centre of the Danish National Research Foundation.

the context of denotational semantics, we shall refer to these languages as *compact* GSOS languages. Their operational semantics will be given in terms of a variation on the standard model of labelled transition systems that takes divergence information into account. This will be done in such a way that the bisimulation preorder is a precongruence with respect to all the operators in the language. In order to obtain this substitutivity result, special care must be taken in interpreting negative premises in GSOS rules; in particular, negative premises will only be interpreted over convergent (or fully specified) processes. Intuitively, this is because, in order to find out what a process can*not* do, we need to know precisely what its capabilities are, and the initial behaviour of a divergent process is only partially specified. A consequence of our choice is that, for example, the rule

$$\frac{x \stackrel{a}{\not\rightarrow}}{odd(x) \stackrel{a}{\rightarrow} odd(x)} \tag{1}$$

cannot be used to derive that $odd(\Omega)$ has an a-labelled transition to itself, where Ω denote the typical totally divergent process with no transitions. Our first main result is that, with our choice of operational semantics for GSOS languages, the bisimulation preorder is substitutive with respect to all language contexts. Moreover, as a consequence of general results established by Abramsky in [1], we are able to give a characterization of the finitely observable (or finitary) part of the bisimulation preorder for every GSOS language. Intuitively, this is the preorder obtained by restricting the bisimulation preorder to observations of finite depth.

We then show how to automatically give a denotational semantics for a GSOS language in terms of Abramsky's domain of synchronization trees $\mathcal{D}$. To this end, it is sufficient to endow Abramsky's model with an appropriate continuous algebra structure in the sense of [8]. This we do by showing how the GSOS rules defining the operational semantics of an operation symbol f of a compact GSOS language can be used to define a continuous function $\mathbf{f}_{\mathcal{D}}$ of the appropriate arity over the domain of synchronization trees $\mathcal{D}$. In defining the semantic counterparts of the operations in a compact GSOS language, we shall rely on a description of the domain $\mathcal{D}$ presented in [10], where it is shown how to reconstruct $\mathcal{D}$ from a suitable preorder over finite synchronization trees. This view of $\mathcal{D}$ will allow us to define each semantic operation $\mathbf{f}_{\mathcal{D}}$ in stepwise fashion from monotonic operations over finite synchronization trees. We hope that this choice will make the presentation more accessible to readers who are unfamiliar with domain theory [13].

As a result of our general framework, we shall then show that the denotational semantics so obtained is guaranteed to be in complete agreement with the chosen behavioural semantics. More precisely, for every compact GSOS language, the denotational semantics produced by the general approach presented in this paper is always fully abstract with respect to the finitary part of the bisimulation preorder.

Due to strict space limitations, this paper contains no proofs, very few technical details, no comparison with related work and no concluding remarks. These may be found in the full version of this paper [3].

2 Preliminaries

We begin by reviewing the basic notions on transition systems and domain theory that will be needed in this study.

2.1 Labelled Transition Systems with Divergence

The operational semantics of the languages considered in this paper will be given in terms of a variation on the model of labelled transition systems that takes divergence information into account. We refer the interested readers to, e.g., [7, 11, 15] for motivation and more information on (variations on) this semantic model for reactive systems.

Definition 1. A *labelled transition system with divergence (lts)* is a quadruple

$$(\mathsf{P}, \mathsf{Lab}, \rightarrow, \uparrow)$$

where: P is a set of *processes*, ranged over by s, t; Lab is a set of *labels*, ranged over by ℓ; $\rightarrow \subseteq \mathsf{P} \times \mathsf{Lab} \times \mathsf{P}$ is a *transition relation*; $\uparrow \subseteq \mathsf{P}$ is a *divergence predicate*, notation $s \uparrow$. As usual, we shall write $s \xrightarrow{\ell} t$ in lieu of $(s, \ell, t) \in \rightarrow$.

We write $s \downarrow$, read "s definitely converges", iff it is not the case that $s \uparrow$. A useful source of examples for labelled transition systems with divergence is the set of finite synchronization trees over a set of labels Lab, denoted by $\mathsf{ST}(\mathsf{Lab})$. These are the sets generated by the following inductive definition:

$$\frac{\{\ell_i \in \mathsf{Lab}, t_i \in \mathsf{ST}(\mathsf{Lab})\}_{i \in I}}{\{\langle \ell_i, t_i \rangle \mid i \in I\}[\cup \{\bot\}] \in \mathsf{ST}(\mathsf{Lab})}$$

where I is a finite index set, and the notation $[\cup\{\bot\}]$ means optional inclusion of $\bot$. The set of finite synchronization trees $\mathsf{ST}(\mathsf{Lab})$ can be turned into a labelled transition system with divergence by stipulating that, for $t \in \mathsf{ST}(\mathsf{Lab})$: $t \uparrow$ iff $\bot$ is in t, and $t \xrightarrow{\ell_i} t_i$ iff $\langle \ell_i, t_i \rangle$ is in t. The behavioural relation over processes that we shall study in this paper is that of *prebisimulation* [11, 7, 15] (also known as *partial bisimulation* [1]).

Definition 2. Let $(\mathsf{P}, \mathsf{Lab}, \rightarrow, \uparrow)$ be an lts. Let $\mathsf{Rel}(\mathsf{P})$ denote the set of binary relations over P. Define the functional $F : \mathsf{Rel}(\mathsf{P}) \rightarrow \mathsf{Rel}(\mathsf{P})$ by:

$$\begin{aligned} F(\mathcal{R}) = \{(s,t) \mid \forall \ell \in \mathsf{Lab} \\ &\bullet\ s \xrightarrow{\ell} s' \Rightarrow \exists t' :\ t \xrightarrow{\ell} t' \text{ and } s' \mathrel{\mathcal{R}} t' \\ &\bullet\ s \downarrow \Rightarrow t \downarrow \text{ and } [t \xrightarrow{\ell} t' \Rightarrow \exists s' :\ s \xrightarrow{\ell} s' \text{ and } s' \mathrel{\mathcal{R}} t']\} \end{aligned}$$

A relation $\mathcal{R}$ is a prebisimulation iff $\mathcal{R} \subseteq F(\mathcal{R})$. We write $s_1 \lesssim s_2$ iff there exists a prebisimulation $\mathcal{R}$ such that $s_1 \mathrel{\mathcal{R}} s_2$.

The relation $\lesssim$ is a preorder over P based on a variation on bisimulation equivalence [12]. Its kernel will be denoted by $\sim$, i.e., $\sim = \lesssim \cap \lesssim^{-1}$. In this study, we shall be interested in relating the notion of prebisimulation to a denotationally defined preorder on processes. As the preorders induced by a denotational semantics are completely determined by how they act on *finite processes*, we shall be interested in comparing them with the "finitely observable", or *finitary*, part of the bisimulation preorder in the sense of, e.g., [7]. The following definition is from [1].

Definition 3. The *finitary preorder* $\lesssim^F$ is defined on any lts by

$$s \lesssim^F s' \Leftrightarrow \forall t \in \mathsf{ST}(\mathsf{Lab}).\ t \lesssim s \Rightarrow t \lesssim s' .$$

An alternative method for using the functional F to obtain a behavioural preorder is to apply it inductively as in [1, Page 165]. The ω-iterate of this inductive construction will be denoted by $\lesssim_\omega$. The preorders $\lesssim$, $\lesssim_\omega$ and $\lesssim^F$ are related thus: $\lesssim \subseteq \lesssim_\omega \subseteq \lesssim^F$. Moreover the inclusions are, in general, strict. The interested reader is referred to [1] for more information on these preorders.

2.2 A Domain Equation for Synchronization Trees

In this section we recall Abramsky's domain equation for synchronization trees, and introduce the background in domain theory that is necessary to understand the paper. The interested reader is referred to, e.g., [13] for more general information on the theory of domains.

The canonical domain we shall use to give a denotational semantics to a class of GSOS languages is the domain of synchronization trees over a countable set of labels Lab considered by Abramsky in his seminal paper [1]. This is defined to be the initial solution $\mathcal{D}(\mathsf{Lab})$ of the domain equation

$$\mathcal{D}(\mathsf{Lab}) \cong (\mathbf{1})_\perp \oplus P[\sum_{\ell \in \mathsf{Lab}} \mathcal{D}(\mathsf{Lab})] \tag{2}$$

where $\mathbf{1}$ is the one point domain, $(\cdot)_\perp$ is lifting, $\oplus$ is coalesced sum, $\sum$ is separated sum, and $P[D]$ denotes the Plotkin powerdomain of D (cf. [13] for details on these domain-theoretic operations). We henceforth omit the parameter Lab as it will always be clear from the context.

To streamline the presentation and make our results more accessible to uninitiated readers, in this study we shall abstract completely from the domain-theoretic description of $\mathcal{D}$ given by (2). Our description of the domain of synchronization trees $\mathcal{D}$ will follow the one given in [10], and we shall rely on results presented in that reference that show how to construct $\mathcal{D}$ starting from a suitable preorder on the set of finite synchronization trees $\mathsf{ST}(\mathsf{Lab})$. Our reconstruction of $\mathcal{D}$ will be given in three steps: First of all, we shall define a preorder $\sqsubseteq$ on the set of synchronization trees $\mathsf{ST}(\mathsf{Lab})$. This preorder will be a reformulation of the Egli-Milner preorder over $\mathsf{ST}(\mathsf{Lab})$ presented in [10]. Secondly, we shall relate the poset of compact elements of $\mathcal{D}$ to the poset of equivalence classes induced by $(\mathsf{ST}(\mathsf{Lab}), \sqsubseteq)$. Finally, we shall use the fact that $\mathcal{D}$ is the ideal completion of its poset of compact elements to relate it to $(\mathsf{ST}(\mathsf{Lab}), \sqsubseteq)$. This approach will allow us to factor the definition of the continuous algebra structure [8] on $\mathcal{D}$ given in Sect. 4 in three similar steps, hopefully making it simpler to understand.

Definition 4. We define $\sqsubseteq$ as the least binary relation over $\mathsf{ST}(\mathsf{Lab})$ satisfying:

$$\begin{aligned} t \sqsubseteq u \text{ if } & (1)\ \langle \ell, t' \rangle \in t \Rightarrow \exists \langle \ell, u' \rangle \in u :\ t' \sqsubseteq u' \text{ and} \\ & (2)\ \bot \in u \Rightarrow \bot \in t \text{ and} \\ & (3)\ \langle \ell, u' \rangle \in u \Rightarrow (\bot \in t \text{ or } \exists \langle \ell, t' \rangle \in t :\ t' \sqsubseteq u') \end{aligned}$$

The relation $\sqsubseteq$ so defined is easily seen to be a preorder over $\mathsf{ST}(\mathsf{Lab})$, whose kernel will be denoted by $\simeq$. We can now relate the preorder of synchronization trees $(\mathsf{ST}(\mathsf{Lab}), \sqsubseteq)$ with the poset of compact elements of $\mathcal{D}$ in a way that will allow us to define, in a canonical way, continuous operations on $\mathcal{D}$ from monotonic ones on $(\mathsf{ST}(\mathsf{Lab}), \sqsubseteq)$. First of all, we recall here that $\mathcal{D}$ is, up to isomorphism, the algebraic complete partial order (cpo) whose poset of compact elements $(\mathcal{K}(\mathcal{D}), \sqsubseteq_{\mathcal{K}(\mathcal{D})})$ is defined in [1, Def. 3.9]. $\mathcal{K}(\mathcal{D})$ is a subset of the set of finite synchronization trees, and the relations $\sqsubseteq$ and $\sqsubseteq_{\mathcal{K}(\mathcal{D})}$ may be shown to coincide over it. As a consequence of this observation, from now on we shall always use $\sqsubseteq$ as our notion of preorder on $\mathcal{K}(\mathcal{D})$.

For a synchronization tree $t = \{\langle \ell_i, t_i \rangle \mid 1 \le i \le n\}[\cup\{\bot\}]$, its recursive convex-closure t^c is inductively defined as follows:

$$t^c \triangleq \mathsf{Con}(\{\langle \ell_i, t_i^c \rangle \mid 1 \le i \le n\}[\cup\{\bot\}]) \tag{3}$$

where Con denotes the convex-closure operation given in [1, Def. 3.2]. It is not difficult to see that, for every $t \in \mathsf{ST}(\mathsf{Lab})$, t^c is a compact element of $\mathcal{D}$. Moreover, the function $(\cdot)^c : (\mathsf{ST}(\mathsf{Lab}), \sqsubseteq) \to (\mathcal{K}(\mathcal{D}), \sqsubseteq)$ is monotonic and maps trees that are related by $\simeq$ to the same compact element of $\mathcal{D}$.

Assume now that $\mathbf{f}_{\mathsf{ST}} : (\mathsf{ST}(\mathsf{Lab}), \sqsubseteq)^l \to (\mathsf{ST}(\mathsf{Lab}), \sqsubseteq)$ is a monotonic function. Using the fact that each element of $\mathcal{K}(\mathcal{D})$ is a synchronization tree, we may naturally use $\mathbf{f}_{\mathsf{ST}}$ to define a function $\mathbf{f}_{\mathcal{K}(\mathcal{D})} : (\mathcal{K}(\mathcal{D}), \sqsubseteq)^l \to (\mathcal{K}(\mathcal{D}), \sqsubseteq)$ as follows:

$$\mathbf{f}_{\mathcal{K}(\mathcal{D})}(\mathbf{d}) \triangleq (\mathbf{f}_{\mathsf{ST}}(\mathbf{d}))^c \ . \tag{4}$$

It is easy to see that the function so defined is guaranteed to be monotonic. This implies that we can use (4) to lift any Σ-preorder structure [10] on $(\mathsf{ST}(\mathsf{Lab}), \sqsubseteq)$ to a Σ-poset structure on $(\mathcal{K}(\mathcal{D}), \sqsubseteq)$ in the sense of [8]. In Sect. 4.2 we shall take advantage of this fact. Finally, from the theory of powerdomains [13], we know that the domain of synchronization trees $\mathcal{D}$ is, up to isomorphism, the ideal completion of the poset of compact elements $\mathcal{K}(\mathcal{D})$. As a result of this observation, we can extend any monotonic function $\mathbf{f}_{\mathcal{K}(\mathcal{D})} : (\mathcal{K}(\mathcal{D}), \sqsubseteq)^l \to (\mathcal{K}(\mathcal{D}), \sqsubseteq)$ to a continuous function $\mathbf{f}_{\mathcal{D}} : (\mathcal{D}, \sqsubseteq_{\mathcal{D}})^l \to (\mathcal{D}, \sqsubseteq_{\mathcal{D}})$ by:

$$\mathbf{f}_{\mathcal{D}}(\mathbf{k}) \triangleq \bigsqcup \{\mathbf{f}_{\mathcal{K}(\mathcal{D})}(\mathbf{d}) \mid \mathbf{d} \in \mathcal{K}(\mathcal{D})^l \text{ and } \mathbf{d} \sqsubseteq_{\mathcal{D}} \mathbf{k}\} \ . \tag{5}$$

The interested reader is invited to consult, e.g., [8, Sect. 3.3] for a discussion of the properties afforded by this canonical extension. In what follows, all we shall need to know is that $\mathbf{f}_{\mathcal{D}}$ is guaranteed to be continuous. Thus (5) can be used to conservatively extend any Σ-po algebra structure on $(\mathcal{K}(\mathcal{D}), \sqsubseteq)$ to a continuous algebra structure on $\mathcal{D}$.

3 GSOS Languages

Let Var be a denumerable set of *meta-variables* ranged over by x, y. A *signature* Σ consists of a set of *operation symbols*, disjoint from Var, together with a function *arity* that assigns a natural number to each operation symbol. Throughout this paper, following the standard lines of algebraic semantics (see, e.g., [8]), we shall assume that signatures contain a distinguished function symbol Ω of arity zero to denote the totally unspecified, or divergent, process, i.e., a process about whose behaviour we have no information. The set $\mathbb{T}(\Sigma, \mathsf{Var})$ of *terms* over Σ and Var (abbreviated to $\mathbb{T}(\Sigma)$ when the set of variables is clear from the context or immaterial) is defined as usual. We shall use $P, Q, \ldots$ to range over terms and the symbol $\equiv$ for the relation of syntactic equality on terms. $\mathrm{T}(\Sigma)$ is the set of *closed* terms over Σ, i.e., terms that do not contain variables. Constants, i.e. terms of the form $f()$, will be abbreviated as f. A Σ*-context* $C[\mathbf{x}]$ is a term in which at most the variables $\mathbf{x}$ appear. $C[\mathbf{P}]$ is $C[\mathbf{x}]$ with x_i replaced by P_i wherever it occurs. Besides terms we have *actions*, elements of some given finite set Act, which is ranged over by a, b, c.

Definition 5. Suppose Σ is a signature. A *GSOS rule* ρ over Σ is an inference rule of the form:

$$\frac{\bigcup_{i=1}^{l}\left\{x_i \stackrel{a_{ij}}{\rightarrow} y_{ij} | 1 \leq j \leq m_i\right\} \;\cup\; \bigcup_{i=1}^{l}\left\{x_i \stackrel{b_{ik}}{\nrightarrow} | 1 \leq k \leq n_i\right\}}{f(x_1, \ldots, x_l) \stackrel{c}{\rightarrow} C[\mathbf{x}, \mathbf{y}]} \qquad (6)$$

where all the variables are distinct, $m_i, n_i \geq 0$, f is an operation symbol from Σ with arity l, $C[\mathbf{x}, \mathbf{y}]$ is a Σ-context, and the a_{ij}, b_{ik}, and c are actions in Act.

The operation symbol f in rules of the form (6) will be referred to as the *principal operation* of the rule. If, for some i, $m_i > 0$ then we say that ρ *tests its* i*-th argument positively.* Similarly if $n_i > 0$ then we say that ρ *tests its* i*-th argument negatively.* An operation f *tests its* i*-th argument positively (resp. negatively)* if it occurs as principal operation of a rule that tests its i-th argument positively (resp. negatively). We say that an operation f *tests its* i*-th argument* if it tests it either positively or negatively.

Definition 6. A *GSOS system* is a pair $G = (\Sigma_G, R_G)$, where Σ_G is a finite signature and R_G is a finite set of GSOS rules over Σ_G containing no rules with Ω as principal operation.

An example of GSOS system, the language $\mathcal{L}$, is presented in Fig. 1. We shall use this concrete language as a running example throughout the paper to illustrate our definitions and results. The language $\mathcal{L}$ is a subset of ACP [5] with action prefixing in lieu of general sequential composition. Its parallel composition operator, denoted by $\|$, is parameterized with respect to a partial, commutative and associative communication function $\gamma : \mathsf{Act} \times \mathsf{Act} \rightharpoonup \mathsf{Act}$. An operation in $\mathcal{L}$ that uses the power of negative premises, at least in the presence of a non-trivial priority structure on actions, is the priority operation θ of Baeten, Bergstra and Klop [4]. In order to define this operation, we assume a given partial ordering relation $>$ on Act. Intuitively,

Signature	*Arity*	*Rules*
δ	0	no rules
Ω	0	no rules
$a.\_$ $(a \in \mathsf{Act})$	1	$a.x \xrightarrow{a} x$
$+$	2	$\frac{x \xrightarrow{a} x'}{x+y \xrightarrow{a} x'}$ $\frac{y \xrightarrow{a} y'}{x+y \xrightarrow{a} y'}$
$\Vert$	2	$\frac{x \xrightarrow{a} x'}{x \Vert y \xrightarrow{a} x' \Vert y}$ $\frac{y \xrightarrow{a} y'}{x \Vert y \xrightarrow{a} x \Vert y'}$ $\frac{x \xrightarrow{a} x', y \xrightarrow{b} y'}{x \Vert y \xrightarrow{c} x' \Vert y'}$ $\gamma(a,b) \simeq c$
θ	1	$\frac{x \xrightarrow{a} x', (\forall b > a) x \stackrel{b}{\nrightarrow}}{\theta(x) \xrightarrow{a} \theta(x')}$

Fig. 1. The language $\mathcal{L}$

$b > a$ is interpreted as "action b has priority over action a". The sub-language of $\mathcal{L}$ consisting only of the operations Ω, δ, $a.\_$ and $+$ will be denoted by $\mathsf{FINTREE}_\Omega$.

GSOS systems have been introduced and studied in depth in [6]. Intuitively, a GSOS system gives a language, whose constructs are the operations in the signature Σ_G, together with a Plotkin-style structural operational semantics [14] for it defined by the set of conditional rules R_G. In this study, the operational semantics of a GSOS system will be given in terms of labelled transition systems with divergence. In order to obtain this novel interpretation, we aim at using the rules in a GSOS system G to define a divergence predicate over terms and a transition relation in such a way that our definitions: (1) specialize to those originally given by Bloom, Istrail and Meyer in their seminal study [6] when divergence is not taken into account; (2) give results that are in agreement with those already presented in the literature when applied to known process description languages; and (3) produce operators that are well-behaved with respect to the notion of prebisimulation, i.e., operations for which prebisimulation is a precongruence.

First of all, we shall use the rules in a GSOS systems to define a divergence (or underspecification) predicate on the set of closed terms over Σ_G. In fact, as is common practice in the literature on process algebras, we shall define the notion of convergence, and use it to define the divergence predicate we are after. Intuitively, a term P is convergent if the set of its initial transitions is fully specified. The basic divergent term is Ω, the totally unspecified process. A term of the form $f(\mathbf{P})$ is convergent iff the set of its initial transitions only depends on those arguments P_is whose initial behaviour is completely known. This informal discussion motivates the following definition.

Definition 7. Let $G = (\Sigma_G, R_G)$ be a GSOS system. The convergence predicate $\downarrow_G$ (abbreviated to $\downarrow$ when the GSOS system G is clear from the context) is the least predicate over $\mathrm{T}(\Sigma_G)$ that satisfies the following clause:

$f(P_1, \ldots, P_l) \downarrow_G$ if $f \neq \Omega$ and, for every argument i of f, if f tests i then $P_i \downarrow_G$.

We write $P \uparrow_G$ iff it is not the case that $P \downarrow_G$.

When applied to the language $\mathcal{L}$, Def. 7 gives the following convergence predicate: (1) $\delta \downarrow$; (2) if $P \downarrow$ and $Q \downarrow$, then $P + Q \downarrow$ and $P \Vert Q \downarrow$; and (3) if $P \downarrow$ then $\theta(P) \downarrow$.

The reader familiar with the literature on prebisimulation over CCS-like languages will have noted the similarity of this definition with those given in, e.g., [9, 7, 1].

We shall now present our non-standard operational semantics for GSOS languages. As stated above, we take as our starting point the original theory developed by Bloom, Istrail and Meyer. However, in the presence of divergence information, we shall interpret negative transition formulae over *convergent processes* only. Intuitively, to know that a process cannot initially perform a given action, we need to find out precisely all the actions that it can perform. If a process is divergent, its set of initial actions is not fully specified; thus we cannot be sure whether such a process satisfies a negative transition formula or not. Informally, the intent of a GSOS rule in our setting is as follows. Suppose that we are wondering whether $f(\mathbf{P})$ is capable of taking a c-step. We look at each rule of the form (6) with principal operation f and action c in turn. We inspect each positive premise $x_i \stackrel{a_{ij}}{\rightarrow} y_{ij}$, checking if P_i is capable of taking an a_{ij}-step for each j and if so calling the a_{ij}-children Q_{ij}. We also check the negative premises; this involves finding out whether P_i is convergent, and, in that case, if P_i is *in*capable of taking a b_{ik}-step for each k. If so, then the rule *fires* and $f(\mathbf{P}) \stackrel{c}{\rightarrow} C[\mathbf{P}, \mathbf{Q}]$. We write $\rightarrow_G$ for the transition relation for G defined in this way. The lts with divergence specified by a GSOS system G is then given by $\mathsf{lts}(G) = (\mathrm{T}(\Sigma_G), \rightarrow_G, \uparrow_G)$. The largest prebisimulation over $\mathsf{lts}(G)$ will be denoted by $\lesssim_G$, and its kernel by $\sim_G$. (The subscript G will be omitted from these relations when this causes no confusion).

Example 1. We exemplify our approach using our running example, the language $\mathcal{L}$, by considering some identities involving simple terms that use the priority operation θ.

The term $\theta(\Omega)$ is divergent, as Ω is. Moreover it does not have any transition because Ω has none. We thus have that $\theta(\Omega) \sim \Omega$.

Consider a term of the form $P \equiv a.\delta + \Omega$, with a a maximal element in the poset $(\mathsf{Act}, >)$, i.e., with a an action with maximal priority. Then the rule for θ with action a has no negative premises, and it can be used to establish the transition $\theta(P) \stackrel{a}{\rightarrow} \theta(\delta)$. Indeed, this is the only transition that is possible from $\theta(P)$. As $\theta(P)$ is divergent, as P is, it is easy to see that $\theta(P) \sim a.\delta + \Omega$.

On the other hand, if a is *not* maximal in the poset $(\mathsf{Act}, >)$, the rule for θ with action a will have at least one negative premise. As P is divergent, that rule cannot be used to derive a transition from the term $\theta(P)$. It thus follows that $\theta(P) \sim \Omega$, if a is not maximal in the poset $(\mathsf{Act}, >)$.

We are now ready to establish the first main result of this paper. Namely, we shall prove that the operations of a GSOS system preserve the semantic notion of prebisimulation.

Theorem 8. *Let G be a GSOS system. Then $\lesssim_G$ is a precongruence for all operation symbols f of G, i.e.,* $(\forall i : P_i \lesssim_G Q_i) \Rightarrow f(\mathbf{P}) \lesssim_G f(\mathbf{Q})$.

3.1 GSOS Languages with Recursion

In this section we consider GSOS languages that may include recursion. Let $G = (\Sigma_G, R_G)$ be a GSOS system, and let PVar be a fresh denumerable set of *process variables* ($X, Y \in \mathsf{PVar}$). The set of recursive terms over Σ_G and PVar, denoted by $\mathsf{REC}(\Sigma_G, \mathsf{PVar})$, is given by the following BNF syntax:

$$P ::= X \mid f(P_1, \ldots, P_l) \mid \mathrm{fix}(X = P)$$

where $X \in \mathsf{PVar}$, f is an operation symbol in Σ_G of arity l and fix is a binding construct. This gives rise to the usual notions of free and bound variables in terms. The set of closed recursive terms (or *programs*) will be denoted by $\mathsf{CREC}(\Sigma_G, \mathsf{PVar})$. We shall assume a standard notion of substitution of terms for free process variables, and use $P\{Q/X\}$ to denote term P in which each free occurrence of X has been replaced by Q, after possibly renaming bound variables in P. We shall now define an operational semantics for the set of programs $\mathsf{CREC}(\Sigma_G, \mathsf{PVar})$ in terms of an lts with divergence, following the techniques presented in Sect. 3. In this study, the operational semantics of recursion will be given by the standard unfolding rule:

$$\frac{x\{\mathrm{fix}(X = x)/X\} \xrightarrow{a} y}{\mathrm{fix}(X = x) \xrightarrow{a} y} \tag{7}$$

This will ensure that recursive terms are interpreted as fixed-points, and that the following equation holds:

$$\mathrm{fix}(X = P) = P\{\mathrm{fix}(X = P)/X\} \ . \tag{8}$$

In order to define the operational semantics of $\mathsf{CREC}(\Sigma_G, \mathsf{PVar})$, we need, first of all, to extend the convergence predicate to $\mathsf{CREC}(\Sigma_G, \mathsf{PVar})$.

Definition 9. The convergence predicate $\downarrow_{\mathrm{Grec}}$ (abbreviated to $\downarrow$ when the GSOS system G is clear from the context) is the least predicate over $\mathsf{CREC}(\Sigma_G, \mathsf{Var})$ that satisfies the following clauses:

1. $f(P_1, \ldots, P_l) \downarrow_{\mathrm{Grec}}$ if $f \neq \Omega$, and for every argument i of f, if f tests i then $P_i \downarrow_{\mathrm{Grec}}$;
2. $\mathrm{fix}(X = P) \downarrow_{\mathrm{Grec}}$ if $P\{\mathrm{fix}(X = P)/X\} \downarrow_{\mathrm{Grec}}$.

Again, we write $P \uparrow_{\mathrm{Grec}}$ iff it is not the case that $P \downarrow_{\mathrm{Grec}}$.

The motivation for the above definition is the following: a term P is divergent if its initial transitions are not fully specified. This occurs either when the initial behaviour of term P depends on underspecified arguments like Ω or in the presence of unguarded recursive definitions. For example, the terms $\mathrm{fix}(X = X)$ and $\mathrm{fix}(X = \mathit{odd}(X))$, where *odd* is the operation given by rule (1), are *not* convergent as the initial behaviour of these processes depends on itself. It is immediate to see that the predicates $\downarrow_G$ and $\downarrow_{Grec}$ coincide over $\mathrm{T}(\Sigma_G)$, the set of recursion-free terms in $\mathsf{CREC}(\Sigma_G, \mathsf{PVar})$.

We shall now show how to associate a transition relation with a GSOS language with recursion by putting the extra structure given by the convergence predicate to good use.

We construct the relation $\rightarrow_{Grec}$ over $\mathsf{CREC}(\Sigma_G, \mathsf{PVar})$ in two steps. In the first step of the construction, we derive the transitions emanating from *convergent terms* by induction on the convergence predicate following the approach outlined in the previous section, and using (7) to derive the transitions of recursive terms. In the second, we use the information about the transitions that are possible for convergent terms to determine the outgoing transitions for all the terms in $\mathsf{CREC}(\Sigma_G, \mathsf{PVar})$. For a divergent term P, a transition $P \xrightarrow{a}_{Grec} Q$ holds iff it is provable from the rules in R_G and those for recursion in the standard sense, with the proviso that every time we need to establish the validity of a negative premise we appeal to the information on the transitions that are possible from convergent terms discovered in the first step of our construction. To exemplify this construction on a pathological case, let us consider the term $\text{fix}(X = \mathit{odd}(X))$, where the operation *odd* is given by rule (1). The operation *odd* is standardly used in the literature to show that negative premises and unguarded recursive definitions can lead to inconsistent specifications. Note, first of all, that $\text{fix}(X = \mathit{odd}(X))$ is a divergent term. It is then easy to see that, because of our requirement that negative premises in rules be interpreted over convergent terms only, rule (1) can never be applied to derive a transition for $\text{fix}(X = \mathit{odd}(X))$. Thus we have that this term has *no* transition and is divergent, i.e., that $\text{fix}(X = \mathit{odd}(X)) \sim \Omega$.

With the above definitions, the operational semantics of a GSOS language with recursion $\mathsf{CREC}(\Sigma_G, \mathsf{PVar})$ is given by the lts with divergence

$$\mathsf{lts}(G_{rec}) = (\mathsf{CREC}(\Sigma_G, \mathsf{PVar}), \mathsf{Act}, \rightarrow_{Grec}, \uparrow_{Grec}) \ .$$

As a corollary of general results by Abramsky, we can give the following general characterization of the finitary bisimulation preorder over $\mathsf{lts}(G_{rec})$ for arbitrary G:

Proposition 10. *The preorders $\lesssim^F$ and $\lesssim_\omega$ coincide over $\mathsf{lts}(G_{rec})$.*

4 Denotational Semantics

In this section we shall present a general technique to give denotational semantics in terms of the Plotkin powerdomain of synchronization trees (see Sect. 2.2) for a class of GSOS languages with recursion. The denotational semantics will be guaranteed to be *fully abstract*, in the sense of Milner and Plotkin, with respect to the finitary part of the prebisimulation relation $\lesssim_\omega$. The languages that we shall consider have the structure of most standard process calculi (see, e.g., [12, 5]); they will consist of a set of operations to build finite, acyclic labelled transition systems and a facility for recursive definitions of behaviours. Thus we shall consider GSOS languages with recursion in which infinite behaviours can only be defined by means of recursive definitions.

We assume that the reader is familiar with the basic notions of ordered and continuous algebras (see, e.g., [8, 10]); however, in what follows we give a quick overview of the way a denotational semantics can be given to a recursive language like $\mathsf{REC}(\Sigma_G, \mathsf{PVar})$ following the standard lines of algebraic semantics [8]. The interested reader is invited to consult [8] for an explanation of the theory.

Let $\mathcal{A}$ be any Σ_G-cpo, i.e., a Σ_G-algebra whose carrier is an algebraic cpo and whose operations are interpreted as continuous functions. A denotational semantics for the language $\mathsf{REC}(\Sigma_G, \mathsf{PVar})$ is given by the mapping $\mathcal{A}[\![\cdot]\!] : \mathsf{REC}(\Sigma_G, \mathsf{PVar}) \rightarrow [\mathrm{ENV}_\mathcal{A} \rightarrow \mathcal{A}]$ defined in, e.g., [8, Def. 4.2.3], where $\mathrm{ENV}_\mathcal{A} = [\mathsf{PVar} \rightarrow \mathcal{A}]$ is the set of

$\mathcal{A}$-environments, ranged over by the meta-variable ρ. For each $P \in \mathsf{CREC}(\Sigma_G, \mathsf{PVar})$, $\mathcal{A}[\![P]\!]\rho$ does not depend on the environment ρ. Hence the denotation of a closed term P will be denoted by $\mathcal{A}[\![P]\!]$. A general result about the semantic mapping $\mathcal{A}[\![\cdot]\!]$ states that, for any $P \in \mathsf{REC}(\Sigma_G, \mathsf{PVar})$, there exists an infinite sequence of *finite approximations* $P^n \in \mathbb{T}(\Sigma_G, \mathsf{PVar})$ $(n \in \mathbb{N})$ such that

$$\mathcal{A}[\![P]\!] = \bigsqcup_{n \geq 0} \mathcal{A}[\![P^n]\!] \ . \tag{9}$$

For any binary relation $\mathcal{R}$ over $\mathsf{CREC}(\Sigma_G, \mathsf{PVar})$, the algebraic part of $\mathcal{R}$, denoted by $\mathcal{R}^A$ is defined as follows [8]:

$$P \ \mathcal{R}^A \ Q \Leftrightarrow \text{for every } P^n \text{, there exists } Q^m \text{ such that } P^n \ \mathcal{R} \ Q^m \ .$$

We say that $\mathcal{R}$ is *algebraic* iff $\mathcal{R}$=$\mathcal{R}^A$. Intuitively, a relation is algebraic if it is completely determined by how it behaves on recursion-free terms. Because of Eqn. 9, the relations over terms induced by a denotational semantics are always algebraic. We shall make use of this fact in the technical developments to follow.

4.1 Compact GSOS Systems

The following notion from [2] will allow us to pin down precisely a class of GSOS operations that map finite processes to finite processes. The semantic counterparts of these operations will have the property of being *compact* in the sense of [10], i.e., of mapping compact elements in the Plotkin powerdomain of synchronization trees to compact elements.

Definition 11. A GSOS rule of the general form (6) is *linear* if each variable occurs at most once in the target and, for each argument i that is tested positively, x_i does not occur in the target and at most one of the y_{ij}'s does. An operation from a GSOS system G is *linear* iff all rules for it are linear. Finally, G itself is *linear* iff it only contains linear rules.

The format of linear rules is a restriction of the general GSOS format in that no copying of arguments is allowed and no argument for which there is a positive premise may appear in the target of a rule. Moreover, there may be possibly many positive premises for an argument x_i in a rule, but at most one of the y_{ij}'s may appear in its target. As far as we know, all the operations occurring in the standard process algebras are linear.

Definition 12 [2]. A GSOS system G is *syntactically well-founded* iff there exists a function w from operation symbols in Σ_G to natural numbers such that, for each rule $\rho \in R_G$ with principal operation symbol f and target $C[\mathbf{x}, \mathbf{y}]$ the following conditions hold:

- if ρ has no positive premises then $W(C[\mathbf{x}, \mathbf{y}]) < w(f)$, and
- $W(C[\mathbf{x}, \mathbf{y}]) \leq w(f)$ otherwise,

where $W : \mathbb{T}(\Sigma_G) \rightarrow \mathbb{N}$ is given by

$$\begin{aligned} W(x) &\triangleq 0 \\ W(f(P_1, \ldots, P_l)) &\triangleq w(f) + W(P_1) + \cdots + W(P_l). \end{aligned}$$

For example, the GSOS system in Fig. 1 is linear and syntactically well-founded. In fact, it is sufficient to assign weight 1 to the action prefixing operations and weight 0 to all the other operations. Syntactic well-foundedness is decidable over GSOS systems (cf. [2, Thm. 6.8]), and, for linear GSOS systems, it is sufficient to guarantee that terms are semantically well-founded in the sense of [2].

Definition 13. A GSOS system is said to be *compact* iff it is linear and syntactically well-founded.

4.2 Full Abstraction for Compact GSOS Systems

Let G be a compact GSOS language. We shall now give a way of defining, for each Σ_G-context $C[\mathbf{x}]$, a function $\mathbf{C}_{\mathsf{ST}}$ over $\mathsf{ST}(\mathsf{Act})$ of the appropriate arity. The definition of $\mathbf{C}_{\mathsf{ST}}$ will be given using the rules in R_G as a guideline. First of all, note that it is sufficient to define semantic operations $\mathbf{f}_{\mathsf{ST}}$ for each $f \in \Sigma_G$, as derived semantic operations can then be obtained by function composition. The definition of the functions $\mathbf{f}_{\mathsf{ST}}$ is given by the inductive construction in Def. 14. Intuitively, the inductive construction of the synchronization tree $\mathbf{f}_{\mathsf{ST}}(\mathbf{t})$ given below is well-founded because, by the compactness of G, whenever the premises of a rule of the form (6) can be met by $\mathbf{t}$, then either the weight of $C[\mathbf{x},\mathbf{y}]$ is strictly smaller than that of f, or the weight of $C[\mathbf{x},\mathbf{y}]$ is the same as that of f, and the sum of the sizes of the arguments of $\mathbf{C}_{\mathsf{ST}}$ has decreased.

Definition 14. Let $G = (\Sigma_G, R_G)$ be a compact GSOS system, and let f be an l-ary operation in Σ_G. We define the operation $\mathbf{f}_{\mathsf{ST}} : \mathsf{ST}(\mathsf{Act})^l \to \mathsf{ST}(\mathsf{Act})$ inductively by stipulating that, for every $t_1, \ldots, t_l \in \mathsf{ST}(\mathsf{Act})$:

- $\perp \in \mathbf{f}_{\mathsf{ST}}(t_1, \ldots, t_l)$ iff $f = \Omega$ or there is an argument i for f such that f tests its i-th argument and $\perp \in t_i$;
- $\langle c, t\rangle \in \mathbf{f}_{\mathsf{ST}}(t_1, \ldots, t_l)$ iff there exist a rule for f of the form (6) and a vector of trees $\mathbf{u} = u_{11} \ldots u_{1m_1} \ldots u_{l1} \ldots u_{lm_l}$ such that:
  1. for all $1 \leq i \leq l$, $1 \leq j \leq m_i$, $\langle a_{ij}, u_{ij}\rangle \in t_i$,
  2. for all $1 \leq i \leq l$, $1 \leq k \leq n_i$, $\perp \notin t_i$ and, for no $u \in \mathsf{ST}(\mathsf{Act})$, $\langle b_{ik}, u\rangle \in t_i$, and
  3. $\mathbf{C}_{\mathsf{ST}}[\mathbf{t}, \mathbf{u}] = t$, where $\mathbf{C}_{\mathsf{ST}}$ denotes the derived semantic operation associated with the Σ_G-context $C[\mathbf{x}, \mathbf{y}]$. If $C[\mathbf{x}]$ is a variable x_i, then $\mathbf{C}_{\mathsf{ST}}[\mathbf{t}] = t_i$.

When applied to the language $\mathcal{L}$, the construction in Def. 14 produces the following functions:

- $\delta_{\mathsf{ST}} = \emptyset$,
- $\Omega_{\mathsf{ST}} = \{\perp\}$,
- for every $t \in \mathsf{ST}(\mathsf{Act})$, $\mathbf{a}_{\mathsf{ST}}(t) = \{\langle a, t\rangle\}$,
- for every $t_1, t_2 \in \mathsf{ST}(\mathsf{Act})$, $t_1 +_{\mathsf{ST}} t_2 = t_1 \cup t_2$,
- for every $t_1, t_2 \in \mathsf{ST}(\mathsf{Act})$, $t_1 \|_{\mathsf{ST}} t_2$ is given by:
  1. $\perp \in t_1 \|_{\mathsf{ST}} t_2$ iff $\perp \in t_1$ or $\perp \in t_2$;
  2. $\langle c, t\rangle \in t_1 \|_{\mathsf{ST}} t_2$ iff one of the following holds:
     (a) there exists $\langle c, t_1'\rangle \in t_1$ such that $t = t_1' \|_{\mathsf{ST}} t_2$, or
     (b) there exists $\langle c, t_2'\rangle \in t_2$ such that $t = t_1 \|_{\mathsf{ST}} t_2'$, or

(c) there exist $\langle a, t_1' \rangle \in t_1$ and $\langle b, t_2' \rangle \in t_2$ such that $c = \gamma(a, b)$ and $t = t_1' \|_{\mathsf{ST}} t_2'$.

- for every $t \in \mathsf{ST}(\mathsf{Act})$, $\theta_{\mathsf{ST}}(t)$ is given by:
  1. $\perp \in \theta_{\mathsf{ST}}(t)$ iff $\perp \in t$,
  2. $\langle c, t_1 \rangle \in \theta_{\mathsf{ST}}(t)$ iff there exists $\langle c, t' \rangle \in t$ such that:
     (a) either c is maximal in $(\mathsf{Act}, >)$ and $\theta_{\mathsf{ST}}(t') = t_1$,
     (b) or c is not maximal in $(\mathsf{Act}, >)$, for no action $b > c$ and t_2 $\langle b, t_2 \rangle \in d$, $\perp \notin t$, and $\theta_{\mathsf{ST}}(t') = t_1$.

We shall now prove that the definition of the operations given in Def. 14 endows the preorder of synchronization trees $\mathsf{ST}(\mathsf{Act})$ with a Σ_G-preorder structure in the sense of [10]. To this end, it is sufficient to prove that each operation f_{ST} is monotonic with respect to the preorder $\sqsubseteq$.

Theorem 15. *Let G be a compact GSOS system, and $f \in \Sigma_G$. Then the function f_{ST} given by the construction in Def. 14 is monotonic with respect to $\sqsubseteq$.*

Because of the above result, the construction of Def. 14 allows us to define, for each operation symbol f in the signature of a compact GSOS system, a monotonic function f_{ST} over $\mathsf{ST}(\mathsf{Act})$ of the appropriate arity. This is exactly what is needed to endow the preorder $(\mathsf{ST}(\mathsf{Act}), \sqsubseteq)$ with the structure of a Σ_G-preorder in the sense of [10]. Using Eqn. 4, we then automatically obtain a Σ_G-poset structure on the poset of compact elements of $\mathcal{D}$. The unique meaning maps from $\mathrm{T}(\Sigma_G)$ to the resulting algebraic structures, denoted by $\mathsf{ST}[\![\cdot]\!]$ and $\mathcal{K}(\mathcal{D})[\![\cdot]\!]$, are related thus:

Lemma 16. *For every $P \in \mathrm{T}(\Sigma_G)$, $(\mathsf{ST}[\![P]\!])^c = \mathcal{K}(\mathcal{D})[\![P]\!]$.*

We now proceed to show that the denotational semantics $\mathcal{K}(\mathcal{D})[\![\cdot]\!]$ for recursion-free terms in $\mathsf{CREC}(\Sigma_G, \mathsf{PVar})$ is fully abstract with respect to the bisimulation preorder.

Theorem 17. *Let G be a compact GSOS system. Then, for all $P, Q \in \mathrm{T}(\Sigma_G)$, $P \precsim Q$ iff $\mathcal{K}(\mathcal{D})[\![P]\!] \sqsubseteq \mathcal{K}(\mathcal{D})[\![Q]\!]$.*

Our aim in the remainder of this section will be to extend the above full abstraction result to the whole of $\mathsf{CREC}(\Sigma_G, \mathsf{PVar})$. In the process of proving this result, we shall establish very general results for compact GSOS languages that have independent interest. First of all, in order to define an interpretation of programs in $\mathsf{CREC}(\Sigma_G, \mathsf{PVar})$ as elements of $\mathcal{D}$, we need to define a continuous Σ_G-algebra structure on $\mathcal{D}$. As $(\mathcal{D}, \sqsubseteq_{\mathcal{D}})$ is, up to isomorphism, the unique algebraic cpo with $(\mathcal{K}(\mathcal{D}), \sqsubseteq)$ as poset of compact elements, this is easily done by using Eqn. 5 to define a continuous function $\mathsf{f}_{\mathcal{D}}$ for each $f \in \Sigma_G$. By the general theory of algebraic semantics (see, e.g., [8]), we then have that, for all $P, Q \in \mathrm{T}(\Sigma_G)$,

$$\mathcal{D}[\![P]\!] \sqsubseteq_{\mathcal{D}} \mathcal{D}[\![Q]\!] \Leftrightarrow \mathcal{K}(\mathcal{D})[\![P]\!] \sqsubseteq \mathcal{K}(\mathcal{D})[\![Q]\!] \ . \tag{10}$$

In view of Thm. 17, our desired full abstraction result will follow if we prove that the behavioural preorder $\precsim_\omega$ is algebraic. This is because, from general properties of denotational interpretations, the relation $\sqsubseteq_{\mathcal{D}}$ is algebraic, and two algebraic relations that coincide over $\mathrm{T}(\Sigma_G)$ do, in fact, coincide over the whole of $\mathsf{CREC}(\Sigma_G, \mathsf{PVar})$. The key to the proof of the algebraicity of $\precsim_\omega$ is the following general theorem providing a partial completeness result for $\precsim$ in the sense of Hennessy [7] for arbitrary compact GSOS systems.

Theorem 18 Partial Completeness. *Let G be a compact GSOS system. Then there exist a compact GSOS system G' and a set of $\Sigma_{G'}$-inequations T such that:*

- *G' disjointly extends G and $\mathsf{FINTREE}_\Omega$ in the sense of [2], and*
- *for all $P \in \mathrm{T}(G')$, $Q \in \mathsf{CREC}(\Sigma_{G'}, \mathsf{Var})$, $P \lesssim Q$ iff $T \cup \{\text{Eqn. } 8\} \vdash P \leq Q$.*

The proof of this theorem is rather involved. It relies on an algorithm for generating the compact GSOS system G' and the inequational theory T over it following the lines of [2]. Apart from its intrinsic interest, the main consequence of Thm. 18 is the following key result, whose proof uses properties of initial continuous algebras in inequational varieties, that essentially states that finite trees are compact elements with respect to the preorder $\lesssim$.

Theorem 19. *Suppose that G is a compact GSOS system. Assume that $t \in \mathsf{ST}(\mathsf{Act})$ and $P \in \mathsf{CREC}(\Sigma_G, \mathsf{Var})$. Then $t \lesssim_{Grec} P$ iff there exists a finite approximation P^n of P such that $t \lesssim_{Grec} P^n$.*

The above result, in conjunction with Propn. 10, allows us to prove that $\lesssim_\omega$ is indeed algebraic.

Theorem 20. *Let G be a compact GSOS system. Then the relation $\lesssim_\omega$ over the labelled transition system with divergence $\mathsf{lts}(Grec)$ is algebraic.*

In light of the above results, we can now show that, for any compact GSOS system G, the denotational semantics for $\mathsf{CREC}(\Sigma_G, \mathsf{PVar})$ is fully abstract with respect to $\lesssim_\omega$.

Theorem 21. *Let G be a compact GSOS system. Then:*

$$\text{for all } P, Q \in \mathsf{CREC}(\Sigma_G, \mathsf{Var}),\ P \lesssim_\omega Q \text{ iff } \mathcal{D}[\![P]\!] \sqsubseteq_{\mathcal{D}} \mathcal{D}[\![Q]\!].$$

References

1. S. Abramsky, *A domain equation for bisimulation*, Information and Computation, 92 (1991), pp. 161–218.
2. L. Aceto, B. Bloom, and F. Vaandrager, *Turning SOS rules into equations*, Information and Computation, 111 (1994), pp. 1–52.
3. L. Aceto and A. Ingólfsdóttir, *CPO models for GSOS languages — Part I: Compact GSOS languages*, Research Report RS-94-40, BRICS (Basic Research in Computer Science, Centre of the Danish National Research Foundation), Department of Mathematics and Computer Science, Aalborg University, December 1994. Available through the WWW by opening the URL `http://www.daimi.aau.dk/BRICS/` and following the links thereof.
4. J. Baeten, J. Bergstra, and J. Klop, *Syntax and defining equations for an interrupt mechanism in process algebra*, Fundamenta Informaticae, IX (1986), pp. 127–168.
5. J. Baeten and W. Weijland, *Process Algebra*, Cambridge Tracts in Theoretical Computer Science 18, Cambridge University Press, 1990.
6. B. Bloom, S. Istrail, and A. Meyer, *Bisimulation can't be traced: preliminary report*, in Conference Record of the Fifteenth Annual ACM Symposium on Principles of Programming Languages, 1988, pp. 229–239. Full version available as Technical Report 90-1150, Department of Computer Science, Cornell University, Ithaca, New York, August 1990. To appear in the *Journal of the ACM*.

7. M. HENNESSY, *A term model for synchronous processes*, Information and Control, 51 (1981), pp. 58–75.
8. ——, *Algebraic Theory of Processes*, MIT Press, Cambridge, Massachusetts, 1988.
9. M. HENNESSY AND G. PLOTKIN, *A term model for CCS*, in 9th Symposium on Mathematical Foundations of Computer Science, P. Dembiński, ed., vol. 88 of Lecture Notes in Computer Science, Springer-Verlag, 1980, pp. 261–274.
10. A. INGÓLFSDÓTTIR, *Semantic Models for Communicating Process with Value-Passing*, PhD thesis, School of Cognitive and Computing Sciences, University of Sussex, June 1994. Computer Science Report 8/94. Also available as Report R–94–2044, Department of Mathematics and Computer Science, Aalborg University.
11. R. MILNER, *A modal characterisation of observable machine behaviour*, in Proceedings CAAP 81, G. Astesiano and C. Bohm, eds., vol. 112 of Lecture Notes in Computer Science, Springer-Verlag, 1981, pp. 25–34.
12. ——, *Communication and Concurrency*, Prentice-Hall International, Englewood Cliffs, 1989.
13. G. PLOTKIN, *Lecture notes in domain theory*, 1981. University of Edinburgh.
14. ——, *A structural approach to operational semantics*, Report DAIMI FN-19, Computer Science Department, Aarhus University, 1981.
15. D. WALKER, *Bisimulation and divergence*, Information and Computation, 85 (1990), pp. 202–241.

Statecharts, Transition Structures and Transformations*

Adriano Peron

Dipartimento di Matematica ed Informatica — Università di Udine
Via Zanon 6 — I-33100 Udine — Italy
E_mail: peron@dimi.uniud.it

Abstract. Statecharts are state-transition machines endowed with hierarchy on states and parallelism on transitions. It is shown that a statechart is described by a pair of relations over transitions (a transition structure), the former describing causality and the other describing a notion of asymmetric independence. A statechart can be effectively constructed from its transition structure. Transition structures corresponding to a subclass of Statecharts are characterized. Natural notions of morphisms among transition structures allow to define classes of statechart transformations which preserve behaviour.

1 Introduction

Statecharts (see [2]) is a graphical specification formalism which enriches state-transition diagrams with a hierarchical structure (i.e., tree-like) on states and with graphical conventions for explicitly representing parallelism and communication among parallel components. In recent years, a great effort has been devoted to semantics of Statecharts (e.g., [3, 4, 1, 7, 5, 8]). A minor attention has been paied to the investigation of equivalence notions and to the related issues of behaviour preserving transformations and "a priori" correct development of specifications. This paper gives a contribution in this sense.

The classical representation of Statecharts emphasizes the structure of the specification (it is a graphical structured formalism), but, if behaviour properties are the main concern, structure might be an useless complication. For this reason we provide a basic representation of a statechart in terms of its set of transitions, a relation of causality and a relation of asymmetric independence on transitions (a *transition structure*). We show that a transition structure is sufficient to describe a statechart and that states, hierarchy on states and representation of parallelism can be derived from the transition structure. In particular, we provide a recursive algorithm which associates, with the transition structure of a statechart Z, a statechart Z' having the same transition structure. In general, the statechart Z' is not isomorphic to Z, since it has minimal

* Partially supported by project ESPRIT Basic Research 8130 LOMAPS and by project CNR 94.01874.CT7 Specifica di Alto Livello e Verifica Formale di Sistemi Digitali.

structure on states. The proposed algorithm is useful for removing redundances in the graphical representation of a statechart. We also characterize transition structures corresponding to "well structured statecharts" -a widely adopted restriction of statecharts (e.g., see [8])- and we call them *good structures*. Good structures are dual with respect to well structured statecharts and it is possible to shift effortless from one formalism to the other.

Since transition structures are simple objects which emphasize behavioural properties of a statecharts, they are a proper representation for studying transformations. We investigate statechart transformations by investigating morphisms of transition structures which preserve behaviour. Implicitly, each notion of morphism defines a class of transformation of statecharts, in the sense that if there is a morphism from the transition structure of a statechart Z to that of Z', then Z can be transformed into Z'. We provide two different notions of morphism which support two meaningful classes of structural transformations: transformations which allow (in some cases) to reshape a statechart into a well structured statechart and a form of top-down refinement.

For the sake of simplicity, we consider statecharts in a version where many communication features are simplified (e.g., we do not consider shared variables and negative events). However, since our main concern is not communication, we stress that the results of this paper does not depend on restricting communication. The semantics we enforce slightly modifies the original one (see [3]).

In section 2 Statecharts, transition structures and semantics are defined. In section 3 the technique for reconstructing a statechart from its transition structure is described and it is proved correct. In section 4 transition structures corresponding to well structured statecharts are characterized. In section 5 notions of behaviour preserving morphisms of transition structures are defined.

2 Statecharts

The graphical convention is that states are depicted as boxes, and the box of a substate of a state b is drawn inside the area of the box of b. States are either of type OR, called *or-states*, or of type AND, called *and-states*. And-states are depicted as boxes whose area is partitioned by dashed lines. Each element of the partition is the root state of a statechart describing a *parallel component* of the and-state. When an or-state is entered, also one and only one of its immediate substates is. When an and-state is entered, all of its immediate substates are. Each non basic or-state has a privileged immediate substate: the *default substate* (graphically, it is the target of a dangling arc). For instance, in Fig.1, L is an and-state whose parallel components are K and J. State B is the default substate of A. Transitions are represented graphically by arrows and are labelled by a pair of sets of events, one representing a "triggering", the other an "action". Events are interpreted as pure signals communicated by the environment. A transition is *enabled* if the set of events of the triggering are currently communicated. When a transition t is performed, the set of events in the action of t are instantaneously communicated, so augmenting the set of events offered by the environment. As

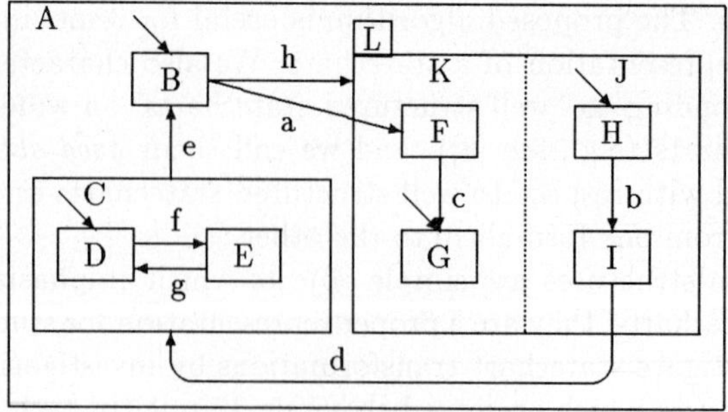

Fig. 1. A statechart.

an example, if transition a in Fig.1 is labelled by a pair $(\{\alpha, \beta\}, \{\gamma\})$, then a is enabled when events α and β are communicated. When transition a is performed, event γ is instantaneously communicated.

Definition 1. A *statechart* Z is a 8-tuple $(B, \rho, \phi, T, in, out, P, \chi, \delta)$, where:

- B is the nonempty finite set of *states*;
- $\rho : B \to 2^B$ is the *hierarchy function* which gives, for each state, the set of its immediate substates; for $s \in B$, $\rho^\star(s)$ denotes the least set $S \subseteq B$ such that $s \in S$ and $\rho(s') \in S$ for all $s' \in S$, and $\rho^+(s)$ denotes the set $\rho^\star(s) - \{s\}$; ρ describes a tree-like structure, namely:
  1. there exists a unique $s \in B$ s.t. $\rho^\star(s) = B$, denoted as $root_Z$;
  2. $s \notin \rho^+(s)$, for all $s \in B$;
  3. if $s' \notin \rho^+(s)$, $s \notin \rho^+(s')$, then $\rho^\star(s) \cap \rho^\star(s') \neq \emptyset$ implies $s = s'$, for all $s, s' \in B$.

  Given two states b and b', *the lowest common ancestor* of b and b', denoted as $\mathcal{L}(b, b')$, is the state $\bar{b} \in B$ such that $\rho^\star(\bar{b}) \supseteq \{b, b'\}$ and, $\bar{b} \in \rho^\star(b'')$, for each b'' with $\rho^\star(b'') \supseteq \{b, b'\}$;
- $\phi : B \to \{AND, OR\}$ is the *state type function*;
- T is a finite set of *transitions*;
- $in : T \to B$ is the function which gives the *target state* of a transition;
- $out : T \to B$ is the function which gives the *source state* of a transition; functions in and out are such that $\phi(\mathcal{L}(t)) = OR$,[2] $in(t) \notin \rho^\star(out(t))$ and $out(t) \notin \rho^\star(in(t))$, for all $t \in T$;
- P is the finite set of *events*;
- $\chi : T \to 2^P \times 2^P$ is the *transition labelling function*; $Ev(t)$ and $Act(t)$ denote the first and the second component of $\chi(t)$, respectively;
- $\delta : B \to B$ is the (partial) *default function* giving, for a non basic or-state, the default substate, i.e., $\delta(b) \in \rho(b)$, for all $\phi(b) = OR$ s.t. $\rho(b) \neq \emptyset$.

[2] $\mathcal{L}(t)$ is a short writing for $\mathcal{L}(in(t), out(t))$.

In the following, we shall write B_Z intending the set of states of statechart Z (and analogously for all the other statechart components). We shall write $\mathcal{L}_Z$ to stress that relation $\mathcal{L}$ is over Z and we omit the index when the context is clear (and analogously for all the other relations we shall define).

When a state b is entered a subset of its substates is entered consistently with the requirement that if an and-state (resp.: an or-state) is entered, then all of its (resp.: exactly one) immediate substates are entered. In particular, one of these sets of states is the one induced by the default function (i.e., the chosen immediate substate of an or-state is its default substate), called *default closure of* b. As an example, the default closure of state L is the set $\{L, K, J, G, H\}$.

For $K \subseteq B_Z$, the *default closure of* K, denoted as $\Downarrow_Z K$, is the least superset of K such that

1. $\rho_Z(d) \subseteq \Downarrow_Z K$, for each and-state $d \in \Downarrow_Z K$,
2. $\delta_Z(d) \in \Downarrow_Z K$, for each or-state $d \in \Downarrow_Z K$ such that $\rho_Z(d) \cap K = \emptyset$.

When the target state b of a transition is entered, states in the default closure of b are entered. When an and-component of an and-state is entered, states in the default closure of all the other components are entered. As an example, when transition a is performed the set of entered states is $\{L, K, F, J, H\}$. In general, when a transition t is performed, the set of entered states is given by the default closure of the set of substates of $\mathcal{L}(t)$ which are ancestors of $in(t)$.

On the transition set we define a *sequentiality relation*. A transition t' *follows* t if the source state of t' belongs to the set of states entered by performing t. Actually, we enrich the set of transitions T by a transition *imp* representing the "start up" of the statechart activities. We can assume that *imp* is a transition without source and leading to the root. The set of states entered by *imp* is the downward closure of the root of the statechart.

Definition 2. Let *imp* be a symbol not in T_Z, called *initial transition*, and let T_Z^i denote $T_Z \cup \{imp\}$. *Sequentiality relation* is $\rightarrow_Z \subseteq T_Z^i \times T_Z$, with

$$t \rightarrow_Z t' \text{ iff } out_Z(t') \in \Downarrow_Z \{b : b \in \rho_Z^+(\mathcal{L}(t)), in_Z(t) \in \rho_Z^\star(b)\}, \text{ for } t, t' \in T_Z$$

$$\text{and } imp \rightarrow_Z t \text{ iff } out_Z(t) \in \Downarrow_Z \{root_Z\}.$$

If $t \in T_Z$, then $t^{\rightarrow_Z}$ denotes the set $\{t' \in T_Z : t \rightarrow_Z t'\}$.

With reference to Fig.1, $imp^{\rightarrow} = e^{\rightarrow} = \{h, a\}$, $a^{\rightarrow} = \{c, b\}$, $c^{\rightarrow} = \emptyset$, $d^{\rightarrow} = \{f, e\}$, $b \rightarrow d$, $f \rightarrow g$, $g \rightarrow f$ and $h \rightarrow b$.

On the transition set we define a *concurrency* relation. Two transition are concurrent if both of their source states can be simultaneously entered. If t and t' are concurrent, then they may be enabled simultaneously (it does not imply that they can be performed simultaneously).

Definition 3. *Concurrency relation* is the symmetric relation $\|_Z \subseteq T_Z \times T_Z$, with $t' \|_Z t''$ and $t'' \|_Z t'$ iff one of the two following constraints is satisfied:

1. there is a transition t such that $t \rightarrow_Z t'$, $t \rightarrow_Z t_1 \rightarrow_Z \dots \rightarrow_Z t_m \rightarrow_Z t''$ and $\mathcal{L}(\mathcal{L}(t_i), out(t')) = out_Z(t')$, for all t_i with $1 \leq i \leq m$;
2. there is a transition t such that $t \rightarrow_Z t_1 \rightarrow_Z \dots \rightarrow_Z t_m \rightarrow_Z t'$ and $t \rightarrow_Z h_1 \rightarrow_Z \dots \rightarrow_Z h_n \rightarrow_Z t''$, with t_i and h_j transitions such that $\mathcal{L}_Z(\mathcal{L}_Z(t_i), \mathcal{L}_Z(h_j))$, $\mathcal{L}_Z(\mathcal{L}_Z(t_i), out(t''))$ and $\mathcal{L}_Z(\mathcal{L}_Z(h_i), out(t'))$ are and-states, for all $1 \leq i \leq m$ and $1 \leq j \leq n$.

With ref. to Fig.1, $a \parallel h$, $b \parallel c$, $d \parallel c$, $f \parallel e$ and $g \parallel e$ and the symmetric cases.

A transition t' is *independent* w.r.t a transition t if t and t' are concurrent and the performance of t does not disable the performance of t' (i.e., the performance of t does not cause exiting the source state of t').

Definition 4. *Independence relation* is $\triangleright_Z \subseteq T_Z \times T_Z$ with $t \triangleright_Z t'$ iff

$$\text{either } \mathcal{L}_Z(\mathcal{L}_Z(t), out_Z(t')) = out_Z(t')$$

$$\text{or } \mathcal{L}_Z(\mathcal{L}_Z(t), out_Z(t')) \text{ is an and-state and } t \parallel_Z t'.$$

With reference to Fig.1, $b \triangleright c$, $c \triangleright b$, $c \triangleright d$, $f \triangleright e$, $g \triangleright e$, and $d \not\triangleright c$, $e \not\triangleright f$ and $e \not\triangleright g$ (the relation $\triangleright$ is not symmetric). If $t \triangleright t'$ and not $t' \triangleright t$, then t' can be seen as being an *interrupt* for t. If $t \triangleright t'$ and $t' \triangleright t$ (we write shortly $t \diamond t'$ and we say that t and t' are *parallel*), then t and t' can be performed, if enabled, in any order as well as in parallel. With reference to Fig.1, transition e is an interrupt for f and g, and d is an interrupt for c. Transitions c and b are parallel.

The *transition structure* of Z is the quadruple

$$\mathcal{TS}(Z) \stackrel{def}{=} (T_Z^i, \rightarrow_Z, \triangleright_Z, \chi_Z).$$

We shall introduce now a slight variant of the standard semantics of Statecharts (see [3]). At each instant of time (a discrete time domain is enforced, for instance natural numbers $\mathbb{N}$) the environment prompts a statechart with a set of events. So, we assume to have a function $Env : \mathbb{N} \rightarrow 2^P$ describing environment. At a fixed instant of time n, a statechart *configuration* is characterized by the set of states which are currently entered and by the set of events communicated at that time. A statechart reacts by simultaneously performing a number of transitions (i.e., a *microstep*) enabled by events $Env(n)$. The effect is that the set of currently entered states is changed and the set $Env(n)$ is augmented by adding events in the action part of the performed transitions. As a consequence, a larger set of transitions might be enabled at time n (than that enabled by $Env(n)$) and a chain reaction might occur (i.e., a sequence of microsteps). Events can be sensed only at the instant of time they have been communicated (i.e., they are instantaneous), and only sets of parallel transitions can be performed instantaneously. Thus, the sequence of microsteps triggered by $Env(n)$ is finite. In our definition, a configuration consists of a set D of transitions and a function describing the environment. Transitions belonging to D are those having source state in the set of currently entered set of states. Semantics is defined only by exploiting the transition structure of a statechart without any direct reference to the notion of state and hierarchy on states.

Definition 5. A *configuration* is a pair $C = (D, Env)$, where $D \subseteq T_Z$ and $Env : \mathbb{N} \to 2^{P_Z}$ is the *environment function*; C is *initial* iff $D = imp^{\to_Z}$.
A transition t is *enabled at time* $\tau \in \mathbb{N}$ in C iff $t \in D$ and $Ev(t) \subseteq Env(\tau)$.
A set $\Psi \subseteq T_Z$ of transitions is a *microstep at time* τ from C iff each transition in Ψ is enabled at time τ in C and $t \diamond t'$, for any $t, t' \in \Psi$ with $t \neq t'$.
For a microstep Ψ at time τ from C, the configuration *reached from* C *by* Ψ is (D', Env'), with:

$$D' = \{t \in D : t' \not\triangleright t, \text{ for all } t' \in \Psi\} \cup \bigcup_{t \in \Psi} t^{\to}$$

$$Env'(n) = \begin{cases} Env(\tau) \cup \bigcup_{t \in \Psi} Act(t) & \text{for } n = \tau \\ Env(n) & \text{for } n \neq \tau. \end{cases}$$

A sequence (possibly null) $\mathcal{S} = \Psi_0.\Psi_1 \ldots \Psi_n$ of pairwise disjoint transition sets such that $t_i \not\triangleright t_j$, for each $t_i \in \Psi_i$ and $t_j \in \Psi_j$ with $0 \leq i < j \leq n$, is a *step at time* τ from a configuration C to a configuration C' iff there exists a sequence $C_0 \ldots C_{n+1}$ of configurations such that $C_0 = C$, $C_{n+1} = C'$, C_{i+1} is reached from C_i by microstep Ψ_i at time τ, for $0 \leq i \leq n$. Step $\mathcal{S}$ is *maximal* iff $\mathcal{S}.\Psi$ is not a step, for each non-empty microstep Ψ from C'.
A sequence $\mathcal{S}_0 \ldots \mathcal{S}_n$, where $\mathcal{S}_i$ is a sequence (possibly null) of transition sets, for $0 \leq i \leq n$, is a *behaviour* from an initial configuration C iff there exists a sequence of configurations $C_0 \ldots C_{n+1}$, with $C_0 = C$ and $\mathcal{S}_i$ is a maximal step at time i from C_i to C_{i+1}, for all $0 \leq i \leq n$.

In the standard semantics (see [3]) a step is a sequence $\Psi_0.\Psi_1 \ldots \Psi_n$ of pairwise disjoint transition sets such that $t_i \diamond t_j$, for each $t_i \in \Psi_i$ and $t_j \in \Psi_j$ with $0 \leq i \leq j \leq n$. With reference to Fig.1, if the transitions f and e (resp.: c and d) are both enabled, then they can be performed in the same step provided that f is performed before e (resp.: b is performed before d). In the classical semantics they cannot be performed in the same step and the choice between them is non-deterministic. As shown in [6], the advantages (with respect to the standard semantics) are that (high-level) transitions can be interpreted as interrupts and that some natural refinement techniques are supported.

3 Statecharts from Transition Structures

In this section we show that a transition structure completely describes a statechart. We present a recursive algorithm which associates, with the transition structure of a statechart Z, a statechart Z' having the same transition structure of Z. Actually, the algorithm is given for a slight restriction of the class of Statecharts, namely, for Statecharts all of whose states are *downward reachable*. A state $b \in B_Z$ is *downward reachable* iff there exists a transition t such that $b \in \Downarrow \{in(t)\}$. But in few pathological cases, a statechart can be transformed into a statechart with downward reachable states. In order to give a recursive definition of the algorithm, we have to extend the notion of Statecharts given in Def.1, thus allowing Statecharts possibly having transitions either without source or without target state (*dangling transitions*). In particular, each state b

in a statechart Z *induces* an (incomplete) statechart whose set of states is $\rho^\star(b)$ and whose set of transitions is

$$\{t \in T_Z : in_Z(t) \in \rho_Z^\star(b) \text{ or } out_Z(t) \in \rho_Z^\star(b)\} \cup \{t \in T_Z : b \in \Downarrow_Z \{in_Z(t)\}\}.$$

The other components are the obvious restrictions of the corresponding components of Z.

As concerns the transition structure $\Omega = (T_\Omega, \rightarrow_\Omega, \triangleright_\Omega, \chi_\Omega)$ of an incomplete statechart Z, we need to distinguish dangling transitions from the others. In particular, we are interested in the following subsets of T_Ω:

1. $K_\Omega \subseteq T_\Omega$ is the set of non dangling transitions;
2. $O_\Omega \subseteq T_\Omega$ is the set of transitions without target;
3. $W_\Omega \subseteq O_\Omega$ is the set of transitions whose source is the root;
4. $I_\Omega \subseteq T_\Omega$ is the set of transitions without source;
5. $U_\Omega \subseteq I_\Omega$ is the set of transitions not having a substate of the root as target.

Note that $T_\Omega = I_\Omega \cup K_\Omega \cup O_\Omega$. Note, also, that if Z is a *complete* statechart (i.e., as in Def.1), then the initial transition *imp* can be regarded as an incomplete transition leading to the root of Z, and so, our convention is that, for $\Omega = \mathcal{TS}(Z)$, $K_\Omega = T_Z$, $I_\Omega = U_\Omega = \{imp\}$, and $O_\Omega = W_\Omega = \emptyset$. Given a transition structure Ω, we associate a pair of symbols $o(t)$ and $i(t)$ with each transition $t \in K_\Omega$, a symbol $i(t)$ with each transition $t \in I_\Omega$, and a symbol $o(t)$ with each transition $t \in O_\Omega$. Symbols $o(t)$ and $i(t)$ represent a source and a target state, respectively, for transition t. Over that set of symbols we define an equivalence relation $\equiv_\Omega$ and we consider the quotient set. If the quotient set is not a singleton, then we associate with Ω a statechart whose root is an or-state. The set of the immediate substates of the root is in one-to-one correspondence with the quotient set. If the quotient set is a singleton, then we associate with Ω a statechart whose root is an and-state and the set of parallel components of the root is in one-to-one correspondence with the quotient set of the set of transition T under an equivalence relation $\approx_\Omega$ (defined below). Each element of the quotient sets under $\equiv_\Omega$ and $\approx_\Omega$ induces a transition structure, and the required statechart can be obtained by recursively applying the outlined step to the transition structures induced by the elements of the quotient set.

Definition 6. For a transition structure Ω, assume that $i, o : T_\Omega \rightarrow M$ are fixed injective and image disjoint maps, with M a suitable alphabet; then, $\equiv_\Omega \subseteq M \times M$ is the least equivalence relation s.t.:

1. if $t^{\rightarrow_\Omega} = t'^{\rightarrow_\Omega} = \emptyset$, then $i(t) \equiv_\Omega i(t')$, for $t, t' \in I_\Omega \cup K_\Omega$;
2. if $t \triangleright_\Omega t'$, then $o(t) \equiv_\Omega o(t')$ and $o(t) \equiv_\Omega i(t)$, for $t, t' \in T_\Omega$;
3. if $t \rightarrow_\Omega t'$, then $i(t) \equiv_\Omega o(t')$, for $t \in I_\Omega \cup K_\Omega$ and $t' \in (O_\Omega - W_\Omega) \cup K_\Omega$;

The quotient set of $\equiv_\Omega$ over $i(I_\Omega \cup K_\Omega) \cup o((O_\Omega - W_\Omega) \cup K_\Omega)$ is denoted by $\mathcal{V}_\Omega$.

Example 1. Let Ω be the transition structure of the statechart of Fig.1, then $I_\Omega = U_\Omega = \{imp\}$, $O_\Omega = \emptyset$ and $K_\Omega = \{a, b, c, d, e, f, g, h\}$.

The quotient set is $V_\Omega = \{v_1, v_2, v_3\}$, with:
$v_1 = \{i(e), i(imp), o(a), o(h)\}$;
$v_2 = \{i(a), i(h), i(c), i(b), o(b), o(c), o(d)\}$;
$v_3 = \{i(d), i(f), i(g), o(f), o(g), o(e)\}$.
A statechart with an or-state root corresponds with Ω.

For a transition structure Ω, each element $v \in V_\Omega$ *induces a transition structure* Ω_v, where

$$T_{\Omega_v} \stackrel{def}{=} \{t \in T_\Omega : \text{ either } i(t) \in v \text{ or } o(t) \in v\}$$

and $\rightarrow_{\Omega_v}$, $\triangleright_{\Omega_v}$, and χ_{Ω_v} are obvious restrictions of $\rightarrow_\Omega$, $\triangleright_\Omega$, and χ_Ω, respectively, to T_{Ω_v}. Moreover,

1. $K_{\Omega_v} \stackrel{def}{=} \{t \in T_\Omega : o(t), i(t) \in v\}$;
2. $O_{\Omega_v} \stackrel{def}{=} \{t \in T_\Omega : o(t) \in v, i(t) \notin v\}$;
3. $W_{\Omega_v} \stackrel{def}{=} \{t \in O_{\Omega_v} : h \triangleright_\Omega t \text{ for all } h \in K_{\Omega_v}, h \rightarrow_\Omega t \text{ for all } h \in I_{\Omega_v}\}$;
4. $I_{\Omega_v} \stackrel{def}{=} \{t \in T_\Omega : o(t) \notin v \text{ and } i(t) \in v\}$;
5. $U_{\Omega_v} \stackrel{def}{=} \begin{cases} \text{if } i(U_\Omega) \cap v \neq \emptyset, \text{ then} \\ U_\Omega \cup \{t : t \in I_{\Omega_v} - U_\Omega, t^{\rightarrow_{\Omega_v}} = h^{\rightarrow_{\Omega_v}}, \text{ for all } h \in U_\Omega\}; \\ \text{otherwise, a maximal set of transitions } V \subseteq I_{\Omega_v} \text{ s.t.} \\ t, h \in V \text{ implies } t^{\rightarrow_{\Omega_v}} = h^{\rightarrow_{\Omega_v}}. \end{cases}$

Example 2. With reference to the quotient set of Ex.1,
$K_{\Omega_{v_1}} = \emptyset$; $O_{\Omega_{v_1}} = W_{\Omega_{v_1}} = \{a, h\}$; $I_{\Omega_{v_1}} = U_{\Omega_{v_1}} = \{e, imp\}$;
$K_{\Omega_{v_2}} = \{c, b\}$; $O_{\Omega_{v_2}} = \{d\}$; $W_{\Omega_{v_2}} = \emptyset$; $I_{\Omega_{v_2}} = \{a, h\}$;
there are two possible choices for $U_{\Omega_{v_2}}$: either $U_{\Omega_{v_2}} = \{a\}$ or $U_{\Omega_{v_2}} = \{h\}$;
$K_{\Omega_{v_3}} = \{f, g\}$; $O_{\Omega_{v_3}} = W_{\Omega_{v_3}} = \{e\}$; $I_{\Omega_{v_3}} = U_{\Omega_{v_3}} = \{d\}$.

The sets O_{Ω_v} and W_{Ω_v} allow us to determine whether the source of a dangling outgoing transition t in Ω_v is the root of the statechart associated with Ω_v (i.e., $t \in W_{\Omega_v}$) or a substate of the root (i.e., $t \in O_{\Omega_v} - W_{\Omega_v}$). The transitions leading to the root of the statechart associated with Ω_v are the ones belonging to $U_{\Omega_v} - U_\Omega$. The default substate of the root is associated with the element $v \in V_\Omega$ such that $U_\Omega \subseteq U_{\Omega_v}$.

We define now the equivalence $\approx_\Omega$.

Definition 7. For a transition structure Ω, $\approx_\Omega \subseteq (T_\Omega - (U_\Omega \cup W_\Omega)) \times (T_\Omega - (U_\Omega \cup W_\Omega))$ is the least equivalence relation s.t.:

1. if $t \rightarrow_\Omega t'$, then $t \approx_\Omega t'$, for $t \in K_\Omega$ and $t' \in (O_\Omega - W_\Omega) \cup K_\Omega$;
2. if either $t_1 \rightarrow_\Omega h$, $t_2 \not\rightarrow_\Omega h$ or $t_2 \rightarrow_\Omega h$, $t_1 \not\rightarrow_\Omega h$, then $t_2 \approx_\Omega h$, for $t_1 \in U_\Omega$, $t_2 \in I_\Omega - U_\Omega$ and $h \in (O_\Omega - W_\Omega) \cup K_\Omega$;
3. if there exists a chain $t_1 \rightarrow_\Omega \ldots \rightarrow_\Omega t_k$ such that $t_1 \in I_\Omega$, $t_i \in K_\Omega$ for $2 \leq i \leq k$, then $t_k \approx_\Omega h$, for all $h \in K_\Omega \cup (O_\Omega - W_\Omega)$ such that $t_1 \rightarrow_\Omega h$ and $t_k \not\triangleright_\Omega h$.

The quotient set of $\approx_\Omega$ is denoted as $\mathcal{A}_\Omega$.

For a transition structure Ω, each element $v \in \mathcal{A}_\Omega$ *induces a transition structure* Ω_v, where $T_{\Omega_v} \stackrel{def}{=} I_\Omega \cup v$ and $\rightarrow_{\Omega_v}$, $\triangleright_{\Omega_v}$, and χ_{Ω_v} are the obvious restrictions of $\rightarrow_\Omega$, $\triangleright_\Omega$, and χ_Ω, respectively, to T_{Ω_v}.
Moreover, $K_{\Omega_v} \stackrel{def}{=} K_\Omega \cap v; O_{\Omega_v} \stackrel{def}{=} O_\Omega \cap v; W_{\Omega_v} \stackrel{def}{=} \emptyset; I_{\Omega_v} \stackrel{def}{=} I_\Omega; U_{\Omega_v} \stackrel{def}{=} I_\Omega - v$.

Example 3. Let Ω' (resp.: Ω'') be the transition structure induced by v_2 (see Ex.1 and Ex.2) with $U_{\Omega_{v_2}} = \{a\}$ (resp.: $U_{\Omega_{v_2}} = \{h\}$). The quotient sets $\mathcal{V}_{\Omega'}$ and $\mathcal{V}_{\Omega''}$ are singletons. The quotient set $\mathcal{A}_{\Omega'}$ (resp.: $\mathcal{A}_{\Omega''}$) has two elements $z_1 = \{h, c\}$ and $z_2 = \{b, d\}$ (resp.: $w_1 = \{a, c\}$ and $w_2 = \{b, d\}$). Moreover, $K_{\Omega'_{z_1}} = K_{\Omega''_{w_1}} = \{c\}$; $K_{\Omega'_{z_2}} = K_{\Omega''_{w_2}} = \{b\}$; $O_{\Omega'_{z_1}} = O_{\Omega''_{w_1}} = \emptyset$; $O_{\Omega'_{z_2}} = W_{\Omega''_{w_2}} = \{d\}$; $I_{\Omega'_{z_1}} = I_{\Omega''_{w_1}} = I_{\Omega'_{z_2}} = I_{\Omega''_{w_2}} = \{h, a\}$; $U_{\Omega'_{z_1}} = \{a\}$; $U_{\Omega''_{w_1}} = \{h\}$; $U_{\Omega'_{z_2}} = U_{\Omega''_{w_2}} = \{a, h\}$.

We define now the algorithm associating statecharts with transition structures. Since the way for defining the set U_{Ω_v}, for $v \in \mathcal{V}_\Omega$, is not unique, more than one statechart can be associated with a transition structure.

Definition 8. For a transition structure Ω, a statechart Z and a symbol *sym*, $\Omega \Rightarrow_{sym} Z$ iff $T_Z^i = T_\Omega$, $\chi_Z = \chi_\Omega$, and

1. if $T_\Omega = U_\Omega \cup W_\Omega$, then $B_Z = \{sym\}$, $\rho_Z = \{(sym, \emptyset)\}$, $\phi_Z = \{(sym, OR)\}$, $in_Z = \delta_Z = \emptyset$ and $out_Z = \{(t, sym) : t \in W_\Omega\}$.
2. if $T_\Omega \neq U_\Omega \cup W_\Omega$ and $\mathcal{V}_\Omega$ is a singleton, then, for $v \in \mathcal{A}_\Omega$,

$$Z_v \text{ is a statechart such that } \Omega_v \Rightarrow_{(sym,v)} Z_v, \text{ and}$$

$B_Z = \{sym\} \cup \bigcup_{v \in \mathcal{A}_\Omega} B_{Z_v}$;
$\rho_Z = \{(sym, sym \times \mathcal{A}_\Omega)\} \cup \bigcup_{v \in \mathcal{A}_\Omega} \rho_{Z_v}$;
$in_Z = \bigcup_{v \in \mathcal{A}_\Omega} in_{Z_v}$ and $out_Z = \bigcup_{v \in \mathcal{A}_\Omega} out_{Z_v} \cup \{(t, sym) : t \in W_\Omega\}$;
$\delta_Z = \bigcup_{v \in \mathcal{A}_\Omega} \delta_{Z_v}$; $\phi_H = \{(sym, AND)\} \cup \bigcup_{v \in \mathcal{A}_\Omega} \phi_{Z_v}$.
3. otherwise, for $v \in \mathcal{V}_\Omega$,

$$Z_v \text{ is a statechart such that } \Omega_v \Rightarrow_{(sym,v)} Z_v, \text{ and}$$

$B_Z = \{sym\} \cup \bigcup_{v \in \mathcal{V}_\Omega} B_{Z_v}$;
$\rho_Z = \{(sym, sym \times \mathcal{V}_\Omega)\} \cup \bigcup_{v \in \mathcal{V}_\Omega} \rho_{Z_v}$;
$in_Z = \{(t, (sym, v)) : t \in U_{\Omega_v} - U_\Omega\} \cup \bigcup_{v \in \mathcal{V}_\Omega} in_{Z_v}$;
$out_Z = \{(t, sym)) : t \in W_\Omega\} \cup \bigcup_{v \in \mathcal{V}_\Omega} out_{Z_v}$;
$\delta_Z = \{(sym, (sym, \overline{v}))\} \cup \bigcup_{v \in \mathcal{V}_\Omega} \delta_{Z_v}$, with $\overline{v} \in \mathcal{V}_\Omega$ s.t. $\overline{v} \cap i(U_\Omega) \neq \emptyset$;
$\phi_Z = \{(sym, OR)\} \cup \bigcup_{v \in \mathcal{V}_\Omega} \phi_{Z_v}$.

For Z the statechart of Fig.1, there are two statecharts Z' and Z'' such that $\mathcal{TS}(Z) \Rightarrow_{sym} Z'$ and $\mathcal{TS}(Z) \Rightarrow_{sym} Z''$: Z' is isomorphic to Z (with ref. to Ex.2, $U_{\Omega_{v_2}} = \{h\}$), and Z'' is represented in Fig.2 (with ref. to Ex.2, $U_{\Omega_{v_2}} = \{a\}$).

Theorem 9. For a (complete) statechart Z with downward reachable states,

$$\mathcal{TS}(Z) \Rightarrow_{sym} Z' \text{ implies } \mathcal{TS}(Z) = \mathcal{TS}(Z').$$

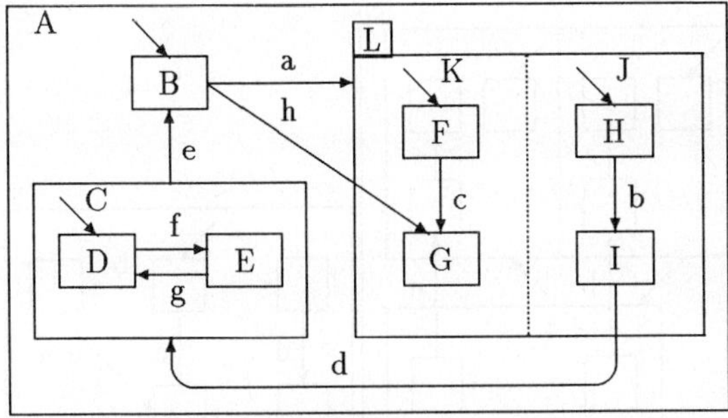

Fig. 2. A statechart built from the transition structure of the one in Fig.1.

Proof. (Sketch) Let Z be a (possibly incomplete) statechart with $\mathcal{TS}(Z) = \Omega$ and let Z' be such that $\Omega \Rightarrow_{sym} Z'$. That Z' is a statechart can be easily checked. We prove, by induction on the definition of relation $\Rightarrow_{sym}$, that, if $\Omega' = \mathcal{TS}(Z)$, then Ω and Ω' are componentwise equal but possibly unequal with respect to component U. (Actually, if Z is complete, then by construction, also Z' is, and $U_\Omega = U_{\Omega'} = \{imp\}$, thus proving the thesis).
(Base) That $\Omega = \Omega'$ immediately follows from construction.
(Inductive step) Assume that $\mathcal{V}_\Omega$ is not a singleton and let Z'_v, for $v \in \mathcal{V}_\Omega$, be the statechart induced by state (sym, v) of Z'. If $\Omega_{Z'_v} = \mathcal{TS}(Z'_v)$, then, by induction hypothesis, we have that Ω_v and $\Omega_{Z'_v}$ are componentwise equal (but possibly unequal with respect to component U). By construction Z' is a statechart having or-state root, and the transition structure of Z' can be obtained from the ones of Z'_v (for $v \in \mathcal{V}_\Omega$) as follows: $T_{\Omega'} = \bigcup_{v \in \mathcal{V}_\Omega} T_{\Omega_v} \cup W_\Omega$; $K_{\Omega'} = \bigcup_{v \in \mathcal{V}_\Omega} K_{\Omega_v} \cup \bigcup_{v,v' \in \mathcal{V}_\Omega} I_{\Omega_v} \cap O_{\Omega_{v'}}$; $O_{\Omega'} = W_\Omega \cup \bigcup_{v \in \mathcal{V}_\Omega} O_{\Omega_v} - \bigcup_{v,v' \in \mathcal{V}_\Omega} I_{\Omega_v} \cap O_{\Omega_{v'}}$; $W_{\Omega'} = W_\Omega$; $I_{\Omega'} = \bigcup_{v \in \mathcal{V}_\Omega} I_{\Omega_v} - \bigcup_{v,v' \in \mathcal{V}_\Omega} I_{\Omega_v} \cap O_{\Omega_{v'}}$; $\rightarrow_{\Omega'} = \bigcup_{v \in \mathcal{V}_\Omega} \rightarrow_{\Omega_v} \cup \{(t,t') : t \in I_{\Omega'}, t' \in W_{\Omega'}\}$; $\triangleright_{\Omega'} = \bigcup_{v \in \mathcal{V}_\Omega} \triangleright_{\Omega_v} \cup \{(t,t') : t \in K_{\Omega'}, t' \in W_{\Omega'}\}$. Now, by exploiting Def.6, it can be easily shown that $T_{\Omega'} = T_\Omega$, $K_{\Omega'} = K_\Omega$ $O_{\Omega'} = O_\Omega$, $I_{\Omega'} = I_\Omega$, $\rightarrow_{\Omega'} = \rightarrow_\Omega$ and $\triangleright_{\Omega'} = \triangleright_\Omega$. (Note that component U_Ω is not referenced in Def.6). Assume now that $\mathcal{V}_\Omega$ is a singleton. It can be proved that $\mathcal{A}_\Omega$ is not a singleton. Let Z'_v, for $v \in \mathcal{A}_\Omega$, be the statechart induced by state (sym, v) of Z'. By induction hypothesis, we have that Ω_v and $\Omega_{Z'_v}$ are componentwise equal (but possibly unequal with respect to component U). Now, Z' is a statechart having and-state root and the transition structure of Z' can be obtained from the ones of Z'_v (for $v \in \mathcal{A}_\Omega$) as follows: $T_{\Omega'} = \bigcup_{v \in \mathcal{A}_\Omega} T_{\Omega_v} \cup W_\Omega$; $K_{\Omega'} = \bigcup_{v \in \mathcal{A}_\Omega} K_{\Omega_v}$; $O_{\Omega'} = \bigcup_{v \in \mathcal{A}_\Omega} O_{\Omega_v} \cup W_\Omega$; $W_{\Omega'} = W_\Omega$; $I_{\Omega'} = I_{\Omega_v}$ (for all $v \in \mathcal{A}_\Omega$); $\rightarrow_{\Omega'} = \bigcup_{v \in \mathcal{A}_\Omega} \rightarrow_{\Omega_v} \cup \{(t,t') : t \in I_{\Omega'}, t' \in W_{\Omega'}\}$; $\triangleright_{\Omega'} = \bigcup_{v \in \mathcal{V}_\Omega} \triangleright_{\Omega_v} \cup \{(t,t') : t \in K_{\Omega_v}, t' \in T_{\Omega_{v'}}$, for some $v \neq v'$ and there is $h \in I_{\Omega'}$ s.t. $h \rightarrow^\star_{\Omega_v} t, h \rightarrow^\star_{\Omega'_v} t'\}$[3]. Now, by exploiting Def.7, it can be easily shown that $T_{\Omega'} = T_\Omega$, $K_{\Omega'} = K_\Omega$ $O_{\Omega'} = O_\Omega$, $\rightarrow_{\Omega'} = \rightarrow_\Omega$ and $\triangleright_{\Omega'} = \triangleright_\Omega$. (Equalities above can be proved by exploiting only points 1 and 3 of Def.7 where U_Ω is not referenced). □

[3] $\rightarrow^\star$ denotes the transitive closure of $\rightarrow$.

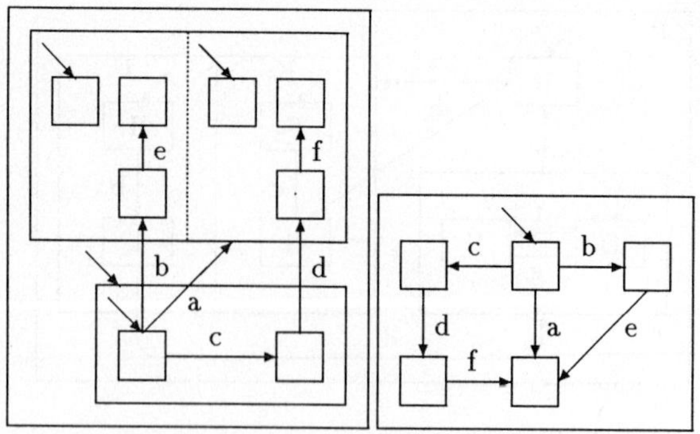

Fig. 3. A statechart Z (on the letf-hand side) and a statechart Z' such that $\mathcal{TS}(Z) \Rightarrow_{sym} Z'$.

In general, two statecharts Z and Z' such that $\mathcal{TS}(Z) \Rightarrow_{sym} Z'$ are not isomorphic. For instance, consider the statecharts Z and Z' of Fig.3. The statechart Z has an and-state though, apparently, no pair of transitions can be performed simultaneously. Since $\mathcal{TS}(Z)$ is an encoding of the behaviour properties of Z, the structural details of Z which do not affect behaviour cannot be recovered in Z'. This suggests that, in general, the algorithm of Def.8 can be exploited for simplifying a statechart by removing its irrelevant structural details.

4 Characterizing Transition Structures for Well Structured Statecharts

In the previous section we have shown that a given statechart can be represented by its transition structure. In general, a quadruple $(T, \rightarrow, \triangleright, \chi)$ (we call it *structure*), where $\rightarrow$ and $\triangleright$ are relations over set T and χ is a function on T, describes a statechart if there is a statechart Z s.t. $\mathcal{TS}(Z) = (T, \rightarrow, \triangleright, \chi)$. We are able to characterize the class of structures which describe *well structured statecharts*. A statechart Z is *well structured* iff

$$in_Z(t), out_Z(t) \in \rho_Z(\mathcal{L}_Z(t)), \text{ for all } t \in T_Z. \tag{1}$$

Transitions of well structured statecharts preserve the hierarchy on states (i.e., no transition crosses borders of boxes depicting states). Well structured statecharts is a proper restriction of the formalism which has been adopted frequently in literature to enjoy a simpler definition of semantics (e.g. see [8]). With reference to Fig.1, the represented statechart is not well structured since transitions a and

d do not satisfy constraint (1). Structures describing well structured statecharts can be axiomatically defined, thus allowing to precisely state the relationship among causality, parallelism and interruptions (i.e., hierarchy) in the formalism.

Definition 10. A 4-tuple $(T, \rightarrow, \triangleright, \chi)$, where T is a finite set, $\rightarrow, \triangleright \subseteq T \times T$ are anti-reflexive relations and $\chi : T \rightarrow 2^P \times 2^P$, for some finite set P, is a *good structure* iff:

1. if $t \rightarrow^* t'$, then $t \not\triangleright t'$[4];
2. there exists t s.t. $t \rightarrow^* t'$, for all $t' \in T - \{t\}$, and $t'' \not\rightarrow t$, for all $t'' \in T$;
3. if $t \rightarrow t'$ and $t \triangleright t''$, then $t' \triangleright t''$;
4. if $t \triangleright t'$ and $t' \not\triangleright t$, then $h \rightarrow t$ and $h \not\triangleright t'$ implies $h \rightarrow t'$;
5. if $t \triangleright t'$, $t' \not\triangleright t$, $t' \triangleright t''$ and $t'' \not\triangleright t'$, then $t \triangleright t''$;
6. if $t \triangleright t'$, $t' \not\triangleright t$ and $t' \diamond t''$ [5], then $t \diamond t''$;
7. if $t \triangleright t'$, $t' \not\triangleright t$ and $t \diamond t''$, then $t'' \triangleright t'$;
8. if $t \rightarrow t'$ and $t \diamond t''$, then $t' \diamond t''$;
9. if $t \rightarrow t'$, $h \rightarrow h'$, $t' \diamond h'$, $t \not\triangleright h'$ and $h \not\triangleright t'$, then $t \rightarrow h'$ and $h \rightarrow t'$;
10. if $t \rightarrow t'$, $h \rightarrow h'$, $t' \diamond h'$, $t \not\triangleright h'$ and $h \diamond t'$, then $t \rightarrow g_1 \rightarrow \ldots \rightarrow g_n \rightarrow h$ and $g_i \diamond t'$;
11. if $t^{\rightarrow} \cap t'^{\rightarrow} \neq \emptyset$, then $t \triangleright h$, for all $h \in t'^{\rightarrow} - t^{\rightarrow}$ and $t' \triangleright h$, for all $h \in t^{\rightarrow} - t'^{\rightarrow}$;
12. if $t \rightarrow h, h', h''$, then $h \triangleright h'$ and $h'' \not\triangleright h'$ implies $h \triangleright h''$;

The properties at points 2, 5 and 6 are satisfied also by the intere class of Statecharts. Good structures are a dual representation, with respect to the classical one, of well structured statechart. It is possible to shift from one representation to the other by exploiting the map $\mathcal{TS}$ and the relation $\Rightarrow_{sym}$.

Theorem 11. A structure Ω is a good structure iff there exists a well structured (downward reachable) statechart such that $\Omega = \mathcal{TS}(Z)$.

Proof. (Sketch) ($\Rightarrow$) It can be shown that the procedure of Def.8 is well defined when it is applied to good structures. In particular, it can be shown that if Ω is a good structure, and $\mathcal{V}_\Omega$ is a singleton, then $\mathcal{A}_\Omega$ is not a singleton, and, if $v \in \mathcal{V}_\Omega$ or $v \in \mathcal{A}_\Omega$, then Ω_v is also a good structure. So, the procedure always terminates and, for each good structure Ω, there exists a statechart Z such that $\Omega \Rightarrow_{sym} Z$. By Th.9, we have that $\Omega = \mathcal{TS}(Z)$. Moreover, it is possible to show, by induction on the definition of relation $\Rightarrow_{sym}$, that Z is well structured.
($\Leftarrow$) It is easy to check that $\mathcal{TS}(Z)$ satisfies the constraints of Def.10. □

5 Morphisms of Transition Structures and Transformations of Statecharts

In this section we show that the investigation of transition structure morphisms is useful for investigating transformations of statecharts which preserve behaviour.

[4] $\rightarrow^*$ denotes the transitive closure of $\rightarrow$.

[5] $t \diamond t'$ is a short writing for $t \triangleright t'$ and $t' \triangleright t$.

A morphism between two transition structures is a map from the transition set of the former to the transition set of the latter which preserves the initial transition, sequentiality and independence relations, and transition labels. We are interested in morphisms which preserve behaviour in the sense that a behaviour corresponding to the former transition structure can be suitably mapped into a behaviour corresponding to the latter and viceversa. Behaviour preserving morphisms induce classes of behaviour preserving transformations over statecharts.

Definition 12. A (partial) map $\omega : T_\Omega \rightarrow T_{\Omega'}$ is a *morphism of transition structures* Ω and Ω', iff:

1. $\omega(imp) = imp$;
2. $t \rightarrow_\Omega t'$ implies $\omega(t) \rightarrow_{\Omega'} \omega(t')$ (whenever $\omega(t)$ and $\omega(t')$ are defined);
3. $t \triangleright_\Omega t'$ implies $\omega(t) \triangleright_{\Omega'} \omega(t')$ (whenever $\omega(t)$ and $\omega(t')$ are defined);
4. $\chi_{\Omega'}(\omega(t)) = \chi_\Omega(t)$ (whenever $\omega(t)$ is defined).

Unless otherwise said, a morphism is assumed to be a total map. Obviously, isomorphisms[6] of transition structures preserve behaviour. For instance, if statecharts Z, Z' and Z'' are such that $\mathcal{TS}(Z) \Rightarrow_{sym} Z'$ and $\mathcal{TS}(Z) \Rightarrow_{sym} Z''$, then their transition structures are isomorphic. In general, isomorphisms induces transformations over statecharts which allow to add (resp.: remove) irrelevant structural details to (resp.: from) a statechart or to suitably change its defaults (and sources of transitions accordingly). Actually, we are interested in morphisms less strict than isomorphisms. For instance, consider the problem of transforming a statechart into a well structured equivalent statechart. Sometimes, a statechart can be transformed into a well structured statechart provided that a number of states and transitions are duplicated (the corresponding transition structures fail to be isomorphic). As an example, see Fig.4 where a transformation of the statechart of Fig.1 is depicted. The transition a of Fig.4 does not violate the constraint 1 but it does in Fig.1. The transformation requires the duplication of transitions b and d. Unfortunately, morphisms as defined in Def.12 do not preserve behaviour, since maximality of steps is not preserved and, so, additional constraints must be considered.

Definition 13. The morphism ω of transition structures Ω and Ω' is called *strong* when,

$$\omega(t^{\rightarrow_\Omega}) = \omega(t)^{\rightarrow_{\Omega'}} \text{for all } t \in T_\Omega \text{ and} \tag{2}$$

$$t \triangleright_\Omega t' \text{ for all } t, t' \in T_\Omega \text{ s.t. } \omega(t) \triangleright_{\Omega'} \omega(t') \text{ and } t \parallel_\Omega t'^{7}. \tag{3}$$

Let us consider the statecharts of Fig.4 and the one of Fig.1. The map ω, from the transitions of the former to the ones of the latter such that $\omega(b) = \omega(b') = b$, $\omega(d) = \omega(d') = c$, and acting as the identity elsewhere, is a strong morphism.

[6] A morphism ω is an *isomorphism* iff it is a bijection and ω^{-1} is also a morphism.

[7] For a statechart Z, the concurrency relation $\parallel_Z$ can be derived from $\Omega = \mathcal{TS}(Z)$ (it suffices to rephrase Def.3 by exploiting relations $\rightarrow_\Omega$ and $\triangleright_\Omega$). So, we write $\parallel_\Omega$ instead of $\parallel_Z$.

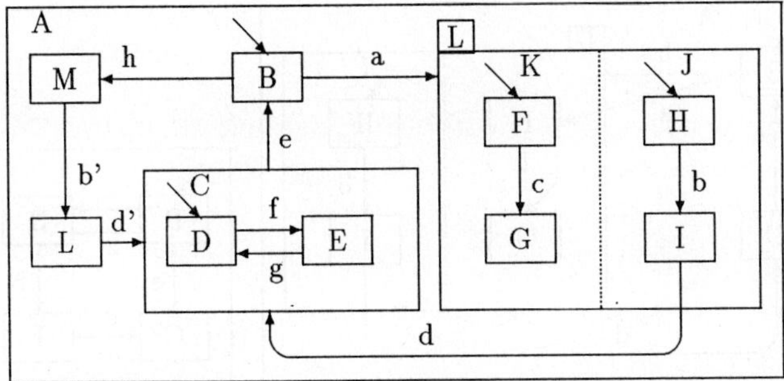

Fig. 4. A statechart admitting a strong morphism from its transition structure to the one of the statechart of Fig.1.

Partial strong morphisms preserve behaviour provided that other constraints are satisfied. In particular, we consider partial morphisms which *preserve causality, choice and communication* in the sense that if a morphism is defined over a transition t, then it is defined over all the transitions causing t, over all the transitions which are concurrent and mutually exclusive with respect to t, and over all the transitions communicating signals enabling t.

Definition 14. A partial morphism ω of transition structures Ω and Ω' *preserves causes* if, for $t, t' \in T_\Omega$ $\omega(t)$ defined and $t' \rightarrow_\Omega t$ implies $\omega(t')$ is defined; ω *preserves choices* if, for $t, t', t'' \in T_\Omega$, that $t \rightarrow_\Omega t'$, $t \rightarrow_\Omega t''$, $\omega(t)$ and $\omega(t')$ are defined and $\omega(t'')$ is not defined implies $t'' \rhd_\Omega t'$;
ω *preserves communication* iff for all $t, t' \in T_\Omega$, $\omega(t)$ undefined and $\omega(t')$ defined implies $Act(t) \cap Ev(t') = \emptyset$.

When a morphism of transition structures Ω and Ω' is partial, we compare the part of the transition structure over which the morphism is defined, with Ω'. Partial morphisms can be exploited for proving the correctness of some refinement techniques. As an example, the statechart of Fig.1 is a refinement of both the statecharts of Fig.5 and the statechart on the left-hand side of figure Fig.5 is a refinement of the one on the right-hand side. The map ω from the set of transitions of the statechart in Fig.1 to the set of the one on the left-hand side (resp.: right-hand side) of Fig.5 such that ω is not defined in f and g (resp.: in f, g and c) and ω is the identity elsewhere, is a strong morphism which preserves causes and choices (in our examples we have not considered transition labels and so we omit the property of preserving communication). A similar morphism can be defined between the transition structures of the two statecharts of Fig.5.

Theorem 15. Let ω be a strong morphism of transition structures Ω and Ω' (resp.: a strong partial morphism which preserve causes, choices and communication), then $\mathcal{S}_0.\mathcal{S}_1 \ldots \mathcal{S}_n$ is a behaviour from a configuration $(imp^{\rightarrow_{\Omega'}}, Env)$ iff there exists a behaviour $\mathcal{S}'_0.\mathcal{S}'_1 \ldots \mathcal{S}'_n$ from $(imp^{\rightarrow_\Omega}, Env)$ such that

$$\mathcal{S}_0.\mathcal{S}_1 \ldots \mathcal{S}_n = \omega(\mathcal{S}'_0).\omega(\mathcal{S}'_1) \ldots \omega(\mathcal{S}'_n).$$

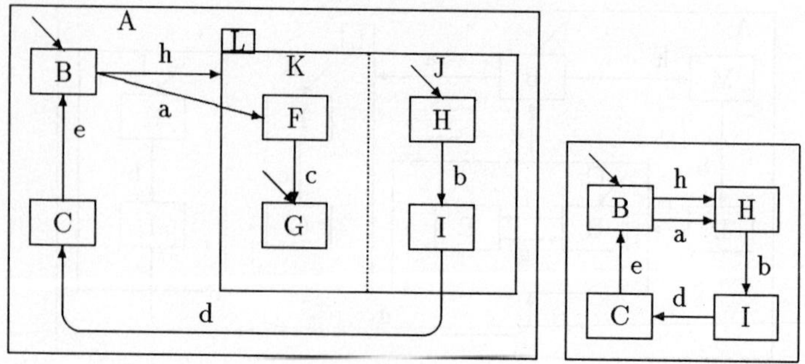

Fig. 5. Two statecharts of which the statechart in Fig.1 is a refinement.

Note that a strong morphism preserves behaviours (in the sense of Th.15) even when the classical semantics is enforced. That is not the case when partial morphisms are considered. For a discussion on the problem we refer to [6].

References

1. von der Beek, M.: A Comparison of Statecharts Variants, LNCS 863, Springer, Berlin, 1994, pp. 128–148.
2. Harel, D.: Statecharts: A Visual Formalism for Complex Systems, Science of Computer Programming **8** (1987), pp. 231–274.
3. Harel, D., Pnueli, A., Schmidt, J., P., Sherman, R.: On the Formal Semantics of Statecharts, Proc. 2nd IEEE Symposium on Logic in Computer Science, IEEE CS Press, New York, 1987, pp. 54–64.
4. Huizing, C., Gerth, R., de Roever, W.P.: Modelling Statechart Behaviour in a Fully Abstract Way, LNCS 299, Springer, Berlin, 1988, pp. 271–294.
5. Peron, A.: Synchronous and Asynchronous Models for Statecharts, Dipartimento di Informatica, Università di Pisa, PhD Thesis, TD 21/93, 1993.
6. Peron, A., Maggiolo-Schettini, A.: Transitions as Interrupts: A New Semantics for Timed Statecharts, LNCS 789, Springer, 1994, Berlin, pp. 806–821.
7. Pnueli, A., Shalev, M.: What is in a Step: On the Semantics of Statecharts, LNCS 525, Springer, 1991, Berlin, pp. 244–464.
8. Uselton, A.C., Smolka S.A.: A Process Algebraic Semantics for Statecharts via State Refinement, Proceedings Working Conference on Programming, Concepts, Methods and Calculi (PROCOMET'94), San Miniato, Italy, 1994, pp. 184–200.

Part III

FASE

An Imperative Object Calculus

Martín Abadi and Luca Cardelli

Digital Equipment Corporation, Systems Research Center

Abstract. We develop an imperative calculus of objects. Its main type constructor is the one for object types, which incorporate variance annotations and Self types. A subtyping relation between object types supports object subsumption. The type system for objects relies on unusual but beneficial assumptions about the possible subtypes of an object type. With the addition of polymorphism, the calculus can express classes and inheritance.

1. Introduction

Object calculi are formalisms at the same level of abstraction as λ-calculi, but based exclusively on objects rather than functions. Unlike λ-calculi, object calculi are designed specifically for clarifying features of object-oriented languages. There is a wide spectrum of relevant object calculi, just as there is a wide spectrum of λ-calculi. One can investigate untyped, simply-typed, and polymorphic calculi, as well as functional and imperative calculi.

In object calculi, as in λ-calculi, a minimal untyped kernel is enriched with derived constructions and with increasingly sophisticated type systems, until language features can be realistically modeled. The compactness of the initial kernel gives conceptual unity to the calculi, and enables formal analysis.

In this paper, we develop an imperative object calculus. It provides a minimal setting in which to study the imperative operational semantics and the delicate typing rules of practical object-oriented languages.

The calculus includes objects, method invocation, method update, and object cloning. Traditionally, an object is seen as a bundle of mutable fields together with a method suite. In our calculus, the method suite is itself mutable, so we can dispense with the fields.

The main type constructor is the one for object types; an object type is a list of method names and method result types. A subtyping relation between object types supports object subsumption, which allows an object to be used where an object with fewer methods is expected. Variance annotations enable flexible subtyping and protection from side effects.

The object type constructor incorporates a notion of Self types. Intuitively, Self is the partially unknown type of the self parameter of each method. Several object-oriented languages have included it in their type systems [18, 22], sometimes with unsound rules [13]. Therefore, it seems important to have a precise understanding of Self. Unfortunately, it has proven hard to reduce Self to more primitive and well-understood notions (see [3, 7, 19] for recent progress). We aim to provide a satisfactory treatment of Self by taking it as primitive and axiomatizing its desired properties.

The treatment of Self types relies on assumptions about the possible subtypes of object types. These assumptions are operationally sound, but would not hold in natural semantic models. We show the necessity of these assumptions in finding satisfactory typings for programs involving Self types.

We consider also bounded type quantifiers for polymorphism. Taken together, objects with imperative features, object types, and polymorphism form a realistic kernel for a programming language. Using these primitives, we account for classes, subclasses, inheritance, method and field specialization in subclasses, parametric method update, and protection from external updates.

A few other object formalisms have been defined and studied. Many of these rely on purely functional models, with an emphasis on types [1, 7, 10, 11, 16, 19-21, 24]. Others deal with imperative features in the context of concurrency; see for example [26]. The works most closely related to ours are that of Eifrig *et al.* on LOOP [14] and that of Bruce *et al.* on PolyTOIL [9]. LOOP and PolyTOIL are typed, imperative, object-oriented languages with procedures, objects, and classes. PolyTOIL takes procedures, objects, and classes as primitive, with fairly complex rules. LOOP is translated into a somewhat simpler calculus. Our calculus is centered on objects; procedures and classes can be defined from them. Despite these differences, we all share the goal of modeling imperative object-oriented languages by precise semantic structures and sound type systems.

This paper is self-contained, but continues our work of [2-5]. The most apparent novelties are the variance annotations, the treatment of Self types, and the representation of classes and inheritance. The new typing features led us to prefer syntactic proof techniques over denotational methods.

In section 2 we give the untyped term syntax of our calculus and its operational semantics. In section 3 we present object types. In section 4 we add bounded universal quantifiers. In section 5 we discuss soundness. In section 6 we consider the typing of some critical examples, and provide a representation of classes and method inheritance.

2. An Untyped Imperative Calculus

We begin with the syntax of an untyped imperative calculus. The initial syntax is minimal, but in sections 2.2, 2.3, and 6.2 we show how to express convenient constructs such as fields, procedures, and classes. We omit how to encode basic data types and control structures, which can be treated much as in [4]. In section 2.5 we give an operational semantics.

2.1 Syntax and Informal Semantics

The evaluation of terms is based on an imperative operational semantics with a store, and generally proceeds deterministically from left to right. The letter ς (sigma) is a binder; it delays evaluation of the term to its right.

Syntax of terms

$a,b ::=$	term
x	variable
$[l_i{=}\varsigma(x_i)b_i \;^{i\in 1..n}]$	object (l_i distinct)
$a.l$	method invocation
$a.l{\Leftarrow}(y, z{=}c)\varsigma(x)b$	method update
$\mathrm{clone}(a)$	cloning

An object is a collection of components $l_i{=}\varsigma(x_i)b_i$, for distinct labels l_i and associated methods $\varsigma(x_i)b_i$; the order of these components does not matter, even for our deterministic operational semantics. Each binder ς binds the self parameter of a method; ς(x)b is a method with self variable x and body b.

A method invocation b.l results in the evaluation of b, followed by the evaluation of the body of the method named l, with the value of b bound to the self variable of the method.

A cloning operation clone(b) produces a new object with the same labels as b, with each component sharing the methods of the corresponding component of b.

The method update construct, a.l⇐(y,z=c)ς(x)b, is best understood by looking at two of its special cases:

Simple method update: a.l⇐ς(x)b

This construct evaluates a, replaces the method named l with the new method ς(x)b, and returns the modified object.

Method update with old self: a.l⇐(y)ς(x)b

This construct is similar to simple method update, but in addition the value of a is bound to the variable y within ς(x)b. Informally, it means y.l⇐ς(x)b where the value of a is bound to y. After the update, when the method l is invoked, y still points to the old value of a, and x points to the current self.

The general method update construct, a.l⇐(y,z=c)ς(x)b, first evaluates a and binds its value to y, then evaluates c and binds its value to z, and finally updates the l method of y and returns the modified object. The variable y may occur in c and b, and the variables z and x may occur in b.

The two special cases above are definable from a.l⇐(y,z=c)ς(x)b:

a.l⇐ς(x)b ≜ a.l⇐(y, z=y)ς(x)b	where y,z ∉ FV(b)
a.l⇐(y)ς(x)b ≜ a.l⇐(y, z=y)ς(x)b	where z ∉ FV(b)

The standard let and sequencing constructs are also definable:

let x = a in b ≜	
([val = ς(y)y.val].val⇐(z, x=a)ς(w)b).val	where z,w ∉ FV(b) and z ∉ FV(a)
a ; b ≜ let x = a in b	where x ∉ FV(b)

Conversely, in an untyped calculus, the construct a.l⇐(y,z=c)ς(x)b can be expressed in terms of let and simple method update, as let y = a in let z = c in y.l⇐ς(x)b. However, the construct a.l⇐(y,z=c)ς(x)b yields better typings, as shown in section 6.1.

2.2 Fields

In our calculus, every component of an object contains a method. However, we can encode fields with eagerly evaluated contents. We write $[l_i{=}b_i\ ^{i\in1..n}, l_j{=}\varsigma(x_j)b_j\ ^{j\in1..m}]$ for an object where $l_i{=}b_i$ are fields and $l_j{=}\varsigma(x_j)b_j$ are methods. We also write a.l:=b for field update, and a.l, as before, for field selection. We abbreviate:

Field notation

$[l_i{=}b_i\ ^{i\in1..n}, l_j{=}\varsigma(x_j)b_j\ ^{j\in1..m}]$	for $y_i \notin FV(b_i\ ^{i\in1..n}, b_j\ ^{j\in1..m})$, y_i distinct, $i\in0..n$
$\triangleq$ let $y_1{=}b_1$ in ... let $y_n{=}b_n$ in $[l_i{=}\varsigma(y_0)y_i\ ^{i\in1..n}, l_j{=}\varsigma(x_j)b_j\ ^{j\in1..m}]$	

a.l:=b	$\triangleq$ a.l⇐(y,z=b)ς(x)z	for y ∉ FV(b), x,y,z distinct

The semantics of an object with fields may depend on the order of its components, because of side-effects in computing contents of fields. The encoding specifies an evaluation order.

By an update, a method can be changed into a field and vice versa. Thus, we use somewhat interchangeably the names selection and invocation.

2.3 Procedures

Our object calculus is so minimal that it does not include procedures, but these can be expressed too. To illustrate this point, we consider informally an imperative call-by-value λ-calculus that includes abstraction, application, and assignment to λ-bound variables. For example, assuming arithmetic primitives, (λ(x) x:=x+1)(3) is a term yielding 4. We translate this λ-calculus into our object calculus:

Translation of procedures

$⟪x⟫_\rho$	$\triangleq$	ρ(x) if x∈dom(ρ), and x otherwise
$⟪x{:=}a⟫_\rho$	$\triangleq$	$x.arg{:=}⟪a⟫_\rho$
$⟪\lambda(x)b⟫_\rho$	$\triangleq$	$[arg = \varsigma(x)x.arg,\ val = \varsigma(x)⟪b⟫_{\rho\{x \leftarrow x.arg\}}]$
$⟪b(a)⟫_\rho$	$\triangleq$	$(clone(⟪b⟫_\rho).arg{:=}⟪a⟫_\rho).val$

In the translation, an environment ρ maps each variable x either to x.arg if x is λ-bound, or to x if x is a free variable. A λ-abstraction is translated to an object with an arg component, for storing the argument, and a val method, for executing the body. The arg component is initially set to a divergent method, and is filled with an argument upon procedure call. A call activates the val method that can then access the argument through self as x.arg. An assignment x:=a updates x.arg, where the argument is stored (assuming that x is λ-bound). A procedure needs to be cloned when it is called; the clone provides a fresh location in which to store the argument of the call, preventing interference with other calls of the same procedure. Such interference would derail recursive invocations.

2.4 A Small Example

We give a trivial example as a notation drill. We use fields, procedures, and booleans in defining a memory cell with get, set, and dup (duplicate) components:

let m = [get = false, set = ς(self) λ(b) self.get:=b, dup = ς(self) clone(self)]
in m.set(true); m.get   yields true

2.5 Operational Semantics

We now give an operational semantics for the basic calculus of section 2.1; the semantics relates terms to results in a global store. Object terms reduce to object results $[l_i{=}\iota_i\ ^{i\in 1..n}]$ consisting of sequences of store locations, one location for each object component. In order to stay close to standard implementation techniques, we avoid using formal substitutions during reduction: we describe a semantics based on stacks and closures. A stack $\mathcal{S}$ associates variables with results; a closure $\langle \varsigma(x)b, S\rangle$ is a pair of a method and a stack that is used for the reduction of the method body. A store maps locations ι to method closures; we write stores in the form $\iota_i \mapsto \langle \varsigma(x_i)b_i, S_i\rangle^{\, i\in 1..n}$. We let $\sigma.\iota \leftarrow m$ denote the result of writing m in the ι location of σ.

The operational semantics is expressed in terms of a relation that relates a store σ, a stack S, a term b, a result v, and another store σ'. This relation is written $\sigma \bullet S \vdash b \rightsquigarrow v \bullet \sigma'$, and it means that with the store σ and the stack S, the term b reduces to a result v, yielding an updated store σ'; the stack does not change.

Notation

ι		store location	(e.g., an integer)
v	::=	$[l_i = \iota_i^{\; i\in 1..n}]$	object result	(l_i distinct)
σ	::=	$\iota_i \mapsto \langle \varsigma(x_i)b_i, S_i\rangle^{\, i\in 1..n}$	store	(ι_i distinct)
S	::=	$x_i \mapsto v_i^{\; i\in 1..n}$	stack	(x_i distinct)

Well-formed store judgment: $\sigma \vdash \diamond$

(Store $\emptyset$)

$$\frac{}{\emptyset \vdash \diamond}$$

(Store ι)

$$\frac{\sigma \bullet S \vdash \diamond \qquad \iota \notin dom(\sigma)}{\sigma, \iota \mapsto \langle \varsigma(x)b, S\rangle \vdash \diamond}$$

Well-formed stack judgment: $\sigma \bullet S \vdash \diamond$

(Stack $\emptyset$)

$$\frac{\sigma \vdash \diamond}{\sigma \bullet \emptyset \vdash \diamond}$$

(Stack x) (l_i, ι_i distinct)

$$\frac{\sigma \bullet S \vdash \diamond \qquad x \notin dom(S) \quad \iota_i \in dom(\sigma) \qquad \forall i \in 1..n}{\sigma \bullet S, x \mapsto [l_i = \iota_i^{\; i\in 1..n}] \vdash \diamond}$$

Term reduction judgment: $\sigma \bullet S \vdash a \rightsquigarrow v \bullet \sigma'$

(Red x)

$$\frac{\sigma \bullet S', x \mapsto v, S'' \vdash \diamond}{\sigma \bullet S', x \mapsto v, S'' \vdash x \rightsquigarrow v \bullet \sigma}$$

(Red Object) (l_i, ι_i distinct)

$$\frac{\sigma \bullet S \vdash \diamond \qquad \iota_i \notin dom(\sigma) \qquad \forall i \in 1..n}{\sigma \bullet S \vdash [l_i = \varsigma(x_i)b_i^{\; i\in 1..n}] \rightsquigarrow [l_i = \iota_i^{\; i\in 1..n}] \bullet (\sigma, \iota_i \mapsto \langle \varsigma(x_i)b_i, S\rangle^{\, i\in 1..n})}$$

(Red Select)

$$\frac{\begin{array}{c}\sigma \bullet S \vdash a \rightsquigarrow [l_i = \iota_i^{\; i\in 1..n}] \bullet \sigma' \qquad \sigma'(\iota_j) = \langle \varsigma(x_j)b_j, S'\rangle \qquad x_j \notin dom(S') \qquad j \in 1..n \\ \sigma' \bullet S', x_j \mapsto [l_i = \iota_i^{\; i\in 1..n}] \vdash b_j \rightsquigarrow v \bullet \sigma''\end{array}}{\sigma \bullet S \vdash a.l_j \rightsquigarrow v \bullet \sigma''}$$

(Red Update)

$$\frac{\sigma\bullet S \vdash a \leadsto [l_i{=}\iota_i{}^{i\in 1..n}]\bullet\sigma' \qquad \iota_j{\in}dom(\sigma') \qquad j{\in}1..n \qquad \sigma'\bullet S,\ y{\mapsto}[l_i{=}\iota_i{}^{i\in 1..n}] \vdash c \leadsto v\bullet\sigma''}{\sigma\bullet S \vdash a.l_j{\Leftarrow}(y,\ z{=}c)\varsigma(x)b \leadsto [l_i{=}\iota_i{}^{i\in 1..n}]\bullet \sigma''.\iota_j{\leftarrow}\langle\varsigma(x)b,\ (S,\ y{\mapsto}[l_i{=}\iota_i{}^{i\in 1..n}],\ z{\mapsto}v)\rangle}$$

(Red Clone) (ι'_i distinct)

$$\frac{\sigma\bullet S \vdash a \leadsto [l_i{=}\iota_i{}^{i\in 1..n}]\bullet\sigma' \qquad \iota_i \in dom(\sigma') \qquad \iota'_i \notin dom(\sigma) \qquad \forall i{\in}1..n}{\sigma\bullet S \vdash clone(a) \leadsto [l_i{=}\iota'_i{}^{i\in 1..n}]\bullet(\sigma',\ \iota'_i{\mapsto}\sigma'(\iota_i){}^{i\in 1..n})}$$

A variable reduces to the result it denotes in the current stack. An object reduces to a result consisting of a fresh collection of locations; the store is extended to associate method closures to those locations. A selection operation $a.l_j$ first reduces the object a to a result, then activates the appropriate method closure. An update operation $a.l_j{\Leftarrow}(y,z{=}c)\varsigma(x)b$ first reduces the object a to the final result; next, with y bound to that result, it reduces the term c to another result; finally, it updates the appropriate store location with a closure consisting of the new method $\varsigma(x)b$ and a stack binding y and z. A clone operation reduces its object to a result; then it allocates a fresh collection of locations that are associated to the existing method closures from the object.

We illustrate method update, and the creation of loops through the store, by the reduction of the term $[l{=}\varsigma(x)x.l{:=}x].l$, that is, $[l{=}\varsigma(x)x.l{\Leftarrow}(y,z{=}x)\varsigma(w)z].l$:

$$\emptyset\bullet\emptyset \vdash [l{=}\varsigma(x)x.l{\Leftarrow}(y,z{=}x)\varsigma(w)z].l \leadsto [l{=}0]\bullet\sigma$$

$$\text{where} \quad \sigma \equiv 0{\mapsto}\langle\varsigma(w)z,\ (x{\mapsto}[l{=}0],\ y{\mapsto}[l{=}0],\ z{\mapsto}[l{=}0])\rangle$$

The store σ contains a loop, because it maps the index 0 to a closure that binds the variable z to a value that contains index 0. Hence, an attempt to read out the result of $[l{=}\varsigma(x)x.l{:=}x].l$ by "inlining" the store and stack mappings would produce the infinite term $[l{=}\varsigma(w)[l{=}\varsigma(w)[l{=}\varsigma(w)...]]]$.

3. Typing

In this section we develop a type system for the calculus of section 2. We have the following syntax of types:

Syntax of types

A,B ::=	type
X	type variable
Top	the biggest type
$Obj(X)[l_i\upsilon_i{:}B_i\{X\}^{i\in 1..n}]$	object type ($\upsilon_i \in \{^-,^o,^+\}$, l_i distinct)

Let $A \equiv Obj(X)[l_i\upsilon_i{:}B_i\{X\}^{i\in 1..n}]$. The binder Obj binds a Self type named X, which is known to be a subtype of A. Then A is the type of those objects with methods named $l_i{}^{i\in 1..n}$ having self parameters of type X, and with corresponding result types $B_i\{X\}$. The type X may occur only covariantly in the result types B_i. This covariance requirement is necessary for the soundness of our rules; covariance is defined precisely below.

Each υ_i is a variance annotation; it is one of the symbols $^-$, ^{o}, and $^+$, for contravariance, invariance, and covariance, respectively. Covariant components allow covariant subtyping, but prevent update. Symmetrically, contravariant components allow contravariant subtyping, but prevent invocation. Invariant components can be both invoked and updated; by subtyping, they can be regarded as either covariant or contravariant. Therefore, variance annotations support flexible subtyping and a form of protection.

The rules for our object calculus are given next. The first three groups of rules concern typing environments, types, and the subtyping relation. The final group concerns typing of terms: there is one rule for each construct in the calculus; in addition, a subsumption rule connects term typing with subtyping.

Well-formed environment judgment: $E \vdash \diamond$

(Env ø)
$$\frac{}{\emptyset \vdash \diamond}$$

(Env x)
$$\frac{E \vdash A \quad x \notin dom(E)}{E,x{:}A \vdash \diamond}$$

(Env X<:)
$$\frac{E \vdash A \quad X \notin dom(E)}{E,X{<:}A \vdash \diamond}$$

Well-formed type judgment: $E \vdash A$

(Type X<:)
$$\frac{E',X{<:}A,E'' \vdash \diamond}{E',X{<:}A,E'' \vdash X}$$

(Type Top)
$$\frac{E \vdash \diamond}{E \vdash Top}$$

(Type Object) (l_i distinct, $\upsilon_i \in \{^o,^-,^+\}$)
$$\frac{E,X{<:}Top \vdash B_i\{X^+\} \quad \forall i \in 1..n}{E \vdash Obj(X)[l_i\upsilon_i{:}B_i\{X\}^{\ i \in 1..n}]}$$

Formally, $B\{X^+\}$ indicates that X occurs only covariantly in B; that is, either B is a variable (possibly X), or B≡Top, or $B \equiv Obj(Y)[l_i\upsilon_i{:}B_i^{\ i \in 1..n}]$ and either Y≡X or for each $\upsilon_i \equiv^+$ we have $B_i\{X^+\}$, for each $\upsilon_i \equiv^-$ we have $B_i\{X^-\}$, and for each $\upsilon_i \equiv^o$ we have $X \notin FV(B_i)$. Similarly, $B\{X^-\}$ indicates that X occurs only contravariantly in B; that is, either B is a variable different from X, or B≡Top, or $B \equiv Obj(Y)[l_i\upsilon_i{:}B_i^{\ i \in 1..n}]$ and either Y≡X or for each $\upsilon_i \equiv^+$ we have $B_i\{X^-\}$, for each $\upsilon_i \equiv^-$ we have $B_i\{X^+\}$, and for each $\upsilon_i \equiv^o$ we have $X \notin FV(B_i)$.

The formation rule for object types (Type Object) requires that all the component types be covariant in Self. According to the definition of covariant occurrences, more than one Self type may be active in a given context, as in the type $Obj(X)[l^o{:}\ Obj(Y)[m^+{:}X,\ n^o{:}Y]]$.

By convention, any omitted υ's are taken to be equal to ^{o}. We regard a simple object type $[l_i{:}B_i^{\ i \in 1..n}]$ (as defined in [4]) as an abbreviation for $Obj(X)[l_i^o{:}B_i^{\ i \in 1..n}]$, where X does not appear in any B_i.

Subtyping judgments: $E \vdash A <: B,\ \ E \vdash \upsilon A <: \upsilon B$

(Sub Refl)
$$\frac{E \vdash A}{E \vdash A <: A}$$

(Sub Trans)
$$\frac{E \vdash A <: B \quad E \vdash B <: C}{E \vdash A <: C}$$

(Sub X)
$$\frac{E',X{<:}A,E'' \vdash \diamond}{E',X{<:}A,E'' \vdash X{<:}A}$$

(Sub Top)
$$\frac{E \vdash A}{E \vdash A <: Top}$$

(Sub Object)

$$\frac{E,Y{<:}Obj(X)[l_i \upsilon_i{:}B_i\{X\}^{\,i\in 1..n+m}] \vdash \upsilon_i\, B_i\{Y\} <: \upsilon_i'\, B_i'\{Y\} \qquad \forall i\in 1..n}{E \vdash Obj(X)[l_i \upsilon_i{:}B_i\{X\}^{\,i\in 1..n+m}] <: Obj(X)[l_i \upsilon_i'{:}B_i'\{X\}^{\,i\in 1..n}]}$$

(Sub Invariant) (Sub Covariant) (Sub Contravariant)

$$\frac{E \vdash B}{E \vdash {}^{o}B <: {}^{o}B} \qquad \frac{E \vdash B <: B' \quad \upsilon\in\{^o,^+\}}{E \vdash \upsilon\, B <: {}^{+}B'} \qquad \frac{E \vdash B' <: B \quad \upsilon\in\{^o,^-\}}{E \vdash \upsilon\, B <: {}^{-}B'}$$

The subtyping rule for object types (Sub Object) says, to a first approximation, that a longer object type on the left is a subtype of a shorter one on the right. The antecedents operate under the assumption that Self is a subtype of the longer type.

Because of the variance annotations we use an auxiliary judgment, $E \vdash \upsilon\, B <: \upsilon'\, B'$, for inclusion of components with variance. The rules say:

- (Sub Object) Components that occur both on the left and on the right are handled by the other three rules. For components that occur only on the left, the component types must be well-formed.
- (Sub Invariant) An invariant component on the right requires an identical one on the left.
- (Sub Covariant) A covariant component type on the right can be a supertype of a corresponding component type on the left, either covariant or invariant. Intuitively, an invariant component can be regarded as covariant.
- (Sub Contravariant) A contravariant component type on the right can be a subtype of a corresponding component type on the left, either contravariant or invariant. Intuitively, an invariant component can be regarded as contravariant.

The type Obj(X)[...] can be viewed as a recursive type, but with differences in subtyping that are crucial for object-oriented applications. The subtyping rule for object types (Sub Object), with all components invariant, would read:

$$\frac{E,X{<:}Top \vdash B_i\{X^+\} \qquad \forall i\in 1..n+m}{E \vdash Obj(X)[l_i{:}B_i\{X\}^{\,i\in 1..n+m}] <: Obj(X)[l_i{:}B_i\{X\}^{\,i\in 1..n}]}$$

An analogous rule would be unsound with recursive types instead of Self types [6].

Term typing judgment: $E \vdash a : A$

(Val Subsumption) (Val x)

$$\frac{E \vdash a : A \qquad E \vdash A <: B}{E \vdash a : B} \qquad \frac{E',x{:}A,E'' \vdash \diamond}{E',x{:}A,E'' \vdash x{:}A}$$

(Val Object) (where $A \equiv Obj(X)[l_i \upsilon_i{:}B_i\{X\}^{\,i\in 1..n}]$)

$$\frac{E, x_i{:}A \vdash b_i : B_i\{A\} \qquad \forall i\in 1..n}{E \vdash [l_i{=}\varsigma(x_i)b_i^{\,i\in 1..n}] : A}$$

(Val Select) (where $A' \equiv Obj(X)[l_i\upsilon_i{:}B_i\{X\}^{i\in 1..n}]$)

$$\frac{E \vdash a : A \quad E \vdash A <: A' \quad \upsilon_j \in \{^{\circ},^{+}\} \quad j \in 1..n}{E \vdash a.l_j : B_j\{A\}}$$

(Val Update) (where $A' \equiv Obj(X)[l_i\upsilon_i{:}B_i\{X\}^{i\in 1..n}]$)

$$\frac{\begin{array}{c}E \vdash a : A \quad E \vdash A <: A' \quad E, Y<:A, y{:}Y \vdash c : C \\ E, Y<:A, y{:}Y, z{:}C, x{:}Y \vdash b : B_j\{Y\} \quad \upsilon_j \in \{^{\circ},^{-}\} \quad j \in 1..n\end{array}}{E \vdash a.l_j \Leftarrow (y, z{=}c)\varsigma(x)b : A}$$

(Val Clone) (where $A' \equiv Obj(X)[l_i\upsilon_i{:}B_i\{X\}^{i\in 1..n}]$)

$$\frac{E \vdash a : A \quad E \vdash A <: A'}{E \vdash clone(a) : A}$$

The typing rules are largely the same ones we would have for a functional calculus; the main novelty is the construct for method update. Because of the eager evaluation associated with imperative semantics, there is a need for a construct that can express sequential evaluation. This construct is combined with method update to obtain sufficiently general typings.

To preserve soundness, the rules for selection and update are restricted: selection cannot operate on contravariant components, while update cannot operate on covariant components.

A remarkable aspect of our type system is that the rules (Val Select), (Val Update), and (Val Clone) are based on structural assumptions about the universe of types (cf. [3]). These assumptions are operationally valid, but would not hold in natural semantic models. For example, the update rule implies that if x:X and X<:A' where A' is a given object type with an invariant component l:B, then we may update l in x with a term b of type B yielding an updated object of type X, and not just A'. This rule is based on the assumption that any X<:A' is closed under updating of l with elements of B. The closure property holds in a model only if any subtype of A' allows the result of l to be any element of B. Intuitively, this condition may fail because a subtype of A' may be a subset with l:B' for B' strictly included in B. Operationally, the closure property holds because any possible instance of X in the course of a computation is a closed object type that, being a subtype of A', has a component l of type exactly B.

Rules based on structural assumptions (structural rules, for short) are critical for Self types; they are required for typing programs satisfactorily. Structural rules allow methods to act parametrically over any X<:A', where X is the Self type and A' is a given object type. In section 6 we demonstrate the power of structural rules by examples, and by our representation of classes and inheritance. We can prove that structural rules are sound for our operational semantics (see section 5).

4. Self and Polymorphism

Self types produce an expressive type system, sufficient for interesting examples. However, this type system still lacks facilities for type parameterization. Type parameterization has useful interactions with objects; in particular, it supports method reuse and inheritance, as we show in section 6. To allow for parameterization, we add bounded universal quantifiers [12].

First we extend the syntax of terms. We add two new forms. We write λ()b for a type abstraction and a() for a type application. In typed calculi, it is common to find λ(X<:A)b and a(A) instead. However, we are already committed to an untyped operational semantics, so we strip the types from those terms. Technically, we adopt λ()b, instead of dropping λ() altogether, in order to distinguish the elements of quantified types from those of object types. The distinction greatly simplifies case analysis in proofs.

Additional syntax of terms

a,b ::=	term
. . .	(as before)
λ()b	type abstraction
a()	type application

This choice of syntax affects the operational semantics. In particular, a closure $\langle\lambda()b,S\rangle$, consisting of a type abstraction and a stack, is a result:

Additional results

v ::=	result
. . .	(as before)
$\langle\lambda()b,S\rangle$	type abstraction result

We add two rules to the operational semantics. According to these rules, evaluation stops at type abstractions and is triggered again by type applications. This is a sensible semantics of polymorphism, particularly in presence of side-effects.

Additional term reductions

(Red Fun2)

$$\frac{\sigma{\cdot}S \vdash \diamond}{\sigma{\cdot}S \vdash \lambda()b \leadsto \langle\lambda()b,S\rangle{\cdot}\sigma}$$

(Red Appl2)

$$\frac{\sigma{\cdot}S \vdash a \leadsto \langle\lambda()b,S'\rangle{\cdot}\sigma' \qquad \sigma'{\cdot}S' \vdash b \leadsto v{\cdot}\sigma''}{\sigma{\cdot}S \vdash a() \leadsto v{\cdot}\sigma''}$$

The typing rules for bounded universal quantifiers are:

Additional typing rules

(Type All<:)

$$\frac{E,X{<:}A \vdash B}{E \vdash \forall(X{<:}A)B}$$

(Sub All)

$$\frac{E \vdash A' <: A \qquad E,X{<:}A' \vdash B <: B'}{E \vdash \forall(X{<:}A)B <: \forall(X{<:}A')B'}$$

(Val Fun2<:)

$$\frac{E,X{<:}A \vdash b : B}{E \vdash \lambda()b : \forall(X{<:}A)B}$$

(Val Appl2<:)

$$\frac{E \vdash b : \forall(X{<:}A)B\{X\} \qquad E \vdash A'{<:}A}{E \vdash b() : B\{A'\}}$$

The variance of quantifiers, implied by (Sub All), is the usual one: $\forall(X<:A)B$ is contravariant in the bound (A) and covariant in the body (B).

5. Soundness

Our technique for proving typing soundness is an extension of Harper's [15], but using closures and stacks instead of formal substitutions (see [17, 23, 25] for related techniques). This approach yields a manageable proof for a realistic implementation strategy, and deals easily with typing rules that seem hard to justify denotationally. Our soundness result covers subtyping and polymorphism in the presence of side-effects.

Here we present only a simple statement of a subject reduction theorem: additional definitions are needed for a proper formulation of the induction hypothesis.

Subject Reduction Theorem

If $\emptyset \vdash a : Obj(X)[l_i \upsilon_i : B_i \ ^{i \in 1..n}]$ and $\emptyset \cdot \emptyset \vdash a \leadsto v \cdot \sigma$ then v is an object result.

If $\emptyset \vdash a : \forall(X<:A)B$ and $\emptyset \cdot \emptyset \vdash a \leadsto v \cdot \sigma$ then v is a type abstraction result.

The proof is an extension of the one given in [5] for an imperative calculus with a simpler type structure. It is based on store types [23], and on judgments for typing a result with respect to a store type, and for typing a stack of closed types and a stack of results with respect to a typing environment.

6. Applications

We study some challenging examples. Then we show that quantifiers are useful for factoring out methods as generic procedures, and we describe how collections of generic procedures can be organized into classes and subclasses.

6.1 Typing Challenges and Solutions

We examine some delicate typing issues in the context of simple examples. We use procedures, as defined in section 2.3, and booleans. Procedure types can be defined as:

$$A \to B \triangleq [arg^{-}:A, val^{+}:B]$$

The variance annotations yield the expected contravariant/covariant subtyping rule for procedure types. The typing of procedures relies on the inclusion $[arg^{o}: A, val^{o}: B] <: A \to B$.

- We define the type of memory cells with a get field and with a set method. Given a boolean, the set method stores it in the cell and returns the modified cell. For get, we use a method. (Using a field, with the encoding of section 2.2, leads to simpler code but makes it harder to check the typings of the examples against the rules.)

$$Mem \triangleq Obj(X)[get:Bool, set:Bool \to X]$$

$$m: Mem \triangleq [get = \varsigma(x)\ false, set = \varsigma(x)\ \lambda(b)\ x.get \Leftarrow \varsigma(z)\ b]$$

- Interesting uses of (Val Update) are required when updating methods that return a value of type Self. Here we update the method set with a method that updates get to $\varsigma(z)$false:

m.set ⇐ ς(x) λ(b) x.get ⇐ ς(z) false : Mem

To obtain this typing using (Val Update), we give type Y to x.get⇐ς(z)false for an arbitrary Y<:Mem, parametrically in Y.

- With quantifiers, we can define "parametric pre-methods" as polymorphic procedures that can later be used in updating. The method previously used for updating m.set, for example, can be isolated as a procedure of type ∀(X<:Mem)X→X:

λ() λ(m) m.set ⇐ ς(x) λ(b) x.get ⇐ ς(z) false : ∀(X<:Mem)X→X

The derivation makes an essential use of the structural subtyping assumption in (Val Update); without it we would obtain at best the type ∀(X<:Mem)X→Mem.

- It is natural to expect both components of Mem to be protected against external update. To this end we can use covariance annotations, which block (Val Update). Take:

ProtectedMem ≜ Obj(X)[get⁺:Bool, set⁺:Bool→X]

Since Mem <: ProtectedMem, any memory cell can be subsumed into ProtectedMem and thus protected against updating from the outside. However, after subsumption, the set method can still update the get field because it was originally typechecked with X equal to Mem.

- Consider a type of memory cells with a duplicate method, as in section 2.4.

MemDup ≜ Obj(X)[get:Bool, set:Bool→X, dup:X]

We have MemDup <: Mem, thanks to the subtyping rule for object types. This subtyping would have failed had we used recursive type instead of Self types [4].

- Consider now a type of memory cells with backup and restore methods, and a candidate implementation:

MemBk ≜ Obj(X)[restore:X, backup:X, get:Bool, set:Bool→X]

o ≜ [restore = ς(self) self, backup = ς(self) self.restore := clone(self),

get = ... , set = ...]

The initial restore method is set to return the current memory cell. Whenever the backup method is invoked, it places a clone of self into restore. Note that backup saves the self that is current at backup-invocation time, not the self that will be current at restore-invocation time.

The untyped behavior of backup and restore are the desired ones, but o cannot be given the type MemBk. We can see why by expanding the definition of :=, obtaining:

backup = ς(self) self.restore ⇐ (y, z=clone(self)) ς(x) z

In typing self.restore⇐(y,z=clone(self))ς(x)z, we have self:MemBk and z:MemBk as well. The update requires that for an arbitrary Y<:MemBk we be able to show that z:Y. This cannot be achieved.

The following alternative code has the same problem if we assume the obvious typing rule for let:

backup $=$ ς(self) let z = clone(self) in self.restore ⇐ ς(x) z

Therefore, for typing this example, it is not sufficient to adopt let and simple update as separate primitives.

The solution to this typing problem requires the general method update construct:

backup = ς(self) self.restore ⇐ (y, z=clone(y)) ς(x) z

In typing self.restore⇐(y,z=clone(y))ς(x)z, we have self:MemBk. For an arbitrary Y<:MemBk, the update rule assigns to y the type Y. Therefore, clone(y) has type Y by (Val Clone), and hence z has the required type Y.

Note that this typing problem manifests itself with field update, and is not a consequence of allowing method update. It arises from the combination of Self and eager evaluation, when a component of a type that depends on Self is updated.

6.2 Classes as Collections of Pre-Methods

As shown in section 6.1, types of the form ∀(X<:A)X→B{X} (with B{X} covariant in X) arise naturally for methods used in updating. In our type system, these types contain useful elements because of our structural assumptions. In contrast, they have no interesting elements in standard models of subtyping; see [8].

Types of this form can be used for defining classes as collections of pre-methods, where a pre-method is a procedure that is later used to construct a method. Each pre-method must work for all possible subclasses, parametrically in self, so that it can be inherited and instantiated to any of these subclasses. This is precisely what a type of the form ∀(X<:A)X→ B{X} expresses.

We associate a class type Class(A) to each object type A. (We make the components of Class(A) invariant, for simplicity.)

If $\quad A \equiv \mathrm{Obj}(X)[l_i \upsilon_i{:}B_i\{X\}^{\,i\in 1..n}]$

then $\quad \mathrm{Class}(A) \triangleq [\mathrm{new}{:}A,\ l_i{:}\forall(X{<:}A)X\to B_i\{X\}^{\,i\in 1..n}]$.

A class c of type Class(A) consists of a particular collection of pre-methods l_i of the appropriate types, along with a method, called new, for constructing new objects. The implementation of new is uniform for all classes: it produces an object of type A by collecting all the pre-methods of the class and applying them to the self of the new object.

$$c : \mathrm{Class}(A) \triangleq [\mathrm{new} = \varsigma(z)\ [l_i{=}\varsigma(x)\ z.l_i()(x)^{\,i\in 1..n}],\ l_1 = ...,\ ...\ ,\ l_n = ...\ ]$$

The methods l_i do not normally use the self of the class, but new does. For example:

Class(Mem) ≡
    [new: Mem,
    get: ∀(X<:Mem) X→Bool,
    set: ∀(X<:Mem) X→Bool→X]

memClass: Class(Mem) $\triangleq$

[new = ς(z) [get = ς(x) z.get()(x), set = ς(x) z.set()(x)],

get = λ() λ(x) false,

set = λ() λ(x) λ(b) x.get:=b]

m : Mem $\triangleq$ memClass.new

We can now consider the inheritance relation between classes. Suppose that we have another type $A' \equiv Obj(X)[l_i \upsilon'_i{:}B'_i\{X\}^{\,i\in 1..n+m}] <: A$, and a corresponding class type $Class(A') \equiv [new{:}A', l_i{:}\forall(X<:A')X\to B'_i\{X\}^{\,i\in 1..n+m}]$. For all $i\in 1..n$, we say that:

l_i is inheritable from Class(A) to Class(A') iff $X<:A'$ implies $B_i\{X\}<:B'_i\{X\}$

When l_i is inheritable, we have $\forall(X<:A)X\to B_i\{X\} <: \forall(X<:A')X\to B'_i\{X\}$. So, if c:Class(A) and l_i is inheritable, we obtain $c.l_i : \forall(X<:A')X\to B'_i\{X\}$ by subsumption. Then, $c.l_i$ has the correct type to be reused when building a class c':Class(A'). That is, it can be inherited. For example, get and set are inheritable from Class(Mem) to Class(MemDup):

Class(MemDup) $\equiv$

[new: MemDup,

get: $\forall$(X<:MemDup) X$\to$Bool,

set: $\forall$(X<:MemDup) X$\to$Bool$\to$X,

dup: $\forall$(X<:MemDup) X$\to$X]

memDupClass: Class(MemDup) $\triangleq$

[new = ς(z) [get = ς(x) z.get()(x), set = ς(x) z.set()(x), dup = ς(x) z.dup()(x)],

get = memClass.get,

set = memClass.set,

dup = λ() λ(x) clone(x)]

The inheritability condition holds for any invariant component l_i, since in this case $B_i\{X\}\equiv B'_i\{X\}$. For contravariance, if $A' \equiv Obj(X)[l_i^-{:}B_i'\{X\}, ...]$ and $A \equiv Obj(X)[l_i^-{:}B_i\{X\}, ...]$ with $A'<:A$, then $X<:A'$ always implies $B_i\{X\}<:B_i'\{X\}$. Thus, inheritability of contravariant components is also guaranteed.

Covariant components do not necessarily correspond to inheritable pre-methods. For example, if $A' \equiv [l^+{:}Nat]$ and $A \equiv [l^+{:}Int]$ with Nat<:Int, and c : [new:A, l:$\forall$(X<:A)X$\to$Int], then c.l cannot be inherited into Class(A') $\equiv$ [new:A', l:$\forall$(X<:A')X$\to$Nat], because it would produce a bad result. However, a class c' : Class(A') can include a different method for l with result type Nat: this corresponds to method specialization on overriding.

In conclusion, covariant components induce mild restrictions in subclassing. Invariant and contravariant components induce no restrictions. In practice, inheritability is expected between a class type C and another class type C' obtained as an extension of C (so that C' and C have identical common components). In this case, inheritability trivially holds for components of any variance.

7. Conclusions

We have described a basic calculus for objects and their types. It includes a sound type system with Self types within an imperative framework. Classes and inheritance arise from object types and polymorphic types. Because of its compactness and expressiveness, this calculus is appealing as a kernel for object-oriented languages that include subsumption and Self types.

References

[1] Abadi, M., **Baby Modula-3 and a theory of objects**. *Journal of Functional Programming* **4**(2), 249-283. 1994.

[2] Abadi, M. and L. Cardelli, **A semantics of object types**. *Proc. IEEE Symposium on Logic in Computer Science*, 332-341. 1994.

[3] Abadi, M. and L. Cardelli, **A theory of primitive objects: second-order systems**. *Proc. ESOP'94 - European Symposium on Programming*. Springer-Verlag. 1994.

[4] Abadi, M. and L. Cardelli, **A theory of primitive objects: untyped and first-order systems**. *Proc. Theoretical Aspects of Computer Software*. Springer-Verlag. 1994.

[5] Abadi, M. and L. Cardelli, **An imperative object calculus: basic typing and soundness**. *Proc. Second ACM SIGPLAN Workshop on State in Programming Languages*, 19-32. Technical Report UIUCDCS-R-95-1900, University of Illinois at Urbana Champaign. 1995.

[6] Amadio, R.M. and L. Cardelli, **Subtyping recursive types**. *ACM Transactions on Programming Languages and Systems* **15**(4), 575-631. 1993.

[7] Bruce, K.B., **A paradigmatic object-oriented programming language: design, static typing and semantics**. *Journal of Functional Programming* **4**(2), 127-206. 1994.

[8] Bruce, K.B. and G. Longo, **A modest model of records, inheritance and bounded quantification**. *Information and Computation* **87**(1/2), 196-240. 1990.

[9] Bruce, K.B., A. Schuett, and R. van Gent, **PolyTOIL: a type-safe polymorphic object-oriented language.** Williams College. 1994.

[10] Cardelli, L., **Extensible records in a pure calculus of subtyping**. In *Theoretical Aspects of Object-Oriented Programming,* C.A. Gunter and J.C. Mitchell, ed. MIT Press. 373-425. 1994.

[11] Cardelli, L. and J.C. Mitchell, **Operations on records**. *Mathematical Structures in Computer Science* **1**(1), 3-48. 1991.

[12] Cardelli, L., J.C. Mitchell, S. Martini, and A. Scedrov, **An extension of system F with subtyping**. *Information and Computation* **109**(1-2), 4-56. 1994.

[13] Cook, W.R., **A proposal for making Eiffel type-safe**. *Proc. European Conference of Object-Oriented Programming*, 57-72. 1989.

[14] Eifrig, J., S. Smith, V. Trifonov, and A. Zwarico, **An interpretation of typed OOP in a language with state**. *Lisp and Symbolic Computation.* (to appear). 1995.

[15] Harper, R., **A simplified account of polymorphic references.** *Information Processing Letters* **51**(4). 1994.

[16] Harper, R. and B. Pierce, **A record calculus based on symmetric concatenation**. *Proc. 18th Annual ACM Symposium on Principles of Programming Languages*. 1991.

[17] Leroy, X., **Polymorphic typing of an algorithmic language**. Rapport de Recherche no.1778 (Ph.D Thesis). INRIA. 1992.

[18] Meyer, B., **Object-oriented software construction**. Prentice Hall. 1988.

[19] Mitchell, J.C., F. Honsell, and K. Fisher, **A lambda calculus of objects and method specialization**. *Proc. 8th Annual IEEE Symposium on Logic in Computer Science*. 1993.

[20] Pierce, B.C. and D.N. Turner, **Simple type-theoretic foundations for object-oriented programming**. *Journal of Functional Programming* **4**(2), 207-247. 1994.

[21] Rémy, D., **Typechecking records and variants in a natural extension of ML**. *Proc. 16th Annual ACM Symposium on Principles of Programming Languages*, 77-88. 1989.

[22] Szypersky, C., S. Omohundro, and S. Murer, **Engineering a programming language: the type and class system of Sather**. TR-93-064. ICSI, Berkeley. 1993.

[23] Tofte, M., **Type inference for polymorphic references**. *Information and Computation* **89**, 1-34. 1990.

[24] Wand, M., **Type inference for record concatenation and multiple inheritance**. *Proc. 4th Annual IEEE Symposium on Logic in Computer Science*, 92-97. 1989.

[25] Wright, A.K. and M. Felleisen, **A syntactic approach to type soundness**. *Information and Computation* **115**(1), 38-94. 1994.

[26] Yonezawa, A. and M. Tokoro, ed. **Object-oriented concurrent programming**. MIT Press. 1987.

A Refinement of Import/Export Declarations in Modular Logic Programming and its Semantics

Isambo Karali and Constantin Halatsis

Department of Informatics, University of Athens

Abstract. Encapsulation constructs with import/export declarations is the structuring facility offered in most commercial Prolog systems. However, real-life applications have shown to require a finer information exchange between encapsulated pieces of code. In this paper, a refinement of import/export declarations for modules of logic programs is presented. This offers a stricter form of communication between the modules and a larger variety of visibility states of their predicates, the standard approaches being special cases of it. The semantics of this module system has been examined and model-theoretic, fixpoint and operational ones are given and have been proved to be equivalent. Instead of using other logics, all these semantics extend the ones of Horn clause logic using concepts commonly used in it. In addition, the module system has been naturally transformed to Horn clause logic exploiting the distinction of the predicates within a module according to the interface declarations of this module. A form of equivalence with the other semantics of the system is given. In addition, the employed transformation has provided us with a basis for a preprocessor based implementation of the module system.

1 Introduction

The declarative style of logic programming [14] via its implementation as Prolog [8, 22] facilitates the software development phase and has become a favorite platform for a large variety of advanced applications (artificial intelligence applications, expert systems, scheduling applications etc.). Thus, a variety of Prolog implementations incorporated also an ecapsulation mechanism. At the same time, much work is being carried out in providing logic programming with a structuring mechanism with formal foundations which fits elegantly in the underlying theory, since one of the main advantages of logic programming is its clear semantics. As stated in [7], two main lines of research exist towards this direction: program composition and linguistic extensions. The former has been inspired from the work in [20] where an algebra for logic programs is introduced. Logic programs are the elements of this algebra and a variety of operators performs program composition. Various researchers [15, 11, 5, 1] have worked in this area. The module support with import/export interfaces, which is also the case of commercial Prolog systems, is a special case of this approach and provides a fine-grained program composition. On the other hand, linguistic extensions, first appearing in [16], extend the syntax of Horn clauses by allowing implications as goals. This approach offers a rich expressive power, but its application areas are still under investigation. In the area of linguistic extensions, the work of contextual logic programming [17] is an eminent one. The work in [16] uses intuitionistic logic to formulate the introduced ideas. Other logics are also used for a module concept in logic programming in a variety of works.

The module system presented and examined in this paper is the result of the effort to make a structuring tool for large applications which require encapsulation and complicated interconnections. It provides privacy, abstraction and name clashes avoidance. The presented system relies on the area of module support with import/export declarations and it can be said to extend the functionality in predicate visibility of [10]. The encapsulation affects predicates only. Although coming out from practical needs, our module system has been given a model-theoretic, a fixpoint as well as an operational semantics, all proved to be equivalent. The semantics has been concentrated on modelling the environment of a module with respect to other modules that form the surrounding system. Instead of relying on other logics, all these semantics extend the standard semantics of Horn clause programs [23] naturally and smoothly to capture the introduced extension. In the employed formalism, modules are a kind of first order theories which differ from classical ones in that the encapsulation and the interfaces qualify the predicates. Commonly used and widely understood concepts such as Herbrand interpretations and models as well as the immediate consequence operator have been found to be sufficient to form the means of the semantics of this module system. Nevertheless, a transformation of the module system to Horn clause logic has been also defined and a sort of equivalence with the other semantics of the system has been proved. A preprocessor implementation of the module system is based on this transformation [13]. The preprocessor extends the standard Prolog functionality so that to take the module system into account. Modular Prolog programs are mapped to flat Prolog code by the preprocessor which is coded in Prolog itself.

In this paper, firstly, the module system is briefly presented. Its model-theoretic, fixpoint and operational semantics follow. The transformation of the module system to Horn clause logic comes next. In all cases, the equivalence relation is stated. Proofs of all theorems can be found in [12]. Finally, related work is included and comments on the presented module system are made.

2 The Module System

In this section, firstly, the module system is briefly presented from the Prolog programmer's point of view. Secondly, the system's formal framework is introduced.

A module encapsulates a set of Prolog procedures that form its *body* and exchanges information with other modules via *interface declarations.* As *home module* of an interface declaration, we consider the module where this declaration appears. A *module header* of the form *:-module(ModuleName)*, where *Module Name* is a constant, introduces a module with name *ModuleName* and denotes that the interface declarations as well as the Prolog code that follow until the end-of-file mark or another module header form the module.

The interface declarations carry out the following. A module is allowed to declare via its interface all or some of its predicates *global* to the system, i.e. visible everywhere, "its predicates" referring to the ones defined in this module. In addition, it can declare them *exported to* specified modules or to all the modules of the system. Furthermore, a module may *import* predicates, at the extensional level, *from* specific modules. In this case, to achieve usability, the other module must export the predicates to the home module of the import declaration. Moreover, a module may *merge* procedure results *from* other modules, specific or not, with its own ones. Again an export declaration in the other module must export the procedure to the home module of the merge declaration. The order of the merged results is not ensured and depends on the order of the module loading. When a merge declaration within a module refers to a predicate, the module is not allowed to declare this predicate exported or global. No more than one module should declare the same predicate global. In case a predicate exists in an export declaration it is not allowed to appear in a global one in the home module of the export declaration. If more than one merge or import declarations within a module refer to the same predicate, the declaration that appears last is considered. The preceding ones are ignored. The interface declarations are processed at compile time and cannot change at run time.

No space outside the modules exists. The concept of *worlds* is effectively supported. That is to say, the top level loop executes within the environment of a module and all predicates visible to this module are visible and usable in the top level loop.

In order to determine which procedure definition is addressed when a predicate appears within a module, *visibility states* are introduced and define the effect of the interface declarations.

Definition 1. A predicate can fall into one and only one of the following *visibility states* within a module:

merged iff a merge declaration exists in this module and refers to this predicate

local iff the above does not hold and there is a definition for this predicate in this module

imported iff none of the above holds and there is an import declaration in this module that refers to this predicate

possibly_global iff none of the above holds

In the formalism of the module system presented in this paper, pure logic programming and definite program clauses are assumed. The terminology used in [14] is adopted. Modules are considered as a kind of first order theories, namely *module First Order Theories* (*m-FOTs*). Each module is a m-FOT. A m-FOT differs from a Horn clause theory in that:

1. It includes a constant identifying the m-FOT which corresponds to the name of the module.
2. Predicates in a m-FOT do not belong to a flat set. The set of predicate symbols is substituted by a 4-tuple $P = (M, L, I, GO)$. Each of the M, L, I, GO correspond to the merged, local, imported and possibly_global predicates. L is further refined to $L = (H, E, GI)$, i.e. hidden, exported and declared global predicates. A hidden predicate in a module is a local predicate which is neither exported nor declared global in this module. All M, H, E, GI, I and GO sets contain predicates distinct from each other. As expected, M, E and I combine the predicates with the modules that the interface declarations relate them to. To illustrate this, consider the case of the merged predicates within a module m. M is a finite set of (mms, mp) pairs and (mpr) elements where mms is a finite set of constants other than m and mp, mpr are predicates. An (mms, mp) pair in M denotes that mp is a predicate merged from the modules in mms, though (mpr) denotes that the predicate mpr is merged from all the modules. As, in the following, a set of modules will be considered, the module name will be used to identify the predicate sets among the various modules, i.e. $E(m)$ represents the exported predicates of the module m.
3. As far as the program clauses of the m-FOTs are concerned, only predicates from M or L should appear in their heads.

A (V, F) pair where V is a finite or denumerably infinite set of variables and F a finite set of function symbols is assumed to be global to all the m-FOTs. The module system affects predicates only. The m-FOTs are, then, reduced to a triple $(m, P, Progr)$ where m is the constant which identifies the m-FOT and P is as previously described. $Progr$ is a finite set of program clauses which forms the module's program and corresponds to the module's body.

Consider

$$\begin{aligned}
Merged(m) &= \{p|(p) \in M(m)\} \cup \{p|(ms, p) \in M(m)\} \\
Local(m) &= H(m) \cup \{p|(p) \in E(m)\} \cup \{p|(m', p) \in E(m)\} \cup GI(m) \\
Imported(m) &= \{p|(m', p) \in I(m)\} \\
PGlobal(m) &= GO(m) \\
Using(m) &= Merged(m) \cup Local(m) \cup Imported(m) \cup PGlobal(m)
\end{aligned}$$

Moreover,

$$\begin{aligned}
M(m, m') &= \{p|(ms, p) \in M(m) \ and \ m' \in ms\} \cup \{p|(p) \in M(m)\} \\
I(m, m') &= \{p|(m', p) \in I(m)\} \\
E(m, m') &= \{p|(m', p) \in E(m)\} \cup \{p|(p) \in E(m)\}
\end{aligned}$$

3 Model-Theoretic Semantics

In this section, a model-theoretic semantics of the module system is given. This is based on Herbrand interpretations and provides a minimal model as model intersections.

The work in this paper is concentrated on the semantics of a module *surrounded by* a set of modules. The reason is that every formula is associated with a module, as there is no space outside the modules. Thus, in this section, we try to model what holds with respect to this module which, certainly, depends on what holds to other modules.

Definition 2. Consider a m-FOT $(m, P, Progr)$. Then, a set

$$\begin{aligned} SW(m) = \{(m_i, P_i, Progr_i) \mid 1 \leq i \leq n, n \in \mathrm{N},\ (m_i, P_i, Progr_i)\ a\ m\text{-}FOT, \\ m_i \neq m, GI(m_i) \neq GI(m)\ and \\ \forall j\ such\ that\ 1 \leq j \leq n, j \neq i : m_i \neq m_j, GI(m_i) \neq GI(m_j)\} \end{aligned}$$

where N is the set of natural numbers, is called a *surrounding world* of m and *m is surrounded by $SW(m)$ (sym: m srd $SW(m)$)*

From now on, the triple representing a m-FOT and the constant identifying it will be used interchangeably.

The concepts of Herbrand Universe (U) and Herbrand Base of the language for a m-FOT, as well as the one of interpretations are left unchanged. Herbrand interpretations are considered. Nevertheless, a Herbrand Base is referred as *m-Herbrand Base* (*m-B*), because predicates are module dependent and, for a m-FOT m, it is built over the predicates in $Using(m)$. What changes, however, is the concept of truth value of an atomic formula. As all formulae and programs in the module system are addressed with respect to a module, they will be referred to as *m-formulae* and *m-programs*, respectively. Moreover, consider that for a m-atomic formula $A = p(t_1, \ldots, t_n)$, it is $pred(A) = p$. Then, if a m-atomic formula of a module involves a local predicate, it is the module's responsibility to assign the truth value to it. This is partially the case for merged predicates. Otherwise, it is a matter of interface declarations and of other module information. For instance, if the predicate of a m-atomic formula A of a module m is possibly_global, i.e. $pred(A) \in GO(m)$, then this formula will be true if there exists another module m' in the surrounding world which declares $pred(A)$ global, i.e. $pred(A) \in GI(m')$, and A is true within m'. Informally speaking, truthity of a ground m-atomic formula of a module is again identical to membership to an interpretation. However, which module's interpretation is considered depends on the visibility state of the formula's predicate within this module.

Definition 3. Consider a m-FOT m_0 *srd* $SW(m_0) = \{m_1, \ldots, m_n\}, n \in \mathrm{N}$, an interpretation I_0 of m_0 and $Is = \{I_i | 1 \leq i \leq n, I_i : interpretation\ of\ m_i \in SW(m_0)\}$. Then, a ground m-atomic formula A of m_0 is *true in interpretation I_0 surrounded by Is of $SW(m_0)$ (sym: true in I_0 srd Is)* iff

1. $pred(A) \in Merged(m_0)$ and
   either $A \in I_0$ or
   $\exists m_i \in SW(m_0) : pred(A) \in M(m_0, m_i) \cap E(m_i, m_0)$ and $A \in I_i$ where $I_i \in Is$ is the interpretation of m_i.
2. $pred(A) \in Local(m_0)$ and $A \in I_0$.

3. $pred(A) \in Imported(m_0)$ and
$\exists m_i \in SW(m_0) : pred(A) \in I(m_0, m_i) \cap E(m_i, m_0)$ and $A \in I_i$ where $I_i \in Is$ is the interpretation of m_i.
4. $pred(A) \in PGlobal(m_0)$ and $\exists m_i \in SW(m_0) : pred(A) \in GI(m_i)$ and $A \in I_i$ where $I_i \in Is$ is the interpretation of m_i.

Assuming this definition, the definition of the truth value of m-atomic formulae and m-clauses is kept the same as it is for first order atomic formulae and Horn clauses. Considering the null formula Δ, it can be said that it is true everywhere.

As mentioned before, the approach is concentrated on examining what holds in a module with respect to what holds in some other modules. Thus, it is natural and useful to restrict these other modules to the information relevant to this central module only. In other words, considering a m_0 *srd* $SW(m_0)$, the surrounding world $SW(m_0)$ is restricted to $SW'(m_0)$ by restricting each module m_i in $SW(m_0)$. Each module in the surrounding world is restricted to these interface declarations and code only that are used either directly by m_0 or indirectly by some other module restriction. If, after the reduction, a module is empty, it is not included in $SW'(m_0)$ at all. In terms of the formalism previously presented, for each $(m_i, (M, (H, E, GI), I, GO), Progr) \in SW(m_0)$, if its restriction is not empty, it is denoted as $(m_i, (M', (H', E', GI'), I', GO'), Progr')$ where E', GI' and $Progr'$ contain only the "useful" information for m_0 and the other module restrictions. H', M', I' and GO' contain predicates that appear in $Progr'$. The construction of $SW'(m_0)$ can be carried out in a systematic way.

The restriction of the surrounding world is followed in the concept of models. A model for a module m_0 surrounded by $SW(m_0)$ should model m_0 taking into account all requested information from $SW(m_0)$. In addition, $SW'(m_0)$ should be modelled as well. A model in our framework consists of an interpretation of the central module which is considered with respect to a set of interpretations, one for each module of the surrounding world.

Considering a central module surrounded by a set of modules contrasts to other approaches [17, 6, 2] where a set of units is considered as a world and effort is made to model such a world. In these approaches, all units are treated uniformly thus the formalism becomes more compact. However, our intention is to model the environment of one module. Thus, if we tried to model this central module and its surrounding world uniformly as a set of modules, we wouldn't be complete. The reason is that some candidate models would have been rejected because they don't model the whole information, although some of it is irrelevant to the central module. Thus, considering the concept of the surrounding world and restricting it have been found necessary.

Definition 4. Consider a m-FOT m_0 *srd* $SW(m_0) = \{m_1, \ldots, m_n\}, n \in \mathrm{N}$, an interpretation M_0 of m_0 and $Ms = \{M_i | 1 \le i \le n, M_i : \textit{interpretation of } m_i \in SW(m_0)\}$. Then, M_0 *srd* Ms is a *model for* m_0 *srd* $SW(m_0)$ *(sym, also:* M_0 *model for* m_0 *srd* Ms *of* $SW(m_0)$*)* iff all the following hold:

1. Every m-clause of the m-program of m_0 is true in M_0 *srd* Ms.

2. $\forall m_i \in SW'(m_0)$ and $\forall$ m-atomic formula A of m_i such that $pred(A) \in Accord\_set(m_0, m_i)$, the following holds: if $A \in M_i \in Ms$ and M_i is the interpretation of m_i then $A \in M_0$ where:

$$\begin{aligned}Accord\_set(m_0, m_i) = &(M(m_0, m_i) \cap E'(m_i, m_0)) \cup \\ &(I(m_0, m_i) \cap E'(m_i, m_0)) \cup \\ &(GO(m_0) \cap GI'(m_i))\end{aligned}$$

and

$$E'(m_i, m_0) = \{p | (m_0, p) \in E'(m_i)\} \cup \{p | (p) \in E'(m_i)\}$$

Informally speaking, the accordance set of m_0 to m_i represents the predicates that m_0 asks from m_i and m_i offers to m_0.

3. Items 1 and 2 hold $\forall m_i \in SW'(m_0)$, considering the m_i srd $(SW'(m_0) - \{m_i\}) \cup \{m_0\}$ and the M_i srd $(Ms - \{M_i\}) \cup \{M_0\}$ where $M_i \in Ms$ is the interpretation of m_i.

Proposition 5. *Let M_0 srd Ms be a model for m_0 srd $SW(m_0)$ and A a ground m-atomic formula of m_0. Then, A true in M_0 srd $Ms \Rightarrow A \in M_0$.*

Definition 6. Let m_0 *srd* $SW(m_0)$ and F either a m-atomic formula of m_0 or a m-clause of m_0. Then, F is a *logical consequence of m_0 srd $SW(m_0)$* iff $\forall M_0$ *srd* Ms model for m_0 *srd* $SW(m_0)$, F is true in M_0 *srd* Ms.

Definition 7. Let M_0 *srd* Ms, M_0' *srd* Ms' be models for m_0 *srd* $SW(m_0) = \{m_1, \ldots, m_n\}, n \in$ N. Then M_0 *srd* $Ms \leq M_0'$ *srd* Ms' iff $M_0 \subseteq M_0'$ and $\forall i$ such that $1 \leq i \leq n$: $M_i \subseteq M_i'$, where $M_i \in Ms, M_i' \in Ms'$ are the interpretations of $m_i \in SW(m_0)$. Thus, a partial order is defined on the set of models of a m_0 *srd* $SW(m_0)$.

Proposition 8. *The m-Herbrand base is a model for a m-FOT surrounded by the m-Herbrand bases of the surrounding world. Thus, the set of models for a m-FOT surrounded by other m-FOTs is nonempty.*

Theorem 9. *Let $M1_0$ srd $M1s$, $M2_0$ srd $M2s$ be models for m_0 srd $SW(m_0) = \{m_1, \ldots, m_n\}, n \in N$. Then $M_0 = M1_0 \cap M2_0$ is a model for m_0 srd Ms of $SW(m_0)$, where $Ms = \{M1_i \cap M2_i | 1 \leq i \leq n, M1_i \in M1s, M2_i \in M2s$ and $M1_i, M2_i$ the interpretations of $m_i \in SW(m_0)\}$.*

Proposition 10. *Let m_0 srd $SW(m_0) = \{m_1, \ldots, m_n\}, n \in N$. Let $Models = \{M_0$ srd $Ms | M_0$ srd Ms is a model for m_0 srd $SW(m_0)\}$. Then, M_{MIN} srd $M_{MIN}s$ where*

$$\begin{aligned}M_{MIN} &= \cap\{M_0 | M_0 \; srd \; Ms \in Models\} \text{ and} \\ M_{MIN}s &= \{M_i | 1 \leq i \leq n, \\ &\quad M_i = \cap\{Ms_i | Ms_i \in Ms, \; M_0 \; srd \; Ms \in Models \text{ and} \\ &\quad Ms_i \text{ is the interpretation of } m_i \in SW(m_0)\}\}\end{aligned}$$

is the minimal model for m_0 srd $SW(m_0)$ (with respect to the defined partial order).

4 Fixpoint Semantics

In this section, a fixpoint semantics of the module system is given in terms of a continuous transformation associated with a module surrounded by a surrounding world. The transformation's least fixpoint involves the minimal model of the system into consideration. The employed transformation can be considered as an extension of the immediate consequence operator introduced in [23].

Definition 11. Let m_0 *srd* $SW(m_0) = \{m_1, \ldots, m_n\}, n \in \mathrm{N}$.
Let $m\text{-}B(m_i)$ denote the m-Herbrand base of the m-FOT m_i, $0 \leq i \leq n$.
Let $Lat = \{(I_0, Is) | I_0 \subseteq m\text{-}B(m_0), Is = \{I_i | 1 \leq i \leq n, I_i \subseteq m\text{-}B(m_i)\}\}$.
Then, consider a transformation $T : Lat \longrightarrow Lat$ such that $T : (I_0, Is) \mapsto (I_0', Is')$ where:

$$\begin{aligned} I_0' = \{A | A \in m\text{-}B(m_0), \exists C\ &ground\ instance\ of\ a\ clause\ in\ Progr(m_0) : \\ &C \equiv A\text{:-}A_1, \ldots, A_k\ and\ A_1, \ldots, A_k\ true\ in\ I_0\ srd\ Is, k \geq 0\} \cup \\ &\{A | A \in I_j', 1 \leq j \leq n, pred(A) \in Accord\_set(m_0, m_j)\} \end{aligned}$$

$$\begin{aligned} I_i' = \{A | A \in m\text{-}B(m_i), \exists C\ &ground\ instance\ of\ a\ clause\ in\ Progr'(m_i) : \\ &C \equiv A\text{:-}A_1, \ldots, A_k\ and\ A_1, \ldots, A_k\ true\ in\ I_i\ srd\ (Is - \{I_i\}) \cup \{I_0\}, k \geq 0\} \\ &\cup \\ &\{A | A \in I_j',\ 0 \leq j \leq n, j \neq i, pred(A) \in Accord\_set(m_i, m_j), m_i \in SW'(m_0)\} \end{aligned}$$

or

$I_i' = I_i$, *if* $m_i \notin SW'(m_0)$
and $Is' = \{I_i' | 1 \leq i \leq n\}$

Lat is a complete lattice with partial order $\leq$ such that $(I_0, Is) \leq (I_0', Is')$ iff $I_0 \subseteq I_0'$ and $\forall i$ such that $1 \leq i \leq n$: $I_i \subseteq I_i'$, where $I_i \in Is, I_i' \in Is'$ are interpretations of $m_i \in SW(m_0)$. In other words, the order defined for models is extended to interpretations. If $X \subseteq Lat$, then

$$lub(X) = (\cup_{(I_0,Is) \in X} I_0, \{Un_i | 1 \leq i \leq n\ and\ Un_i = \cup_{(I_0,Is) \in X\ and\ I_i \in Is} I_i\})$$
$$glb(X) = (\cap_{(I_0,Is) \in X} I_0, \{Int_i | 1 \leq i \leq n\ and\ Int_i = \cap_{(I_0,Is) \in X\ and\ I_i \in Is} I_i\})$$

Theorem 12. *Let* m_0 *srd* $SW(m_0)$ *and* T *as previously defined.* T *is continuous.*

Theorem 13. *Consider* m_0 *srd* $SW(m_0) = \{m_1, \ldots, m_n\}, n \in N$.
Then, I_0 *srd* Is *is a model for* m_0 *srd* $SW(m_0) \Rightarrow T((I_0, Is)) \leq (I_0, Is)$

Corollary 14. *Let* m_0 *srd* $SW(m_0)$ *and* M_{MIN} *srd* $M_{MIN}s$ *its minimal model.*
Then, $lfp(T) \leq (M_{MIN}, M_{MIN}s)$.

Theorem 15. *Consider* m_0 *srd* $SW(m_0) = \{m_1, \ldots, m_n\}, n \in N$.
Then, $T((I_0, Is)) = (I_0, Is) \Rightarrow I_0$ *srd* Is *is a model for* m_0 *srd* $SW(m_0)$.

Corollary 16. *Let* m_0 *srd* $SW(m_0)$ *and* M_{MIN} *srd* $M_{MIN}s$ *its minimal model.*
Then, $(M_{MIN}, M_{MIN}s) \leq lfp(T)$.

Corollary 17 Equivalence. *Let* m_0 *srd* $SW(m_0)$ *and* M_{MIN} *srd* $M_{MIN}s$ *its minimal model.*
Then, $(M_{MIN}, M_{MIN}s) = lfp(T) = T \uparrow \omega$.

5 Operational Semantics

In this section the operational behaviour of the module system is presented. More precisely, the concept of derivability of a m-formula from a module surrounded by a surrounding world is expressed in terms of a set of inference rules, adopting a frequently used framework. The notation m_0 srd $SW(m_0) \vdash F[\theta]$ is used to denote that there is a derivation of F from m_0 srd $SW(m_0)$ with substitution θ, where F is a m-formula of m_0 such as the null formula, a m-atomic formula or conjunction of these. The inference rules are of the form:

$$\frac{Assumption}{Conclusion}$$

Such a rule states that *Conclusion* holds whenever *Assumption* holds. In the following, ε denotes the identity substitution and θ, σ are substitutions. Moreover, A is a m-atomic formula of m_0 and Gs is a conjunction of those. The result of applying θ to A is written $A\theta$.

Null Formula

$$\frac{}{m_0 \ srd \ SW(m_0) \vdash \Delta[\varepsilon]}$$

Conjunction

$$\frac{m_0 \ srd \ SW(m_0) \vdash A[\theta] \wedge m_0 \ srd \ SW(m_0) \vdash Gs\theta[\sigma]}{m_0 \ srd \ SW(m_0) \vdash (A, Gs)[\theta\sigma]}$$

m-Atomic Formula(I)

$$\frac{\exists A_0 \text{:-} B_0 \in Progr(m_0) \wedge \theta = mgu(A, A_0) \wedge m_0 \ srd \ SW(m_0) \vdash B_0\theta[\sigma]}{m_0 \ srd \ SW(m_0) \vdash A[\theta\sigma]}$$

m-Atomic Formula(II)

$$\frac{\begin{array}{l}\exists m_i \in SW'(m_0) : pred(A) \in Accord\_set(m_0, m_i) \wedge \\ m_i \ srd \ (SW'(m_0) - \{m_i\}) \cup \{m_0\} \vdash A[\theta]\end{array}}{m_0 \ srd \ SW(m_0) \vdash A[\theta]}$$

Actually, it is only the last rule that corresponds to the extension introduced by the module system and expresses the change in the proof environment that is carried out when an "external" predicate appears in a m-atomic formula.

With respect to the model-theoretic semantics previously presented, the following relations hold.

Theorem 18. *Consider* m_0 *srd* $SW(m_0)$ *and* A *a ground m-formula of* m_0. *Then,* m_0 *srd* $SW(m_0) \vdash A \Rightarrow A$ *is true in* M_0 *srd* Ms, $\forall M_0$ *srd* Ms *model for* m_0 *srd* $SW(m_0)$.

Theorem 19. *Consider* m_0 *srd* $SW(m_0)$ *and* A *a ground m-formula of* m_0. *Then,* A *is true in* M_{MIN} *srd* $M_{MIN}s \Rightarrow m_0$ *srd* $SW(m_0) \vdash A$, *where* M_{MIN} *srd* $M_{MIN}s$ *is the minimal model of* m_0 *srd* $SW(m_0)$.

Corollary 20 Equivalence. *Consider* m_0 *srd* $SW(m_0)$ *and* A *a ground m-atomic formula of* m_0. *Then,* A *is a logical consequence of* m_0 *srd* $SW(m_0)$ $\Leftrightarrow m_0$ *srd* $SW(m_0) \vdash A$.

6 Transformation to Horn Clause Logic

The previously presented module system can be easily transformed to Horn clause logic. Each module may be mapped onto a flat Horn clause program. Thus, a module surrounded by a surrounding world is mapped onto a Horn clause theory that is the union of the images of the modules of the system. Each m-clause in a module's body is mapped onto a Horn clause. Every m-atomic formula of the m-clause is substituted by an atomic formula according to the visibility state of the predicate of the m-atomic formula within this module. The interface declarations of a module are mapped onto Horn clauses that provide a link between the inter-module atomic formulae.

The mapping of the m-atomic formulae is defined as follows.

Definition 21.

$$map: \; M\text{-}FOTs \times M\text{-}atomic\text{-}formulae \;\longrightarrow\; atomic\text{-}formulae$$

where *M-FOTs* is the set of m-FOTs, *M-atomic-formulae* is the set of m-atomic formulae, *atomic-formulae* is the set of first order atomic formulae and *map* is defined in the following way:

$$\begin{array}{ll} map(mn, Atom) = m(mn, Atom), & if\ pred(Atom) \in Merged(mn) \\ map(mn, Atom) = l(mn, Atom), & if\ pred(Atom) \in Local(mn) \\ map(mn, Atom) = e(mn, otherm, Atom), & if\ pred(Atom) \in Imported(mn) \\ map(mn, Atom) = g(Atom), & if\ pred(Atom) \in PGlobal(mn) \end{array}$$

where mn is a m-FOT, $Atom$ a m-atomic formula of mn and $otherm$ is a m-FOT such that $pred(Atom) \in I(mn, otherm)$.

The mapping is extended to m-clauses and m-programs by considering the image of each m-atomic formula in the m-clause and the image of each m-clause in the m-program.

As previously mentioned, the interface declarations provide a set of clauses which derive as follows.

Definition 22. Consider a m-FOT $(mn, P, Progr)$ and (V, F) a pair of variables and function symbols global to the whole system. *Interface_clauses(mn)* is a set of clauses such that:

1. $\forall(em, prd) \in E(mn), \exists$ an interface clause which is:
$$e(em, mn, Atom) \; :- \; l(mn, Atom)$$
where $Atom = prd(t_1, \ldots, t_n)$, n is the arity of prd and $t_1, \ldots, t_n \in V$.
2. $\forall(prd) \in E(mn), \exists$ an interface clause which is:
$$e(em, mn, Atom) \; :- \; l(mn, Atom)$$
where $Atom$ as above and $em \in V$.
3. $\forall(mms, prd) \in M(mn)$ and $\forall mm \in mms$, $\exists$ an interface clause which is:
$$m(mn, Atom) \; :- \; e(mn, mm, Atom)$$
where $Atom$ as above.
4. $\forall(prd) \in M(mn), \exists$ an interface clause which is:
$$m(mn, Atom) \; :- \; e(mn, mm, Atom)$$
where $Atom$ as above and $mm \in V$.
5. $\forall prd \in GI(mn), \exists$ an interface clause which is:
$$g(Atom) \; :- \; l(mn, Atom)$$
where $Atom$ as above.

Then, considering the above definitions, the mapping is also extended to m-FOTs in the following way.

Definition 23. Assuming (V, F) a pair of variables and function symbols global to the system, each m-FOT $(mn, P, Progr)$ is mapped onto a Horn clause theory with function symbols $F' = F \cup Using(mn)$, variables V and program $Progr' = map(mn, Progr) \cup Interface\_clauses(mn)$. The set of predicate symbols is $P' = \{m, l, e, g\}$ where m,l are 2-ary predicate symbols, e a 3-ary predicate symbol and g is a unary predicate symbol.

To comment on the mapping, it can be said that it exploits and reflects the distinction of the predicates among the various modules as well as within a module according to the interface declarations of this module. Moreover, it achieves parameterization with respect to the modules of the surrounding world by transforming a module body independently from any other module's transformation. In addition, it treats interfaces separately from any code. Techniques employed in other work, where structuring extensions have been introduced to logic programming and have been mapped onto flat code [1, 17, 18, 19, 21, 9], are not sufficient or relevant to our case. A straightforward predicate renaming can be deduced from the substitution of the m-atomic formulae performed by the mapping.

It is interesting to see the relation of the mapping with the other semantics of the module system. More precisely, the relation with the model-thoretic semantics has been investigated.

Consider m_0 srd $SW(m_0)$ where m_0 is $(m_0, (M, (H, E, GI), I, GO), Progr)$. Then, reduce its E and GI sets to their elements which contain predicates used by $SW'(m_0)$ and add the remaining elements to H. At the same time, for both the modified m_0 as well as all modules in $SW'(m_0)$, eliminate the concept of "all" modules from the interfaces by explicitly enumerating the modules in $SW'(m_0) \cup \{m_0\}$ (minus the home module of the interface). Then, consider $P1_{RESTR}$ to be the program of $map(m_0) \cup (\cup_{m \in SW'(m_0)} map(m))$ where m_0 srd $SW'(m_0)$ is modified as previously described. From $P1_{RESTR}$ derive P_{RESTR} by substituting each pair of clauses:

$$m(InM, Atom)\ :-\ e(InM, FromM, Atom)$$

and

$$e(InM, FromM, Atom)\ :-\ l(FromM, Atom)$$

by the clause

$$m(InM, Atom)\ :-\ l(FromM, Atom)$$

where InM, $FromM$ are module names and $Atom$ an atomic formula. If a merge interface clause cannot be paired, it is not included in P_{RESTR}.

Considering m_0 srd $SW(m_0)$ and P_{RESTR} derived as previously described, the following theorems have been proved.

Theorem 24. *Let m_0 srd $SW(m_0)$ and Atom a m-atomic formula of m_0. Then, Atom logical consequence of m_0 srd $SW(m_0) \Leftrightarrow \forall(map(m_0, Atom))$ logical consequence of P_{RESTR}.*

Theorem 25. *Let P_{RESTR} as previously defined and MOD a Herbrand model for P_{RESTR}. Consider*

$$MOD_{RESTR}(m_i) = \{Atom | Atom \in MOD,\ \exists Atom' \text{ a m-atomic formula of } m_i \text{ such that } map(m_i, Atom') = Atom\},$$

$\forall m_i \in SW'(m_0) \cup \{m_0\}$.
Consider also

$$MODm(m_i) = \{Atom' | Atom' \text{ is a m-atomic formula of } m_i \text{ such that } map(m_i, Atom') \in MOD_{RESTR}(m_i)\},\ \forall m_i \in SW'(m_0) \cup \{m_0\}$$
$$MODm(m_i) = \emptyset,\ \forall m_i \in SW(m_0) - SW'(m_0)$$

Thus, $map(m_i, MODm(m_i)) = MOD_{RESTR}(m_i), \forall m_i \in SW'(m_0) \cup \{m_0\}$. Then, $MODm(m_0)$ is a model for m_0 srd MODms of $SW(m_0)$ where $MODms = \{MODm(m_i) | m_i \in SW(m_0)\}$.

Theorem 26 Minimal Model Characterization in Terms of the Mapping.

Consider M_{MIN}, the minimal model of P_{RESTR}. Then, $M_{MIN}m(m_0)$ srd $M_{MIN}ms$ is the minimal model for m_0 srd $SW(m_0)$.

7 Related Work and Discussion

There is also other work related to import/export program composition. The work of [20] should be mentioned where an algebra for building logic programs out of pieces is introduced. The elementary terms of the algebra are breeze blocks and building bricks. The building bricks are logic programs. The breeze blocks (include/exclude/rename) correspond to import/export lists of conventional module systems. Breeze blocks are considered as functions on predicate symbols. Building bricks are given a meaning as a monotone map from interpretations to interpretations. In [1], the introduced union, intersection and encapsulation operations are used to define two operators as powerful as import/export relations at the extensional level. Logic modules with import/export interfaces are studied in [11] within the framework of the abstract semantics they introduce. A logic module is a quadruple (P, Im, Ex, Int). Im, Ex and Int are disjoint sets of the imported, exported and internal predicates, respectively. P is a logic program with no clause having head with a predicate in Im. However, in their approach the intensional view is adopted, i.e. program clauses are imported/exported.

In [4] composition of logic programs is modelled by the composition of the admissible Herbrand models of the programs. Admissibility of a model is considered under an admissible set of hypotheses where each of them occurs in the body of a clause of the program. A hypothesis is an element of the Herbrand base of the program. Then, a Herbrand model is the admissible Herbrand model under these hypotheses if and only if it is the minimal model of the union of the program and these hypotheses. Admissible models are claimed to model even logic modules with import/export declarations and modules with import declarations have been studied in [3]. The concept of the surrounding world of our approach can be parameterized in terms of the concept of the hypotheses. Nevertheless, the conditions for admissibility of hypotheses must change to meet the enhanced requirements of the visibility states. At the same time, the admissible model's definition can be compared with the model concept presented in Sect. 3. However, only one admissible model is considered under some hypotheses, though more than one models are considered for a m-FOT surrounded by a surrounding world. Actually, the approach presented in [4] seems very interesting and it is in our near future work to try to abstract (parameterize) the semantics of our module system either by adopting and adjusting this approach or by developing a new one inspired from that work.

To comment on our module system, the following can be said. It can support complicated interconnections among a set of modules which is something that is needed in various application areas. In addition, higher encapsulation structures can be built on top of the existing module system according to the requirements of the specific application. Moreover, the module system can offer the encapsulation required in various advanced application areas, such as multi-agent systems, as well as in sophisticated platforms, such as task oriented languages. Another advantage is that information may be distributed since the module system may collect it to form a single block. Furthermore, incremental module loading and unloading makes the system useful for the debugging phase. The system, although inspired from practical needs, has formal semantics which smoothly and naturally extends the ones of Horn clause logic. More precisely, standard model-theory [23] based on Herbrand interpretations and models as well as the immediate consequence operator have been suitably adjusted. What is more is that, no migration to other logics is required. In addition, the operational semantics extends the SLD-resolution by a simple rule that performs environment change, when required. A single module with no interfaces is a special case of the approach ($SW(m_0) = \emptyset$). Moreover, the approach taken is such that if a larger variety of interface declarations is needed, it can be extended by increasing the number of visibility states. The semantics can be easily adjusted to model the new system. Standard import/export declarations can be considered a special case of the approach. Visibility states are the pivot in the transformation of modular programs into flat code, implemented as a preprocessor. The preprocessor is written in Prolog, thus an integrated system can be derived. A form of equivalence with the other semantics of the system has been also provided for the transformation. The semantics given to the system can also model the world of the top level loop execution when various modules are loaded to the system. This is formalized as a central module surrounded by a surrounding world. The central module provides the environment of the top level loop execution and the surrounding world corresponds to the set of the loaded modules.

8 Conclusions

In this paper, a module system for logic programming was presented. This module system provides a finer program composition than import/export declarations and has been found useful to be a structuring tool in various application areas. This work showed that such a module system, although coming out from practice, has clear model-theoretic, fixpoint and operational semantics extending the ones of Horn clause logic using simple, well-known and widely understood concepts. In all the approaches we consider a central module surrounded by a surrounding world of other modules. In addition, modular logic programs are mapped to flat ones and this mapping provides a basis for a preprocessor implementation of the module system which meets the requirement of independent transformation. Equivalence relations have been proved for all the approaches of the semantics of the module system.

References

1. A. Brogi. *Program Composition in Computational Logic.* PhD thesis, Università di Pisa, 1993.
2. A. Brogi, E. Lamma, and P. Mello. A general framework for structuring logic programs. Technical Report 4/1, CNR Progetto Finalizzato Sistemi Informatici e Calcolo Parallelo, 1990.

3. A. Brogi, E. Lamma, and P. Mello. Composing open logic programs. *Journal of Logic and Computation*, 3(91-11:4):1–25, 1992.
4. A. Brogi, E. Lamma, and P. Mello. Compositional model-theoretic semantics for logic programs. *New Generation Computing*, 11:1–21, 1992.
5. A. Brogi, P. Mancarella, D. Pedreschi, and F. Turini. Composition operators for logic theories. In J. W. Lloyd, editor, *Proceedings of the Computational Logic Symposium*, pages 117–134, November 1990.
6. M. Bugliesi. A declarative view of inheritance in logic programming. In *Joint International Conference and Symposium on Logic Programming*, pages 112–127, 1992.
7. M. Bugliesi, E. Lamma, and P. Mello. Modularity in logic programming. *Journal of Logic Programming*, 19,20:443–502, 1994.
8. W. F. Clocksin and C. S. Mellish. *Programming in Prolog*. Springer-Verlag, second edition, 1984.
9. R. Dietrich. A preprocessor based module system for Prolog. In *TAPSOFT'89 International Joint Conference on Theory and Practice in Software Development*, volume 2, pages 126–139, 1989.
10. *ECL^iPS^e: User Manual*, March 1993.
11. H. Gaifman and E. Shapiro. Fully abstract compositional semantics for logic programs. In *6th Conference on Principles of Programming Languages*, pages 134–142, 1989.
12. I. Karali and C. Halatsis. The semantics of a module support for logic programming. Technical report, Department of Informatics, University of Athens, 1993.
13. I. Karali, E. Pelecanos, and C. Halatsis. A versatile module system for Prolog mapped to flat Prolog. In *ACM Symposium on Applied Computing*, pages 578–585, 1993.
14. J. W. Lloyd. *Foundations of Logic Programming*. Springer-Verlag, 1987.
15. P. Mancarella and D. Pedreschi. An algebra for logic programs. In *5th International Conference in Logic Programming*, pages 1006–1023, 1988.
16. D. Miller. A theory of modules for logic programming. In *Proceedings of the 1986 Symposium on Logic Programming*, pages 106–114, 1986.
17. L. Monteiro and A. Porto. Contextual logic programming. In *6th International Conference in Logic Programming*, pages 284–299, 1989.
18. L. Monteiro and A. Porto. A transformational view of inheritance in logic programming. In *7th International Conference in Logic Programming*, pages 481–494, 1990.
19. Y. Moscowitz and E. Shapiro. Lexical logic programs. In *8th International Symposium in Logic Programming*, pages 349–363, 1991.
20. R. O'Keefe. Towards an algebra for constructing logic programs. In *IEEE Symposium on Logic Programming*, pages 152–160, 1985.
21. D. T. Sannella and L. A. Wallen. A calculus for the construction of modular Prolog programs. *Journal of Logic Programming*, 12(1):147–177, January 1992.
22. L. Sterling and E. Shapiro. *The Art of Prolog*. MIT Press, 1986.
23. M. Van Emden and A. Kowalski. The semantics of predicate logic as a programming language. *Journal of the Association for Computing Machinery*, 23:733–742, 1976.

Strictness and Totality Analysis with Conjunction

Kirsten Lackner Solberg

Computer Science Department
Aarhus University, Denmark
e-mail: kls@daimi.aau.dk

Abstract. We extend the strictness and totality analysis of [12] by allowing conjunction at all levels rather than at the top-level. We prove the strictness and totality analysis correct with respect to a denotational semantics and finally construct an algorithm for inferring the strictness and totality properties.

1 Introduction

Strictness analysis has proved useful in the implementation of lazy functional languages like Miranda, Lazy ML and Haskell: when a function is strict it is safe to evaluate its argument before performing the function call. Totality analysis has not been adopted so widely: if the argument to a function is known to terminate then it is safe to evaluate it before performing the function call [9].

In the literature there are several approaches to the specification of strictness analysis: abstract interpretation (e.g. [10, 3]), projection analysis (e.g. [14]) and inference based methods (e.g. [2, 6, 7, 8, 15]). Totality analysis has received much less attention and has primarily been specified using abstract interpretation [10, 1]. It can be regarded as an approximation to time complexity analysis; most literature performing such developments consider eager languages but [11] considers lazy languages.

The paper [12] presents an inference system for performing strictness *and* totality analysis. The inference system is an extension of the usual type system in that we introduce three annotations on types σ:

- $\mathbf{b}^{\sigma}$: the value has type σ and is definitely $\bot$,
- $\mathbf{n}^{\sigma}$: the value has type σ and is definitely *not* $\bot$, and
- $\top^{\sigma}$: the value has type σ and it can be any value.

Annotated types can be constructed using the function type constructor and (top-level) conjunction. As an example a function may have the annotated type $(\mathbf{n}^{\mathtt{Int}} \to \mathbf{n}^{\mathtt{Int}}) \wedge (\mathbf{b}^{\mathtt{Int}} \to \mathbf{b}^{\mathtt{Int}})$ which means that given a terminating argument the function will definitely terminate and given a non-terminating argument it will definitely not terminate. Thus we capture the strictness as well as the totality of the function. Strictness and totality information can also be combined as in $(\mathbf{n}^{\mathtt{Int}} \to \mathbf{n}^{\mathtt{Int}} \to \mathbf{n}^{\mathtt{Int}}) \wedge (\mathbf{b}^{\mathtt{Int}} \to \mathbf{n}^{\mathtt{Int}} \to \mathbf{n}^{\mathtt{Int}}) \wedge (\mathbf{n}^{\mathtt{Int}} \to \mathbf{b}^{\mathtt{Int}} \to \mathbf{n}^{\mathtt{Int}}) \wedge (\mathbf{b}^{\mathtt{Int}} \to \mathbf{b}^{\mathtt{Int}} \to \mathbf{b}^{\mathtt{Int}})$ which will be the annotated type of McCarthy's ambiguity operator.

The strictness and totality analysis in [12] is defined by an inference system and proven sound with respect to a natural-style operational semantics. The proof is long and detailed because in order to reason about fixpoints it is necessary to introduce new terms which include information about how many times the fixpoint was allowed to be unfolded. In a denotational semantics it is easy to reason about fixpoints since there is no need for new terms; all the denotations are already included. In this paper we will extend the analysis of [12] with unrestricted conjunction and we will prove this analysis sound with respect to a denotational semantics. Finally we will construct an algorithm for inferring the strictness and totality properties. There are two different ways of constructing inference algorithms: one is to calculate all the information that can be inferred; the other is to check if a given property can be inferred. We choose the latter since it is often the case that we are only interested in knowing if a term possesses one particular property and we thus expect this approach to lead to more efficient implementations.

Overview Section 2 presents the standard type inference rules and the denotational semantics for our simply-typed lazy lambda calculus. In section 3 we define the strictness and totality properties and the analysis of [12] is restated. In section 4 the analysis is proven correct with respect to the denotational semantics. Finally in Section 5 we construct an algorithm for strictness and totality property inference.

2 Syntax and Semantics

This section introduces the simply-typed lazy λ-calculus with constants and fixpoints. We first define the syntax and typing rules for the language, and then we define the lazy semantics by means of a denotational semantics.

2.1 The Language

The types, $\tau \in \mathrm{T}$, are either base types or function types

$$\tau ::= \mathtt{B} \mid \tau \rightarrow \tau$$

where the base types (i.e. the `B`'s) include `Bool` and `Int`. The terms, $\mathtt{e} \in \mathrm{E}$, of the simply-typed λ-calculus are

$$\mathtt{e} ::= \mathtt{x}^{\tau} \mid \lambda \mathtt{x}^{\tau}.\mathtt{e} \mid \mathtt{e}\ \mathtt{e} \mid \mathtt{fix}\ \mathtt{e} \mid \mathtt{if}\ \mathtt{e}\ \mathtt{then}\ \mathtt{e}\ \mathtt{else}\ \mathtt{e} \mid \mathtt{c}$$

where the constants (i.e. the `c`'s) include `true` and `false` of type `Bool`, and all the integers of type `Int`. In this paper we have chosen to annotate the variables with their type.

We are only considering terms that are typeable according to the type inference rules defined in Figure 1. To all the constants `c` there is a unique type $\tau_{\mathtt{c}}$. The free variables in the term `e` is the set FV(`e`) and substitution on terms $\mathtt{e}[\mathtt{e}_2/\mathtt{x}]$ is defined as usual.

$$[\text{var}]_T \frac{}{\vdash \mathtt{x}^\tau : \tau} \qquad [\text{const}]_T \frac{}{\vdash \mathtt{c} : \tau_{\mathtt{c}}}$$

$$[\text{abs}]_T \frac{\vdash \mathtt{e} : \tau}{\vdash \lambda \mathtt{x}^\sigma . \mathtt{e} : \sigma \to \tau} \qquad [\text{app}]_T \frac{\vdash \mathtt{e}_1 : \sigma \to \tau \quad \vdash \mathtt{e}_2 : \sigma}{\vdash \mathtt{e}_1\ \mathtt{e}_2 : \tau}$$

$$[\text{if}]_T \frac{\vdash \mathtt{e}_1 : \mathtt{Bool} \quad \vdash \mathtt{e}_2 : \tau \quad \vdash \mathtt{e}_3 : \tau}{\vdash \mathtt{if}\ \mathtt{e}_1\ \mathtt{then}\ \mathtt{e}_2\ \mathtt{else}\ \mathtt{e}_3 : \tau} \qquad [\text{fix}]_T \frac{\vdash \mathtt{e} : \sigma \to \sigma}{\vdash \mathtt{fix}\ \mathtt{e} : \sigma}$$

Fig. 1. Type inference

2.2 The Semantics

The reason for choosing a lazy semantics is to capture the semantics of "real-life" lazy functional programming languages like Miranda [13] in contrast to most other papers on strictness analysis ([3, 5]). The semantics in [12] is a natural-style operational semantics where the terms are evaluated to weak head normal form (abbreviated WHNF), i.e. to constants or lambda-abstractions. Here we will define the semantics as a denotational semantics. We have a type-indexed family of domains:

$$D_B = B_\perp$$
$$D_{\sigma \to \tau} = (D_\sigma \to_{\text{cont}} D_\tau)_\perp$$

We need the two functions $\mathtt{up}$ and $\mathtt{dn}$ to get from a domain to the lifted domain and back again. We also need an environment ρ that assigns denotations to variables. This is a partial function from variables to the disjoint union of the domains. The environment is type-preserving, that is if $\rho\,(\mathtt{x}^\tau)$ is defined then it is a member of D_τ. Now the semantics assigns denotations to terms, meaning that if we have $\vdash \mathtt{e} : \tau$, then $[\![\mathtt{e}]\!]$ is a partial function from environments to D_τ (Figure 2). For each constant, $\mathtt{c}$, there is a unique predefined denotation c.

3 The Analysis

We will assume that the terms are annotated with their types. We define the strictness and totality logic $\mathcal{L}_\tau^{\text{ST}}$ as follows:

$$\mathbf{n}^\tau, \mathbf{b}^\tau, \mathrm{T}^\tau \in \mathcal{L}_\tau^{\text{ST}} \qquad \frac{\phi^\tau \in \mathcal{L}_\tau^{\text{ST}} \quad \psi^\tau \in \mathcal{L}_\tau^{\text{ST}}}{\phi^\tau \wedge \psi^\tau \in \mathcal{L}_\tau^{\text{ST}}}$$

$$\frac{\psi^\tau \in \mathcal{L}_\tau^{\text{ST}}}{\downarrow(\psi^\tau) \in \mathcal{L}_\tau^{\text{ST}}} \qquad \frac{\phi^\tau \in \mathcal{L}_\tau^{\text{ST}} \quad \psi^\sigma \in \mathcal{L}_\sigma^{\text{ST}}}{\phi^\tau \to \psi^\sigma \in \mathcal{L}_{\tau \to \sigma}^{\text{ST}}}$$

The idea is that $\mathcal{L}_\tau^{\text{ST}}$ is the properties that a term of type τ may possess. We relate a subset of D_τ to each property ϕ^τ (Figure 3). For this we need to take the downwards closure of a subset of the domains:

$$\mathtt{dc}(X) = \{d' \mid \exists d \in X : d' \leq d\}$$

$$
\begin{aligned}
[\![\mathtt{x}^\tau]\!]\,\rho &= \rho\,(\mathtt{x}^\tau)\\
[\![\lambda\mathtt{x}^\tau\,.\,\mathtt{e}]\!]\,\rho &= \mathtt{up}(\lambda d\,.\,[\![\mathtt{e}]\!]\ \rho[d/\mathtt{x}^\tau])\\
[\![\mathtt{e}_1\ \mathtt{e}_2]\!]\,\rho &= \mathtt{dn}([\![\mathtt{e}_1]\!]\,\rho)([\![\mathtt{e}_2]\!]\,\rho)\\
[\![\mathtt{fix}\ \ \mathtt{e}]\!]\,\rho &= \sqcup_n d_n \text{where}\\
&\qquad d_0 = \bot\\
&\qquad d_{n+1} = \mathtt{dn}([\![\mathtt{e}]\!]\,\rho)d_n\\
[\![\mathtt{if}\ \mathtt{e}_1\ \mathtt{then}\ \mathtt{e}_2\ \mathtt{else}\ \mathtt{e}_3]\!]\,\rho &= \begin{cases} \bot, & \text{if } [\![\mathtt{e}_1]\!]\,\rho = \bot_{D_{\mathtt{Bool}}}\\ [\![\mathtt{e}_2]\!]\,\rho, & \text{if } [\![\mathtt{e}_1]\!]\,\rho = \mathtt{true}\\ [\![\mathtt{e}_3]\!]\,\rho, & \text{if } [\![\mathtt{e}_1]\!]\,\rho = \mathtt{false}\end{cases}\\
[\![\mathtt{c}]\!]\,\rho &= c
\end{aligned}
$$

Fig. 2. Denotational semantics for the λ-calculus

$$
\begin{aligned}
[\![\mathbf{n}^\tau]\!] &= D_\tau \setminus \{\bot_{D_\tau}\}\\
[\![\mathbf{b}^\tau]\!] &= \{\bot_{D_\tau}\}\\
[\![\top^\tau]\!] &= D_\tau\\
[\![\phi^\tau \to \psi^\sigma]\!] &= \{f \in D_{\tau\to\sigma} \mid \mathtt{dn}(f)\ [\![\phi^\tau]\!] \subseteq [\![\psi^\sigma]\!]\}\\
[\![\psi^\sigma \wedge \phi^\sigma]\!] &= [\![\psi^\sigma]\!] \cap [\![\phi^\sigma]\!]\\
[\![\downarrow(\psi^\sigma)]\!] &= \mathtt{dc}([\![\psi^\sigma]\!])
\end{aligned}
$$

Fig. 3. The meaning of the properties

The idea is that a term with the strictness and totality property $\mathbf{n}^\tau$ is a term of type τ and it has a denotation in $D_\tau\setminus\{\bot_{D_\tau}\}$ i.e. the term has a non-bottom denotation. A term with the strictness and totality property $\mathbf{b}^\tau$ has the type τ and it has the denotation $\bot_{D_\tau}$, i.e. it is bottom. For terms with the strictness and totality property $\top^\tau$ we only know that it has the type τ. A term with strictness and totality property $\phi^\tau \to \psi^\sigma$ will have the type $\tau \to \sigma$ and will, when applied to another term with the strictness and totality property ϕ^τ, yield a term with strictness and totality property ψ^σ. A term with the strictness and totality property $\phi^\tau \wedge \psi^\tau$ is a term with both properties, ϕ^τ and ψ^τ. The set of terms with property $\downarrow(\phi^\tau)$ is the set of term with property ϕ^τ and including bottom; but whenever ϕ^τ is empty so is $\downarrow(\phi^\tau)$. The $\downarrow(\phi^\tau)$-property is used to express the fact that the functions we are considering are monotonic, see the rule [monotone] in Figure 4.

An empty property is a property possessed by no term. One example is $(\mathbf{n}^\tau \wedge \mathbf{b}^\tau)$ since a term cannot both terminate and not terminate.

Most terms possess more than one strictness and totality property; as an example consider the strictness and totality properties of $\lambda \mathtt{x}^{\mathtt{Int}}.7$ which includes

$$\top^{\mathtt{Int}} \to \mathtt{Int}, \mathbf{n}^{\mathtt{Int}} \to \mathtt{Int}, \top^{\mathtt{Int}} \to \mathbf{n}^{\mathtt{Int}}, \mathbf{n}^{\mathtt{Int}} \to \mathbf{n}^{\mathtt{Int}}$$

among others. Some of them are redundant and to express this we define coercions between the strictness and totality properties: $\psi^{\mathcal{T}} \leq_{\mathrm{ST}} \phi^{\mathcal{T}}$ may only hold if all terms of strictness and totality property $\psi^{\mathcal{T}}$ also have the strictness and totality property $\phi^{\mathcal{T}}$ (assuming the types are the same).

The coercion relation $\leq_{\mathrm{ST}}$ defined in Figure 4 is reflexive, transitive, and anti-monotone in contravariant position. We will write $\equiv$ for the equivalence induced by $\leq_{\mathrm{ST}}$, i.e. $\psi^{\mathcal{T}} \equiv \phi^{\mathcal{T}}$ if and only if $\psi^{\mathcal{T}} \leq_{\mathrm{ST}} \phi^{\mathcal{T}}$ and $\phi^{\mathcal{T}} \leq_{\mathrm{ST}} \psi^{\mathcal{T}}$. The rule [top1] expresses that the strictness and totality property $\top^{\tau}$ includes all the terms of type τ. One axiom derived from the rule [top1] is

$$\top^{\tau} \to \top^{\sigma} \leq_{\mathrm{ST}} \top^{\tau \to \sigma} \tag{1}$$

Axiom (1) then motivates rule [top2] because when combined they yield

$$\top^{\tau \to \sigma} \equiv \top^{\tau} \to \top^{\sigma}$$

The rule [monotone] ensures that we live in a universe of monotone function: if we know less about the argument to a function, then we should know less about the result as well. We can infer

$$\mathbf{n}^{\mathcal{T}} \to \mathbf{b}^{\mathcal{T}} \leq_{\mathrm{ST}} \top^{\mathcal{T}} \to \mathbf{b}^{\mathcal{T}}$$

using the [monotone]-rule. This is used in order to infer the type

$$(\mathbf{n}^{\mathcal{T}} \to \mathbf{b}^{\mathcal{T}}) \to \top^{\mathcal{T}} \to \mathbf{b}^{\mathcal{T}}$$

for `twice`.

We would like the $\downarrow(\psi)$ properties to be equivalent to properties without any $\downarrow(\psi')$. We have

$$\downarrow(\mathbf{n}^{\sigma}) \equiv \top^{\sigma} \qquad \downarrow(\top^{\sigma}) \equiv \top^{\sigma}$$
$$\downarrow(\mathbf{b}^{\sigma}) \equiv \mathbf{b}^{\sigma} \qquad \downarrow(\psi \to \phi) \equiv \psi \to \downarrow(\phi)$$

but only

$$\downarrow(\psi \wedge \phi) \leq_{\mathrm{ST}} \downarrow(\psi) \wedge \downarrow(\phi)$$

The reason for introducing $\downarrow(\psi)$ in the first place was to be able to express the monotonicity-rule. The advantage of having an equivalence between properties with $\downarrow$ and properties without $\downarrow$ is that we can forget all about $\downarrow(\phi)$-properties since they are equivalent to another property without any $\downarrow(\phi)$-properties and the world will look nicer.

Now we can turn to the analysis defined in Figure 5. The list A of assumptions gives strictness and totality properties to the free variables. We shall assume that all the variables in the list are distinct. For each constant `c`, we assume that a strictness and

$$[\text{ref}]\ \frac{}{\psi \leq_{ST} \psi} \qquad [\text{trans}]\ \frac{\psi \leq_{ST} \phi \quad \phi \leq_{ST} \chi}{\psi \leq_{ST} \chi}$$

$$[\rightarrow]\ \frac{\psi' \leq_{ST} \psi \quad \phi \leq_{ST} \phi'}{\psi \rightarrow \phi \leq_{ST} \psi' \rightarrow \phi'}$$

$$[\text{top1}]\ \frac{}{\phi^{\tau} \leq_{ST} \top^{\tau}} \qquad [\text{top2}]\ \frac{}{\top^{\tau} \rightarrow {}^{\sigma} \leq_{ST} \top^{\tau} \rightarrow \top^{\sigma}}$$

$$[\text{bot}]\ \frac{}{\mathbf{b}^{\tau} \rightarrow {}^{\sigma} \leq_{ST} \top^{\tau} \rightarrow \mathbf{b}^{\sigma}}$$

$$[\text{notbot}]\ \frac{}{\mathbf{n}^{\tau} \rightarrow \mathbf{n}^{\sigma} \leq_{ST} \mathbf{n}^{\tau} \rightarrow {}^{\sigma}}$$

$$[\downarrow 1]\ \frac{}{\phi \leq_{ST} \downarrow(\phi)} \qquad [\downarrow 2]\ \frac{\psi \leq_{ST} \phi}{\downarrow(\psi) \leq_{ST} \downarrow(\phi)}$$

$$[\downarrow 3]\ \frac{}{\top^{\tau} \leq_{ST} \downarrow(\mathbf{n}^{\tau})} \qquad [\downarrow 4]\ \frac{}{\downarrow(\mathbf{b}^{\tau}) \leq_{ST} \mathbf{b}^{\tau}}$$

$$[\downarrow 5]\ \frac{}{\downarrow(\downarrow(\psi)) \leq_{ST} \downarrow(\psi)} \qquad [\downarrow 6]\ \frac{}{\downarrow(\psi \wedge \phi) \leq_{ST} \downarrow(\psi) \wedge \downarrow(\phi)}$$

$$[\downarrow 7]\ \frac{}{\downarrow(\psi \rightarrow \phi) \equiv \psi \rightarrow \downarrow(\phi)}$$

$$[\text{monotone}]\ \frac{}{\psi \rightarrow \phi \leq_{ST} \downarrow(\psi) \rightarrow \downarrow(\phi)}$$

$$[\wedge 1]\ \frac{}{\psi \wedge \phi \leq_{ST} \psi} \qquad [\wedge 2]\ \frac{}{\psi \wedge \phi \leq_{ST} \phi}$$

$$[\wedge]\ \frac{\chi \leq_{ST} \psi \quad \chi \leq_{ST} \phi}{\chi \leq_{ST} \psi \wedge \phi}$$

$$[\rightarrow \wedge]\ \frac{}{(\psi \rightarrow \phi') \wedge (\psi \rightarrow \phi'') \leq_{ST} \psi \rightarrow (\phi' \wedge \phi'')}$$

Fig. 4. Coercions between strictness and totality properties

totality property is specified $\phi_{\mathtt{C}}$; as an example for the successor function we have $\phi_{\mathtt{succ}} = (\mathbf{n}^{\mathtt{Int}} \rightarrow \mathbf{n}^{\mathtt{Int}}) \wedge (\mathbf{b}^{\mathtt{Int}} \rightarrow \mathbf{b}^{\mathtt{Int}})$. The remaining properties can be coerced from this strictness and totality property:

$$\phi_{\mathtt{succ}} \leq_{ST} \top^{\mathtt{Int}} \rightarrow {}^{\mathtt{Int}}$$
$$\phi_{\mathtt{succ}} \leq_{ST} \top^{\mathtt{Int}} \rightarrow \top^{\mathtt{Int}}$$
$$\phi_{\mathtt{succ}} \leq_{ST} \mathbf{n}^{\mathtt{Int}} \rightarrow \top^{\mathtt{Int}}$$
etc.

The rules [var], [abs], [app], and [const] are straightforward. There are three rules for conditional — depending on whether the test is of strictness and totality property $\mathbf{b}^{\mathtt{Bool}}$, $\mathbf{n}^{\mathtt{Bool}}$, or $\top^{\mathtt{Bool}}$.

$$[\text{var}]\ \frac{}{\mathtt{A} \vdash \mathtt{x}^{\tau} : \phi^{\tau}} \text{ if } \mathtt{x}^{\tau} : \phi^{\tau} \in \mathtt{A}$$

$$[\text{abs}]\ \frac{\mathtt{A}, \mathtt{x} : \phi^{\sigma} \vdash \mathtt{e} : \psi^{\tau}}{\mathtt{A} \vdash \lambda \mathtt{x}^{\sigma}.\mathtt{e} : (\phi^{\sigma} \to \psi^{\tau}) \wedge \mathbf{n}^{\sigma \to \tau}}$$

$$[\text{app}]\ \frac{\mathtt{A} \vdash \mathtt{e}_1 : \psi^{\sigma} \to \phi^{\tau} \quad \mathtt{A} \vdash \mathtt{e}_2 : \psi^{\sigma}}{\mathtt{A} \vdash \mathtt{e}_1\ \mathtt{e}_2 : \phi^{\tau}}$$

$$[\text{if1}]\ \frac{\mathtt{A} \vdash \mathtt{e}_1 : \mathbf{b}^{\mathtt{Bool}} \quad \mathtt{A} \vdash \mathtt{e}_2 : \psi^{\sigma} \quad \mathtt{A} \vdash \mathtt{e}_3 : \psi^{\sigma}}{\mathtt{A} \vdash \mathtt{if}\ \mathtt{e}_1\ \mathtt{then}\ \mathtt{e}_2\ \mathtt{else}\ \mathtt{e}_3 : \mathbf{b}^{\sigma}}$$

$$[\text{if2}]\ \frac{\mathtt{A} \vdash \mathtt{e}_1 : \mathbf{n}^{\mathtt{Bool}} \quad \mathtt{A} \vdash \mathtt{e}_2 : \psi^{\sigma} \quad \mathtt{A} \vdash \mathtt{e}_3 : \psi^{\sigma}}{\mathtt{A} \vdash \mathtt{if}\ \mathtt{e}_1\ \mathtt{then}\ \mathtt{e}_2\ \mathtt{else}\ \mathtt{e}_3 : \psi^{\sigma}}$$

$$[\text{if3}]\ \frac{\mathtt{A} \vdash \mathtt{e}_1 : \top^{\mathtt{Bool}} \quad \mathtt{A} \vdash \mathtt{e}_2 : \psi^{\sigma} \quad \mathtt{A} \vdash \mathtt{e}_3 : \psi^{\sigma}}{\mathtt{A} \vdash \mathtt{if}\ \mathtt{e}_1\ \mathtt{then}\ \mathtt{e}_2\ \mathtt{else}\ \mathtt{e}_3 : \psi^{\sigma}} \text{ if BOT}(\psi^{\sigma})$$

$$[\text{fix}]\ \frac{\mathtt{A} \vdash \mathtt{e} : \psi_1^{\sigma} \to \psi_2^{\sigma} \wedge \psi_2^{\sigma} \to \psi_3^{\sigma} \wedge \cdots \wedge \psi_{n-1}^{\sigma} \to \psi_n^{\sigma}}{\mathtt{A} \vdash \mathtt{fix}\ \mathtt{e} : \psi_n^{\sigma}} \quad \text{if} \begin{cases} \text{BOT}(\psi_1^{\sigma}), \\ \exists p, q : p < q \wedge \\ \psi_q^{\sigma} \leq_{\text{ST}} \psi_p^{\sigma} \end{cases}$$

$$[\text{const}]\ \frac{}{\mathtt{A} \vdash \mathtt{c} : \psi_{\mathtt{C}}}$$

$$[\text{coer}]\ \frac{\mathtt{A} \vdash \mathtt{e} : \psi^{\sigma}}{\mathtt{A} \vdash \mathtt{e} : \phi^{\sigma}} \text{ if } \psi^{\sigma} \leq_{\text{ST}} \phi^{\sigma} \qquad [\text{conj}]\ \frac{\mathtt{A} \vdash \mathtt{e} : \psi^{\sigma} \quad \mathtt{A} \vdash \mathtt{e} : \phi^{\sigma}}{\mathtt{A} \vdash \mathtt{e} : \psi^{\sigma} \wedge \phi^{\sigma}}$$

Fig. 5. Strictness and Totality Property Inference

The predicate BOT defined by

$$\begin{aligned} &\text{BOT}(\mathbf{n}^{\sigma}) = \mathtt{ff} && \text{BOT}(\top^{\sigma}) = \mathtt{tt} \\ &\text{BOT}(\mathbf{b}^{\sigma}) = \mathtt{tt} && \text{BOT}(\downarrow(\phi)) = \text{BOT}(\phi) \\ &\text{BOT}(\psi \to \phi) = \text{BOT}(\phi) \\ &\text{BOT}(\psi \wedge \phi) = \text{BOT}(\psi) \wedge \text{BOT}(\phi) \end{aligned}$$

is true for the strictness and totality property ψ^{τ} whenever it is guaranteed that bottom can be described by the property ψ^{τ}. The reason for *not* taking BOT($\downarrow(\phi)$) be to true is that ϕ may be empty and therefore also $\downarrow(\phi)$ may be empty. However, the definition of BOT($\downarrow(\phi)$) that we have adopted is not as precise as one would wish. (An example of which is when $\phi = \mathbf{n}^{\sigma}$.)

The rule [coer] allows to change the strictness and totality property to a greater property. It is quite useful as a preparation for applying the rule [if3], i.e. whenever BOT(ϕ) is not true we can coerce ϕ to a property ϕ' so that BOT(ϕ') is true.

From the rule [fix] the two more intuitive rules

$$[\text{fix1}]\ \frac{\mathtt{A} \vdash \mathtt{e} : \psi^{\sigma} \to \psi^{\sigma}}{\mathtt{A} \vdash \mathtt{fix}\ \mathtt{e} : \psi^{\sigma}} \text{ if BOT}(\psi^{\sigma})$$

and

$$[\text{fix2}]\ \frac{A \vdash \texttt{e} : \psi^{\sigma} \ \rightarrow \ \phi^{\sigma}}{A \vdash \texttt{fix e} : \phi^{\sigma}} \text{ if BOT}(\psi^{\sigma}) \text{ and } \phi^{\sigma} \ \leq_{\text{ST}} \ \psi^{\sigma}$$

are easily derived. The rule [fix] itself can be explained as follows: first we have to ensure that the strictness and totality property ψ_1^{σ} can describe bottom in order to be able to start the iteration towards the fixpoint. After the first iteration the term has the property ψ_2^{σ} and after the second the strictness and totality property ψ_3^{σ}, etc. When we reach iteration number $q-1$ we can apply the rule [coer] because we have $\psi_q^{\sigma} \ \leq_{\text{ST}} \ \psi_p^{\sigma}$ and the term has the property ψ_p^{σ}. In this way we can go on as long as necessary to calculate the fixpoint. Finally we are allowed to iterate $n-q$ times more to get the property ψ_n^{σ} for the fixpoint.

Example 1
We can infer $\vdash \texttt{fix}\ \lambda \texttt{x}_{\texttt{Int}}.\texttt{x}_{\texttt{Int}} : \mathbf{b}^{\texttt{Int}}$ which is more precise than the information $\top^{\texttt{Int}}$ obtained by [15]; in [16] it can be done. In the systems of [2, 6, 7, 16] one can infer the property $\top^{\texttt{Int}}$ for the term $\texttt{fix}\ \lambda \texttt{x}^{\texttt{Int}}.7$ whereas we can infer the more precise property $\mathbf{n}^{\texttt{Int}}$. In this system (as well as those of [12, 2, 6, 7, 16]) it is possible to infer the property

$$(\mathbf{b}^{\texttt{Int}} \rightarrow \top^{\texttt{Int}} \rightarrow \top^{\texttt{Int}} \rightarrow \mathbf{b}^{\texttt{Int}}) \wedge (\top^{\texttt{Int}} \rightarrow \mathbf{b}^{\texttt{Int}} \rightarrow \top^{\texttt{Int}} \rightarrow \mathbf{b}^{\texttt{Int}})$$

for the term

```
fix λf.(λx.λy.λz.if z = 0 then z + y else f y x (z - 1))
```

that way beyond the techniques of [8].
The term[1] `twice g` where

$$\texttt{twice} = \lambda \texttt{f}.\lambda \texttt{x}.\texttt{f (f x)}$$
$$\texttt{g} = \lambda \texttt{y}.\lambda \texttt{x}.\texttt{+ x (y (fix } \lambda \texttt{x.x))}$$

will have the strictness and totality property

$$(\top^{\texttt{Int}} \rightarrow \top^{\texttt{Int}}) \rightarrow \top^{\texttt{Int}} \rightarrow \mathbf{b}^{\texttt{Int}}$$

However, we are *not* able to prove it using the analysis in [12], because we need full power of conjunction in order to construct the proof-tree. The reason is that we need to infer that `twice` has the property

$$((\phi \rightarrow \psi) \wedge (\psi \rightarrow \chi)) \rightarrow (\phi \rightarrow \chi)$$

for any ϕ, ψ, and χ but this is not a well-formed conjunction type in [12]. □

Note that this analysis and the analysis in [12] only differ in the use of conjunction.

[1] Thanks to Nick Benton for pointing to this example

4 Soundness

In this section we will sketch the proof for soundness of the analysis (Figure 5) with respect to the denotational semantics (Figure 2). For the details see the author's forthcoming PhD Thesis.

Definition 2
A subset X of a domain D_σ is *limit closed* if whenever $d_0 \sqsubseteq d_1 \sqsubseteq \cdots$ is a chain in D_σ and $\forall i : d_i \in X$ then $\sqcup_i d_i \in X$ and it is *convex* if whenever $d_1 \sqsubseteq d_2 \sqsubseteq d_3 \in D_\sigma$ and $d_1 \in X$ and $d_3 \in X$ then $d_2 \in X$. □

First we prove that each $[\![\psi^\sigma]\!]$ is a limit-closed and convex subset of D_σ and convex:

Proposition 3 *Limit closed subsets*
$[\![\psi^\sigma]\!]$ is a limit closed and convex subset of D_σ □

Proof We assume that $d_0 \sqsubseteq d_1 \sqsubseteq \cdots$ is a chain in D_σ such that for all i we have $d_i \in [\![\psi^\sigma]\!]$, then we show by induction on the property ψ^σ that $\sqcup_i d_i \in [\![\psi^\sigma]\!]$ holds. And we assume that $d_1 \sqsubseteq d_2 \sqsubseteq d_3$ and both d_1 and d_3 is in $[\![\psi^\sigma]\!]$, then we show by induction on the property ψ^σ that d_2 is in $[\![\psi^\sigma]\!]$. We omit the details. ■

The predicate BOT is sound but it is not complete. Without properties of the form $\downarrow(\phi)$ and un-restricted conjunction or without conjunction we would have an bi-implication in Lemma 4 below. The reason is that ϕ can be an empty property, due to the conjunctions, and hence we cannot define BOT($\downarrow(\phi)$) to be true always — although it is true for all non-empty properties.

Lemma 4
$(\mathrm{BOT}(\psi^\sigma) = \mathtt{tt}) \Rightarrow (\bot_{D_\sigma} \in [\![\psi^\sigma]\!])$ □

Proof We assume that BOT(ψ^σ) is true and then we prove by induction on ψ^σ that $\bot_{D_\sigma} \in [\![\psi^\sigma]\!]$ holds. We omit the details. ■

Next we want to prove that the coercion rules are sound:

Lemma 5 *Soundness of coercions*
If $\psi^\sigma \leq_{\mathrm{ST}} \phi^\sigma$ then $[\![\psi^\sigma]\!] \subseteq [\![\phi^\sigma]\!]$ □

Proof We assume $\psi^\sigma \leq_{\mathrm{ST}} \phi^\sigma$ and then we prove by induction on the proof-tree for $\psi^\sigma \leq_{\mathrm{ST}} \phi^\sigma$ that $[\![\psi^\sigma]\!] \subseteq [\![\phi^\sigma]\!]$ holds. We omit the details. ■

The validity predicate $\models$ is defined for denotations and properties and extended to environments:

Definition 6 *Validity*
$d \models \psi^\sigma \Leftrightarrow (d \in [\![\psi^\sigma]\!])$
For environments we define
$\rho \models A \Leftrightarrow (\mathrm{dom}(A) = \mathrm{dom}(\rho) \wedge \forall\, x^\sigma \in \mathrm{dom}(\rho) : \rho\,(x^\sigma) \models A(x^\sigma))$ □

In the operational world [12] we did not introduce $\downarrow(\phi)$-types as part of the syntax. This is due to the difficulties in defining validity for $\downarrow(\phi)$-types in the operational setting.

Now soundness is:

Proposition 7 *Soundness*
$A \vdash e : \psi^\sigma \Rightarrow (\forall\, \rho : \rho \models A \Rightarrow [\![e]\!]\,\rho \models \psi^\sigma)$ □

Proof We assume $A \vdash e : \psi^\sigma$ and $\rho \models A$ then we show by induction on the proof-tree for $A \vdash e : \psi^\sigma$ that $[\![e]\!]\,\rho \models \psi^\sigma$ holds. We omit the details. ■

In the domain D_σ there are elements d to which there is no term that has d as its standard denotation. In the operational setting all the "meanings" are terms themselves so in order to express properties about the partial results of the fixpoints we find it convenient to introduce special terms approximating the fixpoint. This complicates the soundness proof in the operational setting.

5 Algorithm for Strictness and Totality Property Inference

One way to construct an algorithm for strictness and totality property inference — for both the un-restricted and restricted [12] case — is to follow the *most general type* approach by Hankin and Le Métayer [4]. For a given environment and term the algorithm will find *all* the strictness and totality properties that can be inferred for the term. Often we are only interested in knowing if a term possesses one particular property and not all of them, so this approach seems like using a sledge hammer to crack a nut. We follow the *lazy type* approach of Hankin and Le Métayer [4] where only the information necessary to answer *one* question is calculated.

The algorithm is constructed as follows:

- Make the inference system structural in the term and property. This is achieved by integrating the rule [coer] into all the appropriate rules and axioms.
- Introduce the lazy properties.
- Extract an algorithm from the lazy property inference system.

5.1 Structural Strictness and Totality Inference System

We define an inference system without a coercion rule but where the other rules have the coercion built in.

The coercion-rule maybe needed after the rules [var], [const], [if1], and [abs]. For the [abs]-rule we generate all the possible rules:

$$[\text{abs1}_S]\ \frac{}{A \vdash_S \lambda x^\sigma.e : \mathbf{n}^{\sigma\to\tau}} \qquad [\text{abs2}_S]\ \frac{}{A \vdash_S \lambda x^\sigma.e : \top^{\sigma\to\tau}}$$

$$[\text{abs3}_S]\ \frac{A \vdash_S \lambda x^\sigma.e : \phi^\sigma \to \psi^\tau}{A \vdash_S \lambda x^\sigma.e : \downarrow(\phi^\sigma) \to \downarrow(\psi^\tau)} \qquad [\text{abs4}_S]\ \frac{A, x : \phi^\sigma \vdash_S e : \psi^\tau}{A \vdash_S \lambda x^\sigma.e : \phi^\sigma \to \psi^\tau}$$

$$[\text{abs5}_S]\ \frac{A \vdash_S \lambda x^\sigma.e : \phi^\sigma \to \downarrow(\psi^\tau)}{A \vdash_S \lambda x^\sigma.e : \downarrow(\phi^\sigma \to \psi^\tau)}$$

The last rule can be stated more generally as

$$[\text{down}_S]\ \frac{A \vdash_S e : \text{exdown}'(\phi)}{A \vdash_S e : \downarrow(\phi)}$$

where we define the functions exdown and exdown′:

$$\begin{array}{llll}
\mathtt{exdown}(\mathbf{n}^\sigma) & = \top^\sigma & \mathtt{exdown}(\mathbf{b}^\sigma) & = \mathbf{b}^\sigma \\
\mathtt{exdown}(\top^\sigma) & = \top^\sigma & \mathtt{exdown}(\phi \rightarrow \psi) & = \phi \rightarrow \downarrow(\psi) \\
\mathtt{exdown}(\phi \wedge \psi) & = \downarrow(\phi) \wedge \downarrow(\psi) & \mathtt{exdown}(\downarrow(\phi)) & = \downarrow(\phi) \\
\mathtt{exdown}'(\phi \wedge \psi) & = \phi \wedge \psi & \mathtt{exdown}'(\phi) & = \mathtt{exdown}(\phi)
\end{array}$$

The functions moves the $\downarrow$ inwards one level using the coercion rules. The difference between exdown and exdown′ is on conjunction: we have

Fact 8
$(\downarrow(\phi) \ \leq_{\mathrm{L}} \ \mathtt{exdown}(\phi)) \wedge (\mathtt{exdown}'(\phi) \ \leq_{\mathrm{L}} \ \downarrow(\phi))$ □

Proof We will show $(\downarrow(\phi) \ \leq_{\mathrm{L}} \ \mathtt{exdown}(\phi))$ and $(\mathtt{exdown}'(\phi) \ \leq_{\mathrm{L}} \ \downarrow(\phi))$ by induction on the property ϕ. ■

The rest of the rules ([app], [if2], [if3], [fix], and [conj]) are unchanged. Since the terms are typed therefore no more terms can be typed using these rules than using Figure 5. The reason for changing the presentation is that we are interested in doing as little as possible to check that a term has a given property. In the definition of the analysis (Figure 5) we were looking at the idea of the analysis.

The new structural strictness and property inference system is sound with respect to the strictness and totality inference system:

Lemma 9
$\mathrm{A} \vdash_{\mathrm{S}} \mathtt{e} : \psi \Rightarrow \mathrm{A} \vdash \mathtt{e} : \psi$ □

Proof We show that the rules in the structural inference system can be derived in the non-structural inference system. ■

5.2 Lazy Property Inference System

Following the lazy type approach by Hankin and Le Métayer [4] we now introduce the lazy properties:

$$\mathbf{n}^\tau, \mathbf{b}^\tau, \top^\tau, (\mathrm{A}, \mathtt{e}) \in \mathcal{L}^{\mathrm{L}}_\tau \qquad \frac{\phi^\tau \in \mathcal{L}^{\mathrm{L}}_\tau \quad \psi^\tau \in \mathcal{L}^{\mathrm{L}}_\tau}{\phi^\tau \wedge \psi^\tau \in \mathcal{L}^{\mathrm{L}}_\tau}$$

$$\frac{\psi^\tau \in \mathcal{L}^{\mathrm{L}}_\tau}{\downarrow(\psi^\tau) \in \mathcal{L}^{\mathrm{L}}_\tau} \qquad \frac{\phi^\tau \in \mathcal{L}^{\mathrm{L}}_\tau \quad \psi^\sigma \in \mathcal{L}^{\mathrm{L}}_\sigma}{\phi^\tau \rightarrow \psi^\sigma \in \mathcal{L}^{\mathrm{L}}_{\tau \rightarrow \sigma}}$$

The property $(\mathrm{A}, \mathtt{e})$ is a shorthand (un-evaluated property) for the conjunction of all the properties ϕ that can be inferred for e using the environment A. The function expand maps lazy properties to strictness and totality properties due to [4]:

$$\begin{array}{ll}
\mathtt{expand} & :: \mathcal{L}^{\mathrm{L}}_\tau \rightarrow \mathcal{L}^{\mathrm{ST}}_\tau \\
\mathtt{expand}(\mathbf{n}^\tau) & = \mathbf{n}^\tau \\
\mathtt{expand}(\mathbf{b}^\tau) & = \mathbf{b}^\tau \\
\mathtt{expand}(\top^\tau) & = \top^\tau \\
\mathtt{expand}(\downarrow(\phi)) & = \downarrow(\mathtt{expand}(\phi)) \\
\mathtt{expand}(\phi \rightarrow \psi) & = \mathtt{expand}(\phi) \rightarrow \ \mathtt{expand}(\psi) \\
\mathtt{expand}(\phi \wedge \psi) & = \mathtt{expand}(\phi) \wedge \mathtt{expand}(\psi) \\
\mathtt{expand}((\mathrm{A}, \mathtt{e})) & = \bigwedge \{\phi \mid \mathtt{expand}(\mathrm{A}) \vdash_{\mathrm{S}} \mathtt{e} : \phi\}
\end{array}$$

and the function is extended to environments in a component-wise manner. The predicate BOT on lazy properties is defined by

$$\mathrm{BOT}((\mathrm{A}, \mathtt{e})) = \mathrm{BOT}(\mathtt{expand}((\mathrm{A}, \mathtt{e})))$$

We need two new rules for relating the lazy properties:

$$[\mathrm{env_L}]\ \frac{\mathrm{A} \vdash_{\mathrm{L}} \mathtt{e} : \phi}{(\mathrm{A}, \mathtt{e}) \leq_{\mathrm{L}} \phi} \text{ if } \phi \neq (\mathrm{A}', \mathtt{e}') \quad [\mathrm{env_R}]\ \frac{\forall \phi : \mathrm{A} \vdash_{\mathrm{L}} \mathtt{e} : \phi \Rightarrow (\psi \leq_{\mathrm{L}} \phi)}{\psi \leq_{\mathrm{L}} (\mathrm{A}, \mathtt{e})}$$

The lazy properties are useful in the application rule:

$$[\mathrm{app_L}]\ \frac{\mathrm{A} \vdash_{\mathrm{S}} \mathtt{e}_1 : (\mathrm{A}, \mathtt{e}_2) \rightarrow \phi^{\tau}}{\mathrm{A} \vdash_{\mathrm{S}} \mathtt{e}_1\ \mathtt{e}_2 : \phi^{\tau}}$$

In the [if1]-rule we no longer construct proof-trees for $\mathtt{e}_2$ and $\mathtt{e}_3$:

$$[\mathrm{if1_L}]\ \frac{\mathrm{A} \vdash_{\mathrm{S}} \mathtt{e}_1 : \mathbf{b}^{\mathtt{Bool}} \quad \mathbf{b}^{\sigma} \leq_{\mathrm{ST}} \psi}{\mathrm{A} \vdash_{\mathrm{S}} \mathtt{if}\ \mathtt{e}_1\ \mathtt{then}\ \mathtt{e}_2\ \mathtt{else}\ \mathtt{e}_3 : \psi}$$

All the other rules remain the same.

The lazy property inference system is sound with respect to the structural strictness and totality inference system:

Lemma 10
$(((\phi \leq_{\mathrm{L}} \psi) \wedge \mathrm{A} \vdash_{\mathrm{L}} \mathtt{e} : \phi') \Rightarrow$
$((\mathtt{expand}(\phi) \leq_{\mathrm{ST}} \mathtt{expand}(\psi)) \wedge \mathtt{expand}(\mathrm{A}) \vdash_{\mathrm{S}} \mathtt{e} : \mathtt{expand}(\phi')))$ □

Proof
Suppose $\phi \leq_{\mathrm{L}} \psi$ and $\mathrm{A} \vdash_{\mathrm{L}} \mathtt{e} : \phi$, then we will show $\mathtt{expand}(\phi) \leq_{\mathrm{ST}} \mathtt{expand}(\psi)$ and $\mathtt{expand}(\mathrm{A}) \vdash_{\mathrm{S}} \mathtt{e} : \mathtt{expand}(\phi)$ by simultaneous induction on the proof-tree for $\leq_{\mathrm{L}}$ and $\vdash_{\mathrm{L}}$.

The reason that we have to do simultaneous induction on $\leq_{\mathrm{L}}$ and $\vdash_{\mathrm{L}}$ is that $\leq_{\mathrm{L}}$ depends on $\vdash_{\mathrm{L}}$ (in [$\mathrm{env_L}$] and [$\mathrm{env_R}$]) and not only $\vdash_{\mathrm{L}}$ depending on $\leq_{\mathrm{L}}$ (in [$\mathrm{var_L}$], [$\mathrm{if1_L}$], [$\mathrm{const_L}$]) as in the other inference systems. We omit the details. ■

5.3 The Lazy Property Inference Algorithm

Finally the last step is to extract the algorithm $\mathcal{T}$ (see Figure 6) for lazy property inference from the lazy property inference system. The function $\mathcal{ALL}(\sigma)$ gives a list of all the strictness and totality properties of the type σ. When the function $\mathcal{T}$ is applied to a list it gives back the list of all those strictness and totality properties for which the function is true; the function $\mathcal{ISCHAIN}(\phi)$ applied to a list of properties gives back the list of those properties that are chains with the property ϕ as the last one and BOT of the first is true. The algorithm for checking the coercions is displayed in Figure 7 and 8. The algorithms are sound with respect to the lazy property inference system:

Lemma 11
$(\mathcal{T}(\mathrm{A}, \mathtt{e}, \phi') = \mathtt{tt} \wedge \mathcal{I}(\phi, \psi) = \mathtt{tt}) \Rightarrow (\mathrm{A} \vdash_{\mathrm{L}} \mathtt{e} : \phi' \wedge (\phi \leq_{\mathrm{L}} \psi))$ □

$$
\begin{aligned}
&\mathcal{T}(\mathrm{A}, \mathtt{e}, \phi \wedge \psi) &&= \mathcal{T}(\mathrm{A}, \mathtt{e}, \phi) \wedge \mathcal{T}(\mathrm{A}, \mathtt{e}, \psi)\\
&\mathcal{T}(\mathrm{A}, \lambda \mathtt{x}^{\sigma}.\mathtt{e}, \mathbf{n}^{\sigma \to \tau}) &&= \mathtt{tt}\\
&\mathcal{T}(\mathrm{A}, \lambda \mathtt{x}^{\sigma}.\mathtt{e}, \top^{\sigma \to \tau}) &&= \mathtt{tt}\\
&\mathcal{T}(\mathrm{A}, \lambda \mathtt{x}^{\sigma}.\mathtt{e}, \mathbf{b}^{\sigma \to \tau}) &&= \mathtt{ff}\\
&\mathcal{T}(\mathrm{A}, \lambda \mathtt{x}^{\sigma}.\mathtt{e}, \downarrow(\phi) \to \downarrow(\psi)) &&= \mathcal{T}((\mathtt{x}^{\sigma} : \phi) : \mathrm{A}, \mathtt{e}, \psi) \vee \mathcal{T}((\mathtt{x}^{\sigma} : \downarrow(\phi)) : \mathrm{A}, \mathtt{e}, \downarrow(\psi))\\
&\mathcal{T}(\mathrm{A}, \lambda \mathtt{x}^{\sigma}.\mathtt{e}, \phi \to \psi) &&= \mathcal{T}((\mathtt{x}^{\sigma} : \phi) : \mathrm{A}, \mathtt{e}, \psi)\\
&\mathcal{T}(\mathrm{A}, \mathtt{e}_1\, \mathtt{e}_2, \psi) &&= \mathcal{T}(\mathrm{A}, \mathtt{e}_1, (\mathrm{A}, \mathtt{e}_2) \to \psi)\\
&\mathcal{T}(\mathrm{A}, \mathtt{x}^{\sigma}, \psi) &&= \mathcal{I}(\mathrm{A}(\mathtt{x}^{\sigma}), \psi)\\
&\mathcal{T}(\mathrm{A}, \mathtt{if}\ \mathtt{e}_1\ \mathtt{then}\ \mathtt{e}_2\ \mathtt{else}\ \mathtt{e}_3, \phi) &&= (\mathcal{T}(\mathrm{A}, \mathtt{e}_1, \mathbf{b}^{\mathrm{Bool}}) \wedge \mathcal{I}(\mathbf{b}^{\sigma}, \phi)) \vee\\
& &&\quad (\mathcal{T}(\mathrm{A}, \mathtt{e}_2, \phi) \wedge \mathcal{T}(\mathrm{A}, \mathtt{e}_3, \phi)) \wedge\\
& &&\quad (\mathcal{T}(\mathrm{A}, \mathtt{e}_1, \mathbf{n}^{\mathrm{Bool}}) \vee (\mathcal{T}(\mathrm{A}, \mathtt{e}_1, \top^{\mathrm{Bool}}) \wedge \mathrm{BOT}(\phi)))\\
&\mathcal{T}(\mathrm{A}, \mathtt{c}, \phi) &&= \mathcal{I}(\psi_{\mathtt{C}}, \phi)\\
&\mathcal{T}(\mathrm{A}, \mathtt{fix}\ \mathtt{e}, \phi) &&= \mathcal{FIX}(\mathrm{A}, \mathtt{e}, \phi)\\
&\mathcal{T}(\mathrm{A}, \mathtt{e}, \downarrow(\phi)) &&= \mathcal{T}(\mathrm{A}, \mathtt{e}, \mathrm{exdown}'(\phi))\\
&\mathcal{FIX}(\mathrm{A}, \mathtt{e}, \phi^{\sigma}) &&= \mathrm{let}\ l1 = \mathcal{T}(\mathrm{A}, \mathtt{e}, \mathcal{ALL}(\sigma))\\
& &&\qquad\ l2 = \mathcal{ISCHAIN}(\phi^{\sigma}, l1)\\
& &&\quad \mathrm{in}\ l2 \neq [\,]
\end{aligned}
$$

Fig. 6. Lazy Property Inference Algorithm

$$
\begin{aligned}
&\mathcal{I}(\phi^{\sigma}, \psi^{\tau}) &&= \mathtt{ff} &&\mathcal{I}(\phi, \phi) &&= \mathtt{tt}\\
&\mathcal{I}(\phi, \top^{\sigma}) &&= \mathtt{tt} &&\mathcal{I}(\mathbf{n}^{\sigma}, \mathbf{b}^{\sigma}) &&= \mathtt{ff}\\
&\mathcal{I}(\mathbf{b}^{\sigma}, \mathbf{n}^{\sigma}) &&= \mathtt{ff} &&\mathcal{I}(\top^{\sigma}, \mathbf{n}^{\sigma}) &&= \mathtt{ff}\\
&\mathcal{I}(\top^{\sigma}, \mathbf{b}^{\sigma}) &&= \mathtt{ff} &&\mathcal{I}(\downarrow(\mathbf{b}^{\sigma}), \mathbf{b}^{\sigma}) &&= \mathtt{tt}\\
&\mathcal{I}(\phi \to \psi, \mathbf{b}^{\sigma \to \tau}) &&= \mathtt{ff} &&\mathcal{I}(\downarrow(\phi), \mathbf{n}^{\sigma}) &&= \mathtt{ff}\\
&\mathcal{I}(\phi', \phi \wedge \psi) &&= \mathcal{I}(\phi', \phi) \wedge \mathcal{I}(\phi', \psi) &&\mathcal{I}(\phi \to \psi, \mathbf{n}^{\sigma \to \tau}) &&= \mathcal{I}(\mathbf{n}^{\sigma}, \phi) \wedge \mathcal{I}(\psi, \mathbf{n}^{\tau})\\
&\mathcal{I}(\phi \wedge \psi, \mathbf{n}^{\sigma}) &&= \mathcal{I}(\phi, \mathbf{n}^{\sigma}) \vee \mathcal{I}(\psi, \mathbf{n}^{\sigma}) &&\mathcal{I}(\phi \wedge \psi, \mathbf{b}^{\sigma}) &&= \mathcal{I}(\phi, \mathbf{b}^{\sigma}) \vee \mathcal{I}(\psi, \mathbf{b}^{\sigma})\\
&\mathcal{I}(\mathbf{n}^{\sigma \to \tau}, \phi \to \psi) &&= \mathcal{I}(\top^{\tau}, \psi) &&\mathcal{I}(\mathbf{b}^{\sigma \to \tau}, \phi \to \psi) &&= \mathcal{I}(\top^{\tau}, \psi) \vee \mathcal{I}(\mathbf{b}^{\tau}, \psi)\\
&\mathcal{I}(\top^{\sigma \to \tau}, \phi \to \psi) &&= \mathcal{I}(\top^{\tau}, \psi) &&\mathcal{I}(\mathbf{n}^{\sigma}, \downarrow(\phi)) &&= \mathcal{I}(\mathbf{n}^{\sigma}, \phi)\\
&\mathcal{I}(\mathbf{b}^{\sigma}, \downarrow(\phi)) &&= \mathcal{I}(\mathbf{b}^{\sigma}, \phi) \vee (\phi = \mathbf{n}^{\sigma}) &&\mathcal{I}(\top^{\sigma}, \downarrow(\phi)) &&= \mathcal{I}(\top^{\sigma}, \phi) \vee (\phi = \mathbf{n}^{\sigma})\\
&\mathcal{I}(\phi \to \psi, \downarrow(\phi')) &&= \mathcal{I}(\phi \to \psi, \phi') && &&
\end{aligned}
$$

Fig. 7. Lazy Coercion Inference Algorithm (Part 1)

Proof We will assume that both $\mathcal{T}(\mathrm{A}, \mathtt{e}, \phi')$ and $\mathcal{I}(\phi, \psi)$ are true and then we will prove $\mathrm{A} \vdash_{\mathrm{L}} \mathtt{e} : \phi'$ and $\phi \leq_{\mathrm{L}} \psi$ by induction on e, ϕ', and ψ. We omit the details. ■

Finally we have that the inference algorithm is sound with respect to the strictness and totality property inference system:

Theorem 12
$\mathcal{T}(\mathrm{A}, \mathtt{e}, \phi) \Rightarrow \mathtt{expand(A)} \vdash \mathtt{e} : \mathtt{expand}(\phi)$ □

Proof This is a consequence of Lemma 9, 10, and 11. ■

The inference algorithm is not complete. Consider the term, e, $\lambda \mathtt{x}.(\mathtt{fix}\ \lambda \mathtt{x}.\mathtt{x})$

$$
\begin{aligned}
\mathcal{I}(\phi^\sigma \to \psi^\tau, \phi'^\sigma \to \psi'^\tau) &= (\mathcal{I}(\phi', \phi) \wedge \mathcal{I}(\psi, \psi')) \vee (\mathcal{I}(\phi', \downarrow(\phi)) \wedge \mathcal{I}(\downarrow(\psi), \psi')) \vee \\
&\quad \mathcal{I}(\top^\tau, \psi') \\
\mathcal{I}(\downarrow(\phi), \downarrow(\psi)) &= \mathcal{I}(\phi, \psi) \vee \mathcal{I}(\mathtt{exdown}(\phi), \downarrow(\psi)) \vee \mathcal{I}(\downarrow(\phi), \mathtt{exdown}'(\psi)) \\
&\quad \vee \mathcal{I}(\mathtt{exdown}(\phi), \mathtt{exdown}'(\psi)) \\
\mathcal{I}(\phi \wedge \psi, \phi' \to \psi') &= \mathcal{I}(\phi, \phi' \to \psi') \vee \mathcal{I}(\psi, \phi' \to \psi') \vee \mathcal{I}(\top^\tau, \psi') \\
\mathcal{I}(\downarrow(\phi), \phi'^\sigma \to \psi'^\tau) &= \mathcal{I}(\top^\tau, \psi') \vee (\phi = \mathbf{b}^{\sigma \to \tau} \wedge \mathcal{I}(\mathbf{b}^\tau, \psi')) \vee \\
&\quad (\phi = \phi'' \to \psi'' \wedge \mathcal{I}(\phi'' \to \downarrow(\psi''), \phi' \to \psi')) \vee \\
&\quad (\phi = (\phi'' \wedge \psi'') \wedge \mathcal{I}(\downarrow(\phi'') \wedge \downarrow(\psi''), \phi' \to \psi')) \\
\mathcal{I}(\phi \wedge \psi, \downarrow(\phi')) &= \mathcal{I}(\phi \wedge \psi, \phi') \vee \mathcal{I}(\phi, \downarrow(\phi')) \vee \mathcal{I}(\psi, \downarrow(\phi')) \\
\mathcal{I}((\mathrm{A}, \mathtt{e}), \phi) &= \mathcal{T}(\mathrm{A}, \mathtt{e}, \phi) \\
\mathcal{I}(\psi^\sigma, (\mathrm{A}, \mathtt{e})) &= \mathcal{C}(\mathcal{ALL}(\sigma), \mathrm{A}, \mathtt{e}, \psi) \\
\mathcal{C}([\,], \mathrm{A}, \mathtt{e}, \psi) &= \mathtt{tt} \\
\mathcal{C}(\psi{:}l, \mathrm{A}, \mathtt{e}, \phi) &= \begin{cases} \mathcal{I}(\phi, \psi) \wedge \mathcal{C}(l, \mathrm{A}, \mathtt{e}, \phi), & \text{if } \mathcal{T}(\mathrm{A}, \mathtt{e}, \psi) \\ \mathcal{C}(l, \mathrm{A}, \mathtt{e}, \phi), & \text{otherwise} \end{cases}
\end{aligned}
$$

Fig. 8. Lazy Coercion Inference Algorithm (Part 2)

and the property, ϕ, $\downarrow((\mathbf{n}^\sigma \to \mathbf{n}^\tau) \wedge (\mathbf{n}^\sigma \to \top^\tau))$. In the analysis (Figure 5) we can construct a proof-tree for $\emptyset \vdash \mathtt{e} : \phi$. However, it is not possible to infer

$$\emptyset \vdash \mathtt{e} : (\mathbf{n}^\sigma \to \mathbf{n}^\tau) \wedge (\mathbf{n}^\sigma \to \top^\tau)$$

The algorithm will do as follows:

$$
\begin{aligned}
\mathcal{T}(\emptyset, \mathtt{e}, \phi) &= \mathcal{T}(\emptyset, \mathtt{e}, (\mathbf{n}^\sigma \to \mathbf{n}^\tau) \wedge (\mathbf{n}^\sigma \to \top^\tau)) \\
&= \mathcal{T}(\emptyset, \mathtt{e}, (\mathbf{n}^\sigma \to \mathbf{n}^\tau)) \wedge \mathcal{T}(\emptyset, \mathtt{e}, (\mathbf{n}^\sigma \to \top^\tau)) \\
&= \mathtt{ff} \wedge \mathtt{tt} = \mathtt{ff}
\end{aligned}
$$

The problem is that $\downarrow(\phi \wedge \psi)$ is not equivalent to $\phi \wedge \psi$. More work is needed to find a sound *and* complete inference algorithm.

6 Conclusion

We have restated the strictness and totality analysis of [12] and removed the restriction that conjunction may only occur at the top-level. We have proven the strictness and totality analysis correct with respect to a denotational semantics. Finally we have constructed an algorithm for inferring the strictness and totality properties by following the lazy types approach of [4].

Acknowledgement The author has been funded by Odense University, Denmark. I would like to thank LOMAPS (Esprit Basic Research) and DART (Danish Science Research Council) for partial support. Part of the research was carried out while visiting Cambridge University, England; the visit was supported by the Danish Research Academy. I am grateful to Nick Benton, David Wright, Hanne Riis Nielson and Flemming Nielson for interesting discussions.

References

1. Samson Abramsky. Abstract interpretation, logical relations and Kan extensions. *Journal of Logic and Computation*, 1(1):5–39, 1990.
2. Nick Benton. *Strictness Analysis of Functional Programs*. PhD thesis, University of Cambridge, 1993. Available as Technical Report No. 309.
3. Geoffrey L. Burn, Chris Hankin, and Samson Abramsky. Strictness Analysis for Higher-order Functions. *Science of Computer Programming*, 7:249–278, 1986.
4. Chris Hankin and Daniel Le Métayer. Deriving algorithms from type inference systems: Application to strictness analysis. In *Proceedings of POPL'94*, pages 202 – 212, 1994.
5. Chris Hankin and Daniel Le Métayer. A Type-based framework for Program Analysis. In *Proceedings of SAS'94*, LNCS 864, pages 380–394, 1994.
6. Thomas P. Jensen. Strictness analysis in logical form. In *Proceedings of FPCA'91*, LNCS 523, pages 352 – 366, 1991.
7. Thomas P. Jensen. Disjunctive strictness analysis. In *Proceedings of LICS'92*, pages 174 – 185, 1992.
8. Tsung-Min Kuo and Prateek Mishra. Strictness analysis: A new perspective based on type inference. In *Proceedings of FPCA'89*, pages 260 – 272. ACM Press, 1989.
9. Alan Mycroft. The theory and practice of transforming call-by-need into call-by-value. In *Proceedings of the 4th International Symposium on Programming*, LNCS 83, pages 269–281, 1980.
10. Alan Mycroft. *Abstract Interpretation and Optimising Transformation for Applicative programs*. PhD thesis, University of Edinburgh, Scotland, 1981.
11. David Sands. Complexity analysis for a lazy higher-order language. In *Proceedings of ESOP'90*, LNCS 432, pages 361–376, 1990.
12. Kirsten Lackner Solberg, Hanne Riis Nielson, and Flemming Nielson. Strictness and totality analysis. In *Proceedings of SAS'94*, LNCS 864, pages 408 – 422, 1994.
13. D. A. Turner. Miranda: A non-strict functional language with polymorphic types. In *Proceedings of FPCA'85*, LNCS 201, pages 1 – 16, 1985.
14. Phil Wadler and John Hughes. Projections for strictness analysis. In *Proceedings of FPCA'87*, LNCS 27, 1987.
15. David A. Wright. A new technique for strictness analysis. In *Proceedings TAPSOFT'91*, LNCS 494, pages 260 – 272. Springer Verlag, 1991.
16. David A. Wright. *Reduction Types and Intensionality in the Lambda-Calculus*. PhD thesis, University of Tasmania, 1992.

Generic Techniques for Source-Level Debugging and Dynamic Program Slicing

Frank Tip*

CWI, P.O. Box 94079, 1090 GB Amsterdam, The Netherlands

tip@cwi.nl

Abstract. Algebraic specifications have been used successfully as a formal basis for software development. This paper discusses how the *origin* and *dynamic dependence* relations implicitly defined by an algebraic specification can be used to define powerful language-specific tools. In particular, the generation of tools for source-level debugging and dynamic program slicing from specifications of interpreters will be addressed.

1 Introduction

Algebraic specifications [4] have been used successfully for the generation of a variety of software development tools, such as typecheckers [9], interpreters [10], and program analysis tools [11, 12, 21]. The present paper discusses how two previously developed language-independent techniques, origin tracking [8] and dynamic dependence tracking [13], can be used to derive powerful language-specific debugging tools from algebraic specifications of interpreters. In particular, we show that—in addition to "standard" debugger features such as single-stepping, state inspection, and breakpoints—a variation of dynamic program slicing [1, 17] can be defined with surprisingly little effort. The main contribution of this paper is to show that the information required to construct such debugging tools is to a very large extent *language-independent* and *implicitly* present in a language's specification.

We assume that specifications are executed by conditional term rewriting [16]. Specifically, an algebraic specification of an interpreter expresses the execution of a program as the rewriting of a term consisting of a function `execute` applied to the abstract syntax tree (AST) of that program. Rewriting this term produces a sequence of terms that effectively represent the consecutive internal states of the interpreter. Origin tracking is a method for tracing occurrences of the *same* subterm in a sequence of terms, and is used for the definition of single-stepping and breakpoints. Dependence tracking establishes certain minimal dependence relations between terms in a rewriting sequence, and is used to obtain dynamic slices.

2 Specification of an interpreter

We illustrate our ideas by way of a simple language **L** that features assignments, **if** statements, **while** statements, and statement sequences. **L**-expressions are constructed

* Supported in part by the European Union under ESPRIT project # 5399 (Compiler Generation for Parallel Machines—COMPARE).

from constants, variables, arithmetic operators '+', '-', and '*', and the equality test operator '='. Fig. 1 shows an algebraic specification of an **L**-interpreter. The execution of an **L**-program P corresponds to the *rewriting* of the *term* `execute(`t_P`)` according to this specification, where t_P is the term that constitutes the AST of P; this will ultimately result in a (term that represents a) list containing the final value of each variable.

/* top-level function for execution of programs */

[L1] execute(**declare** *DeclSeq* **begin** *StatSeq* **end**) = exec(*StatSeq*, create(*DeclSeq*, ϵ_e))

/* functions for creation and manipulation of environments */

[L2] create(ϵ_d, *Env*) = *Env*
[L3] create(*Var*;*DeclSeq*, *Env*) = create(*DeclSeq*, *Var* $\mapsto$ 0; *Env*)
[L4] lookup(*Var* $\mapsto$ *Constant*;*Env*, *Var*) = *Constant*
[L5] lookup(*Var* $\mapsto$ *Constant*;*Env*, *Var'*) = lookup(*Env*, *Var'*) **when** *Var* $\neq$ *Var'*
[L6] update(*Var* $\mapsto$ *Constant*;*Env*, *Var*, *Constant'*) = *Var* $\mapsto$ *Constant'*;*Env*
[L7] update(*Var* $\mapsto$ *Constant*;*Env*, *Var'*, *Constant'*) = *Var* $\mapsto$ *Constant*; update(*Env*, *Var'*, *Constant'*) **when** *Var* $\neq$ *Var'*

/* evaluation of expressions */

[L8] eval(*Constant*, *Env*) = *Constant*
[L9] eval(*Var*, *Env*) = lookup(*Var*, *Env*)
[L10] eval((*Exp* + *Exp'*), *Env*) = intadd(eval(*Exp*, *Env*), eval(*Exp'*, *Env*))
[L11] eval((*Exp* - *Exp'*), *Env*) = intsub(eval(*Exp*, *Env*), eval(*Exp'*, *Env*))
[L12] eval((*Exp* * *Exp'*), *Env*) = intmul(eval(*Exp*, *Env*), eval(*Exp'*, *Env*))
[L13] eval((*Exp* = *Exp'*), *Env*) = inteq(eval(*Exp*, *Env*), eval(*Exp'*, *Env*))

/* execution of (lists of) statements */

[L14] exec(ϵ_s, *Env*) = *Env*
[L15] exec(*Var* := *Exp*;*StatSeq*, *Env*) = exec(*StatSeq*, update(*Env*, *Var*, eval(*Exp*, *Env*)))
[L16] exec(**if** *Exp* **then** *StatSeq* **else** *StatSeq'* **end**;*StatSeq''*, *Env*) = exec(*StatSeq''*, exec(*StatSeq*, *Env*))
when eval(*Exp*, *Env*) $\neq$ 0
[L17] exec(**if** *Exp* **then** *StatSeq* **else** *StatSeq'* **end**;*StatSeq''*, *Env*) = exec(*StatSeq''*, exec(*StatSeq'*, *Env*))
when eval(*Exp*, *Env*) = 0
[L18] exec(**while** *Exp* **do** *StatSeq* **end**; *StatSeq'*, *Env*) = exec(**while** *Exp* **do** *StatSeq* **end**; *StatSeq'*, exec(*StatSeq*, *Env*))
when eval(*Exp*, *Env*) $\neq$ 0
[L19] exec(**while** *Exp* **do** *StatSeq* **end**; *StatSeq'*, *Env*) = exec(*StatSeq'*, *Env*)
when eval(*Exp*, *Env*) = 0

Fig. 1. Algebraic specification of an **L**-interpreter.

Term rewriting is a cyclic process where each cycle involves determining a subterm t and a rule $l = r$ such that t and l match. This is the case if a substitution σ can be found that maps every variable X in l to a term $\sigma(X)$ such that $t \equiv \sigma(l)$ (σ distributes over function symbols). For rewrite rules without conditions, the cycle is completed by replacing t by the instantiated right-hand side $\sigma(r)$. A term for which no rule is applicable to any of its subterms is called a *normal form*; the process of rewriting a term to its normal form (if it exists) is referred to as *normalizing*. A conditional rewrite rule (e.g., **[L16]**) is only applicable if all its conditions succeed; this is determined by instantiating and normalizing the left-hand side and the right-hand side of each condition. Positive conditions (of the form $t_1 = t_2$) succeed iff the resulting normal forms are syntactically equal, negative conditions ($t_1 \neq t_2$) if they are syntactically different.

The specification of Fig. 1 is based on the manipulation of an environment, i.e., a list containing the current value of each variable. **[L1]** defines the top-level function `execute` in terms of two other functions, `create` and `exec`. The former, `create`, uses the declarations of the program to create an initial environment, where each variable has the value `0` (**[L2]** and **[L3]**)[2]. The latter, `exec`, specifies the execution of a list of statements; it "uses" the functions `lookup` (**[L4]**–**[L5]**) for retrieving a value from an environment, and `update` (**[L6]**–**[L7]**) for updating the value of a variable in an environment. Rules **[L8]**–**[L13]** define a recursive function `eval` for evaluating **L**-expressions. The specification of the primitive operations `intadd`, `intsub`, `intmul`, and `inteq` is omitted here. **[L14]** states that executing the empty list of statements does not affect the environment. In **[L15]**–**[L19]**, the cases are specified where the statement list is non-empty. **[L15]** defines the execution of an assignment in terms of the evaluation of its right-hand side expression, and an update of the environment. In **[L16]**–**[L17]** the execution of a non-empty statement list beginning with an **if–then–else** construct is defined by conditional rules; **[L16]** and **[L17]** correspond to situations where the control predicate evaluates to any non-zero value and zero, respectively. The execution of a **while** statement is specified in a similar way (**[L18]**–**[L19]**).

Fig. 2 (**a**) shows an example **L**-program. By applying the equations of Fig. 1, the environment of Fig. 2 (**b**) is produced.

```
declare
  i; s; p;
begin
  i := 5;
  s := 0;
  p := 1;
  while i do
    s := (s + i);
    p := (p * i);
    i := (i - 1);
  end;
end
```

(**a**)

```
p ↦ 120;
s ↦ 15;
i ↦ 0;
```

(**b**)

Fig. 2. (**a**) Example **L**-program. (**b**) Environment obtained by executing the program of (**a**) according to the specification of Fig. 1.

3 Basic techniques

In this section, we will briefly present origin tracking and dynamic dependence tracking. Due to space limitations, only an informal description of these techniques is presented here; the reader is referred to [8, 13, 21] for formal definitions.

3.1 Origin tracking

In the discussion below, it is assumed that a term S is rewritten to a term T in zero or more steps: $S \rightarrow^* T$. In [8, 21], the origin relation is formally defined as a relation

[2] This specification assumes that every variable is properly declared.

between subterms of S and subterms of T; associated with every subterm T' of T is a set of subterms, *OriginOf*(T'), of the initial term S—the *origin of* T'. The principal properties of the origin relation are that: (i) relations involve *equal* terms (in the sense of rewriting): for each subterm $S' \in$ *OriginOf*(T') we have that $S' \rightarrow^* T'$, and that (ii) relations are defined in an inductive manner. For a reduction of length zero, the origin relation is the identity relation; for a multi-step reduction $S \rightarrow^* T \xrightarrow{r} U$, the origin of a subterm U' of U is defined in terms of the origins of subterms of T, and the structure of the applied rule, r.

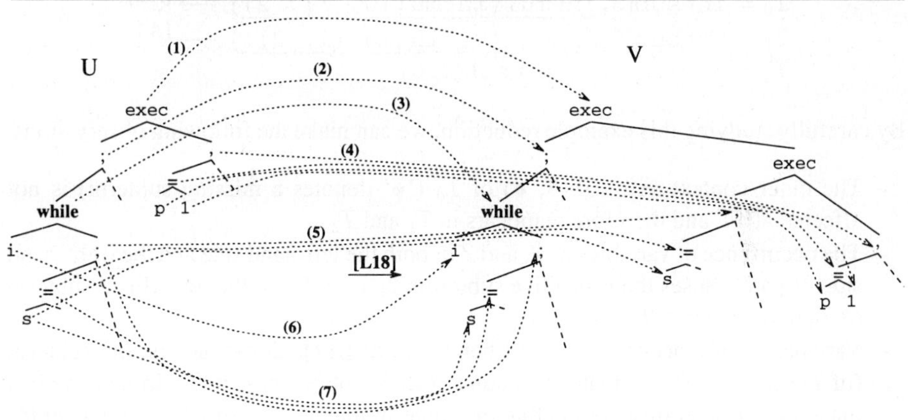

Fig. 3. Origin relations.

As an example, Fig. 3 depicts an application of **[L18]** to a **while**-term. Dotted lines in the figure indicate origin relations. The relation labeled **(1)** is the relation between the roots of U and V—such a relation is always present. Variables that occur in both the left-hand side and the right-hand side of **[L18]** cause more origin relations to appear—variable *Exp* gives rise to the relation labeled **(6)**, variable *StatSeq* to the sets of relations labeled **(5)** and **(7)**, and variable *Env* to the relations labeled **(4)**. The relation labeled **(3)** is caused by the occurrence of a *subterm* **while** *Exp* **do** *StatSeq* **end** in both the left-hand side and the right-hand side of **[L18]**. Relation **(2)** is also caused by a common subterm.

Note that the rightmost `exec` function symbol in term V is not related to any symbol in U—its origin is the empty set. In general, a term will have a non-empty origin if it was derived directly from a subterm of the initial term (here: the program's AST). In [8, 21], a number of sufficient constraints on specifications is stated that guarantee that origin sets of subterms with a specific root function symbol, or of a specific sort, contain at least one, or exactly one element. The specification of Fig. 1 satisfies the constraints necessary to guarantee that each "statement" subterm will have an origin set containing exactly one element. For specifications that do not conform to these constraints, the origin relation of [7, Chapter 7] may be used, which is applicable to any specification of a compositional nature.

3.2 Dynamic dependence tracking

Consider thc following simple rules for integer arithmetic:

[A1] `intmul(0,`X`)` $=$ `0`
[A2] `intmul(intmul(`X`,` Y`),`Z`)` $=$ `intmul(`X`, intmul(`Y`,` Z`))`

By applying these rules, the term `intsub(3, intmul(intmul(0, 1), 2))` may be rewritten as follows (subterms affected by rule applications are underlined):

$$\begin{array}{ll} T_0 = \texttt{intsub(3,}\underline{\texttt{intmul(intmul(0, 1), 2)}}\texttt{)} & \longrightarrow \textbf{[A2]} \\ T_1 = \texttt{intsub(3,}\underline{\texttt{intmul(0, intmul(1, 2))}}\texttt{)} & \longrightarrow \textbf{[A1]} \\ T_2 = \texttt{intsub(3,0)} & \end{array}$$

By carefully studying this example reduction, we can make the following observations:

- The outer context `intsub(3,` $\bullet$`)` of T_0 ('$\bullet$' denotes a missing subterm) is not affected at all, and therefore reappears in T_1 and T_2.
- The occurrence of variables X, Y, and Z in both the left-hand side and the right-hand side of **[A2]** causes the respective subterms `0`, `1`, and `2` of the underlined subterm of T_0 to reappear in T_1.
- Variable X only occurs in the left-hand side of **[A1]**. Consequently, the subterm (of T_1) `intmul(1, 2)` matched against X does not reappear in T_2. In fact, we can make the stronger observation that the subterm matched against X is *irrelevant* for producing the constant `0` in T_2: the "creation" of this subterm `0` only requires the presence of the context `intmul(0,` $\bullet$`)` in T_1.

The above observations are the cornerstones of the dynamic dependence relation of [13, 21]. Notions of *creation* and *residuation* are defined for single rewrite-steps. The former involves function symbols produced by rewrite rules whereas the latter corresponds to situations where symbols are copied, erased, or not affected by rewrite rules[3]. Fig. 4 shows all residuation and creation relations for the example reduction discussed above.

Roughly speaking, the dynamic dependence relation for a multi-step reduction ρ consists of the transitive closure of creation and residuation relations for the individual rewrite steps in ρ. In [13, 21], the dynamic dependence relation is defined as a relation on *contexts*, i.e., connected sets of function symbols in a term. The fact that C is a *subcontext* of a term T is denoted $C \sqsubseteq T$. For any reduction ρ that transforms a term T into a term T', a *term slice* with respect to some $C' \sqsubseteq T'$ is defined as the subcontext $C \sqsubseteq T$ that is found by tracing back the dynamic dependence relations from C'. The term slice C satisfies the following properties:

1. C can be rewritten to a term $D' \sqsupseteq C'$ via a reduction ρ', and
2. ρ' is a subreduction of the original reduction ρ. Intuitively, ρ' contains a subset of the rule applications in ρ.

[3] The notions of creation and residuation become more complicated in the presence of so-called *left-nonlinear* rules and *collapse rules*. This is discussed at greater length in [13, 21].

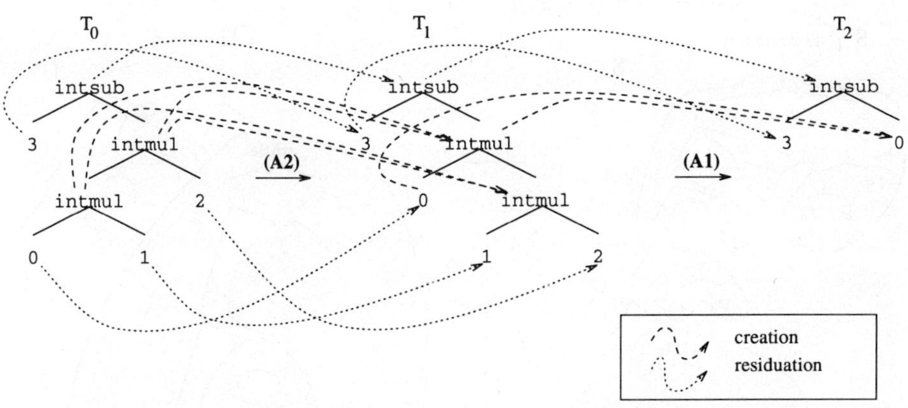

Fig. 4. Example of creation and residuation relations.

In cases where no confusion arises, we will write $C = \mathit{SliceOf}(C')$ to indicate that C is the term slice with respect to C' for some reduction $\rho : T {\rightarrow}^{*} T'$, $C \sqsubseteq T$, and $C' \sqsubseteq T'$.

Returning to the example, we can determine the term slice with respect to the entire term T_2 by tracing back all creation and residuation relations to T_0; the reader may verify that *SliceOf*(`intsub(3, 0)`) = `intsub(3, intmul(intmul(0, •), •))`.

3.3 Application to specifications of interpreters

Fig. 5 depicts some of the relations established by origin tracking and dynamic dependence tracking as a result of executing the program of Fig. 2. The figure shows the initial term S, the final term T and an intermediate term U that occur in the process of executing the program according to the specification of Fig. 1. The intermediate term U corresponds to the situation where the **while** loop is entered for the first time.

Subterms of U and S that are related by the origin relation are indicated by dotted lines in Fig. 5. Also shown in Fig. 5 is a subcontext S' of S that is related to the subterm U' of U via the dynamic dependence relation. Observe that S' *excludes* the right-hand sides of two of the assignment statements in the program. One of the key properties of the dynamic dependence relation is that replacing these right-hand sides by *any* **L**-expression will yield a term that can be rewritten (via a subreduction of `r`) to a term that contains a subcontext `p` $\mapsto$ `1`.

Although origin and dependence relations are computed in a similar manner, using similar information as input, the nature of these relations is different. This is mainly due to the fact that these relations were designed with different objectives in mind. Origin information always involves *equal* terms. In the example of Fig. 5, origin track-

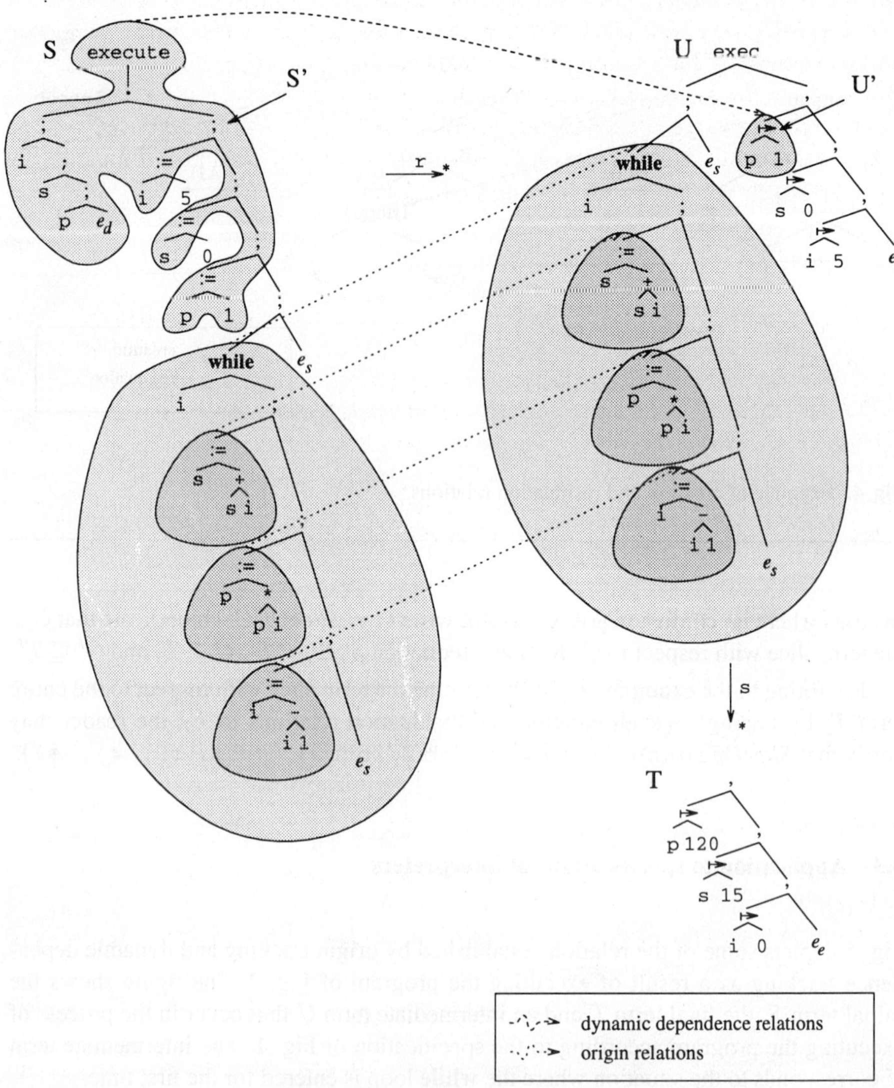

Fig. 5. Illustration of origin and dynamic dependence relations.

ing establishes relations between a number of syntactically[4] equal terms; in this case corresponding to the statements of the program. Equality (via convertibility of terms) also plays an important role in the notion of dependence tracking. Dynamic dependence

[4] For the purpose of debugging, origin relations rarely involve terms that are not syntactically equal. Examples of origin relations involving terms not syntactically equal are mainly to be found in the area of error-reporting [10, 9, 7].

relations are in principle defined for any subcontext of any term that occurs in a rewriting process: associated with a subcontext s is the minimal subcontext of the initial term that was necessary for "creating" a term that contains s. In the sequel, we are primarily interested in the dynamic dependence relations for subcontexts that represent values computed by a program (such as the subterm U' in Fig. 5). It will be shown below that for these subcontexts, the dynamic dependence relation will compute information that is similar to the notion of a dynamic program slice [1, 17].

3.4 Implementation

Origin tracking and dynamic dependence tracking have been implemented in the rewrite engine of the ASF+SDF Meta-environment [15]. All function symbols of all terms that arise in a rewriting process are *annotated* with their associated origin and dependence information; this information is efficiently represented by way of bit-vectors. Whenever a rewrite rule is applied to a term t, and a new term t' is created, origin and dependence information is *propagated* from t to t'. These propagations are expressed in terms of operations on sets. In [21], it is argued that the cost of performing these propagation steps is at worst linear in the size of the initial term of the reduction.

4 Definition of debugger features

Below, we describe how a number of debugger features can be defined using the techniques of the previous section. We will primarily concentrate on the mechanisms needed for *defining* debugger features, and ignore issues related to a debugger's user-interface.

4.1 Single stepping/visualization

Step-wise execution of a program at the source code level is the basic feature of any debugger.

Observe that in the specification of Fig. 1, the execution of a statement corresponds to the rewriting of a term of the following form:

exec(*Stat*;*StatList*, *Env*)

where *Stat* represents any statement, *StatList* any list of statements, and *Env* any environment. Consequently, the fact that *some* statement is executed can be detected by matching the above *pattern* against the current redex[5].

Origin tracking can be used to determine *which* statement is currently being executed. We assume that the rewriting process is suspended whenever a redex T *matches* the above pattern. At this point, the subterm T' of T that is matched against variable *Stat* is determined. The origin of T', *OriginOf*(T'), will consist of the subtree of the program's AST that represents the currently executed statement. Thus, program execution can be visualized at the source level by highlighting this subterm of the AST.

[5] We will use the term "redex" (short for reducible expression) to denote the subterm that has been matched against some equation. For conditional rules, it is assumed that no conditions have been evaluated yet.

4.2 Breakpoints

Another standard source-level debugger feature is the *breakpoint*. The idea is that the user selects a statement s in the program, and execution continues until s is reached.

A breakpoint on a statement s can be implemented as follows. Let T_s be the subterm of the AST that corresponds to s. Then the rewriting process should be suspended when: (i) a redex T matches the pattern exec(*Stat*;*StatList*, *Env*) (indicating that *some* statement is being executed), and (ii) $T_s \in \mathit{OriginOf}(T')$, where T' is the subterm of T matched against variable *Stat*.

4.3 State inspection

At any moment that execution is suspended, either while single-stepping or due to a breakpoint, one may wish to inspect the values of variables or, more generally, arbitrary source-level expressions.

State inspection may be implemented as follows. We assume that execution was suspended at the moment that some statement was executed, i.e., a redex T matches the pattern exec(*Stat*;*StatList*, *Env*) Let T_z be the subterm of T that was matched against variable *Env*. Then an arbitrary source-level expression e (with an AST T_e) can be evaluated by *rewriting* the term eval(T_e, T_z) according to the specification of Fig. 1. The result of this rewriting process will be a term representing the "current" value of expression e.

4.4 Watchpoints

Watchpoints [18] are a generalization of breakpoints. The user supplies a source-level expression e (with AST T_e), and execution continues until the value of e changes.

A watchpoint may be implemented as follows. First, an initial value u (with AST T_u) of expression e is computed (using the technique of Sec. 4.3) and stored by the debugger. Whenever a statement is executed, the current value v (with AST T_v) of e is determined and is compared with u by rewriting a term inteq(T_u, T_v). Execution (i.e., the rewriting process) is suspended when this test fails (i.e., yields the value zero).

4.5 Data breakpoints

A *data breakpoint* [22] is yet another variation on the breakpoint theme. A data breakpoint on a variable v (with AST T_v) is effective when v is referenced (or modified).

Data breakpoints can be implemented by suspending the rewriting process when a redex matches the pattern lookup($T_v \mapsto$ *Constant*;*Env*, T_v) (for a data breakpoint on a reference to v), or update($T_v \mapsto$ *Constant*;*Env*, T_v, *Constant'*) (for a data breakpoint on an update to v).

4.6 Call stack inspection

In the presence of procedures, the notion of an "environment" needs to be generalized to a stack of activation records, where each record contains the values of the local variables and parameters for a procedure call. Call-stack inspection can be defined in way that is similar to the techniques of Sec. 4.3, by visualizing the procedure calls in each record. One can easily imagine a tool that allows interactive traversal of the stack of activation records, and enables one to inspect the values of arbitrary source-level expressions in each scope.

5 Dynamic program slicing

Myriad variations on the notion of a *dynamic program slice* [1, 17] can be found in the literature [20]. For the purposes of this paper, we define a *dynamic slice with respect to the current value of a variable* v to be the parts of the program that are necessary for obtaining the current value of v. To see why dynamic slicing is useful for debugging, consider a situation where an incorrect value is computed for v—only the statements in the dynamic slice with respect to v had an effect on the value of v. This allows one to ignore many statements in the process of localizing a bug[6].

Below we pursue a two-phase approach for computing dynamic slices. Sec. 5.1 discusses the nature of the "raw" information provided by the dynamic dependence relation of Sec. 3.2. In Sec. 5.2, we present an heuristic approach for post-processing this information, in order to obtain dynamic slices similar to those of [1, 17].

5.1 Pure term slices

We assume that execution is suspended at a moment that some statement was executed, i.e., a redex T matches the pattern `exec(`*Stat*`;` *StatList*`,` *Env*`)`. Let T_z be the subterm of T matched against *Env*, and let T_p be the subterm of T_z that constitutes the variable-value pair for variable x. Then, the dynamic dependence relation of Sec. 3.2 will associate with T_p a minimal set of function symbols, *SliceOf*(T_p), in the program's AST.

Fig. 6 (**a**) shows a (textual representation of) the term slice that is determined for the final value of variable `p` as obtained by executing the example program of Fig. 2. Observe that the two holes in this term slice can be replaced by *any* **L**-expression without affecting the computation of the value `120` for variable `p`.

One may wonder why the assignments to variable `s` are not completely omitted in the term slice of Fig. 6 (**a**). This is best understood by keeping in mind that *any* hole in a term slice may be replaced by *any* syntactically valid **L**-term. Note that the assignments to `s` cannot be replaced by any other assignment; e.g., they can certainly not be replaced by any assignment to `p`.

5.2 Post-processing of term slices

While term slices provide information that is semantically sound, they may contain a certain amount of "clutter", in the form of uninteresting information. An example of such information are the two partial assignments to `s` in the term slice of Fig. 6 (**a**).

[6] Even in cases where a statement is missing inadvertently, dynamic slices may provide useful information. In such a case, it is likely that more statements show up in the slice than one would expect.

```
declare
  i; s; p;
begin
  i := 5;
  s := ●;
  p := 1;
  while i do
    s := ●;
    p := (p * i);
    i := (i - 1);
  end;
end
```

(a)

```
declare
  i; s; p;
begin
  i := 5;
  p := 1;
  while i do
    p := (p * i);
    i := (i - 1);
  end;
end
```

(b)

Fig. 6. **(a)** Term slice with respect to the final value of p. **(b)** Post-processed slice with respect to the final value of p.

In order obtain dynamic slices similar to those in [1, 17], one may *post-process* term slices by: (i) transforming any statement whose right-hand side is irrelevant into an irrelevant statement (rule **[P1]**), and (ii) removing irrelevant statements from statement lists (rule **[P2]**). A specification of this post-processing is shown in Fig. 7. Rewriting the term slice of Fig. 6 **(a)** according to this specification yields the slice of Fig. 6 **(b)**.

[P1] *Var* := ● = ●
[P2] ● ; *StatSeq* = *StatSeq*

Fig. 7. Specification for post-processing of term slices.

The specification of Fig. 7 is minimal—it only removes irrelevant assignments. In practice, one would like more sophisticated post-processing that, for example, removes all irrelevant declarations from the program. Post-processing becomes nontrivial in the presence of procedures, where situations may occur in which different parameters are omitted at different call sites.

6 Practical experience

To a large extent, the ideas in this paper have been implemented using the ASF+SDF Meta-environment [15], a programming environment generator. In particular, origin tracking, dynamic dependence tracking, and the matching of language-specific patterns have been implemented successfully.

Fig. 8 shows some snapshots of a language-specific single-stepping tool for the language CLaX [10, 19], a substantial subset of Pascal that features procedures with nested scopes, unstructured control flow, and multi-dimensional arrays. This tool has been implemented according to the techniques of Sec. 4.1.

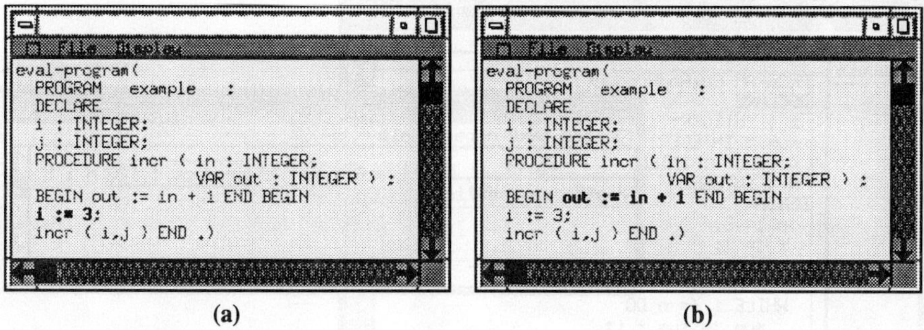

Fig. 8. Generated language-specific single-stepping tool.

Fig. 9 shows a screen dump of a dynamic slicing tool for the language CLaX, that was created using the technique of Sec. 5. In this figure, the dynamic slice with respect to the final value of variable `product` is shown, both in pure "term slice" form (here, '<?>' indicates a missing subterm), and in post-processed form.

7 Related work

The work that is most closely related to ours was done in the context of the PSG system [3]. A generator for language-specific debuggers was described in [2]. Language-specific compilers are generated by compiling denotational semantics definitions to a functional language. A standard, language-independent interpreter is used to execute the generated functional language fragments. The behavior of a debugger is specified using a set of built-in debugging concepts. In particular, trace functions are provided for the visualization of execution. Other notions enable one to inspect the state of the interpreter, and to define breakpoints. Bahlke et al. write that 'correspondences between the AST and the terms of the functional language are established in both directions'. These correspondences are used to determine a language-specific notion of a step. However, the nature of these "correspondences" is not described, making it impossible to conclude how powerful these correspondences are, or what constraints on specifications they imply[7]. By contrast, our method for keeping track of correspondences, origin tracking [8], is well-defined, and has proven to be sufficiently powerful for realistic languages [19]. A second difference between the work by Bahlke et al. is the information that is used to define debugger features. In our approach, debugger features are defined in terms of specification-level patterns in conjunction with language-independent origin information. That is, the specification of the interpreter and the specification of debugger features are uniform. It is unclear to what extent the debugging concepts of [2] are similar to the interpreter's specification. Finally, Bahlke et al. do not consider more advanced debugger features such as watchpoints, data breakpoints, and dynamic slices.

[7] The subset of Pascal that is considered in [2] does not contain **goto** statements. It is unclear what complications these statements would cause.

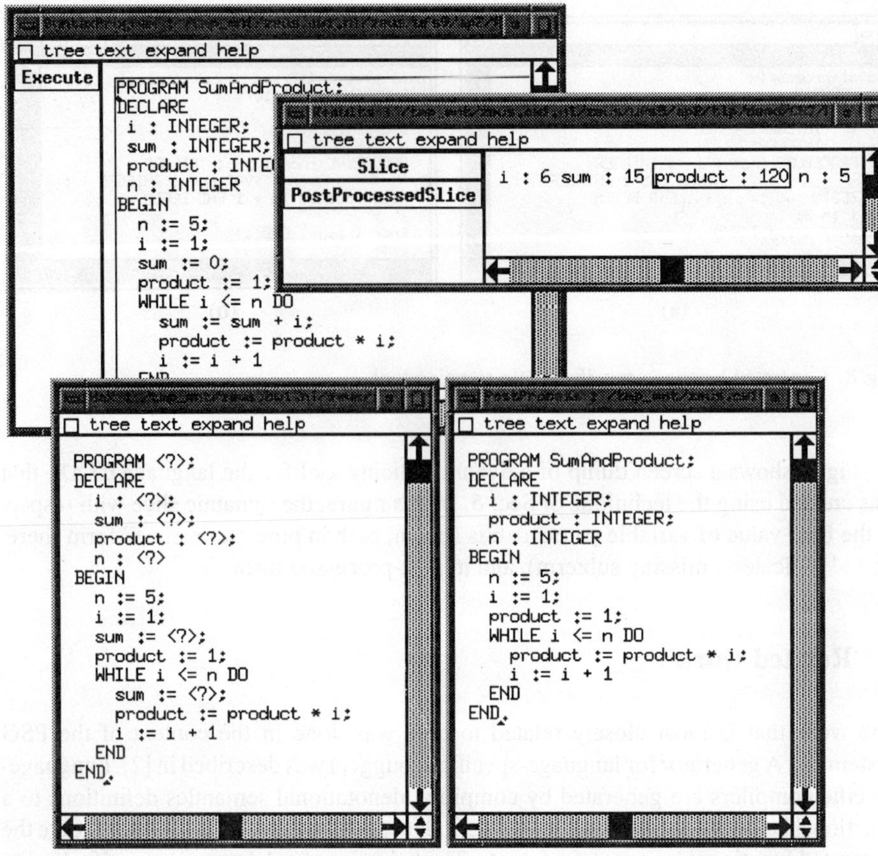

Fig. 9. Generated language-specific dynamic slicing tool.

Bertot [6] contributes a technique called *subject tracking* to the specification language Typol, which is based on natural semantics [14], for animation and debugging purposes. A key property of Typol specifications is that the meaning of a language construct is expressed in terms of its sub-constructs. A special variable, *Subject*, serves to indicate the language construct currently processed. This variable may be manipulated by the specification writer, when different animation or debugging behavior is required. Bertot does not consider other debugger features besides single-stepping, animation, and simple breakpoints.

Berry [5] presents an approach where animators are generated from structured operational semantics definitions. These specifications are augmented with *semantic display rules* that determine how to perform animation when a particular semantic rule is being processed. Various views of the execution of a program can be obtained by defining the appropriate display rules. Static views consist of parts of the AST of a program, and dynamic views are constructed from the program state during execution. As an example of a dynamic view, the evaluation of a control predicate may be visualized as the actual truth value it obtains during execution. Although Berry considers highly sophisticated animation features, he does not consider debugger features such as breakpoints and dynamic program slices.

8 Conclusions and future work

We have presented a generic approach for deriving debugging and dynamic program slicing tools from algebraic specifications. The main conclusion of this paper is that the information needed for implementing such tools is to a very large extent *language-independent* and *implicitly* present in the language's specification. The three "building blocks" we used to define debugger features are:

1. matching of patterns,
2. rewriting of terms, and
3. computation of origin/dependence information.

The first two items consist of functionality that is, at least in principle, already provided by any rewriting engine. As was described in Sec. 3, the information used in the third item can be computed automatically, as a side-effect of rewriting.

The only additional *language-dependent* information that is required to define debugging and slicing features consists of the specification of a set of language-specific patterns, and the actions that should be performed when a match with such a pattern occurs.

The emphasis of this paper has been on generic techniques for constructing debugging tools; we have ignored all aspects that have to do with user-interfacing. In the future, we plan to develop a formalism in which one can *specify* such tools together with their user-interfaces.

Acknowledgments

I am grateful to Paul Klint and T.B. Dinesh for their comments on a draft of this paper.

References

1. AGRAWAL, H., AND HORGAN, J. Dynamic program slicing. In *Proceedings of the ACM SIGPLAN'90 Conference on Programming Language Design and Implementation* (1990), pp. 246–256. *SIGPLAN Notices* 25(6).
2. BAHLKE, R., MORITZ, B., AND SNELTING, G. A generator of language-specific debugging systems. In *Proceedings of the ACM SIGPLAN'87 Symposium on Interpreters and Interpretive Techniques* (1987), pp. 92–101. SIGPLAN Notices 22(7).
3. BAHLKE, R., AND SNELTING, G. The PSG system: from formal language definitions to interactive programming environments. *ACM Transactions on Programming Languages and Systems 8*, 4 (1986), 547–576.
4. BERGSTRA, J., HEERING, J., AND KLINT, P., Eds. *Algebraic Specification.* ACM Press Frontier Series. The ACM Press in co-operation with Addison-Wesley, 1989.

5. BERRY, D. *Generating Program Animators from Programming Language Semantics.* PhD thesis, University of Edinburgh, 1991.
6. BERTOT, Y. Occurrences in debugger specifications. In *Proceedings of the ACM SIGPLAN'91 Conference on Programming Language Design and Implementation* (1991), pp. 327–337. *SIGPLAN Notices* 26(6).
7. DEURSEN, A. V. *Executable Language Definitions—Case Studies and Origin Tracking Techniques.* PhD thesis, University of Amsterdam, 1994.
8. DEURSEN, A. V., KLINT, P., AND TIP, F. Origin tracking. *Journal of Symbolic Computation 15* (1993), 523–545.
9. DINESH, T. Type checking revisited: Modular error handling. In *International Workshop on Semantics of Specification Languages* (1993).
10. DINESH, T., AND TIP, F. Animators and error reporters for generated programming environments. Report CS-R9253, Centrum voor Wiskunde en Informatica (CWI), Amsterdam, 1992.
11. FIELD, J. A simple rewriting semantics for realistic imperative programs and its application to program analysis. In *Proceedings of the ACM SIGPLAN Workshop on Partial Evaluation and Semantics-Based Program Manipulation* (1992), pp. 98–107. Published as Yale University Technical Report YALEU/DCS/RR–909.
12. FIELD, J., RAMALINGAM, G., AND TIP, F. Parametric program slicing. In *Conference Record of the Twenty-Second ACM Symposium on Principles of Programming Languages* (San Francisco, CA, 1995). To appear.
13. FIELD, J., AND TIP, F. Dynamic dependence in term rewriting systems and its application to program slicing. In *Proceedings of the Sixth International Symposium on Programming Language Implementation and Logic Programming* (1994), M. Hermenegildo and J. Penjam, Eds., vol. 844, Springer-Verlag, pp. 415–431.
14. KAHN, G. Natural semantics. In *Fourth Annual Symposium on Theoretical Aspects of Computer Science* (1987), F. Brandenburg, G. Vidal-Naquet, and M. Wirsing, Eds., vol. 247 of *LNCS*, Springer-Verlag, pp. 22–39.
15. KLINT, P. A meta-environment for generating programming environments. *ACM Transactions on Software Engineering and Methodology* 2, 2 (1993), 176–201.
16. KLOP, J. Term rewriting systems. In *Handbook of Logic in Computer Science, Volume 2. Background: Computational Structures*, S. Abramsky, D. Gabbay, and T. Maibaum, Eds. Oxford University Press, 1992, pp. 1–116.
17. KOREL, B., AND LASKI, J. Dynamic slicing of computer programs. *Journal of Systems and Software 13* (1990), 187–195.
18. STALLMAN, R., AND PESCH, R. *Using GDB, A guide to the GNU Source-Level Debugger.* Free Software Foundation/Cygnus Support, 1991. Version 4.0.
19. TIP, F. Animators for generated programming environments. In *Proceedings of the First International Workshop on Automated and Algorithmic Debugging* (1993), P. Fritzson, Ed., vol. 749 of *LNCS*, Springer-Verlag, pp. 241–254.
20. TIP, F. A survey of program slicing techniques. Report CS-R9438, Centrum voor Wiskunde en Informatica (CWI), 1994.
21. TIP, F. *Generation of Program Analysis Tools.* PhD thesis, University of Amsterdam, 1995.
22. WAHBE, R., LUCCO, S., AND GRAHAM, S. Practical data breakpoints: Design and implementation. In *Proceedings of the ACM SIGPLAN'93 Conference on Programming Language Design and Implementation* (Albuquerque, NM, 1993), pp. 1–12. *SIGPLAN Notices* 28(6).

Reasoning with Executable Specifications

Yves Bertot and Ranan Fraer

INRIA – Sophia Antipolis,
2004, route des Lucioles,
06902 Sophia Antipolis, France
e-mail: {bertot,rfraer}@sophia.inria.fr

Abstract. Starting from the specification of a small imperative programming language, and the description of two program transformations on this language, we formally prove the correctness of these transformations. The formal specifications are given in a single format, and can be compiled into both executable tools and collections of definitions to reason about into a theorem prover. This work is a case study of an environment integrating executable tool generation and formal reasoning on these tools.

1 Introduction

Two important areas of computer science have shown some interest in formal specifications of programming languages. One area is that of programming environment generators like Centaur [Jac92], the Synthesizer Generator [RT88], or ASF+SDF [Kli93] where one is interested in deriving programming tools from an abstract description of the programming language. Users of the programming environment generators can thus provide short descriptions of tools, which are then obtained by some compilation process from these descriptions.

In the other area interested in formal specifications, the central tool is a proof tool like Coq [DFH+93], HOL [MT92], or Elf [Pfe89] rather than a programming environment. Here, the actual derivation of programming tools is less relevant than the ease with which one can describe a programming language, feed this description to a theorem proving system, and get this theorem proving system to produce a proof for statements about the language.

Because of the distance between these two areas, there is no insurance that the same notion of "formal specification" is shared by speakers from all sides. The work described in these notes attempts to unite the two sides: we are going to provide formal specifications that will be both integrated in practical programming environments and abstract enough to reason about formally. In this respect we follow Berry's "What you prove is what you execute" principle [Ber89]. The result of our work is a practical environment where users can edit, run and debug programs and trigger transformations by clicking the mouse. The same environment also provides support for proof checked by a machine. We used Centaur et Coq to realize the experiment described in this paper.

2 Related work

A wide variety of programming environment generators use formal descriptions of programming languages. The best known systems use Attribute Grammars, Conditional Rewriting Systems or Natural Semantics. Only in rare cases does the specification formalism adapt to some kind of formal proof.

Attribute Grammars, used in the Synthesizer Generator, exemplify the case of specification formalisms where the formal convenience is sacrificed to efficiency. Attribute Grammars can be compiled into very efficient programs, with good incrementality properties (incrementality is the holy grail of interactive environments). However, Attribute Grammars are limited in scope, so that language designers are left on their own to describe key aspects of their language's environment like dynamic semantics. When it comes to formal reasoning, the situation is even worse, as to our knowledge the only work done in this direction is by Reetz and Kropf [RK94] but their approach is very limited in scope.

Conditional Rewriting Systems, used in ASF+SDF, may be more adapted to formal reasoning than attribute grammars, but, to our knowledge there are no experiments done on coupling ASF+SDF with proof tools.

The specification formalism we use in Centaur is often referred to as Natural Semantics [Kah87]. It draws upon earlier work of Plotkin who introduced Structured Operational Semantics [Plo81]. This style of specification is well suited to execution, as it can easily be related with Prolog, Attribute Grammars or functional evaluation. However, this style of specification is also suitable for formal reasoning, as it has its foundations in meta-mathematics and logics. The natural semantics is widely used for the formal description of type systems or program execution.

Another area of related work is formal semantics and proof tools. The work closest to the experience described in this document is that of Pfenning and Rohwedder [PR92]. They use the LF Logical Framework [HHP91] to specify the meta-theory of deductive systems and the meta-language Elf to implement it. Our study improves on their results in two respects: first, we present an integrated environment, where exactly the *same* specification is executed to perform transformations and to *mechanically* produce the necessary theorem prover input; second, Coq provides general tools related to inductive definitions as in [PM93], while in LF the induction principle is not internalized in the system. A drawback of our approach with respect to theirs is that we are not able to use higher order abstract syntax. Despeyroux and Hirschowitz are currently doing research in this direction [DH94]. However, they prove properties of functional languages, and it is unclear whether higher order abstract syntax can also be useful in reasoning about imperative languages.

There are also case studies using HOL for reasoning about semantic properties of programming languages. Very close to our work is [RN91], where Roxas and Newey study simple program transformations on roughly the same programming language. However, they do not have a complete environment and they do not use induction (as they prove only the correctness of local transformation rules).

Camilleri and Zammit [CZ94] study a way to execute formal specifications inside the theorem prover HOL, and to use this symbolic execution as a proof tool. This kind of tool could have been useful in our experiment.

Recently, Buth presented a transformation of operational and denotational semantics definitions into rewrite rules [But94]. These rules can be used as proof input by the Larch Prover [GJ93]. As the transformation is automatic this approach is similar to ours. However Buth doesn't provide a tool for executing the semantic specifications.

3 Starting little

In this section, we present the formal specification of a small imperative programming language, little, that only handles boolean and integer values.

3.1 Syntactic specifications

The abstract syntax describes how to construct syntactic trees for the programs of a language, while the concrete syntax describes their textual form. The abstract syntax consists of *sorts* and *operators*. Operators represent primitive tree patterns, while sorts represent tree categories, for instance instructions or expressions. Each sort is defined as the set of head operators accepted for trees in this sort. The syntactic description of the main part of the language is as follows, where operators are given in lower case characters and sorts are in upper case.

```
program   -> DECLS INST ;         PROGRAM  ::= program ;
decls   -> DECL + ... ;          DECLS   ::= decls ;
decl   -> ID VAL ;               DECL   ::= decl ;
assign   -> ID EXP ;             INST   ::= assign sequence if while ;
sequence   -> INST * ... ;       SEQUENCE   ::= sequence ;
if -> EXP INST INST ;
while  -> EXP INST ;
```

This description states that a program is made of a list of declarations and an instruction. Each declaration assigns an initial value to some variable of the program. An instruction can be an assignment, an if conditional instruction, a while loop or a sequence of instructions. In the following we will often use skip as a shorthand for sequence[].

The abstract syntax description of a language can be used to implement a structure editor for this language. This tool provides a more user-friendly environment for editing programs in this language. We can also give specifications for other tools of the environment, like a pretty-printer to a more readable textual form and a parser that allows editing fragments of programs as text.

3.2 Semantic Specifications

We describe semantic aspects of the programming language in a natural semantics style [Kah87]. More exactly we define relations between abstract syntax trees and provide inference rules for proving instances of these relations. These inference rules have the following form:

$$\frac{premise_1 \quad \cdots \quad premise_n}{conclusion}$$

The meaning of such a rule is that the conclusion holds if all the premises hold. There is an implicit universal quantification for all the variables occurring in the rule.

Dynamic Semantics We can use this kind of inference rules to specify the *dynamic semantics* of programming languages. We do this with a judgement of the form

$$dynamics(\vdash P \rightarrow D)$$

that states that the execution of program P terminates and returns a list of declarations D, a judgement of the form

$$exec(D \vdash I \rightarrow D')$$

that states that the execution of an instruction I in the environment D terminates and returns a list of declarations D', a judgement of the form

$$eval(D \vdash E \mapsto V)$$

that states that the evaluation of expression E in the environment D returns the value V, and a judgement of the form

$$update(id, V \vdash D \rightarrow D_1)$$

stating that we obtain the new environment D_1 from the environment D by associating the value V to the identifier *id*.

For instance, the rule describing the execution of a program has the following form:

$$\frac{exec(D \vdash I \rightarrow D')}{dynamics(\vdash \mathsf{program}(D, I) \rightarrow D')} \quad (1)$$

This rule says that if the execution of I terminates in the environment D and returns the environment D' then the execution of $\mathsf{program}(D, I)$ terminates and returns the same environment. The rule describing the execution of an assignment has the following form:

$$\frac{eval(D \vdash E \mapsto V) \qquad update(id, V \vdash D \rightarrow D_1)}{exec(D \vdash \mathsf{assign}(id, E) \rightarrow D_1)} \quad (2)$$

It states that to execute an assignment we evaluate the expression E and associate the obtained value V to the identifier *id* in the new environment.

The rule describing the execution of a sequence of instructions has the following form:

$$\frac{exec(D \vdash I_1 \rightarrow D_1) \qquad exec(D_1 \vdash I_2 \rightarrow D_2)}{exec(D \vdash \mathsf{sequence}[I_1 . I_2] \rightarrow D_2)} \quad (3)$$

It states that the execution of the two instructions has to terminate for the execution of a sequence of two instructions to terminate, and it gives the relation between the various computed environments.

Compiling the dynamic semantics specification into a Prolog program yields an interpreter that can be used to run programs [Des84]. If the programming environment generator also provides subject tracking and breakpointing facilities, a complete debugger can also be derived from this specification [Ber91].

Static Semantics In the same way that we specified the execution of programs, we can express the property that programs respect a type discipline. We will consider a program to be *well typed* if every variable used in the program is declared in the initial list of declarations and if all subsequent uses of this variable are coherent with its declaration. The specification of the static semantics can be described with Natural Semantics rules and compiled into a type-checker for the programs of the language. In the case of static semantics, the target language of the compilation may also be Attribute Grammars [Att88], so that an incremental evaluation of static properties may be achieved.

4 Program transformations

We distinguish two important classes of transformations. Global transformations require a full pass on the program; local ones replace a piece of code with another. In this section we will study a global transformation, constant propagation, and a local one, code simplification.

4.1 Constant propagation

Constant propagation builds on a data flow analysis technique used by compilers in the optimization phase. Its goal is to discover variables whose value is constant on all possible executions and propagate these values as far as possible in the program. For example, this transformation can perform relevant simplifications on a program fragment that has the following form:

```
a := true;
if a then
 begin  x := 2; y := z + (x + 4); z := x + y; end
else
 x := 0
```

and replace it with the following equivalent fragment, inferring the way the conditional instruction and the various assignments will be performed.

```
y:= z + 6; z:= 2 + y; a:= true; x:= 2;
```

As before, we specify constant propagation by describing a number of judgements on programs, instructions, expressions, etc. The idea is to compute in each point of the program a list of bindings associating some variables with their values at that point whenever these values are the same for every possible execution of the program. We use meta-variables named B, B' to denote such lists.

We have a judgement

$$propagate\_program(P \rightarrow P')$$

that states that the program P' is the result of constant propagation applied to the program P.

We also have a judgement

$$propagation(B \vdash I \rightarrow I' + B')$$

that states that the instruction I' is obtained from the instruction I by simplifying it with respect to the bindings given by B and that B' denotes new bindings derived from B and I. Note that $+$ in judgements is merely a syntactic separator symbol.

The rule used to propagate constants in a program is:

$$\frac{propagation(\mathsf{bindings}[] \vdash I \rightarrow I' + B') \quad conversion(B' \mapsto S')}{propagate\_program(\mathsf{program}(D, I) \rightarrow \mathsf{program}(D, \mathsf{sequence}[I'.S']))} \quad (4)$$

It says that if the body I of the initial program is simplified with respect to the empty list of bindings, giving us the instruction I' and the new list of bindings B', then the new program will have the body $I'; S'$ where S' is the sequence of assignments $(I_1 := V_1); \ldots; (I_n := V_n)$ corresponding to the list of bindings $B' = (I_1, V_1); \ldots; (I_n, V_n)$. We have a judgement

$$propag\_eval(B \vdash E \mapsto E')$$

that states that the expression E' is obtained from the expression E by simplifying it with respect to a list of bindings of values to variables given by B.

We have a judgement

$$partial\_update(id \backslash val \vdash B \rightarrow B')$$

that states that B' is the same list of bindings as B except that it maps the identifier id to the value val.

We also have a judgement

$$remove(id \vdash B \rightarrow B')$$

that states that B' is the same list of bindings as B except that it does not associate any value to the identifier id.

For instance, the rules describing constant propagation over assignments have the following form:

$$\frac{propag\_eval(B \vdash E \mapsto val) \quad partial\_update(id \backslash val \vdash B \rightarrow B')}{propagation(B \vdash \mathsf{assign}(id, E) \rightarrow \mathsf{skip} + B')} \quad (5)$$

$$\frac{propag\_eval(B \vdash E \mapsto E') \quad remove(id \vdash B \rightarrow B')}{propagation(B \vdash \textsf{assign}(id, E) \rightarrow \textsf{assign}(id, E') + B')} \tag{6}$$

provided E' is not a value

The first rule states that if the expression E simplifies to a value val in the context of the list of bindings B and if updating the list B with the couple (id, val) yields the new list B', then the assignment $\textsf{assign}(id, E)$ reduces to an empty instruction together with the list B'. This rule is valid only when E simplifies to a fixed value, since **partial_update** is only defined for such immediate values. The second rule states that if the expression E simplifies to another expression E', which is not a fixed value, then the assignment $\textsf{assign}(id, E)$ must be transformed into the assignment $\textsf{assign}(id, E')$ together with a new list of bindings B' where the identifier id is not assigned a value.

The rule describing constant propagation over a sequence of instructions has the following form:

$$\frac{propagation(B \vdash I_1 \rightarrow I_1' + B_1) \quad propagation(B_1 \vdash I_2 \rightarrow I_2' + B_2)}{propagation(B \vdash \textsf{sequence}[I_1.I_2] \rightarrow \textsf{sequence}[I_1'.I_2'] + B_2)} \tag{7}$$

It states that the first instruction is simplified with respect to the initial list of bindings and the second instruction is simplified with respect to the list of bindings resulting from the propagation on the first instruction. This transformation specification can also be compiled to Prolog or Attribute Grammars to obtain an executable tool.

4.2 Code simplification

After constant propagation, programs present some unpleasant characteristics. They contain pieces of useless code like **if(E,skip,skip)**. We use code simplification to get rid of such useless fragments. The specification of this local transformation is divided into two parts. First, we define a judgement

$$replace(I \rightarrow I')$$

expressing that the instruction I is locally replaced with the instruction I'. The following two rules describe how the local replacements are performed:

$$replace(\textsf{if}(E, \textsf{skip}, \textsf{skip}) \rightarrow \textsf{skip}) \tag{8}$$

var $S1$: SEQUENCE

$$\frac{append(S_1 + S_2 = S)}{replace(\textsf{sequence}[S_1, S_2] \rightarrow S)} \tag{9}$$

The first one detects pieces of unused code and suppresses them. The second one restructures some parts of the code into a simpler form. More exactly it flattens a sequence of sequences into one sequence. The variable declaration is used to check that the variable S_1 is already a sequence.

Then we introduce the judgement

$$rewrite(I \to I')$$

as the closure of the relation *replace* under the operators if,while and sequence. Two of the rules defining this judgement are:

$$\frac{replace(I \to I')}{rewrite(I \to I')} \quad (10)$$

$$\frac{rewrite(I \to I')}{rewrite(\mathsf{while}(E, I) \to \mathsf{while}(E, I'))} \quad (11)$$

Finally, code simplification is the transitive closure of the *rewrite* relation.

In an interactive environment, local transformations may be applied on request using the mouse, by selecting the location in the program and the rule to apply in a "Transformation menu". Such transformation menus are easy to define in programming environment generators such as the Cornell Synthesizer Generator or Centaur.

5 Using the Coq proof assistant

Formal specifications of programming languages are objects that one should be able to reason about. The reasoning process can be done informally, but it can also be done formally, in a way that can be mechanically checked, by using a proof assistant like Coq. This proof assistant is a system in itself, *a priori* independent from our programming environment generator, but tools have been developed to increase the cooperation between the two systems. So far, these tools provide the following features:

- Abstract syntax specification and semantic specification can be compiled into data-type declarations and axioms for the Coq system [Ter94],
- Programming tools as found in our programming environment generator can improve the usability of the Coq system and make some proofs easier [BKT92].

The type theory provided by the Coq system seems to be a good candidate for representing programming languages, but the real gain of using this system is in the specialized proof tactics provided for manipulating inductive types.

5.1 Translating Specifications

Translating the Abstract Syntax We illustrate the translation of abstract syntax specifications towards Coq data structures on the example of the language little. All the sorts of the language are merged into one inductive type called little and each operator is translated into a constructor of this type: [1]

[1] Another possibility would be to associate a type to each sort. This approach, requires mutually inductive types in the general case. This feature was not available in Coq at the time of the experiment.

```
Inductive Definition little : Set =
    program : little → little → little
    | assign : little → little → little
    | if : little → little → little → little
    | sequence : little → little → little
    | nul_sequence : little
    | while : little → little → little
    | ...
```

In this definition $A \rightarrow B \rightarrow C$ is read as $A \rightarrow (B \rightarrow C)$. List operators are encoded using two operators, a binary one (**sequence**) and an atomic one (**nul_sequence**).

To forbid the manipulation of exotic terms (not respecting the syntactic constraints) we define the set of sorts of our language, such as **little_PROGRAM** and **little_EXP**, and we define a function **little_is** which takes two arguments, a term t and a sort p and determines whether t is a syntactically correct tree in the sort p.

Translating Semantic Specifications Semantic specifications are translated into collections of axioms. Each inference rule is compiled into a universally quantified formula. For example, the rule describing the execution of an assignment is translated into the following statement:

```
exec_assign : ∀D, E, id, V : little.(eval D E V) ⇒ (update id V D D1) ⇒
              (exec D (assign id E) D1)
```

The statement $\forall x : A.B$ reads as "for all x of type A, B is true". Also, $A \Rightarrow B \Rightarrow C$ is understood as $A \Rightarrow (B \Rightarrow C)$. Coq also supports inductive definitions of relations. Given a collection of statements about a relation, an inductive definition expresses that the defined relation is the *least* relation, in terms of set inclusion, that verifies all these statements. Actually, semantic specifications correspond to inductive definitions. For instance, in the case of our **exec** property, we will write down the following inductive definition:

```
Inductive Definition exec : little → little → little → Prop =
    exec_assign : ∀D, E, id, V : little.(eval D E V) ⇒ (update id V D D1) ⇒
                  (exec D (assign id E) D1)
  | exec_sequence : ∀l1, l2, D, D1, D2 : little.
                      (little_is l2 little_SEQUENCE) ⇒ (exec D l1 D1) ⇒
                      (exec D1 l2 D2) ⇒ (exec D (sequence l1 l2) D2)
  | ...
```

5.2 Proof Methods

The Coq system provides a variety of methods for manipulating inductive definitions. Proof of properties of programs often rely on proofs by induction of various forms [Des86, Win93]. More precisely:

- From the definition of an inductive set the Coq system automatically generates a *structural induction principle.* This principle states that this set is the least one closed under the given operators.
- From the definition of an inductive relation the Coq system automatically generates a *principle of induction on the structure of the proof.* This principle states that this relation is the least one closed under the given axioms and inference rules.

Sometimes a degenerate form of induction is sufficient. For example an argument by cases on the structure of expressions will do when a property is true of all expressions simply by virtue of the different forms expressions can take, without having to use the fact that the property holds for subexpressions.

Thanks to the work of Terrasse [Ter94], the relevant inductive definitions are automatically generated from the specification of the language. In turn, the induction theorems are automatically generated by the Coq system. A precise definition of the translation to Coq and a proof of its correctness is given in [Ter94]. This proof guarantees that correctness proofs in Coq imply correctness of the underlying natural semantics style specifications.

6 Proving transformations correct

Once we have translated the syntactic and semantic specifications into Coq definitions, we can start proving that the given program transformations preserve the meaning of programs.

6.1 Validating the constant propagation

We saw that the execution of a program returns a list of pairs *(variable,value)*. To prove the transformation correct it is enough to show that the execution of the transformed program returns a list that associates the same values to the variables. In fact it is easier to prove a stronger result, namely that the transformed program returns the same list as the initial program.

More exactly, we prove the *soundness* and the *completeness* of the transformation. The soundness property states that there is no result that the transformed program returns but that the initial program cannot return.

$$\forall \mathsf{P}_1, \mathsf{P}_2, \mathsf{D}' : \mathsf{little.}(\mathsf{propagate\_program}\ \mathsf{P}_1\ \mathsf{P}_2) \Rightarrow \\ (\mathsf{dynamics}\ \mathsf{P}_2\ \mathsf{D}') \Rightarrow (\mathsf{dynamics}\ \mathsf{P}_1\ \mathsf{D}')$$

The completeness property states that any result returned by the initial program can also be returned by the transformed program.

$$\forall \mathsf{P}_1, \mathsf{P}_2, \mathsf{D}' : \mathsf{little.}(\mathsf{propagate\_program}\ \mathsf{P}_1\ \mathsf{P}_2) \Rightarrow \\ (\mathsf{dynamics}\ \mathsf{P}_1\ \mathsf{D}') \Rightarrow (\mathsf{dynamics}\ \mathsf{P}_2\ \mathsf{D}')$$

As the proofs of the two properties are very similar we shall limit our presentation only to the proof of the soundness property. Using the rules (1), (4) and (3) the soundness property can be reduced to the following one:

$\forall$I, I', B', S', D, D_1, D' : little.
(propagation nul_bindings I I' B') $\Rightarrow$ (conversion B' S') $\Rightarrow$
(exec D I' D_1) $\Rightarrow$ (exec D_1 S' D') $\Rightarrow$ (exec D I D')

This property is a particular case of a more general one, **propagation_sound**, which has the following statement:

$\forall$I, I', B, B', S, S', D, D_1, D' : little.
(propagation B I I' B') $\Rightarrow$ (wf_bindings B) $\Rightarrow$ (conversion B S) $\Rightarrow$
(conversion B' S') $\Rightarrow$ (exec D I' D_1) $\Rightarrow$ (exec D_1 S' D') $\Rightarrow$
$\exists D_2$: little.(exec D S D_2) $\wedge$ (exec D_2 I D')

What matters here is that we replace **nul_bindings** by a more general value B, with a specific constraint, (wf_bindings B), expressing that the list B contains at most one occurrence of each variable. This kind of generalization step seems difficult to automatize and justifies the use of an interactive proof assistant.

The property **propagation_sound** can be better understood as expressing the commutativity of the following diagram (where the dashed lines represent properties that must be proved):

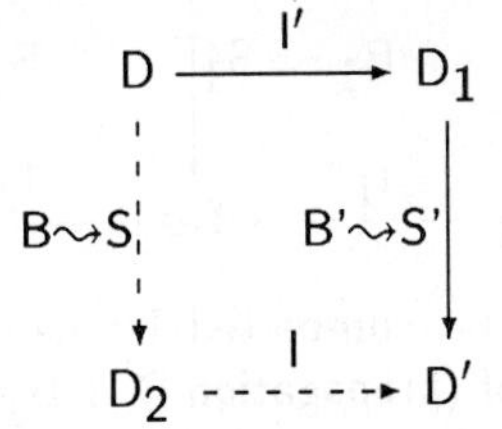

```
        I'
  D ---------> D1
  :            |
B~>S:      B'~>S'
  :            |
  v     I      v
  D2 - - - - > D'
```

For this diagram we have the following assumptions:

- the instruction I' is obtained from the instruction I by simplifying it with respect to the bindings given by B, and B' is a new list of bindings derived from B and I,
- S and S' are sequences of assignments corresponding to the lists of bindings B and B', and
- B is well-formed.

We prove the property **propagation_sound** by induction on the structure of the proof of the hypothesis (propagation B I I' B'), followed by case reasoning on the proof of (exec D I' D_1). We obtain several cases, one for each inference rule given in the definition of the predicate **propagation**.

We present the proof of one of these cases. It is the case corresponding to the rule (7) when I $\equiv$ sequence(I_1, I_2) and I' $\equiv$ sequence(I'_1, I'_2). In this case, we must prove the commutativity of the following diagram:

```
       I'1           I'2
  D ---------> D'1 ---------> D1
  :             :             |
B~>S:     B1~>S1:      B2~>S2 |
  :             :             |
  v     I1      v      I2     v
  D2 - - - - -> D0 - - - - -> D'
```

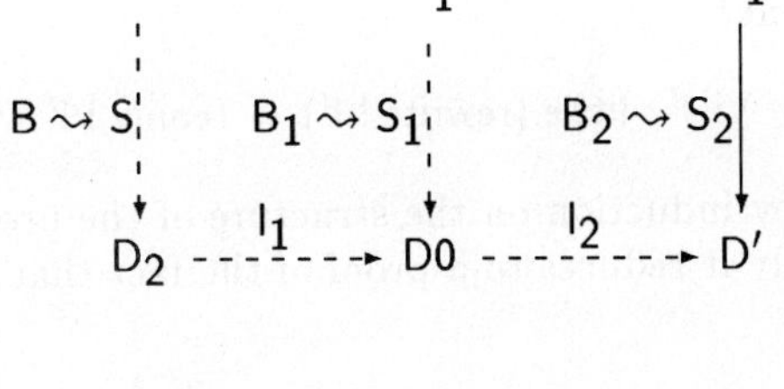

We begin by applying the induction assumption corresponding to the proof of (**propagation** B_1 I_2 B_2 I'_2), where B_1 is the list of bindings obtained by applying the propagation on I_1. We have to show that the list B_1 is well-formed: (**wf_bindings** B_1). We do this by using the assumption that the initial list B is well-formed and applying an auxiliary lemma, **propagate_well_formed** saying that the propagation transforms a well-formed list into another well-formed list:

$$\forall B, I, B', I' : \text{little.}(\textbf{propagation}\ B\ I\ I'\ B') \Rightarrow (\textbf{wf\_bindings}\ B) \Rightarrow (\textbf{wf\_bindings}\ B')$$

Interestingly, **propagation_sound** expresses that the propagation preserves dynamic properties of instructions, while **propagate_well_formed** expresses that the propagation also preserves static properties, like well-formedness. After this first step the intermediary state can be represented by the following partially completed diagram:

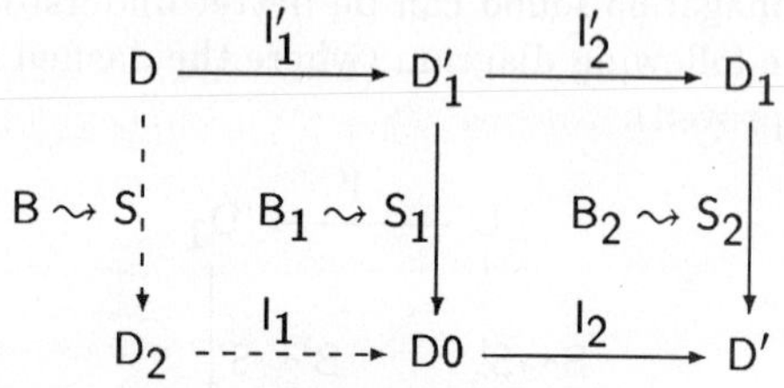

$$\begin{array}{ccccc}
D & \xrightarrow{I'_1} & D'_1 & \xrightarrow{I'_2} & D_1 \\
\Big\downarrow B \rightsquigarrow S' & & \Big\downarrow B_1 \rightsquigarrow S_1 & & \Big\downarrow B_2 \rightsquigarrow S_2 \\
D_2 & \dashrightarrow^{I_1} & D0 & \xrightarrow{I_2} & D'
\end{array}$$

The proof of the case can be completed by using the induction assumption corresponding to the proof of (**propagation** B I1 B_1 I'_1).

6.2 Validating the code simplification

As before we want to prove the soundness and the completeness of the transformation. The proof closely follows the specification of the transformation, being also divided into two parts.

Let us first define the relation **equiv** on the instructions of the language as the equivalence induced by the dynamic semantics:

$$\forall I, I' : \text{little.}(\textbf{equiv}\ I\ I') \stackrel{\text{def}}{=} \forall D, D_1 : \text{little.}(\textbf{exec}\ D\ I\ D_1) \Leftrightarrow (\textbf{exec}\ D\ I'\ D_1)$$

In the first part, we prove that each local replacement transforms an instruction into an equivalent one:

$$\forall I, I' : \text{little.}(\textbf{replace}\ I\ I') \Rightarrow (\textbf{equiv}\ I\ I')$$

In the second part we prove that the relation **rewrite** transforms an instruction into an equivalent one:

$$\forall I, I' : \text{little.}(\textbf{rewrite}\ I\ I') \Rightarrow (\textbf{equiv}\ I\ I')$$

This proof is done by induction on the structure of the proof of the judgement (**rewrite** I I'). Actually it reduces to a proof of the fact that the relation **equiv** is a congruence with respect to the operators **if**, **while** and **sequence**. For instance, one of the subgoals to prove is:

$$\forall \mathsf{I}, \mathsf{I}', \mathsf{E} : \mathsf{little.(equiv\ I\ I')} \Rightarrow \mathsf{(equiv\ (while\ E\ I)\ (while\ E\ I'))}$$

We should stress that the second part of the proof is *generic*, as it can be shared by all the proofs of local transformations.

Another interesting remark about this proof is that it must be done under the assumption that the manipulated programs are well typed. We need this assumption in order to prove that the instructions **skip** and **if** E **then skip else skip** are equivalent. But **skip** can be executed in any environment whereas **if** E **then skip else skip** can only be executed in an environment where E is a boolean expression. This shows the need to prove several facts which relate the static and the dynamic semantics of the language, such as:

- the evaluation of a well typed expression always terminates and returns a value having the same type as the expression.
- types of variables do not change during the execution of a well typed instruction.

7 Conclusions and future work

The work described in this paper aims at providing a uniform environment for the design and study of well defined programming languages. The originality of this work is not in the way formal specifications are executed and integrated in an interactive environment or in the proof techniques that have been used to establish the coherence results between the various specifications. Rather, this work is original as it connects several aspects of formal descriptions of programming languages which have so far been politely ignoring each other. Connecting these various research domains is not only interesting *per se*, it is also relevant when considering the evolution of software engineering tools. First, the wide variety of applications of computer technology leads to the design of numerous special purpose languages for which trustworthy compilers and programming tools are needed. It is sensible to provide tools to the designers of these languages to assist the task of writing these compilers and verifying their correctness. Second, transformation tools can become a major feature of programming environments, since such tools can assist software engineers not only in their task of writing new programs and optimizing them, but also in the task of maintening old software and adapting it to new architectures. The transformations we have studied in our work exemplify two kinds of transformation tools: one performs a complete pass on the program, without interaction from the user, while the other describes a transformation that can be piloted by the engineer in an interactive environment.

This work was very labor intensive, especially due to the lack of programmability of the proof system we used (an old version of Coq). The issue whether this technique will scale up to more powerful languages cannot be fairly estimated before evaluating the progress obtained with a programmable proof system. In this respect we have remarked that many proofs followed a similar pattern which could make them amenable to an automatic treatment. For scaling up to real programming languages it is also important to be able to reuse previous semantic descriptions and proofs as one adds a new feature to the language. We suspect that the work of Felty and Howe [FH94] brings pertinent answers to this problem.

All these problems hide a more general one: compiling semantic specifications to definitions for the proof assistant and then using the proof assistant for manipulating these definitions forces the user down to the lowest level of abstraction. A more user-friendly environment would allow the user to reason directly with the concepts available at the level of the formal specification, or even with concepts available at the level of the programming language. Finding the correct representation for concepts during the proof is an interesting but difficult goal.

References

[Att88] I. Attali. Compiling Typol with Attribute Grammars. In *Programming Language Implementation and Logic Programming*, Orléans, France, 1988. Springer Verlag, LNCS.

[Ber89] G. Berry. Real-time programming: General purpose or special-purpose languages. In G. Ritter, editor, *Information Processing 89*, pages 11–17. Elsevier Science Publishers P.V, 1989.

[Ber91] Y. Bertot. *Une Automatisation du Calcul des Résidus en Sémantique Naturelle.* PhD thesis, Université de Nice-Sophia Antipolis, 1991.

[BKT92] Y. Bertot, G. Kahn, and L. Théry. Real Theorem Provers Deserve Real Interfaces. In *5th ACM Symposium on Software Development Environments*, Washington, 1992. Also available as INRIA Research Report, RR-1684.

[But94] K. Buth. *Techniques for Modelling Structured Operational and Denotational Semantics Definitions with Term Rewriting Systems.* PhD thesis, Christian-Albrechts University, Kiel, 1994.

[CZ94] J. Camilleri and V. Zammit. Symbolic Animation as a Proof Tool. In *HOL Theorem Proving System and its Applications.* Springer-Verlag LNCS 859, 1994.

[Des84] T. Despeyroux. Executable Specifications of Static Semantics. In *International Symposium on Semantics of Data Types*, 1984. Springer-Verlag LNCS 173.

[Des86] J. Despeyroux. Proof of Translation in Natural Semantics. In *Proceedings of the first ACM-IEEE Symp. on Logic In Computer Science, Cambridge, Ma, USA, June 1986*, pages 193–205, 1986. also available as a Research Report RR-514, Inria-Sophia-Antipolis, France, April 1986.

[DFH+93] G. Dowek, A. Felty, H. Herbelin, G. Huet, Ch. Paulin, and B. Werner. The Coq Proof Assistant User's guide, Version 5.8. Technical Report 154, INRIA, Rocquencourt, May 1993.

[DH94] J. Despeyroux and A. Hirschowitz. Higher-Order Abstract Syntax and Induction in Coq. In *Proceedings of the* 5th *Int. Conf. on Logic Programming and Automated Reasoning*, July 1994.

[FH94] A. Felty and D. Howe. Generalization and Reuse of Tactic Proofs. In *Proceedings of the* 5th *Int. Conf. on Logic Programming and Automated Reasoning*, July 1994.

[GJ93] J.V. Guttag and J.J.Horning, editors. *Larch: Languages and Tools for Formal Specification.* Springer-Verlag, 1993.

[HHP91] R. Harper, F. Honsell, and G. Plotkin. A framework for defining logics. Technical Report 162, LFCS, University of Edinburgh, June 1991.

[Jac92] I. Jacobs. The Centaur 1.2 Manual. Technical report, INRIA, Sophia-Antipolis, 1992.

[Kah87] G. Kahn. Natural Semantics. In *Proceedings of the Symp. on Theorical Aspects of Computer Science, Passau, Germany*, 1987. Also available as Research Report RR-601,INRIA, Sophia-Antipolis, February 1987.

[Kli93] Paul Klint. A Meta-environment for Generating Programming Environments. In *ACM Transaction on Software Engineering and Methodology*, number 2 in 2, pages 176–201, 1993.

[MT92] M.J.C. Gordon and T.Melham. *HOL: a Proof Generating System for Higher-order Logic.* Cambridge University Press, 1992.

[Pfe89] F. Pfenning. Elf: A Language for Logic Definition and Verified Meta-Programming. In *Proceedings of the* 4th *International Symposium on Logic in Computer Science*, June 1989.

[Plo81] G.D. Plotkin. A Structural Approach to Operational Semantics. Technical Report DAIMI FN-19, Aarhus, 1981.

[PM93] C. Paulin-Mohring. Inductive Definitions in the System Coq: Rules and Properties. In Mark Bezem and Jan-Friso Groote, editors, *Typed Lambda Calculi and Applications*, pages 328–345. Springer-Verlag, March 1993.

[PR92] F. Pfenning and E. Rohwedder. Implementing the Meta-Theory of Deductive Systems. In D. Kapur, editor, *Proceedings of the* 11th *International Conference on Automated Deduction*, Saratoga Springs, New York, June 1992.

[RK94] R. Reetz and T. Kropf. Simplifying Deep Embedding: A Formalised Code Generator. In *HOL Theorem Proving System and its Applications.* Springer-Verlag LNCS 859, 1994.

[RN91] R. Roxas and M. Newey. Proof of Program Transformations. In *HOL'91, HOL Theorem Proving System and its Applications*, pages 223–230. IEEE Computer Society Press, 1991.

[RT88] T. Reps and T. Teitelbaum. *The Synthesizer Generator: a System for Constructing Language Based Editors.* Springer Verlag, 1988. (third edition).

[Ter94] D. Terrasse. Encoding Natural Semantics in Coq. Submitted to AMAST'95. Also available by anonymous ftp to babar.inria.fr: pub/croap/terrasse:NSinCoq.dvi, 1994.

[Win93] G. Winskel. *The Formal Semantics of Programming Languages, an Introduction.* Foundations of Computing. The MIT Press, 1993.

Calculating Software Generators from Solution Specifications *

Richard B. Kieburtz Francoise Bellegarde
Jef Bell James Hook Jeffrey Lewis Dino Oliva
Tim Sheard Lisa Walton Tong Zhou

Pacific Software Research Center
Oregon Graduate Institute of Science & Technology
PO Box 91000, Portland, OR 97291-1000 USA

1 A technology for automatic program generation

Program generators can substantially reduce the effort needed to produce versions of a common software design that are tailored to particular applications, but the task of designing and implementing a program generator for a new application domain can be formidable. This paper describes a new technology for creating program generators. It is built upon research results in the theory of programming languages, formal semantics, program transformation and compilation. It comprises a suite of translation and transformation tools that constitute a design automation system for software engineering.

In our method, the user's interface to a program generator is a language in which to specify each particular application for which a software module is required. We refer to this specification language as a *domain-specific design language* (DSDL), for it is tailored to the problem domain for which the generator is intended. A DSDL is a specialized, declarative language in which the important, high-level abstractions of the problem domain are directly expressible. Often, a DSDL is just a formalization of a tabular or graphical specification language that engineers in the problem domain have long been using to express detailed designs.

For a DSDL to be used to express input to a program generator, it must have a computational semantics. The requirements that we impose upon the semantics definition for a DSDL are that it be (i) compositional, (ii) effectively computable, and (iii) total. The implementation of a program generator is derived from the semantics of a DSDL through several steps of translation and transformation to obtain satisfactory algorithmic performance and to tailor the implementation to a specific platform and software environment.

Compositionality implies that an implementation can be assembled piecewise from the components of the semantics. Effective computability requires semantic

* The research reported here has been sponsored by the USAF Materiel Command.

functions to be expressed algorithmically. Requiring totality allows the use of equational theories to drive program transformations.

The idea of deriving an implementation for a formally specified language from its semantics was first tried experimentally in the SIS system [19] over 25 years ago. However, at that time, the prospect of a technology to improve the performance of an implementation enough that it would become acceptable for practical use seemed remote. In the intervening years, there have been many discoveries relating to the formal calculation of programs, and it seems time to revisit the ambitious task of automating program generation.

2 Classes of transformations

The compositional style of programming used in designing a computational semantics for a formal specification language is attractive to the designer. However, powerful transformations are necessary to improve efficiency of the programs synthesized from the semantics. Semantics-preserving, fully automatic transformation tools can relieve the software designer from having to consider programming details that tend to obscure high-level concepts relevant to the design itself.

The transformations we have considered fall into four classes, for which distinct implementation strategies seem most appropriate:

1. Parametric transformations are instances of general theorems established by parametricity arguments. They yield equivalences that apply in all datatypes, hence the resulting transformations are type-parametric.
2. Order-reduction transformations replace expressions that use higher-order functions by equivalent expressions using only first-order functions.
3. Algebra-specific transformations are those that depend upon some algebraic laws, such as the associativity and commutativity of a binary operator.
4. Architecture-specific transformations depend upon representation equivalences or properties of the operations of a particular computer architecture. Such transformations typically occur in the code generator of an optimizing compiler.

A compositional programming style introduces many intermediate data structures. When semantic functions are applied directly, their compositions may entail multiple traversals of data structures that represent the abstract syntax of the object language. These problems can be addressed by two parametric transformation strategies:

- fusion or deforestation, in which identical control structures of sequentially applied functions are merged, often allowing an intermediate data structure to be eliminated [25, 8], and
- the tupling, or parallel fusion strategy [6, 9], in which a pair of functions that operate on the same data are transformed into a single function that returns a result pair. Symbolically, this transformation is

$$(f\ x,\ g\ x) \Longrightarrow \langle f,\ g\rangle\ x$$

When applied to traditional functional programs, parametric strategies can require expensive and inexact analysis to determine whether sufficient conditions for their application are satisfied. However, if control structures are explicitly designated when formulating semantic functions and if this information is preserved through the translation process, it can be exploited to drive transformation strategies by pattern matching alone.

Parametric transformations are remarkably effective. However, they do not exploit specific, algebraic properties of functions used in designing a semantics. A property like the associativity and commutativity of multiplication over natural numbers is not paramctric. Associativity is necessary to apply the accumulator-introduction strategy that eliminates recursion in favor of iteration. It can be exploited by transformation systems based on the unfold-fold method [9], but these require human intervention or *ad hoc* heuristics to direct them.

Term-rewriting, using a theory completion process for control, provides a flexible basis for implementing algebra-specific transformations [11, 2]. Such systems perform transformations on first-order programs. Parametric transformation strategies can also be performed by term-rewriting methods. Algebra-specific transformations are more costly and more difficult to automate than parametric transformations but they can have a dramatic impact on the performance of programs. Algorithmic complexity improvement can be obtained through transformations, by a clever use of algebraic laws.

A strategy for order reduction is to generate a specialized version of each higher-order function for each distinct list of functional arguments to which it is applied in a given program. Specialization may increase the size of a program but has no negative impact on its execution time, and often improves it. Generation of an appropriate data structure to represent closures [20, 1] leads to a more general but less straightforward approach for order-reducing transformations.

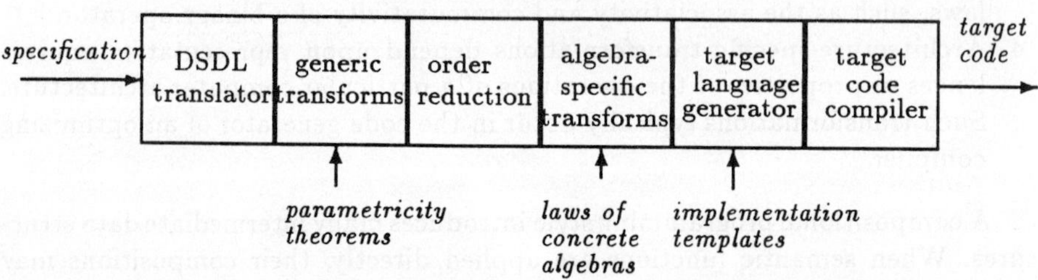

Figure 1—Transformation and translation pipeline

3 Computable denotational semantics

Denotational semantics for programming languages interpret syntax by means of functional expressions such that all constructions are deterministic and composable. Composability implies that the semantics of a syntactic construction is a function of the semantics of its component parts—and of nothing else. To ensure that the semantics of a specification language is computable, its intuitive meaning is formalized in terms of an executable meta-language.

We have designed the ADL language [14] as our preferred meta-language. ADL is an acronym for Algebraic Design Language. It adapts the notion of structure algebras from the mathematics of universal algebras to provide an unusually rich control structure without employing an explicit recursion operator. ADL is a language of total functions, which admits equational reasoning and program transformation by equational rewriting. ADL also incorporates a dual concept of coalgebras, which contribute control structures that correspond naturally to iteration.

3.1 Structure algebras in ADL

Some structure algebras, most notably the algebra of lists, are familiar to functional programmers and have been used by Bird, Meertens and their students [5, 16, 17, 12] to derive programs from logical specifications by formal reasoning. In ADL, structure algebras are first-class entities that can be declared, bound to identifiers and form the basis for ADL control operators. The declarative elements of ADL include *signatures* of algebraic varieties, *algebra specifications* and constant (value) declarations.

Signature declarations do not use explicit recursion, for a signature defines not just a single algebra, but an entire class (or variety) of algebras that share a common structure. For example, the signature declaration for *list* algebras is:

$$\textbf{signature}\ list(a)\ \{\textbf{type}\ c;\ \$nil,\ \$cons\ \textbf{of}\ a * c\}$$

Each algebra in the variety defined by this signature has operators *$nil* and *$cons*. The identifier c, which ranges over all types, designates the *carrier* of an algebra of this variety. For each such algebra, c represents a specific type. The codomain of each operator is the carrier. The domain typing of each operator is specified in the signature. By convention, an operator symbol such as *$nil*, for which no domain typing is given, represents a constant of the carrier type.

An algebra specification binds a type for the carrier and a compatibly typed constant for each operator symbol. An example of a *list*-algebra specification is:

$$\textbf{algebra}\ Sum\_list = list(int)\{c := int;\ \$nil := 0,\ \$cons := (+)\}$$

In this specification, both the type parameter, a, and the carrier have been bound to a common type, *int*; the operator symbol *$nil* has been bound to a constant of type *int* and *$cons* has been bound to the operator that designates *int*-addition.

Another *list*-algebra is a free term algebra, which has as its operators data constructors *nil* and *cons*, and whose carrier is the set of terms constructed by well-typed applications of these operators. The type parameter, a, instantiated to any type, determines a particular instance of a free *list* algebra. Thus the carrier of a free term algebra derived from the variety *list* corresponds exactly to an instance of a *list* datatype in a functional programming language such as

Standard ML [18]. For each variety declared by a signature in an ADL program, its free term algebra functor is implicitly declared.

In ADL, we distinguish two degrees of knowledge of the structure of an algebra. When an algebra is specified as an instance of a declared variety, we know how to form composite functions from it with the combinators described in the following section. This is what we mean by a structure algebra.

If the signature of the variety is not visible or the algebra has not been declared as an instance of a variety, then only its operators and their typings are known. We say that such an algebra is *concrete.* The definitions of operators of a concrete algebra may be invisible, if the algebra has been imported. For example, the type *int* is the carrier of a concrete algebra of integer arithmetic, which is externally specified.

3.2 Control structures in ADL

The expression elements of ADL include variables, constants, function and operator applications, datatype constructions, abstractions and saturated combinator expressions [2]. Of particular interest are the combinator expressions, for these determine all interesting control structures. ADL provides four combinators, *red*, *hom*, *gen* and *cohom*. The first two express control derived from algebras; the second two derive control from coalgebras. We shall only discuss the algebraic control combinators.

The combinator *red* is indexed by a sort name and applied to an algebra specification. Its denotation is then a function from an initial term algebra to the carrier of the specified algebra. For example, the expression

$$sum \doteq red[list]\, Sum\_list \,:\, list(int) \rightarrow int$$

denotes a function that sums the elements of a list of integers. This function is an example of a *list*-algebra homomorphism; the condition that it satisfies is

$$sum\ Nil = 0$$
$$sum\ (cons(x, y)) = x + sum\ y$$

Had *sum* been defined in a language such as SML using explicit recursion, then the homomorphism equations would constitute its declaration. However, recursion is not explicit in ADL, it is instead calculated from the signature declaration given for the variety *list.* The combinator *red* has also been called a catamorphism combinator [17].

[2] The term *combinator* is used here to mean an operator with no dependence on free identifiers and which operates on well-typed expressions in the language to produce a new expression. A combinator expression is *saturated* if all required arguments of the combinator are present.

3.3 A tool for parametric transformations

A parametric transformation schema has an instance for every variety of structure algebra. The quintessential parametric transformation is based upon the Promotion Theorem [15]. This theorem and the transformation derived from it are most easily presented with the help of some notation from category theory.

The data of a signature with type parameter a consists of the domain typings of its operators. We can represent the structure of these data in the category $\mathcal{S}et$ by a coproduct of the domain types of the separate operators. This representation is the object map of a bifunctor, $\mathcal{E}$. For instance, the bifunctor that represents the signature *list* has the object map

$$\mathcal{E}^{list}(a, c) = \mathbf{1} + a \times c$$

where $\mathbf{1}$ is the empty product. A *list*-algebra is represented in this notation by an arrow. For instance, the algebra *Sum_list* is the arrow

$$\mathcal{E}^{list}(int, int) \xrightarrow{\{0, (+)\}} int$$

where the expression enclosed in curly brackets denotes the operation of case analysis of an element of a sum type, with component operators $0 : \mathbf{1} \rightarrow int$ and $(+) : int \times int \rightarrow int$.

The free *list* algebra with parameter type a is the arrow

$$\mathcal{E}^{list}(a, list(a)) \xrightarrow{\mathbf{in}^{list} = \{nil,\ cons\}} list(a)$$

where $\mathbf{in}^{list}$ is the composite operator of the free *list* algebra.

A *list* reduction, $h = red[list]\,\{c;\ f_{nil},\ f_{cons}\}$ satisfies the equations

$$h\ nil = f_{nil} \tag{1}$$

$$h\ (cons(x, y)) = f_{cons}(x,\ h\ y) \tag{2}$$

which can be read from the commuting diagram:

$$\begin{array}{ccc}
\mathcal{E}^{list}(a, list(a)) & \xrightarrow{\mathbf{in}^{list}} & list(a) \\
\Big\downarrow \mathcal{E}^{list}(id_a, h) & & \Big\downarrow h = red[list]\,\{c;\ f_{nil},\ f_{cons}\} \\
\mathcal{E}^{list}(a, c) & \xrightarrow[\{f_{nil},\ f_{cons}\}]{} & c
\end{array}$$

Not only does $red[list]\,\{c;\ f_{nil},\ f_{cons}\}$ satisfy the equations read from the diagram, but it is the unique function for which the diagram commutes.

Moreover, for any variety T, every T-reduction is uniquely determined by a T-algebra specification and satisfies a similar diagram, in which the specific algebraic operators correspond to the T-signature.

Theorem: Promotion.
Let $\{c;\ f\}$ be a $T(a)$ algebra and let $g : c \rightarrow c'$. If there exists a $T(a)$ algebra $\{c';\ \phi\}$ such that $\phi \circ \mathcal{E}^T(id_a,\ g) = g \circ f$ with type $\mathcal{E}^T(a, c) \rightarrow c'$ then $g \circ red[T]\ f = red[T]\ \phi : T(a) \rightarrow c'$.

Proof: Consider the diagram below. The upper square commutes since h is a T-algebra reduction. The lower square commutes as the hypothesis of the theorem. Therefore the outer square commutes, thus the arrow on its right-hand edge is the unique T-algebra reduction determined by the algebra $\{c'\ \phi\}$.

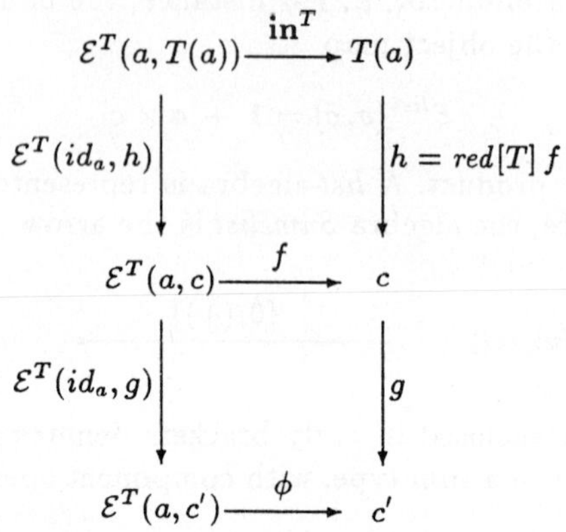

□

The higher-order transformation tool, HOT, uses a clever heuristic tactic to calculate an operator ϕ that satisfies the promotion theorem [21, 22]. The tactic is not complete—it does not always find a candidate if one exists—but it is inexpensive to apply and it often succeeds.

Given the data described in the proof of the Promotion Theorem, HOT introduces a symbol, g', with the assumed law that $g \circ g' = id_{c'}$. A consequence of the assumption is that $\mathcal{E}^T(id_a, g) \circ \mathcal{E}^T(id_a, g') = id_{\mathcal{E}(a,c')}$. Using this deduced law, we derive a representation for ϕ, namely that

$$\phi = g \circ f \circ \mathcal{E}^T(id, g')$$

Now g' is a meaningless symbol, but the expression on the right-hand side of the equation can often be simplified after introducing the detailed structure of f and of the bifunctor $\mathcal{E}^T$, which is derived from the signature T. In the course of simplification, any occurrence of the expression $g \circ g'$ is replaced by $id_{c'}$, which is justified by the assumed law. If, after simplification, the residual expression contains no occurrence of the identifier g', then it represents the operator of a $T(a)$-algebra that was sought. Otherwise, the tactic fails.

4 Order-reduction transformations

Order-reduction transformations remove instances of higher-order functions (applications that include function-typed arguments or which return function-typed results) from a program while preserving its overall semantics. Obviously, this is only possible for programs that calculate ground-typed results from ground-typed data. The order-reduction stage in our translation pipeline consists of a suite of individual algorithms that perform specific order-reduction transformations efficiently. These are:

- A lambda-lifter [13], which removes nested function declarations and explicit abstractions, replacing them by new, closed function declarations. After lambda-lifting, the program contains function definitions of the form $f\ x_1 \ldots x_n = e$ where each of the x_i is a variable and e is either a variable, a constant, an application, or a pattern case analysis.
- Eta-abstraction furnishes abstracted variables as arguments to an unsaturated application of a curried function. It is used to increase the arity of a function definition if its arity does not agree with its typing, and to add dummy arguments to an applicative expression that is unsaturated.
  This transformation sometimes enables an expression in the body of a function declaration to be statically reduced, and is a prerequisite to further steps of function specialization and reduction. This transformation has been studied by Chin and Darlington [7], who refer to it as Algorithm A for higher-order function removal.
- Specializing a function to the arguments found at each of its call sites is a familiar technique for order-reduction (see for instance, Algorithm R of [7]). Specialization occurs in two phases. A naive but efficient algorithm is effective in nearly all cases that arise in practice. For cases that are beyond the scope of the naive algorithm, we have implemented a more general specializer based upon an algorithm due to Reynolds [20].

For example, an application *map sqr x*, can be replaced by the application of a new function, *map_sqr x*, whose definition is gotten by specializing the definition of *map*:

$$map\ f\ nil = nil \qquad map\ f\ (x :: xs) = (f\ x) :: (map\ f\ xs)$$

with respect to the constant *sqr*, obtaining

$$map\_sqr\ nil = nil \qquad map\_sqr\ (x :: xs) = (sqr\ x) :: map\_sqr\ xs$$

A sufficient condition for this technique to work is that the function-typed arguments in a definition are ***variable or constant-only.*** A function-typed argument of a higher-order function F is variable or constant only if in each recursive call in the declaration of F, this argument position is filled either by a variable or by a constant (i.e. a closed expression without free variables). The function *map* is variable-only. Reynolds' algorithm constructs a closure representation for higher-order functions that are not variable-or-constant only.

5 Algebra Specific Transformations

Many transformations are justified in part by the laws of specific algebras. As a logical extension to an ADL module, properties of an imported concrete algebra may be asserted as equational laws. It is these laws on which we base algebra-specific transformations. At the present time, there is no formal verification that the realization of a concrete algebra actually obeys the asserted laws. This gap in verifiability needs attention in the future development of our system.

Common equational laws such as associativity, commutativity, distributivity, unit laws and inverse laws can justify tactics such as recursion elimination, which can sometimes reduce the asymptotic complexity of an algorithm.

Astre is a transformation tool based on rewriting techniques [3]. It is flexible enough so that some tactics can be fully automated. An example is the elimination of structural recursion by accumulator introduction in the presence of an associative operator, which is the familiar *foldr*-to-*foldl* transformation when specialized to *list* algebras.

A rewrite system is a set of rules, ordered pairs of terms, written as $l \rightarrow r$. When a first-order functional program is expressed by a set of mutually recursive pattern-matching equations, it translates into a rewrite system $R0$. The techniques available to transform such a program are simply rewriting and critical pair computation. A critical pair is the result of an *overlap* between the left-hand sides of two rules $g \rightarrow d$ and $l \rightarrow r$. An overlap exists if there is a position ω in l such that $l|_\omega$ and g are unifiable with the most general unifier σ (after renaming the two rules so that their respective sets of variables are disjoint). A *critical pair* is the (new) equation $\sigma(l[\omega \leftarrow \sigma(d)]) = \sigma(r)$ where the notation $t[\omega \leftarrow u]$ denotes the replacement in t of the subterm at position ω by u. Rewriting allows both folding and unfolding of definitions, depending upon the orientation of the equations as rules. Critical pair computation performs both instantiation and unfolding and hence can implement transformations by the unfold/fold technique. This has been called *synthesis by completion* [10, 11].

In Astre, synthesis by completion is used as a mechanism to transform R_0 into a sequence of rewrite systems $R_1, R_2, \ldots, R_n$ to get from a functional program P_0 to a new, semantically equivalent program P_n that is more efficient. Astre translates R_n into an SML program in which functions are presented by a set of mutually recursive equations with pattern-matching arguments.

A fully automated transformation system needs additional techniques, including:

- a mechanism that introduces new function definitions to form *synthesis rules*. Critical pair computations with synthesis rules are the basis of many transformations. Synthesis rules were called *eureka* rules in the fold/unfold methodology because they depended upon the insight of a clever user.
- a mechanism to orient critical pairs into rewrite rules and to control critical pair production so that it generates a complete definition of the synthesized function. Astre orients critical pairs into rules as required by the transformation strategy. It guarantees that termination of the rewrite system is

preserved during the synthesis. Astre carefully controls the production of critical pairs to ensure that the completion process does not diverge [4].

Consider, for example, the function that reverses the elements of a list. It is translated into the following rewrite system:

$$reverse(nil) \rightarrow nil \tag{3}$$
$$reverse(x :: xs) \rightarrow reverse(xs) \mathbin{@} [x] \tag{4}$$

where @ is a concrete algebra operator that is associative and has *nil* as right and left unit. A simple analysis discovers that the recursive call $reverse(xs)$ in the right-hand side of (4) occurs under the associative operator @. In this case, it introduces automatically a synthesis rule $reverse(x) \mathbin{@} u \rightarrow g(x, u)$. This synthesis rule reduces the right-hand side of (4), yielding $reverse(x :: xs) \rightarrow g(xs, [x])$. Critical pair computation with the right unit law, $x \mathbin{@} nil \rightarrow x$, gives the pair $(reverse(x), g(x, nil))$, which yields a new definition of *reverse*:

$$reverse(x) \rightarrow g(x, nil) \tag{$*$}$$

Critical pair computation with associativity gives the equation:

$$g(x, u) \mathbin{@} z = g(x, u \mathbin{@} z) \tag{$**$}$$

Critical pair computations with (3) and $(*)$ return pairs: $(nil \mathbin{@} u, g(nil, u))$, and $(g(xs, [x]) \mathbin{@} u, g(x :: xs, u))$. The left-hand side of the first pair reduces into u by rewriting with the left unit law, $nil \mathbin{@} x \rightarrow x$. The left-hand side of the second pair reduces by rewriting with equation $(**)$ conveniently oriented into the rule $g(x, u) \mathbin{@} z \rightarrow g(x, u \mathbin{@} z)$. The result is $reverse(xs) \mathbin{@} ([x] \mathbin{@} u)$, which further reduces with the synthesis rule itself into $g(xs, [x] \mathbin{@} u)$. The system has discovered the definition of g:

$$g(nil, u) \rightarrow u \tag{5}$$
$$g(x :: xs, u) \rightarrow g(xs, [x] \mathbin{@} u) \tag{6}$$

which is tail recursive. Use of another law of @: $[x] \mathbin{@} y \rightarrow x :: y$, reduces the left-hand side of (6) into $g(x :: xs) \rightarrow g(xs, x :: u)$. The new definition of *reverse* no longer refers to @:

$$reverse(x) \rightarrow g(x, nil) \qquad g(nil, u) \rightarrow u \qquad g(x :: xs, u) \rightarrow g(xs, x :: u)$$

This derivation is replicated each time a recursive call occurs under an associative operator with left and right unit.

6 Generating implementations

Following several stages of transformation, our system produces a first-order SML program that is functionally equivalent to the computational semantics of a sentence in the DSDL that a user has written. This program can be compiled by an SML compiler to produce an executable software module. To execute this module, the run-time support for SML needs to be present, however. Often, the requirements imposed by a software architecture, a target platform for the software, or standards adopted by a software organization dictate a specific form of implementation. To provide for alternate implementations, a back-end tool called the *Program Instantiator* generates target code to meet requirements imposed on a desired implementation.

The Program Instantiator (abbreviated PI) is based upon earlier research by Dennis Volpano [23, 24]. It is driven by several parameters of an implementation, which include:

- the target programming language in which an implementation is to be coded;
- templates in the target language that realize implementations of the concrete algebras used in a program;
- target language templates that provide a standard implementation of free term algebras and of the case discrimination on data constructors;
- templates for function calls and module headers in the target language.

The PI also interprets an environment specification that provides the types and structure of data and control interfaces with a host software architecture. The output of the PI is a module (or modules) in the syntax of the specified target language that implements the first-order SML program given it as input. The PI is currently the least mature of the tools in the translation pipeline and several issues remain to be resolved. These include:

* duplicate function declarations. There is currently no test for function definitions that are identical, up to renaming, and hence could be identified.
* heap storage management. The PI does not currently generate a general-purpose garbage collector. It performs storage allocation in blocks that can be collected entirely when the data they contain are no longer accessible.
* special scoping restrictions. Some possible target languages ('C', for instance) impose restrictions on the declarations of nested scopes. The PI does not currently provide for such restrictions.

7 Implementing the pipeline

The translation and transformation tools described in the preceding sections have all been implemented in Standard ML (SML) [18] except for Astre, the term-rewriting transformation tool, which is implemented in CAML. Furthermore, a restricted sublanguage of SML is used for the intermediate representation of programs as they are passed through the pipeline. An abstract syntax representation of SML is used internally by each tool. This representation is unique to the transformation pipeline and has little in common with the internal representation used by the SML/NJ compiler, for instance.

Use of SML language technology has been an important factor in the success of the project during the fifteen months in which most of the tool development occurred. It has allowed substantial code reuse among tools, and has simplified integration and testing procedures.

8 An application generator

The design method we have described here has been applied to design a software component generator for message translation and validation (MTV). This application arises in military command and control systems, with automatic teller machines in banking and with point-of-sale terminals for retail stores. A central controller receives messages encoded as byte-strings from remote sensors or terminals. It must validate each message and translate it into an internal format for further analysis and response. A controller may serve several sensors, each of which generates messages in a different format. An MTV module is required for each message format. It analyzes a string of bytes given as input to check whether it has the expected structure, reports errors if the input is not a valid message, and translates the input into a data structure representing the contents of the message if the input is valid.

Under current practice, an engineer receives a message specification in the form of an *interface control document* (ICD). An ICD is a semi-formal description of the string-encoded format of the message. It gives the maximum expected length of a message, followed by a field-by-field description of its contents. Field descriptions may themselves have internal structure. For example, a date field will contain a day, month and year. A field may represent various types of data. For example, a field may represent an altitude if it consists only of digits or a location if it contains alphabetic characters. An ICD can also specify constraints on valid messages; these are expressed informally in natural language. We have designed a Message Specification Language (MSL), which is a formal, domain-specific design language for the MTV application.

For the MTV domain the essential abstractions are the internal and external representations of messages. They are related by translation functions that map between them. A logical representation in which both intra- and inter-field constraints are imposed is introduced as an intermediate representation. From the logical representation, a controller can derive the necessary internal representation. There is also a "user" representation, which is an Ascii string in a format readable by humans. It is used for logging messages received by a controller or for manual entry of a message.

A software module for MTV consists of six components:

- two functions that check the formats of external or user messages,
- two functions that translate between external and internal formats, and
- two functions that translate between user and internal formats.

The MSL language describes the logical structure of a message, the translation action that parses a message, scaling of numeric values, and any constraints imposed on the values of fields. From these descriptions, the MSL translator and the transformation pipeline generate the required six functions as an Ada package.

8.1 The Message Specification Language

To use the MTV generator, an engineer specifies the logical structure of a message as a logical type in MSL. In the example that follows, square brackets enclose the components of a labeled sum. Labeled sums are types for variant records. Labeled products are types for records, but they are not illustrated here.

```
(* Type declarations *)
type Confidence_type = [High, Medium, Low, No];

type Alt_or_TC_type = [Altitude: integer(1..99),
                       Track_confidence: Confidence_type,
                       No_value_or_Alt_less_than_1000];
```

The engineer also specifies the translation map in one direction: from external to logical. This specifies an external message reader (EXR). For the field types shown above, the external reader declarations are:

```
(* Action declarations *)
EXRaction to_Confidence = [High: Asc 2 | "HH",
                           Medium: Asc 2 | "MM",
                           Low: Asc 2 | "LL",
                           No: Asc 2 | "NN"];

EXRaction to_Alt_or_TC = [Altitude: Asc2Int 2,
                          Track_confidence: to_Confidence,
                          No_value_or_Alt_less_than_1000: Skip 0
                         ] @ Delim "/"; (* field separator "/" *)
```

Message reader declarations are a fundamental syntactic construct in MSL, and are given semantics in its formal definition. The semantics makes use of the structure implicit in the types declared for the corresponding fields. Primitive translation functions such as `Asc2Int` provide basic translation actions. For example, `Asc2Int 2` reads two Ascii characters (which must be numerals) and produces an integer value.

From the specification of an external message reader, the MSL translator not only compiles a message parser that produces a logical representation, but also infers the inverse mapping from logical to external representation and the logical to user mappings. For either the external to logical or the user to logical translation, the semantics must prescribe checking of constraints on values of fields in the message. Constraints are of two kinds:

- Subrange specifications on an individual field. These are specified in a field type and are translated as range checks;
- Inter-field dependencies. These can involve conjunctions or disjunctions of boolean-valued expressions that refer to values in different fields.

A generator for MTV modules has been implemented with the technology described in this paper and evaluated in an experiment whose results will be reported elsewhere.

9 Conclusions

We have successfully demonstrated an automated transformation system that compiles practical software modules from the semantic specification of a domain-specific application design language. The integrated suite of transformation and translation tools represents a new level of design automation for software. Although there is much more that can be done to further improve the performance of generated code, the prototype system demonstrates the feasibility of this approach.

The implementation of type-parametric theorems as transformation tactics for HOT has not been done before. It remains to be seen whether algebra-specific transformations can be incorporated in the same tool by referring to a database of algebraic laws. In the current system, algebra-specific transformations are performed by term-rewriting, which is an entirely different paradigm.

Acknowledgements

We wish to acknowledge the generous help of Andrew Tolmach, who shared with us his extensive knowledge and valuable insight of Standard ML language technology, and of Satnam Singh, who furnished expert advice on Ada code generation issues. We are grateful to Laura McKinney and Alexei Kotov, who provided management and measurement of our project, essential to its success.

References

1. J. M. Bell and J. Hook. Defunctionalization of typed programs. Technical report, Department of Computer Science and Engineering, Oregon Graduate Institute, Feb. 1994.
2. F. Bellegarde. Program transformation and rewriting. In *Proceedings of the fourth conference on Rewriting Techniques and Applications*, vol. 488 of *LNCS*, pages 226–239, Berlin, 1991. Springer-Verlag.
3. F. Bellegarde. A transformation system combining partial evaluation with term rewriting. In *Higher Order Algebra, Logic and Term Rewriting (HOA '93)*, vol. 816 of *Lecture Notes in Computer Science*, pages 40–58. Springer-Verlag, Sept. 1993.
4. F. Bellegarde. Termination issues in automated syntheses. Submitted to RTA95, Sept. 1994.
5. R. S. Bird. An introduction to the theory of lists. In M. Broy, editor, *Logic of Programming and Calculi of Discrete Design*, vol. 36 of *NATO Series F*. Springer-Verlag, 1986.
6. W. Burge. *Recursive Programming Techniques*. Addison-Wesley, 1975.
7. W. Chin and J. Darlington. Higher-order removal: A modular approach. Unpublished work, 1993.
8. W.-N. Chin. Safe fusion of functional expressions. In *Proc. of 1992 ACM Conf. on Lisp and Functional Programming*, pages 11–20, June 1992.
9. J. Darlington and R. Burstall. A system which automatically improves programs. *Acta Informatica*, 6(1):41–60, 1976.
10. N. Dershowitz. Synthesis by completion. In *Proceedings of the Ninth International Joint Conference on Artificial Intelligence*, pages 208–214, Los Angeles, 1985.

11. N. Dershowitz. Completion and its applications. In *Resolution of Equations in Algebraic Structures.* Academic Press, New York, 1988.
12. M. M. Fokkinga. *Law and Order in Algorithmics.* PhD thesis, University of Twente, Twente, The Netherlands, Feb. 1992.
13. T. Johnsson. Lambda lifting: transforming programs to recursive equations. In J.-P. Jouannaud, editor, *Functiona Programming Languages and Computer Architecture*, vol. 201 of *Lecture Notes in Computer Science*, pages 190–203. Springer Verlag, 1985.
14. R. B. Kieburtz and J. Lewis. Algebraic Design Language—Preliminary definition. Technical report, Pacific Software Research Center, Oregon Graduate Institute of Science & Technology, Jan. 1994.
15. G. Malcolm. Homomorphisms and promotability. In J. L. A. van de Snepscheut, editor, *Mathematics of Program Construction*, vol. 375 of *Lecture Notes in Computer Science*, pages 335–347. Springer-Verlag, June 1989.
16. L. Meertens. Algorithmics—towards programming as a mathematical activity. In *Proc. of the CWI Symbposium on Mathematics and Computer Science*, pages 289–334. North-Holland, 1986.
17. E. Meijer, M. Fokkinga, and R. Paterson. Functional programming with bananas, lenses, envelopes and barbed wire. In *Proc. of 5th ACM Conf. on Functional Programming Languages and Computer Architecture*, vol. 523 of *Lecture Notes in Computer Science*, pages 124–144. Springer-Verlag, Aug. 1991.
18. R. Milner, M. Tofte, and R. Harper. *The Definition of Standard ML.* MIT Press, Cambridge, Massachusetts, 1990.
19. P. D. Mosses. Sis—semantics implementation system: reference manual and user guide. Technical Report DAIMI MD-30, Computer Science Department, University of Aarhus, 1979.
20. J. C. Reynolds. Definitional interpreters for higher-order programming languages. In *ACM National Conference*, pages 717–740. ACM, 1972.
21. T. Sheard. Optimizing algebraic programs. Technical Report OGI-CSE-94-004, Oregon Graduate Institute of Science & Technology, Jan. 1994.
22. T. Sheard and L. Fegaras. A fold for all seasons. In *Proceedings of the conference on Functional Programming and Computer Architecture*, Copenhagen, June 1993.
23. D. Volpano and R. B. Kieburtz. Software templates. In *Proceedings Eighth International Conference on Software Engineering*, pages 55–60. IEEE Computer Society, Aug. 1985.
24. D. Volpano and R. B. Kieburtz. The templates approach to software reuse. In T. J. Biggersstaff and A. J. Perlis, editors, *Software Reusability*, pages 247–255. ACM Press, 1989.
25. P. Wadler. Deforestation: Transforming programs to eliminate trees. In *2nd European Symposium on Programming ESOP'88*, vol. 300 of *LNCS*. pages 344-358, Springer-Verlag, 1988.

Comparing Flow-based Binding-time Analyses

Jens Palsberg

Computer Science Department, Aarhus University
Ny Munkegade, DK–8000 Aarhus C, Denmark
palsberg@daimi.aau.dk

Abstract. Binding-time analyses based on flow analysis have been presented by Bondorf, Consel, Bondorf and Jørgensen, and Schwartzbach and the present author. The analyses are formulated in radically different ways, making comparison non-trivial.
In this paper we demonstrate how to compare such analyses. We prove that the first and the fourth analyses can be specified by constraint systems of a particular form, enabling direct comparison. As corollaries, we get that Bondorf's analysis is more conservative than ours, that both analyses can be performed in cubic time, and that the core of Bondorf's analysis is correct. Our comparison is of analyses that apply to the pure λ-calculus.

1 Our Results

We present a constraint-based technique for comparing flow-based binding-time analyses. Binding-time analysis is used in most partial evaluators. The analysis divides the computations in a source program into "static" computations (to be performed by the partial evaluator) and "dynamic" computations (to be performed in the partially evaluated program).

Several binding-time analyses of untyped higher-order languages such as Scheme use a flow analysis to obtain information about higher-order control flow. Such analyses have been presented by Bondorf [2], Consel [4], Bondorf and Jørgensen [3], and Schwartzbach and the present author [11]. The analyses are formulated in radically different ways, as follows:

- **Bondorf.** Flow analysis is performed first, by abstract interpretation; and binding-time analysis is then performed by another abstract interpretation, using the computed flow information.
- **Consel.** Flow and binding-time information are computed by a single abstract interpretation.
- **Bondorf and Jørgensen.** Flow analysis is performed first, by solving a constraint system; binding-time analysis is then performed by solving another constraint system.
- **Palsberg and Schwartzbach (PS).** Binding-time analysis is performed by searching for an output which satisfies a certain predicate. The predicate is formulated using constraint systems where variables range over a combination of flow and binding-time information.

Comparison of these analyses is non-trivial and until now an open problem.

In this paper we demonstrate how to compare such analyses. We concentrate on comparing the analysis of Bondorf with the analysis of PS. To enable comparison, we restrict Bondorf's analysis to the pure λ-calculus. We prove that both analyses can be specified by so-called SF-systems (SF = "Separate Flow"). This leads to the direct comparison:

$$\text{Bondorf} \iff \text{Bondorf as SF-system} \stackrel{\text{direct compar.}}{\Longrightarrow} \text{PS as SF-system} \iff \text{PS}$$

An SF-system is a form of constraint system that uses both variables ranging over flow information and variables ranging over binding-time information. The two SF-systems for the analyses of Bondorf and PS are both derived from the program to be analyzed and both contain a subsystem that specifies flow analysis. As corollaries of the two equivalence proofs, we get:

- **Comparison.** Bondorf's analysis is more conservative than that of Schwartzbach and me, because for all programs the latter SF-system is a subset of the former;
- **Efficiency.** Both analyses can be performed in cubic time, because every SF-system can be solved in cubic time; and
- **Correctness.** The core of Bondorf's analysis is correct, because the SF-system can be connected to a known correctness result for binding-time analysis.

These results demonstrate the benefits of formulating flow-based binding-time analyses as SF-systems.

2 Example

We now illustrate the idea of flow-based binding-time analysis, the notion of an SF-system, and the similarities and differences between the binding-time analysis of Bondorf and that of PS.

Consider the λ-term $(\lambda x.xx)(y)$. Throughout we assume that free variables, in this case y, correspond to dynamic information. The task of a binding-time analysis is to assign either Stat (static) or Dyn (dynamic) to each subterm. This information can then be used to annotate the λ-term.

Following Bondorf [2] and others, we label all abstractions and applications. Variables will also be labeled: if a variable is bound, then it is labeled with the label of the λ that binds it, and if it is free, then with an arbitrary label. By introducing an explicit application symbol, we get the following abstract syntax for the above λ-term.

$$(\lambda^1 x.x^1 \mathbin{@_2} x^1) \mathbin{@_3} y^4$$

For this particular λ-term, there are two possible ways of annotating consistently:

$$(\lambda^1 x.x^1 \mathbin{\underline{@}_2} x^1) \mathbin{@_3} y^4 \tag{1}$$

$$(\underline{\lambda}^1 x.x^1 \ @_2\ x^1)\ \underline{@}_3\ y^4 \qquad (2)$$

Here, underlining means "dynamic" and no underlining means "static". Annotated λ-terms are called 2-level λ-terms. Consistency means that no static computation can depend on the result of a dynamic computation [8].

Notice that only abstraction and application symbols can be annotated. We do not need to annotate variables because a free variable is dynamic and the binding-time of a bound variable is the same as that of the λ that binds it.

Bondorf's binding-time analysis yields information which when used for annotation leads to (2). The binding-time analysis of PS leads to (1). Thus, in this particular case, Bondorf's analysis is more conservative. One of our theorems says that Bondorf's analysis always leads to the same or more underlinings compared the analysis of PS.

An SF-system is a form of constraint system that uses both variables ranging over flow information and variables ranging over binding-time information. Our equivalence theorems say that both of the analyses of Bondorf and PS can be formulated as SF-systems.

The two SF-systems for the analyses of Bondorf and PS are both derived from the program to be analyzed and both contain a subsystem that specifies flow analysis. One of our theorems says that for every λ-term, the SF-systems for the analyses of Bondorf and PS have identical subsystems for flow analysis. In the case of the above λ-term, this subsystem is as follows.

$$\begin{array}{ll}
\text{From } \lambda^1 & \{1\} \subseteq [\![\lambda^1]\!] \\
\text{From } @_2 \text{ and } \lambda^1 & \left\{ \begin{array}{l} \{1\} \subseteq [\![\nu^1]\!] \Rightarrow [\![\nu^1]\!] \subseteq [\![\nu^1]\!] \\ \{1\} \subseteq [\![\nu^1]\!] \Rightarrow [\![@_2]\!] \subseteq [\![@_2]\!] \end{array} \right. \\
\text{From } @_3 \text{ and } \lambda^1 & \left\{ \begin{array}{l} \{1\} \subseteq [\![\lambda^1]\!] \Rightarrow [\![\nu^4]\!] \subseteq [\![\nu^1]\!] \\ \{1\} \subseteq [\![\lambda^1]\!] \Rightarrow [\![@_2]\!] \subseteq [\![@_3]\!] \end{array} \right.
\end{array}$$

Symbols of the forms $[\![\nu^l]\!]$, $[\![\lambda^l]\!]$, and $[\![@_i]\!]$ are meta-variables ranging over flow information, that is, sets of labels. They relate to variables with label l, abstractions with label l, and applications with label i, respectively.

To the left of the constraints, we have indicated from where they arise. The first constraint says that an abstraction may evaluate to an abstraction with the same label. The rest of the constraints comes in pairs. For each application point $@_i$ and each abstraction with label l there are two constraints of the form:

$$\begin{array}{lll}
\{l\} \subseteq \text{"meta-var. for operator of } @_i\text{"} & \Rightarrow & \text{"meta-var. for operand of } @_i\text{"} \subseteq [\![\nu^l]\!] \\
\{l\} \subseteq \text{"meta-var. for operator of } @_i\text{"} & \Rightarrow & \text{"meta-var. for body of abst."} \subseteq [\![@_i]\!]
\end{array}$$

Such pairs of constraints can be read as:

- **The first constraint.** If the function part of $@_i$ evaluates to an abstraction with label l, then the bound variable of that abstraction may be substituted with anything to which the argument part of $@_i$ can evaluate.

- **The second constraint.** If the function part of $@_i$ evaluates to an abstraction with label l, then anything to which the body of the abstraction may evaluate is also a possible result of evaluating the whole application $@_i$.

In a solution of the constraint system, meta-variables are assigned flow information. The minimal solution of the above constraint system is the mapping L where:

$$L[\![\lambda^1]\!] = \{1\}$$
$$L[\![\nu^1]\!] = L[\![\nu^4]\!] = L[\![@_2]\!] = L[\![@_3]\!] = \emptyset$$

This L says that the only subterm that can evaluate to an abstraction is the abstraction with label 1.

Although the SF-systems for the analyses of Bondorf and PS have the same subsystem for specifying flow analysis, they are not the same. One of our theorems says that for all λ-terms, the SF-system for the analysis of Bondorf is a superset of the SF-system for the analysis of PS. The SF-system for the PS analysis of the above λ-term contains the following constraints in addition to those already presented.

$$\begin{array}{ll}
\text{From } @_3 & [\![@_3]\!]_b = \mathsf{Dyn} \\
\text{From } y^4 & [\![\nu^4]\!]_b = \mathsf{Dyn} \\
\text{From } \lambda^1 & [\![\lambda^1]\!]_b = \mathsf{Dyn} \Rightarrow [\![\nu^1]\!]_b = [\![@_2]\!]_b = \mathsf{Dyn} \\
\text{From } @_2 & [\![\nu^1]\!]_b = \mathsf{Dyn} \Rightarrow [\![\nu^1]\!]_b = [\![@_2]\!]_b = \mathsf{Dyn} \\
\text{From } @_3 & [\![\lambda^1]\!]_b = \mathsf{Dyn} \Rightarrow [\![\nu^4]\!]_b = [\![@_3]\!]_b = \mathsf{Dyn} \\
\text{From } @_2 \text{ and } \lambda^1 & \left\{ \begin{array}{l} \{1\} \subseteq [\![\nu^1]\!] \Rightarrow [\![\nu^1]\!]_b = [\![\nu^1]\!]_b \\ \{1\} \subseteq [\![\nu^1]\!] \Rightarrow [\![@_2]\!]_b = [\![@_2]\!]_b \end{array} \right. \\
\text{From } @_3 \text{ and } \lambda^1 & \left\{ \begin{array}{l} \{1\} \subseteq [\![\lambda^1]\!] \Rightarrow [\![\nu^4]\!]_b = [\![\nu^1]\!]_b \\ \{1\} \subseteq [\![\lambda^1]\!] \Rightarrow [\![@_2]\!]_b = [\![@_3]\!]_b \end{array} \right.
\end{array}$$

Meta-variables with b as subscript range over binding-time information, that is, the set $\{\mathsf{Stat}, \mathsf{Dyn}\}$, where $\mathsf{Stat} \leq \mathsf{Dyn}$. To the left of the constraints, we have indicated from where they arise. The constraints can be informally read as follows.

- The first constraint says that the partial evaluator must produce a program.
- The second constraint says that the variable y^4 corresponds to dynamic information.
- The third constraint says that if an abstraction gets classified as dynamic, then so should its bound variable and its body.
- The fourth and fifth constraints say that if the function part of an application gets classified as dynamic, then so should the argument part and the whole application.
- The rest of the constraints come in pairs. They involve both variables ranging over flow information and variables ranging over binding-time information. These constraints are similar to the ones used in the subsystem for flow analysis. The key difference is that the binding-times of the actual and the

formal parameter should be equal, and so should the binding-times of the body of the abstraction and of the application.

The minimal solution of this SF-system is a pair of mappings (L, M), where L was presented above and M is as follows.

$$M[\![\lambda^1]\!]_b = \mathsf{Stat}$$
$$M[\![\nu^1]\!]_b = M[\![\nu^4]\!]_b = M[\![@_2]\!]_b = M[\![@_3]\!]_b = \mathsf{Dyn}$$

The SF-system for Bondorf's analysis of the above λ-term contains in addition the following two constraints.

$$\text{From } @_2 \ [\![\nu^1]\!]_b = \mathsf{Dyn} \Rightarrow \ [\![\nu^1]\!]_b = \mathsf{Dyn}$$
$$\text{From } @_3 \ [\![\nu^4]\!]_b = \mathsf{Dyn} \Rightarrow \ [\![\lambda^1]\!]_b = \mathsf{Dyn}$$

The constraints can be informally read as follows.

- If the argument part of an application gets classified as dynamic, then so should the function part.

The minimal solution of this SF-system is a pair of mappings (L, M'), where L was presented above and M' is as follows.

$$M'[\![\lambda^1]\!]_b = M'[\![\nu^1]\!]_b = M'[\![\nu^4]\!]_b = M'[\![@_2]\!]_b = M'[\![@_3]\!]_b = \mathsf{Dyn}$$

The minimal solution of an SF-system can be computed in cubic time. Previously, no complexity analysis has been given for the analysis of Bondorf, and the best-known algorithm for the analysis of PS has so far been one with worst-case exponential running time [11].

Our equivalence proofs makes it possible to relate Bondorf's analysis to a known correctness result for binding-time analysis [8]. We thereby obtain the first proof of correctness for the core of Bondorf's analysis.

In the following section we recall from [7] a constraint system that specifies flow analysis. In Section 4 we define SF-systems and we present the two SF-systems that are equivalent to the analyses of Bondorf and PS. Finally in Section 5 we recall the original definitions of Bondorf's and PS's analyses and we give equivalence proofs that relate them to the SF-systems.

3 Flow Analysis

We now present the flow analysis which is a subsystem of both the SF-system for Bondorf's analysis and the SF-system for the analysis of PS. Recall the λ-calculus [1].

Definition 1. The language of λ-terms has an abstract syntax which is defined by the grammar:

$$
\begin{array}{rll}
E ::= & x^l & \text{(variable)} \\
| & \lambda^l x.E & \text{(abstraction)} \\
| & E_1 \mathbin{@_i} E_2 & \text{(application)}
\end{array}
$$

The labels on variables, abstraction symbols, and application symbols have no semantic impact; they mark program points. The label on a bound variable is the same as that on the λ that binds it. Labels are drawn from the infinite set Label. The labels and the application symbols are not part of the concrete syntax.

The abstract domain for flow analysis of a λ-term E is called $\mathsf{CMap}(E)$ and is defined as follows.

Definition 2. A meta-variable is of one of the forms $[\![\nu^l]\!]$, $[\![\lambda^l]\!]$, and $[\![@_i]\!]$. The set of all meta-variables is denoted $\mathsf{Metavar}$. A λ-term is assigned a meta-variable by the function var, which maps x^l to $[\![\nu^l]\!]$, $\lambda^l x.E$ to $[\![\lambda^l]\!]$, and $E_1 \mathbin{@_i} E_2$ to $[\![@_i]\!]$.

For a λ-term E, $\mathsf{Lab}(E)$ is the set of labels on abstractions (but not applications) occurring in E. Notice that $\mathsf{Lab}(E)$ is finite. The set $\mathsf{CSet}(E)$ is the powerset of $\mathsf{Lab}(E)$; $\mathsf{CSet}(E)$ with the inclusion ordering is a complete lattice. The set $\mathsf{CMap}(E)$ consists of the total functions from $\mathsf{Metavar}$ to $\mathsf{CSet}(E)$. The set $\mathsf{CMap}(E)$ with point-wise ordering, written $\leq$, is a complete lattice where least upper bound is written $\sqcup$.

The following flow analysis uses a constraint system. It has been used by Schwartzbach and the present author in [9, 10], and in [7] is was proved equivalent to the flow analysis of Bondorf [2], which in turn is based on Sestoft's [13]. Flow analysis is called closure analysis in some papers, including [2, 7].

For a λ-term E, the constraint system is a finite set of conditional clauses over inclusions of the form $P \subseteq P'$, where P and P' are either meta-variables or elements of $\mathsf{CSet}(E)$. A *solution* of such a system is an element of $\mathsf{CMap}(E)$ that satisfies all constraints.

The constraint system is defined in terms of the program to be analyzed. We need *not* assume that all labels are distinct.

The set $R(E_1 \mathbin{@_i} E_2, \lambda^l x.E)$ consists of the two elements
$\{l\} \subseteq \mathsf{var}(E_1) \Rightarrow \mathsf{var}(E_2) \subseteq [\![\nu^l]\!]$
$\{l\} \subseteq \mathsf{var}(E_1) \Rightarrow \mathsf{var}(E) \subseteq [\![@_i]\!]$
For a λ-term E, the constraint system $C(E)$ is the union of the following sets of constraints.

- For every $\lambda^l x.F$ in E, the singleton constraint set consisting of $\{l\} \subseteq [\![\lambda^l]\!]$.
- For every $E_1 \mathbin{@_i} E_2$ in E and for every $\lambda^l x.F$ in E, the set $R(E_1 \mathbin{@_i} E_2, \lambda^l x.F)$.

Each $C(E)$ has a least solution namely the pointwise intersection of all solutions.

We can now do flow analysis of E by computing a solution of $C(E)$. The canonical choice of solution is of course the least one.

4 Flow-based Binding-time Analysis

The output of a binding-time analysis can be presented as an *annotated* version of the analyzed term. In the annotated term, all dynamic abstractions and applications are underlined. The language of annotated terms is usually called a 2-level λ-calculus [6] and is defined as follows.

Definition 3. The language of 2-level λ-terms is defined by the grammar:

$$
\begin{array}{lll}
W ::= & x^l & \text{(variable)} \\
 & \mid \lambda^l x.W & \text{(static abstraction)} \\
 & \mid W_1 \mathbin{@_i} W_2 & \text{(static application)} \\
 & \mid \underline{\lambda}^l x.W & \text{(dynamic abstraction)} \\
 & \mid W_1 \mathbin{\underline{@}_i} W_2 & \text{(dynamic application)}
\end{array}
$$

The language of 2-level λ-terms is partially ordered by $\sqsubseteq$ as follows. Given 2-level λ-terms W and W', $W \sqsubseteq W'$ if and only if they are equal except for underlinings and W' has the same and possibly more underlinings than W. For example, $(\lambda^1 x.x^1 \mathbin{\underline{@}_2} x^1) \mathbin{@_3} y^4 \sqsubseteq (\underline{\lambda}^1 x.x^1 \mathbin{\underline{@}_2} x^1) \mathbin{\underline{@}_3} y^4$. Notice that $\sqsubseteq$ admits greatest lower bounds for terms that are equal except for underlinings.

The abstract domain for the binding-time analysis of a λ-term E is called $\mathsf{BMap}(E)$ and is defined as follows.

Definition 4. Let $\mathsf{BVal} = \{\mathsf{Stat}, \mathsf{Dyn}\}$. The set BVal is totally ordered by $\leq$ so that $\mathsf{Stat} \leq \mathsf{Dyn}$. For clarity, let $\mathsf{Metavar}_b$ be a copy of Metavar where elements are written with b as subscript. The function var_b maps λ-terms to meta-variables with subscript b. The set BMap consists of the total functions from $\mathsf{Metavar}_b$ to BVal. The set BEnv contains each function in BMap when restricted to meta-variables of the form $[\![\nu^l]\!]_b$. Both BMap and BEnv with point-wise ordering, written $\leq$, are complete lattices where least upper bound is written $\sqcup$. The function $\langle V \mapsto S\rangle$ maps the meta-variable V to the value S and maps all other meta-variables to Stat. Finally, we define $\mathit{upd}\ V\ S\ L = \langle V \mapsto S\rangle \sqcup L$.

Given a λ-term E and $M \in \mathsf{BMap}$, we can annotate E by the following function T_M.

$$T_M(x) = x$$

$$T_M(\lambda^l x.E) = \begin{cases} \lambda^l x.T_M(E) & \text{if } M[\![\lambda^l]\!]_b = \mathsf{Stat} \\ \underline{\lambda}^l x.T_M(E) & \text{if } M[\![\lambda^l]\!]_b = \mathsf{Dyn} \end{cases}$$

$$T_M(E_1 \mathbin{@_i} E_2) = \begin{cases} T_M(E_1) \mathbin{@_i} T_M(E_2) & \text{if } M(\mathsf{var}_b(E_1)) = \mathsf{Stat} \\ T_M(E_1) \mathbin{\underline{@}_i} T_M(E_2) & \text{if } M(\mathsf{var}_b(E_1)) = \mathsf{Dyn} \end{cases}$$

Lemma 5. *Let E be a λ-term and let $M, M' \in \mathsf{BMap}$. If $M \leq M'$, then $T_M(E) \sqsubseteq T_{M'}(E)$.*

Proof. Immediate.

We can now define the notion of an SF-system.

Definition 6. An *SF-system* is a finite set of constraints over two disjoint copies of Metavar. The first copy of Metavar is denoted $\mathsf{Metavar}_c$ and the second copy is denoted $\mathsf{Metavar}_b$. Elements of $\mathsf{Metavar}_c$ are written without subscript and elements of $\mathsf{Metavar}_b$ are written with b as subscript. A constraint is a conditional clause of the following form:

- The hypotheses are either of the form $\{l\} \subseteq V$ where $V \in \mathsf{Metavar}_c$, or of the form $V_b = \mathsf{Dyn}$ where $V_b \in \mathsf{Metavar}_b$.
- The conclusion is either of the form $P \subseteq P'$ where $P, P' \in \mathsf{CSet}(E) \cup \mathsf{Metavar}_c$ for some E, or of the form $P_b = P'_b$ where $P_b, P'_b \in \mathsf{BVal} \cup \mathsf{Metavar}_b$.

A *solution* for an SF-system is a pair of mappings (L, M) such that all constraints are satisfied when elements of $\mathsf{Metavar}_c$ are mapped to a value by L and elements of $\mathsf{Metavar}_b$ are mapped to a value by M. The desired binding-time information is then the mapping M.

Each SF-system has a least solution namely the component-wise greatest lower bound of all solutions. The least solution of an SF-system can be computed in cubic time using a straightforward modification of the algorithm in [9] (see also [12, Chapter 5]).

Given a λ-term E, the following SF-system yields a binding-time analysis of E.

For a λ-term E, the constraint system $B(E)$ is the union of $C(E)$ and the following sets of constraints.

- The singleton set consisting of $\mathsf{var}_b(E) = \mathsf{Dyn}$.
- For every free variable x^l of E, the singleton set consisting of $[\![\nu^l]\!]_b = \mathsf{Dyn}$.
- For every $\lambda^l x.F$ in E, the set consisting of $[\![\lambda^l]\!]_b = \mathsf{Dyn} \Rightarrow [\![\nu^l]\!]_b = \mathsf{var}_b(F) = \mathsf{Dyn}$.
- For every $E_1 \mathbin{@_i} E_2$ in E, the set consisting of $\mathsf{var}_b(E_1) = \mathsf{Dyn} \Rightarrow \mathsf{var}_b(E_2) = [\![@_i]\!]_b = \mathsf{Dyn}$.
- For every $E_1 \mathbin{@_i} E_2$ in E and for every $\lambda^l x.F$ in E, the set consisting of
  $\{l\} \subseteq \mathsf{var}(E_1) \Rightarrow \mathsf{var}_b(E_2) = [\![\nu^l]\!]_b$
  $\{l\} \subseteq \mathsf{var}(E_1) \Rightarrow \mathsf{var}_b(F) = [\![@_i]\!]_b$

We can now do binding-time analysis of E by computing a solution of $B(E)$. The canonical choice of solution is of course the least one.

In the next section we will prove that this binding-time analysis is equivalent to that of PS. We will also prove that the analysis of Bondorf is equivalent to the following modified analysis.

For a λ-term E, the constraint system $B'(E)$ is the union of $B(E)$ and the following sets of constraints.

- For every $E_1 \mathbin{@_i} E_2$ in E, the singleton set consisting of $\mathsf{var}_b(E_2) = \mathsf{Dyn} \Rightarrow \mathsf{var}_b(E_1) = \mathsf{Dyn}$.

Fact 7 *Bondorf's analysis is more conservative than the analysis of PS.*

Proof. Clearly, if $B'(E)$ is solvable, then so is $B(E)$. So if (L, M) is the least solution of $B(E)$ and (L', M') is the least solution of $B'(E)$, then $M \leq M'$, and by Lemma 5, $T_M(E) \sqsubseteq T_{M'}(E)$.

5 Equivalence Proofs

5.1 Bondorf's Analysis

The Original Formulation We recall the binding-time analysis of Bondorf [2], with a few minor changes in the notation compared to his presentation. The analysis assumes that all labels are distinct. Bondorf's definition was originally given for a subset of Scheme; we have restricted it to the λ-calculus.

We will use the notation that if $\lambda^l x.E$ is a subterm of the term to be analyzed, then the partial function *body* maps the label l to E. We define $\mu_E^{input} = \langle \mathsf{var}(E) \mapsto \mathsf{Dyn} \rangle$ and we define $\rho_E^{input} = \langle x_1 \mapsto \mathsf{Dyn} \rangle \sqcup \ldots \sqcup \langle x_n \mapsto \mathsf{Dyn} \rangle$, where $x_1 \ldots x_n$ are the free variables of E.

Bondorf's analysis proceeds by first computing flow information by an abstract interpretation. In a previous paper [7] we proved that Bondorf's flow analysis is equivalent to computing the least solution of the constraint system $C(E)$. So for a λ-term E, suppose that $C(E)$ has least solution L.

We follow Bondorf in using an auxiliary function raise, defined as follows.

$$\mathsf{raise} : \mathsf{Metavar} \to \mathsf{BMap} \to \mathsf{BEnv} \to \mathsf{BMap} \times \mathsf{BEnv}$$
$$\mathsf{raise}\ k\mu\rho = (\mu, \rho) \sqcup (\textstyle\bigsqcup_{l \in L(k)} (\mathit{upd}\ [\![\lambda^l]\!]\ \mathsf{Dyn}\ \mu, \mathit{upd}\ [\![\nu^l]\!]\ \mathsf{Dyn}\ \rho))$$

Here follows Bondorf's binding-time analysis of E.

$$\mathsf{Bt} : (E : \Lambda) \to \mathsf{BMap} \times \mathsf{BEnv}$$
$$\mathsf{Bt}(E) = \mathit{fix}(\lambda(\mu, \rho).(\mu_E^{input}, \rho_E^{input}) \sqcup \mathsf{bt}(E)\mu\rho)$$

$b, \mathsf{bt} : (E : \Lambda) \to \mathsf{BMap} \to \mathsf{BEnv} \to \mathsf{BMap} \times \mathsf{BEnv}$

$\mathsf{bt}(E)\mu\rho =$ let (μ', ρ') be $b(E)\mu\rho$ in
let k be $\mathsf{var}(E)$ in
if $\mu'(k) = \mathsf{Dyn}$
then raise $k\ \mu'\rho'$
else (μ', ρ')

$b(x^l)\mu\rho = (\mathit{upd}\ [\![\nu^l]\!]\ \rho[\![\nu^l]\!]\ \mu, \rho)$

$b(\lambda^l x.E)\mu\rho =$ let (μ', ρ') be $\mathsf{bt}(E)\mu\rho$ in
if $\mu'([\![\lambda^l]\!]) = \mathsf{Dyn}$
then raise $\mathsf{var}(E)\ \mu'\rho'$
else (μ', ρ')

$b(E_1 \mathbin{@_i} E_2)\mu\rho =$
let (μ', ρ') be $(\mathsf{bt}(E_1)\mu\rho) \sqcup (\mathsf{bt}(E_2)\mu\rho)$ in

let c be $L(\mathsf{var}(E_1))$ in
let μ'' be
$\quad upd\ [\![@_i]\!]\ (\mu'(\mathsf{var}(E_1)) \sqcup \mu'(\mathsf{var}(E_2)) \sqcup \sqcup_{l \in c} \mu'(\mathsf{var}(body(l))))\ \mu'$ in
let ρ'' be $\rho' \sqcup (\sqcup_{l \in c} (upd\ [\![\nu^l]\!]\ \mu'(\mathsf{var}(E_2)))\ \rho'))$ in
if $\mu''(\mathsf{var}(E_1)) = \mathsf{Dyn}$
then raise $\mathsf{var}(E_2)\ \mu''\rho''$
else (μ'', ρ'')

We can now do binding-time analysis of E by computing $fst(\mathsf{Bt}(E))$.

A Simpler Definition Bondorf's definition can be simplified considerably. To see why, consider the second component of $\mathsf{BMap} \times \mathsf{BEnv}$. This component is updated only in $b(E_1\ @_i\ E_2)\mu\rho$ and read only in $b(x^l)\mu\rho$. The key observation is that both these operations can be done on the first component instead. Thus, we can omit the use of BEnv. By rewriting Bondorf's definition according to this observation, we arrive at the definition below. We use the auxiliary function newraise which is defined as follows.

$$\mathsf{newraise} : \mathsf{Metavar} \rightarrow \mathsf{Metavar} \rightarrow \mathsf{BMap} \rightarrow \mathsf{BMap}$$
$$\mathsf{newraise}\ kk'\mu = \text{if } \mu(k) = \mathsf{Dyn} \text{ then } \mu \sqcup (\bigsqcup_{l \in L(k')} (\langle [\![\lambda^l]\!] \mapsto \mathsf{Dyn}\rangle \sqcup \langle [\![\nu^l]\!] \mapsto \mathsf{Dyn}\rangle)) \text{ else } \mu$$

As with Bondorf's definition, we assume that all labels are distinct.

$$\mathsf{bta}, m : (E : \Lambda) \rightarrow \mathsf{BMap} \rightarrow \mathsf{BMap}$$
$$\mathsf{bta}(E)\mu = \mathsf{newraise}\ \mathsf{var}(E)\ \mathsf{var}(E)\ (m(E)\mu)$$
$$m(x^l)\mu = \mu$$
$$m(\lambda^l x.E)\mu = (\mathsf{bta}(E)\mu) \sqcup (\mathsf{newraise}\ [\![\lambda^l]\!]\ \mathsf{var}(E)\ \mu)$$
$$m(E_1\ @_i\ E_2)\mu = (\mathsf{bta}(E_1)\mu) \sqcup (\mathsf{bta}(E_2)\mu) \sqcup \bigsqcup_{l \in L(\mathsf{var}(E_1))} (\langle [\![\nu^l]\!] \mapsto \mu(\mathsf{var}(E_2))\rangle \sqcup \langle [\![@_i]\!] \mapsto \mu(\mathsf{var}(body(l)))\rangle) \sqcup (\mathsf{newraise}\ \mathsf{var}(E_1)\ \mathsf{var}(E_2)\ \mu) \sqcup \langle [\![@_i]\!] \mapsto \mu(\mathsf{var}(E_1)) \sqcup \mu(\mathsf{var}(E_2))\rangle$$

We can now do binding-time analysis of E by computing

$$fix(\lambda\mu.\mu^{input} \sqcup \rho^{input} \sqcup \mathsf{bta}(E)\mu)\ .$$

A key question is: is the simpler definition equivalent to Bondorf's? We might attempt to prove this using fixed point induction, but we find it much easier to prove that both of them are equivalent to the SF-system presented in the previous section.

Equivalence For every λ-term E where all labels are distinct, we now prove the equivalence of the binding-time analysis of Bondorf, the simplified definition of his analysis, and the analysis specified by the SF-system $B'(E)$. We will use the standard terminology that μ is a *postfixed point* of $m(E)$ if $m(E)\mu \leq \mu$.

Lemma 8. *For every λ-term E, the following properties hold:*

- *If μ is a postfixed point of $\mathsf{bta}(E)$, then so is it of $m(E)$.*
- *If μ is a postfixed point of $\mathsf{bta}(E)$, then so is it of $\mathsf{bta}(F)$ for every subterm F of E.*
- *If μ is a postfixed point of $m(E)$, then so is it of $m(F)$ for every subterm F of E.*

Proof. By induction on the structure of E.

Lemma 9. *$B'(E)$ has least solution $(L, fix(\lambda\mu.\mu^{input} \sqcup \rho^{input} \sqcup \mathsf{bta}(E)\mu))$.*

Proof. We prove a stronger property: the solutions of $B'(E)$ that are of the form (L, M) are exactly the postfixed points of $(L, \lambda\mu.\mu^{input} \sqcup \rho^{input} \sqcup \mathsf{bta}(E)\mu)$. The proof of this involves repeated use of Lemma 8 and is analogous to the proof of [7, Lemma 5]; we omit the details.

Lemma 10. *$B'(E)$ has least solution $(L, fst(\mathsf{Bt}(E)))$.*

Proof. Similar to the proof of Lemma 9.

Theorem 11. *For every λ-term E, the three binding-time analyses defined in Section 5.1.1, 5.1.2, and by the SF-system $B'(E)$ are equivalent.*

Proof. Combine Lemmas 9 and 10.

5.2 The Well-annotatedness Predicate

The Original Formulation We recall the binding-time analysis of Schwartzbach and me [11, 8], with a few minor changes in the notation compared to the previous presentations.

First, we introduce two new forms of meta-variables. A meta-variable is of one of the forms $[\![\nu^l]\!]$, $[\![\lambda^l]\!]$, $[\![@_i]\!]$, $[\![\underline{\lambda}^l]\!]$, and $[\![\underline{@}_i]\!]$. The set of all such meta-variables is denoted $\mathsf{Metavar2}$. A 2-level λ-term is assigned a meta-variable by the function var, which maps x^l to $[\![\nu^l]\!]$, $\lambda^l x.W$ to $[\![\lambda^l]\!]$, $W_1 \; @_i \; W_2$ to $[\![@_i]\!]$, $\underline{\lambda}^l x.W$ to $[\![\underline{\lambda}^l]\!]$, and $W_1 \; \underline{@}_i \; W_2$ to $[\![@_i]\!]$. (Notice that var is an extension of the previously defined function var that operates on λ-terms.)

To define if a 2-level λ-term W is *well-annotated,* we use an abstract domain $\mathsf{DMap}(W)$ which is defined as follows.

Definition 12. For a 2-level λ-term W, $\mathsf{Lab}(W)$ is the set of labels on static abstractions occurring in W. Notice that $\mathsf{Lab}(W)$ is finite. The set $\mathsf{CSet}(W)$ is the powerset of $\mathsf{Lab}(W)$; $\mathsf{CSet}(W)$ with the inclusion ordering is a complete lattice.

Notice that these definitions of $\mathsf{Lab}(W)$ and $\mathsf{CSet}(W)$ extend the previously given ones. We then define $D(W) = \mathsf{CSet}(W) \cup \{\mathsf{Dyn}\}$. The set $D(W)$ is partially ordered by $\leq$ such that if d and d' are sets and $d \subseteq d'$, then $d \leq d'$. Notice that $D(W)$ is *not* a lattice, since Dyn is incomparable to all other elements of $D(W)$. The set $\mathsf{DMap}(W)$ consists of the total functions from Metavar2 to $D(W)$.

A 2-level λ-term W is said to be well-annotated if the constraint system $WA(W)$ below is solvable. The constraint system is a finite set of conditional clauses over inequalities of the form $P \leq P'$, where P and P' are either meta-variables or elements of $D(W)$. A *solution* of such a system is an element of $\mathsf{DMap}(W)$ that satisfies all constraints.

The constraint system is defined in terms of the λ-term to be analyzed. We need *not* assume that all labels are distinct.

For a 2-level λ-term W, the constraint system $WA(W)$ is the union of the following sets of constraints.

- The singleton set consisting of $\mathsf{var}(W) = \mathsf{Dyn}$.
- For every free variable x^l of W, the singleton set consisting of $[\![\nu^l]\!] = \mathsf{Dyn}$.
- For every $\lambda^l x.W'$ in W, the singleton set consisting of $\{l\} \leq [\![\lambda^l]\!]$.
- For every $W_1 \mathbin{@_i} W_2$ in W, the singleton set consisting of $\emptyset \leq \mathsf{var}(W_1)$.
- For every $W_1 \mathbin{@_i} W_2$ in W and for every $\lambda^l.W'$ in W, the set consisting of the two constraints
  $\{l\} \leq \mathsf{var}(W_1) \Rightarrow \mathsf{var}(W_2) \leq [\![\nu^l]\!]$
  $\{l\} \leq \mathsf{var}(W_1) \Rightarrow \mathsf{var}(W') \leq [\![@_i]\!]$
- For every $\underline{\lambda}^l x.W'$ in W, the set consisting of $[\![\underline{\lambda}^l]\!] = [\![\nu^l]\!] = \mathsf{var}(W') = \mathsf{Dyn}$.
- For every $W_1 \mathbin{\underline{@}_i} W_2$ in W, the set consisting of $\mathsf{var}(W_1) = \mathsf{var}(W_2) = [\![\underline{@}_i]\!] = \mathsf{Dyn}$.

Fact 13 *For all λ-terms, there is a $\sqsubseteq$-least well-annotated version.*

Proof. See [11].

We can now do binding-time analysis of a λ-term by computing the $\sqsubseteq$-least well-annotated version.

Equivalence For every λ-term E, we now prove the equivalence of the binding-time analysis of PS, and the analysis specified by the SF-system $B(E)$

We will use the notation that if W is a 2-level λ-term, then $\hat{W}$ is the λ-term which is equal to W except that all underlinings have been removed. Moreover, for a 2-level λ-term W, we will write $\mathsf{DLab}(W)$ for the set of labels on dynamic abstractions occurring in W.

Theorem 14. *Let E be a λ-term. Let W be an annotated version of E. $WA(W)$ is solvable if and only if $B(E)$ has a solution (L, M) and $T_M(E) = W$.*

Proof. Let E be λ-term. Suppose first $B(E)$ has solution (L, M). We will prove that $WA(T_M(E))$ is solvable. Construct $S \in \mathsf{DMap}(T_M(E))$ as follows. For each subterm F in E, define

$$S(\mathsf{var}(T_M(F))) = \begin{cases} L(\mathsf{var}(F)) \text{ if } M(\mathsf{var}_b(F)) = \mathsf{Stat} \\ \mathsf{Dyn} \qquad\quad \text{if } M(\mathsf{var}_b(F)) = \mathsf{Dyn} \end{cases}$$

On the remainder of its domain, S yields Dyn. It is straightforward to check that $WA(T_M(E))$ has solution S.

Suppose then that W is an annotated version of E and suppose that $WA(W)$ has solution S. Construct L as follows. For each subterm W' of W, define

$$L(\mathsf{var}(\hat{W}')) = \begin{cases} S(\mathsf{var}(W')) \text{ if } S(\mathsf{var}(W')) \geq \emptyset \\ \mathsf{DLab}(W') \;\text{ if } S(\mathsf{var}(W')) = \mathsf{Dyn} \end{cases}$$

On the remainder of its domain, L yields $\emptyset$.

Construct then M as follows. For each subterm W' of W, define

$$M(\mathsf{var}_b(\hat{W}')) = \begin{cases} \mathsf{Stat} \text{ if } S(\mathsf{var}(W')) \geq \emptyset \\ \mathsf{Dyn} \text{ if } S(\mathsf{var}(W')) = \mathsf{Dyn} \end{cases}$$

On the remainder of its domain, M yields Stat. Clearly, $T_M(\hat{W}) = W$. It is straightforward to check that $B(\hat{W})$ has solution (L, M).

Theorem 15. *Let E be a λ-term and suppose $B(E)$ has least solution (L, M). Then $T_M(E)$ is the least well-annotated version of E.*

Proof. By Theorem 14, $T_M(E)$ is well-annotated. Let W_l be the least well-annotated version of E. By Theorem 14, choose (L', M') so that $B(E)$ has solution (L', M') and $T_{M'}(E) = W_l$. We have $M \leq M'$ so by Lemma 5, we then get that $T_M(E) \sqsubseteq W_l$. From W_l and $T_M(E)$ being well-annotated and from W_l being the least of the well-annotated versions of E, we get that $W_l \sqsubseteq T_M(E)$. In conclusion, $T_M(E) = W_l$.

From Theorem 15 follows the desired result:

Theorem 16. *For every λ-term E, the binding-time analyses defined in Section 5.2.1 and by the SF-system $B(E)$ are equivalent.*

In previous work [8], we proved that any binding-time analysis that always produces well-annotated 2-level terms is correct. Since for every λ-term E, we have $B(E) \subseteq B'(E)$, the least solution (L, M) of $B'(E)$ is also a solution of $B(E)$. By Theorem 14, $T_M(E)$ is well-annotated. We thus get that Bondorf's analysis, when restricted to the pure λ-calculus, is correct.

6 Concluding Remarks

In a previous paper [11], we proved that the type inference based binding-time analysis of Gomard [5] is more conservative than the analysis of PS. In the papers [8, 11] we emphasized that the analysis of PS was originally intended to capture the outputs of the binding-time analyses of Bondorf and Consel. With the result of this paper, it is now clarified that the analyses of Bondorf is more conservative than the analysis of PS. In future work, we would like to make comparisons with also the analyses of Consel and of Bondorf and Jørgensen.

Acknowledgement. The author thanks Paul Steckler, Mitchell Wand, and the anonymous referees for helpful comments on a draft of the paper. The results of this paper were obtained at Northeastern University, Boston. The author is currently hosted by BRICS, Basic Research in Computer Science, Centre of the Danish National Research Foundation.

References

1. Henk P. Barendregt. *The Lambda Calculus: Its Syntax and Semantics.* North-Holland, 1981.
2. Anders Bondorf. Automatic autoprojection of higher order recursive equations. *Science of Computer Programming*, 17(1–3):3–34, December 1991.
3. Anders Bondorf and Jesper Jørgensen. Efficient analyses for realistic off-line partial evaluation. *Journal of Functional Programming*, 3(3):315–346, 1993.
4. Charles Consel. Binding time analysis for higher order untyped functional languages. In *Proc. ACM Conference on Lisp and Functional Programming*, pages 264–272, 1990.
5. Carsten K. Gomard. Partial type inference for untyped functional programs. In *Proc. ACM Conference on Lisp and Functional Programming*, pages 282–287, 1990.
6. Hanne R. Nielson and Flemming Nielson. Automatic binding time analysis for a typed λ-calculus. *Science of Computer Programming*, 10:139–176, 1988.
7. Jens Palsberg. Closure analysis in constraint form. *ACM Transactions on Programming Languages and Systems.* To appear. Also in Proc. CAAP'94, Colloquium on Trees in Algebra and Programming, Springer-Verlag (*LNCS* 787), pages 276–290, Edinburgh, Scotland, April 1994.
8. Jens Palsberg. Correctness of binding-time analysis. *Journal of Functional Programming*, 3(3):347–363, 1993.
9. Jens Palsberg and Michael I. Schwartzbach. Safety analysis versus type inference. *Information and Computation.* To appear.
10. Jens Palsberg and Michael I. Schwartzbach. Safety analysis versus type inference for partial types. *Information Processing Letters*, 43:175–180, 1992.
11. Jens Palsberg and Michael I. Schwartzbach. Binding-time analysis: Abstract interpretation versus type inference. In *Proc. ICCL'94, Fifth IEEE International Conference on Computer Languages*, pages 289–298, Toulouse, France, May 1994.
12. Jens Palsberg and Michael I. Schwartzbach. *Object-Oriented Type Systems.* John Wiley & Sons, 1994.
13. Peter Sestoft. Replacing function parameters by global variables. Master's thesis, DIKU, University of Copenhagen, September 1989.

Can you Trust your Data?

Peter Ørbæk
poe@daimi.aau.dk

BRICS*

Abstract. A new program analysis is presented, and two compile time methods for this analysis are given. The analysis attempts to answer the question: "Given some trustworthy and some untrustworthy input, can we trust the value of a given variable after execution of some code". The analyses are based on an abstract interpretation framework and a constraint generation framework respectively. The analyses are proved safe with respect to an instrumented semantics. We explicitly deal with a language with pointers and possible aliasing problems. The constraint based analysis is related *directly* to the abstract interpretation and therefore indirectly to the instrumented semantics.

1 Introduction

This paper discusses a static program analysis that can be used to check that the validity of data is only promoted to higher levels of trust in a conscious and controlled fashion.
It is important to stress that the purpose of the analyses is *not* to improve run-time performance, but to give warnings to the programmer whenever untrustworthy data are being unduly trusted.
In the rest of the paper we try to motivate the need for a trust analysis. We give an instrumented semantics for a simple first order language with pointers, in effect keeping track of the trustworthiness of data at run-time. Then an abstract interpretation is presented, approximating the analysis statically. Finally, in order to gain separate analysis of separate program modules as well as better time complexity, a constraint based analysis is presented. The constraint based analysis is proved to be a safe approximation of the abstract interpretation.

2 Motivation

Many computer systems handle information of various levels of trustworthiness. Whereas the contents of the company database can usually be trusted, the input gathered via a modem, or from a part-time secretary may not be trusted as much, and data validation and authentication routines must ensure the validity of data before it is promoted to a higher level of trust and entered into the database.
That there is a need for some method to control the propagation of trust in real-life computer programs is witnessed for example by the security hole recently found in the Unix `sendmail` program [1]. `Sendmail` is the mail forwarding program running on the majority of Unix machines on the Internet. The security hole allowed one to give the program a certain devious input (in an e-mail message) that would result in having

* Basic Research in Computer Science,Dept. of Comp. Sci., University of Aarhus, Denmark, Centre of the Danish National Research Foundation.

arbitrary commands executed on the machine with superuser privileges. Had an analysis like the one described in this paper been run on the sendmail sources it is likely that such a breach in security could have been noticed in advance. See below.

As an example of the kind of analysis envisioned, Perl [8] implements "taint" checks at run-time to help ensure that untrustworthy values are not put in places (such as a process' user-id) where only trusted data should go. This "tainting" is very closely related to the instrumented semantics given below.

We aim at finding a *static* program analysis, i.e. an analysis run only once when a program is compiled, such that the programmer is warned if and when data is promoted from untrustworthy to trustworthy in an uncontrolled fashion. Clearly there will be a need to promote data from untrusted to trusted, but with the envisioned analysis we can guarantee that the promotion takes place in an explicit and conscious way.

In [3, 4] Denning and Denning present a flow analysis for what they call "secure information flow". Their analysis in a sense solves the dual of the problem attacked in this paper. Their aim is to prevent privileged information from leaking out of a trusted computer system, whereas "trust analysis" aims at preventing untrustworthy information from entering into a trusted computer system.

2.1 The Sendmail example

Inside the sendmail C code there is a routine, deliver(), that delivers an e-mail message to an address:

```
void deliver(MSG m, ADR a, ...) {
   ...
   setuid(a.uid);
   ...
}
```

For some addresses, the uid field makes no sense and is uninitialized. In current sources, the ADR structure contains a bit that should be set just when the uid field is valid, and this bit is tested in several places at run-time before the uid field is used. The security hole existed because the programmer had forgotten to insert enough of these checks and consequently, under certain circumstances one was able to circumvent the checks and gain superuser privileges.

With a trust analysis, a reasonable choice is to make the setuid() system-call accept only trusted values, as it sets the user-id of the current process. This forces a.uid to be a trusted value for compilation of deliver() to succeed. One would then have just *one* place, namely in a validation procedure, where the value of an address' uid field is promoted to trusted.

```
ADR validate_address(ADR a) {
   ADR a1;
   ... some validation, fill in appropriate parts of a1.
   ... we may now trust the contents of a.uid.
   a1.uid = trust(a.uid);
   return a1;
}
```

The trust analyzer will now be able to ensure the programmer that only trusted values are passed to `setuid()`. And all the run-time checks on the validity bit are no longer needed as the trust checks are wholly static.

3 The `While` language

Since a large part of security conscious programs today are written in C, a stripped down imperative C-like language with pointers is explored. The abstract syntax for the language is defined by the following BNF:

$$
\begin{aligned}
I &::= \mathit{variable\ names} \\
P &::= \mathsf{deref}\ P \mid I \\
E &::= P \mid E + E \mid \ldots \mid \mathit{const} \mid \mathsf{addr}\ I \mid \mathsf{trust}\ E \mid \mathsf{distrust}\ E \\
S &::= \mathsf{while}\ E\ \mathsf{do}\ S \mid S; S \mid P\ := E
\end{aligned}
$$

Informally, I denotes identifiers, P denotes pointer expressions, E denotes arithmetic and boolean expressions and S denotes statements. Initially the language included first order procedures, but due to lack of space and since they can be added on in a straightforward way they have been left out. How to do this is briefly discussed in Section 7.
We assume programs are *strongly typed* (i.e. like in Pascal), but leave out type declarations such as int or bool as the only thing that matters for our purpose is whether a variable contains a pointer or a scalar (non-pointer) value.
Deref dereferences pointers. If-statements can be emulated by while loops. This saves a syntactic construct.
Notation: The following conventions are used for meta-syntactic variables: i ranges over identifiers I; e, e_1 and e_2 range over expressions E; p range over pointer expressions P and s, s_1 and s_2 range over statements S.

4 Instrumented Semantics

In order to keep track the trustworthiness of values at run-time, we give an instrumented semantics that associate each value with a flag telling whether the value can be trusted or not. This is to be taken as the *definition* of the desired analysis.
Below are the definitions of the semantic domains. *Addr* is the set of possible addresses in memory. The set of possible program values, *Val*, includes at least integers, booleans and addresses. Environments (*Env*) map identifiers to addresses. Note that environments are assumed to be *injective*.
By strong typing we can assume that trust _ is applied to scalar values only. This will be important for the constraint generation analysis. *Notation:* The memory $M[v/a]$ is as M except that the address a is mapped to the value v, and similarly for environments.

$$
\begin{aligned}
\mathit{Tr} &= \{\bot, \top\} \\
\mathit{Val}_I &= \mathit{Val} \times \mathit{Tr} \\
\mathit{Mem}_I &= \mathit{Addr} \rightarrow \mathit{Val}_I \\
\mathcal{E}_I &: E \rightarrow \mathit{Env} \rightarrow \mathit{Mem}_I \rightarrow \mathit{Val}_I \\
\mathcal{S}_I &: S \rightarrow \mathit{Env} \rightarrow \mathit{Mem}_I \rightarrow \mathit{Tr} \rightarrow \mathit{Mem}_I
\end{aligned}
$$

$$addr_I : P \to Env \to Mem_I \to Addr$$
$$M_I \in Mem_I$$

We equip the set *Tr* with a total ordering ($\leq$) such that $\bot \leq \top$ in order to make it a lattice. The least upper bound operation on this lattice will be denoted by $\vee$, which will also be used to denote the *lub* of environments by point-wise extension. The idea is that $\bot$ corresponds to trusted data, and $\top$ corresponds to untrusted data. *Notation:* $\langle \cdot, \cdot \rangle$ forms Cartesian products and π_n is the n'th projection. t ranges over *Tr* and v over *Val*.

$$\begin{aligned}
\mathcal{E}_I\ i\ A\ M_I &= M_I(A(i)) \\
\mathcal{E}_I\ [\![\mathsf{addr}\ i]\!]\ A\ M_I &= \langle A(i), \bot \rangle \\
\mathcal{E}_I\ [\![\mathsf{deref}\ p]\!]\ A\ M_I &= \mathsf{let}\ \langle v, t \rangle = \mathcal{E}_I\ p\ A\ M_I\ \mathsf{in} \\
&\quad\ \langle \pi_1(M_I(v)),\ t \vee \pi_2(M_I(v)) \rangle \\
\mathcal{E}_I\ [\![e_1 + e_2]\!]\ A\ M_I &= (\mathcal{E}_I\ e_1\ A\ M_I)\hat{+}(\mathcal{E}_I\ e_2\ A\ M_I) \\
\mathcal{E}_I\ [\![\mathsf{trust}\ e]\!]\ A\ M_I &= \langle \mathcal{E}_I\ e\ A\ M_I, \bot \rangle \\
\mathcal{E}_I\ [\![\mathsf{distrust}\ e]\!]\ A\ M_I &= \langle \mathcal{E}_I\ e\ A\ M_I, \top \rangle \\
\mathcal{E}_I\ const\ A\ M_I &= \langle const, \bot \rangle \\
\langle v_1, t_1 \rangle \hat{+} \langle v_2, t_2 \rangle &= \langle v_1 + v_2, t_1 \vee t_2 \rangle
\end{aligned}$$

The last parameter to $\mathcal{S}_I$ is used in connection with while loops, the reason being that if the condition in the loop cannot be trusted, then all variables assigned in the loop can no longer be trusted as they may depend on the number of iterations taken.

$$\begin{aligned}
addr_I\ i\ A\ M_I &= A(i) \\
addr_I\ [\![\mathsf{deref}\ p]\!]\ A\ M_I &= \pi_1(M_I(addr_I\ p\ A\ M_I))
\end{aligned}$$

$$\begin{aligned}
\mathcal{S}_I\ [\![\mathsf{while}\ e\ \mathsf{do}\ s]\!]\ A\ M_I\ t &= \mathsf{let}\ \langle v, t' \rangle = \mathcal{E}_I\ e\ A\ M_I\ \mathsf{in} \\
&\quad\ \mathsf{if}\ v\ \mathsf{then} \\
&\quad\quad \mathcal{S}_I\ [\![\mathsf{while}\ e\ \mathsf{do}\ s]\!]\ A\ (\mathcal{S}_I\ s\ A\ M_I\ (t \vee t'))\ t \\
&\quad\ \mathsf{else}\ M_I \\
\mathcal{S}_I\ [\![p\ := \ e]\!]\ A\ M_I\ t &= \mathsf{let}\ \langle v, t' \rangle = \mathcal{E}_I\ e\ A\ M_I\ \mathsf{in} \\
&\quad\ M_I[\langle v, t \vee t' \rangle / (addr_I\ p\ A\ M_I)] \\
\mathcal{S}_I\ [\![s_1; s_2]\!]\ A\ M_I\ t &= \mathcal{S}_I\ s_2\ A\ (\mathcal{S}_I\ s_1\ A\ M_I\ t)\ t
\end{aligned}$$

5 Abstract Interpretation

The instrumented semantics has the drawback that it propagates the trust of variables only at run-time. Below is presented an abstract interpretation [2] of the language computing an approximation to the trust tags and not the actual values.
Since the actual values are not known during the abstract interpretation neither are the addresses, hence environments and memories are collapsed into abstract environments mapping identifiers directly to "trust signatures". *Notation:* 2^I denotes the set of subsets of I.

$$
\begin{aligned}
Val_A &= Tr \cup 2^I \\
Env_A &= I \rightarrow Val_A \\
\mathcal{E}_A &: E \rightarrow Env_A \rightarrow Val_A \\
\mathcal{S}_A &: S \rightarrow Env_A \rightarrow Tr \rightarrow Env_A \\
addr_A &: P \rightarrow Env_A \rightarrow 2^I \\
asg &: Val_A \rightarrow Env_A \rightarrow Val_A \rightarrow Env_A \\
M_A &\in Mem_I \\
v &\in Val_A \\
A_A &\in Env_A
\end{aligned}
$$

We extend the total ordering on *Tr* to a partial ordering on Val_A such that
$\forall v \in Val_A : \bot \leq v \leq \top$ and $a,\, b \in 2^I \Rightarrow (a \leq b \iff a \subseteq b)$.
This makes Val_A a complete lattice, and for any finite collection of programs, finite as well. $\vee$ is used for least upper bound on this lattice too.
The idea is that $\bot$ corresponds to trusted scalars. A set of identifiers corresponds to a trusted pointer that may point to any of the variables mentioned in the set. $\top$ corresponds to untrusted values of any kind. Letting abstract environments map identifiers to sets of identifiers, instead of keeping both information about the pointer and the data pointed to in the abstract environment, is done to handle pointer aliasing. *Notation:* For brevity, define $A_A(\top) = \top$, and for $a \subseteq I$ let $A_A(a) = \bigcup\{A_A(i) \mid i \in a\}$.

$$
\begin{aligned}
\mathcal{E}_A\ i\ A_A &= A_A(i) \\
\mathcal{E}_A\ [\![\mathsf{addr}\ i]\!]\ A_A &= \{i\} \\
\mathcal{E}_A\ [\![\mathsf{deref}\ p]\!]\ A_A &= \bigvee A_A(\mathcal{E}_A\ p\ A_A) \\
\mathcal{E}_A\ [\![e_1 + e_2]\!]\ A_A &= (\mathcal{E}_A\ e_1\ A_A) \vee (\mathcal{E}_A\ e_2\ A_A) \\
\mathcal{E}_A\ [\![\mathsf{trust}\ e]\!]\ A_A &= \bot \\
\mathcal{E}_A\ [\![\mathsf{distrust}\ e]\!]\ A_A &= \top \\
\mathcal{E}_A\ const\ A_A &= \bot
\end{aligned}
$$

The auxiliary *asg* function monotonically assigns a new trust value to a set of identifiers in an abstract environment. $addr_A\ p\ A_A$ yields the set of variables that might be assigned to when p is the left hand side of an assignment. *Notation: dom(M)* denotes the domain of the map M.

$$
\begin{aligned}
asg\ t\ A_A\ \top &= \{(i \mapsto \top) \mid i \in dom(A_A)\} \\
asg\ t\ A_A\ s &= \{(i \mapsto A_A(i) \vee t) \mid i \in s\} \\
&\quad \cup \{(i \mapsto A_A(i)) \mid i \in dom(A_A) \setminus s\} \\
addr_A\ i\ A_A &= \{i\} \\
addr_A\ [\![\mathsf{deref}\ p]\!]\ A_A &= \bigvee A_A(addr_A\ p\ A_A)
\end{aligned}
$$

$$\mathcal{S}_A \,[\![\text{while } e \text{ do } s]\!]\, A_A\, t = \text{let } A'_A = \mathcal{S}_A\ s\ A_A\ (t \vee \mathcal{E}_A\ e\ A_A)$$
$$\text{in if } A'_A \leq A_A \text{ then } A_A \text{ else } \mathcal{S}_A \,[\![\text{while } e \text{ do } s]\!]\, A'_A\ t$$
$$\mathcal{S}_A \,[\![p := e]\!]\, A_A\, t = asg\ (\mathcal{E}_A\ e\ A_A \vee t)\ A_A\ (addr_A\ p\ A_A)$$
$$\mathcal{S}_A \,[\![s_1; s_2]\!]\, A_A\, t = \mathcal{S}_A\ s_2\ (\mathcal{S}_A\ s_1\ A_A\ t)\ t$$

To relate the instrumented and abstract semantics an ordering between instrumented and abstract values is defined relative to an environment:

$$A \vdash \langle v, t \rangle \sqsubseteq a$$

if and only if $a = \bot \Rightarrow t = \bot$ and $a \subseteq I \Rightarrow (t = \bot \ and \ v \in A(a))$.
Informally, the first implication means that if the abstract semantics says that a value is a trustworthy scalar then indeed it is marked trusted in the instrumented semantics. The second implication means that if the abstract semantics thinks a value is a pointer to one of the variables in a set a then by the instrumented semantics the value is indeed trustworthy and is a pointer to one of the variables in the set a.
The relation is extended to relate combined instrumented memories and environments with abstract environments like this:

$$M_I \circ A \sqsubseteq A_A$$

if and only if $dom(M_I \circ A) = dom(A_A)$ and $A \vdash (M_I \circ A)(i) \sqsubseteq A_A(i)$ for all variables $i \in dom(A_A)$
We relate the abstract interpretation to the instrumented semantics in the following way:

Proposition 1 Safety. *If a statement is executed in an environment A and a memory M_I by the instrumented semantics, and the abstract environment A_A is a safe approximation of A and M_I then the result of the abstract interpretation is a safe approximation of the memory resulting from the instrumented semantics. Formally: If*

$$\mathcal{S}_I\ s\ A\ M_I\ t \ = \ M', \quad M_I \circ A \sqsubseteq A_A, \quad \mathcal{S}_A\ s\ A_A\ t_A \ = \ A' \ \ and \ \ t \leq t_A$$

then $M' \circ A \sqsubseteq A'$.

Proof. See Appendix A.
The abstract interpretation terminates. It is clear that $\mathcal{E}_A$ terminates as it is defined inductively in the (finite) structure of expressions, and no fixpoints are computed. The only possibility for $\mathcal{S}_A$ to diverge would be in the while case where a fixpoint is computed, but by Lemma 6 the fixpoint is computed of a monotone function over a lattice of finite height, hence the fixpoint can be found in finite time by iteration.
If we let n denote the number of distinct variables used in a program, let l denote the number of statements and expressions, and let m denote the greatest depth of while-loop nests in the program, the number of least upper bound operations on Val_A executed by the abstract interpretation will be in $O((n+l)^{2m})$. In the worst case, the least upper bound operation on Val_A can be computed in $O(n)$ time. This sounds worse than it really is. For ordinary programs m will be a small constant, and the complexity of analyzing a while-loop is at most $O(n_b^2)$ times the complexity of analyzing the loop body. Here n_b is the number of *pointer* variables occurring in the body of the loop.

If procedures are added to the language, fixpoints need to be computed for each procedure call, hence the time complexity will be even worse in that case.
Apart from the time complexity, the main drawback of the abstract interpretation analysis is that it needs the world to be closed; that is, the analysis cannot be run for each program module separately. In the next section a separable constraint based analysis is presented.

6 Constraint Generation

- Or else, what follows?
- Bloody constraint!...

William Shakespeare: Henry V, Act II, Scene 4.

The constraint generator is going to associate three constraint variables to each program variable. A solution to the generated set of constraints will assign an appropriate trust value for the program variable to one of these constraint variables.
The constraint analysis constructs constraints from any sequence of statements. This is more general than simply allowing for separate analysis of individual functions, since any sequence of statements can be (partly) analyzed out of context. This might for example be useful with an advanced module system like the Beta fragment system [7].
For the purpose of this article, a program consists of a top fragment that includes zero or more fragments which may again include smaller fragments and so on. The inclusion ordering of the fragments form a directed acyclic graph (DAG), as a single fragment may be included more than once, but we disallow circular dependencies.
Fragments are supposed to be analyzed in a bottom-up fashion, first analyzing the leaf fragments that include no other fragments, then analyzing fragments that include only leaf fragments and so on. In effect, the fragments are treated in reverse topological order.
The domains used in the definition of the constraint generation analysis are defined below:

$$
\begin{aligned}
V &::= I \mid \nabla I \mid \Delta I \\
\delta, \eta &: V \to V \\
N &: P \to V \\
Ct &= (V \cup Tr) \times V \\
C &= 2^{Ct} \\
\mathcal{E}_S &: E \to C \times V \\
\mathcal{S}_S &: S \to C \times 2^V \\
G &\in V
\end{aligned}
$$

V is the set of constraint variables. For an identifier i, Δi, and ∇i are simply constraint variables. The intuition is that whereas i will hold the trustworthiness of the value of the program variable i, Δi will hold the trust of all the values reachable by dereferencing i any number of times. Constraint variables ∇i are used to hold the trust of addr terms.
G is a special constraint variable corresponding to the global trustworthiness of a memory. That is, if a value is assigned to the target of an untrusted pointer then that value could end up anywhere, and the trustworthiness of the entire memory is corrupted.
The pair $\langle s, t\rangle \in Ct$ codes the constraint $s \leq t$. For readability we write $\{s \leq t\}$ for such a constraint and $\{s = t\}$ as an abbreviation for $\{s \leq t, t \leq s\}$. The generated constraints will be of the form $\{variable\ or\ constant\ \leq\ variable\}$ over the two element lattice

$\{\bot, \top\}$, hence they can be solved by simple constraint propagation in linear time. The existence of a solution is guaranteed since assigning $\top$ to all constraint variables will satisfy the generated constraints.
We assume that any set of constraints include the constraints $\{i \leq \Delta i\}$ for all identifiers i.
The function δ on V "dereferences" constraint variables:

$$\begin{aligned} \delta\ \nabla i &= i \\ \delta\ i &= \Delta i \\ \delta\ \Delta i &= \Delta i \end{aligned}$$

The function η "safely" takes the address of a constraint variable.

$$\begin{aligned} \eta\ \nabla i &= \nabla i \\ \eta\ i &= \nabla i \\ \eta\ \Delta i &= \Delta i \end{aligned}$$

The map N generates constraint variables from pointer expressions P:

$$\begin{aligned} N\ i &= i \\ N[\![\mathsf{deref}\ p]\!] &= \delta N(p) \end{aligned}$$

$\mathcal{E}_S$ generates constraints for expressions together with the variable corresponding to the given expression. In each case n denotes a freshly created constraint variable.

$$\begin{aligned} \mathcal{E}_S\ i &= \langle \emptyset, i \rangle \\ \mathcal{E}_S[\![\mathsf{addr}\ i]\!] &= \langle \emptyset, \nabla i \rangle \\ \mathcal{E}_S[\![\mathsf{deref}\ p]\!] &= \mathsf{let}\ \langle c, v \rangle = \mathcal{E}_S\ p \\ &\quad\ \mathsf{in}\ \langle c, \delta v \rangle \\ \mathcal{E}_S\ [\![e_1 + e_2]\!] &= \mathsf{let}\ \langle c_1, v_1 \rangle = \mathcal{E}_S\ e_1 \\ &\qquad\quad \langle c_2, v_2 \rangle = \mathcal{E}_S\ e_2 \\ &\quad\ \mathsf{in}\ \langle c_1 \cup c_2 \cup \{v_1 \leq n,\ v_2 \leq n\},\ n \rangle \\ \mathcal{E}_S[\![\mathsf{trust}\ e]\!] &= \langle \emptyset, n \rangle \\ \mathcal{E}_S[\![\mathsf{distrust}\ e]\!] &= \langle \{\top \leq n\}, n \rangle \\ \mathcal{E}_S\ \mathit{const} &= \langle \emptyset, n \rangle \end{aligned}$$

$\mathcal{S}_S$ generates constraints for statements. The second part of the result is the set of constraint variables corresponding to variables assigned to within the statement. This is used to generate additional constraints for while-loops such that variables assigned to in the loop body are trusted only if the condition of the loop is.

$$\begin{aligned} \mathcal{S}_S[\![\mathsf{while}\ e\ \mathsf{do}\ s]\!] &= \mathsf{let}\ \langle c_e, v \rangle = \mathcal{E}_S\ e \\ &\qquad\quad \langle c_s, a \rangle = \mathcal{S}_S\ s \\ &\quad\ \mathsf{in}\ \langle c_s \cup c_e \cup \{v \leq x \mid x \in a\},\ a \rangle \end{aligned}$$

$$\mathcal{S}_S[\![p := e]\!] = \text{let } \langle c_e, v\rangle = \mathcal{E}_S\ e$$
$$\text{in } \langle c_e \cup \{v \le N(p),\ \delta N(p) = \delta v, \eta N(p) \le G\},\ \{N(p)\}\rangle$$
$$\mathcal{S}_S[\![s_1; s_2]\!] = \text{let } \langle c_1, a_1\rangle = \mathcal{S}_S\ s_1$$
$$\langle c_2, a_2\rangle = \mathcal{S}_S\ s_2$$
$$\text{in } \langle c_1 \cup c_2,\ a_1 \cup a_2\rangle$$

A solution to the generated constraints (called a *model*) is a map m giving values to the constraint variables such that the constraints c are fulfilled, this is written $m \models c$. Formally: $m \models c$ if and only if

$$\forall \langle s, t\rangle \in c :\ m(s) \le m(t).$$

It is clear that if $m \models c_1 \cup c_2$ then $m \models c_1$ and $m \models c_2$.
We will consider only a subset of all possible models for a set of constraints, namely so-called *coherent* models. A model m is coherent if it satisfies

$$m(a) \le m(b)\ \Rightarrow\ m(\delta a) \le m(\delta b).$$

It is clear that the model that assigns $\top$ to all variables is a coherent model, hence the existence of a coherent model is assured.
Coherent models and abstract environments can be related to each other in the following way: We write $A_A \sqsubseteq m$ if and only if

$$A_A(i) = \top\ \Rightarrow\ m(i) = \top$$

and

$$a \in A_A(i)\ \Rightarrow\ m(\Delta i) = m(a),$$

or, alternatively $m(G) = \top$.
An intuitive view of the above is that in order for a model to be a safe approximation of an abstract environment, it must assign conservative trust-values to all variables, and if a pointer p can point to a number of variables then the constraint variable Δp must be equated to the trust-values of all these variables.
The constraint generation analysis is related to the abstract interpretation by the following safety statement:

Proposition 2. *If*

$$\langle c, v\rangle = \mathcal{S}_S\ s,$$
$$m \models c, \textit{ and } m \textit{ is coherent}$$
$$A_A \sqsubseteq m,$$
$$\forall x \in v\ :\ t \le m(x),$$
$$A'_A = \mathcal{S}_A\ s\ A_A\ t$$

then $A'_A \sqsubseteq m$.

Proof. See Appendix B.
The constraint generation analysis is strictly weaker than the abstract interpretation in the sense that more variables are treated as untrusted, as is demonstrated by the following example:

Program	New constraint
p := addr j	$\{\nabla j \leq p,\ \Delta p = j\}$
p := addr i	$\{\nabla i \leq p,\ \Delta p = i\}$
i := distrust 8	$\{\top \leq i\}$
k := deref p	$\{\Delta p \leq k,\ \Delta k = \Delta p\}$

Remember that the following constraint is implicitly assumed: $\{p \leq \Delta p\}$. In the abstract interpretation, only i will be marked untrusted at the end, whereas in the constraint analysis the trust of i and j are linked by equality since p may point to both[2].
Generating the constraints for a program of size n takes $O(n^2)$ time in the worst case assuming that the addition of a single constraint can be done in constant time. The constraints, being of such simple nature, may be solved by value propagation in linear time in the number of constraints. All in all constraint generation and (partial) solving can be done in quadratic time in the size of the program fragment.

7 Extensions

By treating arrays as one logical variable, the analysis is able to handle arrays as well as scalar data. This means that the analysis cannot know that some elements of an array are trusted and some are not. Either all elements are trusted or none are. This tradeoff is necessary for the abstract and constraint analyses since they are unable to compute actual offsets in the array. This tradeoff in accuracy is the same as encountered in set-based analysis [5].
Records or structs can be handled by treating each field of the record as a separate variable.
Extending the language with first order procedures is simple enough. The abstract interpretation will simply model the procedure calls directly and compute fixed points in case of recursion. The constraint generation will first compute constraints for the body of a procedure and for each call add constraints matching formal and actual parameters. By copying the constraints generated for the body we can achieve a polyvariant analysis such that a particular call of the procedure with an untrustworthy argument does not influence other calls of that procedure.
A "check for trusted value" construct that will raise an error when an untrusted value is given as parameter is easily added to the language, but makes the semantics larger and a bit more complicated as it has to deal with abnormal termination. The relation between the instrumented and abstract interpretation must state that if the instrumented semantics says that a program will fail then the abstract interpretation will too. Extending the constraint generation analysis with the "check" construct means that there will only be a model for the generated constraints if all checks are met.

[2] As remarked by one of the referees, it might be possible to detect some of these situations as p is *dead* after the first assignment, so one might remove the constraints added in the first line from the final constraints and thereby get a better solution. This effect might also be achieved by removing assignments to dead variables before trust analysis.

Extending the analysis to languages with higher order functions while still catering for pointers and mutable data seems to be more complicated and is left for future research. The concept of trust can be extended to multiple levels of trust, so that instead of a binary lattice of trust values, a lattice with longer chains was used. For the instrumented semantics and the constraint generation, this is a straightforward generalization. For the abstract interpretation, the abstract domain is changed such that all "very trusted" pointers are below the "lesser trusted" pointers all of which are below $\top$.

8 Conclusion

We have argued that the analysis of the trustworthiness of data is a useful program analysis in security conscious settings, and we have given two static analyses for this purpose, one based on abstract interpretation, and another constraint analysis that facilitates separate analysis of program modules at the cost of slightly less accuracy.
The analyses have been proved safe with respect to an instrumented semantics that has served as the definition of the goal of the analysis.
The main contribution of this paper is thought to be the introduction of the concept of trust analysis, and the application of it to a language with pointers and mutable data
Currently, work is in progress together with Jens Palsberg to formulate trust analysis for a higher order language with polymorphic functions in terms of a type inference system. There are some similarities between binding-time analysis [6] and trust analysis in this case, but there are also significant differences. Most notably, in binding-time analysis: if an argument is used by a function that expects a dynamic argument, the argument itself has to be marked dynamic, and the "dynamicness" propagates back through the argument. Not so in trust analysis. There the argument can be "lifted" from trusted to untrusted in that place without affecting other parts of the program.
Acknowledgments: The author wants to thank Jens Palsberg, Peter D. Mosses and Neil D. Jones for reading earlier drafts of this paper and giving useful comments. Also the anonymous referees provided useful feedback.

A Safety of Abstract Interpretation

Fact 1 *If $a \leq b$ and $b \in s \subseteq Val_A$ then $a \leq \bigvee s$.*

Fact 2 *If $A \vdash v \sqsubseteq a$ and $a \leq b$ then $A \vdash v \sqsubseteq b$.*

Lemma 3. *If $M_I \circ A \sqsubseteq A_A$ then $A \vdash \mathcal{E}_I\ e\ A\ M_I \sqsubseteq \mathcal{E}_A\ e\ A_A$.*

Proof. By structural induction on e. We proceed with a case analysis:

- $e = i$: Show $A \vdash M_I(A(i)) \sqsubseteq A_A(i)$ which follows from the definition of $\sqsubseteq$.
- $e = [\![\mathsf{addr}\ i]\!]$: Show $A \vdash \langle A(i), \bot\rangle \sqsubseteq \{i\}$, and clearly $A(i) \in A(\{i\})$.
- $e = [\![\mathsf{deref}\ p]\!]$: Let $\langle v, t\rangle = \mathcal{E}_I\ p\ A\ M_I$ and $a = \mathcal{E}_A\ p\ A_A$, show:

$$A \vdash \langle \pi_1(M_I(v)), t \vee \pi_2(M_I(v))\rangle \sqsubseteq \bigvee A_A(a).$$

By induction, $A \vdash \langle v, t\rangle \sqsubseteq a$. By strong typing we can assume that v is indeed a pointer and that either $a = \top$ or $a \subseteq I$. In the first case the desired inequality holds trivially. In the second case we know that $v \in A(a)$, and also that $t = \bot$. Assume that $v = A(a_0),\ a_0 \in a$. As $M_I \circ A \sqsubseteq A_A$, $A \vdash M_I(v) \sqsubseteq A_A(a_0)$, and using Fact 1 and Fact 2 we get the result.

- $e = [\![e_1 + e_2]\!]$: By induction,

$$A \vdash \ (\langle v_1, t_1\rangle \ = \mathcal{E}_I\ e_1\ A\ M_I) \sqsubseteq \mathcal{E}_A\ e_1\ A_A = a_1,$$

$$A \vdash \ (\langle v_2, t_2\rangle \ = \mathcal{E}_I\ e_2\ A\ M_I) \sqsubseteq \mathcal{E}_A\ e_2\ A_A = a_2.$$

  Show $A \vdash \ \langle v_1 + v_2, t_1 \vee t_2\rangle \ \sqsubseteq \ a_1 \vee a_2$. If one of $\{a_1, a_2\}$ is $\top$, the result is trivial. If they are both $\bot$, both t_1 and t_2 must be too.
- $e = [\![\mathsf{trust}\ e']\!]$: Show $A \vdash \langle \mathcal{E}_I\ e'\ A\ M_I,\ \bot\rangle \sqsubseteq \bot$. This follows directly from the definition of $\sqsubseteq$.
- $e = [\![\mathsf{distrust}\ e']\!]$: Trivial from the definitions.
- $e = const$: Show $A \vdash \langle const, \bot\rangle \sqsubseteq \bot$, which is trivial.

Lemma 4. *If $M_I \circ A \sqsubseteq A_A$ then*

$$A \vdash \langle addr_I\ p\ A\ M_I,\ \bot\rangle \sqsubseteq addr_A\ p\ A_A$$

Proof. By structural induction in p.

- $p = i$: Show $A \vdash \langle A(i), \bot\rangle \sqsubseteq \{i\}$ which follows directly from the definition of $\sqsubseteq$.
- $p = [\![\mathsf{deref}\ p']\!]$: Show $A \vdash \langle \pi_1(M_I(addr_I\ p'\ A\ M_I)), \bot\rangle \sqsubseteq \bigvee A_A(addr_A\ p'\ A_A)$. By induction: $A \vdash \langle addr_I\ p'\ A\ M_I,\ \bot\rangle \sqsubseteq addr_A\ p'\ A_A$. If $addr_A\ p'\ A_A \ = \ \top$ the result is trivial. If $addr_A\ p'\ A_A = s \subseteq I$ then there is an identifier $a_0 \in s$ such that $A(a_0) = addr_I\ p'\ A\ M_I$. Thus $A \vdash M_I(A(a_0)) \sqsubseteq A_A(a_0)$ by the assumption that $M_I \circ A \sqsubseteq A_A$, and via Fact 1 and 2 the result follows.

Lemma 5. *$\mathcal{E}_A$ is monotone in its second argument:*

$$A_A \leq A'_A \ \Rightarrow\ \mathcal{E}_A\ e\ A_A \leq \mathcal{E}_A\ e\ A'_A.$$

Proof. Trivial by structural induction in e.

Lemma 6. *S_A is monotone in its second argument:*

$$A_A \leq A'_A \ \Rightarrow\ S_A\ s\ A_A\ t \leq S_A\ s\ A'_A\ t$$

Proof. By structural induction in s.

Proof of Proposition 1 (Safety). We want to prove the following: If

$$S_I\ s\ A\ M_I\ t \ = \ M', \ \ M_I \circ A \sqsubseteq A_A, \ \ S_A\ s\ A_A\ t_A \ = \ A'_A \ \ and \ \ t \leq t_A$$

then $M' \circ A \sqsubseteq A'_A$.
The proof is by induction in the number of calls of S_I. We proceed by a case analysis of the syntax of s:

- $s = [\![\mathsf{while}\ e\ \mathsf{do}\ s']\!]$: By Lemma 3, monotonicity of $\mathcal{E}_A$ and Fact 2 we know that $A \vdash \mathcal{E}_I\ e\ A\ M_I \sqsubseteq \mathcal{E}_A\ e\ A_A$.
  If v is false (in the definition of $\mathcal{S}_I$) the result follows from monotonicity.
  Otherwise, let $\langle v, t' \rangle = \mathcal{E}_I\ e\ A\ M_I$, $M'' = \mathcal{S}_I\ s'\ A\ M_I\ (t \vee t')$ and $A''_A = \mathcal{S}_A\ s'\ A_A\ (t_A \vee \mathcal{E}_A\ e\ A_A)$. By the above fact on e we can apply induction and get $M'' \circ A \sqsubseteq A''_A$.
  Now we have $M' = \mathcal{S}_I\ [\![\mathsf{while}\ e\ \mathsf{do}\ s']\!]\ A\ M''\ t$ and

$$A'_A = \mathcal{S}_A\ [\![\mathsf{while}\ e\ \mathsf{do}\ s']\!]\ A_A\ t_A = \mathcal{S}_A\ [\![\mathsf{while}\ e\ \mathsf{do}\ s']\!]\ A''_A\ t_A.$$

  By induction we get $M' \circ A \sqsubseteq A'_A$.
- $s = [\![p := e]\!]$: Let $\langle v, t' \rangle = \mathcal{E}_I\ e\ A\ M_I$, $v_A = \mathcal{E}_A\ e\ A_A$, $a = addr_I\ p\ A\ M_I$ and $a_A = addr_A\ p\ A_A$. We need to show:

$$M_I[\langle v, t \vee t' \rangle / a] \circ A \sqsubseteq asg\ (v_A \vee t_A)\ A_A\ a_A.$$

  If $a_A = \top$ then this follows directly from the definition of asg. Otherwise by Lemma 4 we have $A \vdash \langle a, \bot \rangle \sqsubseteq a_A$, hence there exists an $a_0 \in a_A$ such that $A(a_0) = a$. It is enough to ensure the inequality at a_0 since this is the only point where the left hand side is different from $M_I \circ A$ and asg is clearly monotone in the second argument so by Fact 2 the inequality holds automatically everywhere else. Evaluating we get:

$$(asg\ (v_A \vee t_A)\ A_A\ a_A)(a_0) = (v_A \vee t_A \vee A_A(a_0)).$$

  and

$$(M_I[\langle v, t \vee t' \rangle / a] \circ A)(a_0) = \langle v, t \vee t' \rangle.$$

  By Lemma 3 we know that $A \vdash \langle v, t' \rangle \sqsubseteq v_A$. All that remains to show is: $A \vdash \langle v, t \vee t' \rangle \sqsubseteq v_A \vee t_A \vee A_A(a_0)$ which follows from Fact 1.
- $s = [\![s_1; s_2]\!]$: This case follows immediately by two applications of induction.

B Safety of Constraint Generation

Lemma 7 Addresses. *If m is a coherent model, $m(G) = \bot$ and $A_A \sqsubseteq m$ then these two implications hold:*

$$a \in addr_A\ p\ A_A \subseteq I \Rightarrow m(a) = m(N(p))$$

and

$$addr_A\ p\ A_A = \top \Rightarrow \top = m(\eta N(p)) \leq m(N(p)).$$

Proof. By structural induction in p.
- $p = i$: $addr_A\ i\ A_A = \{i\}$ and $m(i) = m(N(p)) = m(i)$.
- $p = [\![\mathsf{deref}\ p']\!]$: Note that $m(N(p')) \leq m(\eta N(p))$. First assume $a \in addr_A\ p\ A_A = \bigvee A_A(addr_A\ p'\ A_A) \subseteq I$. By induction, $b \in addr_A\ p'\ A_A \Rightarrow m(b) = m(N(p'))$. Since m is coherent, $m(\delta b) = m(\delta N(p')) = m(N(p))$. Also, as $A_A \sqsubseteq m$: $m(\delta b) = m(\Delta b) = m(a)$. Combining the equalities we get the desired result.
  Secondly, suppose $\bigvee A_A(addr_A\ p'\ A_A) = \top$. Either $addr_A\ p'\ A_A = \top$ in which case induction yields $\top = m(N(p')) \leq m(\delta N(p')) = m(N(p))$, or there is some $b_0 \in addr_A\ p'\ A_A$ such that $A_A(b_0) = \top$. Since m is a safe approximation of A_A this means $m(b_0) = \top$. By induction $m(b) = m(N(p'))$ for all $b \in addr_A\ p'\ A_A$ so we get $\top = m(b_0) = m(N(p')) \leq m(N(p))$ which is the required result.

Lemma 8 Expressions. *The constraints generated for expressions safely approximate the abstract interpretation of expressions.*
Suppose $\langle c, v\rangle = \mathcal{E}_S\ e$, *$m$ is a coherent model of c*, $A_A \sqsubseteq m$ *and* $a = \mathcal{E}_A\ e\ A_A$ *then the following implications hold:*

$$a = \top \Rightarrow m(v) = \top$$

and

$$a_0 \in a \subseteq I \Rightarrow m(a_0) = m(\delta v).$$

Proof. By structural induction in e.

- $e = i$: $\mathcal{E}_A\ i\ A_A = A_A(i)$ and $\langle c, v\rangle = \langle\emptyset, i\rangle$ by definition. If $A_A(i) = \top$ then $m(i) = m(v) = \top$ as $A_A \sqsubseteq m$. If $a_0 \in A_A(i)$ then $m(\Delta i) = m(\delta i) = m(a_0)$ by the same reason.
- $e = [\![\mathsf{addr}\ i]\!]$: $\langle c, v\rangle = \langle\emptyset, \nabla i\rangle$ and $a = \{i\}$. What is required to prove thus is $m(a_0) = m(\delta v) = m(i)$ for $a_0 \in \{i\}$ which is clear.
- $e = [\![\mathsf{deref}\ p]\!]$: $\langle c, v_p\rangle = \mathcal{E}_S\ p$, $v = \delta v_p$ and $a = \bigvee A_A(\mathcal{E}_A\ p\ A_A)$.
  If $a = \top$ then either $\mathcal{E}_A\ p\ A_A = \top$ and by induction $\top = m(v_p) \leq m(\delta v_p) = m(v)$, or $\mathcal{E}_A\ p\ A_A \subseteq I$ in which case there is some $a_0 \in \mathcal{E}_A\ p\ A_A$ such that $A_A(a_0) = \top$. As $A_A \sqsubseteq m$ this means that $m(a_0) = \top$. By induction $\top = m(a_0) = m(\delta v_p) = m(v)$.
  If $a_0 \in a \subseteq I$ then we must show $m(a_0) = m(\delta v)$. By induction $m(a_0') = m(\delta v_p)$ for all $a_0' \in \mathcal{E}_A\ p\ A_A \subseteq I$. $a_0 = A_A(a_0')$ for some such a_0' thus since $A_A \sqsubseteq m$, $m(\Delta a_0') = m(a_0)$ and since m is coherent:

$$m(a_0') = m(\delta v_p) = m(v) \Rightarrow m(a_0) = m(\delta a_0') = m(\delta v).$$

- $e = [\![e_1 {+} e_2]\!]$: Let $\langle c_1, v_1\rangle = \mathcal{E}_S\ e_1$ and $\langle c_2, v_2\rangle = \mathcal{E}_S\ e_2$. We have $c = c_1 \cup c_2 \cup \{v_1 \leq v, v_2 \leq v\}$ and by induction the implications hold for the two subexpressions. Suppose $a = \top$: This means that $\mathcal{E}_A\ e_j\ A_A = \top$ for some $j \in \{1,2\}$ and by induction this means that $m(v_j) = \top$ and by definition of c we get $m(v) = \top$.
  By strong typing, the abstract value for the expression must be either $\top$ or $\bot$ so this concludes the case.
- $e = [\![\mathsf{trust}\ e']\!]$: We have $a = \bot$ so the implications hold vacuously.
- $e = [\![\mathsf{distrust}\ e']\!]$: We have $a = \top$ and $c = \{\top \leq v\}$ hence $m(v) = \top$ as required.
- $e = \mathit{const}$: We have $a = \bot$ so the implications hold vacuously.

Proof of Proposition 2. We want to prove the following: If

$$\langle c, v\rangle = \mathcal{S}_S\ s, \tag{1}$$
$$m \models c, \text{ and } m \text{ is coherent} \tag{2}$$
$$A_A \sqsubseteq m, \tag{3}$$
$$\forall x \in v : t \leq m(x), \tag{4}$$
$$A_A' = \mathcal{S}_A\ s\ A_A\ t \tag{5}$$

then $A_A' \sqsubseteq m$.
We proceed by induction in the number of calls to $\mathcal{S}_A$. If $m(G) = \top$ then the final inequality holds regardless of A_A', so assume $m(G) = \bot$. A case analysis follows:

- $s = [\![\mathsf{while}\ e\ \mathsf{do}\ s']\!]$: Let $\langle c_e, v_e \rangle = \mathcal{E}_S\ e$ and $\langle c_s, v_s \rangle = \mathcal{S}_S\ s'$. By definition of c: $x \in v_s \Rightarrow m(v_e) \leq m(x)$ and by Lemma 8 $\mathcal{E}_A\ e\ A_A = \top \Rightarrow m(v_e) = \top$ thus by (4) $\forall x \in v_s : t \vee \mathcal{E}_A\ e\ A_A \leq m(x)$. We can now apply induction on s' and get $A'_A = \mathcal{S}_A\ s'\ A_A\ (t \vee \mathcal{E}_A\ e\ A_A) \sqsubseteq m$. If this is the same as A_A we are done. Otherwise we apply induction once more and get the result.
- $s = [\![p\ := \ e]\!]$: If $addr_A\ p\ A_A = \top$ then by Lemma 7, $\top = m(\eta N(p)) \leq m(G)$ so in that case $A'_A \sqsubseteq m$ by definition of $\sqsubseteq$.
  Now suppose $a_0 \in a = addr_A\ p\ A_A \subseteq I$. A'_A differs from A_A only on the set a by definition of *asg*. Let $\langle c_e, v_e \rangle = \mathcal{E}_S\ e$ and $a_e = \mathcal{E}_A\ e\ A_A$.
  If $A'_A(a_0) = t \vee A_A(a_0) \vee a_e = \top$ we must show $m(a_0) = \top$. By (4) $t \leq m(N(p)) = m(a_0)$ where that last equality comes from Lemma 7. By (3) $A_A(a_0) = \top \Rightarrow m(a_0) = \top$. By Lemma 8 $a_e = \top \Rightarrow m(v_e) = \top$, and by definition of c, $m(v_e) \leq m(v) = m(N(p)) = m(a_0)$, using Lemma 7 last. For $A'_A(a_0)$ to be $\top$ at least one of the parts of the above disjunction must be $\top$ (by definition of the Val_A lattice) and by the inequalities, $m(a_0) = \top$ in all cases.
  If $A'_A(a_0) = t \vee A_A(a_0) \vee a_e \subseteq I$ then we must show that $a' \in A'_A(a_0) \Rightarrow m(\Delta a_0) = m(a')$. a' cannot belong to t as $t \in Tr$. If $a' \in A_A(a_0)$ then (3) secures the result. Otherwise, if $a' \in a_e$ then by Lemma 8 $m(a') = m(\delta v_e) = m(\delta N(p))$ where the last equality stems from the definition of c. By Lemma 7 and coherence $m(\delta N(p)) = m(\delta a_0) = m(\Delta a_0)$.
- $s = [\![s_1; s_2]\!]$: Let $A''_A = \mathcal{S}_A\ s_1\ A_A\ t$ and $\langle c_1, v_1 \rangle = \mathcal{S}_S\ s_1$. Now $c_1 \subseteq c$ and $v_1 \subseteq v$ by definition of $\mathcal{S}_S$, so by induction we get $A''_A \sqsubseteq m$. With this and equivalent considerations as above we can apply induction to A''_A and s_2 and get $A'_A \sqsubseteq m$ as required.

References

1. CERT Advisory 94:12 Sendmail Vulnerability. Technical report, CERT, 1994. URL: ftp://ftp.cert.org/.
2. P. Cousot and R. Cousot. Abstract Interpretation: A Unified Lattice Model for Static Analysis of Programs by Construction or Approximation of Fixpoints. In *Conference Proceedings of the Fourth ACM Symposium on Principles of Programming Languages*, pages 238–252, Los Angeles, January 1977.
3. D. E. Denning. A Lattice Model of Secure Information Flow. *Communications of the ACM*, 19(5):236–242, May 1976.
4. D. E. Denning and P. J. Denning. Certifications of Programs for Secure Information Flow. *Communications of the ACM*, 20(7):504–512, July 1977.
5. N. Heintze. Set-Based Analysis of ML Programs. Technical Report CMU-CS-93-193, CMU School of Computer Science, 1993. URL: ftp://reports.adm.cs.cmu.edu/usr/anon/1993/CMU-CS-93-193.ps.
6. F. Henglein and C. Mossin. Polymorphic Binding-Time Analysis. In D. Sannella, editor, *Proceedings of the 1994 European Symposium on Programming (ESOP'94)*, volume 788 of LNCS, pages 287–301. Springer-Verlag, April 1994.
7. J. L. Knudsen, M. Löfgren, O. L. Madsen, and B. Magnusson. *Object Oriented Environments: The Mjølner Approach*. Prentice-Hall, 1993. ISBN 0-13-009291-6.
8. L. Wall and R. L. Schwartz. *Programming Perl*. O'Reilly and Associates, 1991.

Static and Dynamic Processor Allocation for Higher-Order Concurrent Languages*

Hanne Riis Nielson, Flemming Nielson

Computer Science Department, Aarhus University, Denmark.

e-mail:{hrnielson,fnielson}@daimi.aau.dk

Abstract. Starting from the process algebra for Concurrent ML we develop two program analyses that facilitate the intelligent placement of processes on processors. Both analyses are obtained by augmenting an inference system for counting the number of channels created, the number of input and output operations performed, and the number of processes spawned by the execution of a Concurrent ML program. One analysis provides information useful for making a static decision about processor allocation; to this end it accumulates the communication cost for all processes with the same label. The other analysis provides information useful for making a dynamic decision about processor allocation; to this end it determines the maximum communication cost among processes with the same label. We prove the soundness of the inference system and the two analyses and demonstrate how to implement them; the latter amounts to transforming the syntax-directed inference problems to instances of syntax-free equation solving problems.

1 Introduction

Higher-order concurrent languages as CML [15] and FACILE [5] offer primitives for the dynamic creation of processes and channels. A distributed implementation of these languages immediately raises the problem of processor allocation. The efficiency of the implementation will depend upon how well the *network configuration* matches the *communication topology* of the program – and here it is important which processes reside on which processors. When deciding this it will be useful to know:

- Which channels will be used by the process for input and output operations and how many times will the operations be performed?

*The full paper appears as DAIMI-PB 483 and electronic copies are obtainable via `http://www.daimi.aau.dk/~bra8130/LOMAPS.html` using WWW.

- Which channels and processes will be created by the process and how many instances will be generated?

As an example, two processes that frequently communicate with one another should be allocated on processors in the network so as to ensure a low communication overhead.

In CML and FACILE processes and channels are created dynamically and this leads to a distinction between two different processor allocation schemes:

- *Static processor allocation*: At compile-time it is decided where all instances of a process will reside at run-time.
- *Dynamic processor allocation*: At run-time it is decided where the individual instances of a process will reside.

The first scheme is the simpler one and it is used in the current distributed implementation of FACILE; finer grain control over parallelism may be achieved using the second scheme [17].

What has been accomplished. In this paper we present *analyses providing information for static and dynamic processor allocation* of CML programs. We shall follow the approach of [12] and develop the analyses in two stages. In the *first stage* we extract the communication behaviour of the CML program following [12] that develops a type and behaviour inference system for expressing the communication capabilities of programs in CML. As was already indicated in [11] the behaviours may be regarded as terms in a process algebra (like CCS or CSP); however the process algebra of behaviours is specifically designed so as to capture those aspects of communication that are relevant for the efficient implementation of programs in CML.

In the *second stage* we then analyse the behaviours so as to obtain information for static and dynamic processor allocation. To prepare for this we first develop an analysis that uses simple ideas from abstract interpretation to count for *each behaviour* the number of channels created, the number of input and output operations performed and the number of processes spawned. To provide information for static and dynamic processor allocation we then differentiate the information with respect to *labels* associated with the `fork` operations of the CML program; these labels will identify all instances of a given process and *for each label* we count the number of channels created, the number of input and output operations performed and the number of processes spawned. The central observation is now that for the *static* allocation scheme we *accumulate* the requirements of the individual instances whereas for the *dynamic* allocation scheme we take the *maximum* of the individual instance requirements.

Comparison with other work. First we want to stress that our approach to processor allocation is that of *static program analysis* rather than, say, heuristics based on profiling as is often found in the literature on implementation of concurrent languages.

In the literature there are only few program analyses for combined functional and concurrent languages. An extension of SML with Linda communication primitives is studied in [3] and, based on the corresponding process algebra, an analysis is presented that provides useful information for the placement of processes on a finite number of processors. A functional language with communication via shared variables is studied in [8] and its communication patterns are analysed, again with the goal of producing useful information for processor (and storage) allocation. Also a couple of program analyses have been developed for concurrent languages with an imperative facet. The papers [4, 7, 14] all present reachability analyses for concurrent programs with a statically determined communication topology; only [14] shows how this restriction can be lifted to allow communication in the style of the π-calculus. Finally, [10] presents an analysis determining the number of communications on each channel connecting two processes in a CSP-like language.

2 Behaviours

Full details of the syntax of CML are not necessary for the developments of the present paper. It will suffice to introduce a running example and to use it to motivate the process algebra of CML.

Example 2.1 Suppose we want to define a program `pipe [f1,f2,f3] in out` that constructs a pipeline of processes: the sequence of inputs is taken over channel `in`, the sequence of outputs is produced over channel `out` and the functions `f1`, `f2`, `f3` (and the identity function `id` defined by `fn x => x`) are applied in turn. To achieve concurrency we want separate processes for each of the functions `f1`, `f2`, `f3` (and `id`). This system might be depicted graphically as follows:

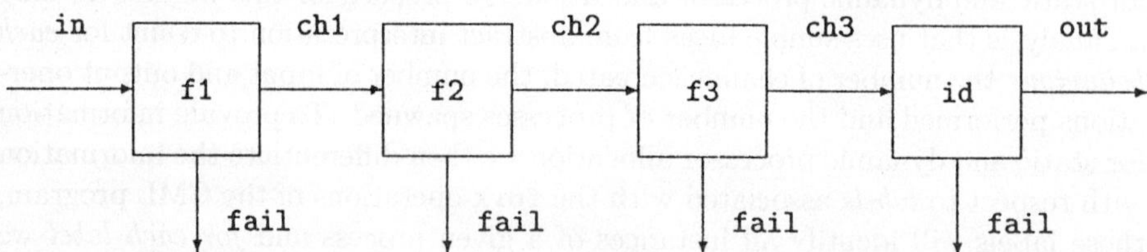

Here `ch1`, `ch2`, and `ch3` are new internal channels for interconnecting the processes; and `fail` is a channel over which failure of operation may be reported.

Taking the second process as an example it may be created by the CML expression `node f2 ch1 ch2` where the function `node` is given by

```
fn f => fn in => fn out =>
fork_π (rec loop d =>
          sync (choose [wrap (receive in,
                                        fn x => sync (send (out, f x));
```

```
                                loop d),
                    send(fail,())]))
```

Here `f` is the function to be applied, `in` is the input channel and `out` is the output channel. The function $\texttt{fork}_\pi$ creates a new process labelled π that performs as described by the recursive function `loop` that takes the dummy parameter `d`. In each recursive call the function may either report failure by `send(fail,())` or it may perform one step of the processing: receive the input by means of `receive in`, take the value `x` received and transmit the modified value `f x` by means of `send(out,f x)` after which the process repeats itself by means of `loop d`. The primitive `choose` allows to perform an unspecified choice between the two communication possibilities and `wrap` allows to modify a communication by postprocessing the value received or transmitted. The `sync` primitive enforces synchronisation at the right points and we refer to [15] for a discussion of the language design issues involved in this; once we have arrived at the process algebra such considerations will be of little importance to us.

The overall construction of the network of processes is then the task of the `pipe` function defined by

```
rec pipe fs => fn in => fn out =>
if isnil fs
then node (fn x => x) in out
else let ch = channel ()
     in (node (hd fs) in ch; pipe (tl fs) ch out)
```

Here `fs` is the list of functions to be applied, `in` is the input channel, and `out` is the output channel. If the list of functions is empty we connect `in` and `out` by means of a process that applies the identity function; otherwise we create a new internal channel by means of `channel ()` and then we create the process for the first function in the list and then recurse on the remainder of the list. □

The process algebra of CML [12] allows to give succinct representations of the communications taking place in CML programs. The terms of the process algebra are called *behaviours*, denoted $b \in \mathbf{Beh}$, and are given by

$$b \quad ::= \quad \epsilon \mid L!t \mid L?t \mid t \text{ CHAN}_L \mid \beta \mid \text{FORK}_L\ b \mid b_1; b_2 \mid b_1 + b_2 \mid \text{REC}\beta.\, b$$

where $L \subseteq$ **Labels** is a non-empty and finite set of program labels. The behaviour ϵ is associated with the pure functional computations of CML. The behaviours $L!t$ and $L?t$ are associated with sending and receiving values of type t over channels with label in L, the behaviour t CHAN_L is associated with creating a new channel with label in L and over which values of type t can be communicated, and the behaviour $\text{FORK}_L\ b$ is associated with creating a new process with behaviour b and with label in L. Together these behaviours constitute the *atomic behaviours*, denoted $p \in \mathbf{ABeh}$, as may be expressed by setting

$$p \quad ::= \quad \epsilon \mid L!t \mid L?t \mid t \text{ CHAN}_L \mid \text{FORK}_L\ b$$

Finally, behaviours may be composed by sequencing (as in $b_1; b_2$) and internal choice (as in $b_1 + b_2$) and we use *behaviour variables* together with an explicit REC construct to express recursive behaviours.

The structure of the types, denoted $t \in \mathbf{Typ}$, shall be of little concern to us in this paper and we shall therefore leave it mostly unspecified (but see [12]); however, we need to state that $\alpha\ \mathtt{chan}_L$ is the type of a channel with label in L over which elements of type α may be communicated. Since types might conceivably contain behaviours the notion of free variables needs to be replaced by a notion of exposed variables: we shall say that a behaviour variable β is *exposed* in a behaviour b if it has a free occurrence that is not a subterm of any type mentioned in b.

Example 2.2 Assuming that `fail` is a channel of type $\mathtt{unit\ chan}_L$ the type inference system of [12] can be used to prove that `pipe` has type t where

$$t = (\alpha \ \rightarrow^{\beta} \alpha)\ \mathtt{list} \rightarrow^{\epsilon} \alpha\ \mathtt{chan}_{L_1} \rightarrow^{\epsilon} \alpha\ \mathtt{chan}_{L_2} \rightarrow^{b} \mathtt{unit}$$

$$\begin{aligned} b = {} & \text{REC}\beta'.(\text{FORK}_\pi(\text{REC}\beta''.(L_1?\alpha; \epsilon; L_2!\alpha; \beta'' + L!\mathtt{unit})) \\ & +\alpha\ \text{CHAN}_{L_1}; \text{FORK}_\pi(\text{REC}\beta''.(L_1?\alpha; \beta; L_2!\alpha; \beta'' + L!\mathtt{unit})); \beta') \end{aligned}$$

Thus the behaviour expresses directly that the `pipe` function is recursively defined and that it either spawns a single process or creates a channel, spawns a process and recurses. The spawned processes will all be recursive and they will either report failure over a channel in L and terminate, or else input over a channel in L_1, do something (as expressed by ϵ and β), output over a channel in L_2 and recurse. □

The *semantics* of behaviours is defined by a transition relation of the form

$$PB \Longrightarrow^{a}_{ps} PB'$$

where PB and PB' are mappings from process identifiers to *closed* behaviours and the special symbol $\surd$ denoting termination. Furthermore, a is an action that takes place and ps is a list of the processes that take part in the action. The *actions* rather closely correspond to atomic behaviours and are given by

$$a ::= \epsilon \mid L!t?L \mid t\ \text{CHAN}_L \mid \text{FORK}_L\ b$$

If the transition $PB \Longrightarrow^{a}_{ps} PB'$ has $a = \epsilon$ this means that *one* of the behaviours in PB performed some internal computation that *did not* involve communication; in other words it performed the atomic behaviour ϵ. If $a = L!t?L$ this means that *two* disctinct behaviours performed a communication: one performed the atomic behaviour $L!t$ and the other the atomic behaviour $L?t$. Finally if $a = \text{CHAN}_L$ or $a = \text{FORK}_L$ this means that *one* of the behaviours in PB allocated a new channel or forked a new process. Since we have covered all possibilities of atomic behaviours we have also covered all possibilities of actions. We refer to [12] for the precise details of the semantics as these are of little importance for the development of the analyses.

3 Value Spaces

In the analyses we want to predict the number of times certain events may happen. The precision as well as the complexity of the analyses will depend upon how we count so we shall parameterise the formulation of the analyses on our notion of counting.

This amounts to abstracting the non-negative integers **N** by a complete lattice (**Abs**, $\sqsubseteq$). As usual we write $\bot$ for the least element, $\top$ for the greatest element, $\bigsqcup$ and $\sqcup$ for least upper bounds by a function and $\sqcap$ for greatest lower bounds. The abstraction is expressed

$\mathcal{R} : \mathbf{N} \to_m \mathbf{Abs}$ that is strict (has $\mathcal{R}(0) = \bot$) and monotone (has $\mathcal{R}(n_1) \sqsubseteq \mathcal{R}(n_2)$ whenever $n_1 \leq n_2$); hence the ordering on the natural numbers is reflected in the abstract values. Three elements of **Abs** are of particular interest and we shall introduce special syntax for them:

$$\text{O} = \mathcal{R}(0) = \bot \qquad\qquad \text{I} = \mathcal{R}(1) \qquad\qquad \text{M} = \top$$

We cannot expect our notion of counting to be precisely reflected by **Abs**; indeed it is likely that we shall allow to identify for example $\mathcal{R}(2)$ and $\mathcal{R}(3)$ and perhaps even $\mathcal{R}(1)$ and $\mathcal{R}(2)$. However, we shall ensure throughout that no identifications involve $\mathcal{R}(0)$ by demanding that $\mathcal{R}^{-1}(\text{O}) = \{0\}$ so that O really represents "did not happen".

We shall be interested in two binary operations on the non-negative integers. One is the operation of *maximum*: $\max\{n_1, n_2\}$ is the larger of n_1 and n_2. In **Abs** we shall use the binary least upper bound operation to express the maximum operation. Indeed $\mathcal{R}(\max\{n_1, n_2\}) = \mathcal{R}(n_1) \sqcup \mathcal{R}(n_2)$ holds by monotonicity of $\mathcal{R}$ as do the laws $n_1 \sqsubseteq n_1 \sqcup n_2$, $n_2 \sqsubseteq n_1 \sqcup n_2$ and $n \sqcup n = n$. As a consequence $n_1 \sqcup n_2 = \text{O}$ iff both n_1 and n_2 equal O.

The other operation is *addition*: $n_1 + n_2$ is the sum of n_1 and n_2. In **Abs** we shall have to define a function $\oplus$ and demand that (**Abs**, $\oplus$, O) is an Abelian *monoid* with $\oplus$ monotone. This ensures that we have the associative law $n_1 \oplus (n_2 \oplus n_3) = (n_1 \oplus n_2) \oplus n_3$, the absorption laws $n \oplus \text{O} = \text{O} \oplus n = n$, the commutative law $n_1 \oplus n_2 = n_2 \oplus n_1$ and by monotonicity we have also the laws $n_1 \sqsubseteq n_1 \oplus n_2$ and $n_2 \sqsubseteq n_1 \oplus n_2$. As a consequence $n_1 \oplus n_2 = \text{O}$ iff both n_1 and n_2 equal O. To ensure that $\oplus$ models addition on the integers we impose the condition $\forall n_1, n_2.\ \mathcal{R}(n_1 + n_2) \sqsubseteq \mathcal{R}(n_1) \oplus \mathcal{R}(n_2)$ that is common in abstract interpretation.

Definition 3.1 A *value space* is a structure (**Abs**, $\sqsubseteq$, O, I, M, $\oplus$, $\mathcal{R}$) as detailed above. It is an *atomic value space* if I is an atom (that is $\text{O} \sqsubseteq n \sqsubseteq \text{I}$ implies that $\text{O} = n$ or $\text{I} = n$).

Example 3.2 One possibility is to use $\mathbf{A3} = \{\text{O}, \text{I}, \text{M}\}$ and define $\sqsubseteq$ by $\text{O} \sqsubseteq \text{I} \sqsubseteq \text{M}$. The abstraction function $\mathcal{R}$ will then map 0 to O, 1 to I and all other numbers to M. The operations $\sqcup$ and $\oplus$ can then be given by the following tables:

$\sqcup$	O	I	M
O	O	I	M
I	I	I	M
M	M	M	M

$\oplus$	O	I	M
O	O	I	M
I	I	M	M
M	M	M	M

This defines an atomic value space. □

For two value spaces ($\mathbf{Abs}'$, $\sqsubseteq'$, O', I', M', $\oplus'$, $\mathcal{R}'$) and ($\mathbf{Abs}''$, $\sqsubseteq''$, O'', I'', M'', $\oplus''$, $\mathcal{R}''$) we may construct their *cartesian product* ($\mathbf{Abs}$, $\sqsubseteq$, O, I, M, $\oplus$, $\mathcal{R}$) by setting $\mathbf{Abs} = \mathbf{Abs}' \times \mathbf{Abs}''$ and by defining $\sqsubseteq$, O, I, M, $\oplus$ and $\mathcal{R}$ componentwise.

For a value space ($\mathbf{Abs}'$, $\sqsubseteq'$, O', I', M', $\oplus'$, $\mathcal{R}'$) and a non-empty set E of *events* we may construct the *indexed value space* (or function space) ($\mathbf{Abs}$, $\sqsubseteq$, O, I, M, $\oplus$, $\mathcal{R}$) by setting $\mathbf{Abs} = E \to \mathbf{Abs}'$ (the set of total functions from E to $\mathbf{Abs}'$) and by defining $\sqsubseteq$, O, I, M, $\oplus$ and $\mathcal{R}$ componentwise.

4 Counting the Behaviours

For a given behaviour b and value space $\mathbf{Abs}$ we may ask the following four questions:

how many times are channels labelled by L created?

how many times do channels labelled by L participate in input?

how many times do channels labelled by L participate in output?

and how many times are processes labelled by L generated?

To answer these questions we define an inference system with formulae

$$benv \vdash b : A$$

where $\mathbf{LabSet} = \mathcal{P}_f(\mathbf{Labels})$ is the set of finite and non-empty subsets of $\mathbf{Labels}$ and $A \in \mathbf{LabSet} \to_f \mathbf{Abs}$ records the required information.

In this section we shall define the inference system for answering all four questions simultaneously. Hence we let $\mathbf{Abs}$ be the four-fold cartesian product $\mathbf{Ab}^4$ of an atomic value space $\mathbf{Ab}$; we shall leave the formulation parameterised on the choice of $\mathbf{Ab}$ but a useful candidate is the three-element value space $\mathbf{A3}$ of Example 3.2 and this will be the choice in all examples.

The idea is that $A(L) = (n_c, n_i, n_o, n_f)$ means that channels labelled by L are created at most n_c times, that channels labelled by L participate in at most n_i input operations, that channels labelled by L participate in at most n_o output operations, and that processes labelled by L are generated at most n_f times. The behaviour environment $benv$ then associates each behaviour variable with an element of $\mathbf{LabSet} \to_f \mathbf{Abs}$.

The analysis is defined in Table 1. We use [ ] as a shorthand for $\lambda L.(\text{O},\text{O},\text{O},\text{O})$ and $[L \mapsto \vec{n}]$ as a shorthand for $\lambda L'.\left\{ \begin{array}{ll} (\text{O},\text{O},\text{O},\text{O}) & \text{if } L' \neq L \\ \vec{n} & \text{if } L' = L \end{array} \right\}$. Note that I

$$benv \vdash \epsilon : [\,]$$

$$benv \vdash L!t : [L \mapsto (\text{o},\text{o},\text{I},\text{o})] \qquad benv \vdash L?t : [L \mapsto (\text{o},\text{I},\text{o},\text{o})]$$

$$benv \vdash t \text{ CHAN}_L : [L \mapsto (\text{I},\text{o},\text{o},\text{o})] \qquad \frac{benv \vdash b : A}{benv \vdash \text{FORK}_L\ b : [L \mapsto (\text{o},\text{o},\text{o},\text{I})] \oplus A}$$

$$\frac{benv \vdash b_1 : A_1 \quad benv \vdash b_2 : A_2}{benv \vdash b_1; b_2 : A_1 \oplus A_2} \qquad \frac{benv \vdash b_1 : A_1 \quad benv \vdash b_2 : A_2}{benv \vdash b_1 + b_2 : A_1 \sqcup A_2}$$

$$\frac{benv[\beta \mapsto A] \vdash b : A}{benv \vdash \text{REC } \beta.\ b : A} \qquad benv \vdash \beta : A \quad \text{if } benv(\beta) = A$$

Table 1: Analysis of behaviours

denotes the designated "one"-element in each copy of **Ab** since it is the atoms $(\text{I},\text{o},\text{o},\text{o})$, $(\text{o},\text{I},\text{o},\text{o})$, $(\text{o},\text{o},\text{I},\text{o})$, and $(\text{o},\text{o},\text{o},\text{I})$ that are useful for increasing the count. In the rule for FORK_L we are deliberately incorporating the effects of the forked process; to avoid doing so simply remove the "$\oplus A$" component. The rules for sequencing, choice, and behaviour variables are straightforward given the developments of the previous section.

Example 4.1 For the `pipe` function of Examples 2.1 and 2.2 the analysis will give the following information (read "M" as "many"):

L_1: M channels created and M inputs performed
L_2: M outputs performed
L: M outputs performed
π: M processes created

While this is evidently correct it also seems pretty uninformative; yet we shall see that this simple analysis suffices for developing more informative analyses for static and dynamic processor allocation. □

To formally express the correctness of the analysis we need a few definitions. Given a list X of actions define:

$$\text{COUNT}(X) = \lambda L.(CC(X,L), CI(X,L), CO(X,L), CF(X,L))$$

$CC(X,L)$: the number of elements of the form $t \text{ CHAN}_L$ in X,
$CI(X,L)$: the number of elements of the form $L'!t?L$ in X,
$CO(X,L)$: the number of elements of the form $L!t?L'$ in X, and
$CF(X,L)$: the number of elements of the form $\text{FORK}_L\ b$ in X.

The formal version of our explanations above about the intentions with the analysis then amounts to the following soundness result:

Theorem 4.2 If $\emptyset \vdash b : A$ and $[pi_0 \mapsto b] \Longrightarrow^{a_1}_{ps_1} \cdots \Longrightarrow^{a_k}_{ps_k} PB$ then we have

$$\mathcal{E}[\![B : \varpi : \epsilon]\!] = \{\langle\varpi\rangle = [\,]\}$$

$$\mathcal{E}[\![B : \varpi : L!t]\!] = \{\langle\varpi\rangle = [L \mapsto (\text{o},\text{o},\text{I},\text{o})]\}$$

$$\mathcal{E}[\![B : \varpi : L?t]\!] = \{\langle\varpi\rangle = [L \mapsto (\text{o},\text{I},\text{o},\text{o})]\}$$

$$\mathcal{E}[\![B : \varpi : t\ \text{CHAN}_L]\!] = \{\langle\varpi\rangle = [L \mapsto (\text{I},\text{o},\text{o},\text{o})]\}$$

$$\mathcal{E}[\![B : \varpi : \text{FORK}_L\ b]\!] = \{\langle\varpi\rangle = [L \mapsto (\text{o},\text{o},\text{o},\text{I})] \oplus \langle\varpi 1\rangle\} \cup \mathcal{E}[\![B : \varpi 1 : b]\!]$$

$$\mathcal{E}[\![B : \varpi : b_1; b_2]\!] = \{\langle\varpi\rangle = \langle\varpi 1\rangle \oplus \langle\varpi 2\rangle\} \cup \mathcal{E}[\![B : \varpi 1 : b_1]\!] \cup \mathcal{E}[\![B : \varpi 2 : b_2]\!]$$

$$\mathcal{E}[\![B : \varpi : b_1 + b_2]\!] = \{\langle\varpi\rangle = \langle\varpi 1\rangle \sqcup \langle\varpi 2\rangle\} \cup \mathcal{E}[\![B : \varpi 1 : b_1]\!] \cup \mathcal{E}[\![B : \varpi 2 : b_2]\!]$$

$$\mathcal{E}[\![B : \varpi : \beta]\!] = \{\langle\varpi\rangle = \langle\beta\rangle\}$$

$$\mathcal{E}[\![B : \varpi : \text{REC}\ \beta.\ b]\!] = \text{CLOSE}^{\varpi}_{\beta}(\ \{\langle\varpi\rangle = \langle\varpi 1\rangle,\ \langle\varpi\rangle = \langle\beta\rangle\} \cup \mathcal{E}[\![B : \varpi 1 : b]\!]\ )$$

Table 2: Constructing the equation system

$$\mathcal{R}^*(\text{COUNT}[a_1, \cdots, a_k]) \sqsubseteq A.$$

where $\mathcal{R}^*(C)(L) = (\mathcal{R}(c), \mathcal{R}(i), \mathcal{R}(o), \mathcal{R}(f))$ if $C(L) = (c, i, o, f)$. □

5 Implementation

It is well-known that compositional specifications of program analyses (whether as abstract interpretations or annotated type systems) are not the most efficient way of obtaining the actual solutions. We therefore demonstrate how the inference problem may be transformed to an equation solving problem that is independent of the syntax of our process algebra and where standard algorithmic techniques may be applied. This approach also carries over to the inference systems for processor allocation developed subsequently.

The first step is to generate the set of equations. The function $\mathcal{E}$ for generating the equations for the overall behaviour B achieves this by the call $\mathcal{E}[\![B : \varepsilon : b]\!]$ where ε denotes the empty tree-address. In general $B : \varpi : b$ indicates that the subtree of B rooted at ϖ is of the form b and the result of $\mathcal{E}[\![B : \varpi : b]\!]$ is the set of equations produced for b. The formal definition is given in Table 2.

The key idea is that $\mathcal{E}[\![B : \varpi : b]\!]$ operates with *flow variables* of the form $\langle\varpi'\rangle$ and $\langle\beta'\rangle$. We maintain the invariant that all ϖ' occurring in $\mathcal{E}[\![B : \varpi : b]\!]$ are (possibly empty) prolongations of ϖ and that all β' occurring in $\mathcal{E}[\![B : \varpi : b]\!]$ are exposed in b. To maintain this invariant in the case of recursion we define

$$\text{CLOSE}^{\varpi}_{\beta}(\mathbf{E}) = \{\ (L[\langle\varpi\rangle/\langle\beta\rangle] = R[\langle\varpi\rangle/\langle\beta\rangle])\ \mid\ (L = R) \in \mathbf{E}\}.$$

Terms of the equations are formal terms over the flow variables (that range over the complete lattice **LabSet** → **Abs**), the operations ⊕ and ⊔ and the constants (that are elements of the complete lattice **LabSet** $\rightarrow$ **Abs**). Thus all terms are monotonic in their free flow variables. A *solution* to a set **E** of equations is a partial function σ from flow variables to **LabSet** $\rightarrow$ **Abs** such that all flow variables in **E** are in the domain of σ and such that all equations $(L = R)$ of **E** have $\sigma(L) = \sigma(R)$ where σ is extended to formal terms in the obvious way. We write $\sigma \models \mathbf{E}$ whenever this is the case.

Theorem 5.1 $[\,] \vdash b : A$ iff $\exists\sigma.\ \sigma \models \mathcal{E}[\![b : \varepsilon : b]\!]\ \wedge\ \sigma(\langle\varepsilon\rangle) = A$. □

Corollary 5.2 The least (or greatest) A such that $[\,] \vdash b : A$ is $\sigma(\langle\varepsilon\rangle)$ for the least (or greatest) σ such that $\sigma \models \mathcal{E}[\![b : \varepsilon : b]\!]$. □

We have now transformed our inference problem to a form where the standard algorithmic techniques [2, 6, 9, 16] can be exploited.

6 Static Processor Allocation

The idea behind the static processor allocation is that all processes with the *same* label will be placed on the *same* processor and we would therefore like to know what requirements this puts on the processor. To obtain such information we shall extend the simple counting analysis of Section 4 to associate information with the *process labels* mentioned in a given behaviour b. For each process label L_a we therefore ask the four questions of Section 4 accumulating the *total* information for all processes with label L_a: how many times are channels labelled by L created, how many times do channels labelled by L participate in input, how many times do channels labelled by L participate in output, and how many times are processes labelled by L generated?

Example 6.1 Let us return to the `pipe` function of Examples 2.1 and 2.2 and suppose that we want to perform *static processor allocation*. This means that *all* instances of the processes labelled π will reside on the *same* processor. The analysis should therefore estimate the *total* requirements of these processes as follows:

main:	L_1:	M channels created	π:	L_1:	M inputs performed
	π:	M processes created		L_2:	M outputs performed
				L:	M outputs performed

Note that even though each process labelled by π can only communicate once over L we can generate many such processes and their combined behaviour is to communicate many times over L. It follows from this analysis that the main program does not in itself communicate over L_2 or L and that the processes do not by themselves spawn new processes.

Now suppose we have a network of three processors **P1**, **P2** and **P3** such that there are communication links between any pairs of distinct processors. One

$$benv \vdash t \text{ CHAN}_L : [L \mapsto (\text{I}, \text{O}, \text{O}, \text{O})] \ \& \ [\,]$$

$$\frac{benv \vdash b : A \ \& \ P}{benv \vdash \text{FORK}_L \ b : [L \mapsto (\text{O}, \text{O}, \text{O}, \text{I})] \ \& \ ([L \mapsto A] \oplus P)}$$

$$\frac{benv \vdash b_1 : A_1 \ \& \ P_1 \quad benv \vdash b_2 : A_2 \ \& \ P_2}{benv \vdash b_1; b_2 : A_1 \oplus A_2 \ \& \ P_1 \oplus P_2}$$

$$\frac{benv \vdash b_1 : A_1 \ \& \ P_1 \quad benv \vdash b_2 : A_2 \ \& \ P_2}{benv \vdash b_1 + b_2 : A_1 \sqcup A_2 \ \& \ P_1 \sqcup P_2}$$

$$\frac{benv[\beta \mapsto A \ \& \ P] \vdash b : A \ \& \ P}{benv \vdash \text{REC } \beta.\, b : A \ \& \ P}$$

$$benv \vdash \beta : A \ \& \ P \qquad \text{if } benv(\beta) = A \ \& \ P$$

Table 3: Analysis for static process allocation (selected clauses)

way to place our processes is to place the main program on **P1** and all the processes labelled π on **P2**. This requires support for multitasking on **P2** and for multiplexing (over L_1) on **P1** and **P2**. □

The analysis (specified in Table 3) is obtained by modifying the inference system of Section 4 to have formulae

$$benv \vdash b : A \ \& \ P$$

where $A \in \mathbf{LabSet} \rightarrow_f \mathbf{Abs}$ as before and the new ingredient is

$$P : \mathbf{LabSet} \rightarrow_f (\mathbf{LabSet} \rightarrow_f \mathbf{Abs})$$

The idea is that if some process is labelled L_a then $P(L_a)$ describes the *total* requirements of all processes labelled by L_a. The behaviour environment *benv* is an extension of that of Section 4 in that it associates pairs $A \ \& \ P$ with the behaviour variables. Note that in the rule for FORK_L we have removed the "$\oplus A$" component from the local effect; instead it is incorporated in the global effect for L.

To express the correctness of the analysis we need to keep track of the relationship between the process identifiers and the associated labels. So let *penv* be a mapping from process identifiers to elements L_a of **LabSet**. We shall say that *penv* respects the derivation sequence $PB \Longrightarrow^{a_1}_{ps_1} \cdots \Longrightarrow^{a_k}_{ps_k} PB'$ if whenever (a_i, ps_i) have the form $(\text{FORK}_L \ b, (pi_1, pi_2))$ then $penv(pi_2) = L$; this ensures that the newly created process (pi_2) indeed has a label (in L) as reported by the semantics.

We can now redefine the function COUNT of Section 4. Given a list $\mathcal{X}$ of pairs of actions and lists of process identifiers define

$$\text{COUNT}^{penv}(\mathcal{X}) = \lambda L_a.\lambda L.(CC_{L_a}(\mathcal{X}, L), CI_{L_a}(\mathcal{X}, L), CO_{L_a}(\mathcal{X}, L), CF_{L_a}(\mathcal{X}, L))$$

$CC_{L_a}(\mathcal{X}, L)$: the number of elements of the form (t CHAN$_L, pi$) in $\mathcal{X}$ where $penv(pi) = L_a$,

$CI_{L_a}(\mathcal{X}, L)$: the number of elements of the form $(L'!t?L, (pi', pi))$ in $\mathcal{X}$, where $penv(pi) = L_a$,

$CO_{L_a}(\mathcal{X}, L)$: the number of elements of the form $(L!t?L', (pi, pi'))$ in $\mathcal{X}$, where $penv(pi) = L_a$, and

$CF_{L_a}(\mathcal{X}, L)$: the number of elements of the form (FORK$_L b, (pi, pi')$) in $\mathcal{X}$ where $penv(pi) = L_a$.

Soundness of the analysis then amounts to:

Theorem 6.2 Assume that $\emptyset \vdash b : A \;\&\; P$ and $[pi_0 \mapsto b] \Longrightarrow^{a_1}_{ps_1} \cdots \Longrightarrow^{a_k}_{ps_k} PB$ and let $penv$ be a mapping from process identifiers to elements of **LabSet** respecting the above derivation sequence and such that $penv(pi_0) = L_0$. We then have

$$\mathcal{R}^*(\mathrm{COUNT}^{penv}[(a_1, ps_1), \cdots, (a_k, ps_k)]) \sqsubseteq (P \oplus [L_0 \mapsto A])$$

where $\mathcal{R}^*(C)(L_a)(L) = (\mathcal{R}(c), \mathcal{R}(i), \mathcal{R}(o), \mathcal{R}(f))$ if $C(L_a)(L) = (c, i, o, f)$. □

Note that the lefthand side of the inequality counts the number of operations for all processes whose labels is given (by L_a); hence our information is useful for static processor allocation.

To obtain an efficient implementation of the analysis it is once more profitable to generate an equation system. This is hardly any different from the approach of Section 5 except that by now there is even greater scope for decomposing the flow variables into families of flow variables over simpler value spaces.

7 Dynamic Processor Allocation

The idea behind the dynamic processor allocation is that the decision of how to place processes on processors is taken dynamically. Again we will be interested in knowing which requirements this puts on the processor but in contrast to the previous section we are only concerned with a single process rather than all processes with a given label. We shall now modify the analysis of Section 6 to associate *worst-case* information with the *process labels* rather than accumulating the total information. For each process label L_a we therefore ask the four questions of Section 4 taking the *maximum* information over all processes with label L_a: how many times are channels labelled by L created, how many times do channels labelled by L participate in input, how many times do channels labelled by L participate in output, and how many times are processes labelled by L generated?

Example 7.1 Let us return to the `pipe` function of Examples 2.1 and 2.2 and suppose that we want to perform *dynamic processor allocation*. This means that all the processes labelled π *need not* reside on the same processor. The analysis

$$\frac{benv \vdash b : A \ \& \ P}{benv \vdash \text{FORK}_L \ b : [L \mapsto (\text{O},\text{O},\text{O},\text{I})] \ \& \ ([L \mapsto A] \sqcup P)}$$

$$\frac{benv \vdash b_1 : A_1 \ \& \ P_1 \quad benv \vdash b_2 : A_2 \ \& \ P_2}{benv \vdash b_1; b_2 : A_1 \oplus A_2 \ \& \ P_1 \sqcup P_2}$$

$$\frac{benv[\beta \mapsto A] \vdash b : A \ \& \ P}{benv \vdash \text{REC} \ \beta. \ b : A \ \& \ P}$$

$$benv \vdash \beta : A \ \& \ [\,] \qquad \text{if } benv(\beta) = A$$

Table 4: Analysis for dynamic process allocation (selected clauses)

should therefore estimate the *maximal* requirements of the instances of these processes as follows:

main:	L_1:	M channels created	π:	L_1:	M inputs performed
	π:	M processes created		L_2:	M outputs performed
				L:	I output performed

Note that now we do record that each individual process labelled by π actually only communicates over L at most once.

Returning to the processor network of Example 6.1 we may allocate the main program on **P1** and the remaining processes on **P2** and **P3** (and possibly **P1** as well): say `f1` and `f3` on **P2** and `f2` and `id` on **P3**. Facilities for multitasking are needed on **P2** and **P3** and facilities for multiplexing on all of **P1**, **P2** and **P3**.

□

The inference system still has formulae

$$benv \vdash b : A \ \& \ P$$

where A and P are as in Section 6 and now *benv* is as in Section 4: it does not incorporate the P component[1]. Most of the axioms and rules are as in Table 3; the modifications are listed in Table 4.

A difference from Section 6 is that now we need to keep track of the individual process identifiers. We therefore redefine the function COUNT^{penv} as follows:

$$\text{COUNT}^{penv}(\mathcal{X}) = \lambda L_a.\lambda L.((CC_{PI}(\mathcal{X}, L), CI_{PI}(\mathcal{X}, L), CO_{PI}(\mathcal{X}, L), CF_{PI}(\mathcal{X}, L))$$
$$\text{where } PI = penv^{-1}(L_a))$$

[1]It could be as in Section 6 as well because we now combine P components using $\sqcup$ rather than $\oplus$.

$CC_{PI}(\mathcal{X}, L)$: the maximum over all $pi \in PI$ of the number of elements of the form $(t \text{ CHAN}_L, pi)$ in $\mathcal{X}$,

$CI_{PI}(\mathcal{X}, L)$: the maximum over all $pi \in PI$ of the number of elements of the form $(L'!t?L, (pi', pi))$ in $\mathcal{X}$,

$CO_{PI}(\mathcal{X}, L)$: the maximum over all $pi \in PI$ of the number of elements of the form $(L!t?L', (pi, pi'))$ in $\mathcal{X}$, and

$CF_{PI}(\mathcal{X}, L)$: the maximum over all $pi \in PI$ of the number of elements of the form $(\text{FORK}_L b, (pi, pi'))$ in $\mathcal{X}$.

Soundness of the analysis then amounts to:

Theorem 7.2 Assume that $\emptyset \vdash b : A \& P$ and $[pi_0 \mapsto b] \Longrightarrow^{a_1}_{ps_1} \cdots \Longrightarrow^{a_k}_{ps_k} PB$ and let *penv* be a mapping from process identifiers to elements of **LabSet** respecting the above derivation sequence and such that $penv(pi_0) = L_0$. We then have

$$\mathcal{R}^*(\text{COUNT}^{penv}[(a_1, ps_1), \cdots, (a_k, ps_k)]) \sqsubseteq (P \sqcup [L_0 \mapsto A])$$

where $\mathcal{R}^*$ is as in Theorem 6.2. □

Note that the lefthand side of the inequality gives the maximum number of operations over all processes with a given label; hence our information is useful for dynamic processor allocation.

To obtain an efficient implementation of the analysis it is once more profitable to generate an equation system and the remarks at the end of the previous section still apply.

8 Conclusion

The specifications of the analyses for static and dynamic allocation have much in common; the major difference of course being that for static processor allocation we *accumulate* the total numbers whereas for dynamic processor allocation we calculate the *maximum*; a minor difference being that for the static analysis it was crucial to let behaviour environments include the P component whereas for the dynamic analysis this was hardly of any importance.

Acknowledgements. We would like to thank Torben Amtoft for many interesting discussions. This research has been funded in part by the LOMAPS (ESPRIT BRA) and DART (Danish Science Research Council) projects.

References

[1] T.Amtoft, F.Nielson, H.R.Nielson: Type and behaviour reconstruction for higher-order concurrent programs. Manuscript.

[2] J.Cai, R.Paige: Program Derivation by Fixed Point Computation. *Science of Computer Programming* **11**, pp. 197–261, 1989.

[3] R. Cridlig, E.Goubault: Semantics and analysis of Linda-based languages. *Proc. Static Analysis*, Springer Lecture Notes in Computer Science **724**, 1993.

[4] C.E.McDowell: A practical algorithm for static analysis of parallel programs. *Journal of parallel and distributed computing* **6**, 1989.

[5] A.Giacalone, P.Mishra, S.Prasad: Operational and Algebraic Semantics for Facile: a Symmetric Integration of Concurrent and Functional Programming. *Proc. ICALP'90*, Springer Lecture Notes in Computer Science **443**, 1990.

[6] M.S.Hecht: *Flow Analysis of Computer Programs*, North-Holland, 1977.

[7] Y.-C.Hung, G.-H.Chen: Reverse reachability analysis: a new technique for deadlock detection on communicating finite state machines. *Software — Practice and Experience* **23**, 1993.

[8] S.Jagannathan, S.Week: Analysing stores and references in a parallel symbolic language. *Proc. L&FP*, 1994.

[9] M.Jourdan, D.Parigot: Techniques for Improving Grammar Flow Analysis. *Proc. ESOP'90*, Springer Lecture Notes in Computer Science **432**, pp. 240–255, 1990.

[10] N. Mercouroff: An algorithm for analysing communicating processes. *Proc. of MFPS*, Springer Lecture Notes in Computer Science **598**, 1992.

[11] F.Nielson, H.R.Nielson: From CML to Process Algebras. *Proc. CONCUR'93*, Springer Lecture Notes in Computer Science **715**, 1993.

[12] H.R.Nielson, F.Nielson: Higher-Order Concurrent Programs with Finite Communication Topology. *Proc. POPL'94*, pp. 84–97, ACM Press, 1994.

[13] F.Nielson, H.R.Nielson: Constraints for Polymorphic Behaviours for Concurrent ML. *Proc. CCL'94*, Springer Lecture Notes in Computer Science **845**, 1994.

[14] J.H.Reif, S.A.Smolka: Dataflow analysis of distributed communicating processes. *International Journal of Parallel Programs* **19**, 1990.

[15] J.R.Reppy: Concurrent ML: Design, Application and Semantics. Springer Lecture Notes in Computer Science **693**, pp. 165–198, 1993.

[16] R.Tarjan: Iterative Algorithms for Global Flow Analysis. In J.Traub (ed.), *Algorithms and Complexity*, pp. 91–102, Academic Press, 1976.

[17] B.Thomsen. Personal communication, May 1994.

Mechanized inductive proof of properties of a simple code optimizer

Alfons GESER

Universität Passau, Lehrstuhl für Programmiersysteme, D-94030 Passau
Phone: +49 851 509 353, E-mail: geser@fmi.uni-passau.de

Abstract. We demonstrate how mechanical proofs of properties of a simple code generator and a partial evaluator can be done by term rewriting induction. We yield proofs that the code generator is correct and that the partial evaluator produces equivalent, optimal, shorter code. We treat a case of disequations and show how comparisons can be done adequately.

1 Introduction

Although much effort has been devoted to automation of inductive reasoning, only a few trivial theorems can be proven fully automatically. It appears difficult enough to improve effectiveness and to increase the degree of automation of mechanical inductive proving for a strongly restricted domain of application. We restrict ourselves to claims and axioms that are universally quantified equations which can be directed so that they form a term rewriting system. We perform proofs by "implicit induction" [1]. We feed the prover a few lemmas, the way people use e.g. the Boyer/Moore theorem prover [4] very successfully.

The case study we are reporting, is a continuation of work that began in 1987. Rudolf Berghammer, Herbert Ehler, and Hans Zierer (BEZ, for short) gave an algebraic specification, using 59 term rewriting rules, of a code generator and partial evaluator for arithmetic expressions [3]. They proved correctness of the code generator and of the partial evaluator. They encoded parts of the proof such that they could employ RAP [11], a rapid prototyping tool for algebraic specifications. RAP uses a narrowing procedure to perform case analysis, and simplifies intermediate goals by rewriting. As it is not an inductive prover, inductive hypotheses had to be encoded as additional axioms, with the inductive variables as Skolem constants. As a further consequence, case analyses had to be provided explicitly by the user. In spite of these shortcomings, the case study was an obvious success as it illustrated a successful formal proof plan.

This encouraged Heinrich Hußmann, Ulrich Fraus, and the author to develop an inductive prover, TIP [7]. This tool essentially uses the data structures and algorithms RAP uses, and moreover manages inductive hypotheses. This paper is a summary of the author's experience proving BEZ's and two further claims using TIP. The extended system consists of 78 rewrite rules.

2 Related Work

Among the other studies which use algebraic methods to verify code generators, there are to mention: J. Strother Moore's KIT project, a very ambitious formal verification, using the Boyer/Moore prover, of a real life compiler for an abstract machine. William Young proved correctness of the code generator [19]. Compared to the KIT project, our approach is small scale. But it offers more automation as our prover needs no induction hints.

> "The key to the proof (*of the essential lemma for correctness of the code generator – A.G.*) is formulating the induction such that the inductive hypotheses fit together to yield a proof of the theorem for PROG2. Some measure of the complexity of the induction is that the induction hint, given in the form of a definition in the Boyer-Moore logic, has 12 parameters and is over 250 lines long."([19], p. 510)

The "algebraic alternative", surveyed in [16], uses homomorphism properties to guide the correctness proof. We do not follow this peculiar technique as we are interested in inductive proofs in a more general setting.

With the RAP and TIP tools, a number of other medium size case studies have been done, e.g. the formal specification of an industrial 8-bit microprocessor [9] (225 rewrite rules). Christian Rank formalized a code generator from a small functional language to a stack machine [14]. Heinrich Hußmann [13] analyzed the treatment of recursive function definitions, and attacked the problems of partiality and nontermination by a variant of fixed point induction.

3 A Short View to Theory

We assume that the reader is familiar with the essentials of algebraic specification and term rewriting. For surveys see [17] and [5], respectively. We will deal with hierarchical systems of simply typed first-order term rewriting systems.

A *term rewriting system* is a pair (Σ, R) where Σ is a signature (often omitted), and R is any (usually finite) binary relation on terms. The elements of R are called *rewrite rules*, and are written $l \rightarrow r$. The *rewrite relation*, $\rightarrow_R$, is defined as the smallest relation that contains R and is closed under instantiation by substitutions and under contexts. This mirrors the universal quantification of variables and the congruence property, respectively, of the described *semantic equality*, $\leftrightarrow_R^*$, the equivalence closure of $\rightarrow_R$. A term t from which some rewrite step $t \rightarrow_R u$ starts, is called *(R-)reducible*. In this case the subterm of t which is replaced is called the *redex*. If there is a derivation $s \rightarrow_R^* t$ where t is not reducible, then t is called a *normal form* of s.

A term rewriting system R is called *terminating* if no infinite derivation $t_1 \rightarrow_R t_2 \rightarrow_R \ldots$ exists. R is called *confluent* if for all terms s, t, $s \leftrightarrow_R^* t$ implies $s \rightarrow_R^* \leftarrow_R^* t$. That is, in a confluent term rewriting system, two terms are semantically equal only if they can be rewritten to a common descendant term. As it is well-known, for terminating, confluent term rewriting systems semantic equality is decidable: $s \leftrightarrow_R^* t$ if and only if, $R(s) = R(t)$, where $R(s)$ denotes the unique normal form of s. Moreover, confluent rewriting systems guarantee for conservativity of extensions, and so (together with sufficient completeness, see below) for a clean hierarchy of specifications.

3.1 Inductive Theorems

Let us just recall briefly the theory of inductive proving in term rewriting. A term is called *ground* if it contains no variable. A term t is called *ground reducible* if every ground instance of t is reducible. Given a term rewriting system R, an equation $s \equiv t$ is called an *inductive theorem* if $s\sigma \leftrightarrow_R^* t\sigma$ holds for every substitution σ where both $s\sigma$ and $t\sigma$ are ground. A rewrite rule $s \to t$, which is an oriented equation, may likewise be called an inductive theorem. Let π be a position of a function symbol in l'. Then a *critical pair* of $l \to r$ below $l' \to r'$ at position π is, provided it exists, a pair of terms (c, p) if, roughly speaking, $c \leftarrow_{l \to r} t \to_{l' \to r'} p$ is most general (up to renaming of variables) among the forking derivations $\leftarrow_{l \to r} t' \to_{l' \to r'}$ where in t' the redex position of $\to_{l \to r}$ is at position π below the redex position of $\to_{l' \to r'}$. The term t in this derivation is called the *trigger* of the critical pair.

We employ a simplified version of Theorem 1 of Hofbauer/Kutsche to prove by implicit induction that a set H of claims are inductive theorems on a set R of axioms. The clue of the method is that both axioms and inductive claims are viewed as terminating term rewriting rules.

Theorem 1 [12]. *Let R and H be term rewriting systems such that*

1. *$R \cup H$ is terminating,*
2. *the left hand side of each rule in H is ground R-reducible,*
3. *every critical pair (c, p) of rules in R below rules in H satisfies*

$$c \to_{R \cup H}^* \leftarrow_{R \cup H}^* p \; .$$

Then H is a set of inductive theorems.

R may also include some previously proven lemmas. H is during the proof also used as the set of inductive hypotheses. Like in the Knuth/Bendix completion procedure, critical pairs which do not "join" are entered as new members into H.

Laurent Fribourg [8] has observed that condition (3) may be restricted to the set of critical pairs at position π, provided that π is *completely superposable*, i.e. the triggers formed by the critical pairs at π cover all ground instances of the left hand sides of H rules. If there is a completely superposable position then obviously (2) holds as well.

Computing the critical pairs of R rules below H rules is nothing but performing R-narrowing steps on H equations at the left hand side. In effect each serves to establish a *finite case analysis*. We will therefore call a position π in H where a critical pair exists, a *case analysis redex*. Instead of "π is completely superposable" we will rather say that π offers a *complete case analysis.* If a case analysis is not complete, one of the missing cases may yield a counterexample.

In practice, function symbols are partitioned into constructors and evaluators. An evaluator symbol f is called *completely defined* if every term of the form $f(c_1, \ldots, c_n)$ where each c_i is a ground constructor term, is reducible. This property can be checked statically. If every evaluator is completely defined and no constructor term is reducible then *innermost* case analysis redexes are always completely superposable. Otherwise, we have to check on the spot that the respective case analysis is complete.

Typing takes care for the notion of a correctly typed term. One may commonly ignore typing information. However we wish to stress that ground reducibility and complete definedness mark an important exception. Obviously one would like to prove $x + y = y + x$ for all ground terms x, y of type `Nat`, but not for ground terms of other sorts, as e.g. `Stack`. In view of this, ground reducibility should not require $\texttt{empty} + \texttt{push}(0, \texttt{empty})$ to be reducible. For space reasons we do not develop theory for this question; we only take care that we get reducibility of *correctly typed* ground terms, which we feel should work. A point in favour of our conjecture is that complete definedness for correctly typed ground terms, together with termination, entails *sufficient completeness.*

3.2 Comparisons and Bi-rewriting

It is the common policy of the algebraic specification community to express every predicate other than equality by a Boolean valued function. While this encoding keeps the approach simple, it turns out very ineffective for the case of *transitive* binary relations. The basic idea behind the "bi-rewriting" approach of Jorge Levy and Jaume Agustí [15] is now to treat orders analogous to equality. Leo Bachmair and Harald Ganzinger extended it to the case of clausal reasoning [2].

An order $\leq$ is axiomatized by two sets, L and R, of term rewriting rules. The first, L, defines rewrite steps $s \rightarrow_L t$, such that $s \leq t$ holds. R, dually, defines rewrite steps $s \rightarrow_R t$ such that $s \geq t$ holds. Here we abuse notation: There may be function symbols in the signature which are interpreted as non-monotonic functions. Hence $\rightarrow_L$ and $\rightarrow_R$ need not be closed under contexts, and so are no proper rewrite relations. We define $\rightarrow_L$ and $\rightarrow_R$ to be the closure of L and R, respectively, under substitution (only). Rewrite steps thus may only be applied at the top of a term. To take into account equality, a congruence, we consider a third rewrite system, S, where $\rightarrow_S$ denotes the closure under contexts and substitution of S, as usual. So $\leq =_{\text{def}} (\rightarrow_L \cup \leftarrow_R \cup \leftrightarrow_S)^*$.

In practice a formal comparison of two terms, s and t, proceeds as follows. Term s is rewritten using L and S rules, and t is rewritten using R and S rules, to a common term. The name L is chosen to indicate that L rules may be applied only at the left hand side of a goal $s \leq t$. This rewriting process terminates if $\rightarrow_L \cup \rightarrow_R \cup \rightarrow_S$ is wellfounded.

This leads to a straightforward extension of theorem 1 towards comparisons. To this end, let the set of axioms and the set of claims each be partitioned into three subsets, indexed by L, R, and S, respectively.

Theorem 2 Bi-rewriting induction. *Let A_L, A_R, A_S, H_L, H_R, and H_S be term rewriting systems, and let $L =_{\text{def}} A_L \cup H_L$, $R =_{\text{def}} A_R \cup H_R$, $S =_{\text{def}} A_S \cup H_S$. Suppose that*

1. $\rightarrow_L \cup \rightarrow_R \cup \rightarrow_S$ *is wellfounded,*
2. *the left hand side of each rule in $H_L \cup H_R \cup H_S$ is ground A_S-reducible,*
3. *every critical pair (c, p) of rules in A_S below rules in H_S satisfies*

$$c \rightarrow_S^* \leftarrow_S^* p \ ,$$

4. *every critical pair (c, p) of rules in A_S below rules in H_L, and every critical pair (p, c) of rules in A_S below rules in H_R satisfies*

$$c \, (\rightarrow_S \cup \rightarrow_L)^* (\leftarrow_S \cup \leftarrow_R)^* \, p \ ,$$

Then H_S is a set of inductive theorems, and $s\sigma \, (\leftrightarrow_S \cup \rightarrow_L \cup \leftarrow_R)^* \, t\sigma$ holds for all $s \rightarrow t$ in L and all $t \rightarrow s$ in R, and for all substitutions σ where both $s\sigma$ and $t\sigma$ are ground.

We omit the proof.

4 The Specification

Now let us speak shortly about the specification of the code generator and the partial evaluator. We follow closely the specification given by BEZ [3]. Likewise, we use the input language of the specification tools RAP and TIP [6]. For the complete specification text cf. the workshop version [10]. An ASCII file is available, too; see Section 5 for details.

4.1 The Compiler

Assume given a small programming language for arithmetic expressions, by the following context free grammar.

Op ::= "+" | "−" | "*" Expr ::= `Nat` | `Id` | Expr Op Expr

Here `Nat` and `Id` denote the set of natural numbers and of identifiers, respectively. With specifications given for numbers (`NAT`) and identifiers (`ID`), this grammar is easily translated into the a specification module `EXPRESSION` of arithmetic expressions.

Next one specifies an abstract data type module `ENVIRONMENT` for environments, i.e. finite mappings from identifiers to numbers. This gives one the means to speak about *source semantics*, specified formally in the module `SSEMANTICS`. The semantic mapping is specified as a function `func ssem: (Env,Expr)Nat`, by induction on the structure of arithmetic expressions. We take for granted that `NAT` contains definitions for the standard operations + (`add`), − (`sub`), and * (`mult`).

Module INSTRUCTION enumerates the set of instructions to the stack machine. There are instructions to push a number (NSTORE(n)) or to push the value of an identifier (ISTORE(i)), and one per arithmetic operator (ADD, SUB, MUL), where e.g. ADD replaces the two topmost values on the stack by their sum value.

Stack machine programs, i.e. sequences of instructions, are modelled in module SEQUINSTRUCTION. The module defines constructor functions empty for the empty sequence, prefix for addition of an element to the left, and some evaluator functions, e.g. conc for concatenation. To BEZ's version, we add a function length, to be able to express length decrease in THM4 below, and functions bottom, upper, to obtain the last element of a sequence, and the rest of the sequence, respectively. The latter will be useful at the specification of the partial evaluator.

Then the target semantics TSEMANTICS, i.e. the stack machine interpreter, is modelled, based on a straightforward specification of stacks of natural numbers. The target semantics is given by a function tsem: (Env, SequInstr) Nat, specified using an auxiliary function ts: (Env,SequInstr,Stack)Stack by structural induction on the syntax of the target program.

The compiler module COMPILER introduces a function symbol compile: (Expr) SequInstr by induction on the structure of expressions.

Correctness of the compiler means that under any environment e, the target semantics applied to the compiled source program a yields the same value as the source semantics does. Our correctness claim reads as follows.[1]

(THM1) $\texttt{tsem(e, compile(a))} = \texttt{ssem(e, a)}$.

In subsection 5.1 we report on our TIP proof session for THM1.

4.2 The Partial Evaluator

There is a straightforward idea to partially evaluate target programs. Every pattern of the form

```
prefix(NSTORE(m), prefix(NSTORE(n), prefix(ADD, s)))
```

may be rewritten to the shorter form prefix(add(m, n), s), and likewise for SUB and MUL[2]. Let pev: (SequInstr) SequInstr be the function that iteratively replaces every occurrence of a pattern by its *contractum*. As BEZ mention, there is an obvious first order specification for pev, viz.

(1)

$\forall$ l, s : SequInstr, m, n : Nat.

pev(conc(l, prefix(NSTORE(m), prefix(NSTORE(n), prefix(ADD, s))))) =
pev(conc(l, prefix(NSTORE(add(m, n)), s)))

[1] In order to save space, and to drop information which is redundant for the reader, we will not use full TIP syntax, but a more compact representation.

[2] In their final version, BEZ dropped optimization of SUB and MUL patterns. We stay with their report version.

for ADD, and likewise for SUB and MUL, together with

(2) $\forall$ t : SequInstr. OPTIMAL(t) $\Longrightarrow$ pev(t) = t

where OPTIMAL is a predicate on SequInstr defined by

OPTIMAL(t) $\Longleftrightarrow$
  ($\neg\exists$ l, s : SequInstr, m, n : Nat
    t = conc(l, prefix(NSTORE(m), prefix(NSTORE(n), prefix(ADD, s)))) $\vee$
    t = conc(l, prefix(NSTORE(m), prefix(NSTORE(n), prefix(SUB, s)))) $\vee$
    t = conc(l, prefix(NSTORE(m), prefix(NSTORE(n), prefix(MUL, s)))))

Remark. Indeed pev is specified *uniquely* this way. This is proven by induction on the length of t. As a lemma, one needs to prove that contraction of an optimizable pattern does not destroy any other optimizable pattern.

In spite of the problem of expressiveness, we wish to stay reasoning within the framework of equations and rewriting. Our plan is as follows. We adopt BEZ's "algorithmic specification" of pev, given as a term rewriting system in module PARTEVAL. Then we prove by that pev satisfies certain equational properties derived from (1) and (2).

pev is based on an auxiliary function, pv. Given a split (l, s) of the target program, pv scans for an occurrence of a pattern at the start of the right half, s. One may distinguish whether the sequence s is too short to have a pattern, or whether it begins with a proper part of the pattern but does not continue accordingly, or whether s indeed begins with the pattern. In the latter case, after contraction of the pattern, one must be aware of a new pattern that is formed using the rightmost instruction of the left half, l.

In [3] the latter axioms have a form that is not satisfactory.

```
pv(postfix(l,x),prefix(NSTORE(m),prefix(NSTORE(n),prefix(ADD,s))))
-> pv(l,prefix(x,prefix(NSTORE(add(m,n)),s)))
```

Their left hand sides violate the constructor discipline: postfix(l,x) should be a constructor term, but postfix is not a constructor. Even worse, confluence does not hold. To fix this, we add access functions bottom and upper to SEQUINSTRUCTION. Then we replace postfix(l,x) by prefix(x',l') on the left hand side, and l by upper(prefix(l',x')) and x by bottom(prefix(l',x')), respectively, on the right hand side. Thus we get:

```
pv(prefix(x',l'),prefix(NSTORE(m),prefix(NSTORE(n),prefix(ADD,s))))
-> pv(upper(prefix(x',l')),
      prefix(bottom(prefix(x',l')),prefix(NSTORE(add(m,n)),s)))
```

Interesting to note, the new rewrite system is still terminating, although a semantic path order is necessary to prove it.

A basic theorem says that the partial evaluator preserves the semantics of a target program. The proof session for this theorem is reported in subsection 5.2.

(THM2) tsem(e, pev(s)) = tsem(e, s)

4.3 More about the Partial Evaluator

If PARTEVAL satisfies (1) and (2), then it satisfies THM2 as an inductive consequence. But THM2 does not imply (1) and (2). It is therefore advisable to prove further properties to increase confidence. We will prove that pev yields optimal instruction sequences, and decreases the length of an instruction sequence.

First we introduce a specification OPTIMALITY for a Boolean valued function optimal: (SequInstr) Bool, whose purpose is to internalize the predicate OPTIMAL.

(3) $\quad \forall$t : SequInstr. $\quad$ optimal(t) = true $\iff$ OPTIMAL(t)

To define optimal by a term rewriting system we borrow the recursive structure from function pv. We should be able to prove the following claim, a consequence of (1), (2), and (3). The proof session is reported in subsection 5.3.

(THM3) $\qquad$ optimal(pev(s)) = true

Still it may be the case that optimal is not the wanted optimality predicate — it might be constantly true, for instance. There is a way to achieve sure knowledge. Show that optimal(s) does not rewrite to true for any s that contains an optimizable pattern. We cannot prove a negation by rewriting, but we can prove that optimal(s) yields false in that case. For the proof session see subsection 5.4.

(OPT)
optimal(conc(t, prefix(NSTORE(m), prefix(NSTORE(n), prefix(ADD, s)))))
= false

In order to derive a disequality, we employ confluence. Our rewriting system is confluent; and by confluence, a term cannot have two distinct normal forms, true and false. So we get

(4) $\quad \forall$ t : SequInstr. $\quad$ optimal(t) = true $\implies$ OPTIMAL(t) ,

which is not yet the characterization (3) that we wanted but sufficient, together with theorem THM3, to imply

$\forall$ t : SequInstr. $\quad$ OPTIMAL(pev(t)) .

Even a function pev that satisfies both THM2 and THM3, may fail to satisfy (2), for it may change an optimal instruction sequence to another optimal one. Such a function may even increase the code size as follows.

```
pev(prefix(ISTORE(i),prefix(NSTORE(3),prefix(MUL,emptysequ)))) =
prefix(ISTORE(i),prefix(ISTORE(i),prefix(ISTORE(i),
                              prefix(ADD,prefix(ADD,emptysequ)))))
```

Regarding this it is interesting to learn that our partial evaluator does not increase code lengths. We report on our experience in subsection 5.5.

(THM4) $\qquad$ length(pev(s)) $\leq$ length(s)

5 Proof Sessions

We used TIP with a peculiar choice of settings. Basically we orient every hypothesis and every lemma from left to right, just as the rewrite rules of the specification. We take care in each case that this orientation preserves termination of the induced rewriting relation. As a consequence, rewriting induction may correctly be applied, i.e. application of an inductive hypothesis needs not to be justified explicitly.

As steps are performed in a terminating way, we may drop some amount of user control. We have achieved good results switching the default "debug" mode off, but switching "interactive" mode on. In effect the user is only asked to select one of the offered case analysis redexes. Experience has shown that the success of a proof attempt strongly depends on the chosen redex position. Although the default *innermost* redex is most convenient, proof attempts using innermost redexes exclusively may fail; see lemma `CRIT` in section 5.2. Usually we succeeded when we chose the *outermost* redex provided that upon inspection the case analysis offered was complete.

The reader is encouraged to redo the sessions. The TIP system and the source text of this case study are available via anonymous FTP from server `forwiss.uni-passau.de` in directory `pub/local/tip`. Put in your home directory a copy of the settings file `tiprc.rewind` and rename it to `.tiprc`, to have TIP do rewriting induction by default. To start TIP, enter the command `tip comp.tip`. After the start, the input file `comp.tip` containing the specification text together with the inductive claims is read, and a check is made for termination and constructor totality.

Below we report how each proof is done in practice. We put stress on the way one is guided to the proof. For an overview of the dependence relation among the lemmas consult figure 1.

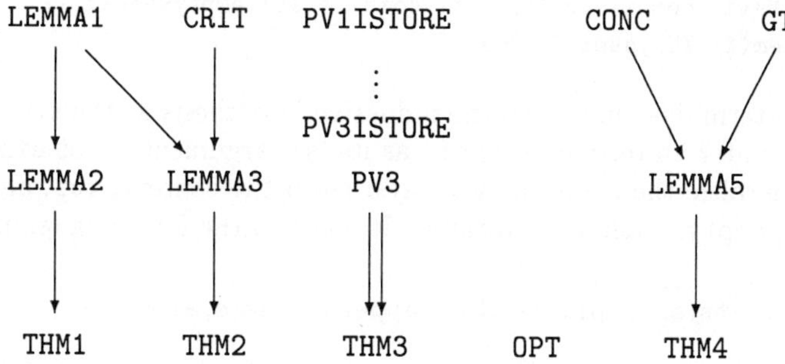

Fig. 1. The Proof Hierarchy

5.1 THM1

Having started TIP, we enter the proof session by typing `prove THM1`, then `go` to switch off the "debug" mode. The TIP system offers a case analysis redex,

```
? POSSIBLE INDUCTION REDEX:
top(ts(X1,compile(X2),emptystack)) = ssem(X1,X2) ,
```

which is acceptable[3]. The next offer shows that the proof is likely not to work.

```
? POSSIBLE INDUCTION REDEX:
top(ts(X1,conc(conc(compile(X5),compile(X6)),prefix(ADD,emptysequ)),
      emptystack))
= add(ssem(X1,X5),ssem(X1,X6))
```

We find ourselves faced with an equation where two `conc` symbols prevent the inductive hypothesis from application. As soon as we try to continue the proof attempt, even more `conc` symbols appear. We better find some lemma to get rid of the `conc` symbols. Now it is human intuition to find out that the execution of a concatenated sequence of instruction leads to the same state as subsequent execution of the parts.

(LEMMA1) $\quad ts(e, conc(s,t), k) = ts(e, t, ts(e, s, k))$

TIP can prove `LEMMA1` automatically. On demand it writes a proof documentation which is boring but fairly readable.

When we try to prove `THM1`, this time assuming `LEMMA1`[4], we are faced with a new problem.

```
? POSSIBLE INDUCTION REDEX:
add(top(pop(ts(X1,compile(X6),ts(X1,compile(X5),emptystack)))),
    top(ts(X1,compile(X6),ts(X1,compile(X5),emptystack))))
= add(ssem(X1,X5),ssem(X1,X6))
```

The inner `ts` term does not fit to the inductive hypothesis as the symbol `top` is missing. The outer `ts` term does not fit as its last argument is not `emptystack`. So let us generalize the claim in two ways: Drop the context, `top`, and replace the subterm, `emptystack`, by a variable. It leads to the following lemma.

(LEMMA2) $\quad ts(e, compile(a), k) = append(ssem(e, a), k)$

It is now straightforward to prove `THM1` by `LEMMA2`, and to prove `LEMMA2` by `LEMMA1`.

---

[3] TIP uses internal variable names of the form `X1`, `X2`, etc.

[4] In TIP, start a new session and type `enter lemma /assumed LEMMA1` .

5.2 THM2

Trying to prove claim THM2 without any lemma is soon recognized hopeless. The left hand side, l, of pv(l,s) must be generalized. The necessary lemma,

$$\mathtt{tsem}(\mathtt{e}, \mathtt{pv}(\mathtt{l}, \mathtt{s})) = \mathtt{tsem}(\mathtt{e}, \mathtt{conc}(\mathtt{l}, \mathtt{s})) \ ,$$

is slightly more special than BEZ's

(LEMMA3) $$\mathtt{ts}(\mathtt{e}, \mathtt{pv}(\mathtt{l}, \mathtt{s}), \mathtt{k}) = \mathtt{ts}(\mathtt{e}, \mathtt{s}, \mathtt{ts}(\mathtt{e}, \mathtt{l}, \mathtt{k}))$$

But the proofs are essentially the same. So we will stay with LEMMA3. A proof attempt for LEMMA3 unveils at once that LEMMA1 is needed. With LEMMA1 assumed, we arrive at

```
? POSSIBLE INDUCTION REDEX:
ts(X1,prefix(bottom(prefix(X52,X53)),prefix(NSTORE(add(X54,X55)),X56)),
      ts(X1,upper(prefix(X52,X53)),X4))
= ts(X1,X56,append(add(X54,X55),ts(X1,prefix(X52,X53),X4))) ,
```

which shows us that the prover cannot deal appropriately with the theory of bottom and upper. One would like to try with the equality

(CUB) $$\mathtt{conc}(\mathtt{upper}(\mathtt{prefix}(\mathtt{x}, \mathtt{s})), \mathtt{prefix}(\mathtt{bottom}(\mathtt{prefix}(\mathtt{x}, \mathtt{s})), \mathtt{t})) = \mathtt{prefix}(\mathtt{x}, \mathtt{conc}(\mathtt{s}, \mathtt{t})) \ ,$$

which expresses in a general way that conc is left-inverse to (upper, bottom), which split a nonempty sequence. Using CUB in the proof of LEMMA3, however, produces no recognizable effect. The reason is that the symbol conc of the left hand side is unlikely to appear thanks to the presence of LEMMA1 which we introduced for the purpose to get rid of conc symbols. To have CUB working, one has to take the effect of LEMMA1 into account, i.e. one has to compute the critical pair between LEMMA1 and CUB. This yields the following lemma.

(CRIT)
$$\mathtt{ts}(\mathtt{e}, \mathtt{prefix}(\mathtt{bottom}(\mathtt{prefix}(\mathtt{x}, \mathtt{l})), \mathtt{s}), \mathtt{ts}(\mathtt{e}, \mathtt{upper}(\mathtt{prefix}(\mathtt{x}, \mathtt{l})), \mathtt{k})) = \mathtt{ts}(\mathtt{e}, \mathtt{s}, \mathtt{ts}(\mathtt{e}, \mathtt{prefix}(\mathtt{x}, \mathtt{l}), \mathtt{k}))$$

There are two ways to prove CRIT, either as an immediate consequence of CUB and LEMMA1, or without CUB. We find the latter technically more suggestive. For the proof session, we only remark that the first offer for an inductive redex,

```
ts(X1,prefix(bottom(prefix(X8,X9)),X4),
      ts(X1,prefix(X2,upper(prefix(X8,X9))),X5))
= ts(X1,X4,ts(X1,prefix(X2,prefix(X8,X9)),X5)) ,
```

should be rejected. A good reason to do so is the fact that an occurrence of symbol prefix in the second line prevents the inductive hypothesis from being applied, a fact that is not changed when one accepts this offer. CRIT is a witness that the leftmost-innermost redex selection strategy may fail.

5.3 THM3

Unlike previous claims, THM3 is not straightforward to generalize by one proposition. For example, the conjecture that pv turns an optimal left argument into an optimal result, is wrong.

(THM3A) $\texttt{optimal}(\texttt{pv}(\texttt{l},\texttt{s})) = \texttt{optimal}(\texttt{l})$

The TIP prover, running in "debug mode", finds a counterexample for it. In a nutshell, the intermediate claim

```
optimal(conc(l,prefix(ADD,emptysequ))) = optimal(l)
```

turns out not to hold for the case

```
l = prefix(NSTORE(m),prefix(NSTORE(n),emptysequ))  .
```

The optimal instruction sequence l is supplemented to an instruction sequence which is not optimal, such that pv does not take action for it.

The suggestion we finally followed is guided by syntactic considerations. The trial to prove THM3 leads to an infinite sequence of claims whose left hand sides follow the pattern

```
optimal(pv(prefix(ISTORE(i),l),r) .
```

We know that any prefix of the form ISTORE(i) of the left argument of pv cannot be part of an optimizable pattern. In other words, ISTORE(i) may as well be stripped. Indeed it is routine to prove the following lemma.

(PV1ISTORE) $\texttt{optimal}(\texttt{pv}(\texttt{prefix}(\texttt{ISTORE}(\texttt{i}),\texttt{l}),\texttt{r})) = \texttt{optimal}(\texttt{pv}(\texttt{l},\texttt{r}))$

After trying with this lemma, we learn that another pattern occurs,

```
optimal(pv(prefix(ADD,l),r) .
```

Again we prove a lemma, PV1ADD, to express that the first instruction may be stripped.

Repeating this procedure, one can construct a finite set of lemmas PV1ISTORE, PV1ADD, PV1SUB, PV1MUL, PV2ISTORE, PV2ADD, PV2SUB, PV2MUL, PV3ISTORE, PV3 (three NSTORE instructions at the beginning). Each of these lemmas can be proven for itself, and together they allow to prove THM3. The lemmas mirror the case analysis structure of optimal.

5.4 OPT

The optimality proof is comparatively easy. Basically, one should prefer to choose the case analysis redex at the symbol optimal, provided that this yields a complete case analysis. This holds whenever at least three prefix symbols appear at the top of the argument of optimal.

5.5 THM4

Here the main problem is the adequate treatment of the $\leq$ relation on natural numbers. First let us demonstrate that the naive modelling by a Boolean valued function `le` is not satisfying.

Given a rewriting system for `le` on the naturals, let us attempt to prove the following claim.

(THM4A) $\quad$ `le(length(pev(s)), length(s))` $=$ `true`

During a proof session for THM4A soon problems emerge like those experienced for THM3. It is natural to try the same methods to solve them. One may prove lemma LE1ISTORE for instance.

(LE1ISTORE)

`length(pv(prefix(ISTORE(i), l), s))` $=$ `succ(length(pv(l, s)))`

There is, however, no such lemma for the case

```
length(pv(prefix(NSTORE(m),prefix(NSTORE(n),prefix(NSTORE(p),l)),s))
```

as one cannot predict uniformly how many of the NSTORE symbols `pv` will remove. This leaves to say only that the length decreases when the first NSTORE symbol is stripped from the instruction sequence. At the following claim, one may experience why any proof attempt, even supported by all lemmas LE1ISTORE, ..., LE3ISTORE, must fail.

(LEN) $\quad$ `le(length(pv(emptysequ, prefix(NSTORE(m), s))),`
`succ(length(pv(emptysequ, s))))` $=$ `true`

The offer for a case analysis redex

```
? POSSIBLE INDUCTION REDEX:
le(length(pv(emptysequ,prefix(NSTORE(add(X1,X60)),X61))),
   succ(succ(succ(length(pv(emptysequ,X61)))))) = true
```

indicates that two `succ` symbols prevent TIP from applying the inductive hypothesis. Only an application of the transitivity law for `le` is necessary to close the gap. Transitivity of binary Boolean functions however is not supported by rewriting.[5]

As $\leq$ is a transitive relation, we may also try bi-rewriting induction (theorem 2). All rewrite rules treated so far concern the semantic equality, and so are collected in the set A_S. It is easy to see that the sets A_R and H_L contain the only rule `succ(x)` $\rightarrow$ `x` and `length(pev(s))` $\rightarrow$ `length(s)`, respectively. All other sets are empty.

To simulate bi-rewriting in TIP, we add a new rewrite rule for each comparison as if the comparison symbol were the equality symbol. To supervise that L and R rules and hypotheses are applied correctly, we introduce each rule as a lemma, and we switch TIP to

---

[5] It can be expressed as a *conditional* rewriting rule, but conditional rewriting is far less automatable at the moment.

```
set param hypothesis_usage interlr
set param lemma_usage interlr
```

having the effect that before every application of an inductive hypothesis or lemma, the user is asked whether the intended step should take place.

On these grounds, the axiom for ">" is encoded as an unproven lemma GT, succ(x) = x. Likewise the inductive claim THM4 is encoded as length(pev(s)) = length(s). With that we can prove THM4 using the encoding of the following obvious LEMMA5 (in L),

$$\text{(LEMMA5)} \qquad \texttt{length(pv(l, s))} \leq \texttt{length(conc(l, s))} \ .$$

In the same way, we achieved a proof of LEMMA5 by GT where we use the equational lemma (in S)

$$\text{(CONC)} \qquad \texttt{length(conc(s, t))} = \texttt{add(length(s), length(t))} \ .$$

6 Conclusion

We revisited Berghammer, Ehler, and Zierer's study [3] on automated inductive reasoning. Our inductive prover, TIP, set for term rewriting induction, yields complete proofs with a degree of automation of typically $> 98\%$, which is the number of internal steps divided by the total number of steps.

We extended the case study to show how a negative proposition, and how a comparison can be attacked by rewriting induction.

Acknowledgements. Thanks to Rudi Berghammer and Bettina Buth for giving me the opportunity to present my work in Kiel. I am grateful to Gerald Lüttgen for reading and commenting on a preliminary version.

References

1. Leo Bachmair. Proof by consistency in equational theories. In *3rd Proc. IEEE Symp. Logic in Computer Science*, pages 228–233, July 1988.
2. Leo Bachmair and Harald Ganzinger. Rewrite techniques for transitive relations. Technical Report MPI-I-93-249, Max-Planck-Institut für Informatik, Saarbrücken, Germany, November 1993.
3. Rudolf Berghammer, Herbert Ehler, and Hans Zierer. Towards an algebraic specification of code generation. *Science of Computer Programming*, 11:45–63, 1988. Also as technical report TUM-I8707, June, 1987, Technische Universität München, Germany.
4. Robert S. Boyer and J. Strother Moore. *A computational logic handbook.* Academic Press, 1988.
5. Nachum Dershowitz and Jean-Pierre Jouannaud. Rewrite systems. In Jan van Leeuwen, editor, *Handbook of Theoretical Computer Science, Vol. B*, chapter 6, pages 243–320. Elsevier, 1990.
6. Ulrich Fraus. Inductive theorem proving for algebraic specifications — TIP system user's manual. Technical Report MIP-9401, Universität Passau, Germany, February 1994.

7. Ulrich Fraus and Heinrich Hußmann. Term induction proofs by a generalization of narrowing. In C. Rattray and R. G. Clark, editors, *The Unified Computation Laboratory — Unifying Frameworks, Theories and Tools*, Oxford, UK, 1992. Clarendon Press.
8. Laurent Fribourg. A strong restriction of the inductive completion procedure. *J. Symbolic Computation*, 8(3):253–276, September 1989.
9. Alfons Geser. A specification of the intel 8085 microprocessor — a case study. In *[18]*, pages 347–402, 1987.
10. Alfons Geser. Mechanized inductive proof of properties of a simple code optimizer. In Bettina Buth and Rudolf Berghammer, editors, *Systems for Computer-Aided Specification, Development, and Verification.* Technical report 9416, Universität Kiel, Germany, October 1994.
11. Alfons Geser and Heinrich Hußmann. Experiences with the RAP system — a specification interpreter combining term rewriting and resolution. In Bernard Robinet and Reinhard Wilhelm, editors, *2nd European Symposium on Programming*, pages 339–350. Springer LNCS 213, March 1986.
12. Dieter Hofbauer and Ralf-Detlef Kutsche. Proving inductive theorems based on term rewriting systems. In *Proc. Algebraic and Logic Programing*, pages 180–190, Gaußig, Germany, 1988. Springer LNCS 343.
13. Heinrich Hußmann. A case study towards algebraic specification of code generation. In Maurice Nivat, C. Rattray, Teodor Rus, and Giuseppe Scollo, editors, *Algebraic Methodology and Software Technology 91*, Workshops in Computing, pages 254–263. Springer, 1992.
14. Heinrich Hußmann and Christian Rank. Specification and prototyping of a compiler for a small applicative language. In *[18]*, pages 403–418, 1987.
15. J. Levy and J. Agustí. Bi-rewriting, a term rewriting technique for monotonic order relations. In Claude Kirchner, editor, *Int. Conf. Rewriting Techniques and Applications*, pages 17–31. Springer LNCS 690, 1993.
16. Teodor Rus. Algebraic alternative for compiler construction. In *IMA Conf. on the Unified Computation Laboratory*, pages 144–152, Stirling, Scotland, 1990.
17. Martin Wirsing. Algebraic specification. In J. van Leeuwen, editor, *Formal Models and Semantics, Handbook of Theoretical Computer Science, Vol. B.* Elsevier - The MIT Press, 1990.
18. Martin Wirsing and Jan A. Bergstra. *Algebraic methods: Theory, Tools, and Applications.* Springer LNCS 394, June 1987.
19. William D. Young. A mechanically verified code generator. *J. Automated Reasoning*, 5(4):493–518, 1989.

Describing a Signal Analyzer in the Process Algebra PMC – A Case Study

Henrik Reif Andersen and Michael Mendler

Technical University of Denmark, Department of Computer Science, Building 344, DK-2800 Lyngby, Denmark. E-mail: {hra,mvm}@id.dtu.dk

Abstract. In this paper we take a look at real-time systems from an implementation-oriented perspective. We are interested in the formal description of genuinely distributed systems whose correct functional behaviour depends on real-time constraints. The question of how to combine real-time with distributed processing in a clean and satisfactory way is the object of our investigation.

The approach we wish to advance is based on PMC, an asynchronous process algebra with multiple clocks. The keywords here are 'asynchrony' as the essential feature of distributed computation and the notion of a 'clock' as an elementary real-time mechanism. We base the discussion on an actual industrial product: The Brüel & Kjær 2145 Vehicle Signal Analyzer, an instrument for measuring and analyzing noise generated by cars and other machines with rotating objects. We present an extension of PMC by ML-style value passing and demonstrate its use on a simplified version of the Brüel & Kjær Signal Analyzer.

1 Introduction

The initial motivation for the work reported in this paper stems from an industrial case study pursued by the authors in the context of the CoDesign project at the Department of Computer Science of the Technical University of Denmark, Lyngby. The task of this case study is the formal description and rational reconstruction of a commercial real-time measurement instrument, the Brüel & Kjær 2145 Vehicle Signal Analyzer [9]. Brüel & Kjær, an industrial partner associated with the CoDesign project, is a big Danish manufacturer for measurement equipment and the 2145 is one of the most sophisticated of their products. The instrument — in its portable version — looks roughly as shown in Fig. 1. Its main purpose is to measure and analyze the noise produced by rotating mechanical objects such as car engines or turbines. It is applied in quality check and trouble shooting. As indicated in the figure basically two kinds of data are

[0] The first author has been supported by the Danish Technical Research Council and the second author by the Human Capital and Mobility Network EUROFORM.

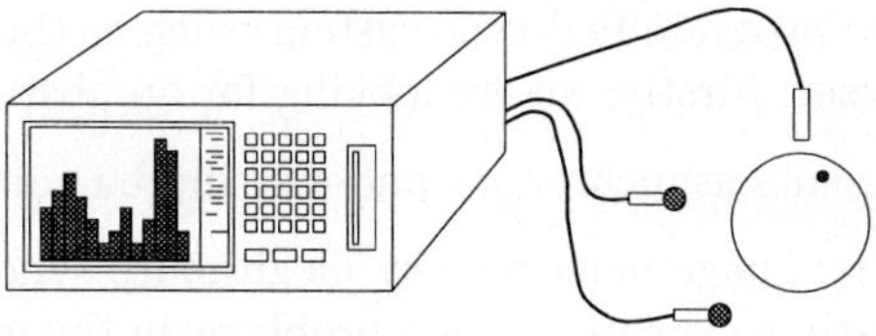

Fig. 1. The Brüel & Kjær 2145 Vehicle Signal Analyzer

processed. The first is tacho information relating to the position, velocity, and acceleration of the rotating object. The second type of information is the sound produced, which is picked up by a number of microphones. The input signals are digitized and undergo fairly involved data processing to extract what is essentially frequency information, but linked up with the rotational data in one way or another.

When one studies the instrument's implementation one recognizes two salient features that must be accounted for by any attempt on a formal description of the instrument. The first is the fact that one is dealing with a truly distributed system, distributed both in terms of hardware as well as in terms of software. Depending on how one counts, one identifies at least four separate and dedicated hardware processors which are independently clocked and which communicate asynchronously. One of these processors runs a real-time operating system which in turn schedules three basic software functions in a quasi-parallel fashion.

The second insight one arrives at rather quickly is that it would be a hopeless undertaking to attempt a precise and complete specification of the instrument's internal timing behaviour. All one can reasonably expect is to capture a few and essential real-time aspects. But what are the essential real-time aspects? Of course, there is the obvious 'What-You-See-Is-What-You-Hear' response time constraint that says that the instrument must be fast enough for the test engineer to be able to relate the display output directly to the noise she or he is hearing. From the users point of view this is certainly a relevant real-time requirement. But there are more subtle and more important real-time constraints relating to the functional correctness of the measurement. In fact, when one talks to the engineers they insist that the main problem they are struggling with is to guarantee internal time consistency: to maintain the original exact time synchrony of the input data within the system, despite the fact that the signals are sampled independently and processed in a distributed fashion, despite the fact that the data split up into different submodules and reconverge later in yet another independently clocked subcomponent; and above all the instrument must be able to measure absolute time with high precision in order to compute the current rotation speed, and relate it to the various signal data for later time-domain processing.

From this discussion we derive two central requirements for a prospective language to describe and program real-time systems such as the Brüel & Kjær 2145 Vehicle Signal Analyzer: Firstly, we are looking for an abstract approach that

- faithfully represents asynchronous and distributed computations.

In other words, our language must not, by illegitimate synchrony assumptions, mask out actual real-time synchronization problems in the implementation. Secondly, in order to master the complexity of the instrument the language

- must not mix up function and quantitative timing unnecessarily.

In other words, we must be able to focus on the essential real-time behaviour and purely functional aspects, and wherever appropriate ignore quantitative timing altogether.

In this paper we wish to put forward the real-time process language PMC [5] which has been conceived to comply with the two requirements above. It is in fact an extreme solution in the sense that in PMC all concurrent computations are asynchronous so that any global synchronization must be specified explicitly by the programmer. Also, PMC takes an extreme stand as regards the second requirement: it focuses on the qualitative aspects of real-time programming and does not attempt to capture quantitative timing, though this could be introduced as a derived concept.

PMC (*Processes with Multiple Clocks*) is an extension of Robin Milner's *Calculus of Communicating Systems* (CCS) by the notion of multiple clocks. Processes in PMC are described by their ability to communicate locally in a handshake fashion and synchronize globally on clocks. Clocks in this context are an elementary mechanism for achieving real-time constraints. They embody an abstract, qualitative, and local notion of time which can be interpreted as referring not only to real hardware clocks as in synchronous circuits, but also to time-out interrupts, global synchronization signals as in MODULA, the ticking of real process time, or the completion signal of a distributed initialization or termination protocol. PMC has a mathematical theory along the lines of CCS; the results obtained concern the formal calculus of PMC, its operational semantics, and complete equational axiomatizations for bisimulation equivalence and observation congruence [4, 3]. In this paper we extend PMC by value-passing using Standard ML [17] and illustrate its application as a programming language on a simplified version of the Brüel & Kjær 2145 Vehicle Signal Analyzer.

As mentioned before PMC is designed for describing truly distributed real-time systems with few but essential real-time constraints. This goal distinguishes it from the usual approaches in the area.

On the one side, PMC does not build in any global synchrony assumption as in the real-time programming languages ESTEREL [7] and LUSTRE [12]. Global synchrony is implicit also in timed process algebras with the so-called *maximal progress property*, which essentially amounts to a globally synchronous, locally asynchronous model of computation. Examples are TPL [14] and TIMED CCS [25]. PMC, in contrast, can deal not only with globally synchronous, locally asynchronous behaviour but also with the more general class of globally asynchronous, locally synchronous behaviour. (A recent proposal for extending ESTEREL to achieve a similar effect can be found in [8].)

On the other side, whereas PMC concentrates on qualitative real-time constraints, the standard pattern of introducing time into process algebras aims at a precise and complete description of a real-time system's quantitative timing. Examples are ATP [21], TIMED CSP [24], BPA$\rho\delta$, and many others [22, 25, 20, 16, 15, 23]. These approaches use a global notion of time and describe the global real-time behaviour of the system quite precisely by inserting explicit delays. This may be necessary in many safety-critical applications, however, for real-time systems such as the Vehicle Signal Analyzer, it is overly realistic, for it implies that rather precise knowledge of the timing behaviour of the implementation is known or assumed; not only for the time-critical parts, but also for the remaining time-irrelevant aspects, which, so we believe, constitute the majority in practice. For instance, in a simple process like

$$P = a;\ b_1;\ \cdots b_n;\ P,$$

which performs an infinite sequence of a actions separated by a sequence of b_i actions, we might want to limit the time between any two a-actions without specifying anything about the intermediate b_i's. The usual formalisms typically require a fixed delay or an interval of delays (as in [16]) to be assigned to each b_i, which means we are imposing unnecessary restrictions on them. In general, this will not be the most helpful solution as it might require almost clairvoyant skills: We must foresee the effects of our compiler and code optimization, have precise knowledge about the properties of our real-time operating system, and finally also of our hardware on which the program eventually is going to run.

2 PMC

In PMC concurrent systems are described by their ability to perform *actions* and synchronize with *clocks*. This dichotomy leads to a notion of transition system which distinguishes between pure action and pure clock transitions. One difference between action and clock transitions is that actions embody local *handshake communication* whereas clocks embody global *broadcast synchronization*. Another is that action transitions are *nondeterministic* in general since they arise from parallel and distributed computations. Clock transitions, in contrast, are *deterministic* since they model the global passage of time. The idea that time passes deterministically is natural and appears to be common in timed process algebras, where it is known as the property of time determinism [22]. PMC was introduced in [5] and its mathematical theory was developed in [4, 3]. In this section we extend PMC by *value-passing* and ML-style *local declarations*, and present a simple operational semantics for *late binding* (see [19]).

As in value-passing CCS [18] we assume a set of process names *Proc*, channel names *Chan* and sets of values $\mathcal{V}$ and value variables *Var*. The semantics we present will be akin to symbolic transition systems [13]. We assume the existence of a *silent* action τ and take the set of *actions* to be $Act =_{\text{def}} \{c? \mid c \in Chan\} \cup \{c!v \mid c \in Chan, v \in \mathcal{V}\} \cup \{\tau\}$. Actions of the form $c?$ are *input actions* and $c!v$ are *output actions.* Note, input actions $c?$ do not carry a concrete value like output actions, they simply represent a commitment to communicate on channel c. This asymmetry between input and output captures the late binding semantics. Finally, in addition to the ordinary actions, PMC assumes a set of *clocks* Clk the elements of which are ranged over by σ.

The syntax of *value expressions* is taken from a subset of Standard ML – roughly the subset characterised by removing exceptions and references leaving us with a side-effect-free functional language. We will not describe this in detail, nor do we get involved with the type system for PMC and the semantics of value expressions. For the purpose of this paper it will be enough simply to refer to a (partial) evaluation relation for expressions. The syntax, type system, and evaluation semantics for expressions may be thought of as being taken over wholesale from Standard ML.

Process terms t are generated by the following grammar:

$$
\begin{aligned}
t ::= {} & \texttt{stop} \\
\mid {} & \alpha; t \\
\mid {} & \texttt{if } e \texttt{ then } t_0 \texttt{ else } t_1 \\
\mid {} & t_0 + t_1 \\
\mid {} & t_0 \parallel t_1 \\
\mid {} & \texttt{restrict } cseq \texttt{ to } t \\
\mid {} & \texttt{timeout } t_0 \texttt{ on } \sigma \texttt{ as } t_1 \\
\mid {} & t \texttt{ allowing } \sigma seq \\
\mid {} & p(eseq) \\
\mid {} & \texttt{let } d \texttt{ in } t \texttt{ end}
\end{aligned}
$$

Roughly, the meaning of the operators, in terms of their ability to perform actions or to take part in clock ticks, is as follows. The process `stop` can do nothing, neither an action nor does it admit any clock to tick. The process $\alpha; t$ performs the prefix α and then behaves as t; it prevents all clocks from ticking, whence it is called 'insistent' prefix. The *prefix* α is either an input, an output or a silent prefix:

$$\alpha ::= c\,?\,x \mid c\,!\,e \mid \tau.$$

The conditional process `if` e `then` t_0 `else` t_1 behaves like t_0 or t_1 depending on the value of the (boolean) expression e. The process $t_0 + t_1$ behaves either as t_0 or t_1, the choice being made by the first action (but *not* by a clock-tick). The concurrent composition $t_0 \parallel t_1$ behaves like t_0 and t_1 executing concurrently, with possible communications. The process `restrict` *cseq* `to` t behaves like t but does not allow input and output actions on any of the channels in $cseq \in Chan^*$. Each one of the processes $t_0 + t_1$, $t_0 \parallel t_1$, and `restrict` *cseq* `to` t takes part in a clock tick by having all of its components t_0, t_1, t take part in it. Finally, `timeout` t_0 `on` σ `as` t_1 behaves like t_0 if an initial action of t_0 is performed or a clock tick different from σ occurs in t_0, however, if σ occurs it behaves like t_1. This timeout operator is inspired by the timeout operator of Nicollin and Sifakis [21] which can be seen as a special case of ours where there is only one clock. The process t `allowing` σseq behaves like t but will take part in any tick from a clock in $\sigma seq \in Clk^*$ without changing state. Process constants can be instantiated as $p(eseq)$ by applying the process name p to a sequence $eseq$ of channel or clock names, or value expressions. The `let` construct introduces local *declarations* like in ML, *i.e.* `let` d `in` t `end` behaves like t in an environment with the binding of identifiers to values, functions and processes as declared by d. We extend the declarations in ML to allow process declarations

$$\texttt{proc}\ p(aseq) = t,$$

where *aseq* is any sequence of channel or clock names, or value variables. Like in Standard ML we use the keyword and to connect mutually recursive declarations. Two syntactic abbreviations will turn out to be useful:

$$\begin{aligned} \texttt{await}\ \sigma;\ t &=_{\text{def}} \texttt{timeout stop on}\ \sigma\ \texttt{as}\ t \\ \alpha\ \texttt{allowing}\ \sigma;\ t &=_{\text{def}} \texttt{let}\ \ \texttt{proc}\ X = \texttt{timeout}\ \alpha;\ t\ \texttt{on}\ \sigma\ \texttt{as}\ X \\ &\qquad\ \texttt{in}\ \ \ X\ \texttt{end} \end{aligned}$$

The first process waits for the clock σ to tick, whereupon it continues as t. The second process is a relaxed prefix, which admits clock σ to tick freely until it performs action α whereupon it continues as t. The `let` construct applies a recursive definition with a fresh process name X, which must not occur free in t.

The semantics of PMC is given as a labelled *transition relation* $\rightarrow$. Labels are taken from the set $\mathcal{L} = Act \cup Clk$. Like in PMC without value-passing [5], a transition with label $l \in \mathcal{L}$ is either a pure action transition, if $l \in Act$, or a pure clock transitions, if $l \in Clk$. The difference is that now actions carry value-passing information, and further that the transitions relates configurations instead of just process terms like in PMC. Configurations are introduced essentially to deal with local declarations `let` d `in` t `end`, *i.e.* with the situation where the processes of a term have different local environments. A *configuration* is either a pair $\langle D, t\rangle$ consisting of a sequence D of declarations and a term t (process or expression), or any of the process operators $op \in \{$`if_then_else_`, $+$, $\|$, `restrict` $\vec{c}$ `to_`, `timeout_on` σ `as_`,`_allowing` $\vec{\sigma}\}$ applied to configurations. For example, $\langle D_0, t_0\rangle \| \langle D_1, t_1\rangle$ and `if` $\langle D, e\rangle$ `then` $\langle D_0, t_0\rangle$ `else` $\langle D_1, t_1\rangle$ are configurations. As usual a configuration will be closed if it contains no free identifiers. We denote the set of configurations by $\mathcal{C}$ and the set of closed configurations by $\mathcal{C}^{cl}$. A *declaration sequence* is a sequence of sets of mutually recursive declarations. In order to handle the late binding of values in input actions we use a special variable name # as a place holder. Let $\mathcal{C}^{\#}$ denote the set of configurations that has at most the free identifier #. Using this notation the transition relation $\rightarrow$ is a subset of $\mathcal{C}^{cl} \times \mathcal{L} \times \mathcal{C}^{\#}$.

We will need to assume that every well-formed syntactic declaration d can be mapped to a sequence of sets of bindings by the map $\hat{}$ as indicated by the following example: If d is

$$\begin{array}{l}\texttt{proc}\ p_1(\vec{x}_1) = t_1\\ \texttt{proc}\ p_2(\vec{x}_2) = t_2\\ \texttt{and}\ \ p_3(\vec{x}_3) = t_3\end{array}$$

then $\hat{d}$ is

$$\{p_2(\vec{x}_2) = t_2,\ p_3(\vec{x}_3) = t_3\}\{p_1(\vec{x}_1) = t_1\},$$

where a sequence is simply constructed by juxtapositioning the elements (using ε for the empty sequence). Hence the first element of the above sequence contains the bindings for p_2 and p_3, the second and last element contains the binding for p_1. Note, in general a declaration sequence D will also contain ordinary ML declarations for constants, functions, *etc.* but since we wish to focus on the PMC-related part, we shall not be bothered by how $\hat{}$ works on pure ML declarations.

For a declaration sequence D we define the partial function of looking up and instantiating the process named p with arguments $\vec{v}$, denoted $D(p)(\vec{v})$, by induction on the length of D: If $D = \varepsilon$, then $D(p)(\vec{v})$ is undefined, otherwise if $D = d\ D'$ we distinguish two cases; if $d = \{p_1(\vec{x}_1) = t_1, \ldots, p_k(\vec{x}_k) = t_k\}$ and $p = p_i$ for some $1 \leq i \leq k$, then $D(p)(\vec{v}) = \langle D, t_i[\vec{v}/\vec{x}_i]\rangle$; otherwise, if $p \neq p_i$ for all $1 \leq i \leq k$ then $D(p)(\vec{v}) = D'(p)(\vec{v})$. Hence, $D(p)(\vec{v})$ gives a configuration consisting of the body of p, where the arguments have been instantiated to $\vec{v}$ and a declaration sequence in which to execute the process.

Our operational semantics is parameterized in the ML evaluation relation $\Rightarrow$, where $\langle D, e\rangle \Rightarrow v$ means that in the environment of declaration sequence D, e evaluates to v. Since expressions do not depend on processes the evaluation may safely ignore any process bindings in D. It will be convenient to extend this relation to channel and clock names by stipulating

$$\langle D, c\rangle \Rightarrow c \qquad\qquad \langle D, \sigma\rangle \Rightarrow \sigma.$$

The transition relation is given by the inductive set of rules shown in Fig. 2.

3 A Signal Analyzer in PMC

We are now going to describe a simplified version of the Brüel & Kjær 2145 in PMC where we focus on some of the essential features of the actual instrument illustrating the use of clocks for the distributed programming of a real-time measurement problem. The main simplification consists in picking out only one measurement mode and trigger condition from the many possibilities available in the Brüel & Kjær 2145.

The simplified 2145 measures the noise produced by a large turbine in the run-up phase and at a certain critical rotation angle. The total result of the measurement shall be the peak value in three pre-defined frequency bands together with the velocities at which the peaks occurred. To solve our measurement problem we use the three basic components, Filter, Evaluation, Tacho, shown in Fig. 3. All three modules correspond to hardware components in the Brüel & Kjær 2145's implementation, and the formal description to follow is a (simplified) abstract view of the actual components' functionality.

$$\langle D,\ c\ ?\ x;\ t\rangle \xrightarrow{c?} \langle D,\ t[\#/x]\rangle \qquad \frac{\langle D,\ e\rangle \Rightarrow v}{\langle D,\ c\ !\ e;\ t\rangle \xrightarrow{c!v} \langle D,\ t\rangle}$$

$$\frac{B \Rightarrow \texttt{true} \quad C_0 \xrightarrow{l} C'}{\texttt{if}\ B\ \texttt{then}\ C_0\ \texttt{else}\ C_1 \xrightarrow{l} C'} \qquad \frac{B \Rightarrow \texttt{false} \quad C_1 \xrightarrow{l} C'}{\texttt{if}\ B\ \texttt{then}\ C_0\ \texttt{else}\ C_1 \xrightarrow{l} C'}$$

$$\frac{C_0 \xrightarrow{\alpha} C'}{C_0 + C_1 \xrightarrow{\alpha} C'} \qquad \frac{C_1 \xrightarrow{\alpha} C'}{C_0 + C_1 \xrightarrow{\alpha} C'} \qquad \frac{C_0 \xrightarrow{\sigma} C_0' \quad C_1 \xrightarrow{\sigma} C_1'}{C_0 + C_1 \xrightarrow{\sigma} C_0' + C_1'}$$

$$\frac{C_0 \xrightarrow{\alpha} C_0'}{C_0 \parallel C_1 \xrightarrow{\alpha} C_0' \parallel C_1} \qquad \frac{C_1 \xrightarrow{\alpha} C_1'}{C_0 \parallel C_1 \xrightarrow{\alpha} C_0 \parallel C_1'}$$

$$\frac{C_0 \xrightarrow{\sigma} C_0' \quad C_1 \xrightarrow{\sigma} C_1'}{C_0 \parallel C_1 \xrightarrow{\sigma} C_0' \parallel C_1'}$$

$$\frac{C_0 \xrightarrow{c?} \langle D_0', t_0'\rangle \qquad C_1 \xrightarrow{c!v} C_1'}{C_0 \parallel C_1 \xrightarrow{\tau} \langle D_0', t_0'[v/\#]\rangle \parallel C_1'} \qquad \frac{C_0 \xrightarrow{c!v} C_0' \qquad C_1 \xrightarrow{c?} \langle D_1', t_1'\rangle}{C_0 \parallel C_1 \xrightarrow{\tau} C_0' \parallel \langle D_1', t_1'[v/\#]\rangle}$$

$$\frac{C \xrightarrow{l} C'}{\texttt{restrict}\ \vec{c}\ \texttt{to}\ C \xrightarrow{l} \texttt{restrict}\ \vec{c}\ \texttt{to}\ C'}\ (l = c?, c!v \text{ implies } c \notin \vec{c})$$

$$\frac{C_0 \xrightarrow{l} C'}{\texttt{timeout}\ C_0\ \texttt{on}\ \sigma\ \texttt{as}\ C_1 \xrightarrow{l} C'}\ (l \neq \sigma) \qquad \texttt{timeout}\ C_0\ \texttt{on}\ \sigma\ \texttt{as}\ C_1 \xrightarrow{\sigma} C_1$$

$$\frac{C \xrightarrow{l} C'}{C\ \texttt{allowing}\ \vec{\sigma} \xrightarrow{l} C'\ \texttt{allowing}\ \vec{\sigma}}\ (l \notin \vec{\sigma}) \qquad C\ \texttt{allowing}\ \vec{\sigma} \xrightarrow{\sigma_i} C\ \texttt{allowing}\ \vec{\sigma}$$

$$\frac{C \xrightarrow{l} C'}{\langle D, p(\vec{e})\rangle \xrightarrow{l} C'}\ (\langle D, e_i\rangle \Rightarrow v_i,\ D(p)(\vec{v}) = C)$$

$$\frac{\langle \hat{d}\, D, t\rangle \xrightarrow{l} C}{\langle D, \texttt{let}\ d\ \texttt{in}\ t\ \texttt{end}\rangle \xrightarrow{l} C} \qquad \frac{op(\langle D, t_1\rangle, \ldots, \langle D, t_n\rangle) \xrightarrow{l} C}{\langle D, op(t_1, \ldots, t_n)\rangle \xrightarrow{l} C}$$

Fig. 2. Action and Clock Progress Rules. Recall that α ranges over actions, σ over clocks, l over both, and finally op over {`if_then_else_`, $+$, $\parallel$, `restrict` $\vec{c}$ `to_`, `timeout_on` σ `as_`, `_allowing` $\vec{\sigma}$} in the last rule.

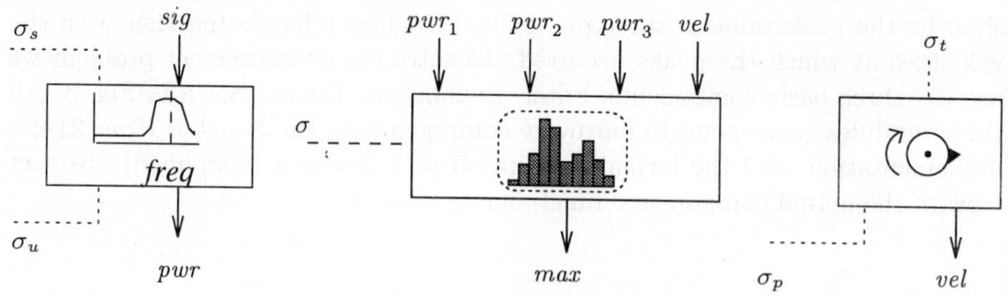

Fig. 3. A Filter, Evaluation, and Tacho Component

The **filter** extracts the average energy of the incoming signal *sig* in a well-defined frequency band, and delivers the square root of this mean value on output *pwr*. There are two clocks associated with the filter characterizing its real-time behaviour. The first one, σ_s is the sampling rate which determines the frequency resolution and the filter's maximal cut-off frequency. In the 2145 this is set at a fixed rate of $65kHz$. The second clock, σ_u, is the update rate on the output side. It is the rate with which the accumulated averaged signal energy is updated on the output to be picked up and evaluated by the system. In general, σ_u may be variable and smaller than the sampling rate depending on the speed of the successive computations or on how fast the frequency information of interest changes over time.

A description of the filter in PMC syntax reads as follows:

```
proc Filter(freq, sig, pwr, σs, σu) =
  restrict r to
    let proc F = await σs; sig ? x; r ? s; r ! filter(freq, x, s); F
        proc R(s, p, o) = timeout
                            timeout
                                  r ? s; R(s, p, o)
                                + r ! s; R(s, p, o)
                                + pwr ! o; R(s, p, o)
                            on σs as R(s, s, o)
                          on σu as R(s, p, p)

    in  R(0, 0, 0) || F allowing σu end
```

The unspecified function *filter*, parametrized by a frequency *freq*, a sample x, and a filter-state s, implements the filtering algorithm. The filter consists of two processes running in parallel and communicating on the internal channel r. The process $R(s,p,o)$ is a register with three state variables, s, p and o. The first component can be set and read along the channel r. The last component holds the current value of the output line of the filter and it can always be read off by the output action *pwr* ! o. At every tick of σ_s the value of s is copied to the second component, and at every tick of σ_u the value of p is copied to the third component becoming the new output of the filter. The register is used by the process F for storing the accumulated mean square of the signal energy. At the beginning of each iteration the process F waits for the next tick of σ_s, reads in the new sample x and retrieves the current value of s from the register. From x and s it computes the new state *filter*$(freq, x, s)$ and updates the register.

The two-phase shifting of states in the register ensures that if a bank of filters is connected to the same σ_s and σ_u, values read from the output lines of different filters between consecutive ticks of σ_u will be consistent. *I.e.* they will be the result of computing the signal energy of the same number of samples. The reader is encouraged to try out a simplified version where the register only contains the state variables s and o and at every tick of σ_u the value of s is copied to o while σ_s is given free by `allowing`. With such filters unsynchronized values can occur: If some of the filters have performed the update of their registers and others not, the values read off are inconsistent.

The **tacho measurement** (the right-hand flow-graph in Fig. 3) computes the current rotation speed from the tacho pulse, which we may view as a variable clock σ_p. To get the velocity from this tacho clock we need to know the amount of time that has passed between any two pulses. This real-time information is implemented by another clock, σ_t, ticking off global system time. In the Brüel & Kjær 2145 this is done by a high-precision free-running timer oscillating at $1MHz$, yielding a $1\mu s$ time resolution. A description of the tacho as a PMC process is as follows:

```
proc Tacho(vel, σp, σt) =
  let proc T(c, e) = timeout
                       timeout
                         vel ! 1/e; T(c, e)
                       on σp as T(0, c)
                     on σt as T(c + 1, e)
  in  T(0, ∞) end
```

The state of the tacho $T(c, e)$ is specified by two parameters. The first one, c, counts the time between pulses, *i.e.* it is incremented with every σ_t and reset with every σ_p tick. The second parameter, e, holds the result count between two pulses; it is updated with σ_p. The current velocity, which is indirectly proportional to the result count can be read at any time with output action *vel* ! $1/e$.

The last module to be specified is the **evaluation** module. A flow-graph for this module is found in Fig. 3. The task of the evaluation is to find the maximum peak energies supplied at its inputs pwr_i, $i = 1, 2, 3$ in the run-up phase of the rotation. The run-up phase is a period of increasing velocity *vel*, beginning with a start value *start* and ending with a pre-defined stop value *stop*. The clock σ serves to separate successive input vectors of synchronous frequency and velocity data. The evaluation module cycles through the states E_{wait}, $E_{comp}\ (m)$, and E_{ready}. In state E_{ready} it is ready to start the next run-up measurement. When the velocity falls below the *start* margin it passes to state E_{wait} where it waits for the velocity to enter the run-up interval [*start*, *stop*]. Then the actual computation state $E_{comp}\ (m)$ is entered. In this state the component reads in consecutive triples of frequency energies from pwr_1, pwr_2, pwr_3 and for each frequency channel memorizes the maximum value found so far along with the corresponding velocity. This computation is done on the state parameter m, a triple of pairs of maximal energies and corresponding speeds, using an appropriate ML function *max*. We use m_0 for the initial value of the state parameter. In concrete terms the PMC description of this process can be given as follows:

```
proc Eval(pwr₁, pwr₂, pwr₃, max, vel, σ) =
    let proc E_wait      = await σ;
                           pwr₁ ? p₁; pwr₂ ? p₂; pwr₃ ? p₃; vel ? x;
                           if x < start then E_wait
                           else E_comp (max (m₀, p₁, p₂, p₃, x))
        and  E_comp (m)  = await σ;
                           pwr₁ ? p₁; pwr₂ ? p₂; pwr₃ ? p₃; vel ? x;
                           if x > stop then
                              max ! m allowing σ;
                              E_ready
                           else
                              E_comp (max (m, p₁, p₂, p₃, x))
        and  E_ready     = await σ;
                           vel ? x;
                           if x < start then E_wait
                           else E_ready
    in E_ready end
```

A few explanations are in order here. The fact that the sequence of input prefixes $pwr_1?p_1$; $pwr_2?p_2$; $pwr_3?p_3$; $vel?x$; blocks clocks is essential for it makes sure that no tick of σ_u can intercept with the reading of the input lines, so that *Eval* obtains a time consistent view of the input. On the other hand, when the velocity has passed the upper margin, $x > stop$, we may safely allow the environment to run on freely until the results of the previous measurement have been picked up at output *max*. When this happens we prepare ourselves for a new measurement in state E_{ready}. This explains the relaxed prefix $max!m$ `allowing` σ; E_{ready}. The final observation made use of in the above formulation is that in state E_{ready}, where we wait for the velocity to fall below the start margin, we do not need to read in the frequency information, therefore the input action $vel?x$ suffices.

With the three components at hand we may now assemble our instrument as shown in Fig. 4. We take a bank of three filters each one tuned at a specific center frequency and have all filters sample the incoming sound signal by the same sampling rate. This ensures that all filters get a *consistent* view of the signal's shape. This is important as any imprecision in the synchronization of the sampling would result in a distortion of the measured results. Further, we

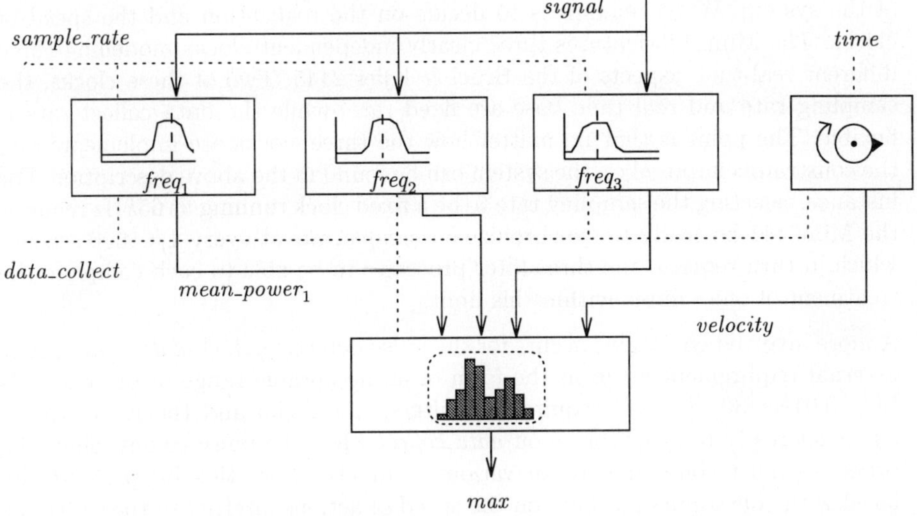

Fig. 4. *Mini2145* – A Simple Version of the 2145 Signal Analyzer

connect the filters' output update rate with the tacho pulse, to obtain a vector of time-synchronous frequency energies and rotation speed relating to a *fixed position* of the rotating turbine. The evaluation module finally uses the velocity to pick out the frequency spectra corresponding to a predefined speed-interval in the run-up phase of the turbine. The PMC description of the overall system is now easily given:

```
proc Mini2145(signal, max, sample_rate, data_collect, time) =
  restrict mean_power1, mean_power2, mean_power3, velocity to

   ( Filter(freq1, signal, mean_power1, sample_rate, data_collect)
   || Filter(freq2, signal, mean_power2, sample_rate, data_collect)
   || Filter(freq3, signal, mean_power3, sample_rate, data_collect)
   ) allowing time

   || Tacho(velocity, data_collect, time)
      allowing sample_rate

   || Eval(mean_power1, mean_power2, mean_power3, max, velocity, data_collect)
      allowing sample_rate, time
```

Although this description contains no explicit timing constraints, it *does* contain all the information necessary to ensure proper functional real-time behaviour of the system. What remains is to decide on the realization and the speed of clocks. The Mini2145 features three clearly independent clocks modelling three different real-time aspects of the Brüel & Kjær 2145. Two of these clocks, the sampling rate and real time base are fixed rate, while the data collect rate is flexible. The point is that no matter how the three clocks are implemented all the constraints imposed on the system can be found in the above description. For instance, selecting the sampling rate to be a fixed clock running at 65kHz requires the Mini2145 be ready to synchronize on *sample_rate* at every 1/65000 second, which in turn requires the three filter processes to be able to each complete the treatment of one sample within this limit.

A more involved constraint occurs for the pulse detecting clock *data_collect*. Any external requirement given in the form of an acceptable range of pulse speeds (*e.g.* 0.01Hz–30kHz) will require the Filters, the Tacho and the Eval process all to get ready to synchronize on *data_collect* when the pulse comes. Since the processes must communicate on various channels before this happens we are faced with constraints not only on the speed of actions internal to the processes but also on the communications between them.

4 Clocks and Real-Time Constraints

Given that the notion of 'clock' features prominently in our approach it is appropriate to be rigorous about our use of the term, and for that matter, about our view of real-time programming.

In fact, to get the right picture of our approach it is important to realize that the term 'clock' in its strict sense does not refer to the chronometer or an absolute notion of time but to the bell, *i.e.* the audible signal by which we tell the hour. The point we wish to make, of course, is that our use of clocks does not formalize the quantitative aspect of real time but rather the qualitative aspect of real-time, *viz.* that of a global synchronization event. There is indeed some risk of confusion as in the literature on timed semantics 'clocks' sometimes are used as a mechanism for measuring absolute quantitative time in order to time-stamp observations. Examples of such uses are the process algebra CIPA [1] and the timed automata of Alur and Dill [2].

Although, at first glance our approach is somewhat akin to having a discrete time-domain, *viz.* using a single clock to tick off intervals of a global and absolute time, the intended interpretation here is more abstract: In general, PMC processes would use a set of unrelated clocks which *a priori* proceed independently. As mentioned in the beginning, in any actual implementation these clocks may have a variety of different realizations: They could be chosen to be real hardware clocks running at fixed speed, or more relaxed clocks with an allowed range of time-intervals between successive ticks. The fixed clocks *sample_rate* and *time* in the Brüel & Kjær 2145 are examples of the first kind, whereas as the pulse *data_collect* is an example of the second kind. However, some clocks may even run entirely independent while others are derived multiples of a distinguished master clock. But not only may the hardware interpretation apply, also software realizations are adequate: a clock may represent a time-out interrupt, a global synchronization signal, or the completion signal of a distributed initialization or termination protocol.

When we say that clocks are a primitive real-time mechanism then we do suggest that they capture certain properties of real time. There is, however, one crucial property not captured by clocks, and this is the ceaseless progress of time. Real time, as it is usually perceived, is an independent physical parameter that cannot be prevented from continuously proceeding towards infinity. This progress of time cannot be modelled by clocks. A clock in PMC is an internal signal which all components of a system are free to block or synchronize on. In other words, a process may produce a *time-lock* preventing a particular clock from ticking ever again. In PMC time-locks indicate the violation of a real-time constraint. If for example the Mini2145 is put in parallel with a process that occassionally gets into a state where it stops sending new samples on the channel *signal*, the filters will stop the clocks *sample_rate* and *data_collect* indefinitely. Another example occurs in synchronous circuits where a time-lock is produced by feed-back loops that do not contain a clocked register [4].

5 Conclusion and Future Work

The ideas put forward in this paper aim at a qualitative approach to real-time programming that focuses on functional correctness and factors out issues like response time, measurement resolution, and calibration. The approach, which is based on PMC and emphasizes the importance of clocks, was illustrated on the Brüel & Kjær 2145 Vehicle Signal Analyzer.

It is worth to be stressed that we do not propose to ignore quantitative timing altogether. As a matter of fact, in our example analyzer we do have, implicitly, constraints on the implementation of clocks. For instance, the time base clock must be a high-precision fixed-frequency oscillator, for otherwise, the actual rotation speed cannot be computed correctly. Also, the sampling rate must be higher than the update rate, *etc.* Clearly, nothing prevents us from specifying timing properties initially as requirements on the clocks and actions of a design but – so is our thesis – ultimately their satisfaction cannot be determined until the final implementation is developed. For instance, determining the actual frequency of the Mini2145's time-base clock and its precision is an issue of calibration not of programming.

Thus, the approach we follow with PMC is to provide a powerful, high-level operational description language for which satisfaction of timing constraints will be determined from the final machine-executable code. It is our hope that by being very careful in the way the compilation is carried out, we shall be able to lift this information to a higher-level to guide the design by providing analysis information. For instance, by compiling parts of the description and estimating the execution time of this partial code information on clocks may be obtained. Hence, the emphasis is on providing information to the programmer and not to require him to perform detailed calculations on timing requirements. Of course, timed automata [2] and temporal logics such as the Duration Calculus [10] are good candidates for expressing timing requirements but we do not want this information to enter the process description.

The timing of code ultimately depends on the choice of the target machine(s); any attempt to estimate the execution times early in the design must rely on a very carefully designed compilation strategy. We believe that any such strategy should be based on a clear operational semantics of the language that reveals in detail the steps that have to be performed and where choices must be made.

For expressing dynamic behaviour PMC uses the basic constructions of Milner's CCS and for computations on values fragments of Standard ML. Of course, there is a tension between having a rich language and being able to derive real-time faithful implementations. We handle this by allowing a rich language that can be useful for initial high-level descriptions and to run simulations, and only give time-respecting implementations for some reasonable subsets of the language – any future advances in compilation technology could then extend these subsets. The design goal in such a framework is to refine a high-level description into one within one of the executable subsets. All this takes place within the *same* language, which makes possible the co-existence and debugging of descriptions containing both low-level and high-level components.

Acknowledgements

Thanks to A.P. Ravn for his many inspiring comments, to Ole Wahlgreen, Klaus Gram Hansen and Ole Roth at Brüel & Kjær for spending their time explaining the 2145 to the authors, to the Backing Group at ID, and to Manfred Broy. Thanks are due to Rocco De Nicola for inviting Michael Mendler to the University of Rome, La Sapienza where part of this work was carried out.

References

1. L. Aceto and D. Murphy. On the ill-timed but well-caused. In E. Best, editor, *Proc. Concur'93*, pages 97–111. Springer LNCS 715, 1993.
2. R. Alur and D. Dill. The theory of timed automata. In de Bakker et al. [11], pages 45–73.
3. H. R. Andersen and M. Mendler. A complete axiomatization of observation congruence in PMC. Technical Report ID-TR:1993-126, Department of Computer Science, Technical University of Denmark, December 1993.
4. H. R. Andersen and M. Mendler. A process algebra with multiple clocks. Technical Report ID-TR:1993-122, Department of Computer Science, Technical University of Denmark, August 1993.

5. H. R. Andersen and M. Mendler. An asynchronous process algebra with multiple clocks. In D. Sannella, editor, *Programming Languages and Systems – ESOP'94*, pages 58–73. Springer, LNCS 788, 1994.
6. J.C.M. Baeten and J.W. Klop, editors. *Proceedings of CONCUR '90*, volume 458 of *LNCS*. Springer-Verlag, 1990.
7. G. Berry and L. Cosserat. The ESTEREL synchronous programming language and its mathematical semantics. In S. D. Brookes, A. W. Roscoe, and G. Winskel, editors, *Seminar on Concurrency*, pages 389–448. Springer LNCS 197, 1984.
8. G. Berry, S. Ramesh, and R.K. Shyamasundar. Communicating reactive processes. In *Principles of Programming Languages POPL'93*, pages 85–98. ACM, 1993.
9. Brüel & Kjær. *Vehicle Signal Analyzer Type 2145, User Manual Vol. 1*, April 1994.
10. Zhou Chaochen, C. A. R. Hoare, and A. P. Ravn. A calculus of durations. *Information Processing Letters*, 40(5):269–276, 1991.
11. J. W. de Bakker, C. Huizing, W. P. de Roever, and G. Rozenberg, editors. *Real-Time: Theory in Practice*, volume 600 of *LNCS*. Springer-Verlag, 1991.
12. N. Halbwachs, D. Pilaud, F. Ouabdesselam, and A.-C. Glory. Specifying, programming and verifying real-time systems using a synchronous declarative language. In *Workshop on automatic verification methods for finite state systems*, Grenoble, France, June 12–14 1989. Springer LNCS 407.
13. M. Hennessy and H. Lin. Symbolic bisimulations. Technical Report 1/92, University of Sussex, April 1992.
14. M. Hennessy and T. Regan. A process algebra for timed systems. Computer Science Technical Report 91:05, Department of Computer Science, University of Sussex, April 1991. To appear in Information and Computation.
15. Jozef Hooman. *Specification and Compositional Verification of Real-Time Systems.* Number 558 in Lecture Notes in Computer Science. Springer-Verlag, 1991.
16. Chen Liang. An interleaving model for real-time systems. Technical Report ECS-LFCS-91-184, Laboratory for Foundations of Computer Science, University of Edinburgh, November 1991.
17. R. Milner, M. Tofte, and R. Harper. *The Definition of Standard ML.* MIT press, 1990.
18. Robin Milner. *Communication and Concurrency.* Prentice Hall, 1989.
19. Robin Milner, Joachim Parrow, and David Walker. Modal logics for mobile processes. Technical Report SICS/R–91/03–SE, Swedish Institute of Computer Science, 1991.
20. Faron Moller and Chris Tofts. A temporal calculus of communicating systems. In Baeten and Klop [6], pages 401–415.
21. X. Nicollin and J. Sifakis. The algebra of timed processes ATP: theory and application. Technical Report RT-C26, LGI-IMAG, Grenoble, France, December 1990.
22. X. Nicollin and J. Sifakis. An overview and synthesis on timed process algebras. In de Bakker et al. [11], pages 526–548.
23. G. Reed and A. Roscoe. A timed model for communicating sequential processes. In Laurent Kott, editor, *Proceedings of the 13'th ICALP*, pages 314–323. Springer, LNCS 226, 1986.
24. S. Schneider, J. Davies, D.M. Jackson, G.M. Reed, J.N. Reed, and A.W. Roscoe. Timed CSP: Theory and practice. In de Bakker et al. [11], pages 526–548.
25. Yi Wang. Real-time behaviour of asynchronous agents. In Baeten and Klop [6].

A Gentle Introduction to Specification Engineering Using a Case Study in Telecommunications*

Stephan Kleuker**
FB Informatik
University of Oldenburg, P.O. Box 2503
26111 Oldenburg, Germany

Abstract

Software development based on formal methods is the only way to provably correct software. Therefore a method for the development of complex systems in intuitive steps is needed. A suitable solution is the transformational approach where verified semantics-preserving transformation rules are used to come from a first verified specification to the desired system. A problem is that for most industrial applications the system development never terminates because requirements change and new functionalities have to be added to the system.

This paper describes a new approach for the development of extensible specifications in small intuitive steps. New transformation rules are introduced that guarantee that intermediate results of development can be used for further steps.

keywords: extensible systems, formal software development, provably correct software

1 Introduction

Telecommunication networks are highly distributed systems, e.g. in Germany the public telecommunications network contains some thousands of switching systems, and they are required to be highly reliable. It is demanded that every switching system has an expected down time of at the most two hours in 20 years.

These switching systems have usually been built starting from some informal requirements that have changed after some time. Today, the only established way of 'proving the correctness' of a system is extensive testing. Exhaustive testing is not possible because of the complexity of software. An approach is needed for extensible, provably correct software which fulfils given requirements.

Therefore it becomes a key issue to design communication system software that provably and not only arguably meets its requirements. To come to some essential improvements of the current dissatisfying situation, the project *Provably Correct Communication Networks* — abbreviated as CoCoN — was born. CoCoN is the name of a research project carried out in close cooperation between Philips Research

*This research was supported by the Philips Research Laboratories Aachen as part of the project CoCoN (Provably Correct Communication Networks)

**E-mail: Stephan.Kleuker@informatik.uni-oldenburg.de, Tel: +49-441-798-3124

Laboratories Aachen and the Department of Computer Science at the University of Oldenburg. The overall goal of this project is to improve the software quality of future communications systems. More precisely, the aim of the project CoCoN is to support a stepwise and verified development of communication systems from the requirement phase over the specification phase to an implementation. Our method is based on results of the ESPRIT project ProCoS [3, 4, 6] (Provably Correct Systems).

ProCoS is a wide-spectrum verification project where embedded communicating systems are studied at various levels of abstraction ranging from requirements' capture over specification language and programming language down to the machine language. It emphasizes a constructive approach to correctness, using stepwise transformations between specifications, designs, programs, compilers and hardware.

But the application conditions of semantics-preserving transformation rules are often very restrictive. Therefore it is impossible to guarantee that a specification reached in a certain step of development can be transformed in any further step. For large systems lots of calculations must be done to solve this problem.

Specification engineering introduced in this paper is a new approach where each result of intermediate steps can be used without detailed information about further steps. New transformation rules are introduced in this paper that preserve only certain requirements but have less restrictive application conditions. Proofs for other requirements have to be done again where old proof structures can be reused.

Another important disadvantage of stepwise development techniques so far is that extension and change of requirements of systems are not supported.But, most systems have to be extended, i.e. they shall or must fulfil new, additional requirements not known at the time they were designed. One example is the ever increasing demand for the fast and flexible introduction of new value-added services and new features into private as well as into public telecommunications networks. Intelligent networks (IN) [1, 12], personal communications and computer-supported telecommunications applications (CSTA) are just a few areas from which these services are emerging. Adding more and more services to the telecommunications network must be supported by a stepwise development of specifications.

Specification engineering can be used for the addition of new complex sequences of communications to existing systems. Other approaches for an *incremental* design of systems like [10, 22] describe only the development of asynchronous protocols with the restriction that new communications are added one at a time.

The example in the next section is an intermediate result of a stepwise development of a complete simple call handling. This result is used in CoCoN as a starting point for the introduction of correct value added services. The initial steps of a stepwise development with the transformational approach are left out here, they can be found in [14]. These stages include a development initiated by an informal description of the problem and the development of formal requirements in trace logic [23] that the system must fulfil. A specification (or program) is called correct (or verified) with respect to a set of formal requirements if it is proven that it fulfils each requirement. The complete method including the idea of specification engineering which is introduced in the following sections is sketched in the conclusions.

The next section presents a specification of a distributed call handling with finite automata. It follows an informal introduction to the extension of systems with specification engineering which leads to an extension theorem. The fourth section discusses the application of specification engineering in a specification language which is more powerful than finite automata. The conclusions contain a short summary of the CoCoN approach and possible further steps.

2 Specification with finite automata

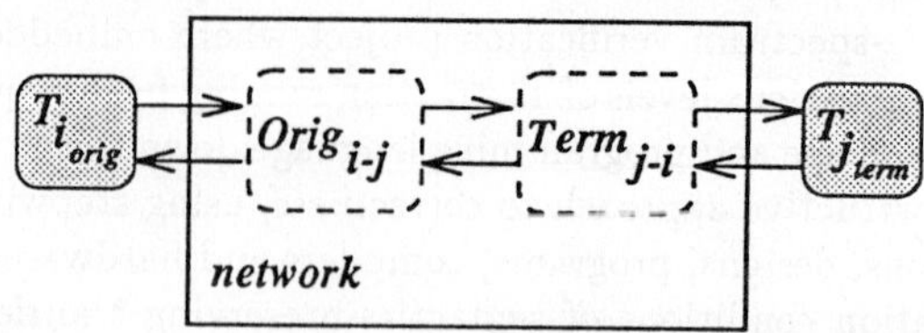

Figure 1: Example of a representation of a call from telephone T_i to telephone T_j

This section introduces a simple sort of call handling as a case study for a system that should be extensible. Finite automata are used as specification language through the following sections. Because the semantics of many specification languages is based on extended automata (or transition systems) it is possible to transfer our extension algorithm presented in the next section to other languages.

The systems in our case study are non-terminating and we assume that if a process (represented by an automaton) terminates it returns to its initial state immediately. It is possible to rewrite the following text for systems based on other types of automata.

In our example, automata are used to describe each telephone and the representation of a call in the network. A call between two sides i and j consists of four automata: $T_{i_{orig}}$ for the originating side telephone, $Orig_{i-j}$ for a representation of the originating side in the network, $Term_{j-i}$ for a representation of a call from i to j in the network and $T_{j_{term}}$ for the terminating side telephone. This situation is sketched in figure 1. Note that one telephone T_i is represented by the two automata $T_{i_{orig}}$ and $T_{i_{term}}$. This specification is an intermediate result of a development after a decomposition of the process *network*.

The interfaces (communications between the automata) and their informal meaning are given in table 1 for communications between the network and the telephone (the first letter indicates either the originating or the terminating side) and in table 2 for communications between the two processes representing a call in the network (each communication starts with a small letter, here an subscript ij is used for messages from i to j).

The specification for each process is given in figure 2 (superscript ^{o} for initiated by originating and superscript ^{t} for initiated by terminating side). Each communication is marked to show whether it is an input ($> c$) or output ($c >$). Each automaton starts in its initial state, marked by an initial arrow at the top. A communication can only happen if it is possible as the next communication by the sender and the receiver (fully synchronized communications). The automaton changes its state to the following state after performing a communication. If a process described by an automaton terminates (no communication can follow) it returns to its initial state immediately. These final states and the first state can be seen as equal or connected by an ε-arc between them. There is no graphical presentation of this fact because it is the same for each automaton and we can emphasize that an automaton 'terminates' if no communication can follow.

from an originating side $T_{i_{orig}}$ to a process $Orig_{i-j}$ that represents a part of a call from i to j inside the process *network*:	
$Osetup_i$	(Capital letter O for originating) initial message to the network
$Oinformation_i$	transmission of the complete number of terminating side
$Odiscon_i^u$	originating side initiates call termination (^{u} for "from user")
$Odiscompl_i^n$	originating side acknowledges a call termination signal from network (indicated by ^{n})
from $Orig_{i-j}$ to $T_{i_{orig}}$:	
$Oabort_i$	Call is aborted by some reason like no free line or called side is busy
$Oalerting_i$	network indicates that it rings at terminating side
$Oconnect_i$	terminating side has gone off-hook
$Odiscon_i^n$	network indicates that terminating side has gone on-hook
$Odiscompl_i^u$	network acknowledges a call termination signal from originating side
From $T_{j_{term}}$ to $Term_{j-i}$ and vice versa the dual communications to the explained ones.	

Table 1: Communications between network and telephone

$setup_{i,j}$	the initial message between the new processes
$abort_{i,j}$	for an abort of a call
$alert_{i,j}$	for ringing at the terminating side
$connect_{i,j}$	for a completed connection
$discon_{i,j}$	for disconnect initiated
$discompl_{i,j}$	for disconnect complete (acknowledge)

Table 2: Communications between originating and terminating part in the network

There exist two automata for each possible call in the specification, called $Orig_{i-j}$ and $Term_{j-i}$ ($i \neq j, 1 \leq i, j \leq n$). This parametrization with i, j is a possibility to work with a dynamic number of processes (calls) in a static model.

Our first specification describes a call under the assumption that no intermediate call termination is possible. This assumption was made to arrive at a first small and easily verifiable specification.

The following definitions are used to formalize the behaviour of communicating automata (with close relation to e.g. CSP [13]).

Definition (syntax of an automaton): An *automaton* $A = (Com, Q, \delta, q_0)$ consists of four parts, a finite set Com of *communications* ($Comm(A) = Com$), a finite set Q of states ($States(A) = Q$), a partial function $\delta : Q \times Com \rightarrow Q$ which describes for a given state, and a communication the next state and the initial state $q_0 \in Q$.

A trace is possible in one automaton if there exists one sequence of states in the automaton where the connecting arcs are marked by the trace. A state where no communication can follow (termination) is called a *return state.*

Definition (possible traces and return states): A *trace* is an element of Com^*. We use t as typical letter for traces. The transition function δ is extended in the usual way from a single communication to traces (Let ε be the empty word, $\delta(q, \varepsilon) = q$, $\delta(q, t.t') = \delta(\delta(q, t), t')$, t, t' are traces). A trace t is *possible* in A iff $\delta(q_0, t)$ is defined.
The set $return(A) \subseteq States(A)$ denotes the set of states in which A immediately returns to its initial state ($return(A) = \{q \in States(A) | \forall c \in Comm(A) \bullet \delta(q, c) \text{ is not defined}\}$), e.g. $return(T_{i_{orig}}) = \{7\}$. The projection $\cdot \downarrow \cdot$ projects a trace on a set of communications, e.g. $a.c.b.c \downarrow \{a, b\} = a.b$.

As mentioned before there exists one automaton for each possible call in the network. Therefore we have to formalize how these automata work together to describe the whole system. The possibility of a trace in a parallel composition of two or more automata requires synchronization on common symbols and is formalized as follows:

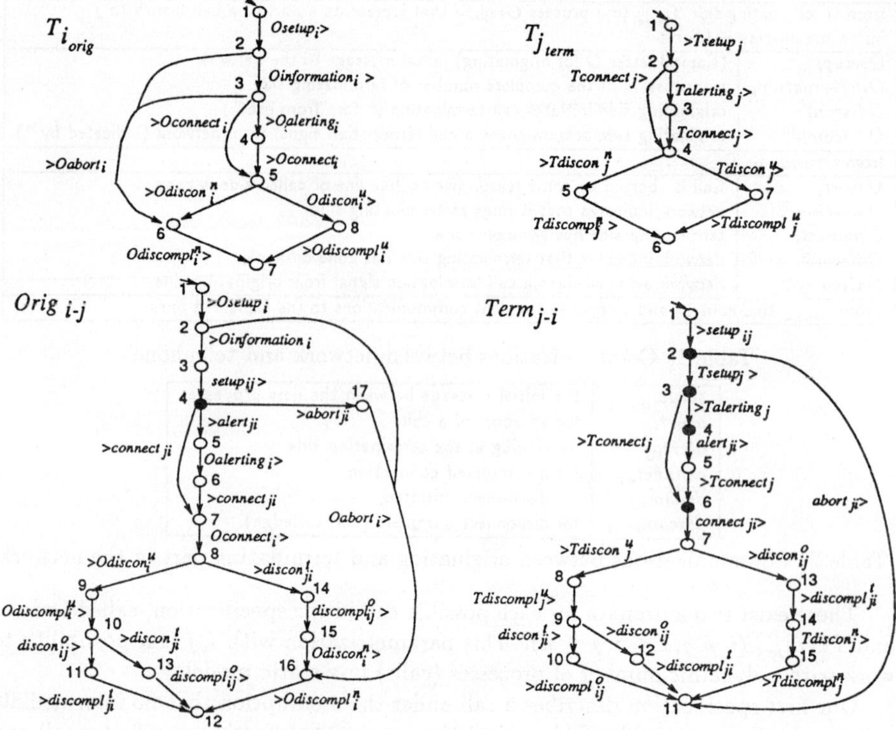

Figure 2: Specification of a distributed call

Definition (parallel composition): Let $A_i = (Com_i, Q_i, \delta_i, q_{0_i})$, $1 \leq i \leq n$ be automata. A trace $tr \in (\bigcup_{i=1}^{n} Com_i)^*$ is possible in a *parallel composition* $A_1 \| A_2 \| \ldots \| A_n$ iff $tr \downarrow Com_i$ is possible in each automaton A_i.
Formally: $\forall 1 \leq i \leq n \; \exists q_i \in Q_i \bullet \; \delta_i(q_{0_i}, tr \downarrow Com_i) = q_i$
Example: A trace $Osetup_i.Oinformation_i.setup_{ij}.alert_{ji}.Oalerting_i$ is possible in $T_{i_{orig}} \| Orig_{i-j}$, but not $Osetup_i.Oinformation_i.Oalerting_i$.
For each communication $c \in Comm(A_i) \cap Comm(A_j)$ a function $from(c)$ determines the sender and $to(c)$ of the receiver, e.g. $from(Osetup_i) = T_{i_{orig}}$, $to(Tsetup_j) = T_{j_{term}}$.

Two different processes in the network describing two different calls need not be synchronized because they are independent of each other. If we take two traces of these calls they can be mixed in any possible form to come to a new trace describing the two calls at the same time. The mixture of traces is called *merging.* The mixture of two or more automata is called *interleaving.* Therefore an interleaving operator for automata is defined. A trace is possible in an interleaving of n automata iff it is a mixture of traces each of which is possible in one of the automata. The difference between interleaving and parallel operator is that no synchronization has to take place.

Definition (interleaving): Let $A_i = (Com_i, Q_i, \delta_i, q_{0_i})$, $1 \leq i \leq n$ **be automata. A trace** $tr \in (\bigcup_{i=1}^{n} Com_i)^*$ is possible in an *interleaving* $A_1 \| A_2 \| \ldots \| A_n$ iff
$\forall 1 \leq i \leq n \; \exists t_1 \in Com_1, \ldots, t_n \in Com_n \bullet \; (\exists q_i \in Q_i \bullet \; \delta_i(q_{0_i}, t_i) = q_i)$
$\wedge \; tr \in merge(t_1, \ldots, t_n)$.
merge is defined as: Let t_i be traces. Then
$merge(t_1, ..., t_n) = \{a_{11}.a_{21}.\ldots.a_{n1}.a_{12}.a_{22}.\ldots.a_{n2}.\ldots.a_{1k}.a_{2k}\ldots.a_{nk} |$
$a_{ij} \in Com_i \cup \{\varepsilon\} \wedge t_i = a_{i1}.\ldots.a_{ik}\}$
Example: $merge(a.b, c.d) = \{a.b.c.d, a.c.b.d, a.c.d.b, c.a.d.b, c.a.b.d, c.d.a.b\}$

A telephone is described by two automata, one for the originating and one for the terminating side. These automata are used alternatively, because in the simple call handling a telephone can either be the originating or terminating side. Therefore a third operator describes the alternative of n automata. A trace is possible in an alternative iff it is possible in one of the automata.

Definition (alternative): Let $A_i = (Com_i, Q_i, \delta_i, q_{0_i})$, $1 \leq i \leq n$ be automata. A trace $tr \in (\bigcup_{i=1}^{n} Com_i)^*$ is possible in an *alternative* $A_1 + A_2 + \ldots + A_n$ iff tr is possible in one automaton. Formally: $\exists 1 \leq i \leq n \; \exists q_i \in Q_i \bullet \; \delta_i(q_{0_i}, tr) = q_i$
Example: $Osetup_i.Oinformation_i$ is possible in $T_{i_{orig}} + T_{i_{term}}$ but not $Osetup_i.Tsetup_i$.

The underlying automata of the described processes can be summarized with the previous remarks as:

Example: Specification with finite automata.
A telephone T_i is $T_i = T_{i_{orig}} + T_{i_{term}}$. The network is $network = \big\|_{i=1}^{n} \big\|_{j=1, j \neq i}^{n} Call_{i-j}$.
The simple switching system is $SSS = T_1 \| \ldots \| T_n \| network$.

This specification describes all possible behaviours because each possible call and each set of possible active calls at the same time is described by the specification. Note that there are traces possible in the specification that are not desired for the final program. Therefore the automata describe a superset of the desired traces. Non-desired traces are omitted with an extension of the specification with local variables (for details see section 4).

The following definitions are used in the next section to describe the extension of systems and the resulting consequences for each subautomaton.

A relation between states of different processes is defined which is used to introduce our transformation rules. The idea is to formalize that if a certain subprocess is in the state p another subprocess might be in the state q.

Informally, q_i is in *K-relation*[1] to q_j iff it exists a possible trace t in S_i to q_i and it is possible to construct a trace t' out of t to q_j in S_j in the following way: The same communications of t w.r.t. $Comm(S_i) \cap Comm(S_j)$ have to be used to produce t' but communications of $Comm(S_j) - Comm(S_i)$ can be added anywhere in t'.

Definition (K-related states): Let $S = S_1 \| \ldots \| S_n$ be a composition of n automata, S_i, S_j $(i \neq j)$ be two parts of S that are directly connected (i.e. with $Comm(S_i) \cap Comm(S_j) \neq \emptyset$) with initial states q_{0_i} and q_{0_j}, q_i a state of S_i and q_j be a state of S_j. Then q_j is in *K-relation* to q_i (abbreviated $q_i \; {}^{S_i}\mathsf{K}^{S_j} \; q_j$) iff
$\exists t, t' \bullet \; \delta_i(q_{0_i}, t) = q_i \; \wedge \; \delta_j(q_{0_j}, t') = q_j$
$\wedge \; t \downarrow (Comm(S_i) \cap Comm(S_j)) = t' \downarrow (Comm(S_i) \cap Comm(S_j)))$

[1] K for German "Kommunikation"

Example: If we look at the processes $Orig_{i-j}$ and $Term_{j-i}$ we observe that $4\ {}^{Orig_{i-j}}\mathsf{K}^{Term_{j-i}}\ 2$, $4\ {}^{Orig_{i-j}}\mathsf{K}^{Term_{j-i}}\ 3$, $4\ {}^{Orig_{i-j}}\mathsf{K}^{Term_{j-i}}\ 4$, $4\ {}^{Orig_{i-j}}\mathsf{K}^{Term_{j-i}}\ 6$ (these states are marked black in figure 2) because after a trace $Osetup_i.Oinformation_i.setup_{ij}$ in $Orig_{i-j}$ there are some communications in $Term_{j-i}$ after $setup_{ij}$ that are independent from $Orig_{i-j}$. It follows that if $Orig_{i-j}$ is in the state 4 then $Term_{j-i}$ could be in one of the states of $\{2,3,4,6\}$.

Remark: If we observe the state space of S (the Cartesian product of the state spaces of the sub-systems) a state $(q_1,\ldots,q_n)$ can only be reached when for all $1 \leq i,j \leq n$ $q_i\ \mathsf{K}^*\ q_j$ holds, where K^* is the transitive, irreflexive closure of all K-relations.

One basic requirement which a parallel non-terminating system must fulfil is deadlock-freedom, i.e. there shall always be a possibility that a new communication can happen. The following definition of deadlock freedom is more restrictive because it ensures that after each possible trace t a new communication of each automaton of a parallel system can happen in the future.

Definition (deadlock freedom): Let $S = S_1 \parallel \ldots \parallel S_n$ be a parallel composition of automata, δ_S be the transition function and q_{0_S} be the initial state of S. Then S is called *deadlock free* iff
$\forall t \bullet\ (\delta_S(q_{0_S}, t) \text{ defined} \Rightarrow (\forall 1 \leq i \leq n\ \exists t' \bullet\ (\delta_S(q_{0_S}, t.t') \text{ defined } \wedge t' \downarrow Comm(S_i) \neq \varepsilon)))$

3 The extension algorithm

The overall idea to develop verified specifications in small steps leads to the transformational approach. Verified semantics-preserving transformation rules are used to come from a first verified specification by applying these rules to the desired system. If a specification fulfils a requirement then each result of the transformation will fulfil this requirement, too. Verified transformations are used in projects like the Munich CIP [19] and the ESPRIT basic research actions ProCoS I and II.

Case studies [6, 17] document that transformations are a suitable approach in system design. But for larger examples the question arises how to come to a first verified specification which guarantees that all desired transformation rules with their restricting application criteria can be applied in later steps. Another question is what happens to the transformational approach if system requirements are changed or new features shall be added to the system. Therefore we concentrate on a new additional technique in the following text which ensures that results of any development step can be used for further developments.

New transformation rules are added in our approach which guarantee that certain requirements are still fulfilled but can change the overall semantics. Proofs for requirements that are not guaranteed by the new rules have to be done again. But practice shows that large parts of proofs done in previous steps can be reused. The big advantage of our approach is that we come to less restrictive application conditions for the transformation rules.

We illustrate our approach with our telephone example. Suppose we wish to drop the assumption that a user cannot terminate a call at any time. We use new transformation rules of specification engineering for additional features to add possibilities of call termination.

New features are introduced by taking two states of an existing automaton of one subprocess and connecting them with a new (added) trace. Then, each related state of

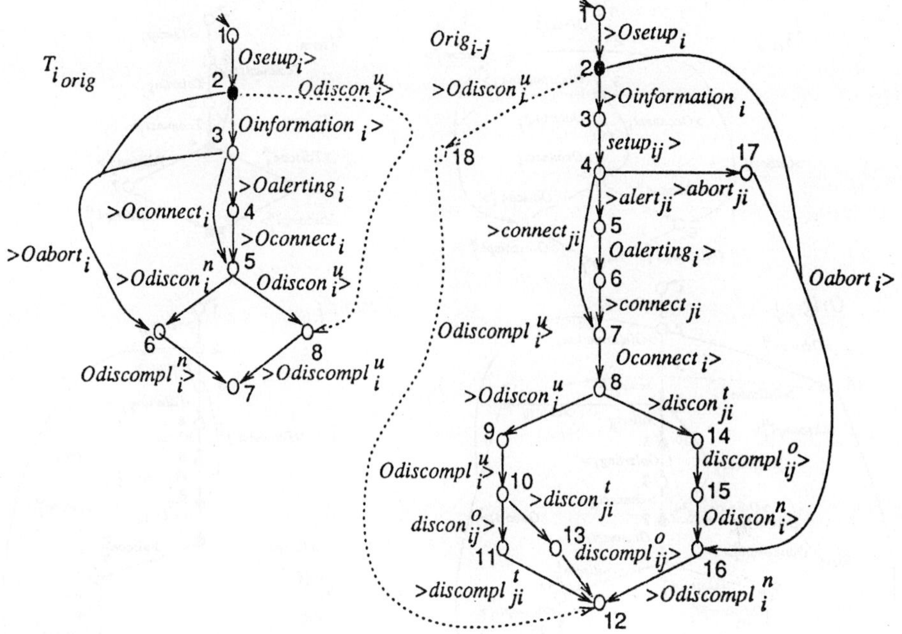

Figure 3: A first extension of the call termination at the originating side

the other automata of other subprocesses is calculated to make the new trace possible and to guarantee that no new deadlocks are introduced.

A new trace is added to the system in the following way: First, we choose a state of $T_{i_{orig}}$ where a new call termination ($Odiscon_i^u$) shall be possible. Then we calculate which states of $Orig_{i-j}$, $Term_{j-i}$ and $T_{j_{term}}$ are influenced. Finally, we have to extend the system in each calculated state with a new trace to a return state to guarantee that our system is deadlock free again. This extension is repeated for each possible call termination. We give an introduction to this idea of stepwise engineering by two extensions of our example:

Example 1: We want to add a new call termination to the originating side $T_{i_{orig}}$. A trace $t_1 = Odiscon_i^u.Odiscompl_i^u$ shall be possible in the state 2 to the return state 7 to indicate a new possible call termination. (The first communication of the new trace is the dotted arrow in $T_{i_{orig}}$ in figure 3. If it is possible to use old parts of an automaton then not the whole new trace is drawn in the automata. Instead of adding t_1 from state 2 to 7 only the trace $Odiscon_i^u$ is added from 2 to 8 because $Odiscompl_i^u$ is the only possible next communication in state 8.) We calculate for state 2 the set of K_related states of $Orig_{i-j}$ which contains only state 2. The trace t_1 is added from state 2 to the return state 12 by introducing a new state 18. Then we calculate for state 2 of $Orig_{i-j}$ the set of K_related states of $Term_{j-i}$ which contains only the initial state. Therefore nothing must be changed in $Term_{j-i}$ because this process could not 'recognize' (is not influenced) that the new trace happens. The new system is deadlock free again with an additional call termination possibility.

Example 2: We add a call-termination to state 3 of $T_{i_{orig}}$. If $T_{i_{orig}}$ reaches the

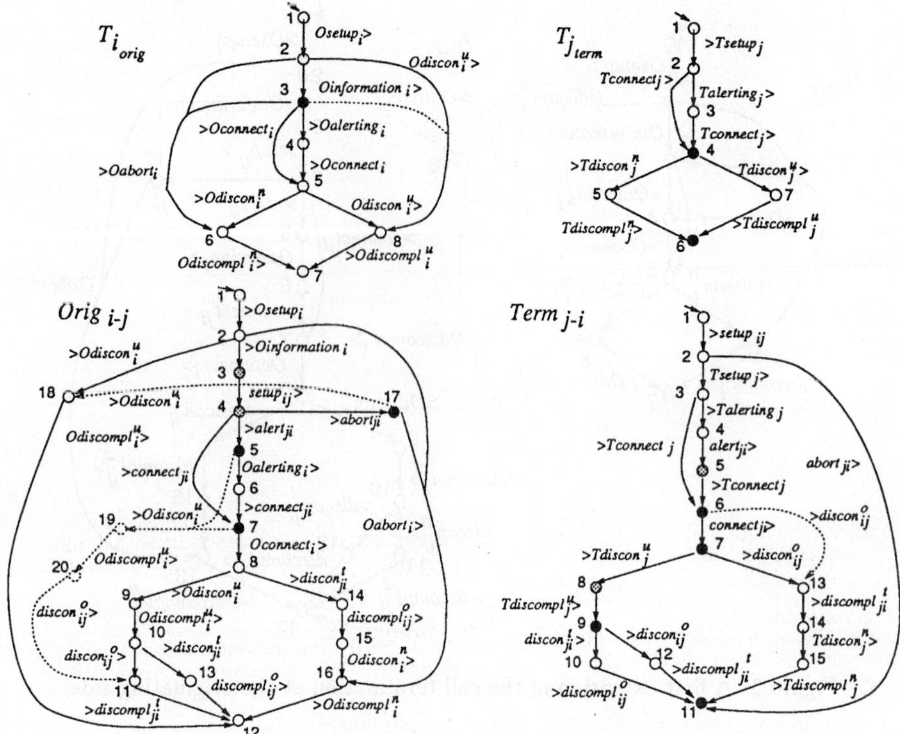

Figure 4: Another extension of the call termination

the state 3 the trace

$$t_2 = Odiscon_i^u.Odiscompl_i^u.discon_{ij}^o.discompl_{ji}^t.Tdiscon_j^n.Tdiscompl_j^n$$

describing a call termination through the system shall be possible. The extension steps are documented in figure 4. The trace $Odiscon_i^u.Odiscompl_i^u$ ($= t_2 \downarrow Comm(T_{i_{orig}})$) connects state 3 and the return state 7 in $T_{i_{orig}}$. The set of K_related states for state 3 of $T_{i_{orig}}$ in $Orig_{i-j}$ is $\{3,4,5,7,17\}$. Following the basic idea we have to add $t_2 \downarrow Comm(Orig_{i-j})$ to each of these states. But some optimization is possible. First we can observe that in states 3 and 4 (dotted in figure 4) no communication with $T_{i_{orig}}$ can follow. Therefore communications from $T_{i_{orig}}$ can be ignored without running into deadlocks and no traces are added in the states 3 and 4.

Remark: This optimization can be added to the algorithm for calculating K_related states. Note that this optimization need not be done but leads to smaller extended systems.

For state 17 we calculate $17\,^{Orig_{i-j}}\mathsf{K}^{Term_{j-i}}\,11$ as the only K_related state in $Term_{j-i}$. But 11 is a return state and therefore $Term_{i-j}$ needs no information about the new call termination in this case. Therefore only the trace $Odiscon_i^u.Odiscompl_i^u$ is added from state 17 to 12 in $Orig_{i-j}$.

The complete trace $t_2 \downarrow Comm(Orig_{i-j})$ is added to the states 5 and 7 of $Orig_{i-j}$. Next, we calculate for the states 5 and 7 the set of K_related states of $Term_{j-i}$ which is $\{5,6,7,8,9\}$. For the states 5 and 8 it holds again that no communication with the previous automaton ($Orig_{i-j}$) can follow. Therefore no trace is added for these states. For state 9 we calculate $9^{Term_{j-i}}\mathsf{K}^{T_{j_{term}}}6$ as the only K_related state in $T_{j_{term}}$. This is a return state and therefore no information about the call termination needs to be sent to $T_{j_{term}}$. Therefore only a trace $discon^o_{ij}.discompl^t_{ji}$ is added from state 9 to 11. (This trace already exists, nothing must be changed in the automaton.) The trace $t_2 \downarrow Comm(Term_{j-i})$ is added to the states 6 and 7 of $Term_{j-i}$.

The state 4 of $T_{j_{term}}$ is the only K_related state for the states 6 and 7 of $Term_{j-i}$. The trace $t_2 \downarrow Comm(T_{j_{term}})$ is added from 4 to 6. The new system is deadlock free again with an additional call termination possibility. □

The extension ideas used in the examples are formalized in general terms. Throughout the following text $S = S_1 \parallel S_2 \parallel \ldots \parallel S_n$ will always be a parallel composition of n automata, $t = c_1.c_2.\ldots.c_m$ a trace over $\bigcup_{j=1}^{n} Comm(S_j)$, $c_1 \in Comm(S_1)$, z_1 a state of S_1. (We will define an extension of S_1 in z_1 with t. Since $\parallel$ is commutative S_1 can be an arbitrary component of S.)

Traces are added that describe one path through the system initiated in one certain state of one automaton. These traces have to fulfil certain requirements such that an extension of the automata is possible. This is formalized as follows. It exists for each trace t which is used for an extension a sequence of 'related automata'. This sequence consists of the names of the sender and the receiver of each communication. The formal definition is:

Definition (index sequence of a trace): Let be S and t be as described above. The related *index sequence* of t in S is: $s(t) := (from(c_1), to(c_1)).\ldots.(from(c_m), to(c_m))$
Example: $t = Odiscon^u_i.Odiscompl^u_i$, $s(t) = (T_{i_{orig}}, Orig_{i-j}).(Orig_{i-j}, T_{i_{orig}})$.

Sometimes it is simpler to reference the index of an automaton rather than the complete name. Now, the new example $s(t) = (1,2).(3,2).(1,3).(x,y)$ $(1 \leq, x, y, \leq n)$ is analyzed. If we extend S with a trace t (with $s(t)$ as described before) then we begin with a calculation of K-related states in S_2 of the extended state in S_1 (refering to the first pair $(1,2)$). The next calculation is done for K-related states of S_2 in S_3. The automata S_1 and S_3 are involved in the next communication (pair $(1,3)$). These automata are already extended and therefore no new calculation is needed. The next communication belongs to the automata S_x and S_y.

If $\{x,y\} \subseteq \{1,2,3\}$ then no calculation of states which have to be extended is needed. If $x \in \{1,2,3\}$ and $y \notin \{1,2,3\}$ (or $y \in \{1,2,3\}$ and $x \notin \{1,2,3\}$) then it is possible to calculate the states of S_y (S_x) which have to be extended from S_x (S_y). If $x \notin \{1,2,3\}$ and $y \notin \{1,2,3\}$ then it is impossible to calculate for the related communication which states of S_x and S_y have to be extended. There is no relation to the previous communications of t. (It must be guaranteed that $\{x,y\} \cap \{1,2,3,2,1,3\} = \{x,y\} \cap \{1,2,3\} \neq \emptyset$ holds.) Therefore such traces shall be omitted. This is done by the following definition.

Definition (traces that can be used for extensions): Let S and t be as described above. A trace t fulfils the *one-path-condition* (abbreviated $opc_S(t)$) for a system S iff

$$\forall 2 \leq j \leq m \bullet \{to(c_j), from(c_j)\} \cap (\bigcup_{k=1}^{j-1} \{to(c_k), from(c_k)\}) \neq \emptyset$$

From now on we assume $opc_S(t)$. We calculate step by step for each communication in t the set R_j of states of S_j of K_related states of the next processes that have to be extended. A set I collects the indices of automata that have been extended. Automata in I do not have to be extended for t again because they already 'know' that the system is performing the new trace. We can describe the extension algorithm which calculates the states that have to be extended in the following way:

An algorithm for calculating the sets of states that have to be extended
Input: $S = S_1 \parallel S_2 \parallel \ldots \parallel S_n$, $t = c_1.c_2.\ldots.c_m$, $z_1 \in State(S_1)$.
Output: $R_1 \subseteq States(S_1), \ldots, R_n \subseteq States(S_n)$ sets of states of each automaton which have to be extended with a new trace (a part of t).
Internal variable: I is the set of indices of the automata which are already observed.

$R_1 := \{z_1\}$;
$I := \{1\}$;
for $j = 1$ to m do
  if $from(c_j) \notin I$ then ⌈ $R_{from(c_j)} :=$ K_related $(R_{to(c_j)}, S_{to(c_j)}, S_{from(c_j)})$;
    $I := I \cup \{from(c_j)\}$ ⌋
  elsif $to(c_j) \notin I$ then ⌈ $R_{to(c_j)} :=$ K_related $(R_{from(c_j)}, S_{from(c_j)}, S_{to(c_j)})$;
    $I := I \cup \{to(c_j)\}$ ⌋

Note that $from(c_j) \notin I \wedge to(c_j) \notin I$ is always false because of $opc_S(t)$. It is possible to optimize interactively (in dialogue with the specifier) the computation of K_related to determine which states should be extended.

The optimizations mentioned in the examples could happen if the K_related states are calculated. They should be done with an interactive tool which asks the user in each case whether (s)he wants an optimization. Two typical optimization criteria are: If $x\,{}^A\mathsf{K}^B\,y$ is calculated then if y is initial or return state of B or if the intersection of the next possible communications in y with $Comm(A)$ is empty then y needs not be added to the calculated set of K_related states.

It might happen that not every automaton S_j is directly related to t ($t \downarrow Comm(S_j) = \varepsilon$) but the new trace may influence S_j. Therefore we first assume that after performing the algorithm $I = \{1, 2, \ldots, n\}$ holds and present after the extension theorem a general solution.

The next definition describes an extension of an automaton, i.e. that a new trace is added between two existing states. A state z cannot be extended if the first communication of the new trace is possible in z (to preserve the determinism of δ the assumption (*) is made).

Definition (adding a trace to an automaton): Let $T = (Com, Q, \delta, q_0)$ be an automaton, $c_j \in Com$ $(1 \leq j \leq s)$, $t = c_1.\ldots.c_s$ a trace, $z \in Q - return(T)$ and $y \in return(T)$ states, (*) $\delta(z, c_1)$ is not defined,
let $\widetilde{z_1}, \ldots, \widetilde{z_{s-1}}$ be distinct, no elements of Q (new states used to make t possible).
The automaton $T' = (Com, Q \cup \{\widetilde{z_1}, \ldots, \widetilde{z_{s-1}}\}, \delta', q_0)$ is derived from S by adding the following trace to δ of T in δ': $\overset{z}{\bullet} \xrightarrow{c_1} \overset{\widetilde{z_1}}{\bullet} \xrightarrow{c_2} \overset{\widetilde{z_2}}{\bullet} \ldots \overset{\widetilde{z_{s-1}}}{\bullet} \xrightarrow{c_s} \overset{y}{\bullet}$
Then T' is called *extension* of T in z with t (short: $T' = ext(T, z, t)$).

Note that y can be any return state of the automaton. It is easy to extend the definition from a state z to a set of states R by stepwise adding the trace to each state of R. The following theorem proves the correctness of a typical new transformation rule of specification engineering for the extension of distributed systems.

Extension Theorem: Let S, t, S_1, z_i be as declared above. Let R_j $(1 \leq j \leq n)$ be the sets of states computed by the extension algorithm. Let be $S'_j = ext(S_j, R_j, t \downarrow Comm(S_j))$ $(1 \leq j \leq n)$ and $S' = S'_1 \parallel S'_2 \parallel \ldots \parallel S'_n$. Then the following holds:
(i) If S is deadlock free then S' is, too.
(ii) If a trace t' is possible in S then it is possible in S', too.

Proof sketch: (i): If the new trace is initiated in S_i then each related automaton will get the possibility to work off the new trace because K_related states are extended and therefore the information about the new trace is propagated to the whole system. No mixture of old traces and new traces is possible because of the deterministic extension. The one-path-condition guarantees that there is only one initial point for the new trace and no other automaton as S_i can start the new trace. Therefore no new deadlocks are possible in S'. (ii): Traces are only added to the old automata therefore all traces of S are possible in S'.

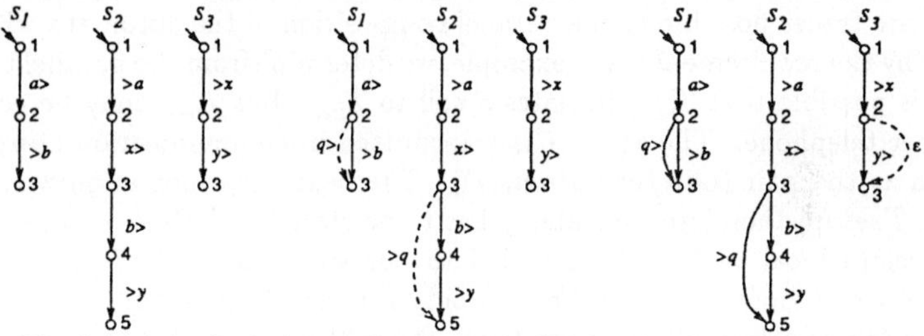

The initial deadlock free system is on the left-hand side. The extended system (with ignoring S_3) with a deadlock after $a.x.q.a$ is in the middle. The right-hand side shows the final extended deadlock free system.

Figure 5: An extension where not every automata is directly influenced

For $I \neq \{1, 2, \ldots, n\}$ we have to calculate the related states and add a trace ε from these states to a return state. The related states are the intersection of the other K_related states. Therefore we have to compute the sets of related states of the automata S_j with $j \notin I$. These sets are (unique) solutions for the following equations:

$$\forall j \in \{1, 2, \ldots, n\} - I \bullet \ R_j = \bigcap_{k=1}^{n} \mathsf{K\_related}(R_k, S_k, S_j)$$

A trace ε can be added to an automaton T with initial state q_o in a state z if

$$\forall c \in Comm(T) \bullet \ \delta(z, c) \text{ defined} \Rightarrow \delta(q_o, c) \text{ not defined}$$

holds. This condition guarantees a deterministic behaviour because if T is in the state z it is distinguishable whether the following communication leads from state z or from state q_0 to another state. A small additional example is given in figure 5.

The system $S_1 \parallel S_2 \parallel S_3$ is deadlock free. A trace q is added to S_1 and S_2. This trace is initiated in state 2 of S_1. From $2 \,{}^{S_1}\mathsf{K}^{S_2}\, 2$ and $2 \,{}^{S_1}\mathsf{K}^{S_2}\, 3$ follows that state 3 is extended. (State 2 needs no extension because no communication with S_1 can follow.) There is no communication w.r.t. S_3 in t but S_3 is influenced. If S_3 is not extended then the system is after the trace $a.x.q.a$ in a deadlock (S_2 is in the state 2 and S_3 in the state 2). If we do the calculations mentioned above we get: $R_1 = \{2\}, R_2 = \{3\}$, $\mathsf{K\_related}(R_1, S_1, S_3) = \{1, 2, 3\}, \mathsf{K\_related}(R_2, S_2, S_3) = \{2\}$ and $R_3 = \{1, 2, 3\} \cap \{2\} = \{2\}$. The initial communication x of S_3 is not possible in the state 2 and therefore a trace ε can be added from the state 2 to the state 1.

Many optimizations of the Extension theorem (some are mentioned in the examples) are possible. If we use a different definition of possible traces then we have to take care of states where the new traces end (return states are a rather simple example). But this theorem is the starting point for the stepwise development of large verified and extensible specifications. Future research will lead to descriptions of the optimizations mentioned above. Note that closely related algorithms can be written to delete traces or add alternatives (or regular languages) to existing systems.

4 Applying specification engineering to a specification language

Although finite automata are useful to describe communicating processes they are not powerful enough to describe certain dependencies. Therefore we only use automata to describe a superset of all possible traces. A restriction on this set must be imposed in the next step.

The requirements developed earlier (e.g. given in [14]) are analyzed to determine if there are traces possible in the parallel composition of the automata which are not allowed by the requirements. For example, we determine from the parallel composition that it is possible that $T_{i_{orig}}$ initiates a call to $T_{j_{term}}$ but $T_{i_{orig}}$ may be connected to any other telephone. The value j is transmitted in communication $Oinformation_i$ (written as the pair $(Oinformation_i, j)$). The next communication w.r.t. this call shall be $Tsetup_j$ therefore the value j has to be stored and $Tsetup_j$ activated.

Therefore local variables are added to our specification. We can then formulate that a communication can happen only if a certain pre-condition over the local variables (an *enable-predicate*) is fulfilled. After the execution of a communication a post-condition (an *effect-predicate*) where values of local variables may change must be fulfilled. Local variables are introduced for each process to formulate these predicates.

In our example Boolean variables $setup[i]$, $1 \leq i \leq n$, are used, one for each telephone inside the process *network*. Their initial values are *false*. If a communication $(Osetup_i, j)$ happens, the value of $setup[j]$ is set to *true*. The communication $Tsetup_j$ is possible only if the value of $setup[j]$ is *true*. The value of $setup[j]$ is *false* after the communication $Tsetup_j$ is executed.

A *communication-assertion* is added for each communication (we refer to a communicated value which is transmitted by a communication c by writing @c.), e.g.:

com $Oinformation_i$ write *setup* when *true* then $setup[@Oinformation_i]'$
com $Tsetup_j$ write *setup* when $setup[j]$ then $\neg setup[j]'$

Automata and communication assertions are summarized by the specification language SL [18] developed in the ProCoS. In the ProCoS project it has been shown that SL specifications can be transformed into occam-like programs [20, 21].

If we want to use our extension technique from the previous chapter, local variables have to be taken into account. Certain conditions for the enable predicates of communications of new traces must be fulfilled. Sometimes, new local variables have to be introduced to describe changes caused by a new trace. One idea is to transform the idea of superposition of UNITY [9] to SL. Further transformation rules are developed that are only possible with local variables because situations that may lead to deadlocks can be excluded by certain enable predicates over local variables. Due to lack of space only this general information can be given.

The idea of specification engineering can be used for many other specification languages whose semantics is based on transition systems. Typical examples are SDL [2] and LOTOS [15] which are widely used in the telecommunication area.

The specification engineering approach is used in SL for a stepwise development of a verified complex description of a typical call handling. This call handling is closely related to a *Basic Call State Model* [8, 11] of the ITU-T (former CCITT) standardization committee which is a suitable starting point for the development of value added services. Therefore specification engineering presents an intuitive technique for a system designer to extend specifications in small verifiable steps.

5 Conclusions and final remarks

The transformational approach of ProCoS [18, 20] with verified semantics-preserving transformation rules is extended by a new kind of transformation rules only preserving several requirements. The extension is useful because semantics-preserving rules have very restrictive application conditions and are often not suitable for system extensions.

step	name of phase	related subjects
1	requirement engineering	informal description informal requirements formal requirements
2	initial specification	typical system behaviour superset of all possibilities restriction verification
3	specification engineering	decomposition extension of functionality transformation verification of new parts

Table 3: Phases in the development of extendable systems

Specification engineering is a way to come to large verified specifications by small intuitive steps. In contrast to other formal methods the wish for extendable systems is integrated. Basic ideas of specification engineering can be transferred to other languages based on extended finite state machines. Future research will cover possibilities and limitations of this idea.

Typical phases of the development of extensible systems in the transformational approach with specification engineering are summarized in table 3. The way to come to a first verified specification are steps 1 and 2. An extension of a system deals with a sequence of steps 1 and 3.

Formal proofs have to be done on computers. In ProCoS many transformation rules from SL to OCCAM are implemented and verified [5]. These rules are used in an interactive system. Tools have to be built for software engineers that support specification engineering and proofs that requirements are fulfilled. Here, reuseability of proofs will be an important part.

Next design steps will lead to a new service management process for value added services. We try to develop a simple method that explains how new services can be added to the system with a guarantee that no requirements are violated. The interplay between different services, so called *feature interaction* [7], will be one important research topic.

Acknowledgements. The author thanks M. Elixmann, A. Kehne, H. Tjabben of Philips Research Laboratories Aachen and He Jifeng, E.-R. Olderog, M. Schenke and the other members of the ProCoS Group in Oldenburg for helpful discussions.

References

[1] S. Abramowski et al., CCITT Intelligent Network Capability Set-1: Concepts and Limitations, Philips Research Laboratories Aachen, Technical Report, November 1993

[2] F. Belina, D. Hogrefe, The CCITT-Specification and Description Language SDL, Computer Networks and ISDN Systems 16 (1988/89) 311-341, North-Holland

[3] D. Bjørner, H. Langmaack, C.A.R. Hoare, ProCoS I Final Deliverable, ProCoS Technical Report ID/DTH db 13/1, January 1993

[4] D. Bjørner et al., A ProCoS project description: ESPRIT BRA 3104, Bulletin of the EATCS, 39:60-73, 1989

[5] J. Bohn, H. Hungar, Traverdi - Transformation and Verification of Distributed Systems, in M. Broy, S. Jähnichen, (eds.): KORSO, Correct Software by Formal Methods, to appear in LNCS (Springer-Verlag)

[6] J.Bowen et al., Developing Correct Systems, 5th EuroMicro Workshop on Real-Time Systems, Oulu, Finland, 1993, (IEEE Computer Society Press) 176-187

[7] E.J. Cameron et al., A Feature-Interaction Benchmark for IN and Beyond, IEEE Communications Magazine, March 1993

[8] CCITT Recommendations Q.1200: Intelligent Networks, final version, WP XI/4. Geneva. March 1992

[9] K.M.Chandy, J. Misra, Parallel Program Design, Addison-Wesley, 1988

[10] D. Y. Chao, D. T. Wang, An Interactive Tool for Design, Simulation, Verification, and Synthesis of Protocols, Software - Practice and Experience, Vol. 24(8), 1994

[11] J.M. Duran, J. Visser, International Standards for Intelligent Networks, IEEE Communications Magazine, February 1992

[12] J.J. Garrahan et al., Intelligent Network Overview, IEEE Communications Magazine, March 1993

[13] C.A.R. Hoare, Communicating Sequential Processes, Prentice-Hall, London, 1985

[14] S. Kleuker, Provably Correct Communication Networks (CoCoN) (Draft Version), Philips Research Laboratories Aachen, Technical Report, 1123/95, 1995,

[15] L. Logrippo, M. Faci, M. Haj-Hussein, An Introduction to LOTOS, Computer Networks and ISDN Systems 23 (1992) 325-342, North-Holland

[16] E.-R. Olderog, Towards a Design Calculus for Communicating Programs, LNCS 527 (Springer-Verlag), p. 61-77, 1991

[17] E.-R. Olderog, S. Rössig, A Case study in Transformational Design on Concurrent Systems, in M.-C. Gaudel, J.-P. Jouannaud, eds., Proc. TAPSOFT '93, LNCS (Springer-Verlag), 1993

[18] E.-R. Olderog et al., ProCoS at Oldenburg: The Interface between Specification Language and OCCAM-like Programming Language. Technical Report, Bericht 3/92, Univ. Oldenburg, Fachbereich Informatik, 1992

[19] H. A. Partsch, Specification and Transformation of Programs, Springer-Verlag, 1990

[20] S. Rössig, A Transformational Approach to the Design of Communicating Systems, PhD thesis, University of Oldenburg, 1994

[21] S. Rössig, M. Schenke, Specification and Stepwise Development of Communicating Systems, LNCS 551 (Springer-Verlag), 1991

[22] P. Zafiropulo et al., Towards Analyzing and Synthesizing Protocols, IEEE Transactions on Communications, Vol COM-28, No. 4, April 1980

[23] J. Zwiers, Compositionality, Concurrency and Partial Correctness - Proof Theories for Networks of Processes and Their Relationship, LNCS 321 (Springer-Verlag), 1989

Precise Interprocedural Dataflow Analysis with Applications to Constant Propagation[1]

Mooly Sagiv,[2] *Thomas Reps, and Susan Horwitz*
Computer Sciences Department, University of Wisconsin-Madison
1210 West Dayton Street, Madison, WI 53706 USA
Electronic mail: {sagiv, reps, horwitz}@cs.wisc.edu

ABSTRACT This paper concerns interprocedural dataflow-analysis problems in which the dataflow information at a program point is represented by an environment (i.e., a mapping from symbols to values), and the effect of a program operation is represented by a distributive environment transformer. We present an efficient dynamic-programming algorithm that produces precise solutions.
The method is applied to solve precisely and efficiently two (decidable) variants of the interprocedural constant-propagation problem: *copy constant propagation* and *linear constant propagation*. The former interprets program statements of the form $x := 7$ and $x := y$. The latter also interprets statements of the form $x := 5 * y + 17$.

1 Introduction

This paper concerns how to find precise solutions to a large class of interprocedural dataflow-analysis problems in polynomial time. Of the problems to which our techniques apply, several variants of the *interprocedural constant-propagation problem* stand out as being of particular importance.

In contrast with *intra*procedural dataflow analysis, where "precise" means "meet-over-all-paths" [Kil73], a precise *inter*procedural dataflow-analysis algorithm must provide the "meet-over-all-*valid*-paths" solution. (A path is *valid* if it respects the fact that when a procedure finishes it returns to the site of the most recent call [SP81, Cal88, LR91, KS92, Rep94, RSH94, RHS95].) In this paper, we show how to find the meet-over-all-valid-paths solution for a certain class of dataflow problems in which the dataflow facts are maps ("environments") from some finite set of symbols D to some (possibly infinite) set of values L (i.e., the dataflow facts are members of $Env(D, L)$), and the dataflow functions ("environment transformers" in $Env(D, L) \xrightarrow{d} Env(D, L)$) distribute over the meet operator of $Env(D, L)$. We call this set of dataflow problems the *I*nterprocedural *D*istributive *E*nvironment problems (or IDE problems, for short).

The contributions of this paper can be summarized as follows:

- We introduce a **compact graph representation of distributive environment transformers.**
- We present a **dynamic-programming algorithm** for finding meet-over-all-valid-paths solutions. For general IDE problems the algorithm will not necessarily terminate. However, we identify a subset of IDE problems for which the algorithm does terminate and runs in time $O(ED^3)$, where E is the number of edges in the program's control-flow graph.
- We study two natural variants of the constant-propagation problem: copy-constant propagation [FL88] and linear-constant propagation, which extends copy constant propagation by interpreting statements of the form $x = a * y + b$, where a and b are

---

[1]This work was supported in part by a David and Lucile Packard Fellowship for Science and Engineering, by the National Science Foundation under grants CCR-8958530 and CCR-9100424, by the Defense Advanced Research Projects Agency under ARPA Order No. 8856 (monitored by the Office of Naval Research under contract N00014-92-J-1937), by the Air Force Office of Scientific Research under grant AFOSR-91-0308, and by a grant from Xerox Corporate Research. Part of this work was done while the authors were visiting the University of Copenhagen.

[2]On leave from IBM Scientific Center, Haifa, Israel.

The environment transformers associated with edges out of call and exit nodes reflect the assignments of actual to formal parameters, and vice versa (for call-by-value-result parameters). For example, the transformer associated with edge $n1 \rightarrow s_P$ in the supergraph of Figure 1 is $\lambda env.env[a \rightarrow 7]$. Aliasing (e.g., due to pointers or reference parameters) can be handled conservatively; if x and y might be aliased before the statement $x := 5$, then the corresponding environment transformer would be $\lambda env.env[x \rightarrow 5][y \rightarrow (5 \sqcap env(y))]$.

Linear constant propagation handles assignments of the form $x := c$ and $x := c_1 * y + c_2$ where c, c_1, and c_2 are literals or user-defined constants. The environment transformers associated with these assignment statements are of the form: $\lambda env.env[x \rightarrow c]$, and $\lambda env.env[x \rightarrow c_1 * env(y) + c_2]$, respectively.

For other assignment statements, for example: $x := y + z$, the associated environment transformer is: $\lambda env.env[x \rightarrow \perp]$. This transformer is a safe approximation to the actual semantics of the assignment; the transformer that exactly corresponds to the semantics, $\lambda env.env[x \rightarrow env(y) + env(z)]$, cannot be used in the IDE framework because it is not distributive. □

3.5 The Meet Over All Valid Paths Solution

Definition 3.9 *Let* $IP = (G^*, D, L, M)$ *be an IDE problem instance. The* **meet-over-all-valid-paths** *solution of IP for a given node* $n \in N^*$*, denoted by* MVP_n*, is defined as follows:* $MVP_n \stackrel{\text{def}}{=} \sqcap_{q \in VP(s_{main}, n)} M(q)(\Omega)$*, where M is extended to paths by composition, i.e.,* $M([\,]) = \lambda env.env$ *and* $M([e_1, e_2, \ldots, e_j]) \stackrel{\text{def}}{=} M(e_j) \circ M(e_{j-1}) \circ \cdots \circ M(e_2) \circ M(e_1)$*.* □

In an IDE problem, the environment transformer associated with an intraprocedural edge e represents a safe approximation to the actual semantics of the code at the source of e. Functions on call-to-return-site edges extract (from the dataflow information valid immediately before the call) dataflow information about local variables that must be re-established after the return from the call. Functions on exit-to-return-site edges extract dataflow information that is both valid at the exit site of the called procedure and relevant to the calling procedure.

Note that call-to-return-site edges introduce some additional paths in the supergraph that do not correspond to standard program-execution paths. The intuition behind the IDE framework is that the interprocedurally valid paths of Definition 3.3 correspond to "paths of action" for particular *subsets* of the runtime entities (e.g., global variables). The path function along a particular path contributes only *part* of the dataflow information that reflects what happens during the corresponding run-time execution. The facts for other subsets of the runtime entities (e.g., local variables) are handled by different "trajectories", for example, paths that take "short-cuts" via call-to-return-site edges.

4 Using Graphs to Represent Environment Transformers

One of the keys to the efficiency of our dataflow-analysis algorithm is the use of a *pointwise* representation of environment transformers. In this section, we show that every distributive environment transformer $t: Env(D, L) \xrightarrow{d} Env(D, L)$ can be represented using a set of functions $F_t = \{f_{d',d} | d', d \in D \cup \{\Lambda\}\}$, each of type $L \rightarrow L$. Function $f_{\Lambda,d}$ is used to represent the effects on symbol d that are independent of the argument environment. Function $f_{d',d}$ captures the effect that the value of symbol d' in the argument environment has on the value of symbol d in the result environment; if d does not depend on d', then $f_{d',d} = \lambda l.\top$. For any symbol d, the value of $t(env)(d)$ can be determined by taking the meet of the values of $D + 1$ individual function applications: $t(env)(d) = f_{\Lambda,d}(\top) \sqcap (\sqcap_{d' \in D} f_{d',d}((env)(d')))$.

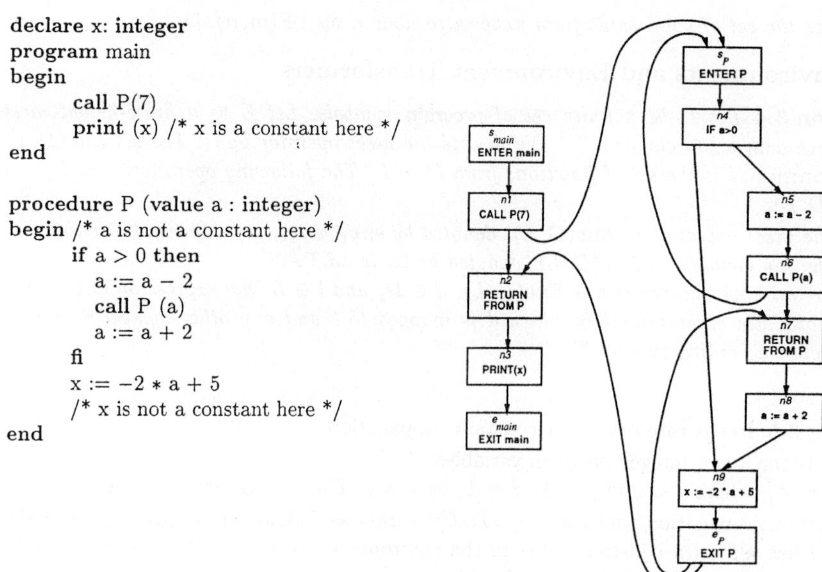

FIGURE 1. An example program and its supergraph G^*.

- An intraprocedural **call-to-return-site** edge from c to r;
- An interprocedural **call-to-start** edge from c to the start node of the called procedure;
- An interprocedural **exit-to-return-site** edge from the exit node of the called procedure to r.

The call-to-return-site edges are included so that we can handle programs with local variables and parameters; the dataflow functions on call-to-return-site and exit-to-return-site edges permit the information about local variables that holds at the call site to be combined with the information about global variables that holds at the end of the called procedure.

Example 3.1 Figure 1 shows an example program and its supergraph. □

3.2 Interprocedural Paths

Definition 3.2 *A* **path** *of length j from node m to node n is a (possibly empty) sequence of j edges, which will be denoted by $[e_1, e_2, \ldots, e_j]$, s.t., for all i, $1 \le i \le j-1$, the target of edge e_i is the source of edge e_{i+1}. Path concatenation is denoted by $\|$.* □

The notion of an "(interprocedurally) valid path" captures the idea that some paths in G^* do not respect the fact that when a procedure finishes, control is transfered to the site of the most recent call. A "same-level valid path" is a valid path that starts and ends in the same procedure, and in which every call has a corresponding return.

Definition 3.3 *The sets of* **same-level valid paths** *and* **valid paths** *in G^* are defined inductively as follows:*

- *The empty path is a* **same-level valid path** *(and therefore a* **valid path***).*
- *Path $p \| e$ is a* **valid path** *if either e is not an exit-to-return-site edge and p is valid or e is an exit-to-return-site edge and $p = p_h \| e_c \| p_t$ where p_t is a same-level valid path, p_h is a valid path, and the source node of e_c is the call node that matches the return-site node at the target of e. Such a path is a* **same-level valid path** *if p_h is also a same-level valid path.*

We denote the set of valid paths from node m to node n by $VP(m,n)$. □

3.3 Environments and Environment Transformers

Definition 3.4 *Let D be a finite set of program symbols. Let L be a finite-height meet semi-lattice with a top element $\top$.*[3] *We denote the meet operator by $\sqcap$. The set $Env(D,L)$ of* **environments** *is the set of functions from D to L. The following operations are defined on $Env(D,L)$:*

- *The meet operator on $Env(D,L)$, denoted by $env_1 \sqcap env_2$, is $\lambda d.(env_1(d) \sqcap env_2(d))$.*
- *The top element in $Env(D,L)$, denoted by Ω, is $\lambda d.\top$.*
- *For an environment $env \in Env(D,L)$, $d \in D$, and $l \in L$, the expression $env[d \to l]$ denotes the environment in which d is mapped to l and any other symbol $d' \neq d$ is mapped according to $env(d')$.*

□

Example 3.5 In the case of integer constant propagation:

- D is the set of integer program variables.
- $L = Z_{\perp}^{\top}$ where $x \sqsubseteq y$ iff $y = \top$, $x = \perp$, or $x = y$. Thus the height of $Z_{\perp}^{\top}$ is 3.

In a constant-propagation problem, $Env(D,L)$ is used as follows: If $env(d) \in Z$ then the variable d has a known constant value in the environment env; the value $\perp$ denotes non-constant and $\top$ denotes an unknown value. □

Definition 3.6 *An environment transformer $t\colon Env(D,L) \to Env(D,L)$ is* **distributive** *(denoted by $t\colon Env(D,L) \xrightarrow{d} Env(D,L)$) iff for every $env_1, env_2, \ldots \in Env(D,L)$, and $d \in D$, $(t(\sqcap_i env_i))(d) = \sqcap_i (t(env_i))(d)$. Note that this equality must also hold for infinite sets of environments.* □

3.4 The Dataflow Functions

A dataflow problem is specified by annotating each edge e of G^* with an environment transformer that captures the effect of the program operation at the source of e.

Definition 3.7 *An instance of an* **interprocedural distributive environment problem** *(or* **IDE problem** *for short) is a four-tuple, $IP = (G^*, D, L, M)$, where:*

- *G^* is a supergraph.*
- *D and L are as defined in* Definition 3.4.
- *$M\colon E^* \to (Env(D,L) \xrightarrow{d} Env(D,L))$ is an assignment of distributive environment transformers to the edges of G^*.*

□

Example 3.8 In the case of linear constant propagation, the interesting environment transformers are those associated with edges whose sources are start nodes, call nodes, exit nodes, or nodes that represent assignment statements.

Whether edges out of start nodes have non-identity environment transformers depends on the semantics of the programming language. For example, these edges' environment transformers may reflect the fact that a procedure's local variables are uninitialized at the start of the procedure; that is, the transformers would be: $\lambda env.env[x_1 \to \perp][x_2 \to \perp]\ldots[x_n \to \perp]$ for all local variables x_i. The environment transformers for the edges out of the start node for the program's main procedure may also reflect the fact that global variables are uninitialized when the program is started. For example, the environment transformer associated with edge $s_{main} \to n1$ in the supergraph of Figure 1 is: $\lambda env.\lambda d.\perp$.

[3] Hence, L is also complete and has a least element, denoted by $\perp$.

literals or user-defined constants. The IDE problems that correspond to both of these variants fall into the above-mentioned subset; consequently, our techniques **solve all instances of these constant-propagation problems in time $O(E\,\mathrm{MaxVisible}^3)$**, where "MaxVisible" is the maximum number of variables visible in any procedure of the program. The algorithms obtained in this way improve on the well-known constant-propagation work from Rice [CCKT86, GT93] in two ways:

- The Rice algorithm is not precise for recursive programs. (In fact, it may fall into an infinite loop when applied to recursive programs).
- Because of limitations in the way "return jump functions" are generated, the Rice algorithm does not even yield precise answers for all non-recursive programs.

In contrast, our algorithm yields **precise results, for both recursive and non-recursive programs.**

- Our dataflow-analysis algorithm has been implemented and used to analyze C programs. Preliminary experimental results are reported in Section 6.

The remainder of the paper is organized as follows: In Section 2 we introduce the copy constant-propagation and linear constant-propagation problems. Linear constant propagation is used in subsequent sections to illustrate our ideas. In Section 3 we define the class of IDE problems. In Section 4, we define the compact graph representation of distributive environment transformers and show how to use these graphs to find the meet-over-all-valid-paths solution to a dataflow problem. Section 5 presents our dynamic-programming algorithm. In Section 5.4, we discuss the application of our approach to the copy constant-propagation and linear constant-propagation problems. Preliminary experiments in which our algorithm has been applied to perform linear constant propagation on C programs are reported in Section 6. Section 7 discusses related work. Section 8 gives an overview of how the work has been extended to perform demand-driven dataflow analysis.

2 Distributive Constant-Propagation Problems

There are (at least) two important variants of the constant-propagation problem that fit into the framework presented in this paper: copy constant propagation and linear constant propagation. In copy constant propagation, a variable x is discovered to be constant either if it is assigned a constant value (e.g., $x := 3$) or if it is assigned the value of another variable that is itself constant (e.g., $y := 3$; $x := y$). All other forms of assignment (e.g., $x := y + 1$) are (conservatively) assumed to make x non-constant.

Linear constant propagation identifies a superset of the instances of constant variables found by copy constant propagation. Variable x is discovered to be constant either if it is assigned a constant value (e.g., $x := 3$) or if it is assigned a value that is a linear function of one variable that is itself constant (e.g., $y := 3$; $x := 2 * y + 5$). All other forms of assignment are assumed to make x non-constant.

3 The IDE Framework

3.1 Program Representation

A program is represented using a directed graph $G^* = (N^*, E^*)$ called a **supergraph**. G^* consists of a collection of flowgraphs $G_1, G_2, \ldots$ (one for each procedure), one of which, G_{main}, represents the program's main procedure. Each flowgraph G_p has a unique **start** node s_p, and a unique **exit** node e_p. The other nodes of the flowgraph represent statements and predicates of the program in the usual way, except that a procedure call is represented by two nodes, a **call** node and a **return-site** node.

In addition to the ordinary intraprocedural edges that connect the nodes of the individual flowgraphs, for each procedure call, represented by call-node c and return-site node r, G^* has three edges:

It is convenient to represent t as a graph with $2(D+1)$ nodes and at most $(D+1)^2$ edges, where each edge $d' \to d$ is annotated with the function $f_{d',d}$ as described above. (An edge function $\lambda l.\top$ does not contribute to the final value of a symbol; therefore, the edges that would normally be annotated with that function can be omitted from the graph.)

In this section we show that the meet-over-all-valid-paths solution in G^* can be found by finding the "meet-over-all-realizable-paths" solution of a related problem in a graph $G^{\#}_{IP}$ obtained by pasting together the representation graphs for every control flow edge in G^*.

4.1 A Pointwise Representation of Environment Transformers

Definition 4.1 *Let* $t\colon Env(D,L) \xrightarrow{d} Env(D,L)$ *be an environment transformer and let* $\Lambda \notin D$. *The* **pointwise representation** *of* t, *denoted by* $R_t\colon (D \cup \{\Lambda\}) \times (D \cup \{\Lambda\}) \to (L \to L)$, *is defined by:*

$$R_t(d',d) \stackrel{\text{def}}{=} \begin{cases} id & d' = d = \Lambda \\ \lambda l.t(\Omega)(d) & d' = \Lambda, d \in D \\ \lambda l.\top & d', d \in D \wedge \forall l.t(\Omega[d' \to l])(d) = t(\Omega)(d) \\ id & d', d \in D \wedge \forall l.t(\Omega[d' \to l])(d) = t(\Omega)(d) \sqcap l \\ \lambda l.\begin{cases} \top & l = \top \\ t(\Omega[d' \to l])(d) & o.w. \end{cases} & o.w. \end{cases}$$

Also, for a given representation $R_t\colon (D \cup \{\Lambda\}) \times (D \cup \{\Lambda\}) \to (L \to L)$, *the* **interpretation** *of* R_t, $[\![R_t]\!]\colon Env(D,L) \xrightarrow{d} Env(D,L)$ *is the distributive environment transformer defined by*

$$[\![R_t]\!](env)(d) \stackrel{\text{def}}{=} R_t(\Lambda,d)(\top) \sqcap (\sqcap_{d' \in D} R_t(d',d)(env(d'))) \quad (1)$$

□

Example 4.2 Figure 2 shows the pointwise representations of the environment transformers for linear constant propagation for the supergraph of Figure 1. □

The intuition behind the definition of R_t is that "macro-function" t is broken down into "micro-functions" that are basically of the form $\lambda l.t(\Omega[d' \to l])(d)$. More precisely, all micro-functions $R_t(d',d)$, where $d' \neq \Lambda$, are co-strict variants of $\lambda l.t(\Omega[d' \to l])(d)$. The micro-functions $R_t(\Lambda,d)$ are the only non-co-strict micro-functions; they play a role similar to the "gen" sets of gen-kill problems. The top function is used whenever possible, i.e., when $\lambda l.t(\Omega[d' \to l])(d)$ is equal to $R_t(\Lambda,d)$ and thus does not contribute to the right-hand side of (1). Finally, the identity function is used whenever possible, i.e., when the right-hand side of (1) will have the same value when id is substituted for $\lambda l.t(\Omega[d' \to l])(d)$.

Theorem 4.3 *For every* $t\colon Env(D,L) \xrightarrow{d} Env(D,L)$, $t = [\![R_t]\!]$. □

Pointwise representations are closed under composition, as captured by the following definition and theorem.

Definition 4.4 *The* **composition** $R_{t_1}; R_{t_2}$ *of pointwise representations* $R_{t_1}, R_{t_2}\colon (D \cup \{\Lambda\} \times (D \cup \{\Lambda\}) \to (L \to L)$ *is defined by:* $(R_{t_1}; R_{t_2})(d',d)(l) \stackrel{\text{def}}{=} \sqcap_{z \in D \cup \{\Lambda\}} R_{t_2}(z,d)(R_{t_1}(d',z)(l))$.

□

Theorem 4.5 *For all* $t_1, t_2, \ldots, t_n\colon Env(D,L) \to Env(D,L)$,
$[\![R_{t_1}; R_{t_2}; \cdots; R_{t_n}]\!] = t_n \, o \, t_{n-1} \, o \cdots o \, t_1$. □

Definition 4.4 means that $R_{t_1}; R_{t_2}$ yields another representation graph. Theorem 4.5 means that the composition of several environment transformers can be represented by a single representation graph. That is, environment transformers are "compressible": there is a bound on the size of the graph needed to represent any such function **as well as the compositions of such functions!**

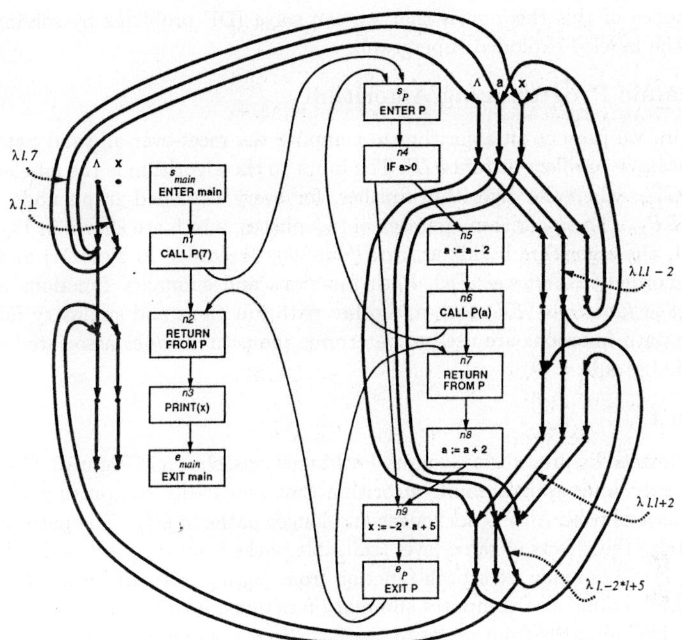

FIGURE 2. The labeled exploded supergraph for the running example program for the linear constant-propagation problem. The edge functions are all $\lambda l.l$ except where indicated.

4.2 The Labeled Exploded Supergraph

Definition 4.6 *Let $IP = (G^*, D, L, M)$ be an IDE problem instance. The* **labeled exploded supergraph** *of IP is a directed graph $G^\#_{IP} = (N^\#, E^\#)$ where $N^\# \stackrel{\text{def}}{=} N^* \times (D \cup \{\Lambda\})$ and $E^\# \stackrel{\text{def}}{=} \{\langle m, d' \rangle \to \langle n, d \rangle \mid m \to n \in E^*, R_{M(m \to n)}(d', d) \neq \lambda l.\top\}$. Edge labels are given by a function $EdgeFn$: $E^\# \to (L \to L)$ defined to be: $EdgeFn(\langle m, d' \rangle \to \langle n, d \rangle) \stackrel{\text{def}}{=} R_{M(m \to n)}(d', d)$.*

A path p in $G^\#_{IP}$ is a **realizable path** *if the corresponding path in G^* is a valid path. We denote the set of realizable paths from an exploded-graph node em to an exploded-graph node en by $RP(em, en)$.* **Same-level realizable paths** *are defined similarly.* □

Example 4.7 Figure 2 contains the exploded supergraph for the running example program labeled with the non-identity *EdgeFn* functions. □

Definition 4.8 *Let $IP = (G^*, D, L, M)$ be an IDE problem instance. The* **meet-over-all-realizable-paths** *solution of IP for a given exploded node $en \in N^\#$, denoted by MRP_{en}, is defined as follows:*

$$MRP_{en} \stackrel{\text{def}}{=} \sqcap_{q \in RP(\langle s_{main}, \Lambda \rangle, en)} PathFn(q)(\top)$$

where PathFn is EdgeFn extended to paths by composition. □

We now state the theorem that is the basis for our algorithm for solving IDE problems:

Theorem 4.9 *For every $n \in N^*$ and $d \in D$, $MVP_n(d) = MRP_{\langle n,d \rangle}$.* □

The consequence of this theorem is that we can solve IDE problems by solving a related problem on the labeled exploded supergraph.

5 A Dynamic Programming Algorithm

In this section, we present an algorithm to compute the meet-over-all-valid-paths solution to a given dataflow problem instance *IP*. The input to the algorithm is the labeled exploded supergraph $G^{\#}_{IP}$; when the algorithm finishes, for every exploded-graph node $en \in N^{\#}$, $val(en) = MRP_{en}$. The algorithm operates in two phases, which are shown in Figures 3 and 4. In Phase I, the algorithm builds up *path functions* (recorded in *PathFn*) and *summary functions* (recorded in *SummaryFn*). Path functions and summary functions are defined in terms of *edge functions* (*EdgeFn*), and other path functions and summary functions. In Phase II, the path functions are used to determine the actual *values* associated with nodes of the exploded graph.

5.1 Phase I

Phase I is performed by procedure ComputePathFunctions, shown in Figure 3. ComputePathFunctions is a dynamic-programming algorithm that repeatedly computes path functions, which are functions from L to L, for longer and longer paths in $G^{\#}_{IP}$. The path functions to $\langle n, d\rangle$ summarize the effects of same-level realizable paths from the start node of n's procedure p to $\langle n, d\rangle$. There may be a path function from $\langle s_p, d'\rangle$ to $\langle n, d\rangle$ for all $d' \in D \cup \{\Lambda\}$. ComputePathFunctions also computes summary functions, which summarize the effects of same-level realizable paths from nodes of the form $\langle c, d'\rangle$, where c is a call node, to $\langle r, d\rangle$, where r is the corresponding return-site node.

ComputePathFunctions is a worklist algorithm that computes successively better approximations to the path and summary functions. It starts by initializing path and summary functions to $\lambda l.\top$. The worklist is initialized to contain the path from $\langle s_{main}, \Lambda\rangle$ to $\langle s_{main}, \Lambda\rangle$, and the path function for that path is initialized to the identity function, *id*. On each iteration of the main loop, the algorithm determines better approximations to path and summary functions.

To reduce the amount of work performed, ComputePathFunctions uses an idea similar to the "minimal-function-graph" approach [JM86]: Only after a path function for a path from a node of the form $\langle s_p, d_1\rangle$ to a node of the form $\langle c, d_2\rangle$ has been processed, where c is a call on procedure q, will a path from $\langle s_q, d_3\rangle$ to $\langle s_q, d_3\rangle$ be put on the worklist — and then only if edge $\langle c, d_2\rangle \rightarrow \langle s_q, d_3\rangle$ is in $E^{\#}$.

5.2 Phase II

Phase II is performed by procedure ComputeValues, shown in Figure 4. In this phase, the path functions are used to determine the actual *MRP* values associated with nodes of the exploded graph. Phase II consists of two sub-phases:

(i) An iterative algorithm is used to propagate values from the start node of the main procedure to all other start nodes and all call nodes. To compute a new approximation to the value at start node $\langle s_p, d\rangle$, $EdgeFn(en, \langle s_p, d\rangle)$ is applied to the current approximation at all nodes *en* associated with calls to p. To compute a new approximation to the value at call node $\langle c, d\rangle$ in procedure q, $PathFn(\langle s_q, d'\rangle, \langle c, d\rangle)$ is applied to the current approximations at all nodes $\langle s_q, d'\rangle$.

(ii) Values are computed for all nodes $\langle n, d\rangle$ that are neither start nor call nodes. This is done by applying $PathFn(\langle s_p, d'\rangle, \langle n, d\rangle)$ to $MRP(\langle s_p, d'\rangle)$ for all d' (where p is the procedure that contains n), and taking the meet of the resulting values.

Note that $val(\langle s_{main}, \Lambda\rangle)$ is initialized to $\perp$ in Phase II(i). As a result $\perp$ is propagated to all nodes of the form $\langle n, \Lambda\rangle$. Because the function on an edge from one of these nodes to

```
procedure ComputePathFunctions()
begin
  for all ⟨s_p, d'⟩, ⟨m, d⟩ such that m occurs in procedure p and d', d ∈ D ∪ {Λ} do
    PathFn(⟨s_p, d'⟩, ⟨m, d⟩) = λl.⊤ od
  for all corresponding call-return pairs c, r and d', d ∈ D ∪ {Λ} do
    SummaryFn(⟨c, d'⟩, ⟨r, d⟩) = λl.⊤ od
  WorkList:= {⟨s_main, Λ⟩ → ⟨s_main, Λ⟩}
  PathFn(⟨s_main, Λ⟩ → ⟨s_main, Λ⟩) := id
  while WorkList ≠ ∅ do
     Select and remove an edge ⟨s_p, d_1⟩ → ⟨n, d_2⟩ from WorkList
     let f = PathFn(⟨s_p, d_1⟩ → ⟨n, d_2⟩)
     switch(n)
        case n is a call node in p, calling a procedure q:
           for each d_3 s.t. ⟨n, d_2⟩ → ⟨s_q, d_3⟩ ∈ E# do
              Propagate (⟨s_q, d_3⟩ → ⟨s_q, d_3⟩, id) od
           let r be the return-site node that corresponds to n
           for each d_3 s.t. e = ⟨n, d_2⟩ → ⟨r, d_3⟩ ∈ E# do
              Propagate(⟨s_p, d_1⟩ → ⟨r, d_3⟩, EdgeFn(e) o f) od
           for each d_3 s.t. f_3 = SummaryFn(⟨n, d_2⟩ → ⟨r, d_3⟩) ≠ λl.⊤ do
              Propagate(⟨s_p, d_1⟩ → ⟨r, d_3⟩, f_3 o f) od endcase
        case n is the exit node of p:
           for each call node c that calls p with corresponding return-site node r do
              for each d_4, d_5 s.t. ⟨c, d_4⟩ → ⟨s_p, d_1⟩ ∈ E# and ⟨e_p, d_2⟩ → ⟨r, d_5⟩ ∈ E# do
                 let f_4 = EdgeFn(⟨c, d_4⟩ → ⟨s_p, d_1⟩) and
                     f_5 = EdgeFn(⟨e_p, d_2⟩ → ⟨r, d_5⟩) and
                     f' = (f_5 o f o f_4)⊓SummaryFn(⟨c, d_4⟩ → ⟨r, d_5⟩)
                 if f' ≠ SummaryFn(⟨c, d_4⟩ → ⟨r, d_5⟩) then
                   SummaryFn(⟨c, d_4⟩ → ⟨r, d_5⟩) := f'
                   let s_q be the start node of c's procedure
                   for each d_3 s.t. f_3 = PathFn(⟨s_q, d_3⟩ → ⟨c, d_4⟩) ≠ λl.⊤ do
                      Propagate(⟨s_q, d_3⟩ → ⟨r, d_5⟩, f' o f_3) od fi od od endcase
        default:
           for each ⟨m, d_3⟩ s.t. ⟨n, d_2⟩ → ⟨m, d_3⟩ ∈ E# do
              Propagate(⟨s_p, d_1⟩ → ⟨m, d_3⟩, EdgeFn(⟨n, d_2⟩ → ⟨m, d_3⟩) o f) od endcase
     end switch od
end
procedure Propagate(e, f)
begin
  let f' = f⊓PathFn(e)
  if f' ≠ PathFn(e) then
    PathFn(e) := f'
    Insert e into WorkList fi
end
```

FIGURE 3. The algorithm for Phase I.

```
procedure ComputeValues()
begin
   /* Phase II(i) */
   for each en ∈ N# do val(en) := ⊤ od
   val((s_main, Λ)) := ⊥
   WorkList := {(s_main, Λ)}
   while WorkList ≠ ∅ do
      Select and remove an exploded-graph node ⟨n, d⟩ from WorkList
      switch(n)
         case n is the start node of p:
            for each c that is a call node inside p do
               for each d' s.t. f' = PathFn(⟨n, d⟩ → ⟨c, d'⟩) ≠ λl.⊤ do
                  PropagateValue(⟨c, d'⟩, f'(val(⟨s_p, d⟩))) od od endcase
         case n is a call node in p, calling a procedure q:
            for each d' s.t. ⟨n, d⟩ → ⟨s_q, d'⟩ ∈ E# do
               PropagateValue(⟨s_q, d'⟩, EdgeFn(⟨n, d⟩ → ⟨s_q, d'⟩)(val(⟨n, d⟩))) od endcase
      end switch od
   /* Phase II(ii) */
   for each node n, in a procedure p, that is not a call or a start node do
      for each d', d s.t. f' = PathFn(⟨s_p, d'⟩ → ⟨n, d⟩) ≠ λl.⊤ do
         val(⟨n, d⟩) := val(⟨n, d⟩) ⊓ f'(val(⟨s_p, d'⟩)) od od
end
procedure PropagateValue(en, v)
begin
   let v' = v ⊓ val(en)
   if v' ≠ val(en) then
      val(en) := v'
      Insert en into WorkList fi
end
```

FIGURE 4. The algorithm for Phase II.

a non-Λ node *em* is always a constant function (see Definition 4.1), the $\perp$ value at $\langle n, \Lambda\rangle$ cannot affect the value at *em*.

Example 5.1 When applied to the exploded graph of Figure 2, our algorithm discovers that x has the constant value -9 at node $n3$ (the print statement in the main procedure), and that a does *not* have a constant value at node s_P (the start node of procedure P). During Phase I, the algorithm computes the following relevant path and summary functions: $PathFn(\langle s_P, a\rangle \rightarrow \langle n6, a\rangle) = \lambda l.l - 2$, $PathFn(\langle s_P, a\rangle \rightarrow \langle e_P, x\rangle) = \lambda l. -2 * l + 5$, $SummaryFn(\langle n1, \Lambda\rangle \rightarrow \langle n2, x\rangle) = \lambda l. -9$, $PathFn(\langle s_{main}, \Lambda\rangle \rightarrow \langle n2, x\rangle) = \lambda l. -9$, and $PathFn(\langle s_{main}, \Lambda\rangle \rightarrow \langle n3, x\rangle) = \lambda l. -9$.

During Phase II(i), values are propagated as follows to discover that a is not constant at node s_P: $val(\langle s_{main}, \Lambda\rangle) := \perp$, $val(\langle n1, \Lambda\rangle) := \perp$, $val(\langle s_P, a\rangle) := 7$, $val(\langle n6, a\rangle) := 5$, $val(\langle s_P, a\rangle) := 5 \sqcap 7 = \perp$.

During Phase II(ii), $PathFn(\langle s_{main}, \Lambda\rangle \rightarrow \langle n3, x\rangle)$ is applied to $val(\langle s_{main}, \Lambda\rangle)$, producing the value -9. □

5.3 Termination and Cost Issues

The algorithm of the previous section does not terminate for all IDE problems; however, it does terminate for all copy constant-propagation problems, all linear constant-propagation problems, and, in general, for all problems for which the space F of value-transformer functions contains no infinite decreasing chains. (Note that it is possible to construct infinite decreasing chains even in certain distributive variants of constant propagation [SP81, page 206].)

The cost of the algorithm is dominated by the cost of Phase I. This phase can be carried out particularly efficiently if there exists a way of representing the functions such that the functional operations can be computed in unit-time.

These termination and cost issues motivate the following definition:

Definition 5.2 *A class of value-transformer functions $F \subseteq L \to L$ has an* **efficient representation** *if*

- *$id \in F$ and F is closed under functional meet and composition.*
- *F has a finite height (under the pointwise ordering).*
- *There is a representation scheme for F with the following properties:*

Apply: *Given a representation for a function $f \in F$, for every $l \in L$, $f(l)$ can be computed in constant time.*[4]

Composition: *Given the representations for any two functions $f_1, f_2 \in F$, a representation for the function $f_1 \circ f_2 \in F$ can be computed in constant time.*

Meet: *Given the representations for any two functions $f_1, f_2 \in F$, a representation for the function $f_1 \sqcap f_2 \in F$ can be computed in constant time.*

EQU: *Given the representations for any two functions $f_1, f_2 \in F$, it is possible to test in constant time whether $f_1 = f_2$.*

Storage: *There is a constant bound on the storage needed for the representation of any function $f \in F$.*

An IDE problem instance $IP = (G^*, D, L, M)$ is **efficiently representable** *if for every $e \in E^*$, and $d', d \in D$, $R_{M(e)}(d', d) \in F$ for some class of functions F that has an efficient representation.* □

Note that in the above definition we do not impose any restrictions on $R_{M(e)}(d', d)$ when either d' or d is Λ. This is based on the assumption that the constant functions and the identity function can always be represented in an efficient manner. (Similarly, we assume that $\lambda l.\top$ can always be represented in an efficient manner.)

In describing the cost of the algorithm it is convenient to introduce the notions of *path edge* and *summary edge*. A path edge is a pair of exploded-graph nodes whose path function is not equal to $\lambda l.\top$; likewise, a summary edge is a pair of exploded-graph nodes whose summary function is not equal to $\lambda l.\top$.

The source of a path edge is a node of the form $\langle s, d\rangle$, where s is the start node of some procedure; thus, there can be at most $D + 1$ path-edge sources in each procedure. Each iteration of Phase I extends a known path edge by composing it with (the function of) either an $E^\#$ edge or a summary edge. There are at most $O(ED^2)$ such edges. Because each edge e can be used in the operation "extend a path along edge e" once for every path-edge source, there are at most $O(ED^3)$ such composition steps.

For each path edge and summary edge from an exploded node $\langle n, \Lambda\rangle$, the path-function value can change at most height of L times. Similarly, path edges and summary edges emanating from other exploded nodes $\langle n, d\rangle$, $d \in D$, can change at most height of F times. Consequently, the total cost of Phase I, and thus of the entire algorithm, is bounded by $O(ED^3)$ (where the constant of proportionality depends on the heights of L and F.)

5.4 Some Efficiently Representable IDE Problems

Copy Constant Propagation

In copy constant propagation, all of the constant functions $\lambda l.c$ are associated with edges of the form $\langle m, \Lambda\rangle \to \langle n, d\rangle$. The only functions on "non-Λ" edges are identity functions. Since

[4] We assume a uniform-cost measure, rather than a logarithmic-cost measure; e.g., operations on integers can be performed in constant time.

$id \, o \, id = id$ and $id \sqcap id = id$, the class $F = \{id\}$ is trivially a class of functions that has an efficient representation.

Linear Constant Propagation

Linear constant propagation can be handled using the set of functions $F_{lc} = \{\lambda l.(a*l+b) \sqcap c \mid a \in Z-\{0\}, b \in Z, \text{and } c \in Z_{\perp}^{\top}\}$. (The functions where $a = 0$ are the constant functions, and, as in copy constant propagation, these are all associated with "Λ" edges.) Every function $f \in F_{lc}$ can be represented by a triple (a, b, c) where $a \in Z - \{0\}$, $b \in Z$, and $c \in Z_{\perp}^{\top}$ where:

$$f = \lambda l. \begin{cases} \top & l = \top \\ (a * l + b) \sqcap c & \text{otherwise} \end{cases}$$

F_{lc} has an efficient representation because:

- $id \in F_{lc}$
- Longest chains in F_{lc} have the form: $\lambda l.(a * l + b) \sqsupset \lambda l.(a * l + b) \sqcap c \sqsupset \lambda l.\perp$, for some $a, b, c \in Z$.
- The four representation requirements are met:

  Apply: Trivial.
  Meet:

$$(a_1, b_1, c_1) \sqcap (a_2, b_2, c_2) = \begin{cases} (a_1, b_1, c_1 \sqcap c_2) & a_1 = a_2, b_1 = b_2 \\ (a_1, b_1, c) & c = (a_1 * l_0 + b_1) \sqcap c_1 \sqcap c_2, \text{ where} \\ & l_0 = (b_1 - b_2)/(a_2 - a_1) \in Z \\ (1, 0, \perp) & \text{o.w.} \end{cases}$$

  Composition: $(a_1, b_1, c_1) \, o \, (a_2, b_2, c_2) = ((a_1 a_2), (a_1 b_2 + b_1), ((a_1 c_2 + b_1) \sqcap c_1))$. Here it is assumed that $x * \top = \top * x = x + \top = \top + x = \top$ for $x \in Z$.

  EQU: All representations except that of $\lambda l.\perp$ are unique. Any two triples in which $c = \perp$ represents $\lambda l.\perp$. However, equality can still be tested in unit time.

The third component c is needed so that the meet of two functions can be represented. For example, consider the code fragment **if** $\cdots$ **then** $y := 5 * x - 7$ **else** $y := 3 * x + 1$ **fi**. Variable y is only constant after the **if** when the initial value of x is 4, and in this case y's value is 13. Therefore, the meet of the functions in the then- and else-branches for y in terms of x is represented by $(5, -7, 13)$.

Linear constant propagation can be also performed on real numbers $R_{\perp}^{\top}$. In this case, the meet operation is slightly simpler because there no need to test whether $a_2 - a_1$ divides $b_1 - b_2$ evenly — only that $a_2 \neq a_1$ if $b_2 \neq b_1$.

6 Preliminary Experiments

We have carried out a preliminary study to determine the feasibility of the dynamic-programming algorithm and to compare its accuracy and time requirements with those of the naive algorithm that considers *all* paths rather than just the realizable paths. (The latter approach is still safe, but may be less accurate than the algorithm that considers only realizable paths. For example, for the program in Figure 1, variable x would not be identified as a constant at the print statement in procedure *main*.) The two algorithms were implemented in C and used with a front end that analyzes a C program and generates the corresponding exploded supergraph for the integer linear constant-propagation problem. (Pointers were handled conservatively; every assignment through a pointer was considered to kill all variables to which the "&" operator is applied somewhere in the program; all uses through pointers were considered non-constant.) The study used five C programs taken from the SPEC integer benchmark suite [SPE92]. Tests were carried out on a Sun SPARCstation 20 Model 61 with 64 MB of RAM.

Example	Lines of code: Source	Lines of code: Preprocessed	Procedures	Calls	N	E	D
compress	1503	657	15	28	1329	1464	77
eqntott	3454	2570	61	211	4015	4266	57
gcc.cpp	7037	4079	71	306	6492	7344	91
li	7741	6054	356	1707	13286	12648	56
sc	8515	7378	151	682	12366	13157	150

TABLE 1. Sizes of the input programs.

Example	Dynamic Programming: Time	Dynamic Programming: Constants	Dynamic Programming: Lines/sec.	Naive Algorithm: Time	Naive Algorithm: Constants	Naive Algorithm: Lines/sec.
compress	2.3 + .57	82	524	.91 + .40	50	1147
eqntott	4.53 + 1.59	9	564	2.42 + .14	9	1349
gcc.cpp	14.2 + 6.58	37	339	8.1 + .28	29	840
li	51.69 + 43.23	2	81	9.96 + .34	2	752
sc	47.91 + 43.12	78	94	20.4 + 1.13	72	395

TABLE 2. CPU times and number of constants discovered.

Table 1 gives information about code size (lines of source code and lines of preprocessed source code) and the parameters that characterize the size of the control-flow graphs. Table 2 compares the cost and accuracy of the dynamic-programming algorithm and the naive algorithm. The running times are "user cpu-time" + "system cpu-time" (in seconds) for the algorithms once the exploded supergraph is constructed. The columns labeled "Constants" indicate the number of right-hand-side variable uses that were found to be constant. "Lines/sec." indicates the number of lines of source code processed per second.

7 Related Work

The IDE framework is based on earlier interprocedural dataflow-analysis frameworks defined by Sharir and Pnueli [SP81] and Knoop and Steffen [KS92], as well as the *interprocedural, finite, distributive, subset framework* (or *IFDS framework*, for short) that we proposed earlier [RSH94, RHS95]. The IDE framework is basically the Sharir-Pnueli framework with three modifications:

(i) The dataflow domain is restricted to be a domain of environments.
(ii) The dataflow functions are restricted to be distributive environment transformers.
(iii) The edge from a call node to the corresponding return-site node can have an associated dataflow function.

Conditions (i) and (ii) are restrictions that make the IDE framework less general than the full Sharir-Pnueli framework. Condition (iii), however, generalizes the Sharir-Pnueli framework and permits it to cover programming languages in which recursive procedures have local variables and parameters (which the Sharir-Pnueli framework does not). A different generalization to handle recursive procedures with local variables and parameters was proposed by Knoop and Steffen [KS92].

The IDE framework is a strict generalization of the IFDS framework proposed in [RSH94, RHS95]. In IFDS problems, the set of dataflow facts D is a finite set and the dataflow functions (which are in $2^D \rightarrow 2^D$) distribute over the meet operator (either union or intersection, depending on the problem). Some IDE problems can be encoded as IFDS problems; however, an IDE problem in which L is infinite — such as the linear constant-propagation problem — cannot be translated into an IFDS problem. Consequently, this paper strictly extends the class of interprocedural dataflow-analysis problems known to be solvable in polynomial time. However, even when L is finite, the algorithm presented in this paper will perform much better than the algorithm for IFDS problems for many kinds of problems. For example, in the case of copy constant propagation, in any given problem instance the size of L is no larger than the number of constant literals in the program. The IDE version of copy constant propagation involves environments of size D, where D is the set of program variables; by contrast, the IFDS version involves subsets of $D \times L$. For some C programs that we investigated (of around 1,300 lines), the IFDS version ran out of virtual memory, whereas the IDE version finished in a few seconds.

The algorithm for solving IDE problems yields an efficient polynomial algorithm for determining precise (i.e., meet-over-all-valid-paths) solutions. For both copy constant propagation and linear constant propagation, there are several antecedents. A version of interprocedural copy constant propagation was developed at Rice and has been in use for many years. The algorithm is described in [CCKT86], and studies of how the algorithm performs in practice on Fortran programs were carried out by Grove and Torczon [GT93]. However, the Rice algorithm has two potential drawbacks that our algorithm does not have:

- The Rice algorithm is not precise for recursive programs. (In fact, it may fall into an infinite loop when applied to recursive programs.)
- Because of limitations in the way "return jump functions" are generated, the Rice algorithm does not yield precise answers for all non-recursive programs.

We have also shown in this paper how to solve linear constant-propagation problems, which in general find a superset of the instances of constant variables found by copy constant propagation. Several others have also examined classes of constant-propagation problems more general than copy constant propagation [Kar76, SK91, GT93, MS93].

8 Demand Dataflow Analysis

We have developed and implemented a demand algorithm for the IDE framework. The demand algorithm finds the value of a given symbol $d \in D$ at a given control flow graph node $n \in N^*$. Because of space limitations we confine ourselves to a brief summary of this work.

The demand algorithm is similar to the dynamic-programming algorithm of Section 5; however, in the demand algorithm, path functions are computed during a backwards traversal of $G^{\#}_{IP}$ (i.e., edges are traversed from target to source). The relationship between the demand algorithm and the algorithm of Section 5 is similar to the relationship that holds for IFDS problems between the demand algorithm of [RSH94, HRS95] and the exhaustive algorithm of [RSH94, RHS95].

A different approach to obtaining demand versions of interprocedural dataflow-analysis algorithms has been investigated by Duesterwald, Gupta, and Soffa [DGS95]. In their approach, for each query a set of dataflow equations is set up on the flow graph (but as if all edges were reversed). The flow functions on the reverse graph are the (approximate) inverses of the forward flow functions. These equations are then solved using a demand-driven fixed-point-finding procedure.

Our demand algorithm has the following advantages over the algorithm given by Duesterwald, Gupta, and Soffa:

(1) Their algorithm only applies when L has a *finite number of elements*, whereas we require only that L and F be of *finite height*. For example, linear constant propagation, where L has an infinite number of elements, is outside the class of problems handled by their algorithm.

(2) Instead of computing the value of d at n, their algorithm answers queries of the form "Is the value of d at $n \sqsupseteq l$?" for a given value $l \in L$. In linear constant propagation, there is no way to use queries of this form to find the constant value of a given variable.

(3) When restricted to IFDS problems, the worst-case cost of the Duesterwald-Gupta-Soffa

technique is $O(E\,D\,2^D)$. In contrast, the worst-case cost of our demand algorithm is $O(E\,D^3)$.

Duesterwald, Gupta, and Soffa also give a specialized algorithm that, for copy constant propagation, remedies problems (2) and (3).

References

[Cal88] D. Callahan. The program summary graph and flow-sensitive interprocedural data flow analysis. In *SIGPLAN Conference on Programming Languages Design and Implementation*, pages 47–56, 1988.

[CCKT86] D. Callahan, K.D. Cooper, K. Kennedy, and L. Torczon. Interprocedural constant propagation. In *SIGPLAN Symposium on Compiler Construction*, pages 152–161, 1986.

[DGS95] E. Duesterwald, R. Gupta, and M.L. Soffa. Demand-driven computation of interprocedural data flow. In *ACM Symposium on Principles of Programming Languages*, pages 37–48, 1995.

[FL88] C.N. Fischer and R.J. LeBlanc. *Crafting a Compiler.* Benjamin/Cummings Publishing Company, Inc., Menlo Park, CA, 1988.

[GT93] D. Grove and L. Torczon. A study of jump function implementations. In *SIGPLAN Conference on Programming Languages Design and Implementation*, pages 90–99, 1993.

[HRS95] S. Horwitz, T. Reps, and M. Sagiv. Demand interprocedural dataflow analysis. Unpublished manuscript, 1995.

[JM86] N.D. Jones and A. Mycroft. Data flow analysis of applicative programs using minimal function graphs. In *ACM Symposium on Principles of Programming Languages*, pages 296–306, 1986.

[Kar76] M. Karr. Affine relationship among variables of a program. *Acta Inf.*, 6:133–151, 1976.

[Kil73] G.A. Kildall. A unified approach to global program optimization. In *ACM Symposium on Principles of Programming Languages*, pages 194–206, 1973.

[KS92] J. Knoop and B. Steffen. The interprocedural coincidence theorem. In *International Conference on Compiler Construction*, pages 125–140, 1992.

[LR91] W. Landi and B.G. Ryder. Pointer induced aliasing: A problem classification. In *ACM Symposium on Principles of Programming Languages*, pages 93–103, 1991.

[MS93] R. Metzger and S. Stroud. Interprocedural constant propagation: An empirical study. *ACM Letters on Programming Languages and Systems*, 2, 1993.

[Rep94] T. Reps. Solving demand versions of interprocedural analysis problems. In *International Conference on Compiler Construction*, pages 389–403, 1994.

[RHS95] T. Reps, S. Horwitz, and M. Sagiv. Precise interprocedural dataflow analysis via graph reachability. In *ACM Symposium on Principles of Programming Languages*, pages 49–61, 1995.

[RSH94] T. Reps, M. Sagiv, and S. Horwitz. Interprocedural dataflow analysis via graph reachability. Technical Report TR 94-14, Datalogisk Institut, University of Copenhagen, 1994.

[SK91] B. Steffen and J. Knoop. Finite constants: Characterizations of a new decidable set of constants. *Theoretical Computer Science*, 80(2):303–318, 1991.

[SP81] M. Sharir and A. Pnueli. Two approaches for interprocedural data flow analysis. In S.S. Muchnick and N.D. Jones, editors, *Program Flow Analysis: Theory and Applications*, chapter 7, pages 189–234. Prentice-Hall, 1981.

[SPE92] SPEC Component CPU Integer Release 2/1992 (Cint92). Standard Performance Evaluation Corporation (SPEC), Fairfax, VA, 1992.

Formal Specification and Prototyping of a Program Specializer

Sandrine Blazy, Philippe Facon
CEDRIC IIE
18 allée Jean Rostand
91025 Evry Cedex, France
{blazy, facon}@iie.cnam.fr

Abstract. This paper reports on the use of formal specifications in the development of a software maintenance tool for specializing imperative programs, which have become very complex due to extensive modifications. The tool is specified in terms of inference rules and operates by induction on the abstract syntax. The correctness of these rules is proved using rule induction. A Prolog prototype has been derived for Fortran programs, using the Centaur programming environment.
Keywords: structured operational semantics, VDM, software maintenance, program specialization, proof of correctness, rule induction, Centaur.

1 Introduction

We have developed an original technique for specializing programs which are too difficult to maintain because they are too general. These programs are written in an imperative language (noted L in the sequel of this paper). This technique aims at understanding old programs, which have become very complex due to extensive modifications. From a given program and some form of restriction of its usage (e.g. the knowledge of some specific values of its input variables), this technique provides a simplified program, which behaves like the initial one when used according to the restriction. This approach is particularly well adapted to programs which have evolved as their application domains increase continually.

Our technique is a variant of partial evaluation, a well known technique that has been used for optimization and to derive compilers from interpreters [10]. Partial evaluation of a subject program P with respect to input variables $x_1, ..., x_m, y_1, ..., y_n$ for the values $x_1 = c_1, ..., x_m = c_m$ gives a residual program P', whose input variables are $y_1, ..., y_n$ and the executions of $P(c_1, ..., c_m, y_1, ..., y_n)$ and $P'(y_1, ..., y_n)$ produce the same results. Such a program is obtained by replacing variables by their constant values, by propagating constant values, and by modifying statements, for instance replacing each alternative whose condition simplifies to a constant value by the corresponding branch or unfolding loops when possible. But, our aim differs from the one of traditional partial evaluation. We do not try to optimize code but to improve its readability, mainly by simplifying it. For example, we never expand loops.

In another paper we have explained the aim and use of our tool [3], but not it's development. Here we will instead focus on the formal concepts we have used for developing it. Residual programs are used during maintenance. They are either visualized to locate anomalies while debugging or used as independent programs, instead of the initial ones. Thus, our tool - as software maintenance tool - must introduce absolutely no unforeseen changes in programs. Therefore, we have first to formally specify the specializer, then to prove the correctness of that specification with respect to the standard semantics, and eventually (third step) to prove the correctness of the implemented tool with respect to the specialization rules. We will develop here only the first two steps of the process. Indeed, from that specification, a Prolog prototype has been almost systematically derived by using the Centaur programming environment [4]. An industrial tool is being developed from that specification.

Our specification is expressed by inference rules operating on the abstract syntax of the language L. More precisely, we have used the natural semantics formalism [9], augmented with some VDM [8] operators. Natural semantics has its origin in the work of G.Plotkin ([7], [11]). Under the name "structured operational semantics", he gives inference rules as a direct formalization of an intuitive operational semantics: his rules define inductively the transitions of an abstract interpreter. Natural semantics extends that work by applying the same idea (use of a formal system) to different kinds of semantic analysis (not only interpretation, but also typing, translation, etc.)

This paper is organized as follows. First, we detail in section 2 some inference rules that formally specify our specializer. Next, section 3 presents proofs of correctness of our specializer rules with respect to the dynamic semantics of the imperative language L. Section 4 explains how we have prototyped our specializer and gives some quantitative results about the implementation of a prototype for specializing Fortran programs. Section 5 presents conclusions and future work.

2 Inference Rules for Specialization

2.1 The Specialization Strategy

As explained in the introduction, we want to specialize a program for readability purposes, not for optimization ones, that is we want only to simplify it. What does it mean to simplify a program in that context? We believe that to remove useless code is always beneficial to program understanding. In that case the objective is compatible with that of program optimization (dead code elimination [2]), but this is certainly not the case in general. On the other hand, the replacement of (occurences of) variables by their values is not so obvious. The benefit depends on what these variables mean for the user: variables like PI, TAX_RATE, etc. are likely to be kept in the code; on the contrary, intermediate variables used only to decompose some computations may be not so meaningful for the user, and he may prefer to have them removed.

Replacing variables by their values may lead to dead code (by making the assignments to these variables useless) and thus gives more opportunities to remove code. However, this is certainly not a sufficient reason to do systematic replacement. Of course, even when there is no replacement, the known value of a variable is kept in the environment of our simplification rules, as it can give opportunities to remove useless code, for instance if the condition of an alternative may be evaluated thanks to that knowledge (and thus a branch may be removed).

The benefit of replacement depends not only on the kind of variable but also on the kind of user: a user who knows the application program well may prefer to keep the variables the meaning of which is already known to him; a user trying to understand an application program he does not know at all may prefer to see as few variables as possible. In fact, our experiments have shown that the system must be very flexible in that respect. Thus, our system works as follows. There are three options: no replacement, systematic replacement, and each replacement depending on the user.

To specify the partial evaluation, we use inference rules operating on the L abstract syntax. The following part of this section first presents rules defining both the constant propagation process and the simplification process. Then, a third part details the rules for partial evaluation of statements. These new rules combine the propagation rules and the simplification rules. Note that these techniques are not new, but we specify and use them in a novel way. In this paper, we present only the rules for assignment and alternative statements. The other rules can be found in [3].

2.2 Propagation and Simplification Rules

In the following, we use sequents such as $H \overset{propag}{\vdash} I{:}H'$ (propagation), $H \overset{simpl}{\vdash} I \rightarrow I'$ (simplification), and the combination of both $H \overset{PE}{\vdash} I \mapsto I', H'$ (propagation and simplification). In these sequents:

- H is the environment associating values to variables whose values are known before executing I. It is modelled by a VDM-like map [8], shown as a collection of pairs contained in set braces such as {variable → constant, ...}, where no two pairs have the same first elements. Our system initializes such maps by the list of variables and their initial values, supplied by the user.
- I is a statement (expressed in a linear form of the abstract syntax of L).
- I' is the simplified statement under the hypothesis H.
- H' is H which has been modified by the execution of I.
- The superscript of the turnstile such as *propag*, *simpl* or *PE* denotes the set of rules the sequent belongs to.

In the sequents exhibited in this paper, we use the map operators *dom*, ∪, ∩, =, † and ⩤.

- The domain operator *dom* yields the set of the first elements of the pairs in the map.
- The union operator ∪ yields the union of maps whose domains are disjoint (in VDM, this operator is undefined if the domains overlap).
- The intersection operator ∩ of two maps yields the pairs common to both maps.
- The equality operator = of two maps yields *true* if and only if each pair of one map is a pair of the other map (and reciprocally).
- The map override operator † whose operands are two maps, yields a map which contains all of the pairs from the second map and those pairs of the first map whose first elements are not in the domain of the second map.
- When applied to a set and a map, the map deletion operator ⩤ yields those pairs in

the map whose first elements are not in the set.

The examples of Figure 1 illustrate these definitions of map operators.

$$m = \{X \to 5, B \to true\} \qquad dom(m) = \{X, B\}$$
$$m \cup \{Y \to 7\} = \{Y \to 7, X \to 5, B \to true\}$$
$$\{B\} ⩤ m = \{X \to 5\}$$
$$m \cap \{X \to 5, B \to false\} = \{X \to 5\}$$
$$n = \{C \to false, X \to 8\} \qquad m \dagger n = \{X \to 8, B \to true, C \to false\}$$
$$n \dagger m = \{X \to 5, B \to true, C \to false\}$$

Fig. 1. Some map operators

We have written some inference rules to explain how sequents are obtained from other sequents. Propagation rules are a special case of program verification rules: they perform only forward analysis and they propagate only equalities between variables and constants. Figure 2 presents six of the eight simplification and propagation rules for alternatives. If the condition C of an alternative evaluates to true, then:

- the environment H' resulting from the propagation of H through the alternative is obtained by propagating H through the statements I_1 of the then-branch (first rule: propagation),
- the simplification of the alternative is the simplification of its then-branch (second rule: simplification).

In the same way, there are two rules for an alternative whose condition evaluates to false (in these rules "true" becomes "false", "I_1" becomes "I_2", and "then" becomes "else"). Since these rules are very similar to the first two rules, they do not appear in Figure 5. They are shown with partial evaluation rules in Figure 4.

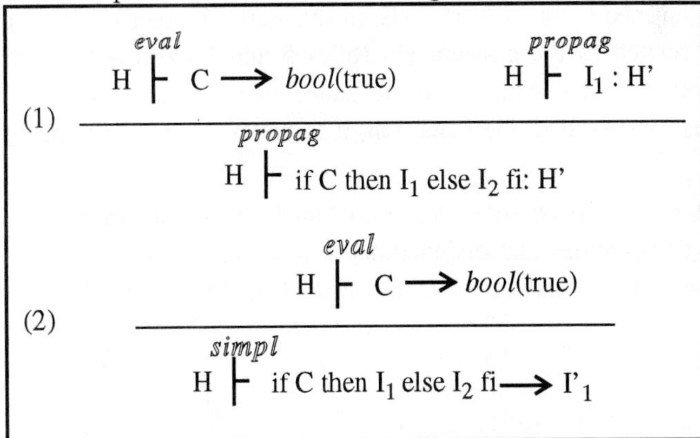

Fig. 2 (begin) Propagation and simplification rules for alternatives

If the condition C of an alternative is only partially evaluated to C', the propagation and the simplification proceed along both branches of the alternative:

- the propagation of H through the then-branch I_j leads to an environment H_j, j=1,2.

The intersection of both environments is the final environment: if a variable has the same value in both environments H_1 and H_2, that value is kept in the final environment, otherwise it is removed from the final environment (third rule: propagation).

- the simplification of the alternative yields the alternative whose condition is the partially evaluated condition C' and whose branches are the simplified branches of the initial alternative (fourth rule: simplification).

$$(3)\ \frac{H \overset{eval}{\vdash} C \longrightarrow C' \quad C' \neq bool(B) \quad H \overset{propag}{\vdash} I_1 : H_1 \quad H \overset{propag}{\vdash} I_2 : H_2}{H \overset{propag}{\vdash} \text{if C then } I_1 \text{ else } I_2 \text{ fi: } H_1 \cap H_2}$$

$$(4)\ \frac{H \overset{eval}{\vdash} C \longrightarrow C' \quad C' \neq bool(B) \quad H \overset{simpl}{\vdash} I_1 \longrightarrow I'_1 \quad H \overset{simpl}{\vdash} I_2 \longrightarrow I'_2}{H \overset{simpl}{\vdash} \text{if C then } I_1 \text{ else } I_2 \text{ fi} \longrightarrow \text{if C' then I'1 else } I'_2 \text{ fi}}$$

Fig. 2 (cont'd) Propagation and simplification rules for alternatives

The fifth rule of Figure 2 is a propagation rule. It shows that information can sometimes be derived from the equality tests that control alternatives. If the condition of an alternative is expressed as an equality such as X=E, where X is a variable that does not belong to the domain of the environment H and E evaluates to a constant N, then the pair (X, N) is added to the environment related to the then-branch.

Since the statements *if X≠E then I_1 else I_2 fi* and *if X=E then I_2 else I_1 fi* are semantically equivalent, there is a corresponding rule (sixth rule) for a condition of an alternative expressed as an inequality such as X≠E: in that case, the pair (X,N) is added to the environment related to the else-branch. Rules 5 and 6 express that only equalities between variables and constants can be added to the environment. Thus, if other information is expressed in the condition, it is not taken into account by the partial evaluator.

Rules 5 and 6 have been generalized to conditions of alternatives expressed as conjunctions of equalities and disjunctions of inequalities (rules 5' and 6'). In these rules, we have used generalized AND (denoted $\underset{i=1,n}{\wedge}$) and OR (denoted $\underset{i=1,n}{\vee}$).

$$\frac{H \overset{eval}{\vdash} E \longrightarrow number(N) \quad X \notin dom(H) \quad H \cup \{X \rightarrow N\} \overset{propag}{\vdash} I_1 : H_1 \quad H \overset{propag}{\vdash} I_2 : H_2}{H \overset{propag}{\vdash} \text{if } (X = E) \text{ then } I_1 \text{ else } I_2 \text{ fi: } H_1 \cap H_2} \quad (5)$$

$$\frac{H \overset{eval}{\vdash} E \longrightarrow number(N) \quad X \notin dom(H) \quad H \overset{propag}{\vdash} I_1 : H_1 \quad H \cup \{X \rightarrow N\} \overset{propag}{\vdash} I_2 : H_2}{H \overset{propag}{\vdash} \text{if } (X \neq E) \text{ then } I_1 \text{ else } I_2 \text{ fi: } H_1 \cap H_2} \quad (6)$$

$$\frac{\begin{array}{c} \forall i, H \overset{eval}{\vdash} E_i \longrightarrow number(N_i) \\ \forall i, X_i \notin dom(H) \quad H \bigcup_{i=1,n} \{Xi \rightarrow Ni\} \overset{propag}{\vdash} I_1 : H_1 \quad H \overset{propag}{\vdash} I_2 : H_2 \end{array}}{H \overset{propag}{\vdash} \text{if } (\bigwedge_{i=1,n} Xi = Ei) \text{ then } I_1 \text{ else } I_2 \text{ fi: } H_1 \cap H_2} \quad (5')$$

$$\frac{\begin{array}{c} \forall i, H \overset{eval}{\vdash} E_i \longrightarrow number(N_i) \\ \forall i, X_i \notin dom(H) \quad H \overset{propag}{\vdash} I_1 : H_1 \quad H \bigcup_{i=1,n} \{Xi \rightarrow Ni\} \overset{propag}{\vdash} I_2 : H_2 \end{array}}{H \overset{propag}{\vdash} \text{if } (\bigvee_{i=1,n} Xi \neq Ei) \text{ then } I_1 \text{ else } I_2 \text{ fi: } H_1 \cap H_2} \quad (6')$$

Fig. 2-(end) Propagation and simplification rules for alternatives

Since the simplification is performed in the context of the propagation, and the propagation uses the simplification of expressions, we have chosen to combine propagation and simplification in our rules.

2.3 Combined Rules

For every FORTRAN statement, we have written rules that describe the combination of the propagation and simplification systems. This combination $\twoheadrightarrow$ of these two systems is defined by:

$$H \overset{PE}{\vdash} I \twoheadrightarrow I', H' \quad \text{iff} \quad H \overset{propag}{\vdash} I{:}H' \quad \text{and} \quad H \overset{simpl}{\vdash} I \rightarrow I'$$

From this rule, we may define inductively the $\twoheadrightarrow$relation. For instance, Figure 3 specifies the rules for partial evaluation of assignments. The ***eval*** notation refers to the formal system of rules which simplifies the expressions.

If the expression E evaluates to a numerical constant N, the environment H is modified: the value of X is N whether X had already a value in H or not. With the kind of propagation we perform, the assignment X := E can be removed only if all possible uses of that occurrence of X do not use another value of X. For instance, in the sequence

X := 2; if CODE ≠ 5 then X := X+1 fi; Y := X,

the value 2 of X is propagated in the expression X+1 but the assignment X:=2 can not be removed because in the assignment Y:=X, X comes either from X:=2 (value 2) or from X:=X+1 (value 3). Thus, that sequence is only simplified to

X := 2; if CODE ≠ 5 then X := 3 fi; Y := X.

To eliminate assignments that become useless after the partial evaluation, we use classical dead code elimination algorithms [2]. Thus, elimination of redundant assignments is performed in a separate optimization phase.

If E is only partially evaluable into E', the expression E is modified as part of the assignment X:= E and the variable X is removed from the environment if it was in it, because its value has become unknown.

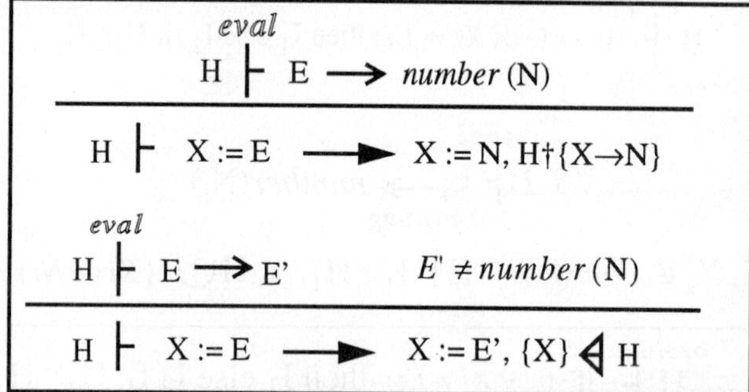

Fig. 3. Partial evaluation of assignments

The following examples illustrate these two cases. In *Ex.1*, as the value of the variable A is known, the new value of the assigned variable C is introduced in the environment. We suppose that the assignment C := A+1 can be removed from the reduced program. In *Ex.2*, after the partial evaluation of the expression A+B, the value of C has become unknown. Such a case only happens when A and B do not have both constant values.

Ex.1 $\{A \rightarrow 1, C \rightarrow 4\} \vdash C := A + 1 \longrightarrow$ skip, $\{A \rightarrow 1, C \rightarrow 2\}$

Ex.2 $\{A \rightarrow 1, C \rightarrow 2\} \vdash C := A + B \longrightarrow C := 1 + B, \{A \rightarrow 1\}$

The rules for partial evaluation of alternatives are defined in Figure 4. If the condition C of an alternative evaluates to a logical constant, this alternative can be simplified to the corresponding simplified branch. If C is only partially evaluated to C', the partial evaluation proceeds along both branches of the alternative and the final environment is the intersection of the two environments resulting from the simplification of both branches (as explained previously, Fig. 2, rule (4)).

$$\frac{H \overset{eval}{\vdash} C \rightarrow bool\,(\text{false}) \qquad H \vdash I_2 \longrightarrow I'_2, H'}{H \vdash \text{if } C \text{ then } I_1 \text{ else } I_2 \text{ fi} \longrightarrow I'_2, H'}$$

$$\frac{H \overset{eval}{\vdash} C \rightarrow bool\,(\text{true}) \qquad H \vdash I_1 \longrightarrow I'_1, H'}{H \vdash \text{if } C \text{ then } I_1 \text{ else } I_2 \text{ fi} \longrightarrow I'_1, H'}$$

$$\frac{H \overset{eval}{\vdash} C \rightarrow C' \qquad C' \neq bool(B) \qquad H \vdash I_1 \longrightarrow I'_1, H'_1 \qquad H \vdash I_2 \longrightarrow I'_2, H'_2}{H \vdash \text{if } C \text{ then } I_1 \text{ else } I_2 \text{ fi} \longrightarrow \text{if } C' \text{ then } I'_1 \text{ else } I'_2 \text{ fi}, H'_1 \cap H'_2}$$

Fig. 4. Partial evaluation of alternatives

3 Correctness of the Partial Evaluation

Our aim in this section is to show how to prove that the specialization presented above is correct, with respect to the dynamic semantics of L, given in the natural semantics formalism.

We will show that this is expressed by two inference rules, one expressing soundness (each result of the residual program is correct with respect to the initial program) and one expressing "R-completeness" (each correct result is computed by the residual program too). We use the term "R-completeness" (result-completeness) to avoid confusion with the completely different notion of specialization completeness (i.e. no further specialization could be done, which is not an issue here). As both programs are deterministic, we could have only one rule using equality, but the demonstration of our two rules is not more complicated and is more general (being also applicable for non-deterministic programs). Examples of proofs for the assignment and alternative statements are detailed in this section.

3.1 Rules Proving Soundness and R-completeness

To prove the simplification, we need a formal dynamic semantics of L and we must prove the soundness and R-completeness of the simplification rules with respect to that dynamic semantics. To express this dynamic semantics, we use the same formalism (natural semantics [9]) as for simplification. Thus, the semantic rules we give have to generate theorems of the form $H \overset{sem}{\vdash} I: H'$, meaning that in environment H, the execution of statement I leads to the environment H' (or the evaluation of expression I gives value H'). These rules are themselves not proved: they are supposed to define ex nihilo the semantics of L, as G.Plotkin [11] and G.Kahn [9] did for languages like ML.

To prove these rules would mean to have another formal semantics (e.g. a denotational one) and prove that the rules are sound and complete with respect to it. But there is no such official semantics for any imperative language. Thus that proof would rather be a proof of consistency between two dynamic semantics we give. That is outside the scope of our work: we want to prove consistency between simplification and dynamic semantics, not between two dynamic semantics.

Now how can we prove that the specialization system is sound and R-complete with respect to the dynamic semantics system? Instead of the usual situation, that is a formal system and an intended model, we have two formal systems: the specialization system (noted $\mathbb{PE}$) and the dynamic semantics system (noted sem). A program P is simplified to P' under hypothesis H_0 on some input variables if and only if $Ho \vdash P \rightarrow P'$ is a theorem of the specialization system.

Let us call H the environment containing the values of the remaining input variables. Thus, $H_0 \cup H$ is the environment containing the values of all input variables. With that initial environment, P' evaluates to H' if and only if $Ho \cup H \overset{sem}{\vdash} P' : H'$ is a theorem of the dynamic semantics (sem) system. In a similar way, P evaluates to H' if and only if $Ho \cup H \overset{sem}{\vdash} P : H'$ is a theorem of the sem system

Now, soundness of specialization with respect to dynamic semantics means that each result computed by the residual program is computed by the initial program. That is, for each P, P', H_0, H, H': if P is simplified to P' under hypothesis H_0 and P' executes to H' under hypothesis $H_0 \cup H$, then P executes to H'under hypothesis $H_0 \cup H$. Thus soundness of simplification with respect to dynamic semantics is formally expressed by the first rule of Figure 5.

R-completeness of simplification with respect to dynamic semantics means that each result computed by the initial program P is computed by the residual program P'. Thus, it is expressed by the second inference rule of Figure 5. In fact, our approach to prove simplification is very close to the approach of [5] to prove the correctness of translators: in that paper, dynamic semantics and translation are both given by formal systems and the correctness of the translation with respect to dynamic semantics of source and object languages is also formalized by inference rules (that are proved by induction on the length of the proof; here we will use rule induction instead).

Note that both rules are not the most restricting rules (for instance their initial environment is $Ho \cup H$ and not only H, to allow partial simplification).

$$\frac{Ho \vdash P \rightarrow P' \qquad Ho \cup H \overset{sem}{\vdash} P' : H'}{Ho \cup H \overset{sem}{\vdash} P : H'} \quad \textit{(soundness)}$$

$$\frac{Ho \vdash P \rightarrow P' \qquad Ho \cup H \overset{sem}{\vdash} P : H'}{Ho \cup H \overset{sem}{\vdash} P' : H'} \quad \textit{(R-completeness)}$$

Fig. 5. Correctness of the program simplification

To prove both rules of Figure 5 concerning programs, we prove that they hold for any statement we specialize (remember that we do not analyze data declarations). Thus, we have to prove that both rules of Figure 6 hold. In these rules, I denotes a statement and I' denotes the corresponding specialized statement.

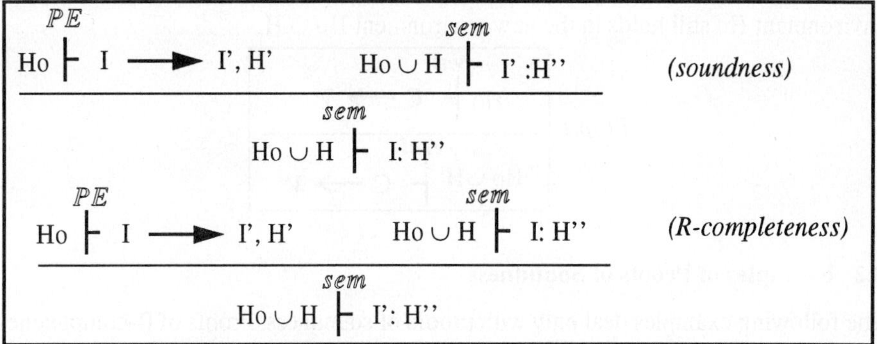

Fig. 6. Correctness of the statements partial evaluation

The dynamic semantics of L has been formalized by the *sem* system. The dynamic semantics rules for assignments and alternatives are propagation rules, as shown in Figure 7. For that reason, in the *sem* system, we have overloaded the ":" symbol representing the system *propag*, instead of using a new symbol.

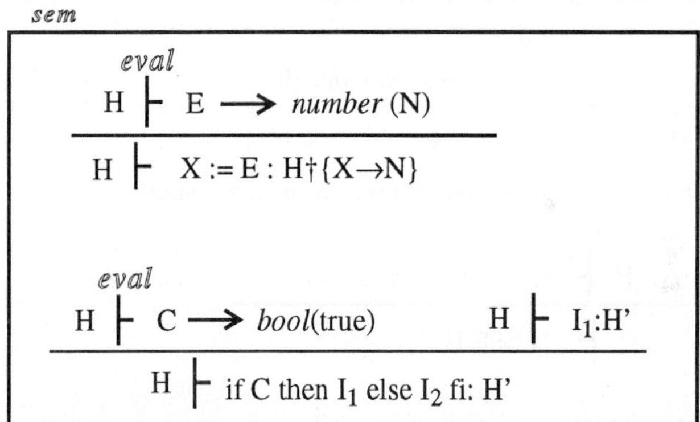

Fig. 7. Dynamic semantics rules for assignments and alternatives

To prove the validity of the R-completeness and soundness rules, we use rule induction on the partial evaluation, and on the dynamic semantics. Indeed, the *PE* and *sem* systems have been defined inductively.

Our inductive hypothesis for soundness is the following property Π_s, defined as follows: $\Pi_s\,(Ho,I,I',H') \Leftrightarrow (\forall\, Ho,I,I',H' \mid Ho \vdash^{PE} I \longrightarrow I', H' :$

$$(\forall\, H,H''\ Ho \cup H \vdash^{sem} I': H'' \Rightarrow Ho \cup H \vdash^{sem} I: H'')).$$

The inductive hypothesis Π_c for R-completeness is defined in a similar way. The rule induction operating on a formal system (either *PE* or *sem*) states that quadruples are only obtained by the rules belonging to this formal system.

To construct our proof trees we use property *Prop.1*, which states that if some (variable, value) pairs are added to an environment Ho, what had been already proved in this environment Ho still holds in the new environment Ho ∪ H.

$$Prop.1 \quad \frac{Ho \vdash^{eval} C \rightarrow V}{Ho \cup H \vdash^{eval} C \rightarrow V}$$

3.2 Examples of Proofs of Soundness

The following examples deal only with proofs of soundness. Proofs of R-completeness are similar. We start with treating simple statements, which are not composed of other statements. They form the basic cases of the proof. Figure 8 shows a proof of such a statement. The possible removal of assignment does not appear in the proof tree, since it is performed during a dead code elimination phase, subsequently to the evaluation of the expression of the assignment.

If we assume that the partial evaluation rule

$$\frac{H \vdash^{eval} E \rightarrow number\ (N)}{H \vdash X := E \longrightarrow X := N,\ H\dagger\{X \rightarrow N\}}$$

holds, and by the rule of the sem system about assignment:

$$\frac{H \vdash^{eval} E \rightarrow number\ (N)}{H \vdash X := E\ H\dagger\{X \rightarrow N\}}$$

then for any H_0 and H'' such that Ho ∪ H ⊢ X:=N : H'',
we have, H'' = (Ho ∪ H)†{X→N}, *thus proving that the following proof tree holds:*

$$\frac{\dfrac{H \vdash^{eval} E \rightarrow number\ (N)}{Ho \cup H \vdash^{eval} E \rightarrow number\ (N)}\ Prop.1}{Ho \cup H \vdash X := E \longrightarrow X := N,\ H\dagger\{X \rightarrow N\}}\ \textit{rule for the assignment belonging to the sem system}$$

thus proving that Π_s *(H, X:=E, X:=N,* H†{X→N}*) holds.*

Fig. 8. Proof of soundness of an assignment partial evaluation

Once simple statements have been proved, we have to prove that the soundness rule holds for composite statements. Figure 10 shows a proof of soundness for an alternative whose condition evaluates to true. There is a similar proof for the case when the condition evaluates to false.

If we assume that the rule

$$\frac{Ho \overset{eval}{\vdash} C \longrightarrow bool(\text{true}) \qquad Ho \overset{PE}{\vdash} I_1 \longrightarrow I'_1, H'}{Ho \overset{PE}{\vdash} \text{if C then } I_1 \text{ else } I_2 \text{ fi} \longrightarrow I'_1, H'}$$

and the inductive hypothesis Π_s *(H,*I_1*,*I'_1*,H') hold, then we can deduce that:*

$$(\forall H_0, H'': \quad Ho \cup H \overset{sem}{\vdash} I'_1 : H'' \Rightarrow Ho \cup H \overset{sem}{\vdash} I_1 : H'').$$

Furthermore, the dynamic semantics of the if statement states that

$$\frac{H \overset{eval}{\vdash} C \longrightarrow bool(\text{true}) \qquad H \vdash I_1 : H'}{H \vdash \text{if C then } I_1 \text{ else } I_2 \text{ fi}: H'}$$

Then, we can state that:

$$(\forall Ho, H'': \quad Ho \cup H \overset{sem}{\vdash} I'_1 : H'' \Rightarrow \quad Ho \cup H \overset{sem}{\vdash} \text{if C then } I_1 \text{ else } I_2 \text{ fi}: H'').$$

thus proving that Π_s *(H, if C then I1else I2 fi,* I'_1*,H') holds.*

Fig. 9. Proof of soundness of an alternative whose condition evaluates to true

4 Implementation of a Prototype

This section describes the overall architecture of our specializer. Then, it gives quantitative results measured for a Fortran specializer.

4.1 Architecture of the Specializer

The specialization rules are very close to the ones we have implemented in the Centaur/L environment. The Centaur system [4] is a generic programming environment parametrized by the syntax and semantics of programming languages. When provided with the description of a particular programming language, including its syntax and semantics, Centaur produces a language specific environment. The resulting environment consists of a structured editor, an interpreter/debugger and other tools, together with an uniform graphical interface. Furthermore, in Centaur, program texts are represented by abstract syntax trees. The textual (or graphical) representation of abstract syntax trees nodes may be specified by pretty-printing rules. Centaur provides a default representation.

We have used such a resulting environment, Centaur/L, to build our specializer. From Centaur/L we have implemented an environment for specialization of programs written in L. Figure 10 shows the overall architecture of this environment, where Centaur/L is represented by the grey part.

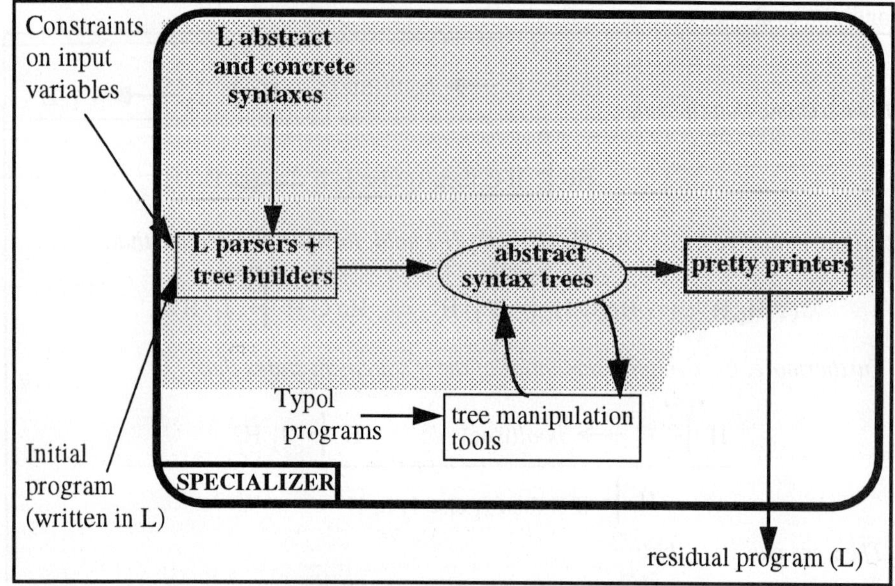

Fig. 10. The Centaur/L environment

From a Centaur/L environment, we have written Typol programs to implement our specification rules. Typol is a language for specifying the semantic aspects of languages; it is included in Centaur, so that the system is not restricted to manipulations that are based solely on syntax. Typol is an implementation of natural semantics. It can be used to specify and implement static semantics, dynamic semantics and translations. Typol programs are compiled into Prolog code. When executing these programs, Prolog is used as the engine of the deductive system.

Figure 11 shows two examples of Typol rules: a rule specializing an assignment whose expression does not evaluate to a constant value (1) and a rule specializing an alternative in its else-branch (2). These rules show Prolog primitives implementing map operators (their identifiers are italicized), nodes of abstract syntax trees (they are written in bold), and calls to Typol programs (their printing stands out in relief).

eval (H |- E -> E') & nonvar (E') & *deletion* (H, X, H')

-- (1)

Env |- **ass** (**name** X, E) -> **ass** (**name** X, E'), Env' ;

eval (H |- E -> **logic_cst** E') & false (E') & H |- I2 -> I2', H'

-- (2)

H |- **struct_if** (Tag, E, I1, I2) -> **l_stat**[I2'], H' ;

Fig. 11. Some Typol rules for assignments and alternatives

4.2 Quantitative Results for Fortran Programs

We have chosen Fortran to implement our technique for specializing imperative programs because Fortran is still widespread in scientific programming. We have exhibited a large class of scientific applications our approach is particularly well adapted to. We have written about 200 Typol rules to implement a Fortran specializer. 10 rules express how to reach abstract syntax nodes representing simplifiable statements. 90 rules perform the normalization of expressions. Among the 100 rules for simplification, 60 rules implement the simplification of expressions. The 40 other rules implement the statements simplification. We have written about 25 Prolog predicates to implement the VDM operators we have used to specify the simplification. Thus, these operators are used in Typol rules as in the formal specification of the simplification.

The partial evaluator may analyze any Fortran program, but it simplifies only a subset of Fortran 77. This subset is a recommended standard for developping the scientific applications we have studied. For instance, it does not analyze any goto statement (they are not recommended), but only goto statements that implement specific control structures (e.g. a while-loop).

The average initial length of programs or subroutines we have analyzed is 100 lines of FORTRAN code, which is lengthier than the recommended length (60-70 lines). The reduction rate amounts from 25% to 80% of lines of code. That length reduction is obtained mostly by removal of code which is useless in the given context. Thus, it implies a direct improvement in readability. This reduction is specially important when there is a large number of assignments and conditionals. This is the case for most subroutines implementing mathematical algorithms. For subroutines whose main purpose is editing results or calling other subroutines, the reduction is generally not so important.

5 Conclusion

We have used partial evaluation for programs which are difficult to maintain because they are too general. We have formally specified our specialization with inference rules expressed in the natural semantics formalism and augmented with some VDM operators. We have shown how to prove by rule induction the correctness of our formal system, given the standard semantics of the programming language.

A protoype has been derived from this specification. We are now focusing on an industrial implementation of this prototype. This tool will be used by maintainers at the EDF, the national French company that provides and distributes electricity to the whole country. It will be developed by CEDRIC IIE and Simulog, a company that provided us with some basic tools including Centaur/Fortran. To obtain an insdustrial tool from the current prototype, we will take into account new operators from Fortran 90. Most of this work will consist first in adding new language concepts, that is new abstract syntax operators, and seconly in defining for each new operator how the specialization rules are modified.

Furthermore, the formal specification of our specializer is used as a reference document between people involved in the development of the specializer. It allows us to:

- express the real semantics of each languge construct we simplify,
- define precisely what are the interesting simplifications of statements,
- exhibit and prove the specialization rules. With all extensions we take into account, the whole proof become rather tedious. Thus, we expect to use a theorem prover as COQ [6].

References

1. *FORTRAN.* ANSI standard X3.9, 1978.
2. A.Aho, R.Sethi, J.Ullman, *Compilers*. Addison-Wesley eds., 1986.
3. S.Blazy, P.Facon *SFAC, a tool for program comprehension by specialization* IEEE Workshop on program comprehension, Washington, November 1994.
4. *Centaur 1.1 documentation.* INRIA, January 1990.
5. J.Despeyroux, *Proof of translation in natural semantics*. Symposium on Logic in Computer Science, Cambridge USA, June 86.
6. G.Dowek et al. *The Coq proof assistant user's guide* INRIA report 134, December 1991.
7. M.Hennessy, *The semantics of programming languages*. Wiley eds., 1990.
8. C.B.Jones, *Systematic software development using VDM*. Prentice-Hall, 2nd eds., 1990.
9. G.Kahn, *Natural semantics*. Proceedings of STACS'87, Lecture Notes in Computer Science, vol.247, March 1987.
10. U.Meyer, *Techniques for evaluation of imperative languages*. ACM SIGSOFT, March 1991, pp.94-105.
11. G. Plotkin, *A structural approach to operational semantics*. Report DAIMI FN-19, University of Aarhus, 1981.

Proving the Correctness of Recursion-Based Automatic Program Transformations

David Sands

DIKU, University of Copenhagen *

Abstract This paper shows how the *Improvement Theorem*—a semantic condition for the total correctness of program transformation on higher-order functional programs—has practical value in proving the correctness of automatic techniques, including deforestation and supercompilation. This is aided by a novel formulation (and generalisation) of deforestation-like transformations, which also greatly adds to the modularity of the proof with respect to extensions to both the language and the transformation rules.

1 Introduction

Transformation of recursive programs Source-to-source transformation methods for functional programs, such as *partial evaluation* [JGS93] and *deforestation* [Wad90,Chi90], perform equivalence preserving modifications to the definitions in a given program. These methods fall in to a class which have been called called *generative set transformations* [PS83]: transformations built from a small set of rules which gain their power from their compound and selective application. The classic example of this (informal) class is Burstall and Darlington's unfold-fold method [BD77]; many automatic transformations of this class can be viewed as specialised instances of unfold-fold rules.

These methods improve the efficiency of programs by performing local optimisations, thus transferring run-time computations to compile-time. In order to compound the effect of these relatively simple local optimisations (in order to get a speedup of more than an additive constant factor), it is desirable that such transformations have the ability to introduce recursion. Transformations such as deforestation (a functional form of loop-fusion) and partial evaluation (and analogous transformations on logic programs) have this capability via a process of selectively memoising previously encountered expressions, and introducing recursion according to a "*déjà vu*" principal [JGS93].

The Problem of Correctness Program transformations should preserve the the *extensional* meaning of programs in order to be of any practical value. In this case we say that the transformation is *correct.*

One might say that there are two problems with correctness – the first being that it has not been widely recognised as a problem! Because the individual transformation components often represent quite simple operations on programs and are obviously meaning-preserving, confidence in the correctness of such transformation methods or systems is high. The problem with this view, for transformations that can introduce recursion, is that correctness cannot be argued by simply showing that the basic transformation steps are meaning-preserving. Yet this problem (exemplified below) runs contrary to many informal (and some formal) arguments which are used in attempts to justify correctness of particular transformation methods.

* Universitetsparken 1, 2100 København Ø; dave@diku.dk

To take a concrete (but contrived) example to illustrate this point, consider the following transformation (where $\triangleq$ denotes a function definition, and $\cong$ is semantic equivalence with respect to the current definition):

$$\boxed{f\ x \triangleq x + 42} \xrightarrow[\text{using } 42 \cong f\ 0]{\text{transform}} \boxed{f\ x \triangleq x + f\ 0}$$

This example fits into the framework of the unfold-fold method (first apply the *law* $42 \cong 0 + 42$, and *fold* $0 + 42$ to get $f\ 0$), and thus illustrates the well-known fact that, in general, unfold-fold transformations preserve only partial correctness. It also serves as a reminder that one cannot argue correctness of a transformation method by simply showing that it can be recast as an unfold-fold transformation.

A Solution, in Principal To obtain total correctness without losing the local, stepwise character of program transformation, it is clear that a stronger condition than extensional equivalence is necessary. In [Sa95a] we present such a condition, *improvement*, and show that if the local steps of a transformation are improvements (in a formal sense) then the transformation will be correct, and, *a fortiori*, yield an "improved" program. The method applies to call-by-name and call-by-value functional languages, including higher-order functions and lazy data structures. In [Sa95a] the improvement theorem was used to design a method for restricting the unfold-fold method, such that correctness (and improvement) are guaranteed. It is also claimed that the improvement theorem has practical value in proving the correctness of more automatic transformation methods (without need for restrictions).

In this paper we substantiate this claim.

A Solution, in Practice We consider two "automatic" program transformations to illustrate the application of the improvement theorem.

The first application [which we only have space to outline] is to a simple systematisation (due to Wadler [Wad89]) of a well-known transformation to eliminate instances of the concatenate operator from functional programs. With only minor changes in the presentation, the improvement theorem is directly applicable, and thus correctness and improvement are guaranteed.

The main application of the improvement theorem illustrated in this paper is more involved. We provide a total correctness proof for an automatic transformation based on a higher-order variant of the deforestation method [Wad90] (which implies the correctness of the transformations performed by the well-known first-order algorithm). To reason about the folding process, and to apply the improvement theorem, we need to reformulate the usual inductive style of definition to provide a *stepwise* account. With this new formulation (extended naturally to deal with higher-order functions) the proof of correctness[2] becomes strikingly simple, since it amounts to showing that each "step" is an improvement; the proof is robust with respect to the folding strategy, and is modular with respect to the transformation steps, so we also consider a generalisation of the "positive supercompilation" rule from [SGJ94]. To our knowledge this is the first proof of correctness for the results of recursive deforestation (for a first-order language or otherwise) which explicitly considers the essential folding steps.

[2] This does not consider termination aspects of deforestation *algorithms*, although we expect that the stepwise formulation will also be useful here.

Related Work In the study of the correctness issues (in program transformation of the kind addressed in this paper) it is typical to *ignore* the folding or memoisation aspects of the algorithms. This often because the correctness issues studied relate to the transformation *algorithm* rather than the correctness of the resulting program. For example, studies of correctness in partial evaluation [Gom92][Pal93][Wan93] [CK93] ignore the memoisation aspects entirely and deal with the orthogonal issue of the correctness of *binding time analysis*, which controls *where* transformation occurs in a program. Transformations considered by Steckler [Ste94] are quite orthogonal to the ones studied here, since they concern local optimisations which are (only) justified by dataflow properties of the program in which they are performed. To the author's knowledge, the only other correctness proofs (of which we are aware) for automatic transformations of recursive programs which use some form of folding are in the study of related logic-program transformation, eg. [LS91] [Kom92]. For an extensive comparison of the improvement theorem with other general techniques for correct transformations, see [Sa95b].

The remainder of the paper is organised as follows. **Section 2** deals with syntax, operational semantics and definition of operational approximation and equivalence for a higher-order functional language. In **Section 3** the definition and properties of improvement are given, and the improvement theorem is stated. **Section 4** outlines the application of the improvement theorem to a concatenate-elimination transformation. **Section 5** applies the improvement theorem to prove correctness of the deforestation-like transformations.

2 Preliminaries

We summarise some of the notation used in specifying the language and its operational semantics. The subject of this study will be an untyped higher-order non-strict functional language with lazy data-constructors. Our technical results will be specific to this language (and its call-by-name operational semantics), but the inclusion of a strict application operator and arbitrary strict primitive functions (which could include constructors and destructors for strict data structures) should be sufficient to convince the reader that similar results carry over to call-by-value languages.

We assume a flat set of mutually recursive function definitions of the form $\mathtt{f}\, x_1 \ldots x_{\alpha_\mathtt{f}} \triangleq e_\mathtt{f}$ where $\alpha_\mathtt{f}$, the arity of function $\mathtt{f}$, is greater than zero. (For an indexed set of functions we will sometimes refer to the arity by index, $\alpha_\mathtt{i}$, rather than function name.) $\mathtt{f}$, $\mathtt{g}$, $\mathtt{h}$ ..., range over function names, $x, y, z \ldots$ over variables and e, e_1, $e_2 \ldots$ over expressions. The syntax of expressions is as follows:

$$
\begin{array}{lll}
e = x \mid \mathtt{f} \mid e_1\, e_2 & & \text{(Variable; Function name; Application)} \\
\quad \mid e_1 @ e_2 & & \text{(Strict application)} \\
\quad \mid \mathtt{case}\ e\ \mathtt{of} & & \text{(Case expressions)} \\
\qquad c_1(\vec{x}_1) : e_1 \ldots c_n(\vec{x}_n) : e_n & & \\
\quad \mid c(\vec{e}) & & \text{(Constructor expressions and constants)} \\
\quad \mid p(\vec{e}) & & \text{(Strict primitive functions)}
\end{array}
$$

The expression written $e\{\vec{e'}/\vec{x}\}$ will denote simultaneous (capture-free) substitution of a sequence of expressions $\vec{e'}$ for free occurrences of a sequence of variables $\vec{x}$, respectively, in the expression e. The term $\text{FV}(e)$ will denote the free variables of expression e. Sometimes we will (informally) write substitutions of the form $\{\vec{e}/\vec{\mathtt{g}}\}$ to represent the replacement of occurrences of function symbols $\vec{\mathtt{g}}$ by expressions $\vec{e}$. A *context*, ranged over by C, C_1, etc. is an expression with zero or more "holes", $[\,]$, in the place of some subexpressions; $C[e]$ is the expression produced by replacing the holes with expression e. Contrasting with substitution, occurrences of free variables in e may become bound in $C[e]$; if $C[e]$ is closed then we say it is a *closing context* (for e).

Operational Semantics The operational semantics defines an evaluation relation (a partial function) $\Downarrow$. If $e{\Downarrow}w$ for some closed expression e then we say that *e evaluates to weak head normal form w*, or *e converges*. The weak head normal forms, $w, w_1, w_2, \ldots \in \text{WHNF}$ are just the constructor-expressions $c(\vec{e})$, and the partially applied functions, $\mathtt{f}\,e_1 \ldots e_k$, $0 \leq k < \alpha_{\mathtt{f}}$. For a given closed e, if there is no such w then we say the *e diverges*. We make no finer distinctions between divergent expressions, so "errors" and "loops" are identified. The operational semantics is a standard call-by-name one, and $\Downarrow$ is defined in terms of a one-step evaluation relation using the notion of a *reduction context* [FFK87]. Reduction contexts, ranged over by $I\!R$, are contexts containing a single hole which is used to identify the next expression to be evaluated (reduced).

Definition 2.1 *A reduction context $I\!R$ is given inductively by the following grammar*

$$I\!R = [\,] \mid I\!R\ e \mid I\!R@e \mid w@I\!R \mid \texttt{case}\ I\!R\ \texttt{of}\ c_1(\vec{x}_1) : e_1 \ldots c_n(\vec{x}_n) : e_n \ \mid p(\vec{c}, I\!R, \vec{e})$$

Now we define the one step reduction relation on closed expressions. We assume that each primitive function p is given meaning by a partial function $[\![p]\!]$ from vectors of constants (according to the arity of p) to the constants (nullary constructors). We do not need to specify the exact set of primitive functions; it will suffice to note that they are strict—all operands must evaluate to constants before the result of an application, if any, can be returned— and are only defined over constants, not over arbitrary weak head normal forms.

Definition 2.2 *One-step reduction $\mapsto$ is the least relation on closed expressions satisfying the rules given in Figure 1.*

$$
\begin{array}{rll}
I\!R[\mathtt{f}\ e_1 \ldots e_{\alpha_{\mathtt{f}}}] & \mapsto I\!R[e_{\mathtt{f}}\{e_1 \cdots e_{\alpha_{\mathtt{f}}}/x_1 \ldots x_{\alpha_{\mathtt{f}}}\}] & (*) \\
I\!R[w@w'] & \mapsto I\!R[w\ w'] & \\
I\!R[\texttt{case}\ c_i(\vec{e})\ \texttt{of} \ldots c_i(\vec{x}_i) : e_i \ldots] & \mapsto I\!R[e_i\{\vec{e}/\vec{x}_i\}] & \\
I\!R[p(\vec{c})] & \mapsto I\!R[c'] & (\textit{if } [\![p]\!]\vec{c} = c')
\end{array}
$$

Fig. 1. *One-step reduction rules*

In each rule of the form $I\!R[e] \mapsto I\!R[e']$ in Figure 1, the expression e is referred to as a *redex*. The one step evaluation relation is deterministic; this relies on the fact that if $e_1 \mapsto e_2$ then e_1 can be uniquely factored into a reduction context $I\!R$ and a redex e' such that $e_1 = I\!R[e']$.

Definition 2.3 *Closed expression e converges to weak head normal form w, $e{\Downarrow}w$, if and only if $e \mapsto^* w$ (where $\mapsto^*$ is the transitive reflexive closure of $\mapsto$).*

From this we define the standard notions of operational approximation and equivalence. The operational approximation we use is the standard Morris-style contextual ordering, or *observational approximation* eg. [Plo75].The notion of "observation" we take is just the fact of convergence, as in the lazy lambda calculus [Abr90]. Operational equivalence equates two expressions if and only if in all closing contexts they give rise to the same observation - ie. either they both converge, or they both diverge[3].

Definition 2.4 *(i) e* observationally approximates *e', $e \precsim e'$, if for all contexts C such that $C[e]$, $C[e']$ are closed, if $C[e]{\Downarrow}$ then $C[e']{\Downarrow}$.*
(ii) e is observationally equivalent *to e', $e \cong e'$, if $e \precsim e'$ and $e' \precsim e$.*

3 Improvement

In this section we outline the main technical result from [Sa95a], which says that if transformation steps are guided by certain optimisation concerns (a fairly natural condition for a transformation), then correctness of the transformation follows.

The above notion of optimisation is based on a formal *improvement-theory.* Roughly speaking, improvement is a refinement of operational approximation which says that an expression e is improved by e' if, in all closing contexts, computation using e' is no less efficient than when using e, in terms of the number of non-primitive function calls computed. From the point of view of program transformation, the important property of improvement is that it is substitutive—an expression can be improved by improving a sub-expression. For reasoning about the improvement relation a more tractable formulation and some related proof techniques are used.

The *improvement theorem* shows that if e is improved by e' (in addition to e being operationally equivalent to e') then a transformation which replaces e by e' (potentially introducing recursion) is totally correct; in addition this guarantees that the transformed program is a formal improvement over the original. (Notice that in the example in the introduction, replacement of 42 by the equivalent term $f\ 0$ is not an improvement since the latter requires evaluation of an additional function call).

Definition 3.1 *Closed expression e converges in n ($\in I\!N$) -steps to weak head normal form w, $e{\Downarrow}^n w$ if $e{\Downarrow}w$, and this computation requires n reductions of non-primitive functions (rule (*), Fig. 1).*

We will be convenient to adopt the following abbreviations:

- $e{\Downarrow}^n \stackrel{\text{def}}{=} \exists w.\, e{\Downarrow}^n w$ • $e{\Downarrow}^{n \leq m} \stackrel{\text{def}}{=} e{\Downarrow}^n \ \&\ n \leq m$ • $e{\Downarrow}^{\leq m} \stackrel{\text{def}}{=} \exists n.\, e{\Downarrow}^{n \leq m}$

Now improvement is defined in an analogous way to observational approximation:

---

[3] For this language if we choose to observe more – such as the actual constructor produced – or if we choose to observe only convergence to a constant rather than any WHNF, the observational approximation and equivalence relations will be unchanged.

Definition 3.2 *(Improvement)* e is improved by e', $e \gtrsim e'$, *if for all contexts C such that $C[e]$, $C[e']$ are closed, if $C[e]\Downarrow^n$ then $C[e']\Downarrow^{\leq n}$.*

It can be seen that $\gtrsim$ is a *precongruence* (transitive, reflexive, closed under contexts, ie. $e \gtrsim e' \Rightarrow C[e] \gtrsim C[e']$) and is a refinement of operational approximation, ie. $e \gtrsim e' \Rightarrow e \sqsubseteq e'$.

3.1 The Improvement Theorem

We are now able to state the improvement theorem. For the purposes of the formal statement, transformation is viewed as the introduction of some *new* functions from a given set of definitions, so the transformation from a program consisting of a single function $\mathtt{f}\,x \triangleq e$ to a new version $\mathtt{f}\,x \triangleq e'$ will be represented by the derivation of a new function $\mathtt{g}\,x \triangleq e'\{\mathtt{g}/\mathtt{f}\}$. In this way we do not need to explicitly parameterise operational equivalence and improvement by the intended set of function definitions.

Theorem 3.3 ([Sa95a]) *Given a set of function definitions, $\{\mathtt{f}_i\, x_1 \ldots x_{\alpha i} \triangleq e_i\}_{i\in I}$ and a set $\{e'_i\}_{i\in I}$ such that $\mathrm{FV}(e'_i) \subseteq \{x_1 \ldots x_{\alpha i}\}$,*

if $e_i \gtrsim e'_i$ then $\mathtt{f}_i \gtrsim \mathtt{g}_i$ where $\vec{\mathtt{g}}$ are new functions: $\{\mathtt{g}_i\, x_1 \ldots x_{\alpha i} \triangleq e'_i\{\vec{\mathtt{g}}/\vec{\mathtt{f}}\}\}_{i\in I}$

The "standard" partial correctness result (see eg. [Kot78][Cou79]), which follows easily from a least fixed-point theorem for $\sqsubseteq$, (the full details are given in [Sa95b]) says that if $\mathtt{f}\,x \triangleq e$ and $e \cong e'$ then $\mathtt{g} \sqsubseteq \mathtt{f}$ where $\mathtt{g}\,x \triangleq e'\{\mathtt{g}/\mathtt{f}\}$. Combining this with the improvement theorem, we get a condition for total correctness for transformations which are built by (repeated) application of a set of source-to-source transformations to the bodies of function definitions:

Corollary 3.4 *If the basic steps of a transformation are equivalence-preserving, and are also contained in the improvement relation (with respect to the original definitions) then the resulting transformation will be correct, an moreover, the resulting program will be an improvement over the original.*

3.2 Proving Improvement

Finding a more tractable characterisation of improvement (than that provided by Def. 3.2) is essential in establishing improvement laws (and in the proof of the improvement theorem). The characterisation we use says that two expressions are in the improvement relation if and only if they are contained in a certain kind of *simulation* relation. This is a form of *context lemma* eg. [Abr90,How89], and the proof of the characterisation uses previous technical results concerning a more general class of improvement relations [San91].

Definition 3.5 *A relation $\mathcal{IR}$ on closed expressions is an* improvement simulation *if for all e, e', whenever $e\,\mathcal{IR}\,e'$, if $e\Downarrow^n w_1$ then $e'\Downarrow^{\leq n} w_2$ for some w_2 such that either:*

(i) $w_1 \equiv c(e_1 \ldots e_n)$, $w_2 \equiv c(e'_1 \ldots e'_n)$, and $e_i\,\mathcal{IR}\,e'_i$, $(i \in 1 \ldots n)$, or

(ii) $w_1 \in$ Closures[4], $w_2 \in$ Closures, and for all closed e_0, $(w_1\, e_0)\,\mathcal{IR}\,(w_2\, e_0)$

[4] *Closures* is the set of function-valued results, ie. partially applied functions.

So, intuitively, if an improvement-simulation relates e to e', then if e converges, e' does so at least as efficiently, and yields a "similar" result, whose "components" are related by that improvement-simulation.

The key to reasoning about the improvement relation is the fact that $\underset{\sim}{\triangleright}$, restricted to closed expressions, is itself an improvement simulation (and is in fact the *maximal* improvement simulation). Furthermore, improvement on open expressions can be characterised in terms of improvement on all closed instances. This is summarised in the following:

Lemma 3.6 (Improvement Context-Lemma) *For all e, e', $e \underset{\sim}{\triangleright} e'$ if and only if there exists an improvement simulation $\mathcal{IR}$ such that for all closing substitutions σ, $e\sigma \; \mathcal{IR} \; e'\sigma$.*

The lemma provides a basic proof technique, sometimes called *co-induction*:

> to show that $e \underset{\sim}{\triangleright} e'$ it is sufficient to find an improvement-simulation containing each closed instance of the pair.

We conclude the section with some example laws which follow directly from this characterisation, or can be proved by exhibiting appropriate improvement simulations:

Proposition 3.7 (i) $e \mapsto e' \Rightarrow e \underset{\sim}{\triangleright} e'$ $\quad(ii)$ $\mathtt{f}\,x \underset{\sim}{\triangleright} e$ *if* $\mathtt{f}\,x \triangleq e$

$$(iii)\quad \mathbb{R}[\mathtt{case}\;x\;\mathtt{of} \qquad \underset{\sim}{\triangleright}\; \mathtt{case}\;x\;\mathtt{of}$$
$$c_1(\vec{y}_1) : e_1 \qquad\qquad c_1(\vec{y}_1) : \mathbb{R}[e_1]$$
$$\ldots \qquad\qquad \ldots$$
$$c_n(\vec{y}_n) : e_n] \qquad\qquad c_n(\vec{y}_n) : \mathbb{R}[e_n]$$

The first rule follows easily by showing that the relation containing (e, e') together with all syntactic equivalences is an improvement simulation. It is also easy to see that if the reduction step is not the function call case $(*)$, then $e' \underset{\sim}{\triangleright} e$ also holds. (ii) says that *unfolding* is an improvement; this is just a consequence of (i), since each closed instance is in the one-step reduction relation. For the third law we construct a simulation relation in the manner of the first case, and reason from the operational semantics.

4 A Simple Application

The simplest illustration of the application of the improvement theorem is to the verification of the correctness (and improvement) of a mechanisable transformation which aims to eliminate calls to the concatenate (or *append*) function. The effects of the transformation are well-known, such as the transformation of a naïve quadratic-time reverse function into a linear-time equivalent. The systematic definition of the transformation used is due to Wadler [Wad89]. Wadler's formulation of this well known transformation is completely mechanisable, and the transformation "algorithm" always terminates. Unlike many other mechanisable transformations (such as deforestation and partial evaluation), it can improve the asymptotic complexity of some programs.

After some initial definitions have been constructed, the core of the transformation is a set of rewrite rules which are applied exhaustively to the program. Without any essential change to the definition of the transformation, we have obtained a strikingly simple proof of correctness by showing that all of the rewrites are improvements.

[The details are omitted for lack of space—see [Sa95b]]

5 Deforestation and Positive Supercompilation

Deforestation [Wad90] is a transformation developed for first-order lazy functional programs, which aims to eliminate the construction of intermediate data structures (eg. trees, and hence the name). The aim of the transformation is the symbolic fusion of code which produces some data structure with the code which consumes it. The general aims of the transformation are well known in the transformation literature as a form of loop fusion; deforestation is an attempt to make this transformation systematic and thereby mechanisable.

The deforestation algorithm is described by simple expression-level transformation of the expressions in a program, plus implicit (but essential) folding steps, whereby previously encountered expressions are identified, and recursion is introduced. The main body of work on this transformation concerns the restriction of the transformation steps so that, assuming folding, the algorithm terminates [FW88,Chi90,Sø94a]. Other work considers extensions of the algorithm to richer languages eg. higher-order functions [MW92], and extensions to enable more powerful transformations [SGJ94].

The contributions of this section are:

- a new stepwise formulation of the deforestation transformation;
- a natural generalisation to higher-order functions;
- a correctness proof which includes folding steps, and shows that any folding strategy based on the transformation history (not excluding the possibility of mutual recursion) is correct.

Regarding the correctness of the transformed programs, Wadler originally argued that the expression level transformation is obviously correct (since it essentially uses just unfolding and simplifications which eliminate constructors). This fact is proved for a certain weak form of equivalence in [Sø94b] (unfortunately the "weakness" in question is that the equivalence relation is not closed under arbitrary substitution, so is not a congruence). But these properties, whilst necessary, do not in themselves imply correctness of the resulting programs, because the transformation uses a memoisation process to implement folding[5]. What remains to be achieved, and what we achieve in the remainder of this section, is to show that the resulting programs are equivalent to the originals – and in particular in the presence of folding.

The Deforestation Transformation

In most work studying deforestation (or fusion/driving), the language is a first-order subset of the language presented here, including just case-expressions (or equivalently, definition by pattern-matching) and recursive function calls. We will generalise this to a higher-order language but we will omit primitive function and strict application to simplify the presentation. The results of transformation using this generalisation are not substantially different from those achieved by Marlow and Wadler [MW92], but the presentation is more concise; in some sense this extension of the deforestation method to deal with higher-order functions is the canonical one, stemming from the fact that, in addition to the case-reduction context, the language now has an application reduction context ($\mathbb{R}\, e$), plus an

[5] Non recursion based approaches to deforestation [GLJ93] [SF93] do not encounter this problem, but cannot handle recursive definitions.

additional set of weak head normal forms—the partially applied functions. A similar generalisation is given by Nielsen and Sørensen [NH94], where they study the relationship to partial evaluation.

For reasons of space we do not present the original recursive formulation of the deforestation algorithm.

5.1 Stepwise Deforestation

For the most part the folding process is left *implicit* in the definition of the transformation. But from the point of view of proving total correctness this is the meat of the problem. Combining folding with the standard deforestation algorithm is notationally rather complicated. In essence, the steps of the transformation must be sequentialised in some way, and a "memo-table" of terms encountered so-far must be threaded through the transformation. However, such a description commits the method to using a particular "transformation order" – eg. should the sub-expressions in the term $c(e_1 \ldots e_n)$ be transformed left-to-right, breadth-first, or as is usual in the implicit definitions, independently. Not all transformation orders will lead to the same transformed program, but from the point of view of the correctness of the resulting programs, these issues are orthogonal.

We will prove correctness for a finer-grained description of the transformation (than is usually given) via a *one-step deforestation relation* on terms, analogous to the one-step reduction relation ($\mapsto$). This is based on a novel combination of *reduction contexts* (as implicit in earlier formulations of deforestation [FW88]) and *passive contexts* which enable transformations to be pushed deeper into a term.

Unlike the one-step reduction relation, the transformation rules we specify are not deterministic. This is because the resulting correctness results do not depend on the the transformation order; any strategies of applying the given rules (eg. breadth-first to obtain more possible folds) including restrictions (eg. to improve termination behaviour on a wider class of programs) will give correct programs. Folding can be described simply in terms of the transformation history - the sequences of expressions rewritten (and new function definitions introduced). A second benefit of the new presentation will be that additional rules can be added and the correctness proof will be completely modular.

The basic deforestation rules are presented in Figure 2. To simplify presentation, we define a class of *simple dynamic expressions* – these are variables or variables applied to some expressions. Using this we define the *passive contexts.* These are the contexts which take no further part in the transformation and allow the transformations to be pushed further into an expression.

Definition 5.1

(i) The simple dynamic expressions, *ranged over by d are given by $d = x \mid d\,e$.*

(ii) The passive contexts, *ranged over by $I\!P$, are single-holed contexts given by*

$$I\!P = [\,] \;\mid\; \texttt{case}\; d\; \texttt{of} \ldots c_n(\vec{x}_i) : I\!P \ldots \;\mid\; c(\ldots I\!P \ldots)$$

Recall that the reduction contexts for this subset of the language are given by

$$I\!R = [\,] \;\mid\; \texttt{case}\; I\!R\; \texttt{of}\; c_1(\vec{x}_1) : e_1 \ldots c_n(\vec{x}_n) : e_n \;\mid\; I\!R\, e$$

$$\mathbb{P}.\mathbb{R}[\mathtt{f}\ e_1 \ldots e_{\alpha_{\mathtt{f}}}] \rightsquigarrow \mathbb{P}[\mathtt{f}^\diamond\ y_1 \ldots y_n] \qquad (d1)$$
$$\textit{where } \{y_1 \ldots y_n\} = \mathrm{FV}(\mathbb{R}[\mathtt{f}\ e_1 \ldots e_{\alpha_{\mathtt{f}}}])$$
$$\textit{and } \mathtt{f}^\diamond\ y_1 \ldots y_n \triangleq \mathbb{R}[e_{\mathtt{f}}\{e_1 \ldots e_{\alpha_{\mathtt{f}}}/x_1 \ldots x_{\alpha_{\mathtt{f}}}\}]$$

$$\mathbb{P}.\mathbb{R}[\mathtt{case}\ c_i(\vec{e})\ \mathtt{of} \ldots c_i(\vec{x}_i) : e_i \ldots] \rightsquigarrow \mathbb{P}.\mathbb{R}[e_i\{\vec{e}/\vec{x}_i\}] \qquad (d2)$$

$$\mathbb{P}.\mathbb{R}[\mathtt{case}\ d\ \mathtt{of}\ c_1(\vec{x}_1) : e_1 \ldots c_n(\vec{x}_n) : e_n] \qquad (d3)$$
$$\rightsquigarrow \mathbb{P}[\mathtt{case}\ d\ \mathtt{of}\ c_1(\vec{x}_1) : \mathbb{R}[e_1] \ldots c_n(\vec{x}_n) : \mathbb{R}[e_n]]$$

$$\mathbb{P}.\mathbb{R}[\mathtt{f}\ e_1 \ldots e_{\alpha_{\mathtt{f}}-k}] \rightsquigarrow \mathbb{P}.\mathbb{R}[\mathtt{f}^\diamond\ y_1 \ldots y_j] \qquad (d4)$$
$$\textit{where } \{y_1 \ldots y_j\} = \mathrm{FV}(e_1 \ldots e_{\alpha_{\mathtt{f}}-k})$$
$$\textit{and } \mathtt{f}^\diamond\ y_1 \ldots y_j\ z_1 \ldots z_k \triangleq e_{\mathtt{f}}\{e_1 \ldots e_{\alpha_{\mathtt{f}}-k}\ z_1 \ldots z_k/x_1 \ldots x_{\alpha_{\mathtt{f}}}\}$$

Fig. 2. One-Step Deforestation Rules

We write $\mathbb{P}.\mathbb{R}$ to denote the composition of passive and reduction contexts, so $\mathbb{P}.\mathbb{R}[e]$ will denote the term $\mathbb{P}[\mathbb{R}[e]]$. Note that contexts $\mathbb{P}.\mathbb{R}$ include both the passive and the reduction contexts.

Some comments are appropriate. The rules essentially mimic the action of the operational semantics, but for terms containing free variables. Rule **(d1)** unfolds a function call occurring in a reduction context; the result of the unfolding of the call in the reduction context is represented indirectly by the introduction of a new function definition (introduced for the purpose of folding, in case this expression is re-encountered). It is assumed that new function names are fresh. Rule **(d2)** is the standard case-reduction rule from the operational semantics. Rule **(d3)** is the "propagate-context" rule. Here a case expression, with an un-resolvable (dynamic) test, occurs in a reduction position, and so the reduction context is pushed into the branches. This is the generalisation of the "case-case" law in the original formulation of deforestation. Rule **(d4)** is the case of a partially applied function where we force an unfolding via an auxiliary function.

The role of the passive context is to allow the rules to drive deeper into a term, in the situation where the outer layer of the term cannot be transformed further. For example, if the outermost construct of the term is an un-resolvable case expression, then transformation can proceed to the branches.

Applying the Rules in Deforestation The deforestation algorithm begins with a top level expression, e_0, which represents the program (containing some free variables) to be transformed.

The one step deforestation rules can implement the deforestation process by applying them in the following manner. First abstract the free variables from e_0 to form a new (non-recursive) definition $\mathtt{f}_0^\diamond\ \vec{x} \triangleq e_0$. Maintaining a distinction between the original functions in the program (ranged over by $\mathtt{f}, \mathtt{g} \ldots$), and the new functions introduced by the transformation steps (henceforth ranged over by $\mathtt{f}^\diamond, \mathtt{g}^\diamond \ldots$) including $\mathtt{f}_0^\diamond$, transform the right-hand sides of the new functions by repeated (nondeterministic) application of the rules *but never applying rule* (*d*1) *in order to unfold a new function.* Rule (d3) is not applied when $\mathbb{R} = [\,]$, since in this case the rule is the identity, and rule (d4) is not used if $\mathbb{R}$ is an application context.

Folding in Deforestation In order to get the above algorithm to terminate in some non trivial cases we need to add folding, or memoization[6]. Both rules (d1) and (d4) introduce new function definitions (without these rules termination would be assured, but uninteresting). The basic idea is to use a memo-table, which is accumulated during the transformation, to enable (d1) and (d4) to make use of previously defined functions.

When there is a possibility of applying the rule $(d1)$ to an expression of the form $\mathbb{P}.\mathbb{R}[\mathtt{f}\ e_1 \ldots e_{\alpha_\mathtt{f}}]$ then we look into the memo-list. If there is an entry $\langle \mathbb{R}'[\mathtt{f}\ e'_1 \ldots e'_{\alpha_\mathtt{f}}], \mathtt{f}^\diamond \vec{y}\rangle$ such that $\mathbb{R}'[\mathtt{f}\ e'_1 \ldots e'_{\alpha_\mathtt{f}}]\theta \equiv \mathbb{R}[\mathtt{f}\ e_1 \ldots e_{\alpha_\mathtt{f}}]$ where θ is a *renaming* (a substitution mapping variables to variables) then we transform $\mathbb{P}.\mathbb{R}[\mathtt{f}\ e_1 \ldots e_{\alpha_\mathtt{f}}]$ to $\mathbb{P}[(\mathtt{f}^\diamond \vec{y})\theta]$. Otherwise we apply the rule as normal, introducing a new function name $\mathtt{f}^\diamond$, and add the pair $\langle \mathbb{R}[\mathtt{f}\ e_1 \ldots e_{\alpha_\mathtt{f}}], \mathtt{f}^\diamond \vec{y}\rangle$ to the memo-table. We memoise use of rule $(d4)$ in the same way.

Example 5.2 Consider the following definitions:

$$
\begin{aligned}
\mathtt{filter}\ p\ xs &\triangleq \mathtt{case}\ xs\ \mathtt{of} \\
&\qquad nil : \mathtt{nil} \\
&\qquad cons(y, ys) : \mathtt{case}\ p\ y\ \mathtt{of} \\
&\qquad\qquad true : \mathtt{cons}(y, \mathtt{filter}\ p\ ys) \\
&\qquad\qquad false : \mathtt{filter}\ p\ ys \\
\mathtt{map}\ f\ xs &\triangleq \mathtt{case}\ xs\ \mathtt{of} \\
&\qquad nil : \mathtt{nil} \\
&\qquad cons(z, zs) : \mathtt{cons}((f\ z), \mathtt{map}\ f\ zs) \\
\mathtt{compose} f\ g\ x &\triangleq f\ (g\ x)
\end{aligned}
$$

Writing `compose` in the usual infix style ($e \circ e' \equiv \mathtt{compose}\, e\, e'$) we wish to transform the initial definition:

$$\mathtt{f}_0^\diamond\ f\ p \triangleq (\mathtt{map} f) \circ (\mathtt{filter}\, p)$$

Now we transform the right hand side of the initial definition and the right-hand sides of subsequently introduced definitions. The initial transformation steps are given in Fig. 3; each derivation step ($\rightsquigarrow$) refers to the right-hand side of the preceding definition.

After these steps the transformation can proceed to the two occurrences of the sub-term $\mathtt{filter}\ p\ (\mathtt{map} f\ zs))$ (both of which occur in passive contexts) — but these expressions (modulo renaming) have been encountered above at the first application of rule $(d1)$ (and therefore would occur in the memo-table), so

[6] Although with this stepwise formulation we can simply stop the transformation at any point and we have a well-formed program.

$$(\texttt{filter}\,p)\circ(\texttt{map}\,f) \overset{d4}{\leadsto} \texttt{f}_1^\circ\,p\,f \quad \textit{where}$$

$$\begin{array}{l}
\texttt{f}_1^\circ\,p\,f\,xs \triangleq \texttt{filter}\,p\,(\texttt{map}\,f\,xs) \\
\quad \overset{d1}{\leadsto} \texttt{f}_2^\circ\,p\,f\,xs \quad \textit{where} \\
\texttt{f}_2^\circ\,p\,f\,xs \triangleq \texttt{case}\,(\texttt{map}\,f\,xs)\ \texttt{of} \\
\qquad \textit{nil} : \texttt{nil} \\
\qquad \textit{cons}(y, ys) : \texttt{case}\ p\ y\ \texttt{of} \\
\qquad\qquad \textit{true} : \texttt{cons}(y, \texttt{filter}\ p\ ys) \\
\qquad\qquad \textit{false} : \texttt{filter}\ p\ ys \\
\quad \overset{d1}{\leadsto} \texttt{f}_3^\circ\,p\,f\,xs \quad \textit{where} \\
\texttt{f}_3^\circ\,p\,f\,xs \triangleq \texttt{case}\,(\,\texttt{case}\ xs\ \texttt{of} \\
\qquad\qquad \textit{nil} : \texttt{nil} \\
\qquad\qquad \textit{cons}(z, zs) : \texttt{cons}((f\ z), \texttt{map}\,f\ zs))\ \texttt{of} \\
\qquad \textit{nil} : \texttt{nil} \\
\qquad \textit{cons}(y, ys) : \texttt{case}\ p\ y\ \texttt{of} \\
\qquad\qquad \textit{true} : \texttt{cons}(y, \texttt{filter}\ p\ ys) \\
\qquad\qquad \textit{false} : \texttt{filter}\ p\ ys \\
\quad \overset{d3\,d2\,d2}{\leadsto\leadsto\leadsto} \\
\quad \texttt{case}\ xs\ \texttt{of} \\
\qquad \textit{nil} : \texttt{nil} \\
\qquad \textit{cons}(z, zs) : \texttt{case}\ p\ (f\ z)\ \texttt{of} \\
\qquad\qquad \textit{true} : \texttt{cons}((f\ z), \texttt{filter}\ p\ (\texttt{map}\,f\ zs)) \\
\qquad\qquad \textit{false} : \texttt{filter}\ p\ (\texttt{map}\,f\ zs)
\end{array}$$

Fig. 3. Initial Deforestation Steps

we "fold", introducing a recursive calls to $\texttt{f}_2^\circ$, obtaining:

$$\begin{array}{ll}
\texttt{f}_1^\circ\,p\,f\,xs \triangleq \texttt{f}_2^\circ\,p\,f\,xs & \texttt{f}_3^\circ p\,f\,xs \triangleq \texttt{case}\ xs\ \texttt{of} \\
\texttt{f}_2^\circ\,p\,f\,xs \triangleq \texttt{f}_3^\circ\,p\,f\,xs & \quad \textit{nil} : \texttt{nil} \\
& \quad \textit{cons}(z, zs) : \texttt{case}\ p\ (f\ z)\ \texttt{of} \\
& \qquad \textit{true} : \texttt{cons}((f\ z), \texttt{f}_2^\circ\,p\,f\,zs) \\
& \qquad \textit{false} : \texttt{f}_2^\circ\,p\,f\,zs
\end{array}$$

As is usual, we can eliminate the trivial intermediate functions $\texttt{f}_1^\circ$ and $\texttt{f}_2^\circ$ by *post-unfolding* [JGS93].

5.2 Correctness

Using the improvement theorem, to prove correctness it will be sufficient to prove that each transformation step is an improvement. This property holds because, as observed by Chin [Chi90], each new function call introduced by the transformation comes together with an unfolding step. This is, in turn, sufficient to justify the folding steps, since these are guaranteed to be improvements.

Proposition 5.3 *$e \leadsto e'$ implies $e \trianglerighteq e'$.*

PROOF. Straightforward using the congruence properties of improvement. □

There are generally considered to be three aspects to the correctness of deforestation [Sø94b]: (i) termination of the algorithm, (ii) correctness of the resulting program, and (iii) non degradation of efficiency. It is not difficult to construct example programs for which the procedure does not terminate, so the effort in point (i) must be, eg., to find some syntactic characterisation of the programs for which the algorithm terminates (such a "treeless form") These issue is outside the scope of this paper. The improvement theorem deals with aspects (ii) and to some extent (iii); from the previous proposition it is a small step to show that the transformation yields equivalent programs, and these will be, formally, equally efficient (in terms of $\underset{\sim}{\trianglerighteq}$) under call-by-name evaluation.

Proposition 5.4 *Deforestation yields totally correct programs in that any result of applying the deforestation steps (including folding) to a program will result in an improved program.*

PROOF. From the previous proposition, the basic steps are all in the improvement relation. Clearly they are also operational equivalences. Taking a "virtual" view of the transformation [TS84] in which we consider that the initial definitions of the new functions (introduced by the transformation steps) are already present at the beginning of the transformation, then the folding steps are essentially no different from any other rule: they replace an expression by an improved one. So by corollary 3.4 the result of the transformation equivalent to, and an improvement over, the original. □

On Efficiency Improvement relates to call-by-name. Under a call-by-need implementation the usual restrictions of the transformation seem sufficient to regain the improvement result under call-by-need. These restrictions are that only functions which are *linear* in their arguments should be transformed — see [Wad90], [Chi90]. Alternatively, duplication of sub-expressions (eg. Example 5.2 (fz) is duplicated in $\mathtt{f}_3^\circ$) can be avoided by the use of let-bindings, in the obvious way.

On Robustness The correctness proof is dependent on the fact that the individual steps (and hence the folding steps) are improvements, but not on the overall structure of the transformation. This means that the application of the transformation steps can be constrained, for example by use of annotations (eg. "blazing" from [Wad90]) without any additional proof obligation. Similarly, given any particular sequentialisation of the transformation steps, the memoisation process can be arbitrarily constrained in terms of both lookups and writes. In this sense any memoisation strategy is covered.

It also means that we can add or replace transformation rules to increase the power of the method (eg. allowing folding to take advantage of more general expressions) and the only property that needs to be verified is that the new rule is an improvement. Language extensions, such as addition of primitive functions, are easily incorporated by extending the classes of dynamic expressions, passive and reduction contexts appropriately, and by adding any new reduction rules from the operational semantics.

5.3 Driving and Positive Supercompilation

In terms of transformational power (but ignoring termination issues) Turchin's *driving* techniques [Tur86] subsume deforestation. This increased power is due, in part, to increased information-propagation in the transformation. Propagation of the so-called "positive" information [GK93] can be easily added to the the one-step deforestation rules along the lines of [SGJ94]. The basic idea is that when a case-expression has a variable in the test position, as in case y of $\ldots c_i(\vec{x}_i) : e_i \ldots$, within the ith branch we know that free occurrences of y are equivalent to $c_i(\vec{x}_i)$. The effect of "positive information propagation" is achieved by substituting $c_i(\vec{x}_i)$ for all free occurrences of y in e_i. The transformation seems trivial, but cannot be achieved by preprocessing because it is applied to terms generated on the fly by earlier unfolding steps. The effect of this extra power is illustrated in [SGJ94].

We achieve the natural higher order variant of this transformation rule by generalising the propagation from the single variable case, to any free occurrences of a simple dynamic expression d (Def. 5.1). Positive information propagation is implemented by adding the following rule.

Definition 5.5 *Define the following transformation rule* (**d5**)*:*

$$\mathbb{P}.\mathbb{R}[\texttt{case}\ d\ \texttt{of}\ \ldots c_i(\vec{x}_i) : e\{^d/_z\}\ldots] \rightsquigarrow \mathbb{P}.\mathbb{R}[\texttt{case}\ d\ \texttt{of}\ \ldots c_i(\vec{x}_i) : e\{^{c_i(\vec{x}_i)}/_z\}\ldots]$$

where we assume the free variables in d and $\vec{x}_i$ are all distinct, and that we allow renaming of bound variables in a term.

Proposition 5.6 $e \overset{d5}{\rightsquigarrow} e'$ *implies* $e \gtrsim e'$

PROOF. Straightforward using the fact that $e_1 \Downarrow e_2$ implies $e_1 \gtrsim e_2$, together with congruence properties of improvement. □

In conclusion we mention an additional feature of Turchin's supercompilation, namely *generalisation*. This is a familiar concept in inductive proofs, and has a fairly direct analogy in program transformation (see eg. [BD77] [Tur86]), where in order to be able to fold one must proceed by transforming a more general function. In the transformation studied here we can model generalisation as follows. Rule ($d1$) abstracts the free variables from a term and introduces a new function which replaces the term. Generalisation is enabled if we allow abstraction of sub-terms other than just the free variables, thereby creating a *more general* new function $\mathtt{f}^\diamond$. (We leave a discussion of *what* should be abstracted to a long version of the paper.) There is a corresponding generalisation of the folding process. The correctness of these variations are also easily proved from the congruence properties of the improvement relation.

ACKNOWLEDGEMENTS Thanks to Robert Glück, John Hatcliff, Morten Heiner Sørensen, Kristian Nielson and Phil Wadler for a number of invaluable discussions and feedback on earlier drafts, and to the referees for suggesting a number of clarifications and improvements.

References

[Abr90] S. Abramsky. The lazy lambda calculus. In *Research Topics in Functional Programming*. Addison Wesley, 1990.

[BD77] R. Burstall and J. Darlington. A transformation system for developing recursive programs. *JACM*, 24:44–67, January 1977.

[Chi90] W. N. Chin. *Automatic Methods for Program Transformation*. PhD thesis, Imperial College, 1990.

[CK93] C. Consel and S. Khoo. On-line and off-line partial evaluation: Semantic specification and correctness proofs. Tech. Report, Yale, April 1993.

[Cou79] B. Courcelle. Infinite trees in normal form and recursive equations having a unique solution. *Math. Systems Theory*, 13:131–180, 1979.

[FFK87] M. Felleisen, D. Friedman, and E. Kohlbecker. A syntactic theory of sequential control. *TCS*, 52:205–237, 1987.

[FW88] A. Ferguson and P. Wadler. When will deforestation stop. In *1988 Glasgow Workshop on Functional Programming*, Research Rep. 89/R4, 1988.

[GK93] R. Glück and A. V. Klimov. Occam's razor in metacomputation: the notion of a perfect process tree. In *Static Analysis Syposium*, *LNCS* 724, 1993.

[GLJ93] A. Gill, J. Launchbury, and S. Peyton Jones. A short cut to deforestation. In *FPCA '93*. ACM Press, 1993.

[Gom92] C. Gomard. A self-applicable partial evaluator for the lambda calculus: correctness and pragmatics. *ACM TOPLAS*, 14(2):147–172, 1992.

[How89] D. J. Howe. Equality in lazy computation systems. In *4th LICS*. IEEE, 1989.

[JGS93] N. D. Jones, C. Gomard, and P. Sestoft. *Partial Evaluation and Automatic Program Generation*. Prentice-Hall, 1993.

[Kom92] J. Komorowski. An introduction to partial deduction. In *Third Int. Workshop on Meta-Programming in Logic*, *LNCS* 649, 1992.

[Kot78] L. Kott. About transformation system: A theoretical study. In B. Robinet, editor, *Program Transformations*. Dunod, 1978.

[LS91] J. W. Lloyd and J. Shepherdson. Partial evaluation in logic programming. *J. Logic Programming*, 3–4(11), 1991.

[MW92] S. Marlow and P. Wadler. Deforestation for higher-order functions. In *Functional Programming, Glasgow 1992*, Springer Workshop Series, 1992.

[NH94] K. Nielsen and M. Heine Sørensen Deforestation, partial exaluation and evaluation orders. Unpublished, DIKU, Copenhagen, 1994.

[Pal93] J. Palsberg. Correctness of binding time analysis. *J. Functional Programming*, 3(3), 1993.

[Plo75] G. D. Plotkin. Call-by-name, Call-by-value and the λ-calculus. *TCS*, 1(1):125–159, 1975.

[PS83] P. Partsch and R. Steinbruggen. Program transformation systems. *Computing Surveys*, 15:199–236, 1983.

[San91] D. Sands. Operational theories of improvement in functional languages (extended abstract). In *Fourth Glasgow Workshop on Functional Programming*, Springer Workshop Series, 1991.

[Sa95a] D. Sands. Total correctness by local improvement in program transformation. In *22nd POPL*. ACM Press, 1995.

[Sa95b] D. Sands. Total correctness by local improvement in the transformation of functional programs. DIKU, University of Copenhagen, 48pages, January 1995.

[SF93] T. Sheard and L. Fegaras. A fold for all seasons. In *FPCA '93*. ACM Press, 1993.

[SGJ94] M. H. Sørensen, R. Glück, and N. D. Jones. Towards unifying partial evaluation, deforestation, supercompilation, and GPC. In *ESOP'94*. LNCS 788, Springer Verlag, 1994.

[Sø94a] M H Sørensen. A grammar-based data-flow analysis to stop deforestation. In *CAAP'94*, LNCS 787, 1994.

[Sø94b] M H Sørensen. Turchin's supercompiler revisited: An operational theory of positive information propagation. Master's thesis, DIKU, University of Copenhagen, (RR 94/9) 1994.

[Ste94] P. Steckler. *Correct Higher-Order Program Transformations*. PhD thesis, Northeastern University, Boston, 1994.

[TS84] H. Tamaki and T. Sato. Unfold/-fold transformation of logic programs. In*2nd Int. Logic Programming Conf.*, 1984.

[Tur86] V. F. Turchin. The concept of a supercompiler. *ToPLaS*, 8:292–325, July 1986.

[Wad89] P. Wadler. The concatenate vanishes. University of Glasgow. Unpublished (preliminary version circulated on the fp mailing list, 1987), November 1989.

[Wad90] P. Wadler. Deforestation: transforming programs to eliminate trees. *TCS*, 73:231–248, 1990. (Preliminary version in ESOP 88, LNCS 300).

[Wan93] M. Wand. Specifying the correctness of binding time analysis. *J. Functional Programming*, 3(3), 1993.

Reactive System Specification and Refinement

K. Lano

Dept. of Computing, Imperial College, 180 Queens Gate, London SW7 2BZ.

Abstract. This paper describes formal approaches for reactive and real time system specification and development, using a process of systematic translation from statechart descriptions of a system into a specification language utilising real time logic (RTL), and refinement within this language. Alternative implementation strategies using synchronisation constraints and synchronisation code are also provided, together with examples of development using the approach.

The approach provides a unitary formalism which combines statecharts, RTL and temporal logic. Animation and proof tools are also briefly described.

1 Introduction

Software applications whose main purpose is to interact in real time with external systems or devices are termed 'reactive systems'. Examples include chemical process control systems, or patient monitoring systems, in which response to external events is a major part of the system requirements, and the timing of these responses is also critical. More generally, many safety critical systems are reactive or real time systems, for which formal specifications are becoming more frequently required by standards. Thus a formal language capable of treating issues of process scheduling, timing, concurrent execution and interrupts, and of supporting reasoning about such aspects at a suitable level of abstraction, is highly desirable.

In this context the use of an object-oriented paradigm is appropriate: objects may correspond to reactive components whose behaviour can be specified in isolation, or with real world concepts or entities, such as particular controlled devices, thus enabling a systematic tracing of requirements through specifications to code to be performed, supporting validation, assessment and maintenance.

The formal specification language Z^{++} [10, 6, 8] will be considered as the basis for a real time specification language. This paper extends the Z^{++} language by allowing the use of RTL formulae in the `HISTORY` clause of a class. In contrast to VDM^{++} [10], this formalism is more orientated towards *discrete event systems* rather than continuous variable dynamic systems [14]. However, the formalism presented here could be used as a unifying semantics for much of VDM^{++}, and was initially defined to serve this purpose.

Section 2 gives the syntax of Z^{++} specifications, together with examples. Section 3 summarises the temporal logic formalism used in the paper. Section 4 describes the development process intended to be used with the language, and summarises the steps in this process. Section 5 introduces a refinement technique using semaphores to implement synchronisation constraints, and Section 6 describes refinement using *synchronisation code* [13].

2 Z++/RTL Syntax

2.1 Classes

A Z++ specification consists of a collection of *class* definitions, including generic classes. A schematic Z++ class is of the form:

```
CLASS  C[TypeParameters]
EXTENDS Ancestors
TYPES
  Tdefs
FUNCTIONS
  Axdefs
OWNS
  c
INVARIANT
  Inv_C
OPERATIONS
  [*] m  :  IN  →  OUT;
  ....
RETURNS
  r  :  IN  →  OUT;
  ....
ACTIONS
   Pre_m,C  &
         [*] m x y    ==>    Def_m,C;
  ....
HISTORY  H_C
END CLASS
```

Each of the clauses in the body of a class definition are optional, although an ACTIONS clause requires an OPERATIONS clause. The **TypeParameters** are a list (possibly empty) of *generic* type parameters used in the class definition. The EXTENDS list is the set of previously defined classes that are inherited by this class. Local types, functions and constants can be defined in the TYPES and FUNCTIONS clauses. The OWNS list gives attribute declarations. The INVARIANT specifies time-invariant properties of the internal state. The default invariant is **true**.

The ACTIONS list gives the definitions of the various operations that can be performed on instances of the object. The default action for a method, if no action for it is listed, is the completely non-deterministic operation on the state of the class and its parameter types. Input parameters are listed before the output parameters in the action definitions. Z predicates, method invocations and the B0 procedural code constructs of Abrial's B Notation [11] can be used to define methods. Operations are given explicit preconditions by the notations

```
Pre_m,C &                    m x y   ==>
   m x y   ==>   Def_m,C   or     PRE Pre_m,C  THEN  Def_m,C  END
```

The default precondition is **true**. Methods with a preceeding $*$ are *internal actions* and are discussed further below. The HISTORY of a class is an RTL predicate, the forms of which are given in Section 3.

Details of the reference semantics of Z^{++} are given in [6]. Essentially a class name **C**, when used as a type, denotes a countably infinite set @**C** of references to objects of **C**. A function

$$*_C : @C \rightarrowtail State_C$$

then obtains actual object values (elements of the implicit state schema of **C**) from these references. $\overline{C}$ denotes dom $*_C$, the set of existing objects of **C**.

An operation New_C creates a new instance of **C** and modifies the set of existing instances of **C** (and those of each identified supertype of **C**). A declaration **a** : **C** in the OWNS list of another class is interpreted as **a** : @**C**.

2.2 Specification Examples

Examples of properties which may be expressed in an abstract declarative manner using Z^{++}/RTL formulae are: "**m** initiates every **t** seconds, and in the order of its requests":

$$\forall i : \mathbb{N}_1 \bullet \uparrow(m(x), i+1) = \uparrow(m(x), i) + t$$

$\uparrow(m(x), i)$ denotes the time that the **i**-th request for invocation of **m(x)** received by the current object begins to execute, whilst $\dagger(\uparrow m(x), i)$ denotes the **i**-th time of the form $\uparrow(m(x), j)$. These may be different if invocations are not initiated in the order that they are received by an object. The 'shortest job first' protocol is stated:

$$\forall i, j : \mathbb{N}_1 \mid \rightarrow(m, i) \leq \uparrow(m, j) \bullet$$
$$f((m, i).x) < f((m, j).x) \Rightarrow \uparrow(m, i) \leq \uparrow(m, j)$$

That is, if **(m, j)** has not already started execution by the time the request for **(m, i)** arrives, then **(m, i)** will be started first if it has a smaller value of some priority assigning function **f** on parameter(s) **x**.

Liveness and fairness constraints can also be stated. An example of a complete (but highly abstract) Z^{++} class is a binary semaphore:

```
CLASS Semaphore
OPERATIONS
  signal : →;
  release : →
HISTORY
  #fin(signal) ≥ #act(release) ∧
  #fin(release) + 1 ≥ #act(signal)
END CLASS
```

self_mutex({signal, release}) and **mutex({signal, release})** follow from the remainder of the history constraint, which is implicitly quantified by a $\Box^{\tau}$ operator.

3 Z++/RTL Logic

3.1 Logic

Events

- For each method **m** of **C**: $\uparrow\mathbf{m(e)}$, $\downarrow\mathbf{m(e)}$, $\rightarrow\mathbf{m(e)}$ for $\mathbf{e} \in \mathbf{IN}$, denoting the initiation, termination and the arrival of a request at the object class, respectively, of an invocation instance of **m(e)**;
- θ := **true**, θ := **false** for a predicate θ without modal operators, which denote the events of this predicate becoming true or false, respectively.

These events, together with events of the form $\leftarrow(\mathbf{n(x1), a})$ for $\mathbf{a : S}$ a supplier object to **C**, and **n** a method of **S** (the sending of a request for **a** to execute **n(x1)**), are collectively referred to as $\mathbf{BasicEvent_C}$. The complete set of events of **C** also include the following:

- $\uparrow(\mathbf{n(x1), a})$, $\downarrow(\mathbf{n(x1), a})$, $\rightarrow(\mathbf{n(x1), a})$ where **a** and **n** are as above;
- $\leftarrow(\mathbf{n(x1), a, b})$ where both **a** and **b** are supplier objects to **C**, $\mathbf{a : S}$, and **n** is a method of **S**.

The complete collection of events of **C** is denoted by $\mathbf{Event_C}$.

Terms For a given class **C**, the following terms can occur in the formulae of its RTL language:

1. variables $\mathbf{v_i}$: $\mathbf{i} \in \mathbb{N}$ – only variables can be quantified over;
2. attributes of the class, its ancestors and supertypes;
3. $\mathbf{f(e_1, \ldots, e_n)}$ for an **n**-ary function symbol **f** and terms $\mathbf{e_1}, \ldots, \mathbf{e_n}$, and other Z expressions in terms and schema texts;
4. $\dagger\mathbf{e}$ where **e** is an *event occurrence* $(\mathbf{E, i})$, where **E** is in $\mathbf{Event_C}$ – the time of the **i**-th occurrence of **E**, $\mathbf{i} : \mathbb{N}_1$;
5. $\mathbf{Op(m(e), i)}$ where $\mathbf{m} \in \underline{\mathbf{methods}}(\mathbf{C})$, **e** in the input type of **m**, $\mathbf{i} : \mathbb{N}_1$ and $\mathbf{Op} \in \{\uparrow, \downarrow, \rightarrow\}$, and $\leftarrow((\mathbf{m(e), a}), \mathbf{i})$ for a supplier object $\mathbf{a : D}$ and method **m** of **D**;
6. $\mathbf{e} \circledast \mathbf{t}$ and $\bigcirc\mathbf{e}$ where **e** is a term, **t** a time-valued term – the value of **e** at **t** and at the next method initiation, respectively;
7. **#act(m(e))**, **#fin(m(e))**, **#req(m(e))**, **#req(m)**, **#fin(m)**, **#act(m)** for $\mathbf{m} \in \underline{\mathbf{methods}}(\mathbf{C})$;
8. **self**.

$\#\mathbf{req(m)}$ is the number of requests for $\mathbf{m}$ received by the current object up to the present time, $\#\mathbf{act(m)}$ the number of initiations of execution of $\mathbf{m}$ and $\#\mathbf{fin(m)}$ the number of terminations of $\mathbf{m}$.

Time-valued terms are arithmetic combinations of terms of the form 4 or 5 and elements of $\mathbb{N}$. The time domain satisfies the axioms of the set of non-negative elements of a totally ordered topological ring, with addition operation $+$ and unit 0, and multiplication operation $*$ with unit 1. Thus $\mathbb{N} \subseteq \mathbf{TIME}$ can be assumed. Quantification over $\mathbf{TIME}$ is not allowed.

Relativised versions $\#\mathbf{act(m(e), a)}$, etc of event counters for suppliers $\mathbf{a} : \mathbf{D}$ to $\mathbf{C}$ are also included, as are attributes $\mathbf{a.att}$ of such suppliers.

In addition, method names $\mathbf{m}$ from supertypes $\mathbf{D}$ of $\mathbf{C}$ can be used in its events. They will be interpreted (if unambiguous) as $\phi(\mathbf{m})$ in the semantics of the language, where $\mathbf{D} \sqsubseteq_{\phi,\mathbf{R}} \mathbf{C}$ is asserted in the specification.

$\overline{\mathbf{A}}$ and $*_{\mathbf{A}}$ can be referred to, for any class $\mathbf{A}$ in the specification. This enables control over object sharing and aliasing.

Formulae For any class $\mathbf{C}$ the following are the formulae in its RTL language.

1. $\mathbf{P}(\mathbf{e}_1, \ldots, \mathbf{e_n})$ for an $\mathbf{n}$-ary predicate symbol $\mathbf{P}$ and terms $\mathbf{e}_1, \ldots, \mathbf{e_n}$;
2. $\phi \wedge \psi$, $\phi \vee \psi$, $\phi \Rightarrow \psi$, $\neg\, \phi$ for formulae ϕ and ψ;
3. $\phi \circledcirc \mathbf{t}$ for formulae ϕ and time-valued terms $\mathbf{t}$ – "ϕ holds at time $\mathbf{t}$";
4. $\forall \mathbf{SD} \bullet \phi$, $\exists \mathbf{SD} \bullet \phi$ for declarations $\mathbf{SD}$ and formulae ϕ;
5. $\Box^{\tau}\theta$, $\Box\theta$ and $\bigcirc\theta$ for formulae θ;
6. $\diamond^{\tau}\theta$, $\diamond\theta$ for formulae θ;
7. $\mathbf{enabled(m)}$ and $\mathbf{enabled(m(e))}$ for methods $\mathbf{m}$, $\mathbf{e}$ in the input type of $\mathbf{m}$, and $\mathbf{enabled(m, a)}$ for suppliers $\mathbf{a}$ of $\mathbf{C}$.

$\Box\psi$ denotes that ψ holds at all times of the form $\uparrow(\mathbf{m}, \mathbf{i})$ for $\mathbf{m}$ a method of $\mathbf{C}$ which are at or greater than the present time. $\bigcirc\psi$ denotes that ψ holds at the next time of the form $\uparrow(\mathbf{m}, \mathbf{i})$ (if there is any). In contrast $\Box^{\tau}$ and $\diamond^{\tau}$ refer to all present and future times.

Axioms Only selected axioms will be presented here. A full list, together with details of the semantics and a proof of soundness, is contained in [7]. The axioms include those of classical predicate logic in this language, and the axioms of the Z mathematical toolkit. Of particular importance is a *frame* axiom which asserts that attributes of $\mathbf{C}$ can only change in value if a method of $\mathbf{C}$ is currently executing – it is a form of *locality* property in the sense of [4].

The `ACTIONS` specification of a method $\mathbf{m}$ is interpreted as:

$$\mathbf{(xi)} : \forall \mathbf{e} : \mathbf{IN};\ \mathbf{i} : \mathbb{N}_1 \bullet \mathbf{Pre_{m,C}} \circledcirc \uparrow(\mathbf{m(e)}, \mathbf{i}) \Rightarrow \\ \mathbf{Def_{m,C}}[\mathbf{v} \circledast \downarrow(\mathbf{m(e)}, \mathbf{i})/\mathbf{v}'] \circledcirc \uparrow(\mathbf{m(e)}, \mathbf{i})$$

where the appropriate versions $(\mathbf{m(e),i).x_j}$ of formal input or output parameters are used in $\mathbf{Pre_{m,C}}$ or $\mathbf{Def_{m,C}}$.

Axioms of linear temporal logic (LTL) [15] hold in this formalism, including the induction scheme:

$$\phi \circledcirc \mathbf{min}(\{\dagger(\uparrow \mathbf{m}_1, 1), \ldots, \dagger(\uparrow \mathbf{m_n}, 1)\}) \wedge \Box(\phi \Rightarrow \bigcirc\phi) \Rightarrow \Box\phi$$

which holds for each LTL formula ϕ, where $\underline{\mathbf{methods}}(\mathbf{C}) = \{\mathbf{m}_1, \ldots, \mathbf{m_n}\}$.

In [7] it is shown that a version of Manna-Pnueli logic [14] is provable from Z^{++}/RTL, and that Z^{++}/RTL is conservative over Manna-Pnueli logic.

Abbreviations $\underline{\mathbf{methods}}(\mathbf{C})$ abbreviates the set of methods of a class $\mathbf{C}$, including inherited methods.

$\mathbf{\#active(m)}$ abbreviates $\mathbf{\#act(m)} - \mathbf{\#fin(m)}$, the number of currently active instances of $\mathbf{m}$. $\mathbf{\#waiting(m)}$ abbreviates $\mathbf{\#req(m)} - \mathbf{\#act(m)}$, the number of instances of $\mathbf{m}$ awaiting execution.

$\mathbf{delay(m,i)}$ abbreviates $\uparrow(\mathbf{m,i}) - \rightarrow(\mathbf{m,i})$. $\mathbf{duration(m,i)}$ abbreviates $\downarrow(\mathbf{m,i}) - \uparrow(\mathbf{m,i})$. $\mathbf{mutex}(\{\mathbf{m}_1, \ldots, \mathbf{m_n}\})$ abbreviates the assertion

$$\mathbf{\#active(m_1)} = \sum_{\mathbf{i}=1}^{\mathbf{n}} \mathbf{\#active(m_i)} \vee \ldots \vee$$
$$\mathbf{\#active(m_n)} = \sum_{\mathbf{i}=1}^{\mathbf{n}} \mathbf{\#active(m_i)}$$

$\mathbf{self\_mutex}(\{\mathbf{m}_1, \ldots, \mathbf{m_n}\})$ abbreviates $\mathbf{\#active(m_1)} \leq 1 \wedge \ldots \wedge \mathbf{\#active(m_n)} \leq 1$.

$\underline{\mathbf{m}}$ abbreviates $\mathbf{\#active(m)} > 0$.

$\mathbf{fires(t,i)}$ denotes $\neg\ (\mathbf{false} \circledcirc \uparrow(\mathbf{t,i}))$, that is, the object exists at this time point.

A *durative method* $\mathbf{m}$ is a method which satisfies $\mathbf{durative(m)}$: $\forall \mathbf{i} : \mathbb{N}_1 \bullet \downarrow(\mathbf{m,i}) > \uparrow(\mathbf{m,i})$. A *durative class* is a class all of whose methods are durative. For such a class, the property $\forall \mathbf{i} : \mathbb{N}_1 \bullet \underline{\mathbf{m}} \circledcirc \uparrow(\mathbf{m,i})$ holds for each method $\mathbf{m}$.

3.2 Semantics

A model Ω of a Z^{++}/RTL specification $\mathbf{S}$ consists of a family $(@\mathbf{C})_{\mathbf{C} \in \underline{\mathbf{classes\_of}}(\mathbf{S})}$ of countably infinite sets of object references for each class $\mathbf{C}$ of $\mathbf{S}$, and a family $(\Omega_\mathbf{C})_{\mathbf{C} \in \underline{\mathbf{classes\_of}}(\mathbf{S})}$ with typing $\Omega_\mathbf{C} : @\mathbf{C} \rightarrow \mathbf{Object_C}$ where $\mathbf{Object_C}$ is the set of pairs $\beta = (\alpha, \sigma)$ with the type

$$(\alpha, \sigma) : (\mathbf{BasicEvent_C} * \mathbb{N}_1 \rightarrow \mathbf{TIME}) \times (\mathbf{TIME} \twoheadrightarrow \mathbf{State}^\beta_\mathbf{C})$$

which satisfy a set of conditions corresponding to basic properties of events. $\mathbf{State}^\beta_\mathbf{C}$ is $\mathbf{State_C}$ with each declaration $\mathbf{att} : \mathbf{T}$ of $\mathbf{C}$ replaced by $\mathbf{att} : \mathbf{T}^\beta$.

α assigns a time (not necessarily in the lifetime of the object) to each occurrence of an event of $\mathbf{C}$, and σ gives the state of the object at each time point in its history. From these the value of terms and formulae of $\mathcal{L}_\mathbf{C}$ can be computed at each time point.

4 Development Process

The development process envisaged for the use of the language for real time systems is as follows:

1. *requirements capture and analysis* of the problem, using a structured method suitable for real time problems, such as OMT [16];
2. *formalisation* of structured method notations in Z++/RTL, using systematic processes for the translation of object classes in OMT into Z++ classes (similar to the processes for B AMN described in [11]) and statecharts into history constraints. The abstract declarative nature of RTL allows fairness, liveness and safety constraints to be stated in an implementation-independent manner;
3. *refinement* of Z++/RTL specifications into implementation-oriented classes, making use of reusable specified components and the code of these components;
4. *implementation* of classes using classes which contain procedural code, with timing information derived from a particular execution environment being used to prove the final refinement step.

In the following sections stages 2, 3 and 4 will be illustrated using a small example. Larger applications are given in [7, 8].

4.1 Formalisation of OMT Analysis Models

Integrating formal and structured methods has a number of advantages as a development approach: it can make use of the complementary strengths of these two techniques, and it can make use of existing software engineering expertise, rather than attempting to replace it. A recent survey on the use of formal methods in industry reported that 31% of those companies using formal methods were using them in conjunction with structured methods [2].

Object Models There are two main models which form the input to the formalisation process. The first is the *Object Model* which describes the entities involved in the system, and their attributes, operations and the relationships between them (including inheritance or subtyping). An object model describing a railway station consisting of a set of track sections is shown in Fig. 1.

These models are used to build an initial outline specification, which will later be enhanced by consideration of the dynamic model, and by the addition of semantic detail which could not be expressed in the structured models.

The formalisation process is as follows:

1. For each entity C in the object model, create a Z++ object class **C**;
2. Each attribute of C becomes an attribute of **C**, with corresponding type;

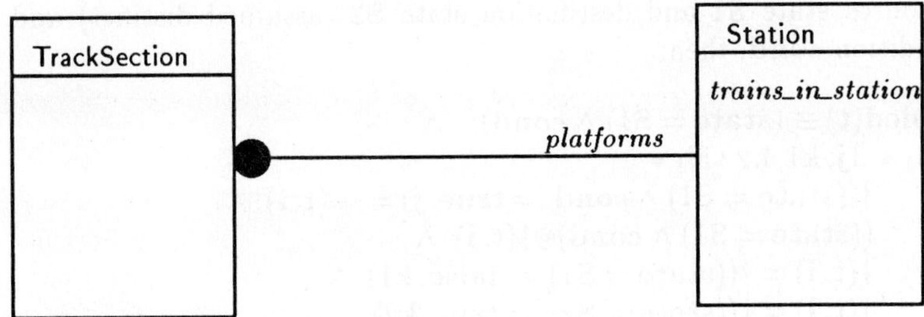

Fig. 1. Object Model of Station

3. Each association r between entities C and D is examined to determine if both directions of the association are required in the final system. The required directions are then formalised as attributes $\mathbf{r}_1$ of $\mathbf{C}$, of type $\mathbf{D}$ (in the case of a many-one or one-one association from C to D), or of type $\mathbb{F}(\mathbf{D})$ or seq($\mathbf{D}$) (in the case of an unordered or ordered many-many or one-many association from C to D, respectively). Similarly for the inverse map $\mathbf{r}_2$ from $\mathbf{D}$ to $\mathbf{C}$, if this is required;
4. If D inherits from C, then the clause `EXTENDS` $\mathbf{C}$ is placed in the header of $\mathbf{D}$. Conformant subtypes are expressed via suitable $\sqsubseteq$ assertions;
5. Operations are translated into outline specifications of operations, with however all signatures completed;
6. Formalisation of all assertions on an object model can be attempted, using the `INVARIANT` and `HISTORY` components of a class.

Dynamic Model For reactive systems the dynamic model, based upon Harel statecharts, is the most significant analysis model. Here we will consider extensions of statecharts to include time bounds on transitions. The formalisation process for dynamic models is:

1. Condition triggered transitions and anonymous (automatic) transitions are formalised as operations which are internally invoked, whilst event-triggered transitions are formalised as operations which are invokable from other objects;
2. states are formalised as elements of an enumerated set, and an attribute of this type is defined to record the current state. Methods formalising a transition modify this variable appropriately;
3. time bounds $[\mathbf{l}, \mathbf{u}]$ on transition $\mathbf{t}$ are expressed via the formula $\forall \mathbf{i} : \mathbb{N}_1 \bullet \mathbf{fires}(\mathbf{t}, \mathbf{i}) \Rightarrow \mathbf{l} \leq \mathbf{delay}(\mathbf{t}, \mathbf{i}) \leq \mathbf{u}$;

4. if **t** has source state **S1** and destination state **S2** (assumed distinct) and guard condition **cond**, then:

$$
\begin{aligned}
&(\mathbf{enabled(t)} \equiv (\mathbf{state} = \mathbf{S1}) \wedge \mathbf{cond}) \quad \wedge \\
&\forall \mathbf{i} : \mathbb{N}_1 \bullet \exists \mathbf{j}, \mathbf{k1}, \mathbf{k2} : \mathbb{N}_1 \bullet \\
&\qquad \dagger((\mathbf{state} = \mathbf{S1}) \wedge \mathbf{cond} := \mathbf{true}, \mathbf{j}) = \rightarrow(\mathbf{t}, \mathbf{i}) \wedge \\
&\qquad ((\mathbf{state} = \mathbf{S1}) \wedge \mathbf{cond}) \circledcirc \uparrow(\mathbf{t}, \mathbf{i}) \wedge \\
&\qquad \downarrow(\mathbf{t}, \mathbf{i}) = \dagger((\mathbf{state} = \mathbf{S1}) := \mathbf{false}, \mathbf{k1}) \wedge \\
&\qquad \downarrow(\mathbf{t}, \mathbf{i}) = \dagger((\mathbf{state} = \mathbf{S2}) := \mathbf{true}, \mathbf{k2})
\end{aligned}
$$

If **t** is durative (in particular if $\mathbf{S1} \neq \mathbf{S2}$) then the LTL properties

$$\Box(\underline{\mathbf{t}} \Rightarrow \bigcirc(\mathbf{state} = \mathbf{S2})) \qquad \Box(\underline{\mathbf{t}} \Rightarrow \mathbf{state} = \mathbf{S1})$$

can be derived (if **t** has no other source or destination);

5. if **t** has an associated action **act** on supplier object **a**, then:

$$\forall \mathbf{i} : \mathbb{N}_1 \bullet \exists \mathbf{k3} : \mathbb{N}_1 \bullet \uparrow(\mathbf{t}, \mathbf{i}) = \leftarrow((\mathbf{act}, \mathbf{a}), \mathbf{k3})$$

6. event triggered transitions are formalised in the same way, however clause 4 is replaced by:

$$
\begin{aligned}
&\mathbf{enabled(t(p))} \equiv (\mathbf{state} = \mathbf{S1}) \quad \wedge \\
&\forall \mathbf{i} : \mathbb{N}_1 \bullet \exists \mathbf{j} : \mathbb{N}_1 \bullet \\
&\qquad (\mathbf{state} = \mathbf{S1}) \circledcirc \dagger(\mathbf{event(p)}, \mathbf{j}) \wedge \\
&\qquad \dagger(\mathbf{event(p)}, \mathbf{j}) = \rightarrow(\mathbf{t(p)}, \mathbf{i}) \wedge \\
&\qquad (\mathbf{state} = \mathbf{S1}) \circledcirc \uparrow(\mathbf{t(p)}, \mathbf{i})
\end{aligned}
$$

Each class corresponding to a statechart is mutex and self-mutex. In addition there are liveness constraints asserting that any non-terminal state must eventually be exited, and constraints asserting that states can only become true as a result of a transition into them. If there are no self-transitions on **S1** then the assertion $\Box(\mathbf{state} = \mathbf{S1} \Rightarrow \underline{\mathbf{t_1}} \vee \ldots \vee \underline{\mathbf{t_n}})$ states that **S1** can only be exited via transitions $\mathbf{t_1}, \ldots, \mathbf{t_n}$.

For example, consider the statechart of track sections shown in Fig. 2.

A *track section* is a defined contiguous segment of track which can be occupied by at most one train at any time. In addition, it may be closed (eg, for engineering work) so that no trains may enter the section. A train will take a minimum of 60 seconds to clear a track section, and a closed track section will be closed for a minimum of 120 seconds. The corresponding outline class, with a state variable **tstate : TState** is:

```
CLASS TrackSection
TYPES
  TState ::= closed | free | blocked
OWNS
  tstate : TState
```

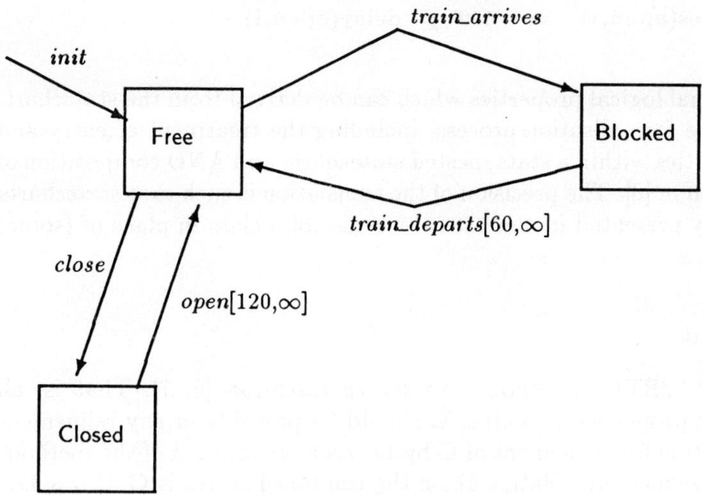

Fig. 2. Statechart of **TrackSection**

```
OPERATIONS
  init : →;
  train_arrives : →;
  train_departs : →;
  open : →;
  close : →
ACTIONS
  init ==>
          tstate' = free;

  train_arrives ==>
          tstate' = blocked;

  train_departs ==>
          tstate' = free;

  open ==>
          tstate' = free;

  close ==>
          tstate' = closed
HISTORY
  mutex({ init, train_arrives, train_departs, open, close }) ∧
  self_mutex({ init, train_arrives, train_departs, open, close }) ∧
  □(train_arrives ⇒ tstate = free) ∧
  □(train_departs ⇒ tstate = blocked) ∧
  □(open ⇒ tstate = closed) ∧
  □(close ⇒ tstate = free) ∧
  ∀ i : ℕ1 • fires(train_departs, i) ⇒ 60 ≤ delay(train_departs, i) ∧
```

$\forall$ **i** : $\mathbb{N}_1$ • **fires(open, i)** $\Rightarrow$ 120 $\leq$ **delay(open, i)**
`END CLASS`

There are additional logical properties which can be derived from the statechart. More detail on the formalisation process, including the treatment of entry and exit actions, activities within a state, nested statecharts and AND composition of statecharts is given in [8]. The precision of the translation is such that statecharts could be explicitly presented in the `HISTORY` clause of a class in place of (some) temporal assertions.

4.2 Refinement

Refinement in Z++/RTL corresponds to *theory extension* [6, 7]. That is, all specified dynamic properties of a class **C** should be provable in any refinement **D** of **C**. The notation for refinement of **C** by **D**, via a renaming ϕ of the methods of **C**, and a data refinement relation **R** on the combined states is $\mathbf{C} \sqsubseteq_{\phi,\mathbf{R}} \mathbf{D}$.

Subtyping of classes is equated with class refinement, in contrast to [12], although the roles of subtyping and refinement within the development process are clearly distinguished. Alternative concepts of refinement, related to *operational compatibility* [3], and strictly stronger than subtyping, are discussed in [7].

4.3 Implementation

In the final refinement of a subsystem, a restricted language is used, in which methods are defined using constructs corresponding to procedural code structures, and in which types are restricted to be arrays, strings, object reference types or scalars.

This language *preserves refinement* in the sense that if a class **D** is a client of a class **C**, and $\mathbf{C}_1$ refines **C**, then substituting $\mathbf{C}_1$ for **C** in **D** to produce a class $\mathbf{D}_1$ implies that $\mathbf{D}_1$ refines **D**. This supports compositional (separate) development of subsystems. It is also direct to implement such classes in an object-oriented programming language such as C++. Timing specifications for such implementations can be derived from the timing specifications of the hardware which is the ultimate destination of the compilation process.

The RTL language is extended by times $\uparrow(\mathbf{s}, \mathbf{i})$, $\downarrow(\mathbf{s}, \mathbf{i})$ and $\rightarrow(\mathbf{s}, \mathbf{i})$ for each statement occurrence **s** of the implementation language in **C**. These denote respectively start, end, and request times for the **i**-th invocation of **s** within an instance of **C**.

These times are assumed in general to be non-negative real numbers. The approach of [5] is used: For each primitive operation **op**, which is one of: **gaddr** (get an address), **stor** (store a value in an address), **eval(e)** (evaluate expression **e**), **decl(T)** (define storage for a variable of type **T**), **brt**, **brtloop** (branch on true), **brf**, **brfloop** (branch on false), there are corresponding *sets* **T(op)** of possible durations for this operation.

$\mathbf{T(op)}$ should always be a small finite set, thus allowing reasoning by case analysis. The definition of $\mathbf{T}$ will vary between destination processor architectures. An operation $\dotplus$ performs addition of such sets, ie: $\mathbf{S} \dotplus \mathbf{T} = \{\mathbf{s}+\mathbf{t} \mid \mathbf{s} \in \mathbf{S} \wedge \mathbf{t} \in \mathbf{T}\}$. An example of the timing rules is:

Assignment The behaviour of assignment is given by:

$$\rightarrow(\mathbf{x} := \mathbf{e}, \mathbf{i}) = \uparrow(\mathbf{x} := \mathbf{e}, \mathbf{i})$$
$$\downarrow(\mathbf{x} := \mathbf{e}, \mathbf{i}) - \uparrow(\mathbf{x} := \mathbf{e}, \mathbf{i}) \in \mathbf{T(gaddr)} \dotplus \mathbf{T(stor)} \dotplus \mathbf{T(eval(e))}$$

That is, there is no delay in executing the assignment after its request, and its duration is a sum of possible durations for its constituent steps.

5 Development Using Semaphores

A general approach for the refinement of classes with non-trivial synchronisation constraints is to utilise classes, such as semaphores, which provide specific synchronisation facilities. That is, a class **C** with synchronisation requirements expressed in its `HISTORY` clause will be refined by a class **C_1** which has a supplier class **S** whose properties can be used to prove the requirements of **C**. **C_1** itself may not need to contain any synchronisation mechanisms.

An example is the case where it is required that a particular method **m** is self-mutex (Fig. 3). Synchronisation constraints of **C** are implemented using a

<pre>CLASS C
OWNS
  ...
OPERATIONS
  m : X → Y;
  ...
ACTIONS
  m x y   ==>   Def_m;
  ...
HISTORY
  self_mutex({ m })
END CLASS</pre>
	<pre>CLASS C_1
	OWNS
	  s : Semaphore;
	  ...
	OPERATIONS
	  m : X → Y;
	  ...
	ACTIONS
	  m x y ==>
	          BEGIN
	            s.signal;
	            Code;
	            s.release
	          END;
	  ...
	END CLASS</pre>

Fig. 3. Refinement Using Semaphores

Semaphore instance, where **Code** implements the state transitions defined in $\mathbf{Def_m}$. The refinement is formally provable because:

$$\begin{aligned}\mathbf{\#active(m)} &= \mathbf{\#act(m)} - \mathbf{\#fin(m)} \\ &= \mathbf{\#act(signal, s)} - \mathbf{\#fin(release, s)} \leq 1\end{aligned}$$

from the history constraint of **Semaphore**.

Other examples are given in [8], including a development of the dining philosophers problem using this approach.

6 Refinement Using Synchronisation Code

An alternative refinement route, which allows synchronisation and fairness requirements expressed in a Z^{++} specification to be discharged, makes use of the concept of *synchronisation code* [13]. This involves the definition of state transformations on *synchronisation variables* which are performed at event occurrences. An event is either the creation of an object, a reception of a request for a method execution, the start of an execution of a method, or the termination of execution of a method. Thus the approach is consistent with the Z^{++}/RTL formalism, and with statecharts.

Synchronisation variables and functions over these are then used to control the permission to execute methods via permission guards.

The refinement of a class (at the end of a data and procedural refinement process) into a C++ class with synchronisation code can be formally checked by an induction over events. This induction will be that the abstract declarative history constraint of the Z^{++} class is always true at each event time, with respect to the translation between Z^{++} and C++ variables.

As an example, consider the specification that requests of **m** are served in a first-come, first-served manner (FCFS):

```
CLASS C
OPERATIONS
  m : →
HISTORY
  ∀ i, j : ℕ₁ | →(m,i) < →(m,j) • ↑(m,i) ≤ ↑(m,j)
END CLASS
```

An appropriate extended C++ class is (following [13]):

```
class C{
  m() {}
synchronisation
  int clk;
  int arr_time local to m;

  start(C) --> clk = 0;
  arrival(m) --> this_inv.arr_time = clk++;

  m: there_is_no(p in waiting(m): p.arr_time < this_inv.arr_time);
}
```

The final clause here asserts that the **this_inv** invocation instance of **m** cannot initiate execution unless the priority condition holds for this instance.

We can relate these two versions of $\mathbf{C}$ as follows. The concrete expression `this_inv.arr_time` refers to a local (synchronisation) variable of a specific instance $(\mathbf{m}, \mathbf{i})$ of an invocation of $\mathbf{m}$. This can be formalised as $(\mathbf{m}, \mathbf{i}).\mathbf{arr\_time}$. From the code it follows that: $(\mathbf{m}, \mathbf{i}).\mathbf{arr\_time} = \mathbf{clk} \circledast \rightarrow (\mathbf{m}, \mathbf{i})$.

By induction on events it can be shown that this value is also

$$\mathbf{previous\_requests}(\mathbf{m}, \rightarrow(\mathbf{m}, \mathbf{i})) \;=\; \#\{\mathbf{j} : \mathbb{N}_1 \mid \rightarrow(\mathbf{m}, \mathbf{j}) < \rightarrow(\mathbf{m}, \mathbf{i})\}$$

(The only relevant events are those listed in the concrete class, and it is assumed that object creation occurs before any $(\mathbf{m}, \mathbf{i})$ invocation.)

The set $\mathbf{waiting}(\mathbf{m})$ of outstanding invocation instances of $\mathbf{m}$ has the formal counterpart $\mathbf{waiting\_instances}(\mathbf{m}, \mathbf{t}) = \{\mathbf{i} : \mathbb{N}_1 \mid \rightarrow(\mathbf{m}, \mathbf{i}) \leq \mathbf{t} \land \neg\, (\uparrow(\mathbf{m}, \mathbf{i}) \leq \mathbf{t})\}$ for each time-valued term $\mathbf{t}$.

Therefore the concrete guard has corresponding formal permission requirement

$$\begin{array}{l} \forall \mathbf{i} : \mathbb{N}_1 \bullet \\ \quad (\neg\, \exists\, \mathbf{pind} : \mathbb{N}_1 \mid \mathbf{pind} \in \mathbf{waiting\_instances}(\mathbf{m}, \uparrow(\mathbf{m}, \mathbf{i})) \bullet \\ \qquad \mathbf{previous\_requests}(\mathbf{m}, \rightarrow(\mathbf{m}, \mathbf{pind})) < \\ \qquad\qquad \mathbf{previous\_requests}(\mathbf{m}, \rightarrow(\mathbf{m}, \mathbf{i})))\circledast\uparrow(\mathbf{m}, \mathbf{i}) \end{array}$$

Given this, it is impossible for there to be $\mathbf{pind} < \mathbf{i}$ with $\rightarrow(\mathbf{m}, \mathbf{pind}) < \rightarrow(\mathbf{m}, \mathbf{i})$ but $\uparrow(\mathbf{m}, \mathbf{i}) < \uparrow(\mathbf{m}, \mathbf{pind})$.

Assume otherwise. Then $\mathbf{pind} \in \mathbf{waiting\_instances}(\mathbf{m}, \uparrow(\mathbf{m}, \mathbf{i}))$. But

$$\mathbf{previous\_requests}(\mathbf{m}, \rightarrow(\mathbf{m}, \mathbf{pind})) < \mathbf{previous\_requests}(\mathbf{m}, \rightarrow(\mathbf{m}, \mathbf{i}))$$

since $\mathbf{pind}$ is a member of the second set and not the first (and $\mathbf{previous\_requests}(\mathbf{m}, \mathbf{t})$ is monotonically increasing with $\mathbf{t}$), contradicting the guard for $\mathbf{m}$.

Tools

Animation and proof tools have been developed for this formalism. Animation is based upon the checking of proposed scenarios expressed as sequences of events. The tool allows a sequence of events and corresponding times to be incrementally constructed, checking permission guards, duration and delay constraints, synchronisation constraints involving event counters, and mutual exclusion properties. Post-states are generated from pre-states, with user interaction being required if there is non-determinism in the method specification [9].

Conclusions

This paper has detailed development processes for real time system development which integrate structured and formal methods in an object-oriented framework, and which combine the benefits of these methods. The proposed formalism provides many of the facilities of real time formalisms such as interval logic [1] or RTTL [14] without excessive notational overhead.

References

1. J. F. Allen: *Maintaining knowledge about temporal intervals*, *CACM*, 26(11):832–843, November 1983.
2. S. Austin, G. I. Parkin: *Formal Methods: A Survey*, National Physical Laboratory, Queens Road, Teddington, Middlesex, TW11 0LW, March 1993.
3. R. Duke, P. King P, G. Smith: *Formalising Behavioural Compatibility for Reactive Object-oriented Systems*, in **Proc 14th Australian Compt. Sci. Conf. (ACSC-14)**, 1991.
4. J. Fiadeiro, T. Maibaum: *Sometimes "Tomorrow" is "Sometime"*, in **Temporal Logic**, D. M. Gabbay and H. J. Ohlbach (editors), LNAI 827, Springer-Verlag 1994, 48–66.
5. C. Fidge: *Proof Obligations for Real-Time Refinement*, **Proceedings of 6th Refinement Workshop**, Springer-Verlag Workshops in Computing, 1994.
6. K. Lano: *Refinement in Object-oriented Specification Languages*, **Proceedings of 6th Refinement Workshop**, Springer-Verlag Workshops in Computing, 1994.
7. K. Lano: *Formal Object-oriented Specification of Real Time Systems*, Dept. of Computing, Imperial College, 1994.
8. K. Lano: *Software Specification and Development in* Z^{++}, to appear in **The Z Handbook**, J. Bowen and M. Hinchey (eds.), McGraw-Hill 1995.
9. K. Lano: *Reasoning Techniques in* VDM^{++}, AFRODITE project report AFRO/IC/KL/RT/V1, Dept. of Computing, Imperial College, 1994.
10. K. Lano, H. Haughton: **Object-oriented Specification Case Studies**, Prentice Hall, 1993.
11. K. Lano, H. Haughton: *Improving the Process of System Specification and Refinement in B*, **Proceedings of 6th Refinement Workshop**, Springer-Verlag Workshops in Computing, 1994.
12. B. Liskov, J. Wing: *Family Values: A Behavioral Notion of Subtyping*, School of Computer Science, Carnegie Mellon University, report CMU-CS-93-187, 1993.
13. C. McHale, S. Baker, B. Walsh, A. Donnelly: *Synchronisation Variables*, Amadeus Project report TCD-CS-94-01, University of Dublin, 1994.
14. J. S. Ostroff: **Temporal Logic for Real-Time Systems**, John Wiley, 1989.
15. A. Pnueli: *Applications of Temporal Logic to the Specification and Verification of Reactive Systems: A Survey of Current Trends*, **Current Trends in Concurrency**, de Bakker J., de Roever W.-P., Rozenberg G. (Eds), Springer-Verlag Lecture Notes in Computer Science, Vol. 224, 1986.
16. J. Rumbaugh, M. Blaha, W. Premerlani, F. Eddy, W. Lorensen, **Object-Oriented Modelling and Design**, Prentice-Hall International, 1991.

Measuring Concurrency of Regular Distributed Computations

Cyrille Bareau[1], Benoît Caillaud[2], Claude Jard[1]
René Thoraval[3]
E-mail: {name}@irisa.fr

[1] IRISA, Campus de Beaulieu, 35042 Rennes cedex, France
[2] LFCS, JCMB, King's Buildings, The University of Edinburgh, Edinburgh, EH9 3JZ, UK
[3] Université de Nantes, Section Informatique, 2 rue de la Houssinière 44072 Nantes cedex 03, France

Abstract. In this paper we present a concurrency measure that is especially adapted to distributed programs that exhibit regular run-time behaviours, including many programs that are obtained by automatic parallelization of sequential code. This measure is based on the antichain lattice of the partial order that models the distributed execution under consideration. We show the conditions under which the measure is computable on an infinite execution that is the repetition of a finite pattern. There, the measure can be computed by considering only a bounded number of patterns, the bound being at most the number of processors.

1 Introduction

The trend towards the use of distributed memory parallel machines is very evident. However, their programming environments have to be significantly improved, especially in the field we are mainly interested in: semi-automated distribution of sequential code for scientific computing. Indeed, programmers need sophisticated performance evaluation tools. However, there is no well-accepted "complexity" criterion for distributed programs, for the behaviours of asynchronous message-passing programs are not yet sufficiently understood. It is also very difficult to design tools that can give relevant performance information from static analysis of distributed code.

A research axis is to study runs of a distributed program instead of the program itself. Especially, it needs to define concurrency measures, i.e. measures that can help reveal the synchronization structure of a computation, as opposed to the traditional ones (message count, for instance) which only give quantitative information about the computation. For this it is now usual to take a distributed execution as a partially ordered set of events that are causally related by process sequentiality and interprocess communication [14]. As far as we know, the first concurrency measure that takes account of causality was proposed by Charron-Bost [5], followed by [9, 11, 16].

It is shown in [11] that either these measures are too inaccurate or their computational complexity makes them impracticable. It is also important to observe that these measures only deal with finite runs. Although executions of reactive programs are usually infinite. Further, executions of distributed programs for scientific applications, even finite, are usually very long. Nevertheless, [5] and [11] give some encouraging results. The measure in [5] is shown to behave well with respect to a particular kind of concatenation operator on computations. On the other hand, the work in [11] shows that there is some hope of obtaining practical concurrency measures for particular classes of executions (for instance, [11] considers executions that can be modeled as so-called interval orders).

We address several closely related problems. First, is it possible to define a measure that gives significant values even in the case of infinite executions? And if such a measure exists, does there exist a class of infinite computations for which the measure can be computed? Naturally, if such computations do exist, they must exhibit some kind of regularity that the measure must take into account. Moreover, as an infinite execution can be seen as a limit of a sequence of finite ones, the computation of the measure should not depend on the size of the order that models an execution: it must only depend on the size of a bounded subset of this order.

In this paper we give a first positive answer to these problems. We define a concurrency measure and a class of executions that exhibit a particular kind of regularity: an execution in this class can be modeled as either an infinite or a finite repetition of a finite elementary order we call a *basic pattern*. If this pattern is well connected, we establish for any regular execution (even infinite) that our measure is bounded and can be computed merely from a bounded number of repetitions of this basic pattern. Such an execution is said to be *well-synchronized*. Finally, we show that this property is of interest for semi-automated distribution of sequential programs.

Paper Organization. We first describe the formal framework used throughout the paper and present a model of an execution of a distributed program as a labeled poset.

We then define our concurrency measure μ on a distributed execution. It is expressed in terms of the antichain lattice of the associated labeled poset. Measure μ associates a value with each event in the execution. An event with a small value denotes a strong synchronization, that is, an execution bottleneck.

We then formally define regular executions and well-synchronization. For a regular well-synchronized execution, we show that μ is bounded, reflects regularity and can be computed on at most $2N-1$ repetitions of the basic pattern (where N is the number of processes). This enables the definition of a measure μ_∞ on the events of the basic pattern. In the case of very long or infinite executions, the computation of this measure suffices to determine μ on almost the whole execution. We also show that the antichain lattice of the infinite repetition of the pattern is regular enough so that μ_∞ can be computed on at most N repetitions of this pattern.

We then compare μ with other measures from the literature.

Finally, we show that our measure is especially relevant for automatically distributed programs.

An extended version of this paper, with more detailed proofs, is available as a technical report [3].

2 Framework

2.1 Definitions and Notations

For an introduction to poset theory see for instance [6].

A set E associated with a partial order relation $\preceq$ is called a *partially ordered set* (*poset* for short) and is denoted by $\mathcal{E} = \langle E, \preceq \rangle$. Let $x, y \in E$: we say that x and y are *comparable* in $\mathcal{E}$ when either $x \preceq y$ or $y \preceq x$, otherwise x and y are said to be *incomparable*, denoted by $x \| y$ (as usual, $x \preceq y \wedge x \neq y$ is denoted by $x \prec y$). A *chain* (resp. an *antichain*) in $\mathcal{E}$ is a subset A of E such that every pair of distinct elements of A are comparable (resp. incomparable). Letting $A \subseteq E$, $\max(A) = \{e \in A \mid \forall f \in A, e \not\prec f\}$ is the set of *maximal* elements in A. The *width* of $\mathcal{E}$ is the maximum number of elements in an antichain in $\mathcal{E}$. The *covering relation* of $\preceq$ is denoted by $-\!\!\prec$, i.e. $e -\!\!\prec f$ (f covers e) $\Leftrightarrow$ ($e \prec f$ and $\nexists g$, $e \prec g \prec f$). For each element e of E, we define $\downarrow e = \{f \in E \mid f \preceq e\}$ (the set of predecessors of e), and for each subset F of E, $\downarrow F = \bigcup_{f \in F} (\downarrow f)$.

The *Hasse diagram* of a poset $\mathcal{E}$ is the directed graph whose vertices are the elements of E and the arcs are the elements of $-\!\!\prec$ (usually, the direction of the arcs is not represented by arrows but must be read bottom-up).

We define a labeled poset Θ as a tuple $\langle E, \preceq, L, \pi \rangle$ consisting of a non-empty poset $\langle E, \preceq \rangle$ of finite width and with no infinitely decreasing chain, a non-empty set L of labels and a labeling function $\pi : E \longrightarrow L$.

The set of antichains of Θ is denoted by $\mathcal{A}(\Theta)$. This set is known to be a distributive lattice when equipped with the partial order $\sqsubseteq$ defined as follows: $\forall A, B \in \mathcal{A}(\Theta)$, $A \sqsubseteq B \iff \downarrow A \subseteq \downarrow B$. Moreover it is easy to show that:

Lemma 1. *Let Θ be a labeled poset. Then $\forall A, B \in \mathcal{A}(\Theta)$,*
$$B \text{ covers } A \iff A \sqsubseteq B \text{ and } |\downarrow B \setminus \downarrow A| = 1$$

Then we can define $\mathcal{G}(\Theta) = \langle \mathcal{A}(\Theta), \Gamma(\Theta) \rangle$ where $\Gamma(\Theta) \subseteq \mathcal{A}(\Theta) \times E \times \mathcal{A}(\Theta)$ is the set of edges (A, e, B) such that B covers A and $(\downarrow B) \setminus (\downarrow A) = \{e\}$. We call this graph the labeled Hasse diagram of $\langle \mathcal{A}(\Theta), \sqsubseteq \rangle$.

2.2 Discrete Model of a Distributed Computation

Let us consider a computation of a distributed program, that is, a parallel run of a family $(P_i)_{i \in \{1,\ldots,N\}}$ of N sequential processes that communicate by asynchronously exchanging messages. Let P denote the set $\{1, \ldots, N\}$.

We define a discrete model of this computation as a labeled poset $\Theta = \langle E, \preceq, P, \pi \rangle$ that we will call a *distributed order* in the sequel. The elements of E are significant events that occur during the computation. The partial order $\preceq$ indicates how these events are causally related (causality is based on process sequentiality and interprocess communication). The labeling function $\pi : E \longrightarrow P$ associates with each event the identifier of the process it occurs on.

Process Sequentiality. $\pi^{-1}(\{i\})$ denotes the set of events that occur on any given process P_i. Since P_i runs sequentially, any two events of $\pi^{-1}(\{i\})$ are causally related, that is, $\pi^{-1}(\{i\})$ is modeled as a chain. Thus, the family $(\pi^{-1}(\{i\}))_{i \in P}$ is a N-chain decomposition of the labeled poset Θ, the width of which is therefore no more than N.

Concurrency. As we intend to measure concurrency throughout a computation, we are interested to know how far processes can simultaneously proceed at any given point in it. In the context of our discrete model Θ of a computation, that means we are interested in all the sets of events that are causally unconnected, i.e. the antichains of Θ.

Thus, the distributive lattice $\mathcal{A}(\Theta)$ of antichains of Θ well describes the dynamics of concurrency throughout the computation. Moreover, as the behaviours $(\pi^{-1}(\{i\}))_{i\in P}$ of the processes constitute a N-chain decomposition of Θ, this lattice can be given a graphical representation (see Fig. 1), for its Hasse diagram can be embedded into a N-dimensional grid with one dimension per process.

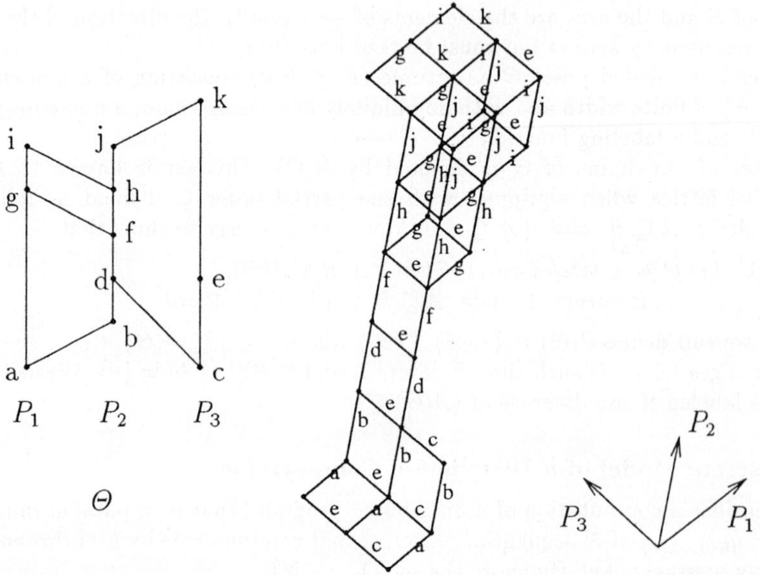

Fig. 1. Hasse diagram of a distributed execution Θ on 3 processors and its graph $\mathcal{G}(\Theta)$

The left part of Fig. 1 shows the Hasse diagram of a computation Θ of a distributed program consisting of three processes P_1, P_2 and P_3. Its middle part illustrates $\mathcal{A}(\Theta)$ by showing the labeled directed graph $\mathcal{G}(\Theta)$ (each direction in the graph corresponds to a processor, as shown in the right part). In this graph, a path from the bottom to the top represents a linear extension of Θ.

3 A Concurrency Measure on the Antichain Lattice

3.1 Definition

The intuition underlying our measure is that the degree of concurrency of an event e is related to "what can happen simultaneously with e". The first idea is to count the number of processors ready to work, i.e. those that are not blocked waiting for e. However this criterion is not accurate enough: for example, it does not enable us to distinguish between events e and h although e is clearly more concurrent than h (e is completely independent on the run of processors P_1 and P_2, whereas h blocks the execution of events i, j, k, therefore the other processors). This idea can be refined by computing the number of antichains containing e, i.e. the number of configurations where the processor that performs e works in parallel with other processors (this is a refinement of a global indicator proposed by Charron-Bost [5]).

Definition 2. Let Θ be a distributed order $\langle E, \preceq, P, \pi \rangle$. For each event e of E:

1. $C_\Theta(e) = \{f \in E \mid f \,\|\, e\}$ is the set of events that are concurrent with e.
2. $\mathcal{A}_\Theta(e) = \{A \in \mathcal{A}(\Theta) \mid e \in A\}$ is the set of antichains that contain e.

The concurrency measure $\mu_\Theta : E \longrightarrow \mathbb{N} \cup \{\omega\}$ is defined as follows:

$$\forall e \in E, \quad \mu_\Theta(e) = |\mathcal{A}_\Theta(e)|$$

A large value of $\mu_\Theta(e)$ (we write $\mu(e)$ when no confusion is possible) means that many things may happen between the first and the last place where e can occur, that is, e has a great "latency" before actually occurring, and therefore is "very concurrent". In contrast, a little value means that this latency is very short: e is in fact a point of strong synchronization, a "bottleneck".

In the execution of Fig. 1, events g and h for instance have respectively h, e, j, k and g, e as concurrent events; $\mu(h) = |\mathcal{A}_\Theta(h)| = |\{\{h\}, \{h, e\}, \{h, g\}, \{h, e, g\}\}| = 4$ and $\mu(g) = |\{\{g\}, \{g, e\}, \{g, h\}, \{g, e, h\}, \{g, j\}, \{g, e, j\}, \{g, k\}\}| = 7$. The following table gives the values for all events of the execution:

a	b	c	d	e	f	g	h	i	j	k
3	3	3	2	12	2	7	4	5	5	3

In Figure 1, we can see on the lattice that, for instance, events d and f strongly synchronize the execution: nothing happens on processor P_1 simultaneously, and only e can occur on P_3. In contrast, e does not depend on the computation on processors P_1 and P_2 and therefore is very concurrent because there are several possible configurations where it can be executed.

3.2 Computation

In the previous section, we define the measure of an event e in terms of the set of antichains that contain it. To compute this measure, we need to count the edges labeled by e in the labeled Hasse diagram $\mathcal{G}(\Theta)$ of the lattice of the execution:

Proposition 3. *Let Θ be a distributed order and $e \in E$. Then*

$$\mu_\Theta(e) = |\{B \in \mathcal{A}(\Theta) \mid \exists A \in \mathcal{A}(\Theta), (A, e, B) \in \Gamma(\Theta)\}|$$

Proof. From Lemma 1, clearly $\forall A, B \in \mathcal{A}(\Theta), \forall e \in E, (A, e, B) \in \Gamma(\Theta)$ iff $A = \max((\downarrow B) \setminus \{e\})$. Then $\mathcal{A}_\Theta(e) = \{B \in \mathcal{A}(\Theta) \mid \exists A \in \mathcal{A}(\Theta), (A, e, B) \in \Gamma(\Theta)\}$. □

This is computationally equivalent to the problem of counting the antichains of an order, which is known to be #P-complete.

This leads us to look for executions for which the number of antichains to be counted does not depend on the length of the execution.

4 Regular and Well-synchronized Executions

The aim of this section is to study a particular class of regular executions: executions which are finite or infinite repetitions of an elementary one (for instance a loop-body). We will show that for a subclass of these executions, μ is computable even in the infinite case by only taking into account at most N (the number of processes) repetitions of a basic "pattern".

4.1 Regular Executions

Definition 4 Regular distributed order. Let $p \in \mathbb{N}^+ \cup \{\omega\}$ and $\Theta = \langle E, \leq, P, \pi \rangle$ be a finite distributed order. Let $E_p = \bigcup_{i \in [0,p[} \varphi_i(E)$ where $(\varphi_i(E))_{i \in [0,p[}$ is a sequence of mutually disjoint isomorphic copies of E. The distributed order $\Theta_p = \langle E_p, \leq_p, P, \pi_p \rangle$ is defined up to order-isomorphism by:

- $\forall i \in [0, p[,\ \pi_p \circ \varphi_i = \pi$
- $\leq_p$ is the least order relation on $E_p \times E_p$ such that:
  - $\forall i \in [0, p[, \forall e, f \in E,\ \varphi_i(e) \leq_p \varphi_i(f) \Longleftrightarrow e \leq f$
  - $\forall i, j \in [0, p[, \forall e, f \in E,\ (\pi(e) = \pi(f)) \wedge (i < j) \Longrightarrow \varphi_i(e) \leq_p \varphi_j(f)$

We say that a distributed order Φ is regular if there exists $p \in \mathbb{N}^+ \cup \{\omega\}$ and a finite distributed order Θ such that Φ is order isomorphic to Θ_p.

When in the sequel we consider a regular distributed order Θ_p, $\leq_p$ and π_p are denoted by $\leq$ and π for the sake of clarity. To speak about events of Θ_p more conveniently, we identify $\varphi_0(E)$ with E and we use $\lambda : E_p \longrightarrow E_p$ defined as follows: $\forall e \in E, \forall i \in [0, p-1[, \lambda(\varphi_i(e)) = \varphi_{i+1}(e)$. This allows us to use the non-negative powers of λ instead of φ_i because $\forall e \in E, \forall i \in [0, p[, \varphi_i(e) = \lambda^i(e)$ (see Fig 2.(1) for a very simple example) and, as λ is clearly injective, its negative powers can also be used. Moreover, λ has the following property:

Lemma 5. *Let Θ_p be a regular distributed order. Then $\forall e, f \in E, \forall i, j \in [1, p[$,*

$$\lambda^{i-1}(e) \preceq \lambda^{j-1}(f) \Longleftrightarrow \lambda^i(e) \preceq \lambda^j(f)$$

In other words, λ preserves the order relation $\preceq$: it is an order isomorphism from $\bigcup_{i \in [0,p-1[} \lambda^i(E)$ onto $\bigcup_{i \in [1,p[} \lambda^i(E)$. On the Hasse diagram of Θ_p, λ is represented as a "one pattern upward shift". Therefore the Hasse diagram of Θ_p is invariant by pattern-wise translations.

Proof. Let $e, f \in E$ and $i, j \in [1, p[$ such that $\lambda^{i-1}(e) \preceq \lambda^{j-1}(f)$. Then there exists a finite path $\lambda^{i-1}(e) = e_0 -\!\!\prec e_1 -\!\!\prec \ldots -\!\!\prec e_h = \lambda^{j-1}(f)$. From Def. 4, we clearly have $\forall k \in [0, h-1],\ \lambda(e_k) -\!\!\prec \lambda(e_{k+1})$, hence the result. □

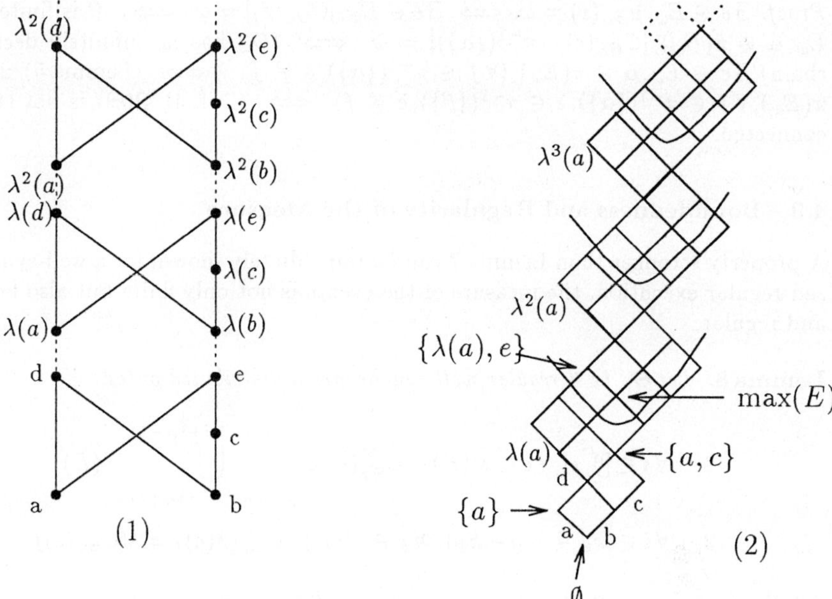

Fig. 2. Notations for regular executions

4.2 Well-synchronized Executions

For a given event e, the number of events that are incomparable with e in an infinite execution can be *a priori* infinite, and so $\mu(e) = \omega$. It is however interesting to see if there exists infinite regular executions for which all events have finite measures.

We will show (Lemma 7) that this property is related to the communication scheme of the basic pattern. We first introduce the notion of *communication graph* of a distributed order.

Definition 6. We call communication graph of a distributed order Θ the quotient of its Hasse diagram by the equivalence relation induced by π^{-1}, i.e. the directed graph $\mathcal{Q}(\Theta) = \langle V, C \rangle$ where:

- $V = \pi(E)$
- $C = \{(\alpha, \beta) \in V \times V \mid \exists\, e \in \pi^{-1}(\{\alpha\}), f \in \pi^{-1}(\{\beta\}),\ e \prec f\}$

A distributed order Θ whose associated communication graph is strongly connected is said to be well-synchronized. The diameter of $\mathcal{Q}(\Theta)$ is then denoted by $k_\Theta - 1$.

Note that $k_\Theta \in [1, N]$, N being the number of processes.

Lemma 7. *Let Θ be a finite distributed order. The concurrency measure μ_{Θ_ω} of any event in $\Theta_\omega = \langle E_\omega, \preceq_\omega, P, \pi_\omega \rangle$ is finite if and only if Θ is well-synchronized.*

Proof. $\exists e \in E_\omega, \mu_{\Theta_\omega}(e) = \omega \iff \exists e \in E_\omega, |C_{\Theta_\omega}(e)| = \omega \iff$ (P is finite) $\exists e \in E_\omega, \alpha \in \pi(E_\omega), |C_{\Theta_\omega}(e) \cap \pi^{-1}(\{\alpha\})| = \omega \iff$ (Θ_ω has no infinitely decreasing chain) $\exists e \in E_\omega, \alpha \in \pi(E_\omega), (\forall f \in \pi^{-1}(\{\alpha\}), e \not\preceq f) \iff$ (Lemma 5) $\exists \alpha, \beta \in \pi(E_\omega), \forall f \in \pi^{-1}(\{\alpha\}), e \in \pi^{-1}(\{\beta\}), e \not\preceq f) \iff$ (Def. 4) $\mathcal{Q}(\Theta)$ is not strongly connected. □

4.3 Boundedness and Regularity of the Measure

A property stronger than Lemma 7 can be immediately shown: for a well-synchronized regular execution, the measure of the events is not only finite but also bounded and regular.

Lemma 8. *Let Θ_p be a regular well-synchronized distributed order.*

1. $$\forall i \in [0, p[, \forall e \in \lambda^i(E), \quad C_{\Theta_p}(e) \subseteq \bigcup_{j=\max(0,i-k_\Theta+1)}^{\min(p-1,i+k_\Theta-1)} \lambda^j(E)$$
2. $$\forall i \in [k_\Theta - 1, p - k_\Theta[, \; \forall e \in \lambda^i(E), \; C_{\Theta_p}(\lambda(e)) = \lambda(C_{\Theta_p}(e))$$

Proof. 1. Let $i \in [0, p[$, $e \in \lambda^i(E)$, $j \in [i + k_\Theta, p[$, and $f \in \lambda^j(E)$. From Def. 6, since the diameter of $\mathcal{Q}(\Theta)$ is $k_\Theta - 1$: $\exists e' \in \lambda^{i+1}(E), \pi(e') = \pi(e)$ and $\exists f' \in \lambda^{i+k_\Theta-1}(E), \pi(f') = \pi(f)$ such that $e' \preceq f'$. From Def. 4, $e \preceq e'$ and $f' \preceq f$, hence e and f are comparable. Similarly, $\forall j$, $0 \le j \le i - k_\Theta$, $\forall f \in \lambda^j(E)$, $f \preceq e$.
2. Routine application of Lemmas 8(1) and 5. □

The measure clearly is bounded: $\forall e \in E$, $\mu(e) \le |\mathcal{A}(\Theta_{2k_\Theta-1})|$. By Lemma 5, it is also regular: $\forall i, j \in [k_\Theta - 1, p - k_\Theta + 1[$, $\forall e \in E$: $\mu_{\Theta_p}(\lambda^i(e)) = \mu_{\Theta_p}(\lambda^j(e))$.

Moreover, μ can be computed on $\mathcal{A}(\Theta_{2k_\Theta-1})$ (even in the case of infinite executions), thus taking at most $2N - 1$ patterns into account (N being the number of processes). For infinite or very long regular well-synchronized executions whose basic patterns have reasonable sizes, μ can be realistically computed.

We have implemented the computation of μ in our distributed environment [12] based on the Estelle specification language. This environment provides a mechanism of vectorial clocks [15], that are traced "on line". These traces are used as input for our algorithm of construction of the antichain lattice of an order [7, 13]. When given as input a linear extension of $\Theta_{2k_\Theta-1}$, this algorithm has a time complexity of $\mathcal{O}(|\mathcal{A}(\Theta_{2k_\Theta-1})| + |\Gamma(\Theta_{2k_\Theta-1})| + N \times |\Theta_{2k_\Theta-1}|^2)$.

The fact that μ reflects regularity makes useful the definition of a measure μ_∞ on the basic pattern:

Definition 9. Let Θ be a finite, well-synchronized distributed order, we write:
$$\forall e \in E, \quad \mu_\infty(e) = \mu_{\Theta_\omega}(\lambda^{k_\Theta-1}(e))$$

As clearly, $\forall e \in E$, $\mu_\infty(e) = \mu_{\Theta_{2k_\Theta-1}}(\lambda^{k_\Theta-1}(e))$, μ_∞ can also be computed on $\mathcal{A}(\Theta_{2k_\Theta-1})$.

We also have a stronger result on μ_∞: it can be computed on a subgraph of the labeled Hasse diagram $\mathcal{G}(\Theta_{k_\Theta})$ of $\mathcal{A}(\Theta_{k_\Theta})$, that is, by only taking account of at most

N repetitions of the basic pattern [4]. This result does not significantly improve the complexity of the computation of μ_∞ (which becomes in N instead of $2N-1$) but enlights the regular structure of the antichain lattice. We briefly present the way to obtain this result, without any proofs nor algorithms (see [3] for details).

4.4 Computation of μ_∞

Let Θ_ω be a regular well-synchronized distributed order.

Regularity. We show in [3] that the labeled Hasse diagram $\mathcal{G}(\Theta_\omega)$ of its antichain lattice $\mathcal{A}(\Theta_\omega)$ is regular.

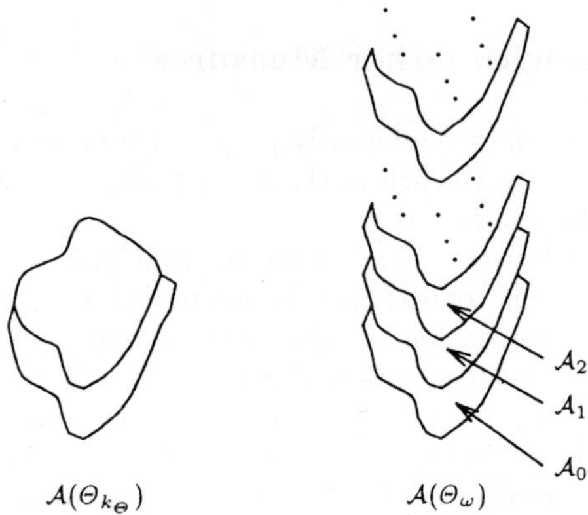

Fig. 3. Hasse diagram of $\mathcal{A}(\Theta_\omega)$

First, we define a partition $(\mathcal{A}_i)_{i\in\mathbb{N}}$ of $\mathcal{A}(\Theta_\omega)$ where $\mathcal{A}_0$ denotes the set $\{A \in \mathcal{A}(\Theta_\omega) \mid A \not\sqsubseteq \max(E)\}$ and for any $i \in \mathbb{N}^+$, $\mathcal{A}_i = \{A \in \mathcal{A}(\Theta_\omega) \mid \lambda^{i-1}(\max(E)) \sqsubseteq A \wedge \lambda^i(\max(E)) \not\sqsubseteq A\}$ (see Fig. 3). Similarly, we define a partition $(\Gamma_i)_{i\in\mathbb{N}}$ of $\Gamma(\Theta_\omega)$: for any $i \in \mathbb{N}$, Γ_i denotes the set $\{(A, e, B) \in \Gamma(\Theta_\omega) \mid A \in \mathcal{A}_i\}$. Finally, we denote by $\mathcal{G}_0$ the subgraph of $\mathcal{G}(\Theta_\omega)$ whose set of vertices is $\mathcal{A}_0 \cup \{B \in \mathcal{A}_1 \mid B \cap \max(E) \neq \emptyset\}$ and whose set of edges is Γ_0.

Lemma 10. *For any $i \in \mathbb{N}$,*

1. *There exists is a one-to-one mapping Λ_i of $\mathcal{A}_0$ onto $\mathcal{A}_i$.*
2. *There exists a one-to-one mapping $\tilde{\Lambda}_i$ of Γ_0 onto Γ_i such that $\forall (A, e, B) \in \Gamma_0$, $\tilde{\Lambda}_i(A, e, B) = (\Lambda_i(A), \lambda^i(e), \Lambda_i(B))$.*

[4] Clearly, μ_∞ cannot be computed on $\mathcal{G}(\Theta_p)$ where $0 < p < k_\Theta$.

Clearly, the set of vertices of $\mathcal{G}_0$ is included in $\cup_{i\in[0,k_\Theta[}\lambda^i(E)$. Hence $\mathcal{G}_0$ is a subgraph of $\mathcal{G}(\Theta_{k_\Theta})$. Then Lemma 10 shows that all the information about $\mathcal{G}(\Theta_\omega)$ is contained into the subgraph $\mathcal{G}_0$ of $\mathcal{G}(\Theta_{k_\Theta})$. Consequently, we can compute μ_∞ by only taking $\mathcal{G}_0$ into account.

Computation. In [3] we show how to compute μ_∞ on $\mathcal{G}_0$:

Proposition 11. $\forall e \in E$,

$$\mu_\infty(e) = |\{(A, f, B) \in \Gamma_0 \mid \exists i \in \mathbb{N}, f = \lambda^i(e)\}|$$

This proposition gives us a new algorithm for the computation of μ_∞. It relies on the computation of the subgraph $\mathcal{G}_0$ of $\mathcal{G}(\Theta_{k_\Theta})$ instead of the computation of $\mathcal{G}(\Theta_{2k_\Theta-1})$ (see subsection 4.3). Its time complexity is the same as for the computation of $\mathcal{G}(\Theta_{k_\Theta})$, that is $\mathcal{O}(|\mathcal{A}(\Theta_{k_\Theta})| + |\Gamma(\Theta_{k_\Theta})| + N \times |\Theta_{k_\Theta}|^2)$ [7, 13] where $k_\Theta \leq N$ (recall N is the number of processes).

5 Comparison with Other Measures

In this section, we present some recently proposed concurrency measures. We show that ours is comparable with each of them, especially if we study the behaviour in case of infinite regular executions.

At first, we present two "global" measures that give a single value to quantify a whole execution. In our context (see section 6), we are not interested in such an approach for it does not enable the detection of bottlenecks (although it can be suitable for other distributed programming problems). However, note that a "local" measure (that associates a value with each event of an execution) can be derived from a global one. The following measures are local ones. They are computed directly on the order of an execution, not on the antichain lattice; the advantage is a better complexity (polynomial in the number of events), but the drawback is that they are less accurate, and not suited to infinite well-synchronized regular executions.

Charron-Bost [5] As far as we know, this is the first attempt to take into account, for a concurrency measure, the causal structure of an execution. In our notation, this measure is:

$$m(\Theta) = \frac{|\mathcal{A}(\Theta)| - |E| - 1}{c(\Theta) - |E| - 1}$$

where $c(\Theta)$ is the number of antichains in a totally concurrent execution (i.e. any two events with distinct labels are incomparable) with as many processes and as many events per process as in Θ, that is to say $c(\Theta) = \prod_{i=1,N}(|\pi^{-1}(\{i\})|+1)$. In fact, μ is quite similar to m: the idea is to count the number of antichains in an execution. The difference is that μ is a global measure and that it is normalized: it ranges from 0 in the worst case ($|E|+1$ is the number of antichains of a totally sequential execution) to 1 in the best (a totally concurrent execution). But this normalization is unsuited to the infinite case: $c(\Theta_p) = \prod_{i=1,N}(p|\pi^{-1}(\{i\})|+1) = p^N \prod_{i=1,N}(|\pi^{-1}(\{i\})| + 1/p)$, hence for a well-synchronized execution:

$$m(\Theta_p) = \frac{(p - k_\Theta + 1)\,|\mathcal{A}_0| + |\mathcal{A}(\Theta_{k_\Theta}) \setminus \mathcal{A}_0| - p|E| - 1}{p^N \prod_{i=1,N}(|\pi^{-1}(\{i\})| + 1/p) - p|E| - 1} \Rightarrow m(\Theta_\omega) = 0$$

Habib et al. [11] They propose a "worst-case-measure" of the concurrency of an execution: the minimal size of the maximal (for inclusion) antichains of its associated poset. It can be seen as the number of processors that can proceed during the worst bottleneck of the execution.
This measure could be made local by computing for each event e the minimal size of the maximal antichains that contain e. As this measure depends on the antichains of a poset, it is obvious from our framework and results that such a derived measure presents the same regularity properties as ours. The difference with our measure is that we consider all the antichains which contain an event, whereas they only consider the maximal antichains.

Fidge [9] Fidge proposes a local measure, that he extends to a global one. The measure β of an event e in an execution Θ is defined as follows:

$$\beta(e) = \frac{|\downarrow e| - 1 - h(e)}{|\downarrow e| - 1 - a}$$

(Fidge proposes two closely related measures, whether $a = 1$ or $a = 1/N$). $h(e)$ is the "height" of e, i.e. the length of the longest chain ending by e. If we consider a well-synchronized regular execution Θ_ω, we can easily prove that β converges:

$$\forall e, \quad \lim_{p \to \infty} \beta(\lambda^p(e)) = \frac{|E| - h(E)}{|E|}$$

We obtain a finite and computable measure. But it does not preserve regularity and for infinite executions, the measure is identical for almost all events.

Raynal et al. [16] This measure is a variant of Fidge's one:

$$\alpha(e) = \frac{|\downarrow e| - 1 - h(e)}{v(\downarrow e) - 1 - h(e)}$$

where $v(\downarrow e)$ is defined as the "volume" of the causal past of e, i.e. $v(\downarrow e) = \sum_{i=1}^{N}(h(e_i) + 1)$ with $e_{\pi(e)} = e$ and for all $i \neq \pi(e)$, e_i is the maximum of the predecessors of e in $\pi^{-1}(\{i\})$. For well-synchronized executions, α converges as well:

$$\lim_{p \to \infty} \alpha(\lambda^p(e)) = \frac{|E| - h(E)}{v(E) - h(E)}$$

We have computed these measures on a kernel of the Jacobi algorithm, automatically distributed on five processors. The results are presented in Fig. 4.

The values for μ must be read on the right vertical axis, and the values for the three other measures (α, β, m) on the left axis: from 0 to 1 because these measures are normalized. Therefore, for comparison sake, the exact values are not to be taken into account, but only the variations of the graph. Charron-Bost's measure m is also presented on this graph, but the plots are in fact the values $m(\Theta_p)$, Θ being the pattern observed on this execution.

This diagram clearly shows that our measure remains relevant when time flows, whereas the others converge to a single value.

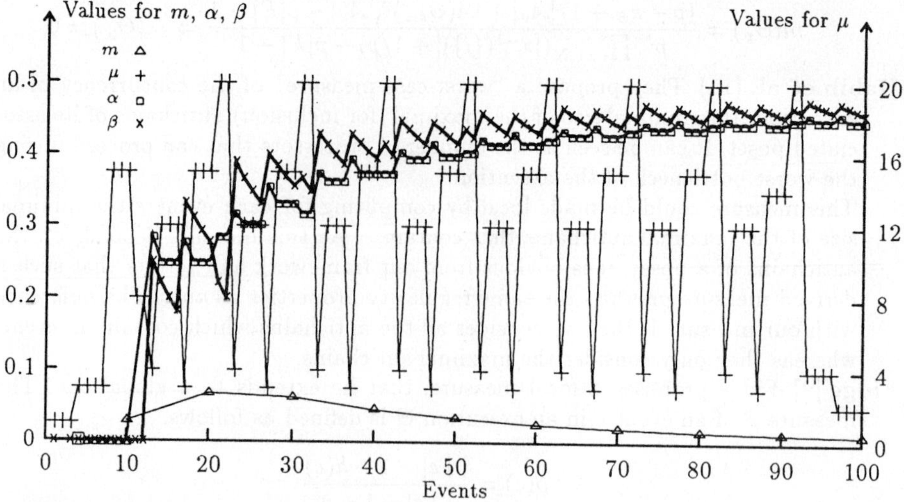

Fig. 4. Measures for the Jacobi algorithm.

6 Use in Automated Distribution of Sequential Programs

6.1 Motivation

Much research is being done on efficient sequential code distribution techniques (see for instance [17]). Our work originates with the practical problem of evaluating automatically distributed programs.

To automatically parallelize a sequential program for a distributed memory parallel computer, compiling directives must be given. For a data-driven distribution technique, the key directive is to specify a data distribution, that is, to indicate how data structures are to be decomposed and mapped onto the network of processes.

A programmer needs tools that help him to select a good distribution of the data structures of a source program. That is, he must be able to evaluate quantitatively and qualitatively the executions of the distributed code that can be generated given a data decomposition. For instance, he needs to determine the fragments of the source code for which a data decomposition is unsuitable. For this, a tool that only measures the average degree of concurrency of a distributed execution is clearly inadequate.

To be efficient enough the tools to be designed should be able to produce relevant outcomes without having to entirely run a generated parallel program. In other words, tools are needed that can collect as much relevant information as possible by efficient static analyses [8] of a source code and of an associated data decomposition.

Semi-automatic distribution is used in application fields (scientific computing) where source codes are generally composed of loops operating on arrays [10]. In fact, available compilers are inefficient when a source program is not regular.

Applying a distribution technique does not affect syntactic regularity. First, generated codes are SPMD (Single Program Multiple Data) [4]: the control structure of each generated process is a copy of that of the source program. Second, data distribution rules are regular as well: arrays, for instance, are decomposed into blocks of contiguous rows or blocks of contiguous columns.

6.2 Detection of Regular Well-synchronized Executions

We deal with programs that are mainly composed of loops operating on arrays. Data distribution is expressed by a distribution function that associates with each array element the processor on which it is located, called its owner ([1]).

From an intuitive point of view, it is clear that the loops of a parallelized program may lead to regular executions, i.e. the finite repetition of the same distributed order. The idea is to consider as the "basic pattern" the distributed order corresponding to the execution of one step of the loop. Then, an execution is actually regular (in the sense of section 4) if *each* step of the loop produces this pattern.

There is repetition of a pattern from one step of the a loop to another if the same events are observed on each processor, as well as the same comparabilities between events. To check this, we have to look at each array reference. For all values of the loop index, this reference must correspond to array elements that are owned by the same processor. Two possibilities arise: the index is not *syntactically* used in the reference, (for instance the external loop of the Jacobi relaxation algorithm), or it is syntactically used but not *semantically* (its value has no incidence on the result of the determination of the owners).

Checking this is not statically possible in the general case. However, in practice, the distribution function and the expressions in array references are often affine. Therefore compile-time checking is possible in some cases.

Considering a regular execution, it is easy to detect if it is well-synchronized or not: it suffices to execute one step of the loop, build the communication graph, and check its connexity.

We have not made an exhaustive study of benchmark programs, but we have found programs whose runtime behaviours are regular and well-synchronized. For example, Jacobi-like programs (walking n times through a matrix, updating each time the values by a function of the neighboring values) satisfy this property whatever the data distribution is, and many linear algebra programs also satisfy it but only for particular data distributions.

7 Conclusion

The contribution we have presented in this paper originates with the practical problem of evaluating the synchronizations of a distributed program running on a network of processors. We are faced with such a problem in the field of automatic parallelization of sequential programs for distributed memory computers (high performance computing).

In this field the generated programs are weakly deterministic [2] and are often control static ones, for which studying one particular execution of a program gives information on the exact quantity of parallelism extracted by the compiler/parallelizer. Another salient feature of the run-time behaviours of these programs is their regularity.

Consecutively, we have been interested in a concurrency measure that would take regularity into account. We have defined a measure that associates a value with each event of an execution. In the case of a regular and well-synchronized execution, this value remains bounded even if the execution is infinite. This is not the case with other measures in the literature, that ultimately associate the same value with all events that occur, although some of them could be extended to take the well-synchronization into account as we have done for that of Charron-Bost. Our measure is therefore relevant whatever the length of the execution is and can be computed from the basic pattern of the execution by taking at most N repetitions of this pattern into account, where N is the number of processors.

To obtain this result, we used partial order theory. A distributed execution is modeled as the causality partial order between events. The degree of synchronization is captured by counting the number of antichains that contain a given event. This theory has proved useful, providing us with an adequate framework to describe the regularity of an execution.

The computation of our measure has been integrated in a parallelization environment developed in our research team [1]. Its exploitation is at the planning stage.

Acknowledgments

This work was partially supported by the project Trace of the French Ministère de l'Enseignement Supérieur et de la Recherche.

References

1. F. André, O. Chéron, and J-L. Pazat. Compiling Sequential Programs for Distributed Memory Parallel Computers with Pandore II. In Jack J. Dongarra and Bernard Tourancheau, editors, *Environments and Tools for Parallel Scientific Computing*, pages 293–308, Elsevier Science Publishers B.V., 1993.
2. C. Bareau, B. Caillaud, C. Jard, and R. Thoraval. Correctness of automated distribution of sequential programs. In A. Bode, M. Reeve, and G. Wolf, editors, *PARLE'93*, pages 517–528, LNCS 694, Springer Verlag, June 1993.
3. C. Bareau, B. Caillaud, C. Jard, and R. Thoraval. *Measuring Concurrency of Regular Distributed Computations.* Research Report 882, Irisa, Rennes, France, October 1994.
4. D. Callahan and K. Kennedy. Compiling programs for distributed-memory multiprocessors. *Journal of Supercomputing*, 2:151–169, 1988.
5. B. Charron-Bost. Combinatorics and Geometry of Consistent Cuts : Application to Concurrency Theory. In Bernard and Raynal, editors, *Int. Workshop on Parallel and Distributed Algorithms*, pages 45–56, Springer Verlag, Nice, France, 1989.
6. B.A. Davey and Priestley H.A. *Introduction to Lattices and Order.* Cambridge University Press, 1990.

7. C. Diehl, C. Jard, and J.X. Rampon. Reachability analysis on distributed executions. In JP. Jouannaud MC. Gaudel, editor, *Proc. TAPSOFT,93 LNCS 668*, pages 629–643, Springer–Verlag, Orsay, Paris, April 1993.
8. T. Fahringer, R. Blasko, and H.P. Zima. Automatic Performance Prediction to Support Parallelization of Fortran Programs for Massively Parallel Systems. In *Proc. of the '92 International Conference on Supercomputing*, pages 347–356, ACM press, July 1992.
9. C.J. Fidge. A simple run–time concurrency measure. In *Proceedings of the 3rd Australian Transputer and OCCAM User Group Conference*, pages 92–101, 1990.
10. G.H. Golub and C.F. Van Loan. *Matrix computations.* The Johns Hopkins University Press, second edition, 1990.
11. M. Habib, M. Morvan, and J.X. Rampon. Remarks on some concurrency measures. In *Graph–Theoretic Concepts in Computer Science*, pages 221–238, LNCS 484, june 1990.
12. C. Jard and J.-M. Jézéquel. ECHIDNA, an Estelle-compiler to prototype protocols on distributed computers. *Concurrency Practice and Experience*, 4(5):377–397, 1992.
13. C. Jard, G.V. Jourdan, and J.X. Rampon. *Some On–Lines Computations of the Ideal Lattice of Posets.* Research Report 773, IRISA, December 1993.
14. L. Lamport. Time, clocks and the ordering of events in a distributed system. *Communications of the ACM*, 21(7):558–565, July 1978.
15. F. Mattern. Virtual time and global states of distributed systems. In Cosnard, Quinton, Raynal, and Robert, editors, *Proc. Int. Workshop on Parallel and Distributed Algorithms Bonas, France, Oct. 1988*, North Holland, 1989.
16. M. Raynal, M. Mizuno, and M.-L. Neilsen. A synchronization and concurrency measure for distributed computations. In *12th IEEE Int. Conf. on Distributed Computing Systems*, pages 657–664, Yokokama, June 1992.
17. H. Sips. 4th Int. Workshop on Compilers for Parallel Computers. Sips, H. Editor. Delft, 13-16 december. Delft University of Technology, 1993.

Non-speculative and Upward Invocation of Continuations in a Parallel Language

Luc Moreau*

Institut d'Electricité Montefiore, B28. Université de Liège, Sart-Tilman, 4000 Liège, Belgium. moreau@montefiore.ulg.ac.be

Abstract. A method of preserving the sequential semantics in parallel programs with first-class continuations is to invoke continuations non-speculatively. This method, which prevents a continuation from being invoked as long as its invocation can infringe the sequential semantics, reduces parallelism by the severe conditions that it imposes, especially on upward uses. In this paper, we present new conditions for invoking continuations in an upward way and both preserving the sequential semantics and providing parallelism. This new approach is formalised in the PCKS-machine, which is proved to be correct by showing that it has the same observational equivalence theory as the sequential semantics.

1 Introduction

The continuation of an expression is the computation that remains to be performed after evaluating this expression [16]. Some programming languages like Scheme [14], or SML of New Jersey [1] provide the user with two facilities to act on the interpreter continuation: the capture and the invocation. The capture of a continuation consists in packaging up the current continuation as a first-class object so that it can be passed to or returned by functions like any other object. The invocation of a continuation discards the current continuation and resumes the computation with the invoked continuation.

Parallelism can be added to a language by some annotations that specify which expressions should be evaluated in parallel [7]. These annotations are required to be *transparent*; that is, parallel programs must return the same results as in the absence of annotations.

Parallelism and first-class continuations can prevent the annotations for parallelism from being transparent. Indeed, as continuations explicitly encode the evaluation order, it is possible to write continuation-based programs that depend on this order. Since parallelism changes the evaluation order, combining both parallelism and first-class continuations can result in non-deterministic programs, which is in opposition to the definition of transparent annotations.

Previously [12, 10, 11], we proposed to invoke continuations *non-speculatively* in order to preserve the transparency property. A continuation is invoked non-speculatively if its invocation can be performed only when it is proved not to infringe the sequential semantics. The non-speculative approach essentially consists in waiting for some expressions to be evaluated before actually invoking the continuation; these expressions are the ones that are evaluated before the invocation in the

* This work was supported in part by the Belgian Incentive Program "Information Technology" - Computer Science of the future, initiated by the Belgian State - Prime Minister's Office - Science Policy Office. The scientific responsibility is assumed by its author.

sequential order. This method of invocation preserves the transparency property of annotations, but it imposes such drastic conditions on continuation invocations that it can seriously reduce parallelism in programs.

One usually distinguishes two usages of continuations [8]. If the invoked continuation is a prefix of the current continuation, the invocation is *downward*; otherwise, it is *upward*. A downward invocation simply consists in discarding a suffix of the current continuation, i.e. it corresponds to an escape. In order to provide more parallelism, we devised [12, 10, 11] a mechanism able to reduce the number of expressions for which a value had to be waited before a downward invocation of a continuation. However, this mechanism [12, 10, 11] still imposes so severe conditions on upward uses that it can reduce parallelism.

In this paper, we propose new conditions for invoking continuations in an upward way without losing parallelism, but still preserving the transparency property. The essence of our new approach relies on the observation that many uses of continuations remain local to a part of a program; for instance, when the use of a continuation (creation, invocation, storage) remains limited to a function. In such circumstances, there is no need to coordinate the invocation of the continuation with expressions that are evaluated in parallel in a part of the program that is unreachable by the continuation.

The original contributions of this paper are the following:

- We propose a new version of the PCKS-machine, an abstract machine that evaluates parallel functional programs with first-class continuations. The machine recognises upward uses of continuations and provides parallelism in such cases, while retaining the non-speculative approach for invocation. This abstract machine formalises the semantics of continuations is an annotation-based parallel language and can be regarded as a guideline for an implementation.
- We prove the correctness of the machine: the PCKS-machine returns the same result for a program as a sequential machine would do for the same program without annotations. Put differently, the semantics implemented by the PCKS-machine guarantees the transparency of annotations for parallelism.
  The proof essentially consists in proving that the observational equivalence theories of the PCKS-machine and of the sequential machine are the same. The proofs differs from the one in [10] and is much simpler.

This paper is organised as follows. We present Felleisen and Friedman's CK-machine, an abstract machine that evaluates sequential functional programs with first-class continuations. After giving the intuition of the annotations for parallelism fork and pcall, we present the PCKS-machine, and its non-speculative approach to continuations invocation. The basic approach is then modified to recognise the upward use. In Section 5, we state some properties of the machine and prove its correctness. A comparison with related work and a conclusion end this paper.

2 The CK-Machine

The set of terms accepted by the CK-machine [4, 6] is denoted by Λ_{ck} and is defined as follows, where x is taken from a set of variables $Vars$ and a from a set of constants $Csts$.

$$
\begin{aligned}
M &::= V \mid (M\ M) && \text{(Terms)}\\
V &::= c \mid x \mid (\lambda x.M) \mid \langle p, \kappa \rangle && \text{(Values)}\\
c &::= \mathsf{callcc} \mid a && \text{(Constants)}\\
\kappa &::= \textbf{(init)} \mid (\kappa\ \textbf{fun}\ V) \mid (\kappa\ \textbf{arg}\ M) && \text{(Continuation Code)}
\end{aligned}
$$

Terms can be *values* or *applications* $(M_1\ M_2)$ composed of an operator M_1 and an operand M_2. Values can be *constants*, *variables*, *abstractions* $(\lambda x.M)$, or *continuation points* $\langle p, \kappa\rangle$. A continuation point represents a first-class continuation; p is a tag that identifies all continuation points and κ is a *continuation code*. Constants either belong to a set of constants $Csts$ or are the distinguished constant callcc. A continuation code is an abstract data type that represents the rest of the computation in the CK-machine; its meaning will be described below. We adopt Barendregt's convention and terminology [2]. In an abstraction $(\lambda x.M)$, a variable x in M occurs *bound*; variables that are not bound by an abstraction are *free*. We define a *program* as a term without free variables.

Felleisen and Friedman [4, 6] introduced the CK-machine, an abstract machine that is characterised by two components: a control string C and a continuation K. A *configuration* of the CK-machine is a pair $\langle M, \kappa\rangle$, where the term M of Λ_{ck} is the *control string*, and the *continuation code* κ represents the rest of the computation, i.e. what remains to be performed after evaluating the control string M. An example of program annotated for parallelism can be found in [10].

In order to evaluate a term M with the CK-machine, we begin the computation with the *initial configuration* $\langle M, (\mathbf{init})\rangle$, and we end the computation when a *terminal configuration* is reached; such a terminal configuration is of the form $\langle V, (\mathbf{init})\rangle$. Transitions between configurations follow Definition 1.

Definition 1 (CK-machine)

$$\langle (M\ N), \kappa\rangle \overset{ck}{\mapsto} \langle M, (\kappa\ \mathbf{arg}\ N)\rangle \qquad \text{(operator)}$$

$$\langle V, (\kappa\ \mathbf{arg}\ N)\rangle \overset{ck}{\mapsto} \langle N, (\kappa\ \mathbf{fun}\ V)\rangle \qquad \text{(operand)}$$

$$\langle V, (\kappa\ \mathbf{fun}\ (\lambda x.M))\rangle \overset{ck}{\mapsto} \langle M\{V/x\}, \kappa\rangle \qquad (\beta_v)$$

$$\langle b, (\kappa\ \mathbf{fun}\ a)\rangle \overset{ck}{\mapsto} \langle \delta(a,b), \kappa\rangle \quad \text{if } \delta(a,b) \text{ is defined, and } a, b \in Csts. \qquad (\delta)$$

$$\langle V, (\kappa\ \mathbf{fun}\ \mathsf{callcc})\rangle \overset{ck}{\mapsto} \langle \langle p, \kappa\rangle, (\kappa\ \mathbf{fun}\ V)\rangle \qquad \text{(capture)}$$

$$\langle V, (\kappa\ \mathbf{fun}\ \langle p, \kappa_0\rangle)\rangle \overset{ck}{\mapsto} \langle V, \kappa_0\rangle \qquad \text{(invoke)}$$

□

Rules operator and operand force a left-to-right evaluation order of components of applications, using the continuation codes **fun** and **arg** which explicitly indicate the part of an application that is already evaluated or remains to be evaluated. The four last rules deal with similar configurations, whose continuation code is of the form $(\kappa\ \mathbf{fun}\ V)$, denoting that the value of the operator is V, and whose control string is a value, which is the value of the operand. We say that the value of the operator is ready to be applied on the value of the operand. Rules (β_v) and (δ) perform the β_v and δ-reductions as in Plotkin's λ_v-calculus [13]. When the value of the operator is the constant callcc, rule capture packages up the current continuation κ as a continuation point $\langle p, \kappa\rangle$ and generates a configuration where the value of the operand is ready to be applied on the continuation point. Continuation points are first-class values that can be used like regular abstractions: rule invoke describes the behaviour of the CK-machine when a continuation point is applied on a value, which is usually called *invoking a continuation*. We see that κ, the continuation of the call of $\langle p, \kappa_0\rangle$ on V, is replaced by the invoked continuation κ_0.

We can abstract the evaluation process of the CK-machine by a function.

Definition 2 ($\mathsf{eval}_{\mathsf{ck}}$) Let M and V be a term and a value of Λ_{ck}. The evaluation function $\mathsf{eval}_{\mathsf{ck}}$ is defined for M, written $\mathsf{eval}_{\mathsf{ck}}(M) = V$, if there are some transitions from the initial configuration to a final configuration of the CK-machine: $\langle M, (\textbf{init})\rangle \overset{ck}{\mapsto}^* \langle V, (\textbf{init})\rangle$, where $\overset{ck}{\mapsto}^*$ denotes the reflexive, transitive closure of $\overset{ck}{\mapsto}$. □

3 Parallelism: pcall and fork

We accept two annotations for parallelism: pcall and fork. An expression (pcall M N) means that the terms M and N should be evaluated in parallel; afterwards, the value of M should be applied to the value of N. Hence, the pcall annotation provides a fork-and-join type of parallelism.

The second annotation fork takes one argument and must appear in a sequence. A sequence is a construct of the form (`begin` M N), which is an abbreviation for $((\lambda d.N)\ M)$ with d not free in N ($d \notin FV(N)$). The expression (`begin` (fork M) N) means that the terms M and N should be evaluated in parallel, and the value of the sequence is the value of N.

Both pcall and fork must be transparent: the expressions (pcall M N) and (`begin` (fork M) N) must be indistinguishable from (M N) and (`begin` M N), respectively. Furthermore, we define the expression (`begin` (fork M) N) as (pcall (`begin` M $(\lambda u.u)$) N). In the sequel, we shall only consider the annotation pcall.

4 The PCKS-Machine

The PCKS-machine [10, 11] is an abstract machine that evaluates parallel functional programs with first-class continuations. This machine consists of a set of processes running in parallel (P), where each process is a represented by a CK configuration, and of a store (S) which specifies the coordination between the different processes.

The set of terms accepted by the PCKS-machine is called Λ_{pcks} and is defined by extending the grammar of Λ_{ck} as follows, with α ranging over a set of locations *Loc*.

$$\begin{aligned} M &::= \ldots \mid (\mathsf{pcall}\ M\ M) \\ \kappa &::= \ldots \mid (\kappa\ \textbf{left}(\alpha_m, \alpha_n, M)) \mid (\kappa\ \textbf{right}(\alpha_m, \alpha_n)) \mid (\textbf{stop}) \end{aligned}$$

The set Λ_{pcks} extends the set Λ_{ck} with a *parallel application* (pcall M_1 M_2) composed of an operator M_1 and an operand M_2. The behaviour of the three new continuation codes is explained below in the set of transitions of the PCKS-machine.

A *configuration* of the PCKS-machine consists of a set of *processes* and a *store*. We distinguish two kinds of processes.

1. An *active process* is represented by a named CK-configuration $\langle M, \kappa\rangle_n$, where M is a control string, i.e. a term of Λ_{pcks}, κ a continuation code, and n a *process name* taken from a set of process identifiers *Pid*.
2. A *dead process* is represented by a special CK-configuration $\langle \ddagger, (\textbf{stop})\rangle_n$, where the control string is the distinguished symbol $\ddagger$ and n is a process name of the set *Pid*.

A store binds *locations* to their *contents*. Locations model addresses in a real computer and are taken from a set *Loc*. Their content can be empty, can contain a value, or can contain a special data structure, whose role will be explained in the sequel. We shall use the letter p to range over processes, P over sets of processes, n over names of processes ($n \in Pid$), and α over locations ($\alpha \in Loc$).

A configuration $\mathcal{M}$ of PCKS-machine consists of a set of processes P and a store σ, and is written $\langle P, \sigma \rangle$. In order to evaluate a term M with the PCKS-machine, we begin the computation with an *initial configuration*, which is composed of a single process $\langle M, (\mathbf{init}) \rangle_{n_0}$ and an empty store. We end the computation when a *final configuration* is reached, i.e. when a process is of the form $\langle V, (\mathbf{init}) \rangle_n$. We can observe that an initial or a final configuration of the PCKS-machine contains a process that is an initial or a final configuration of the CK-machine, respectively.

In order to specify the legal transitions between configurations of the PCKS-machine, we first define a relation, called the *CKS-transition*, which can be applied to a process (represented by a CK-configuration) and a store (S).

Definition 3 (CKS-transition) A CKS-transition is a relation $\langle p, \sigma_1 \rangle \overset{cks}{\mapsto} \langle P, \sigma_2 \rangle$, which associates a process p and a store σ_1 with a set of processes P and a store σ_2. A CKS-transition is assumed to be performed *atomically*. □

Unlike a CK-transition, the applicability of a CKS-transition can depend on the content of the store, and a CKS-transition can update the store (hence the returned store σ_2). Furthermore, a CKS-transition produces a *set* of processes, instead of a single process, because new processes can be created (by the pcall-construct).

In Definition 4, parallelism in the PCKS-machine is modelled by an interleaving semantics. Then, the evaluation relation of the machine is formalised.

Definition 4 (PCKS-transition) There is a transition between a PCKS configuration $\mathcal{M}_1 \equiv \langle P_1, \sigma_1 \rangle$ and a PCKS-configuration $\mathcal{M}_2 \equiv \langle P_2, \sigma_2 \rangle$, written $\mathcal{M}_1 \overset{PCKS}{\mapsto} \mathcal{M}_2$ if there exists a process p and a set of process P such that $\langle p, \sigma_1 \rangle \overset{cks}{\mapsto} \langle P, \sigma_2 \rangle$ with $p \in P_1$ and $P_2 \equiv P_1 \setminus \{p\} \cup P$. Furthermore, transitions performed by processes are supposed to be *atomic*. □

Definition 5 ($\mathsf{eval}_{\mathsf{pcks}}$) Let M and V be a program and a value of Λ_{pcks}. The evaluation function is defined for M, written $\mathsf{eval}_{\mathsf{pcks}}(M) = V$, if there exists a final configuration $\mathcal{M}_f$ that contains a process $\langle V, (\mathbf{init}) \rangle_n$, and such that, for the initial configuration $\mathcal{M}_i \equiv \langle \{ \langle M, (\mathbf{init}) \rangle_{n_0} \}, \emptyset \rangle$, we have $\mathcal{M}_i \overset{PCKS^*}{\mapsto} \mathcal{M}_f$, where $\overset{PCKS^*}{\mapsto}$ denotes the reflexive, transitive closure of $\overset{PCKS}{\mapsto}$. □

It remains to define the CKS-transitions. The first four transitions of the CK-machine (Definition 1) remains valid in the PCKS-machine. Now, let us see how a process that is evaluating a parallel application is transformed. As indicated by rule pcall in Definition 6, a new process, with a name n_i, is created to evaluate the operand N, while the process that was evaluating the parallel application has to evaluate the operator M. The continuation κ of the process evaluating the parallel application is extended with a new continuation code for each process: **left** for the process evaluating the operator and **right** for the one evaluating the operand. Furthermore, two locations α_m and α_n are allocated; these locations are intended to receive the values of the operator and of the operand, respectively. Since they explicitly appear in the continuation codes **left** and **right**, they can be accessed by the processes evaluating the operator and the operand.

Definition 6

$$\langle(\mathsf{pcall}\ M\ N),\kappa\rangle_n \overset{cks}{\longmapsto} \langle M,(\kappa\ \mathbf{left}(\alpha_m,\alpha_n,N))\rangle_n, \langle N,(\kappa\ \mathbf{right}(\alpha_m,\alpha_n))\rangle_{n_i} \quad (\mathsf{pcall})$$
$$\text{with a fresh } \alpha_m \in Loc, \text{ a fresh } \alpha_n \in Loc, \text{ a new } n_i \in Pid$$

$$\langle V,(\kappa\ \mathbf{right}(\alpha_m,\alpha_n))\rangle_n \overset{cks}{\longmapsto} \langle \ddagger,(\mathbf{stop})\rangle_n;\sigma(\alpha_n)\leftarrow V \quad \text{if } \sigma(\alpha_m)=\perp \quad (\mathsf{stop}_r)$$

$$\langle V,(\kappa\ \mathbf{right}(\alpha_m,\alpha_n))\rangle_n \overset{cks}{\longmapsto} \langle V,(\kappa\ \mathbf{fun}\ \sigma(\alpha_m))\rangle_n;\sigma(\alpha_n)\leftarrow V \quad \text{if } \sigma(\alpha_m)\neq\perp \quad (\mathsf{ret}_r)$$

$$\langle V,(\kappa\ \mathbf{left}(\alpha_m,\alpha_n,N))\rangle_n \overset{cks}{\longmapsto} \langle \ddagger,(\mathbf{stop})\rangle_n;\sigma(\alpha_m)\leftarrow V \quad \text{if } \sigma(\alpha_m)=\perp \wedge \sigma(\alpha_n)=\perp \quad (\mathsf{stop}_l)$$

$$\langle V,(\kappa\ \mathbf{left}(\alpha_m,\alpha_n,N))\rangle_n \overset{cks}{\longmapsto} \langle \sigma(\alpha_n),(\kappa\ \mathbf{fun}\ V)\rangle_n;\sigma(\alpha_m)\leftarrow V \quad (\mathsf{ret\text{-}1}_l)$$
$$\text{if } \sigma(\alpha_m)=\perp \wedge \mathit{value?}(\sigma(\alpha_n))$$

$$\langle V,(\kappa\ \mathbf{left}(\alpha_m,\alpha_n,N))\rangle_n \overset{cks}{\longmapsto} \langle N,(\kappa\ \mathbf{fun}\ V)\rangle_n \quad \text{if } \sigma(\alpha_m)\neq\perp \quad (\mathsf{ret\text{-}n}_l)$$

□

A process knows that it has evaluated the operand of a parallel application, because its control string is a value and its continuation is a code **right**. It can access the content of the location α_m that appears in its continuation. If location α_m is empty (rule stop_r), it means that the operator is not evaluated yet, and the application cannot be performed: so, the process evaluating the operand must be stopped, which is represented by the dead process $\langle \ddagger, (\mathbf{stop})\rangle_n$. On the contrary, if the location α_m contains a value, this value is the value of the operator, and it can be applied to the value of the operand as indicated by ret_r. In both cases, the location α_n is updated with the value of the operand.

Symmetrically, a process knows that it has evaluated the operator of a parallel application, because its control string is a value and its continuation is a code **left**. It must be stopped if location α_n is empty. If location α_n contains a value, two cases must be distinguished.

1. The operator is evaluated for the first time, which can be observed by the fact that location α_m is empty (cfr. rule $\mathsf{ret\text{-}1}_l$). Then, the value of the operator can be applied on the value of the operand, after updating the location α_m with the value of the operator.
2. The operator has already been evaluated, which can be observed by the fact that location α_m is not empty (cfr. rule $\mathsf{ret\text{-}n}_l$). In order to preserve the sequential semantics, the operand must be re-evaluated. Such a case corresponds to rule operand which forces the operand of a sequential application to be re-evaluated. The operand N of the parallel application can be retrieved from the code **left** of the continuation where it explicitly appears.

So, locations α_m and α_n are used to coordinate the processes evaluating the operator and the operand. The location α_m is aimed at receiving the first value of the operator, while the location α_n is intended to receive the value of the operand. Definition 7 displays the CKS-transitions related to continuations.

Definition 7

$$\langle V,(\kappa\ \mathbf{fun}\ \mathsf{callcc})\rangle_n \overset{cks}{\longmapsto} \langle\langle p,\kappa\rangle,(\kappa\ \mathbf{fun}\ V)\rangle_n \quad (\mathsf{capture})$$

$$\langle V,((\mathbf{init})\ \mathbf{fun}\ \langle p,\kappa\rangle)\rangle_n \overset{cks}{\longmapsto} \langle V,\kappa\rangle_n \quad (\mathsf{invoke}_{init})$$

$$\langle V,((\kappa_1\ \mathbf{fun}\ V')\ \mathbf{fun}\ \langle p,\kappa\rangle)\rangle_n \overset{cks}{\longmapsto} \langle V,(\kappa_1\ \mathbf{fun}\ \langle p,\kappa\rangle)\rangle_n \quad (\mathsf{prune}_f)$$

$$\langle V,((\kappa_1\ \mathbf{arg}\ N)\ \mathbf{fun}\ \langle p,\kappa\rangle)\rangle_n \overset{cks}{\longmapsto} \langle V,(\kappa_1\ \mathbf{fun}\ \langle p,\kappa\rangle)\rangle_n \quad (\mathsf{prune}_a)$$

$$\langle V, ((\kappa_1\ \mathbf{left}(\alpha_m, \alpha_n, N))\ \mathbf{fun}\ \langle p, \kappa\rangle)\rangle_n \overset{cks}{\mapsto} \langle V, (\kappa_1\ \mathbf{fun}\ \langle p, \kappa\rangle)\rangle_n \qquad (\mathsf{prune}_l)$$

$$\langle V, ((\kappa_1\ \mathbf{right}(\alpha_m, \alpha_n))\ \mathbf{fun}\ \langle p, \kappa\rangle)\rangle_n \overset{cks}{\mapsto} \langle V, (\kappa_1\ \mathbf{fun}\ \langle p, \kappa\rangle)\rangle_n \quad \text{if } \sigma(\alpha_m) \neq \perp \qquad (\mathsf{prune}_r)$$

$$\langle V, ((\kappa_1\ \mathbf{right}(\alpha_m, \alpha_n))\ \mathbf{fun}\ \langle p, \kappa\rangle)\rangle_n \overset{cks}{\mapsto} \langle \ddagger, (\mathbf{stop})\rangle_n; \sigma(\alpha_n) \leftarrow \mathbf{suspend}(\langle p, \kappa\rangle, V) \quad \text{if } \sigma(\alpha_m) = \perp \qquad (\mathsf{suspend}_r)$$

$$\langle V, (\kappa\ \mathbf{left}(\alpha_m, \alpha_n, N))\rangle_n \overset{cks}{\mapsto} \langle V', (\kappa\ \mathbf{fun}\ \langle p, \kappa_0\rangle)\rangle_n; \sigma(\alpha_m) \leftarrow V \quad \text{if } \sigma(\alpha_m) = \perp \wedge \text{ if } \sigma(\alpha_n) = \mathbf{suspend}(\langle p, \kappa_0\rangle, V') \qquad (\mathsf{resume}_r)$$

□

Rule capture of the CK-machine is still valid in the PCKS-machine, but rule invoke becomes unsound. Indeed, rule invoke, as designed in the CK-machine, can replace the current continuation by an invoked continuation in a *single* transition; used in the PCKS-machine, invoke would be able to replace a current continuation with a code **right** by the invoked continuation even though the operator corresponding to the code **right** has not returned a value. Since the PCKS-machine must compute the same results as the CK-machine, we replace rule invoke by three rules invoke_{init}, prune_f, and prune_a. A single transition invoke of the CK-machine will be simulated by a sequence of prune_f and prune_a followed by invoke_{init} in the PCKS-machine[2]. A rule like prune_f (and similarly for prune_a) is said to prune the continuation of a process; indeed, the process continuation before transition $((\kappa_1\ \mathbf{fun}\ V')\ \mathbf{fun}\ \langle p, \kappa\rangle)$ is shortened to $(\kappa_1\ \mathbf{fun}\ \langle p, \kappa\rangle)$. A succession of prune_f and prune_a forms the *abortive phase* where the continuation code of the process is pruned until invoke_{init} can be used. We can observe that invoke_{init} is an instance of invoke with κ replaced by **(init)**.

The mode of invocation of continuations in the PCKS-machine is said to be *non-speculative* because a continuation is invoked only if its invocation does not infringe the sequential semantics. Let us examine how such a mode of invocation behaves in the presence of **left** and **right**. According to rule prune_l, a continuation code **left** can always be pruned. Indeed, a process $\langle V, ((\kappa_1\ \mathbf{left}(\alpha_m, \alpha_n, N))\ \mathbf{fun}\ \langle p, \kappa\rangle)\rangle_n$ evaluates the operator of a parallel application; since the operator is evaluated before the operand in a CK-machine, a continuation can always be invoked in the operator.

Symmetrically, if the operator of a parallel application is already evaluated and the operand invokes a continuation, the code **right** can be pruned as specified by rule prune_r, because the execution of the PCKS-machine follows the CK-execution. On the contrary, if the operator of a parallel application is not yet evaluated when the operand invokes a continuation, the code **right** cannot be pruned if the sequential semantics must be preserved; in such a case, rule $\mathsf{suspend}_r$ *suspends* the invocation of the continuation, by storing in α_n a data-structure containing the continuation and the value, and by stopping the process. The invocation of the continuation can be resumed as soon as the process that was evaluating the operator yields its value, as specified by rule resume_r.

The rules of Definitions 1 (four first rules), 6, 7 specify a machine that evaluates parallel programs with first-class continuations, while preserving the sequential semantics. Unfortunately, in order to preserve the sequential semantics, rule $\mathsf{suspend}_r$ imposes so drastic conditions on the invocation of continuations that it can seriously reduce parallelism in a parallel program with first-class continuations.

---

[2] By a simple reorganisation of the continuation of a process in two components, several continuation codes **arg** and **fun** can be pruned in a single step as in the CK-machine [11].

In the CK-machine, invoking a continuation replaces the current continuation by the invoked continuation. In many usages of continuations, the invoked continuation and the current continuation have a common prefix (in the worst case, the common prefix is simply the initial continuation **init**). Hence, invoking a continuation is equivalent to replacing a suffix of the current continuation by a suffix of the invoked continuation. We can say that the invocation of a continuation has a *local* effect on the computation because it only changes a suffix of the current continuation and leaves the prefix unchanged.

In the PCKS-machine, instead of suspending the invocation of a continuation in the operand of a parallel application when the operator has not yielded a value, we can immediately reinstate the invoked continuation if the current continuation is a prefix of it. (This corresponds to a local use of the continuation.) Let us define the relation "is prefix of" on continuations.

Definition 8 (Extension and Prefix) A continuation κ_1 is a *"one-step" extension* of a continuation κ_2, written $\kappa_1 \sqsupset \kappa_2$, if one of the following equality[3] holds.

$$\kappa_1 \equiv (\kappa_2 \ \mathbf{fun}\ V) \qquad \kappa_1 \equiv (\kappa_2 \ \mathbf{arg}\ N)$$
$$\kappa_1 \equiv (\kappa_2 \ \mathbf{left}\ (\alpha_m, \alpha_n, N)) \quad \kappa_1 \equiv (\kappa_2 \ \mathbf{right}\ (\alpha_m, \alpha_n))$$

The relation *extension* is the reflexive, transitive closure of *"one-step" extension* and is written $\kappa_1 \sqsupseteq \kappa_2$. We also say that k_2 is a *prefix* of k_1 if $\kappa_1 \sqsupseteq \kappa_2$. □

Rule $\mathsf{suspend}_r$ of Definition 7 should be replaced by the rules of Definition 9. Now, if the invoked continuation is not an extension of the current continuation, it must be suspended by rule $\mathsf{suspend}_r$. Otherwise, rule invoke_{up} reinstates the invoked continuation, while preserving the sequential semantics.

Definition 9

$$\langle V, ((\kappa_1 \ \mathbf{right}(\alpha_m, \alpha_n)) \ \mathbf{fun}\ \langle p, \kappa \rangle)\rangle_n \overset{cks}{\mapsto} \langle \ddagger, (\mathbf{stop})\rangle_n ; \sigma(\alpha_n) \leftarrow \mathbf{suspend}(\langle p, \kappa \rangle, V) \quad (\mathsf{suspend}_r)$$
$$\text{if } \sigma(\alpha_m) = \bot \land \kappa \not\sqsupseteq (\kappa_1 \ \mathbf{right}(\alpha_m, \alpha_n))$$
$$\langle V, ((\kappa_1 \ \mathbf{right}(\alpha_m, \alpha_n)) \ \mathbf{fun}\ \langle p, \kappa \rangle)\rangle_n \overset{cks}{\mapsto} \langle V, \kappa \rangle_n \quad (\mathsf{invoke}_{up})$$
$$\text{if } \sigma(\alpha_m) = \bot \land \kappa \sqsupseteq (\kappa_1 \ \mathbf{right}(\alpha_m, \alpha_n))$$

□

Thanks to the rules of Definition 9, the PCKS-machine not only evaluates parallel programs using first-class continuations, but also preserves parallelism in the program, by avoiding to suspend local upward invocations. Invocations can be suspended only in the presence of race conditions that might not preserve the sequential result.

5 Properties

Our goal is to prove the soundness of the PCKS-machine with respect to the sequential semantics, which is implemented by the CK-machine. First, we define a translation that removes the annotations for parallelism in a parallel program, i.e. which returns the sequential version of a program.

[3] The relation $\sqsupseteq$ uses the syntactic equality on terms and continuation codes. In practice, the reorganisation of the continuation in two components, as suggested in footnote 2, can be used for improving the efficiency of $\sqsupseteq$.

Definition 10 (Sequential Version of a Term) The sequential version of a term M of Λ_{pcks} is a term $\mathcal{S}[\![M]\!]$ of Λ_{ck}, defined as follows[4].

$$\begin{aligned}
\mathcal{S}[\![(M\ N)]\!] &= (\mathcal{S}[\![M]\!]\ \mathcal{S}[\![N]\!]) & \mathcal{S}[\![(\mathbf{init})]\!]^c &= (\mathbf{init})\\
\mathcal{S}[\![(\mathsf{pcall}\ M\ N)]\!] &= (\mathcal{S}[\![M]\!]\ \mathcal{S}[\![N]\!]) & \mathcal{S}[\![(\kappa\ \mathbf{fun}\ V)]\!]^c &= (\mathcal{S}[\![\kappa]\!]^c\ \mathbf{fun}\ \mathcal{S}[\![V]\!])\\
\mathcal{S}[\![\lambda x.M]\!] &= \lambda x.\mathcal{S}[\![M]\!] & \mathcal{S}[\![(\kappa\ \mathbf{arg}\ N)]\!]^c &= (\mathcal{S}[\![\kappa]\!]^c\ \mathbf{arg}\ \mathcal{S}[\![N]\!])\\
\mathcal{S}[\![\langle p, \kappa\rangle]\!] &= \langle p, \mathcal{S}[\![\kappa]\!]^c\rangle\\
\mathcal{S}[\![x]\!] &= x, \text{ for } x \in Csts \text{ or } \in Vars
\end{aligned}$$

□

The major result of this section is the following theorem, which states that the observational equivalence theories of the CK-machine and PCKS-machine are the same.

Theorem 11 *Let M be a term of Λ_{pcks} and $\mathcal{S}[\![M]\!]$ its sequential version.*

$$\mathsf{eval}_{\mathsf{ck}}(\mathcal{S}[\![M]\!]) = V \ \textit{ iff } \ \mathsf{eval}_{\mathsf{pcks}}(M) = V'.$$

□

In the sequel, we present the intuition of the proof. The transition pcall creates a new active process to evaluate the operand of a parallel application. Such an operand is evaluated *in advance of* the sequential order. The evaluation of the operand remains in advance of the sequential order as long as the operator is being evaluated. In order to identify the computations that are in advance of the sequential order, we simply have to detect all the pcall transitions that were executed for which the location α_m is empty, i.e. the operator is not evaluated yet. On the other hand, there is a single computation that is *not* in advance of the sequential order: it is the process that follows the left-to-right evaluation order. Let us call this process the *mandatory* process and all other processes *speculative*.

In order to uniformly characterise the different kinds of computations (speculative or mandatory), we introduce the concept of *target*. Each computation evaluating an expression is characterised by the continuation of this expression and the location where to store the value of this expression. Intuitively, a *target* is a pair (location, continuation) for a computation. First, let us slightly change the definition of a final configuration of the PCKS-machine. We assume that the special location 0 is allocated to receive the final value of the whole computation. We add an extra rule to the PCKS-machine, called init, which stores the final result into location 0. A PCKS-configuration will be said to be final if it contains a value in location 0.

$$\langle V, (\mathbf{init})\rangle_n \rightarrow \langle \ddagger, (\mathbf{stop})\rangle_n; \sigma(0) \leftarrow V \qquad (\mathsf{init})$$

Now, we can define the notion of target.

Definition 12 (Target) Let $\mathcal{M} \equiv \langle P, \sigma\rangle$ be a configuration of the PCKS-Machine. A target is a pair $\langle \alpha, \kappa\rangle$ containing a location α and a continuation κ, characterising a computation evaluating an expression with a continuation κ, and whose value is intended to be stored in α. The set of targets of a configuration $\mathcal{M}$ is defined as follows.

- The pair $\langle 0, (\mathbf{init})\rangle$ is a target of $\mathcal{M}$.
- If there are two locations α_m and α_n that were allocated by a transition pcall, such that the location α_m is empty, $\sigma(\alpha_m) = \bot$, then the pair $\langle \alpha_n, (\kappa\ \mathbf{right}(\alpha_m, \alpha_n))\rangle$ is a target of $\mathcal{M}$.

□

[4] The translation is not defined for continuation codes **left** and **right** because it is meaningless to consider such codes independently of a store of the PCKS-machine.

The target $\langle 0, (\mathbf{init})\rangle$ is said to be *mandatory*, while the others are *speculative*. A target $\langle \alpha, \kappa\rangle$ is *active* if $\sigma(\alpha) = \perp$. Each active process can be uniquely associated with an active target. For this purpose, we define a new relation, called *sequential extension*, which is a subset of the relation *extension*.

Definition 13 (Sequential Extension) Let σ be the store of a given PCKS-configuration. A continuation κ_1 is a *"one-step" sequential extension* of a continuation κ_2 (with respect to σ), written $\kappa_1 \sqsupset^s_\sigma \kappa_2$, if one of the following equation holds.

$$\begin{array}{lll} \kappa_1 \equiv (\kappa_2\ \mathbf{fun}\ V) & \kappa_1 \equiv (\kappa_2\ \mathbf{arg}\ N) & \\ \kappa_1 \equiv (\kappa_2\ \mathbf{left}\ (\alpha_m, \alpha_n, N)) & \kappa_1 \equiv (\kappa_2\ \mathbf{right}\ (\alpha_m, \alpha_n)) & \text{if } \sigma(\alpha_m) \neq \perp \end{array}$$

The relation *sequential extension* is the reflexive, transitive closure of *"one-step" sequential extension* and is written $\kappa_1 \sqsupseteq^s_\sigma \kappa_2$. □

The active target associated with an active process can be obtained by the following Definition, and it is easy to prove that there is a unique active process that is associated with each active target.

Definition 14 Let $\mathcal{M} \equiv \langle P, \sigma\rangle$ be a configuration of the PCKS-machine. Let $g \equiv \langle \alpha, \kappa\rangle$ be a target of $\mathcal{M}$. The active process $\langle M, \kappa'\rangle_n$ of P is *associated* with target g if $\kappa' \sqsupseteq^s_\sigma \kappa$. We also say that the target of a continuation κ' is $g \equiv \langle \alpha, \kappa\rangle$ if $\kappa' \sqsupseteq^s_\sigma \kappa$. □

In order to prove the soundness of the PCKS-machine, we proceed in two steps. First, we define a translation of a PCKS-machine configuration into a term of Sabry and Felleisen's λ_v-C-calculus [15]. Second, we prove that for any transition of the PCKS-machine between two configurations $\mathcal{M}_1$ and $\mathcal{M}_2$, the translations of $\mathcal{M}_1$ and $\mathcal{M}_2$ are provably equal in the λ_v-C-calculus.

First, we define the translation of a configuration of the PCKS-machine. A configuration will be translated into a *set* of terms, one term for each target of the machine. The translation of a configuration uses a process translation function $\mathcal{P}^\rho_\sigma[\![\ ]\!]$, a term translation function $\mathcal{T}^\rho_\sigma[\![\ ]\!]$, and a continuation translation function $\mathcal{C}^\rho_\sigma[\![\ ,]\!]$, specified in Definitions 16, 17. By convention, we shall use the letter x to range over user variables, k to range over variables associated with targets, and v to range over variables for continuations. The sets of these variables are supposed to be disjoined.

Definition 15 (Machine Translation) Let $\mathcal{M} \equiv \langle P, \sigma\rangle$ be a PCKS-configuration. Let $\{g_1, \ldots, g_n\}$ be the targets of the machine, and let be $\{k_1, \ldots, k_n\}$ be fresh variables. Let ρ be an environment mapping each target g_i to variable k_i. The translation of the machine $\mathcal{M}$ is a set of terms, obtained as follows for each target g_i.

1. If target g_i is active, then let $\langle M, \kappa\rangle$ be its associated active process. The translation of $\mathcal{M}$ contains the term $\mathsf{callcc}\lambda k_i.\mathcal{P}^\rho_\sigma[\![\langle M, \kappa\rangle]\!]$.
2. If target g_i is not active, then let M be the content of its non empty location α_i. The translation of $\mathcal{M}$ contains the term $\mathsf{callcc}\lambda k_i.\mathcal{T}^\rho_\sigma[\![M]\!]$.

□

Let us define the function that translates a process. It uses the term and the continuation translation functions, which are mutually recursive.

Definition 16 (Process Translation) Let $\mathcal{M} \equiv \langle P, \sigma\rangle$ be a configuration of the PCKS machine, with ρ a function mapping each target g_i of $\mathcal{M}$ to a fresh variable k_i. The translation of a process $\langle M, \kappa\rangle_n$, written $\mathcal{P}^\rho_\sigma[\![\langle M, \kappa\rangle_n]\!]$, is defined as $\mathcal{C}^\rho_\sigma[\![\kappa, \mathcal{T}^\rho_\sigma[\![M]\!]]\!]$, where $\mathcal{T}^\rho_\sigma[\![M]\!]$ and $\mathcal{C}^\rho_\sigma[\![\kappa,\ ]\!]$ are the translations of M and κ. □

Definition 17 (Term and Continuation Translation) Let $\mathcal{M} \equiv \langle P, \sigma \rangle$ be a configuration of the PCKS machine, with ρ a function mapping each target g_i of $\mathcal{M}$ to a fresh variable k_i. The translation of a term M, written $\mathcal{T}_\sigma^\rho[\![M]\!]$, is defined as follows.

$$\mathcal{T}_\sigma^\rho[\![(\text{pcall } M\ N)]\!] = (\mathcal{T}_\sigma^\rho[\![M]\!]\ \mathcal{T}_\sigma^\rho[\![N]\!]) \qquad \mathcal{T}_\sigma^\rho[\![\lambda x.M]\!] = \lambda x.\mathcal{T}_\sigma^\rho[\![M]\!]$$
$$\mathcal{T}_\sigma^\rho[\![(M\ N)]\!] = (\mathcal{T}_\sigma^\rho[\![M]\!]\ \mathcal{T}_\sigma^\rho[\![N]\!]) \qquad \mathcal{T}_\sigma^\rho[\![x]\!] = x \text{ if } x \in Csts \text{ or } \in Vars$$
$$\mathcal{T}_\sigma^\rho[\![\mathbf{suspend}(\langle p, \kappa \rangle, V)]\!] = (\mathcal{T}_\sigma^\rho[\![\langle p, \kappa \rangle]\!]\ \mathcal{T}_\sigma^\rho[\![V]\!])$$
$$\mathcal{T}_\sigma^\rho[\![\langle p, \kappa \rangle]\!] = \lambda v.\mathcal{A}\ (k_i\ \mathcal{C}_\sigma^\rho[\![\kappa, v]\!]) \text{ with } k_i = \rho(g_i) \text{ if } g_i \equiv \langle \alpha_i, \kappa_i \rangle, \kappa \sqsupseteq_\sigma^s \kappa_i$$

The translation of a continuation κ for a term M, written $\mathcal{C}_\sigma^\rho[\![\kappa, M]\!]$, is defined as:

$$\mathcal{C}_\sigma^\rho[\![(\mathbf{init}), M]\!] = M$$
$$\mathcal{C}_\sigma^\rho[\![(\kappa\ \mathbf{arg}\ N), M]\!] = \mathcal{C}_\sigma^\rho[\![\kappa, (M\ \mathcal{T}_\sigma^\rho[\![N]\!])]\!]$$
$$\mathcal{C}_\sigma^\rho[\![(\kappa\ \mathbf{fun}\ V), M]\!] = \mathcal{C}_\sigma^\rho[\![\kappa, (\mathcal{T}_\sigma^\rho[\![V]\!]\ M)]\!]$$
$$\mathcal{C}_\sigma^\rho[\![(\kappa\ \mathbf{left}(\alpha_m, \alpha_n, N)), M]\!] = \mathcal{C}_\sigma^\rho[\![\kappa, (M\ \mathcal{T}_\sigma^\rho[\![N]\!])]\!]$$
$$\mathcal{C}_\sigma^\rho[\![(\kappa\ \mathbf{right}(\alpha_m, \alpha_n)), M]\!] = \mathcal{C}_\sigma^\rho[\![\kappa, (\mathcal{T}_\sigma^\rho[\![\sigma(\alpha_m)]\!]\ M)]\!] \quad \text{if } \sigma(\alpha_m) \neq \bot$$
$$\mathcal{C}_\sigma^\rho[\![(\kappa\ \mathbf{right}(\alpha_m, \alpha_n)), M]\!] = M \quad \text{if } \sigma(\alpha_m) = \bot$$

□

Lemma 18 states that for any transition between two configurations of the PCKS-machine, terms that result from the translation of the configurations and that correspond to a same target are provably equal in the λ_v-C-calculus.

Lemma 18 Let $\mathcal{M}_t \equiv \langle P_t, \sigma_t \rangle$ be a PCKS-configuration obtained after t transitions. Let $\{g_1, \ldots, g_{n_t}\}$ be the targets of the machine. Let e_{i_t} be the term that appears in the translation of $\mathcal{M}$ for target g_{i_t}. For any configuration $\mathcal{M}_s \equiv \langle P_s, \sigma_s \rangle$ obtained after s transitions, with $s \leq t$. Let e_{i_s} be the term associated with target g_{i_s} in the translation of $\mathcal{M}_s$, such that $g_{i_s} \equiv g_{i_t}$.

The terms e_{i_s} and e_{i_t} satisfy λ_v-$C \vdash e_{i_s}\{c_u/k_u\}^* = e_{i_t}$ for any k_u such that $\exists \rho_u,\ \rho_s(g_u) = k_u, \rho_t(g_u) = \bot$, and $c_u = \mathcal{T}_{\sigma_t}^{\rho_t}[\![\langle p, \kappa_u \rangle]\!]$. □

Proofs of Theorem 11 and Lemma 18 can be found in Section 9.

6 Related Work

This paper extends previous results [12, 10, 11] by devising a new criterion for invoking continuations, which preserves the sequential semantics and provides parallelism for upward uses.

Another annotation for parallelism is `future` [7]; its semantics in a purely function language was stated by Flanagan and Felleisen [5]. They use this semantics to statically analyse programs in order to perform a "touch optimisation", i.e. to remove the touch operator when it can be predicted at compile-time that its argument is never a placeholder. We could apply similar optimisations to improve programs efficiency by predicting that an application site always invokes a "local" continuation, i.e. a continuation that satisfies the side-condition of invoke_{up}.

Research on the interaction of `future` and continuations were mainly concerned with the implementation. Halstead [7, page 19] gives three criteria for the semantics of parallel constructs and continuations in a parallel Scheme. We list them here:

1. Programs using `call/cc` without constructs for parallelism should return the same results in a parallel implementation as in a sequential one.

2. Programs that use continuations exclusively in the single-use style should yield the same results as in sequential Scheme, even if a parallel construct is wrapped around arbitrary expressions.
3. Programs should yield the same results as in sequential Scheme, even if a parallel construct is wrapped around arbitrary subexpressions, with no restrictions on how continuations are used.

Our semantics satisfy these conditions. The first criterion is proved by the following proposition: let M be a program of Λ_{ck}, $\mathsf{eval}_{\mathsf{pcks}}(M) = \mathsf{eval}_{\mathsf{ck}}(M)$. The second and third criterion are satisfied by Theorem 11. Rule **ret-1**$_l$ deals with the single-use style, while $\mathsf{ret\text{-}n}_l$ with the multiple-use.

Katz and Weise [9] proposed a implementation technique to provide a transparent `future` annotation for a language with first-class continuation; this technique was successfully implemented by Feeley [3]. In Katz and Weise's approach, continuations are invoked speculatively; that is, they are invoked as soon as possible, without verifying whether their invocation preserves the sequential semantics. In addition, in order to preserve the transparency of the annotation `future`, processes are threaded by a *legitimacy* link. A process is *legitimate* if the code it is executing would have been executed by a sequential implementation in the absence of parallelism. A result is legitimate if it is returned by a legitimate process.

In an implementation where continuations are invoked speculatively, one can expect more speed up, at least theoretically, but more unnecessary computations might be performed than in an implementation with non-speculative invocations. Hence, the non-speculative approach allows the user to have a better control on speculative computations. Furthermore, in the non-speculative approach, a first-class continuation encodes the partial order that must be respected to preserve the sequential semantics. So, first-class continuations can be seen as control operators for synchronising computations; a program illustrating this property can be found in [10].

7 Conclusion

In this paper, we have presented the PCKS-machine, an abstract machine that is able to evaluate parallel functional programs with first-class continuations. This machine is sound with respect to the sequential semantics. In the PCKS-machine, continuations are invoked non-speculatively, i.e. their invocations are allowed only if they do not infringe the sequential semantics. Although this mode of invocation intuitively seems to reduce parallelism by very stringent conditions, the PCKS-machine proves that parallelism can be preserved in programs with first-class continuations. The PCKS-Machine can be considered as a guideline for implementation of continuations in an annotation-based parallel language.

8 Acknowledgement

I am grateful to Daniel Ribbens and the anonymous referees for their helpful comments.

9 Appendix: Proofs

Proof Lemma 18. We proceed by induction on the number of transitions t and by case on the last transition. First, we consider the transitions that do not change the sets of targets and for which the translations of $\mathcal{M}_s$ and $\mathcal{M}_t$ are the same (init, $\mathsf{ret\text{-}n}_l$, stop_r, $\mathsf{ret\text{-}n}_l$, ret_r, operator, operand, $\mathsf{suspend}_r$).

(ret-n$_l$) $\rho_s = \rho_t$ and $\sigma_s = \sigma_t$. Let g_i be the target of $\langle V, (\kappa\ \mathbf{left}\ (\alpha_m, \alpha_n, N))\rangle$ with $\rho_s(g_i) = \rho_t(g_i) = k_i$. There exists an evaluation context $E[\ ]$, such that $e_{is} \equiv \mathsf{callcc}\lambda k_i.E[\mathcal{T}^{\rho_s}_{\sigma_s}[\![V]\!]\ \mathcal{T}^{\rho_s}_{\sigma_s}[\![N]\!]] \equiv e_{it} \equiv \mathsf{callcc}\lambda k_i.E[\mathcal{T}^{\rho_t}_{\sigma_t}[\![V]\!]\ \mathcal{T}^{\rho_t}_{\sigma_t}[\![N]\!]]$.

Some rules do not change the set of targets and correspond to a reduction in the λ_v-C-calculus (β_v, capture, δ, prune$_f$, prune$_a$, prune$_l$, prune$_r$). For instance,

(capture) $\rho_s = \rho_t$ and $\sigma_s = \sigma_t$. Let g_i be the target of $\langle\langle p, \kappa\rangle, (\kappa\ \mathbf{fun}\ V)\rangle$, with $\rho_s(g_i) = \rho_t(g_i) = k_i$. There exists an evaluation context $E[\ ]$, such that $e_{is} \equiv \mathsf{callcc}\lambda k_i.E[\mathsf{callcc}\ \mathcal{T}^{\rho_s}_{\sigma_s}[\![V]\!]]$ and $e_{it} \equiv \mathsf{callcc}\lambda k_i.E[\mathcal{T}^{\rho_t}_{\sigma_t}[\![V]\!]\ \mathcal{T}^{\rho_t}_{\sigma_t}[\![\langle p, \kappa\rangle]\!]]$. Furthermore, $\mathcal{T}^{\rho_t}_{\sigma_t}[\![\langle p, \kappa\rangle]\!] \equiv \lambda v.\mathcal{A}(k_i\ \mathcal{C}^{\rho_t}_{\sigma_t}[\![\kappa, v]\!]) \equiv \lambda v.\mathcal{A}(k_i\ E[v])$ because the evaluation context $E[\ ]$ was defined as $E[\ ] \equiv \mathcal{C}^{\rho_s}_{\sigma_s}[\![\kappa, [\ ]]\!] \equiv \mathcal{C}^{\rho_t}_{\sigma_t}[\![\kappa, [\ ]]\!]$.

$$e_{is} = e_{it} \equiv \mathsf{callcc}\lambda k_i.E[\mathcal{T}^{\rho_s}_{\sigma_s}[\![V]\!]\ \lambda v.\mathcal{A}(k_i\ E[v])] \text{ by } (C_{lift}) \text{ and } (C_{idem})$$

Rule pcall creates a new target.

(pcall) This rule creates a new target $g_x \equiv \langle \alpha_n, \kappa_x\rangle$, with $\kappa_x \equiv (\kappa\ \mathbf{right}\ (\alpha_m, \alpha_n))$. So, we have $\rho_t = \rho_s[g_x \leftarrow k_x]$ and $\sigma_t = \sigma_s[\alpha_m \leftarrow \bot][\alpha_n \leftarrow \bot]$.
In the configuration $\mathcal{M}_t$, there is no other target with a continuation κ_x because α_m and α_n were freshly allocated. We have $e_{xt} \equiv \mathsf{callcc}\lambda k_x.\mathcal{T}^{\rho_t}_{\sigma_t}[\![N]\!]$, with k_x the fresh variable associated with target g_x. So, $k_x \notin FV(\mathcal{T}^{\rho_t}_{\sigma_t}[\![N]\!])$.
Let g_i be the target of $\langle(\mathsf{pcall}\ M\ N), \kappa\rangle$, with $\rho_s(g_i) = \rho_t(g_i) = k_i$. There exists an evaluation context $E[\ ]$, such that $e_{is} \equiv \mathsf{callcc}\lambda k_i.E[\mathcal{T}^{\rho_s}_{\sigma_s}[\![M]\!]\ \mathcal{T}^{\rho_s}_{\sigma_s}[\![N]\!]] \equiv e_{it} \equiv \mathsf{callcc}\lambda k_i.E[\mathcal{T}^{\rho_t}_{\sigma_t}[\![M]\!]\ \mathcal{T}^{\rho_t}_{\sigma_t}[\![N]\!]]$

A target g_j in $\mathcal{M}_s$ disappears after application of rules ret-1$_l$, stop$_l$, ret-1$_l$, resume$_r$. Here, we use the inductive hypothesis. For instance,

(ret-1$_l$) Let g_i be the target of $\langle V, (\kappa\ \mathbf{left}\ (\alpha_m, \alpha_n, N))\rangle$ with $\rho_s(g_i) = k_i$. Let g_j be the target with continuation $(\kappa\ \mathbf{right}(\alpha_m, \alpha_n))$ in configuration $\mathcal{M}_s$. After transition, target g_j disappears in $\mathcal{M}_t$. We have that $\forall g \neq g_j, \rho_t(g) = \rho_s(g)$, and that $\rho_s(g_j) = k_j$, but $\rho_t(g_j)$ is not defined. $\sigma_t = \sigma_s[\alpha_m \leftarrow V]$. There exists an evaluation context $E[\ ]$, such that

$$e_{is} \equiv \mathsf{callcc}\lambda k_i.E[\mathcal{T}^{\rho_s}_{\sigma_s}[\![V]\!]\ \mathcal{T}^{\rho_s}_{\sigma_s}[\![N]\!]] \text{ and } e_{it} \equiv \mathsf{callcc}\lambda k_i.E[\mathcal{T}^{\rho_t}_{\sigma_t}[\![V]\!]\ \mathcal{T}^{\rho_t}_{\sigma_t}[\![\sigma_t(\alpha_n)]\!]]$$

In $\mathcal{M}_s$, the term associated with target g_j is $e_{j_s} \equiv \mathsf{callcc}\lambda k_j.\mathcal{T}^{\rho_s}_{\sigma_s}[\![\sigma_s(\alpha_n)]\!]$. We can find a transition pcall that has allocated locations α_m and α_n. Let s' be this transition. By inductive hypothesis and by Lemma 19, we have that

$$\mathsf{callcc}\lambda k_j.\mathcal{T}^{\rho_{s'}}_{\sigma_{s'}}[\![N]\!]\{c_u/k_v\}^* = \mathsf{callcc}\lambda k_j.\mathcal{T}^{\rho_s}_{\sigma_s}[\![N]\!] = \mathsf{callcc}\lambda k_j.\mathcal{T}^{\rho_s}_{\sigma_s}[\![\sigma_s(\alpha_n)]\!]$$

with $k_j \notin FV(\mathcal{T}^{\rho_s}_{\sigma_s}[\![N]\!])$, with k_u, k_v such that $\exists g_u, g_v, \rho_{s'}(g_u) = \rho_s(g_u) = k_u$, $\rho_{s'}(g_v) = k_v, \rho_{s'}(g_v) = \bot$, with $\kappa_v \sqsupseteq^s_{\sigma_t} \kappa_u$, and $c_u \equiv \mathcal{T}^{\rho_t}_{\sigma_t}[\![\langle p, \kappa_v\rangle]\!]$. So,

$$\begin{aligned}
e_{is} &\equiv \mathsf{callcc}\lambda k_i.E[\mathcal{T}^{\rho_s}_{\sigma_s}[\![V]\!]\ \mathcal{T}^{\rho_s}_{\sigma_s}[\![N]\!]] \\
&= \mathsf{callcc}\lambda k_i.E[\mathcal{T}^{\rho_s}_{\sigma_s}[\![V]\!]\ \mathsf{callcc}\lambda k_j.\mathcal{T}^{\rho_s}_{\sigma_s}[\![N]\!]] \text{ by } (C_{elim}) \\
&= \mathsf{callcc}\lambda k_i.E[\mathcal{T}^{\rho_s}_{\sigma_s}[\![V]\!]\ \mathsf{callcc}\lambda k_j.\mathcal{T}^{\rho_s}_{\sigma_s}[\![\sigma_s(\alpha_n)]\!]] \text{ by Inductive Hypothesis} \\
&= \mathsf{callcc}\lambda k_i.E[\mathcal{T}^{\rho_s}_{\sigma_s}[\![V]\!]\ ((\lambda k_j.\mathcal{T}^{\rho_s}_{\sigma_s}[\![\sigma_s(\alpha_n)]\!])\ (\lambda v.\mathcal{A}(k_i E[\mathcal{T}^{\rho_s}_{\sigma_s}[\![V]\!]\ v])))] \\
&\qquad \text{by } (C_{lift}) \text{ and } (C_{idem}) \\
&= \mathsf{callcc}\lambda k_i.E[\mathcal{T}^{\rho_s}_{\sigma_s}[\![V]\!]\ (\mathcal{T}^{\rho_s}_{\sigma_s}[\![\sigma(\alpha_n)]\!]\{(\lambda v.\mathcal{A}(k_i E[\mathcal{T}^{\rho_s}_{\sigma_s}[\![V]\!]\ v]))/k_j\})] \text{ by } (\beta_v) \\
&= \mathsf{callcc}\lambda k_i.E[\mathcal{T}^{\rho_t}_{\sigma_t}[\![V]\!]\ \mathcal{T}^{\rho_t}_{\sigma_t}[\![\sigma_t(\alpha_n)]\!]] \equiv e_{it} \text{ by Lemma 19}
\end{aligned}$$

We have $\mathcal{T}^{\rho_s}_{\sigma_s}[\![V]\!] \equiv \mathcal{T}^{\rho_t}_{\sigma_t}[\![V]\!]$ because the targets of any continuation point in F are the same in $\mathcal{M}_s$ and $\mathcal{M}_t$ (put differently, there is no continuation point in F with a target g_j, by Lemma 20).
Although the content of α_n has not changed during the transition, the translation $\mathcal{T}^{\rho_t}_{\sigma_t}[\![\sigma(\alpha_n)]\!]$ differs from $\mathcal{T}^{\rho_s}_{\sigma_s}[\![\sigma(\alpha_n)]\!]$ because g_j is no longer a target in $\mathcal{M}_t$. Each continuation that belongs to target g_j in configuration $\mathcal{M}_s$ belongs to target g_i in configuration $\mathcal{M}_t$.
Now, let us consider any term e_{us} which is not associated with targets g_i or g_j. We have $e_{us}\{(\lambda v.\mathcal{A}(k_i E[\mathcal{T}^{\rho_s}_{\sigma_s}[\![V]\!]\ v]))/k_j\} = e_{ut}$ by Lemma 19.

Both invoke$_{init}$ and invoke$_{up}$ rely on Lemma 20, and their soundness is proved by C_{cur}. For instance,

(invoke$_{up}$) $\rho_s = \rho_t$ and $\sigma_s = \sigma_t$. Let $g_i \equiv \langle \alpha_i, \kappa_i \rangle$ be the target of $\langle V, ((\kappa_1\ \mathbf{right}(\alpha_m, \alpha_n))\ \mathbf{fun}\langle p, \kappa \rangle) \rangle$, with $\kappa_i \equiv (\kappa_1\ \mathbf{right}(\alpha_m, \alpha_n))$ and $\rho_s(g_i) = \rho_t(g_i) = k_i$.
By Lemma 20, since $\langle p, \kappa \rangle$ is accessible by the process, the target $g_j \equiv \langle \alpha_j, \kappa_j \rangle$ of κ must be an ancestor of target g_i. So, we have $\kappa \sqsupseteq^s_{\sigma_s} \kappa_j$, and $\kappa \sqsupseteq \kappa_i \sqsupseteq \kappa_j$. Therefore, we have $\kappa \sqsupseteq^s_{\sigma_s} \kappa_i \sqsupseteq^s_{\sigma_s} \kappa_j$. Since κ_i and κ_j are both continuations of targets, $\kappa_i \equiv \kappa_j$. Hence, there exists an evaluation context $E[\ ]$, such that

$$\begin{aligned} e_{is} &\equiv \mathsf{callcc}\lambda k_i.(\mathcal{T}^{\rho_s}_{\sigma_s}[\![\langle p, \kappa \rangle]\!]\ \mathcal{T}^{\rho_s}_{\sigma_s}[\![V]\!]) \equiv \mathsf{callcc}\lambda k_i.((\lambda v.\mathcal{A}k_i(E[v]))\ \mathcal{T}^{\rho_s}_{\sigma_s}[\![V]\!]) \\ &= \mathsf{callcc}\lambda k_i.(E[\mathcal{T}^{\rho_s}_{\sigma_s}[\![V]\!]]) \text{ by } (\beta_v) \text{ and } (C_{cur}) \quad \equiv e_{it} \end{aligned}$$

□

Lemma 19 For all $M \in \Lambda_{pcks}$, for all g_u, g_v such that $\rho_s(g_u) = \rho_t(g_u) = k_u$, and $\rho_s(g_v) = k_v$ but $\rho_t(g_v)$ is undefined,

$$\mathcal{T}^{\rho_s}_{\sigma_s}[\![M]\!]\{c_u/k_v\}^* = \mathcal{T}^{\rho_t}_{\sigma_t}[\![M]\!]$$

with $c_u \equiv \mathcal{T}^{\rho_t}_{\sigma_t}[\![\langle p, \kappa_v \rangle]\!]$, $\kappa_v \sqsupseteq^s_{\sigma_t} \kappa_u$, and $\{c_u/k_v\}^*$ denoting the substitution of all k_v by c_u. □

Proof Lemma 19. By induction on the size of M. The interesting case is the continuation point. Let $g_i \equiv \langle \alpha_i, \kappa_i \rangle$ be the target of κ in $\mathcal{M}_s$, $\kappa \sqsupseteq^s_{\sigma_s} \kappa_i$, and let $g_j \equiv \langle \alpha_j, \kappa_j \rangle$ be the target of κ in $\mathcal{M}_t$, $\kappa \sqsupseteq^s_{\sigma_t} \kappa_j$, with $\kappa_i \sqsupseteq^s_{\sigma_t} \kappa_j$.

$$\begin{aligned} &\mathcal{T}^{\rho_s}_{\sigma_s}[\![\langle p, \kappa \rangle]\!]\{c_u/k_v\}^* \\ &\equiv (\lambda v.\mathcal{A}(k_i\{c_u/k_v\}^*\ \mathcal{C}^{\rho_s}_{\sigma_s}[\![\kappa, v]\!]\{c_u/k_v\}^*)) \equiv (\lambda v.\mathcal{A}(c_j\ \mathcal{C}^{\rho_s}_{\sigma_s}[\![\kappa, v]\!]\{c_u/k_v\}^*)) \\ &\equiv (\lambda v.\mathcal{A}((\lambda v.\mathcal{A}(k_j\ \mathcal{C}^{\rho_t}_{\sigma_t}[\![\kappa_i, v]\!]))\ \mathcal{C}^{\rho_s}_{\sigma_s}[\![\kappa, v]\!]\{c_u/k_v\}^*)) \\ &= (\lambda v.\mathcal{A}((\lambda v.\mathcal{A}(k_j\ \mathcal{C}^{\rho_t}_{\sigma_t}[\![\kappa_i, v]\!]))\ E'[v]))\ (*), \text{ by IH} \\ &= (\lambda v.\mathcal{A}(k_j \mathcal{C}^{\rho_t}_{\sigma_t}[\![\kappa_i, E'[v]]\!])) \text{ by } \beta'_\Omega \text{ and abort} \\ &= (\lambda v.\mathcal{A}(k_j \mathcal{C}^{\rho_t}_{\sigma_t}[\![\kappa, v]\!])) \text{ by dfn. of } \mathcal{C}^{\rho_t}_{\sigma_t}[\![\kappa, v]\!] \quad \equiv \mathcal{T}^{\rho_t}_{\sigma_t}[\![\langle p, \kappa \rangle]\!] \end{aligned}$$

(*) $E'[\ ]$ is obtained by replacing in $E[\ ] \equiv \mathcal{C}^{\rho_t}_{\sigma_t}[\![\kappa_i, [\ ]]\!]$ all terms that have a free variable k_v : $E'[\ ] \equiv E[\ ]\{\mathcal{T}^{\rho_t}_{\sigma_t}[\![N]\!]/\mathcal{T}^{\rho_s}_{\sigma_s}[\![N]\!]\}$. □

Let us prove that the target of a continuation is always an ancestor of the target of a process that can access it.

Lemma 20 If $\langle p, \kappa \rangle$ is a subexpression of M in process $\langle M, \kappa' \rangle$. Let κ_i be the continuation of the target of κ, and let κ'_i be the continuation of the target of κ'. Then $\kappa'_i \sqsupseteq \kappa_i$. □

Sketch of Proof of Theorem 11

If $\mathsf{eval}_{\mathsf{pcks}}(M) = V$, we know that $\lambda_v\text{-}C \vdash \mathcal{T}^\rho_\sigma[\![M]\!] = \mathcal{T}^\rho_\sigma[\![V]\!]$ by Lemma 18. So $\mathsf{eval}_{\mathsf{vc}}(\mathcal{S}[\![M]\!])$ is defined. By Felleisen and Friedman's Corollary 5.8 and Theorem 5.1 [4], $\mathsf{eval}_{\mathsf{ck}}(\mathcal{S}[\![M]\!])$.

Symmetrically, if $\mathsf{eval}_{\mathsf{ck}}(\mathcal{S}[\![M]\!])$ is defined, then $\mathsf{eval}_{\mathsf{pcks}}(M)$ is also defined because the PCKS-machine is able to simulate the CK-machine by always reducing the mandatory process. □

References

1. Andrew W. Appel and David B. MacQueen. Standard ML of New Jersey. In Jan Maluszyński and Martin Wirsing, editors, *Third International Symposium on Programming Language Implementation and Logic Programming*, number 528 in Lecture Notes in Computer Science, pages 1–13, Passau, Germany, August 1991.
2. Henk P. Barendregt. *The Lambda Calculus: Its Syntax and Semantics*, volume 103 of *Studies in Logic and the Foundations of Mathematics*. North-Holland, 1984.
3. Marc Feeley. *An Efficient and General Implementation of Futures on Large Scale Shared-Memory Multiprocessors*. PhD thesis, Brandeis University, 1993.
4. Matthias Felleisen and Daniel P. Friedman. Control Operators, the SECD-Machine and the λ-Calculus. In M. Wirsing, editor, *Formal Description of Programming Concepts III*, pages 193–217, Amsterdam, 1986. Elsevier Science Publishers.
5. Cormac Flanagan and Matthias Felleisen. The Semantics of Future and Its Use in Program Optimization. In *Proceedings of the Twenty Second Annual ACM SIGACT-SIGPLAN Symposium on Principles of Programming Languages*, January 1995.
6. Cormac Flanagan, Amr Sabry, Bruce F. Duba, and Matthias Felleisen. The Essence of Compiling with Continuations. In *Proc. SIGPLAN '93 Conference on Programming Language Design and Implementation*, SIGPLAN Notices, Vol. 28, pages 237–247, 1993.
7. Robert H. Halstead, Jr. New Ideas in Parallel Lisp : Language Design, Implementation. In T. Ito and Robert H. Halstead, editors, *Parallel Lisp : Languages and Systems. US/Japan Workshop on Parallel Lisp. Japan.*, number 441 in Lecture Notes in Computer Science, pages 2–57. Springer-Verlag, 1990.
8. Christopher T. Haynes, Daniel P. Friedman, and Mitchell Wand. Obtaining Coroutines with Continuations. *Comput. Lang.*, 11(3/4):143–153, 1986.
9. Morry Katz and Daniel Weise. Continuing Into the Future: On the Interaction of Futures and First-Class Continuations. In *Proceedings of the 1990 ACM Conference on Lisp and Functional Programming*, pages 176–184, June 1990.
10. Luc Moreau. The PCKS-machine. An Abstract Machine for Sound Evaluation of Parallel Functional Programs with First-Class Continuations. In *European Symposium on Programming (ESOP'94)*, number 788 in Lecture Notes in Computer Science, pages 424–438, Edinburgh, Scotland, April 1994. Springer-Verlag.
11. Luc Moreau. *Sound Evaluation of Parallel Functional Programs with First-Class Continuations*. PhD thesis, University of Liège, June 1994. Also available by anonymous ftp from `ftp.montefiore.ulg.ac.be` in directory `pub/moreau`.
12. Luc Moreau and Daniel Ribbens. Sound Rules for Parallel Evaluation of a Functional Language with callcc. In *ACM conference on Functional Programming and Computer Architecture (FPCA'93)*, pages 125–135, Copenhagen, June 1993.
13. Gordon D. Plotkin. Call-by-Name, Call-by-Value and the λ-Calculus. *Theoretical Computer Science*, pages 125–159, 1975.
14. Jonathan Rees and William Clinger, editors. Revised^4 Report on the Algorithmic Language Scheme. *Lisp Pointers*, 4(3):1–55, July-September 1991.
15. Amr Sabry and Matthias Felleisen. Reasoning about Programs in Continuation-Passing Style. *Lisp and Symbolic and Computation, Special Issue on Continuations*, 6(3/4):289–360, November 1993.
16. Christopher Strachey and Christopher P. Wadsworth. A Mathematical Semantics for Handling Full Jumps. Technical Monography PRG-11, Oxford University Computing Laboratory, Programming Research Group, Oxford, England, 1974.

A Model Inference System for Generic Specification with Application to Code Sharing

Didier Bert, Catherine Oriat

LGI - IMAG, BP 53, 38041 Grenoble Cedex 9, France
e-mail: {Didier.Bert,Catherine.Oriat}@imag.fr

Abstract. This paper presents a model inference system to control instantiation of generic modules. Generic parameters are specified by properties which represent classes of modules sharing some common features. Just as type checking consists in verifying that an expression is well typed, *model checking* allows to detect whether a (possibly generic) instantiation of a generic module is valid, i.e. whether the instantiation module is a *model* of the parameterizing property. Equality of instances can be derived from a canonical representation of modules. At last, we show how the code of generic modules can be shared for all instances of modules.

1 Introduction

Genericity is a useful feature for specification languages, and for programming languages alike, because it allows to reuse already written packages by instantiating them on various ways, thus limits the risk of bugs and reduces software costs. When a generic module is instantiated and imported into another module, one has to check that the instantiation is valid, i.e. that the instantiation module is a *model* of the formal part. For that, one can either rely on the syntax, i.e. on the theory defined by the modules, or on the semantics of the modules in the given specification language. In the first case one has to prove that some formulae are theorems in the theory. This problem is semi-decidable if the semantics is purely loose, but is undecidable if we work in an initial semantics [14]. In the second case, one has to check properties on classes of algebras, which is hard to do automatically. Consequently, in almost all specification languages (e.g. PLUSS [11, 6, 7], ACT-TWO [9], OBJ [10, 12], ...), such verifications are left to the user.

In this paper, we show that such verifications can partly be done automatically. We describe the model inference system used by the specification language LPG to control instantiation of generic modules. LPG (Langage de Programmation Générique, i.e. language for generic programming) is a specification language developed at the IMAG Institute by Didier Bert and Rachid Echahed [4, 5]. LPG allows on the one hand to define and combine generic components of specifications, and on the other hand to make prototypes thanks to an evaluation tool. There is also a solver of goals associating functional and logic programming.

In LPG, generic *modules* are parameterized by *properties*. The semantics of LPG mixes loose and initial features: the semantics of a property is a class of algebras, while the semantics of a generic module is a free functor. An LPG module can be instantiated by another one only if the other module *is a model* of the required property. Properties and modules are related by *constraints.* These constraints are similar those given by Ehrig and Mahr [9] in that they put restrictions on classes of algebras. However, they differ in several points: firstly, Ehrig and Mahr only consider inclusion of specifications, whereas we consider any morphism in LPG. Secondly, for Ehrig and Mahr, the initial (or free) semantics of a specification is stated at the time of its importation. In other words a specification `boolean` can be imported once with a loose semantics, and once with an initial semantics. In LPG, the semantics of a unit is stated once for all at the time of its definition. Thirdly, and this is the original feature of LPG we want to stress in this paper, the language provides an inference system to generate new constraints from declared ones.

This inference system can be compared to type systems used for programming languages: just as types allow to control utilizations of variables, constraints allow to control instantiations of modules. There is one important difference though: constraints apply at the level of units, and are therefore category theoretic (i.e. formulated with morphisms) rather than set theoretic (i.e. formulated with membership or inclusion). In particular, there are various ways a module can be a model of a property.

Such verifications for modules already exist in some programming languages. For instance in Ada [1], homology rules are used to check the validity of instantiations; e.g. with *private* and *limited* types. In Ada, these rules apply to one type only. In contrast, M. V. Aponte proposed a type system for checking SML modules [2], based on unification and sharing, and which performs verifications w.r.t. the whole specification of the generic part of a module. In this approach, verifications are based on the names of types and functions, and therefore there are not various ways an SML-structure (i.e. a module) can match an SML-signature (i.e. a property).

Constraints allow us to reason locally about units. The semantics of algebraic specification languages often seems complicated because it is global, i.e. one has to know the semantics of all imported units to know the semantics of the current unit. Making constraints explicit does not change the semantics, but allows to make safe deductions without having to be aware of all importations at the same time. The inference system presented in this paper is sound with respect to the algebraic semantics of the language. Note that it is not complete, and *cannot* be complete with respect to this semantics. One reason is that we work in initial algebras, and therefore it is impossible to deduce all semantically true statements from any deductive system. All we can do is to rely on the user's declarations, and make safe deductions.

The paper is organized as follows: section 2 and 3 present LPG units and constraints. In section 4 we describe the inference system which allows to deduce new constraints, and thus checks the validity of instantiations. In section 5 we show the representation used for instances of generic modules. This representation allows to share imported modules consistently. Section 6 presents the compilation of modules. In contrast to languages such as Ada [1] or C++ [13], generic modules are compiled only once in LPG, all the instantiations sharing the same code. This is an interesting feature for a prototyping language, because it reduces compilation times a lot when developing highly generic programs.

2 The Language Constructions

The LPG language has two kinds of units, namely *properties* and *modules*. LPG modules allow to define abstract data types, and more generally to group together a set of types and operators logically related. LPG modules can be generic, i.e. parameterized by a set of types and operators. The generic part of a module is itself an LPG unit, and is called the *property required by the module*. LPG units are composed of a *signature* and a set of formulae, which are conditional equations. In modules, the equations may be oriented; in this case they can be compiled and executed by the evaluation tool.

```
module BOOLEAN
types boolean
constructors
   true, false : boolean
operators
   not : boolean -> boolean
   and : boolean, boolean -> boolean
   or  : boolean, boolean -> boolean
equations
   not(true) ==> false
   not(false) ==> true
   and(true,x) ==> x
   and(false,x) ==> false
   or(true,x) ==> true
   or(false,x) ==> x
```

```
property ANY
types any

property DISCRETE
types t
operators first, last : t
          next : t -> t

property MONOID
types t
operators e : t
          op : t,t -> t
equations
   op(e,x) == x
   op(x,e) == x
   op(x,op(y,z)) == op(op(x,y),z)
```

Fig. 1. Simple examples of modules and properties

Figure 1 shows some simple examples of LPG units: the module BOOLEAN, the properties ANY (specifying a single type any), DISCRETE and MONOID. Figure 2 defines the generic module of lists, parameterized by the property ANY.

```
module LIST requires ANY[elem]
types list
constructors nil : list ;  cons : elem,list -> list
operators head : list -> elem ;  tail : list -> list
equations head(cons(e,l)) ==> e ;  tail(cons(e,l)) ==> l
```

Fig. 2. Generic module of lists

Given a module M which requires a property P, there is an injective signature morphism from P to M, which is merely a renaming of the types and operators of the property P into the module M. These morphisms are noted $P \xhookrightarrow{r} M$. The module of lists is noted $\texttt{ANY} \xhookrightarrow{r} \texttt{LIST}$, where r is the morphism $\{\texttt{any} \mapsto \texttt{elem}\}$. r is given in the module `LIST` by the statement **`requires`** `ANY[elem]`.

A non generic module M (such as `BOOLEAN` for instance) can be considered as a generic module $\Phi \xhookrightarrow{\phi_M} M$ parameterized by the empty property Φ, which contains no types nor operators. ϕ_M is the only morphism from Φ to M. (Categorically speaking, Φ is the initial object of the category of signatures.)

We suppose the reader is familiar with basic concepts of algebraic specification (see e.g. [8]). The class of algebras which satisfy a unit U together with homomorphisms is a category noted $Alg\,(U)$. If $m : U_1 \rightarrow U_2$ is a signature morphism, then there is a forgetful functor $\mathcal{U}_m : Alg\,(U_2) \rightarrow Alg\,(U_1)$, and a free functor left adjoint to $\mathcal{U}_m$, $\mathcal{F}_m : Alg\,(U_1) \rightarrow Alg\,(U_2)$. We do not define the whole semantics of LPG here, but only present the features which are relevant for this paper. For a complete description of the semantics of LPG, see [15].

Definition 1. (semantics of a property) The semantics of a property P is a class of algebras $mod\,(P)$, which satisfy the specification P, i.e.: $mod\,(P) \subseteq Alg\,(P)$. The semantics of a property need not be the whole class $Alg\,(P)$ because some algebras may be left out to preserve imported modules.

Definition 2. (semantics of a module) The semantics of a module $P \xhookrightarrow{r} M$ is the free functor $\mathcal{F}_r : Alg\,(P) \rightarrow Alg\,(M)$. The free functor associates to each algebra of $Alg\,(P)$ the algebra freely generated on M. This functor must be strongly persistent on algebras of $mod\,(P)$, i.e.: for all algebras A of $mod\,(P)$, $\mathcal{U}_r(\mathcal{F}_r(A)) = A$.

This condition expresses that previously defined units must be preserved, i.e. that introducing a new module does not change the semantics of old units. Let 1 be the only algebra satisfying the empty property Φ. When a module is not generic, i.e. when P is the empty property, then $\mathcal{F}_r(1)$ is the initial algebra.

3 Constraints

There are five kinds of constraints relating LPG units, namely *model*, *satisfaction*, *combination*, *importation of a module into a property*, and *into a module*. A constraint is composed of a signature morphism and of a semantic condition, which states the validity of the constraint.

Definition 3. (model constraint) A module $P \xhookrightarrow{r} M$ is a *model* of a property P_1 if there is a signature morphism $P_1 \xrightarrow{m} M$ and if the formulae of P_1 hold (through the translation induced by m) in M.

$$\mathrm{Model}\,(P_1 \xrightarrow{m} M) \overset{\mathrm{def}}{\Leftrightarrow} \mathcal{U}_m(\mathcal{F}_r(mod\,(P))) \subseteq mod\,(P_1)$$

For instance, we can express that the module BOOLEAN is a model of the property ANY with the following declaration of model (written in the module BOOLEAN):

```
models ANY[boolean]
```

This declaration defines the signature morphism {any ↦ boolean} from ANY to BOOLEAN. As there is no equation in the property ANY, nothing else has to be checked. In the same way, we can define different models of DISCRETE with natural numbers, for instance the natural numbers from 1 to 10 with the successor operator; or natural numbers from 49 to 0, with the predecessor operator.

```
models DISCRETE[natural,1,10,succ], DISCRETE[natural,49,0,pred]
```

We can also express that the module BOOLEAN is a model of MONOID:

```
models MONOID[boolean,true,and], MONOID[boolean,false,or]
```

Definition 4. (satisfaction constraint) A property P_2 *satisfies* a property P_1 if there is a signature morphism $P_1 \xrightarrow{s} P_2$ and if any module which is a model of P_2 is (through the translation induced by s) a model of P_1.

$$\mathrm{Sat}\,(P_1 \xrightarrow{s} P_2) \overset{\mathrm{def}}{\Leftrightarrow} \mathcal{U}_s(mod\,(P_2)) \subseteq mod\,(P_1) \;\Leftrightarrow\; mod\,(P_2) \subseteq \mathcal{U}_s^{-1}(mod\,(P_1))$$

For instance, we can state that the property MONOID satisfies ANY, with the declaration **satisfies** ANY[t] in the unit MONOID. The declaration states that there is a morphism ANY $\xrightarrow{s}$ MONOID $=$ {any ↦ t}, such that any model of MONOID is a model of ANY.

Combination. Properties can be *combined*, i.e. put together to form a new property. Figure 3 shows a property specifying any type and a discrete type.

```
property ANY+DISCRETE
combines ANY[elem], DISCRETE[index,first,last,next]
```

Fig. 3. Property ANY+DISCRETE

The combination constraint states that any model of ANY+DISCRETE is a model of ANY and is a model of DISCRETE (i.e. ANY+DISCRETE satisfies ANY and DISCRETE). Conversely, any two models of ANY and DISCRETE allow to construct a model of ANY+DISCRETE.

In this example, the "union" of both properties happens to be disjoint, i.e. no symbol of type nor operator appears twice. We can for instance specify a property ANY_DISCRETE, where the type of ANY and the type of DISCRETE are shared. We thus specify a class of modules with *one* type which is a model of both ANY and DISCRETE. Then any two models of ANY and DISCRETE *which share this type* allow to construct a model of ANY_DISCRETE.

Definition 5. (combination constraint) A property P is a combination of the properties $P_1, P_2, \ldots P_k$ w.r.t. the morphisms $P_i \xrightarrow{c_i} P$, $\forall i \in \{1, \ldots k\}$ if models of $P_1, P_2, \ldots P_k$ which share the same types and operators as specified in P allow to construct a model of P.

$$\text{Comb}\,(P_1, \ldots P_k \xrightarrow{c_1, \ldots c_k} P) \overset{\text{def}}{\Leftrightarrow} mod\,(P) = \bigcap_{i=1}^{k} \mathcal{U}_{c_i}^{-1}(mod\,(P_i))$$

$$\Leftrightarrow \begin{cases} \forall i \in \{1, \ldots k\},\ \mathcal{U}_{c_i}(mod\,(P)) \subseteq mod\,(P_i) \\ \forall A \in Alg\,(P),\ (\forall i \in \{1, \ldots k\},\ \mathcal{U}_{c_i}(A) \in mod\,(P_i)) \Rightarrow A \in mod\,(P) \end{cases}$$

Importation and Instantiation. Once a generic module has been defined, it is possible to use it in another unit. This is called importation into a module or into a property. When a module is imported, its formal part (i.e. the signature contained in its required property) must be instantiated, either with actual, or formal parameters, or both. This instantiation defines a signature morphism from the imported module to the currently defined unit.

We define on figure 4 a module called `VECTOR`, parameterized by the property `ANY+DISCRETE`. The property `ANY` gives the type of information stored in a *vector*, and the property `DISCRETE` defines the index. We are not concerned here with the actual representation of vectors, therefore we only specify two operations: `store` which assigns a new value to an index, and `get` which picks up the value associated to an index. From now on, the axiomatization of operators is omitted.

```
module VECTOR requires ANY+DISCRETE[t,index,first,last,next]
types vector
operators store : vector, index, t -> vector
          get : vector, index -> t
```

Fig. 4. Part of the module `VECTOR`

Then we may define vectors of integers with some new operations. For that, we have to import the module `INTEGER` containing integer values as well as usual operations on them. This module no longer requires a type for the information stored, so it is only parameterized by the property `DISCRETE`.

```
module INTEGER_VECTOR requires DISCRETE[index,first,last,next]
imports INTEGER, VECTOR[integer,index,first,last,next]
operators scalar_prod : vector, vector -> integer
```

Fig. 5. Module of vectors of integers

Another example: given a binary operator on the type `t`, we can define a binary operator on vectors. The module figure 6 defines a null vector and a sum of vectors, given a null element `e` and an associative binary operator `op`. Note that we have also stated that vectors with these two operators form a monoid.

```
module VECTOR_SUM requires MONOID+DISCRETE[t,e,op,index,first,last,next]
imports VECTOR[t,index,first,last,next]
operators null_vect : vector ;  sum_vect : vector, vector -> vector
models MONOID[vector,null_vect,sum_vect]
```

Fig. 6. Vectors with a binary operator

In example 5, the type `vector` refers to the type *vector of integers*, whereas in example 6 it refers to *vector of t*. There is no confusion because the module `VECTOR` is only imported once in each module. If we want to import a module several times (with different instantiations) in a module, we have to name the instantiated modules:

```
INTEGER_V = VECTOR[integer,index,first,last,next]
      T_V = VECTOR[t,index,first,last,next]
```

and then to refer to the types and operators as `INTEGER_V.vector`, `T_V.vector`, `INTEGER_V.store` and so on.

The originality of LPG is that not any importation is valid. For instance, the importation `imports LIST[integer]` is valid only if the module `INTEGER` is a model of the property `ANY` with the morphism $\{$`any` $\mapsto$ `integer`$\}$. This can be the case either if the user has defined such a model with the declaration `models ANY[integer]`, or if the system can deduce it from other declarations, using the inference system presented next section. For instance, if `INTEGER` is a model of `MONOID`, and if `MONOID` satisfies `ANY`, then `INTEGER` is a model of `ANY`.

The examples we have presented here are importations of a module into another module. It is also possible to import a module into a property.

Definition 6. (constraint of importation of a module into a module) Let $P_1 \xhookrightarrow{r_1} M_1$ and $P_2 \xhookrightarrow{r_2} M_2$ be two modules. $P_1 \xhookrightarrow{r_1} M_1$ is imported into $P_2 \xhookrightarrow{r_2} M_2$ with the morphism $M_1 \xrightarrow{i} M_2$ if:

$$\text{Import\_M}\,(M_1 \xrightarrow{i} M_2) \overset{\text{def}}{\Leftrightarrow} \mathcal{U}_i(\mathcal{F}_{r_2}(mod\,(P_2))) \subseteq \mathcal{F}_{r_1}(mod\,(P_1))$$

$$\Leftrightarrow \begin{cases} \text{Model}\,(P_1 \xrightarrow{i o r_1} M_2) \\ \forall A_2 \in mod\,(P_2),\ \mathcal{U}_i(\mathcal{F}_{r_2}(A_2)) = \mathcal{F}_{r_1}(\mathcal{U}_{r_1}(\mathcal{U}_i(\mathcal{F}_{r_2}(A_2)))) \qquad (\mathcal{H}_M) \end{cases}$$

The morphism i expresses the *instantiation* of the generic part of the module $P_1 \xhookrightarrow{r_1} M_1$ with a part of the module $P_2 \xhookrightarrow{r_2} M_2$, and the *inclusion* of the non generic part of $P_1 \xhookrightarrow{r_1} M_1$ into $P_2 \xhookrightarrow{r_2} M_2$.

Definition 7. (constraint of importation of a module into a property) Let $P_1 \xhookrightarrow{r_1} M_1$ be a module, P_2 be a property. $P_1 \xhookrightarrow{r_1} M_1$ is imported into P_2 with the morphism $M_1 \xrightarrow{i} P_2$ if:

$$\text{Import\_P}\,(M_1 \xrightarrow{i} P_2) \overset{\text{def}}{\Leftrightarrow} \mathcal{U}_i(mod\,(P_2)) \subseteq \mathcal{F}_{r_1}(mod\,(P_1))$$

$$\Leftrightarrow \begin{cases} \text{Sat}\,(P_1 \xrightarrow{i o r_1} P_2) \\ \forall A_2 \in mod\,(P_2),\ \mathcal{U}_i(A_2) = \mathcal{F}_{r_1}(\mathcal{U}_{r_1}(\mathcal{U}_i(A_2))) \qquad (\mathcal{H}_P) \end{cases}$$

4 Inference Rules for Model Checking

In this section, we describe the rules which allow to combine constraints to build new ones, and thus provide an inference system of constraints. Every declaration of a model, satisfaction or combination constraint gives a corresponding axiom. The user must check that these axioms are semantically correct, i.e. that the associated semantic condition is satisfied.

$$\{\mathcal{H}_M\}\frac{\text{Model}\,(P_1 \xrightarrow{ior_1} M_2)}{\text{Import\_M}\,(M_1 \xrightarrow{i} M_2)} \quad (\text{IM}) \qquad \{\mathcal{H}_P\}\frac{\text{Sat}\,(P_1 \xrightarrow{ior_1} P_2)}{\text{Import\_P}\,(M_1 \xrightarrow{i} P_2)} \quad (\text{IP})$$

$$\frac{}{\text{Sat}\,(\Phi \xrightarrow{\phi_P} P)} \;(1) \qquad \frac{}{\text{Model}\,(\Phi \xrightarrow{\phi_M} M)} \;(2) \qquad \frac{}{\text{Model}\,(P \xrightarrow{r} M)} \;(3)$$

$$\frac{\text{Sat}\,(P_1 \xrightarrow{s_1} P_2)\ ;\ \text{Sat}\,(P_2 \xrightarrow{s_2} P_3)}{\text{Sat}\,(P_1 \xrightarrow{s_2 \circ s_1} P_3)} \quad (4)$$

$$\frac{\text{Sat}\,(P_1 \xrightarrow{s} P_2)\ ;\ \text{Model}\,(P_2 \xrightarrow{m} M)}{\text{Model}\,(P_1 \xrightarrow{m o s} M)} \quad (5)$$

$$\frac{\text{Model}\,(P \xrightarrow{m} M_1)\ ;\ \text{Import\_M}\,(M_1 \xrightarrow{i} M_2)}{\text{Model}\,(P \xrightarrow{iom} M_2)} \quad (6)$$

$$\frac{\text{Model}\,(P_1 \xrightarrow{m} M_2)\ ;\ \text{Import\_P}\,(M_2 \xrightarrow{i} P_3)}{\text{Sat}\,(P_1 \xrightarrow{iom} P_3)} \quad (7)$$

$$\frac{\text{Comb}\,(P_1, \ldots P_k \xrightarrow{c_1, \ldots c_k} P)}{\forall j \in \{1, \ldots k\},\ \text{Sat}\,(P_j \xrightarrow{c_j} P)} \quad (8)$$

$$\frac{\text{Comb}\,(P_1, \ldots P_k \xrightarrow{c_1, \ldots c_k} P)\ ;\ \forall j \in \{1, \ldots k\},\ \text{Sat}\,(P_j \xrightarrow{s o c_j} P')}{\text{Sat}\,(P \xrightarrow{s} P')} \quad (9)$$

$$\frac{\text{Comb}\,(P_1, \ldots P_k \xrightarrow{c_1, \ldots c_k} P)\ ;\ \forall j \in \{1, \ldots k\},\ \text{Model}\,(P_j \xrightarrow{m o c_j} M')}{\text{Model}\,(P \xrightarrow{m} M')} \quad (10)$$

Fig. 7. Main inference rules

Figure 7 shows the set of *main rules* used by the system. Properties are noted P, P_1, P_2, ... Modules such as $P \overset{r}{\hookrightarrow} M$, $P_1 \overset{r_1}{\hookrightarrow} M_1$, $P_2 \overset{r_2}{\hookrightarrow} M_2$, ... are just noted M, M_1, M_2, ... The rules (IM) and (IP) are associated to declarations of importations. Their application is conditioned by the hypothesis $\mathcal{H}_M$ or $\mathcal{H}_P$, which must be checked by the user. The other rules are not associated with any hypothesis, which means that their application is always possible. Axioms 1 and 2 state that any property P satisfies the empty property Φ, and that any module $P \overset{r}{\hookrightarrow} M$ is a model of Φ. As Φ is initial, the morphisms ϕ_P and ϕ_M are unique. Axiom 3 expresses that a module $P \overset{r}{\hookrightarrow} M$ is a model of its own property P, with the morphism r. In particular, if two modules are parameterized by the same property, then one can instantiate one module with the formal part of the other one. Rules 4 to 7 are composition rules. Rules 8 to 10 are related to the `combines` constraint.

$$\frac{\text{Import\_P}\,(M \xrightarrow{i} P_1)\ ;\ \text{Sat}\,(P_1 \xrightarrow{s} P_2)}{\text{Import\_P}\,(M \xrightarrow{s \circ i} P_2)} \tag{11}$$

$$\frac{\text{Import\_P}\,(M \xrightarrow{i} P_1)\ ;\ \text{Model}\,(P_1 \xrightarrow{m} M_2)}{\text{Import\_M}\,(M \xrightarrow{m \circ i} M_2)} \tag{12}$$

$$\frac{\text{Import\_M}\,(M_1 \xrightarrow{i_1} M_2)\ ;\ \text{Import\_P}\,(M_2 \xrightarrow{i_2} P_3)}{\text{Import\_P}\,(M_1 \xrightarrow{i_2 \circ i_1} P_3)} \tag{13}$$

$$\frac{\text{Import\_M}\,(M_1 \xrightarrow{i_1} M_2)\ ;\ \text{Import\_M}\,(M_2 \xrightarrow{i_2} M_3)}{\text{Import\_M}\,(M_1 \xrightarrow{i_2 \circ i_1} M_3)} \tag{14}$$

Fig. 8. Derived inference rules

These rules are actually used by the LPG system. One can note that we have not considered all possible compositions. The remaining compositions are described in figure 8. These *derived* rules are not used by the system, because we have the following result:

Theorem 8. *Any proof involving derived rules can be transformed into a proof only involving main rules.*

Proof. Any introduction of an Import_P constraint is preceded by a satisfaction constraint, and any Import_M constraint is preceded by a model constraint. This allows to get rid of all derived rules, from the axioms to the conclusion.

Theorem 9. *The inference system is sound with respect to the semantics.*

This result means that provided the conditions associated to declaration axioms and rules (IM, IP) are satisfied, the constraints deduced by the inference system are semantically correct.

Examples of Deductions. In this paragraph, we reconsider the examples of importations given in the previous section and prove their validity using the inference system.

The importation of a non generic module into a module or into a property is always valid in the system, provided that the corresponding condition $\mathcal{H}_M$ or $\mathcal{H}_P$ is satisfied. This can be shown by using rule (2) followed by rule (IM), or by using rule (1) followed by rule (IP). In particular, the importation of the module `INTEGER` into `INTEGER_VECTOR` (figure 5) is valid.

Let us now consider the importation of `VECTOR` into `INTEGER_VECTOR` (figure 5), as well as the importation of `VECTOR` into `VECTOR_SUM` (figure 6). We are going to take shorter notation, in order to be able to draw the proofs.

Properties		Modules	
ANY	A	INTEGER	I
DISCRETE	D	VECTOR	$AD \xhookrightarrow{r_1} V$
MONOID	M	INTEGER_VECTOR	$D \xhookrightarrow{r_2} IV$
ANY+DISCRETE	AD	VECTOR_SUM	$MD \xhookrightarrow{r_3} VS$
MONOID+DISCRETE	MD		

$$\dfrac{\mathrm{Comb}\,(A, D \xrightarrow{c_1,c_2} AD) \quad \dfrac{\dfrac{\mathrm{Model}\,(A \xrightarrow{m} I) \quad \mathrm{Import\_M}\,(I \xrightarrow{i_1} IV)}{\mathrm{Model}\,(A \xrightarrow{i_1 \circ m} IV)}\;(6)}{\mathrm{Model}\,(A \xrightarrow{i \circ r_1 \circ c_1} IV)}\;(=) \quad \dfrac{\dfrac{}{\mathrm{Model}\,(D \xrightarrow{r_2} IV)}\;(3)}{\mathrm{Model}\,(D \xrightarrow{i \circ r_1 \circ c_2} IV)}\;(=)}{\dfrac{\mathrm{Model}\,(AD \xrightarrow{i \circ r_1} IV)}{\mathrm{Import\_M}\,(V \xrightarrow{i} IV)}\;(\mathrm{IM})}\;(10)$$

$$\dfrac{\mathrm{Sat}\,(A \xrightarrow{s} M) \quad \dfrac{\dfrac{\mathrm{Comb}\,(M, D \xrightarrow{c'_1,c'_2} MD)}{\mathrm{Sat}\,(M \xrightarrow{c'_1} MD)}\;(8) \quad \dfrac{}{\mathrm{Model}\,(MD \xrightarrow{r_3} VS)}\;(3)}{\mathrm{Model}\,(M \xrightarrow{r_3 \circ c'_1} VS)}\;(5)}{\dfrac{\mathrm{Model}\,(A \xrightarrow{r_3 \circ c'_1 \circ s} VS)}{\mathrm{Model}\,(A \xrightarrow{i' \circ r_1 \circ c_1} VS)}\;(=)}\;(5)$$

$$\dfrac{\dfrac{\mathrm{Comb}\,(M, D \xrightarrow{c'_1,c'_2} MD)}{\mathrm{Sat}\,(D \xrightarrow{c'_2} MD)}\;(8) \quad \dfrac{}{\mathrm{Model}\,(MD \xrightarrow{r_3} VS)}\;(3)}{\dfrac{\mathrm{Model}\,(D \xrightarrow{r_3 \circ c'_2} VS)}{\mathrm{Model}\,(D \xrightarrow{i' \circ r_1 \circ c_2} VS)}\;(=)}\;(5)$$

$$\dfrac{\mathrm{Comb}\,(A, D \xrightarrow{c_1,c_2} AD) \quad \mathrm{Model}\,(A \xrightarrow{i' \circ r_1 \circ c_1} VS) \quad \mathrm{Model}\,(D \xrightarrow{i' \circ r_1 \circ c_2} VS)}{\dfrac{\mathrm{Model}\,(AD \xrightarrow{i' \circ r_1} VS)}{\mathrm{Import\_M}\,(V \xrightarrow{i'} VS)}\;(\mathrm{IM})}\;(10)$$

Fig. 9. Proofs of importations

We suppose the user has declared the following constraints:
INTEGER is a model of ANY: Model $(A \xrightarrow{m} I)$. MONOID satisfies ANY: Sat $(A \xrightarrow{s} I)$.
ANY+DISCRETE is a combination of ANY and DISCRETE: Comb $(A, D \xrightarrow{c_1,c_2} AD)$; and MONOID+DISCRETE of MONOID and DISCRETE: Comb $(M, D \xrightarrow{c'_1,c'_2} MD)$.

The importation of INTEGER into INTEGER_VECTOR is noted Import_M $(I \xrightarrow{i_1} IV)$.

The proofs that Import_M $(V \xrightarrow{i} IV)$ and Import_M $(V \xrightarrow{i'} VS)$ are valid are shown figure 9. Note that we use a rule called (=) which means that we use an equality between morphisms. Indeed we have $i_1 \circ m = i \circ r_1 \circ c_1$, $r_2 = i \circ r_1 \circ c_2$, $r_3 \circ c'_1 \circ s = i' \circ r_1 \circ c_1$, and $r_3 \circ c'_2 = i' \circ r_1 \circ c_2$. This rule appears here mainly to clarify the proofs. It is not used as such by the system which works with an internal representation of morphisms as a set of pairs, and not with a symbolic notation.

5 Representation of Imported Modules

When a module is instantiated and imported, there is no creation of a new module. For instance when we write

```
imports T_V = VECTOR[t,index,i1,in,s]
        T_V2 = VECTOR[t,index,i1,in,s]
```

T_V and T_V2 represent the same module, and in particular, T_V.vector and T_V2.vector refer to the same type.

This implies that instantiations can be done in various orders, as shown figure 10: the names INT_MAT1 and INT_MAT2 refer to the same module. We thus have an equality of modules which is stronger than equality of names, in the sense that two modules with different names may be equal. The equality is of course extended to types and operators. This allows to make multiple enrichments: we may for instance make an enrichment of VECTOR by importing two different enrichments ENRICH_VECTOR1 and ENRICH_VECTOR2. The common part of both modules (i.e. the module VECTOR) will be shared correctly.

```
module ENRICH_VECTOR requires ANY+DISCRETE[t,ind,i1,in,s]
imports INTEGER
        T_V = VECTOR[t,ind,i1,in,s]
        T_MAT = VECTOR[T_V.vector,ind,i1,in,s]
        INT_V = VECTOR[integer,ind,i1,in,s]
        INT_MAT1 = T_MAT[integer,ind,i1,in,s]
        INT_MAT2 = VECTOR[INT_V.vector,ind,i1,in,s]
```

Fig. 10. Example of instantiations

To achieve this, modules are encoded with two pieces of information: first the origin module (i.e. the module we want to import), and secondly the morphism from the required property of the origin module to the current module. That way, named intermediary modules used for clarification are never stored in the system. Similarly, types and operators are encoded with three pieces of information: their name, the module they come from and the morphism from the required property of the origin module to the current module. For instance, addition on integers is coded as + = $\langle$+, INTEGER, $\{\}\rangle$, where $\{\}$ is of course the initial morphism $\Phi \xrightarrow{\phi_I} I$. Let now m be the morphism

$m = \{$ elem $\mapsto$ integer, index $\mapsto$ ind, first $\mapsto$ i1, last $\mapsto$ in, next $\mapsto$ s$\}$:

INT_V.vector = $\langle$vector, VECTOR, $m\rangle$
INT_MAT1.store = INT_MAT2.store =
$\langle$ store, VECTOR, $\{$ elem $\mapsto \langle$ vector, VECTOR, m $\rangle$,
index $\mapsto$ ind, first $\mapsto$ i1, last $\mapsto$ in, next $\mapsto$ s $\}\rangle$

6 Compilation of Modules

The representation of imported modules allows to perform fast code generation for operators of generic modules. The point is to share the code of generic operators with all their instantiations. So, code generation is modular and avoids multiple copies of the common parts. Notice that copying the code of generic modules can be an option for run-time optimization, as for on-line generation of the code of procedure bodies. In this section, we give insights on principles of code generation without too many details about the generated code.

The execution abstract machine for generic operators is constituted of the usual components of such machines, i.e. return-address stack (`r-st`), parameters and memory stack (`m-st`) and evaluation stack (`v-st`). It can also deal with exception recovery mechanism and handling contexts. The technique presented here is independent from these features.

Compiling generic operators requires the introduction of a new stack to perform generic parameter bindings. At run-time, only generic parameters with dynamic behaviour have to be stored in this stack, which is called generic parameter stack (or `g-st`). For example, we assume that types have only a static scope and do not need to be represented in the g-stack. The dynamic part of a property P is noted $dyn(P)$. In the framework presented in the paper, $dyn(P)$ is the list of operators of P. So, for a generic module $P \overset{r}{\hookrightarrow} M$ the g-stack is intended to represent the morphism which binds formal operators of $dyn(P)$ to effective functions. The morphism i restricted to the operators of $dyn(P)$ is noted $dyn(i)$. Its cardinality is written $\#(dyn(P))$.

The compilation procedure *compile* is presented for an expression in a generic module $P \overset{r}{\hookrightarrow} M$. It takes an expression and produces the corresponding code for a machine with a state ⟨`v-st,m-st,r-st,g-st`⟩. Operations on stacks and other macro-commands for the abstract machine are defined figure 11. At run-time, the result of the evaluation of an expression is always at the top of the evaluation stack: `v-st`. Moreover, the elements at the top of `g-st` are the addresses of the effective functions bound to the formal operators of P. The convention adopted here is that identifiers of the compiling procedure are in italic type style whereas generated macrocode is in type-written type style. The procedure *gen* generate a macro-instruction for the abstract machine. All generating procedure can be used as functions. In this case, the value returned is the address of (or a reference to) the beginning of the generated code. In this text, address variables are "logical" variables, because they can be used before having been assigned to. If this happens, these variables are flagged by "^{b}" (for "before").

```
compile (f(e1, ..., en)) =
    compile (e1);                    -- code for evaluating e1
    gen ("m-st.push(v-st.rtop)");    -- the value of e1 will be kept in m-st
    ...;
    compile (en);                    -- code for evaluating en
    gen ("m-st.push(v-st.rtop)");    -- the value of en will be at the top of m-st
    compile_op (f, 0);               -- code for the call of f
    gen ("m-st.pop(n)");             -- code to remove the arguments of f
```

For a stack object `st` the following operations are available in the abstract machine:

`st.push(x)`	push `x` at the top of `st`
`st.top`	return the value of the top of `st`
`st.pop`	remove the top element of `st`
`st.pop(n)`	remove n elements at the top of `st`
`st.rtop`	return `top(st)` and also perform `pop(st)`
`st.elem(n)`	return the element of `st` at offset n from the top. `st.elem(0)` is the same as `st.top`.

The following macro instructions are used in the paper:

`call(f)`	push the address of the next statement onto `r-st` and jump to the address of the beginning of code of `f`.
`fcall(i)`	push the address of the next statement onto `r-st` and jump to the address of `g-st.elem(i)`. Notice that `i` is a constant.
`return`	perform `r-st.rtop` and jump to this address.
`jump_to(a)`	go to the given address `a`.

Fig. 11. Operations of the abstract machine

For example, if f is a function with n parameters the code generation corresponding to the use of the variable x_i in the body of f is:

compile (x_i) = *gen* ("`v-st.push(m-st.elem(`$n-i$`))`");

Now, let us consider the procedure *compile_op* (f, k). k is an integer giving the depth in the g-stack where the binding morphism of the current module $P \xhookrightarrow{r} M$ is. For the call above, the depth is clearly 0. Three cases have to be considered.
1. f is declared in M and is not a formal operator of the required property:

compile_op (f, k) = *gen* ("`call(`f`)`");

2. f is declared in $P \xhookrightarrow{r} M$ and is a formal operator, at rank j in the list of operators. The address of the effective operator is in the g-stack:

compile_op (f, k) = *gen* ("`fcall(`$\#(dyn(P)) - j$`)`");

3. f is declared in the module $P_1 \xhookrightarrow{r_1} M_1$, imported in M: Import_M $(M_1 \xrightarrow{i} M)$.

compile_op (f, k) =
  install_generic_context $(dyn(i \circ r_1), k)$;
  gen ("`call(`f`)`");
  gen ("`g-st.pop(`$\#(dyn(P_1))$`)`"); -- restore the generic context

The installation of the generic context consists in pushing onto the g-stack the addresses of pieces of code performing calls to each effective parameter. So, the first step is to develop the installation for each operator:

install_generic_context $(\{o_1 \mapsto f_1, \ldots, o_l \mapsto f_l\}, k)$ =
  compile_par $(\{o_1 \mapsto f_1\}, k)$;
  ...
  compile_par $(\{o_l \mapsto f_l\}, k)$;

Now, for each binding, two cases occur: either the target operator f_j is an effective operator (in the module M) and then, we have to generate the call to f_j as a thunk and to push the address of this thunk on the g-stack, or the target is a

formal operator in M, say o'_i and then, at run-time, the address of the effective operator bound to o'_i will be already in the g-stack at a given offset from the top. In the first case, the depth of the morphism of the current required property P must be increased by the cardinality of the binding morphism of P_1. These two cases are presented below:
1. The target f_j is effective:

compile_par $(\{o_j \mapsto f_j\}, k) =$
    gen ("jump_to(*link_address*^{b})");
    thunk_address := *compile_op* $(f_j, k + \#(dyn(P_1)))$;
    gen ("return");
    link_address := *gen* ("g-st.push(*thunk_address*)");

2. The target o'_i is formal in M. The address to be fetched is at $\#(dyn(P)) - i$ from the top of g-st of the evaluation context of M. This top is at depth k, and has been modified by the installation of the generic context of the new call. So, the right address depends on the values of k and j, and is computed by the function *fetch*:

compile_par$(\{o_j \mapsto o'_i\}$,k) =
    gen("g-st.push(g-st.elem(*fetch* $(\#(dyn(P)) - i, k, j)$))");

In this paper, we do not develop the proof of correctness of code generation. That can be done by showing that for each ground expression e, the semantics of the evaluation of e is equivalent to the result of evaluation of the compiled code of e with the abstract machine presented here.

The main characteristics of this code generation is that installation of a generic context (parameters in the g-stack) is done only for context changes and not for each call of generic operators as in higher-order functional programming. For example, all the local calls inside a generic module (including recursive calls) have no overhead with respect to non generic calls. In the same way, optimization is possible if there exist several consecutive calls with the same effective generic context, or for calls of operators of imported modules if they have the same list of formal operators as the current module. Last point, this implementation has been carried out successfully for the LPG language. The compilation technique presented here can be applied to languages with generic units if the effective generic context of any module M_1 imported into a module M_2 can be related to the generic context of M_2 (by the morphism $i \circ r_1$).

7 Conclusion

We propose a model inference system to check the validity of instantiation of generic modules. This system is based upon constraints relating whole units. We think these relationships are suitable for modules, whereas other notions such as subtyping or type hierarchies are more adapted to single types. We have shown that the rules of the system are sound with respect to the algebraic semantics of the language. The LPG language allows to instantiate modules either with formal or actual parameters, or both, thus provides partial instantiation at the level of modules. It is possible to define multiple enrichments with consistent sharing of submodules, in spite of renaming possibilities, thanks to a canonical form for types and operators of imported modules. From a practical point of view, all instances of a generic module share the same code, which is interesting for prototyping, specially for highly generic programs with a lot of code reuse.

References

1. *Reference Manual of the Programming Language Ada.* ANSI/MIL-STD 1815A, 1983.
2. M. V. Aponte. Extending record typing to type parametric modules with sharing. In *20th Symposium on Principles of Programming Languages*, 1993.
3. G. Bernot and M. Bidoit. Proving correctness of algebraically specified software: Modularity and observability issues. In *Proceedings of AMAST'91*. Springer-Verlag, 1991.
4. D. Bert and R. Echahed. Design and implementation of a generic, logic and functional programming language. In *Proceedings of ESOP'86*, number 213 in LNCS, pages 119–132. Springer-Verlag, 1986.
5. D. Bert et al. Reference manual of the specification language LPG. Technical Report 59, LIFIA, mars 1990. Anonymous ftp at `imag.fr`, in `/pub/SCOP/LPG/NewSun4/man_lpg.dvi`.
6. M. Bidoit. The stratified loose approach: A generalization of initial and loose semantics. Technical Report 402, Université d'Orsay, France, 1988.
7. C. Choppy. About the "correctness" and "adequacy" of PLUSS specifications. In *Recent Trends in Data Type Specifications*, number 785 in LNCS, pages 128–143. Springer-Verlag, 1992.
8. H. Ehrig and B. Mahr. *Fundamentals of algebraic specification 1. Equations and initial semantics*, volume 6 of *EATCS Monographs on Theoretical Computer Science*. Springer-Verlag, 1985.
9. H. Ehrig and B. Mahr. *Fundamentals of algebraic specification 2. Module Specifications and Constraints*, volume 21 of *EATCS Monographs on Theoretical Computer Science*. Springer-Verlag, 1990.
10. K. Futatsugi, J.A. Goguen, J.-P. Jouannaud, and J. Meseguer. Principles of OBJ2. In *Proc. Principles of Programming Languages*, pages 52–66, 1985.
11. M.-C. Gaudel. A first introduction to PLUSS. Technical report, Université d'Orsay, France, 1984.
12. J.A. Goguen, C. Kirchner, H. Kirchner, A. Mégrelis, J. Meseguer, and T. Winkler. An introduction to OBJ3. In *Proceedings of the 1st International Workshop on Conditional Term Rewriting Systems*, number 308 in LNCS, pages 258–263. Springer-Verlag, 1987.
13. S. B. Lippman. *C++ Primer*. Addison-Wesley, 1992.
14. F. Nourani. On induction for programming logic. *EATCS Bulletin*, 13:51–63, 1981.
15. J.C. Reynaud. Sémantique de LPG. Research Report 651 I IMAG, LIFIA, mars 1987.

Relations as Abstract Datatypes: An Institution to Specify Relations between Algebras *

Hubert Baumeister

Max-Planck-Institut für Informatik
Im Stadtwald, 66123 Saarbrücken, Germany
hubert@mpi-sb.mpg.de

Abstract. One way to view the execution state of an imperative program is as a many sorted algebra. Program variables are (constant) functions and their types are sorts. The execution of a program defines a relation between the state of the program (algebra) before and after the execution of the program. In this paper we shall define an institution for the specification of relations between structures of some base institution (eg. the institution of equational logic or first order predicate logic). Sets of structures over a common signature, abstract datatypes, in this institution denote relations between structures of the base institution. This makes it possible to apply a rich repertoire of existing techniques for specifying abstract datatypes to the specification of relations. This paper tries to narrow the gap between algebraic specification languages like Clear, ASL or Act-One and model theoretic based specification languages like Z, VDM-SL or the Larch Interface language.

1 Introduction

States consisting of variables $x_1 \dots x_n$ of sort $s_1 \dots s_m$ can be seen as algebras over a many sorted signature $\Sigma = \langle S, Op \rangle$ having sorts $S = \{ s_i \mid i = 1 \dots m \}$ and operations $Op = \{ x_i : s_i \mid i = 1 \dots n, s_i \in S \}$, possibly satisfying some state invariants.

As an example consider the specification of a birthday book, taken from the Z reference manual [17]. The goal is to specify a system to record people's birthdays. The state of a birthday book consists of *known*, a set of names of peoples whose birthdays are recorded, and *birthday*, a set of associations of names to dates. The state invariant is that *known* is exactly the set of names occuring as a first component in the elements of *birthday*. Using a notation adapted from Z, the state of a birthday book is described by the specification *Birthdaybook*

* The research described in this paper was supported by the German Ministry for Research and Technology (Bundesministerium für Forschung und Technologie) under grant ITS 9103 and by the ESPRIT Basic Research Working Group 6112 COMPASS (A Comprehensive Algebraic Approach to System Specification and Development).

$$
\begin{array}{|l}
\hline
\textit{Birthdaybook} \\
\textit{Env} \\
\textit{known} : \textit{SETOFNAME} \\
\textit{birthday} : \textit{SETOFBBENTRY} \\
\hline
\forall n : \textit{NAME} \quad n \in \textit{known} \quad \text{iff} \\
\qquad \exists\, \textit{entry} : \textit{BBENTRY} \quad \textit{entry} \in \textit{birthday} \quad \text{and} \quad \textit{name}(\textit{entry}) = n \\
\hline
\end{array}
$$

Birthdaybook is based on the specification *Env*

$$
\begin{array}{|l}
\hline
\textit{Env} \\
\textit{BBEntry} \\
\textit{Set}(\textit{Name})[\textit{SETOFNAME} \leftarrow \textit{SET}] \\
\textit{Set}(\textit{BBEntry})[\textit{SETOFBBENTRY} \leftarrow \textit{SET}] \\
\hline
\end{array}
$$

and *BBEntry*

$$
\begin{array}{|l}
\hline
\textit{BBEntry} \\
\textit{Name}, \textit{Date} \\
\textit{bbEntry} : \textit{NAME} \times \textit{DATE} \rightarrow \textit{BBENTRY} \\
\textit{name} : \textit{BBENTRY} \rightarrow \textit{NAME} \\
\textit{date} : \textit{BBENTRY} \rightarrow \textit{DATE} \\
\hline
\textit{name}(\textit{bbEntry}(n, d)) = n \\
\textit{date}(\textit{bbEntry}(n, d)) = d \\
\hline
\end{array}
$$

and where the specifications *Name* and *Date* merely define the sorts *NAME* and *DATE*. $\textit{Set}(\textit{Name})[\textit{SETOFNAME} \leftarrow \textit{SET}]$ is the notation for the application of the parameterized specification *Set* to the specification *Name* and then renaming the sort *SET* in the result to *SETOFNAME*.[2] Algebras satisfying the *Birthdaybook* specification are possible states of a birthday book.

Operations modifying the state of a system are interpreted as functions on algebras or, more generally, as relations between algebras. For example, the operation *AddBirthday*(*name*: *NAME*; *date*: *DATE*) adds a new entry to the birthday book if the birthday for *name* is not already known. More precisely, $\textit{AddBirthday}(n, d)$ defines, for a name n and a date d, a relation between *Birthdaybook* algebras A and B such that $\textit{known}^B = \textit{known}^A \cup \{n\}$, $\textit{birthday}^B = \textit{birthday}^A \cup \{\textit{bbEntry}^A(n, d)\}$ and such that A and B, when restricted to their environment, the specification *Env*, coincide.

More formally we may define specifications

$$
\begin{array}{|l}
\hline
\textit{AddBirthdayIn} \\
\textit{Birthdaybook} \\
\textit{name?} : \textit{NAME} \\
\textit{date?} : \textit{DATE} \\
\hline
\end{array}
$$

[2] We allow for operations to have the same name, as long as they can be distinguished by their types. For instance the *insert* operations from $\textit{Set}(\textit{Name})[\textit{SETOFNAME} \leftarrow \textit{SET}]$ and $\textit{Set}(\textit{BBEntry})[\textit{SETOFBBENTRY} \leftarrow \textit{SET}]$ are considered different.

and

$$\begin{array}{|l}\hline \textit{AddBirthdayOut} \\ \textit{Birthdaybook} \\ \hline \end{array}$$

and consider *AddBirthday* as a relation between *AddBirthdayIn* algebras A and *AddBirthdayOut* algebras B satisfying $A|_{Env} = B|_{Env}$ and the equations

$$known^B = known^A \cup \{name?^A\} \quad \text{and}$$

$$birthday^B = birthday^A \cup \{bbEntry^A(name?^A, date?^A)\}.$$

The additional constants *name*? and *date*? in *AddBirthdayIn* model the input parameters of the operation *AddBirthday*. In case *AddBirthday* is supposed to deliver a result $x!$ of sort s, a constant $x! : s$ is added to *AddBirthdayOut*. Next we observe that A and B can be extended to an algebra C, a model of

$$\begin{array}{|l}\hline \textit{AddBirthday} \\ \textit{AddBirthdayIn} \\ \textit{AddBirthdayOut}[known' \leftarrow known, birthday' \leftarrow birthday] \\ \hline name? \notin known \\ birthday' = insert(bbEntry(name?, date?), birthday) \\ \hline \end{array}$$

such that

$$C|_{AddBirthdayIn} = A \quad \text{and} \quad C|_{AddBirthdayOut} = B.$$

Note, that there is no need to include an axiom of the form

$$known' = insert(name?, known)$$

explicitly in *AddBirthday* because this is a consequence of the axiom

$$birthday' = insert(bbEntry(name?, date?), birthday)$$

together with the axioms of *Birthdaybook*.

On the other hand, the specification *AddBirthday* defines a relation R between states of birthday book (models of *Birthdaybook*) by

$$A \; R \; B \quad \text{iff} \quad \exists\, C \quad C \models AddBirthday, \; C|_\iota = A \quad \text{and} \quad C|_\sigma = B,$$

where ι is the inclusion of *Birthdaybook* into *AddBirthday* and σ is a morphism from *Birthdaybook* to *AddBirthday* mapping *known* to *known'* and *birthday* to *birthday'*. Therefore, relations between algebras can be regarded as sets of algebras specified using standard abstract datatypes techniques.

In the rest of this paper we shall define an institution $\mathcal{R}_{\mathbf{D}}$ over some base institution $\mathcal{I}$ such that sets of formulas in this institution denote relations between structures from $\mathcal{I}$, which formally are abstract datatypes in the institution $\mathcal{R}_{\mathbf{D}}$. Abstract datatypes are pairs $\langle \Sigma, M \rangle$, where Σ is a signature and M a set of Σ-structures. We shall show that this institution inherits some nice properties from its base institution, like for example a cocomplete category of signatures and amalgamation, which implies extension.

2 Preliminaries

2.1 Institutions

The notion of an institution was introduced by Goguen and Burstall to define the semantics of the specification language Clear [3] independent of an underlying logic. Here we will only recall the definition of institutions, for more details see the paper by Goguen and Burstall [10]. An institution $\mathcal{I} = \langle SIGN, Mod, Sen, \models\rangle$ consists of

- a category of *signatures* $SIGN$,
- a functor $Mod: SIGN \to CAT^{op}$ assigning to each signature Σ the category of Σ-structures and to each signature morphism $\sigma: \Sigma \to \Sigma'$ a forgetful functor $Mod(\sigma): Mod(\Sigma') \to Mod(\Sigma)$,[3]
- a functor $Sen: SIGN \to SET$, assigning to each signature Σ the set of Σ-*formulas* and to each signature morphism $\sigma: \Sigma \to \Sigma'$ a translation $Sen(\sigma)$ of Σ-formulas to Σ'-formulas,[4] and
- a family of *satisfaction relations* $(\models_\Sigma \subseteq Mod(\Sigma) \times Sen(\Sigma))_{\Sigma \in SIGN}$ indicating whether a Σ-formula f is valid in a Σ-structure m ($m \models_\Sigma f$ or for short $m \models f$)

where the *satisfaction condition* holds: for all signature morphisms $\sigma: \Sigma \to \Sigma'$, formulas $f \in Sen(\Sigma)$ and structures $m' \in Mod(\Sigma')$

$$m'|_\sigma \models f \quad \text{iff} \quad \mathrm{m}' \models \sigma(\mathrm{f})$$

Each institution has associated two categories $PRES_\mathcal{I}$ and $ADT_\mathcal{I}$. The objects of $PRES_\mathcal{I}$ are pairs $\langle \Sigma, F\rangle$ where Σ is a signature from $SIGN$ and F a set of Σ-formulas. Morphisms $\sigma: \langle \Sigma, F\rangle \to \langle \Sigma', F'\rangle$ in $PRES_\mathcal{I}$ are signature morphisms such that $F' \models \sigma(F)$. In $ADT_\mathcal{I}$ objects are pairs $\langle \Sigma, M\rangle$ where M is a set of Σ-structures and morphisms $\sigma: \langle \Sigma, M\rangle \to \langle \Sigma', M'\rangle$ are signature morphisms such that $M'|_\sigma \subseteq M$. There are also forgetful functors $Sig^p: PRES_\mathcal{I} \to SIGN$ and $Sig^a: ADT_\mathcal{I} \to SIGN$ defined by

$$Sig^p(\langle \Sigma, F\rangle) = Sig^a(\langle \Sigma, M\rangle) = \Sigma \quad \text{and} \quad Sig^p(\sigma) = Sig^a(\sigma) = \sigma$$

It is known (eg. [15, 2]) that the functors Sig^p and Sig^a create (finite) (co)limits and that as a consequence $PRES_\mathcal{I}$ and $ADT_\mathcal{I}$ are (finitely) (co)complete if the category of signatures $SIGN$ is.

Objects in $PRES_\mathcal{I}$ can be thought of as *specifying* or *presenting* objects in $ADT_\mathcal{I}$, which are called *abstract datatypes*. Thus, there is a semantics function $sem: PRES_\mathcal{I} \to ADT_\mathcal{I}$ associating to a presentation $\langle \Sigma, F\rangle$ an abstract datatype $\langle \Sigma', M'\rangle$. Two commonly used semantic functions are *loose* and *initial*, where

$$loose(\langle \Sigma, F\rangle) = \langle \Sigma, \{\, m \in Mod(\Sigma) \mid m \models F \,\}\rangle$$

and $initial(\langle \Sigma, F\rangle) = \langle \Sigma, M\rangle$ with M the set of all objects that are initial in the full subcategory of $Mod(\Sigma)$ whose objects satisfy F.

[3] The application of $Mod(\sigma)$ to a Σ'-structure m' will be written as $m'|_\sigma$. If σ is understood from the the context we may write $m'|_\Sigma$ instead.

[4] The application of $Sen(\sigma)$ to a formula f will be abbreviated by $\sigma(f)$.

2.2 Limits and Colimits

This section defines the notations used in this paper for limits and colimits in categories. For a definition of limits and colimits refer, for example, to the book of MacLane [14].

We use the notation $\prod_{\mathbf{I}} F$ to denote the limit object of the functor $F: \mathbf{I} \to \mathbf{C}$, if it exists, and π_i^F, or π_i if there is no ambiguity, for the projections $\pi_i^F: \prod_{\mathbf{I}} F \to F(i)$. If $G: \mathbf{I} \to \mathbf{C}$ is another functor with a limit and $\tau: F \Rightarrow G$ is a natural transformation, then $\prod_{\mathbf{I}} \tau$ denotes the unique morphism from the limit object $\prod_{\mathbf{I}} F$ to the limit object $\prod_{\mathbf{I}} G$ such that for all $i \in \mathbf{I}$ the following diagram commutes

$$\begin{array}{ccc} \prod_{\mathbf{I}} F & \xrightarrow{\prod_{\mathbf{I}} \tau} & \prod_{\mathbf{I}} G \\ {\scriptstyle \pi_i^F} \downarrow & & \downarrow {\scriptstyle \pi_i^G} \\ F(i) & \xrightarrow[\tau_i]{} & G(i) \end{array}$$

The colimit object of a functor $F: \mathbf{I} \to \mathbf{C}$ is denoted by $\sum_{\mathbf{I}} F$ and ι_i^F, or ι_i, denotes the inclusions $\iota_i^F: F(i) \to \sum_{\mathbf{I}} F$. If $G: \mathbf{I} \to \mathbf{C}$ is another functor with a colimit and $\tau: F \Rightarrow G$ is a natural transformation, then $\sum_{\mathbf{I}} \tau$ denotes the unique morphism from the colimit object $\sum_{\mathbf{I}} F$ to the colimit object $\sum_{\mathbf{I}} G$ such that for all $i \in \mathbf{I}$ the following diagram commutes

$$\begin{array}{ccc} \sum_{\mathbf{I}} F & \xrightarrow{\sum_{\mathbf{I}} \tau} & \sum_{\mathbf{I}} G \\ {\scriptstyle \iota_i^F} \uparrow & & \uparrow {\scriptstyle \iota_i^G} \\ F(i) & \xrightarrow[\tau_i]{} & G(i) \end{array}$$

3 Binary Relations

Before presenting the general construction in section 4 we shall illustrate the construction using binary relations. Let us assume we are given an institution $\mathcal{I} = \langle SIGN, Mod, Sen, \models \rangle$ and let $\Theta = \langle \Sigma_1, \Sigma_2 \rangle$ be a pair of signatures from $SIGN$. A (binary) relation R of type Θ is a subset M of the cartesian product of $Mod(\Sigma_1)$ and $Mod(\Sigma_2)$. A morphism $\alpha: R \to S$ from a relation R of type Θ^R to a relation S of type Θ^S is a pair of signature morphisms $\alpha_1: \Sigma_1^R \to \Sigma_1^S$ and $\alpha_2: \Sigma_2^R \to \Sigma_2^S$ such that whenever $m_1 \; S \; m_2$ then $m_1|_{\alpha_1} \; R \; m_2|_{\alpha_2}$. The category REL of binary relations has relations as objects and morphisms between relations as arrows.

To specify objects from REL we need to define a notion of formulas together with a satisfaction relation between formulas and elements of the cartesian product of $Mod(\Sigma_1)$ and $Mod(\Sigma_2)$. A possible definition of such formulas is as elements of the disjoint union of $Sen(\Sigma_1)$ and $Sen(\Sigma_2)$. Then for a pair $\langle m_1, m_2 \rangle$ of $Mod(\Sigma_1) \times Mod(\Sigma_2)$ and a formula f of $Sen(\Sigma_1) + Sen(\Sigma_2)$ we define

$$\langle m_1, m_2 \rangle \models^{REL} f \quad \text{iff} \quad \begin{cases} m_1 \models f \text{ if } f \in Sen(\Sigma_1) \\ m_2 \models f \text{ if } f \in Sen(\Sigma_2) \end{cases}$$

However, with this definition it is not possible to write a formula similar to

$$birthday' = insert(bbEntry(name?, date?), birthday)$$

from the *AddBirthday* example because this formula is neither a formula over the signature of *AddBirthdayIn* nor a formula over the signature of *AddBirthdayOut*, instead, it is a formula over the disjoint union of the signatures of *AddBirthdayIn* and *AddBirthdayOut*.

Therefore, we are interested in formulas f from $Scn(\Sigma_1 + \Sigma_2)$. Now we have the problem to define the satisfaction relation between pairs $\langle m_1, m_2 \rangle$ and formulas f. In the institution of first order logic, and many other interesting institutions, there is a one to one correspondence between pairs of algebras from $Mod(\Sigma_1) \times Mod(\Sigma_2)$ and algebras from $Mod(\Sigma_1 + \Sigma_2)$. A $\Sigma_1 + \Sigma_2$-algebra m defines a pair of Σ_1- and Σ_2-algebras by $\langle m|_{\Sigma_1}, m|_{\Sigma_2} \rangle$ and each pair $\langle m_1, m_2 \rangle$ defines an algebra $m_1 + m_2$ such that the interpretation of a symbol s (a sort, function or predicate symbol) from $\Sigma_1 + \Sigma_2$ in $m_1 + m_2$ is the interpretation of s in m_1 if s originates from Σ_1 or the interpretation of s in m_2 otherwise. This makes it possible to define

$$\langle m_1, m_2 \rangle \models^{REL} f \quad \text{iff} \quad m_1 + m_2 \models f.$$

Given a set of formulas F from $Sen(\Sigma_1 + \Sigma_2)$ a pair $Sp = \langle \Theta, F \rangle$ defines a relation by

$$m_1 \; Sp \; m_2 \quad \text{iff} \quad \forall f \in F : \langle m_1, m_2 \rangle \models^{REL} f.$$

The category of specifications of binary relations, *RELSPEC*, has as objects pairs $Sp = \langle \Theta, F \rangle$ and as arrows $\alpha: Sp_R \to Sp_S$ signature morphisms $\alpha: \Sigma_1^R + \Sigma_2^R \to \Sigma_1^S + \Sigma_2^S$ such that $F^S \models^{REL} \alpha(F^R)$.

There is a functor *Rel* from *RELSPEC* to *REL* mapping specifications of binary relations to binary relations defined by

$$Rel(\langle \Theta, F \rangle) = \langle \Theta, \{ \langle m_1, m_2 \rangle \mid \langle m_1, m_2 \rangle \models^{REL} F \} \rangle \quad \text{and}$$

$$Rel(\alpha: Sp_R \to Sp_S) = \alpha: Rel(Sp_R) \to Rel(Sp_S).$$

The domain of a binary relation $R = \langle \Theta, M \rangle$ in *REL* is given by

$$dom(R) = \{ m_1 \mid \langle m_1, m_2 \rangle \in M \}$$

and its codomain by

$$cod(R) = \{ m_2 \mid \langle m_1, m_2 \rangle \in M \}.$$

3.1 Binary Relations as Abstract Datatypes

In this section we shall define an institution $\mathcal{R}_2$ such that the category of abstract datatypes[5] ADT_2 (cf. section 2.1) in this institution is the category of binary relations REL and the category of presentations $PRES_2$ is the category of specifications of binary relations $RELSPEC$. The construction of $\mathcal{R}_2$ is parameterized by an institution $\mathcal{I}$. To define the satisfaction relation of $\mathcal{R}_2$ we require that $SIGN$ has coproducts and that Mod preserves them. Now the institution

$$\mathcal{R}_2 = \langle RSIGN2, RMod2, RSen2, \models^{\mathcal{R}_2} \rangle$$

is given by:

$$RSIGN2 = SIGN^{\mathbf{2}},$$

$$RMod2(\Theta: \mathbf{2} \to SIGN) = \prod_{\mathbf{2}} \Theta; Mod \qquad RMod2(\alpha: \Theta^R \Rightarrow \Theta^S) = \prod_{\mathbf{2}} \alpha; Mod$$

$$RSen2(\Theta) = Sen(\sum_{\mathbf{2}} \Theta) \qquad RSen2(\alpha) = Sen(\sum_{\mathbf{2}} \alpha)$$

$$m \models^{\mathcal{R}_2} f \quad \text{iff} \quad m \models f$$

The category $\mathbf{2}$ is the discrete category having only 1 and 2 as objects and the identities as arrows.

Objects in ADT_2 are pairs $R = \langle \Theta, M \rangle$, where Θ is an element of $RSIGN2$ and M is a subset of $RMod2(\Theta)$. Θ is a functor from $\mathbf{2}$ to $SIGN$ and thus, a pair of signatures $\langle \Theta(1), \Theta(2) \rangle$ from $SIGN \times SIGN$. Since $RMod2(\Theta)$ is $Mod(\Theta(1)) \times Mod(\Theta(2))$, elements of $M \subseteq RMod2(\Theta)$ are pairs $\langle m_1, m_2 \rangle$.

An arrow $\alpha: \Theta^R \Rightarrow \Theta^S$ in $RSIGN2$ is a natural transformation between functors from $\mathbf{2}$ to $SIGN$ and thus, just a pair of signature morphisms α_i from $\Theta^R(i)$ to $\Theta^S(i)$ $(i = 1, 2)$. The application of $RMod2$ to an arrow α of $RSIGN2$ yields the pair of functors $\langle Mod(\alpha_1), Mod(\alpha_2) \rangle$.

Thus an arrow $\alpha: \langle \Theta^R, M^R \rangle \to \langle \Theta^S, M^S \rangle$ in ADT_2 is a morphism α from Θ^R to Θ^S in $RSIGN2$ such that $\langle m_1|_{\alpha_1}, m_2|_{\alpha_2} \rangle \in M^R$ for all $\langle m_1, m_2 \rangle \in M^S$ or, whenever $m_1 \; S \; m_2$ then $m_1|_{\alpha_1} \; R \; m_2|_{\alpha_2}$.

Since $SIGN$ has coproducts, the object $\sum_{\mathbf{2}} \Theta = \Theta(1) + \Theta(2)$ exists for any object Θ in $RSIGN2$. Moreover, since Mod preserves coproducts

$$Mod(\Theta(1) + \Theta(2)) = Mod(\Theta(1)) \times Mod(\Theta(2)) = RMod2(\Theta).$$

Therefore each m in $RMod2(\Theta)$ is also in $Mod(\Theta(1) + \Theta(2))$ and each formula f in $RSen2(\Theta)$ is an element of $Sen(\Theta(1) + \Theta(2))$. Thus the satisfaction relation $m \models^{\mathcal{R}_2} f$ iff $m \models f$ is well defined.

[5] To avoid subscripts of subscripts we write ADT_2 instead of $ADT_{\mathcal{R}_2}$.

4 An Institution to Specify Relations Between Algebras

The institution $\mathcal{R}_\mathbf{2}$ is based on the discrete category $\mathbf{2}$. However, the construction of $\mathcal{R}_\mathbf{2}$ did not depend on the specific properties of $\mathbf{2}$. In fact, the same construction can be used to define an institution

$$\mathcal{R}_\mathbf{D} = \langle RSIGND, RModD, RSenD, \models^{\mathcal{R}_D} \rangle$$

based on an arbitrary category $\mathbf{D}$, provided that *SIGN* is cocomplete with respect to diagrams of shape $\mathbf{D}$ and that *Mod* preserves the colimit of diagrams of shape $\mathbf{D}$:

$$RSIGND = SIGN^{\mathbf{D}}$$

$$RModD(\Theta : \mathbf{D} \to SIGN) = \prod_{\mathbf{D}} \Theta; Mod \qquad RModD(\alpha : \Theta^R \Rightarrow \Theta^S) = \prod_{\mathbf{D}} \alpha; Mod$$

$$RSenD(\Theta) = Sen(\sum_{\mathbf{D}} \Theta) \qquad RSenD(\alpha) = Sen(\sum_{\mathbf{D}} \alpha)$$

$$m \models^{\mathcal{R}_D} f \quad \text{iff} \quad m \models f$$

The following easy facts hold:

- $\mathcal{R}_\mathbf{D}$ is an institution,
- *RSIGND* is (finitely) cocomplete if *SIGN* is and
- *RModD* preserves (finite) colimits if *Mod* preserves them.

Objects in $ADT_\mathbf{D}$ are typed relations of arity $\mathbf{D}$. Let, for example, $\mathbf{D}$ be the discrete category $\mathbf{K}_n$ generated by the set $\{1, \ldots, n\}$. An object Θ of $RSIGNK_n$ is an n-tuple $\Sigma_1, \ldots, \Sigma_n$ of signatures from *SIGN* and objects in $RModK_n(\Theta)$ are n-tuples $m_1, \ldots, m_n$ such that $m_i \in Mod(\Sigma_i)$. Thus an object $R = \langle \Theta, M \rangle$ in $ADT_{\mathbf{K}_n}$ is an n-ary relation $R \subseteq Mod(\Sigma_1) \times \ldots \times Mod(\Sigma_n)$.

Now let $\mathbf{D}$ have an arrow $g: d \to d'$ other than the identity. Together with signatures $\Theta(d) = \Sigma_d$ and $\Theta(d') = \Sigma_{d'}$ objects Θ in *RSIGND* also provide a signature morphism $\Theta(g) = \sigma: \Sigma_d \to \Sigma_{d'}$. This imposes on objects m from $RModD(\Theta)$ the restriction that

$$\pi_{d'}(m)|_\sigma = m_{d'}|_\sigma = m_d = \pi_d(m)$$

5 Relations with Shared Parts

We are interested in binary relations R, such that, if $m_1 \; R \; m_2$ then m_1 and m_2 are persistent extensions of some algebra, like an algebra providing some base types such as *bool* and *nat*. This type of relation can be modeled by a three place relation R given by a set $M \subseteq Mod(\Sigma_1) \times Mod(\Sigma_0) \times Mod(\Sigma_2)$ with the requirement that for all $\langle m_1, m_0, m_2 \rangle$ from M

$$m_1|_{\sigma_1} = m_0 = m_2|_{\sigma_2},$$

where $\sigma_i: \Sigma_0 \to \Sigma_i$ $(i = 1, 2)$ define the parts that Σ_1 and Σ_2 have in common.

The type of R is given by a functor Θ from $\mathbf{3}$ to $SIGN$, where $\mathbf{3}$ is the category freely generated by the diagram

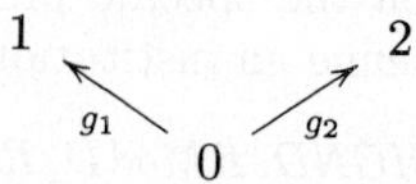

such that $\Theta(1) = \Sigma_1$, $\Theta(0) = \Sigma_0$, $\Theta(2) = \Sigma_2$, $\Theta(g_1) = \sigma_1$ and $\Theta(g_2) = \sigma_2$. The set M is a subset of the objects of the pullback $\prod_{\mathbf{3}} \Theta; Mod$ of the following diagram in CAT

$$\begin{array}{ccccc} & & \prod_{\mathbf{3}} \Theta; Mod & & \\ & \swarrow^{\pi_1} & \downarrow^{\pi_0} & \searrow^{\pi_2} & \\ Mod(\Theta(1)) & & & & Mod(\Theta(2)) \\ & \searrow_{Mod(\sigma_1)} & & \swarrow_{Mod(\sigma_2)} & \\ & & Mod(\Theta(0)) & & \end{array}$$

Since the above diagram commutes in CAT, for any object m and morphism $h: m \to m'$ in $\prod_{\mathbf{3}} \Sigma; Mod$ we have

$$\pi_1(m)|_{\sigma_1} = m_1|_{\sigma_1} = m_0 = m_2|_{\sigma_2} = \pi_2(m)|_{\sigma_2} \quad \text{and}$$

$$\pi_1(h)|_{\sigma_1} = h_1|_{\sigma_1} = h_0 = h_2|_{\sigma_2} = \pi_2(h)|_{\sigma_2}.$$

For objects $R = \langle \Theta, M \rangle$ in the category of abstract datatypes of the institution $\mathcal{R}_{\mathbf{3}}$ we define

$$m_1 \; R \; m_2 \quad \text{iff} \quad \exists\, m \in M : \pi_1(m) = m_1 \text{ and } \pi_2(m) = m_2$$

which gives us that whenever $m_1 \; R \; m_2$ then $m_1|_{\Theta(g_1)} = m_2|_{\Theta(g_2)}$.

Formulas in $RSen3(\Theta)$ are formulas over the pushout $\sum_{\mathbf{3}} \Theta$ of the following diagram in $SIGN$

$$\begin{array}{ccccc} & & \sum_{\mathbf{3}} \Theta & & \\ & \nearrow^{\iota_1} & & \nwarrow^{\iota_2} & \\ \Theta(1) & & \text{po} & & \Theta(2) \\ & \nwarrow_{\Theta(g_1)} & & \nearrow_{\Theta(g_2)} & \\ & & \Theta(0) & & \end{array}$$

Here we have to require that $SIGN$ has all pushouts and that Mod preserves them, which is equivalent for the institution $\mathcal{I}$ to have amalgamation [7, 2, 5].

As an example the *AddBirthday* specification is given as an object of $PRES_{\mathbf{3}}$ for first oder logic with equality as the base institution. The following functor $\Theta: \mathbf{3} \to SIGN$ is the signature of *AddBirthday*:

$$
\begin{array}{lll}
\Theta(0) & = \textbf{sorts} & \mathit{NAME}, \mathit{DATE}, \mathit{BBENTRY}, \\
& & \mathit{SETOFNAME}, \mathit{SETOFBBENTRY} \\
& \quad\textbf{ops} & \mathit{bbentry}\colon \mathit{NAME} \times \mathit{DATE} \to \mathit{BBENTRY} \\
& & \mathit{name}\colon \mathit{BBENTRY} \to \mathit{NAME} \\
& & \mathit{date}\colon \mathit{BBENTRY} \to \mathit{DATE} \\
& & \mathit{insert}\colon \mathit{NAME} \times \mathit{SETOFNAME} \to \mathit{SETOFNAME} \\
& & \mathit{insert}\colon \mathit{NAME} \times \mathit{SETOFBBENTRY} \to \mathit{SETOFBBENTRY} \\
& & \ldots \\
\Theta(1) & = \Theta(0) + & \\
& \quad\textbf{ops} & \mathit{known} : \mathit{SETOFNAME} \\
& & \mathit{birthday} : \mathit{SETOFBBENTRY} \\
& & \mathit{name?} : \mathit{NAME} \\
& & \mathit{date?} : \mathit{DATE} \\
\Theta(2) & = \Theta(0) + & \\
& \quad\textbf{ops} & \mathit{known} : \mathit{SETOFNAME} \\
& & \mathit{birthday} : \mathit{SETOFBBENTRY} \\
\sum_{\mathbf{3}} \Theta & = \Theta(0) + & \\
& \quad\textbf{ops} & \mathit{known} : \mathit{SETOFNAME} \\
& & \mathit{birthday} : \mathit{SETOFBBENTRY} \\
& & \mathit{known}' : \mathit{SETOFNAME} \\
& & \mathit{birthday}' : \mathit{SETOFBBENTRY} \\
& & \mathit{name?} : \mathit{NAME} \\
& & \mathit{date?} : \mathit{DATE}
\end{array}
$$

$\Theta(g_1)$, $\Theta(g_2)$ and ι_1 are the corresponding inclusion of signatures and ι_2 maps *birthday* to *birthday'* and *known* to *known'* and is the identity on all other symbols. The axioms of *AddBirthday* are formulas in $RSen3(\Theta) = Sen(\sum_{\mathbf{3}} \Theta)$:

$$
\begin{array}{l}
\mathit{name}(\mathit{bbEntry}(n, d)) = n \\
\mathit{date}(\mathit{bbEntry}(n, d)) = d \\
\ldots \text{ (all the axioms for } \mathit{Set}(\mathit{Name}) \text{ and } \mathit{Set}(\mathit{BBEntry})) \\
\forall\, n : \mathit{NAME} \quad n \in \mathit{known} \quad \text{iff} \\
\qquad\qquad \exists\, \mathit{entry} : \mathit{BBENTRY} \quad \mathit{entry} \in \mathit{birthday} \quad \text{and} \quad \mathit{name}(\mathit{entry}) = n \\
\forall\, n : \mathit{NAME} \quad n \in \mathit{known}' \quad \text{iff} \\
\qquad\qquad \exists\, \mathit{entry} : \mathit{BBENTRY} \quad \mathit{entry} \in \mathit{birthday}' \quad \text{and} \quad \mathit{name}(\mathit{entry}) = n \\
\mathit{name?} \notin \mathit{known} \\
\mathit{birthday}' = \mathit{insert}(\mathit{bbEntry}(\mathit{name?}, \mathit{date?}), \mathit{birthday})
\end{array}
$$

For an algebra m of $RMod3(\Theta)$ satisfying *AddBirthday* it holds that, among others,

$$\mathit{birthday}'^{m} = \mathit{insert}^{m}(\mathit{bbEntry}^{m}(\mathit{name?}^{m}, \mathit{date?}^{m}), \mathit{birthday}^{m}).$$

Since m is a persistent extension of m_1 and m_2, which in turn are persistent extensions of m_0, this is equivalent to

$$\mathit{birthday}^{m_2} = \mathit{insert}^{m_0}(\mathit{bbEntry}^{m_0}(\mathit{name?}^{m_1}, \mathit{date?}^{m_1}), \mathit{birthday}^{m_1}).$$

When writing specifications of relations it is convenient to use instead of functors $\Theta\colon \mathbf{D} \to \mathit{SIGN}$ functors $\Theta\colon \mathbf{D} \to \mathit{PRES}_{\mathcal{I}}$ as the type of relations. We have done this in section 1, where we gave *AddBirthdayIn*, *Env* and *AddBirthdayOut* as specifications instead of just giving their signatures and including their axioms (eg. the axioms for the environment or the state invariant of *BirthdayBook*) in the set of formulas defining *AddBirthday*, as we have done in this section. This can be achieved by using the institution $\mathcal{PI} = \langle PRES_{\mathcal{I}}, PMod, Sig^p; Sen, \models \rangle$ built from an institution $\mathcal{I}$ as the base institution of $\mathcal{R}_{\mathbf{D}}$ instead of $\mathcal{I}$ itself. Here $PMod(\langle \Theta, F \rangle)$ yields the full subcategory of $Mod(\Theta)$ whose objects satisfy F.

6 Specifications with Auxiliary Symbols

In some cases we would like to use auxiliary sort or function symbols in the specification of relations. For example let $\Theta(1)$ and $\Theta(2)$ be enrichments of $\Theta(0)$ by a new sort s. To define how the interpretation of sort s in m_1 is related to the interpretation of sort s in m_2 an auxiliary function $f: \iota_1(s) \to \iota_2(s)$ may be needed. For example to require that s^{m_1} is isomorphic to a subset of s^{m_2} we provide the formula $\forall x, y : f(x) = f(y) \Rightarrow x = y$. However, this formula can not be written in any of the institutions $\mathcal{R}_{\mathbf{2}}$ and $\mathcal{R}_{\mathbf{3}}$ because formulas in these institutions are only allowed to use the symbols from $\Theta(1)$ and $\Theta(2)$.

A solution to this problem is to use $\mathcal{R}_{\mathbf{4}}$, where $\mathbf{4}$ is the category freely generated by

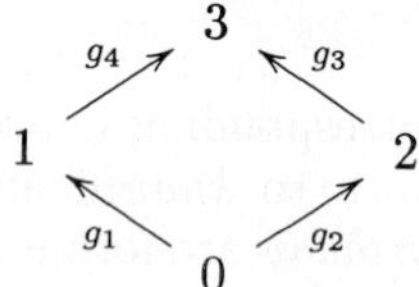

and the equation $g_1; g_4 = g_2; g_3$. Now the function $f: \iota_1(s) \to \iota_2(s)$ can be defined in $\Theta(3)$. It is easy to prove that for a functor $\Theta: \mathbf{4} \to SIGN$ from $RSIGN4$ the colimit $\sum_{\mathbf{4}} \Theta$ is isomorphic to $\Theta(3)$. This holds for any category $\mathbf{D}$ with a terminal object $d_\top$. Thus by providing $\Theta(3)$ one defines exactly the symbols one can use in the specification of relations. Most likely $\Theta(3)$ will be an extension of the pushout of $\Theta(g_1)$ and $\Theta(g_2)$ by auxiliary sort and function symbols, but it is also possible that $\Theta(3)$, $\Theta(1)$ and $\Theta(2)$ coincide.

Objects $Sp = \langle \Theta, F \rangle$ in $PRES_{\mathbf{4}}$ define binary relations by

$$m_1 \; Sp \; m_2 \quad \text{iff} \quad \exists\, m \models^{\mathcal{R}_4} F : \pi_1(m) = m_1 \text{ and } \pi_2(m) = m_2.$$

6.1 Composition of Binary Relations

Using $\mathcal{R}_{\mathbf{4}}$ has also the advantage that $PRES_{\mathbf{4}}$ is closed under the composition of binary relations. If Sp_R and Sp_S are viewed as binary relations and $Sp_R; Sp_S$ is defined in the usual set theoretic way then there exists an object Sp_T of $PRES_{\mathbf{4}}$ defining the same binary relation as $Sp_R; Sp_S$. This, depending on the expressiveness of the base institution $\mathcal{I}$, does not hold, in general, for the composition of relations in $PRES_{\mathbf{2/3}}$ (see below).

Let $Sp_R = \langle\Theta^R, F^R\rangle$ and $Sp_S = \langle\Theta^S, F^S\rangle$ be specifications in *PRES*$_\mathbf{4}$. If $\Theta^R(g_2) = \Theta^S(g_1)$ then the composition $Sp_R; Sp_S = \langle\Theta^T, F^T\rangle$ is defined. The type of $Sp_R; Sp_S$ is given by the following diagram in *SIGN*

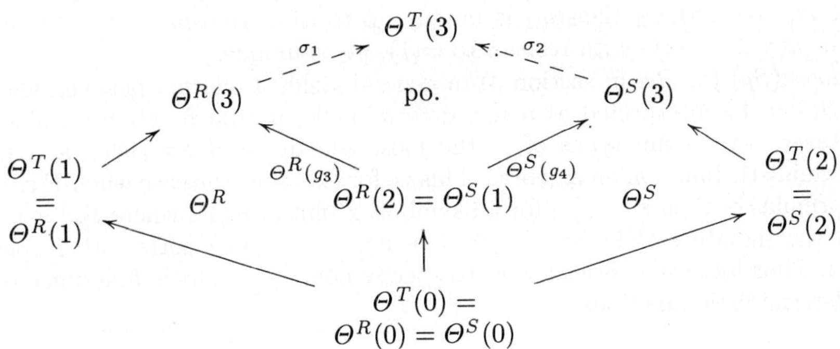

and $F^T = \sigma_1(F^R) \cup \sigma_2(F^S)$.

Theorem. $m_1\ Sp_R; Sp_S\ m_2$ iff $\exists\, n : m_1\ Sp_R\ n$ and $n\ Sp_S\ m_2$

As an example consider the specifications Sp_R and Sp_S such that $\Theta^R(g_2) = \Theta^S(g_1)$ and $\Theta^R(1) = \Theta^S(1) = \Theta^S(2)$ is an enrichment of $\Theta(0)$ by a constant $x : s$. Let F^R contain the formula $x = f(x')$ and F^S the formula $x'' = g(x')$, where f and g are functions defined in $\Theta^R(0)$. For $Sp_R; Sp_S = \langle\Theta^T, F^T\rangle$ as an object of *PRES*$_\mathbf{4}$ the type Θ^T contains the auxiliary symbol $x' : s$ in $\Theta^T(3)$ together with $x : s$ from $\Theta^T(1) = \Theta^R(1)$ and $x'' : s$ from $\Theta^T(2) = \Theta^S(2)$ and F^T equals $\{x = f(x'), x'' = g(x')\}$.

However, to define $Sp_R; Sp_S = \langle\Theta^T, F^T\rangle$ in *PRES*$_\mathbf{3}$ we do not have the possibility to use the auxiliary symbol $x' : s$, therefore we have to find a set of formulas equivalent to the conjunction of $x = f(x')$ and $x'' = g(x')$ only using the symbols x, x'', f and g. Provided that the base institution $\mathcal{I}$ allows to use existential quantifiers we can use $\{\exists\, x' : x = f(x') \wedge x'' = g(x')\}$. In general, it may not be possible to find such a set of formulas.

7 Semantics

Which relation $\langle\Theta, M\rangle$ from ADT_i is denoted by the presentation $\langle\Theta, F\rangle$ in *PRES*$_i$ ($i = \mathbf{2}, \mathbf{3}, \mathbf{4}$)? This is a question about the semantics function

$$sem\colon PRES_i \to ADT_i.$$

Common semantics are *initial* and *loose* from section 2. However, *initial* is not appropriate since all models of *initial*(*Sp*) are isomorphic, and thus, if m_1 *initial*(*Sp*) m_2 and m_1' *initial*(*Sp*) m_2', then m_1 is isomorphic to m_1' and m_2 is isomorphic to m_2'.

Another possible semantics is *free*. If *free*($\langle\Theta, F\rangle$) $= \langle\Theta, M\rangle$ then structures m in M are required to be free extensions of $m|_{\iota_1}$ (or $m|_{\Theta(g_4)}$ in case of $\mathcal{R}_4$) with respect to the full subcategory of $Mod(\sum_i \Theta)$ ($i = \mathbf{2}, \mathbf{3}, \mathbf{4}$) given by $\{ m \mid m \models F \}$ (cf. Goguen and Burstall [10] and Baumeister [2]). *free*(Sp) can be considered as denoting a partial function from structures of $Mod(\Theta(1))$ to structures of $Mod(\Theta(2))$ in the sense that, if for some m_1 there exists m_2 such that m_1 *free*(Sp) m_2 then m_2 is unique up to isomorphism. If $\sum_i \Theta$ does not define any new sorts with respect to $\Theta(1)$, m_2 is unique.

loose(Sp) (or *Rel* in section 3) in general yields a relation between algebras which can be interpreted as a non-deterministic, partial function on algebras. However, for certain types of F the loose semantics of Sp yields a (partial) deterministic function on algebras. This is, for example, the case when F consists of formulas of type $x' = t[x]$ for all symbols x' not in $\Theta(1)$, where $t[x]$ is a term over the signature $\Theta(1)$, and $\sum_i \Theta$ does not contain new sorts with respect to $\Theta(1)$. Thus loose semantics allows to specify non deterministic functions as well as deterministic functions.

8 Related Work

It is not new or surprising to view states as algebras. For example, Ganzinger [9] and Gurevich [11] use this view to define an algebraic semantics of programming languages. Ganzinger defines the semantics of while-programs to be the composition of a free functor and a forgetful functor on algebras representing the state of the program. In principle we have three specifications. $Spec_{base}$ is the specification of some base types defining the domain over which the variables range. $Spec_X$ is a conservative extension of $Spec_{base}$ containing constants of the form $x : s$ denoting the variables of the program. Each program p determines a specification $Spec^p_{X \cup X'}$, which is an enrichment of $Spec_X$ that contains for each $x : s$ in $Spec_X$ a constant $x' : s$ and contains for example in the case where p is the assignment statement $x := t$ the formula $x' = t$. The semantics of a program p is given by T_p; U_σ, where $T_p\colon Alg(Spec_X) \to Alg(Spec^p_{X \cup X'})$ is the left adjoint to the forgetful functor U with respect to the inclusion of $Spec_X$ in $Spec^p_{X \cup X'}$ and $U_\sigma\colon Alg(Spec^p_{X \cup X'}) \to Alg(Spec_X)$ is the forgetful functor for the signature morphism σ that takes each $x : s$ in $Spec_X$ to $x' : s$ in $Spec^p_{X \cup X'}$. In general T_p will be a persistent functor, however, if p does not terminate then $(T_p;\ U)(A) \neq A$. This approach corresponds to using the *free* semantics of section 7 with objects $Sp_p = \langle \Theta, F \rangle$ from $PRES_\mathbf{3}$ such that $\Theta(0) = Spec_{base}$, $\Theta(1) = \Theta(2) = Spec_X$ and $\langle \sum_\mathbf{3} \Theta, F \rangle = Spec^p_{X \cup X'}$. The only difference is that in our approach, in the case of non-termination, *free*(Sp_p), seen as a function, is undefined; this is the reason why *free* is defined by using free extensions instead of a free functor. Ganzinger's results can be used in two ways. First, we have new operations at hand to build relations from relations, like the conditional and while construct; on the other hand, the semantics of while-programs have the same semantic domain as their specifications, objects in $ADT_\mathbf{3}$. This provides us with a connection of specifications of state transformations to their implementation by imperative programs within the same framework.

In the evolving algebra approach of Gurevich [11] a transformation of an algebra A to an algebra B over the same signature is given by a set of guarded local function updates of the form **if** b **then** $f(\mathbf{t}) := t_0$. The problem in translating these updates in our framework to formulas over $RSen2(\Theta)$ for some object $Sp = \langle \Theta, F \rangle$ from $PRES_2$ is the treatment of conflicting updates, eg. $f(a) := true$ and $f(a) := false$. Gurevich chooses one of the updates non deterministicly and discards the others, while in our approach all updates have to be satisfied. This means that some values have to be equated (eg. $true = false$) or the relation, viewed as a (non-deterministic) function, is not defined for some algebras. The algebras of Gurevich have only one sort called the superuniverse containing two distinguished elements *true* and *false*. Different sorts (universes) are modeled by using characteristic functions on the superuniverse. This allows to model the evolution of sorts just by changing the interpretation of their characteristic functions without having to change the interpretation of the superuniverse.

In the implicit state approach of Dauchy and Gaudel [4] states are enrichments of the datatypes used in the system by access functions. Modifiers are functors on states built from elementary modifiers by sequential and indifferent composition and using conditionals. Elementary modifiers $\mu\text{-}ac(\pi, t)$, for some accessor function ac and terms π and t over the signature of states, can be translated into our framework as the formula

$$\forall \mathbf{x}(\exists \mathbf{y} : (\pi = \mathbf{x} \Rightarrow ac'(\mathbf{x}) = t) \quad \vee \quad \forall \mathbf{y} : (\pi \neq \mathbf{x} \Rightarrow ac'(\mathbf{x}) = ac(\mathbf{x}))),$$

where $\mathbf{y}$ is the vector of variables occuring free in π and t. This is a formula in F, where $Sp = \langle \Theta, F \rangle$ is an object of $PRES_3$, $\Theta(1) = \Theta(2)$ contains the accessor function ac and $\Theta(0)$ is the specification of the used datatypes. Now, for a structure m satisfying Sp, it holds that

$$ac^{m_2}(\mathbf{v}) = \begin{cases} \rho^*(t) & \text{if } \rho^*(\pi) = \mathbf{v} \text{ for a variable assignment } \rho\colon X \to m_1 \\ ac^{m_1}(\mathbf{v}) & \text{else} \end{cases}$$

This means, that $loose(Sp)$ defines a function on algebras corresponding to the semantics of the elementary modifiers of Dauchy and Gaudel. Sequential composition of modifiers is given by the composition of relations in $PRES_3$ and ADT_3 and indifferent composition can be described by colimits in $PRES_3$ and ADT_3, respectively.

In all the above approaches the stress is on *constructing* transformations of algebras rather than on specifying these transformations in a possibly *non-constructive* way. In our approach we are able to specify how the states before and after a transformation are related and not necessarily how this relation is established (eg. by while-programs, local function updates or modifiers).

D-oids are a model theoretic approach by Astesiano and Zucca [1] to define dynamic datatypes. D-oids consist of a set of algebras over some signature together with a set of dynamic operations. A dynamic operation associates to an algebra A and a set of values from A an algebra B, a family of functions from the carrier sets of A to the carrier sets of B, the tracking map $f\colon A \Rightarrow B$, and possibly a return value from B. However, Astesiano and Zucca do not have a method to specify their dynamic datatypes yet.

All the previous approaches keep the interpretation of sorts fixed, allowing only for the interpretation of function symbols to change. This is not required by the d-oids approach. The tracking map f is responsible for relating the elements of the sort whose interpretation has changed in B and also for the elements of those sorts that did not change. In our approach there is the possibility to include new sorts in $\Theta(1)$ and $\Theta(2)$ and functions f_i in $\Theta(3)$, $f_i\colon s_i \to s_i'$, for new sorts s_i in $\Theta(1)$ and $\Theta(2)$, and $f_i\colon s_i \to s_i$, for sorts s_i in $\Theta(0)$. The functions f_i can be seen as defining the tracking map of dynamic operations.

An approach similar to d-oids is the informal proposal for dynamic abstract datatypes by Ehrig and Orejas [8]. The instant structure specification, a conservative extension of some value type specification, is intended to model class sorts and attribute functions of objects. A dynamic operation denotes for a model A of the instant structure specification, together with a set of values from A, a set of transformations from A to some other instant algebra B. Given a specification $Sp = \langle \Theta, F \rangle$ in $PRES_{\mathbf{4}}$, a value type specification corresponds to $\Theta(0)$, an instant structure specification, roughly, to $\Theta(1)$ and $\Theta(2)$ and certain classes of transformations could be modeled using function symbols $f\colon s \to s'$ and $f\colon s \to s$ in $\Theta(3)$. Then a dynamic operation is an object $R = \langle \Theta^R, M^R \rangle$ of $ADT_{\mathbf{4}}$ such that $M^R \models^{\mathcal{R}_4} F$.

9 Conclusion

In this paper we have defined a family of institutions in which abstract datatypes have an interpretation as relations between structures from some base institution. We have achieved two things. First we have a model theory of typed relations, which are objects in $ADT_{\mathbf{2}}$, and for typed relations respecting a common environment, objects in $ADT_{\mathbf{3}}$. Since relations are abstract datatypes in certain institutions methods for the construction of abstract datatypes in an arbitrary institution, like eg. various forms of parameterization, can be used to also construct relations, see for example the work of Goguen and Burstall [3, 10], Sannella, Wirsing and Tarlecki [16, 15], Ehrig and others [6]. However, further investigation is needed into whether these constructions are appropriate for constructing relations and which additional constructions, eg. the composition of relations, are needed.

The second achievement of this paper is a specification method for relations between algebras within the theory of abstract datatypes resembling the methods used in specification languages like Z [17], VDM-SL [13] and Larch [12]. Future research has to show how far the resemblance between the presented method and Z, VDM-SL and Larch extends. One could image that the two tiered approach of Larch for some programming language can be given full a semantics within this framework. The base institution is given by the Larch Shared Language; Larch Interface Language specifications are objects in $PRES_{\mathbf{4}}$, which have a denotation as objects in $ADT_{\mathbf{3}}$, and the results of Ganzinger [9] can be used to define the semantics of the programs again as objects of $ADT_{\mathbf{3}}$, which can then be checked to see if they implement the specification.

Colimits in $SIGN$ and therefore in $ADT_{\mathbf{D}}$ and $PRES_{\mathbf{D}}$ allow us to combine smaller states to larger ones and to extend relations from the smaller states to relations on the larger ones. Also colimits allow us to combine several relations on one state as one relation on the same state. This corresponds to a parallel composition of relations instead of a sequential one defined by the composition of relations in section 6.1.

The interpretation of abstract data types as relations fails when it comes to refinement. The refinement of abstract datatypes does not correspond to the refinement of relations if relations are viewed as non-deterministic functions. The refinement of one abstract datatype by another is an abstract datatype morphism, while R refines to S with respect to a signature morphism $\alpha\colon \Theta^R \rightarrow \Theta^S$ iff. $dom(R) \subseteq dom(S)|_\alpha$ and $\alpha\colon R \rightarrow S|_{\alpha(dom(R))}$ is a morphism between relations. $S|_{\alpha(dom(R))}$ denotes the restriction of S to the domain $\alpha(dom(R))$.

References

1. Egidio Astesiano and Elena Zucca. D-oids: A model for dynamic data-types. *Mathematical Structures in Computer Science*, 1994. to appear.
2. Hubert Baumeister. Unifying initial and loose semantics of parameterized specifications in an arbitrary institution. In *Proceedings Tapsoft/CAAP, Brighton, UK*, number 493 in LNCS, pages 103–120. Springer, April 1991.
3. R. M. Burstall and J. A. Goguen. The semantics of Clear, a specification language, February 1980.
4. P. Dauchy and M.-C. Gaudel. Algebraic specifications with implicit state, February 1994.
5. R. Diaconescu, J. Goguen, and P. Stefaneas. Logical support for modularisation. Programming Research Group, Oxford University, August 1991.
6. H. Ehrig, P. Pepper, and F. Orejas. On recent trends in algebraic specification. In *Proceedings ICALP, Stresa, Italy*, number 372 in LNCS, pages 263–288. Springer, July 1989.
7. Hartmut Ehrig and Bernd Mahr. *Fundamentals of Algebraic Specification 1: Equations and initial Semantics.* Number 6 in EATCS Monographs on Theoretical Computer Science. Springer, 1985.
8. Hartmut Ehrig and Fernando Orejas. Dynamic abstract data types, an informal proposal. *Bulletin of the EATCS*, (53):162–169, June 1994.
9. Harald Ganzinger. Programs as transformations of algebraic theories (extended abstract). *Informatik Fachberichte*, 50:22–41, 1981.
10. J. A. Goguen and R. Burstall. Institutions: Abstract model theory for specification and programming. *Journal of the Association for Computing Machinery*, 39(1):95–146, January 1992.
11. Yuri Gurevich. Evolving algebras: An attempt to discover semantics. *Bulletin of the EATCS*, (43):264–284, February 1991.
12. J. V. Guttag, J. J. Horning, and J. M. Wing. Larch in five easy pieces. Report 5, DEC Systems Research Center, July 1985.
13. Cliff B. Jones. *Systematic Software Development Using VDM.* International series in computer science. Prentice Hall, New York, 2sd edition, 1990.
14. Saunders Mac Lane. *Categories for the working mathematician.* Graduated Texts in Mathematics. Springer, 4th edition, 1988.
15. Donald Sannella and Andrzej Tarlecki. Specifications in an arbitrary institution. *Information and Computation*, 76(2/3):165–210, February/March 1988.
16. Donald Sannella and Martin Wirsing. A kernel language for algebraic specification. Internal Report CSR-131-83, University of Edinburgh, September 1983.
17. J. Michael Spivey. *The Z Notation: A Reference Manual.* International series in computer science. Prentice Hall, New York, 2nd edition, 1992.

Performance-Oriented Formal Specifications — the LotoTis Approach

Ina Schieferdecker

GMD FOKUS, Hardenbergplatz 2, D-10623 Berlin
tel: +49 30 254 99 170, e-mail: ina@fokus.gmd.de,
http://www.fokus.gmd.de/htbin/info/minos/ina

Abstract. The paper presents the performance-oriented, Lotos extension LotoTis. LotoTis allows us to specify performance-oriented behavior via quantified time, quantified nondeterminism, quantified parallelism, and action monitoring. It offers a set of refinement rules from Lotos to LotoTis. Therefore, LotoTis supports the standard conform development of performance-oriented specifications from existing Lotos specifications.

1 Performance Evaluation based on Formal Specifications

In the mid eighties [10] there was already recognized that specifying performance requirements can be as important as specifying functional requirements of distributed systems. However, formal specification techniques covered so far primarily functional aspects for the investigation of the functional correctness of distributed systems. Hence, it was (and is still) not unusual that a system is fully implemented or at least implemented as a prototype before any attempt is made to investigate its performance. However, costly re-prototyping or re-implementation can be avoided, if performance could be predicted from the specification of a distributed system. A framework, which supports functional and performance-oriented behavior specification, and which allows us to evaluate performance from that specification would offer major advantages. For this purpose, new concepts have to be incorporated into formal specification techniques. Only recently, there had been published some proposals that close the gap between formal specification and performance evaluation [1].

This paper presents the LotoTis approach that is a newly-designed performance-oriented formal description technique (FDT). Its main advantage is the upward compatibility with Lotos that is one of the internationally standardized FDTs [5]. After introducing the main concepts of LotoTis, we present the language and give an insight into its semantics. The most important properties of LotoTis are given. The paper finishes with a methodology based on the Lotos/LotoTis framework that supports the development of standard conform prototypes and the prediction of their performance.

2 The LOTOTIS Approach

In order to develop a useful and adequate FDT for performance evaluation, we have to identify the aspects of distributed systems which influence their performance. The starting point is to consider a distributed system as being composed of a number of tasks. The execution of system is the parallel and/or sequentially ordered execution of the tasks. Every task realizes a certain functionality. Besides their functional behavior, tasks are

- time-consuming,
- request resources for their execution, and
- have priorities in access to these resources.

For obvious reasons, the precondition for any performance evaluation is the possibility to express the time consumption of tasks. This leads us to the concept of *quantified time*. The availability of resources influences the grade of parallelism in a distributed system and therefore its performance. Thus, a concept of *quantified parallelism* is required. Furthermore, distributed systems are inherently nondeterministic due to their complexity and the unpredictable behavior of their environment. Formal specifications represent nondeterminism by means of choices between several possible subsequent behaviors. For the sake of performance evaluation, we have to quantify these choices explicitly. Hence, we have to have a concept of *quantified nondeterminism*. Last but not least, performance characteristics of a distributed system are determined by the execution of tasks and the time distances between them. They can only be determined if the execution of tasks is observable from outside of the system. A concept of *monitoring* is required in order to make observable any task of interest — independent of whether this task is externally visible or internally hidden.

We decided to incorporate these concepts into LOTOS [5] — the Language of Temporal Ordering Specification. It is based on process algebras (CCS, CSP) and algebraic data type specifications (ACT ONE). Another origin of LOTOTIS is TIS — the Timed Interacting Systems Approach ([14],[12]).

2.1 The Notion of Structured Actions

The main feature of LOTOTIS are *structured actions*, which replace classic actions used in process algebras. While classic actions represent task functionalities, structured action with their action parameters represent also performance characteristics of tasks. These action parameters make the performance-oriented modeling of distributed systems conceptually easy. There are no separate modeling features for time, priorities, resources, and monitoring. All these features belong to the notion of a structured action. The parameters of a structured action `a(t,p,r,m)` are the following:

1. The interaction time **t** defines the length of an interaction with synchronization partners[1]. The interaction time makes structured actions in general non-instantaneous, so that they describe true-concurrent behavior.
2. The priority **p** orders simultaneously enabled actions and determines the subsequent behavior. In addition, the access to resources is adjusted by priorities.
3. The set of resources **r** has to be allocated before any interaction[2]. In addition to action priorities, resource disciplines determine the order of resource allocations.
4. The monitoring signal **m** makes action occurrences observable from outside. Whenever an action attached with a monitoring signal starts its interaction period, the monitoring signal offers the signal identifier and the current, absolute time to the environment.

The behavior of structured actions is explained for three basic cases, which are (1) a single structured action, (2) the synchronization of structured actions, and (3) the interleaving of structured actions.

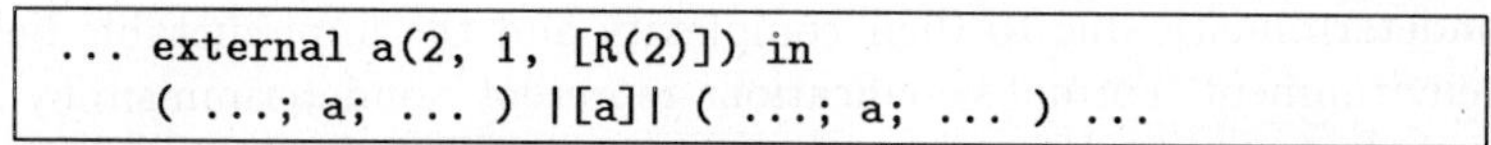

```
... external a(2, 1, [R(2)]) in
( ...; a; ... ) |[a]| ( ...; a; ... ) ...
```

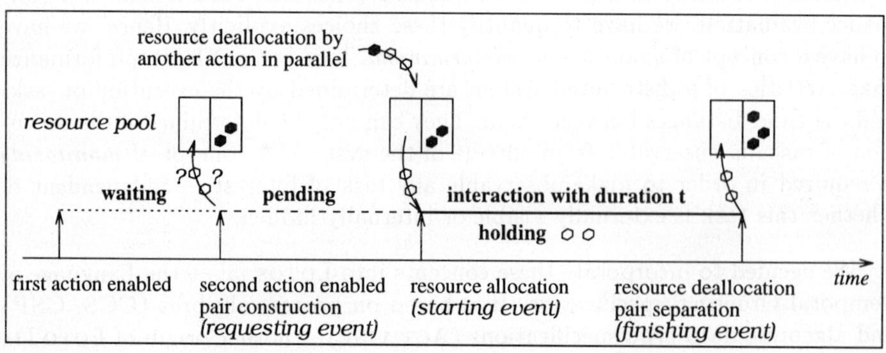

Fig. 1. Synchronization of Structured Actions

Single action Whenever a structured action is enabled it tries to allocate needed resources **r** immediately. A — not explicitly specified — pending period until the successful resource allocation may occur. Resources are assigned to

[1] A structured action without any synchronization can be considered to be a special case of synchronizing structured actions.

[2] Although resources and the resource management during system execution could be represented by additional processes and data types, we adopt the use of explicit resources as a very concise and succinct modeling feature.

```
... external a(0, 3, [R]), b(0, 2, [R]), c(0, 1, [R]) in
    ( a; ... ||| b; ... ||| c; ... )
```

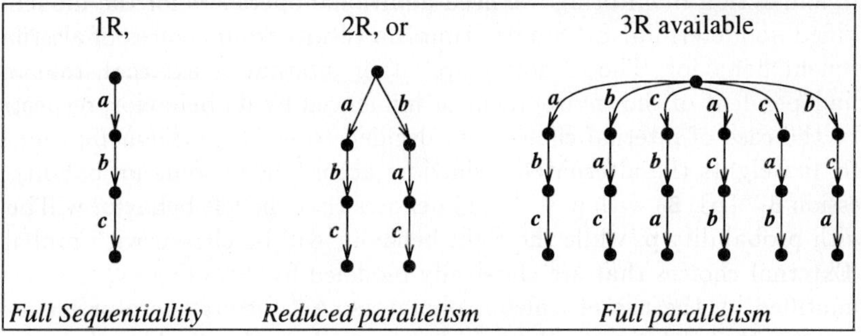

Fig. 2. Independent Structured Actions

pending actions on an all-or-nothing principle, meaning that either all needed resources are assigned, or no assignment takes place. If possible, pending actions are assigned resources without any delay. Resources are assigned on the action priority `p` and the resource discipline[3] basis. After resource allocation the interaction period starts immediately. The monitoring signal `m` informs the environment about the begin of the interaction period. The duration of the interaction period is determined by the interaction time `t`. Resources are occupied throughout the interaction period.

Synchronization Figure 1 depicts the synchronization of two structured actions `a` with interaction time `2`, priority `1`, and two requested resources of type `R`. Synchronization partners become in general enabled at a different point in time. Thus, one action `a` becomes enabled earlier than the other one and has to wait for its synchronization partner before requesting resources. There is a — not explicitly specified — waiting period for synchronization partners. Eventually, both actions are enabled and form an action tuple. This action tuple behaves like a single action: it requests resources, waits for the resource allocation, interacts, and deallocates resources.

Independence Independent structured actions, i.e. parallel composed structured actions without synchronization, allow us to model full parallelism, reduced parallelism, and full sequentiality. Figure 2 gives three independent, instantaneous structured actions `a`, `b`, and `c`. Each of them needs one resource `R`. The grade of parallelism is determined by the number of available resources `R`. The three cases — at most one `R`, two `R`, and at least three `R` — could be also depicted as `1. {a,b,c}`, `2. {a,b}`, `{c}` and `3. {a}`, `{b}`, `{c}`, where actions in parenthesis denote the parallel execution of actions while commata denote their sequential ordering.

---

[3] For time being, we restrict ourselves to the case of `fifo` (first in first out).

2.2 Performance-Oriented Operators

While structured actions can be used to model quantified time, quantified parallelism, and action monitoring, we need additional operators for the modeling of quantified nondeterminism. Nondeterminism results from choices of alternative, subsequent behavior. Those choices are either internal or external, that means fully independent of the environment or influenced by its behavior, respectively.

For the case of internal choices, we decided to use a *probabilistic choice operator*. It weights the alternative behaviors according to some probability. The expression B_1 [p] B_2 with p $\in$ [0,1] denotes that the left behavior will be chosen with probability p, while the right behavior will be chosen with probability 1-p. External choices that are classically modeled by disabling expressions, can be quantified by the use of timeout operators. A timeout operator has a time parameter t that determines the time point at which the disabling behavior expression is enabled. We distinguish between two forms of the timeout operator — the *hard timeout* and the *soft timeout*. While in the first case the disabling always occurs after time t, the disabling in the second case only occurs if the behavior expression to be disabled has not yet successfully started the interaction period of its first action. If the left behavior is fast enough to start an interaction before time t has passed it cannot be disabled anymore. In both cases, the timeout cannot occur if the behavior expression to be disabled has terminated before time t.

Please note that potential nondeterminism still exists. In particular, at time t when both the disabling behavior expression and the behavior expression to be disabled are able to execute actions with the same priority, it is undetermined which of them is chosen. Secondly, although the access to resources is adjusted by the assignment of priorities to actions and resource disciplines to resources, there is still the possibility that two equally prioritrized actions request resources at the same point in time.

2.3 Definition of LOTOTIS

LOTOTIS is LOTOS extended with

1. structured actions that incorporate time, priorities, resources, and monitoring signals,
2. probabilistic choice operator, and
3. timeout operators.

The LOTOTIS syntax is given in Table 1. The new LOTOTIS constructs are marked with ->. A LOTOTIS specification defines the time domain to be discrete or dense. Global available resources are declared on top of the specification. Additionally, each process definition may contain a resource declaration of locally available resources — those resources can only be accessed from process internal actions. Global resources cannot be accessed from internal actions of a locally defined process. Therefore, resources can only be allocated by actions declared on the same level as the resources themselves. Every structured action is explicitly

```
   specification:
     specification-symbol specification-identifier formal-parameter-list
     global-type-definitions
->   [time-decl][resource-symbol resource-decls][external-action-decls]
     behavior definition-block endspecification-symbol
-> time-decl:        time-symbol time-domain in-symbol
-> time-domain:      discrete | dense
-> resource-decls: resource-identifier '[' resource-number
                     [',' resource-discipline] ']' [',' resource-decls]
-> action-decls:     action-identifier '(' interaction-time [',' priority
                     [',' resource-request [',' monitoring-signal]]] ')'
                     [',' action-decls]
-> external-action-decls: external-symbol action-decls in-symbol
   process-definition:
     process-symbol process-identifier formal-parameter-list define-symbol
->   [resource-symbol resource-decls]
     definition-block endprocess-symbol
   behavior-expression: ...
->   | hide-symbol action-decls in-symbol
->   | behavior-expression ''[['' probability '']]'' behavior-expression
->   | behavior-expression ''[['' time '']>'' behavior-expression
->   | behavior-expression ''[['' time ''>>'' behavior-expression
     | ...
```

Table 1. The Syntax of LotoTis

declared by the use of the external operator (for external gates) or by the use of the hide operator (for internal actions). It is not mandatory to define all parameters of a structured action; default assumptions are zero duration, zero priority, no requested resources, and no monitoring signal.

LotoTis operators are used to specify complex behavior composed of structured actions, **stop**, **exit**, and process instances. The result of such compositions are behavior expressions which describe the behavior of a process or a complete system. An overview about the LotoTis operators is given in Table 2.

We distinguish between basic LotoTis and full LotoTis. Basic LotoTis has no data part. Full LotoTis is basic LotoTis extended with data dependencies. It incorporates algebraic data type specifications and the definition of data dependencies in the behavior part. Most importantly, we can use the data part for setting parameters of structured actions and for setting parameters of performance-oriented operators during system execution. It allows us to model the dynamic change of performance characteristics during system run. The additional features of full LotoTis are explained in Table 3. They are similar to those features of full Lotos. A good introduction and guidelines for their use can be found in [2].

Operator	Comment
External: **external** $g_1(..), .., g_n(..)$**in** $\mathcal{B}$	The external operator declares external gates $g_1, \ldots, g_n$ of a LotoTis specification with their parameters.
Hide: **hide** $a_1(..), .., a_n(..)$**in** $\mathcal{B}$	The hide operator declares internal, hidden structured actions $a_1, .., a_n$ with their parameters. These actions are unobservable outside of $\mathcal{B}$.
Action Prefix: $a; \mathcal{B}$	$\mathcal{B}$ becomes enabled after the interaction a has been completed.
Enabling: $\mathcal{B}_1 \gg \mathcal{B}_2$	$\mathcal{B}_2$ becomes enabled after the successful termination of $\mathcal{B}_1$ via the **exit** process.
Parallel Composition: $\mathcal{B}_1 \vert [g_1, .., g_n] \vert \mathcal{B}_2$	$\mathcal{B}_1$ and $\mathcal{B}_2$ are executed in parallel and interact in their gates $g_1, \ldots, g_n$.
Full Synchronization: $\mathcal{B}_1 \vert\vert \mathcal{B}_2$	$\mathcal{B}_1$ and $\mathcal{B}_2$ become are executed in parallel. They interact in their externally visible actions.
Interleaving: $\mathcal{B}_1 \vert\vert\vert \mathcal{B}_2$	$\mathcal{B}_1$ and $\mathcal{B}_2$ are executed in parallel and fully independently, i.e. without any interaction.
Choice: $\mathcal{B}_1 [] \mathcal{B}_2$	Provided that both behavior expressions are potentially able to execute their first action, only one — either $\mathcal{B}_1$ or $\mathcal{B}_2$ — is chosen. The choice is being made nondeterministically.
Probabilistic Choice: $\mathcal{B}_1 [[p]] \mathcal{B}_2$	Either $\mathcal{B}_1$ or $\mathcal{B}_2$ becomes enabled. The choice is being made randomly, with probabilities p for $\mathcal{B}_1$ and $1-p$ for $\mathcal{B}_2$, respectively. This choice does not take into account whether a behavior expression is potentially able to execute its first action or not. It may happen, that a deadlocked behavior expression is being enabled — this cannot happen with the pure choice operator.
Disabling: $\mathcal{B}_1 [> \mathcal{B}_2$	$\mathcal{B}_1$ becomes enabled immediately. $\mathcal{B}_2$ may disable $\mathcal{B}_1$ at arbitrary time, unless $\mathcal{B}_1$ has already terminated.
Soft Timeout: $\mathcal{B}_1 [[t]> \mathcal{B}_2$	$\mathcal{B}_1$ becomes enabled immediately. $\mathcal{B}_2$ disables $\mathcal{B}_1$ at (relative) time t unless $\mathcal{B}_1$ has not yet started an interaction or has not yet terminated. If $\mathcal{B}_1$ started an interaction before time t it "survives", the disabling becomes impossible.
Hard Timeout: $\mathcal{B}_1 [[t \gg \mathcal{B}_2$	$\mathcal{B}_1$ becomes enabled immediately. $\mathcal{B}_2$ disables $\mathcal{B}_1$ at (relative) time t unless $\mathcal{B}_1$ has not yet terminated. Please note, that in contrast to the soft timeout operator $\mathcal{B}_2$ may disable $\mathcal{B}_1$ also within interaction periods. In that case synchronization partners of the disabled interaction of $\mathcal{B}_1$ are deadlocked as they are waiting for the disabled synchronization partner to finish the common interaction period.

Table 2. Basic LotoTis Operators

Feature	Comment
Value offer: $a\,!v$	Action a offers value v.
Variable offer: $a\,?x : type$	Action a offers variable x and requests a value for x.
Parameterized process: **process** $P[g_1, .., g_n]$ $(x_1 : t_1, .., x_m : t_m)$ .. **endproc**	Process P has formal parameters $x_1, \ldots, x_m$ of type $t_1, \ldots, t_m$, respectively. They are actualized when P is instantiated.
Parameterized exit: **exit**$(x, ..)$	Upon successful termination, a list of data values is offered to the subsequent behavior.
Parameterized sequential composition: **exit**$(x, ..) \gg$ **accept**$x_1 : t_1, ..$ **in**B	The exit values are passed to the subsequent behavior.
Local value definition: **let** $x : t = v, ..$ **in**B	Variable x of type t is bounded to value v in $\mathcal{B}$.
Guards: $[g]->\mathcal{B}$	Behavior $\mathcal{B}$ is enabled only if the guard g can be evaluated to true.

Table 3. Additional Full LOTOTIS Features

2.4 The Formal Semantics of LOTOTIS

Due to the true concurrent behavior of LOTOTIS, standard LOTOS semantics is definitely inappropriate for defining LOTOTIS. Instead, we use an intermediate specification language which has instantaneous actions and a concept of time prefixing. Thus, time-consuming, structured LOTOTIS actions can be represented as sequences of instantaneous actions with time consumption in between.

The LOTOTIS semantics is defined in two steps:

$$\text{LOTOTIS} \xrightarrow{trans} \text{GENIUS} \xrightarrow{TDS} SLTS.$$

The intermediate specification language is called GENIUS. Roughly speaking, GENIUS is LOTOS with time, priorities, probabilities, monitoring, and time prefix, probabilistic choice, and timeout operators. GENIUS is an upward compatible extension of LOTOS in the sense that it extends LOTOS with additional features while preserving the original LOTOS semantics. LOTOTIS is GENIUS with structured actions and resources. LOTOTIS is transformed to GENIUS in order to define the LOTOTIS semantics. The transformation allows us to consider LOTOTIS to be an upward compatible extension of LOTOS.

The transformation function *trans* maps every syntactically correct LOTOTIS specification L to a GENIUS specification $trans(L)$. Besides the mapping of structured LOTOTIS actions, the transformation from LOTOTIS to GENIUS is used for the explicit definition of the LOTOTIS resource management. This is defined in terms of additional processes and data types contained in $trans(L)$. The formal semantics of GENIUS is defined by an operational semantics. The transition derivation system *TDS* maps *trans*(*L*) to a class of structured labeled transitions systems *SLTS*(*trans*(*L*)) representing the behavior of *L*.

In order to give an insight into the LOTOTIS semantics definition, Fig. 3 and Fig. 4 present parts of the LOTOTIS to GENIUS transformation and inference rules for GENIUS operators, respectively. The complete LOTOTIS semantics definition is contained in [11].

```
trans(...
hide
  a(0,1,[R],ma),
  b(1,3,[R],mb),
  c(0,2,[R],mc)
in a; exit
  |||
  b; c; exit
...)
```

↦

```
...
( a !at_r ?x:Nat; a !at_s !x; a !at_f !x; exit)
|||
( b !at_r ?x:Nat; b !at_s !x; (1). b !at_f !x;
  c !at_r ?x:Nat; c !at_s !x; c !at_f !x; exit)
...
```

Fig. 3. Mapping of LOTOTIS Actions to GENIUS Actions

The mapping of structured LOTOTIS actions to instantaneous GENIUS actions is exemplarily given in Fig. 3. A structured LOTOTIS action is defined by a sequence of requesting, starting, and finishing GENIUS action. At the requesting action `a !at_r ?x:Nat` the action `a` waits for all its synchronization partners. During the synchronization within this GENIUS action, there is assigned an unique identification number `x` for the tuple of actions. This number is known by all synchronization partners, so that they are the only one that are able to synchronize in the respective starting, requesting, and finishing actions. After the resource request in `a !at_r ?x:Nat`, the tuple of actions willing to synchronize becomes pending until successful resource allocation. The time point of synchronization in `a !at_s !x` marks the successful resource allocation and initiates the start of the interaction period. The duration of the interaction period is defined by means of the time prefix operator. If the structured action is instantaneous (its interaction time is 0), no time prefix is used. The end of the interaction time is marked by a finishing action `a !at_f !x`, which immediately causes all allocated resources to be released. You may wonder, why there is no direct reflection of the other action parameters. In fact, the information on requested resources and monitoring signals is transferred to another process called `Collector` being one of the additional processes for the resource management.

Exemplarily for the transition derivation system of GENIUS we present the axioms for the GENIUS time prefix operator and the inferences for the GENIUS timeout operators. The inferences uses the set **max**$\mathcal{B}$ containing all GENIUS actions with maximal priority that are enabled in $\mathcal{B}$[4]. Thus, the priority order

[4] A GENIUS specification defines a priority for every action. The special action χ represents the passage of time and has lowest priority.

of actions is extended to a priority order on behavior expressions.

Soft Timeout

$$\frac{\mathcal{B}_1\,_{|t} \xrightarrow{g} \mathcal{B}'_1\,_{|t} \text{ and } name(g) \notin \{g_1, \ldots, g_n, \delta, \chi\} \text{and } g \in \mathbf{max}\mathcal{B}_1}{\mathcal{B}_1[g_1, \ldots, g_n[l]\rangle \mathcal{B}_2\,_{|t} \xrightarrow{g} \mathcal{B}'_1[g_1, \ldots, g_n[l]\rangle \mathcal{B}_2\,_{|t}} \qquad (\text{*evolving*})$$

$$\frac{\mathcal{B}_1\,_{|t} \xrightarrow{g} \mathcal{B}'_1\,_{|t} \text{ and } name(g) \in \{g_1, \ldots, g_n, \delta\} \text{ and } g \in \mathbf{max}\mathcal{B}_1}{\mathcal{B}_1[g_1, \ldots, g_n[l]\rangle \mathcal{B}_2\,_{|t} \xrightarrow{g} \mathcal{B}'_1\,_{|t}} \qquad (\text{*saving*})$$

$$\frac{\mathcal{B}_1\,_{|t} \xrightarrow{\chi[l']} \mathcal{B}'_1\,_{|t} \text{ and } \chi \in \mathbf{max}\mathcal{B}_1 \text{ and } l' < l}{\mathcal{B}_1[g_1, \ldots, g_n[l]\rangle \mathcal{B}_2\,_{|t} \xrightarrow{\chi[l']} \mathcal{B}'_1[g_1, \ldots, g_n[l]\rangle \mathcal{B}_2\,_{|t+l'}} \qquad (\text{*passage of time*})$$

$$\frac{\mathcal{B}_1\,_{|t} \xrightarrow{\chi[l']} \mathcal{B}'_1\,_{|t} \text{ and } \chi \in \mathbf{max}\mathcal{B}_1 \text{ and } l' = l}{\mathcal{B}_1[g_1, \ldots, g_n[l]\rangle \mathcal{B}_2\,_{|t} \xrightarrow{\chi[l']} \mathcal{B}_2\,_{|t+l'}} \qquad (\text{*timeout*})$$

Hard Timeout

$$\frac{\mathcal{B}_1[[l]\rangle \mathcal{B}_2\,_{|t} \xrightarrow{g} \mathcal{B}'_{|t'} \text{ and } g \in \mathbf{max}(\mathcal{B}_1[[l]\rangle \mathcal{B}_2)}{\mathcal{B}_1[[l \gg \mathcal{B}_2\,_{|t} \xrightarrow{g} \mathcal{B}'_{|t'}}$$

Fig. 4. The GENIUS Timeout Operators

Likewise to an untimed disable operator, the soft timeout operator represents situations, where the left behavior expression may be disrupted by some exceptional circumstances. However, these exceptions can disable the behavior expression on the left only after time l, i.e. only at a well-defined moment of time. In addition, the left behavior expression cannot be disrupted any more if it executes one of the saving actions $g_1, \ldots, g_n$ or if it terminates. A LOTOTIS soft timeout operator is transformed to a GENIUS soft timeout operator where the saving actions are the respective starts of interaction periods of those LOTOTIS structured actions that are contained in the left hand behavior expression. The hard timeout operator models hard deadlines. Whenever the left behavior expression has not terminated until the hard deadline expires, the timeout will occur and will disrupt the left behavior expression. The hard timeout operator is a special case of the soft timeout operator, since no saving actions exist for the behavior expression on the left. A LOTOTIS hard timeout operator is transformed one-to-one to a GENIUS hard timeout operator.

2.5 The refinement relation between LOTOS and LOTOTIS

The refinement of LOTOTIS and LOTOS is defined as follows. A LOTOTIS specification $\mathcal{B}_2$ refines a LOTOS specification $\mathcal{B}_1$, denoted by $\mathcal{B}_1 >> \mathcal{B}_2$, if and only if for every interaction a that is started from $\mathcal{B}_2$, there is an action a that is executed by $\mathcal{B}_1$ and the subsequent behavior expressions stand in the refinement relation, too. Hence we compare the occurrences of external LOTOS actions with the occurrences of corresponding external LOTOTIS interaction periods. In other words, we only compare the observable behavior of both specifications. Hence, the refinement relation between LOTOTIS and LOTOS can be seen as a weak refinement, which abstracts from internal details of the specifications under study. Obviously, the refined behavior is a subset of the original behavior.

	LOTOS construct		LOTOTIS construct
Structuring actions	External gate a of a LOTOS specification with behavior expression $\mathcal{B}$	$\longmapsto$	**time** ... **in** **resource** R[...],... **in** **external** a(t,p,r,m) **in** $\mathcal{B}$
	hidea **in**	$\longmapsto$	**time** ... **in** $\mathcal{B}$ **resource** R[...],... **in** **hide** a(t,p,r,m) **in** $\mathcal{B}$
Quantifying disablings	$\mathcal{B}_1$ [> $\mathcal{B}_2$	$\longmapsto$	$\mathcal{B}_1$ [[t]> $\mathcal{B}_2$ or
		$\longmapsto$	$\mathcal{B}_1$ [[t≫ $\mathcal{B}_2$
Quantifying choices	$\mathcal{B}_1$ [] $\mathcal{B}_2$	$\longmapsto$	$\mathcal{B}_1$ [[p]] $\mathcal{B}_2$

Table 4. Performance Refinement from LOTOS to LOTOTIS

Three refinement rules from LOTOS to LOTOTIS exist (Table 4). Structuring external and/or internal actions comprises the transformation of defining action parameters for a given action — defining its interaction time, its priority, its resources, and/or its monitoring signal. It assumes that the time domain and the used resources are properly declared. Quantifying disablings is the transformation of defining a time parameter for a disabling operator. This reduces the possibilities, when the disruption can occur. The third transformation is the parameterization of choice operators that weights the alternatives of the choice expression with probabilities for their occurrences. The following theorem can be proven.

Theorem 1. *Structuring actions, quantifying disablings, and quantifying choices in a* LOTOS *specification yield* LOTOTIS *specifications, which are refinements of the original* LOTOS *specification.*

Furthermore, if we define the underlying LOTOS specification of a LOTOTIS specification to be the specification that results from omitting all additional

LOTOTIS features (by application of the inverse transformation rules of Table 4), the following lemma holds.

Lemma 2. *Every* LOTOTIS *specification is a refinement of its underlying* LOTOS *specification.*

For a formal proof of the refinement relation as well as of the subsequent LOTOTIS properties please refer to [11].

2.6 Further Properties of LOTOTIS

Upward compatibility of LOTOTIS with LOTOS comprises of two properties:

1. Every LOTOS specification is syntactically a LOTOTIS specifications.
2. The semantics of a LOTOS specification is preserved when it is interpreted as a LOTOTIS specification.

The proof for upward compatibility is mainly based on the fact that the intermediate specification language GENIUS that is used for the LOTOTIS semantics definition, is upward compatible with LOTOS.

Another important aspect of formal specifications is that of their finiteness. Finiteness is often an essential precondition for the application of verification methods. The refinement relation between LOTOTIS and LOTOS allows us to proof the following theorem.

Theorem 3. *Every guarded* LOTOTIS *specification, whose underlying* LOTOS *specification is finite, is finite.*

Therefore, the finiteness conditions for LOTOS yield finiteness conditions for LOTOTIS. The following lemma can be formulated [3].

Lemma 4. *A guarded* LOTOTIS *specification is finite if the following conditions are fulfilled by its underlying* LOTOS *specification.*

1. *It is guarded,*
2. *it does not contain relabeling,*
3. *enabling is never involved within recursive calls in a process and the processes composed sequentially are finite,*
4. *if enabling is present within a recursive call, then at least its left argument is finite and does not contain the recursive call,*
5. *the disabling operator is only an outermost operator and its arguments are finite,*
6. *if disabling is involved in a recursive call then its left argument is finite, and*
7. *there exists no recursive calls within parallel compositions.* •

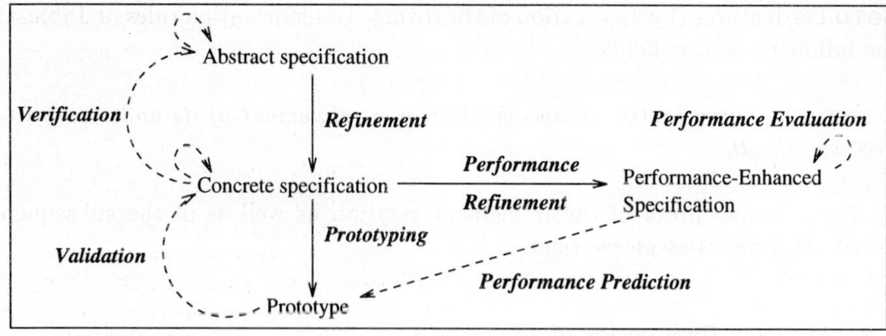

Fig. 5. The Performance-Oriented Prototyping Process

2.7 Predicting the Performance of LOTOS Prototypes

This section presents a methodology for the standard conform development of prototypes of distributed systems whose performance can be predicted in dependence of different execution environments (Fig. 5).

How to develop functionally correct distributed systems from an (untimed) formal service specification down to a system implementation is a well studied area. The development process for distributed systems starts with an abstract specification which reflects the main functionalities (services) offered to the user. Refinement techniques were developed to support the design of formal specifications from abstract to more concrete specifications [2]. A concrete specification describes the mechanisms for realization of the system functionalities. Verification methods are used to proof the functional correctness of these specifications or to proof the functional coincidence between abstract and concrete specifications by means of equivalence or contained-in relations [7]. Afterwards, prototypes are implemented for a first investigation of the system behavior in real environments. Prototype derivation techniques support the (semi)automatic development of prototypes from a concrete, implementation-oriented formal specification [6]. Validation techniques can be used to (semi)formally prove that prototypes (and subsequent implementations) meet their specifications [4].

However, it is still common that the timing behavior and the performance is investigated only when a prototype or a first implementation of the system exist. In the case of inconvenient performance, the whole development process is restarted, what results in long periods of system development, late system delivery, and high costs. Moreover, there will be no guarantee that the newly designed system will have better performance than the first one. Therefore, we suggest to use the technique of performance refinement that has been introduced above for predicting the performance of prototypes of distributed systems. The methodology is based on the LOTOS/LOTOTIS framework. It starts with an abstract functional LOTOS specification of the distributed system. This specification can be refined in order to get a concrete, implementation-oriented LOTOS specification of the system. Afterwards, the concrete specification is enhanced with the performance characteristics of the system tasks in a given execution environment. Let us give two examples for the appropriate parameterization of a specification. Basic real-time parameters of system tasks such as duration of inter-process communication or the access to the storage has to be measured before incorporating them into the specification. Secondly, real resource requirements of system tasks are directly reflected by the resource parameter of structured actions. General rules of how to incorporate performance characteristics of execution environments into formal specification are given in [13]. By applying the performance refinement rules we get a LOTOTIS specification from which we can derive performance measures. We derive simulation models from LOTOTIS specifications. For this purpose, we use the close relationship between transition systems and discrete event systems. A simulation tool is currently under development, where we use our experiences from the TIS simulation tool [13].

Obviously, this is only a first step in order to support the performance-oriented development of distributed systems based on formal specifications. A lot of work has still to be done.

3 Conclusions

This paper resembled the concepts of quantified time, quantified nondeterminism, quantified parallelism, and monitoring to be basic concepts for performance evaluation based on formal specification techniques. Afterwards, it presented structured actions as a powerful concept to describe performance-related issues of distributed systems. We applied structured actions to LOTOS in order to support the standard conform development of distributed systems. The resulting specification technique is called LOTOTIS.

To the author's best knowledge, only two LOTOS extensions [8], [9] are comparable to the one presented in this paper. The first, however, is not a proper extension of LOTOS since it excludes the disabling and enabling operator of LOTOS. The second contains besides a time and a priority/weight concept a concept of random experiments to express stochastic behavior. In that respect, it is more expressive than LOTOTIS since LOTOTIS does not contain any means to specify random variables having certain distribution functions. Both approaches cover quantified time and quantified nondeterminism, but the possibility to express quantified parallelism and action monitoring is not their target. The absence of random variables in LOTOTIS is however lightened by the possibility to express dynamically changing system characteristics by the use of the LOTOTIS data part. In addition, we can see no serious problems when incorporating random variables into LOTOTIS. This would require the extension of the LOTOTIS semantics with aspects from probabilistic theory as it is similar done in [9].

Finally, we presented an approach to predict the performance of distributed systems already during the system design phase. Based on a LOTOS specification of the functional behavior, a performance-enhanced LOTOTIS specification is derived. Simulation models of the LotoTis specification yield the performance estimates of interest. In case of low performance, the distributed system can be re-designed before any prototyping or implementation efforts are spent.

References

1. P. Dembinski. Queueing models for ESTELLE. In *Proc. of the 5th Intern. Conf. on Formal Description Techniques*, pages 73–86, 1993.
2. K.J. Turner (editor). *Using Formal Description Techniques.* John Wiley & Sons, Chichester, 1993.
3. A. Fantechi, S. Gnesi, and G. Mazzarini. How much expressive are LOTOS behaviour expressions? In *Paricipant's Proc. of the Third Intern. Conf. Formal Description Techniques*, pages 9–24, 1990.
4. G.J. Holzmann. *Design and Validation of Computer Protocols.* Prentice Hall Software Series. Prentice-Hall, Englewood Cliffs, New Jersey, 1991.
5. ISO. Information processing systems - open system interconnection - LOTOS - a formal description technique based on the temporal ordering of observational behaviour. ISO/IEC 8807, 1988.
6. Guy Leduc. A framework based on implementation relations for implementing lotos specifications. *Computer Networks and ISDN Systems*, (25):23–41, 1992.
7. F.J. Lin, P.M. Chu, and M.T. Liu. Protocol verification using reachability analysis. *Computer Communication Review*, 17(5):126–135, 1987.
8. M.A. Marsan, A. Bianco, L. Ciminiera, R. Sisto, and A. Valenzano. Integrating performance analysis in the context of LOTOS-based design. In *Proc. of MASCOTS'94*, pages 292–298, 1994.
9. C. Miguel, A. Fernández, J.López, and L. Vidaller. A LOTOS based performance evaluation tool. *Computer Networks and ISDN Systems*, 25(7):791–814, 1993.
10. H. Rudin. Time in formal protocol specification. In *Proc. of the GI/NTG Conf. on Communication in Distributed Systems, Karlsruhe*, pages 575–587, 1985.
11. I. Schieferdecker. *Performance-Oriented Specification of Communication Protocols and Verification of Deterministic Bounds of Their QoS Characteristics.* PhD thesis, Technical University Berlin, 1994. (Upon formal approval).
12. I. Schieferdecker and A. Wolisz. Operational semantics of timed interacting systems: an algebraic performance oriented formal description technique. Technical Report 92/19, Department of Computer Science, Technical University Berlin, 1992.
13. M. Walch. A framework for performance analysis of parallel protocol execution. In *Participant's Proc. of the IFIP Intern. Conf. on Information Networks and Data Communication*, Madeira Island, Portugal, 1994.
14. A. Wolisz. A unified approach to formal specification of communication protocols and analysis of their performance. *Journal of Mathematical Modelling and Simulation in Systems Analysis, Special issue on System Analysis in Informatics*, (1993)(10), 1993.

Part IV

TOOLS

SIGNAL: A Formal Design Environment for Real-Time Systems

EP-ATR Project

IRISA / INRIA, F-35042 RENNES, France, e-mail: Paul.LeGuernic@irisa.fr

The purpose of the EP-ATR Project at IRISA / INRIA-Rennes, is to provide methods and tools for software development, formally founded on a mathematical semantics and model of dynamic systems, integrated within an interactive environment, for the design and implementation of real-time systems. Real time and reactive systems are characterized by their permanent interaction with the external world, the reliability required for their safe execution, their response time and their execution on multi-processor architectures. Targeted application domains feature: aerospace, telecommunications, robotics, signal processing.

Our approach supports a variety of techniques, such as specification, simulation, validation, verification and code generation, all around the synchronous data-flow language SIGNAL, developed at IRISA / INRIA-Rennes. They are integrated into a global software development environment. SIGNAL allows for:

- programming with a user-friendly, interactive graphical interface,
- high-level description of the algorithms, independently of the target hardware, or any implementation consideration,
- reusability of sub-processes through modularity,
- automated analysis of properties, statical as well as dynamical, required to be satisfied for full reliability of the systems,
- automated analysis of the dependencies between sub-processes, for their distribution on multi-processor architectures,
- simulation of the behavior of architectures, of which the components as well as their interactions have been described in SIGNAL,
- automatic code generation and optimization, in portable languages like C and FORTRAN 77,
- hardware / software codesign and generation of VHDL

The SIGNAL environment exists in the INRIA H2 version, developed at IRISA / INRIA-Rennes, and in the CNET / TNI V3 version, which is commercialy available from TNI Inc. (Brest, France). The SYNDEX environment developed at INRIA-Rocquencourt can perform automatic distribution of SIGNAL programs on multiprocessor architectures.

The SIGNAL environment has been experimented in a variety of small and large applications concerning signal processing and the control of complex systems. The SIGNAL environment is demonstrated by the following examples:

- a speech recognition system: this automatic speech-to-phoneme system illustrates the power of the constructs of the language when specifying complex timing behaviours and properties;

- a digital watch: this example of complex automaton, where numerous different modes must be controlled, focuses on the development method, emphasizing modularity and reusability. It is composed of modules (the stopwatch, the alarm, and the watch setup) that could be developed and verified separately.
- a control system for a rail/road crossing: it follows a specification of a real crossing between a road and two railway tracks. It illustrates a general methodology of decomposition into three separate parts: the controller itself, a simulation environment, and a graphical interface, all specified in SIGNAL.
- a robotic vision application (see figure below), where data flow tasks implementing the control laws are sequenced in reaction to event occurrences. This application uses a recent extension to SIGNAL facilitating the specification of the sequencing and hierarchical preemption of data flow tasks.

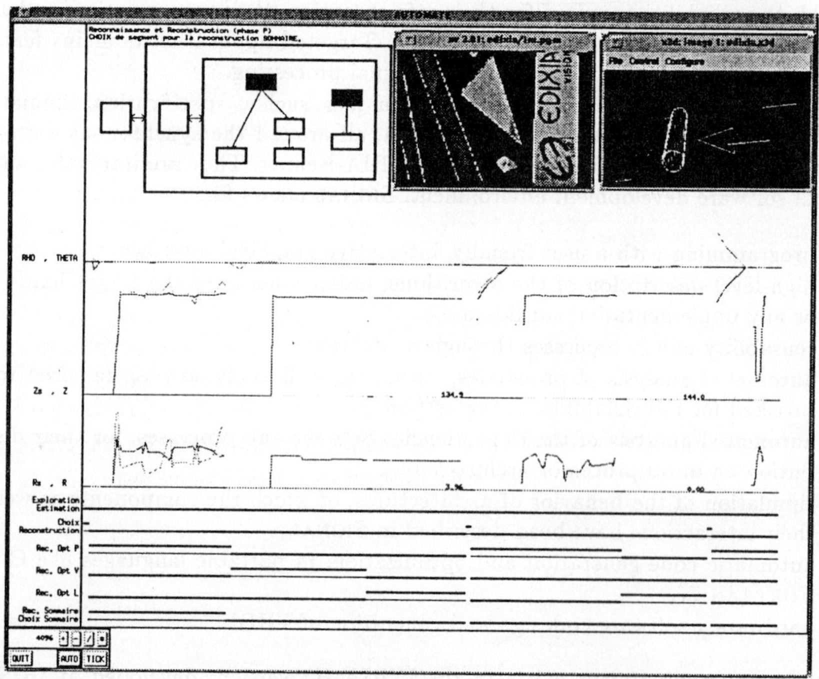

- the specification and verification of a production cell: this is our contribution to a case study proposed by the FZI in Karlsruhe, comparing the application of a variety of formal methods for reactive systems.

The SIGNAL environment and the demonstrations presented run on SUN 4 under SunOS 4.1, and are also availbale for HP 9000 under HP-UX A.B8.

Reference: P. Le Guernic, T. Gautier, M. Le Borgne, C. Le Maire. Programming Real-Time Applications with SIGNAL. *Another look at real-time programming*, special section of *Proceedings of the IEEE*, 79(9), September 1991.

The META-Frame: An Environment for Flexible Tool Management

Bernhard Steffen, Tiziana Margaria, Andreas Claßen

Universität Passau (Germany)
steffen@fmi.uni-passau.de

META-Frame is designed for the flexible management of a *large* library of tools. It supports the semi-automatic construction of application-specific tools from natural language-like 'profiles', as well as the inclusion of new tools into the library, in a way which does not require much expertise. Special care has been taken in the design of an adequate, almost natural-language specification language, a user-friendly graphical interface, a hypertext based navigation tool, the repository management, and in the automation of the synthesis process. This application-independent core has a firm theoretical basis: the synthesis is conceptually based on a model construction algorithm for a linear time temporal logic and supports an advanced form of Meta-level Intelligent Software Synthesis (MISS [SFCM94]). Altogether, META-Frame supports a full synthesis lifecycle (Figure 1) by

1. providing a flexible specification language that captures *local* properties like taxonomic component descriptions and type conditions, and *global* constraints fixing ordering, precedence, eventuality and conditional occurrence,
2. transforming specifications automatically into executable programs by means of a *minimal model generator* for the underlying modal logic (cf. [StMF93]), determining the set of all legal tool compositions satisfying these constraints, which are graphically displayed,
3. supporting the investigation of the alternative legal tool compositions via a hypertext system, which helps the user navigate over the synthesized tool compositions, the taxonomic structure of the repository, and the documentation and code of the tools,
4. selecting on the solution graph suitable tool compositions for direct (interpreted) execution,
5. supporting the classification of satisfactory newly synthesized tools into the repository by proposing an appropriately precomputed default taxonomic classification. These classifications are sufficient for future retrieval, but can also be modified by means of the hypertext system,
6. compiling selected tool compositions for a permanent inclusion in the tool repository. This supports hierarchical tool design.

The experience with META-Frame is very promising: it reveals unexpected alternative solutions and makes the understanding of the available tools and their interaction transparent. Moreover, the possibility of natural language-like specification, the hypertext support of repository navigation, the specific profiles of

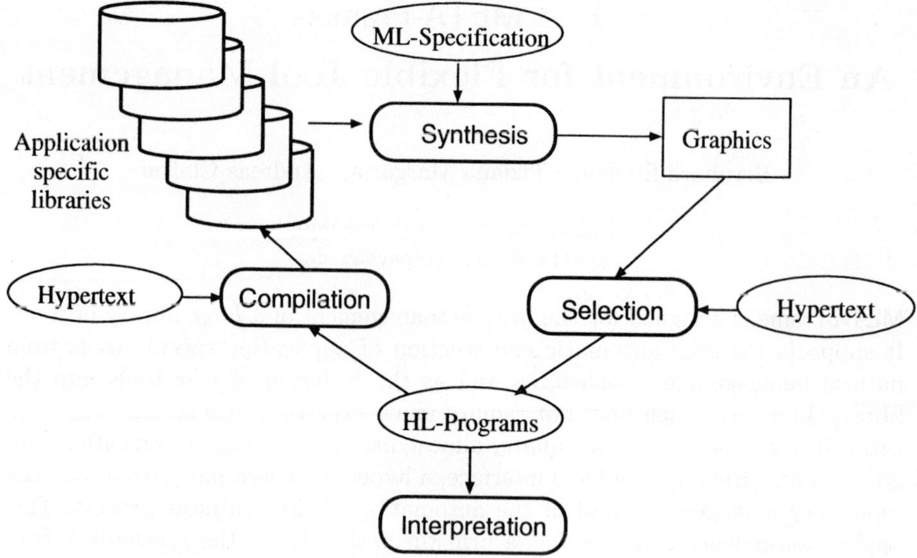

Fig. 1. The META-Frame synthesis lifecycle

the stored tools, and the user friendly graphical interface encourage successful experimentation without requiring much expertise. In fact, one can use META-Frame also as an educational tool to train newcomers in an application field.

As META-Frame is an open system, it can easily be extended and modified to include further tools, to realize a a highly distributed environment where tools are retrieved at need, and to cover other application domains. These properties are particularly important in emerging areas like Hardware/Software codesign, where integration of heterogeneous domains is a key point.

Applications range from the semi-automatic intelligent network programming for advanced telephone services (in cooperation with Siemens Nixdorf, Munich), over the automatic configuration of complex UNIX piping sequences for text and image processing [SFCM94], to the automatic generation of complex tools from a repository of components.

References

[SFCM94] B. Steffen, B. Freitag, A. Claßen, T. Margaria, U. Zukowski: "*Intelligent Software Synthesis in the* DaCapo *Environment*," 6th Nordic Worksh. on Programming Theory, Aarhus (DK), Oct. 1994, BRICS Rep. N.94/6.

[StMF93] B. Steffen, T. Margaria, B. Freitag: "*Module Configuration by Minimal Model Construction*," Techn. Rep. MIP 93-13, Fak. für Mathematik und Informatik, Universität Passau (Germany), Dec. 1993.

STeP: The Stanford Temporal Prover

Zohar Manna, Nikolaj Bjørner, Anca Browne, Edward Chang, Michael Colón, Luca de Alfaro, Harish Devarajan, Arjun Kapur, Jaejin Lee, Henny Sipma and Tomás Uribe

Computer Science Department, Stanford University
Stanford, CA 94305

The Stanford Temporal Prover, STeP, supports the computer-aided formal verification of reactive (and, in particular, concurrent) systems based on temporal specifications. Reactive systems maintain an ongoing interaction with their environment; their specifications are typically expressed as constraints on their behavior over time. Unlike most systems for temporal verification, STeP is not restricted to finite-state systems, but combines model checking with deductive methods to allow the verification of a broad class of systems, including parameterized (N-component) circuit designs, parameterized (N-process) programs, and programs with infinite data domains. In short, STeP has been designed with the objective of combining the expressiveness of deductive methods with the simplicity of model checking.

STeP verifies temporal properties of systems by means of verification rules and verification diagrams. *Verification rules* are used to reduce temporal properties of systems to first-order verification conditions [MP95]. *Verification diagrams* [MP94] provide a visual language for guiding, organizing, and displaying proofs. Verification diagrams allow the user to construct proofs hierarchically, starting from a high-level, intuitive proof sketch and proceeding incrementally, as necessary, through layers of greater detail.

The system implements powerful techniques for automatic *invariant generation*. Deductive verification almost always relies on finding, for a given program and specification, suitably strong (inductive) invariants and intermediate assertions. The user can typically provide an intuitive, high-level invariant, from which the system derives stronger, more detailed, *top-down invariants*. Simultaneously, *bottom-up invariants* are generated automatically by analyzing the program text. By combining these two methods, the system can often deduce sufficiently detailed invariants to carry through the entire verification process.

The system also provides an integrated suite of simplification and decision procedures for automatically checking the validity of a large class of first-order and temporal formulas. This degree of automated deduction is sufficient to handle most of the verification conditions that arise in deductive verification.

An overview of STeP is shown in Figure 1. The main inputs are a reactive system (which can be a hardware or software description) and a property to be proven about the system, represented by a temporal logic formula. Verification can be performed either by the model checker or by deductive means. In the latter case, the proof is typically automatic for safety properties. The proof of progress properties may require user guidance, provided by verification diagrams.

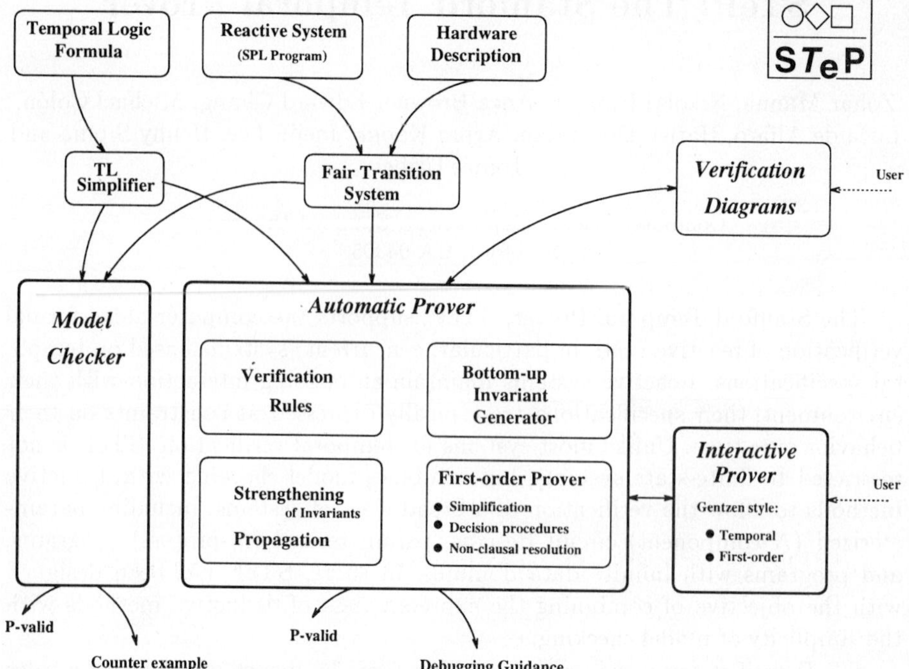

Fig. 1. An overview of the STeP system

In either case, the automatic prover is responsible for generating and proving the required verification conditions. An interactive Gentzen-style theorem prover and a resolution-based prover are available to establish the few verification conditions that are not proved automatically. For a more extensive description of the STeP system and examples of verified programs, the reader is referred to [MAB+94].

STeP is implemented in Standard ML of New Jersey, using CML and eXene for its X-windows user interface. An educational version of the system is currently available. For information on obtaining the system, send e-mail to `step-request@cs.stanford.edu`.

References

[MAB+94] Z. Manna, A. Anuchitanukul, N. Bjørner, A. Browne, E. Chang, M. Colón, L. de Alfaro, H. Devarajan, H. Sipma, and T. Uribe. STeP: the Stanford Temporal Prover. Technical report STAN-CS-TR-94-1518, Computer Science Department, Stanford University, June 1994.

[MP94] Z. Manna and A. Pnueli. Temporal verification diagrams. In *Proc. of the Int. Symp. on Theoretical Aspects of Computer Software*, volume 789 of *LNCS*, pages 726–765. Springer-Verlag, April 1994.

[MP95] Z. Manna and A. Pnueli. *Temporal Verification of Reactive Systems: Safety.* Springer-Verlag, New York, 1995.

The HOL-UNITY verification system

Flemming Andersen Ulla Binau Karsten Nyblad
Kim Dam Petersen Jimmi S. Pettersson

Tele Danmark Research, Lyngsø Allé 2, DK-2970 Hørsholm

Abstract. The HOL-UNITY verification system consists of a collection of tools for specifying and verifying UNITY programs and their properties. All the tools interface the theorem prover HOL for proving the properties of UNITY programs. In this way HOL-UNITY supports mechanised proving of correctness for parallel programs.

Description

A goal of the HOL-UNITY system is the development of aids for the production of reliable software within the telecommunications industry. The present system consists of several tools:

1. A theorem prover, which is actually a mechanisation of the UNITY theory [1, 5] with some extensions in the Cambridge Higher Order Logic theorem prover HOL [2, 3]. The extensions are mainly support for restricted properties similar to Beverly Sanders' subscripted properties [4]. For automatically proving basic UNITY properties (safety and ensures) specialised tactics are implemented in the HOL system.
2. A compiler, which translates UNITY programs, properties, and proofs into HOL representation. The compiler recognises an extended UNITY language, which includes sequential programming constructs, program modules, restricted properties, Chandy and Misra style natural deduction proofs, HOL-style proofs, etc.
3. A graphical tool for developing annotated proof lattices for leadsto properties and translating them into natural deduction style UNITY proofs. Annotated proof lattices are similar to Lamport and Owicki proof lattices but specialised to the UNITY logic, and supplied with annotations which guides the theorem prover in proving the basic properties of the lattices.
4. A compiler for translating verified UNITY programs into executable CC++ (Compositional C++) programs.

The HOL-UNITY system has been used to verify a number of smaller examples such as: mutual exclusion, readers and writers, a two-way arbiter, a lift-control, and a sliding window protocol. All these examples have been exercises towards its application on real problems.

Especially the lift-control example has demonstrated how these tools can be used together for developing a program and property specification, verifying that the program satisfies the required properties, and finally generating an executable program. The lift-control example was developed by first specifying the required properties, and then without taking verification perspectives into consideration the program was specified. This strategy was used to achieve a more realistic scenario for the verification.

The next steps towards realistic applications is the currently on-going task of specifying and verifying an ATM-protocol using the HOL-UNITY tools and the development of tactics for reasoning about service and feature interaction.

Environment: Preferably DecStation 5000/200, but also Sun SPARC, or Sun 3/60 running Ultrix and Standard ML of New Jersey, version 0.93 with 64MB RAM and 150 MB swap

Contact: For further information please email: fa@tdr.dk, or look into WWW URL: http:/www/TDR-Home.html

References

1. K. Mani Chandy and Jayadev Misra. *Parallel Program Design: A Foundation.* Addison–Wesley, 1988.
2. M. J. C. Gordon and T. F. Melham. *Introduction to HOL. A theorem proving environment for higher order logic.* Cambridge University Press, Computer Laboratory, 1993.
3. K. Slind. HOL90 Users Manual. Technical report, 1992.
4. Beverly A. Sanders. Eliminating the Substitution Axiom from UNITY Logic. *Formal Aspects of Computing*, 3(2):189–205, April-June 1991.
5. Flemming Andersen. *A Theorem Prover for UNITY in Higher Order Logic.* PhD thesis, Technical University of Denmark, 1992. Also published as TFL RT 1992-3, Tele Danmark Research, 1992.
6. F. Andersen, K.D. Petersen, and J.S. Pettersson. *Program Verification using HOL-UNITY.* In *Higher Order Logic Theorem Proving and Its Applications, 6th International Workshop, HUG'93*, LNCS 780, pages 1–15, 1993.
7. F. Andersen, K.D. Petersen, and J.S. Pettersson. *A Graphical Tool for Proving Progress.* In *Higher Order Logic Theorem Proving and Its Applications, 7th International Workshop, HUG'94*, LNCS 859, pages 17–32, 1994.
8. F. Andersen, K.D. Petersen, and J.S. Pettersson. *Verification of Software.* Teleteknik, Vol. 1–2, 1993, English Edition. Pages 66–75.
9. U. Binau. *Correct Concurrent Programs: A UNITY design method for Compositional C++ programs.* PhD thesis, Technical University of Denmark, 1994.
10. U. Binau. *Mechanical Verification of a CC++ Mutual Exclusion Program in HOL-UNITY.* Technical report in preparation, Tele Danmark Research, 1994.
11. K.D. Petersen and J.S. Pettersson. *Proving Protocols Correct – Proving Safety and Progress Properties of the Sliding Window Protocol using HOL-UNITY.* Research Report TFL RR 1993-3, Tele Danmark Research, December 1993.

PLATO: A Tool to Assist Programming as Term Rewriting and Theorem Proving

Andre J. Sampaio, Armando M. Haeberer, Claudio T. Prates,
Cristina D. Ururahy, Marcelo F. Frias and Neudson C. Albuquerque

Pontifícia Universidade Católica do Rio de Janeiro, Department of Informatics,
Rua Marquês de São Vicente 225, CEP 22453-900, Rio de Janeiro, RJ, Brazil
e-mails: {andre,armando,terra,ururahy,mfrias,neudson}@inf.puc-rio.br

In this paper we present PLATO, a tool designed for theory presentation construction, theorem proving and formula derivation. It was motivated by equational algebraic theory manipulation needs, nevertheless its aim is software development by program calculation. PLATO has applications in algebra — boolean algebra, relation algebra, etc. — and mathematical logic — as a general framework for theorem proving under different logics —. In the field of software development, we show its application in program calculi construction and in program development under these calculi.

We will consider a programming calculus as being a theory presentation within a given logic. Thus, the task of constructing new calculi can be thought of as one of building new theory presentations. This is true for, in particular, programming calculi based on Relation Algebras, Functional Programming, Fork Algebras, Type Theory and the like.

We will consider a theory presentation as a pair $< \mathcal{T}, \mathcal{F} >$, where $\mathcal{T}$ is a similarity type, i.e., declaration of operation symbols with their arity, and $\mathcal{F}$ is a *finite* set of formulas constituting an axiomatization for that theory.

Constructing Calculi as Theories[1]**.** Since theories are presented as finite sets of axioms, to build from scratch a new theory presentation we must provide the axioms characterizing it. In order to do so the system has a pool of so-called "Platonic" formulas. These are abstract formulas whose semantics is undetermined until one instantiates their operation and relation symbols . Thus, platonic formulas are "incarnated" — the operation and relation symbols occurring in them are binded to the operation and relation symbols in the corresponding similarity type — to give raise to wffs of the theory under development. In order to construct theory presentations PLATO implements, among others, the following operations:

1. *Incarnation of Platonic Formulas*: Allows the addition of new wffs to presentations, for instance, new transformation rules to programming calculi.
2. *Sum of Presentations*: Joins two presentations . The theorems already proved about each presentation are inherited by the target presentation.
3. *Extension and Restriction of Presentations*: Allows addition and deletion of axioms from presentations. This facility is very useful, in mathematics, for con-

[1] The concept of theory manipulation for calculi construction was experimented in Carnaval, a prototype upon which Plato was developed.

structing bigger or smaller classes of models; while in programming, because axioms and theorems represent transformations or construction steps.

Theorem Proving and Software Development. Once a theory presentation is constructed, PLATO can be applied to the process of theorem proving and term manipulation. Keeping in mind our interest in developing software by means of programming calculi, theorem proving is necessary for establishing the correctness of guess steps, while term manipulation is required for performing correct steps. In order to be adequate for programming calculi, the process of theorem proving must have some particular characteristics. During the interactive proof of a theorem, an allowance is made for decisions which are not formally justified. It is useless to formally base a difficult proof step one is unsure will lead to a satisfactory proof of the theorem as a whole. Furthermore, a system that allows guessing, besides *logical proof steps*, also permits to perform *mathematical* proofs.

PLATO has a subsystem that deals with theorem proving and formula derivation. This subsystem allows the performance of guess steps, invoking automatic theorem provers or the interactive theorem prover SYFOM — SYmbolic FOrmula Manipulator. SYFOM is a symbolic manipulation environment based on a rewriting system that allows derivations of formulas and theorem proving under well–defined theory presentations. Its development was motivated by the necessity of dealing, in a clean and organized way, with expressions, rules, axioms and theorems. SYFOM helps the user by suggesting only those axioms and previously proved theorems which are suitable for a determined derivation step.

SYFOM allows to "fold" sub–expressions and "unfold" names of previously folded expressions. It thus makes possible fold/unfold derivation steps in program construction, one of the most important strategies for program development by means of programming calculi. Furthermore, it allows one to choose subexpressions and to continue the derivation process starting from them.

Cases of Study. Currently, there are two cases of study implemented within PLATO. These are, a programming calculus based on Fork Algebras, and an interactive theorem prover for Relation Algebras. Once automatic theorem provers for Relation Algebras and Fork Algebras were implemented, some proof steps take place automatically.

Implementation Issues. PLATO is being developed in HyperCard, Mathematica and plain C. HyperCard, a popular hypertext system for the Apple Macintosh, is used as a man–machine interface generator. Mathematica is a powerful and comprehensive system for mathematical computation. It is used in SYFOM due to its powerful pattern matching mechanism and for its facilities for easy implementation of rewriting rules. Programs written for Mathematica are functionally compatible across a wide variety of hardware platforms. So, a PLATO user will deal with a friendly and customizable interface, which maintains transparency even when accessing SYFOM running on an unknown (and/or remote) hardware platform.

LOFT : a tool for assisting selection of test data sets from algebraic specifications

Bruno Marre

Université de Paris-Sud, Laboratoire de Recherche en Informatique, C.N.R.S. U.R.A. 410, Bâtiment 490, F-91405 Orsay Cedex, France
Phone : (33) 1 69 41 66 32, Email : marre@lri.fr

LOFT (LOgic for Functions and Testing) is a tool allowing to implement test data selection strategies from algebraic specifications. It is the necessary complement of the software testing theory and method proposed at the L.R.I ([1, 2]). We consider positive conditional specifications : the properties of the operations are described by equational Horn clauses. For every axiom, a finite subset of its ground instances is selected by assuming "selection hypotheses" on the program under test. More precisely, it is sufficient to only consider some instances of axioms conclusions such that the premisses are valid ([1, 2]).

In this demonstration we will illustrate the implementation of the selection strategies corresponding to two commonly used selection hypotheses : the regularity and uniformity hypotheses.
A *regularity hypothesis* for a variable occurring in a formula makes it possible to select instances of the formula such that the "size" of the variable substitutions is bounded by some value.
A *uniformity hypothesis* for a variable occurring in a formula makes it possible to select one instance of the formula with any substitution for the variable. Uniformity hypotheses are generalized to set of variables belonging to a subdomain (generally of the validity domain of the formula).

In order to point out sub-domains of an axiom validity domain which are good candidates for uniformity hypotheses, we use a case analysis technique : decomposition by unfolding, i.e. "equal by equal" replacements of the operations occurring in an axiom (introducing one sub-case for each axiom defining the unfolded operation).

The selection of instances corresponding to the above selection hypotheses, as well as the unfolding strategy, can be expressed as a controlled resolution of some equational problem. Thus, the kernel of LOFT is an equational resolution procedure for positive conditional specifications (conditional narrowing). More precisely, LOFT uses an efficient simulation of narrowing through Horn clause resolution : axioms and equational goals are translated into Horn clauses and predicate goals. In order to minimize the size of a narrowing tree, simplification steps of subgoals by rewriting are applied between narrowing steps. Moreover, the strategy adopted for the choice of the occurrence to be narrowed gives priority to occurrences that unify with a minimum number of axioms. This selection rule makes it possible to detect sooner failing computations and decreases the size of a narrowing tree by giving priority to deterministic computations. The completeness of the narrowing procedure is ensured by the use of an efficient and complete strategy : the iterative depth first search strategy.

Two controlled resolution procedures are proposed for the implementation of the unfolding strategy. Both procedures are applied to validity domains described by conjunctions of equations. They return sub-domains expressed by pairs of substitutions and constraints (constraints are conjunction of equations involving operations that are not unfolded).
The first unfolding implementation is activated by the `unfold_std` command which controls the unfolding through an argument list of operations that should not be unfolded. By default, an operation can be unfolded at most one time (in order to ensure termination for recursive definitions). However, it is possible to specify an arbitrary number of unfolding steps.
The other unfolding implementation needs a more deeper understanding of the narrowing procedure. It uses `do_not_unfold` meta clauses specifying which pattern of equation should not be unfolded. This meta control is similar to the "wait" or "delay" directives proposed in some logic programming languages.

For each sort s, LOFT automatically computes a typing function `is_a_s` and a canonical "size" function `alpha_s` (inductively defined w.r.t. the sort generators). They are respectively used for implementations of uniformity selection strategies and regularity selection strategies. The "size" function of a sort computes the number of non constant generators of the sort. A regularity selection strategy for a variable X of sort s bounded by b is implemented as the narrowing of a goal : $alpha\_s(X) \leq b = true$. For the implementation of uniformity selection strategies (on a variable or on a sub-domain), we select the first solution of some goal (a typing goal for uniformity on a variable, or the equations defining the sub-domain for a uniformity on a sub-domain) computed with a random choice strategy for the choice of the axiom to be applied. This particular axiom selection rule allows to compute solutions of a narrowing goal in a non deterministic order. This strategy is activated in LOFT by the "?" command.

LOFT works on Sun4 station under X11. It was developed with the ECLIPSE prolog environment distributed by the ECRC. Its interface is programmed with the Tk/Tcl toolkit. The demonstration of the tool is done on two examples :

- Test data are selected from a specification of sorted lists. This simple example allows to smoothly introduce selection hypotheses and strategies.
- Then, we consider a specification of the door monitoring module of an automatic subway ([3]). We show how to select test data sets allowing to verify the different alarm conditions of this monitoring module.

References

1. Bernot, G. and Gaudel, M.-C. and Marre, B. *Software testing based on formal specifications: a theory and a tool* Software Engineering Journal, Vol.6, Num.6, pp.387-405. November 1991.
2. Gaudel, M.-C. *Testing can be formal, too* Proceedings of TAPSOFT'95. March 1995.
3. Dauchy, P. and Gaudel, M.-C. and Marre, B. *Using algebraic specifications in software testing: a case study on the software of an automatic subway* Journal of Systems and Software, ELSEVIER, Vol.21, Num.3, pp.229-244. June 1993.

The SMoLCS ToolSet *

Egidio Astesiano, Gianna Reggio, Franco Morando **

Dipartimento di Informatica e Scienze dell'Informazione, Università di Genova, Italy

SMoLCS is a formal method, based on algebraic specifications, for specifying *dynamic systems* at different levels of abstraction (from initial requirements till complete design); here by dynamic system we mean a system able to evolve along the time (e.g. a concurrent/parallel/distributed program, a net of computers, a hydro-electric central or an information system).

Formally, a dynamic system is a labelled transition system, which is a triple (S, L, T), where S is a set of states, L a set of labels and T a set of triples (s, l, s'), called transitions, with $s, s' \in S$ and $l \in L$. The states model the intermediate situations of a dynamic system, the labels its possible interactions with the external world and the transitions its possible activity in the sense that each transition corresponds to an action capability. Thus the behaviour of the dynamic system starting from a given state is represented by a labelled transition tree, called execution tree.

Since we need to consider different types of dynamic systems, different ways to compose them and different data structures, we organize all that in an overall algebraic structure, called dynamic algebra. A dynamic algebra is a many-sorted algebra with predicates on a dynamic signature, i.e. a signature where some sorts (dynamic sorts) correspond to states of lts's, and each of them has an associated sort of labels and a ternary predicate corresponding to the transitions.

SMoLCS specifications are pairs consisting of a dynamic signature and a set of axioms, distinguished in: *design specifications* (with conditional axioms and initial semantics), which determine *one* dynamic system by describing abstractly its structure and its activity, including the concurrent cooperations among its components; *requirement specifications* (with axioms of first-order logic extended by temporal combinators and loose semantics) which determine *one class* of dynamic systems by stating their properties, like liveness and safety. Moreover, it is formally defined when a design specification correctly implements a requirement specification. The specifications are written in a user-friendly language METAL, supporting both the design and the requirement level.

A software toolset has been developed to support the development of the SMoLCS specifications, consisting of: a checker of the static correctness of the METAL specifications (METAL-CHECKER); a rapid prototyper (SMoLCS-RP) which, given a design specification of a dynamic system and a state, generates the execution tree starting from such state; and a graphic user interface for SMoLCS-RP (TREE WALKER).

---

* This work has been partly supported by "Progetto Finalizzato Sistemi Informatici e Calcolo Parallelo" of C.N.R. (Italy) and by HCM–Medicis.

** E.Astesiano and G.Reggio have developed the SMoLCS method; F.Morando has developed the basic algorithm for the prototyper and the overall tool architecture.

METAL-CHECKER takes in input a SMoLCS specification and gives the detailed list of errors found during the parsing (lexical, syntax and type errors); it also disambiguates overloadings and signals ambiguous formulae. Moreover it translates a correct specification into the appropriate internal format for SMoLCS-RP, which generates the execution tree starting from a given state. The user may choose different strategies for building the tree. TREE WALKER shows parts of such tree while SMoLCS-RP is still producing it; thus also dynamic systems with infinite execution tree may be investigated.

The generation of the execution tree requires the solution of queries in an algebraic theory with conditional equations and predicates. Usually, these solutions are obtained by using conditional narrowing (CNA) or similar approaches. Such algorithms are unsuitable for our purposes since they tend to fall into endless proofs too frequently; hence we devised a more specialized algorithm called SCNA, which is a restriction of CNA proven to be complete for a meaningful decidable subclass of SMoLCS specifications called separable. SCNA separates logical deduction and functional evaluation to provide an effective complete replacement of CNA. SMoLCS-RP is able to solve, in a reasonable amount of time, systems of equations in the domain of separable specifications. Thus SMoLCS-RP can build the execution tree and also prototype the static subparts of the specifications (data structures) by evaluating operations and predicates on particular arguments.

The TREE WALKER uses Diagram Server (a tool for visualizing graphs, developed by P. Di Battista and his group at the University of Rome) for visualizing the tree topology and the information associated with the nodes and the arcs. The user may in this phase decide which nodes do not need to be further expanded ("frozen" nodes). The frozen nodes may be melted successively and they become eligible for further expansions. The format with which this information is visualized is defined in a highly-parameterized way by means of unparsing schemas allowing to generate an output following the preferences of the user. The toolset has been mainly developed in Prolog, and there is a small part written in C for the interface with Diagram Server. The Prolog code is written for more than 90% following the DEC-10 standard and thus, in principle, it might be easily portable on other Prolog interpreters and compilers. For what concerns the TREE WALKER graphical interface, we have used the Widget set supplied by the Motif interface of the Quintus Prolog V3.1. The toolset has been developed on a HP9000/700 under UNIX HP-UX A.08.07 with Quintus Prolog 3.1 interfaced with Motif 1.0 and X11 Rel. 3. The graphical interface uses, together with Motif, also Diagram Server V1.1; thus in this stage the toolset is available on machines that support Quintus Prolog 3.1 and Diagram Server V1.1.

The toolset software has been developed by F.Morando, A.Capani, F. Parodi, L.Campora and G.Delzanno. A.Giovini († 93) also contributed with F.Morando to the overall architecture.

References and documentations about SMoLCS are available by anonymous ftp at `ftp.disi.unige.it` in the directory `pub/smolcs`; for further information and any question e-mail to `smolcs@disi.unige.it`.

The ASF+SDF Meta-Environment Documentation Tools for Free!

M. G. J. van den Brand and E. Visser

Programming Research Group, University of Amsterdam
Kruislaan 403, NL-1098 SJ Amsterdam, The Netherlands
email: {markvdb,visser}@fwi.uva.nl
www: http://adam.fwi.uva.nl/~{markvdb,visser}/

Introduction Algebraic specifications can be used for the specification of various aspects of programming languages. The executability of the specifications provides not only a mechanism for rapid prototyping, but also tools that can be connected to a programming environment for the language specified.

Over the last 10 years, the programming environments group at CWI and UvA in Amsterdam has conducted research on the generation of programming environments from formal specifications . The main results of this research are:

- The algebraic specification formalism ASF+SDF designed especially for defining the syntax and semantics of (programming) languages [1, 4];
- An interactive Meta-environment for the development and prototyping of programming environments for programming languages [5].

An important consideration in the design of the ASF+SDF formalism and Meta-environment has been the ease of specification of all relevant properties of programming languages: syntax, static semantics, dynamic semantics, transformations, and so on.

The ASF+SDF Formalism ASF+SDF is a combination of the formalisms ASF [1] and SDF [4]. ASF—Algebraic Specification Formalism—supports many-sorted first-order signatures, conditional equations, and modularization. SDF—Syntax Definition Formalism—supports modular definition of lexical and context-free syntax, possibly disambiguated by priorities. In the combination with ASF, the context-free syntax rules in an SDF definition are interpreted as first-order function declarations.

The ASF+SDF Meta-environment The Meta-environment is an interactive environment for the development of ASF+SDF specifications, which can be immediately executed. This is achieved by lazy and incremental generation of scanners and parsers using the SDF parts of the ASF+SDF specification. The equations can be executed as term rewriting systems, which are incrementally updated after modifications in the specifications.

The ASF+SDF Meta-environment has been used in the development of programming environments for several programming languages. To name a few: λ-calculus, Eiffel, Action Semantics, Pascal, Lotos. It has been applied during the development of some commercial products: modeling of financial products and modeling of security constraints for the Dutch Railway Company. It is also used in teaching computer science courses such as Software Engineering and Compiler Construction.

Generation of Documentation Tools A recent extension to the system is a pretty printer generator. Given the SDF definition of a language a pretty printer for this language can be generated [2]. A generated pretty printer can be manually tuned in order to obtain a satisfactory result. The pretty printer works in two phases, it translates the abstract syntax tree of a program into a box expression, which is then translated into text. This approach enables us to obtain documentation tools with little effort for any language for which a specification exists. A translator from boxes to TEX produces code which can be incorporated in TEX or LATEX documents [3]. All components of this tool are specified in ASF+SDF.

Demonstration In the first part of the demonstration we give an overview of the possibilities and functionality of the ASF+SDF Meta-environment. In the second part the generation of a documentation tool for a specific language is explained and the generated tool is demonstrated by giving some examples.

More Information Information on ASF+SDF and the Meta-environment is available through WWW via http://www.cwi.nl/~gipe/[asf+sdf.html]. The meta-environment is part of the Centaur system. The procedure to get centaur is fully explained on WWW page http://www.inria.fr/croap/centaur/get.html. Approximately 35 Mb of disk space is needed. Installation is possible on SunOS4, Solaris, or Silicon Graphics IRIX4/5. Main memory size should be at least 16MB.

References

1. J.A. Bergstra, J. Heering, and P. Klint, editors. *Algebraic Specification.* ACM Press Frontier Series. The ACM Press in co-operation with Addison-Wesley, 1989.
2. M. G. J. van den Brand. Generation of language independent prettyprinters. Technical Report P9327, programming Research Group, University of Amsterdam, Amsterdam, October 1993.
3. Mark van den Brand and Eelco Visser. From Box to TEX: An algebraic approach to the generation of documentation tools. Technical Report P9420, Programming Research Group, University of Amsterdam, July 1994. Available as ftp://ftp.fwi.uva.nl/pub/programming-research/reports/1994/P9420.ps.Z.
4. J. Heering, P.R.H. Hendriks, P. Klint, and J. Rekers. *The syntax definition formalism SDF - reference manual,* version 6 December, 1992. Earlier version in *SIGPLAN Notices,* 24(11):43-75, 1989. Available as ftp: //ftp.cwi.nl /pub/gipe/reports/ SDF-Manual.ps.Z.
5. P. Klint. A meta-environment for generating programming environments. *ACM Transactions on Software Engineering and Methodology,* 2(2):176–201, 1993.

The B-Toolkit Demonstration

B-Core (UK) Ltd.

The Magdalen Centre, The Oxford Science Park, Oxford OX4 4GA, UK

The B-Toolkit is a suite of integrated programs which implement the B-Method for Software Development. The B-Method is a collection of mathematical based techniques which give a formal basis to those activities of Software Development that range from software specification, through design and integration, to code generation and into maintenance.

The B-Toolkit's components tools are implemented in the B Theory Language and is interpreted by the B-Tool. The B Theory language is a special purpose language for writing Software Engineering tools including interactive and automatic proof assistants and other tools where pattern matching, substitution and re-write mechanisms is used (e.g. translators, interpreters and generators).

Technical Description The B-Toolkit and the B-Method underwent eight years of research and development at British Petroleum, and its commercial development is done by B-Core(UK) Ltd. in Oxford. Many aspects of the B-Method have been devised by J.R.Abrial. The B-Toolkit covers many aspects of software engineering, including:

- Syntax and type-checking of specification documents as well as low level design documents, with comprehensive error reporting.
- Verification condition generation which generates the proof-obligations needed to guarantee specification consistency and correctness of refinement.
- Automatic & interactive provers for discharging the verification conditions. Proof listing for visualising how the Automatic prover discharges proof-obligations.
- Specification animation, enabling the specification to be 'run', validated and tested.
- A translator for translating low level design documents into C. Code generation from declarative descriptions, facilitated by a re-usable library of code modules.
- A Library of reusable code modules, which are all accessed and used according to their given specification.
- Rapid prototyping, facilitated by an interface generator, built on the re-usable library.
- Automatic Production, Markup and Indexing of documentation of complete developments.
- Remaking facilities when a source file is altered; the scope of the remake is determined by the toolkit, and the system is rebuilt automatically to its former state, including code, documentation and proofs.

– All tools are fully integrated and designed to run automatically. All tools are activated from a uniform portable comfortable Motif-based control panel which indicates the admissible commands. Help facilities are on-line.

The B-Method The B-Method is a mathematical method belonging to the school of thought known as the "model oriented" approach to software construction.

The notation, in particular the generalised substitution notation used by the B-Method is J.R.Abrial's extension to Dijkstra's calculus of guarded commands. The extension allows you to specify operations in terms of preconditions and postconditions. To the engineer, the formal notation looks like a simple pseudo programming notation. Also, there is no real distinction between the specification notation and the programming notation. The programming notation just appears as a subset of the specification notation.

The method and the notation have been designed together with the B-Toolkit that supports them, so that every aspect of the method has been validated by the genuine possibility of providing significant help to the engineer in using computer based tools to write, verify and maintain software.

Separate (object oriented) techniques within the method support the design of (large) specification and program construction. The complex dependencies within such big systems are automatically controlled by the tools.

The method is based on a series of embedded mathematical notations: the logical notation, the set notation (including the notation for relations, functions and sequences), the Natural Numbers, a substitution notation (predicate transformers), and the Abstract Machine Notation (AMN). The method and the notation is founded on set theory.

Industrial Usage In 1992 BP International conducted an Alpha-test programme for the B-Toolkit. This Alpha-test programme involved 10 industrial sites in Europe. In January 1993, B-Core(UK) Limited started the Beta-test programme on 12 industrial and academic sites. In June 1994 the B-Toolkit became commercially available.

IBM UK has completed the development of a major component for CICS/ESA using the B-Toolkit for specification, proof, design and implementation.

In 1991 BP International developed a Refinery Graphics System for controlling flow of oil within a refinery. The system was 45,000 lines of C of which 28,000 lines was developed using the B-Toolkit. The code generated by the B-Toolkit achieved high reliability and exceptional portability.

GEC Alsthom, Paris, have applied the B-Method to train control systems over the last 4 years. Matra Transport, Paris, has used the B-Toolkit extensively in specification of train control systems over the last 3 years. GEC-Marconi Aveonics is using the B-Toolkit for a pilot project developing embedded control systems. An industrial UK Users Trial Project led by Lloyds Register of Shipping, is providing continuous advice for further development of the B-Toolkit.

Object Oriented Semantics Directed Compiler Generation: A Prototype

Luiz Carlos Castro Guedes[1] Edward Hermann Haeusler[2] José Lucas Rangel[2]

The tool presented here is a prototype of a compiler generator centered on the denotational description of the source language. It is based on an object oriented translation model. This model maps the denotational definition of a programming language into an Object Oriented Programming Language with separated hierarchies for specifications (types) and implementations (classes). The central idea in the model is the mapping from syntactic and semantic domains into types, and from semantic functions into methods of those types. Semantic equations are mapped to the implementation of some of those methods. Its correctness has already been proved and a system prototype implemented. The entire translation process may be summarized by the following table:

Description Components	Examples	Resulting Code
Semantic Domains	δ:D	type tD; class cD;
Syntactic Domains	Δ:Dom	type Dom;
Semantic Functions	$\mathcal{J}$: Dom$\rightarrow$ $D_1 \rightarrow \ldots \rightarrow D_s \rightarrow$ D	type Dom is tD $\mathcal{J}$ (tD_1 δ_1, ..., tD_s δ_s); end;
Semantic Equations	$\mathcal{J}$[[Rule]]$(\delta_1, \delta_2, \ldots, \delta_s) = B$	tD $\mathcal{J}$ (tD_1 δ_1, ..., tD_s δ_s) B_n end;
Syntactic Rules	Rule: $\Delta = \Delta_1\ \Delta_2 \ldots \Delta_m$	class Rule of Dom variables : Dom_1 Δ_1; ... Dom_m Δ_m; methods: tD $\mathcal{J}$ (tD_1 δ_1, ..., tD_s δ_s) B_n end; end;

Table 1 - Translation Process Summary

The compiler generator has two major components: the Tree-Building-Parser Generator (TBPG) and the Denotational Compiler Generator (DCG), see figure 1.

The TBPG was based upon the syntactic analysis ascent method R*S [1], which ignores single production rules in a efficient way, producing smaller derivation trees and, thus, smaller abstract syntax trees (AST).

The DCG reads the standard semantics of the desired compiler input language, ***L***, and produces four files with the declaration of classes and definition of methods produced for either the Syntactic Domains and Semantic ones. Declarations of classes are at the C-style header files *L*.HSY and *L*.HSE and definition of their methods at the files *L*.CSY and *L*.CSE, respectively, where the suffix SY stands for syntactic constructions and SE for semantic ones.

Thus, a compiler (generated for a language L) works in three passes:

1. reading a program written in a language ***L*** and building its AST representation.
2. traversing the AST and producing its denotational representation.
3. compiling the denotational representation and linking it with semantic classes, producing an executable representation of the input program

It is interesting to observe that semantic classes are involved not only at run time, but also at compile time, since the methods of the syntactical classes (classes that correspond to syntactical domains) must know which classes they are generating code for.

[1]Universidade Federal Fluminense
[2]Pontifícia Universidade Católica do Rio de Janeiro
e-mail:{guedes, hermann, rangel}@inf.puc-rio.br
addr: Pontifícia Universidade Católica do Rio de Janeiro, Depto. de Informática, R. Marquês de S. Vicente 225, RDC, 4º andar, Gávea, Rio de Janeiro, RJ, BRAZIL, CEP 22453-900

The DCG prototype (written itself in C++) generates C++ code for classes which represent the denotations of the parts of the source program. Although it does not support separate hierarchies for types and classes, specifications can be written as abstract super-classes. A class that implements a type turns into a sub-class of the abstract class corresponding to the type. C++ seemed the best choice because it is the most powerful language available nowadays capable of simulating separate hierarchies and those functional features required by translation. Its high portability is another outstanding point.

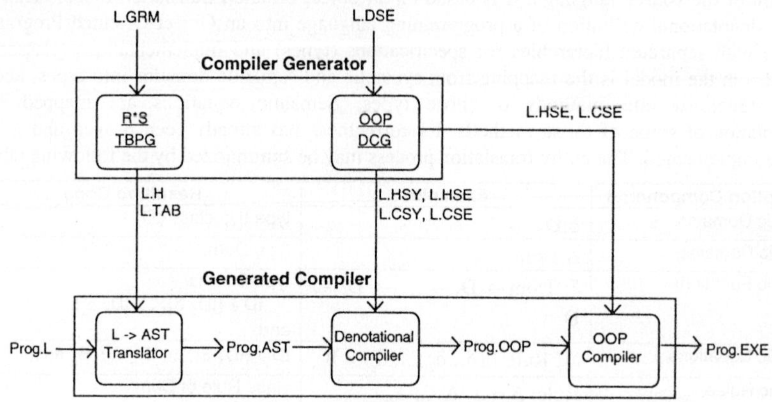

Figure 1 - Compiler Generation Process

Performance tests have shown our system outperforms similar systems [2,3,4,5] and that its produced compilers are just one order of magnitude slower than hand written ones. The great efficiency of the model is a promising step towards the automatic generation of production quality compilers. Thus, a natural and elegant model to translate programming language descriptions into realistic compilers with its correctness guaranteed has been obtained.

	with range checking		without range checking	
	Bubble Sort	Prime Number	Bubble Sort	Prime Number
Turbo Pascal V5.5	7.65 s	6.65 s	1.65 s	3.65 s
Produced Compiler	37 s	49 s	29 s	49 s
Slow-down	4.84	7.37	17.57	13.42

Table 2 - Execution time on the Cx80486 DLC

Table 1 shows execution times for a bubble sort algorithm on a 1000 integers array and for finding the 1000th prime number on a Cx80486 DLC computer with 40MHz of clock.

References

1. Schneider, S.M., "Gramáticas e Reconhecedores R*S(k)", D.Sc. Thesis, Universidade Federal do Rio de Janeiro, Brazil, 1987.
2. Mosses, P.D., "SIS - Semantic Implementation System", Technical Report Daimi MD-30, Computer Science Department, Aarhus University, 1979.
3. Moura, H.; Watt, D.; "Action Transformations in the ACTRESS Compiler Generator"; Compiler Construction - 5th International Conference CC94; Lecture Notes in Computer Science; vol. 786; Springer-Verlag; pp:16-30; 1994
4. Orbaek, P.; "OASIS: An Optimising Action-Based Compiler Generator"; Proceed. of the First International Workshop on ACTION SEMANTICS; Edinburgh, Scotland; 1994; BRICS Notes Series NS-94-1; pp: 99-114.
5. Palsberg, J., "Provably Correct Compiler Generation", Ph.D. Thesis, Aarhus University, Denmark, 1992.

Author Index

Abadi, M., 471
Aceto, L., 439
Albuquerque, N.C., 797
de Alfaro, L., 793
Amadio, R.M., 202
Andersen, F., 795
Andersen, H.R., 620
André, Y., 155
Astesiano, A., 801

B-Core (UK) Ltd., 805
Badouel, E., 364
Bareau, C., 711
Baumeister, H., 756
Bell, J., 546
Bellegarde, F., 546
Bernardinello, L., 364
Bert, D., 741
Bertot, Y., 531
Binau, U., 795
Bjørner, N., 793
Blazy, S., 666
Bloom, S.L., 318
Bossut, F., 155
Brand, M.G.J. van den, 803
Browne, A., 793

Caillaud, B., 711
Cardelli, L., 471
Chang, E., 793
Claßen, A., 791
Colón, M., 793

Dam, M., 202
Darondeau, Ph., 364
Devarajan, H., 793

Ehrig, H., 3
EP-ATR Project, 789
Ésik, Z., 318

Facon, Ph., 666
Floyd, C., 25
Fraer, R., 531
Frias, M.F., 797

Gaudel, M.-C., 82
Geser, A., 605
Goguen, J.A., 62
Guedes, L.C.C., 807

Haeberer, A.M., 797
Haeusler, E.H., 807
Halatsis, C., 486
Hofmann, M., 247
Hook, J., 546
Horwitz, S., 651

Ida, T., 394
Ingólfsdóttir, A., 439

Jančar, P., 349
Jard, C., 711
Jonsson, B., 262

Kapur, A., 793
Karali, I., 486
Karger, B. von, 232
Kieburtz, R.B., 546
Kleuker, S., 636
Kozen, D., 42
Krishna Rao, M.R.K., 379

Lano, K., 696
Lee, J., 793
Lewis, J., 546
Lin, H., 187
Liu, X., 217
Luqi, 62

Mahr, B., 3
Manna, Z., 793
Margaria, T., 791
Marre, B., 799
Meldal, S., 424
Mendler, M., 620
Middeldorp, A., 394
Morando, F., 801
Moreau, L., 726

Nielson, F., 590
Nielson, H.R., 590
Nyblad, K., 795

Okui, S., 394
Oliva, D., 546
Ørbæk, P., 575
Oriat, C., 741

Palsberg, J., 561
Peron, A., 454
Petersen, K.D., 795
Pettersson, J.S., 795
Potthoff, A., 125
Prates, C.T., 797
Pratt, V., 97, 108

Rangel, J.L., 807
Reggio, G., 801
Reps, T., 651

Sagiv, M., 651
Salomaa, K., 140
Sampaio, A.J., 797
Sands, D., 681
Sangiorgi, D., 172
Sannella, D., 247
Sassone, V., 334
Schieferdecker, I., 772
Selivanov, V., 277
Sheard, T., 546
Sipma, H., 793
Solberg, K.L., 501
Steffen, B., 791

Thoraval, R., 711
Tip, F., 516
Tsay, Y.-K., 262

Uribe, T., 793
Ururahy, C.D., 797

Visser, E., 803

Wacrenier, P.-A., 303
Wagner, A., 409
Walicki, M., 424
Walker, D., 217
Walton, L., 546
Wilke, T., 288

Yoo, H., 288

Zhou, T., 546

Springer-Verlag and the Environment

We at Springer-Verlag firmly believe that an international science publisher has a special obligation to the environment, and our corporate policies consistently reflect this conviction.

We also expect our business partners – paper mills, printers, packaging manufacturers, etc. – to commit themselves to using environmentally friendly materials and production processes.

The paper in this book is made from low- or no-chlorine pulp and is acid free, in conformance with international standards for paper permanency.

Lecture Notes in Computer Science

For information about Vols. 1–840
please contact your bookseller or Springer-Verlag

Vol. 841: I. Prívara, B. Rovan, P. Ružička (Eds.), Mathematical Foundations of Computer Science 1994. Proceedings, 1994. X, 628 pages. 1994.

Vol. 842: T. Kloks, Treewidth. IX, 209 pages. 1994.

Vol. 843: A. Szepietowski, Turing Machines with Sublogarithmic Space. VIII, 115 pages. 1994.

Vol. 844: M. Hermenegildo, J. Penjam (Eds.), Programming Language Implementation and Logic Programming. Proceedings, 1994. XII, 469 pages. 1994.

Vol. 845: J.-P. Jouannaud (Ed.), Constraints in Computational Logics. Proceedings, 1994. VIII, 367 pages. 1994.

Vol. 846: D. Shepherd, G. Blair, G. Coulson, N. Davies, F. Garcia (Eds.), Network and Operating System Support for Digital Audio and Video. Proceedings, 1993. VIII, 269 pages. 1994.

Vol. 847: A. L. Ralescu (Ed.) Fuzzy Logic in Artificial Intelligence. Proceedings, 1993. VII, 128 pages. 1994. (Subseries LNAI).

Vol. 848: A. R. Krommer, C. W. Ueberhuber, Numerical Integration on Advanced Computer Systems. XIII, 341 pages. 1994.

Vol. 849: R. W. Hartenstein, M. Z. Servít (Eds.), Field-Programmable Logic. Proceedings, 1994. XI, 434 pages. 1994.

Vol. 850: G. Levi, M. Rodríguez-Artalejo (Eds.), Algebraic and Logic Programming. Proceedings, 1994. VIII, 304 pages. 1994.

Vol. 851: H.-J. Kugler, A. Mullery, N. Niebert (Eds.), Towards a Pan-European Telecommunication Service Infrastructure. Proceedings, 1994. XIII, 582 pages. 1994.

Vol. 852: K. Echtle, D. Hammer, D. Powell (Eds.), Dependable Computing – EDCC-1. Proceedings, 1994. XVII, 618 pages. 1994.

Vol. 853: K. Bolding, L. Snyder (Eds.), Parallel Computer Routing and Communication. Proceedings, 1994. IX, 317 pages. 1994.

Vol. 854: B. Buchberger, J. Volkert (Eds.), Parallel Processing: CONPAR 94 – VAPP VI. Proceedings, 1994. XVI, 893 pages. 1994.

Vol. 855: J. van Leeuwen (Ed.), Algorithms – ESA '94. Proceedings, 1994. X, 510 pages.1994.

Vol. 856: D. Karagiannis (Ed.), Database and Expert Systems Applications. Proceedings, 1994. XVII, 807 pages. 1994.

Vol. 857: G. Tel, P. Vitányi (Eds.), Distributed Algorithms. Proceedings, 1994. X, 370 pages. 1994.

Vol. 858: E. Bertino, S. Urban (Eds.), Object-Oriented Methodologies and Systems. Proceedings, 1994. X, 386 pages. 1994.

Vol. 859: T. F. Melham, J. Camilleri (Eds.), Higher Order Logic Theorem Proving and Its Applications. Proceedings, 1994. IX, 470 pages. 1994.

Vol. 860: W. L. Zagler, G. Busby, R. R. Wagner (Eds.), Computers for Handicapped Persons. Proceedings, 1994. XX, 625 pages. 1994.

Vol: 861: B. Nebel, L. Dreschler-Fischer (Eds.), KI-94: Advances in Artificial Intelligence. Proceedings, 1994. IX, 401 pages. 1994. (Subseries LNAI).

Vol. 862: R. C. Carrasco, J. Oncina (Eds.), Grammatical Inference and Applications. Proceedings, 1994. VIII, 290 pages. 1994. (Subseries LNAI).

Vol. 863: H. Langmaack, W.-P. de Roever, J. Vytopil (Eds.), Formal Techniques in Real-Time and Fault-Tolerant Systems. Proceedings, 1994. XIV, 787 pages. 1994.

Vol. 864: B. Le Charlier (Ed.), Static Analysis. Proceedings, 1994. XII, 465 pages. 1994.

Vol. 865: T. C. Fogarty (Ed.), Evolutionary Computing. Proceedings, 1994. XII, 332 pages. 1994.

Vol. 866: Y. Davidor, H.-P. Schwefel, R. Männer (Eds.), Parallel Problem Solving from Nature - PPSN III. Proceedings, 1994. XV, 642 pages. 1994.

Vol 867: L. Steels, G. Schreiber, W. Van de Velde (Eds.), A Future for Knowledge Acquisition. Proceedings, 1994. XII, 414 pages. 1994. (Subseries LNAI).

Vol. 868: R. Steinmetz (Ed.), Multimedia: Advanced Teleservices and High-Speed Communication Architectures. Proceedings, 1994. IX, 451 pages. 1994.

Vol. 869: Z. W. Raś, Zemankova (Eds.), Methodologies for Intelligent Systems. Proceedings, 1994. X, 613 pages. 1994. (Subseries LNAI).

Vol. 870: J. S. Greenfield, Distributed Programming Paradigms with Cryptography Applications. XI, 182 pages. 1994.

Vol. 871: J. P. Lee, G. G. Grinstein (Eds.), Database Issues for Data Visualization. Proceedings, 1993. XIV, 229 pages. 1994.

Vol. 872: S Arikawa, K. P. Jantke (Eds.), Algorithmic Learning Theory. Proceedings, 1994. XIV, 575 pages. 1994.

Vol. 873: M. Naftalin, T. Denvir, M. Bertran (Eds.), FME '94: Industrial Benefit of Formal Methods. Proceedings, 1994. XI, 723 pages. 1994.

Vol. 874: A. Borning (Ed.), Principles and Practice of Constraint Programming. Proceedings, 1994. IX, 361 pages. 1994.

Vol. 875: D. Gollmann (Ed.), Computer Security – ESORICS 94. Proceedings, 1994. XI, 469 pages. 1994.

Vol. 876: B. Blumenthal, J. Gornostaev, C. Unger (Eds.), Human-Computer Interaction. Proceedings, 1994. IX, 239 pages. 1994.

Vol. 877: L. M. Adleman, M.-D. Huang (Eds.), Algorithmic Number Theory. Proceedings, 1994. IX, 323 pages. 1994.

Vol. 878: T. Ishida; Parallel, Distributed and Multiagent Production Systems. XVII, 166 pages. 1994. (Subseries LNAI).

Vol. 879: J. Dongarra, J. Waśniewski (Eds.), Parallel Scientific Computing. Proceedings, 1994. XI, 566 pages. 1994.

Vol. 880: P. S. Thiagarajan (Ed.), Foundations of Software Technology and Theoretical Computer Science. Proceedings, 1994. XI, 451 pages. 1994.

Vol. 881: P. Loucopoulos (Ed.), Entity-Relationship Approach – ER'94. Proceedings, 1994. XIII, 579 pages. 1994.

Vol. 882: D. Hutchison, A. Danthine, H. Leopold, G. Coulson (Eds.), Multimedia Transport and Teleservices. Proceedings, 1994. XI, 380 pages. 1994.

Vol. 883: L. Fribourg, F. Turini (Eds.), Logic Program Synthesis and Transformation – Meta-Programming in Logic. Proceedings, 1994. IX, 451 pages. 1994.

Vol. 884: J. Nievergelt, T. Roos, H.-J. Schek, P. Widmayer (Eds.), IGIS '94: Geographic Information Systems. Proceedings, 1994. VIII, 292 pages. 19944.

Vol. 885: R. C. Veltkamp, Closed Objects Boundaries from Scattered Points. VIII, 144 pages. 1994.

Vol. 886: M. M. Veloso, Planning and Learning by Analogical Reasoning. XIII, 181 pages. 1994. (Subseries LNAI).

Vol. 887: M. Toussaint (Ed.), Ada in Europe. Proceedings, 1994. XII, 521 pages. 1994.

Vol. 888: S. A. Andersson (Ed.), Analysis of Dynamical and Cognitive Systems. Proceedings, 1993. VII, 260 pages. 1995.

Vol. 889: H. P. Lubich, Towards a CSCW Framework for Scientific Cooperation in Europe. X, 268 pages. 1995.

Vol. 890: M. J. Wooldridge, N. R. Jennings (Eds.), Intelligent Agents. Proceedings, 1994. VIII, 407 pages. 1995. (Subseries LNAI).

Vol. 891: C. Lewerentz, T. Lindner (Eds.), Formal Development of Reactive Systems. XI, 394 pages. 1995.

Vol. 892: K. Pingali, U. Banerjee, D. Gelernter, A. Nicolau, D. Padua (Eds.), Languages and Compilers for Parallel Computing. Proceedings, 1994. XI, 496 pages. 1995.

Vol. 893: G. Gottlob, M. Y. Vardi (Eds.), Database Theory – ICDT '95. Proceedings, 1995. XI, 454 pages. 1995.

Vol. 894: R. Tamassia, I. G. Tollis (Eds.), Graph Drawing. Proceedings, 1994. X, 471 pages. 1995.

Vol. 895: R. L. Ibrahim (Ed.), Software Engineering Education. Proceedings, 1995. XII, 449 pages. 1995.

Vol. 896: R. N. Taylor, J. Coutaz (Eds.), Software Engineering and Human-Computer Interaction. Proceedings, 1994. X, 281 pages. 1995.

Vol. 897: M. Fisher, R. Owens (Eds.), Executable Modal and Temporal Logics. Proceedings, 1993. VII, 180 pages. 1995. (Subseries LNAI).

Vol. 898: P. Steffens (Ed.), Machine Translation and the Lexicon. Proceedings, 1993. X, 251 pages. 1995. (Subseries LNAI).

Vol. 899: W. Banzhaf, F. H. Eeckman (Eds.), Evolution and Biocomputation. VII, 277 pages. 1995.

Vol. 900: E. W. Mayr, C. Puech (Eds.), STACS 95. Proceedings, 1995. XIII, 654 pages. 1995.

Vol. 901: R. Kumar, T. Kropf (Eds.), Theorem Provers in Circuit Design. Proceedings, 1994. VIII, 303 pages. 1995.

Vol. 902: M. Dezani-Ciancaglini, G. Plotkin (Eds.), Typed Lambda Calculi and Applications. Proceedings, 1995. VIII, 443 pages. 1995.

Vol. 903: E. W. Mayr, G. Schmidt, G. Tinhofer (Eds.), Graph-Theoretic Concepts in Computer Science. Proceedings, 1994. IX, 414 pages. 1995.

Vol. 904: P. Vitányi (Ed.), Computational Learning Theory. EuroCOLT'95. Proceedings, 1995. XVII, 415 pages. 1995. (Subseries LNAI).

Vol. 905: N. Ayache (Ed.), Computer Vision, Virtual Reality and Robotics in Medicine. Proceedings, 1995. XIV, 567 pages. 1995.

Vol. 906: E. Astesiano, G. Reggio, A. Tarlecki (Eds.), Recent Trends in Data Type Specification. Proceedings, 1995. VIII, 523 pages. 1995.

Vol. 907: T. Ito, A. Yonezawa (Eds.), Theory and Practice of Parallel Programming. Proceedings, 1995. VIII, 485 pages. 1995.

Vol. 908: J. R. Rao Extensions of the UNITY Methodology: Compositionality, Fairness and Probability in Parallelism. XI, 178 pages. 1995.

Vol. 909: H. Comon, J.-P. Jouannaud (Eds.), Term Rewriting. Proceedings, 1993. VIII, 221 pages. 1995.

Vol. 910: A. Podelski (Ed.), Constraint Programming: Basics and Trends. Proceedings, 1995. XI, 315 pages. 1995.

Vol. 911: R. Baeza-Yates, E. Goles, P. V. Poblete (Eds.), LATIN '95: Theoretical Informatics. Proceedings, 1995. IX, 525 pages. 1995.

Vol. 912: N. Lavrač, S. Wrobel (Eds.), Machine Learning: ECML – 95. Proceedings, 1995. XI, 370 pages. 1995. (Subseries LNAI).

Vol. 913: W. Schäfer (Ed.), Software Process Technology. Proceedings, 1995. IX, 261 pages. 1995.

Vol. 914: J. Hsiang (Ed.), Rewriting Techniques and Applications. Proceedings, 1995. XII, 473 pages. 1995.

Vol. 915: P. D. Mosses, M. Nielsen, M. I. Schwartzbach (Eds.), TAPSOFT '95: Theory and Practice of Software Development. Proceedings, 1995. XV, 810 pages. 1995.

Vol. 916: N. R. Adam, B. K. Bhargava, Y. Yesha (Eds.), Digital Libraries. Proceedings, 1994. XIII, 321 pages. 1995.

Vol. 917: J. Pieprzyk, R. Safavi-Naini (Eds.), Advances in Cryptology - ASIACRYPT '94. Proceedings, 1994. XII, 431 pages. 1995.

Vol. 918: P. Baumgartner, R. Hähnle, J. Posegga (Eds.), Theorem Proving with Analytic Tableaux and Related Methods. Proceedings, 1995. X, 352 pages. 1995. (Subseries LNAI).